# TOI TE MANA

THE ABAKANOWICZ ARTS AND CULTURE COLLECTION

# TOI TE MANA

## AN INDIGENOUS HISTORY OF MĀORI ART

Deidre Brown and Ngarino Ellis, with Jonathan Mane-Wheoki

The University of Chicago Press
Chicago and London

# NGĀ UPOKO — CONTENTS

He kupu whakataki — Preface ... ix

Tīmatanga kōrero — Introduction ... 1

## Part 1 – Te Kete Tuatea ... 17

**1 Ngā momo waka: Moana, migration and Māori** ... 21
Ngarino Ellis

Tā Hekenukumaingāiwi Busby, KNZM MBE (1932–2019) ... 38
Ngarino Ellis

**2 Ngā toi whakairo: The arts of carving** ... 41
Ngarino Ellis

The Taiapa brothers: Carving in the twentieth century ... 62
Ngarino Ellis

Morelli and the nineteenth-century papahou artist ... 66
Ngarino Ellis

Māori art and archaeology ... 70
Deidre Brown

**3 Ngā kākahu: Textiles** ... 73
Ngarino Ellis

Tahuaroa, pākūwhā and hākari: The display and gifting of taonga ... 104
Ngarino Ellis

Tihei mauri ora: The remaking of cloaks from museum collections ... 106
Ngarino Ellis

**4 Ngā whare: Architecture** ... 109
Deidre Brown and Ngarino Ellis

Pakaariki Harrison, QSO (1928–2008) ... 128
Ngarino Ellis

**5 Ngā toi whenua: Rock art** ... 131
Deidre Brown

**6 Ngā taonga o Wharawhara: Body adornment** ... 143
Ngarino Ellis

Areta Wilkinson ... 182
Deidre Brown

Pounamu ... 186
Ngarino Ellis

**7 Mana wāhine, mana tāne, mana takatāpui: Depicting gender in Māori art** ... 189
Ngarino Ellis

Men and weaving ... 200
Ngarino Ellis

## Part 2 – Te Kete Tuauri    203

### 8  Taonga, Māori and museums    207
Ngarino Ellis

Tāngata mamae: The tragic story of Te Maro, Ranginui and Te Kuku    221
Ngarino Ellis

Joseph Banks and the forty brass patu replicas    224
Ngarino Ellis

Tupaia    226
Ngarino Ellis

### 9  Māori art and the Christian missions    229
Deidre Brown

Hongi Hika's self-portraits    250
Deidre Brown

Hone Heke's 'collar'    252
Deidre Brown

He tikanga hōu? Figurative art in Rangitukia in 1838    256
Ngarino Ellis

### 10  The art of utu    259
Deidre Brown

The Mātaatua wharenui    272
Jonathan Mane-Wheoki

### 11  Transforming cultures and traditions: New materials, ideas and technologies    275
Ngarino Ellis

Moko signatures and tino rangatiratanga    292
Ngarino Ellis

Early Māori drawings    296
Deidre Brown

The second age of iron    298
Deidre Brown

### 12  Ngā toi mōrehu: The arts of survival    303
Deidre Brown

Māori flags and banners    324
Deidre Brown

### 13  Ka whawhai tonu mātou: Taonga and museums since 1900    333
Ngarino Ellis

Trick or taonga: The mysterious case of the green-painted patu pora    345
Deidre Brown

Fakes in the collection    347
Ngarino Ellis

Collecting the ancestors    350
Ngarino Ellis

Enrico Giglioli and the taonga collection in the Pigorini National Museum of Prehistory and Ethnography, Rome    353
Ngarino Ellis

## Part 3 – Te Kete Aronui — 355

### 14  The art of social reform: Te Puea, Ngata and Rātana — 359
Deidre Brown

Te Araiteuru pā at the 1906 New Zealand International Exhibition — 386
Deidre Brown

### 15  The emergence of contemporary Māori art 1950–1975 — 391
Jonathan Mane-Wheoki

Oriwa Haddon (1898–1958) — 406
Deidre Brown and Jonathan Mane-Wheoki

Ramai Hayward (1916–2014) — 408
Deidre Brown and Jonathan Mane-Wheoki

Pauline Kahurangi Yearbury (1926–1977) — 412
Deidre Brown

### 16  Urban Māori art and architecture — 415
Deidre Brown

Street art — 433
Deidre Brown

### 17  A new tradition or old disruption? Contemporary Māori exhibitions 1990–2021 — 437
Deidre Brown

Māori architects and architectural designers — 467
Deidre Brown

Māori designers — 477
Deidre Brown

*Māori Moving Image* exhibition — 480
Ngarino Ellis

Wairau Māori Art Gallery: The first public Māori art gallery — 483
Deidre Brown

### 18  Māori art in Western Europe and Australia — 485
Deidre Brown

Ngāti Rānana and Hinemihi — 501
Deidre Brown and Ngarino Ellis

Māori art as a cultural property — 505
Deidre Brown

### 19  Haumi ē! Hui ē! Tāiki ē! Māori and Indigenous art on the global stage — 509
Ngarino Ellis

Ngā taonga uku: Māori ceramicists and clay workers — 525
Deidre Brown

Contemporary Māori clothing — 529
Deidre Brown

Advice to Māori artists — 532
Jonathan Mane-Wheoki

Whakamutunga — Conclusion — 534

Ngā pitopito kōrero — Notes — 538

Kuputaka — Glossary — 567

Rārangi pukapuka — Select bibliography — 573

Kuputohu — Index — 590

This book is dedicated to
Jonathan Mane-Wheoki CNZM
(Ngāpuhi, Te Aupōuri, Ngāti Kurī, 1943–2014)
Collaborator, colleague,
mentor, friend and whanaunga

# HE KUPU WHAKATAKI
## – PREFACE

The rich and varied practices of our Māori ancestors and our contemporaries have led to an engagement with our world through carving, weaving, drawing and oral narratives. Our arts are a source of identity, authority, accommodation, protest, recovery, heritage and, most importantly, pride. This book is an attempt to write an Indigenous story of Māori art that acknowledges it as one of the world's great art traditions. To this end we have adopted a practice that speaks across all art traditions – that of art history. This is not without its challenges in terms of defining what Māori art is (and is not) and how Māori stories should be represented in book form. We should begin by saying that our definition of Māori art is non-negotiable. It is art made by Māori. Just as unequivocal is our position on history. For Māori, time is not a chronology, and therefore our history is not linear, sequential or developmental.

Two events were catalysts for the book. In 2008, the influential Comité International d'Histoire de l'Art (CIHA) debated the revision of art history 'to establish cross-cultural dimensions as fundamental to its scope, method, and vision'.[1] Three years later, the Waitangi Tribunal inquiry into Crown actions that breach the promises made to Māori in the 1840 Te Tiriti o Waitangi[2] released its report into its investigation of Māori cultural property rights, *Ko Aotearoa Tēnei*.[3] The report identified taonga (cultural treasures) as a vital component of mātauranga Māori (Māori knowledge) and stressed that a greater understanding of Māori art – for Māori and non-Māori – is essential for the survival of Māori culture. The three authors of this book have researched, taught and, at times, practised Māori art. The time seemed right to embark on documenting Māori art as a history. In 2012 we began our decade-long research project that has taken us around the country and around the world many times.

Jonathan knew this would be his last project. He became unwell while we were developing the Marsden Fund grant application for *Toi Te Mana*, and about a year after we started the project, he was diagnosed with terminal cancer. This did not stop him from working with us to develop the chapter structure for this book or from writing his contribution to it, while at the same time carrying out his dual roles as professor of fine arts at the Elam School of Fine Arts at the University of Auckland and as head of arts and visual culture at Te Papa Tongarewa Museum of New Zealand. Before he passed away in October 2014, there were many occasions when he spoke with us about why this project was important for Māori and Indigenous art and art historical scholarship. After his death, in his back catalogue of writing we came across a paper he delivered to a symposium on Ralph Hotere at the Auckland Art Gallery in 1998, in which he described the great gaps in current art historical publishing: these included 'the history of the Maori art movement, yet to be written; the grand history of Maori art from the creation stories to the electronic age, yet to be written; an integrated narrative of the visual arts in New Zealand, yet to be written; and the global history of art in the twentieth century'.[4]

Clearly, for Jonathan, *Toi Te Mana* was the project to satisfy the first two objectives, and a contribution to the latter two. This was always going to be an ambitious project that would take many years to complete, even with our combined eight decades of experience in research and teaching in this area. Among the files he left to the project are a number of documents outlining an intention to write fuller biographies of Māori modernists who, he felt, deserved greater recognition – Kāterina Mataira and Pauline Yearbury. In addition, we found two unfinished pieces on Māori artists who were not modernists but who were working in the postwar era – Oriwa Haddon and Ramai Hayward: these two biographies have been finished with additional writing by Deidre and included here. An unfinished chapter on the emergence of contemporary Māori art has been completed according to instructions left by Jonathan: it includes text taken from six other publications he had written, woven together with connecting text by Deidre. Indeed, when we reviewed the large corpus of Jonathan's published articles and unpublished papers it became apparent that the story of postwar Māori art dominated his writing and thinking about Māori art and art in general over many years. He was a Māori modernist himself, as he somewhat modestly acknowledges, and was chosen as a young University of Canterbury art student to exhibit in Buck Nin and Baden Pere's 1966 *New Zealand Maori Culture and the Contemporary Scene* exhibition at the Canterbury Museum. He was the only professional art historian of the Māori modernist period who could write from the point of view of an experienced practitioner. We feel deeply privileged to have worked with him in developing this project, and to be able to include his contribution here.

One of the main goals of this book has been to address the call by Linda Tuhiwai Smith (Ngāti Porou), as a member of the Ngāti Porou Waitangi claimant group Te Haeata, to bring home her own people's 'bits and pieces all over the place', to '[make] us whole again'.[5] We have developed a methodology for this project that brings together kaupapa Māori and art history. As Māori art historians our training and whānau backgrounds have provided us with a unique perspective on the dynamics of Māori art. While we draw on known art historical concepts, we understand these through a Māori lens in which concepts such as whakapapa, whenua and tikanga are central. *Toi Te Mana* promotes a distinctive

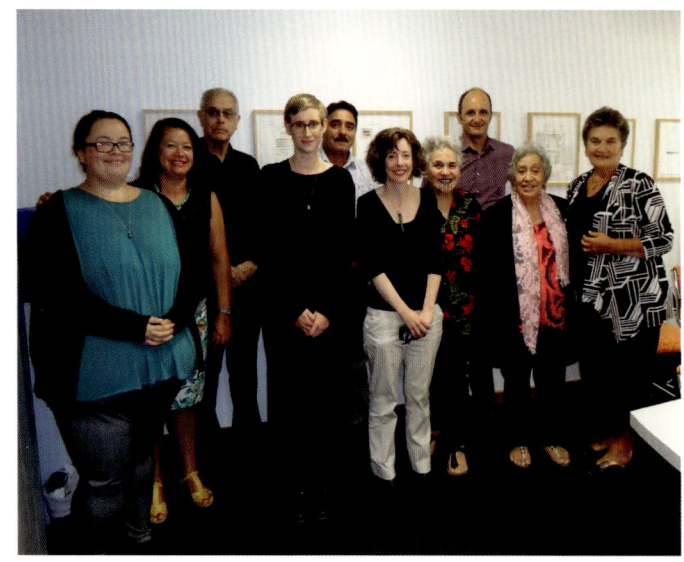

*Toi Te Mana* taumata, March 2014, Waipapa Taumata Rau University of Auckland. From left to right: Elisapeta Heta (*Toi Te Mana* Master's student), Ngarino Ellis, Jonathan Mane-Wheoki, Taarati Taiaroa (*Toi Te Mana* Master's student), Arapata Hakiwai, Deidre Brown, Ngahuia Te Awekotuku, Gerard O'Regan, Kaa Williams and Christina Wirihana. Absent from photograph: Patu Hohepa.

Māori art history whose own values and theories present the wider discipline with other ways of viewing and thinking about art. The rise of global art histories is revolutionary, unsettling linear timelines of art movements centred in Europe and the United States, and instead presenting a matrix of related art forms, techniques, materials and ideas. Taonga Māori reside in over 120 museums around the world, and their lives, as charted in this book, remind us of the importance of imparting knowledge of their history to a wider audience, as well as with those who are ahi kā – who keep the home fires burning.

We were fortunate to have the support of kaumātua (elders) and rangatahi (young people) in our mahi. A taumata – a panel of distinguished experts – comprised of the linguist Patu Hohepa, art historian Ngahuia Te Awekotuku, educationalist Kaa Williams and the expert weaver Christina Wirihana – set us on our early research path. Mentoring early-career researchers is a key aspect of our practice as Māori art historians, ensuring that we grow the next generation of scholars. Two Master's students who worked on the project were instrumental in researching undervalued areas of the Māori art world: Elisapeta Heta (Ngāti Wai, Waikato-Tainui) examined Māori art collectives (2015), and Taarati Taiaroa (Ngāti Tūwharetoa, Ngāti Apa) presented her thesis on a history of Māori art exhibitions (2014); she was also the images editor for this book. Their research is woven throughout the text, particularly in the Kete Aronui section. The project also provided research opportunities for other students who have gone on to forge their own creative careers, including Herman Ang, Amber Ruckes (Ngāi Tūhoe, Ngāti Porou), Justine Treadwell and Stacy Vallis.

Having the opportunity to research and writing about ancestral and contemporary taonga and their makers is a great privilege. We acknowledge the many artists, kaumātua, hapū, iwi, marae, galleries, archives and museums that who have provided access to these taonga and informed our research.

We see ourselves within a whakapapa of Māori art historians. We have been guided in this project by many prominent writers, curators and thinkers from many disciplines, including anthropologists and historians, from the 1980s onwards: Judith Binney, Bernie Kernot, Roger Neich, Mick Pendergrast, Anne Salmond and Nicholas Thomas. Most were Pākehā, but their research focused on Māori perspectives and stories. The work of respected Māori researchers in these fields of study – notably Hirini Moko Mead, Ngahuia Te Awekotuku, Apirana Ngata and Paul Tapsell – was distinct for the insider perspectives that they provided; their tribal identity was inextricably entwined with their academic lives. The Ngāi Tahu archaeologists Gerard O'Regan and Atholl Anderson, Ngāti Toa scholar Ross Calman, and tohunga whakairo Te Warahi Hetaraka were generous in their advice on our rock art, waka/whare, utu and iron chapters and textbox respectively. Special acknowledgement must be given to Mākereti (Maggie) Papakura, whose detailed analysis of the life and art of her Te Arawa people provides what might be considered the first work of Māori art history.

The postgraduate research of Māori students and practitioners in different fields has been invaluable to this project. The work of Dougal Austin, Kriselle Baker, Nigel Borell, Puawai Cairns, Chanel Clarke, Arapata Hakiwai, Elisapeta Heta, Robert Jahnke, Maia Jessop, Rangihīroa Panoho, Lisa Reihana, Huhana Smith, Taarati Taiaroa, Ngahuia Te Awekotuku, Kahutoi Te Kanawa, Areta Wilkinson and Johnson Witehira, as well as of Deidre and Ngarino and others, has provided frameworks and content for *Toi Te Mana,* and has prompted us to keep our standards high and our remit broad.

In opening up the field of Māori art history to include Australia, North America and Europe we have been grateful for information provided to us by Julie Adams, Joshua Bell, Jeremy Coote, Léuli Eshrāghi, Rachel Hand, Jill Hassell, Anita Herle, Maia Jessop, Maarama Kamira, Christopher Philipp, Keren Ruki, Amiria Salmond, John Terrell and Jacqueline Wallace.

Our colleagues in art and architectural history, including Michael Austin, Leonard Bell, Roger Blackley, Peter Brunt, Michael Linzey, Bill McKay, Damian Skinner, Jeremy Treadwell and Patricia Wallace, have given us food for thought in their writings about aspects of Māori art. They have contributed to a growing body of material with a strong art history focus.

The research for this book and its related outputs was generously supported by the Royal Society Te Apārangi's Marsden Fund, and Ngā Pae o te Māramatanga's Publication Support Grant programme. We would like to thank these funders, the reviewers for our proposals, and Waipapa Taumata Rau University of Auckland research support team.

An ambitious book written over many years requires an equally enthusiastic and committed publishing team. Sam Elworthy from Auckland University Press was a supporter of *Toi Te Mana* from the very beginning of the project, and his colleagues Sarah Ell, Lauren Donald, Mairātea Mohi and Katharina Bauer have guided us to the realisation of the book. Special thanks are due to our editor, Gillian Tewsley, with whom we have collaborated on a number of book projects, and Neil Pardington (Kāi Tahu, Kāti Māmoe, Ngāti Kahungunu) who is responsible for the book's beautiful design.

We acknowledge the aroha and tautoko of our whānau for our mahi: our partners Grant and Nepia, and children Maximilian, Oscar, Emere, Hana and Takimoana. They showed extraordinary patience as we undertook a project that took many more years to complete than we had first anticipated.

Finally, we extend our heartfelt gratitude to the Mane-Wheoki whānau, and in particular Jonathan's husband Paul Bushnell, for their support of Jonathan as he continued to work on this book in the last months of his life. Moe mai rā e te Rangatira.

We are proudly Māori art historians: and now we stand aside to let you, the readers, immerse yourselves in the wonderful, exciting and sometimes challenging world of Māori art.

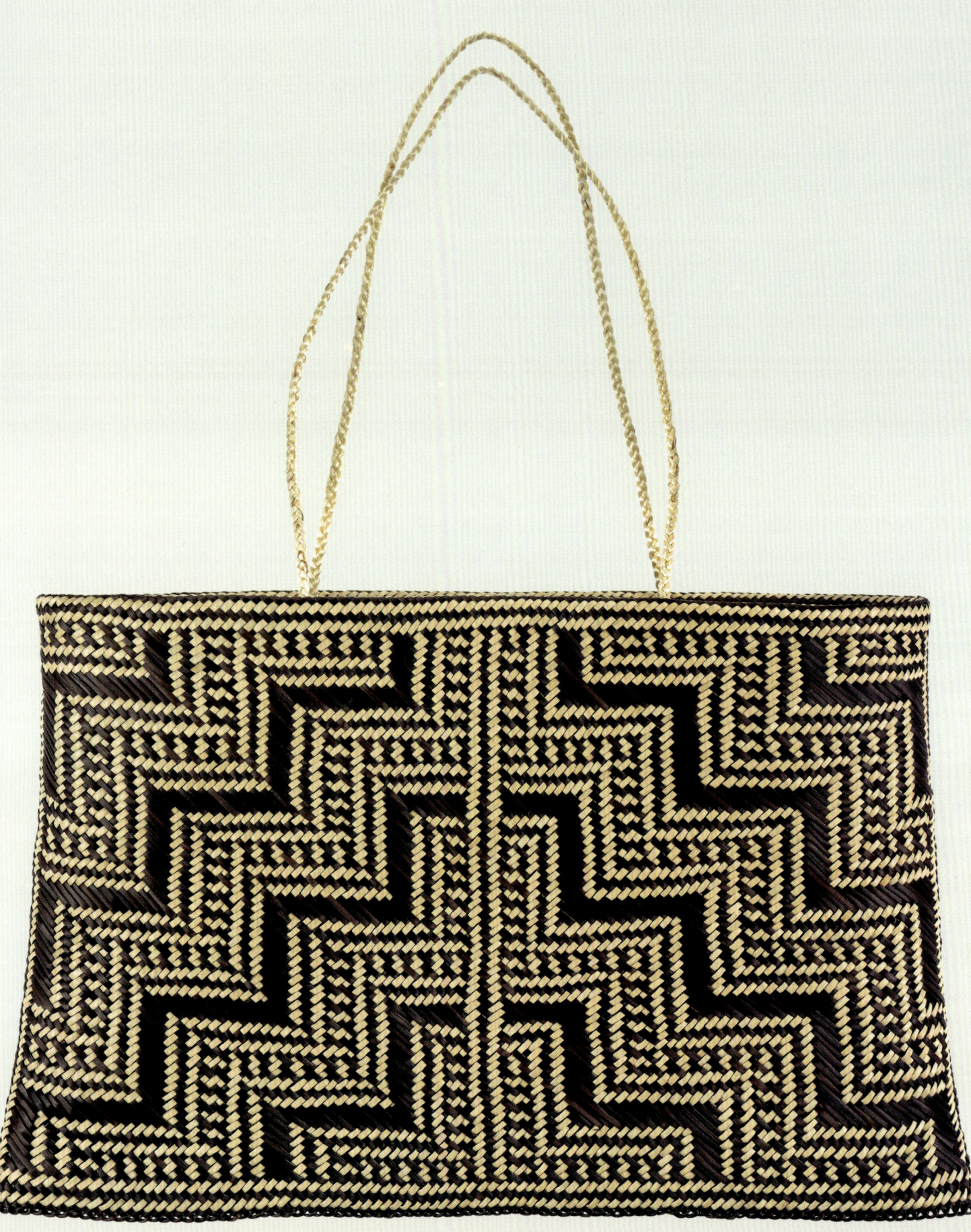

# TĪMATANGA KŌRERO
## – INTRODUCTION

Any history of Māori art begins in darkness, before the separation of Ranginui (the sky father) and Papatūānuku (the earth mother) by their son Tāne. The night is generative, a time in which anything and everything is possible, in which creativity is everywhere. The stories that descend from the separation onwards form the basis for the emergence of different art forms. They are associated with ancestors whose exploits produce ongoing cycles of creativity.

Core narratives stretch from Te Korekore – 'the realm between non-being and being: that is, the realm of potential being'[1] – through to cosmological ancestors, then ancestral stories in the more recent past and on to today. The relationship between ancestors and their deeds attached meaning to art forms: central to this were concepts such as tapu (sacredness), whakapapa (genealogy), tikanga (protocols) and whenua (land). Anglican minister Māori Marsden describes this as a 'woven universe'.[2] The metaphor of weaving is apt here: time moves back and forth, as exemplified in the making of kete (baskets). The act of plaiting or weaving a kete symbolises genealogical ascent and descent, moving back and forth in perpetual cyclical motion across the generations that brings together time as dynamic.

Cosmological and ancestral narratives are central to the story of Māori art. As descendants of Ranginui and Papatūānuku, Māori artists shift back and forth in relation to time. The natural resources they use also have their origins in the lives of atua (gods, supernatural beings) descended from Ranginui and Papatūānuku. These stories are often

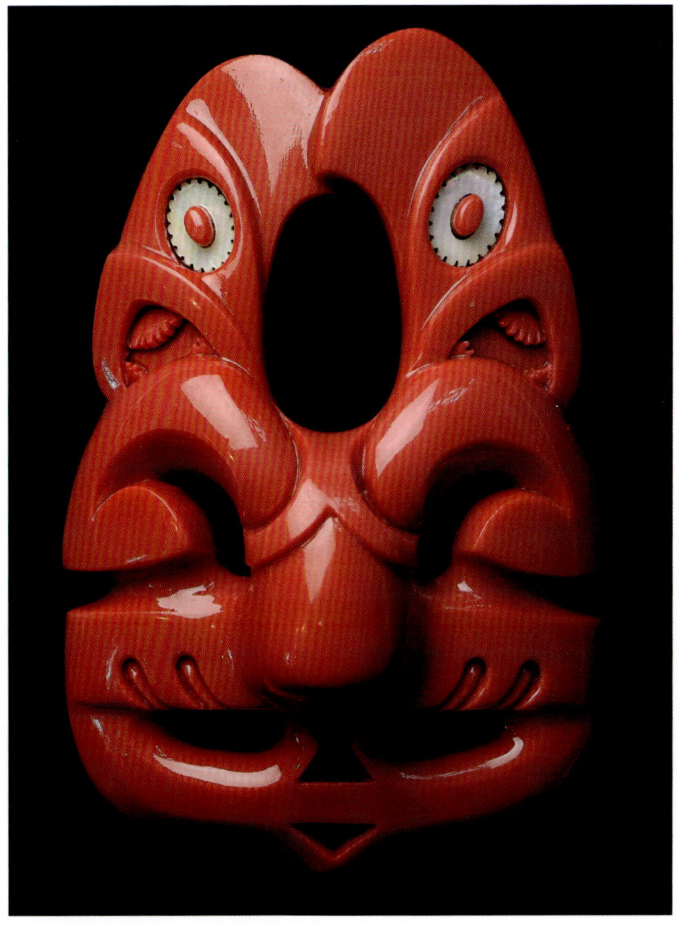

**Rangi Kipa, *Haukura*, 2023**
solid surface media, mother of pearl, photograph by Sam Hartnett, private collection

Opposite: For Te Atiwei Ririnui, the poutama design personifies progression and elevation in the pursuit of higher attainment.
**Te Atiwei Ririnui, *Poutama Ahurewa*, 2020**
kiekie, muka, synthetic dye, Te Papa Tongarewa Museum of New Zealand, ME024648, purchased 2020

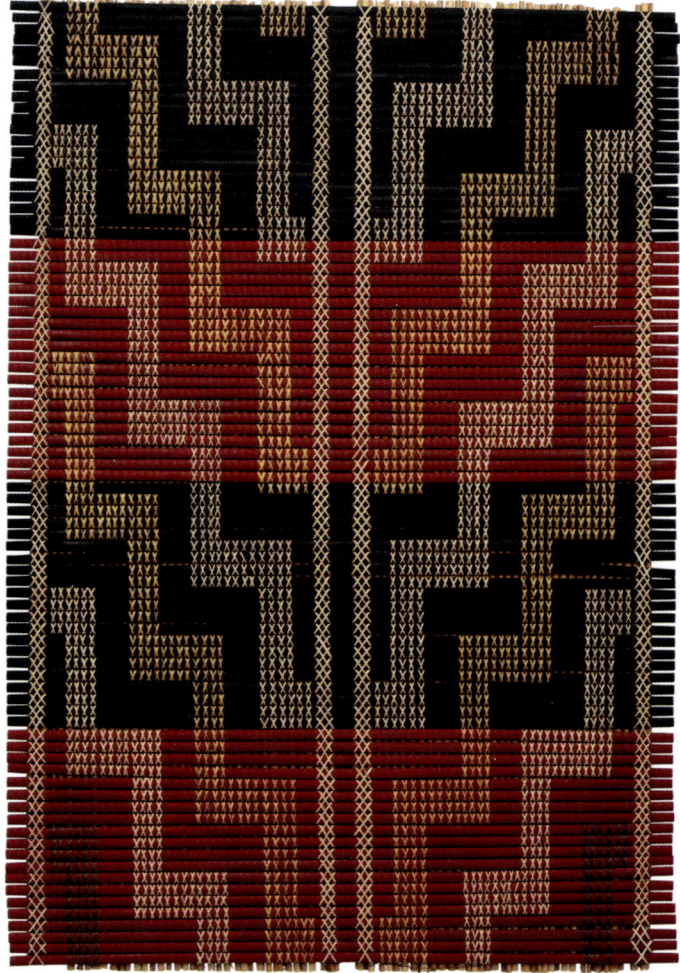

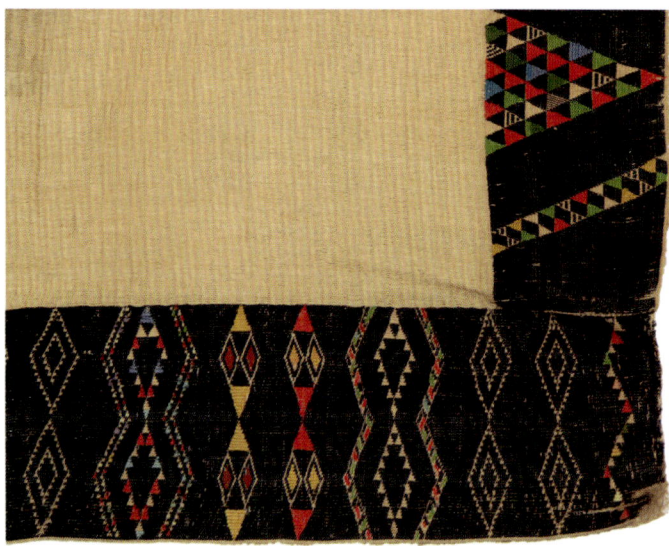

Top: Tukutuku panel featuring the poutama design, currently on display in Waipapa Taumata Rau University of Auckland Clock Tower, woven by students for the foyer of the Māori Adult Education Centre in the 1950s under the instruction of Mere Toka.
Waipapa Taumata Rau University of Auckland Art Collection

Bottom: Paepaeroa (bordered cloak).
Hawke's Bay Museums Trust, Ruawharo Tā-ū-rangi, 39/28

tribally specific; different understandings of stories reflect the ways in which these narratives have been debated and reconsidered through the generations. The account of the origins of pounamu (greenstone) is one example. For those descended from the migratory *Mātaatua* waka around Te Moananui a Toi, the Bay of Plenty, Poutini is the central figure whose children included 'famous greenstone weapons and ornaments'.[3] However Ngāti Porou, who live further east, remember Ngake (also known as Ngahua) in relation to pounamu, out of which the toki (adzes) named Pakitua and Tauira-a-pa were fashioned.[4] These stories reinforce the tribal nature of whakapapa, and that histories are nuanced and multivocal rather than linear and singular.

Oral sources are essential sites of knowledge of the origins of different art forms and materials. Weavers Kahutoi Te Kanawa (Ngāti Maniapoto, Waikato-Tainui, Ngāti Tūwharetoa) and John Turi-Tiakitai, for instance, discuss an oriori (lullaby) composed by Tupai (Te Whānau a Kai) that records the whakapapa of the fibre whītau, also known as muka:

> Ka noho Wai-nui, ka noho i a Rangi
> Puta mai ki waho rā Moana-nui-ā-Kiwa
> Ka maringi kai raro ko Para-whenua-mea
> Nā Moananui e, nā Moanaroa e,
> Nā Tu-i-te-repo, nā Tu-i-te-wao
> Nā Tu-te-hemo-rere, nānā Rangitahuri
> Nāna te whītau, ka roia hei kaka
> Ka mahana i ahau …
>
> The Mighty-waters did abide with the Sky Father
> And unto them was born the Great Ocean of Kiwa
>     [the Pacific]
> Poured down below was the Muddy soil of
>     Mother Earth
> Begotten, too, by the Mighty-ocean were the
>     Open-seas,
> The Oozy-swamp, the forest-swamp
> Tu-te-hemo-rere begat Rangitahuri;
> She grew the flax from which cloaks were woven
> That now keeps me warm …[5]

Artists articulate and activate this history in the making of their artworks. As weavers strip the outer layer of the

TĪMATANGA KŌRERO – INTRODUCTION

harakeke to release the muka to make into dress cloaks, they remember this history and activate these atua to assist them in their work. Karakia are important sites in which these atua are embedded, and are recited at the start and end of each weaving session. In reciting the karakia, these are not simply art materials, but are objects inherently embedded in whakapapa, which brings spiritual meaning to the resources and to what is produced with them.

Indeed, whakapapa is a core methodology in recounting cosmological narratives or pūrākau (ancient stories).[6] Knowledge of art forms was typically passed down through the generations: Kahutoi Te Kanawa credits her mother Diggeress Te Kanawa and her grandmother Rangimārie Hetet, both exquisite weavers, as māreikura, 'female supernatural beings'.[7] Kahutoi describes how both women walked in two worlds, Māori and Pākehā, through which they maintained their knowledge and passion for weaving. Their dedication to keeping the art of weaving alive – by teaching it within and outside of their whānau – influenced Kahutoi's own practice, and encouraged her to think about the knowledge of ancestral practices that they were imparting. As she writes, 'The kaupapa (foundation) of a piece of weaving can be set in one's mind, based on stories, cosmology, signifiers of atua (gods), evolution of time, elements, animals and mammals through the practice of balancing colour and adornment within the structure and process of the making.'[8]

Our knowledge of the histories of Māori art forms tracks back in time to celestial and ancestral narratives. Artists refer to key ancestors, such as Rauru for carving, when they begin their work, binding the present with the past, the ancestors with the living. They create a tapu space in which their art can be made, using protocols set by the ancestors to ensure the safety of their practice, and using materials from the whenua, be they clay, kiekie or kauri, or even factory-made resources. The finished works reinforce the ongoing creative energies that continue to provoke artists to push against boundaries and extend the edges of their practice into other realms. He ao hurihuri – the world turns.

## Ngā kete e toru – the three baskets of knowledge

*Toi Te Mana* is a history of Māori art from its ancestral beginnings to the present day, from the customary arts of whatu (weaving), raranga (plaiting), whakairo rākau (carving) and moko (designs inked on Māori) to contemporary fine arts, craft and design. It explores the art practices that inform how Māori have adorned themselves, their built and natural environments, and exhibition spaces in Aotearoa New Zealand and abroad, as well as the tools, materials, training and methods needed for these forms of expression. Central to the discussion are Māori makers, whose individual and collective histories are examined in relation to their cultural, social and political contexts. The journeys of taonga between Māori communities to facilitate social cohesion, and sometimes out of these communities, by exchange and theft, to collectors and institutions, illustrate the enduring mana and tapu of Māori art, even in challenging circumstances.

*Toi Te Mana* is structured as Ngā Kete e Toru – the three baskets of knowledge. The three kete were recovered from the world above by Tāne, the atua of knowledge and the son of Ranginui and Papatūānuku: he was the main protagonist in the creation of the present world, Te Ao Mārama (the world of light) when he forced his parents apart. Tāne's journey is described as follows:

> Tēnei au te hōkai nei o taku tapuwae
> Ko te hōkai nuku ko te hōkai rangi
> Ko te hōkai a tō tupuna a Tānenui-a-rangi
> Ka pikitia ai ki te rangi tūhāhā ki te Tihi-o-Manono
> Ka rokohina atu rā ko Te Matua-kore anake
> Ka tīkina mai ngā kete o te wānanga
> Ko te kete-tuauri
> Ko te kete-tuatea
> Ko te kete-aronui
> Ka tiritiria ka poupoua
> Ka puta mai iho ko te ira tangata
> Ki te wheiao ki te ao mārama
> Tihei – mauri ora!
>
> This is the journey of sacred footsteps
> Journeyed about the earth, journeyed about the heavens
> The journey of the ancestral god Tānenui-a-rangi
> Who ascended into the heavens to Te Tihi-o-Manono
> Where he found the parentless source
> From there he retrieved the baskets of knowledge
> Te kete-tuauri
> Te kete-tuatea

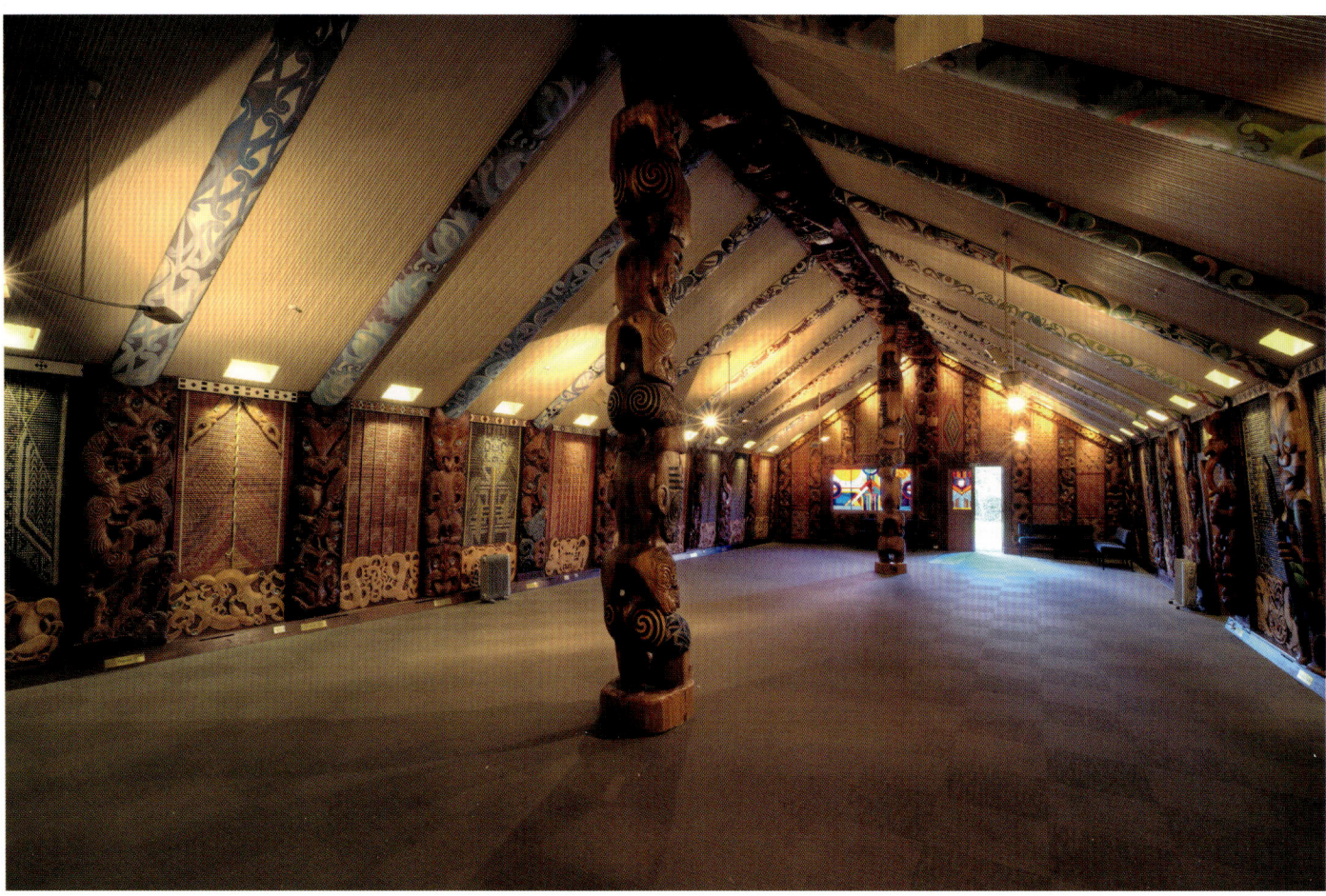

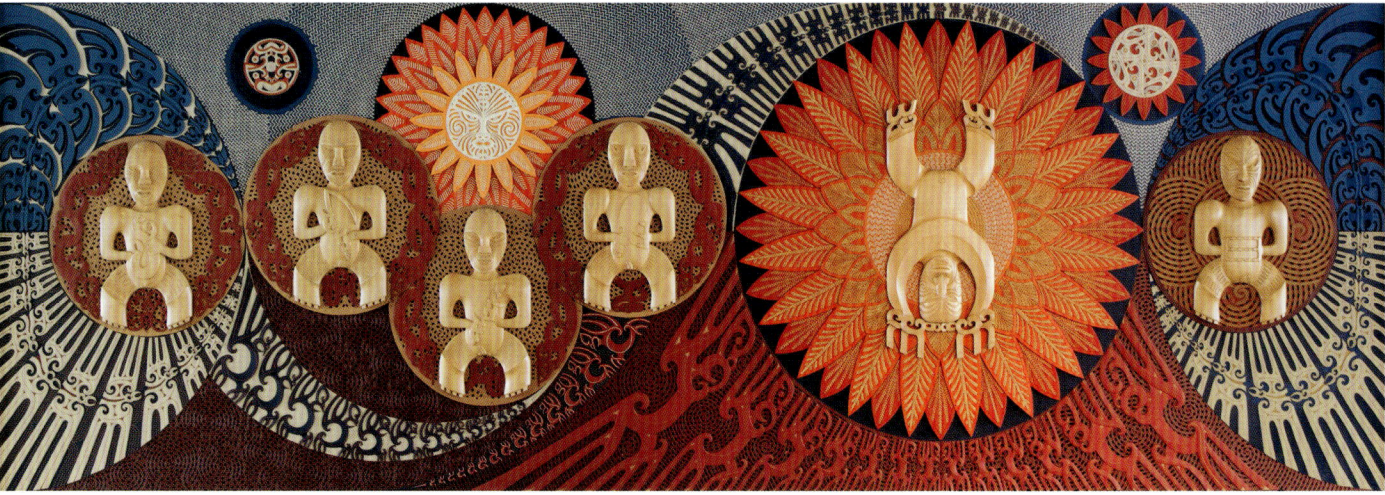

Top: Interior of the whare whakairo Tāne-nui-ā-rangi, Waipapa Marae, Waipapa Taumata Rau University of Auckland. The carving team was led by Pakaariki Harrison, and the whare opened in 1986.
photograph by Godfrey Boehnke

Bottom: **Cliff Whiting,** *Te Wehenga o Rangi rāua ko Papa*, 1969–1974
mixed media, 2590 x 7075mm, National Library of New Zealand
Te Puna Mātauranga o Aotearoa, photograph by Mark Beatty

> Te kete-aronui
> These were distributed and implanted about
>    the earth
> From which came human life
> Growing from dim light to full light
> There was life!⁹

The chapters in *Toi Te Mana* are grouped into these three kete, as defined by Māori Marsden, and extended by us to create definitions of art, although we acknowledge that others have different interpretations of the kete's contents.¹⁰

Te Kete Tuatea, sometimes referred to as 'the basket of light', contains the continuum of Māori art that is from and within the customary world. This art exists in the past, present and future, and it is founded on and informs tikanga. It is represented by the art of waka (as the vessels that bring people and their practices and values to new places), whakairo (carving), kākahu (textiles), whare (architecture), rock art and body adornment. Other accounts of 'customary art' have tended to favour those practices generally performed by men, or have been cisgender and gender-binary in their approach, ignoring quite obvious themes of homosexuality and transsexuality. An important aspect of our art historical practice has been to recognise the role of gender and sexuality in the creation of Māori art through the inclusion of a chapter on this topic.

Te Kete Tuauri, 'the basket of the unknown', contains arts developed out of engagement with Pākehā, and the consequential changing dynamics of Māori relationships with each other as hapū (subtribal), iwi (tribal) and pan-iwi organisations. Pākehā tools, materials and concepts were incorporated into arts that were based in tikanga Māori (customs) and that supported the maintenance of Māori lifeways, despite the impact of colonisation, the New Zealand Wars and consequential land loss. Te Kete Tuauri could be considered the kete of 'survivance' – a term that Gerald Vizenor created to describe strategies used by Indigenous peoples to actively resist colonisation. Art is one of the most important of these strategies.¹¹ This kete contains art from the earliest cross-cultural encounters that has been transformed or translocated by Christianity; exchanged to maintain inter-Māori relationships, resisting Pākehā encroachment; and taken away to form part of museum collections. Art, therefore, is an important strategy that Indigenous peoples employ to actively survive traumatic events and processes that have been their legacy across generations.

The final kete, Aronui, is 'the basket of pursuit': it contains the arts that humans seek. The early twentieth-century architectural movements of Te Puea Hērangi, Apirana Ngata and Tahupōtiki Wiremu Rātana, which sought to reform the social conditions of Māori, can be found in this kete. Their work led to the emergence of contemporary Māori art forms after World War Two with a focus on Māori modernism, and then the schools of artistic thought that followed, through collectives such as Ngā Puna Waihanga and courses in Māori arts at tertiary institutions. The social ruptures caused by Māori urbanisation in the late twentieth century provoked questions about what Māori art is, and who Māori artists and art historians should be; and these were explored in exhibitions of Māori art. At the same time, communities sought to establish their presence in the cities through urban marae; and concerns about cultural loss and empowerment were explored through gritty and direct art – predominantly paint on canvas and (sometimes controversial) public art projects. The final chapters examine the more recent histories of Māori art beyond Aotearoa's shores, as Māori redefine themselves and their creative processes as diasporic communities in Australia and Europe, and as global Indigenous artists showing their work around the world. Māori art is not defined by national borders: it can and does occur all over the world, wherever Māori artists choose to make and exhibit their work.

Textboxes are used liberally as enabling devices in each kete to demonstrate the contribution of pioneering and otherwise influential artists, important or unusual taonga, and critical turning points and events. They assist in disrupting the idea of history as chronology by orientating us towards other histories embedded in personal life stories that span our chapters, narratives of materials and taonga that collapse any distance between the ancestral and contemporary worlds, and moments that redirect our attention.

## Kaupapa – methodology

*Toi Te Mana* is written by, for and about Māori. We have drawn on kaupapa Māori and art history methodologies to create a methodology that is innovative and interdisciplinary and draws on the disciplines of Māori studies, history, art history, archaeology and anthropology. The project has mobilised a multi-pronged approach that is useful for studying Māori art history: a review of the published literature, and research into written accounts of Māori art in books, manuscripts and diaries in archives in Aotearoa New Zealand, such as the Hocken Library Uare Taoka o Hākena and Alexander Turnbull Library, and also overseas, including in the University of Cambridge Museum of Archaeology and Anthropology, the Melbourne Museum, and New York's Metropolitan Museum of Art. We have looked at oral material such as mōteatea (laments), waiata (songs), whakataukī (proverbs) and kōrero tuku iho (ancestral narratives) that now reside in archives. We have worked in museums sourcing taonga long lost from communities, if only physically, as well as those that have travelled through auction houses. We have visited art galleries and talked to artists and curators, to view the art first hand and hear their perspectives of the works.

Western European art history offers many useful approaches that we have used here. Formalism encourages viewers to just look at the 'formal' elements of artwork (including line, colour, composition) to understand and appreciate the work. This is related to the concept of aesthetics – in essence, the choices made by an artist in the making of an artwork. The idea of style is used to identify elements that are similar between artists, and the wānanga (or school) that some of them worked in. These styles were passed down through the generations from an artist to their student. They were usually iwi-specific, and in this way, we can identify the work of a particular iwi, such as Whanganui or Taranaki. An artist's style might change throughout their life, as a result of events such as the New Zealand Wars that might prompt a reconsideration of the purpose and subject matter of an artwork. Biography involves looking at the life of an artist and examining who they worked with: moko practitioners, for example, might work together and learn ideas from each other; the same with weavers. In Te Ao Māori we would extend this collaboration out to taonga tuku iho – treasures handed down from the ancestors, our living ancestors. We can think about biography as whakapapa, a way in which to understand the artist's world and the people they had relationships with. In anthropology this might be called 'the biography of an object' but for us, as Māori, we formulate this according to our tikanga, and whakapapa feels right to us. Related to this, we have considered the historical context in the making and reception of artworks, and we have asked questions such as what were the major events of the period, and who were the main rangatira (chiefs) who were commissioning these works? Patronage is relevant here – the person who paid for the work and would usually have a thing or two to say about its importance. We look, for instance, at how individuals and communities such as Ringatū and the Kīngitanga paid for buildings and other artworks to assert their identity.

We have thought about different theories of art history in the most classic sense. Ideas of feminism have been woven through each chapter as we deliberately sought out women artists and their practices that have often been sidelined in galleries and publications. Why was the first exhibition by Māori women not held until the mid-1980s? And why did we not know until recently that the first Māori to graduate from a tertiary art school was a woman – Pauline Yearbury at Elam School of Fine Arts? Why does the majority of our whakairo today depict men when historically it was the reverse? Queer theory encourages us to look at depictions of those artists from the LGBTQI+ community (chapter 7), for instance, to recuperate their stories as told on taonga such as papahou (treasure boxes) and as envisaged by artists such as Lisa Reihana in her *Dandy* and *Diva* works from *Digital Marae*. Postcolonialism interrogates the power structures around artworks and practices and examines how Indigenous artists have responded to this. The term has been reframed as contemporary artists rework notions of 'post' – as seen in chapter 17, and in the work of curators such as George Hubbard, who has addressed the stereotyping of Māori according to this term. The idea of 'postcolonial' has moved on to 'decolonisation' and 'indigenisation', but in *Toi Te Mana* we take that next step, as pitched by Moana Jackson, of 'reMāorification' of our worlds.[12] While this might be contentious, it is a political situation that addresses our current worldviews as firmly based here in Aotearoa New Zealand.

### An Indigenous art history

Across the world there has been a turn towards the writing of Indigenous art histories by Indigenous art historians, curators and artists. It has always been curious to us how some argue their writing *is* an Indigenous art history if they are not Indigenous themselves. We wonder if they might argue the same if they were based in places like Nigeria or Japan: would they call their works Japanese art history or similar? Jonathan wrote about the changing significance, for artists, of identifying as Indigenous:

> Communities of indigenous artists have also become aware of their counterparts, and the commonalities they share (such as invasion, occupation, subjugation, and the sequestration of resources), in other parts of the world and want to express this in strategies of solidarity and selective resistance to the cultures of their colonisers. The rise of contemporary indigenous art, globally, is a phenomenon of our times.[13]

Further, he describes what makes us distinct: Indigenous people are the descendants of the first or original inhabitants of a geographical territory or region, whose identity is unique and defined by the geographical compass within which they operate, and ancient and ancestral ties to place. Their realities are informed by distinctive cosmological constructs, their sense of the occult in the natural environment, and their shamanistic engagement with it.[14]

Jonathan looked forward to a time when Indigenous peoples might see themselves as a powerful collective comprised of diverse communities with shared experiences that united their otherwise 'unique, local, ancient indigenisms'. The term 'Indigenous' is used throughout our book, and with a capital 'I'. This is a form of identification, just as one might identify as a New Zealander with a capital N and Z.[15]

Throughout our project, we have considered the situation of Māori art history within the wider discipline of art history. We are resistant to seeing it simply as a piece of a 'global art' or 'world art' jigsaw puzzle that, when placed with other art histories, creates a big picture of art across all times and places. The discipline of art history is contestable, its methods are not universally agreed on and its subject matter and participants are not bounded by geography. Still today the field presumes to be centred on Western Europe (and, by extension, the United States and Canada), with the term 'global' used to cover everywhere else. We argue here for the continual shifting of that centre depending on the position of the speaker – as our kaikaranga (callers) and kaikōrero (speakers) do on our marae (complex of space and buildings,

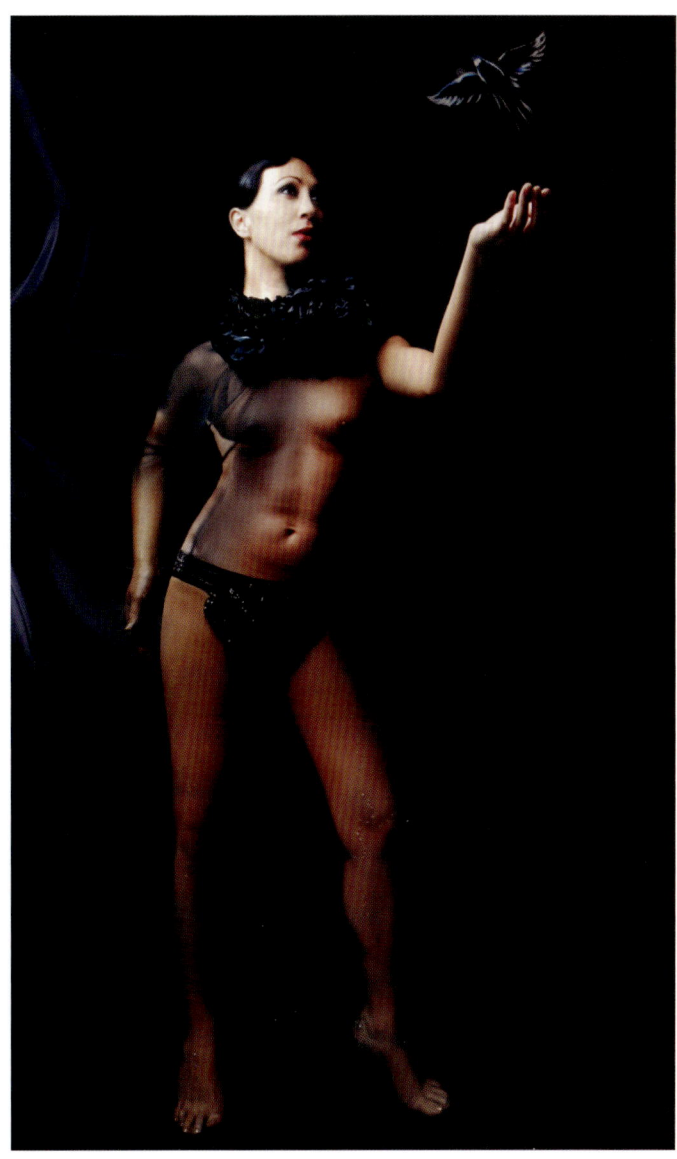

Lisa Reihana, *Diva*, 2007
colour photograph, type C print, 2000 x 1200mm, Te Papa Tongarewa Museum of New Zealand, 0.037194, purchased 2010

including a meeting house). For us in Aotearoa New Zealand, our centre is here, or, even more specifically, wherever our tūrangawaewae – the place where a person has the right to stand, a community of belonging – is located. The uneven funding of 'on-the-ground' art historical research across the world, particularly in Africa, and the politics that suppress particular art genres – for example, Western European-influenced Indigenous art in parts of the Middle East – make a 'global' art project fraught with difficulties. Much Indigenous art history spanning large geographic regions is based on works that are in European and North American collections or exhibitions.

This difference in conceptualising a global art history is evident when comparing who is writing about Māori art and Pacific art now. Art from the wider Pacific is a much larger academic field, dominated by work based on institutional collections, and is yet to benefit from a critical mass of Indigenous voices. In contrast, Māori art history is located within living communities and ancestral landscapes and presents a very different interpretation of art. In this book, we have been more interested in exploring the idea of Indigenous art histories that value Indigenous voices, perspectives and objectives, and making art history more relevant and less Eurocentric.

### Māori art history's history

Māori art history, as a scholarly discipline, was told by anthropologists and archaeologists up until the emergence of Māori art historians in the late twentieth century. Many of these earlier scholars deliberately or otherwise supported contemporary political policies through the ideas they promoted in their writing – policies that resulted in many Māori communities being disenfranchised by the turn of the twentieth century in relation to health, housing, education, land and justice; and, by extension, to taonga Māori being traded, sold, 'gifted' or otherwise taken. Early historians promoted the idea of a hierarchy of Māori artistic 'development' that, they insisted, anticipated the inevitable dying out of the Māori race. This pervasive theory influenced writing about Māori art by non-Māori until recent decades.

We propose a revision of Western-influenced classificatory systems of Māori art, and to look towards an Indigenous dynamic sense of time, and the diversity of art that exists between and behind definitions of practice, oeuvres and canons. Customary Māori art has long been the subject of ethnological inquiry,[16] with the literature consisting largely of monographs and articles on particular artistic[17] and regional[18] practices, or sweeping surveys comprised of collected essays by specialists in different fields.[19] Until the 1990s, Māori art had been largely excluded from New Zealand art historical narratives and only occasionally covered in general surveys of international art history written by European scholars, from Ernst Gombrich's *The Story of Art* first published in 1950 through to Hugh Honour and John Fleming's *A World History of Art* in 1982. Certain groundbreaking books since the 1990s have exploded assumptions about 'traditional art' as a fixed aesthetic and temporal concept, or explored aspects of Māori art with a kaupapa Māori (Māori research) methodology, such as Roger Neich's *Painted Histories: Early Maori Figurative Painting* (1993) and Ngahuia Te Awekotuku and Linda Waimarie Nikora's *Mau Moko: The World of Maori Tattoo* (2007).[20] These provide influential precedents for *Toi Te Mana*. Other authors, in particular Māori anthropologist Hirini Moko Mead and (sometimes problematically) David Simmons, have argued for tribal 'style' categories and developmental chronologies.[21] One of the first evidence-based attempts to create a Māori art history spanning Polynesian arrival to the present day was a developmental style sequence published by Mead in the 1984 *Te Maori* exhibition catalogue.[22] His set of time periods was based on Māori concepts of growth: Ngā Kākano (the seeds), 900–1200CE, art related to arrival and settlement; Te Tīpunga (the growth), 1200–1500, a time when regional practices were established; Te Puāwaitanga (the flowering), 1500–1800, when 'styles' can be attributed to specific ancestors and places; and Te Huringa (the turning), 1800CE to the present. Mead's structuring of the 'prehistoric' sequence into three-century periods may seem arbitrary, but it does loosely fit with radiocarbon dating data available at the time.

The most difficult period to define was Te Huringa: Mead struggled to find a place for contemporary Māori artists and designers working in the Western European idiom with Māori themes. He eventually broke Te Huringa down into two 100-year periods, and he considered excluding art made by Māori but not necessarily building on the art of previous generations. He wrote: 'Māori artists trained in the art schools of the Pākehā are spearheading a movement to change the face of Māori art more radically than ever before. One does not know whether they innovate with love and understanding, or whether they are about to ignite new fires of destruction.'[23] This comment identified a division of opinion within the Māori arts community at the time, between the certainty of a continuing tradition and the uncertainties of also engaging with other art traditions.

The first university-based Māori art historians – Ngahuia Te Awekotuku at Auckland and Jonathan Mane-Wheoki and Ngapine Allen (later Te Ao) at Canterbury – followed an alternative model of historical organisation that tended towards art taxonomies, such as waka building and moko, which contained chronologies and ancestral stories within but not necessarily across practices. The approach we have taken in *Toi Te Mana* is to define Māori art as art made by Māori: eschewing developmental sequences and instead organising bodies of practice conceptually allows the inclusion of diverse, concurrent practices.

What is artistic continuity within the non-linear contexts of Māori time and history? The definition of time that underpins the art history presented here is derived from te reo Māori (the Māori language). Linguist and tribal historian Patu Hohepa has described Māori time as a movable continuum that appears as a three-dimensional model when compared to linear chronologies.[24] This is reflected in parallel, and sometimes intersecting and disrupting understandings of taonga. One thread is organised according to hapū and iwi ways of thinking. Those of us from Ngāti Porou, for example, think of carving as having originated from Ruatepupuke, down through our tupuna (ancestor) Iwirākau and the whare wānanga (school of learning) of legendary carvers whom he inspired in the mid-nineteenth century – Te Kihirini, Hone Taahu, Hone Ngatoto, Riwai Pakerau, Tāmati Ngākaho and Hoani Ngatai; their legacy continued in the work of Pineāmine Taiapa and Hone Taiapa, on to Pakaariki Harrison, and carvers such as Hone McClutchie. While this whakapapa is a lineage, the relativity is not linear: relationships can move up, down and across generations according to the art historian's perspective. Disciplinary boundaries between 'traditional' and 'contemporary', such as Mead's Te Huringa distinctions, dissolve. The task of art history, then, is to navigate us through this complex matrix of time and stories, taking us from one point of understanding to many others. We argue that Māori

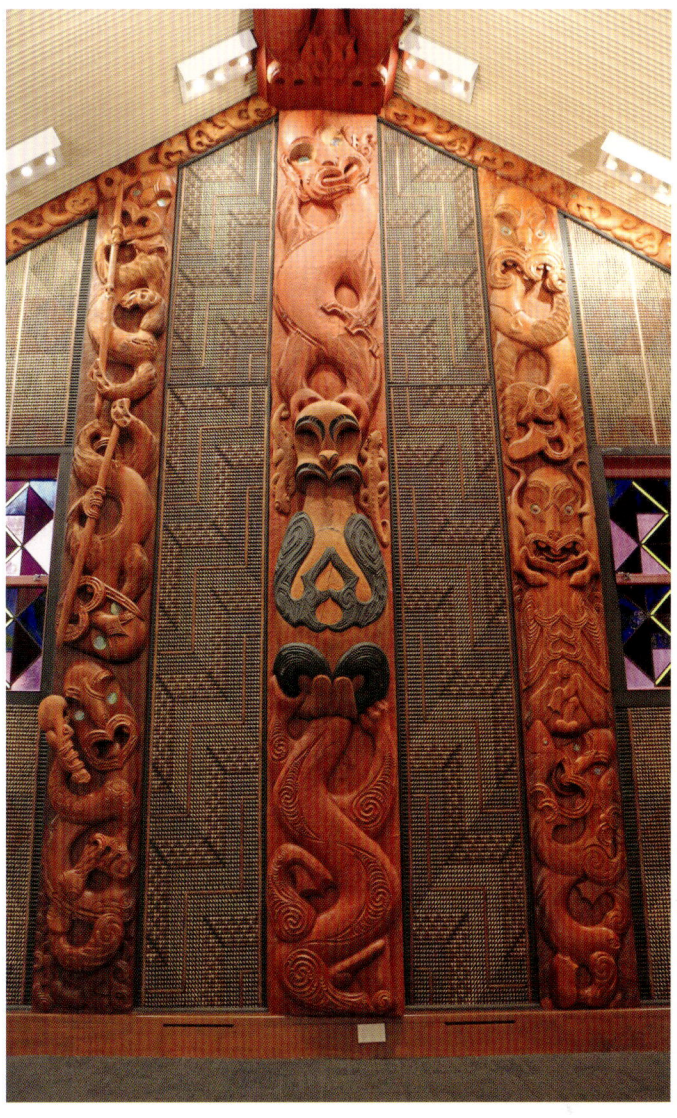

The ancestor Māui is frequently represented in whare whakairo as an ancestor common to all Māori. Here Pakaariki Harrison has carved him on the poutuarongo at the back of Tāne-nui-ā-rangi, Waipapa Marae, Waipapa Taumata Rau University of Auckland, at the moment he attempts to enter Hinenuitepō.
photograph by Lauren Donald

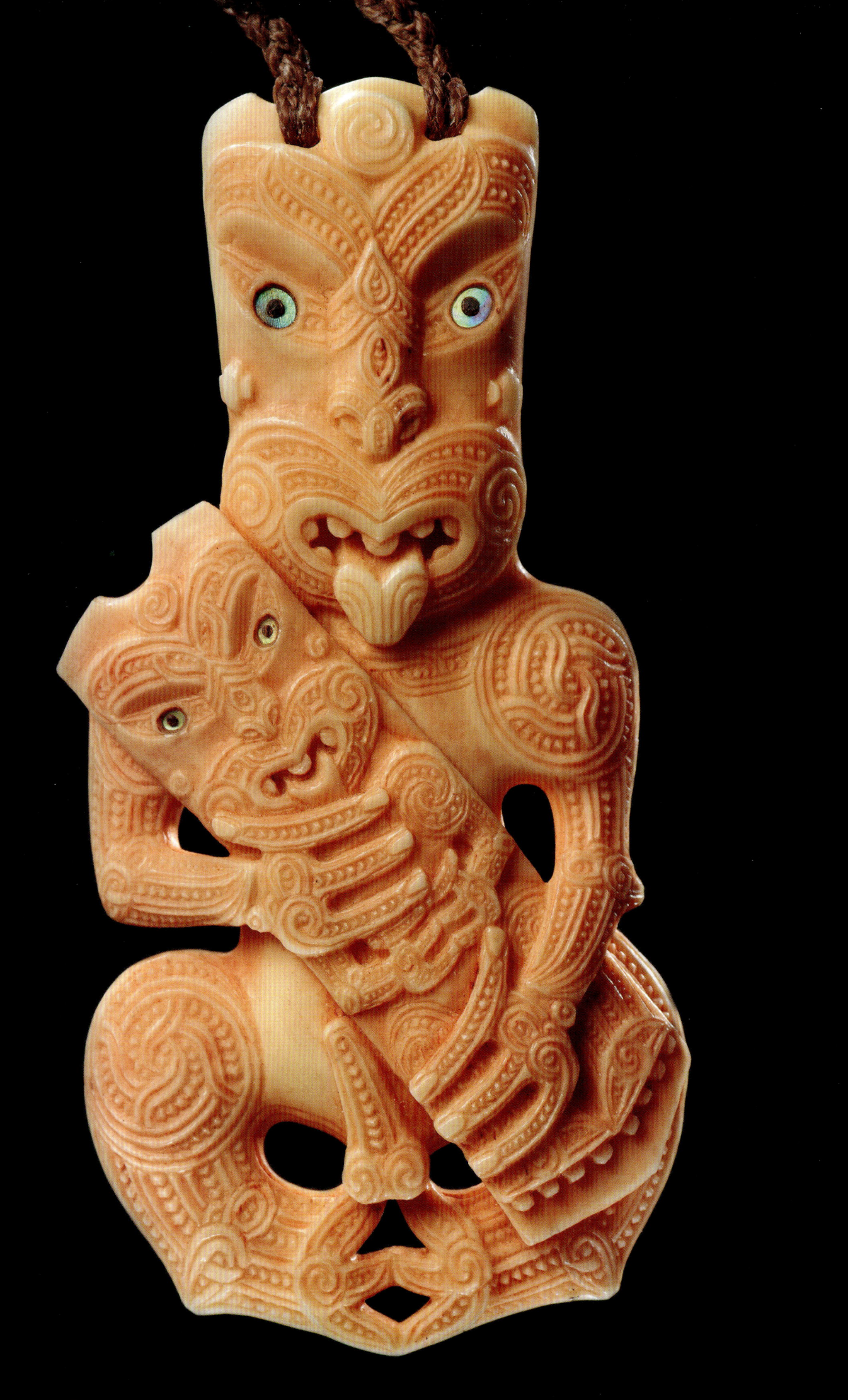

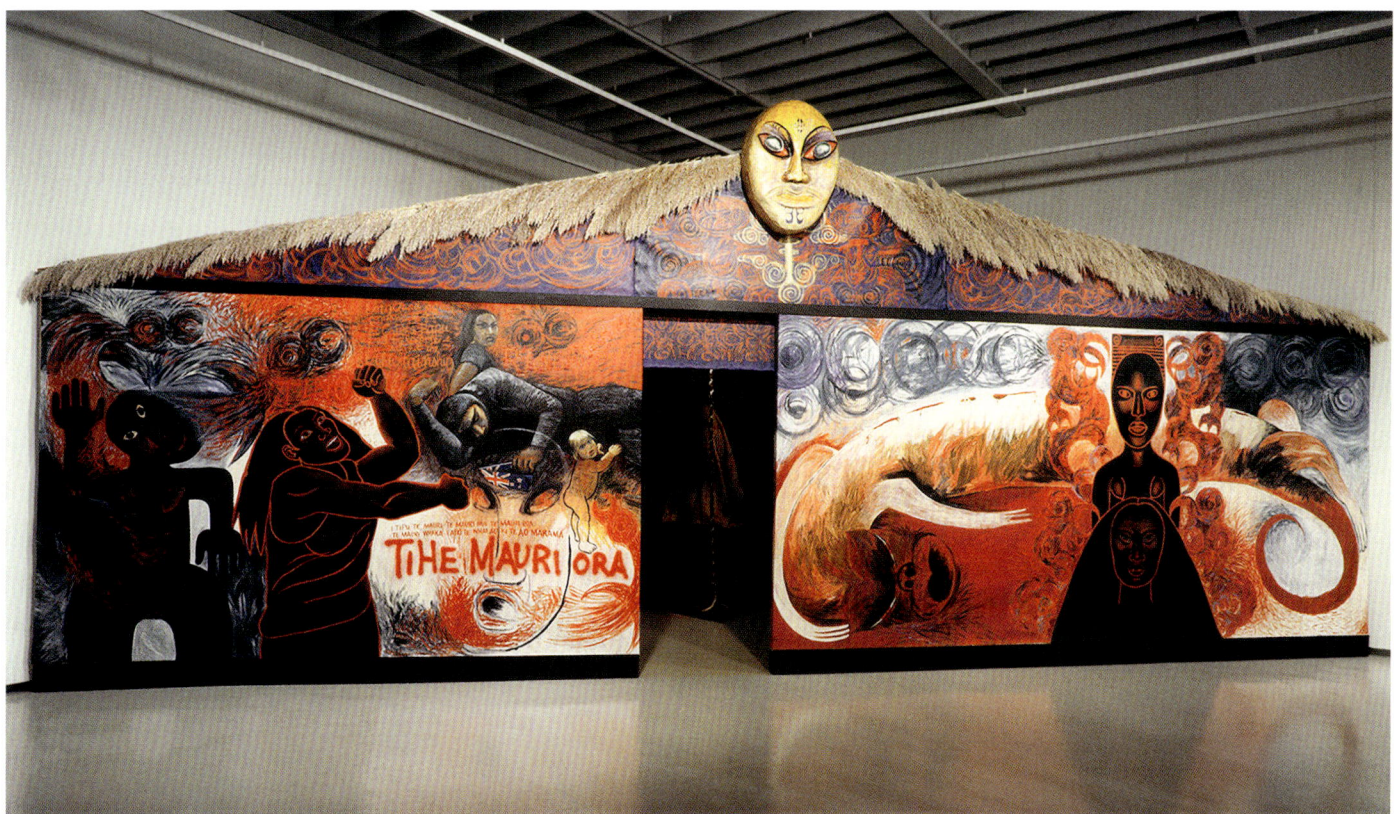

**Haeata, *Hineteiwaiwa te Whare*, as installed in the *Mana Tiriti* exhibition, City Gallery, Wellington, 1990**

mixed media: paint and canvas, wood, customboard, papier-mâché, muslin, photography, cardboard, kākaho, pāua, toetoe, supplejack, harekeke, sand, shells, earth, jute, fibre, stones, harekeke seeds and nikau fronds, photograph by City Gallery, Wellington

art is characterised by change; the role of Māori art history is therefore to understand what these changes are and why they occurred, as well as to record continuities. Indeed, one of the greatest delights in our research has been to document and understand the various and diverse Māori art practices that have operated simultaneously, and to demonstrate that customary Māori art is contemporary art.

Robert Jahnke writes about the 'turning points' that alter the future.[25] While politically most would cite the signing of Te Tiriti o Waitangi, for this book the turning point is the opening of Raharuhi Rukupō's Te Hau ki Tūranga in 1842. The making of this house symbolises the political aspirations of the chief in aligning a number of hapū together. Artistically it broke new ground with the completion of a whare that would have decorations on the inside and the outside, which culturally would orientate the life of the hapū towards a central hub.

Where customary Māori art has featured, in recent years, in impressive exhibitions in the Metropolitan Museum of Art, the Field Museum in Chicago, the British Museum, Musée du Quai Branly in Paris, the Museum Volkenkunde in Leiden, the Netherlands, and in many other international institutions, the emphasis has been on its ethnographic aspect. Museums

Opposite: Hei tiki representing Ruatepupuke holding a poupou (carved post), made by Stacy Gordine, the great-great-nephew of celebrated carvers Pine and Hone Taiapa.

**Stacy Gordine, *Hei Tiki Ruatepupuke*, 2009**

cattle bone, pāua, black goat horn, Te Papa Tongarewa Museum of New Zealand, 2010-0025-1, purchased 2010

in Aotearoa New Zealand and internationally have generated a number of books that contextualise their own collections within Māori culture,[26] and some of these are promoted as surveys of Māori art. These are fundamentally institutional constructs of Māori art history based on collecting. Publications such as *Te Maori* (a companion to the acclaimed eponymous exhibition in 1984–1986) and *Māori: Art and Culture* (first published as the catalogue for a British Museum exhibition, 1996) feature essays by highly regarded scholars but, as a whole, these lack the scope of practice and time that *Toi Te Mana* proposes.[27]

In terms of contemporary 'gallery' art, there are hundreds of catalogues of solo exhibitions and themed group exhibitions examining a range of practices and cultural issues. The major survey publication of contemporary Māori art, *Mataora* (1996), presented an overview of the scene, and presented short profiles of selected artists.[28] The *Taiāwhio* series of interviews with contemporary artists (2002 and 2007), and the *Pūrangiaho* catalogue (2001), accompanied eponymous exhibitions of contemporary Māori art.[29] Julie Paama-Pengelly's *Māori Art and Design: Weaving, Painting, Carving and Architecture* (2010) is important in that it presents one of the first surveys of Māori art written by Māori from an artist's perspective. More recently Rangihīroa Panoho's *Māori Art: History, Architecture, Landscape and Theory* (2015) has provided a diverse range of ideas and concepts with which to consider this field. We believe that their promise invites expansion through the larger and more rigorous examination of Māori art practice that *Toi Te Mana* offers.

## Ngā kupu toi – the language of Māori art

The title *Toi Te Mana* derives from the whakataukī 'Toitū te whenua, toitū te mana, toitū te reo', which instructs us to hold fast (toitū) to our lands, authority and language. 'Toi' is a word that encompasses both art and knowledge. 'Toi te mana' encapsulates all that this book needs to be, a manifesto for the mana of Māori art that can be seen within a wider movement to document and celebrate Māori culture and values.

In *Toi Te Mana*, we lay down some foundational ideas about what a Māori art history might be. As with other ways of looking at art history, it is not merely looking at Māori art that makes it Māori art history. Rather we present here new methods and terminology to help understand, interpret and appreciate Māori art. This may challenge some readers who have been reading other books or have been conditioned through education or the media to think differently. Some words, for instance, we argue cannot and should not be translated into English as the nuances of the practice or concept get lost in translation; examples include moko, tapu and mana. These terms help explain the art that we are examining here. They also firmly ground our viewing in Aotearoa New Zealand. We encourage readers to become confident in using these terms, familiarising themselves with the explanations by Mead, Te Awekotuku, Tapsell and others. We also encourage you to pronounce them properly out of respect for their importance and for the art being discussed.

This book focuses on Māori art, which we define simply as 'art made by Māori'. The politics of this was often played out through exhibitions and writing in the 1980s and 1990s when this idea was challenged, and some argued that those who did not have whakapapa (our definition of being Māori) *could* make Māori art, citing examples such as Gordon Walters and Theo Schoon. Mead was on the other end of a spectrum of voices: he is very specific about his definitions of Māori art and artist, arguing that 'Māori art might be defined as art that looks Māori, feels Māori, is done by Māori following the styles, canons of taste and values of Māori culture.'[30] This is a controversial view. We argue here for a middle ground: for this, we use the concept of a kete that holds Māori art forms and ideas that have survived through colonisation. There are not many, but what *are* in there are very precious: we need to ensure they are kept there, and made only by Māori. One example is moko – an art form that can only be placed by Māori, on Māori. Practitioners have recognised, however, that they need to pay the rent, and that many others are also keen to wear these designs, so they have created a practice they called kirituhi. This may *look* like moko, but it is for non-Māori: it can also speak about the recipient's genealogy (as distinct from whakapapa) and their lives, but it is different. That does not prevent this art from being Māori art – it has been made by Māori – but it is not moko. The story of Māori art is one that diversifies as Māori re-established their connections to the rest of the Pacific and engaged with Europe and other parts of the world, creating new art forms with their own reason for being.

Robyn Kahukiwa, *Hineteiwaiwa*, 2017
acrylic on canvas, 455 x 601mm, private collection

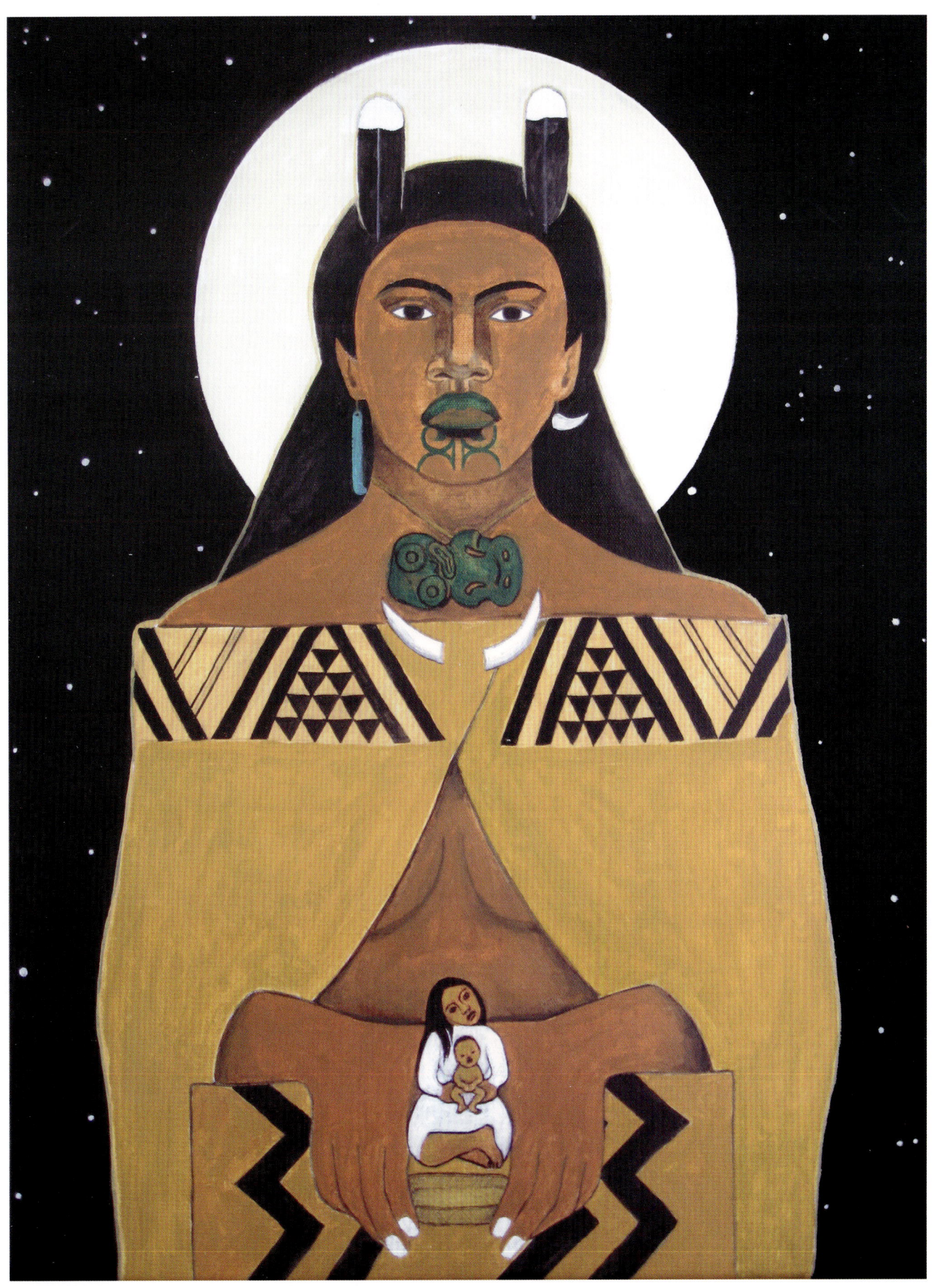

Our research on Māori art practice has identified three recurring themes across these kete: whenua, tikanga and whakapapa. The importance of the whenua in locating Māori as the tangata whenua, the people of the land, and providing the sustenance and materials to make art, as described in Te Kete Tuatea, is brought into sharp focus by the stories of the impact on the art of land loss contained in Te Kete Tuauri. The lamentation of this loss and the struggle to have land returned is demonstrated time and time again through the art in Te Kete Aronui. Artistic change in response to new materials, tools, environments and ideas is a consistent feature in all of the kete, while tikanga, in the form of values, functions and interpretations, remains a constant presence in much of the work. In Te Kete Aronui, we are presented with the situation of artists of Māori descent who have little or no connection to their cultural heritage, and in this book we embrace their contribution as they have whakapapa Māori. Whakapapa pervades all aspects of work in the three kete, through ancestral descent lines, inherited traditions of art, and lineages within whare wānanga and other artistic institutions. The book reveals that whenua, tikanga and whakapapa intersect, overlap and weave together in a multitude of different ways to create an understanding of what Māori art is and what it is to be a Māori artist.

Other key terms are used throughout. Mauri can be explained as a life force that lives around people and all parts of the natural world. The mauri of a person or place can be transferred into a small object to be conveyed into a more permanent and usually larger work later. Te Awekotuku writes of one example of mauri: 'Every piece of the well-dressed Maori's wardrobe had a significance, an essential mauri, or life force, which linked the taonga to the natural world, and in the end, to Papatuanuku herself.'[31] Historian Matutaera (Tuta) Nihoniho (Ngāti Porou, 1850–1914), on the other hand, gave the example of a stone or a piece of wood that was used as a symbol of the mauri of a person.[32] For Waikato-Tainui, the mauri of the ancestor Uenuku was brought to Aotearoa in the form of a stone and the mauri was later transferred into a large carving that bears his name. Ngāi Tahu understand pounamu as having mauri, which is transferred into everything that is made from it, including adornments and weaponry.[33] Mauri surrounds all taonga tuku iho, giving them life.

Mana is a concept of power and authority and was historically inherited, although today it is often achieved through one's actions, such as the contribution of an important artist whose work earns them respect and prestige. There were different types of mana: two of the most important here are mana whenua (rights of the land) and mana tangata (responsibilities of the people). Both are complementary and reinforce a sense of dignity generated from one's actions. A carving, for instance, can gain mana through association with successive kaitiaki (guardians); if these people are well known, then the carving gains in mana. A hei tiki (neck pendant of human form) fashioned from a named toki may have double the mana because of the connection with two primary ancestors after whom they are named.[34]

Taonga tuku iho are often imbued with wairua (spirit). Unlike mauri, wairua is non-physical and flows in and around the world we live in. Taonga naturally have wairua, and their wairua makes them distinct, as Mead explains: 'Today we speak of "taha wairua" that is the spiritual aspect and it is generally acknowledged that a major difference between "artefact" and "taonga" is that there is a taha wairua to the Māori concept.'[35]

Tapu is a way of regulating Māori life and is central to many of the works discussed here. It is a practice that serves to care for and protect people and ensure that balance and harmony are maintained. Some art forms are by their very nature tapu. Moko, for instance, involves the most sacred part of the body – the head – as well as the shedding of blood, and therefore it is essential that tapu restrictions are put in place to ensure the safety of the recipient and of all those involved. Even writing about moko needs to be undertaken in a safe place. Care is taken by reciting karakia (prayers), and ensuring the activity takes place away from areas where food is prepared and consumed. Failure to adhere to these conditions can lead to serious illness or even death. We know of contemporary accounts where this has happened, and therefore we take care in how we practise as Māori art historians.

Taonga tuku iho are central to this book and form a whakapapa of Māori history. Some works are made as objects which become taonga over time due to their association with people and/or specific episodes; indeed, Mead and Tapsell both emphasise the importance of kōrero, mana and tapu in relation to taonga. One example of this is a kahu kiwi (a kiwi feather cloak), now on loan to the Whanganui Regional Museum, which traces its whakapapa from Mere Ngareta (Ngāti Hauiti, Ngāti Apa), who died in 1898. During her lifetime, Ngareta became well known in relation to land sales around Whanganui and she represented her people a number of times in cases brought before the Native Land Court. The kahu kiwi was handed down through the generations, to her great-great-grandsons Richard and John. Richard deposited the cloak with the museum in 1992, probably after his appointment as one of their educators. This kākahu (dress cloak) is distinguished because of its feathers, as well as for the history of the woman whose name is associated with the cloak. In the eyes of her descendants, this is not merely a cloak associated with a tupuna or ancestor – it *is* the tupuna. A taonga tuku iho is addressed as 'grandmother' or 'grandfather', and is the living embodiment of that person.

Other works are taonga right from the moment of their production. They are made to signify relationships or to record events, and are always intended to be treated as taonga. These are usually named and are significant art forms in their own right, such as weaponry, cloaks and adornment. Such taonga are remembered in oral histories. Ngāti Tūwharetoa ariki (high-born chief) Te Heuheu III Iwikau recorded the story of a tribal ear pendant that was so special it was named Kaukau-matua in a mōteatea (lament) he composed in the mid-nineteenth century.[36] Other adornments that were taonga from their inception were Tamore (which belonged to Ngāti Hinemihi, a hapū of Ngāti Maniapoto) and Whakatere-kohukohu (taken by Ngāpuhi leader Hongi Hika during a raid in 1828, and later presented by the Ngāpuhi chief Hone Heke to Governor George Grey).[37]

Legislation has sought to define what taonga might encompass. The Protected Objects Act 1975 protects and regulates the circulation of a range of objects, including 'Taonga tūturu', defined in section 2(1) of the Act as 'an object that — (a) relates to Māori culture, history, or society; and (b) was, or appears to have been, — (i) manufactured or modified in New Zealand by Māori; or (ii) brought into New Zealand by Māori; or (iii) used by Māori; and (c) is more than 50 years old'.[38] Under this definition, we might include contemporary works by artists such as Ralph Hotere, who first exhibited in the late 1950s. Mead and Tapsell's parameters of mana and kōrero would apply to many of Hotere's works, although whether there might be a case for contemporary art to be considered tapu is contentious. The difference in the understandings of what makes something a taonga might change once the Waitangi Tribunal report into the Wai 262 claim, *Ko Aotearoa Tenei*, is actioned: the report recommends 'wide-ranging reforms to laws and policies relating to Māori culture and identity'.[39]

One development we hope to see very soon is Māori art history written in te reo Māori. Our ancestral narratives of Māori art have been passed down to us in our language, and te reo continues to be an important medium for communicating practice in wānanga and institutions where customary arts are taught. It is in te reo that the narratives contained in the art and architecture of wharenui are brought into open discussion during pōwhiri, hui, tangihanga and other marae events. Yet the writing of Māori art history is still predominantly in the language of Pacific explorers, colonisers and collectors – English, French and German. We the authors have been nurturing the next generation of Māori art historians, many of whom have been raised with te reo as their first language, supported by their whānau and in the kōhanga reo and kura kaupapa language nests and schools. Many of these students come from iwi that have a degree of economic and cultural autonomy after settling with the Crown over historic grievances presented to the Waitangi Tribunal. Their perspectives on the story of Māori art may be different to ours as they mature into senior scholars and embark on writing, possibly in te reo, the survey works that will follow *Toi Te Mana*.

*Toi Te Mana* is our koha (gift or offering) to art history, to our ancestors and to all those who are interested in Te Ao Māori. How we have approached the material in this book is shaped by our whakapapa. While we have covered much of the artistic world, we appreciate that there is still much more research to be undertaken. Māori art history offers here a lens through which to understand and conceptualise Māori worlds and, by extension, can contribute nuanced understandings to complex histories of art globally. Though the language and concepts used here are Māori, we encourage readers to question whether they may have relevance for their own art histories.

He iti, ahakoa he pounamu – though it is small, it is significant.

# PART 1
# TE KETE TUATEA

Tāne's epic journey to collect Ngā Kete e Toru brought the knowledges and tikanga that inform creative practice into the mortal world. The story forms one of many celestial and ancestral accounts of art from the Polynesian homeland of Hawaiki in an everlasting cycle of creation, and also in the ancient and contemporary cultural landscapes of Aotearoa. Within this Kete Tuatea, basket of light, are the celestial and ancestral explanations for whakairo (chapter 2), kākahu (chapter 3), and moko and body adornment (chapter 6). The stories feature characters who establish the tikanga of art practice and who perpetuate the karakia and whakapapa that artists need to situate themselves and their work in a complex social and ecological environment.

Ancestral stories describe the Polynesian migrations to Aotearoa, and the great voyaging waka that brought the ancestors to settle this whenua (chapter 1) – the precursors of the elaborately carved waka taua (war canoes) that navigated its islands and waterways. Whakairo rākau (carving) and kōwhaiwhai (decorative patterns on rafters) provide a highly developed visual language for explaining whakapapa and whenua, and in different regions these became differentiated through distinctive hapū and iwi practices and styles. Within these arts remain traces of the Polynesian origins of Māori art, as seen in some of the figurative forms and decorative motifs carved into wood, stone and bone. While art practices could only be sustained in settled communities, toi whenua or rock art (chapter 5) is the enduring reminder of seasonal migrations of Māori hunters and gatherers who sought to draw their world in charcoal and ochre on the surfaces of caves and cliff overhangs.

Textiles and fibre arts were used to create clothing, and to clad whare. Women makers were largely responsible for kākahu, including huru kurī (dogskin cloaks), kahu kiwi, raincapes and sandals – and, of course, kete; whereas the thatch bundles and fibre ropes that were used to bind and clad traditional Māori buildings were mainly made by men. In Te Kete Tuatea, the complementary roles of men, women and LGBTQI+ in the making of Māori art and its stories are explained (chapter 7).

Whereas waka represent movement and journeying, whare represent settlement and belonging (chapter 4). In their many manifestations, from simple wharepuni (sleeping houses) to utilitarian kāuta (cooking sheds) to elaborate pātaka (raised food storehouses) and wharenui (larger houses), these structures sheltered whānau and hapū on their tūrangawaewae. This architecture connected their living inhabitants to the ancestral whenua on which they, and the kāinga (village) as a whole, were located. Pātaka were so closely associated with traditional lifeways that only those that were on sufficiently large Māori landholdings survived beyond the nineteenth century.

Customary Māori art is not unchanging. The arts of Te Kete Tuatea reveal the dynamism of practice and the transformation of forms and concepts as Māori explored and adapted their artistic culture to new environments and materials, while continuing to adhere to tikanga that had its origins in the creation story.

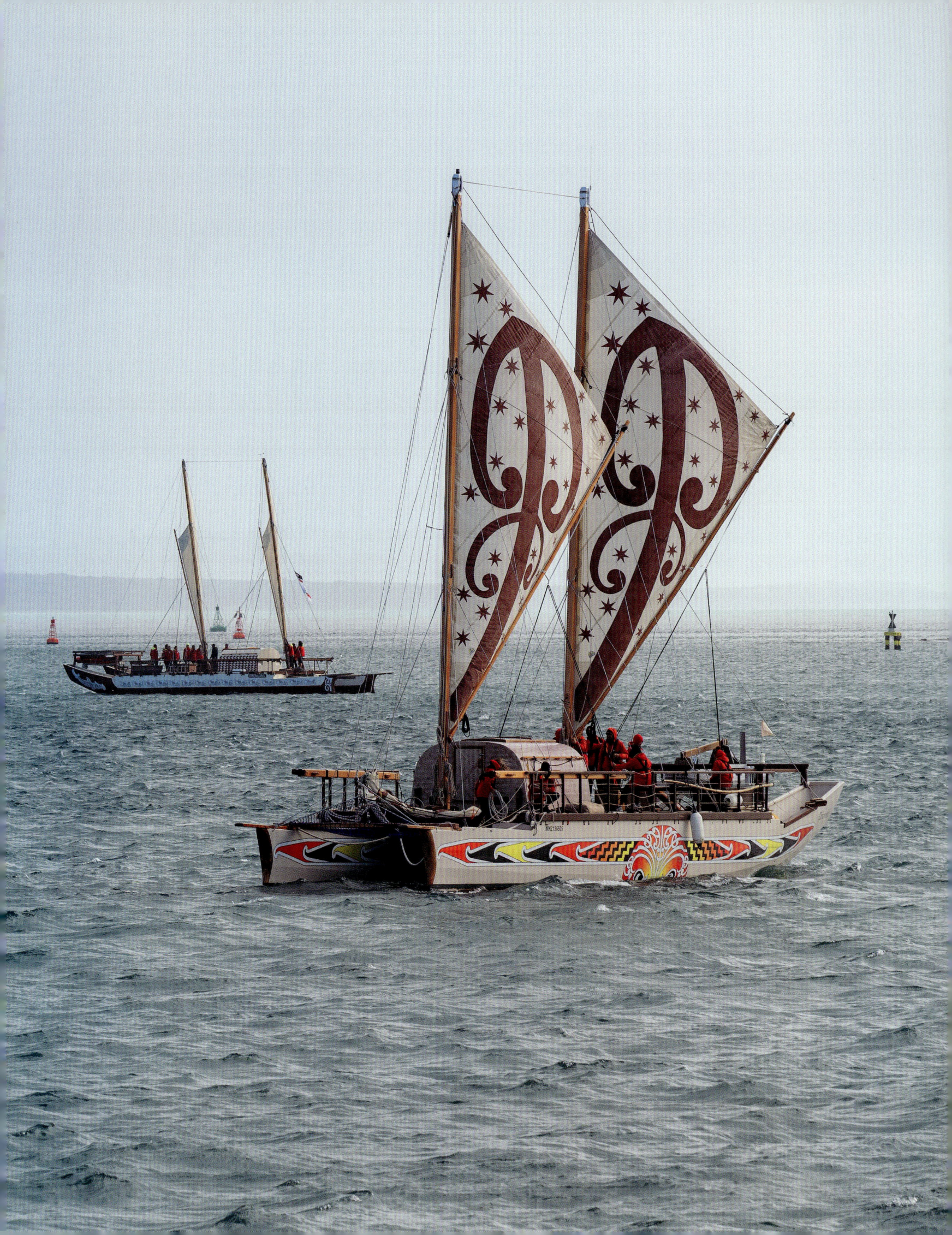

# 1 NGĀ MOMO WAKA
## MOANA, MIGRATION AND MĀORI
### NGARINO ELLIS

*E kutangitangi, e kutangitangi / how the canoe flies*
*E kura tiwaka taua / how the fine paddles sound*
*E kura tiwaka taua / all together!*
*E kura wawawa wai / my grand canoe*
*E kura wawawa wai-i-i! / a treasure of the waters!*[1]

Waka – iwi – hapū – whānau: these concepts shape how we as Māori identify ourselves. They are an integral part of our mihi (greeting) to explain who we are. Waka as canoes are both a physical and a metaphorical manifestation of identity. Māori ancestors travelled from Hawaiki in the Pacific on oceangoing waka pahī, and they created a number of other waka forms for navigating lakes and rivers. In a mihi, descendants of those ancestors identify as a group with the waka their ancestors arrived on. Waka were recorded in several narratives about deities whose vessels are historically significant because of the relationship with those atua.

The rise and fall of different waka traditions mirrors the ebb and flow of Māori culture. Waka taua are an important example. This waka form originated in the 1700s with the rise in inter-hapū warfare, but their construction waned after a hiatus in conflict in the 1850s, when hapū and iwi patrons commissioned carvers to build meeting houses as icons of mana instead. The seizure and destruction of hundreds of waka by colonial forces in the New Zealand Wars, because of their role in maintaining Māori mobility and their cultural significance, reduced the number of active waka in use. From the 1930s the waka taua re-emerged as a statement of survival, driven by influential Māori leaders. From the 1980s, a renaissance in building oceangoing waka and in traditional wayfinding has created exciting opportunities for tohunga tārai waka (expert canoe builders). It has also brought a reconnection with the Pacific, as one example of the ongoing cycles of Māori art through time and space.

### Celestial stories of waka

A number of kōrero tell the origins of waka. One of the best-known cosmological narratives is the story of Māui, who used his grandmother Murirangawhenua's jawbone to fashion a matau (fishhook). He travelled out to sea with his brothers on a waka and hooked a large fish that was later named Te Ika a Māui; this became the North Island, while his waka became Te Wai Pounamu (the South Island), and the punga (anchor stone) became Rakiura (Stewart Island). Other tribal narratives offer alternatives, embedded in their particular landscape: Ngāti Porou maintain that Māui's waka was named *Nukutaimemeha*, which now rests upside down on the top of their ancestral mountain Hikurangi.[2]

For Ngāi Tahu, their tribal lands of the South Island are called Te Waka o Aoraki after their ancestor Aoraki, son of Ranginui and Papatūānuku, who descended from the heavens with three of his brothers to visit their mother. They went fishing but could not catch anything so decided to

*Tairāwhiti* and *Hinemoana* (in the background) at Panepane, Tauranga Moana as part of the opening ceremony to commence Te Hau Kōmaru National Waka Hourua Festival 2021.
Te Ao Mārama – Tauranga City Libraries, photograph by Nathan Pettigrew

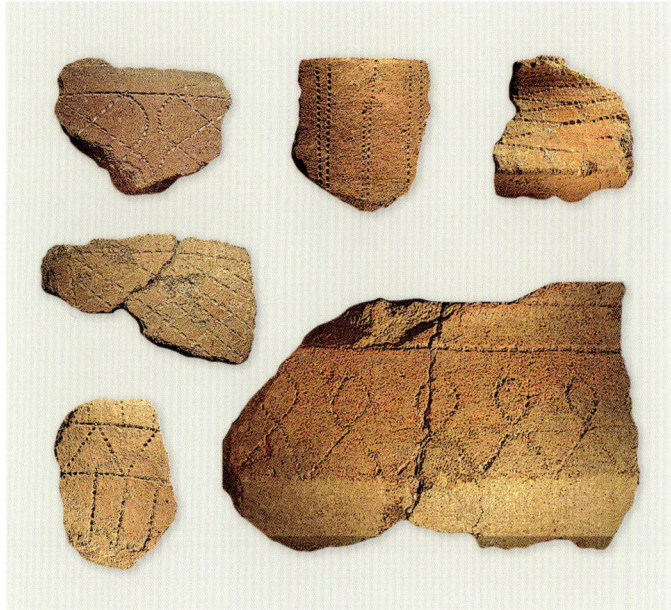

Above: Lapita pottery from the Otea site, Kapa Island, Vava'u, Tonga. Pottery made by Lapita ancestors represents an important cultural marker, which has helped track the migration of Pacific ancestors across Te Moananui a Kiwa.
photograph by David Burley

Right: A number of different styles of sail were used by Pacific ancestors to travel across Te Moananui a Kiwa and down to Aotearoa.
Anderson, *Journal of the Royal Society of New Zealand*, 2017

Opposite: This crowded and probably composite scene reveals a number of activities, including a chief in his dogskin cloak pointing out the direction to paddle, and paddlers in an array of profile poses.
**Sydney Parkinson, *A New Zealand war canoe*, from 'A Collection of Drawings made in the Countries visited by Captain Cook in his First Voyage, 1768–1771'**
British Library, BL747446, Bridgeman Images

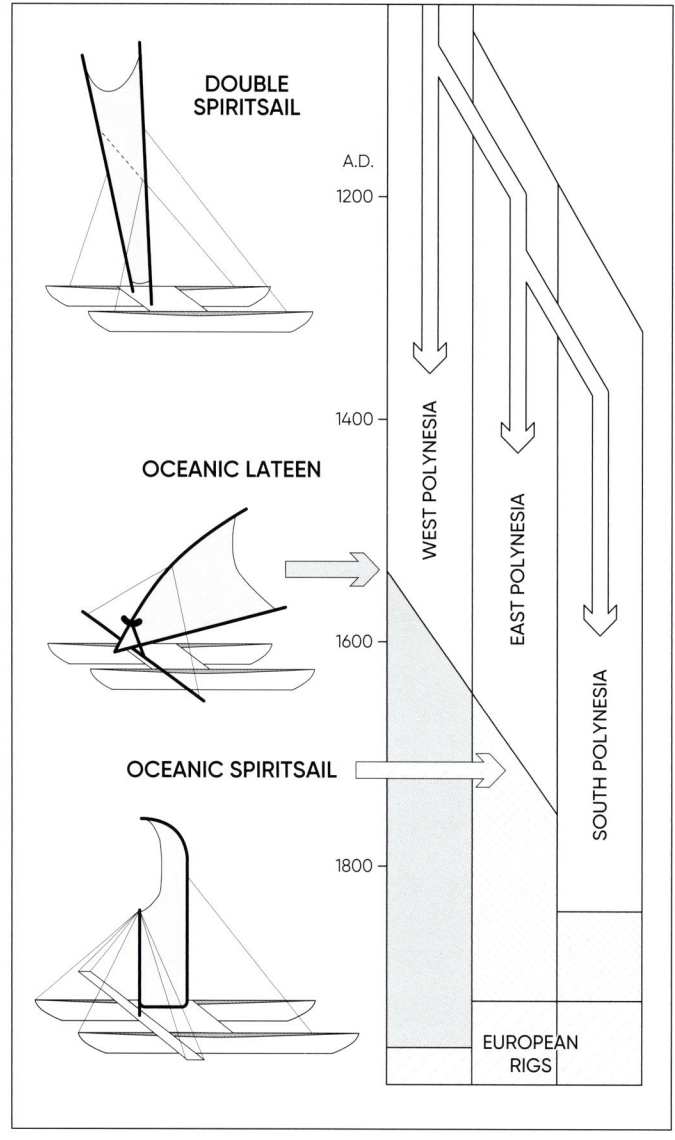

return to their father in the sky. However, the karakia needed to make this transition were chanted incorrectly, which resulted in Aoraki and his brothers unable to return to the heavens. They eventually all turned to stone, thus creating some of the mountains along the spine of the South Island.[3]

These narratives provide an important background for the ancestors who followed. The stories intermingle and remind us that our history is complex and nuanced. The stories are told and retold each time a waka is built, through karakia that are chanted from the beginning, with the cutting down of the tree, through to the final launching of the waka. These narratives are also embedded in the tikanga that surround the actual making of the waka, and they guide those involved to ensure that the values laid down in the narratives are maintained.

From the celestial narratives, we shift to stories from Hawaiki in the Pacific and into Aotearoa. The names of tohunga tārai waka have been recorded through the generations. In Hawaiki there were a number of waka builders who created carved waka pahī. Taranaki narratives record that the tohunga Toto built the great canoe *Aotea*, which was captained by his son-in-law Turi. Some waka that returned to Hawaiki were then recarved and renamed: Kupe travelled to Aotearoa on board the *Matahourua*, and when he returned to Hawaiki the waka was remade fit for Nukutawhiti to bring it back to Aotearoa. Nukutawhiti built a whare wānanga soon after he landed in the Hokianga in the Far North, in order to preserve their traditions. Sometimes these wānanga were physical structures; other times they were metaphorical.

NGĀ MOMO WAKA – MOANA, MIGRATION AND MĀORI

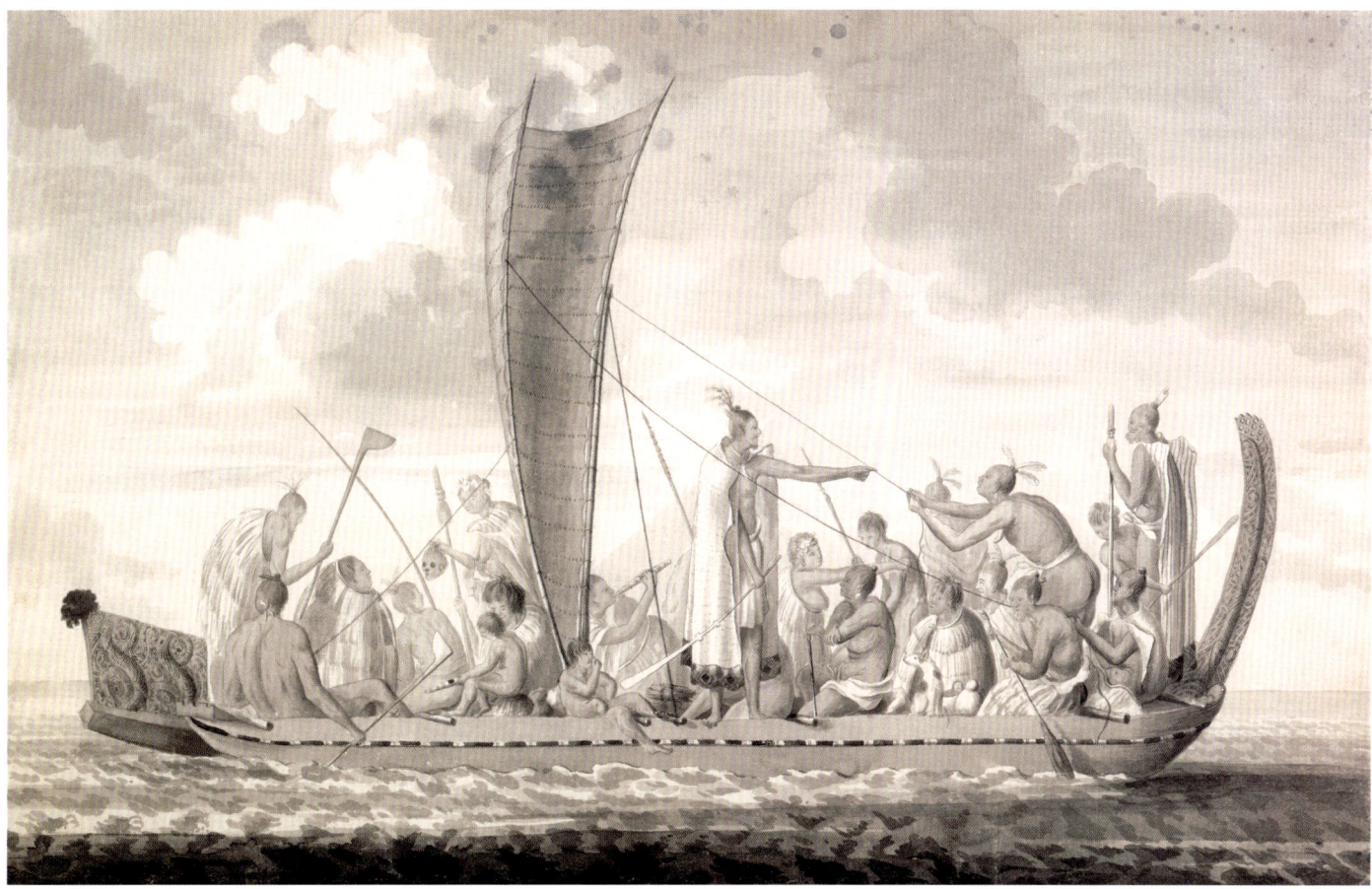

### Archaeological narratives of waka – mana moana

Archaeologists track migrations across the Pacific both eastward and westward. The most accepted narrative locates Māori ancestors in Southeast Asia around 50,000 years ago, from where they travelled in a series of migrations across the Pacific – initially to Australia, New Guinea and the Solomons, and by 1600BCE they had arrived in Melanesia. Archaeologists have identified a particular type of culture that emerged around this time, which they named Lapita after the site in New Caledonia where evidence was first discovered. Over fifty sites have since been identified across 6400km, from c.1600BCE in Fiji to 500BCE in Sāmoa. This Lapita culture produced unique stone adzes, small tattooing chisels, ornaments of shell beads and sharks' teeth and, most importantly, pottery stamped with abstract and figurative designs organised in bands.

But even Lapita culture kept changing. By 300CE there was a distinction between Fiji (in the region that came to be known as Melanesia) and Tonga and Sāmoa (in Polynesia): this was noticeable in stone adzes, fishhooks and personal adornment. Still the people migrated east, arriving in Tahiti and the Cook Islands c.1000CE, and from there further east to the Marquesas and Rapanui Easter Island, north to Hawai'i, and southwest to Aotearoa c.1300CE. In just over a thousand years the world's biggest ocean, covering 16 million sq km, had been peopled.

Waka were used and reused as the ancestors moved across Te Moananui a Kiwa (the Pacific). Over the centuries they reconsidered the most effective styles of canoe for the voyages envisaged. The availability of different materials such as kauri and tōtara prompted different styles of waka.

The connections between people were forged on the ocean. In Papua New Guinea, trade came in many forms, as anthropologists Nicholas Thomas, Susanne Küchler and Lissant Bolton describe: 'Traders never just traded in goods. They also traded in information, in stories and gossip. They learned about the whole region that they visited, and became familiar with the knowledge and practice of its peoples.'[4] In relation to art forms, they note,

> Trade shaped art in the sense that materials, whole objects, motifs and styles travelled. Trade shaped art, too, in the sense that it sometimes transformed local sociality … Art

was also vital to trade. Most obviously, the canoes that materially enabled the trade were works of art, arguably often the greatest works their communities produced.[5]

Tongan Fijian scholar Epeli Hauʻofa[6] provides a useful analogy for understanding and bringing together the broad geographic spread of nations across the Pacific. Rather than thinking about the moana as separating us, he advises, it is better to consider it as bringing us all together. Rather than focusing on the size of landmasses, which to all stretches of the imagination are modest in the context of the ocean they sit in, it is more appropriate to consider the land as a base, and to think about the size of the land as stretching up to the heavens, and down to the core in the earth. He reminds us, too, of the powerful trade lines that flowed through the Pacific, from one community to the next and back. People travelled along these lines, bringing gifts and materials that were exchanged across communities.

### Ancestral narratives of waka hourua

Around 1200CE, Pacific ancestors began travelling to Aotearoa. Kupe was the first voyager, while hunting down a giant octopus on an oceangoing canoe named *Matahourua*. This waka was made up of composite parts, with an extension at either end of the hull (the haumi at the prow and tauropa at the stern), two bailers and an anchor.[7] It was large enough to hold his wife, children and sixty-one crew.[8] When Kupe arrived back in the Pacific his canoe was reshaped and used to make another voyage to Aotearoa, this time captained by Nukutawhiti.[9]

It is still unclear exactly what these oceangoing waka looked like.[10] They have been described as waka pahī or waka hourua (double-hulled sailing canoes), and were either composite or made from a single log. These were highly specialised craft, typically 18–21m long and able to hold at least fifty people, along with animals such as kurī (dogs) and kiore (rats), plants, food and water.

Narratives record specific details of some waka. Whātonga captained a composite canoe named *Te Hawai* (later renamed *Kurahaupō*), which Te Rangi Hīroa described like this: 'The canoe hull had three blunt joins (*haumi tuporo*), 26 thwarts (*taumanu*), two bailing places (*puna wai*), and two anchors. Wash boards (*pairi*) were added to the bow and it was painted with red ochre (*kokowai whenua*) mixed with shark oil.'[11] Each of the thwarts along the sides was named.

Waka hourua were made from two separate logs with extensions on the bow and stern, with a karaho (deck) on top, with a mahau – a small structure covered with mats and tapa (barkcloth) – to give shelter from the elements. The rigging consisted of two toko (masts) to carry the rā (sails). The hull was painted with kōkōwai (red pigment) – a common practice to denote something or someone of mana. Many of these terms are still used today for waka components.[12]

Some waka hourua may have sailed to Aotearoa. Archaeologist Atholl Anderson (Ngāi Tahu) argues that the ancestors employed the double spritsail rig (a sail with two separate masts anchored on the deck) on their waka.[13] The sails were essential to move quickly down from the Pacific to take advantage of a break in the summer tradewinds caused by El Niño events. Māori retained sail technology for at least 600 years after settlement in some areas. Dutch artist Isaack Gilsemans recorded only one of twenty double-hulled waka as having a sail in 1642; and in 1769 Sydney Parkinson, artist on Cook's first voyage, recorded waka hourua with sails further north, in Whakatāne.[14] Sails disappeared from the early nineteenth century: they were revived in the 1970s as part of the rejuvenation of waka culture.

Waka hourua may have been double-outrigger vessels. According to some sources the canoes *Tākitimu*, *Te Arawa* and *Horouta* had double outriggers,[15] and used the ama (outrigger) to stabilise the main hull in heavy weather and rough seas.[16] As with the sail technology, the waka ama did not survive much into the nineteenth century, as other styles of waka addressed community needs better and the large oceangoing waka were no longer required. Only four ama have survived, including two from the South Island. This style has recently been revived, however, as part of the reinvigoration of waka culture.

There are many accounts of aspects of the waka-building process in Hawaiki and the tools used. The toki were given special names and some held particular status within the community. Historian Mere Whaanga (Ngāti Rakaipaaka) describes the adzes used to make the waka *Tākitimu*: 'The adzes of the tohunga were made from stones named Kohurau, Ka-ra, Anewa and pounamu. The most tapu of these was the adze of greenstone called Te Awhiorangi, said to have been used by Tamatea Arikinui to cut the ngaru tupe (breakers) on the *Takitimu*'s voyage to Aotearoa. Other adzes were Te-Whiro-Nui, Rakuraku-o-Tawhaki, Matangirei and Hui-Te-Rangi-Ora.'[17]

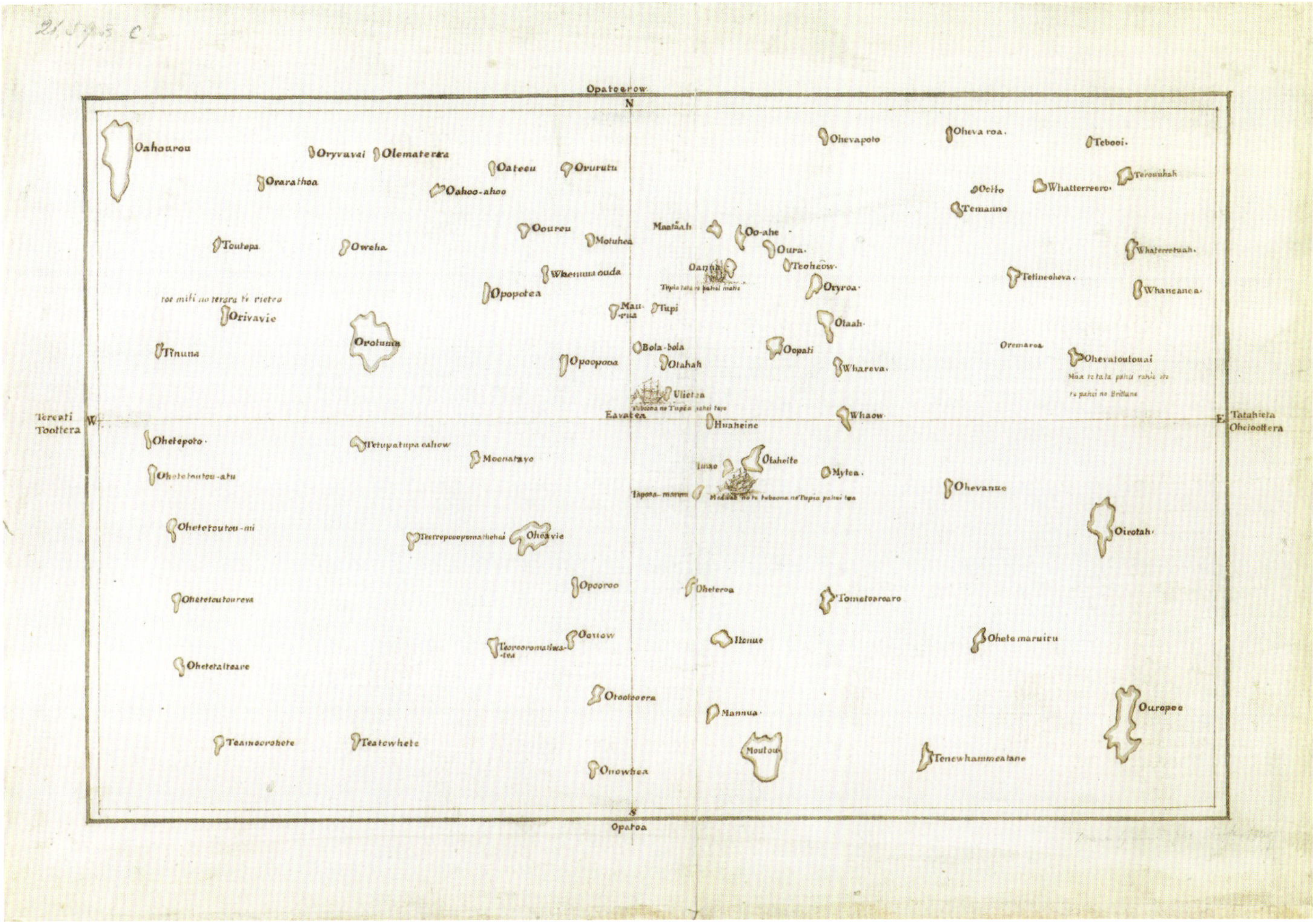

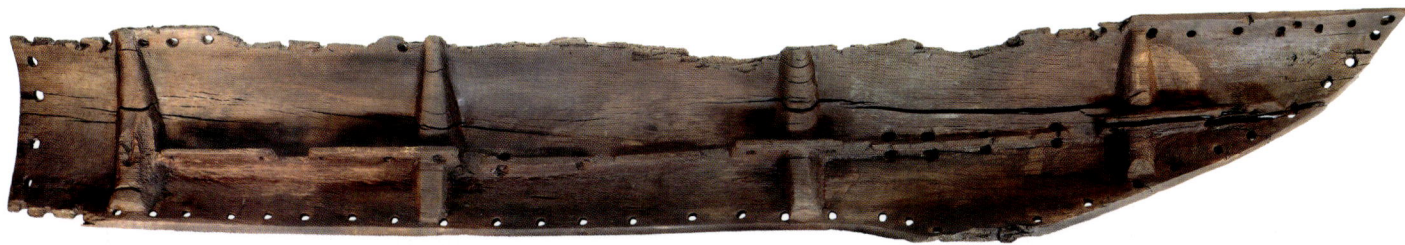

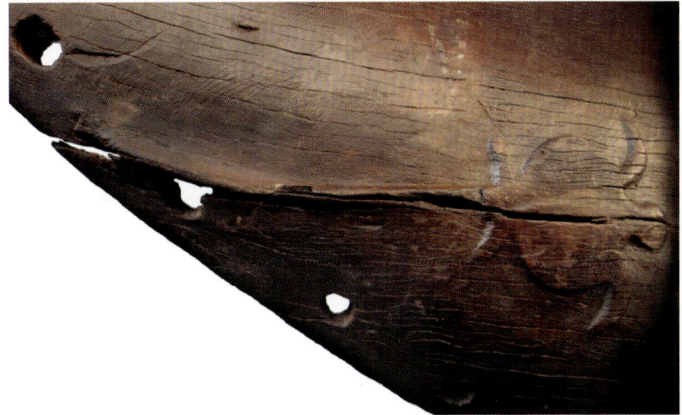

Top: Map drawn by Tupaia (1725–1770), of the Society Islands. This is considered the earliest known drawn map of the Pacific by a Pacific person. It is quite different, of course, to star maps used by those in the Caroline Islands and elsewhere, made of wood, shells and fibre. Its complexity reveals the depth of knowledge in the Pacific of their environment.
British Library, BL3292585, Bridgeman Images

Middle: Lashing holes of the Anaweka waka.
Irwin et al., *Journal of Pacific Archaeology*, 2017

Bottom: Depictions of turtles are extremely rare in Māori art. This example was carved on the exterior of a waka found at Anaweka, on the west coast of the upper South Island. This is the oldest waka found in Aotearoa New Zealand, and dates to c.1400.
Irwin et al., *Journal of Pacific Archaeology*, 2017

Ngāhue was the captain of the *Tāwhiwhirangi* waka, and he was the kaitiaki of the pounamu adze named Te Kaoreore. This adze was used to carve a 40m waka hourua named *Ngārākaurua a Atuamatua* (the two trunks of Atuamatua), after an important ancestor whose sons also made waka and sailed them to Aotearoa, including Houmaitawhiti (father of Tamatekapua).[18]

Paddles were considered sacred in Hawaiki. The ancestor Turi tricked his brother-in-law Taua into fetching the paddles named Rangihoronoa and Kautūkiterangi from the waka named *Taikarairoa*.[19] There were six decorated paddles on the *Tākitimu* waka, possibly not for practical use, but rather for political purposes: rangatira would hold a paddle to symbolise clearly their rank. Bailers and anchors were also often named as part of tying all components of the waka together with those on board.

Not all ancestors arrived in Aotearoa on waka. Paikea (Ngāti Porou) arrived on the back of a tohorā (whale), or, in some versions, *as* a tohorā; and Moerewa (Nukutawhiti's daughter) arrived from the Pacific 'on the back of a taniwha (water demon) named Takauere. This taniwha now resides in Lake Omapere.'[20]

### The earliest waka in Aotearoa

The oldest known surviving waka in Aotearoa was discovered in January 2012 in an estuary at Anaweka on the west coast of the South Island. This pushes back a possible arrival date of Māori in New Zealand to c.1150CE.[21] The hull of the waka is made from local mataī and the caulking is tōtara; the latter has been radiocarbon-dated to 1350–1400CE. Archaeologist Geoff Irwin and others believe that the waka was repaired at around this time using this material, and it may indeed be some 200 years older than this date: they suggest a possible date of at least 1150–1200CE.

A plank from a waka represents a transitional period: the four raised ribs along the length are similar to those on vaka from the Southern Cook Islands and East Polynesia, yet the haumi – the prow or hull extender – is similar to later Māori forms. Holes along the edge were used for lashing to other pieces of the composite waka (since lost). This technique is found in later architectural forms, which suggests that the lashing technique was retained in the practice of builders of waka and whare in Aotearoa (as was the case from the 1800s onwards). Similar canoe pieces have been found, but not from this very early period. In 1997, for example, a piece of decking from a very old waka was found in Rakiura Stewart Island, which is made with similar materials and technology, but with a later dating (fourteenth century). This suggests that haumi may have continued to be made for at least 100–200 years after arrival, before the evolution of the taurapa (carved sternpost) form that is still in use today.

The haumi from Anaweka features a raised carving of a sea turtle on the exterior of the prow. This motif is extremely rare: there are only four Māori objects extant with this design (all in Te Papa Tongarewa). Turtle imagery is important in the Pacific, and is depicted on everything from tatau (tattoo), such as in Tokelau, to string games, rock art and tapa. The depiction of animal forms such as these – and the bonito fish carved into a stone breastplate (chapter 7) – locate the makers firmly in the Pacific. In making these works they are creating visual reminders of their whakapapa, and reinforcing stories that have been passed on down the generations about these animals and the ancestors involved with them.

Waka components show an important transitional step from Pacific geometric-style art to a distinctly Māori curvilinear style. The haumi form of prow changed over several hundred years as different styles of waka emerged as everyday vessels. This resulted in the creation of the tauihu prow with its carved and decorated surfaces that, on a waka taua, are sometimes very elaborate.

A number of haumi reflect experimentations by carvers as they introduced design elements into the prow form. The carver of a waka discovered in four parts in Waitore in Taranaki in 1975 has created a projection of almost 1m out from the bow. The surface is covered in six bands of notched lines – similar to Lapita compositions in the Pacific – and the artist has included two double spirals nicked in with the edge of an adze at the base as a design innovation.[22] On a projection almost at the tip of the haumi is a small bird form, in keeping with the accepted animal imagery of the period 1200–1500CE. The haumi is dated c.1380–1500CE. The notching may have been one strategy to recall generations in the whakapapa, and has been used in at least one other haumi dated 1500–1800, found in the Waikato (Waikato Museum, 1977/60/7).

Further north, at Doubtless Bay, carvers in the 1400s were also trialling new motifs, in particular the manaia, on their

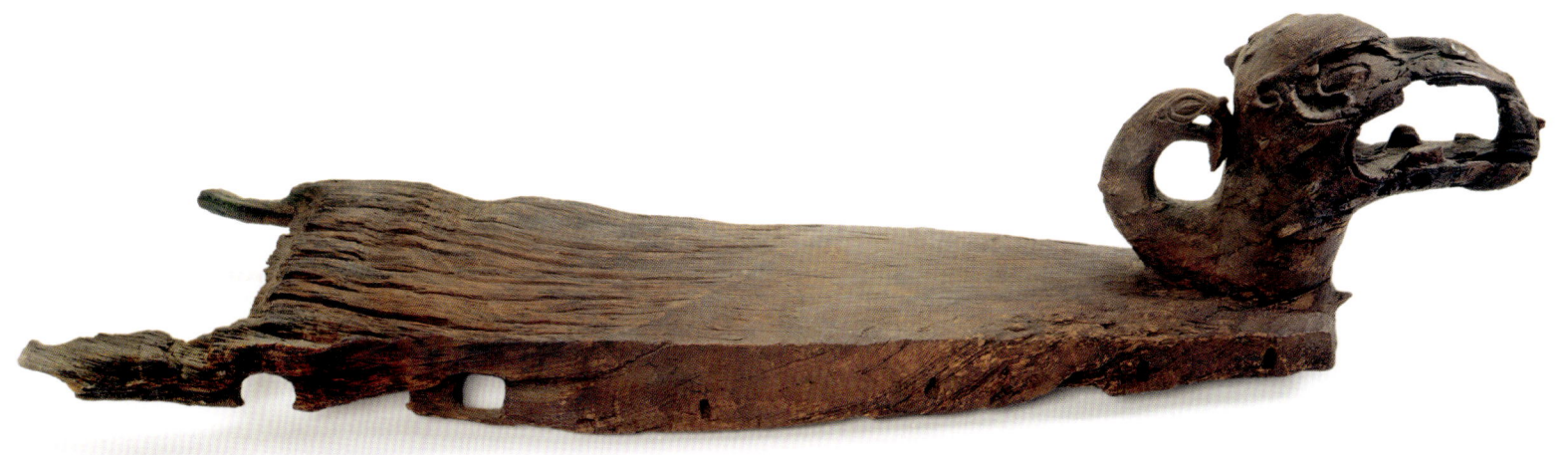

Haumi (bow cover) found near Tokerau Beach, Doubtless Bay.
Its early style manaia are distinctive.
Tāmaki Paenga Hira Auckland War Memorial Museum, AM3078

haumi. The manaia motif represents a spiritual guardian, and is often shown as a beaked figure. Some time between 1200 and 1500, a Ngāti Kahu carver from this area created a prow that included an early-style manaia face with a large mouth with teeth, and a small figure on its back (Auckland Museum, AM3078).[23] At around the same time and place another carver was negotiating how to form the manaia: on a prow that is now also in Auckland Museum (AM35570) the artist has created a metre-long projection, at the end of which is an unusual beaked figure. These haumi would have been attached to either waka ama or waka hourua.

The types of waka that were made changed to reflect changing settlement patterns. As Māori moved from smaller coastal settlements to more established, self-sufficient communities there was less demand for large oceangoing waka. Changes in waka were the result of shifts in use on the one hand, and the availability of materials closer to home. At Te Oneroa Long Bay in Auckland, for instance, hapū swapped adze materials sourced from afar (such as South Island argillites), which had been used to make large waka hourua, to those materials found much closer to home (such as Te Ahumatā obsidian from Great Barrier Island) for making smaller craft.[24] This is evidence of the move towards a more self-sustaining kāinga in which the people did not expect to be building large, oceangoing vessels to travel elsewhere, particularly across the expanse of the Pacific.

From 1500 to 1700 the knowledge and skills to make haumi were transformed into the tauihu and tuere prow forms. At the same time, waka hourua and waka ama were mostly replaced by single-hull canoes. The shift to single-hull vessels was a result of the much wider range of timbers available in Aotearoa, which meant it was possible to build larger canoes.[25] Over time a wider, U-shaped hull emerged from those types found at Anaweka, which impacted on sailing performance.

### Waka in rock art

Rock art in caves and shelters around the country documents the range of waka used through the generations and in different regions. Around the Bay of Plenty a number of carvings into rock depict tauihu, taurapa and spirals, such as at Kaingaroa (west of Murupara) and at Ongare Point.[26] At the Rua Hoata shelter on the Waikato River, ethnologist William Phillipps identified four different types of canoe based on the remarkable fifty-four 'glyphs' etched into the domed roof: a simple dugout canoe; a dugout with raised sides, including one with a tuere-style prow; canoes shown only in outline; and canoes in a 'raised shape'; at least one looked like an outrigger and another like a double canoe.[27] He noted that all the waka prows pointed to the entrance of the shelter. Many of the carvings were covered in moss.

Museum director Gilbert Archey wrote about rock drawings at Arapuni Gorge,[28] which showed a range of waka taua drawn with black charcoal onto the rough surface of two caves. The drawings included many features of the waka taua, including tauihu, taurapa, hull and topstrakes, and four of the canoes had triangular sails.

This brief survey suggests that waka culture was so integral to hapū identity that it was recorded in different techniques in the places they stayed. The presence of sails at Arapuni suggests that this technology was not limited to oceangoing vessels, but may have been used on craft to traverse inland rivers and lakes. The outrigger at Rua Hoata is possibly not so surprising, given the physical and spiritual dominance of the Waikato River and the heavy reliance of people living in the area on the river for getting from place to place, particularly where the water was sometimes turbulent.

### The emergence of new types of waka

Waka were crucial to the early ancestors and through the generations until the late nineteenth century. The waka was their lifeblood – on a physical level, for food gathering and to move warriors, but also as a way of forging and maintaining pivotal relationships, both economic and sociopolitical. In this landscape, the evolution of waka from double canoe to single hull was essential in order to survive. This change took place over at least five hundred years: waka builders were constantly tinkering with design, and shifting notions of power were encapsulated and visually asserted in the making and remaking of waka.

By the 1700s waka builders were making a range of single-hull waka designed to sail rivers and lakes as well as the sea. The smallest were the waka tīwai – about 9m long, these were used on rivers and inland lakes for everyday travel and food gathering, and also in races. The waka tīwai were still in use into the early twentieth century, particularly in remote areas with few roads, where rivers remained integral to ways of life – such as in the Whanganui.

The waka pūhara or kōrari – a flat-bottomed canoe fashioned from bundles of kōrari (the flower stalks of New Zealand flax *Phormium tenax*) – was a popular form of waka in Rēkohu Chatham Islands, where suitable timber was not readily available. These waka could be landed and launched easily on the rocky shores of islands; they were extremely buoyant – if prone to leaks; they were quick to make or remake; and when on shore they could be taken out of the water and dried on the beach. Larger kōrari could measure up to 15m long and carry seventy people; they would be rowed rather than paddled. Smaller kōrari were often only 2.4m long and carried two or three people. Others were used for fishing and food gathering, and also for ceremonies such as burials.

The waka tētē was a seagoing canoe that measured around 15m. Tētē can mean 'chief', which would reflect the owner of the canoe; 'tētē' also refers to the simple carving on the tauihu, which was usually painted red with kōkōwai. A rauawa or topstrake was sometimes attached to give added freeboard, and these were sometimes painted with kōwhaiwhai designs. Waka tētē fulfilled an important function of carrying provisions for leading canoes on war expeditions: waka taua were tapu and so could not carry cooked food, as this would destroy their tapu state. They were also used to ferry people on short expeditions for food gathering.

By the twentieth century waka tētē were no longer being made: they were replaced by motorised boats; and their role in accompanying waka taua became redundant with the cessation of war expeditions. Interestingly, the form was rejuvenated in 2000 when women at Whangaroa in Northland asked tohunga tārai waka Hekenukumaingāiwi (Hec) Busby (Te Rarawa, Ngāti Kahu, 1932–2019) [29] to build them a waka. Hec trained two women carvers in order to establish capacity and reinforce the kaupapa (theme) of mana wāhine (the power and strength of women). The finished canoe was launched under another kaupapa of helping women in family-violence relationships, a very proud moment as it was the first waka tētē to be built within living memory.

### Waka taua – canoes of the people

Over the generations carvers have negotiated changes and challenges to their community's identity through the creation of new types of waka – acting, as artists do, as agents of change. The waka taua was the most visually and symbolically complex of all waka forms, both in terms of the whole canoe, and of the different components. The form emerged some time in the eighteenth century, based on extant canoe parts in museums. Waka taua were the most extravagant canoe in the community, and every rangatira was expected to have at least one.

Waka taua often measured up to 35m long and could hold over a hundred people seated five abreast. The paddlers were led by a kaituki (time-caller), who would check the waves, wind, weather, journey and canoe size, and select the most appropriate chant to motivate them and keep time.

Waka taua were a symbol of group pride, and represented a considerable investment of community resources. The

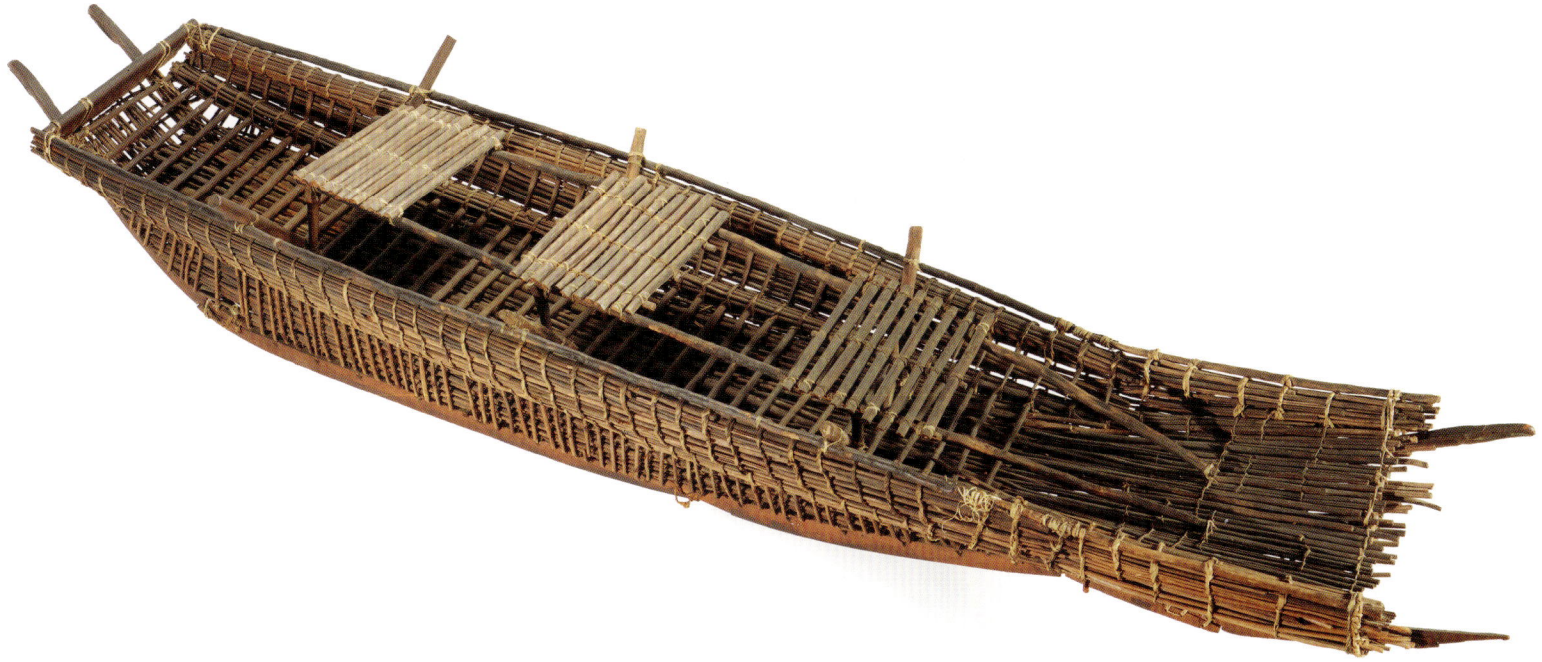

This contemporary waka kōrari has a double hull and flat base, of a style popular in Rēkohu Chatham Islands.
Te Papa Tongarewa Museum of New Zealand, ME012263, gift of Miss A. Shand, 1900

kāinga owned and operated the waka, which represented unity between whānau and hapū. The production of waka taua took many months, if not years, and consumed a tremendous amount of tribal resources. Tōtara and kauri were the most popular timbers. The tohunga tārai waka supervised each stage of the construction and protected all those involved with karakia necessary to ensure that tapu restrictions were not broken. These rules included a prohibition on burning the woodchips from building the waka in cooking fires, no eating around the waka, and a prohibition on women and children being in the vicinity of the waka-building site. The completed waka taua was very precious to the people, and when it was not in use, parts would be unlashed and dismantled, and the hull placed in a wharau or canoe shed near the water.

Carvers gave each part of the waka taua a symbolic function. Carver Pakaariki Harrison (Ngāti Porou, 1928–2008) wrote of the waka taua: 'It portrays the journey through this world from birth to death, the mythical origins of war and stories about the building of waka for this purpose. It is imbued with the genealogies of heaven and earth and the creation as well as the descent lines of illustrious ancestor warriors.'[30]

As each component was named, the tohunga tārai waka would draw together the past and the present. The canoe as a whole represented the riu (body) of Tānemahuta (atua of the forest), and karakia were offered to him when one of his children (a tree) was taken. The prow referred to Tūmatauenga, the deity to whom the war party was dedicated while on their mission.

Until the 1850s some carvers – and/or hapū – were renowned for building waka; others for building whare. With a lull in conflict, few patrons were commissioning new waka, so waka artists focused solely on building meeting houses. Carvers transferred the symbolism of one form onto the other: the central beam (the hull of a waka, or the ridgepole in a whare) was the backbone of an ancestor, and served to link the tauihu (the prow, or the porch carvings) to the taurapa (the sternpost, or the pou tuarongo – the back wall of the whare). The taumanu on which the paddlers sat related to the heke (rafters) in the meeting house, as did the practice of dovetailing composite pieces as a method of building in waka and whare.[31] The mana of a master carver was confirmed and enhanced when he made a whare or a waka: the two forms were related, and ideas and innovations in one were transmitted to the other. These art practices have remained integral in the construction of waka today.

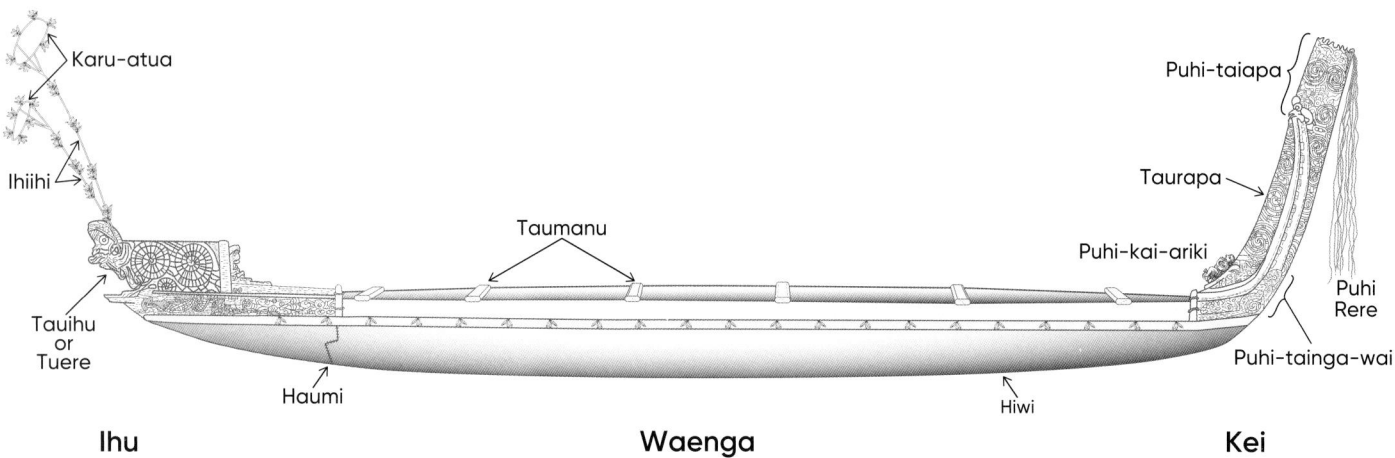

Parts of a waka.
diagram by Tim Nolan/Blackant Mapping Solutions

Each component of the waka taua had a practical and a spiritual role. There were two types of prow – the tauihu and the tuere. The tauihu – also called a pītau-style (spiral) prow[32] – featured one figure facing the crew, and another figure that represented Tūmatauenga (atua of warfare) on the outer edge, pushing his way through the waves. In between these two figures was an upright section with two spirals where a third figure was placed, representing Tāne separating his parents (symbolised as the spirals).

The tuere featured up to three sinuous manaia figures depicted vertically, around which were carved various types of open-fret designs, including takarangi (double spirals) and mata kupenga (fishnet mesh). The tuere type of prow is now very rare – there are only a few examples extant from the North Auckland, Coromandel, Waikato, Bay of Plenty and Tolaga Bay regions.[33] These date to the late eighteenth century; the latest pre-1900 example was one made for the Waikato-Tainui waka taua *Taheretikitiki* in 1882. Roger Neich, in his detailed research on the tuere,[34] argued that it was, in fact, much more prevalent in the late eighteenth century, based on the number depicted in drawings by Sydney Parkinson and Herman Spöring at Tolaga Bay, though Cook and his men reported no sightings of any on their second or third voyages into the Pacific.

The taurapa was attached to the stern of the waka taua. The carving typically featured a manaia figure at the top holding two 'ribs' that extend down to the bottom: in between these are takarangi spirals and other surface decorations, as well as a human figure facing the paddlers. The 'ribs' may represent ira atua (deities) and ira tangata (humankind), and connect all those on board with atua and more recent histories of ancestors, especially when a canoe was named after a specific person. Some taurapa were named, such as Ahimotukura, a taurapa that is associated with Hori Ngakapa Te Whanaunga (Ngāti Whanaunga, Ngāti Pāoa) and was made some time between 1850 and 1880.

Oral accounts provide information about the construction of specific waka taua. In a Te Whānau ā Apanui pātere (song of derision) translated by Kōpu Erueti, Te Waiūrangi refers to the waka taua named *Tonga-ngaua* that was 'fastened with flax leaves [rau harakeke] from Pane-koki. Those *kahika* trees were once his.'[35] Another account, a waiata tangi for Te Ara-Kau Te Umu of Ngāti Rangiwewehi, translated by Rangikauariro, describes the puhi (plumes) at either end of the waka taua.[36] These puhi came from the kererū and tūī, and once they were in place, the canoe was painted with karamea (red ochre pigment) and fluffy white toroa (albatross) feathers were attached: when it is in this state it is said to be 'pīwari' – a thing of beauty. The waiata tangi used the term 'toiere' to describe a 'war canoe with carved stem and stern'. It also noted other types of canoes: 'whakarei' (ornamental) and 'pītau': 'canoe with figurehead ornamented with perforated spiral carving [takarangi]'.

The most important role of the war canoe was to transport taua (war parties) to and from their destination. Thousands of warriors might be involved in a single fleet. Some of the best-known examples were taua led by Ngāpuhi leader Hongi Hika and others in the Bay of Islands in the 1820s, when they left to attack other iwi to the south and southeast. By this time Ngāpuhi carvers were in short supply, and carvers (and moko artists) from Hauraki, Bay of Plenty and the East Coast were captured and brought back to the north as prisoners of war and put to work carving waka.[37] Waka taua might also be used to carry large groups of people on other journeys, such as for celebrations or for trading. They could also be used for fishing: in that case the carved tauihu and taurapa as well as the rauawa would be removed and stored in the wharau.

The waka taua form was a casualty of the New Zealand Wars, as the building of this type of vessel went into a hiatus from the late 1860s until the 1920s. The waka of some iwi, such as Waikato-Tainui, were seized and many were destroyed by the colonial militia in order to shut down an important mode of transport in their tribal rohe and to destroy their sense of iwi identity. It did not work: iwi rallied together and asserted their tribal sovereignty by coming together to construct new symbols of identity, namely the whare whakairo.

One complication in identifying nineteenth-century waka taua is that some were converted into carvings for whare whakairo as that art form became more popular from the 1860s. The house Rangitihi (opened 1872), for instance, incorporates parts of several waka taua that were active in a battle at Te Ariki, Lake Tarawera, in 1853.[38] Neich argues that this practice of reusing timbers from waka taua was fairly common for Ngāti Tarāwhai carvers in the 1870s.[39] Recycling of waka taua occurred before this time, too; and occasionally a waka taua hull was removed and upended to create a memorial when its chiefly owner died.

In the tourism centre of Rotorua, patrons who commissioned work such as waka from carvers put pressure on them to complete their work in a short timeframe. These patrons – both Māori and non-Māori – often had little interest in the tapu restrictions which could apply to reusing earlier work on a later project. They were also dogged in sourcing carvings that could be repurposed in projects such as meeting houses for their tourism ventures. In 1904 the tourism operator Charles Nelson purchased unfinished carvings for one of his architectural enterprises. The original carvings had been made over the period 1871–1878 for Ngāti Rangitihi chief Arama Karaka Mokonuiarangi, and may have been named Ngatitiora.[40] The carvers, Te Amo and his assistants Wero and Aritopuru, used only timbers sourced from the waka *Matire*; Wiremu Te Ohu had taken this canoe, which his brother (and fellow carver) Ānaha Te Rāhui gave to Arama. Both brothers had been taught waka building by their father Te Rāhui and were actively working on commission building them in the 1830s and 1840s. *Te Kura ki Pewhairangi* was another waka that was used in making a meeting house; its name suggests it may have been one of those left behind by Ngāpuhi when they returned home to Pēwhairangi Bay of Islands in 1821. Ānaha Te Rāhui later shifted his practice to focus on carving meeting houses from the 1860s, around which time he became the leader of Ngāti Tarāwhai: he carved Rangitihi (1867–1871) and Tokopikowhakahau (1877) while leading his people.

## Mana tangata – a rejuvenation of waka in the 1930s

By the turn of the twentieth century most waka taua had been destroyed or were lying in pieces in sheds or on riverbanks. A few complete war canoes were in museums; directors and ethnologists actively collected them as part of a trio of Māori art that emerged in the 1870s in tandem with the emergence of new museums: the whare whakairo (which was only just being established), the pātaka (raised food storehouse) and the waka taua. These were considered quintessential examples of Māori art which, according to the museums, was fast disappearing.

One of the best known of these museum-held waka taua is *Te Toki a Tāpiri*. The whakapapa of this waka taua symbolises the relationships across iwi in the nineteenth century. Initially built by Te Waaka Tarakau (Ngāti Matawhāiti) around 1836, the waka was named 'the adze of Tāpiri' after one of the main ancestors of the tribe. Te Waaka worked with Tamati Parangi and Paratene Te Pohoi and a thousand others who were on hand to drag the huge log in stages from the bush to the carving site. When the waka was completed (but not yet carved), Te Waaka gifted it to Te Waaka Perohuka (Ngāti Kaipoho hapū of Rongowhakaata)[41] as thanks for assistance in a battle. (This hapū would, of course, soon be led, in 1840, by master carver extraordinaire Raharuhi Rukupō.) Perohuka presented

Te Waaka with a kākahu named Karamaene in return. He then set to work carving the tauihu, taurapa and rauawa for the waka taua, along with other artists from Rongowhakaata: Tīmoti Rangitotohikura (Tīmoti Totohirangi), Wiremu Te Keteiwi, Patarounu Pakapaka, Natanahira, Toumata and Mahumahu.[42] These carvings today represent the oldest extant models of Ngāti Kaipoho carving.

In 1853, the waka was moved once again. Perohuka gifted the waka to Tāmati Wāka Nene and his brother Patuone (Ngāpuhi) to recognise the state of peace between the iwi after the devastating raids on the area in the 1820s; in response, the two men sent a piebald stallion named Taika (Tiger) – the first horse in the area. The horse was in turn passed on to the original owner of *Te Toki*, thus keeping the relationships across iwi alive. *Te Toki* arrived in Auckland, where it was sold to Kaihau and Te Katipa, two rangatira of Ngāti Te Ata who were based in Waiuku in South Auckland. It is unclear why the waka was in Auckland or why it was sold, given this whakapapa, but certainly the impending warfare with the Crown may have pressed the Auckland chiefs to source a traditional waka taua that could help them in warfare.

In 1863 the Crown confiscated *Te Toki a Tapiri* from Ngāti Te Ata as punishment, even though this iwi had not fought against the Crown. *Te Toki* then lay on a beach in Onehunga, where a British sailor tried to blow it up; although he was unsuccessful, the Crown paid compensation in recognition of this harm. In the ironic play of public politics, the waka was restored in advance of a visit by a representative of the Crown – Prince Alfred, Duke of Edinburgh – and was sailed on the Waitematā harbour in a display of Māori–Crown harmony. After this, *Te Toki* was left in the care of mana whenua Ngāti Whātua ki Ōrākei chief Paora Tūhaere (himself a carver). It was later presented to the New Zealand government in 1885, who gave the waka to Auckland Museum where he stands today.

By the 1930s few waka were being made, and certainly no waka taua. Te Puea Hērangi (Tainui, 1883–1952), a leader from Ngāruawāhia, set out to change this. Piri Poutapu (Ngāti Korokī, 1905–1975) had been raised by Te Puea since childhood, and had moved with her to Ngāruawāhia when she established the settlement in 1921. In the late 1920s Poutapu worked on three projects – Pare Waikato whare, a hostel at Tuakau, and Māhinaarangi meeting house – before Te Puea sent him for formal carving training under Eramiha Kapua at the School of Maori Arts and Crafts. On his return he founded a carving school at Tūrangawaewae, where he revitalised traditional Tainui motifs and designs such as the sinuous taniwha, working from examples in museums as well as old drawings by nineteenth-century artists such as George French Angas.

Ultimately Tainui built three waka taua for the centennial of Te Tiriti o Waitangi: *Te Winika*, *Aotea* (later renamed *Tūmanako*) and *Tākitimu* (later renamed *Te Rangatahi*). *Te Winika* was originally built in the 1830s and belonged to the Kukutai whānau of Ngāti Tamaoho and Ngāti Tipa from the Tuakau region in north Waikato. Tainui dismantled the waka in the 1860s and the most important carvings – the tauihu, taurapa and rauawa – were hidden in Tuakau. The hull was upended and left on the riverbank. Around 1930 Te Puea discovered the hull, which was weathered by then, and it inspired her to set about looking for someone to restore or build seven new waka taua. She conducted a series of hui to find a master carver to lead the *Te Winika* project. At one meeting an old tohunga called Rānui Maupakanga came forward to help and Te Puea asked him to direct the reconstruction. He was assisted by Piri Poutapu. Another assistant on *Te Winika* was Ngāpuhi carver Pita Te Hoe Heperi (1890–1968), son of the renowned waka builder Hohepa, who was just beginning a thirty-year career as a carver.

Maupakanga, Poutapu and Heperi built another waka taua in the 1930s: *Ngātokimatawhaorua* was carved at Kerikeri in the Bay of Islands over a two-year period, to be launched for the 100-year celebration of the signing of Te Tiriti o Waitangi in 1940. Along with Īnia Te Wiata (Ngāti Raukawa, 1915–1971) and Jimmy Kukutai, Poutapu was to spearhead other important waka and whare-building projects in the 1930s and 1940s in the Waikato area.[43]

Eventually only three of Te Puea's seven waka taua were completed: *Te Winika*, *Aotea* and *Tākitimu*, and all three were taken north to represent Tainui at the formal celebrations on 6 February 1940. Their presence was a clear declaration of the tenacity of Tainui to survive despite huge land confiscations as a result of the New Zealand Wars. The waka were also a statement of the enduring mana of the Kīngitanga, and of Te Puea's dynamic leadership.

Piri Poutapu continued to carve and teach new generations about waka culture. Most notably, he encouraged the filming of the remaking of the waka taua *Taheretikitiki II* in 1972, and

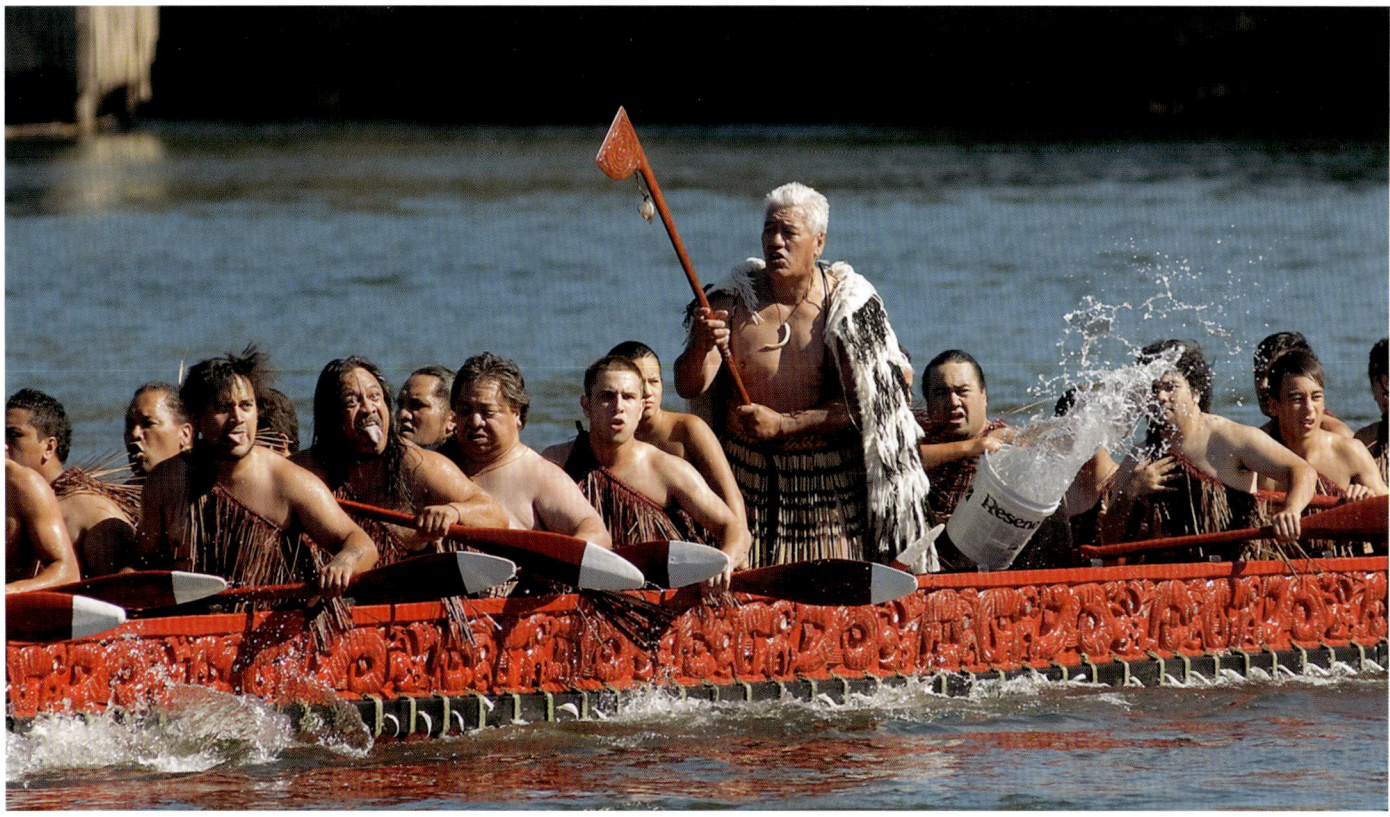

*Te Rangatahi* was one of two waka taua commissioned by Te Puea Hērangi in 1938 for the 1940 Waitangi commemorations. Both *Te Rangatahi* and *Tūmanako* continue to delight crowds, especially for the annual Tūrangawaewae regatta along the Waikato River. Here Karihana Wirihana is captain.
photograph by Jeff Evans

Overleaf: The waka taua *Ngātokimatawhaorua* was built for the commemoration of the signing of Te Tiriti o Waitangi in 1940, and named after a much older waka hourua which travelled from Hawaiki to Hokianga Harbour under the guidance of Nukutawhiti. Today the canoe is housed in a shelter called Te Korowai ō Maikuku, located just down the hill from the Waitangi whare rūnanga built for the same memorial event.
image supplied by Waitangi Limited

he promoted new technologies to aid the building process, such as projecting the drawings onto the timbers to be carved. His legacy is ongoing, not only in the five waka taua that are still in existence today (*Taheretikitiki II*, *Te Winika*, *Ngātokimatawhaorua*, *Aotea* and *Tākitimu*) but also through the careers of some of his students, such as Herekōtuku Leonard Muru (Ngāti Whātua, Tainui, 1937–2018, on *Taheretikitiki II*, launched 1972), Īnia Te Wiata (on Tūrongo meeting house, opened 1936)[44] and Richard (Dick) Tiki Green (Ngāti Maniapoto, 1938–2011, on *Tahere II* and *Te Winika*).

Half a century later, these waka built in the 1930s were very worn, despite renovation on some, such as *Te Winika*. The moment seemed right to assert mana waka – the power and prestige associated with waka. The Kaupapa Waka (Project Canoe) initiative was launched in the late 1980s with the support of the government. The goal was to construct and carve tribal waka taua as a kaupapa towards kotahitanga – bringing people together, Māori and Pākehā. The government contributed $50,000 per waka, and sometimes also a log, towards iwi building or refurbishing a waka to be sailed on Waitangi Day 1990.

Nineteen waka were launched at Waitangi on 6 February 1990. While many of them resembled those we might see in a museum, some iwi took the opportunity to experiment with different symbols, colours, forms and tools – from tōtara logs to fibreglass, chisels to chainsaws. Communities came together to learn about their history, and to choose a theme for their waka.[45]

### The greatness of Te Moananui a Kiwa

In the mid-1970s, communities across the Pacific began investigating a revival of long-distance voyaging in waka hourua. In 1973 Hawaiian artist Herb Kawainui Kāne (1928–2011), anthropologist Ben Finney (1933–2017) and

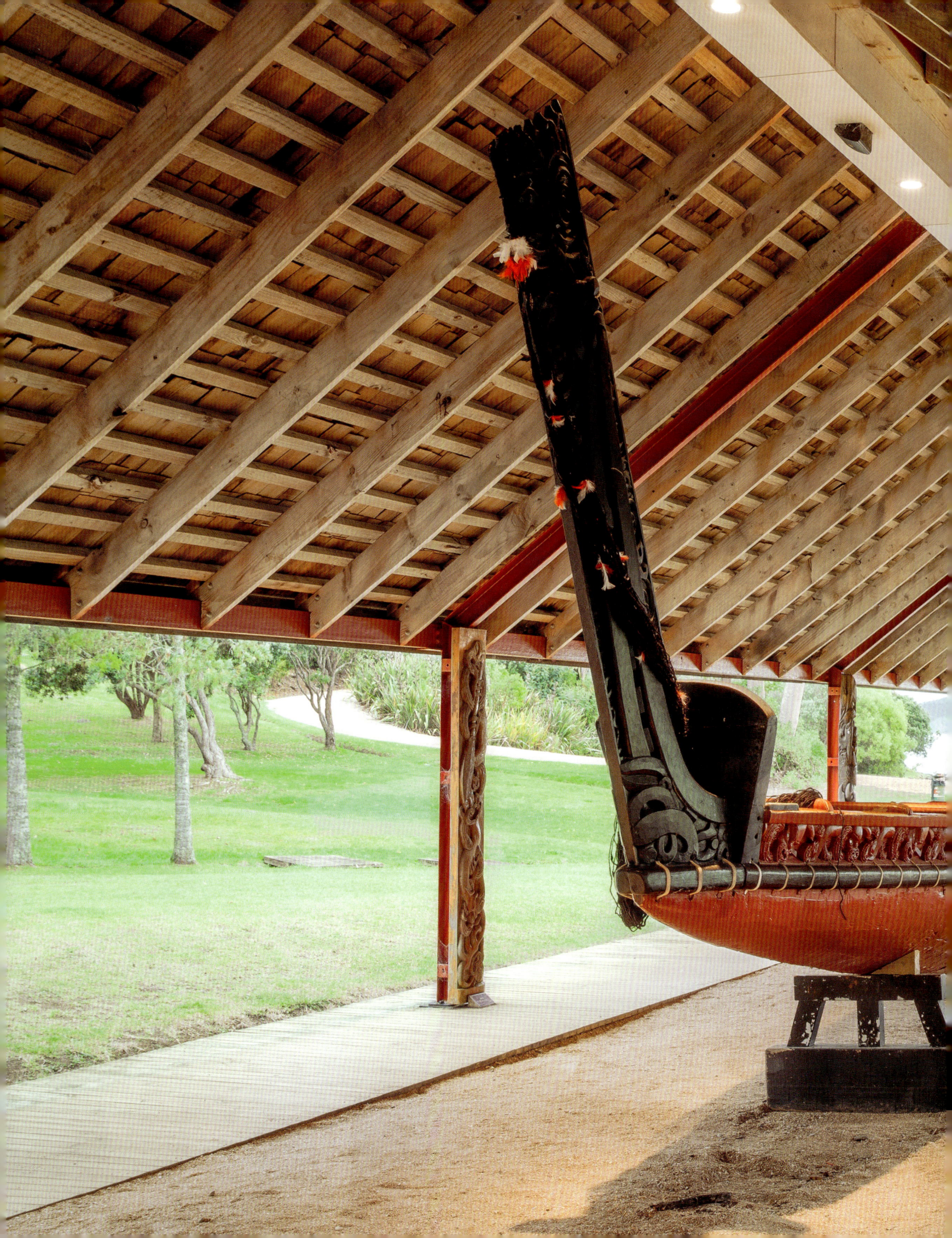

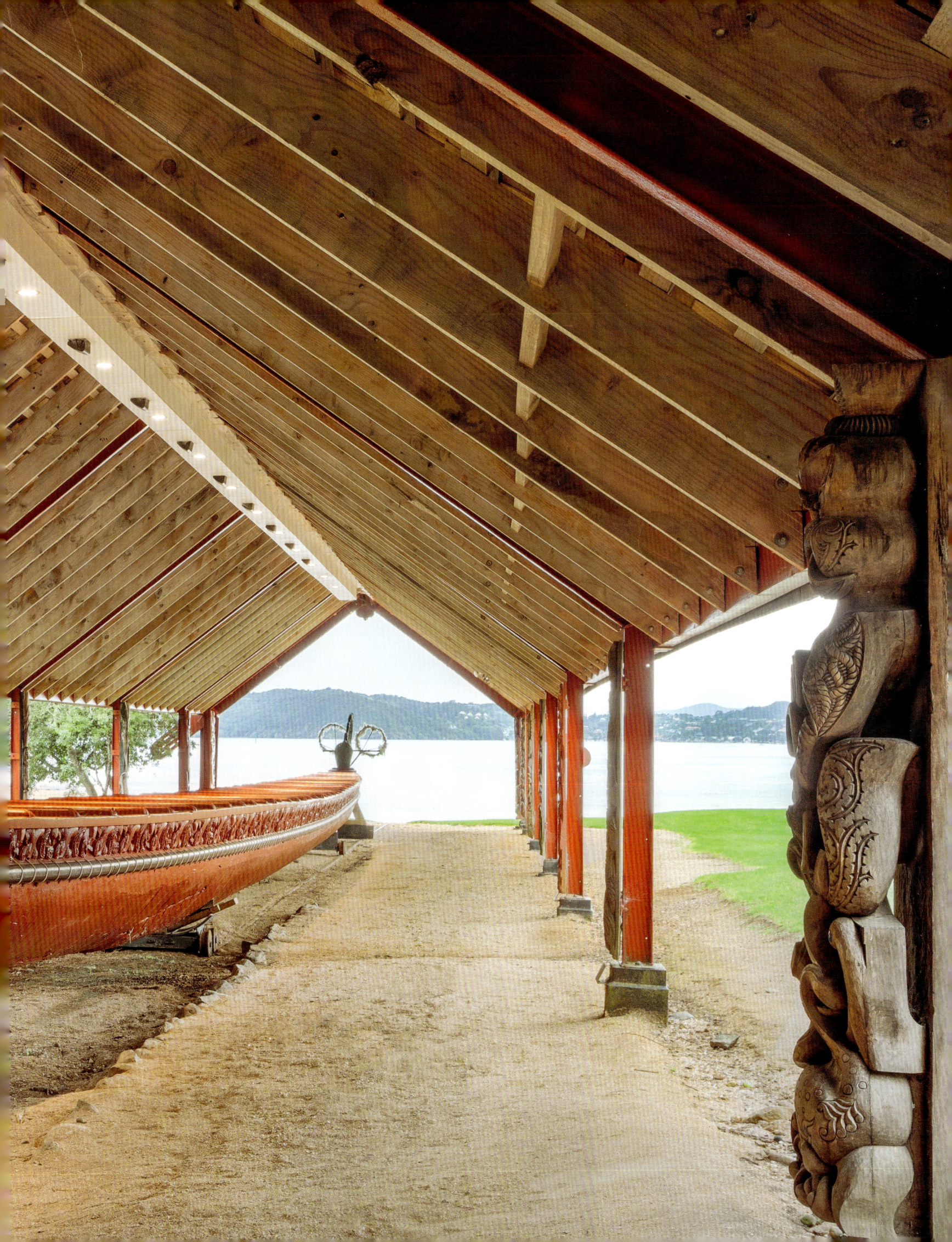

expert waka sailor Tommy Holmes (1945–1993) established the Polynesian Voyaging Society. They were concerned that traditional Polynesian navigational techniques were about to be lost, and they set out to build an oceangoing waka hourua to help revive that tradition and to reconnect across the Pacific. The waka was built in Hawai'i, based on Herb Kāne's design and with input from Finney and others;[46] and they named it *Hōkūle'a* after the star Arcturus, which passed directly over the Hawaiian Islands. Nainoa Thompson became involved with the project in 1974: he had sailed solo from Hawai'i to Tahiti in his twenties, and was studying ocean science at the time *Hōkūle'a* was being built. He trained in the ancient art of navigation with Mau Piailug (1932–2010), one of the last great Pacific navigators, who was based in the island of Satawal in Micronesia. Piailug's teachings were a turning point in Pacific wayfinding: his mātauranga influenced many others around him to learn navigation and, through this, to connect across Te Moananui a Kiwa.

In 1885–1987, *Hōkūle'a* made a hugely important return Voyage of Rediscovery between Hawai'i and Aotearoa. The sheer speed with which travel between islands was made forced many historians to rethink their idea of the power of waka: it took just six weeks to travel from Hawai'i to Rarotonga, and just over two weeks from there to Aotearoa. Many people, including historians, had believed that the Polynesian settlement of Aotearoa was accidental – a myth perpetuated by Charles Goldie and John Louis Steele's painting *The Arrival of the Maoris in New Zealand* (1898), in which Māori are depicted as arriving emaciated from an extended voyage across the Pacific. The *Hōkūle'a* voyage, undertaken using proven ancestral navigational techniques based on the currents and stars and other techniques, confirmed that it would have taken much less time and that it was intentional. This was no drift. The ancestors *wanted* to come here.

### Te Aurere

*Hōkūle'a* was the first of many new waka. The success of its voyages inspired Hekenukumaingāiwi (Hec) Busby to build *Te Aurere*, a waka hourua made from kauri, measuring 17.3m long and 5.4m wide, and able to carry fourteen crew. This would be the first waka hourua made in over 600 years, and it was built for long-haul voyaging.

Busby was a bridge builder in Northland in the early 1970s when he became interested in what was happening in Hawai'i. After Nainoa Thompson stayed with him, it was decided to build a Māori waka hourua. Busby's expertise had been finetuned by working on the restoration of *Ngātokimatawhaorua*, whose maiden voyage he had witnessed as a boy in 1940. He had also built two waka taua – *Mataatua Puhi* and *Te Ika a Maui* – but he called on Thompson for design assistance with the much larger oceangoing vessel.[47]

*Te Aurere*'s maiden voyage was to Rarotonga in 1992, with Mau Piailug as navigator. It was early in the voyaging season, and the waka was battered by storms for days on end. The New Zealand Meteorological Service radioed the crew to sail in a certain direction, but Piailug, relying on his traditional skills and knowledge, suggested another. The decision was made to follow the advice of the meteorologists, and *Te Aurere* ran into an even worse storm. A few days later they encountered foul weather again, but this time the crew decided to follow Piailug's instruction, and they sailed into calmer weather. In 1995 *Te Aurere* sailed from the Marquesas to Hawai'i with several other canoes, including *Tākitimu* and *Te 'Au o Tonga* from Rarotonga, and *Hōkūle'a* and *Hawai'iloa* from Hawai'i. On the return trip, *Te Aurere* sailed non-stop for thirty days from Hawai'i to Rarotonga, and then on to Aotearoa.

Many new canoes have been criticised for not being entirely traditional. *Hōkūle'a*, for example, while the design is based largely on traditional vaka, is made from modern materials such as fibreglass, plywood and resin; *Te 'Au o Tonga* and *Te Aurere* have outboard motors; and most are equipped with radios and satellite navigation instruments. *Hawaiki-nui*, however, has been made using mostly older technology and materials. The waka was carved by Mātahi Avauli Whakataka-Brightwell in the early 1980s under the supervision of Rua Kaika and Kohe Webster: the hulls were hewn from tōtara, lashed together with sennit cord (made from coconut fibre); the bamboo masts supported sails woven from pandanus leaves. The only piece of modern equipment was a radio. In 1985 Whakataka-Brightwell and the Tahitian navigator Francis Cowan sailed *Hawaiki-nui* from Tahiti to Rarotonga, then on to New Zealand.[48] These waka voyages reconnect Māori with their Pacific cousins, and reaffirm the importance of waka as a crucial vessel for the passing on of mātauranga through the generations.

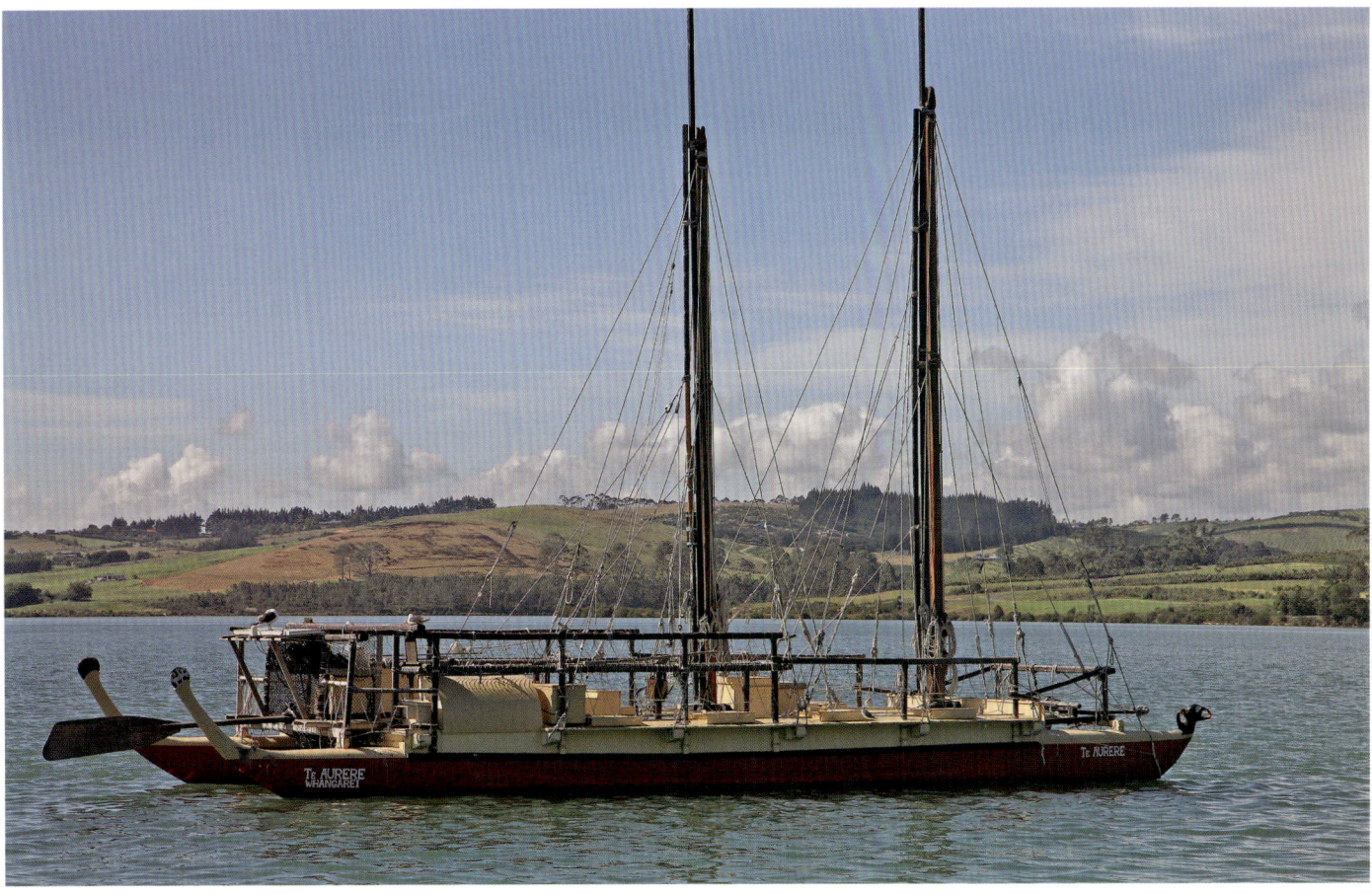

*Te Aurere* was the first waka hourua (oceangoing canoe) built by Hec Busby. Her maiden voyage in 1992 to the Cook Islands reinforced physically the whakapapa links between Māori in both lands.
photograph by W. Bulach

### Waka in the twenty-first century

Waka today are an integral part of iwi cultural identity. They are used for occasions such as Waitangi Day and the celebration of Matariki (the Māori New Year): for the Matariki Festival in Auckland in 2019, for instance, participants could book to view the Matariki star cluster from a traditional waka on the Waitematā harbour; and visitors to the National Maritime Museum in Auckland can board a waka hourua for a trip around the harbour. Waka ama racing is now a popular sport: the first national championships were held in 1990, and the sport now draws over 70 teams for the nationals, and 125 schools and 1700 students for the high school competitions, with almost 60 per cent of participants Māori.

For Waikato-Tainui the annual Tūrangawaewae Regatta, held in March under the mana of Kīngi Tūheitia, head of the Kīngitanga, showcases their tribal waka taua. The day-long event first took place in 1895; today thousands of spectators turn up to enjoy the manaakitanga (hospitality) of Waikato-Tainui and to watch teams racing in waka kōpapa – a distinctly Tainui form of waka that pays homage to Te Puea's aspirations for a fleet of waka on the Waikato River. The regatta is a celebration of the tribal resilience of Waikato-Tainui, and a clear and public proclamation of their mana waka.

Now is an exciting time for the waka community. More research is being undertaken on older examples in museums, contributing to an increased understanding of different styles of waka. On the water, crews are pushing out the horizon by undertaking longer and more difficult voyages across the Pacific, renewing contact between communities with the same ancestors. At the turn of the twentieth century the future of waka was at risk, with no new canoes being built, and older examples residing in museums far away from most Māori. Today, waka are celebrated as a cornerstone of Māori culture, where the sight of groups of war canoes on the water at Auckland or Paihia, or of hundreds of rangatahi on waka ama, is not so much a spectacle as a symbol of resistance and resilience.

# TĀ HEKENUKUMAINGĀIWI BUSBY, KNZM MBE (1932–2019)

## NGARINO ELLIS

In the world of waka, the most influential leader of the twentieth century was carver Tā Hekenukumaingāiwi (Hec) Busby (Te Rarawa, Ngāti Kahu, 1932–2019) who led a team to carve the first voyaging waka in New Zealand in over 600 years. Hec Busby's interest in waka began in the early 1970s while sitting on the beach at Te Tī, Waitangi, watching the waka taua *Ngātokimatawhaorua* being plied around the waters of Paihia on Waitangi Day. By the 1980s his interest had grown into an all-consuming passion. He was inspired by Nainoa Thompson and his work building *Hōkūle'a* (launched 1975). Busby led the team building and carving the first double-hulled waka hourua *Te Aurere*, made specifically for long-haul ocean travel. It was important that they used as many Indigenous materials as possible, from the large kauri (*Agathis australis*) logs to the harakeke (New Zealand flax, *Phormium tenax*) used in the lashings. The waka was 17.4m long and only 5.5m wide, and designed to hold a crew of up to twelve, including a captain and a navigator. *Te Aurere*'s maiden voyage was to Rarotonga in 1992, the first time a waka made in New Zealand had sailed up into the Pacific in over 600 years.

Tā Hec was a great teacher, and he ensured that his knowledge of navigation was transmitted to others in New Zealand, including Jack Thatcher (Ngāti Porou, Te Aitanga a Hauiti, Te Whānau a Tūwhakairiora, Ngāti Awa, Ngāiterangi, Ngāti Ranginui and Ngāti Pukenga) and Stan Conrad (Te Aupōuri). He taught Hemi Eruera (Ngāti Hau, Ngāti Kaharau, Te Uri o Hina) about building waka and together they built several, including the waka taua *Rangimārie* (2004) and the waka tētē *Uerangi* (2005). Eruera has since been appointed tumu (head) of Te Tapuwae o Te Waka, the waka-building arm of the New Zealand Māori Arts and Crafts Institute (NZMACI), and is based in Awanui, Northland.

Tā Hec took several commissions from different iwi who came to him for help to build their waka, including Ngāti Awa ki Whakatāne (*Hine Moana*, 2007) and Ngāti Kahu ki Whangaroa (*Te Au Kaha*, 2001). He worked with other carvers on some of these, notably with Takirirangi Smith (Ngāti Porou) and his students from Whitireia polytechnic in the making of the canoes *Rangimārie* and *Uerangi*.

As with *Hōkūle'a*, *Te Aurere* has become an educational tool to teach about Māori history and voyaging, and the ongoing importance of waka today. On days such as Auckland Anniversary Day, *Te Aurere* ferries passengers around the Waitematā harbour on one-hour trips, when captain Stan Conrad will talk about the history of the waka and about life on board during the many trips he has made as captain on waka hourua. Tā Hec has ensured that his life and work continue through the expertise of his students.

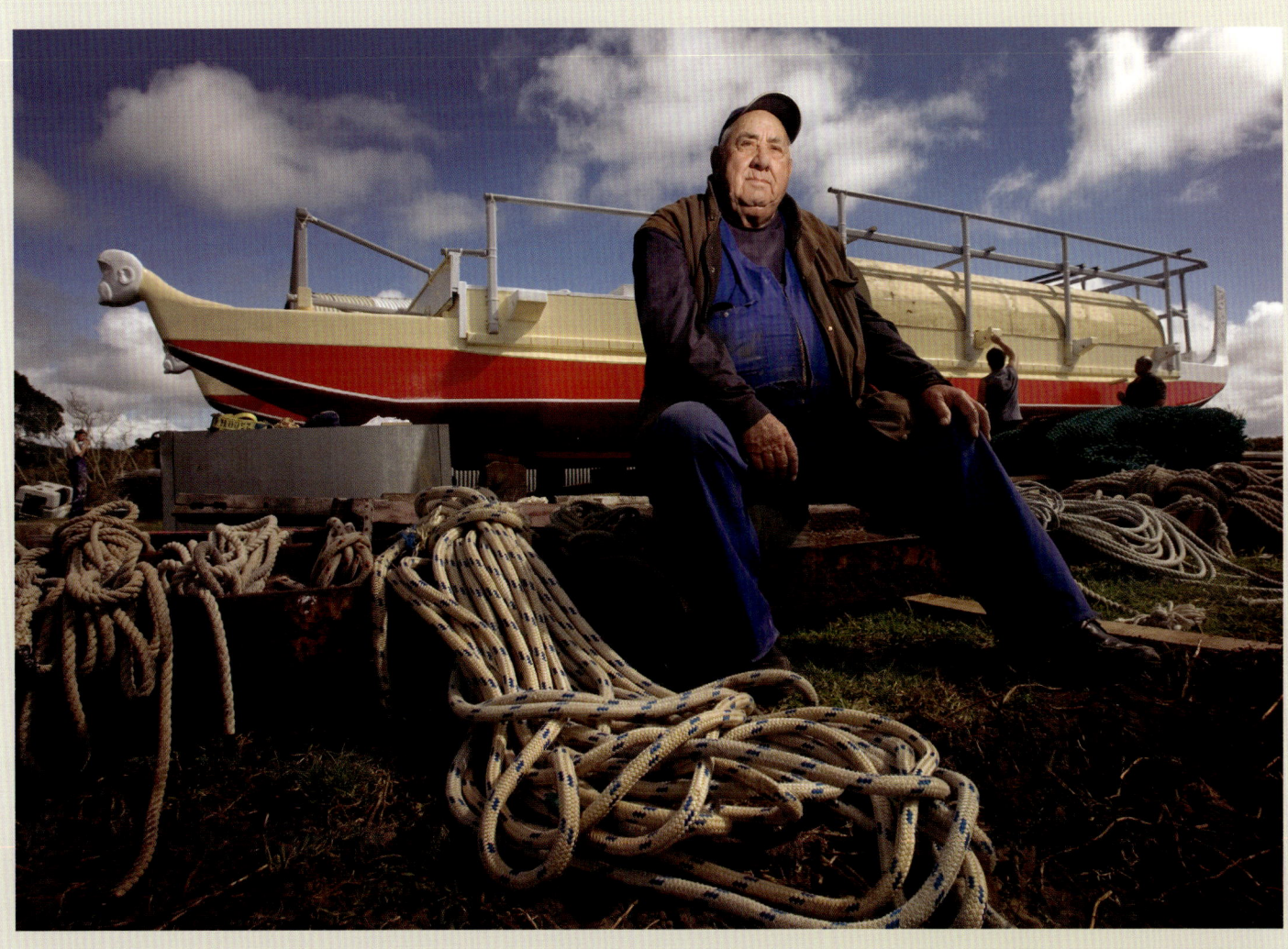

Hekenukumaingāiwi Busby rejuvenated the art of mahi tārai waka (canoe building) in the latter half of the twentieth century. His passion for waka ultimately led to Māori re-engagement with Pacific artists, waka builders and navigators.
*New Zealand Herald*

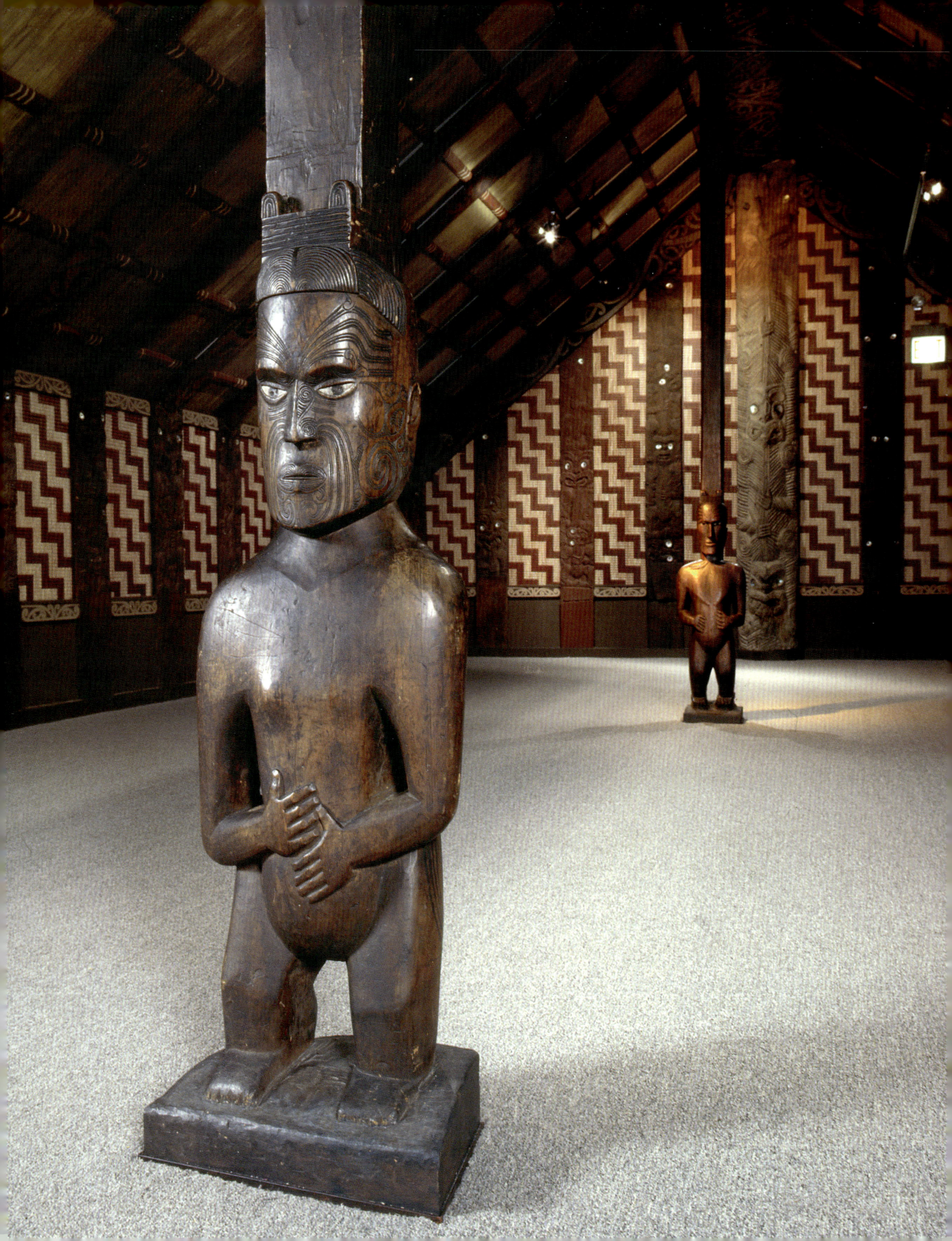

# 2 NGĀ TOI WHAKAIRO
## THE ARTS OF CARVING
### NGARINO ELLIS

*He toi whakairo, he mana tangata.*

*Through artistic excellence, there is human dignity.*

Whakairo is an integral part of who we are as Māori. For hundreds of years, different forms of carving surrounded our ancestors and were a normal part of their visual landscape. These works ranged from waka taua and large, intricately carved pātaka to rākai (adornments). Traditions in whakairo have come to shape what we now know as Māori art. Tohunga whakairo (master carvers) in the past enjoyed a breadth of practice across different media and art forms; they often worked in groups on larger projects, but also by themselves on individual projects, sometimes on commission. The sheer volume of work over the past few centuries is staggering – there are as many as 30,000 taonga in existence today that have been made by carvers,[1] primarily before 1900.

This chapter unravels the history of carving, from Pacific origins through to contemporary practice. It outlines the training of carvers, their styles and motifs and their patrons, and it tracks major shifts in whakairo, largely as a result of external factors. Throughout, important values and concepts of whakairo such as mana, tapu and tikanga have remained central, and artists have continued to experiment with new materials, tools and ideas in their practice.

Poutokomanawa inside Ruatepupuke II today.
photograph by Diane Alexander White and Linda Dorman

### Ngā tūpuna o whakairo – celestial ancestors of carving

There are many stories associated with the origins of carving. One of the earliest relates to the atua Tānemahuta (deity of forests and birds), son of Ranginui and Papatūānuku, who travelled with his brothers to Rangitamaku (the eleventh heaven); they took with them the measurements of a whare that included poupou (carved posts). When Tāne arrived, he and his brother Tangaroa carved a whare whakairo called Huiteananui, described as 'matawhā' (having four windows), including work on the tāhuhu (ridgepole), heke (rafters), maihi (bargeboards) and poutokomanawa (central posts).[2]

Many generations later, stories about Māui referred to houses adorned with whakairo rākau. In one of the first kōrero Māui is asked to prove his whakapapa by his mother Taranga – who thought that he was stillborn and had set him adrift on top of a nest made from her hair. To demonstrate his whakapapa, Māui stood on the tāhuhu of his grandmother Hinenuitepō's house. In this case the tāhuhu is significant as it is, quite literally, the backbone of his grandmother Hinenuitepō. Later in life, Māui fished up the North Island with a matau made from his grandmother's jawbone. However, the 'fish' became stuck in the door of a house belonging to Tonganui;[3] this whare was fully carved with a tāhuhu, heke, maihi and poutokomanawa.

Further down the generations, the ancestral story of Rata provides a model of tikanga in the carving of new works. One day Rata decided to build a waka, but he did not pay homage correctly to Tānemahuta, god of the forests, to ask permission to take one of his 'children'. After he went home for the night, Te Tini-o-te-hakuturi (the multitude of Hakuturi) – all the insects and other forest creatures – returned his waka to its original tree form. This happened on several days in a row until, one night, Rata pretended to leave but hid instead – and saw the creatures resurrecting the tree. At that point he realised it was because he had not recited the proper karakia. The next morning, he began with the appropriate karakia, and *then* cut the tree – and the forest creatures helped him finish his waka. In another version of the story, Rata's mother is Hinetuahōanga, the personification of sandstone. These stories record the names of ancestors, but also provide important moral advice.

For many iwi, Rauru is the paramount ancestor in relation to carving. His life is recorded in a whakairo (a carved surface spiral) called 'Ngā mahi a Rauru ki tahi',[4] and in a number of whakataukī, such as one from Ngāti Kahungunu, which says 'Ngā mahi a Rauru' (The workmanship of Rauru)[5] – referring to Rauru as doing the work of Ruatepupuke, an atua associated with carving from generations earlier. Rauru was the son of Toi, who features in many tribal traditions and may be Toitehuatahi (Toi who was here already) from Hawaiki. Rauru was the father of Whātonga, who later travelled to the East Coast where he initiated a whare wānanga named Taperenui a Whātonga (the local kura kaupapa in Rangitukia at East Cape has taken this name); and on the west coast of the North Island, Ngā Rauru (or Ngā Rauru Kītahi) iwi is named after him. The interweaving of this whakapapa is important as it imbues art history with a distinct Te Ao Māori perspective in which people are central.

## Ancestral narratives of carving

Other narratives merge the celestial with the ancestral, where stories join the generations into a single account. One important example comes from Ūawa Tolaga Bay on the East Coast. The chief Mokena Romio's manuscript connects the deity Ruatepupuke with the ancestor Hīngāngāroa, who lived in the late fifteenth century. He describes how: 'This man, Hingangaroa, was born, grew, and matured. The houseposts brought by Ruatepupuke were shown to him. Later, he erected a house and attached the houseposts to it. Preserved in that house were the models of the manaia, taowaru and many other patterns. When that house was completed Hingangaroa named it Rawheoro [Slow Sun or Rumbling Day].'[6]

This is reinforced in a mōteatea (lament) written by Rangiuia, tohunga of the whare wānanga Te Rāwheoro in the late eighteenth or early nineteenth century:

Me ko Manutangirua, ko Hingangaroa.
Ka tu tona whare, Te Rawheoro, e
Ka tipu te whaihanga, e hika, ki Uawa
Ka riro te whakautu, te Ngaio-tu-ki-Rarotonga,
Ka riro te manaia, ka riro te taowaru;
Ka taka i raro na, i a Apanui e

Who had Manutangirua, whose son was Hingangaroa
He it was who established the house, Te Rawheoro,
And arts and crafts flourished, my son, at Uawa
There came in payment, Te Ngaio-tu-ki-Rarotonga
    [the ngaio tree that stood in Rarotonga]
And there went in exchange the Manaia and Taowaru
    [motifs used in carving]
Passing round thence to the north, Te Apanui,
    [Emerging at Turanga].[7]

This mōteatea records the whakapapa of the whare wānanga ('Manutangirua, whose son was Hingangaroa') and information about the teaching in the school ('arts and crafts flourished'); in particular it records the transmission of specific carving motifs ('manaia and taowaru') and the payment for this knowledge ('There came in payment, Te Ngaio-tu-ki-Rarotonga', a cloak). Here time and worlds are compressed in a single breath – the cloak's name refers to it 'standing' in Rarotonga, thereby activating Pacific ancestral connections, while the carvings on which the whare wānanga was based came from the world of atua. The knowledge of carving was symbolised in the carving motifs taowaru (either a notched surface pattern or a raised central line of carving)[8] and manaia (a spiritual guardian, often shown as a beaked figure), and the balance of male/female art practices is exemplified in the fact that the motifs were exchanged for a cloak, whose name references the Pacific as an ongoing important source of identity.

There are tribal variations of Ruatepupuke's importance: Ngā Pōtiki, based around Tauranga, say that Rua was the 'father of carving', while Ngāti Porou maintain that Rua went to the underworld to obtain carvings. The story begins with Te Manuhauturuki, the son of Ruatepupuke, who was out on the ocean one day when Tangaroa, god of the sea, became angry with him and carried him down to his house, Huiteananui, which was under the sea. Ruatepupuke became worried about his son, and started searching for him. When he found him, Te Manuhauturuki had been transformed into the tekoteko (figurehead) of Tangaroa's house. Incensed, Ruatepupuke killed those belonging to Tangaroa's house, grabbed his son and some of the exterior carvings from the house, and fled home. In doing so he not only avenged the kidnapping of his son, but also brought the knowledge of carving to this world, 'which has been passed down to the present generation'.[9] For carver Pakaariki Harrison, who was trained in history by Pine Taiapa (Ngāti Porou), it was Tangaroa who is essential here:

> As the origin of carving, Tangaroa occupies a very important part as its patron in the ceremonial and ritualistic observances for carved houses and canoes. As a supreme atua of the same status as Tane, Tangaroa was invested with the power of infinity, able to dwell in the past, present, and future simultaneously. He was both constructive and destructive, sacred and profane, positive and negative.[10]

Ngāti Porou named a meeting house after Ruatepupuke; this was built at Tokomaru Bay and opened in 1881. When Mokena Romio, the house's patron, sold the whare in the 1890s to J. F. G. Umlauff, a German ethnographic dealer from Hamburg, he sent a manuscript (maybe in his own hand) with the carvings and other parts of the whare that relayed the story of Ruatepupuke and reinforced the synchronicity of key narratives through the generations.[11] The whare is now in the Field Museum in Chicago.

Ruatepupuke's exploits are embedded in carved designs: human figures are modelled on the internal poupou collected from Tangaroa's house, and the popular manaia form symbolises Te Manuhauturuki when he was transformed into a tekoteko.[12] These narratives do not compete with one another; instead, they reinforce the multivocal nature of the telling of whakapapa.

Carvers recorded other ancestors by creating designs that they named after them. On pātaka, carvers often incised a raised, jagged pattern known as te taratara ā Kae. The design portrays the narrative of Kae, who killed and ate Tutunui, a pet whale belonging to Tinirau. Tinirau sent a group of women assassins to find the culprit. They travelled from village to village until they discovered the thief: they knew it was him when they saw whale meat in his gapped teeth.[13] The barbs of the design are a reference to Kae's crooked teeth: taratara translates as 'barbed, prickly, rough'. Women have agency here as assassins sent to identify and then dispense with the thief. In another telling the women performed a haka, which resulted in the same open-mouthed Kae. This account also furnishes more information about architecture of this early time.

### The archaeological record

The Pacific world was full of carving, tapa and tatau, and ancestors brought these styles to Aotearoa in different variations. Artists created specific forms and added surface designs for spiritual, political, economic or personal reasons. Māori history has been charted in carving; other expressions of culture, such as textiles, have not survived because the materials used to make them have not lasted. Few wood carvings from earlier than the fifteenth century have survived. We know, however, that artists before that time were confident in their tools and in working hard materials, as carved personal ornaments in durable materials such as parāoa (whalebone), pounamu (greenstone) and stone are still in existence today.

Archaeologists and anthropologists have discovered many early carved taonga buried in swamps or placed deliberately in caves. In their study of pre-European taonga buried in wetlands, the anthropologists Caroline Phillips, Dilys Johns and Harry Allen[14] argue that Māori ancestors buried their wooden treasures for many reasons, including sometimes to conceal them temporarily from invading taua – such as the 150 taonga in wood buried at Waitore Point near Pātea, Taranaki, c.1420. For others, burial was a permanent solution – such as at the Kauri Point site, Katikati, western Bay of Plenty (1460–1650), where people deliberately broke hundreds of carved wooden heru (ornamental combs) and then abandoned the site as tapu.[15]

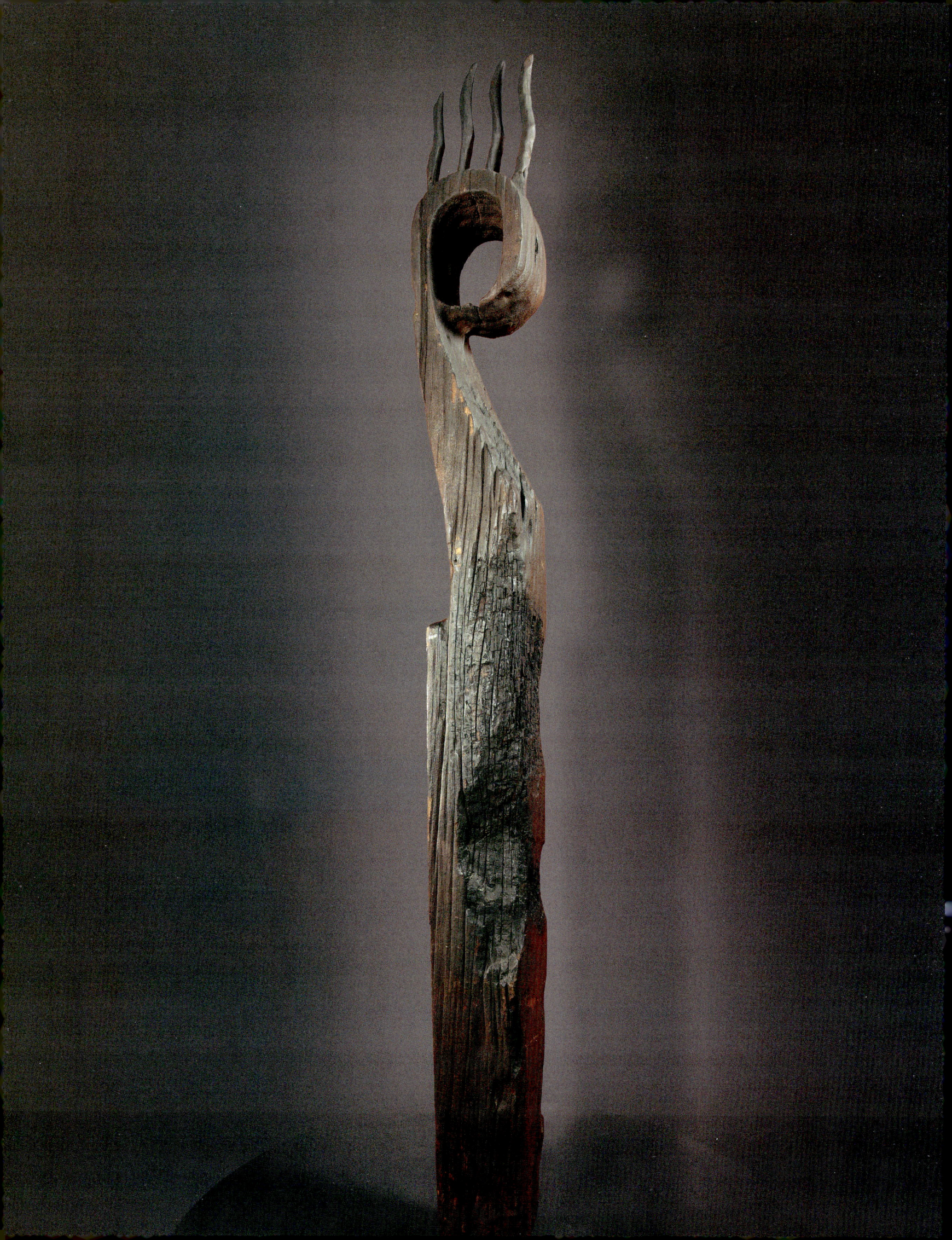

The ancestors brought their Pacific building traditions with them to Aotearoa. Based on archaeological evidence from Palliser Bay and elsewhere, by the late 1300s people in these locations had transformed the fale into whare, using a rectangular floor plan and adding walls to protect from the elements. Pūrākau (oral histories) record several stories about how houses were built in the first arrival period. One example comes from around Kāwhia, where Turi and his people landed and travelled inland to a river they named Pāteanui a Turi (Pātea). At the nearby settlement of Rangitawhi they built a house named Matangirei.[16] Another story – this one from Te Tai Tokerau – records how Nukutawhiti and his brother-in-law Ruanui both arrived in New Zealand and settled on either side of the Hokianga Harbour, where each built a house to establish their mana whenua (their right to be on the land).

These accounts provide the models for later tikanga in relation to building houses, with the need for a formal house opening. They also demonstrate the versatility of the carver as the architect as well as the builder, and the one who makes specific carved elements to embellish the house and to give added meaning and mana.

### Carving motifs

Māori and Pacific carving is based on specific motifs and designs, of which the human figure is the most popular – typically representing an ancestor or an atua. Several favoured examples of carving remind us of the close link between art making in the Pacific and in Aotearoa.

In Tāmaki Paenga Hira Auckland War Memorial Museum is the oldest known wood carving made in New Zealand, since named Tāngonge by Te Rarawa, on whose tribal land the carving was found. Archaeologists have radiocarbon-dated the wood that Tāngonge is made from to c.1400, although it is likely that the actual carving is slightly later. The carving is in an A-B-A composition – A is a manaia, and B is a human figure – and this composition led to its initial interpretation as a lintel. The manaia figures at each end are early examples, with their multi-toothed mouths and 'beaks' facing outwards; next to them, moving inwards, is a series of large chevrons, characteristic of the period. Two features on the carving closely resemble work from the Pacific, especially Tuha'apae (Austral Islands): the notching along the edge, and the shaping of the central male figure, with his triangular head facing forward, and arms and legs in an upraised position.

Drain diggers discovered the carving at Tāngonge lake in Northland in 1920, buried under almost a metre of clay. Both sides of the work are carved. This refutes the idea that he was used as a house lintel; more likely he was a roof combing, similar to those made in New Guinea, or perhaps a gateway figure, as there are holes in the base that would have been used to lash it onto a structure. Tāngonge is asymmetrical: the terminal manaia figures have a different number of teeth. The carving has become central to Te Rarawa's contemporary identity. In 2012 Tāngonge was taken back to the North, where he was greeted with a pōwhiri (welcome ceremony) at Pukepoto Marae, then put on display at Te Ahu heritage centre in Kaitāia for several years before returning to Auckland Museum. Tāngonge featured in the *Oceania* exhibition held at the Royal Academy of Arts, London in 2018, as an icon of Te Rarawa people and an important example of early Māori art.

Deity and ancestral figures were not always depicted naturalistically. At the same time as Te Rarawa ancestors were creating Tāngonge, further south in the Waikato area, Tainui carvers were fortunate to have a tall sculpture from Hawaiki on which to base their works. The carving of Uenukutūwhatu (known as Uenuku) was made c.1500 as the carved manifestation of the mauri stone brought to New Zealand on the *Tainui* waka. Stylistically, Uenuku has strong links to carvings dedicated to Kū, the Hawaiian akua (god) of war, which have similar angled projections at the top. The koru-shaped 'head' suggests Uenuku was made some time after 1500, when koru and spirals were first used in carving. Here the artist has created the deity or mauri as a pou, as if he were a large figure. The kaitiakitanga of the carving currently resides with King Tūheitia, as ariki of Ngāti Apakura, the traditional guardians of Uenukutūwhatu.

The manaia is the second most popular motif, after the human figure, used in carving today. Its origins can be sourced back to Tāngonge, as well as to small taonga where manaia feature, such as heru. The manaia is often presented as a beaked figure, and sometimes is even reduced to simply a beaked face. Carvers often placed manaia on either side of a human figure, reinforcing the manaia's spiritual guardian role.

Waikato-Tainui ancestors brought over the mauri of Uenuku-tuwhatu in a stone from Hawaiki and later transferred it into this wooden carving. The style of the upper projections relate to carvings of the war god Ku in Hawai'i.
Te Awamutu Museum, 2056

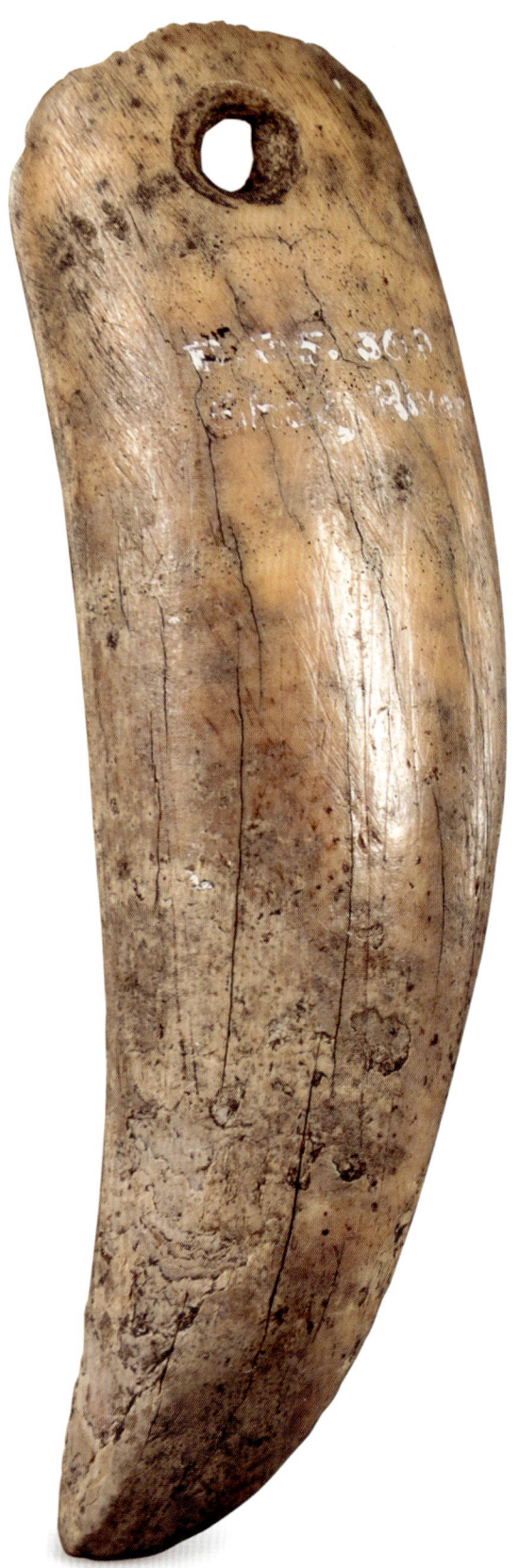

Pakaariki Harrison describes manaia as depicting 'the aura of a chiefly person illustrated in the carving and reflect[ing] the energies and power of his or her divine descent'.[17]

Pacific ancestors also depicted animals in their art, and they brought this practice to Aotearoa, where carvers continued to draw on stories about animals until around 1500. Ngāi Tahu ancestors created a unique image of the kurī – the Polynesian dog: the carving, which was found in Moncks Cave at Ōhikaparuparu (Sumner), dates to around 1500.[18] The carver used native kānuka to create a palm-sized figure, complete with long nose and pricked ears. The tail curls around to touch the body, thereby creating a loop to pass a suspension cord through. Its use is unknown: it may have been a child's toy (given its small size) or a neck ornament (given the suspension hole).

The use of animal imagery in carving evolved between 1200 and 1500. A rei ika (stone pectoral) found in Okains Bay, Banks Peninsula in the South Island depicts a bonito, a fish that is not found in New Zealand waters. Bird imagery can be found on a small rei niho (whale-tooth adornment) from Whangamumu, Northland, as well as on an unfinished bird-shaped bowl from Mōtītī Island in the Bay of Plenty. This latter treasure is particularly unusual as the base has four legs, suggesting it may be a remnant of presentation bowls that were used in the Pacific but were very rare in New Zealand. These examples show that artists across the country were experimenting with different motifs and styles, building on their known repertoire from the Pacific, and challenging themselves to depict the new world around them.

### Styles of carving

By the sixteenth century, distinct styles of carving had emerged; Mead identified ten.[19] Some were based on tribal or waka regions (Horouta o Tākitimu, Mātaatua, Tainui, Te Arawa, Tūwharetoa, Ngāti Kahungunu); others on geographic regions (Hauraki, Te Tai Tokerau, Taranaki, Te Waipounamu). These regions had schools of carving where men learnt a specific style of carving.

We can track the ways in which different tribal styles emerged more broadly by analysing the depiction of human figures. The first is a sinuous style, with a plain body, as can be seen in carvings from Te Tai Tokerau (Northland) and Te Tai Hauāuru (western North Island), as well as some from Te Tai Rawhiti (East Coast). In several examples

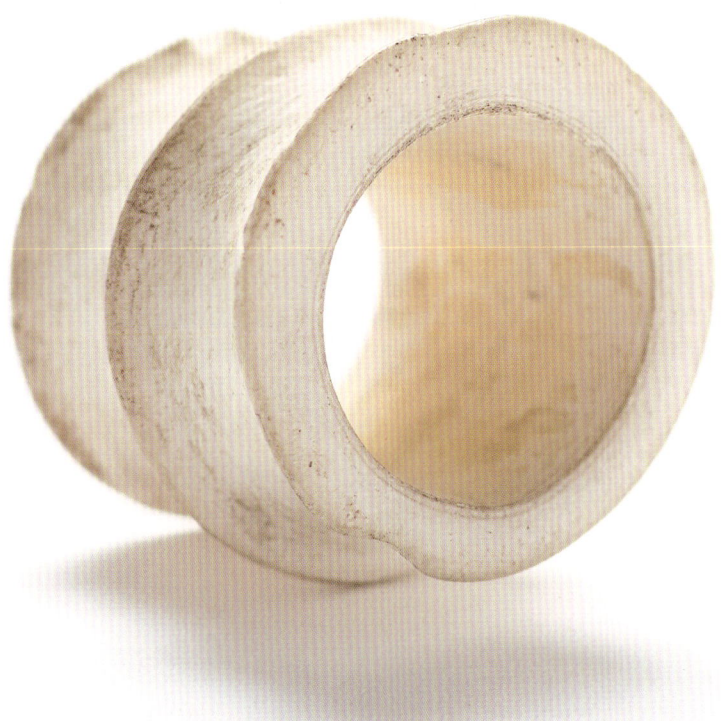

Reels were some of the earliest types of adornments made from malleable materials such as bone, and worn in groups strung on cord around the neck. They were not made past 1600, probably due to a change in fashion.
Te Papa Tongarewa Museum of New Zealand, ME001785, Augustus Hamilton Collection, purchased 1914

Opposite: This rei niho (whale-tooth ornament) found at the Shag River mouth has been hollowed and would have been perforated, ready to be worn around the neck.
Tūhura Otago Museum, D35.369

of epa (a carved panel with a slanted top) from northern Taranaki, Te Ātiawa carvers have created movement in the composition by rendering the human body in a serpentine style, and they have represented three-dimensional space in a two-dimensional form by positioning the claw-like hands coming through the mouth and the arms twisting around the legs. The second style of human figure is square, with the figure depicted frontally, chest facing forward, the hands usually placed on the ribs or on the legs, with the legs carved upright. This style dominated among iwi in the central North Island and on the East Coast.

As iwi migrated around the country, the styles spread too. One example is the ancestor Kahungunu, who spent time in Te Tai Tokerau (where his descendants are Ngāti Kahu) and around the Mahia Peninsula on the East Coast (the tribal seat of Ngāti Kahungunu). The ancestor Awanui also began his life in the North; his descendants migrated southeast (to form Ngāti Awa) and southwest (to form Te Ātiawa). Awanui's people carved waka tūpāpaku (containers to store human bones) in the North in the eighteenth century in a distinctive sinuous style that they took with them when they journeyed south.[20] Awanui's brother was Rauru, and their descendants' styles of carving are closely related. Carvers would have worked together in neighbouring kāinga and pā on major projects such as pātaka, and would have transferred these styles of carving to smaller treasures, such as taonga pūoro (sound instruments) and waka huia (treasure boxes). Understanding whakapapa and the narratives associated with ancestors allows us to understand the emergence and movement of tribal carving styles. The carving traditions of Ngāti Awa and Ngāti Tarāwhai are related through the practice of kai taonga or pākūhā (the presentation of a gift). This consisted of the knowledge of the art of carving being presented by one leader to another. These relationships across the country bound community to community, and were reinforced with the circulation of carvers and with joint carving projects.

### The training of carvers

Carvers were typically rangatira, whose work reinforced ideas of whakapapa and whenua, mana and tapu. Chiefs were expected to have some artistic ability – certainly by the mid-eighteenth century; before this time little is known about the role, status and training of carvers. Often the names of

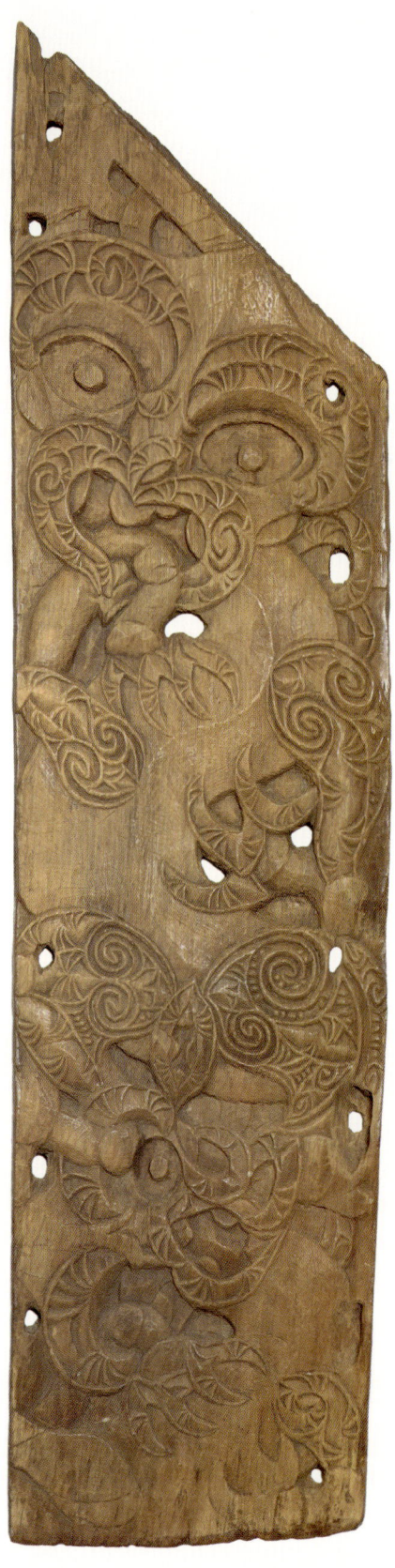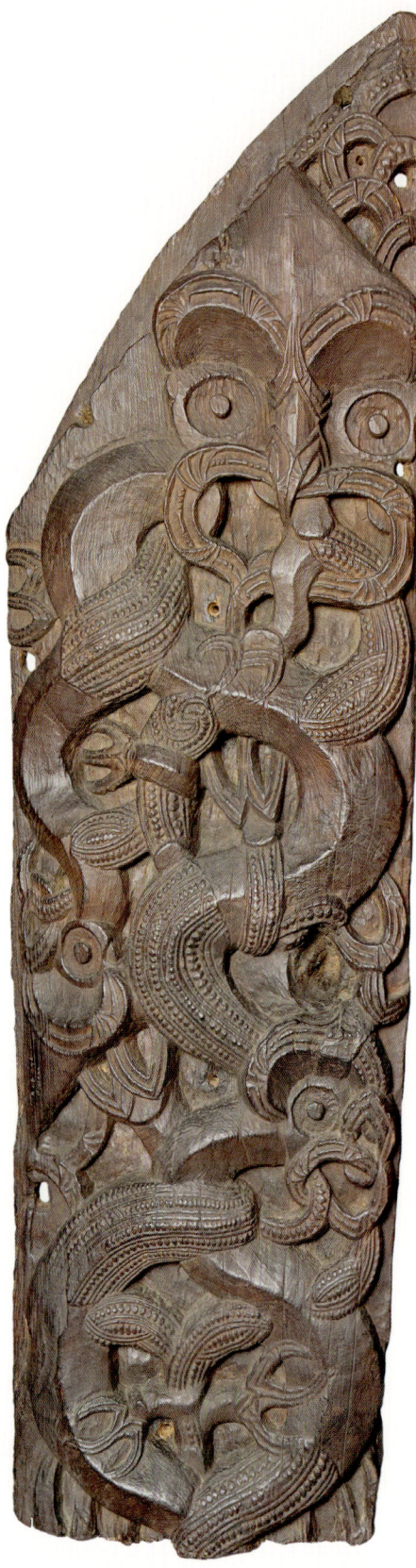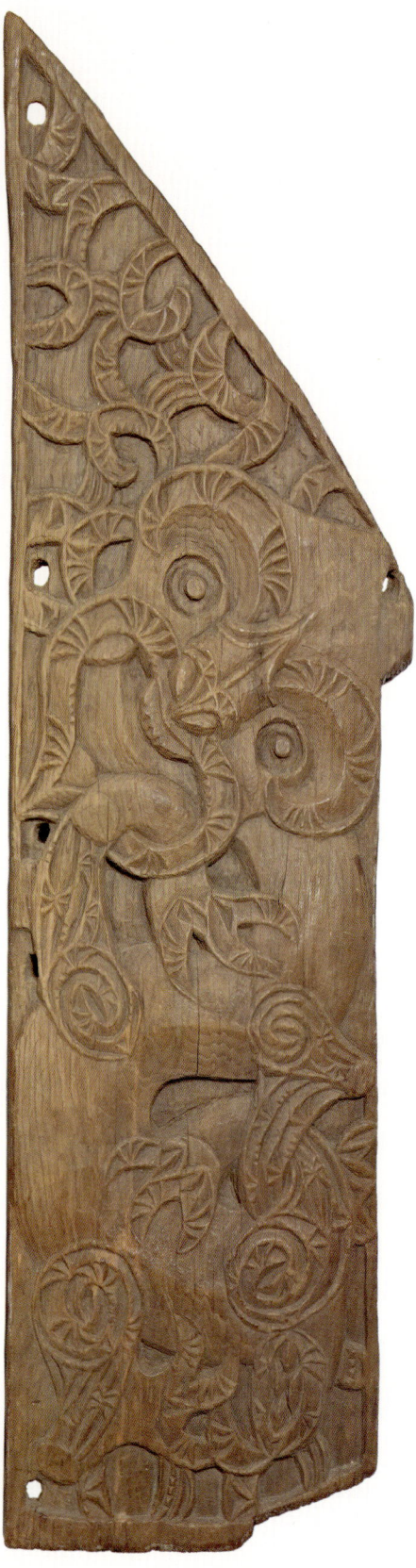

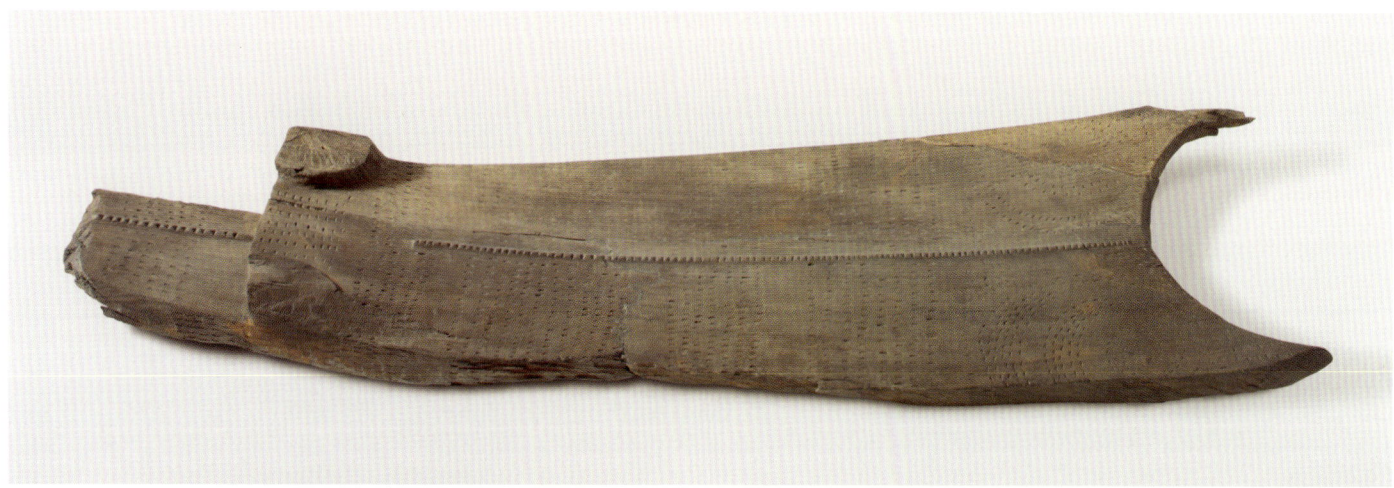

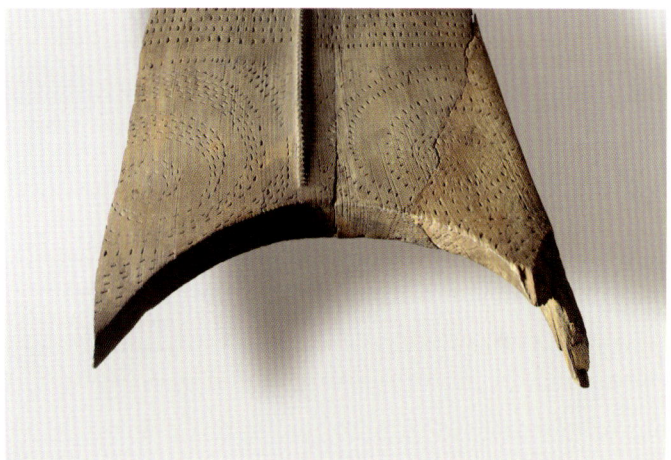
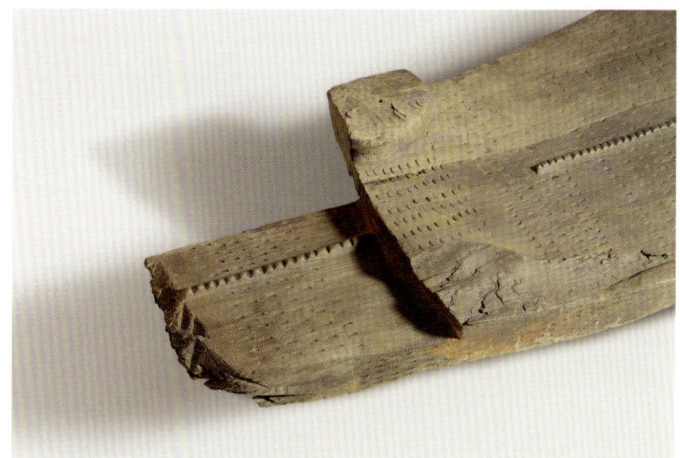

Carving uncovered at Waitore, Taranaki, known as the Waitori haumi. This early form of prow can be read as a transitional carving, as the carver negotiated Pacific geometric styling, alongside a new discovery – the double spiral. The notches may have been made with the edge of a toki.
Aotea Utanganui Museum of South Taranaki, A82.500, Waitore Artefacts Collection, photographs by Richard Wotton

Opposite, left to right: Te Ātiawa carving in the period 1500–1800 was complex and distinctive, with the peaked foreheads, plain bodies, mata kupenga and unaunahi surface designs, claw-like hands, and overall complex composition of the figures.
Puke Ariki, New Plymouth, A77.332

A number of epa made for pātaka have survived from the 1500–1800 period in Taranaki. During this time the pātaka emerged as a unique architectural form to reinforce publicly the mana of the local rangatira and wider hapū. Taranaki carver Te Tuiti-Moeroa carved this epa featuring two primary and two secondary figures.
Puke Ariki, New Plymouth, A77.330

This epa was also carved by Te Tuiti-Moeroa, hidden in the ground, and later found on a private property in Waitara.
Puke Ariki, New Plymouth, A77.331

rangatira are associated with specific carvings, although it is likely that they commissioned the works or were the kaitiaki of them rather than the actual carver. Chiefly sons were taught about the attributes of a leader in the whare wānanga, and this mātauranga was made visually manifest in carvings. In the mid-1850s, Ngāti Rangiwewehi chief Wiremu Maihi Te Rangikāheke described these leadership attributes. At the time, whare wānanga were under threat of closure due to many factors, including shifts in pūmanawa – leadership qualities in the community – and the introduction of literacy. Mead summarised the pūmanawa that Te Rangikāheke identified:

> A chief was expected to be brave, a good warrior, wise in counsel, excellent in keeping the food storehouses full, able at oratory. Good at looking after people (the quality of manaakitanga) and good at art. Especially, he should be able to build or negotiate the building of large houses such as storehouses, chief's houses, cooking sheds and canoes.[21]

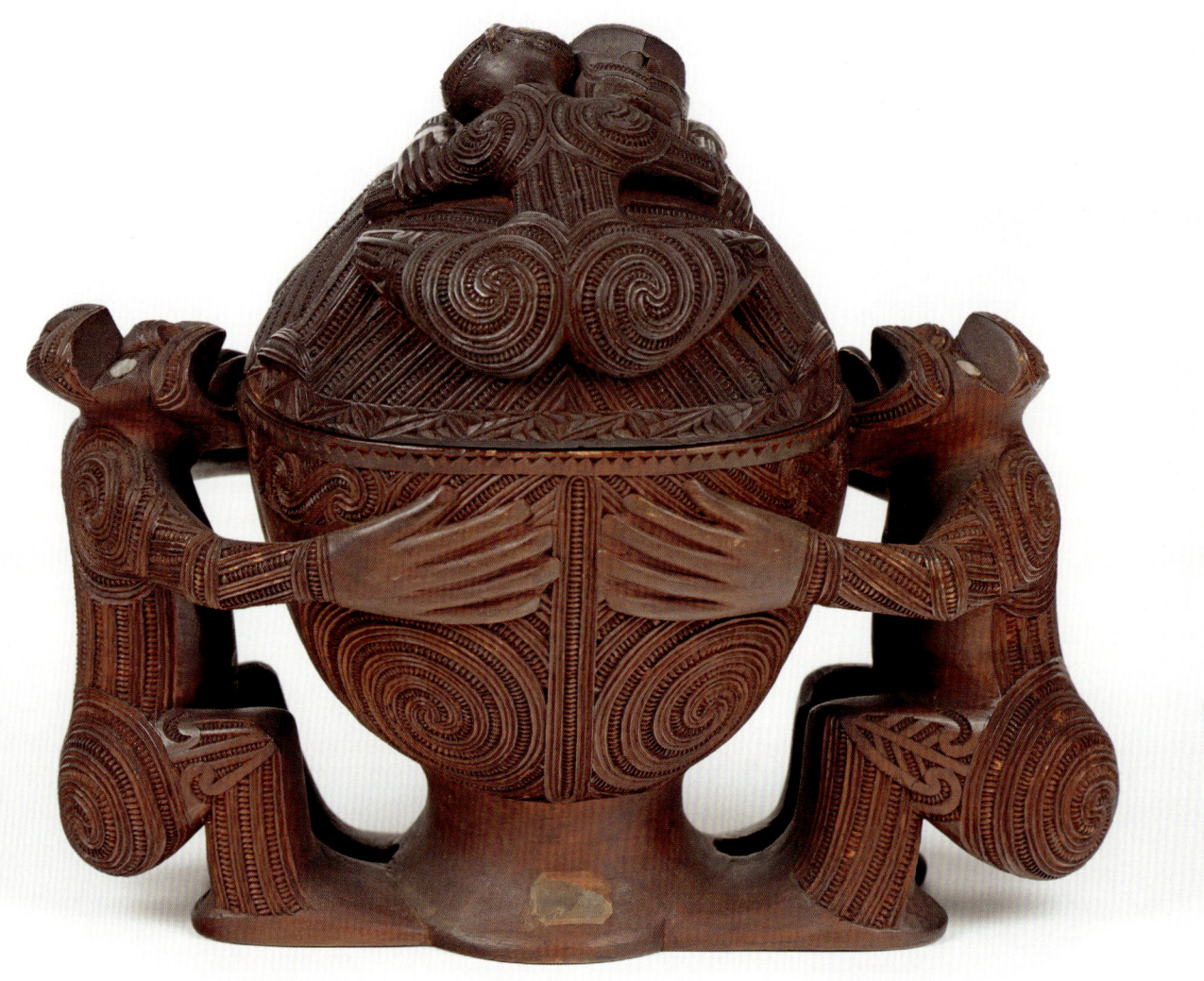

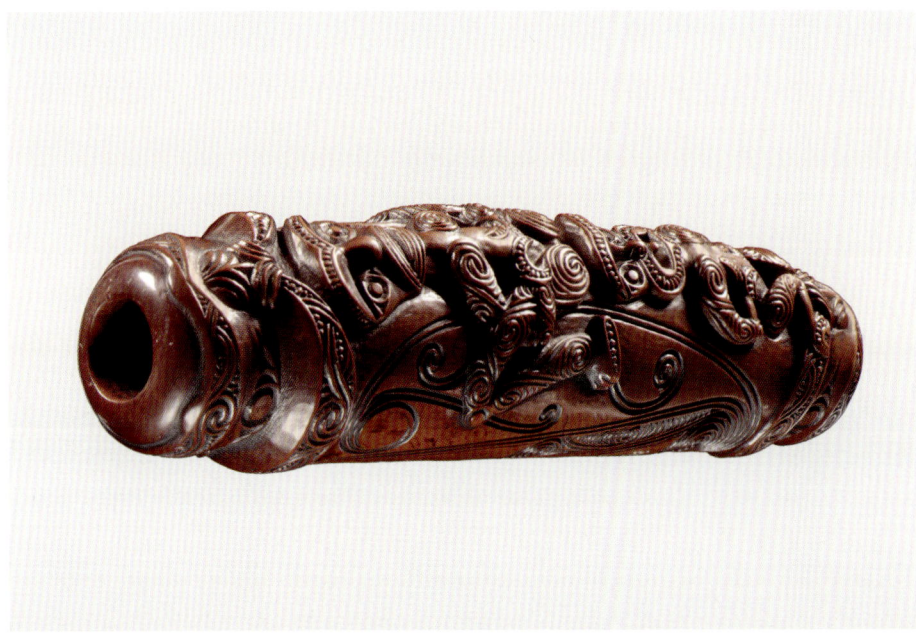

**Above:** Carvers would often practise their hand on smaller objects. Waka huia were popular as treasures made for private spaces, or for presentation to others, especially in the nineteenth century. Ngāti Tarāwhai artist Ānaha Te Rāhui carved two figures 'wrestling' on the lid of at least three kumete in the late nineteenth century: this one is in Auckland Museum, another is in Sydney, and a third in Chicago. The subject matter was apparently a land dispute at Tikitere, Rotorua.
Tāmaki Paenga Hira Auckland War Memorial Museum, 442, 106

**Left:** Kōauau (sound instrument), carver unknown. With further study, it is likely that the distinct style of this carver can be tracked across museum collections.
Te Papa Tongarewa Museum of New Zealand, OL000035, Oldman Collection, gift of the New Zealand Government, 1992

At the whare wānanga, carvers would learn the practical skills of carving, about whao (chisels) and other tools, and also the laws of tapu. Whakairo is a tapu art form, and in making new artworks it was essential that the correct karakia be chanted to protect all those involved – this recalls the story of Rata and the tree. There are a number of kōrero where tapu has been broken, resulting in grave consequences. In the 1870s Te Waru (Ngāti Whāoa) commissioned a house to be built for his wife from Tara Te Awatapu (Ngāti Tarāwhai) and Te Roroa (Ngāti Ranginui). While the whare was still under construction, Te Waru entered the building site smoking a pipe, which was a hara (forbidden action) that could put the state of tapu at risk. A tohunga warned the carvers to stop the project, but Te Waru told them to keep working. Te Waru's wife died soon after, and the carvers put down their tools; but when he remarried he asked them to start carving once more. However, the hara was still there, and his second wife also died. Some time later, Te Waru married once again: two sons were born of this union, but his wife and both children later died. The patron then realised that the project needed to be terminated, and the whakairo were stored away[22] – but still the problems continued. Te Waru was persuaded to sell the carvings to tourism operator Charles Nelson to be installed in another house that was later named Rauru. Both tohunga who were present at the opening to bless that house died shortly afterwards. Rauru was sold in 1904 to the Museum für Völkerkunde in Hamburg, where he still stands today.

Anthropologist Bernie Kernot identified other characteristics that were expected of a chief who became a carver. Some artists were tohunga ahurewa (religious experts), while others acted as military experts (e.g. Tūwharetoa) or as political chiefs.[23] The chief Tūrongo of Tainui, for instance, built a whare as a political move to woo Ruapūtahanga, perhaps for her renowned skills with her taiaha (long staff), named Taukākā.[24] However, he was foiled by his brother Whatihua, and left the incomplete house to move to Mahia Peninsula.

Over the nineteenth century, artists either assumed all of these roles, or none of them, and were only brought in to help out on specific projects. These projects might require extra artists because of the scale of the carving, and in that case, local men would be taught on the job to carry out a range of carving tasks. It was imperative to the mana of the rangatira that the project be carried out to the highest degree of excellence – and expedience. Every chief had some artistic talent, as well as other skills such as negotiation and diplomacy (when working with a community), budgeting (planning costs of materials and labour) and building. Into the twentieth century these roles have been split even further with the increase in building regulations and the specialised skills required of building designers and builders as well as carvers.

Many Ngāti Kahungunu chiefs were noted carvers. Te Hāpuku, for example, was a well-known leader around Mahia Peninsula, but he also knew how to carve.[25] A rākau whakapapa (genealogical staff) now in MTG Hawke's Bay Tai Ahuriri (A.11) is attributed to him.[26] Certainly his pā at Waipukurau on the East Coast held 'carvings of great stature',[27] and he was involved as a patron on the construction of Kahurānaki I at Te Hauke settlement; the whare whakairo was opened in 1877, a year before his death. The carver on this house was Hori Rōpiha, who was helped by twelve people from various hapū of Ngāti Raukawa. This project reinforced a relationship between the iwi, building on an earlier episode whereby Ngāti Raukawa had exchanged Te Hāpuku for a piece of obsidian while he was a prisoner of Waikato in 1824.

Carvers worked alone on various other projects, especially smaller work such as waka huia, taonga pūoro, hoe (paddles) or weapons. Many of the carvers who were active before 1840 are unknown, despite their style of work being very distinctive. The artist of the papahou on page 67, for instance, has a particular way of rendering the single spiral on the hips and buttocks with single haehae (lines); he depicts hands as pincers, and eyes that are elliptical. Similarly there are two waka huia in museums on either side of the Atlantic Ocean, made by the same carver (as yet unnamed): again with elliptical eyes, the unusual kink in the central spirals, and hands through the mouth. Future research may eventually reveal the identities of the carvers, but for now it is enough to gather together the artists' known corpus of works and trace their provenance, to try to isolate a geographic or tribal affiliation and, from there, delve further into the local whakapapa, to attempt to identify a specific individual responsible for the work.

In these larger meeting house or waka projects it is often difficult to identify the specific hand of individual carvers:

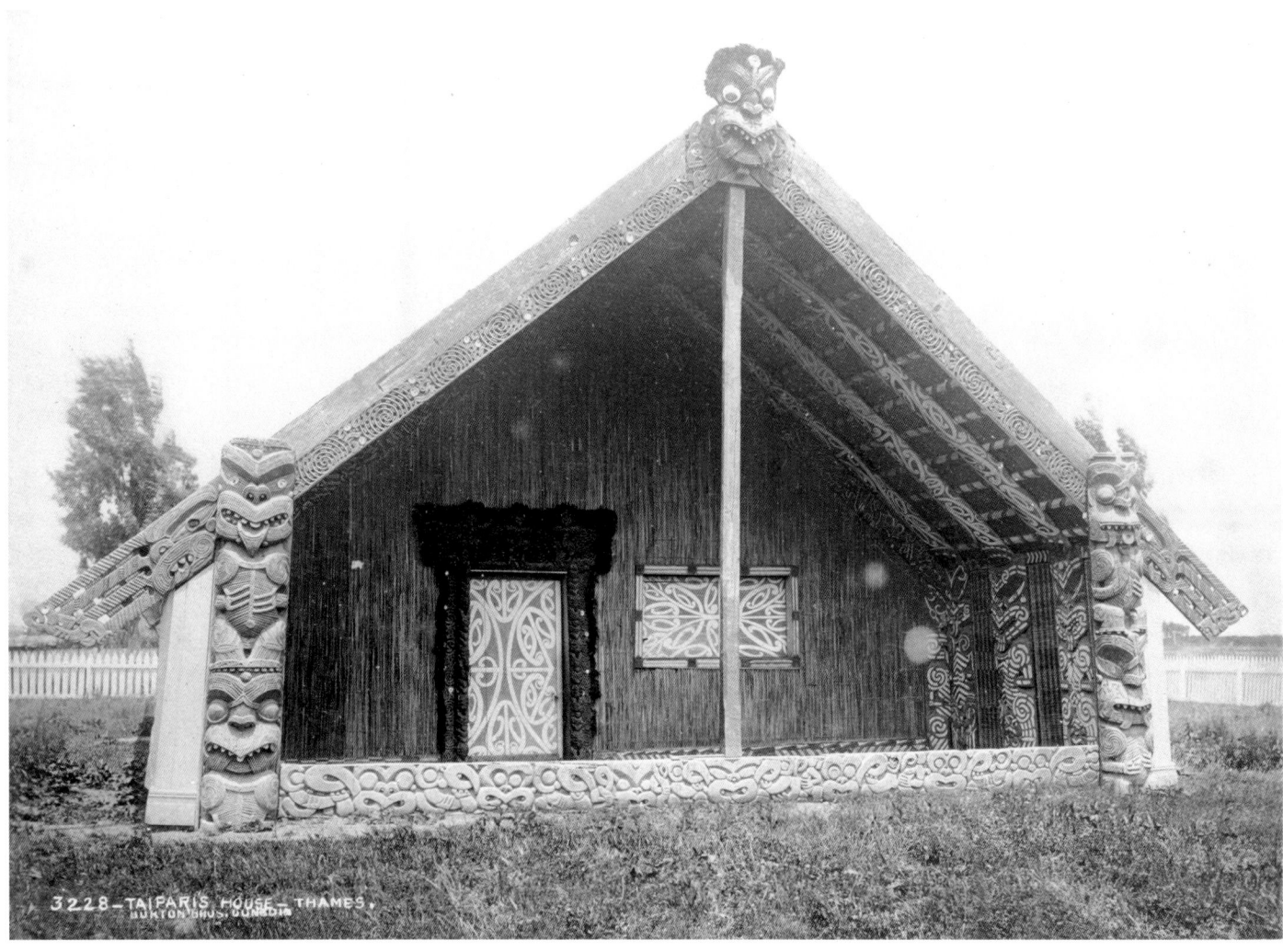

Hotunui was the second meeting house project led by Ngāti Awa after the New Zealand Wars. Built from 1875 to 1878 at Pārāwai near Thames, the carvers drew on connections with other iwi to bring together a team which could create a built design which would relate to their earlier project Mātaatua (1872–1875), which by this time had been taken out of Whakatāne by the colonial government for display in Australia. Hotunui was placed on loan by Ngāti Awa in Auckland Museum for conservation purposes and is now one of the highlights of the Māori Court.
Burton Brothers, 1880s, Alexander Turnbull Library, PA7-05-19

for many of them this might be their only known work, especially if they came from the local community and were there out of necessity. The names of the chiefs Wepiha and Apanui Te Hamaiwaho are typically associated with the projects to construct the wharenui Mātaatua (1872–1875) and Hotunui (1875–1878), but we know that many other carvers worked on these houses; the artists were strategically selected from specific hapū in order to reinforce political and social relationships that were disrupted by the New Zealand Wars. These two projects were also initiated with the kaupapa of reasserting the mana of Ngāti Awa, the primary commissioning iwi, after their previous houses, Te Whare o Rangatapu and Tūpāpakurau, had been destroyed.[28]

> Ko te tohu o te Rangatira he pataka whakairo e tu na i roto i te pa tuwatawata: the sign of a chief is a pātaka that stands in the fortified settlement.[29]

NGĀ TOI WHAKAIRO – THE ARTS OF CARVING

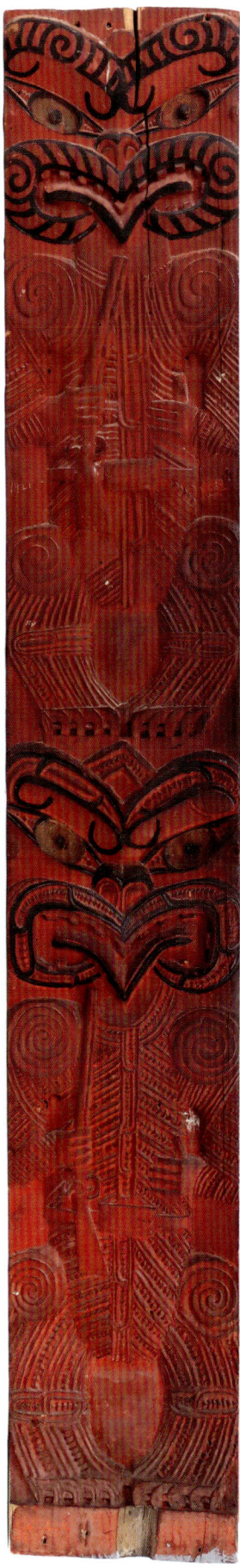

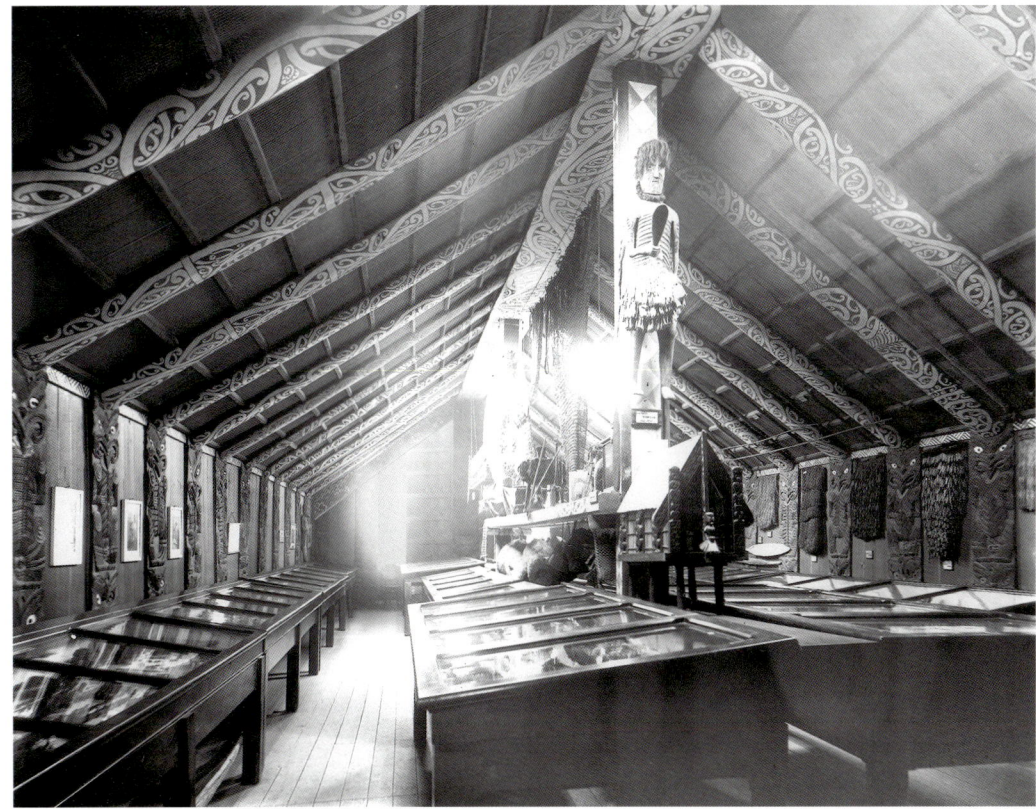

By the late 1870s new modes of teaching novice carvers were required: the whare wānanga, where selected young men were trained as chiefs and carvers, had almost all closed. Indeed, the sheer volume of projects being commissioned across the country required more carvers to be trained than were available, and apprentice carvers were often taught on the job rather than through any chiefly school. Fathers passed on their knowledge to their sons or nephews. Te Amo and his brother Tara Te Awatapu of Ngāti Tarāwhai were both carvers, and may have been taught by their uncle Mahikore.[30] This uncle–nephew method of teaching was found on the East Coast, too: Hoani Ngatai taught his nephew Hare Tokoata, and Hone Taahu taught his nephew Hone Ngatoto. Raharuhi Rukupō and his brother Pera Tawhiti worked together on the meeting house Te Hau ki Tūranga.[31] Sometimes a whole hapū were renowned for their carving: Te Whānau a Hinetapora were known as house builders, for example, and Ngāti Tarāwhai and Ngāti Pikiao as canoe builders.

Tohunga whakairo frequently carved skin as well as wood. Tame Poata (Ngāti Porou) was descended from illustrious tohunga whakairo and tohunga tā moko, including Hīngāngāroa, Īhenga and Tūkaki. He was born

Above: Interior of Ngāti Porou meeting house Hau Te Ana Nui o Tangaroa, in situ at Canterbury Museum.
Canterbury Museum, 19XX.2.4406

Left: Carving by Hone Taahu in 1874 from the meeting house Hau Te Ana Nui o Tangaroa, carved while Taahu was in Christchurch working with Tāmati Ngākaho on contract for Canterbury Museum. Both figures hold guns, referencing the recent troubles in the East Coast area during the New Zealand Wars. Sadly, this house was dismantled by the museum but may be re-erected as part of the redevelopment of the museum in consultation with iwi.
Canterbury Museum, 1874.1.37.2. The museum acknowledges the original commissioning whānau of Henāre Pōtae

| WHĀNAU RELATIONSHIPS IN CARVING | | | | |
| --- | --- | --- | --- | --- |
| Brothers | Father and son | Uncle and nephew | Other relationships | Hapū |
| Raharuhi Rukupō and brother Pera Tawhiti (Rongowhakaata) Te Amo and his brother Tara Te Awatapu (Ngāti Tarāwhai) Riwai Pakerau and his brother Haki Hokopaura (Ngāti Porou) Pine Taiapa and Hone Taiapa (Ngāti Porou) | Te Ngaru Whakapuka and his son Te Ngaru Ranapia Te Rāhui and his son Ānaha Kepa Te Rāhui Neke Kapua and his son Eramiha Neke Kapua (Eramiha's maternal uncle was also a carver, Tene Waitere, Ngāti Tarāwhai) Te Whenuanui and his sons Te Whenuanui Mihaka and Matika (Tūhoe) Apanui Te Hamaiwaho and his son Wepiha Apanui (Ngāti Awa) Hotene and his son Hira Hotene (Ngāti Hokopu) Iwikau Te Heuheu and his son Patatai Te Heuheu (Ngāti Tūwharetoa) Te Whanarere and his son Te Hareti te Whanarere (Ngāti Pikiao) | Hone Taahu and nephew Hone Ngatoto (Ngāti Porou) Hoani Ngatai and nephew Hare Tokoata (Ngāti Porou) Mahikore and nephew Te Amo | *Cousins:* Wero Taroi, Te Amo a Tai and Tara Te Awatapu (Ngāti Tarāwhai) | Ngāti Uepohatu Ngāti Pikiao Ngāti Tarāwhai |

| PAYMENT FOR WHARE WHAKAIRO PROJECTS | | | | | | |
| --- | --- | --- | --- | --- | --- | --- |
| Date | House | Patron/iwi | Number of carvers | Money | Food | Other |
| 1875–1876 | Te Poho o Kahungunu I | Ngāti Kahungunu | 2 + 8 builders | £600 from Ngāpuhi, £500 from Te Waka Takerenui | | |
| 1877 | Kahurānaki I | Te Hāpuku, Ngāti Kahungunu | 13 | £775 | | 5 cartons of tobacco, 3 kākahu, 2 blankets |
| 1878 | Hotunui | Hotereni Taipari, Ngāti Maru | 70 | £1000 | 2 tons flour | |

in 1870 to Te Rangi i Paea (Ngāti Porou) and Thomas Porter, who was a colonel in the colonial forces. Poata did not start carving until he was fifty, in 1920; from that point on, however, he carved skin and wood until he died in 1942.[32] Two of his moko teachers may have been Herewini (Ngāti Porou) and Anaru Makiwhara (Waikato), as both were active at the time and worked with him. Hēni Ngāropi White received her kauae (incised design on the chin) from Poata in Tokomaru Bay in 1911 when she was only twenty-four. She went on to become the matriarch of her whānau. Poata also touched up the kauae on Tiripou Haerewa (Tūhoe) – the first cuts, made by Tarei Tī Wiremu, must have faded.

Te Puea Hērangi encouraged Poata to carve in the 1930s when she was rejuvenating the township of Tūrangawaewae as a centre for the Kīngitanga movement. She had organised for Piri Poutapu and Waka Kereama to train at the School of Maori Arts and Crafts at Rotorua, but she relied on the more experienced Poata to lead major projects. His work included the interior of the whare tūpuna Ngā Tokotoru at Waingaro, west of Ngāruawāhia, and an obelisk in the Tainui Trust Board Headquarters.

## Patronage

The artist and the art patron both had a vested interest in the completion of the final art project. The artist's reputation, as well as any innovative styles, would be confirmed by public acceptance, and could lead to more commissions. For the patron, the launch of the project would be a confirmation of their mana and their ability to fund the creation of other work.

Rangatira organised their community's resources to create a surplus to pay for large group projects such as pātaka (from c.1600) and waka taua (from c.1700). Patrons expected their hapū to support these projects by providing koha (gifts) for the artists, as well as sourcing raw materials (or trading for them) and working alongside the artist. Indeed, without this support the project could not proceed. This ohu style of working as a group was standard practice when undertaking large economic ventures – such as te mahinga kai (gathering seasonal food resources). Neich's identification of 231 nineteenth-century carvers showed that none of them worked alone all the time.[33] Groups in the community would be set specific tasks, such as hauling the timber from the forest. Ngāti Kahungunu chief and carver Te Waaka Perohuka called on a thousand men to haul the huge tōtara log from the bush to his pā Tutamoe, before he shaped it into the hull of a waka taua.³⁴

The community hosted the artist as a demonstration of their manaakitanga, which was one way to uphold the mana of the people. Artists were given the tastiest food and every little comfort possible, sometimes for many months, if not years. At the completion of the project the patron would organise a whakanoa (ritual cleansing) ceremony to lift the tapu of the construction site, and to publicly show off the magnificence of the building and, by extension, the mana of the chief and of the community.

Payment took different forms. Until the introduction of the cash and musket economy, artists were paid in traditional goods such as pounamu, luxury food items, adornments and cloaks. It was imperative that the payment be seen to be more than enough compensation. In 1878, seventy Ngāti Awa carvers refused to accept payment for the three years' work required to complete the Hotunui whare whakairo, as they considered it to be a wedding koha to the carver's sister, Mereana Mokomoko. However, Mokomoko's father-in-law, Wirope Hotereni Taipari, refused to accept this, as his people, Ngāti Maru, were renowned for their generosity: he sent Mokomoko to intercept the party on their way home and give them £1000.³⁵ Taipari also presented 2 tons of flour as part of Mokomoko's dowry at the start of the carving project.³⁶

Patrons relied on their personal and political relationships to source materials and artists for their projects. Pita Te Wharetoroa (Ngāti Hinekura) was the patron (and possibly one of the carvers) of the meeting house Houmaitawhiti at Otaramarae, Lake Rotoiti, which was built in the 1870s using materials from earlier houses as well as a number of disused waka taua. One waka was *Te Mihau o Tiki*, which belonged to Hokohinu; another was *Ahitahunoa*, which belonged to Te Tauhu (the carvings were enough for eight poupou); and the waka *Waipohui*, which had been acquired from Ihakara Te Aukaha and made into an epa (in exchange, Te Aukaha was given a horse named Tauhukura).³⁷ The patron divvied up the workload: some were sent into the bush to acquire timber, others from Ngāti Hinekura were asked to grow food for the workers. The differing stories about who did what in relation to the house reflects the competing political and economic dynamic that characterised this period of rapid change in many communities.

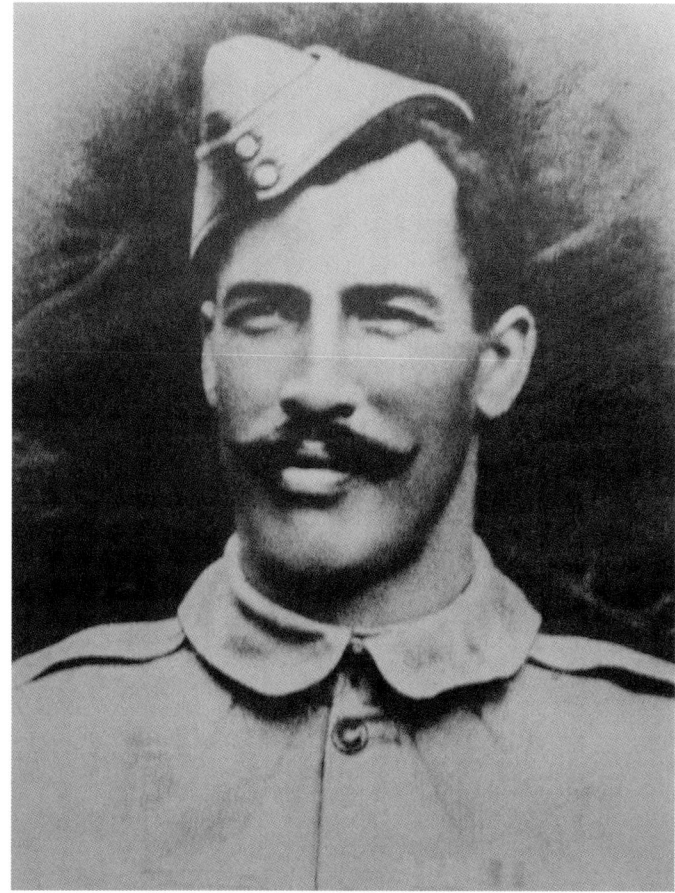

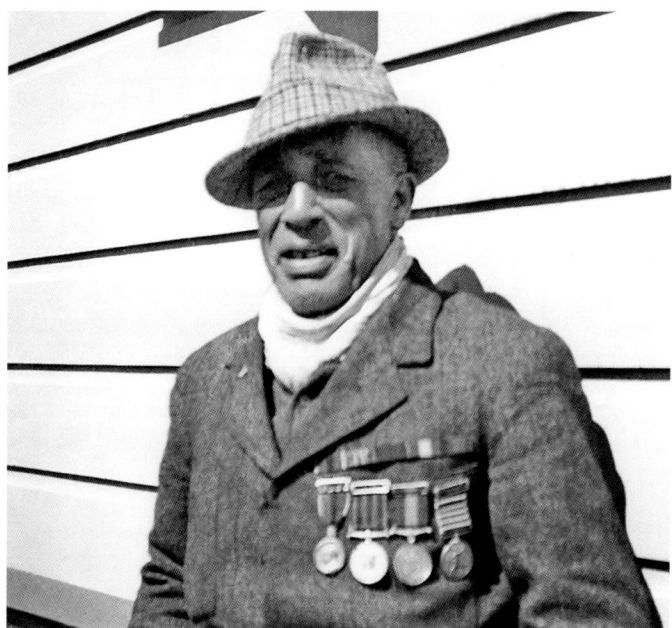

Tame Poata (bottom) was one of the few tohunga tā moko working with both uhi and needles in the 1920s and 1930s. He was highly sought after by wāhine keen to retain the tradition of moko kauae. Poata was also versatile in carving wood, and worked on a number of wharenui. He was, like his father, British army colonel Thomas Porter (top), a soldier, fighting in the South African War, in India and as part of the Pioneer Māori Battalion in World War One.
private collection

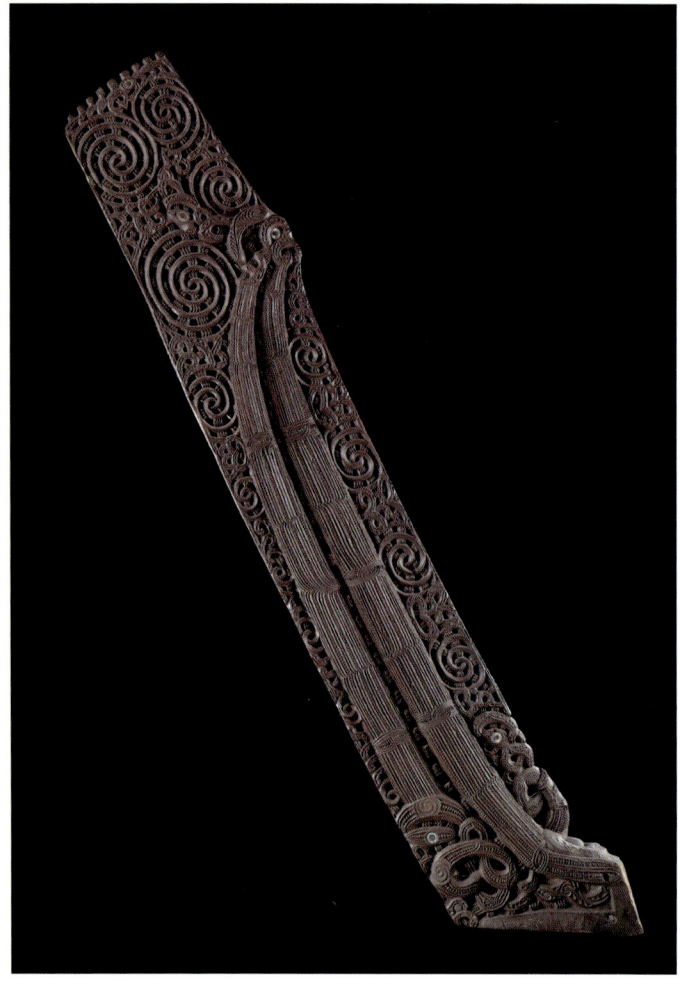

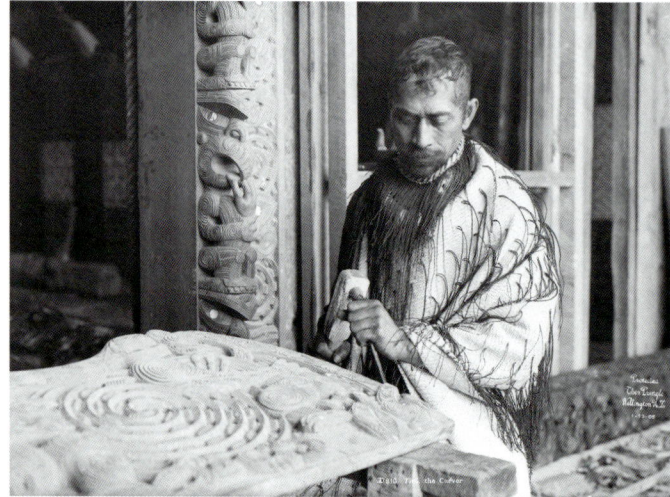

Above: Tene Waitere led new innovations in wood carving in the Rotorua area, taking commissions for wharenui that are now located as far afield as Hamburg, Germany and Surrey, UK.
scenic negatives and prints taken by Thomas Pringle, Alexander Turnbull Library, 1/1-007007-G

Left: Taurapa (canoe stern posts) were significant carvings in themselves, often receiving individual names. This example is *Kahutiaterangi*, and belonged to Te Rauparaha. The waka taua to which this taurapa was attached was used by Ngāti Toa on their expeditions to Kaiapoia pā in the 1820s and 1830s. The waka taua was sold in 1861 to James MacKay, assistant native secretary, and later acquired by the National Publicity Studios, which then gave the taurapa to Te Papa.
Te Papa Tongarewa Museum of New Zealand, ME014331, gift of the National Publicity Studios, 1981

Patrons were also expected to be leaders in terms of setting the artistic parameters of an art project. A patron would approach a certain artist because of their reputation, and knowledge of their previous work; artists, in turn, would work closely with the patron to ensure that their work was in tune with the patron's aspirations. In Tamatekapua whare rūnanga at Ōhinemutu (opened 1872), Te Arawa were keen to visualise their close relationship with the Crown, alongside whom they fought in the New Zealand Wars: initially they intended to have a carving or a painting of Queen Victoria.

Apirana Ngata argued that art could only be made during settled times: in times of war, art was not produced. Another reason may be that military leaders were also lead carvers – and their focus was elsewhere. Carving *was* undertaken during these warring times, however; in fact, it was critical that important treasures were made during this time. Hapū and iwi leaders commissioned waka taua to enhance their military capability. Ngāti Toa, for example, ordered a number of waka taua to be made in the early nineteenth century:

they used one, *Kahutiaterangi*,[38] on their taua to Kaiapoi pā in the 1820s and 1830s. Others have a more complex history: Te Arawa claims association with a taurapa that was part of a waka taua abandoned by Ngāpuhi at Pongakawa when they raided Mokoia Island in 1823 (in Auckland Museum; AM101); the taurapa was presented to Captain Gilbert Mair in 1870.[39]

## Carvers and tourism

Māori carving underwent radical transformation throughout the nineteenth century. A rapidly changing culture led to a rethinking of art traditions. Carvers, as leaders, drove innovation in their communities to respond to these changes; and, as artists, they transferred their skills from one monumental form to another: the waka and pātaka builders of the 1820s became the whare builders of the 1860s. As these different forms emerged, it was the tohunga whakairo who transformed the interpretations of the symbolism of the whole structure and of its components: the takere (keel) of the waka taua became the tāhuhu of the whare whakairo; the practice of naming waka and pātaka after ancestors was transferred to the whare rūnanga. The carver's role as articulator of history was maintained throughout. Artists were agents of change, pushing the boundaries of acceptable forms, styles, colours and materials and supported by patrons ever keen to set a new standard.

A growing tourism industry provided a chance for carvers to earn a living through their art and, at the same time, try out different styles and forms. By the 1890s, many carvers had set down their tools, as commissions dried up and hapū who now had their whare whakairo had no need for (and besides could not afford) other carved projects. In Rotorua, tourism was a primary industry that meant carvers could earn a living by working for communities and, at the same time, for tourism promoters such as Charles Nelson.[40] Ngāti Tarāwhai artists Tene Waitere (1853–1931), Ānaha Te Rāhui and Neke Kapua worked together on commissions from Nelson in 1897 and 1904, carving work for houses that Nelson was having reconfigured (Rauru and Nuku Te Apiapi).

Ngāti Tarāwhai carvers also worked for T. E. Donne in 1902–1910, and were paid five pounds a week for their services. He was the first director of the Department of Tourism and Health Resorts, established in 1901, and he held a 'romantic' view of Māori as a people frozen in time and living in the past. The houses he commissioned, such as Te Wharepuni-a-Māui, were 'purely for entertaining tourists'.[41] Donne commissioned this whare as a miniature house; it was never intended to be used as a wharenui.[42] Once it was completed in 1905, it was transported to the New Zealand International Exhibition in Christchurch, where it stood next to a composite house named Ōhinemutu[43] as a backdrop for performances, ceremonies and re-enactments. Donne was an avid collector, and he 'took' Te Wharepuni-a-Māui with him when he moved to London to be a diplomat. The whare is now on display in the Linden Museum, Stuttgart. Donne also commissioned a model pā to be built at Rotowhio. He directed that the existing pā be dismantled in order to make his pā the sole attraction. However, local Māori were unhappy with Donne's pā, which they described as '"paraka hōia" (soldiers' barracks)'.[44]

The work that carvers made for the tourism market was quite different. The term 'tourist art' has connotations of being cheap and immaterial, yet it is precisely for these audiences that Māori carvers were experimenting with the creation of cross-cultural objects, such as European trinkets with carved surface designs. In this way carvers were able to innovate and, at the same time, fine-tune their skills. Rotorua-based carver Ānaha Te Rāhui was a particularly innovative and prolific artist: he created works for this emerging, mainly Pākehā market, including tobacco pipes and tinder boxes, while at the same time producing traditional whakairo for Māori patrons and for the museums in Auckland and Wellington.[45] Te Rāhui had previously worked on commission – he built and carved waka in the 1840s, when he was in his twenties – but by the 1860s his practice had shifted to making meeting houses, including Rangitihi (1867–1871) and Tokopikowhakahau (1877). Ever responsive to a rapidly expanding tourism market in Rotorua, by the 1890s he was working for Nelson, completing the carvings for the meeting houses Rauru (1897) and Nuku Te Apiapi (1904) and setting them up as tourist ventures.

For carvers today, creating for the tourist market can provide a steady income at a time when long-term projects are thin on the ground. Their work is sold through museums such as Te Papa Tongarewa Museum of New Zealand and Tāmaki Paenga Hira Auckland War Memorial Museum to audiences both local and international; it often supports inhouse exhibitions by enabling visitors to buy contemporary examples of the artworks they have just enjoyed, especially smaller treasures such as waka huia, hoe and weapons.

## Carving in the twentieth century

By the turn of the twentieth century, carvers were operating in a completely different world. There was still work on commission, but their carving was now circulating on the one hand within whānau and, to a lesser extent, ceremonial worlds, and on the other in Pākehā drawing rooms. The works that carvers in Rotorua produced have often been dismissed as simple tourist pieces and have been deemed unworthy of serious scholarly attention. Yet it was just this type of work that enabled many carvers to continue to practice, and if anything, experiment with new forms.

Other artists continued to find work, though irregularly, until the School of Maori Arts and Crafts was founded in the 1920s. This institution taught carving and weaving at a time when these art forms may otherwise have died out due to lack of contemporary practice. The school sent artists to communities who had requested and fundraised to build a meeting house or dining room, and they trained and worked

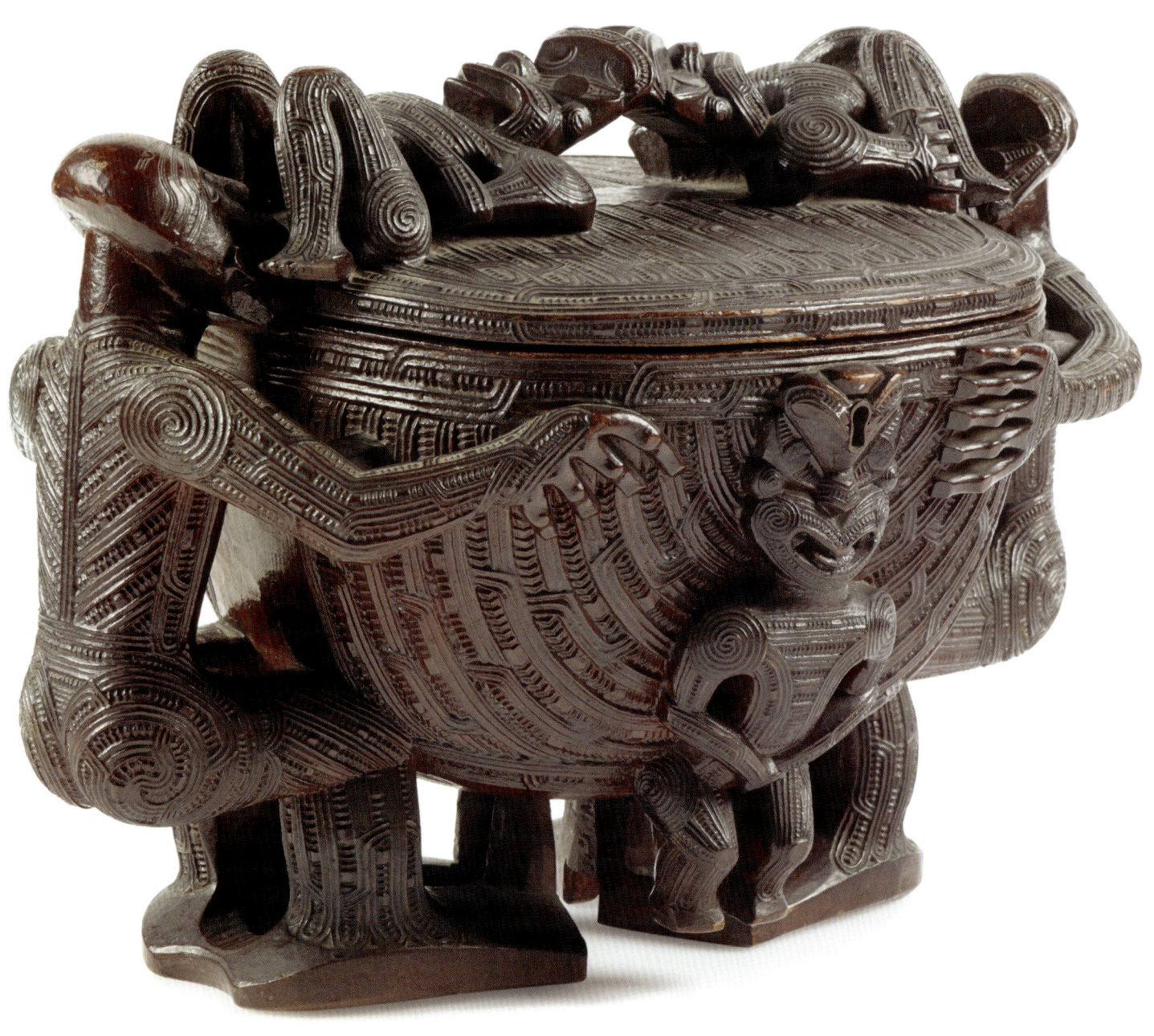

Patoromu Tamatea (Ngāti Pikiao) carved this presentation bowl on commission from Tamihana Te Rauparaha (Ngāti Toa, 1820–1876), son of Te Rauparaha, c.1875. Tamatea made three of these types of kumete between 1865 and 1885, at the end of his artistic career and on the cusp of the emergence of the tourist market. Before this time, he had worked primarily on waka.
Te Papa Tongarewa Museum of New Zealand, ME005222, The Wallace Bequest, gift of Mrs Elsie Chorlton, Mrs Elva Turner, and Mrs Amy Nicholson, 1961

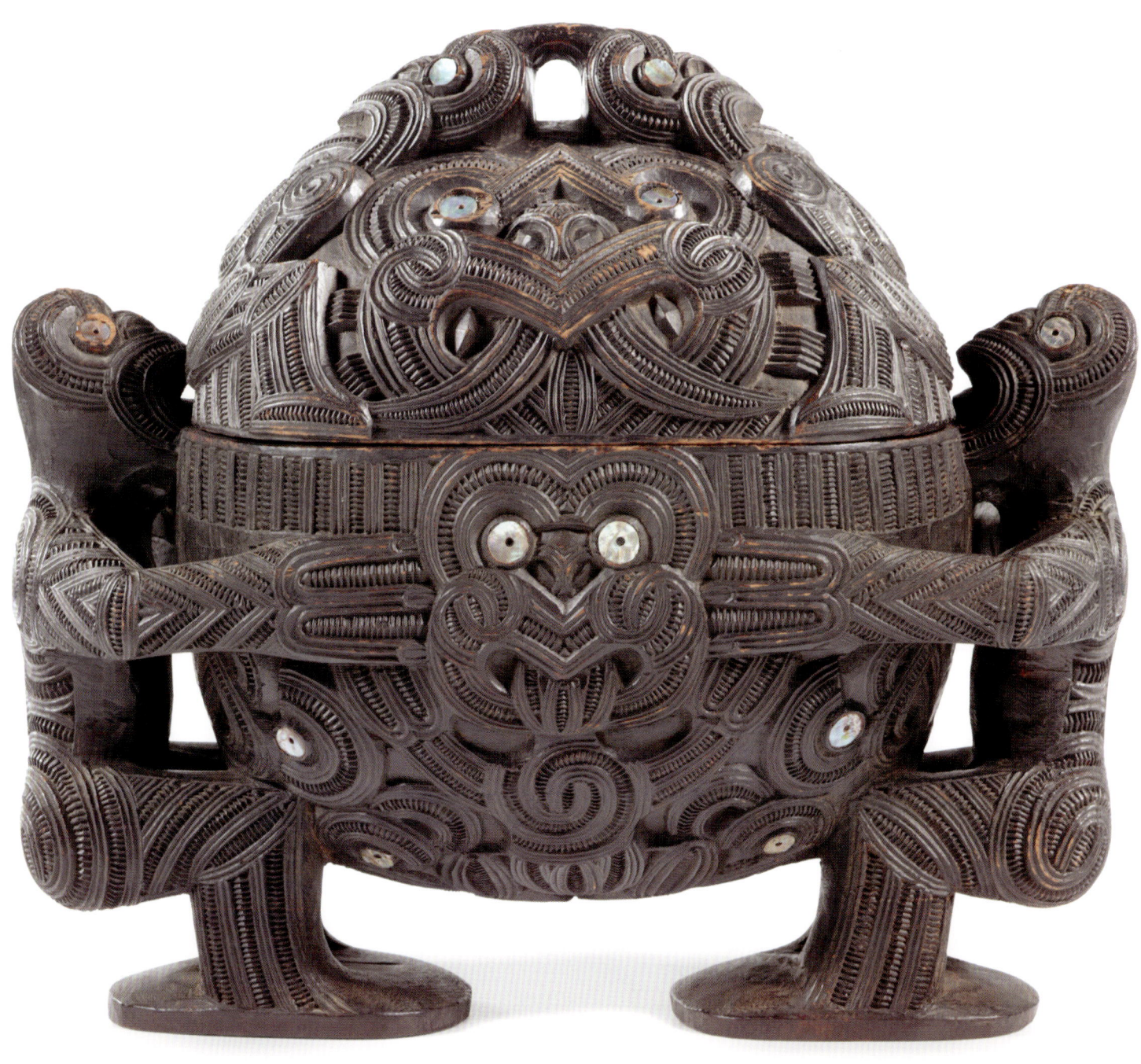

Ānaha Te Rāhui (1822–1913) experimented with a range of new forms which were based on older models for the strong tourist market. These types of kumete are a perfect example – they are similar to pouaka whakairo (larger carved treasure boxes), but with a twist. This example depicts two figures grasping a large, round, lidded bowl. Ornately decorated with surface designs throughout, this type of kumete exemplifies the success with which Māori artists pivoted to different markets and audiences.
Te Papa Tongarewa Museum of New Zealand, ME023133, purchased 2002

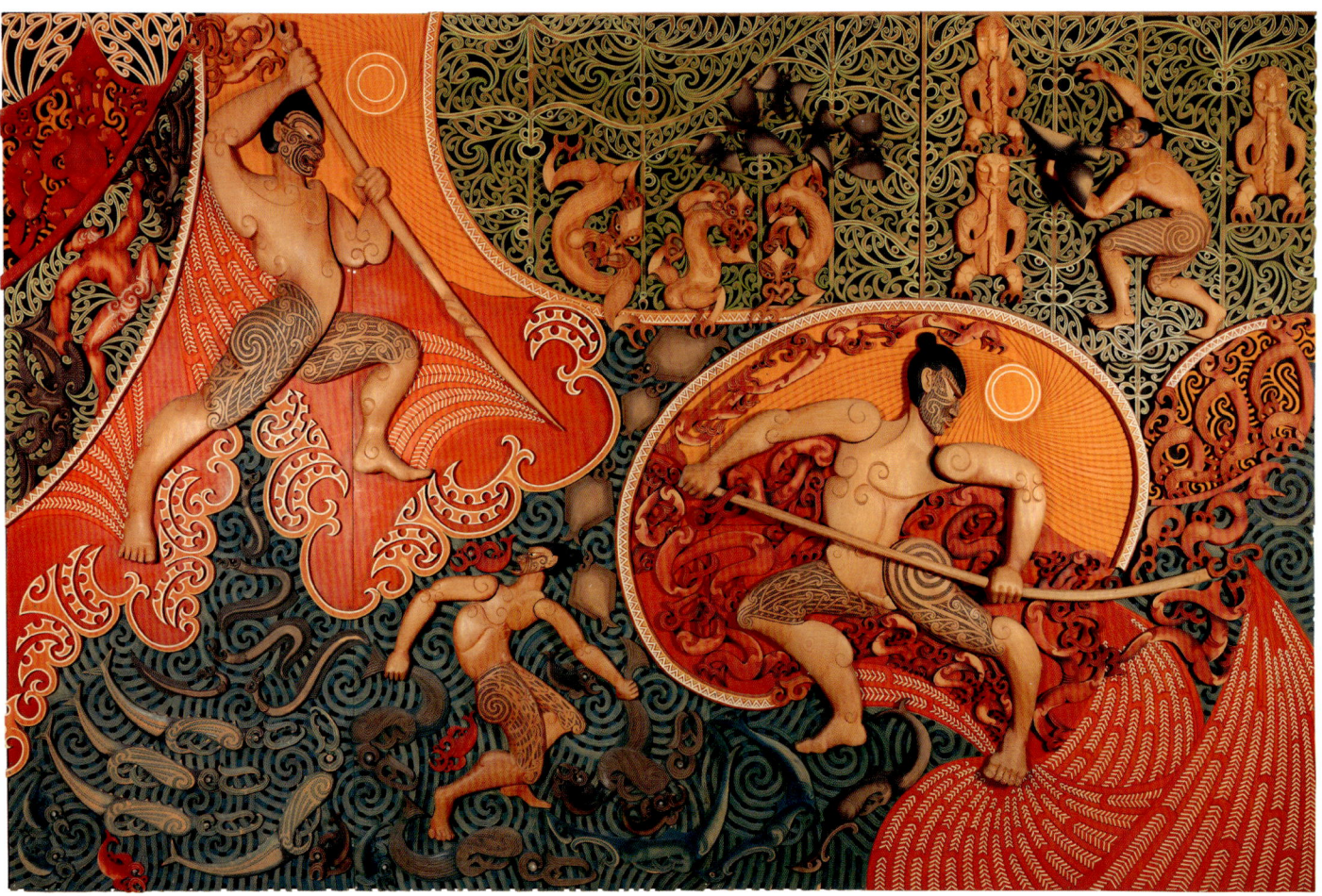

Like carvers before him, Cliff Whiting responded to the changing demands and dynamics of the communities who commissioned work from him.

**Cliff Whiting, *Te Ao o Ngā Atua*, 1988**
Ara Institute of Canterbury

alongside local people to create a finished project over several months. By the 1960s the available work had dried up, and most artists trained in the School of Maori Arts and Crafts (which closed before World War Two) went out to seek more regular employment. Pine Taiapa instigated workshops on Māori art, including carving, for a number of different educational institutions, based at his home in Tikitiki. His brother Hone Taiapa was commissioned to build a house for the Polynesian Cultural Centre in Laʻie, Oʻahu; he was awarded an MBE for services to carving in 1960, and in 1966 he was appointed master carver at the New Zealand Maori Arts and Crafts Institute, which opened in Rotorua in 1963.

In the 1960s the first Māori students were enrolling in tertiary fine arts programmes at the University of Auckland Elam School of Fine Arts and the University of Canterbury School of Fine Arts. These artists began to understand and engage with the world outside their own communities in ways that radically changed the kind of work they were producing. While some, such as Arnold Manaaki Wilson (Ngāi Tūhoe, Ngāti Tarāwhai) and Paratene Matchitt (Te Whānau ā Apanui, Whakatōhea, Ngāti Porou), used familiar carved forms in their work, their perception of how these figures and other motifs might be depicted and their meaning was very different from traditional styles of carving. Indeed, the old carvers were confounded when they first saw this work. Pine Taiapa was surprised at the work on show at a contemporary art exhibition in Hamilton in 1966 but, on reflection, he conceded that the world was wide enough for many kinds of art.

Meanwhile the training of carvers in marae-based arts continued. Some learnt on the job, working alongside older carvers who passed on their skills; many still had Māori as their first language, and were still operating within a customary Māori world. Pakaariki Harrison's journey to being a master carver was very much shaped by Pine Taiapa: as a teenager, he watched Pine carve on a project for his grandmother; and Pine later lived with Harrison to impart his ancestral knowledge while Harrison was at teachers' college. Other students of Pine Taiapa's went on to create contemporary art. Cliff Whiting (Te Whānau ā Apanui, 1936–2017) used his carving training to work on medium-density fibreboard (MDF), a material that was cheap, readily available and easy to use, to make bold and large-scale works that appear both traditional and contemporary at the same time. Pine Taiapa also mentored John Hovell (Ngāti Porou, Ngāpuhi, 1937–2014) who became one of the leading kōwhaiwhai artists of the late twentieth century: he worked on a number of wharenui projects with Harrison, including the dining hall at Te Aute College (1984), Tāne-nui-ā-rangi at Waipapa Marae, University of Auckland (1988), and Harrison's own whānau house Rākairoa at Harataunga, Coromandel (1996).

Two of Hone Taiapa's students are now full-time carvers. James Rickard (Ngāti Koata, Ngāti Hinerupe, Tainui, Ngāti Porou) was one of the first seven students Hone Taiapa taught at the Maori Arts and Crafts Institute: Rickard has worked on thirty marae projects and until 2022 was head tutor at the institute, which is now known as Te Puia. Rangi Hetet (Ngāti Tūwharetoa, Ngāti Maniapoto) descends from the illustrious Hetet artist whānau: his grandmother was Rangimārie Hetet, who led a rejuvenation of weaving from the mid-twentieth century. Rangi Hetet has carved several meeting houses (including his first project, Arohanui ki te Tāngata at Waiwhetū Marae, Lower Hutt, c.1960) and waka taua (including *Te Aniwaniwa* and *Te Raukura*, 1989) as well as regular work on commission. He also founded the Hetet School of Māori Art, which offers instruction in weaving and carving both online and in person with members of the Hetet whānau, including his son-in-law Sam Hauwaho (Tūhoe, Te Aitanga a Hauiti), who is also a carver.

### Carving post-1990

Since the 1990s there has been a resurgence in work for carvers due to a number of factors. As we have seen, the Kaupapa Waka project partially funded iwi to build and carve waka taua to be launched for the 150th anniversary of the signing of Te Tiriti o Waitangi in 1990. Creative New Zealand (CNZ), the main government arts funding body, has provided money for projects to rejuvenate marae, including carved structures onsite, as well as for new buildings.

Contemporary artists are focusing on carved works as their main practice, sometimes stimulating them to create new work after visits to museums, both in New Zealand and overseas. These same museums are commissioning carvers to create works for their displays, such as George Nuku's work in the British Museum, the Museum of Archaeology and Anthropology in Cambridge and the Museum Volkenkunde in Leiden. Māori communities now approach artists to rejuvenate older buildings and continue a practice of contemporary art in the whare, which began in the 1960s with Cliff Whiting and others taking their modern ideas into older buildings to create revolutionary styles of narratives. Robert (Bob) Jahnke (Ngāi Taharora), for instance, was approached by his hapū at Waipiro Bay to create works for the wharekai (dining hall) and to rejuvenate the work on the exterior of the wharenui Iritekura, built by his great-grandfather Riwai Pakerau. His interpretation of the ancestral narratives was shocking to the pakeke (elders), who disagreed with the use of bright blue paint on the exterior of the whare and the size of the genitals on the ancestors inside the wharekai. Jahnke explained that the blue paint related to the importance of the sea for their community, and he was allowed to retain the colour; however, he agreed to alter the depiction of the ancestors' sexuality in line with the pakeke's request.[46]

Building marae and wharenui continues today, though much more slowly, given the huge cost to construct a wharenui. Māori architects and architectural designers are now confident in the arts of the marae, and design meeting houses that are innovative and that push the boundaries of traditional whare. The role of the carver remains the same, it seems: to record the past but also to stretch the limits of artistic creativity.

# THE TAIAPA BROTHERS: CARVING IN THE TWENTIETH CENTURY
NGARINO ELLIS

Pineāmine (Pine) Taiapa (1901–1972) and Hone Taiapa (1911–1979) of Ngāti Porou were two of the most prolific and influential Māori carvers of the twentieth century. The brothers carved over 150 projects across the country between them, and they transformed twentieth-century Māori art with their work.

They were born in Tikitiki, a rural and strongly tribal community on the upper East Coast, at the turn of the twentieth century – a time when MP Apirana Ngata was lobbying for economic reform based on land consolidation schemes. The benefits from these schemes would flow back into the community, who would then celebrate this economic success through building whare whakairo and other forms. As a boy Ngata was withdrawn from Te Aute College to assist in making the tukutuku for his own tribe's meeting house, Porourangi; he later drew on this training when he was teaching tukutuku from the 1920s.

When Ngata realised his vision of a national school of Māori art in 1927 he hand-picked the first interns to go to Rotorua – and Pine Taiapa was top of his list. At this point Pine was enjoying the life of a young man, farming and playing rugby (including touring New Zealand and Australia with the Māori All Blacks). He had been introduced to the world of carving three years earlier, when Ngāti Porou tohunga whakairo Hone Ngatoto had lived with the Taiapa whānau while he was carving the nearby St Mary's Church (opened 1926). Ngata had appointed Ngatoto for this commission. He was the last tohunga whakairo of the Iwirākau whare wānanga of carving; his artistic reputation was renowned on the East Coast, where he had built over twenty houses. Ngatoto was also a close friend of Ngata's father Paratene. Halfway through the church project, Pine began watching Ngatoto as he worked, and practised carving on scraps of wood at the site. So began his life as a carver.

Soon after Pine arrived in Rotorua he was promoted to the role of teacher. He took over from Eramiha Kapua, master of the adze, and local Te Arawa carvers, including Rotohiko Haupapa. Between 1927 and 1939 Pine worked on sixty-four projects, including whare whakairo, wharekai (a new form introduced in the 1920s), and churches and chapels in the North Island – at Ngāruawāhia, Wairoa, Ōtaki and, of course, in communities along the East Coast. By the early 1930s, the school needed more help, and Pine's younger brother Hone was brought in. There was little work at home on the East Coast at the time, during the Depression, and Hone was soon working closely with Pine on projects. As the amount of work increased and his skills expanded, Hone went on to lead his own carving teams.

All the men who trained as carvers at the school also learnt tukutuku and kōwhaiwhai. Museums became central to their education as artists, as many of the older examples of these arts could be found only in museum collections. Barney Christie (Ngāti Kahungunu), for instance, remembered how they were encouraged to stay traditional in their styles, and follow the examples of their ancestors:[1] Ngata reasoned that, once they knew the basics, innovation would follow. When they could not be onsite at museums, they would learn from photographs sent from institutions such as the Dominion Museum in Wellington to Rotorua, where their principal workshop was.[2]

During World War Two the number of commissions did not slow, even though Pine was overseas between 1940 and 1943 as a captain in the Māori Battalion before he was invalided home. Hone was also

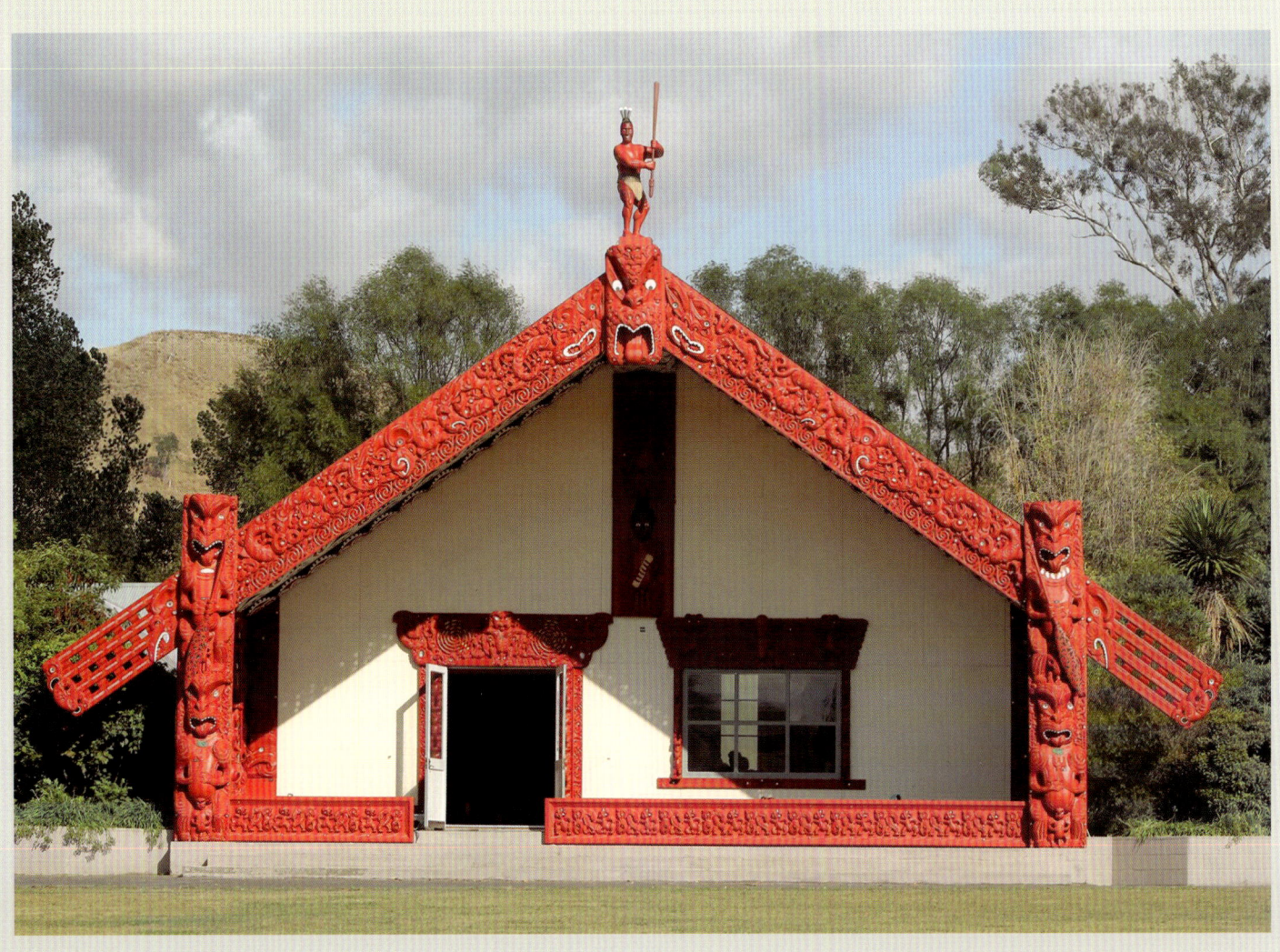

Te Whare o Rangi, the wharenui at Te Aute College carved by Pine Taiapa.
photography by Keri-Lee Maniapoto-Cheer

keen to sign up but Ngata intervened and asked him to wait, in deference to other Ngāti Porou men.

After the war, both brothers took up carving again, though there were fewer commissions and several artists were now reluctant to travel to different communities for months on end with their families. The school's last project was Tāpeka at Waihī Marae in Tokaanu, built for Ngāti Turumākina hapū (opened in 1959). Pine kept carving, but he was also interested in sheep farming, and by the 1960s he had returned permanently to his family farm in Tikitiki. From 1965 he ran a residential Māori arts and crafts school in Tikitiki, which hosted groups from Elam School of Fine Arts (May 1965), Victoria University (August 1965) and the Education Department (January 1967), among others. He also ran workshops in the community, such as at Ardmore Teachers' Training College in Auckland (January 1966), and for iwi in advance of their working on their own whare projects (Ngāti Whātua in May 1965, Ngāti Ranginui in June 1965, and Ngāti Rua).[3]

Pine made a study of tukutuku between 1921 and 1951: he examined panels in whare and museums, recorded the ancestral stories of what he called 'the 12 patterns of traditional usage',[4] and looked at techniques and materials, with the aim of publishing a book as a guide to future projects. He built up a range of written and oral resources, many of them associated with the houses he worked on, including Tūwhakairiora, Hinerupe,[5] Rongomaitāpui,[6] St Mary's war memorial church at Tikitiki,[7] Porourangi[8] and Rongomaianiwaniwa.[9]

Hone, meanwhile, continued to carve. He was appointed the inaugural master carver at the Maori Arts and Crafts Institute in Rotorua in 1967, a position he held until he died in 1979. During this time, he worked on several projects, including two in Auckland, at Hoani Waititi Marae and Ōrākei Marae. He was proud of his students: in 1974 he noted, 'They are starting to get their fingers whereas [before] they were all thumbs.'[10]

Pine and Hone Taiapa's legacy is evident in the architecture that has endured – and in the work of their students, many of whom are leading contemporary artists, among them Sandy Adsett, Cliff Whiting, Lyonel Grant, John Bevan Ford, Rangi Hetet and Pakaariki Harrison – at least twenty-five carvers and 200 tukutuku experts.

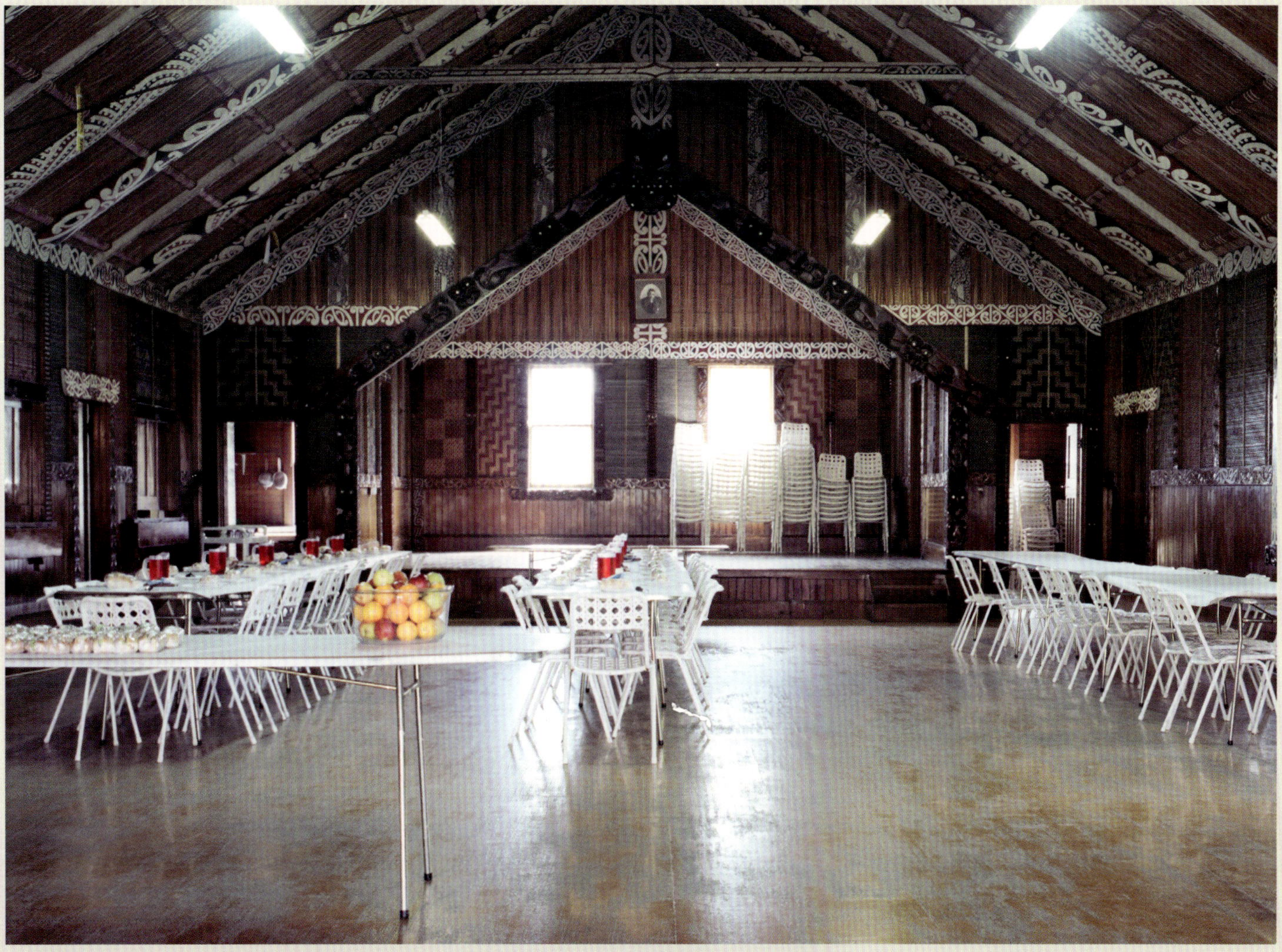

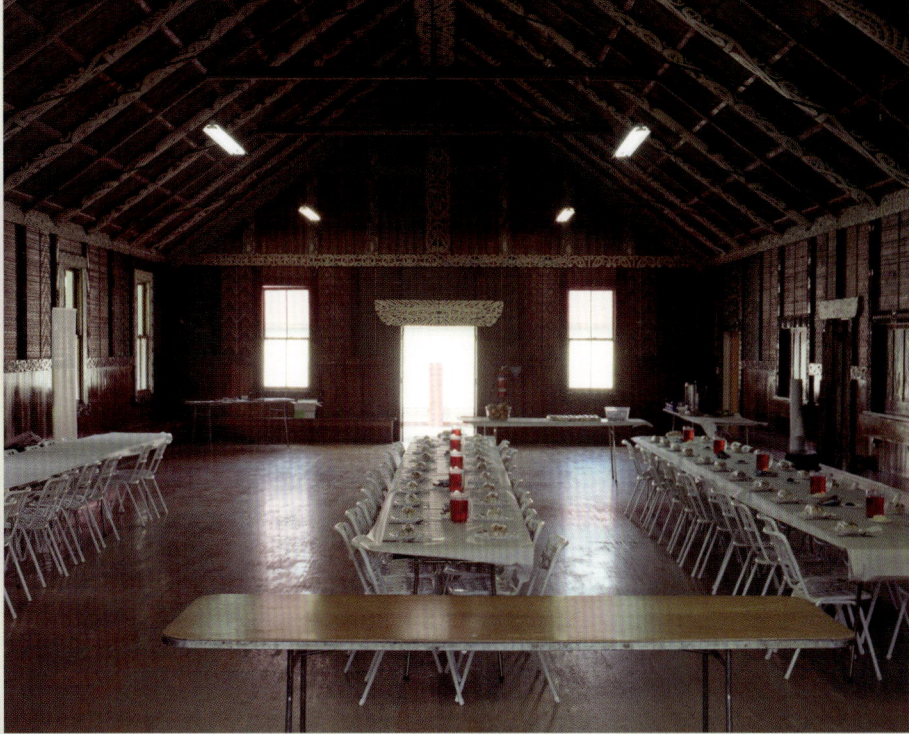

In 1933, Pine Taiapa completed the wharekai Tawhiwhirangi at Rāhui marae, Tikitiki. His first teacher, Hone Ngatoto, had carved the adjacent whare whakairo Rongomaianiwaniwa (opened 1890s), and stayed with Pine's whānau when completing St Mary's Church across the road in 1924–1926.

photographs by Natalie Robertson

# MORELLI AND THE NINETEENTH-CENTURY PAPAHOU ARTIST

NGARINO ELLIS

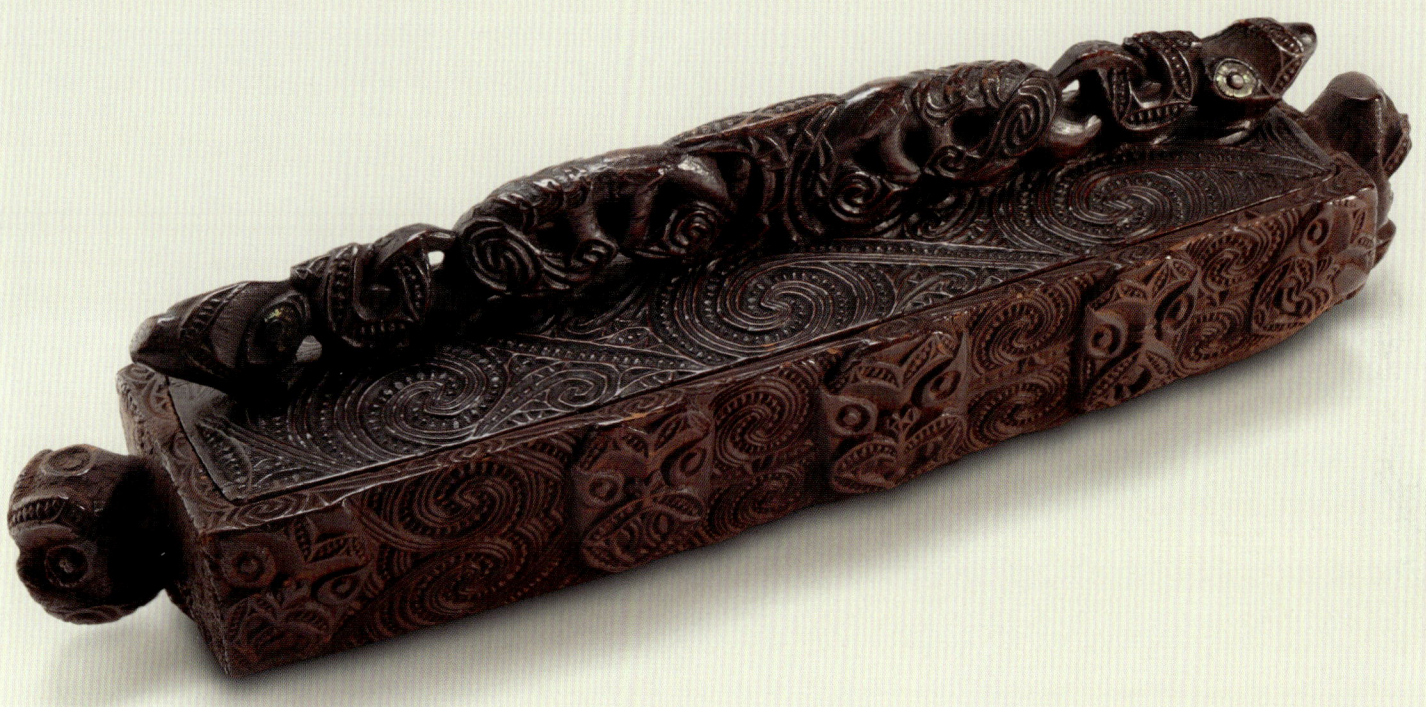

Swiss art historian Giovanni Morelli (1816–1891) believed that all artists had specific ways in which they would create a work – we might call this their style. Morelli encouraged the close examination of small parts of an artwork – such as how an ear is drawn – to help identify or attribute the work to a specific artist. Though Morelli was writing about painters, this technique of visual analysis can be used to identify specific artists' work across different art forms and collections. Using Morelli's system alongside historical research, Roger Neich identified over 250 Māori carvers active in the nineteenth century.[1] Sadly, we have lost the names of most of those whom Neich identified as working before 1900: carvers, weavers, moko practitioners and others. So how might the 'Morelli technique' help us now?

We may not be able to identify the names of specific artists just yet – we need historical research to assist with that – but by using this technique across collections, we can tentatively identify series of works by single artists. This underscores the importance of creating better public awareness and knowledge of museum collections, particularly overseas and especially in countries where English is not the official language.

As an example, using Morelli's method we can identify a single carver who made three papahou some time in the late eighteenth or early nineteenth century. These are currently in Auckland Museum (31512), the Metropolitan Museum of Art in New York (1978.412.755a, b),

This papahou was originally made in the early nineteenth century. It was later purchased by William Oldman, whose taonga collection was sold to the New Zealand government in 1948, which then distributed the works to the four major museums.
Tāmaki Paenga Hira Auckland War Memorial Museum, AM31512, thank you to Starr Ratapu, Māori collections manager, for this information

Stylistically, it appears these three papahou (treasure box) were all carved by the same artist, but are now spread i ngā hau e whā – to the four winds. Each features numerous figures around the base, as well as along the ridge of the lid.
Opposite top:
Metropolitan Museum of Art, New York, 1978, 412.755a, b, The Michael C. Rockefeller Memorial Collection, bequest of Nelson A. Rockefeller, 1960

Opposite bottom:
Museum of Archaeology and Anthropology, University of Cambridge, E 1908.94

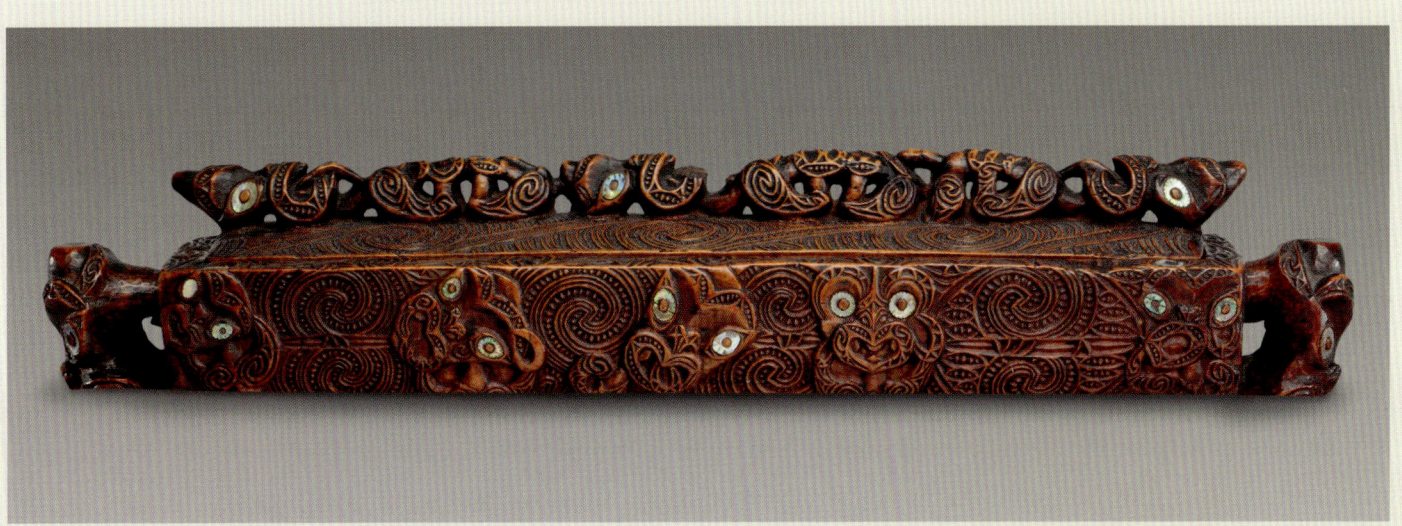
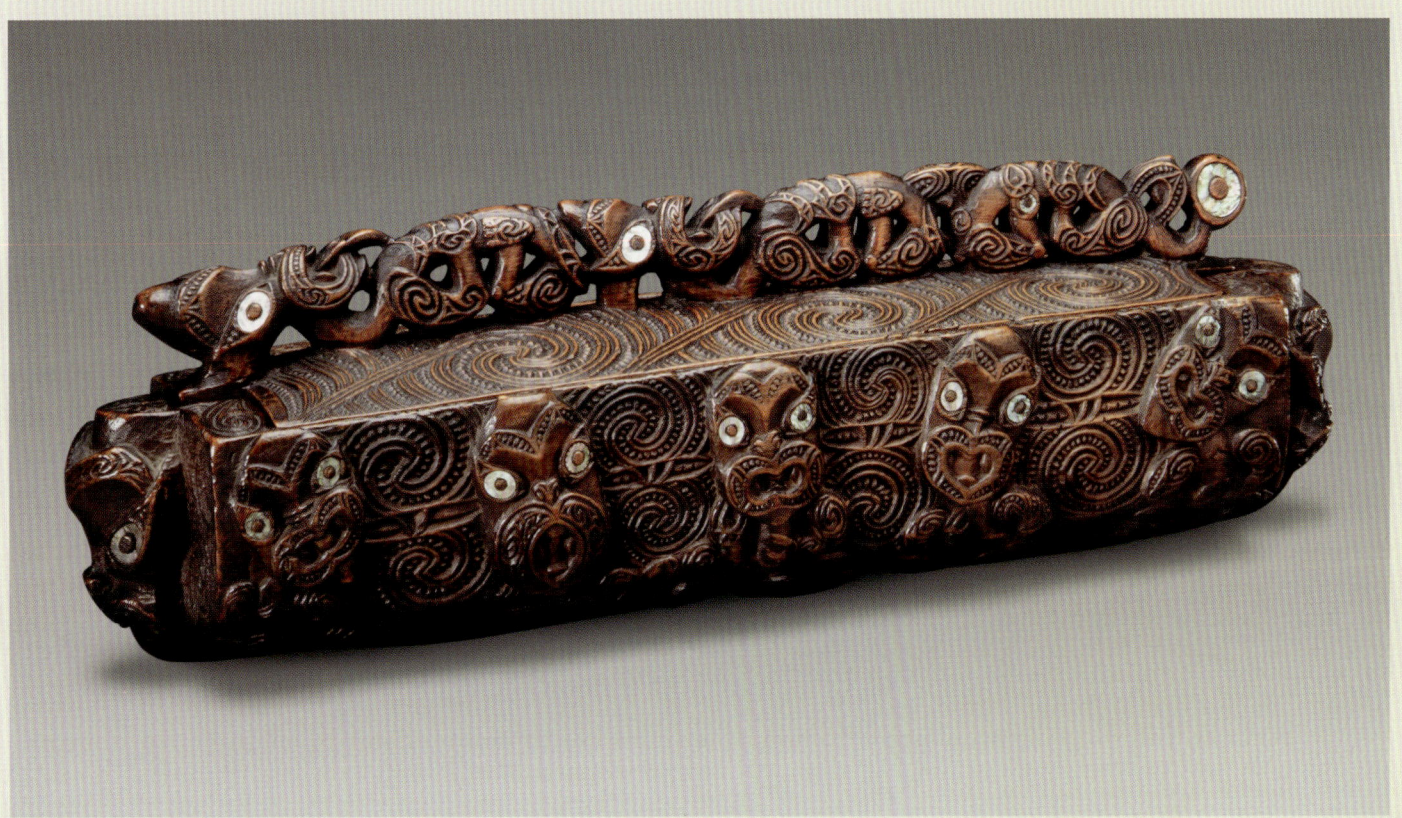

and the Museum of Archaeology and Anthropology, Cambridge (E1908.94). This artist has a distinct style that is recognisable across all three taonga: in particular, each is heavily decorated with a plethora of human faces and figures placed along each side of the base and across the top of the lid. In between them, the artist has carved double spirals with a line of haehae (ridges) enclosing the surface decoration of ritorito or unaunahi (fleur-de-lis-style design). If we look closely, we can see tiny idiosyncrasies of this carver: the centre of the double spirals has a straight angle (instead of a curve); the style of the mouth includes facing ellipses; the eyebrows are made in four sections with a triangle in the middle, perhaps suggesting raised eyebrows; pincer-type hands are often placed in the mouth; and bodies overall are very active and plain.

It is clear that this artist relished carving figures: on the British example there are three figures on the base, four figures and one face on one side and another six figures on the other, as well as three figures on the lid. On the papahou in the Met the carver has included five figures on the base, five figures on either side of the base, and three figures raised on the lid. The papahou in Auckland has five figures on either side of the base, three figures upraised forming a ridge on the lid, and three figures on the base.

Provenance (what we would call whakapapa) is another way of tracking the origins of taonga. This traces the history – the biography – of each taonga. Let us look at our papahou again – the English example usefully has a label pasted onto the bottom of the lid which reads: 'W1908.94.Z6596 [registration number]. Chief's feather box. New Zealand. (Gosport, 1904) * Professor Bevan, 1908.' This provides a date for when the treasure box was circulating across collections between 1904 and 1908; the museum file notes that the papahou was made before 1870 and was acquired from Professor Anthony Ashley Bevan (1859–1933), who was a wealthy professor of Arabic at Cambridge in 1893. He was not known as a collector of Māori or Pacific art, though he was a generous donor to Trinity College at Cambridge, including giving seven waka huia and papahou.

The papahou in the Metropolitan Museum of Art is dated in the museum records to the Bay of Plenty in the eighteenth century; it was gifted by Nelson A. Rockefeller, who had purchased it at auction in 1960 at Sotheby's, New York. Rockefeller was a politician (he was governor of New York and later vice-president of the United States, 1974–1977) and an art collector. He helped found the Museum of Primitive Art in New York in 1954, and donated his growing collection from the Pacific, Africa and the Americas to that institution. He purchased four waka huia in 1979, and bequeathed them all to the Met.[2] The only provenance of the Auckland papahou is that it came as part of the William Oldman Collection after the British collector died in 1949.

Papahou were rectangular in shape, most popular in Northland and Taranaki (they were 'rarely found elsewhere'[3]), and making of them stopped in the 1830s. Neich identified 439 waka huia and papahou in collections, of which seventy-two (16 per cent) were stylistically or historically linked to Northland, and forty-nine (11 per cent) from Taranaki. More recent research reveals that there are at least 465 papahou in collections.[4] But the style of these papahou – how they are carved – defies any easy iwi attribution. Northern and Taranaki carving is usually easily recognisable by the body shape (serpentine in both cases), head style (elongated or peaked), surface decoration and so forth; but none of these aspects is present on these papahou. The similarity between the styles of papahou from Taranaki and Northland may be explained by their close whakapapa links: Taranaki iwi, such as Te Ātiawa, originated in Northland.[5] These may represent an experiment; or perhaps they are the work of an artist from another area who made the papahou, either on commission or as a prisoner of war. Rangatira often would carve only one or two of these containers for their personal use, yet here we have

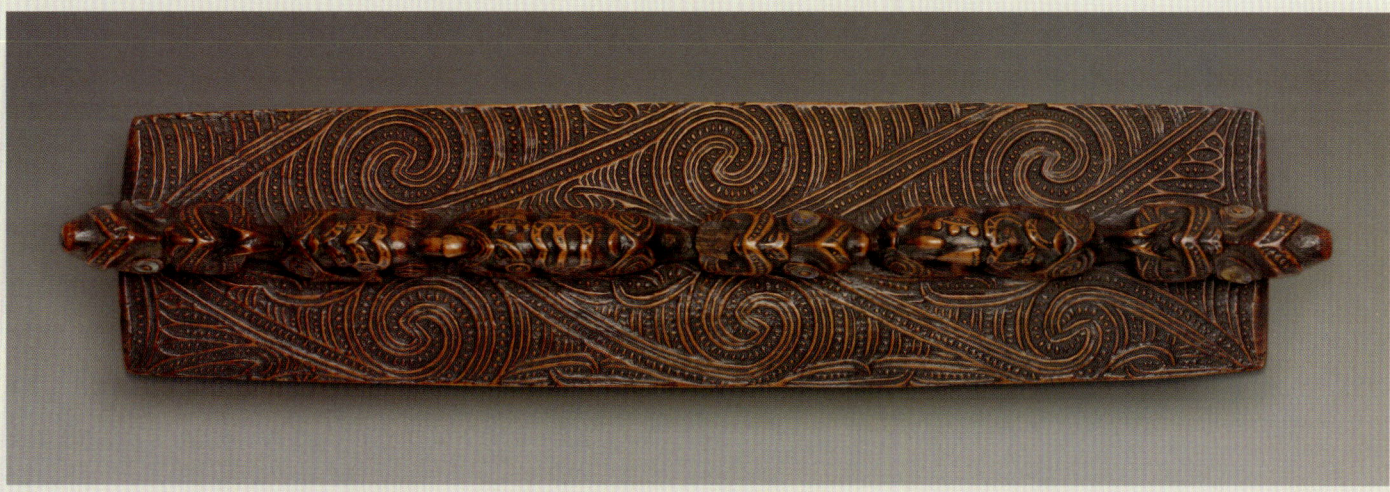

three examples. Each is highly finished, suggesting they were not made for a quick sale to a non-Māori tourist or a collector. Two have been kept for some time on a flat surface, judging by the amount of wear on the base: this suggests that they were purchased in the late nineteenth century and were possibly set on a table or a mantelpiece. It is likely that this artist was an expert in making papahou, and possibly these taonga were traded out of the community or gifted. This would have been pre-1850 however; after that time, size was important and large treasure boxes were commissioned as gifts. One very large example in Melbourne Museum in Australia is an exception; perhaps it was commissioned as a gift to a departing missionary.[6]

Using these art historical methods enables us to investigate these papahou in ways that can give us insights not only into the style of the artist but also the mobility of taonga in the late nineteenth century. With further research, we will be able to attribute to individual artists work on other small taonga, such as taonga pūoro – the pūtōrino (large flute or trumpet) and the kōauau (sound instrument played with the lips) – both of which were often intricately carved and require real expertise with the chisel. Through knowledge of global collections of taonga, we can start to reunite taonga with their communities – if only virtually, initially – as well as seek out at least the iwi who may have a relationship with them, even if we cannot (for now) identify who the carver is.

Triangulating provenance information collected by museums is often futile in identifying a source community for taonga tuku iho. In the case of this papahou, the first named owner was Nelson A. Rockefeller in 1960, though stylistically this papahou was made at least 130 years before.
Metropolitan Museum of Art, New York, 1978.412.755a, b, The Michael C. Rockefeller Memorial Collection, bequest of Nelson A. Rockefeller, 1960

# MĀORI ART AND ARCHAEOLOGY
DEIDRE BROWN

The history of Māori art relies on an understanding of the relationships between taonga Māori from different places and times, and between taonga Māori and people. Some of the earliest taonga Māori still in existence have been recovered through archaeology and the removal practices that pre-date archaeology. Up until recently, archaeology was often undertaken without the consent of Māori communities living at, or with an ancestral connection to, a site, and for many of these communities there is no distinction between looting and archaeological practices.

During the nineteenth and early twentieth centuries, 'relic hunters' and eugenicists plundered many abandoned kāinga and urupā across the country. At Whangaroa and Hokianga, in Northland, Māori burial caves and wāhi tapu were disturbed to take human remains, associated personal items interred with the deceased and waka kōiwi (burial caskets) for research or sale to museums and collectors. This was not without resistance from Māori communities, although most of the removals took place without community knowledge. When Hokianga Māori discovered that a Pākehā shipmaster and one of his passengers disturbed the remains of two tūpuna and their waka kōiwi in 1835, they exacted utu to rectify the transgression of tapu by attempting to raid the Horeke trading station. The situation was settled only by the reinterment of the deceased in new burial cloaks, as well as an utu of blankets, muskets and tobacco from the store.[1]

Waka kōiwi comprise the numerically largest type of taonga Māori from Northland in museum collections and none of them have an acquisition history that would suggest they were acquired with Māori approval.[2] However, Auckland Museum's collection of waka kōiwi from Waimamaku was the basis for the Tai Tokerau-style of carving developed by the School of Māori Arts and Crafts tohunga whakairo, which is still used by tohunga whakairo today.[3] Without knowledge of these taonga Māori, this contemporary regional style would not exist. Most museums now have access restrictions in place for waka kōiwi, and some have been returned to communities.

Along with incidental finds as a result of wetland drainage, archaeology has recovered many early taonga Māori that inform our current understandings of body adornments, weapons, tools, whare and kāinga. The most important archaeological finds from the time of Māori migration to Aotearoa have occurred at the Wairau Bar site, Te Pokohiwi in the Marlborough region, which has been dated to c.1280CE. Excavated graves have yielded the tooth and reel jewellery that demonstrates the formal continuity between Polynesian and early Māori art. Current thinking – based on the wealth and quality of material recovered from graves, middens and other areas at Wairau Bar – suggests that the kāinga may have been an intellectual and artistic centre for a larger network of early kāinga.[4]

From the earliest period of discovery at Wairau Bar, starting with recovery of a skull in 1939, the local Rangitāne iwi opposed the opening of graves and demanded that remains be returned and the digging stop. In return, they had their ancestral claim to the site questioned and found themselves fighting on two fronts: first, to protect the mana, tapu and wairua of the burial sites; and second, to defend their whakapapa links to the tūpuna interred on their land. It was not until the late 1950s, when an ontological turn in archaeology shifted interest to middens rather than graves, that disturbance of the resting places of Wairau Bar ancestors stopped. In 2009, seventy years after the first remains were uncovered, Canterbury Museum returned the waka kōiwi for burial at the Wairau Bar. Taonga removed from Wairau Bar graves remain in museum collections today.[5]

Knowledge about the lifeways and taonga of tūpuna is maintained through kōrero tuku iho (stories passed down through generations). For this reason, communities sometimes see no need for archaeology to occur. Instances when archaeologists argue that their findings 'confirm' kōrero tuku iho can be regarded as condescending by community members who see no need for their ancestral stories to be validated by other means. Archaeological accounts of the past can also conflict with kōrero tuku iho. Contemporary archaeology as generally practised in Aotearoa, including by the rising generation of Māori archaeologists such as Gerard O'Regan and Makere Rika-Heke, is more responsive to these issues and involves community members as consenting authorities, consultants and participants for proposed archaeological investigations. Materials recovered may remain in the hands of community members and be returned to the earth.

Art history still has some way to go in terms of considering the acquisition histories of treasures under discussion as part of the ethical reasoning for research. Responses have ranged from only working with images of grave goods that are already in the public domain, through publication (the 'we cannot "unsee" anything that is already visible' approach), to not specifically addressing or reproducing images of taonga that have been taken from wāhi tapu or similar restricted or prohibited areas. Source communities are increasingly defining the oeuvre – being the content and edges – of Indigenous art history.

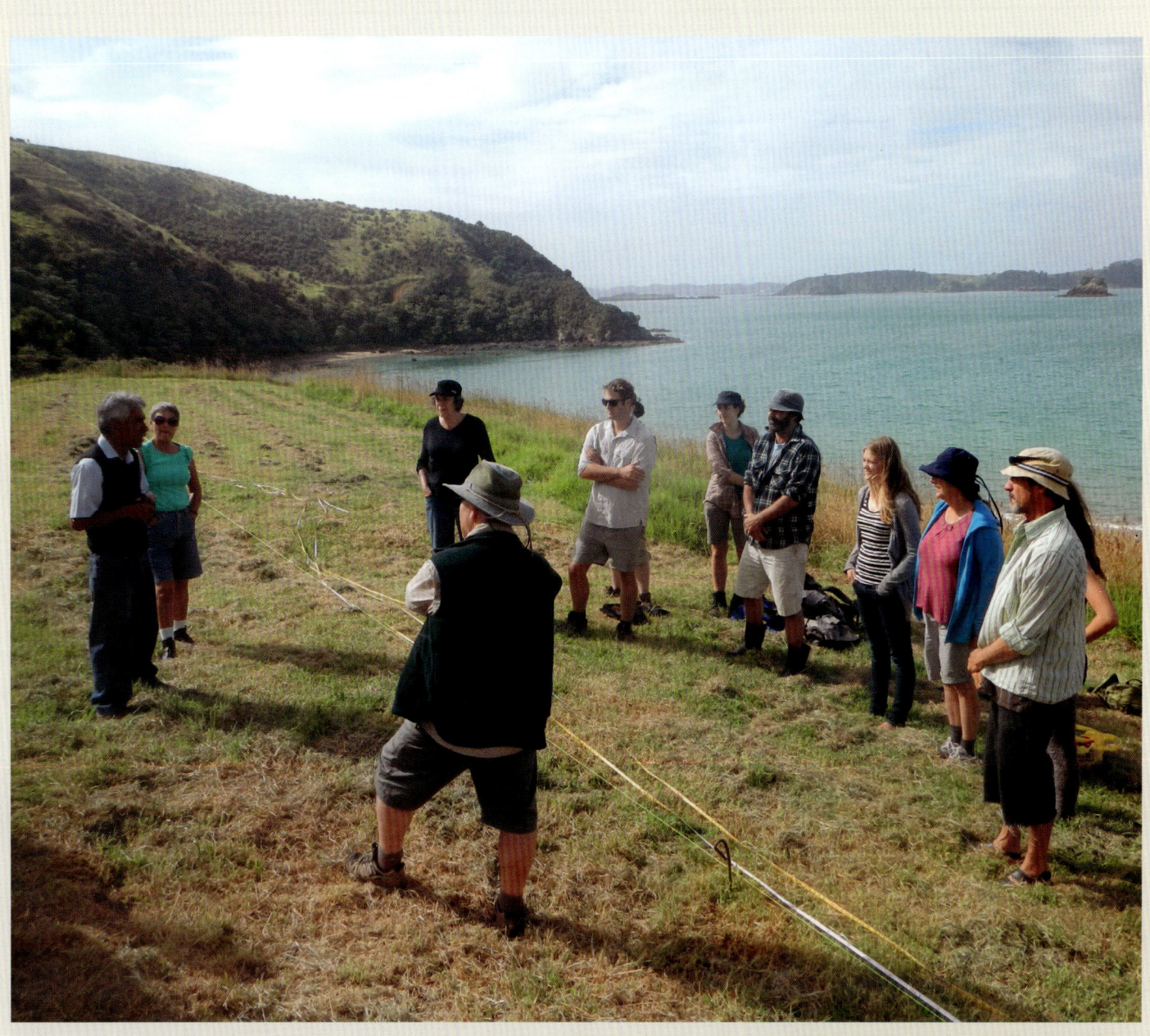

Hugh Rihari (Ngāti Torehina) and Raewyn Ormsby-Rihari (Waikato-Tainui) leading karakia before a University of Otago archaeology team, under the supervision of Ian Smith and Angela Middleton, begin their excavation of a site at Hohi, Bay of Islands in 2013.
photograph courtesy of Andi Blanshard

This remarkable kahu huruhuru features kererū, tūī and kākā feathers which have been arranged in an eye-catching design reminiscent of the roimata toroa pattern.
Tāmaki Paenga Hira Auckland War Memorial Museum, AM19295

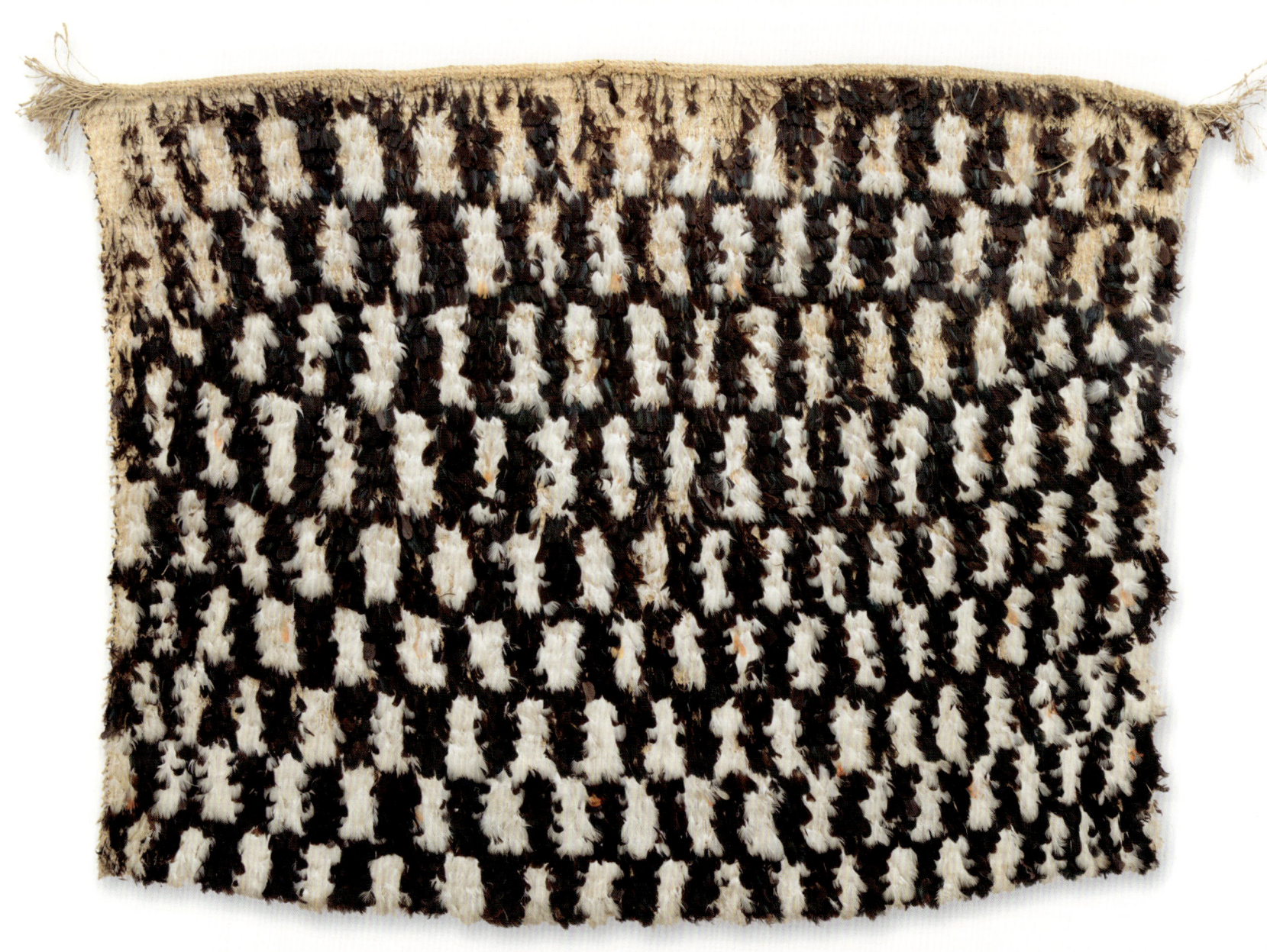

# 3 NGĀ KĀKAHU
## TEXTILES
### NGARINO ELLIS

*Hutia te rito o te harakeke*
*Kei hea te kōmako e kō*
*Kī mai ki ahau*
*He aha te mea nui i te ao?*
*Māku e kī atu*
*He tangata, he tangata, he tangata.*

*If the shoot of the flax is pulled out [and the flax dies]*
*Where will the bellbird sing?*
*If you were to ask me*
*What is the most important thing in the world?*
*I would reply*
*It is people, it is people, it is people.*

This whakataukī provides the kaupapa for this chapter on Māori textiles, especially kākahu (cloaks). In it we delve into the celestial origins of weaving from kōrero tuku iho; how this ancient art spread across Te Moananui a Kiwa from Hawaiki to Aotearoa; through to our ancestors' early textile practices, including the art of making tapa/aute. We examine materials, dyes and attachments before looking at mahi raranga and mahi whatu (plaiting and twining). Finally, we consider the meaning and symbolism of kākahu and the enduring practices through the twentieth century, and provide a snapshot of some contemporary artists, exhibitions and works.

Oral histories recorded in the nineteenth century provide valuable insight into the significance of cloaks. Te Ranginui composed this waiata about two types of kākahu:

**He waiata na Te Ranginui, mo te kakahu kore**

E kai e, te kutu,
E kai e, te tuiau,
E kai e, te tara pake, e tu ki Turamoe ra i a;
Tera te rongo o Paeroa, te hau i raro ra;
Ekore ranei a Te Mui, e whiwhi mai, i tona nei hana,
Hei whakatau ake ki te tangata nei, ki a Te Moko,
Nana i ki mai, He pakaru te ihupuni,
Hoki kau mai a Rangitapuarewa,
Te kai kawe taonga.
Me kawe te hana nei, ki Whakanau,
Ki te wai ra o te hinu oke,
Hei tamata iho, i taku kiri,
Tuku te whero, ki taku tinana i a.[1]

The lice eats,
The flea eats,
The tara pake eats,
And stands to Turamoe there.
That is the feel of Paeroa, the wind there
Te Mui was not able to get a hana [dogskin cloak]
To settle this man, Te Moko
He said to me 'The ihupuni [cloak] is damaged
Give it back to Rangitapuarewa
Who brought the treasure.
You should carry this hana to Whakanau
To the water there for the fat
To revitalise my skin
Take the red to my body, ah.[2]

Te Ranginui describes how Te Mui shamed him by making fun of his torn dogskin cloak (ihupuni). The song suggests that Te Mui tried to replace the cloak but was unable to. Later on Te Ranginui mentions a 'hana', which is a fine cloak smeared with red ochre; the term hana also means to shine or glow, and this must have been the visual effect of the cloak with the pigment on it.[3] The waiata mentions Rangitapuarewa and describes him as a trader who travelled around exchanging goods for taonga, such as the ihupuni referred to in this case. The last two lines describe rubbing hinu (fat) and kōkōwai pigment on the skin to rejuvenate it. Waiata such as these give a window into a world where cloaks circulated within a complex network of relationships: at times they would affirm a relationship; at others kākahu were the reason for the breaking of connections.

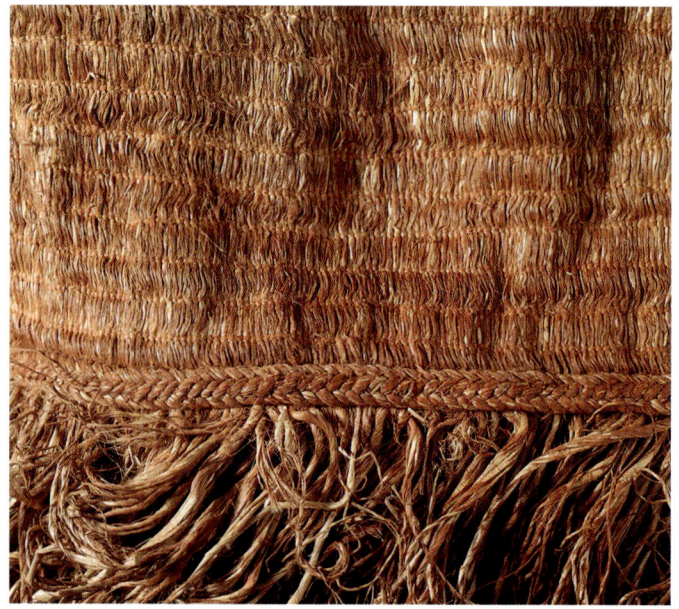

### Archaeological record of textiles

The archaeological record of textiles is often scant, largely because of the tendency for fibre to disintegrate. Where textiles are found, it is often as part of a larger grouping of objects used in a domestic setting, and they have survived because they have been submerged in water or left in dry caves. Weaver Lisa McKendry, a specialist in Māori textiles and customary terminology, researched a collection of nine textile fragments that had been deliberately deposited in a dry rock-shelter at Whakaari pā (Lion Rock, Piha) on the west coast of Auckland. The cache included portions of a patterned whāriki (plaited sleeping or floor mat), a tātua (belt) and at least six different kākahu.[4] One cloak, made from harakeke and kiekie (a native vine, *Freycinetia banksii*), has hukahuka (added tags made of rolled cords) and is 'heavily impregnated with kōkōwai'. Another may be a kōkau, a plain, unadorned cloak, which has 'faint kōkōwai staining' on the fibres.[5] The use of kōkōwai in both cases signals that these were important textiles: the pigment was often applied after a cloak had been made on special occasions, to enhance the mana of the cloak and the wearer. Another textile fragment has a different type of attachment – pōkinikini (cylindrical dried strips of harakeke) – which suggests it may have been a shortened version of a kākahu called a pihepihe.[6] In assessing these fragments against other textiles found in archaeological sites, McKendry notes that technologically the Whakaari pā weaving is quite distinct from elsewhere – the weavers were experimenting with different types of weaves, dyes and attachments – and that, indeed, that these nine textile fragments might represent a tribal style of weaving, just as there are tribal styles of carving.

Probably the earliest known cloak fragment which shows evidence of technology used today in contemporary kākahu has been radiocarbon-dated to the early fifteenth century. In January 2000, archaeologists Dan Witter and Alison Witter found more than a thousand raranga fragments in a rock shelter at Kaitōrete Spit in the South Island.[7] One of the fragments was made using whatu aho pātahi (single-pair twining), which is the most common weaving technique used in kākahu.[8] The fragment, which measures only 120 × 30mm, is made from muka (processed harakeke fibre), which suggests that it was a cloak of some importance. Archaeologist Chris Jacomb described the importance of the discovery of these fragments, which 'demonstrate that Maori ... were already competent in a specialised weaving technology known as whatu aho pātahi – single pair twining ... This find showed us that weaving techniques were well developed very early in Māori history in New Zealand, and these technologies have stood the test of time. They are still used in cloak-making today.'[9]

### Tapa in Aotearoa New Zealand

In the Pacific tapa is made from the stripped bark of three different trees – aute (paper mulberry), breadfruit (*Artocarpus altilis*) and aoa or banyan (*Ficus prolixa*). The bark is beaten until thin, and then decorated with stencils, stamps or freehand in a wide range of colours. Today tapa is used in ceremonial and in domestic life – it holds a crucial ceremonial role in relation to presentation and exchange, and is used both in the Pacific and by diasporic communities as payment for specialist artists and as gifts to visitors. Historically tapa was also used as curtains, bed covers and even mosquito nets.

Māori tribal narratives record the use of aute (tapa): Ngāti Kahungunu, for instance, tell of how their ancestor Kahungunu's hair was decorated with aute, and he wore another piece as an ear ornament; and there is an even earlier reference to a maro aute (apron) in stories about Taranga, mother of Māui. In one story the atua Tāwhaki travelled on a manu aute (a kite made from aute) to the heavens to obtain the baskets of knowledge (though he was thwarted and changed to another mode of transport), and Rahi used a manu aute in his search for his wife Ti Ara, who had been kidnapped by patupaiarehe (fairy folk). Māui was known to have travelled around the country on a manu aute. Later, when aute became rare, only the head of the kite would be made from the bark of the aute tree.

Aute is mentioned in whakataukī, too, such as this one from the Hauraki area: 'He rongo whakamau, me he aute te awhea' (An enduring peace, as the *aute* undisturbed).'[10] Another Hauraki reference is embedded in a mōteatea recorded by ethnologist S. Percy Smith: 'He aha koa au ka mate, tena te aute i whakatokia e au ki te tara o taku whare. / Although I die, there is an aute tree that has been planted by me beside the wall of my house.'[11] Te Rangi Hīroa mentions aute being used in personal names, such as Te Potae Aute, a chief of Ngāti Porou.[12] Herbert Williams, in *A Dictionary of the Maori Language*, includes two words for an ear ornament made from aute – 'kope' and 'turuki' – which suggests that there may have been more than one type.[13] Historian and Native Land Court judge Walter Edward Gudgeon described a Te Arawa whakapakoko atua (deity figure) wrapped in aute in 1823: it was sought after by Ngāpuhi and had been taken from Mokoia Island. Named Ihungaru, the 'figure' was made from a lock of human hair, 'twisted with rope of aute'.[14]

Māori ancestors brought aute from the Pacific as their main source of textiles; however, the plant did not survive the colder climate in Aotearoa, and by the time British and French explorers arrived in the 1760s they saw aute plantations growing only in the Far North. They also

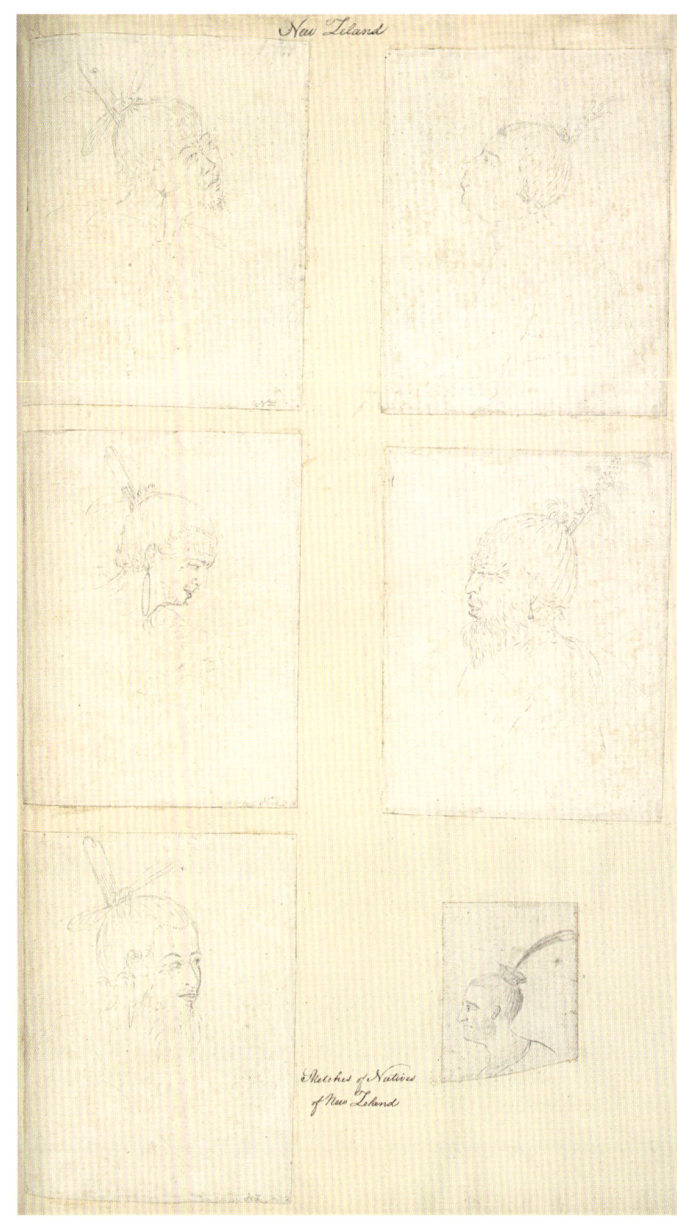

Pencil drawings by Sydney Parkinson, 1769, showing the practice of placing a small piece of tapa in the ear. The location at which the drawings were made is unspecified, but it is likely that it was somewhere in Northland, based on sightings of a small aute (paper mulberry) plantation there.
British Library, Add. 23920, f.61

Opposite: Detail of woven fragment from the inside of a rain cape collected in the eighteenth century by the Cook expedition. The weaver has daubed kōkōwai on the inside as well as on the fringe of the cloak to mark it off as a particularly special example. The Museum of Archaeology and Anthropology in Cambridge, UK has 215 taonga collected by Cook across his three voyages, out of a total of some 2000 treasures he acquired.
Museum of Archaeology and Anthropology, University of Cambridge, D 1924.81

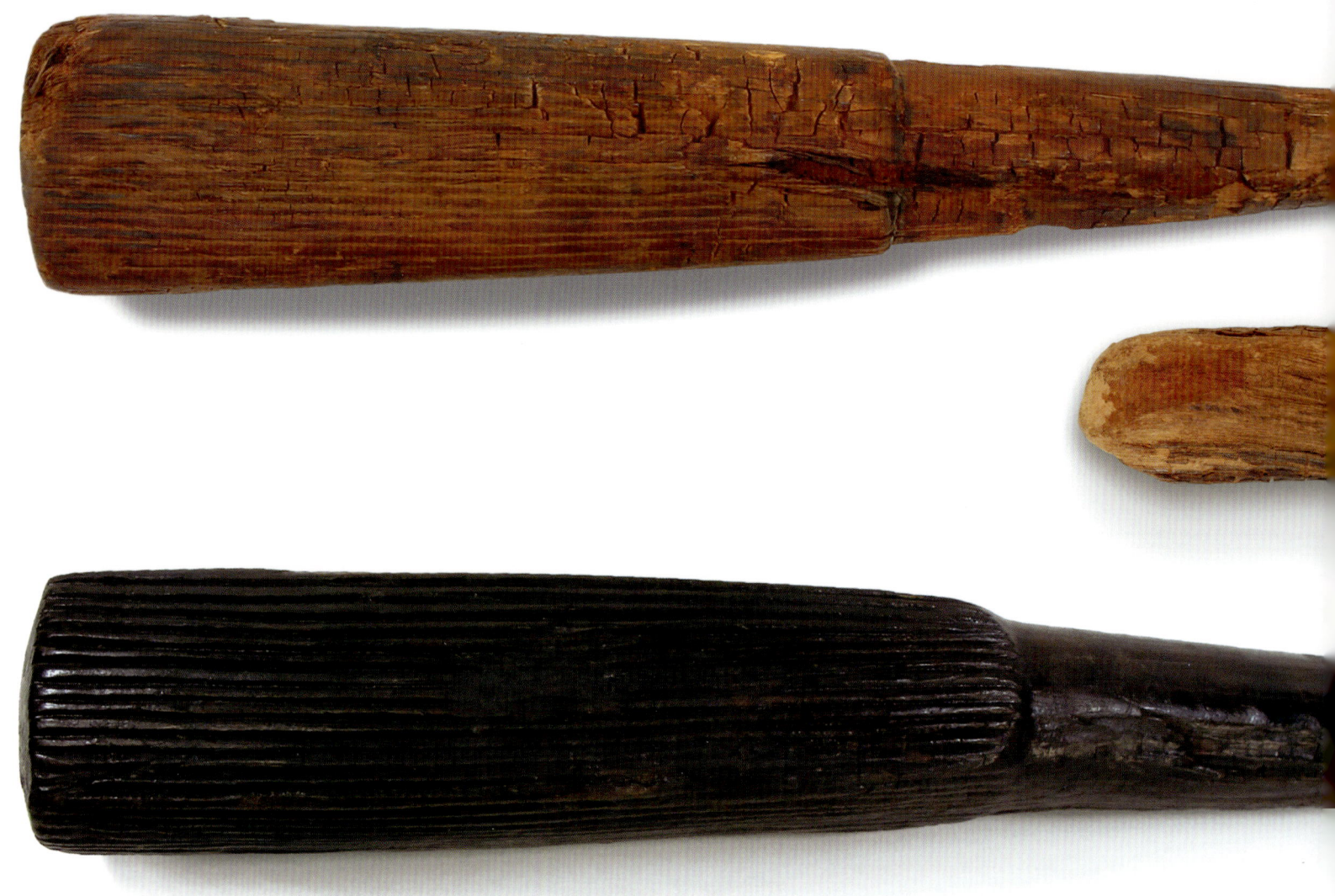

observed Māori wearing palm-sized pieces of aute rolled up and pushed through holes in their ears. Māori were still making aute, presumably using the same techniques as in the Pacific of stripping the bark from the trees and beating it until it was very thin. Joseph Banks, botanist on Cook's first voyage, described Māori tapa in 1769 in the Bay of Islands:

> After this they showed us a great rarity, six plants of what they called aouta [aute], from whence they make cloth like that of Otahite [Tahiti]. The plant proved exactly the same, as the name is the same, Morus papyrifera, Linn. (the Paper Mulberry). The same plant is used by the Chinese to make paper. Whether the climate does not well agree with it I do not know, but they seemed to value it very much; that it was very scarce among them I am inclined to believe, as we have not yet seen among them pieces large enough for any use, but only bits sticking into holes in their ears.[15]

Māori used a range of four-sided carved paoi[16] as tapa beaters. At least fifteen have survived, including one discovered in Auckland in 2015. These examples are made from kauri, rimu and matai, and are stylistically similar to tapa beaters used in the eastern Pacific in the nineteenth century.[17] Some are several hundred years old, which makes them the oldest known tapa beaters globally.[18]

The oral and artefactual evidence points to aute being produced mainly in Northland, Auckland, the Waikato and Hauraki. This is backed up by the fact that the paoi have been found in these areas, as well as in Taranaki. Oral evidence suggests that aute was also grown on the East Coast: the story about Kahungunu is told above; and Matutaera Nihoniho described how aute plantations endured until the time of his grandparents, in around 1800. One rare South Island piece of tapa widens the location where tapa was made and used: a waka huia found in a dry cave in inland Otago was wrapped and lined with tapa and 'hidden in a rock cleft on the Clutha

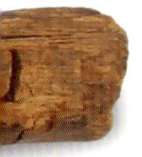
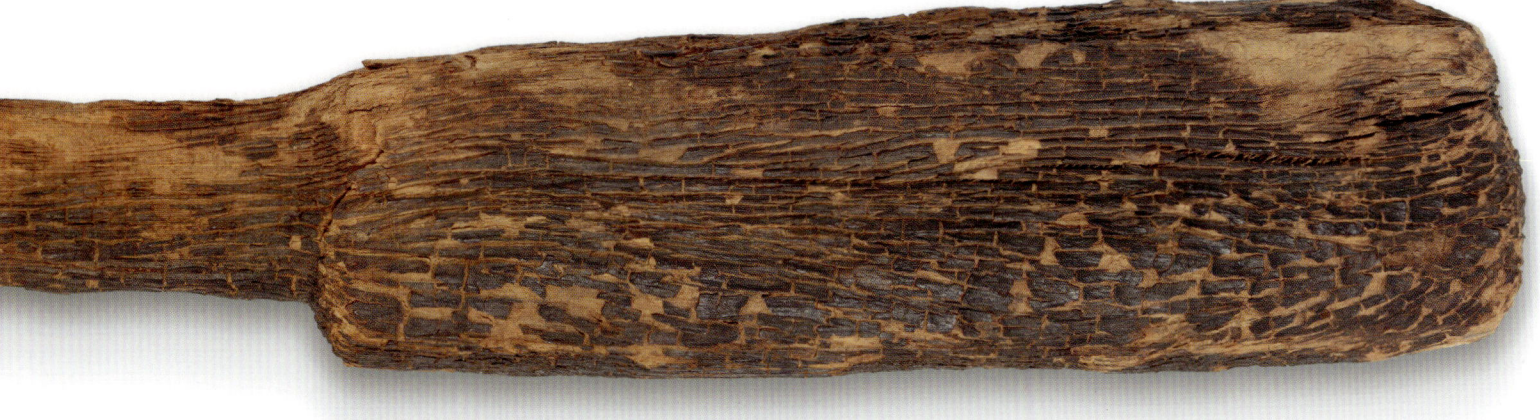

Types of paoi (tapa pounders) – note the different patterns on them. These are some of the only evidence of the practice of Māori making tapa. What makes the paoi distinct from each other is the variation of designs carved into them. The lower paoi shows the haehae (grooves) carved into the wood. Researchers are discovering small amounts of worked aute in the South Island, which challenges the idea that aute was only made in the warm climate of Te Tai Tokerau. Further south, aute was made using houheria (lacebark).
Tāmaki Paenga Hira Auckland War Memorial Museum, from top to bottom: AM8084, AM45305, AM36234

River'.[19] Inside were an astounding number of huia feathers – seventy in total – making this a very precious waka huia.

In the warmer climate of Northland, aute plantations still existed in the early nineteenth century, as this account from the Reverend William Colenso at Kawakawa in the Bay of Islands in 1835 reveals:

> I once saw this plant growing in an old plantation at the head of the Kawakawa River in the Bay of Islands – that was in 1835. There was, however, but one small tree left, which was about six feet high, with few branches, and not many leaves on them, it appeared both aged and unhealthy, and it soon after died. On my finally leaving the Bay of Islands in 1844, to reside in Hawke's Bay, I heard of some aute trees still living at Hokianga. I wrote to a chief of my acquaintance there (E. M. Patuone), who kindly sent me several good cuttings; saying (in a letter) that the plant there was nearly totally destroyed by the cattle of the Europeans. Unfortunately, my removing was so greatly hindered, in not meeting readily with a vessel, and the summer also advancing, that I lost them all.[20]

## Other materials used in textiles

Aotearoa offered a wide variety of materials suitable for making a range of textiles. Harakeke was a welcome substitute for the Pacific pandanus, which struggled to grow in the cold climate of Aotearoa; and it became, as textile historian Patricia Wallace (Ngāti Porou) notes, 'the most wide-spread weaving resource in the country'.[21] Understanding the nuanced nature of naming the Māori world is an important objective of this book: the term 'harakeke' covers the forty-seven known types of this fibre. Though harakeke has often been translated as 'flax' it is actually from a completely different botanical family to the European species. Ignorant of this scientific fact, early Pākehā traders use the term 'flax' as this is what they were familiar with, and the name has in general been retained.

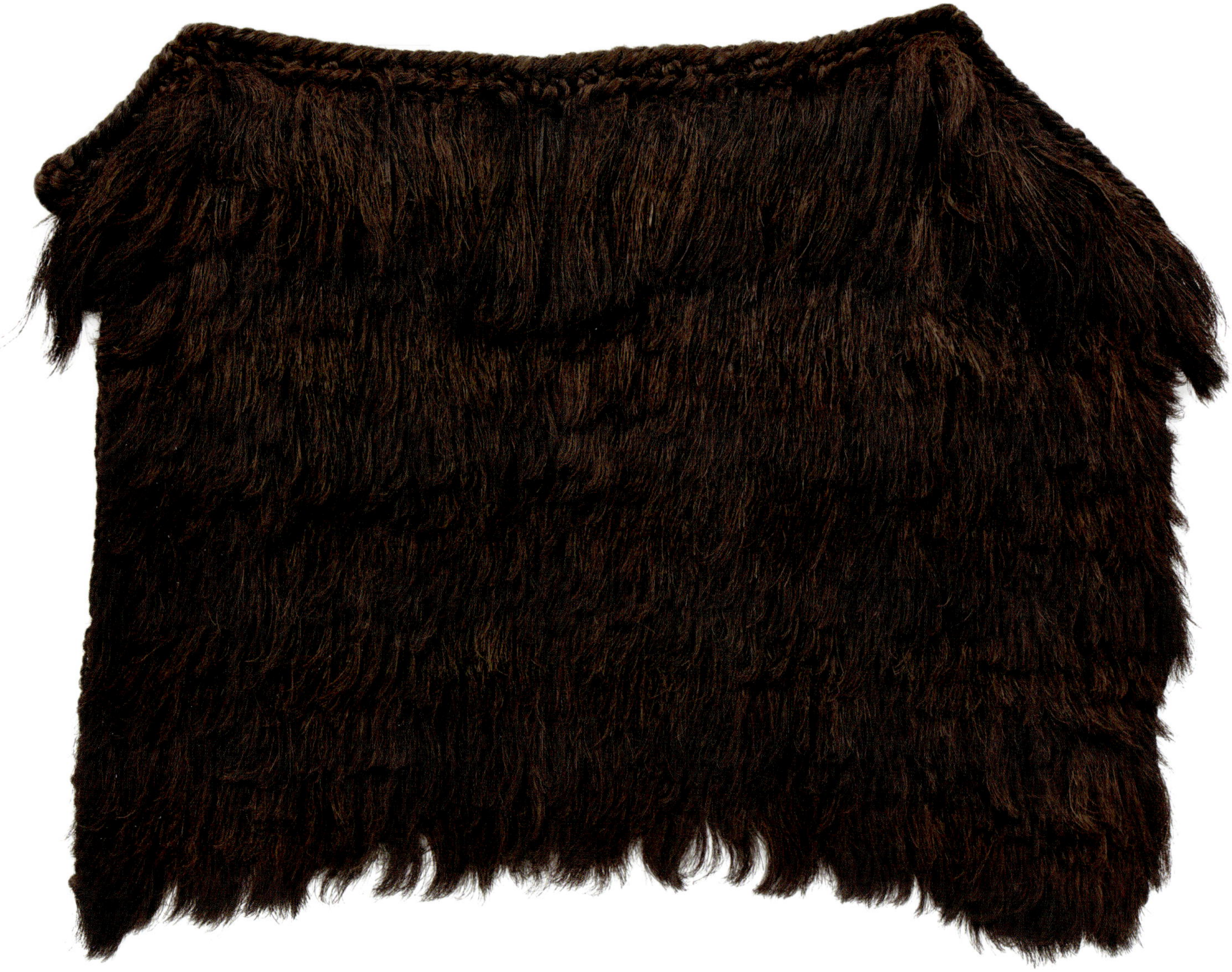

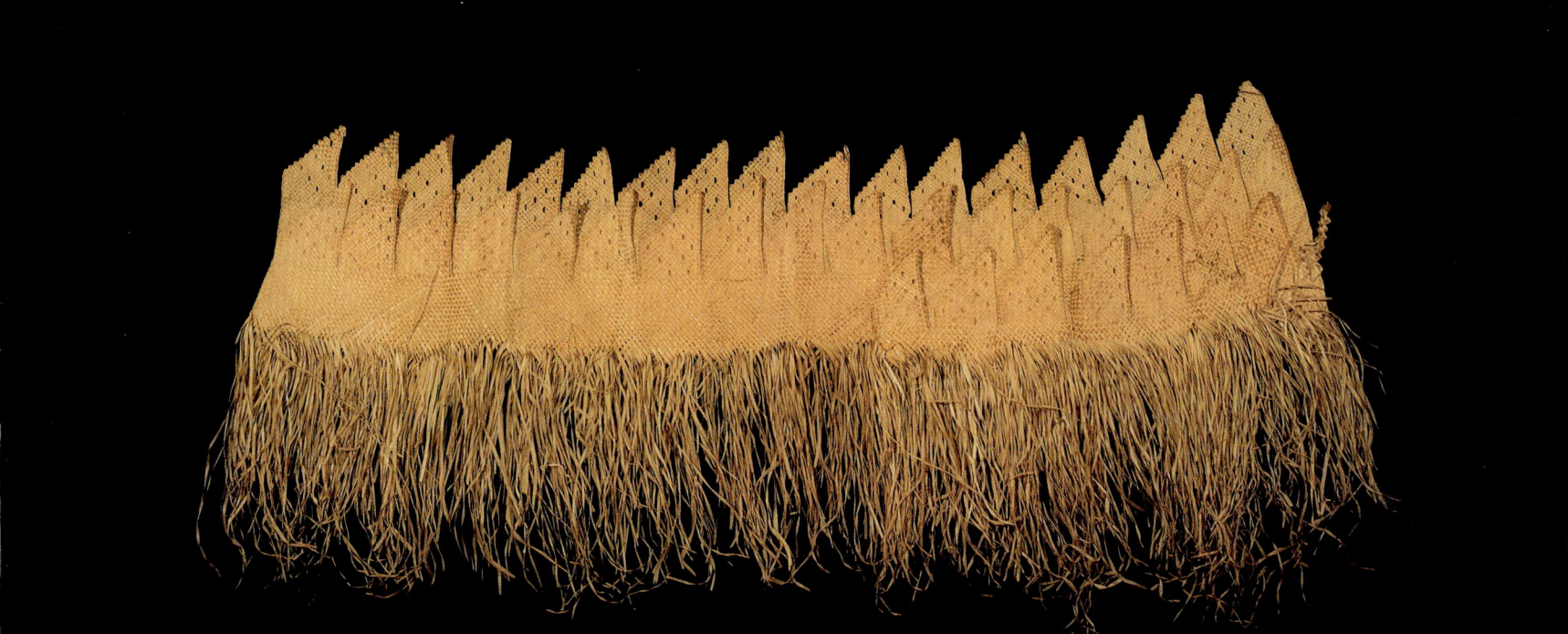

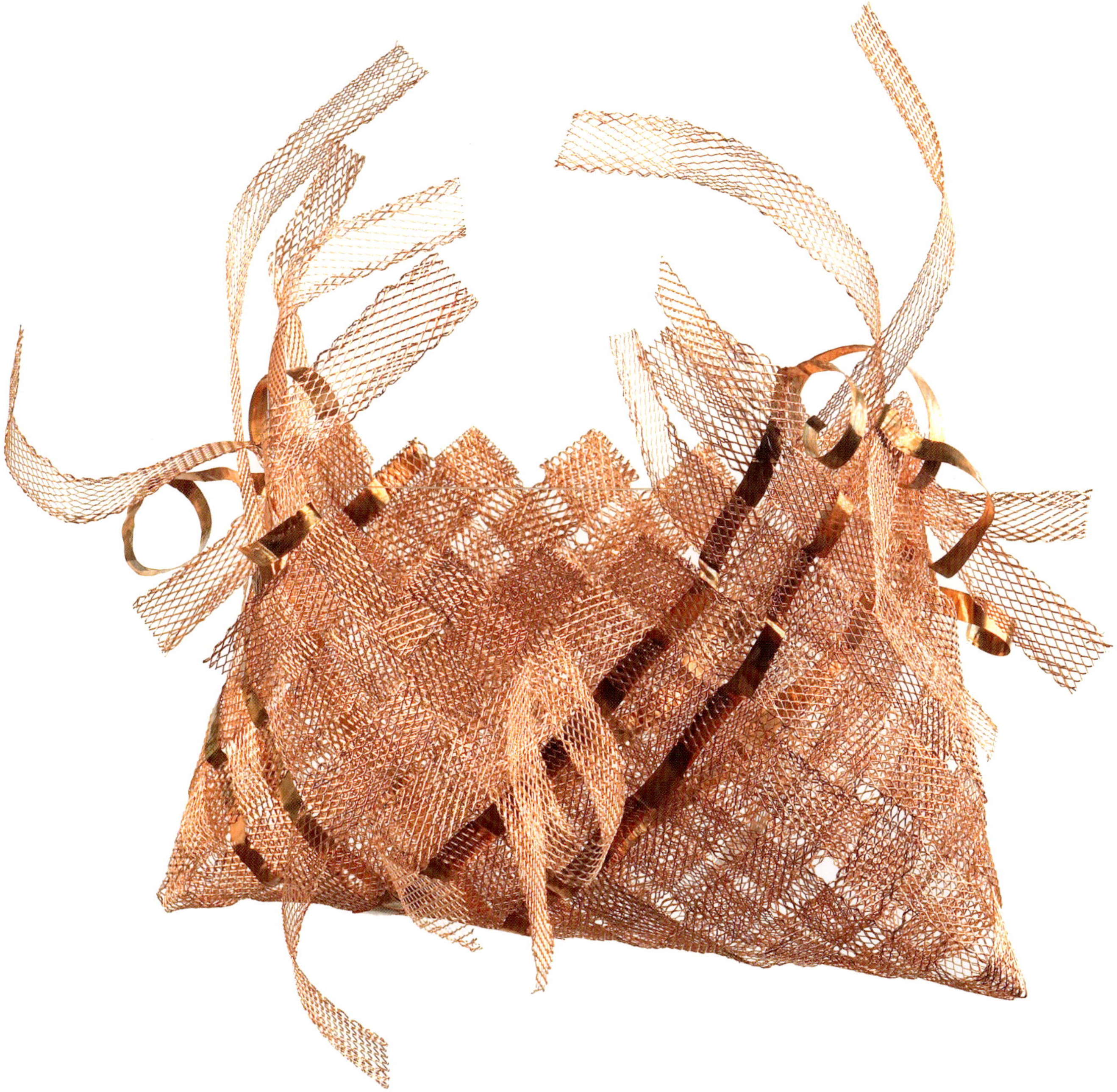

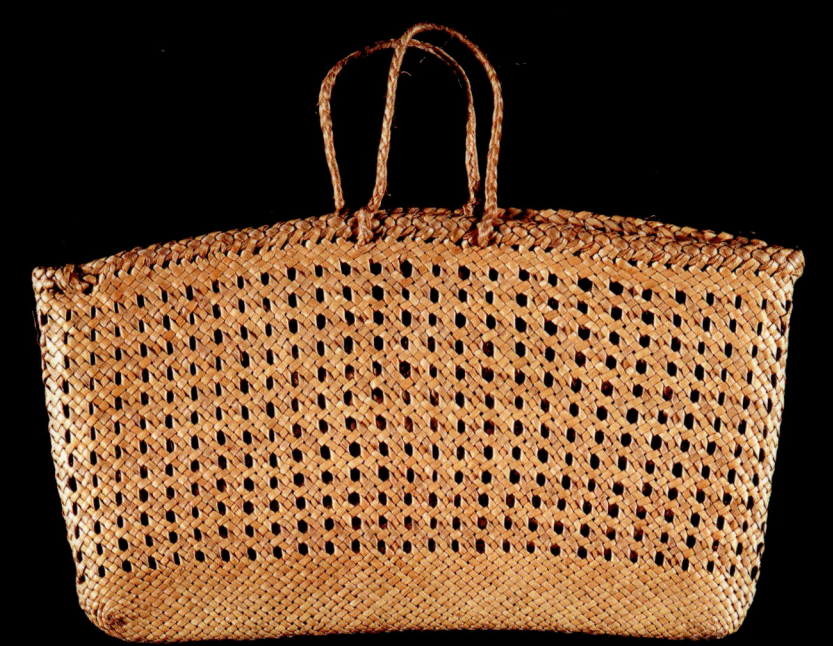

Clockwise from top left:
Kahu tōī (prestigious rain cape) which belonged to Tohi Te Ururangi, a renowned leader of Ngāti Whakaue.
Tāmaki Paenga Hira Auckland War Memorial Museum, 1927.133

**Christina Hurihia Wirihana, *Reflections of Kete Kai*, 1998**
copper mesh, photograph by Norm Heke

Kete whakapuareare with its distinctive spaced composition.
Te Papa Tongarewa Museum of New Zealand, ME000354

Ta'ovala (waist mat) c.1773, a Tongan overskirt with projecting tabs worn by men and women for formal occasions.
Te Papa Tongarewa Museum of New Zealand, FE003021, gift of The Imperial Institute, 1955

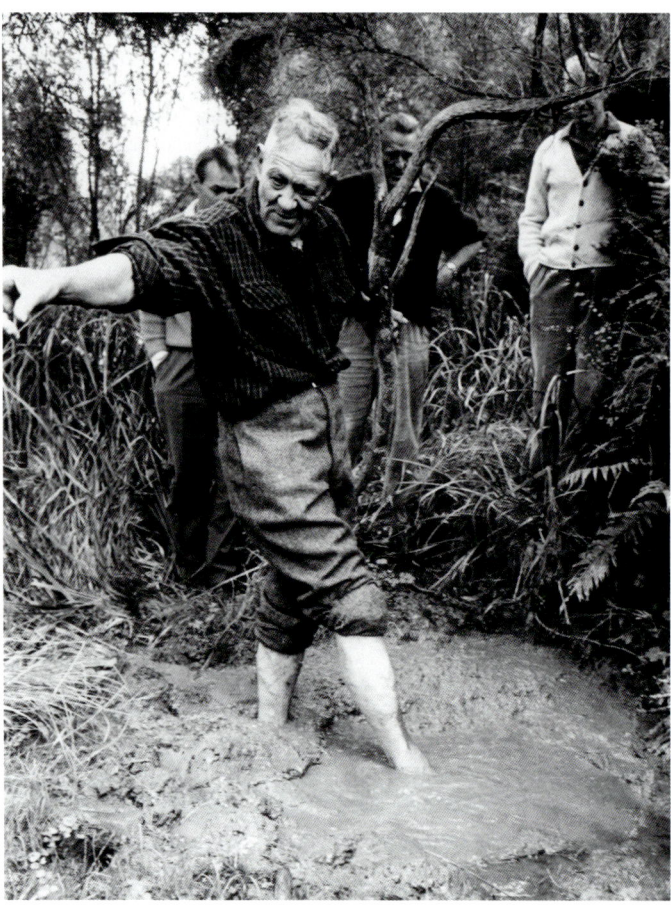

Master carver Pine Taiapa demonstrating the type of paru used at a workshop on the upper East Coast, 1965, for staff and students from Elam School of Fine Arts, including Edward Zagorski (the photographer, here on a Fulbright Scholarship from the University of Illinois). Taiapa was adept at tukutuku, as was Apirana Ngata, a parliamentarian and cultural advocate who himself had been trained in tukutuku as a young boy in the 1870s.
photograph by Edward Zagorski

A number of ancestral narratives link harakeke back into the Pacific. Some plants also had personal names: Ngāti Kahungunu ancestor Tamatea, for instance, landed first in Awanui in the Far North and made his way down the East Coast to arrive at Tauranga, where he 'settled and planted the sacred flax Whara-whara-nui'.[22]

Harakeke types vary in appearance as well as in the quantity and quality of the fibre. The type of harakeke chosen depends on the type of garment and its use. The length of the harakeke strip determines what it will be made into: varieties with long strips and a pleasing colour are best for whāriki, while those with long, strong strips are used in making hīnaki (nets); those with shorter, more flexible strips are better for making kete (baskets).

Other materials besides harakeke are used in textile making. Kiekie was used mainly for rain capes, and to create the patternwork on whāriki, kete and tukutuku panels. Fibre from the leaves of tī kōuka (cabbage tree, *Cordyline australis*), which was stronger and more durable than harakeke, was used to make coarse rain capes, as well as cords and ropes, and the dark leaves of tōī (mountain cabbage tree, *C. indivisa*) were primarily used to make kahu tōī (prestigious cloaks worn by rangatira): the leaves expanded when they were soaked, making the rangatira virtually impervious to attack by an enemy. Pīngao (*Ficinia spiralis*) – a type of sand-binding sedge that grows near the seashore – was valued for its beautiful golden colour, and was used in making kete, whāriki and tukutuku, and sometimes as decoration on rain capes. These materials have endured despite the introduction of new materials such as wool and silk: as weaver Rangimārie Hetet (Ngāti Kinohaku, 1892–1995) insists, 'There is no excuse for not using traditional materials.'[23]

## Dyes and patterns

Textile makers used a range of natural pigments to dye materials. For a black pigment, weaver Diggeress Te Kanawa (Ngāti Maniapoto, Ngāti Kinohaku, 1920–2009) used a two-step process:[24] first the fibre was parboiled in a solution made from the bark of hīnau, which helped the dye to seep in. The fibre was then submerged in paru – a type of mud that was chosen for its dye-fixing qualities; the location of deposits was often a closely held family secret. Red, which was a sacred colour, was achieved by dyeing the fibre or painting the finished garment with kōkōwai. Yellow was derived from the bark and roots of the raurēkau or kanono (*Coprosma grandifolia*): these were boiled, and the fibre was soaked in it before drying. The bark of the tānekaha produced a brown dye, using a two-step process like that for black dye. A fifth colour was that of the natural fibres, which range in hue from white, off-white, cream and beige, through to brown, gold and a deep gold. With the introduction of synthetic dyes, weavers have experimented and innovated in their work with a great array of colours.

Many textiles used patterns to convey messages to the viewer. Weavers enjoyed a repertoire of designs that they used across different woven forms, including tāniko, tukutuku, kete and kākahu. This was part of the visual language that Māori could read and understand. Each pattern conveys an idea or concept. The purapura whetū, for example, refers to a myriad of stars, and the pattern resembles many twinkling dots on a different coloured background. It also refers to the growth of population, which is why Ngāti Toa rangatira Te Rauparaha chose it as the only design for the tukutuku in the church that he commissioned at Ōtaki in the 1850s. Most of the textile patterns resembled objects in the natural world, such as the pātikitiki (flounder) – a diamond-shaped pattern that represented food (fish could be eaten) but also abundance (when the pātikitiki were numerous, there was a sense of abundance for the people). These designs were used across a number of woven forms from kete to tukutuku, reinforcing messages and key ideas in the community.

## Attachments and ornamentation

There are two main techniques used in making textiles: raranga and whatu. Raranga typically uses unprocessed fibre and a folding technique to make mainly domestic and utilitarian garments and other objects: whāriki, kete, rā (canoe sails), tātua, pāraerae (footwear) and kākahu raranga. Whatu is more complex and time-consuming: the fibre is processed then woven using a twisting technique to make a range of garments, especially kākahu.

Tags are small pieces of worked fibre that are attached for practical, aesthetic or ceremonial purposes, and sometimes all three. Historically, rain capes featured a range of different tags made from a variety of materials. Hieke were huge raincapes made with distinctive double tags, made from a single tag that was only partially scraped; it was then folded round and woven in a second time. Sometimes a weaver might add multi-coloured tags for visual effect.

Weavers applied a range of attachments to kākahu. On korowai they used hukahuka (tassels or tags) made from blackened strands of muka, or they would attach kārure (twisted spiral tassels) or ngore (pompoms); eventually cloaks became known as korowai ngore or simply kārure. This showed real experimentation by weavers, and it became popular in the late nineteenth century when the kaitaka form of cloak, with its unadorned body (a feature that made them revered), was set aside as a style in favour of the korowai, with the range of attachments woven onto the base.

Contemporary weavers are still experimenting with different materials and making not only ceremonial kākahu, but also other works to be enjoyed purely for their aesthetic. The maro by Veranoa Hetet (Te Ātiawa, Ngāti Tūwharetoa and Ngāti Maniapoto)[25] uses dyed harakeke and muka with pheasant-feather attachments, and a copper-wire whiri (braid) along the top; the warm colours are offset against the dark, paru-dyed woven base. Native bird feathers are very difficult to obtain today: to access them, weavers are required to apply to the Department of Conservation for permission to gather birds from which to pluck feathers. This is frustrating, given that Te Tiriti o Waitangi guarantees to Māori access to their taonga, and huruhuru (feathers) are certainly taonga.

## Mahi raranga – the art of plaiting

Raranga involves plaiting strips of fibre that are placed diagonally across each other. The strips that go to the left are called aho (weft or sinestrals), and those that go to the right are called whenu (warp or dextrals). This technique was popular in the Pacific, where pandanus leaves were used to make mats and other textiles, and archaeological evidence confirms that the earliest settlers from the Pacific used raranga.

Whāriki were important household items. Utilitarian whāriki were woven in pora (panels) that were then sewn together, for use in different settings: they were placed over soft raupō (bulrush, *Typha orientalis*) matting inside the whare as sleeping mats; placed in the porch to sit on during the day; or used to cover food inside the pātaka. Weaver Erenora Puketapu-Hetet (Te Ātiawa, 1941–2006) identifies specific types of whāriki:[26] tuwhara – a coarse mat used

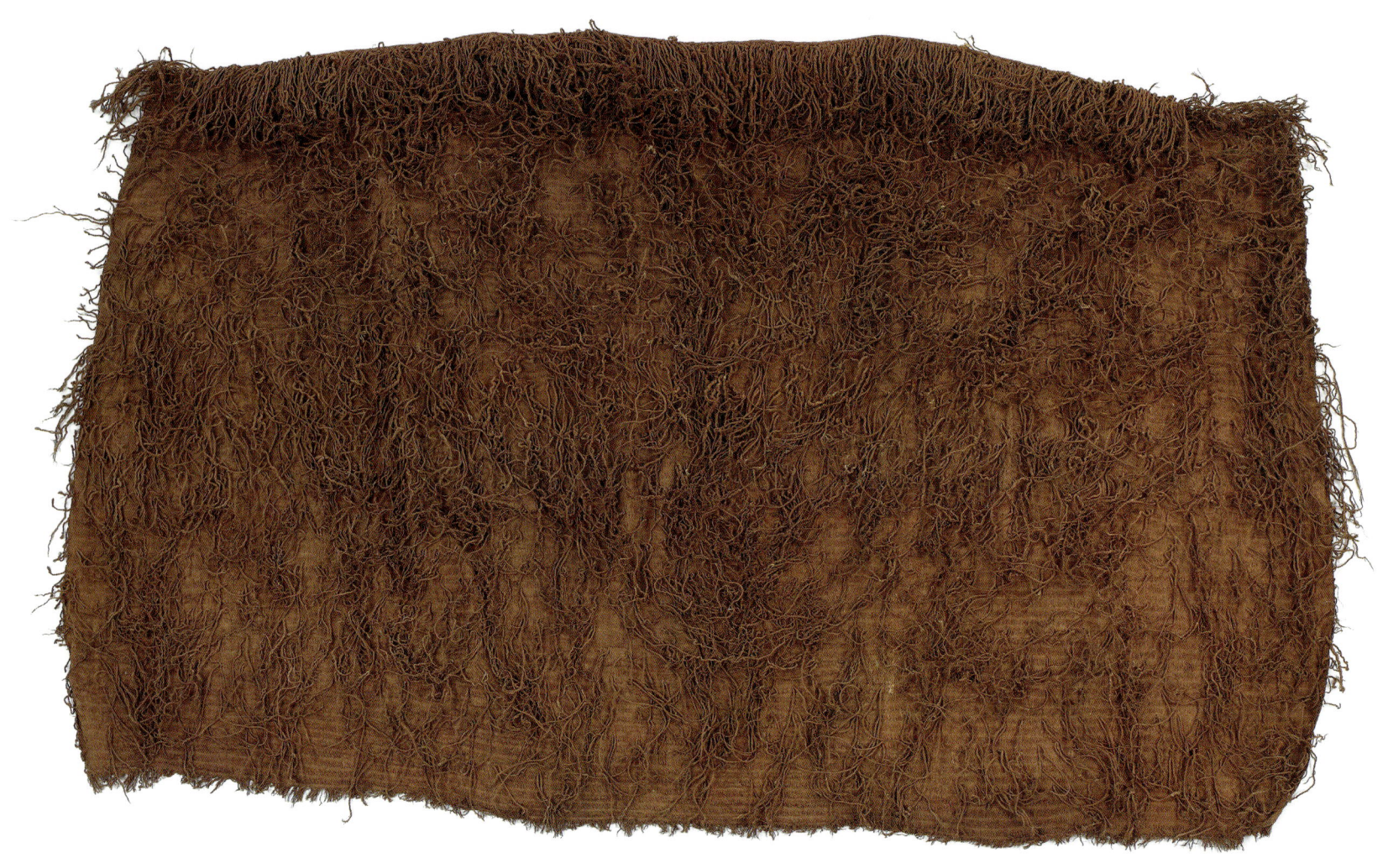

This sequence of images is emblematic of the evolving relationship between Hongi Hika, missionaries and the Crown as mediated by a single kākahu. Maureen Lander undertook extensive research into a red kākahu which Hongi Hika took with him from the Bay of Islands when he travelled with Waikato to England. He is portrayed wearing it in James Barry's 1820 portrait; this may very well be the unusual kākahu with kārure (rolled thrums) painted with kōkōwai currently in the British Museum (above). It was this latter cloak that inspired Lander to create a contemporary version of the kākahu seen at right.
British Museum, Oc1982,Q.712 EOC28231 282636001

Opposite top: **Maureen Lander, *Hongi's Red Cloak – Deconstructed*, as installed in Tell Tails, Alexander Turnbull Library, Wellington, 2015**
photograph by Mark Beatty

Opposite bottom: **James Barry, *The Rev Thomas Kendall and the Maori chiefs Hongi and Waikato*, 1820**
oil on canvas, 720 x 920mm, Alexander Turnbull Library, G-618

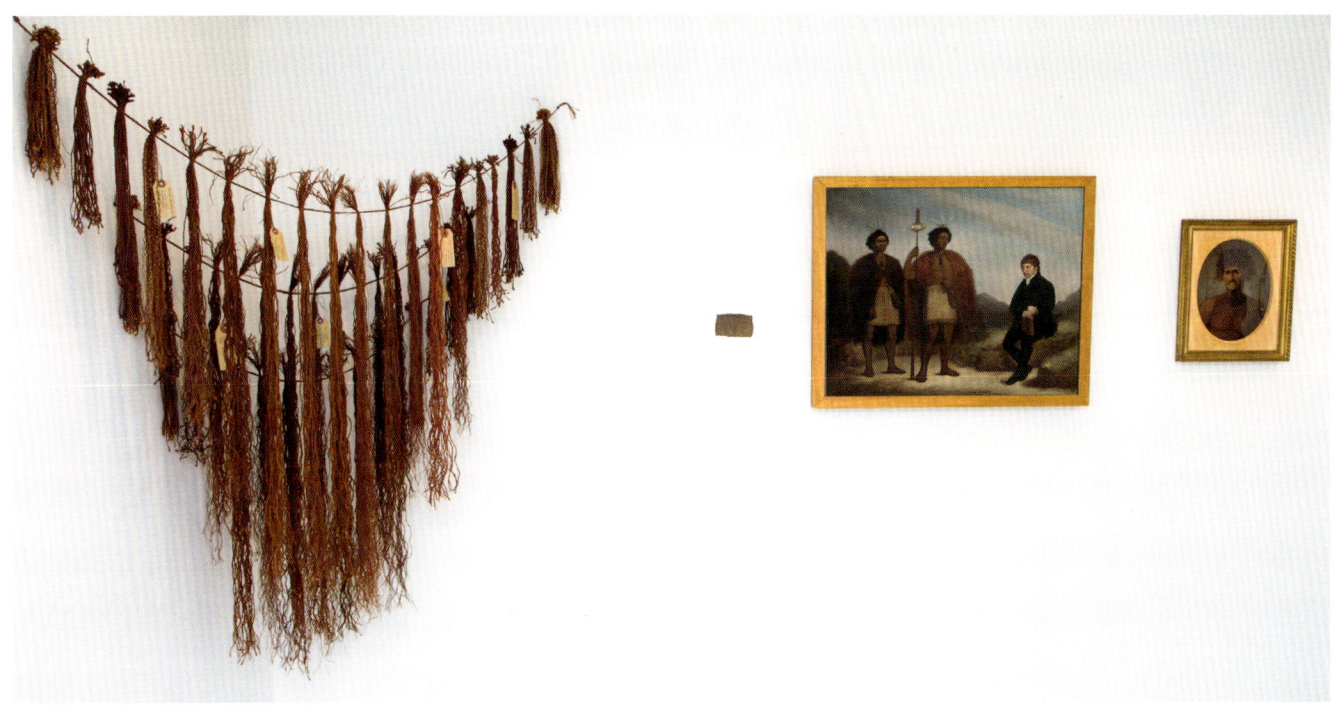

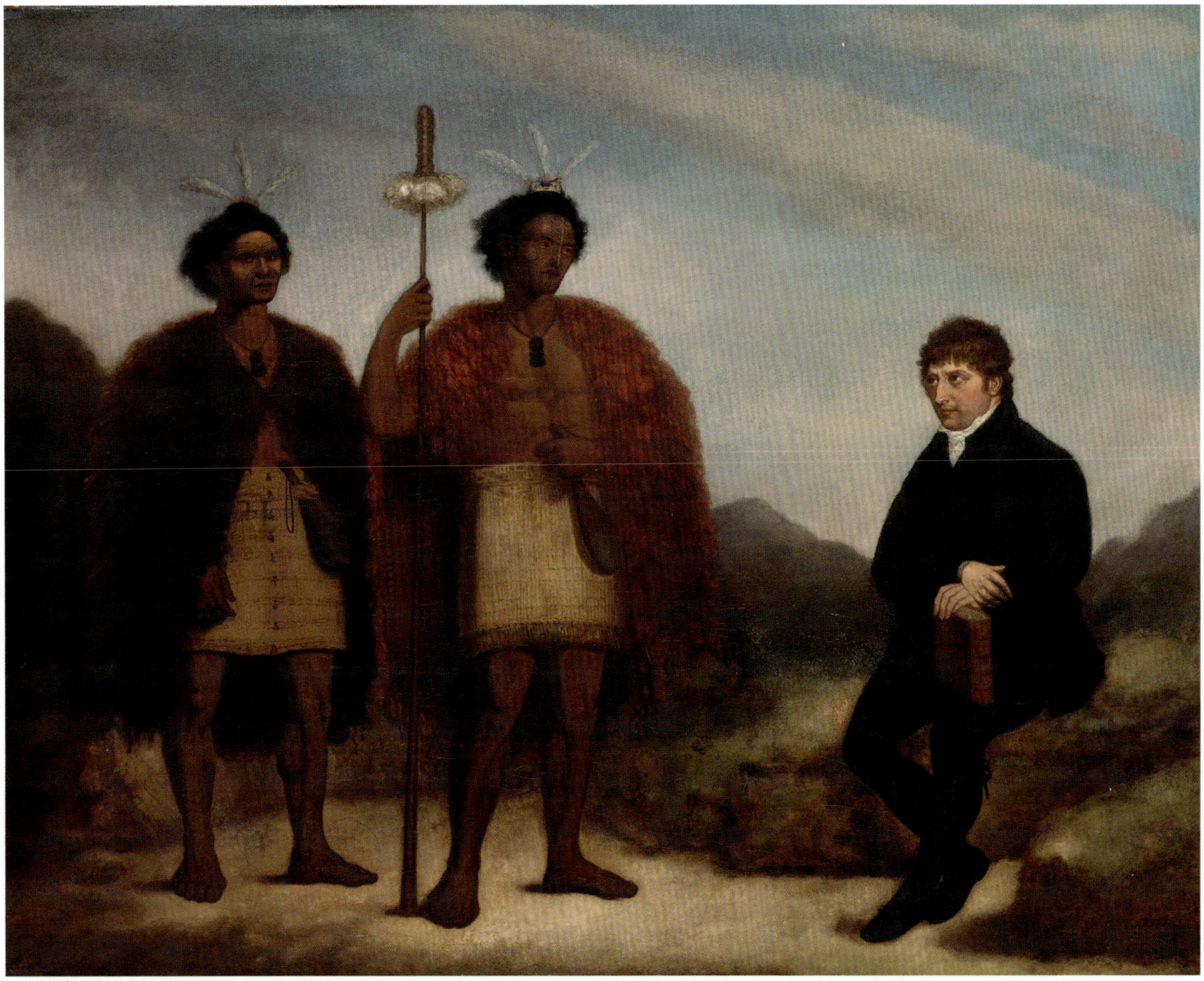

under a fine mat; tīenga or pōrera – a fine kiekie mat, usually patterned; takapau – a finely woven mat used for ceremonies; and takapapa – a mat on which to serve food. There were also whāriki that were patterned and used in more ceremonial ways: in the nineteenth century, as the whare transformed into a communal meeting space, whāriki were placed on the floor; their patterns and placement conveyed important information about the kaitiaki of the house, and whether or not the manuhiri (visitors) were welcome.[27]

Some forms of whāriki had a ceremonial role in marriage celebrations. In a formal tomo (betrothal ceremony) arranged by the elders of both partners, the suitor would sit waiting for his betrothed to join him on a 'tomo mat' – and, by implication, in marriage. This practice continued into the 1920s: on one occasion a contingent of Ngāti Porou produced a tomo mat in the middle of a large gathering of the tribe in Rotorua during the 1920 visit of the Prince of Wales, for the formal betrothal of a young Ngāti Porou nursing student to a suitor (she turned him down).

Mahi raranga was used to make kete. Some kete were utilitarian containers for carrying and storing everything from kūmara to kaimoana: some were made with an open weave, designed to strain out the sand from seafood and soil from kūmara. Food could be placed into kete and lowered into steaming hot water, especially in the geothermal area around Rotorua. Some kete had a special drawstring along the top which could be gathered to stop items falling out; most members of a hapū could whip up one of these practical, functional kete in no time. Today, simple square-shaped containers called kono are often seen in homes to hold everyday objects in and around the marae – everything from cooked food to serviettes in the wharekai.

Kete whakairo (patterned kete) were ceremonial kete used in a number of roles. Some were made to store precious kākahu such as kahu kurī; they would be decorated with feathers and patterned designs to signal this. Some were carried with pride at certain special events and would gain in mana each time they were used. Weavers chose materials that showed the prestige of the kete, such as a light-coloured kiekie or processed muka, and designs that would enhance the mana of the kete whakairo and, by extension, the bearer – and even the occasion. Kete whakairo today are made for personal use, but also for sale – when they can be very elaborate, with unusual types of fibre and complex coloured designs.

Māori also used mahi raranga to make sails – rā, kōmaru, whakawhiti and rāwhara – into the early nineteenth century.[28] There were different types of rā: a whara, for instance, was a 'sail made in a special way for a war canoe';[29] its name possibly derived from the word for pandanus in the Pacific – whara, fala, fara, ara, etc.[30] The names of ancestral sails have been passed down the generations by oral tradition. Mere Whaanga names two that are associated with the voyaging chief Tamatea: Te Haeata o te rangi and Parinuiterā.[31] The sail names may be a reference to aspects of navigation – the sunrise of the day, for instance – and the fact that they have been named suggests they were important taonga in their own right.

The oldest surviving sail is in the British Museum (NZ147). It is in the shape of an isosceles triangle: the two long sides measure 4.35m. The thirteen plaited panels have been stitched together and feature a zigzag design that may have had not only an aesthetic function, to make the sail more beautiful, but also a practical role – to allow wind through the sail. Along the bottom panel is a triangular fringe with attachments of kāhu (hawk) feathers, still mostly intact. There are loops along the two long edges where possibly more kāhu feathers were attached. A fourteenth panel is fastened to one of the long edges and is also decorated with feathers; the purpose of this final panel is most likely as a telltale – a navigational aid to identify wind direction. This sail has recently been the focus of research in which textile conservators Hokimate Harwood (Ngāpuhi) and Catherine Smith and Māori weavers Donna Campbell (Ngāpuhi, Ngāti Ruanui) and Ranui Ngarimu (Ngāi Tahu, Ngāti Mutunga) are working together to discover more about the types of materials and techniques used.

The earliest known drawing of a Māori sail dates to Abel Tasman's week-long visit to New Zealand in 1642. The sketcher and cartographer on the expedition, Isaack Gilsemans, depicts a triangular sail on a double waka; unusually, it is horizontal – in all other drawings of sails they are upright. This may have been a feature used by the local Ngāti Tūmatakōkiri people. A drawing in 1769 by Parkinson shows a twenty-four-panel rā held in place by four guy-ropes on a large and crowded waka taua. There are several recorded sightings of these sails in the nineteenth century – Joel Polack drew a waka with two rā in Tūranganui a Kiwa in 1836, and Tuta Nihoniho mentions seeing them in the same area a

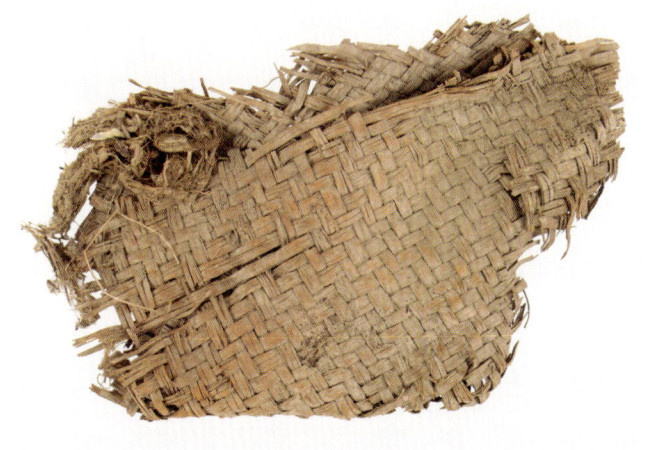
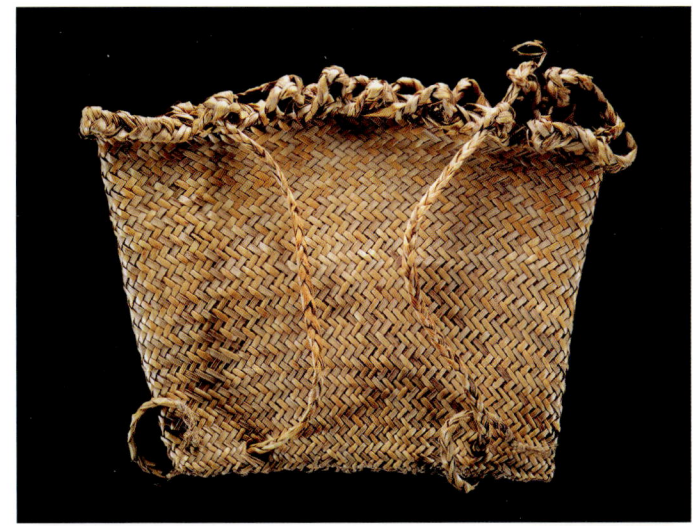
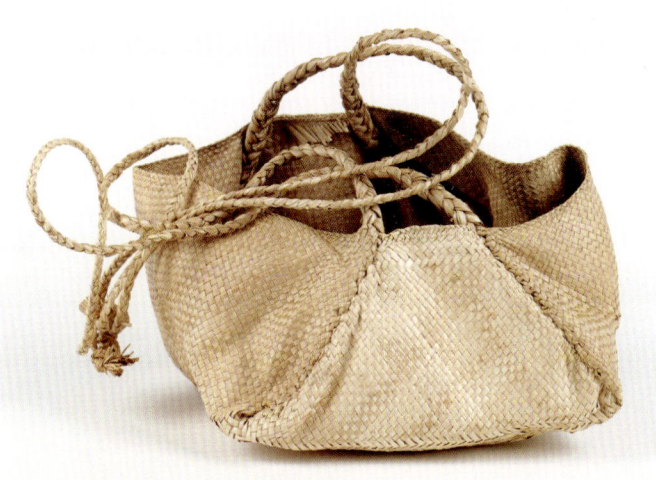
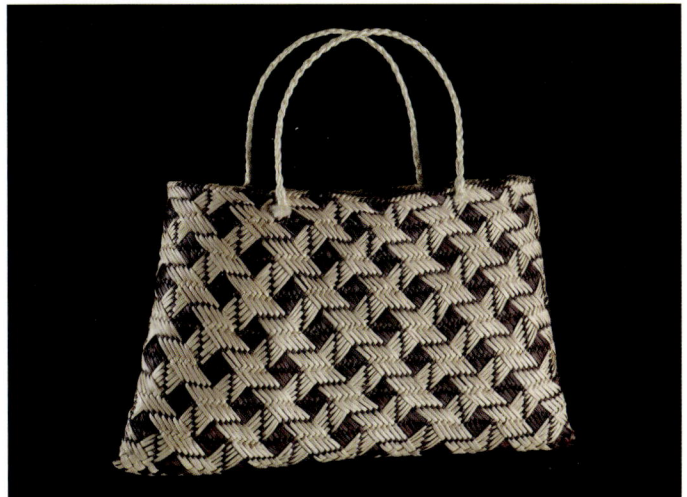
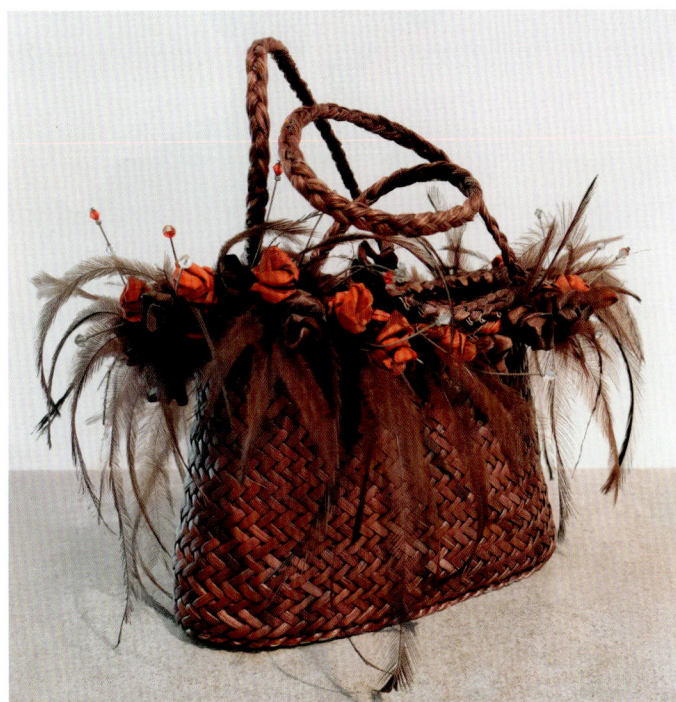

Top left: Raranga fragment from Roxburgh Gorge, Otago.
Tūhura Otago Museum

This kete pukirikiri at top right is a backpack used for carrying gravel to kūmara or taro beds. It is remarkable that such a mundane object was collected in 1907, when many museums and collectors were more interested in kete whakairo. It is very similar to this example at middle left, from the Pentecost Islands, New Hebrides, Vanuatu, made in 1997. Carrying loads in this way was very effective.
Te Papa Tongarewa Museum of New Zealand, ME001757; Tāmaki Paenga Hira Auckland War Memorial Museum, 1992.194

Middle right: **Sonya Snowden**, *Tatai Whetu ki te Rangi*, 2011
kiekie, muka, harakeke, synthetic dyes, Te Papa Tongarewa Museum of New Zealand, ME024141

Bottom: **Jess Paraone**, *Kete Rosebud*, 2010
harakeke, Swarovski crystal, jewellery findings and synthetic dyes, Kura Gallery, photograph by Jess Paraone

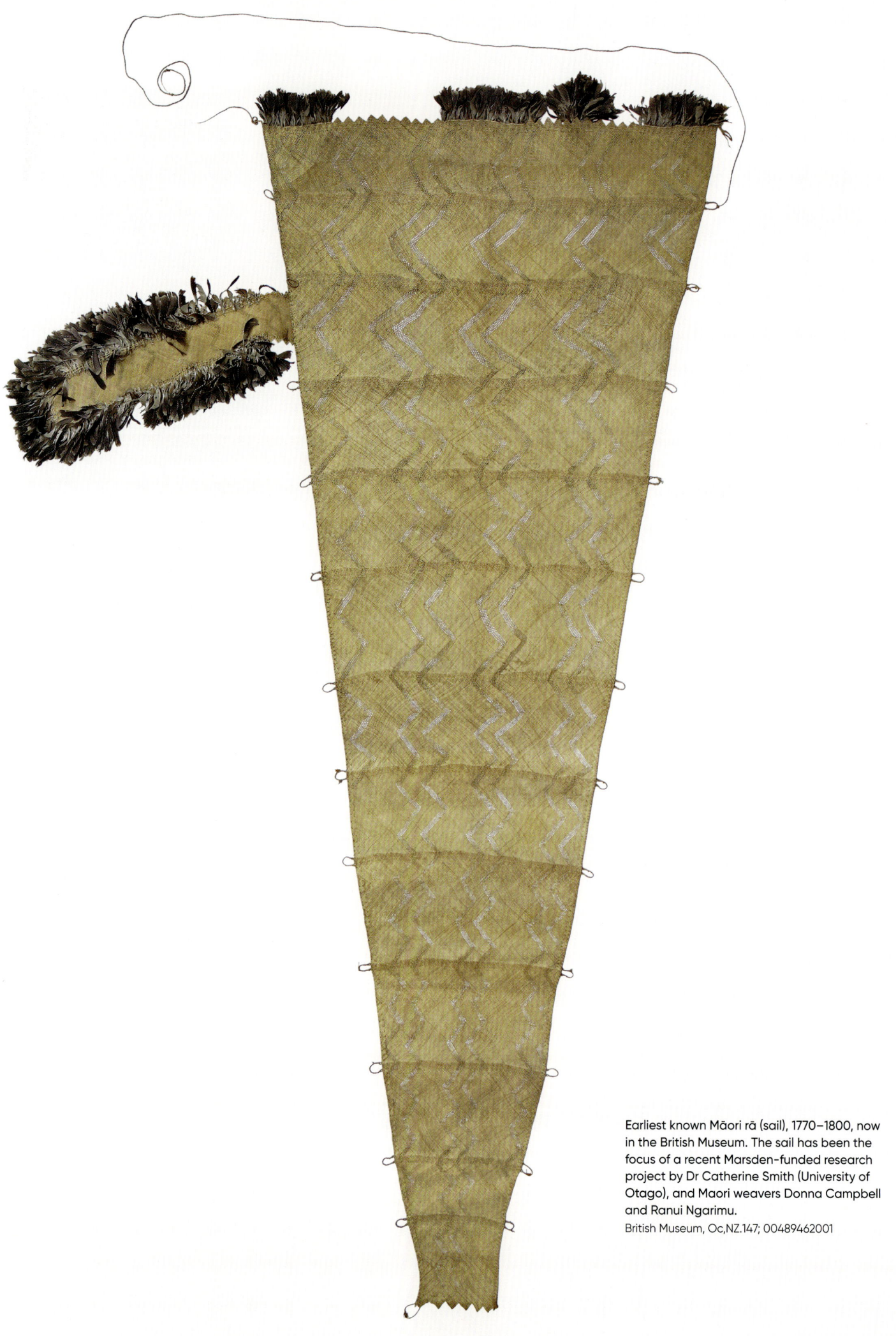

Earliest known Māori rā (sail), 1770–1800, now in the British Museum. The sail has been the focus of a recent Marsden-funded research project by Dr Catherine Smith (University of Otago), and Maori weavers Donna Campbell and Ranui Ngarimu.
British Museum, Oc,NZ.147; 00489462001

generation later – but in general, with the demise of the waka taua, plaited rā were no longer made.

Tātua (woven bands wound round the body for armour and to carry weapons) were made by weaving pīngao (or other materials) into a rectangular sheet that was doubled over to form a pocket; the tātua was tied around the waist using strings attached at either end. There were a number of different versions. One example, collected in 1773 or 1774 by naturalists Johann Reinhold Forster and his son Georg during Cook's second voyage (1772–75), is now in Pitt Rivers Museum (1886.1.1182) as part of a collection of 220 taonga deposited in the museum in 1776.[32] This plain tātua is made using the raranga pūputu (close plaiting) technique,[33] which gives a very dense weave that would have provided protection during hand-to-hand fighting.

Tātua are mentioned in various whakataukī, including:

Te tātua o Hikakawa – *food*
Te tātua o Te Kaha – *red clouds at sunset*
Te tātua o Kahu – *belt of clear sky near the horizon*[34]

Whaanga mentions a 'tātua pūpara' (belt for carrying valuables) – a kind of tātua such as belonged to her ancestor Kahungunu: it held special harakeke that had come from a specific place, which Kahungunu's wife Rongomaiwahine used to adorn his topknot.[35] Elsdon Best illustrates three of these tātua pūpara in his 1941 book *The Maori*: each one is finely woven and decorated with designs in a range of colours. Herbert Williams defines both 'tātua pūpara' and 'tātua whara' interchangeably as 'a girdle in which valuables were carried';[36] and Te Rangi Hīroa describes a tātua kōtara, a plaited war belt.[37] The tātua clearly had an important role in protecting the rangatira in warfare, and would have been ornamented to reflect his status as a chief.

The woven tātua went out of fashion in the late 1800s as Māori opted to wear European clothes instead. The smaller plaited belt lasted until the middle of the nineteenth century, often worn in trousers: two such examples were sold at auction in 2017 in Wellington, made with tāniko weaving and measuring around 90–98cm long. Māori girls at Hukarere Girls' School in Napier practised their tāniko skills in the 1920s by making belts. Today some weavers still make tāniko belts, but also use this form for guitar straps and hat bands worn to celebrate their Māori identity.

The maro – a short, triangular-shaped kilt or apron worn by men and women to cover the genital area – was another popular garment that went out of fashion with the advent of European clothing and values about covering the body. The Ma'ohi of Tahiti made a similar garment, also called maro, described as 'long waist belts of *tapa* which were infused with the power of the gods … generally worn by first-born males who by their ancestry could claim inheritance to the dynasty's kin title'.[38] One of the earliest Māori examples was the maro kōpua – such as an exquisite one the Forsters collected, which was lined with dogskin and ornamented with pāua shell; these types of ornamentation were a strong indication that this was a prestigious garment, probably worn by a rangatira. Other styles of maro were decorated with tāniko borders, and could be double thickness for added protection as body armour; weavers occasionally attached long black hukahuka, although this was unusual. Other maro were more utilitarian: they were made for everyday wear, such as when collecting seafood.

The tū was a belt to which the maro was attached[39] – often decorated with shells and harakeke. Men wore a tū ure, to keep the ure (penis) upright; and women wore a tū kāretu, named for the fragrant kāretu grass (*Hierochloe redolens*) that was attached to the waist cord. Both of these were replaced in the nineteenth century by European drawers (undergarments).

## Mahi whatu – the art of twining

The mahi whatu technique was used primarily to make kākahu. No tools were involved, and no frames; instead, weavers used one or two sets of carved turuturu (weaving pegs), with one end ornately carved and the other end sharpened to a point. The pegs were pushed into the ground, spaced to the width of the intended cloak. The first line woven between the pegs was called te aho tapu (the sacred thread) – which shows the importance of this practice. A series of whenu were woven between the turuturu, and from there the aho were twined from left to right. The cloak was usually woven from the bottom up in this way, leaving the tāniko till last – 'the highest part of Māori craft', according to Rangimārie Hetet.[40] Textile historian Awhina Tamarapa (Ngāti Kahungunu, Ngāti Ruanui, Ngāti Pikiao) identifies two types of kākahu that evolved using the mahi whatu technique – rain capes and some kākahu.[41]

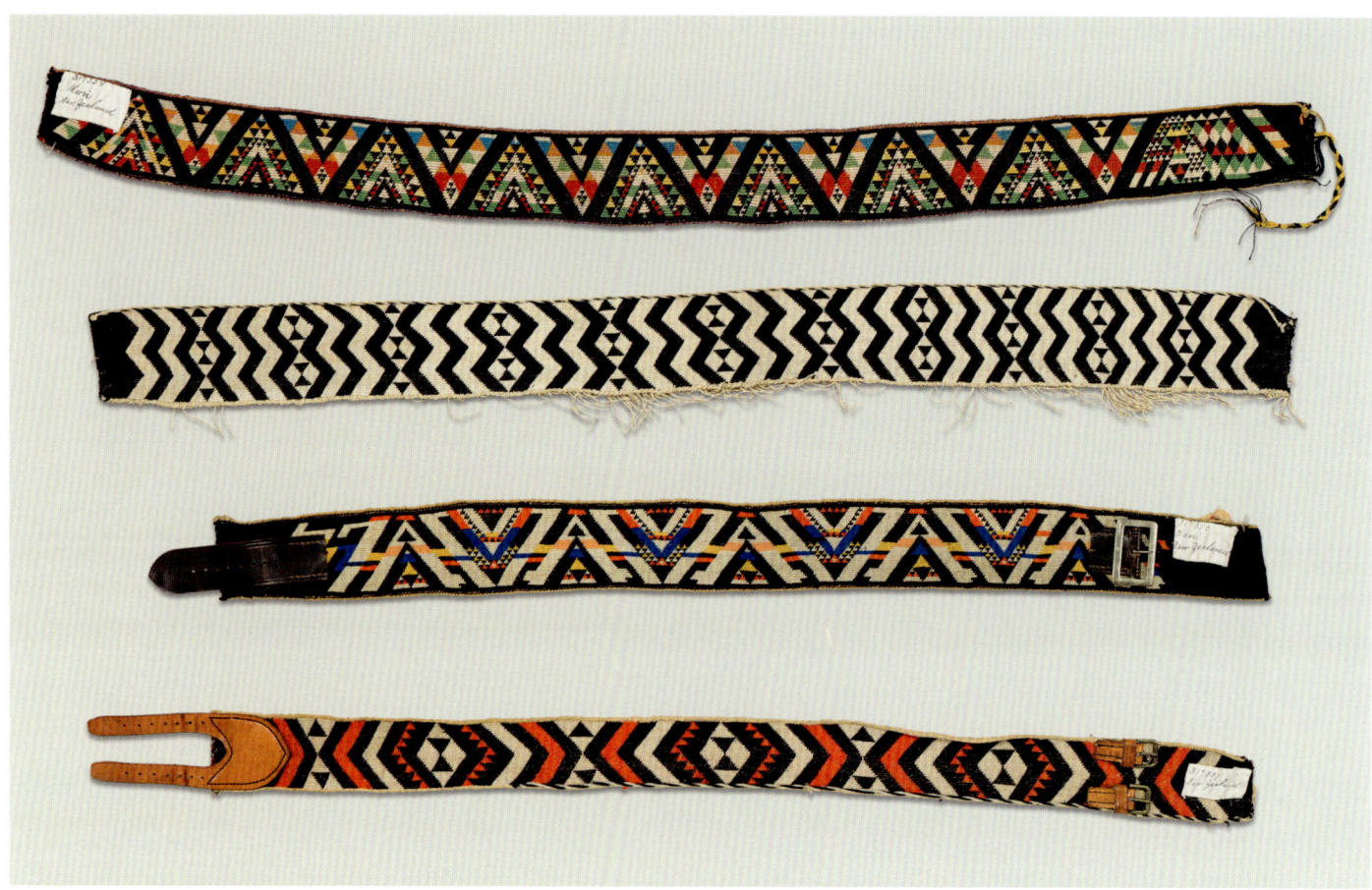

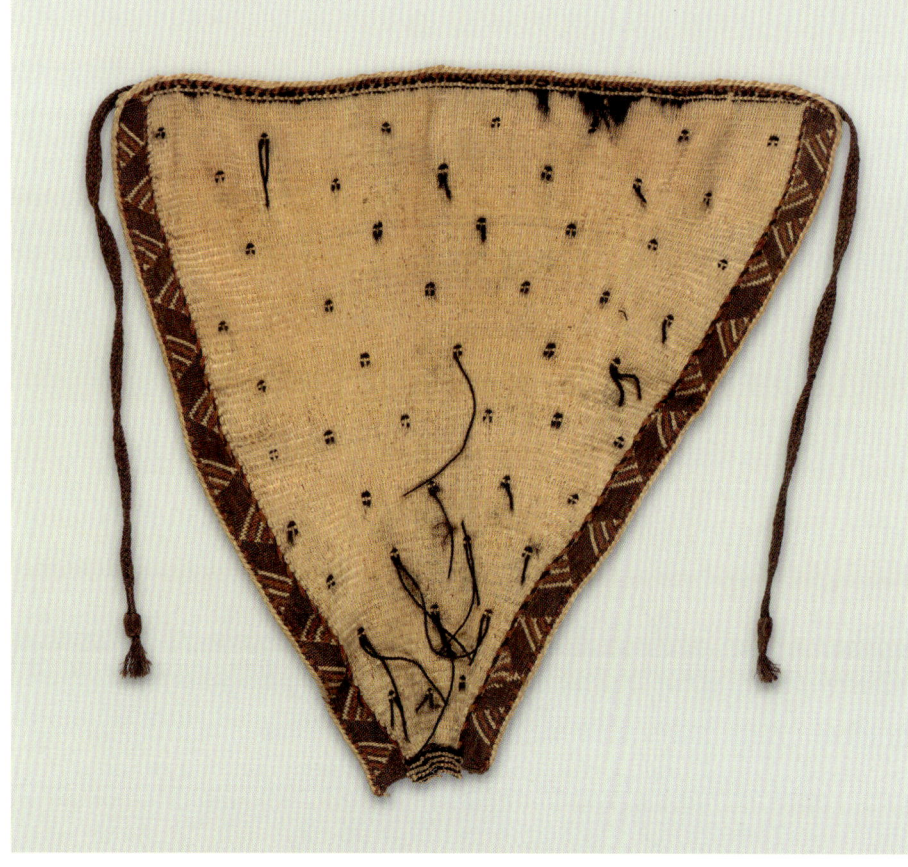

Above: Four of the five tātua in the collection of the Smithsonian National Museum of Natural History, Washington DC.
Smithsonian Institution, E317328, E317329, E317330, E317331, photograph by Donald E. Hurlbert

Left: Maro kōpua (apron) made by a Tūhoe weaver from Ruatāhuna in the late nineteenth or early twentieth century. The tāniko border, close weave and attachments suggest this was made for someone of mana.
Te Papa Tongarewa Museum of New Zealand, ME002836, gift of Alexander Turnbull, 1913

Opposite top: Weaving peg (turuturu), late eighteenth–early nineteenth century.
Metropolitan Museum of Art, New York, 1979.206.1600, The Michael C. Rockefeller Memorial Collection, bequest of Nelson A. Rockefeller, 1979

Opposite bottom: Turuturu were important to hold weaving off the ground. The woman in this photo uses simple uncarved turuturu in the making of her korowai.
Alexander Turnbull Library, 1/1-017334-G

While almost everyone in the community would know basic raranga techniques to make everyday kete, the raranga skills to make kākahu required specialised knowledge and training. Instruction took place in Te Whare Pora – often this was not an actual house; rather, it was a metaphorical term for a space of learning. The learning would begin informally with young girls watching older women and playing with offcuts, before the formal training began. Students learnt practical skills as well as knowledge of the spiritual realm of Hineteiwaiwa, principal atua of weaving; they were taught the tikanga surrounding the gathering of materials, and the protocols associated with weaving practice. As Awhina Tamarapa reminds us: 'These ancestral connections are an integral part of the garment and give the kākahu their immense value.'[42] Weaver Kahutoi Te Kanawa records Mākereti Papakura's incantation:[43]

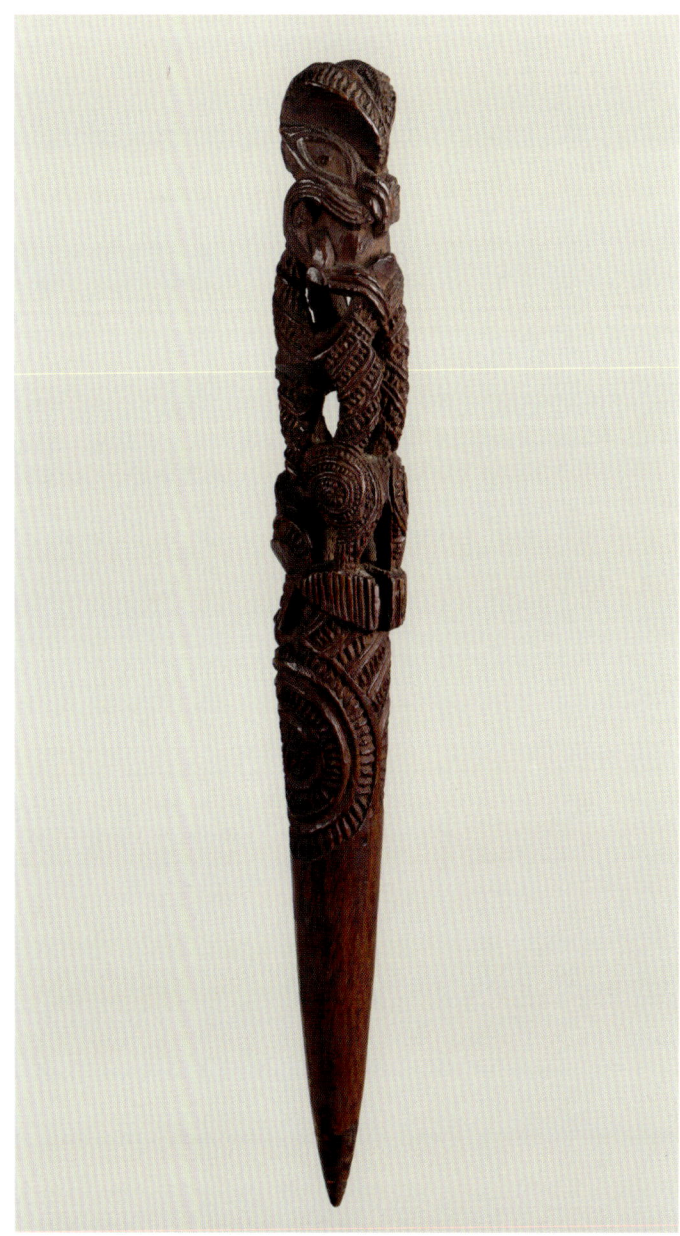

> Tohi ki te wai o Tū
> *Blessed in the sacred waters of Tū*
> Whano koe – tangaengae
> *Go forth in the world – with vigour*
> Ki te mahi kai mau – tangaengae
> *To cook foods for you – with vigour*
> Ki te whatu pueru mou – tangaengae
> *To weave clothing for you – with vigour*

In Te Whare Pora students would learn the two main whatu techniques: whatu aho pātahi (single-pair twining) and whatu aho rua (double-pair twining). Working with single weft was the simplest way of weaving – and is known all round the world – whereas double weft (using two pairs of threads) was a favourite of weavers.

### Types of cloaks and capes

The mahi whatu technique was used to make rain cloaks and capes. In oral narrative, ancestors wore rain capes when they came to Aotearoa from the Pacific. Tamarapa describes them as 'coarse, resilient garments made by attaching strips of various plant material to a whenu (warp thread) base'.[44] Rain capes were practical garments and very thick and heavy, designed to protect the wearer against the elements and the wear and tear of hard labour; and, for warriors, as war capes to deflect attacks.

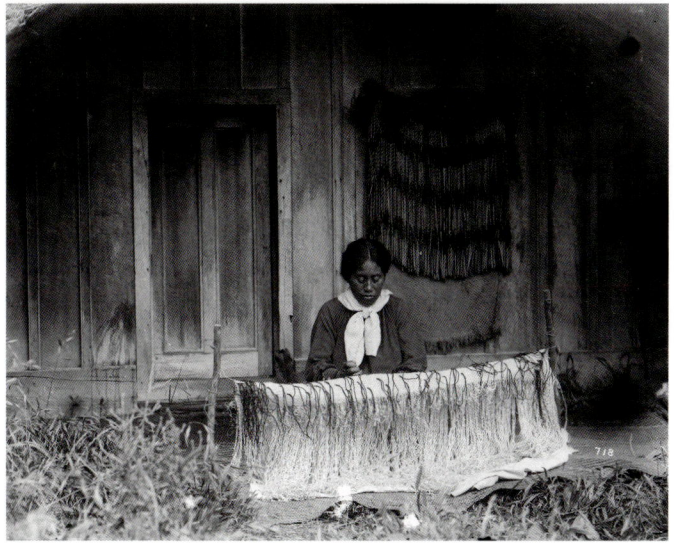

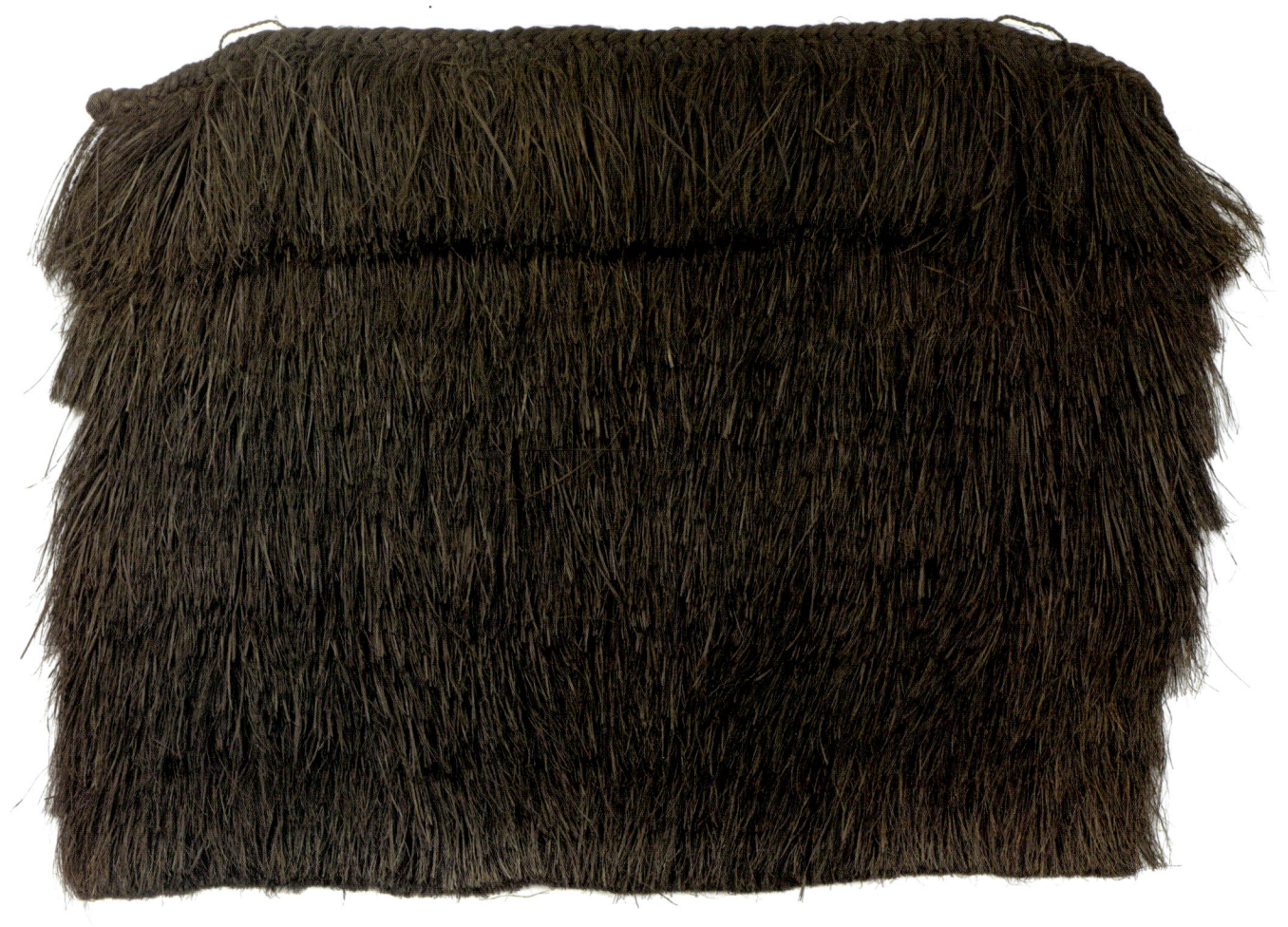

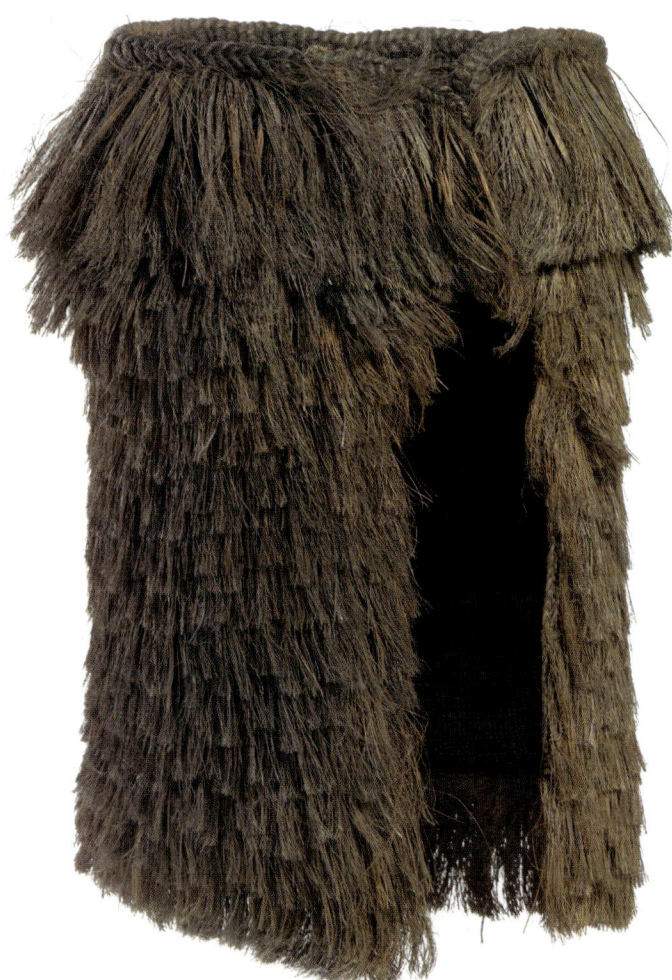

**Above:** Kahu tōī (rain cape), c.1850.
Te Papa Tongarewa Museum of New Zealand, ME001156, Henry Hill Collection, purchased 1905

**Left:** Kahu tōī made of dyed tōī-leaf fibre. This example was made in the early nineteenth century but later taken to England and acquired by the Royal Botanic Gardens, Kew, London, before being passed to the British Museum in 1860.
British Museum, Oc1960,11.70; EOC22624 00416572001

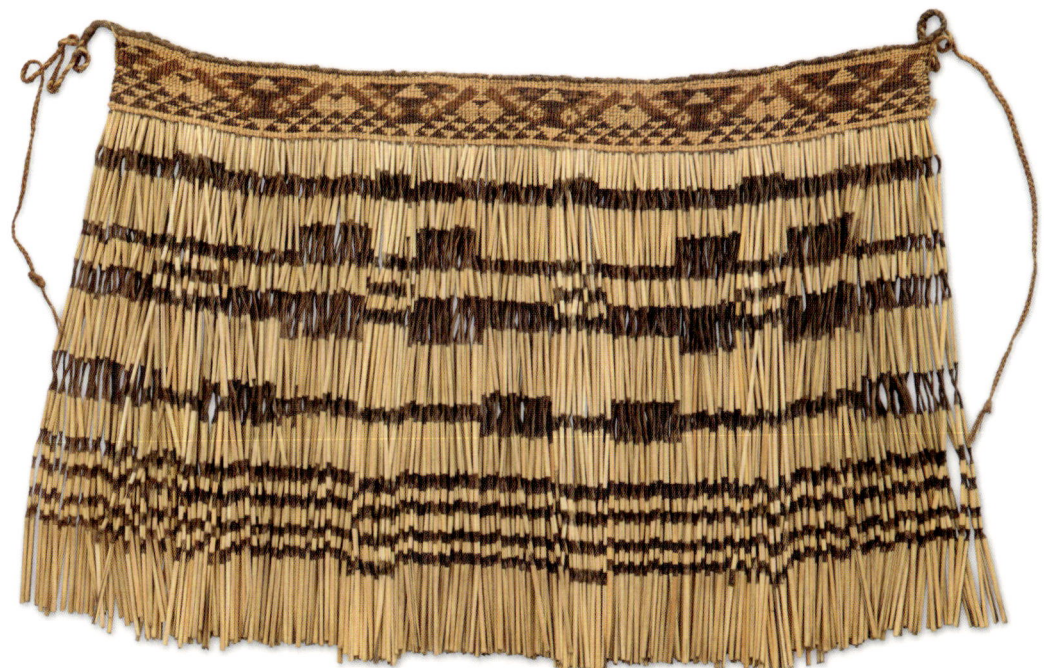

Piupiu with a wide tāniko waistband.
Tāmaki Paenga Hira Auckland War Memorial Museum, AM67888

Rain cloaks, which were more prestigious and formal, were made by twining together partially processed flax strips: these textiles were still in production and use in the early twentieth century in remote areas. The making began with a braided neck, and proceeded down from there. The simplest form was quickly and easily made and just as easily discarded, which may be one reason why so few survive.

The most prestigious form of rain cape was the kahu tōī: these were very valuable and symbolised chieftainship and power. Their significance is evidenced by the fact that they are the only raincape to be given the name 'kahu'.[45] Kahu tōī – named for the material they are made from, the leaves of tōī, the mountain cabbage tree – are distinctive for their rich, lustrous black colour. Often, kahu tōī would be soaked 'in mordant solutions and trodden into paru': this plumped out the fibre, making it impervious to attack and also waterproof, sometimes for years after.[46] One example in Te Papa dates to the mid–late nineteenth century: it has a thick braid around the neck to protect the wearer from attack. Kahu tōī featured goring (inset panels) which ensured a good fit around the shoulders.

The hieke was the largest of the rain capes, reaching from the shoulders to the ankles; it was made using the whatu aho rua technique and was distinguished by the use of double-tag attachments. Te Rangi Hīroa adds that hieke were 'usually dyed black and relief in decoration was obtained by spacing tags of the mountain flax (*Phormium colensoi*) which turn a distinct yellow in colour'.[47] Hieke were used when doing manual labour, and were still being made into the early twentieth century. Recently, weavers such as Te Aue Davis (Ngāti Maniapoto, 1925–2010) have been rejuvenating the art form: in the late 1990s Davis made a hieke (now in Te Papa) from muka, neinei, pīngao, kiekie, bird bone and wood,[48] following directions from a kaumātua at Ōtaua Marae near Kaikohe. Contemporary weavers like Davis today enjoy learning the techniques of earlier artists by examining their cloaks in museum collections: this can give insight into different types of cloaks and techniques, and stimulate innovation and experimentation.

The rāpaki was a knee-length garment worn either around the waist or across the shoulders; sometimes two or three were worn at once. It evolved from the pihepihe type of cloak, with its long, curled attachments and full woven base. It was recognisable for its long, dried pōkinikini, a basic kaupapa (the main body of the cloak) and a thick plaited waistband. Sometimes the pōkinikini were dyed at intervals to create patterns and visual interest.

Over the course of the nineteenth century rāpaki ceased being made: as European clothes became popular, traditional textiles were set aside and worn only on ceremonial occasions. A textile in Auckland Museum (21998) shows the transition from rāpaki to piupiu: the kaupapa is reduced to a broad waistband, and the pōkinikini attachments are longer. Over the next few decades the waistband becomes even narrower, leading to the emergence of the piupiu – the waist-to-knee garment made of dried harakeke strips that kapa haka performers wear. Even the piupiu has changed over time: it has gradually become longer, to at or above the knee; men's versions are often much shorter, similar in shape to a maro.

The kahu kurī was considered to be the most prestigious form of kākahu. Women would make the closely woven kaupapa, and men, sitting either side of the cloak, would attach strips of dogskin and fur, tails and even ears. This shared cloak-making between males and females is unique in kākahu, although of course there were a few male weavers. Men were involved in stripping and preparing the attachments, and they used a special technique that involved tuitui (stitching) rather than weaving them onto the base. Men used this technique in making tukutuku panels, too: the tukutuku panel base was installed during the building process, and later decorated. For both the kahu kurī and the tukutuku, one man would stand on either side of the cloak or the panel and pass through a needle threaded with fibre back and forth between them, creating the design.

There were ten types of dogskin cloaks, including:[49]

- kahu waero, made with long fur from white kurī: these types of dog were so precious that they often slept on special whāriki to ensure the colour of their coats was not sullied
- māhiti: dog's tails were spaced out across a kaupapa that was sometimes dyed
- puahi: skins from white kurī were cut into strips then attached to the kaupapa
- tōpuni: as for the puahi but made with black dogskins (Best); or with alternating black and white dogskins in vertical stripes (Pendergrast)[50]
- ihopuni/ihupuni: Pendergrast uses this term interchangeably with māhiti to describe a cloak made primarily with white dogskin attachments, with darker dogskin used as a border around three sides
- tāpahu: war cloak made from whole dogskins sewn together.

Kaitaka are distinct for their golden, silky kaupapa, which is offset against a dark tāniko border on three sides. Even within this class of textile there were a number of different styles. On the kaitaka pātea the aho ran vertically, and the weaving started from the upper edge. For the kaitaka paepaeroa style of cloak, the aho were horizontal, with the weaving process beginning on the side edge (rather than along one of the long edges).

One of the most rare and precious of cloaks was the kaitaka huaki, where the weaver created two or even three borders that were layered on top of each other. Of the 352 cloaks held in Te Papa, only four are huaki. One example in the British Museum (Q82 Oc.718) dating from the nineteenth century shows real flare, with thick, dark tāniko borders around all edges, and secondary tāniko borders around three of the edges. In addition, the weaver has later sourced goat hair to add on to the kaupapa, perhaps to mimic dog hair, which may have been a precious resource by this time.[51] Unfortunately, there are no details about the date of acquisition, but it is presumed that the huaki was made in the nineteenth century. As kahu kurī went out of production, so too did the involvement of men (in general) with the making of kākahu, certainly up to the late twentieth century.

George French Angas drew korowai (cloaks ornamented with black hukahuka tassels) a number of times in 1844:[52] this suggests that they were contemporaneous with the kahu kurī. The kahu kurī was often worn over the korowai, which indicates a hierarchy of kākahu at the time, in which the outer cloak was the most prestigious one. Korowai emerged as weavers experimented with different attachments on the kākahu. These typically would include kārure or ngore. Kārure is also the name of a specific type of cloak: pākē kārure were waist garments featuring the rolled cords; there were also kākahu kārure, such as the remarkable red-ochre-coloured cloak in the British Museum (BM Ethno. Q82.Oc.712). This

Top: A remarkable and extremely rare kahu waero which Paul Tapsell suggests was possibly presented to Tupaia, and later acquired by Joseph Banks when the Tahitian died. It features bundles of dog-tail hair and a very wide and dark tāniko border over only one edge. The tāniko itself is distinctive, with unusual designs.
Pitt Rivers Museum, University of Oxford, 1886.21.19

Bottom left: Korowai ngore were popular across the North Island from at least the 1840s, including among Ngāti Tuwharetoa (left) and Waikato-Tainui (middle).
**George French Angas, *Te Heuheu & Hiwikau, Tanpo* [sic].**
***Te Kawaw & his nephew Orakai*. J. W. Giles [lith], 1844/1847**
tinted lithograph, hand-coloured, 360 x 550mm, Alexander Turnbull Library, PUBL-0014-56. From George French Angas, *The New Zealanders Illustrated*, Thomas McLean, London, 1847

Bottom right: **George French Angas, *Te Moanaroa (Stephen).***
***Te Awaitaia (William Naylor), Waingaroa*. W. Hawkins [lith], 1844/1847**
tinted lithograph, hand-coloured, 550 x 360mm, Alexander Turnbull Library, PUBL-0014-05. From George French Angas, *The New Zealanders Illustrated*, Thomas McLean, London, 1847

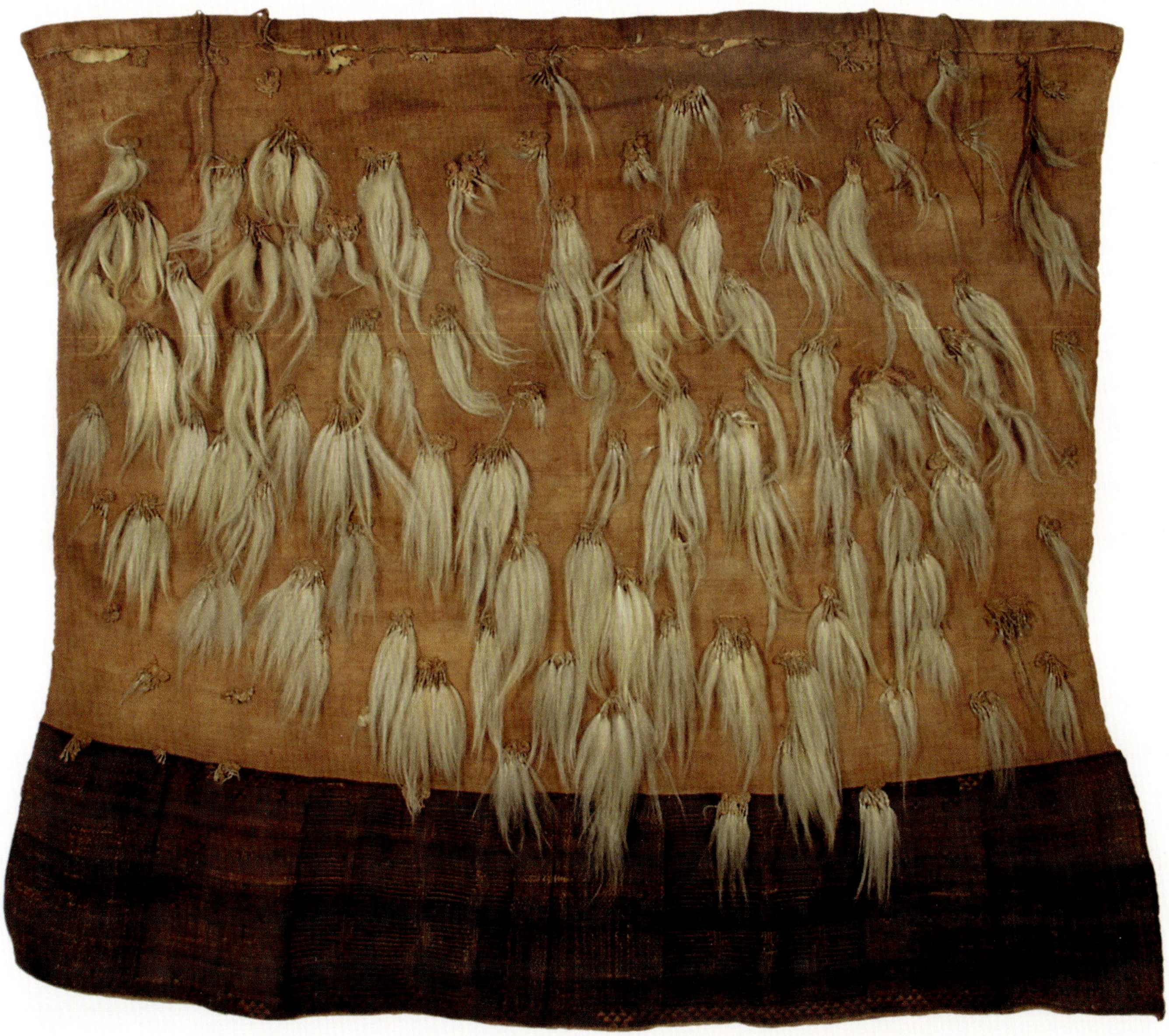

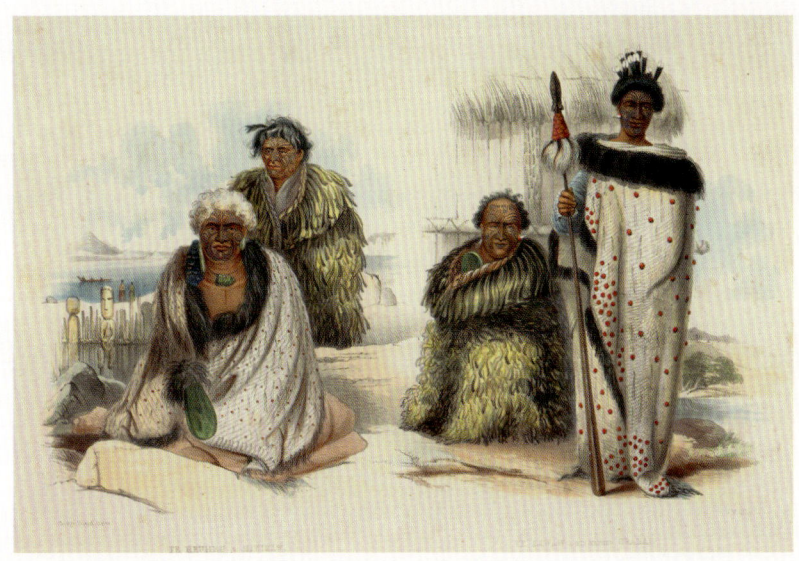
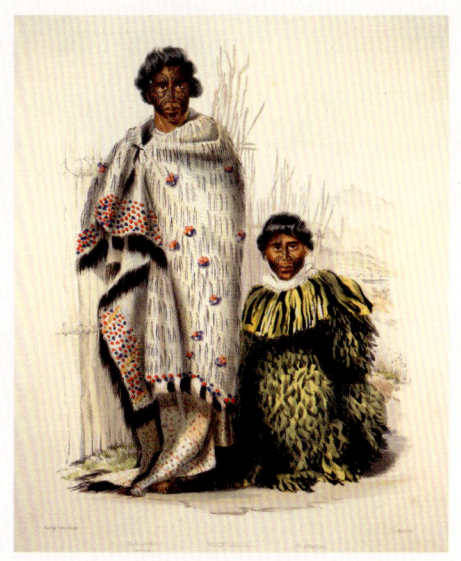

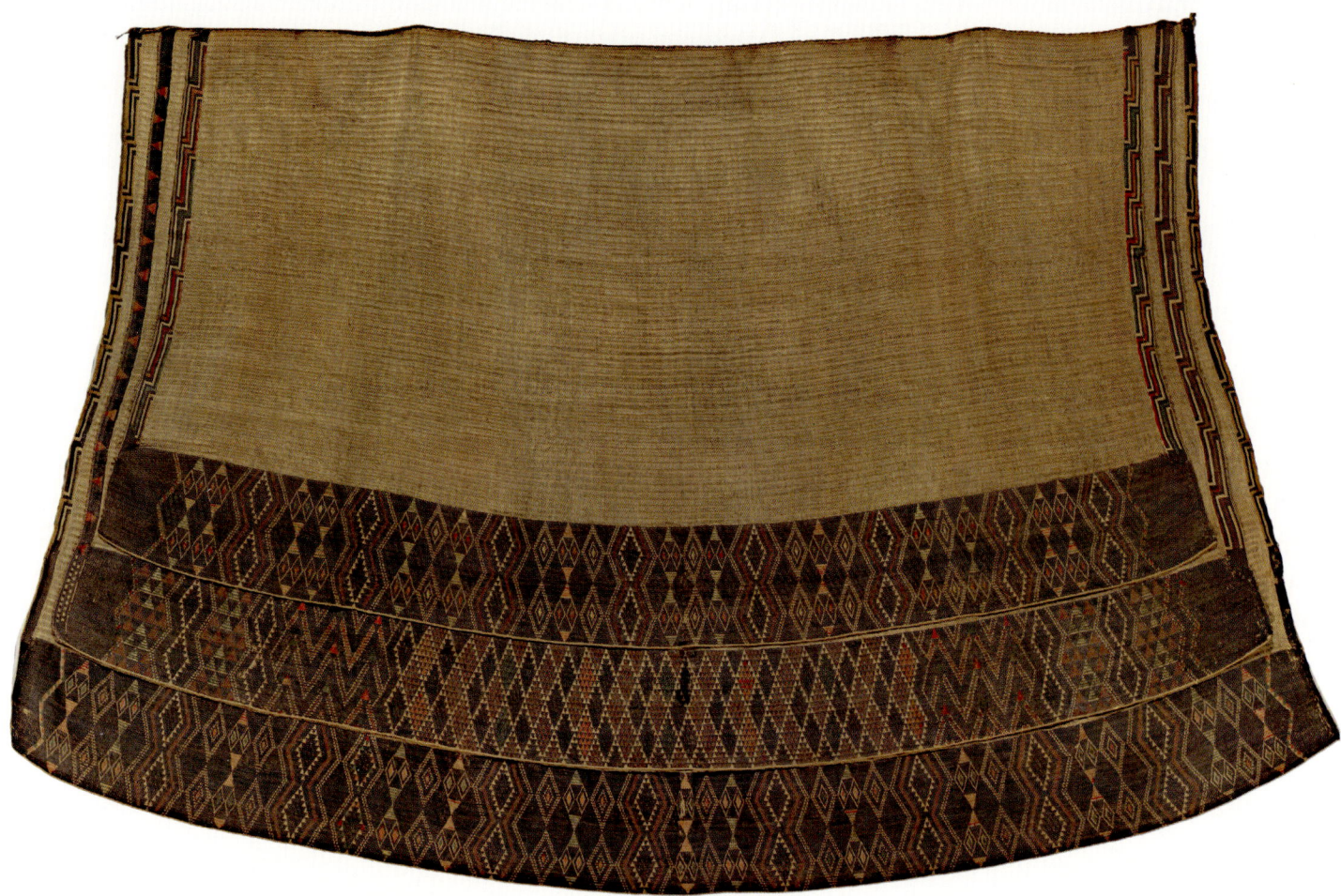

Above: This early nineteenth century kaitaka huaki is particularly unusual, with treble tāniko borders on the lower edge and those on the kauko (sides) featuring a poutama-type pattern which is rarely used.
National Gallery of Australia, 2007.616

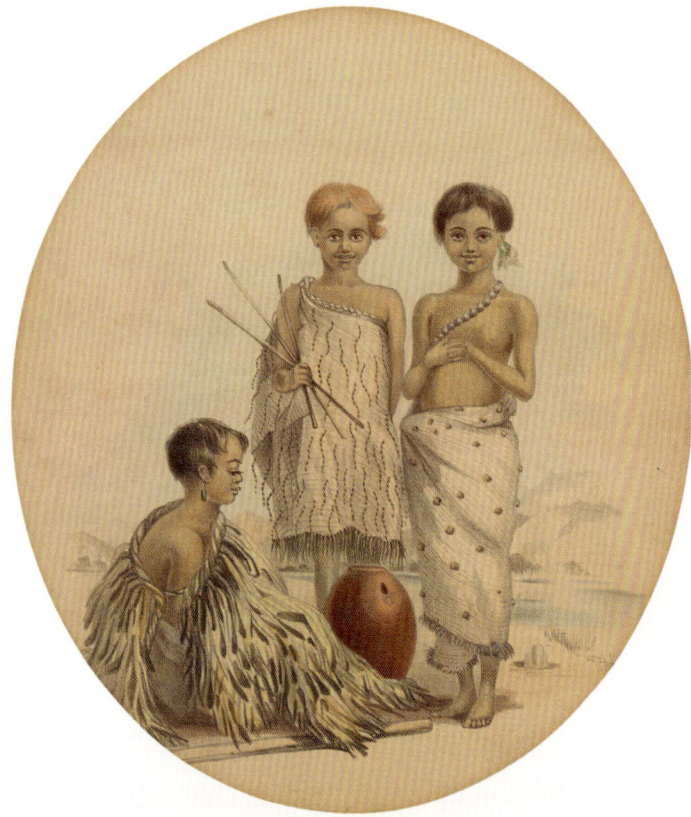

Left: Artist George French Angas described the group pictured here, all of whom were Ngāti Tuwharetoa. The middle boy with light-coloured hair wearing the korowai with its distinctive black hukahuka was one of the sons of the chiefs of Tukanu [Tokaanu], named Tiki 'which means heirloom or treasure'. The boy on the left wearing a raincape was described as 'lame'; he is Papuka, nephew of Te Heuheu, and the girl on the right wearing the korowai ngore is named Tao. Published in Angas's *The New Zealanders Illustrated*, in London in 1847.

**George French Angas, *Children at the boiling springs near Taupo Lake*. Lithograph by Louisa Hawkins, 1847**

lithograph (hand-coloured), 286 x 230mm, Alexander Turnbull Library, A-092-013

large garment has been liberally smeared with kōkōwai which, to this day, still might come off on your fingers, so researchers need to take care. It has since darkened to a deep russet colour, but in its day it must have been a wonderful sight.

Huruhuru have been included as an adornment on kākahu for many centuries. The earliest ancestors from the Pacific brought feather cloaks with them. Hawai'i was settled from a dispersal point in the central Pacific at around the same time as Aotearoa, and it is possible that the importance of using red feathers came with both sets of ancestors across Te Moananui a Kiwa, and was passed down through the generations in similar ways. Stories relate that some early tūpuna were wearing a red headdress when they arrived, which they discarded when they saw the abundance of red-flowering trees lining the shore. As Te Rangi Hīroa recounts:[53]

> Most of the voyagers made their landfall in the Bay of Plenty near Cape Runaway in November or December when the Christmas trees (*pohutukawa*) were in bloom. One of the chiefs, on seeing the scarlet colour of these trees, took off his red feather headdress and hurled it into the sea, saying, 'The chiefly colour of Hawaiki is cast aside for the chiefly red of the new land that welcomes us.'

The earliest known example of a cloak, found draped around a body at a burial site at Lake Hauroko in the South Island, is a kākahu with feathers. The kākahu has been radiocarbon-dated to the seventeenth century, based on kānuka wood also found in the cave.[54] It is made with a very open weave but with no goring or shaping. It is highly unusual, in that the decorations are made from the skins and feathers of kākāpō and kākā, as well as attachments of dogskin and golden, yellow and white dog hair. All of these animals were precious even at this early stage in the settlement of Aotearoa, and to use all of them on a single cloak points to the Hauroko cloak being made for someone of importance.

Kahu huruhuru (feather cloaks) were made from the mid-nineteenth century and were particularly popular with collectors – about one third of Te Papa's cloak collection consists of kahu huruhuru. There was a hierarchy of bird feathers used in cloak-making: at the top was the kākā, whose dark red and light red feathers were highly sought after. Their value was twofold: red was a tapu colour and indicated chieftainship and mana;[55] and the feathers of kākā were highly prized because they were rare. The adornment on kahu kura – a red feather cloak – consisted of the underwing, tail and breast feathers of kākā, woven into a foundation made from muka. These cloaks held an important political role. Weavers Kahutoi Te Kanawa and John Turi-Tiakitai write that kahu kura were 'often referred to as symbols of peace',[56] as in this Waikato-Tainui mōteatea:[57]

> Tākiri mai tea ta i tua, ko tea ata i au e i
> Auē kau au ki te iwi ka ngaro!
> E kore ngaro; he pakū waka nui
> Houhia ki te rongo; horahia ki te kura
>
> Strikes forth the dawn yonder, comes the morn to me
> As I cry in vain for the absent tribes!
> They will not be lost, for the canoe is one of renown.
> End the strife with a peacemaking; spread out the red cloak.

In general, the rarer the bird, the more valuable their feathers. Those of the albino kiwi were especially difficult to acquire and so any cloak made with these was automatically highly prized. Other bird feathers included kākāpō, tūī, kākāriki, weka, pīpīwharauroa (shining cuckoo) and huia. Hokimate Harwood, in her research into 110 pre-1800 cloaks at Te Papa, has identified twenty-seven native bird and eight introduced bird feathers woven into the cloaks:[58] the most popular were brown kiwi (fifty-two), kererū (forty-five), kākā (forty-three) and tūī (thirty-five); the rarest were huia (two), kākāpō (one), ruru (one), kāhu (one) and pīpīwharauroa (one). Diggeress Te Kanawa described how the kahu kiwi were the most valuable cloaks, followed by the kahu kura, and then 'more common were the kāhu weka and kahu kereru'.[59] Huge numbers of birds might be killed for a single cloak: Harwood estimated the number of birds and feathers required to make one kahu huruhuru for Marewaiterangi, the mokopuna (granddaughter) of Tūhoe chief Tūtakangahau: 4800 feathers gathered from six kererū, 5300 feathers from fifty or more tūī, and 2200 feathers from some thirty kākā.[60] These figures seem astounding for a single cloak, and suggest that some trading or storage would have been necessary to gather this number of feathers.

This particular cloak is an important example of the political and social role of kākahu. Marewa died in 1899 at the age of eight or nine from an influenza that swept through Māori communities, decimating many. Her grandfather

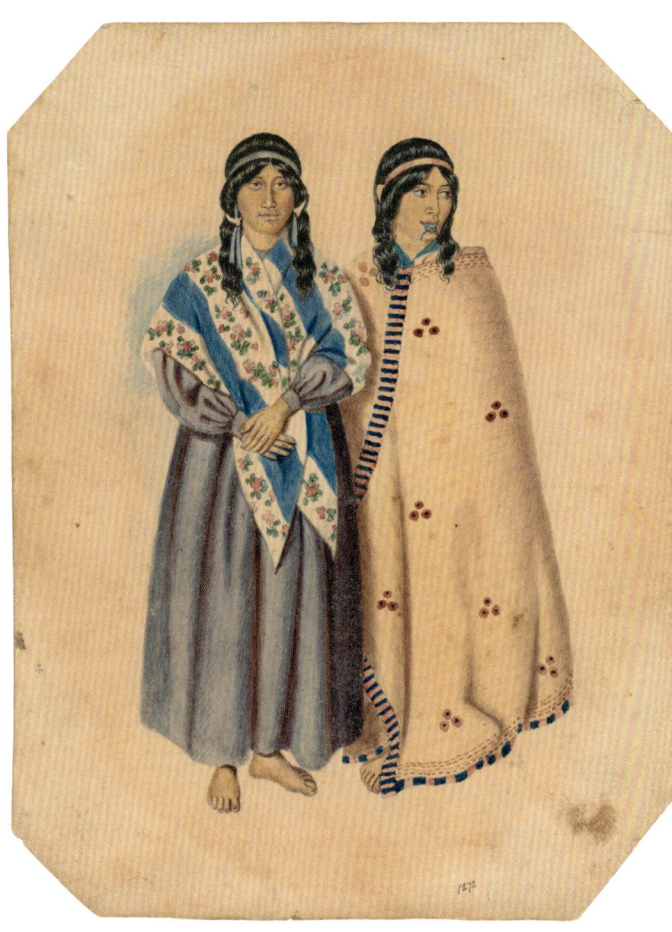

By the time artist Joseph Merrett arrived in New Zealand, many Māori were wearing European clothes all the time, though others would wear them only around mission stations and other Pākehā places, then change into their normal clothes when they got home. Both these girls wear fashionable English hairstyles of the period, with the front of the hair in a middle parting with curls down either side, a headband, and the rest of the hair pulled back into a low bun. Hannah wears a 'mission dress' of presumably coloured calico, with a brightly coloured shawl over the top, while Mary wears a korowai ngore, recognisable with its red-coloured pompoms in groups of three, over her mission dress, which is just visible at the collar.

**Joseph Jenner Merrett, *Hannah and Mary, girls of the Waikato, New Zealand, resident at Mr. Morgan on the Waikato*, c.1840**
pen and wash, 227 x 177mm, National Library of Australia, nla.obj-134588594

Tūtakangahau was a cultural advisor to the ethnographer Elsdon Best; Best was with Marewa when she died, and accompanied her body when she returned home. After the tangi, a tahuaroa ceremony was performed to distribute gifts and, in doing so, cement relationships; as part of this, the cloak was given to Best as a symbol of his friendship with the family. Best later gave the cloak to the Dominion Museum (Te Papa Tongarewa, ME000739).

Harwood has also been examining the ways in which weavers left their signature on a cloak by inserting random feathers, often hidden under others.[61] She has discovered these in at least thirty of the 110 kahu huruhuru. She surmises that these 'were inserted by the maker as an individual mark or memory of an event or person and, in some cases, could indicate the identity of the weaver. They may also provide an indication of the status of the wearer, and the time and environment in which he or she was living.'[62]

### A whakapapa of cloak-making

The four main types of dress cloak – kahu kurī, kaitaka, kahu huruhuru and korowai – were not all made at the same time. When the last kurī died out in the mid-1830s, weavers stopped making whole cloaks with dogskins and fur, and kept their remaining stores of this material for use in tāniko.[63] Kaitaka were similarly set aside in the mid-1850s, probably in response to a change in fashion and a shift to adding attachments such as hukahuka and ngore to the kaupapa, and minimising the wide tāniko borders. By the mid-nineteenth century the korowai and kahu huruhuru took over as the kākahu of choice, though the other forms remained important for ceremonial and political occasions.[64] Changes in textiles over the nineteenth century reflected changes in other art forms, such as carving and architecture. As had happened with the first arrival from the Pacific, artists were rethinking their art forms in response to changes in resources (such as diminishing supplies of aute and dog fur) and a new level of interest in how to visually identify themselves.

Style of dress and how and when certain garments were worn was a visual manifestation of important values in Māori society. Mead identifies two distinct styles of dress.[65] For formal occasions textiles would be chosen for the intricacy and detail of their production, and for particular named cloaks. The wearer might layer their garments to reinforce their social, economic and political status. Preparation took time and energy: according to Mead, men would spend hours putting on their finery to compete with each other; women, too, would take the time to ensure they looked their best, especially for occasions when they needed to wield their own social, economic and political mana. Many of the men were rangatira or ariki – as were women, in some areas. For them, it was a matter of representing their whānau and hapū appropriately. For political events this would have been essential in order to assert the mana of the community; and during tomo and other ceremonies it was crucial to convey a message to others of your personal mana. For informal occasions, on the other hand, people wore everyday working gear such as rain capes or rāpaki.

### Changes in fashion

Styles of dress changed over time. These shifts were often driven by weavers who, through their commissions from rangatira and their individual creativity, would create works that challenged existing ideas. New materials were another impetus for change. Harakeke soon replaced pandanus and aute, but it was never supplanted by European materials that arrived with the first European voyagers. Instead, weavers would embellish existing styles of textiles with wool or silk, to add value (due to the association with Europeans) and aesthetic interest. Weaver Maureen Lander (Te Hikutū, Te Roroa, Ngāpuhi) describes this history: 'Māori weavers had unravelled textiles obtained from the first voyage and reused the yarns in their cloaks by the time the Forsters arrived [in 1772].'[66] Two cloaks in the Pitt Rivers Museum that the Forsters may have collected during Cook's second voyage have small sections made using red wool. Lander identifies different European materials that weavers began using in the eighteenth century, including 'wool, silk, candle-wick, cotton and feathers'.[67] Almost all explorers who visited New Zealand collected cloaks as exemplars of Māori art; there are forty from Cook's voyages alone that are now in English and European collections.[68]

By the 1820s European values of beauty and decorum, promoted in Christian mission stations, began to influence Māori communities living in close proximity; the process was expedited in mission schools, where European gender roles meant that girls were taught domestic skills, especially sewing and mending. Students at the mission schools were expected to dress according to English fashion – the girls in long dresses, and the boys in shirts and breeches. From the 1830s, Christian ideas of propriety were having an influence on personal adornment and, especially, the practice of moko.

Not all communities were the same, however: at one hui at Rangiriri in the Waikato in the 1850s, most of the 2200 attendees were still wearing traditional clothing; this may have been due to the nature of the hui, where wearing finery was an important public statement of a person's allegiance or affiliation. Often communities would retain a garment for hundreds of years, especially if they were living in a place where there was little contact with Europeans and, therefore, little social pressure to conform to European values and dress styles. It is hard to believe that, within 100 years of first contact with Pākehā, most Māori had transitioned to a completely new style of dress.

### Symbolic role of kākahu

Kākahu retained their important symbolic and metaphoric function throughout. As Ngahuia Te Awekotuku writes: 'In Te Ao Māori … korowai are trans-tribal taonga, meaning they often traverse from the tribe of the weaver, to the tribe of the recipients, forging inter-tribal bonds long-lived and remembered; albeit perhaps the taonga are acquired and treated differently from iwi to iwi, throughout the ages.'[69]

Weaver Toi Te Rito Maihi (Ngāti Ipu, Ngāi Te Apata o Ngāti Kahungunu, Ngāti Hao o Tai Tokerau, England, 1937–2022) speaks about the whenu in weaving, which 'is short for whenua', which refers both to 'the whenua, the earth, which sustains us after birth, but whenua is also the placenta that feeds us before birth'. She adds, 'an older name for whenu is Io, the omnipotent one', and when you wear the kākahu it creates 'a connection with all those elements that you live among and … learn from, and you then hand that knowledge on'.[70] Mere Whaanga talks of the *Tākitimu* waka, whose people travelled to Nukutaurua where they decided to settle, and they 'took with them the atua Kahu-kura in the cloak Tawhiri-rangi (a dog-skin cloak belonging to Hau-tu-te-rangi)'.[71]

A cloak would often symbolise a chief's personal mana and tapu.[72] They were and still are used in tangihanga (funerals), when specific cloaks are draped over the coffin to keep the body 'warm'.[73] This is part of the ritual of dressing the body in fine clothes and important adornments. In earlier times, the tūpāpaku (deceased) would be taken to the wāhi tapu and there left to return to the earth; sometimes they were placed in a tree, or in a box on a whatārangi (platform)[74] – these are just some of the more than twenty different burial practices of Māori. Some marae have their own korowai that they place over the tūpāpaku, if the whānau does not have one of their own. It is important that these kākahu are placed appropriately – if they are placed facing as if the person is wearing the cloak they will accompany the body to the urupā (burial site) and be buried with the body – so only some members of the whānau are entrusted with this responsibility.[75] These kākahu are to be used only for this purpose, and cannot be worn by the living[76] (though different iwi have different practices in this respect).[77]

A kaitaka paepaeroa in Te Papa's collection is one example of both spiritual and political roles that a cloak can play. Made in the early nineteenth century by Te Ātiawa, the cloak is distinct for its unusually deep tāniko border. In 1840, it helped save the life of a young immigrant in Wellington called Thomas Wilmor McKenzie. When McKenzie was a boy he explored the interior of a house that was being built for Dr George Evans at Pipitea pā (where Thorndon Quay now stands). Little did he know that the building was still in a state of tapu, as it was unfinished. Te Rira Pōrutu, a chief of Ngāti Hamua and Te Ātiawa, was offended and drew his weapon, the mere pounamu named Horokiwi. However, his daughter-in-law Ruhia Pōrutu rushed over and threw her cloak over the boy, and pleaded for his life. This was a woman's prerogative, and it saved him. McKenzie later became a prominent Wellington citizen and when he died, this cloak was placed over his coffin.[78]

The association of cloaks with specific people added to the mana of both the cloak and the wearer: the cloak literally *was* the person. There are a number of stories like the one above, where this association changes history. Te Rangitopeora of Ngāti Toa was another who claimed a person by throwing her cloak over him. Her lover Te Rātūtonu was sheltering with his Taranaki kin at Tāpuinīkau (near Ōpunake), which was under siege from Te Rangitopeora's brother, Te Rauparaha. She called out to Te Rātūtonu to exit the pā but when he did so, another woman from there, Nekepapa, decided that he should be hers. A race ensued, which ended when Te Rangitopeora threw her dogskin cloak over him, claiming him for herself.[79] Another story comes from the South Island: Pōtahi and his wife Murihaka were looking after the house of Tamaiharanui, a rangatira, and at some point Murihaka decided to try on Tamaiharanui's tōpuni-style dogskin cloak. This was a breach of the owner's tapu, and for this hara (sin) she was killed. This incident led to a series of revenge attacks between Tamaiharanui's people and those of Murihaka, and the feud is now known as Kaihuānga ('eat relations').[80]

## Political value

Kākahu were frequently used in political situations to cement peace, both with other Māori and, later, with Pākehā. In 1822, for example, cloaks played a part in bringing about peace between Ngāpuhi and Ngāi Tūhoe. Ngāpuhi rangatira Pōmare had led two major war parties in 1820 and 1821 along the East Coast; then, in 1822, he sought out Ngāti Awa from the Bay of Plenty south until he arrived in the Ngāi Tūhoe district of Urewera. A delegation of Ngāi Tūhoe met him at Manawaru, where they gifted him with food and three fine cloaks. No fighting ensued, as there had been a symbolic victory.[81] Similarly, Ngāpuhi chief Hongi Hika would sometimes approach an enemy tribe with his taua: he would wave his cloak and show them the toi moko (preserved head) of their relation whom he had captured in battle and killed; if they wept, then war would be averted.[82] Toi moko and other 'gifts' would be exchanged, and the matter settled. Mead also recounts how a cloak would be used to compensate a certain group if they felt that there had been a marriage between two people who were of different social standing – in order to 'restore amicable relations'.[83] Te Ataotū of Ngāi Tahu was captured by Te Rauparaha of Ngāti Toa when his war party attacked Kaiapoi pā, and he and his wife Te Aopaki were taken to Wellington to work for their captor. Later, when they heard that Te Ataotū was going to be sent on to Ngāti Raukawa, the pair decided to escape – but they made it only to Waikanae. There Te Hiko, one of Te Rauparaha's lieutenants, agreed to protect them, having heard of Te Ataotū's warrior skills. However, Te Rauparaha sent Ngāti Raukawa 'some fine cloaks and pounamu'[84] to make amends.

The mere pounamu Horokiwi, which was intended to be used to strike at a Pākehā boy called Thomas McKenzie when he transgressed the tapu of an unfinished wharenui in 1840. However, the strike was deflected when Ruhia Pōrutu threw her paepaeroa, and therefore her mana, over him.
Te Papa Tongarewa Museum of New Zealand, ME015710

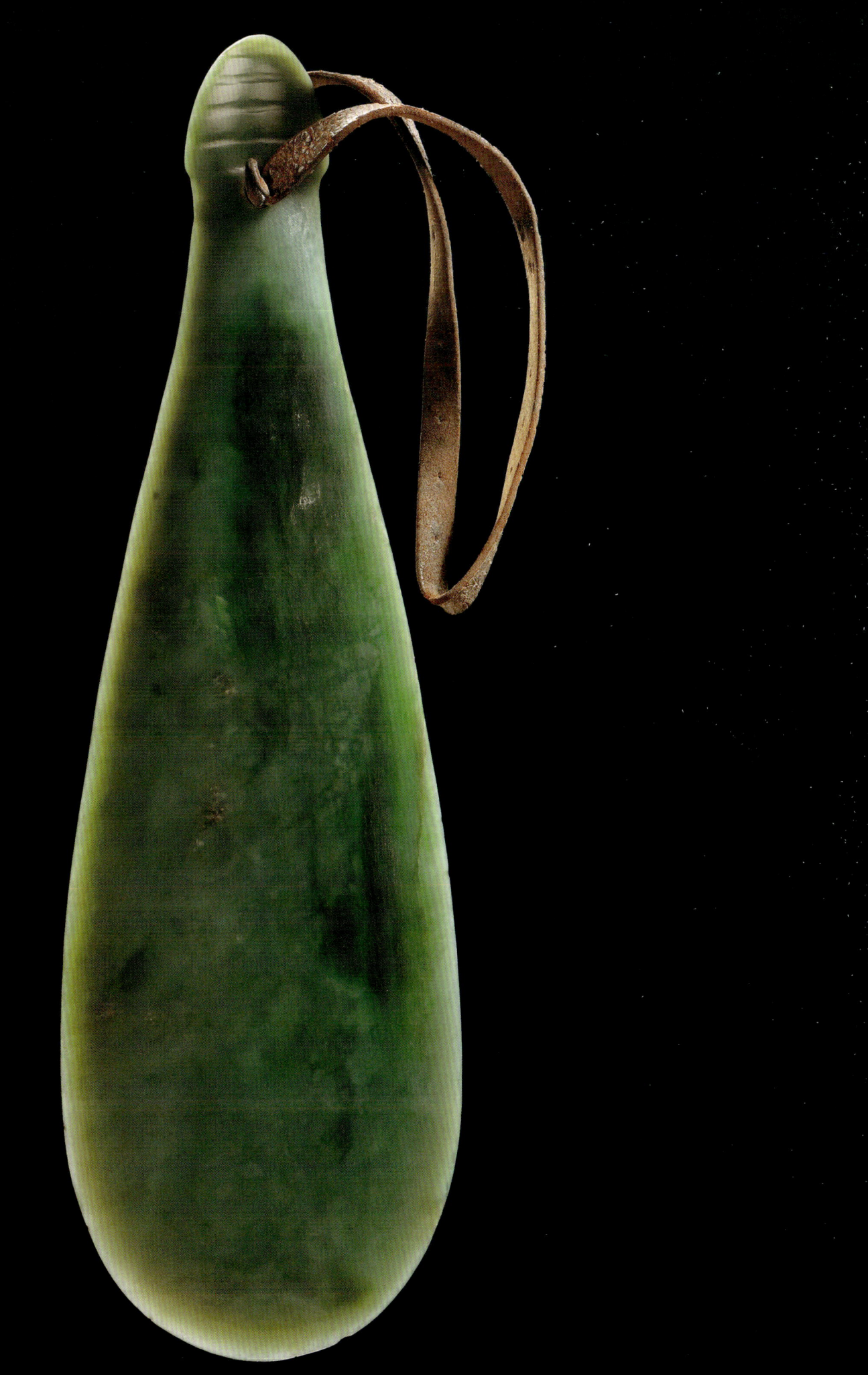

Often kākahu would move back and forth between the donor and a recipient. One example is of three kākahu that Tūhoe gifted to the Crown as part of a larger group of taonga, including two mere pounamu, on 25 September 1870 in order to bind the peace.[85] Just over a hundred years later, in 1988, the Crown was preparing to meet with Tūhoe to address Tūhoe's concerns and, as part of this process, Tūhoe asked for the return of these taonga. Unfortunately, however, they could not be found in collections. This prompted the Crown representative, the retired East Coast MP Duncan MacIntyre, to present his own walking stick (he was seventy-three by this time) to Tūhoe in lieu: in accordance with tikanga, the walking stick was returned to MacIntyre one year later. This to-ing and fro-ing of taonga through the years helped bind together the iwi and the Crown and forge an ongoing relationship.

## Economic value

Rituals of exchange were integral to the balance of mana and tapu in communities across the country. Rangatira maintained this balance with the presentation of gifts, particularly if the items gifted were named taonga and had their own mana. In Hawaiki, the ancestor Turi exchanged a very special named cloak for the *Aotea* waka, which brought his people to Aotearoa, where they settled on the west coast of the North Island. Kaitaka are recorded in oral histories for their symbolic value: Toi Maihi writes of how one kaitaka was exchanged for a single amokura (tail feather of the tawake or red-tailed tropicbird).[86] Cloaks were an appropriate form of recompense for the work of specialists such as moko artists and carvers. At times a cloak might be swapped for a carved taonga seen to be of equal value. While these exchanges might be considered to be part of an economic cycle, they were in fact part of a complicated series of negotiations symbolic of personal and community mana. A well-known example of this is the kaitaka paepaeroa named Karamaene. Ngāti Matawhāiti rangatira Waaka Tarakau presented an uncarved waka, *Te Toki a Tāpiri*, to Te Waaka Perohuka (Rongowhakaata) to acknowledge his support in war,[87] and Perohuka, in return, gave Tarakau the cloak named Karamaene. We know the subsequent history of the waka,[88] but as yet not of the cloak.

In a mōteatea composed for his son Tūterangiwhaitiri, the tohunga Rangiuia mentions a cloak that was whakautu (given in exchange) for knowledge of two carving designs – the taowaru and the manaia:[89]

> Me ko Manutangirua, ko Hingangaroa.
> Ka tu tona whare, Te Rawheoro, e
> Ka tipu te whaihanga, e hika, ki Uawa
> Ka riro te whakautu, te Ngaio-tu-ki-Rarotonga,
> Ka riro te manaia, ka riro te taowaru;
> Ka taka i raro na, i a Apanui e

> Who had Manutangirua, whose son was Hingangaroa
> He it was who established the house, Te Rawheoro,
> And arts and crafts flourished, my son, at Uawa
> There came in payment, Te Ngaio-tu-ki-Rarotonga
>   [the ngaio tree that stood in Rarotonga]
> And there went in exchange the Manaia and Taowaru
>   [motifs used in carving]
> Passing round thence to the north, Te Apanui,
>   [Emerging at Turanga].[90]

The cloak, Te Ngaio tū ki Rarotonga, was described as 'of the finest workmanship, an heirloom which some authorities say came with the migrants from Hawaiki'.[91]

## Rejuvenation of weaving in the twentieth century

Weavers continued to create kākahu for their whānau and communities throughout the difficult period of 1850–1930 when arts such as carving struggled to survive. By the 1950s, however, Māori women were facing new pressures of urbanisation and working outside the home. In some areas, the skills of weaving were not passed on, and lay dormant. While the future of tukutuku was fairly assured – largely because it was taught as an art form at the School of Maori Arts and Crafts – mahi whatu was at risk. The Hetet whānau, based in the central North Island, realised that this was occurring throughout the motu and decided to do something about it. Dame Rangimārie Hetet had learnt the fibre arts from her mother and aunts as a young girl, and passed on her knowledge to her daughter, Diggeress Te Kanawa, who later spoke about what happened:

> Mum and I saw that there were a lot of Maori women who were very good at crafts like crocheting, quilting and knitting. There was nothing they couldn't do. But then when it came to their own craft we realised there wasn't very much known about it.[92]

The Maori Women's Welfare League asked the two women if they would teach weaving to small groups in the King Country. The league was set up in Wellington in 1951 with the aim of preserving Māori culture and enhancing Māori lives through advocacy in relation to housing, health and education (including Māori language).[93] Soon the Hetets began to host hui 'to promote whāriki-making and other weaving traditions'.[94]

Weaving became a way of bringing Māori women together – and Pākehā women who came to learn, too. And as the Hetets taught people from outside their tribal area, the art of weaving became pan-tribal – in the same way as carving had become at the School of Maori Arts and Crafts. Diggeress described how teaching anyone older than yourself or from outside your whānau was restricted, as it was thought that the knowledge of particular designs needed to stay within the confines of specific whānau; however, this needed to change if the art form was going to survive: as Diggeress said, 'there seems to be more demand than ever these days'.[95] Rangimārie and Diggeress carried on weaving and teaching through their whānau venture, Te Ohaki Maori Village and Crafts Centre, which they established at Waitomo in 1982,[96] for ten years. The centre was a place where tourists could 'experience a model Māori village [and] live weaving demonstrations'.[97]

Endeavours such as this were critical to sustaining the different art forms, and they provided a platform for artists to use their skills to earn money for their whānau – a very important aspect of any artistic venture. It also allowed them to work alongside each other and to try out new ideas.

In 1969 Emily Schuster (Tūhourangi, Ngāti Wahiao, Ngāti Hinekura, Tūwharetoa, 1927–1997) became a tutor at Te Rito, the national school of weaving at the New Zealand Maori Arts and Crafts Institute (NZMACI). Schuster was always destined to be an artist: when she was a baby her great-great-uncle, tohunga whakairo Tene Waitere, came to Auckland from Rotorua to ask her parents for the child, and 'after many long hours of discussion' she left Auckland and travelled to Whakarewarewa to be raised there by him.[98] The School of Maori Arts and Crafts had just opened in Rotorua with Waitere as one of the inaugural teachers. Waitere later carved a meeting house for Schuster's birth whānau, which he named Te Aroha o Rongoheikume, after her grandmother. This house is now in Taupō Museum.

Emily's son James Schuster writes about the weaving scene in the 1960s, when Emily was tutoring at Te Rito:

In many areas of Aotearoa, the mātauranga of weaving had been lost when the old weaving experts had passed on without teaching their own whānau or hapū. Mum eventually found that she had to travel away from Rotorua to best share her weaving skills. The courses held in Rotorua had been successful up to a point, but many women [who] were keen to learn could not be away from their big families for more than a week at a time.[99]

With the reinvigoration of the Maori Arts and Crafts Institute, people from around the country could come and study with Schuster and dedicate time to learning the art. Emily's twin daughters Dawn Pahewa and then Edna Pahewa were tumu (head) of Te Rito until 2020. Together with Christina Hurihia Wirihana and John Turi-Tiakitai, Edna worked with Tongan curator and art historian Ane Tonga on the successful exhibition about her mother's work, *Te Ringa Rehe: The Legacy of Emily Schuster* (Rotorua Museum and Art Gallery, 2017).

The practice of weaving kākahu continued to grow well into the twentieth century. In 1983 weavers joined forces with the Maori and South Pacific Arts Council (MASPAC) to establish Aotearoa Moananui a Kiwa Weavers. With changes in funding of the arts, the Māori and Pacific weavers separated, and in 1994 Te Roopu Raranga Whatu o Aotearoa emerged.[100] Te Roopu holds a symposium every two years and, in response to weavers travelling to learn from museum collections overseas, now invites Indigenous weavers internationally to attend.[101] Their focus is on education and professional development and, most importantly, whakawhanaungatanga (establishing relationships) and manaakitanga (hospitality).

There have been other weaving schemes around the country, including one in the 1980s run by the Labour Department through its Project Employment Programme (PEP). Under this scheme, weavers – many of them beginners – made forty-two whāriki at Waiwhetū and Wainuiomata marae,[102] and the tukutuku for Tāne-nui-ā-rangi at the University of Auckland. The PEP scheme also funded local unemployed people to renovate their rural marae.

## Weavers and collections overseas

Many Māori weavers today have travelled overseas to engage with textiles in museum collections to learn different techniques and forms. In 1988, Air New Zealand sponsored Emily Schuster and Diggeress Te Kanawa to spend six weeks with kākahu in museums in England and the United States. Te Kanawa wrote of the experience: 'We saw techniques we hadn't seen before, and we marvelled at the artistry and patience of our ancestors. At times we felt their wairua (spiritual presence) with us, and both felt that one has to look back to look forward.'[103] Her daughter Kahutoi Te Kanawa recalls that Schuster and Diggeress 'were both astonished by the expertise of our past weavers' skills and knowledge. Being of the same work ethic, they would stay up until the early hours of the morning figuring out newly encountered weaving patterns and techniques. They wouldn't give up until they had accomplished the weave or technique.'[104]

Other weavers, such as Maureen Lander, have spent time among overseas collections: this has stimulated their own practice and initiated new works – and, more importantly, built relationships with those museums. As a result, a number of museums have invited Māori weavers to produce art for their collections and to participate in exhibitions. At the Museum of Archaeology and Anthropology in Cambridge, for instance, the exhibition *Pasifika Styles* (2006–2008) included a number of weavers who travelled to work with the Museum's Māori collections and to create works, as well as to run workshops onsite throughout the exhibition.

## Exhibiting kākahu

Exhibitions of Māori textiles became popular from the 1980s. The groundbreaking *Te Maori* exhibition (1984) did not include any kākahu (the curators reasoned that they were too fragile), but in New Zealand, textile historian Mick Pendergrast (1932–2010) curated the small but critical *Feathers and Fibre: A Survey of Traditional and Contemporary Maori Craft* exhibition at Rotorua Museum in 1982. Pendergrast sought to profile the innovation and tradition of woven works, and the exhibition and accompanying catalogue provided a balance to the carved works featured in *Te Maori*. In 1987 Pendergrast curated another exhibition, *Te Aho Tapu*, at Auckland Museum, featuring cloaks held in the museum. Both exhibition catalogues are still an important resource for weavers and kākahu historians today.[105]

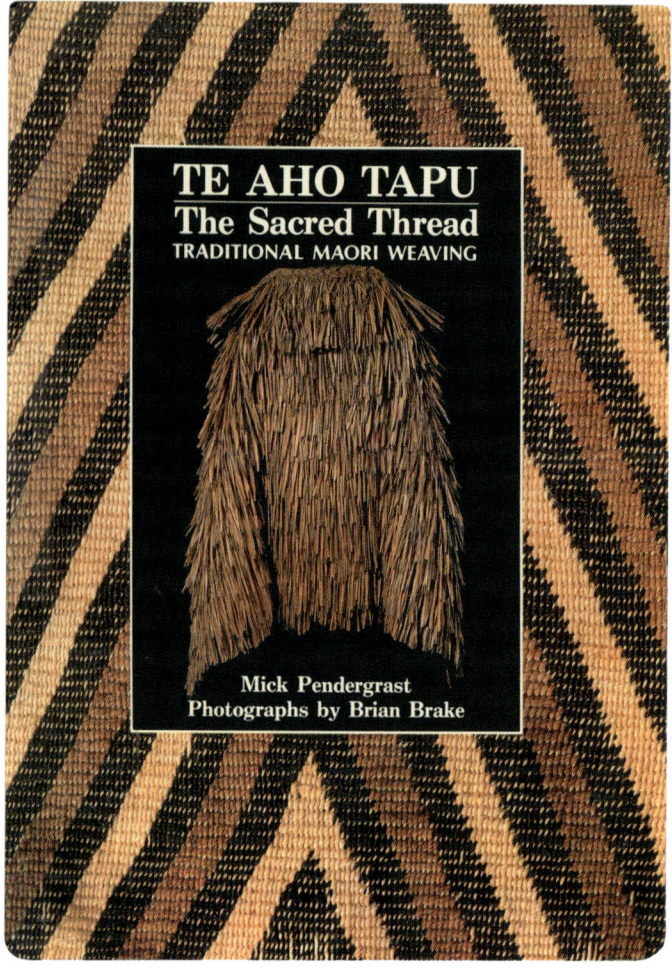

Exhibitions that focus solely on weaving now outnumber those featuring whakairo. They include *Toi Māori: The Eternal Thread – Te Aho Mutunga Kore* (2005), a touring exhibition of the work of forty weavers, curated by Pātaka Art + Museum in conjunction with Toi Māori and Te Roopu Raranga Whatu o Aotearoa; *Kahu Ora – Living Cloaks* (2012) at Te Papa, curated by Awhina Tamarapa, based on the book *Whatu Kākahu: Māori Cloaks* (published in 2011 by Te Papa Press and the National Weavers Collective, and re-released in a second edition in 2019); and *E Ngā Uri Whakatupu Weaving Legacies: Dame Rangimarie Hetet and Diggeress Te Kanawa* (2015) at Waikato Museum. Some dealer galleries feature exhibitions by weavers, such as Te Rongo Kirkwood at Milford Galleries (2015) and Arapeta Ashton at Te Tuhi (2019), and most group exhibitions of Māori art now include weavers as a core group. Each show reinforces the continuum of weaving practice and the status of kākahu as central to Māori art in the twenty-first century.

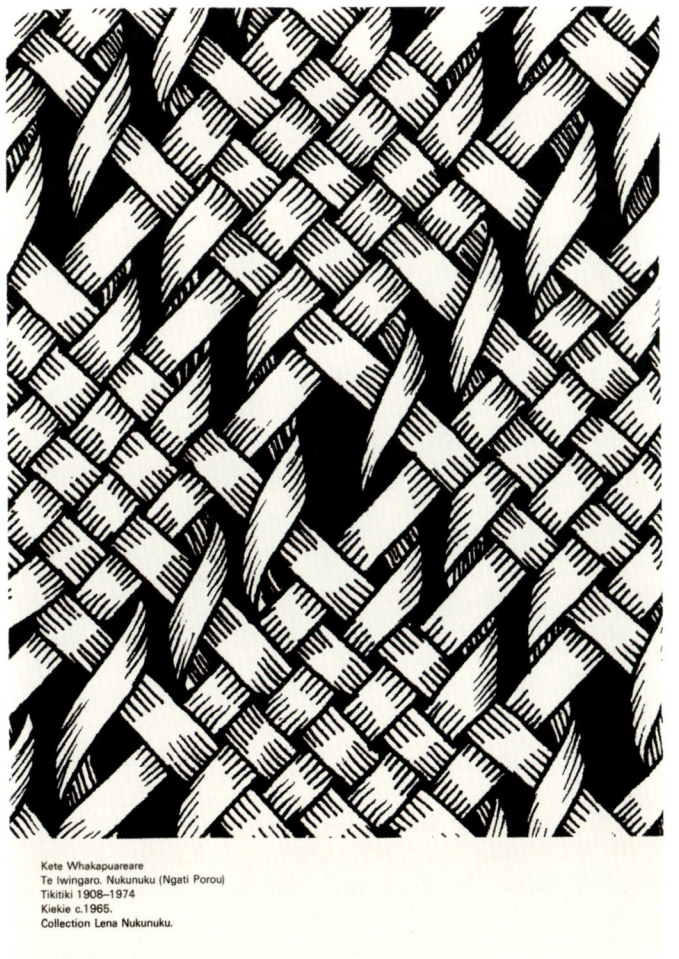

Kete Whakapuareare
Te Iwingaro. Nukunuku (Ngati Porou)
Tikitiki 1908–1974
Kiekie c.1965.
Collection Lena Nukunuku.

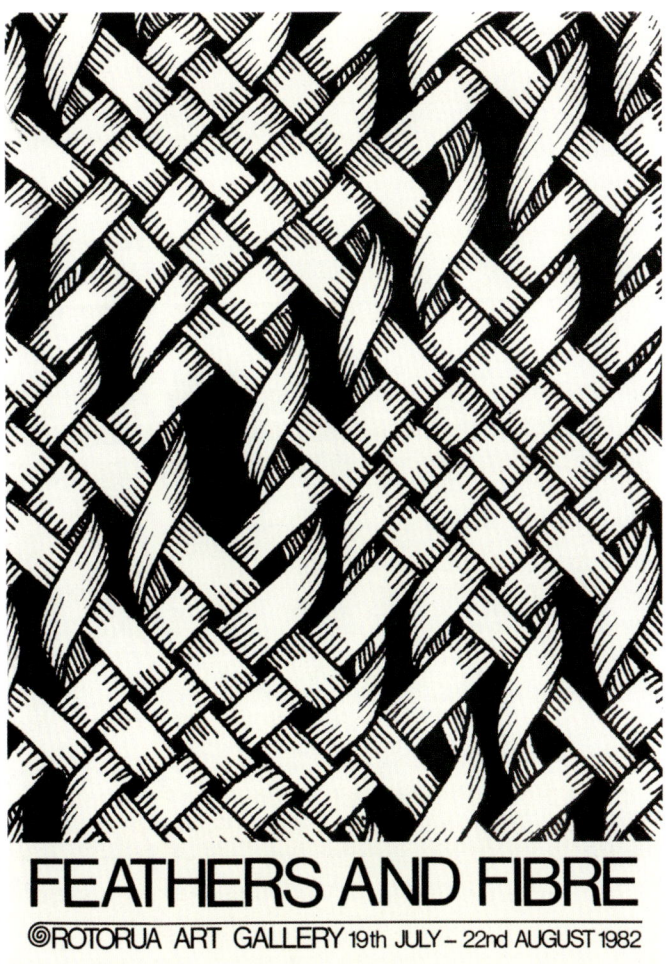

## Textiles in the twenty-first century

Weaving is taught in many different venues and environments today. Some learn the art from others in their whānau in the home or on the marae; others learn through courses at community centres, such as Waitahanui in Taupō, or through tertiary providers such as Te Wānanga o Aotearoa, which offers the year-long Kāwai Raupapa Certificate in Māori and Indigenous Art and a Bachelor of Māori Art (Raranga/Weaving). At Te Rito students study full time for two years. Entrance is highly competitive: students (male and female) must be Māori, and must show some skills in Māori art and design before they are shortlisted. And at the Hetet School of Māori Art students learn online under the guidance of Veranoa Hetet, great-grand-daughter of Rangimārie, and Erenora Puketapu-Hetet, who learnt weaving from Rangimārie. The teachers are renowned weavers in their own right: they often exhibit their own work and are commissioned to create work; Roka Ngarimu-Cameron, for instance, lectures in traditional arts, including weaving,

Full cover of *Feathers and Fibre: A Survey of Traditional and Contemporary Maori Craft* (Rotorua Art Gallery, 1982). The cover features the design 'Kete Whakapuareare' as woven by Te Iwingaro Nukunuku (Ngāti Porou).

Opposite: Cover of *Te Aho Tapu: The Sacred Thread*, by Mick Pendergrast with photographs by Brian Brake (University of Hawai'i Press, 1987).

at the University of Otago. Some weavers explore their practice through academic study: Kahutoi Te Kanawa has a PhD from Waikato University (2022), while Maureen Lander has an Master's in Fine Arts (1993) and was the first Māori woman to gain a Doctorate in Fine Arts at the University of Auckland (2002).

As this book shows, Māori weaving has gone through cycles back and forth across time and space: the need to keep weaving remains.

## TAHUAROA, PĀKŪWHĀ AND HĀKARI: THE DISPLAY AND GIFTING OF TAONGA

NGARINO ELLIS

Cloaks played an important role in display and gifting ceremonies. The tahuaroa ritual sometimes took place after a tangihanga of an important rangatira.[1] Hirini Moko Mead describes the tahuaroa ceremony as 'traditional marriage feast where heaps of food were presented to guests to be consumed on site.'[2] The tahuaroa is similar to the potlatch, a gift-giving ceremony practised by Indigenous peoples on the Pacific Northwest Coast of Canada,[3] where food and goods are distributed by a chief as a sign of their wealth, and also of their generosity and ability to look after their people. Although most examples of tahuaroa witnessed in the nineteenth century involved the presentation of food,[4] at some, cloaks were among the goods to be distributed.

Cloaks played a role in another form of tahuaroa – a blessing ritual for a newborn baby.[5] At this ceremony, a takapau wharenui (great woven mat) would be spread out and two especially fine cloaks placed on top, and after the ritual these would be placed around the father and baby. When they were welcomed back onto the marae, the takapau wharenui would be spread out again, and yet more cloaks placed on top to form the tahuaroa. Mead noted that these ceremonies were no longer followed so strictly, though many whānau have continued with the practice of burying the pito (umbilical cord) and whenua (afterbirth) on their tūrangawaewae.[6]

The pākūwhā was a marriage ceremony carried out when the bride was formally handed over to her husband: it involved a great feast and the presentation of taonga, such as ornaments and cloaks, by the families to the bride and the groom.[7] The quality of the taonga was an important indicator of the value placed by the bride's family on the marriage, and of her personal mana. If the bridal couple were high-born the groom's family might build a whare pākūwhā, a special house for the occasion.[8] Raymond Firth gives a detailed description of a pākūwhā.[9] He stresses the importance of reciprocity during the ceremony, with a great feast expected to follow the speeches, at which large quantities of food that the hosts had stockpiled, sometimes for months, was distributed 'to do honour to their guests'. When the couple's first child was born, it was the turn of the wife's hapū to present food and 'other gifts, fine cloaks, capes, weapons, and ornaments'. In this way, the two hapū would be bound together.

The practice of tahuaroa died out around the end of the nineteenth century as Māori cultural ceremonies were under pressure, and fewer cloaks and ritual foods were being produced. A rare photograph from Whanganui, taken during a tahuaroa ceremony at the tangihanga of rangatira Porokoru Patapu in May 1917, shows a display of at least seventy-five cloaks, mainly korowai and kahu huruhuru. This number is truly remarkable given that kākahu like these were already becoming rare, as weavers did not enjoy much uninterrupted time to make new kākahu because of the war. Such a display of cloaks makes it clear that in this part of Whanganui, large numbers of kākahu were still in private whānau ownership.

Mead describes the hākari taonga as 'a special feast at which taonga were displayed and exchanged'.[10] The taonga were mainly textiles, including cloaks, mats and kete. Guests would present their own taonga to add to those on display by the hosts. The taonga were ritually distributed by calling up different people and formally presenting them with a specific taonga. The missionary William Yate, who was in New Zealand for various periods between 1828 and 1836, described an enormous ritual feast placed in a conical structure around a large tree;[11] and Cuthbert Charles Clarke drew a multi-layered hākari structure that he saw in the Bay of Islands in 1848. While both these hākari featured kai, it is likely that the hosts took the opportunity to also reinforce the relationships of the attendees by the presentation of taonga.

Cloaks and other special treasures often accompanied spiritual ceremonies of birth, death or marriage, as an indicator of the rank of those involved and a signifier of their shifting from one spiritual or political state to another. Many of these cloaks were named, and these associations would enhance the mana of the cloak and, by extension, the wearer. These values continue today: bridal couples will wear cloaks to increase the importance of the occasion, and to bring the lives of those ancestors who are (or were) associated with the cloaks into the ceremony. Cloaks are also still used in tangihanga, where a specific kākahu that is used only for the dead is laid over the coffin – again to enhance the mana of the wearer and to celebrate the person as someone of that marae.

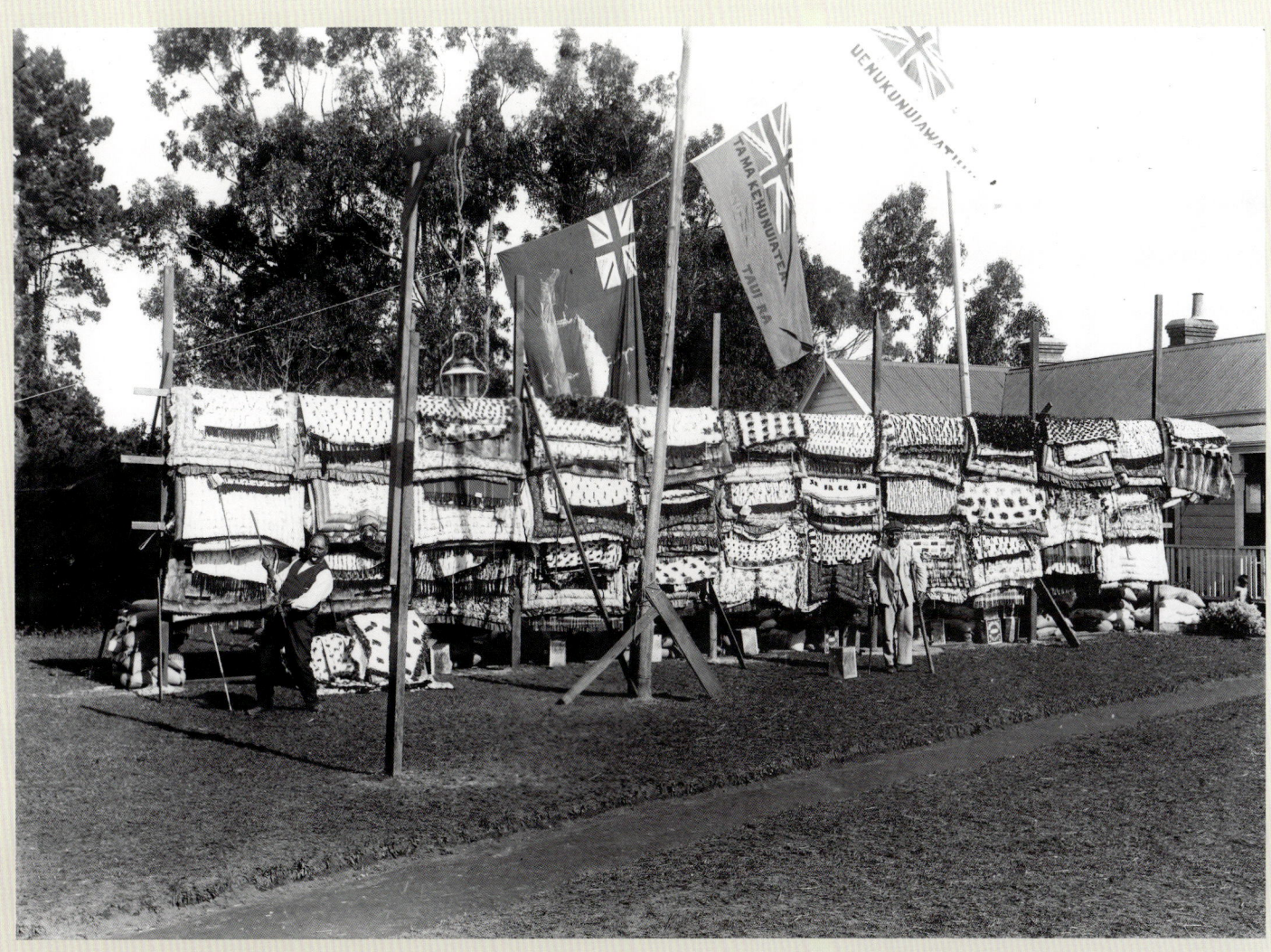

Kākahu and flags are prominently on display in this tahuaroa specially constructed in front of the home of Porokoru Patapu in Putiki Drive, Whanganui, for his tangihanga in 1917. Many of those attending, including the pallbearers, wore kākahu, and the British flag was draped over his body, while a Māori flag was carried in advance of the coffin procession leaving the house.
negatives of Wanganui and district taken by Alfred Martin, Frank Denton and Mark Lampe (Tesla Studios), Alexander Turnbull Library, 1/1-016457-G

# TIHEI MAURI ORA: THE REMAKING OF CLOAKS FROM MUSEUM COLLECTIONS

NGARINO ELLIS

Kākahu in museum collections are made using a wealth of techniques and materials, some of which are now known only because of these collections. While we may be familiar with the four primary types of dress cloaks (korowai, kaitaka, kahu kurī and kahu huruhuru), museum collections reveal a number of techniques and forms that were later set aside in preference to other styles.

The kākahu raranga pūputu is one of these rare kinds of cloak. Examples are scarce in museum collections, and generally date to the late eighteenth and early nineteenth centuries. Kākahu raranga pūputu are, as the name describes, cloaks made using a closely woven raranga technique. The whāriki that form the kaupapa of the cloak are made from a series of pora (panels), joined together to make a single cloak. Textile historian Patricia Te Arapo Wallace, while she was researching the single black-dyed example in Te Papa's collection (ME001685), concluded that these cloaks may be an old, rare, regional style that may have also been known as kōnunu (black flax cape). Another black raranga pūputu in Canterbury Museum is thought to have been made by a Moriori weaver from Rēkohu Chatham Islands.

The kākahu raranga pūputu in the British Museum (Oc1921,1014.18) comprises four woven panels made from undyed and brown harakeke, plaited in a takitahi (one-over, one-under) design, with a fringe attachment along each join. The kākahu came into the museum's collection from the Yorkshire Philosophical Society Museum, which acquired it from a Mr White, who was given the cloak by J. Everett. The British Museum records suggest that White may have been Francis White, who lived in New Zealand from 1835 until 1877. This places the cloak as having been made before 1850. This would align with the dates from the kākahu in Te Papa, which came into the collection in 1914 courtesy of Augustus Hamilton.

Weavers today seek out kākahu in museum collections in order to reconnect with these taonga and the weavers who created them. In February 2018 Māngungu hapū gifted a contemporary kākahu raranga pūputu based on the British Museum model to their kaumātua Whitianga Bedggood on the anniversary of the signing of Te Tiriti o Waitangi. The weaver, Margaret Jackson of Kāpiti, says she was inspired by the British Museum example: 'My cloak, like the original cloak, was woven from harakeke and recreates the distinctive "mūmū" [checkerboard] pattern. It also incorporates some traditional Māori sewing methods that were used on the original garment, reflecting the fact that Maori had developed sewing techniques long before the arrival of European explorers.'[1]

Hamuera Robb (Ngāti Kuia, Ngāti Koata, Ngāti Apa) has been researching forgotten woven forms. His grandmother taught him to weave using wools and cottons, and then his Christchurch whanaunga (relations) gave him further instruction using muka. He went on to study for a Master's in Indigenous knowledge at Te Wānanga o Aotearoa. After discussions with his cousin, historian Peter Meihana, he became interested in rediscovering the textile history of his people, who were based in the Nelson/Marlborough Sounds area.[2] One important group of taonga from this region were collected from Queen Charlotte Sound in 1820 by Fabian Gottlieb von Bellingshausen: the collection, which is now in the Russian Museum of Ethnography in St Petersburg, includes at least forty-two taonga,[3] many of them textiles. Robb was especially interested in a kaitaka huaki, a rare double tāniko-bordered cloak, of which there are few other examples (one is in Te Papa). He considers the kaitaka huaki to be his kaitiaki (guardian), and it has inspired his practice as a weaver to learn more about older techniques.[4]

At present Robb is working on a kaitaka huaki paepaeroa (cloak with double tāniko borders) named Whiria Te Muka Tangata, Whiria Te Muka Whenua. The tāniko on this huaki will be drawn from designs 'transcribed' by an aunty from those seen on the cloaks in the Russian collection and in Te Papa. His materials – muka, paru, tānekaha – come from local sites, and he is liaising with Te Papa conservator Rangi Te Kanawa on this aspect. As Robb describes it: 'What this kakahu represents is a cultural revitalisation of a practice that is somewhat forgotten in some areas and some whānau.'[5] His Kurahaupō people once had an active trade in argillite, and drawings made during visits by Cook (1773, 1774, 1777) and Bellingshausen and Lazarev (1820) in Meretoto Ship Cove depict a settlement whose inhabitants carved waka taua; wore moko,[6] kākahu and adornments made from feathers and human teeth; and had various weapons. Items traded with the Russians in 1820 give an indication of their art practices: mere pounamu, toki, pounamu adornments, waka huia and staffs. Robb is kaitiaki taonga Māori at Nelson Museum, and he regards the process of making the kaitaka as an opportunity for Kurahaupō people to whakawhanaungatanga with their taonga in Russia.

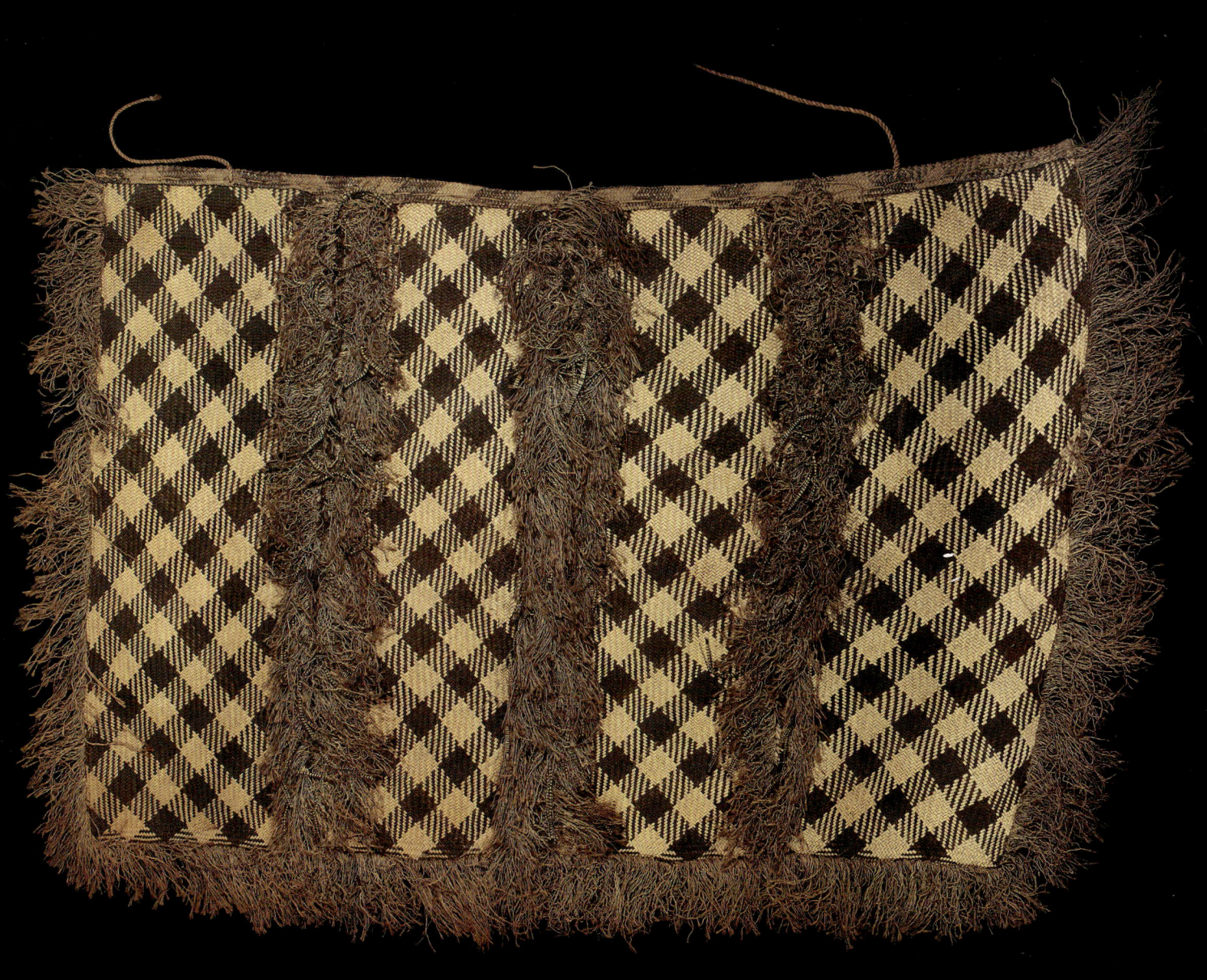

The remaking of styles of kākahu known only from museum collections reflects the ongoing importance of taonga tuku iho for artists today. This example of a kākahu raranga pūputu is made from black and undyed harakeke in four panels, accentuated with a thick fringe along most edges.
British Museum, Oc1921,1014.18, EOC15291 01613468173

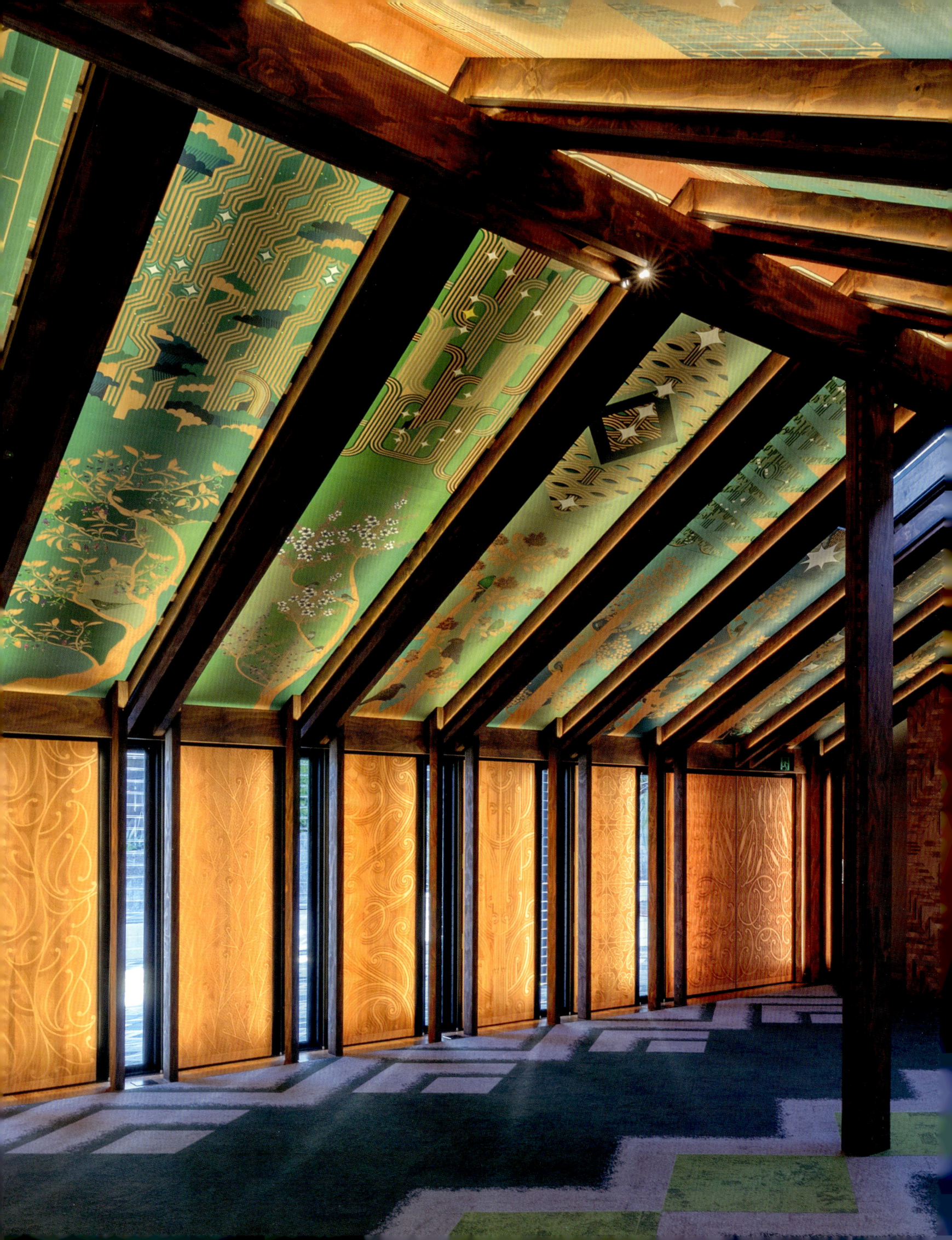

# 4 NGĀ WHARE
## ARCHITECTURE
### DEIDRE BROWN AND NGARINO ELLIS

*He whare maihi tū ki roto ki te pā tūwatawata, he tohu nō te rangatira; whare maihi tū ki te wā ki te paenga, he kai nā te ahi.*

*A carved house standing in a fortified pā is the mark of a well-bred man; a carved house standing in the open, among the cultivations, is food for the fire.*

—Mohi Tūrei, 1913[1]

Whare (buildings), whether on the marae or in the kāinga, represent the whanaungatanga, mauri and rangatiratanga (right to exercise authority, autonomy) of hapū, iwi and, collectively, Māori. Whare design had a strong connection to waka design; this relationship is visible in the corresponding whakairo rākau and kōwhaiwhai of waka and of certain classes of whare, and in waka-rigging technologies that, when transferred to whare, literally pull them together. In this way, the whare can be associated with waterborne migration, exploration and, ultimately, the Polynesian homeland of Hawaiki.

Different types of whare have developed within kāinga according to their function. Among them are: the wharepuni (sleeping house) as a tapu place of sedentary activity and rest; the noa whare kāuta for cooking and informal discussion, which varies widely in construction; the pātaka, a symbol of mana and rangatiratanga through its role as the community storehouse of both noa and tapu resources; and the elaborate whare whakairo form of wharenui, which developed to meet the demands of hapū and iwi

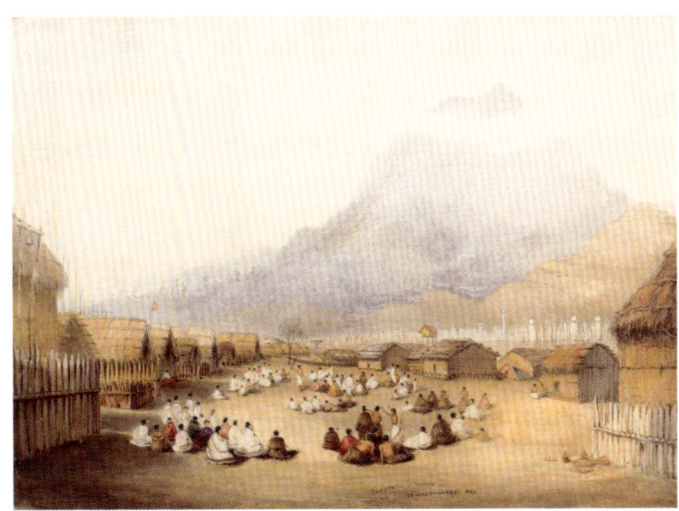

Wharepuni, with long side and front gable entrances, and raised pātaka (centre right), around a marae at Te Wherowhero's village on the Waikato River, with Taupiri mountain in the background.
**George French Angas,** *Tukupoto at Kaitote, Tewherowhero's pah*, **1844**
watercolour and gouache, 232 x 323mm, National Library of Australia, nla.obj-134524320

Opposite: Interior of the wharenui Te Whaioranga o Te Whaiao, Te Rau Karamu Marae, Massey University Pukeahu campus, opened 2021 and designed by Te Kāhui Toi collective and Athfield Architects. The wharenui's design concept is based on the spiritual and natural creation of Te Rākau Tipua (the Cosmic Tree). The integrated concept was created by Te Kāhui Toi, a team of artist-designers, supported by tohunga and tribal leaders, and guided by experts in their specialist knowledge. Artist-designers included Wi Taepa, Saffronn Te Ratana, Ngatai Taepa, Kura Puke, Hemi Macgregor and Stuart Foster. The neighbouring wharekai, Te Whaioranga o te Taiao, features toi whakairo by Israel Tangaroa Birch and Robert Jahnke.
photograph by Russell Kleyn

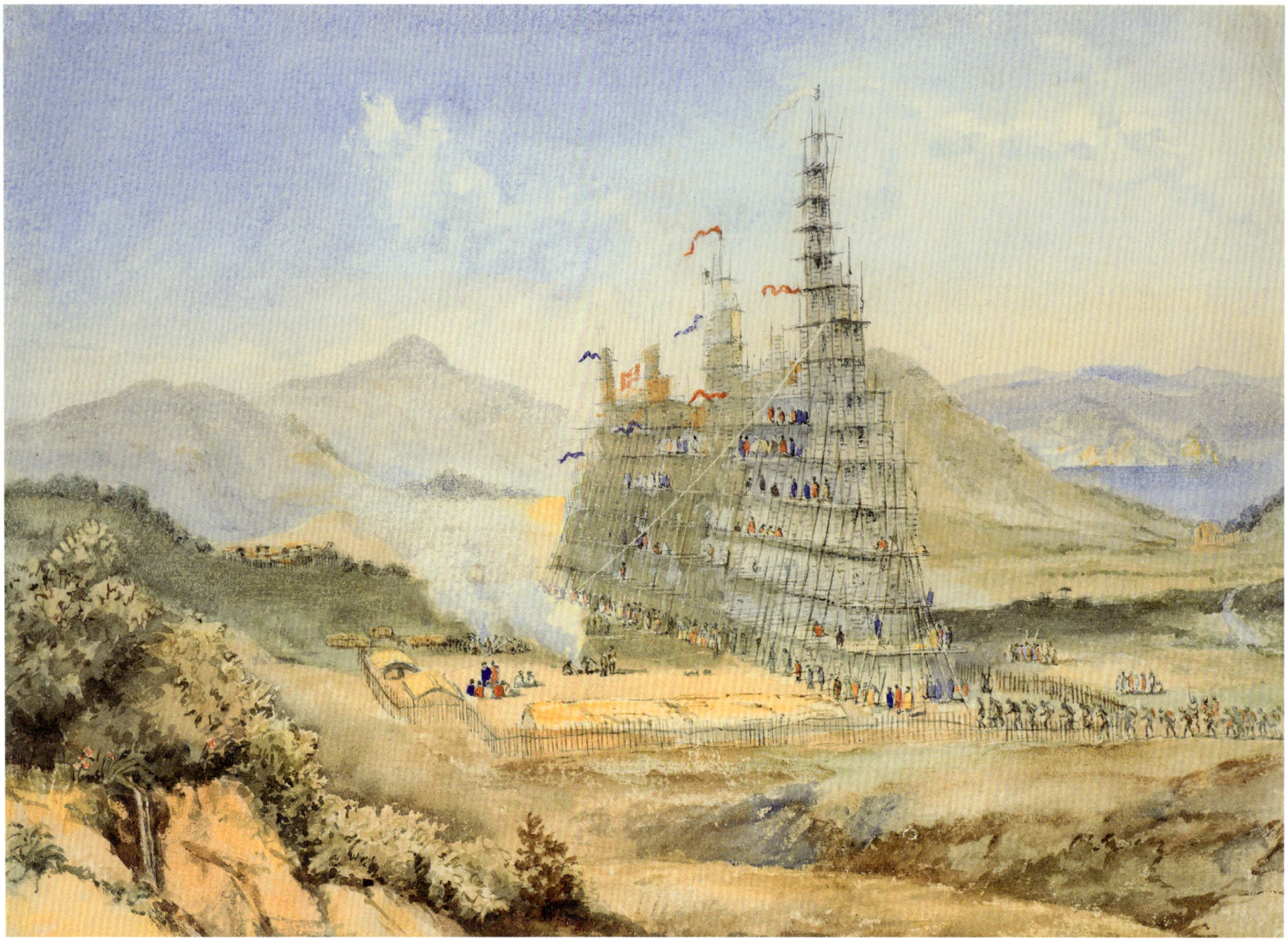

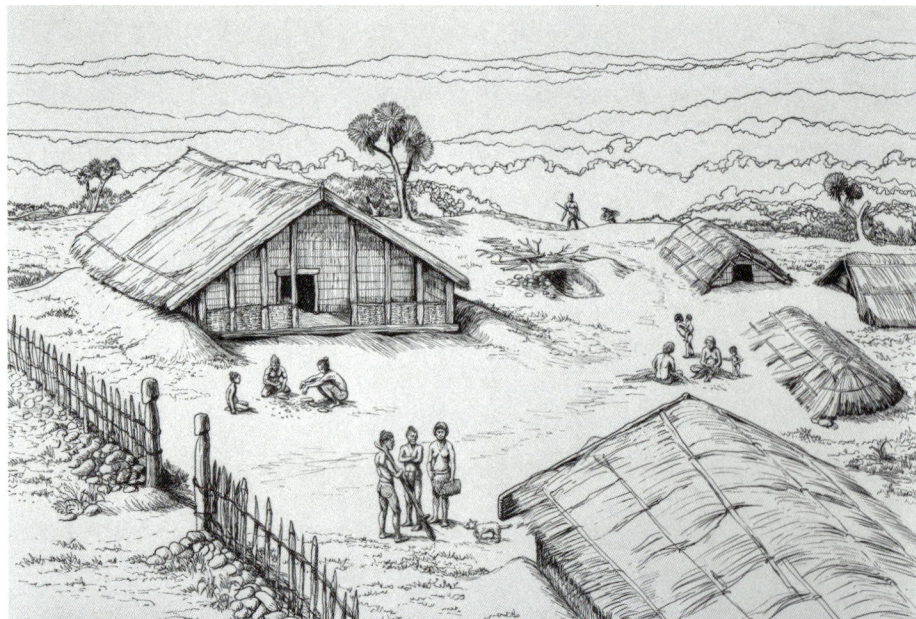

Above: This great stage was built for an 1849 hākari (feast) at Kororāreka (Russell), hosted by Ngāpuhi rangatira Tāmati Wāka Nene, to promote peace between the governor, George Grey, and other Ngāpuhi who had fought against the Crown between 1845 and 1846. Hākari demonstrated manaakitanga (generous hospitality), mana and kaitiakitanga (guardianship) through the stockpiling of food. In nineteenth-century northern New Zealand, hākari food was sometimes displayed to impress on purpose-built structures, such as the one depicted here.

**Captain Richard Oliver, *Feast at the Bay of Islands, September 1849*, c.1849**
watercolour, 375 x 530mm, Te Papa Tongarewa Museum of New Zealand, 1995-0003-1, purchased 1995 with New Zealand Lottery Grants Board funds

Left: Artist's impression of wharepuni with front porches at Moikau, southern Wairarapa.
Te Papa Tongarewa Museum of New Zealand, MA_B.023726, courtesy of Foss Leach

cohesiveness. Linking all of these archetypes together is their relationship within the kāinga, where they surrounded the marae; and outside the kāinga into the wider cultural landscape that provided sustaining resources and the trails, rivers, harbours and seas that led to other kāinga.

Customary whare construction is as much a fibre art as a timber design process. Knowing how to construct a simple whare was an essential skill for most adult male and likely female community members until the mid-nineteenth century. Some practitioners were expert in gathering and processing plant materials, and assembling these elements into an integrated system of load-bearing, weathertight and carefully bundled, stacked and joined architectural elements. For the framing they used the strongest timber to hand relative to the use of the building, from temporary shelters for travelling or hunting and gathering parties, to larger constructions of longevity in kāinga, to the multi-storey hākari stages used for the display of food during massive inter-tribal gatherings, to the larger constructions of longevity in kāinga. The principal external cladding materials, depending on regional availability, were nīkau leaves (*Rhopalostylis sapida*), bundles of raupō (bulrush, *Typha orientalis*), sheets of tōtara bark for roofing and occasionally as cladding, and logs of hardwood and ponga (treefern, *Cyathea dealbata*) embedded in the ground for walls. Knowledge of Polynesian roof thatching most likely informed Māori wall-thatching techniques, although bundling may be a uniquely Māori development.

### Wharepuni

Wharepuni were generally rectangular or circular, gabled buildings that were low to the ground or partially sunken in order to retain the heat from central fires, vented through apertures in the front walls. Some wharepuni raupō from Taranaki were made even more weathertight with mud daub.[2] People had to duck or even crawl to enter the whare, and once inside there was no room to stand up. Photographs from the nineteenth century show that some wharepuni had porches along their long or short front sides, and others did not – this may have been a regional variation. An early wharepuni excavated at Moikau Valley in the southern Wairarapa and dated to 1561CE had a porch.[3] Archaeologists have interpreted different wear patterns on the floor of porches as indications that a wide range of activities probably took place there; they formed an ideal mediating space between smoky, enclosed interiors and an inclement outdoor environment, a perfect solution for a community that may have only recently arrived from the tropics.[4]

Because of the intimate dimensions, the thatched roof of wharepuni was the dominant architectural element: they can be likened to a rain cape suspended on a frame, especially since the techniques used in their construction owed as much to raranga and whatu as to carpentry.[5] The frame was tied together with harakeke or vine lashings; raranga mats were laid over dried grasses as floor covering; thatch bundles were used as insulation in log walls.[6] Interior walls might be lined with whāriki, slim tōtara or rimu battens, or kākaho (stems of toetoe, *Cortaderia* spp.). The nineteenth-century adoption of warmer, layered Victorian-style clothing and woollen blankets as cloaks and bed coverings most likely removed the thermal necessity for sunken dwellings. Māori could now sleep in buildings with larger internal volumes that were also tall enough to stand up in.[7]

With the arrival of European materials, Māori builders began to incorporate joinery such as sash windows and hinged doors, weatherboard cladding, chimneys and iron roofing into their constructions, to the point where traditional wharepuni were being replaced with cottage-style buildings. The rate of change differed depending on the region and the level of contact with Pākehā: as early as the 1840s in the Bay of Islands and as late as the mid-twentieth century in areas distant from Pākehā towns.

The earliest New Zealand governments considered thatched wharepuni a danger and a threat. In 1842 all forms of architecture that used materials such as raupō, nīkau, toetoe, wīwī (native grasses) and kākaho were outlawed within town limits by New Zealand's first building regulation, the Raupo Houses Act 1842, which also imposed a heavy fine on owners of pre-existing thatched or partially thatched whare.[8] The government claimed flammability as the principal concern, but it is likely that the legislation was also an attempt to prevent Māori builders from undercutting the business of Pākehā carpenters in the lucrative settler housing industry, which was rapidly expanding with the influx of British migrants. Wharepuni cost approximately one third of Pākehā light-timber-framed houses to build and were a favoured option for many settlers: they were cost-effective, warm and dry, and were often used as a stop-gap until the inhabitants could afford to build a wooden residence. Thatch was a material closely associated with crofters' housing and tenant farming in Britain – forms of living that settlers had migrated to avoid, and that the British government had actively suppressed through the Highland Clearances.[9]

Te Puea Hērangi made an innovative attempt to sustain raupō architecture in the 1930s but, despite that, the practice all but died out until 2002, when architectural designer Rau Hoskins (Ngāti Hau, Ngāpuhi), artist-designer Carin Wilson (Ngāti Awa, Ngāi Te Rangihouhiri) and a group of Unitec students reclaimed the techniques to build a whare raupō at Whangaruru in Te Tai Tokerau. Four years later, the team built a whare nīkau at Puatahi Marae in the southern Kaipara. 'We had to research the techniques,' Hoskins recalled, 'talk to elders, go into the swamps, experiment with different techniques, improve our approach, and then come up with a finished product that was useful and durable.'[10] The work was challenging and demonstrated the high degree of skills previous generations of builders must have developed in order to construct wharepuni in a matter of days to weeks. More importantly, by walking in the steps of their ancestors, Hoskins, Wilson and their students began to reclaim an ancient knowledge for future generations.

### Whare kāuta

Whare kāuta (known in some areas as whare umu) were buildings used for storage, food preparation and cooking, and were an important space for informal discussion, particularly among women – activities that bind communities and strengthen tikanga.[11] Cooking, as a noa activity, had to be kept separate from sleeping and meeting areas, and this was a distinction that warranted a spatial division of these activities in the kāinga. They ranged in style from open-sided improvised dwellings, to more permanent log-lined structures in kāinga, to large, long buildings built for special events, such as that constructed at Pākirikiri Marae near Tūranga (Gisborne) for the month-long session of the 1894 Kotahitanga Parliament.[12] In an early nineteenth-century account of a whare kāuta near Waikanae, food was suspended from the roof and occupants avoided walking underneath it to avoid violating their personal tapu.[13] Once prepared, food was cooked inside the whare kāuta in a hāngī pit or earth oven. Some kāuta had an ingenious double skin, such as the one at Parihaka, which has an outer wall formed by stacking firewood between ponga logs and a wooden frame; the firewood remained dry under the overhanging thatched eaves until it was required. Government regulations restricting the use of open fires, along with the advent of wharekai, have made these structures an endangered architecture.

### Pātaka

The pātaka was a structure designed to store goods in weatherproof conditions, away from the light. The structure was raised on one or more poles to keep out rodents and rising damp. A clever subfloor construction technique meant the front porch could project out beyond the supporting structure.[14]

A kāinga might have several pātaka, each with a different purpose. Embellished pātaka were carved extensively around the porch and front façade – with kūwaha (doorway/entrance), paepae (porch threshold), maihi (bargeboards), raparapa (end of the maihi) and tekoteko – and contained weapons, fishing equipment, prized garments and other taonga. Their decoration identified their tapu purpose.[15] Pātaka that were unembellished were noa and contained food. Hapū had other names for these structures – in the South Island they were generally called wharepū[16] – and some were given individual names. The whakataukī 'Ko te tohu o te rangatira he pātaka whakairo e tū nā i roto i te pā tūwatawata' (The sign of the chief is a carved pātaka within his fortress) captures the relationship between pātaka and community sustainability, in this case represented by Māori leadership.

Paepae, epa and pare (lintels) from Taranaki pātaka made between 1500 and 1800CE show that a well-developed style had emerged within a few centuries of the first arrivals from the Pacific. This is remarkable, given the unchanging similarity across time in carvings made in the Pacific. It demonstrates a heightened and complex art scene in which carvers were able to innovate on known carving styles and take their whakairo in completely new directions.

The taratara ā Kae surface decoration was a common design on pātaka throughout the country. It represents the story of the ancestor Kae, who stole the sacred whale of Tinirau, named Tutunui, and later killed and ate the whale. When word of this reached Tinirau he sent female assassins to seek out the killer. They arrived in Kae's village

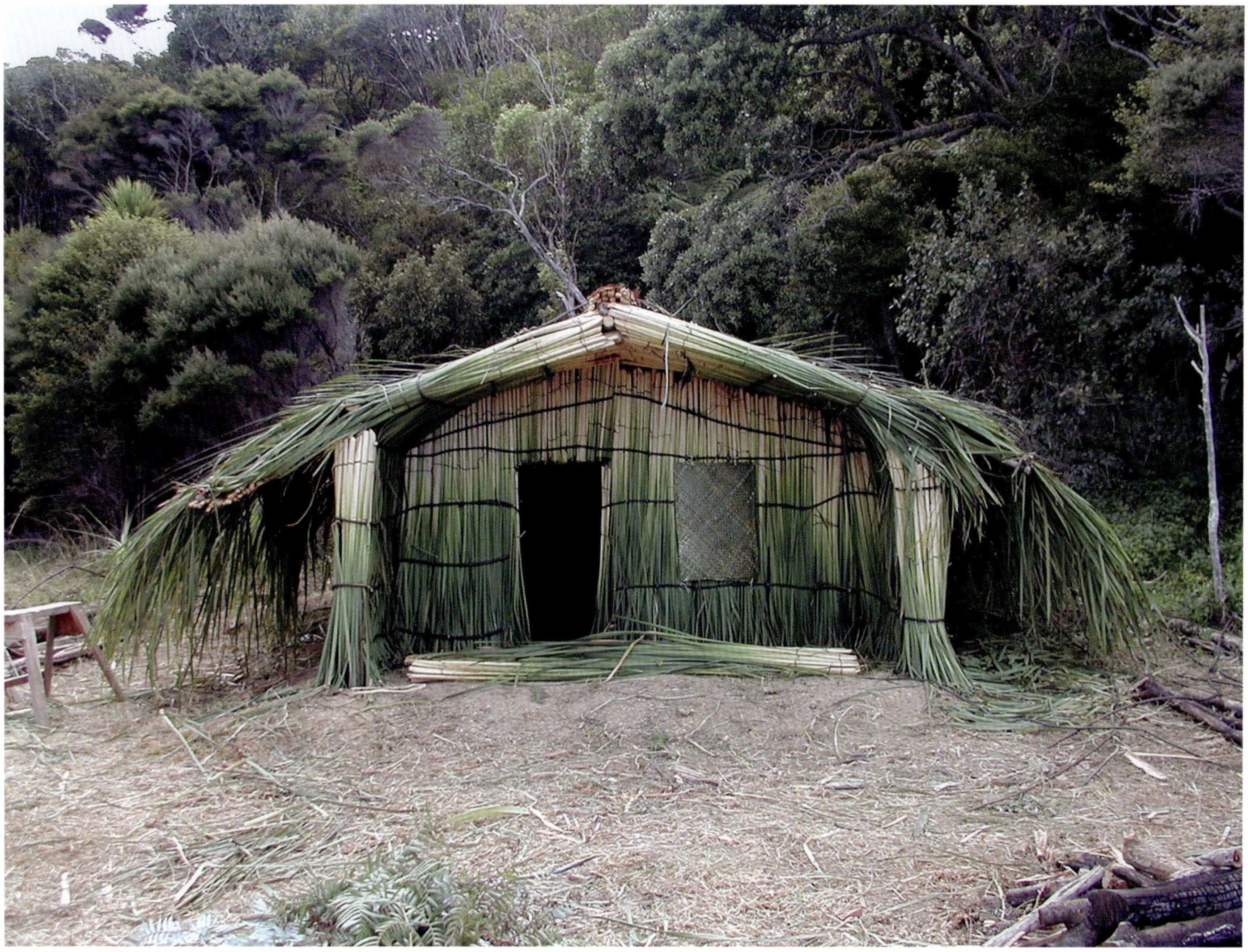

Whare raupō built in 2002 at Te Patunga Bay by Rau Hoskins, Carin Wilson and Unitec students.
photograph by Rau Hoskins

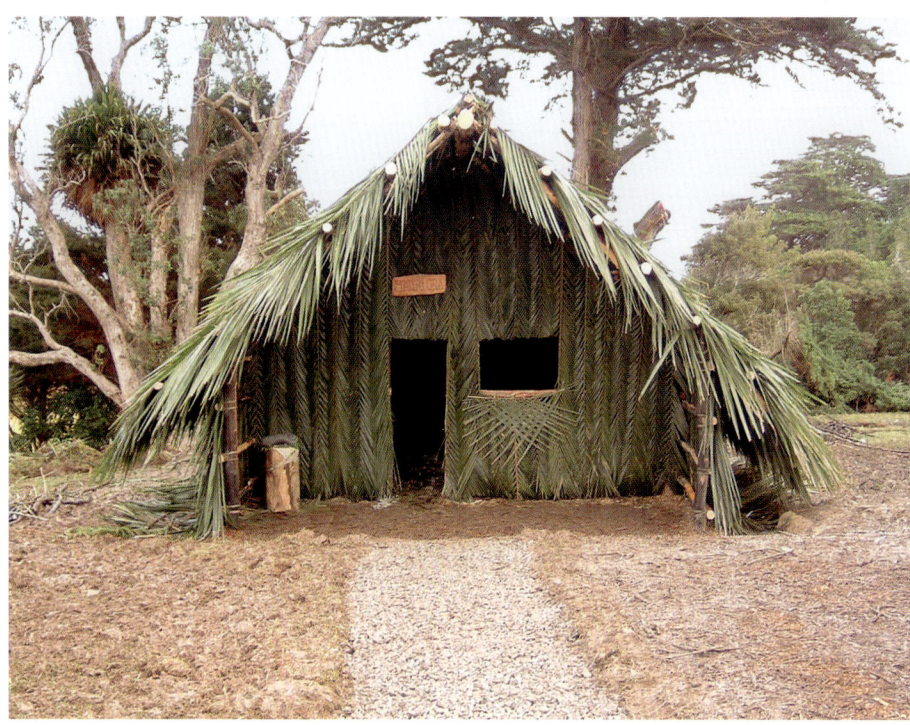

Whare nīkau built in 2006 at Puatahi marae by Rau Hoskins, Carin Wilson and Unitec students.
photograph by Rau Hoskins

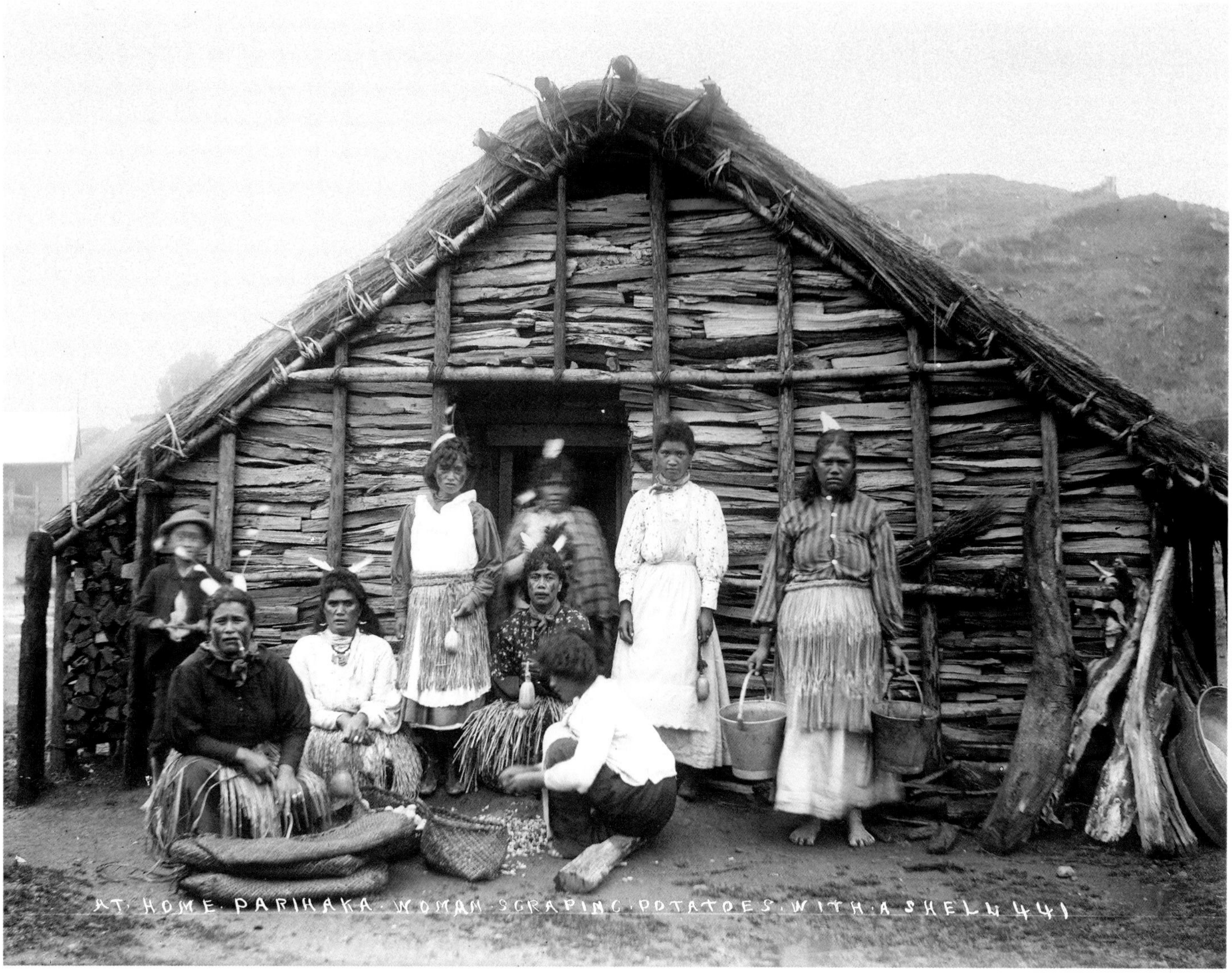

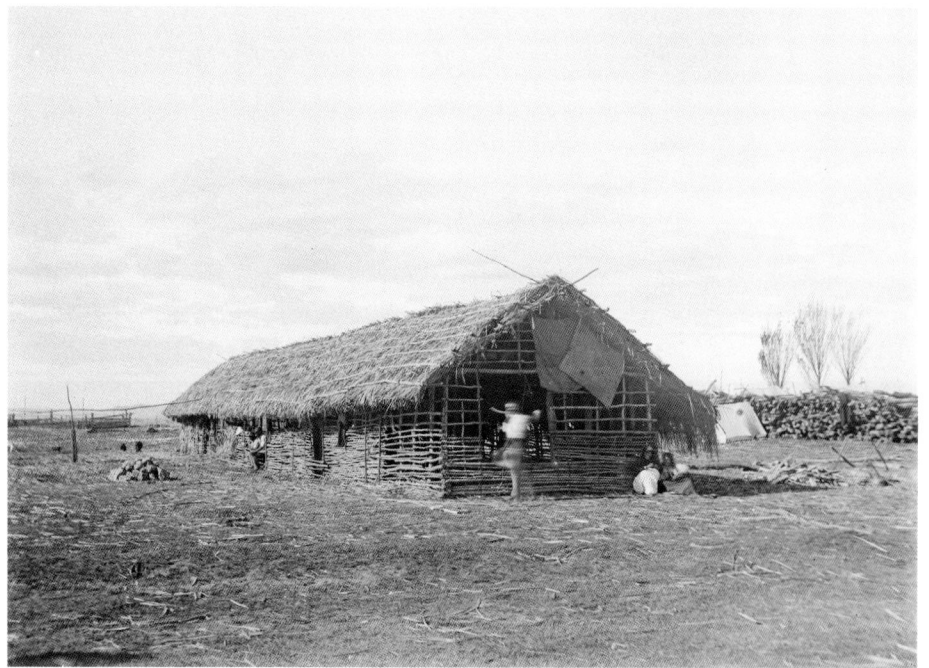

Above: Women gathered outside a kāuta at Parihaka. The firewood for the kāuta is stacked within its walls.
William Andrews Collis, Alexander Turnbull Library, 1/1-012053-G

Left: Kāuta at Pākirikiri pā during the 1894 Kotahitanga Parliament meeting, near Gisborne.
Daneil Manders Beere, Alexander Turnbull Library, 1/4-034258-G

Opposite: Pātaka from Lake Taupō as illustrated by George French Angas in 1844. Angas described them as, top left: a pātaka from Te Pahe on the Waiharikiriki River, used for holding seeds; top right: a pātaka belonging to Tariu at Te Rapa on Lake Taupō; bottom: Te Heuheu's pātaka at Taupō.

**George French Angas, *Whatas, or patukas*. J. W. Giles [lith.], 1847**

tinted lithograph, hand-coloured, 430 x 335mm, Alexander Turnbull Library, PUBL-0014-30, from *The New Zealanders Illustrated*, Thomas McLean, London, 1847

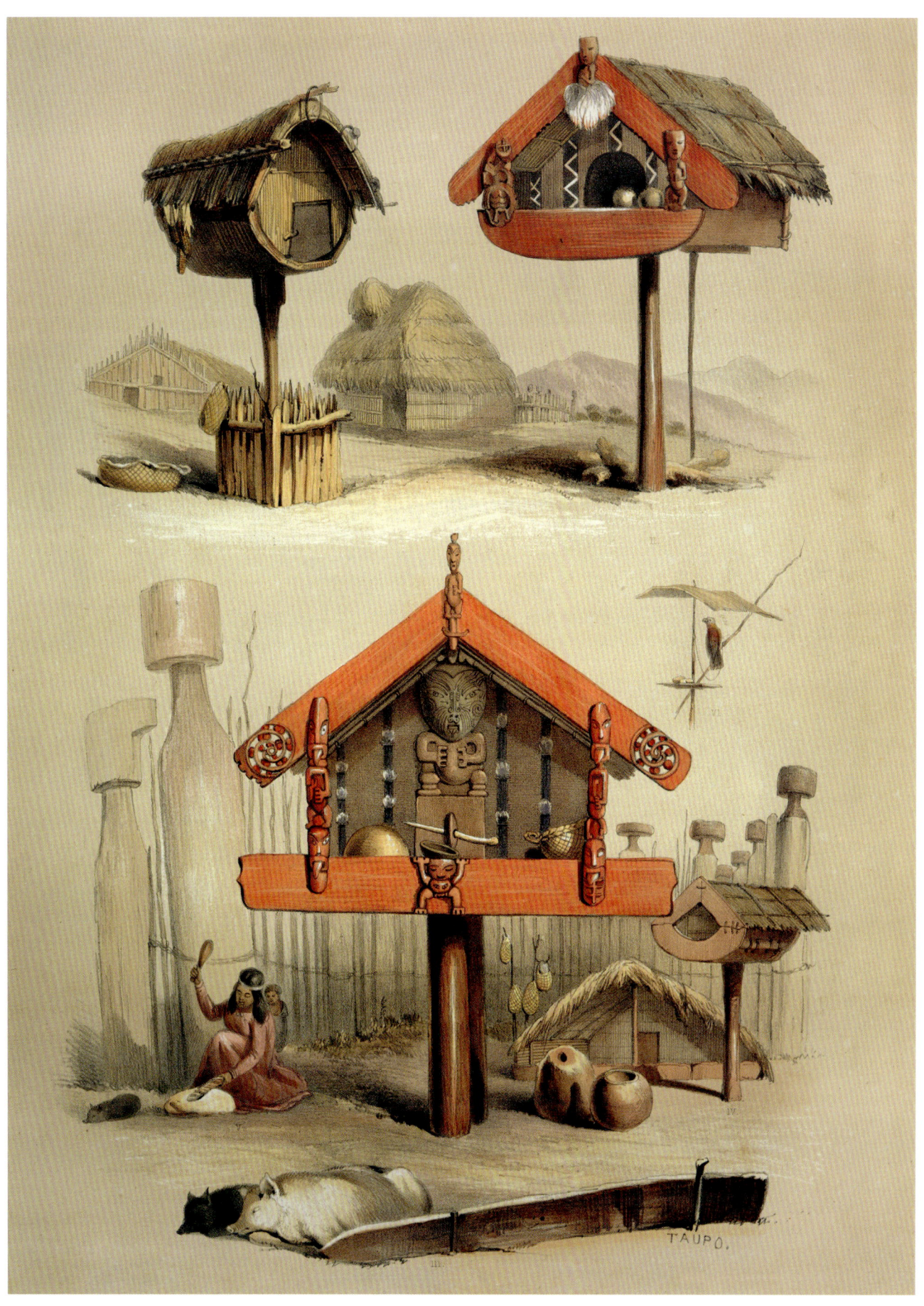

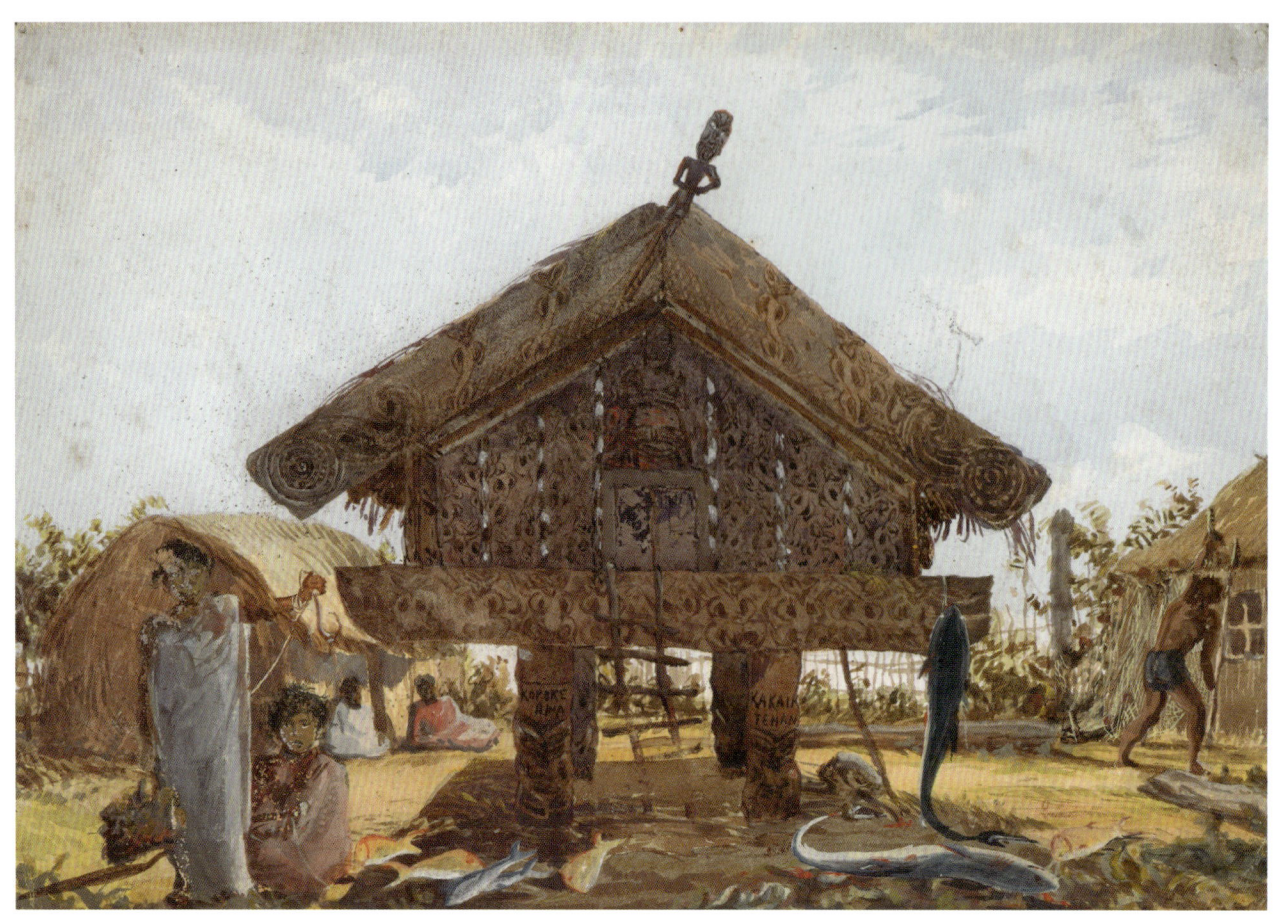
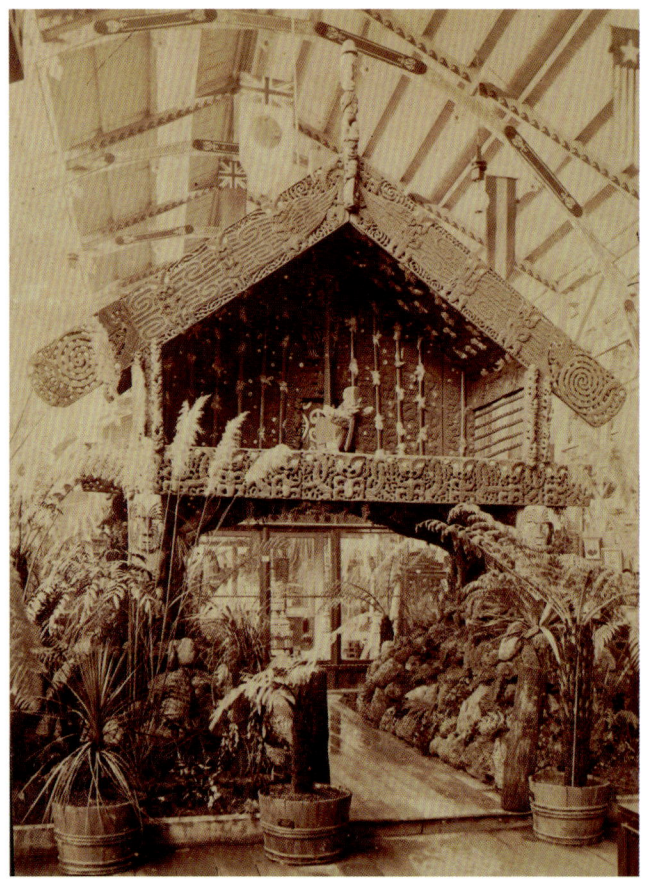
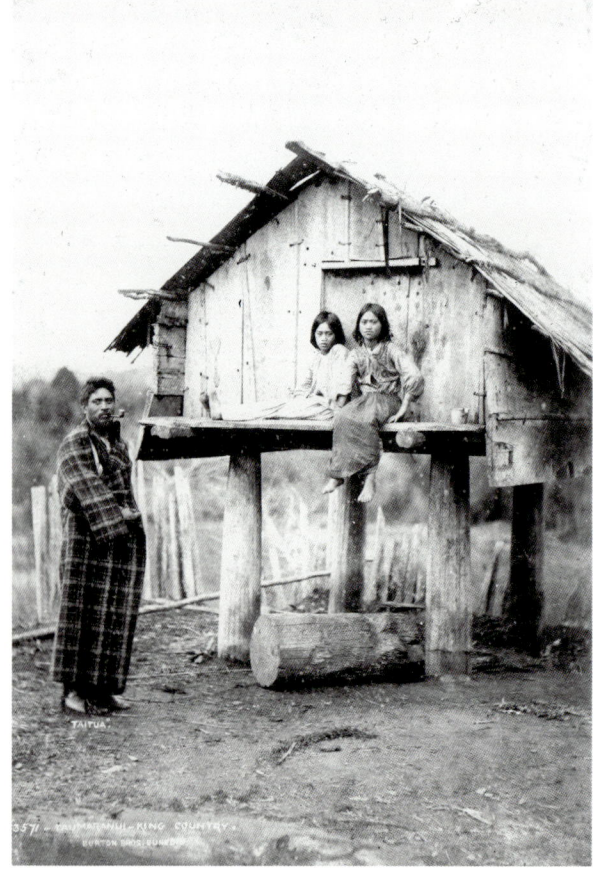

and (according to some versions) proceeded to perform a provocative haka to make Kae laugh, and when he did his crooked (taratara) teeth revealed pieces of whale meat. He was immediately taken back to Tinirau's village, where he was executed.

The taratara ā Kae design is thus an appropriate one on pātaka, which represent values of fertility and abundance. The whale motif is reinforced on the carving of the maihi of the pātaka: often this depicts a whale (shown through a series of spirals) being hauled up the maihi by a series of figures, while at the top of each maihi is another figure, who gathers up the whale with his hands, or in his mouth. A whale in the community meant wealth, not only in terms of the immediate nutritional and material resources – including parāoa (whalebone) for ornaments and weapons – but also for the potential for trading for other goods and services from other communities.

The carver emphasised fertility by depicting a couple entwined on the amo (bargeboard support) or above the doorway. Sexual union was vital for the growth of hapū and iwi, hence its depiction in this prominent position on the most important building in the kāinga. Often these figures represented named ancestors, or the pātaka was named at the time of its formal presentation to the community. On the amo of Te Puawai o Te Arawa (1868–1871, Wero Taroi, Auckland Museum) are couples engaging in sexual union; however, at some point the carving has been censored and the genitals removed.

Uncarved pātaka had a place and purpose in kāinga well into the twentieth century, particularly in areas that were less exposed to Pākehā influence. A survey by Māori built heritage consultant Ambrosia Crum (Ngāpuhi, Ngāti Whātua) identified a strong correlation between pātaka locations and Māori freehold land title, where customary lifeways are maintained.[17] The pātaka that still exist in places along the Whanganui River and within the Tūhoe region owe their survival in part to their remoteness from Pākehā centres, influence and land alienation.

By the 1920s, many Māori communities – and also some Pākehā farmers living in the 'backblocks' – were building forms of pātaka with hybrid construction technologies and materials, including tall doors with fanlights above, fretwork and finials, weatherboard cladding and corrugated-iron roofing.[18] However, the need for pātaka was beginning

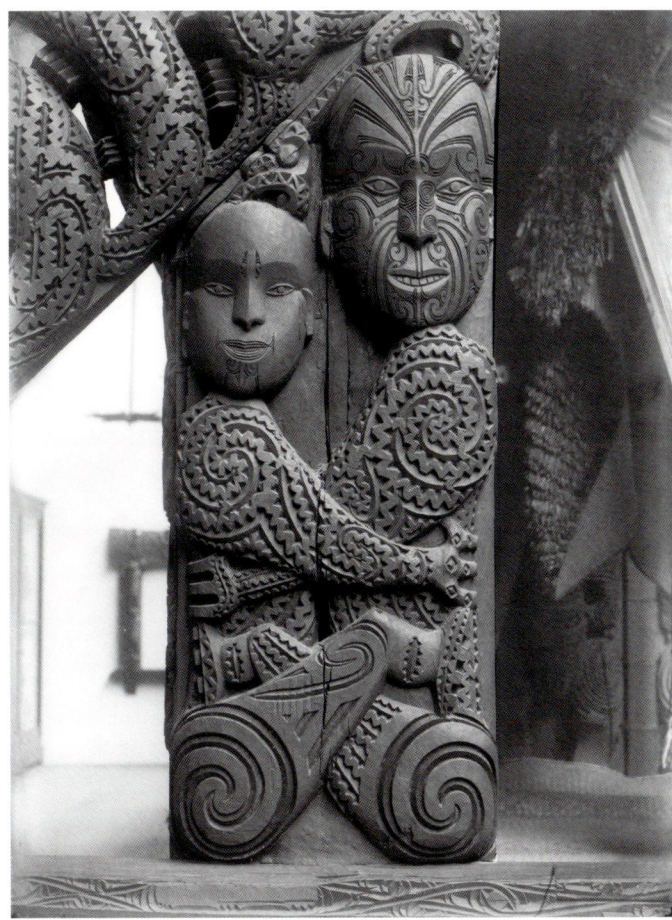

Detail of the left amo from Te Puawai o Te Arawa, opened 1871.
photograph by Josiah Martin, Tāmaki Paenga Hira Auckland War Memorial Museum, PH-1958-1-15415

Opposite: The pātaka drawn by Major General Horatio Robley looks remarkably like Te Tākinga. The photograph at bottom left was taken by John William Lindt in 1888, when Te Tākinga was exhibited at the Melbourne Exhibition. Te Tākinga was carved by Te Hareti Te Whanarere (Ngāti Mākino) c.1850, with metal tools. The carver later gave his pātaka to Te Pokiha Taranui, following a taua due to his indiscretions with Taranui's wife. At some point Te Tākinga was acquired by Gilbert Mair, who sold it to Walter Buller in 1886. Te Tākinga was exhibited in London (1886) and Melbourne (1888), before being given to the Dominion Museum in 1911, following Buller's death in 1906. Some parts of Te Tākinga were re-worked by the Museum's resident carver Thomas Heberley (Te Ātiawa) in the early 1930s.

Opposite top: **Major General Horatio Robley, *Pataka*, 1864**
watercolour, 188 x 278mm, Te Papa Tongarewa Museum of New Zealand, 1992-0035-83

Opposite bottom left: Te Tākinga, photographed by John William Lindt in 1888.
Te Papa Tongarewa Museum of New Zealand, O.022206

Opposite bottom right: Pātaka were still in use as food stores into the 1890s, as seen in this image of Taitua (left) and two young girls at Taumarunui.
Burton Brothers, c.1890, Alexander Turnbull Library, 1/2-091916-F

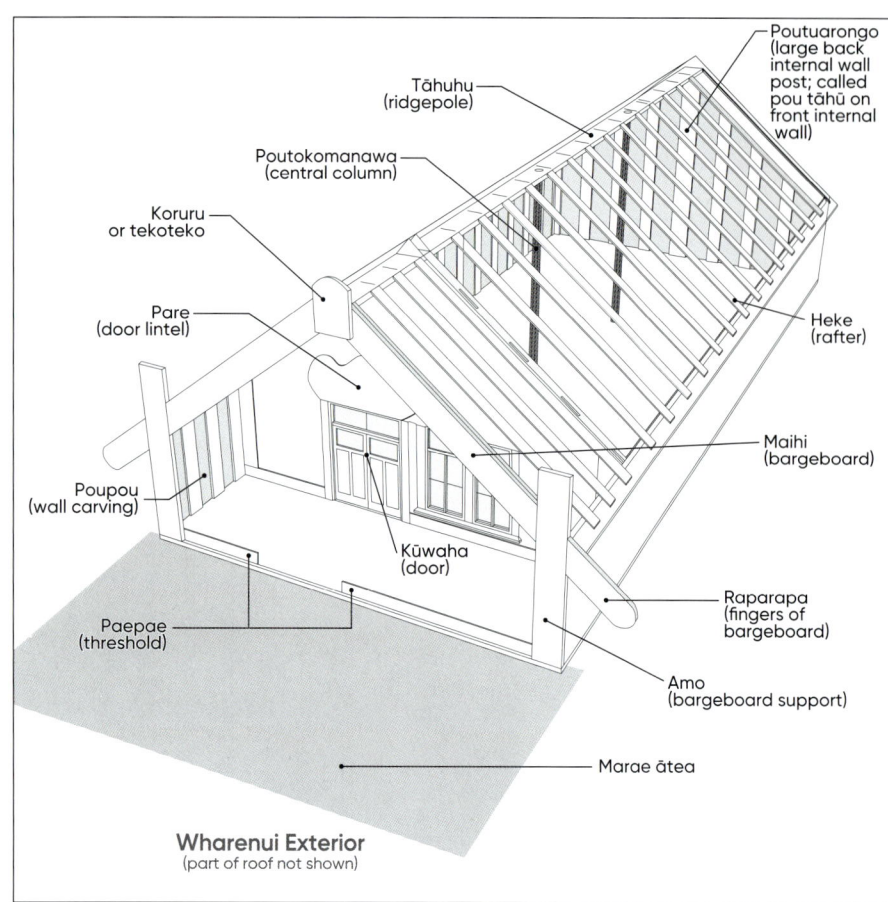

Top: Parts of a wharenui.
diagram by Tim Nolan/Blackant Mapping Solutions

Bottom: Amo carvings from a pātaka in Copenhagen, featuring embracing pairs.
National Museum of Denmark, photograph by Ngarino Ellis

Opposite: Tapeka was a chiefly wharepuni, belonging to Iwikau Te Heuheu, that stood at Waihi near Lake Taupō. The kōkōwai painted on the paepae and maihi was from the nearby geothermal springs at Te Rapa.
**George French Angas, *House of Iwikau, brother of Te Heuheu, and Falls of Ko Waihi at Te Rapa, Taupo Lake*, lithograph by J. W. Giles, 1844**
lithograph in tints, hand-coloured paper, 320 x 233mm, Auckland Art Gallery Toi o Tāmaki, 1987/16/3, purchased with funds from the M. A. Serra Trust, 1987

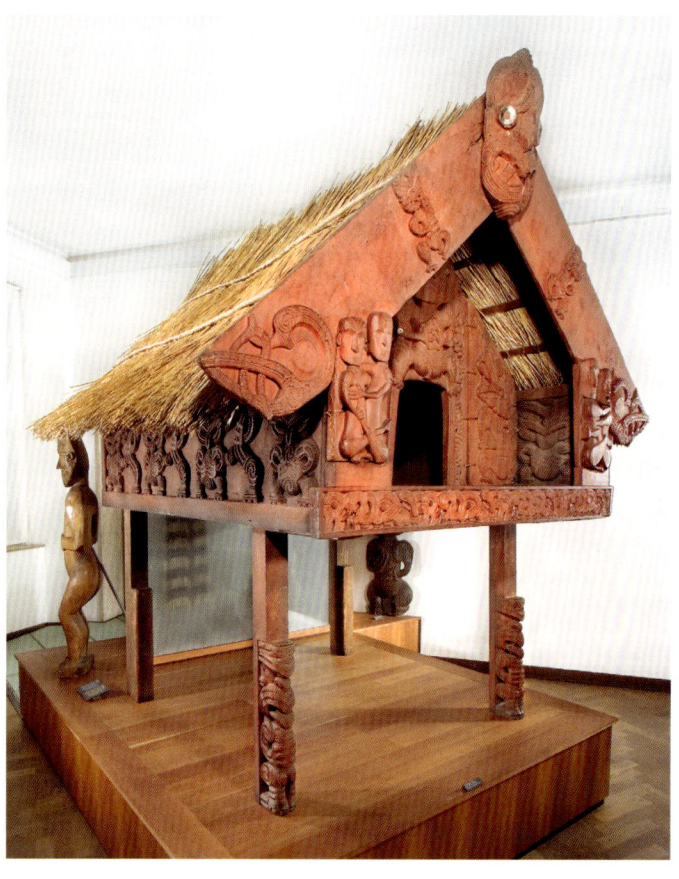

to wane because of a number of factors. Food-gathering expeditions were no longer necessary as the Māori diet gravitated towards flour-based foods such as bread that could be bought from the store or from traders. This change was exacerbated by land loss and reduced landholdings, which made it difficult to maintain traditional ways of food production, hunting and gathering.

Whata, consisting of a pole 6–10m tall holding up a flat floor on which dried foods were stored under coverings, safe from rats, were numerous in South Island kāinga, but by the late nineteenth century were largely gone, and some whānau were on the verge of starvation following land alienation. As Hoani Kahu of Ngāi Tahu noted, 'In former times our whata (storehouses) used to be full of food, but now we do not need storehouses because we have nothing to put in them, through everything being taken by the Europeans.'[19]

By the 1850s, the trade networks that had served to distribute foods and other resources around the country were replaced with routes established to bring foodstuffs and other produce grown in Māori settlements to Pākehā towns. Kitchens became integrated into Māori homes and

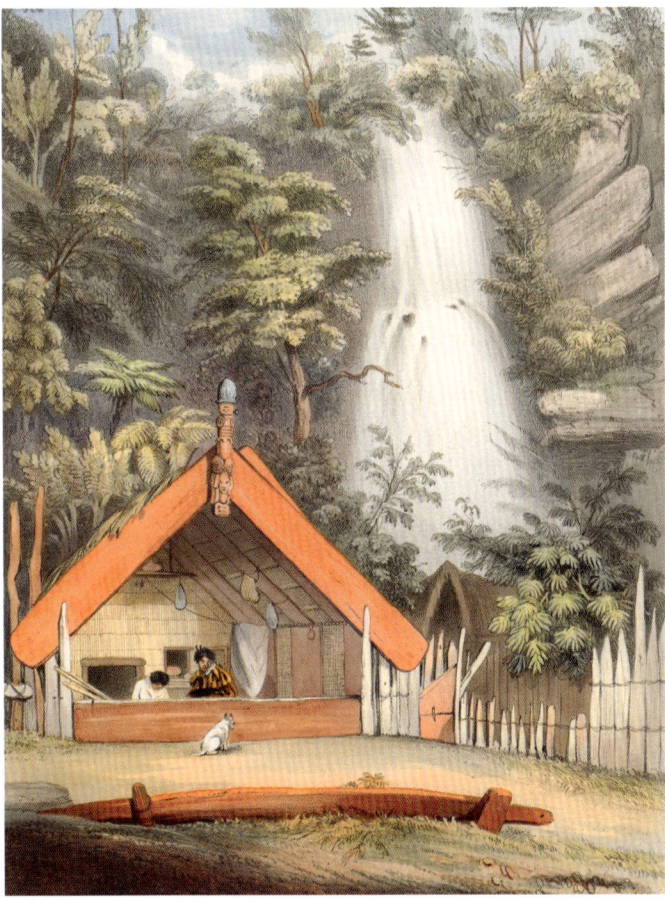

wharekai, and food became a community resource only during functions on the marae. One hundred years later, the unadorned 'food' pātaka as a functional form was no longer relevant and few were being built by Māori for Māori. At least twenty-four have survived to the present day, and some are still in use.[20] Smaller pātaka were still being made on commission as presentation works for museums and private collectors. Pātaka, therefore, can be considered an enduring symbol of rangatiratanga through continued authority over land and maintenance of tikanga-based lifestyles.

Identified closely with rangatiratanga, a series of carved pātaka known collectively as Ngā Pou o te Kīngitanga (the pillars of the kingdom) were built across the western, central and lower North Island in the mid-1850s, during the search for a Māori monarch who would unite all iwi. That search was successful, but by the 1860s and 1870s the social and political value of the carved pātaka – and the time, money and effort that went into their creation – was being re-evaluated. Te Puawai o Te Arawa, for instance, was built in 1868–1871 more as an assertion of the wealth and status of the patron, Te Pokiha Haranui (Ngāti Pikiao), than for any practical purpose.

Many pātaka were destroyed, damaged or plundered for their treasures after settlements were attacked by militia during the New Zealand Wars. In 1863 George Laws of Wairoa wrote to Donald McLean, general government agent in Hawke's Bay: 'The Waikatos have gone to their Kaingas in the Bush, leaving the settlements by the River to be occupied by Opes [other groups] as they arrive. These strangers have emptied the "patakas" and Boxes of all the wearing apparel etc. belonging to the "tangata whenua".'[21]

Communities deemed it prudent to build a type of structure that might better respond to their needs and aspirations, given the huge transformations that were occurring in the aftermath of the New Zealand Wars. Carved pātaka no longer served a contemporary purpose, whereas a wharenui could be used for important events and hui. Carvers who had once been employed on pātaka and waka taua now focused on producing a form that was in many ways an amalgamation of both: the whare whakairo.

## Whare whakairo

The whare whakairo is a community meeting house embellished with whakairo rākau, tukutuku panels and kōwhaiwhai. For Māori, it is the ultimate artistic expression of identity and tūrangawaewae. Whare whakairo began to appear in the eastern regions of the North Island from at least the early 1840s, and their popularity soon spread to communities across the country. Over half of the approximately 1000 marae in use today were established between 1880 and 1950, and most of today's marae have a meeting house – either a whare whakairo or a wharenui or whare rūnanga, which are not carved.[22]

Many writers have considered the origins of the whare whakairo and identified several artistic pathways through which it emerged. For the whare whakairo the carver chose particular styles and stories that were familiar to the community, utilising a decorative tradition established earlier for pātaka, waka taua and chief's houses. Read together, these elements created an architecture of mana that represented rangatiratanga, fecundity, wealth and a community bound by whakapapa.

Typically, whare whakairo, like pātaka and wharepuni, are a gabled building with a porch, with regional variations including the placement of the entrance. Much of the iconography used on pātaka carvings also appears on the whare

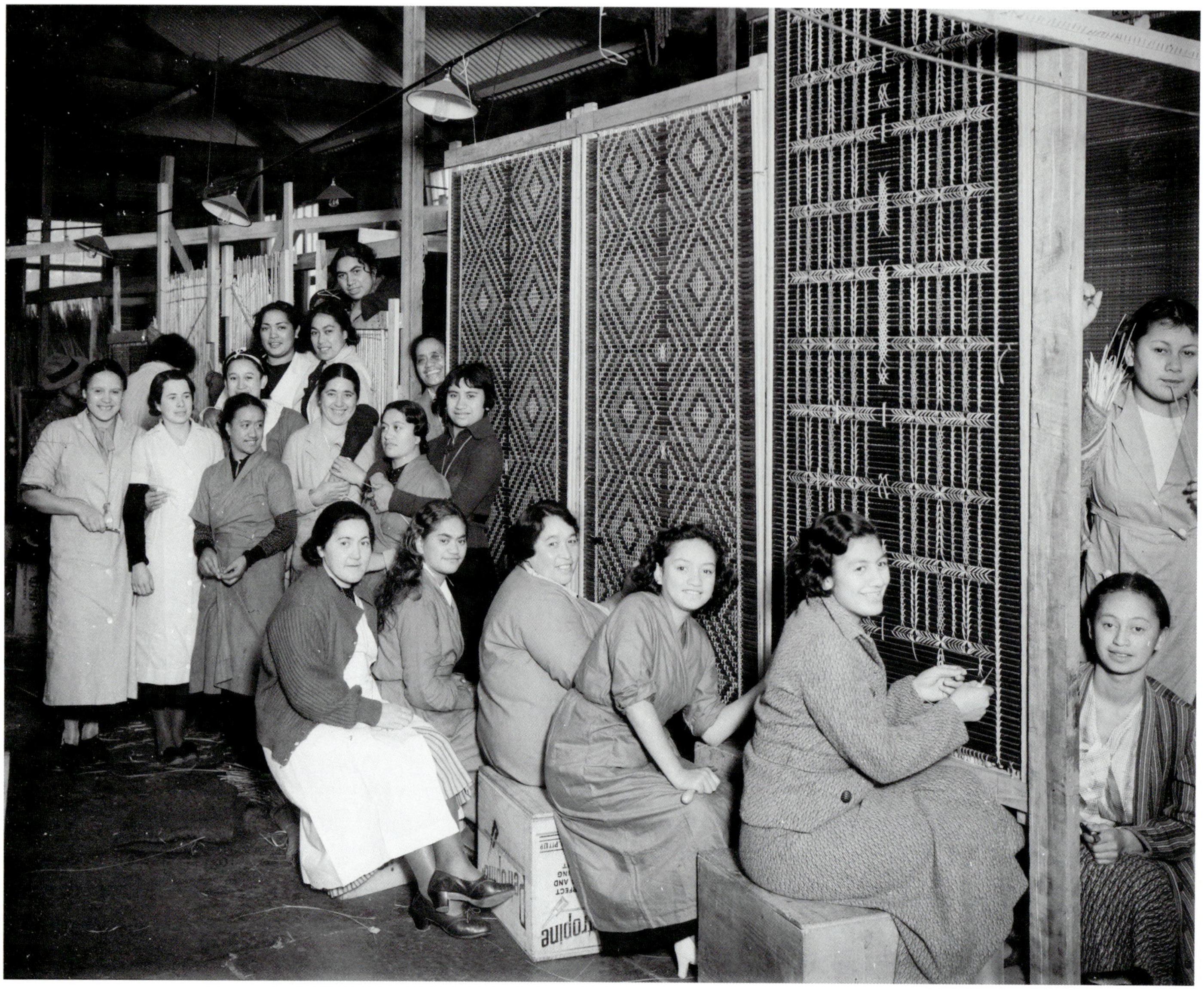

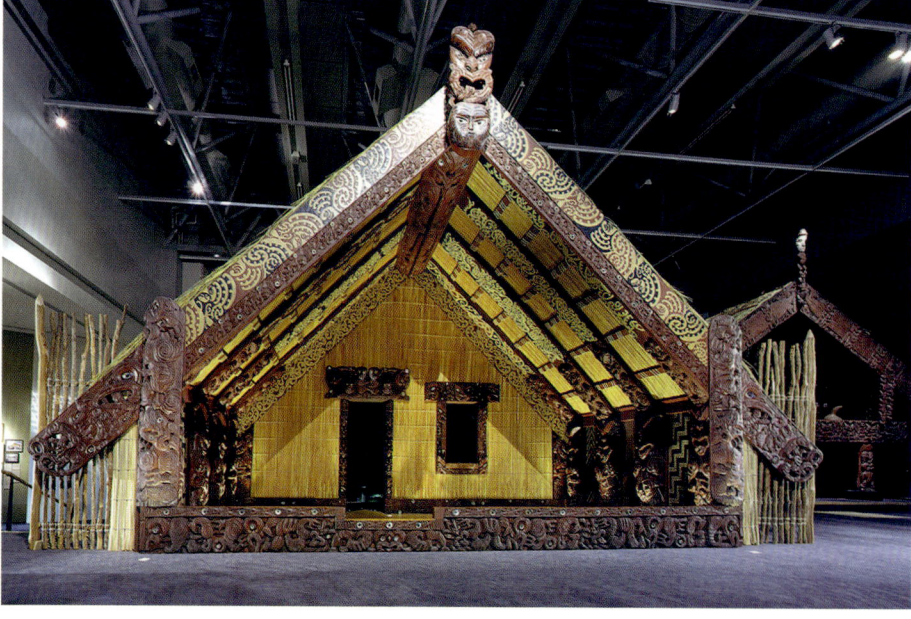

Artists stitching tukutuku panels. This image was almost certainly taken in one of the workshops established by the School of Maori Arts and Crafts, most likely at Wellington's Dominion Museum, in the mid-1930s.
William Hall Raine, Te Papa Tongarewa Museum of New Zealand, B.013046

Te Hau ki Tūranga, built in Tūranga (Gisborne) by Rongowhakaata under the leadership of Raharuhi Rukupō, c.1842. The wharenui was later taken by the government and is shown here at its current location at Te Papa Tongarewa Museum of New Zealand.
Te Papa Tongarewa Museum of New Zealand, B42467

whakairo. Some whare whakairo had whale-derived imagery on maihi, ancestors on amo and repeating tiki (human figure) and manaia sequences across the paepae, and the same pare compositions as on some pātaka.[23] The addition of poupou, or carved wall panels, along the internal walls, illustrating ancestors and atua, was an innovation. Whare whakairo were much longer, wider and taller than wharepuni and could accommodate groups of Māori visitors. This development has sparked debate among scholars as to whether the builders were simulating the scale and congregational aspects of Christian churches or whether these changes occurred independently of external architectural influences.[24] In either case, whare whakairo addressed the need to come together and find agreement across kāinga about responses to Christianity, land sales to Pākehā and other challenges related to colonisation, as well as the finer details of living collectively as iwi and as Māori.

Te Hau ki Tūranga is a surviving example of an early whare whakairo from the East Coast region of the North Island. It was built at Ōrākaiapu pā in Tūranga (Gisborne) under the supervision of the legendary Rongowhakaata tohunga whakairo Raharuhi Rukupō in the early 1840s, a time that coincides with the arrival of the first Christian missionaries to the area and the signing of Te Tiriti o Waitangi. The house, which sits on the cusp of two worlds, was decorated inside and out with a profusion of whakairo rākau, made using metal tools, and kōwhaiwhai patterns painted in rotating sequences along rafters and reflected across rafter pairs, using templates made from Pākehā materials.[25] The real genius of the building, as a device for creating community cohesion, was the inclusion among the carvings of not just local Rongowhakaata ancestors but also those of neighbouring Ngāti Kahungunu, with whom Rongowhakaata wanted to form an alliance. To make the identities of these carved ancestors abundantly clear, the tohunga inscribed their names onto the carvings in the roman typeface familiar to readers of the Bible in Māori. The decorative scheme of the house acted as a visual aid for kaikōrero (orators) in explaining the whakapapa relationships between Rongowhakaata and Ngāti Kahungunu, who were united by their common ancestors and shared histories.[26]

Whare whakairo projects enabled communities to come together to reflect on their history. With the establishment of the Native Land Court in 1862, individuals and hapū were compelled to retell their whakapapa and the history of various parcels of land in order to retain that land. In many cases this provided the impetus for meeting houses to be built in order to assert mana whenua. Carvers were often the kaikōrero in the Native Land Court, and it is possible to see the correlation between the houses they built and kōrero in the courts. Whereas the whakairo rākau on pātaka and waka taua represented the distinctiveness between hapū and iwi, the whare whakairo promised unity and might be regarded as a creative expression of being collectively Māori. Some carvers had originally trained as waka builders – such as Ānaha Te Rāhui, who learnt to carve canoes from his father but, by the 1860s, was carving meeting houses. Chiefs were still commissioning the houses in most cases, though at times a carver might initiate their own meeting house project (usually on a more modest scale), or the community might commission a wharenui. In the late nineteenth century hapū began to conceptualise themselves as iwi, and many made a grand public statement about this identity through the building of large whare whakairo named after their eponymous ancestors and waka, such as Tama Te Kapua for Te Arawa, Porourangi for Ngāti Porou, and Mātaatua for Ngāti Awa.

## Tukutuku

Tukutuku wall panelling, embellished with stitched designs, developed as an art form in its own right within whare whakairo, and entered a period of unrestrained creativity in the late nineteenth century. Te Rangi Hīroa speculated that kākaho wall linings had their origins in Polynesia in the thin vertical timbers made from the pūrau tree that were still in use in Rarotonga in the twentieth century and were known as kākaʻo (kākaho) – the vertical and horizontal toetoe stems or timber battens that, when stitched together, formed panels; these were decorated with paint and complex stitching designs to create tukutuku that lined the ceiling of the whare and the walls between poupou.[27]

Tukutuku patterns were determined by male tohunga until the 1920s, when the invention of the tukutuku frame meant that women could be wholly responsible for the practice off-site. Before this time, a male tohunga would determine the pattern by sitting inside the whare and passing the rākau hei tui (stitching needle) back and forth to an assistant on the outside.[28] Reaching new heights of decorative expression in the whare whakairo, tukutuku

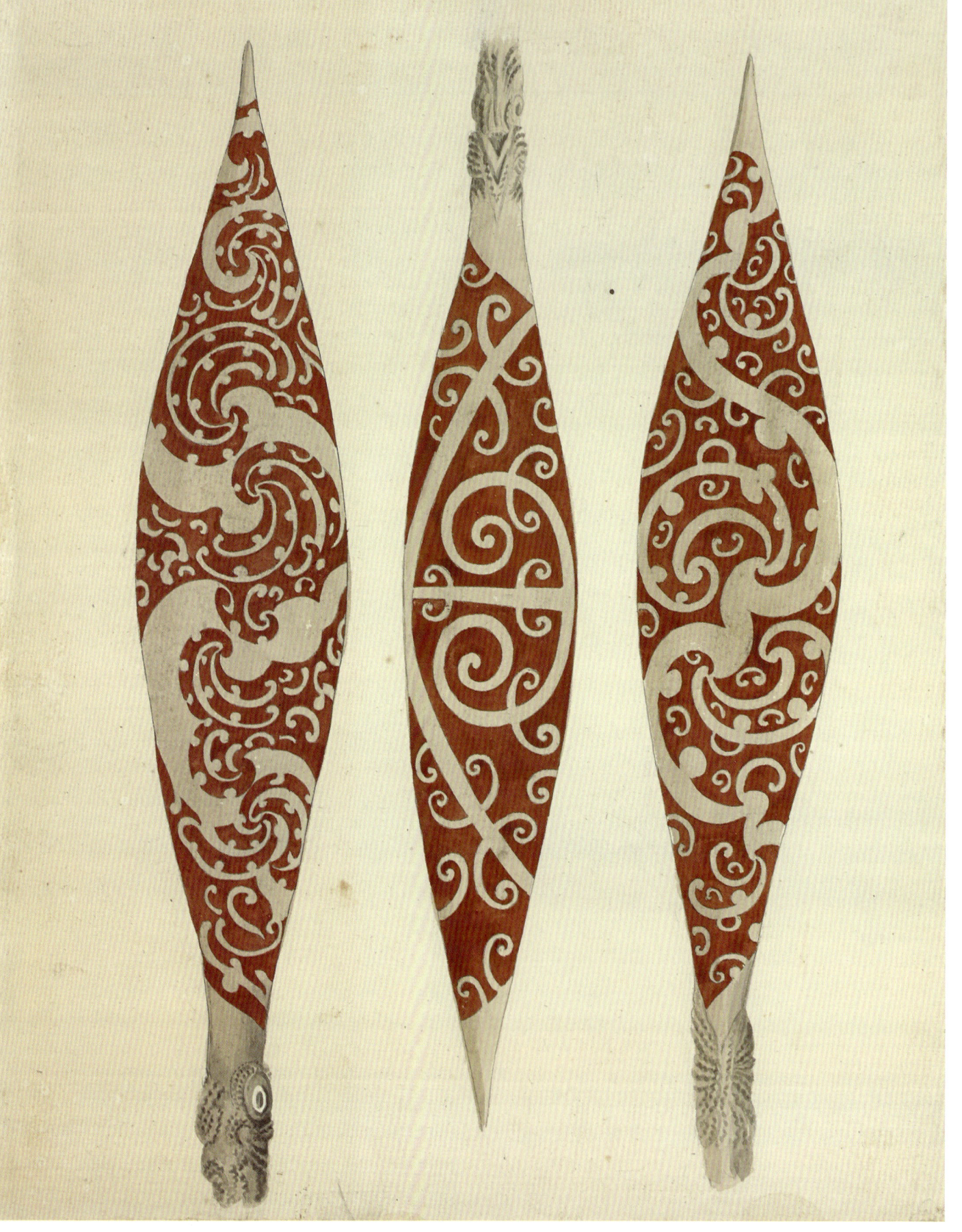

lashings were dyed in different colours and spaced to create larger compositions of repeating and sometimes figurative patterns. Some tukutuku were divided by a tūmatakahuki (vertical stake), which was lashed onto the panel to strengthen the horizontal rods.

Tukutuku was originally practised with a limited number of stitching patterns.[29] One old Whanganui pattern consisted entirely of cross-stitches in one colour; this practice eventually fell out of favour with the introduction of more intricate and complex patterns. A similar pattern has endured, with cross-stitching in alternating red and white; Te Arawa call this pattern mangōroa (Milky Way). Another old pattern was a checkerboard design made of cross-stitches, which Whanganui people call kōwhiti and Te Arawa call roimata (tears).

Tukutuku entered a period of radical transformation from the mid-nineteenth century to the late 1920s as Pākehā embroidery patterns were introduced into stitching designs, and some tukutuku artists began using milled wooden battens and stitching dyed with commercial colours. The School of Maori Arts and Crafts rejected these innovative practices in the late 1920s and 1930s; instead, it revived the use of kākaho and stitching made of harakeke or kiekie (both either sun-bleached or dyed black), or golden pīngao.

### Kōwhaiwhai

Kōwhaiwhai patterns were used in exciting ways with the development of whare whakairo – to embellish tāhuhu and poupou. It was always an art form that denoted mana. Stories abound of its ancestral origins and of the practice being brought into the mortal world by deities such as Whiro and applied to skin as moko, to calabashes (gourds) as incised designs, and painted on waka and hoe.[30] The patterns themselves, while they likely originated from observation of the natural world, developed deeper conceptual meanings through their relationship to other arts, particularly when they complemented and united the decorative scheme of ancestral whakairo rākau and the patterned and figurative elements of tukutuku. The purpose of all of these arts was to inspire oratory that would keep the oral histories of communities alive and bind community members together.

Kōwhaiwhai was a widely practised art applied across a range of art forms. The earliest surviving kōwhaiwhai-decorated taonga is a hoe found in Moncks Cave, Ōhikaparuparu (Sumner), that is thought to be 600 years old:[31] across its blade

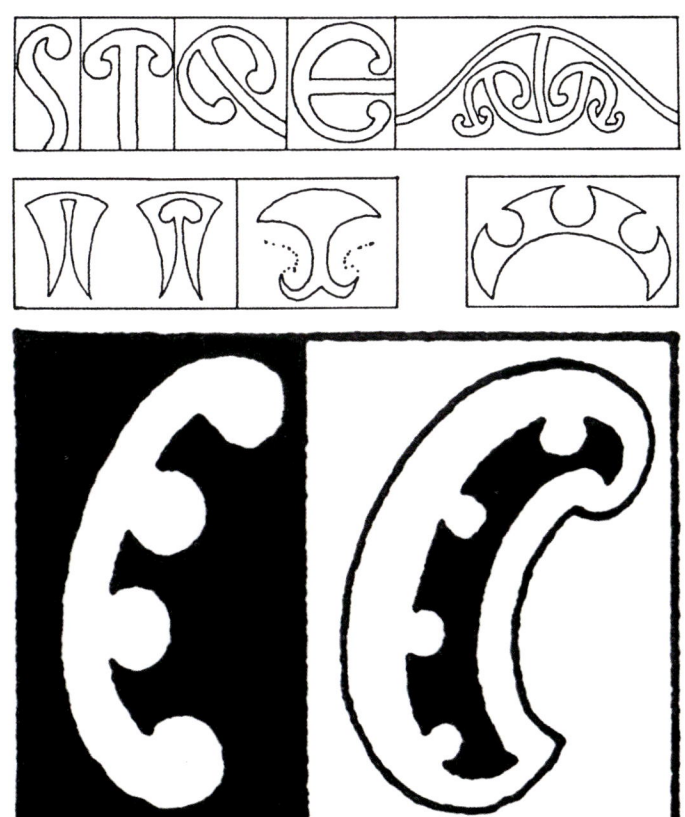

The koru is the fundamental design unit from which all customary kōwhaiwhai is generated. As this diagram shows, combinations of koru and forms created from its negative image produce a wide range of kōwhaiwhai designs.
diagram by Roger Neich from *Painted Histories: Early Maori Figurative Painting*, Auckland University Press, 1993

Opposite: The similarity between the kōwhaiwhai patterns on these hoe, acquired during James Cook's visit to Aotearoa in 1769, and later whare rafters demonstrates the strong decorative relationship between waka and whare. The hoe were possibly a gift by Māori to Tupaia, the Raiatean high priest and navigator travelling with Cook.
British Library, Add. 23920, f.71

is a simple sequence of five bands painted in red ochre. Kōwhaiwhai was already a highly developed art by the time Cook's crew collected hoe with complex painted patterns from the east coast of the North Island in 1769. Seventy years later, kōwhaiwhai of a similar design was painted on the heke in Te Hau ki Tūranga.[32] The patterns on these hoe and heke are remarkably similar and speak to the strong relationship between waka and whare. Kōwhaiwhai painting on architectural elements was a widespread practice by the mid-1840s: it appears on the heke and tāhuhu of a whare whakairo that Puatia built in the Waikato region in the central North Island, and on the same elements in Ngāti Toa leader Te Rangihaeata's whare whakairo on Mana Island, off the west coast of Wellington.[33]

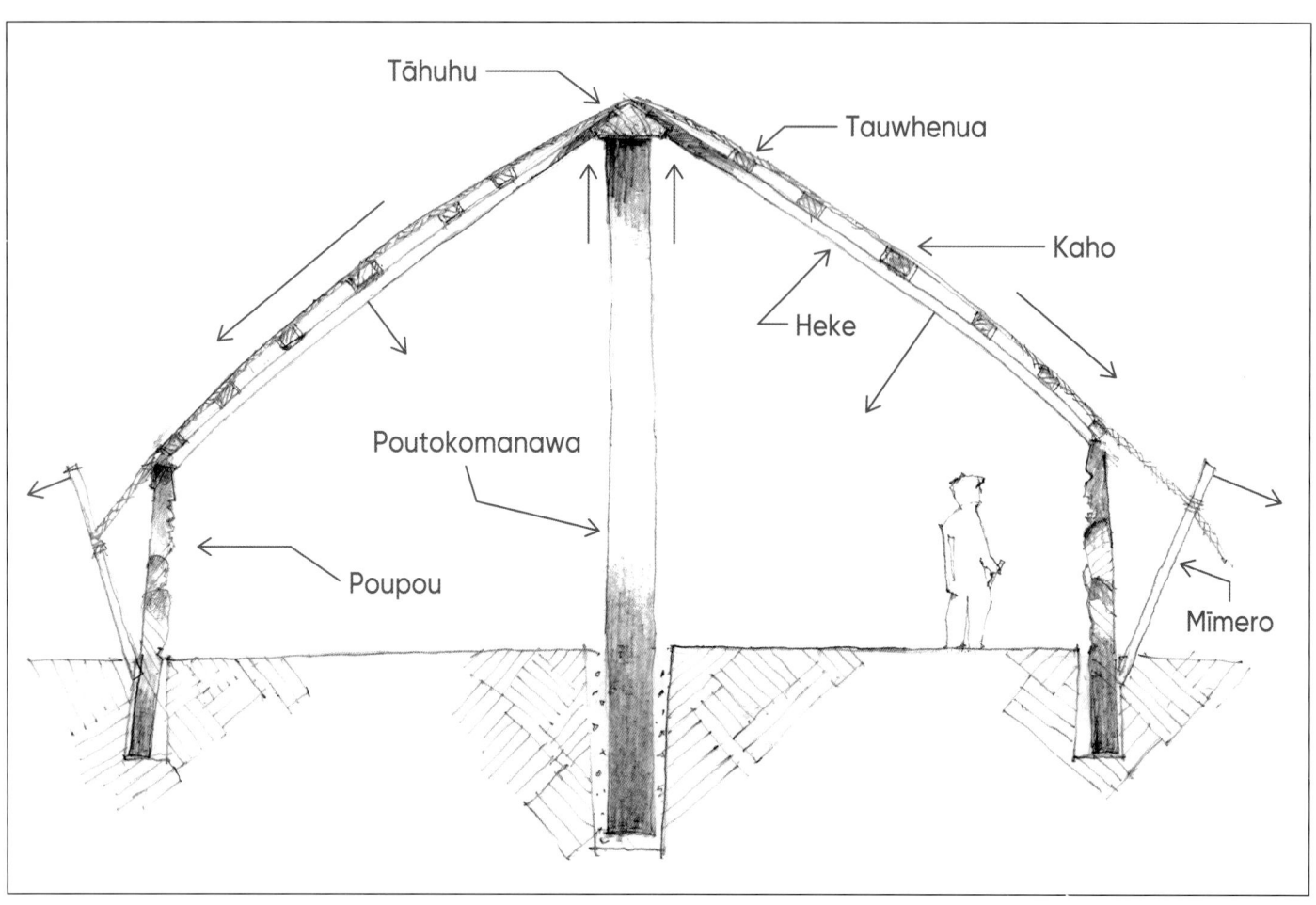

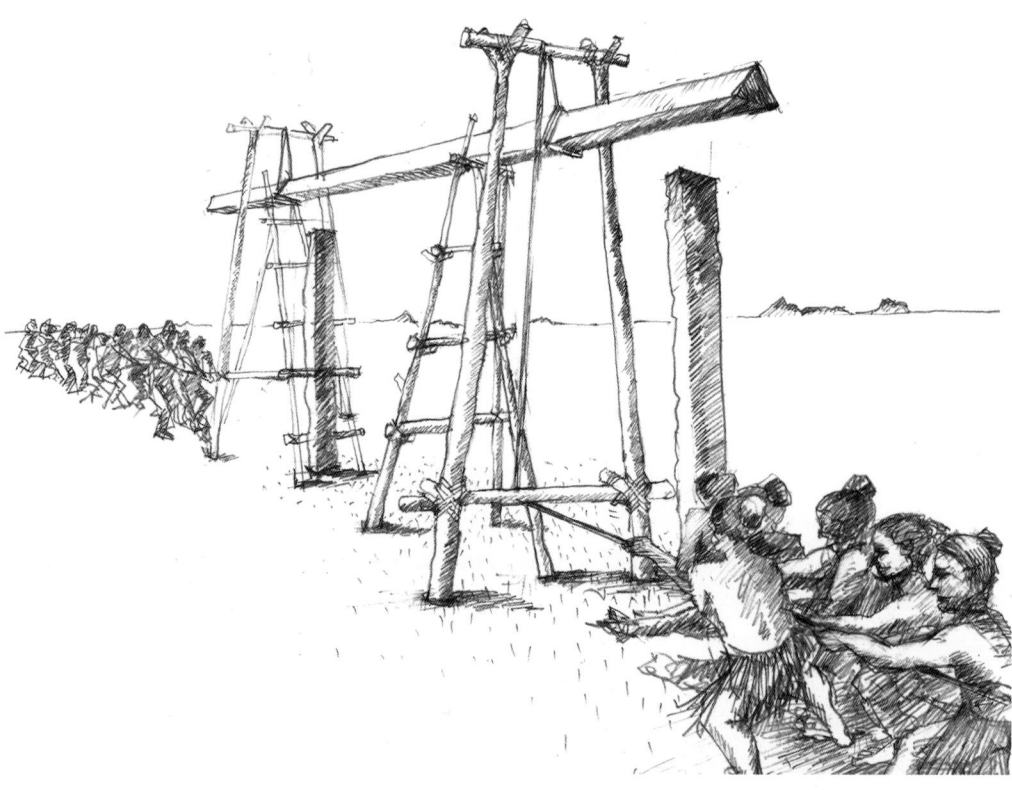

Above: Schematic cross-section of the compressed arched frame of the whare.
Jeremy Treadwell, 2014

Left: A tāhuhu (ridgepole) hoisted into place on top of the main supporting pou (posts).
Jeremy Treadwell, 2014

Opposite: The Ngāti Porou meeting house Ruatepupuke II, carved by Hoani Ngatai in 1880–1881, and now in the Field Museum, Chicago.
photograph by Diane Alexander White and Linda Dorman

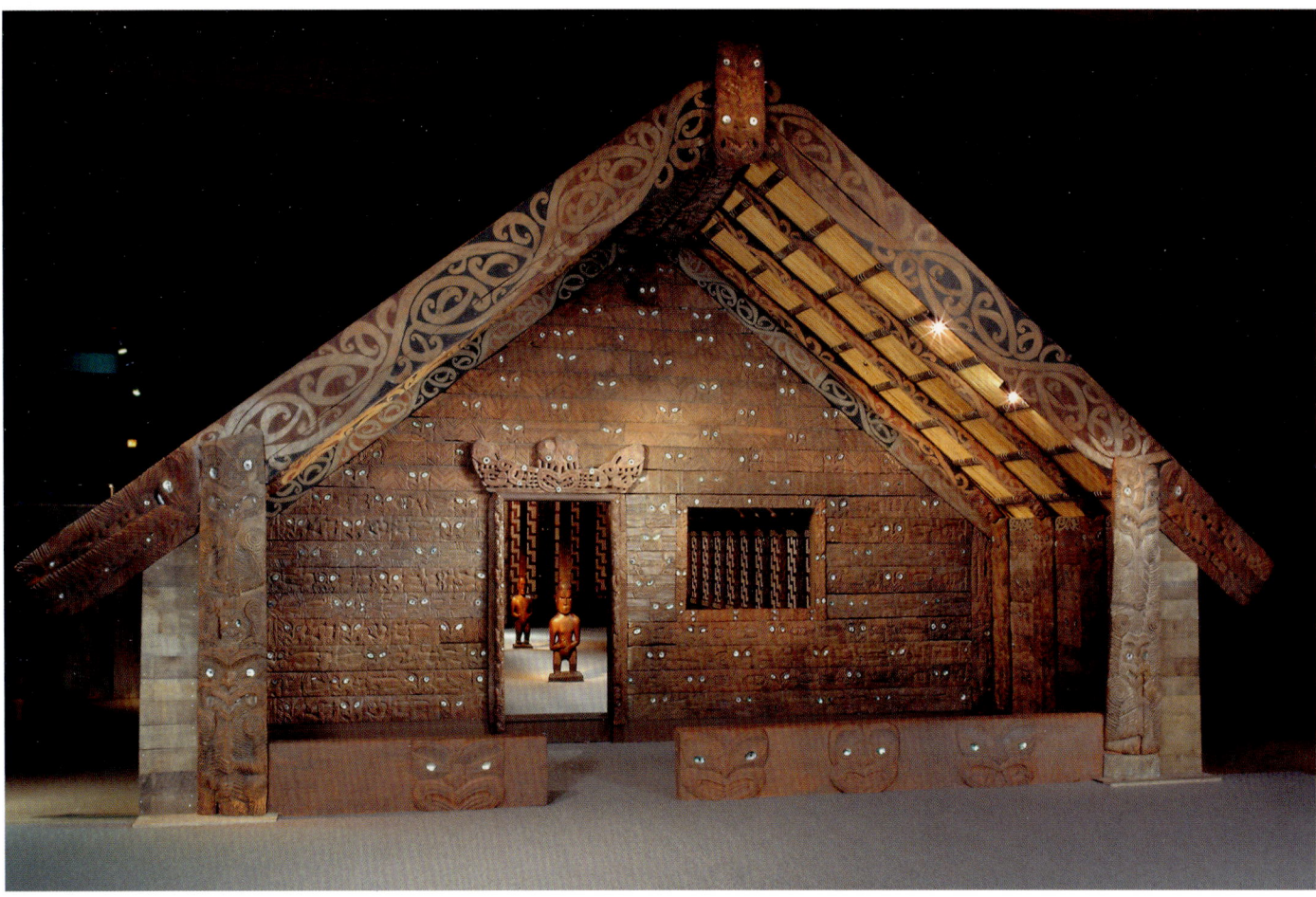

All customary kōwhaiwhai patterns are generated from the same basic design unit, the koru – an unfurling, curved motif terminating in a bulb at one end – and are closely associated with all the metaphors of growth and development inherent in that motif. Complex kōwhaiwhai patterns are created from a single-koru motif; or by using the koru motif as a negative image to construct other designs. For example, the circular indents in the kape (crescent) form are made by the negative space left by the koru bulbs, while its convex edge is created from one continuous koru stalk; the bulbous white areas found around the kape patterns are called ngū (octopus, squid or cuttlefish). Even more complex kōwhaiwhai patterns on heke were achieved through the use of repetition, reflection and rotation: the iterative nature of these compositions alluded to the sequence of generations associated with whakapapa. Kōwhaiwhai thereby manifests the generative nature of the Māori world from its simplest elements to its most intricate expressions.

Before the mid-nineteenth century, architectural kōwhaiwhai patterns were coloured with the same types of red, white and black pigments as those used on carvings, and particular patterns were popular among certain tribes. Pūhoro was a favourite pattern for Te Arawa – based on the moko design on the thigh of a tohunga, Pango Ngawene – and its first use in architecture was in 1870 or 1871.[34] At around this time, kōwhaiwhai underwent a dramatic transformation with the introduction of naturalistic patterns and figurative elements on all internal and porch surfaces of whare. This innovation was inspired by realism in European painting and photography, and the availability of a full colour spectrum of commercial paints. Fifty years later, as with tukutuku, the School of Maori Arts and Crafts promoted restraint and a return to customary patterns on roof elements. However, kōwhaiwhai had been appropriated into Pākehā design by this stage, in everything from art deco buildings to crockery to postage stamps, and it went on to become an important source of inspiration for contemporary Māori artists.

Three types of painters produced architectural kōwhaiwhai. The first were the carvers who were commissioned from other tribes to complete a project and who would practise kōwhaiwhai painting as an art secondary to their carving. The second group were largely untrained local people following the general instructions left by the carvers. The last group were specialist kōwhaiwhai experts who were commissioned from other areas to decorate houses built by other tohunga.[35] In 1897, Herbert Williams recorded one of the few known accounts of how a nineteenth-century kōwhaiwhai artist worked.[36] He noted that kōwhaiwhai artists, like carvers, memorised patterns, and did not carry a stock of drawn patterns from job to job. They would trace the outline of the whole pattern with feather or fibre brushes, or with pencils and chalk, onto the surface of the taonga being decorated, and fill it in with colour afterwards. In the event that the artist overestimated the size of the material, they would not try to squash the design onto the surface, but would draw as much as they could and leave out the edges. This account conflicts somewhat with the suspected use of templates for the kōwhaiwhai on Te Hau ki Tūranga, which shows a variation that suggests the art was far more mutable than Williams observed.

Whakairo rākau, complemented by intricately stitched tukutuku panels and kōwhaiwhai-painted heke and poupou, produced complex decorative schemes that elucidated the ancestral world and cosmological understandings of communities. These meanings found voice through explanatory kōrero that used the embellishments as visual aids. Depending on the whare whakairo, and the kaikōrero explaining its meaning, the internal and external parts of the whare whakairo could embody a founding ancestor; a community's whakapapa (sometimes extending to other groups); or the local conception of a larger Māori world.

### The meaning of whare whakairo

Descent from a founding ancestor is central to hapū and iwi identity. Whare whakairo are often named after ancestors and are designed in their image. The likeness begins with the carved koruru atop the porch gable, representing the ancestor's face. From here, the ancestor's outstretched arms extend as the maihi of the porch, as if to gather in the people, a gesture emphasised by the finger-like protrusions of the carved raparapa or extensions. To complete the metaphor of the face of the building, the door is seen as representing the ancestor's mouth, and any apertures beside the door – in earlier times smoke vents and, later, windows – as the ancestor's eyes. The interior is the poho – the chest or stomach of the ancestor – and this meaning is affirmed in the naming of some whare whakairo as 'Te Poho o [ancestor's name]'. The tāhuhu is the backbone, the heke the ribs and the poutokomanawa the heart.

The whare whakairo may also be read as a whakapapa, starting from a founding ancestor represented as a carved tekoteko figure at the gable apex, from whom descend generations of ancestors, depicted in whakairo rākau or kōwhaiwhai running down the internal face of the tāhuhu and heke, to their descendants on the poupou. Tohunga whakairo generally did not depict living people in their work, and this custom still holds: portraits (paintings or photographs) of recently deceased community members may only be hung on the back wall of the wharenui.

The definition of the back wall as a space associated with death and the atua Hinenuitepō is connected to another conception of the wharenui and the marae complex as representing relationships between complementary elements in Māori cosmology. The front wall of the wharenui, whether carved or uncarved, is associated with life, and the entire building represents the domain of Rongomātāne, the atua of peace, as opposed to the marae ātea, which personifies Rongomātāne's brother Tūmatauenga, the atua of war. Such understandings of the world create the rationale for marae practices and determine all tikanga, from how hau kāinga (the home community) and manuhiri engage across the marae and within a wharenui in a pōwhiri, to tangihanga or any other ritual context – with iwi and hapū variations.

Cosmology determines the physical dynamics of the whare whakairo's structure. Research by architectural historian Jeremy Treadwell has revealed compelling linguistic, narrative and architectural evidence that tāhuhu are conceived of as physically massive elements that represent Ranginui, the primeval sky father.[37] He is hoisted into place by the whare's builders in a re-enactment of the creation story, when Tāne-nui-ā-rangi separated Ranginui from Papatūānuku, the earth mother. The pou that bear the weight of Ranginui represent the burden of their son in maintaining Te Ao Mārama, the mortal world of light, by keeping his parents separated.

Similarly, in the Pacific, the tāhuhu is one of the first structural components to be raised and supported on two posts, creating the gable that defines most of the region's architecture.³⁸ In Sāmoa and Tonga the tāhuhu is short and the ends are rounded, making the plan of the fale almost oval; in Papua New Guinea, the ends of the gable roof are extended up into majestic sweeping points; and in Tuvalu and Kiribati, it is complemented with a hipped 'skirt'. These Pacific origins suggest that the symbolism of the tāhuhu was both physically and cosmologically located in Hawaiki. On the East Coast of the North Island in particular, the tāhuhu is orientated so that the wharenui faces the rising sun, with the associated metaphors of new life. In other parts of Aotearoa, road access is a common determining factor for the orientations of wharenui built in the twentieth century, and streams and harbours – the highways of Māori before horses and cars – for those from the nineteenth. The scale of a wharenui built using customary methods seems to have been largely determined by the labour available to hoist the tāhuhu, some of which were more than 25m long and weighed over 1000kg. Hence, the size of a whare was an indication of the mana of the leaders who commissioned it, and their ability to mobilise the labour and source the materials needed to build it.³⁹

The entire system of tension (in the ropes) and compression (the weight of the building elements) was brought into physical and cosmological balance through an ingenious system of 'post tensioning'. Ropes made of harakeke fibre were lashed through each portal frame, comprising opposing pairs of heke and supporting poupou, then tightened to lock the components and literally pull the house together. In this way, the parts of the wharenui are woven together. This system of post tensioning is related to, and possibly derived from, similar systems used on waka throughout the Pacific for rigging; and to connect strakes and struts to hulls, and outriggers to floats.⁴⁰

The engineering of the whare whakairo was inseparable from the arts, and all of these structural elements – the tāhuhu, heke, poupou and other load-bearing pou – could be carved and painted. Tohunga whakairo Lyonel Grant (Ngāti Pikiao, Ngāti Rangiwewehi, Te Arawa) revived this custom in his Te Ngākau Māhaki whare whakairo project (opened in 2009 at Unitec's Mount Albert campus), in which the carved poupou and heke (which extend to the ground) are structural, rather than applied decorative members.

The wharenui has proved to be a resilient cultural taonga despite the influence of Pākehā culture and building technologies, largely because the marae is so central to Māori cultural identity. The architectural revivals by the School of Maori Arts and Crafts and the Tūrangawaewae carving school in the early twentieth century brought the whare whakairo to the fore once again, particularly as these institutions were closely linked to national and iwi initiatives to promote unity and Māori social reform. A second revival in whare whakairo construction began in the 1970s and gained momentum from the 1980s as urbanisation and land loss prompted Māori to reconsider their relationship to their marae, whether they were in ancestral homelands or newly established in urban centres and institutions. The form of the whare whakairo is so influential that many contemporary Māori architectural design projects are generated from the tikanga and formalism of the whare whakairo.

## Conclusion

The wharepuni, whare kāuta, pātaka and wharenui each contributed to a system of living in kāinga and a network of relationships that strengthened whānau, hapū, iwi and broader Māori relationships. Through their technologies and carved, painted and woven elements, they defined and supported the tikanga of everyday and ritual life, from gender roles to whakapapa, to the tapu and noa dichotomy. These architectures maintained balance within Māori communities. In difficult times, they came to represent the mana and rangatiratanga of hapū and iwi, as seen in the changing fortunes of the pātaka and whare whakairo; yet they were dynamic in their response to new ideas and technologies. The whare and related arts have fluctuated between periods of innovation (as seen in the development of kōwhaiwhai and tukutuku) and conservatism (such as that promoted by the School of Maori Arts and Crafts) to meet the needs of communities. The biggest challenge to whare architecture has been the loss of land to Pākehā, leaving only those pockets of Māori landholdings distant from Pākehā towns as metaphorical 'pātaka' repositories of Māori cultural knowledge, from which later generations of Māori have drawn inspiration in magnificent revival initiatives.

# PAKAARIKI HARRISON, QSO (1928–2008)
NGARINO ELLIS

One of the constant challenges in any art form is succession – who will carry on the ideas and techniques for the next generation. By the early twentieth century this became a very real dilemma, prompting the creation of a national School of Maori Arts and Crafts in 1927. During its operation, many carvers and weavers were trained at the school, but their success depended on constantly seeking new talent across the nation to ensure its continuation.

In the small community of Hiruharama on the East Coast in 1940, a twelve-year-old by the name of Pakaariki Harrison (Ngāti Porou) picked up a chisel and began experimenting with wood – just as the chisel's owner, Pine Taiapa, had done in 1925 during the building of St Mary's Church across the river at Tikitiki. And, just like Pine, Paki thought no one would notice.

Harrison was born in Ruatōria in 1928, the oldest of twenty-one children – a large family even back then. He was whāngaied by his grandmother, the formidable Materoa Reedy, until he was eleven, when he was returned to his parents as they moved the whānau to Harataunga Marae at Kennedy Bay in the Coromandel – an enclave of Ngāti Porou who had been gifted land by the local iwi, as they had been stopping there regularly in the nineteenth century on their trade routes to and from Auckland.

Back on the East Coast in 1940, Harrison became aware of a group of carvers working on a wharekai named Ngā Tamatoa that his grandmother had commissioned. He became interested in the work of Pine and Hone Taiapa, as well as the Rarotongan Charlie Tuarau and local carver Rua Kaika, who worked at Waitangirua. When he went to Te Aute College, a Māori Anglican boarding school in Hawke's Bay, Paki met Pine again: the carver was living there while he worked on the wharenui Te Whare o Rangi. As an old boy of Te Aute, it was natural that Apirana Ngata would select Pine for this job – one of the first projects undertaken by students of the School of Maori Arts and Crafts – and it was also natural that Pine would ask the young Paki to apprentice to him while he was at school. Harrison's formal apprenticeship began when he was sixteen.

Harrison's interest in carving was set aside once he left Te Aute. His beloved grandmother passed away in 1944, and he moved permanently away from the East Coast to be with his father in Harataunga, which became his base for the rest of his life. At the age of twenty-one he enrolled at Auckland Teachers' College, and was later posted to Mangamuka in Te Tai Tokerau, where he met and married Hinemoa Rakena. Over the next few years as they raised their family, the couple moved around the country to different teaching contracts, including at Harataunga and at Manurewa in Auckland.

Harrison's role in schools often included teaching Māori art. His passion for making art grew, and was given a boost when he won a New Zealand Arts Council grant to attend a UNESCO conference in Paris in 1974 to demonstrate carving. Pine had recently died, and his brother Hone was at the Maori Arts and Crafts Institute in Rotorua and unable to attend the conference; he suggested Harrison attend instead. When Harrison returned to New Zealand his doctor diagnosed various health concerns and recommended he take up a different form of employment. Fortunately, his training as a carver could provide a solution when the Otara Maori Catholic Society asked him to build a meeting house. In 1977 his first whare whakairo, Te Waiariki, was opened at Whaiora Marae, Ōtara – the result of three years of intensive work.

He soon received other commissions: in 1983 his Te Poho o Tipene meeting house was opened at Tipene/St Stephen's School in South Auckland, and this was followed by regular carving work, including:

1985 Te Otawhao meeting house, Te Awamutu College
1988 Tāne-nui-ā-rangi meeting house, Waipapa Marae, University of Auckland, with kōwhaiwhai by John Hovell
1996 Rākairoa meeting house, Harataunga Marae, Kennedy Bay, Coromandel, with kōwhaiwhai by John Hovell
1996 Te Wai o Pāoa meeting house, Te Tahawai Marae, Edgewater College, Pakuranga, Auckland
1999 Matukurua meeting house, Manurewa Marae, Clendon, Auckland, with tukutuku by Peter Boyd
1999 Te Kete Uruuru Matua meeting house, Ngā Kete Wānanga Marae, Manukau Institute of Technology, Ōtara.[1]

In 2002 Harrison worked with Te Waka Toi, the Māori Board of Creative New Zealand, to create a trademark called Toi Iho, as a sign of quality and authenticity in Māori art. He and others were concerned at seeing copies of their work and others' being sold in tourist outlets, often for high prices, under the pretence that they were made by Māori. The Toi Iho trademark was awarded to Māori applicants whose work had passed a rigorous quality-check system run by Māori artists, and who would then be able to place the mark next to their work. Māori artists, including performance artists, still use the trademark today, despite Creative New Zealand's withdrawal of support and funding for marketing of the Toi Iho brand.[2]

For Harrison, one of the most significant commissions was for his hau kāinga at Harataunga. The house Rākairoa exemplified the innovation that characterised his work, as well as introducing novel elements in other aspects of the whare whakairo. The kōwhaiwhai work, for example, led by John Hovell (Ngāpuhi, Ngāti Porou), who was raised in Harataunga, is an explosion of colour and form, with birds flying on one side of the ceiling, and sea life depicted on the opposite side. Teaching was an important theme in the house, and with the radical kōwhaiwhai Paki wanted to emphasise to tamariki the importance of the natural world around them. For rangatahi who were searching for their whakapapa, and who were constantly asking him to tell them where they fitted into it, Paki made a board that charted the names of all the main ancestors; he joked that when rangatahi asked about their heritage, he could just point to the board. And fittingly, it was here that Harrison was finally laid to rest in late December 2008.

Paki Harrison's meeting houses stand as exemplars of late-twentieth-century carving, and key spaces for embedding Te Ao Māori in university and secondary school campuses.

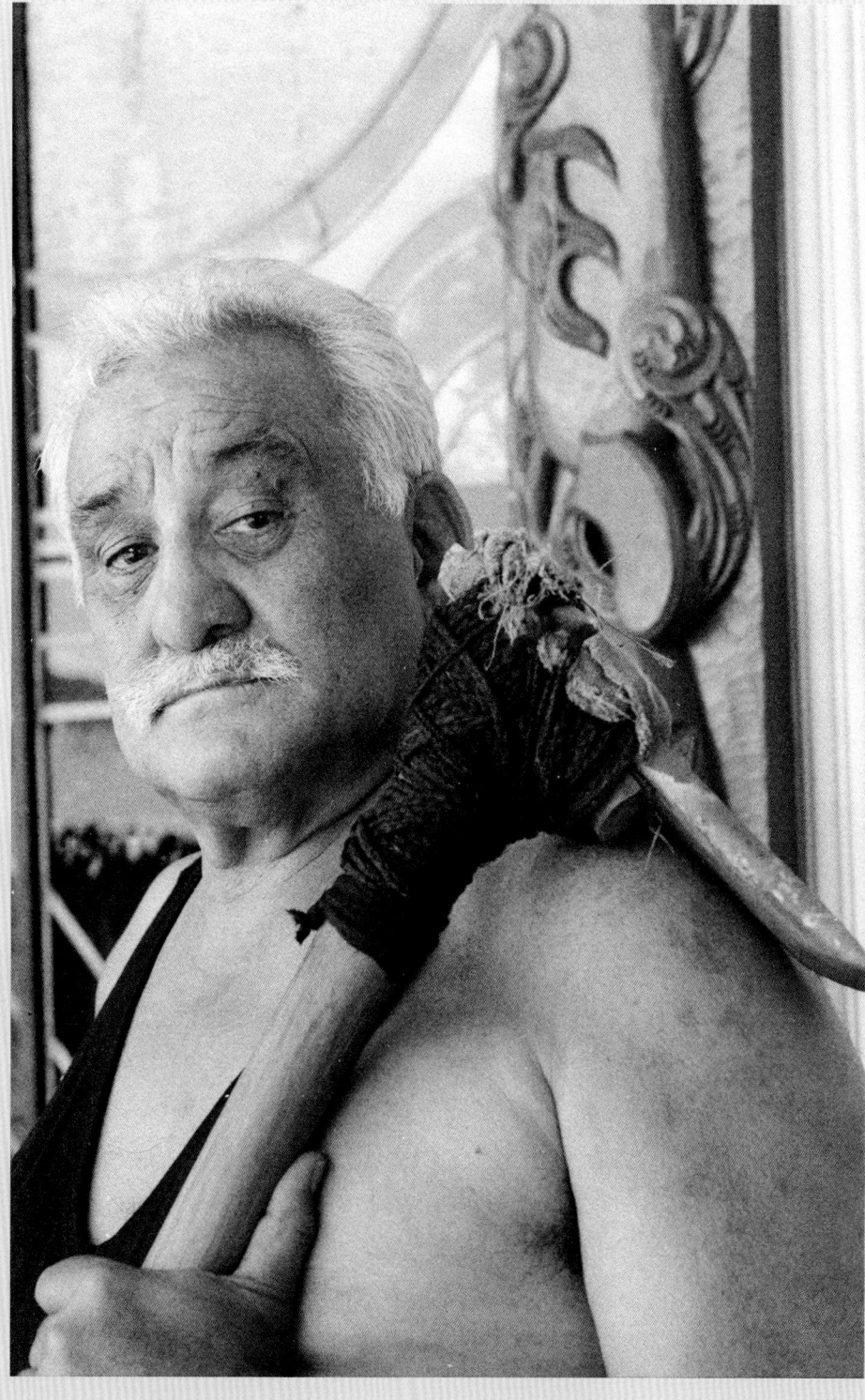

Tohunga whakairo rākau Pakaariki Harrison.
photograph by Sally Tagg

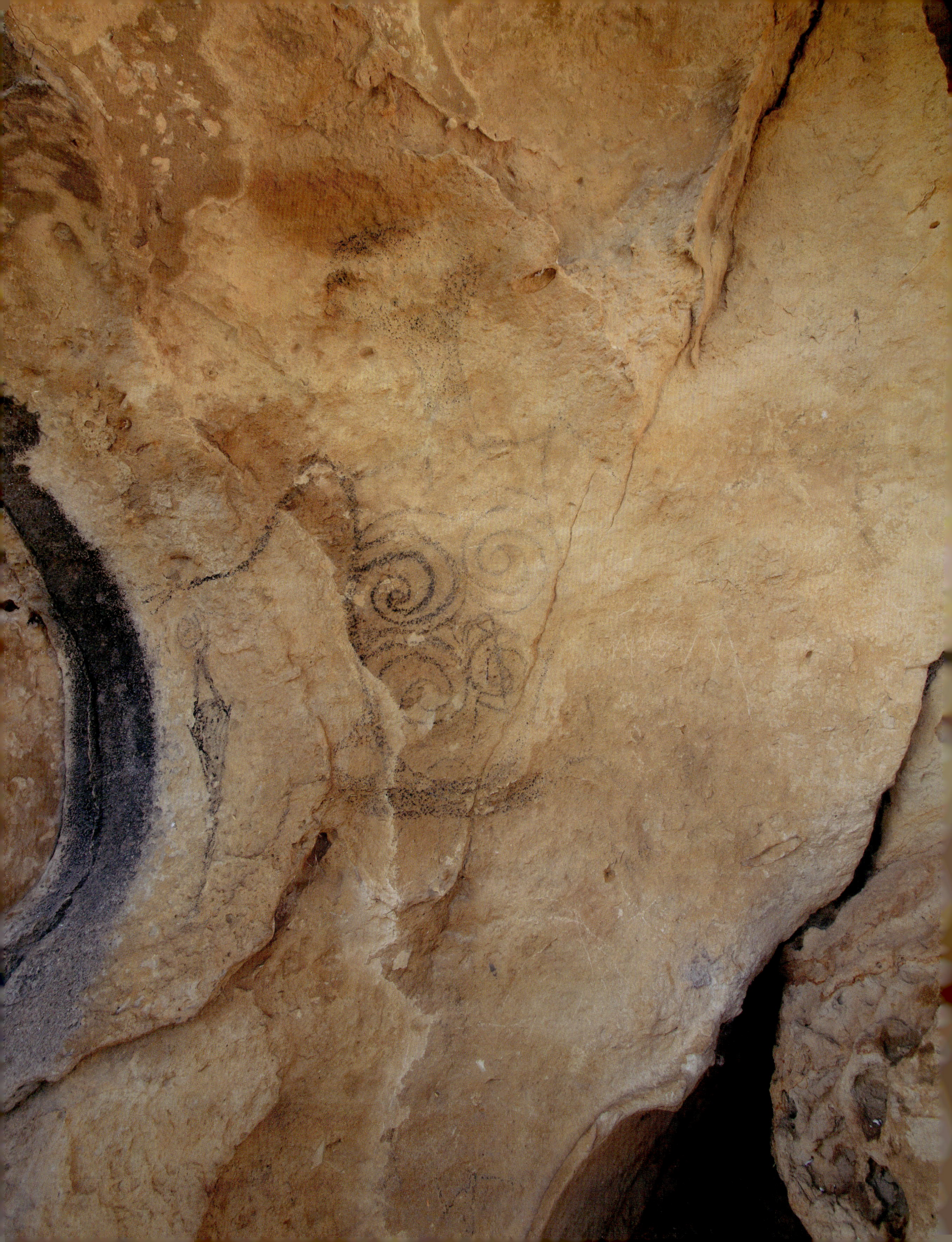

# 5 NGĀ TOI WHENUA
## ROCK ART
### DEIDRE BROWN

*This stone looks
like a little moon
or a small hill
off the white page
and the black text – it
has a whakapapa.*

—Robert Sullivan (Ngāpuhi, Ngāi Tahu),
excerpt from 'He Kohatu Iti'

As Māori travelled across the country, exploring, hunting, gathering and naming its coasts, hinterlands and mountain ranges, they made sense of the landscape by creating rock art. These drawings, paintings and engravings inscribed in the land where the ancestors made them are as much about the activation of place as they are depictions of people, animals, supernatural creatures, objects and patterns. They were part of a Polynesian portable artistic culture that at least in some known cases included storytelling and performance. Rock art changed an initially unexplored landscape into a known one, enabling people returning to sites to understand and contribute to the inhabitation of a place.

Māori practised rock art until the nineteenth century and, with more than 700 sites already identified around the country, it is one of the most prolific and widespread forms of Māori creative expression.[1] Over eighty percent of reported rock art sites are in the South Island, mostly in North Otago and South Canterbury; the sites in the North Island are largely situated within a band across the Coromandel,

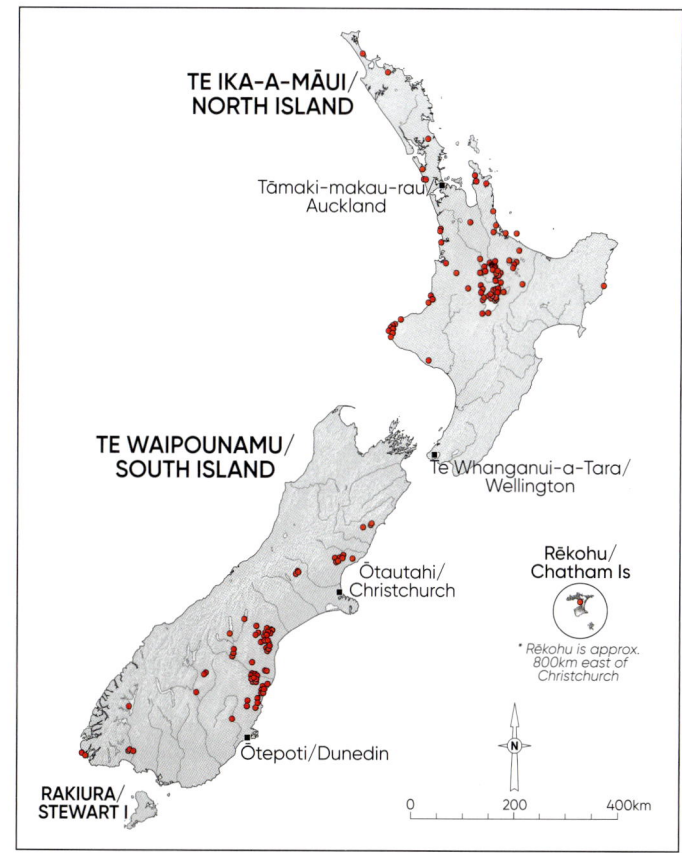

Identified rock art sites in Aotearoa New Zealand.
North island data provided by Gerard O'Regan; South Island data provided by Ngāi Tahu Maōri Rock Art Trust, map by Tim Nolan/Blackant Mapping Solutions

Opposite: Tiki (human forms) are a common subject in South Island Māori rock art. The tiki shown here, on a limestone outcrop at Maerewhenua in Waitaki, is made with black pigment with koru spirals infilling the torso and is holding a long object – perhaps a kete.
photograph by Matthew Hill/Brian Allingham, Ngāi Tahu Maōri Rock Art Trust

130 | 131

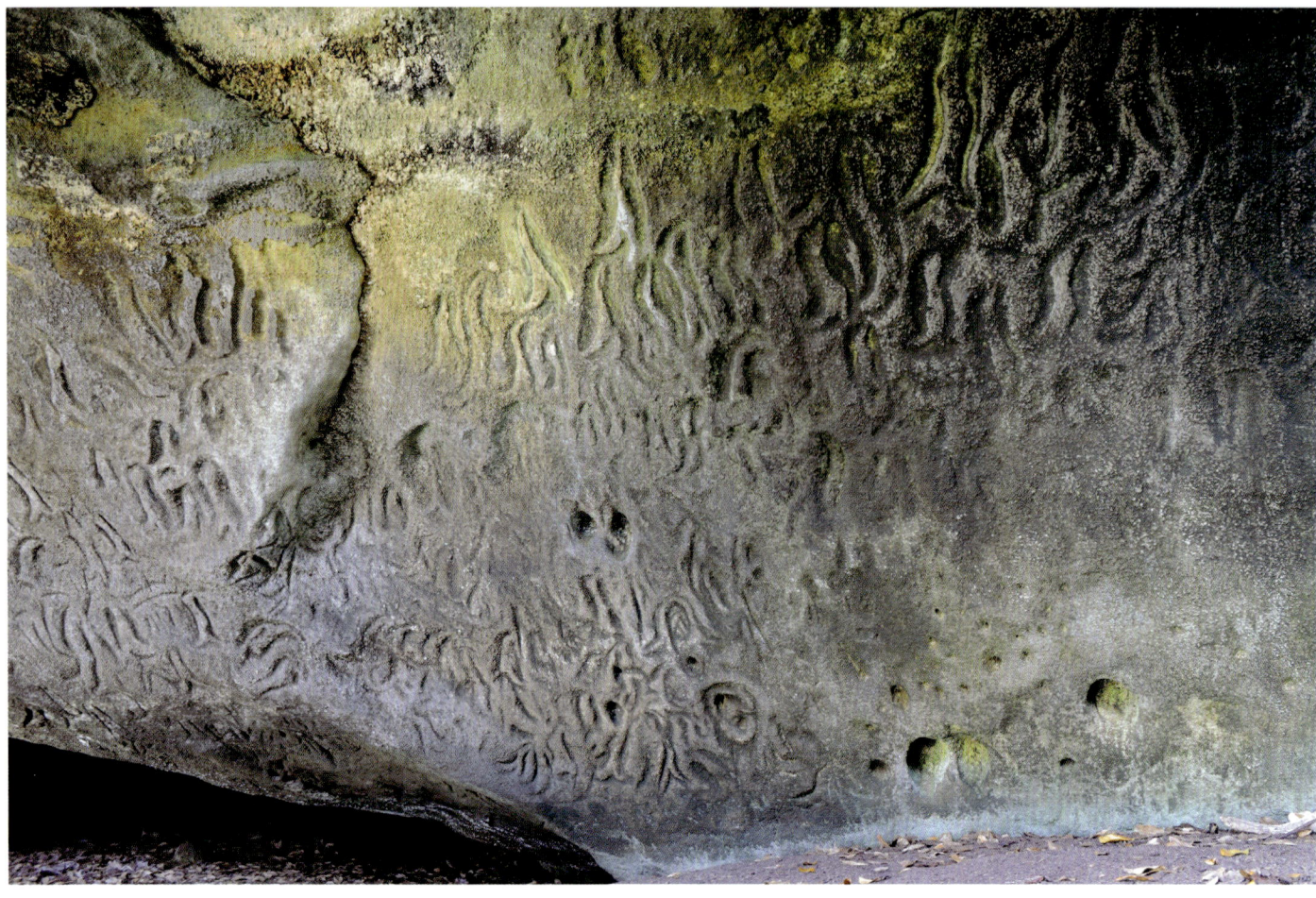

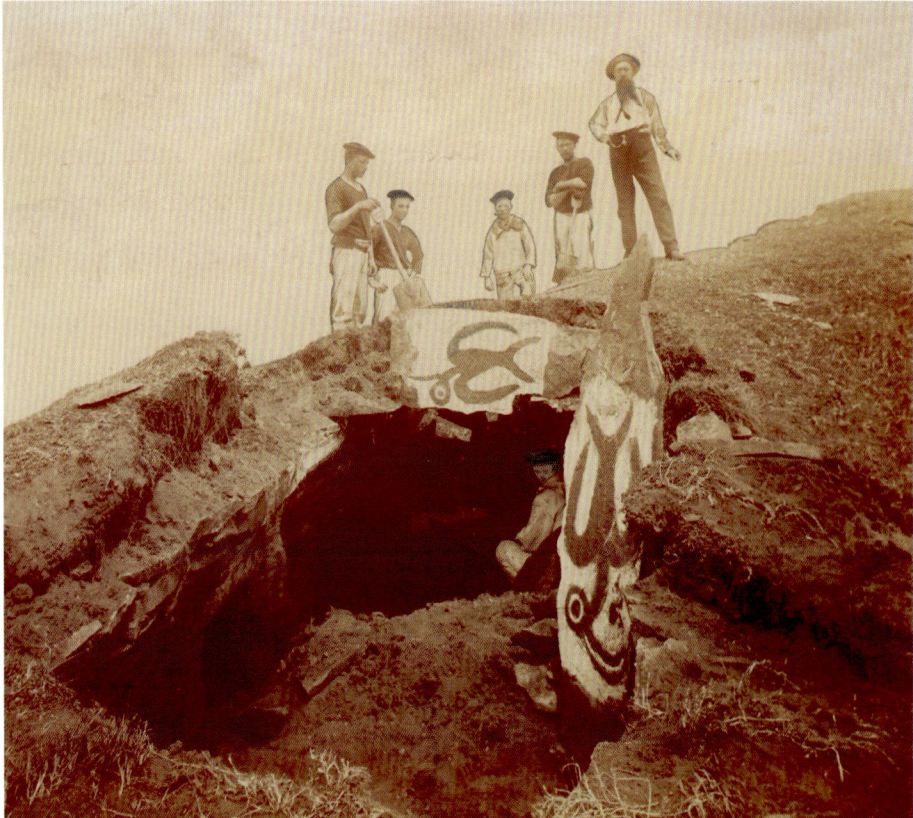

Above: Rock carvings on Te Ana a Nunuku cave, Rēkohu Chatham Islands.
images supplied by Hokotehi Moriori Trust

Left: Rock paintings at 'Orongo, Rapanui Easter Island. This image from 1886 shows them removed from their original stone house.
William J. Thomson and William Edwin Safford, Smithsonian Institution, NAA INV.04952500 OPPS NEG.81-2890

Opposite: Rākau momori, Rēkohu Chatham Islands. Moriori impressed these designs into living kōpī trees.
images supplied by Hokotehi Moriori Trust, photograph by Ashleigh Ryan

Bay of Plenty, Waikato, Taupō and Taranaki regions, and some scattered sites in regions as distant as the Far North and the southern Hawke's Bay.[2] The constrained distribution of the North Island sites, when compared to those in the south, has been variously attributed to the availability of appropriate rock surfaces; preference for the practice by closely related groups (those who speak western Māori dialects); and the limited national scope of archaeological surveys to date.[3] A comprehensive identification and examination of Aotearoa rock art sites is needed before a truly complete analysis of rock art motifs and their meanings can be achieved. Histories for a few rock art sites speak to the significance of the markings but for most only general observations are possible at this point in time.[4]

### Polynesian origins

Rock art was likely brought to Aotearoa as a practice from other parts of Polynesia, where it similarly represents the place associations and lifeways of people, and changed in character as people moved and developed their relationships with the landscape.[5] In his survey of research on Marquesan, Hawaiian, Rapanui and Moriori rock art, archaeologist Gerard O'Regan concluded that the practice was strongly associated with place marking – identifying or signposting or personifying different places such as important landscape features, trails, shelters or tapu areas.[6] Across Polynesia, rock art depicts patterns, faces, birds, bird-headed people and waka; there is regional variation in motifs, but commonalities are also evident.

Moriori rock engraving is a derivative of that wider Polynesian marking practice. The only currently recorded Moriori rock carving sites at Rēkohu Chatham Islands are around Te Whanga lagoon and appear to be stylised seal and bird images. The greatest concentration is at Te Ana a Nunuku (a cave named after an important ancestor), where curvilinear designs have been engraved over earlier, more angular examples.[7] Similar motifs appear on Moriori rākau momori, 'memorial trees', their living trunks culturally marked since at least the eighteenth century with images that also include people and abstract designs. The rākau momori are fruit-bearing kōpī trees that are thought to have been brought to Rēkohu by Moriori ancestors from Aotearoa (where they are known as karaka). They are now under threat from exposure to the weather after surrounding bush was

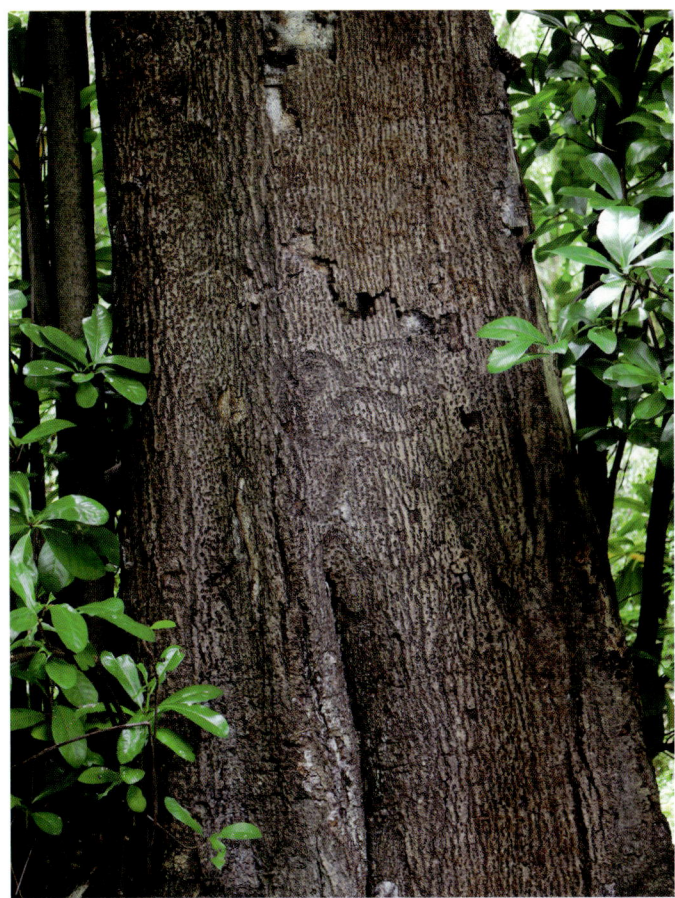

cleared: the number of rākau momori has declined from over 1000 before 1835 to fewer than 200 today.[8]

What is apparent in Rēkohu rock and tree marking – and may be of relevance in Māori rock art – is strong narrative and pictorial associations with ancestors at specific places.[9] The embellishment of inhabitable spaces with rock art is also seen on Rapanui Easter Island, where rock carvings and paintings of birdmen appear on the doorways, walls and ceilings of stone houses at 'Orongo, a site occupied between the eighteenth and nineteenth centuries, if not earlier.[10] It is tempting to speculate that there may be a relationship, through earlier precedents in Central Polynesia, between the 'Orongo stone house images and the manaia embellishments of pātaka and, later, the whare whakairo, although further research is required before these artistic and architectural origins can be confirmed. Indeed, Polynesian rock art research to date suggests that there was a common point of origin for the practice of rock art in the Polynesian home islands, which the ancestors of Māori, Morioricy, Hawaiian and Rapanui people took to the outer islands of Polynesia in order to inhabit, understand and personify landscapes and places.

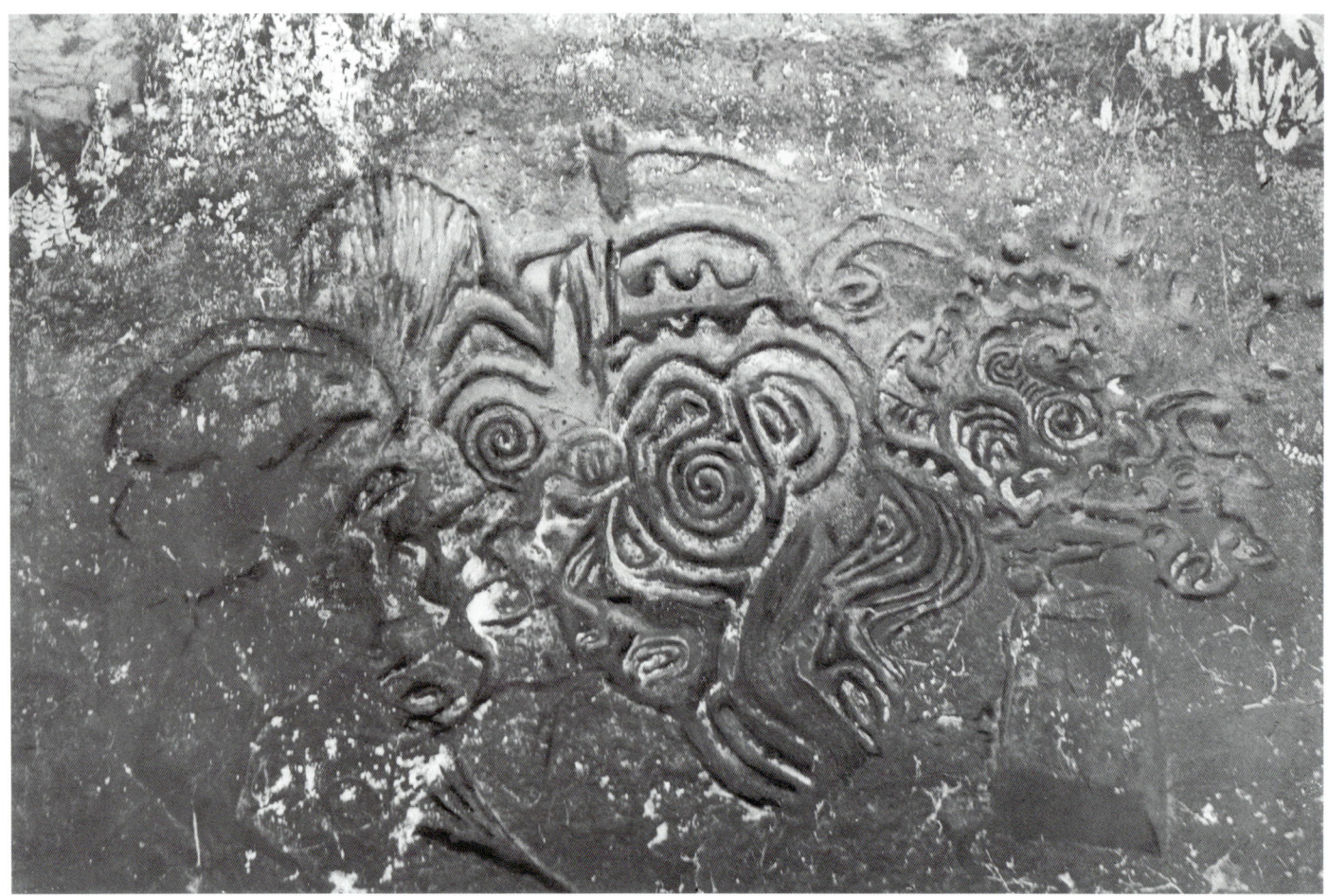

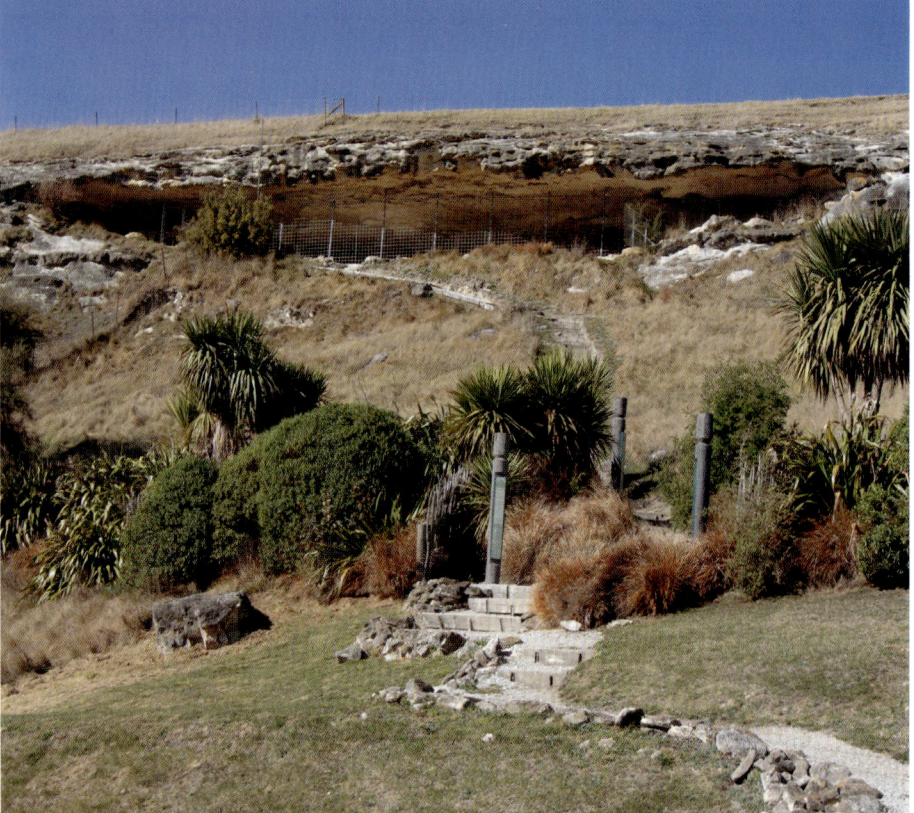

Above: Rock engraving at Kohi Gorge, Waverley, Taranaki.
photograph by Wal Ambrose

Left: Entrance to the Maerewhenua rock shelter site, Waitaki, with the shelter protected by caging visible at the top of the cliff face.
photograph by Matthew Hill, Ngāi Tahu Māori Rock Art Trust

Opposite top: People riding horses and sailing European-style vessels are the subjects of drawings in a small shelter near the larger Takiroa site.
photograph by Yann Pierre Montelle/Brian Allingham, Ngāi Tahu Māori Rock Art Trust

Opposite middle: A fleet of waka, some with fine koru detailing, were engraved into the shelter at Kaingaroa, one of the most well-known North Island rock art sites.
photograph by Wal Ambrose

Opposite bottom: Rock painting of multiple, perhaps an armada, of waka found buried under ash from the 1886 Mount Tarawera eruption.
photograph by Rob Brown

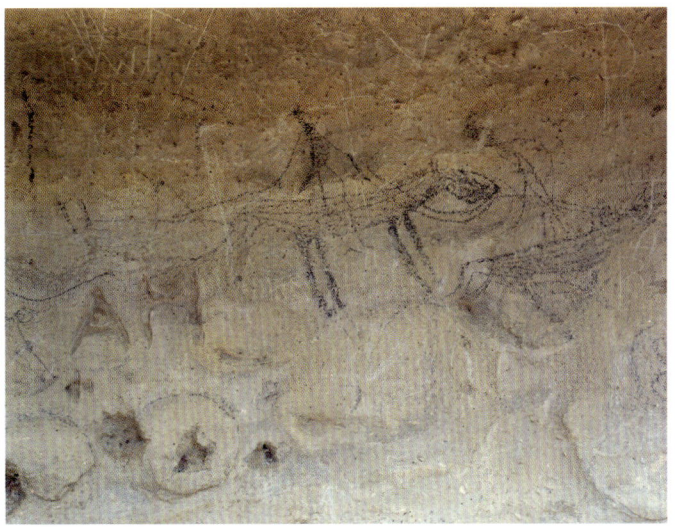
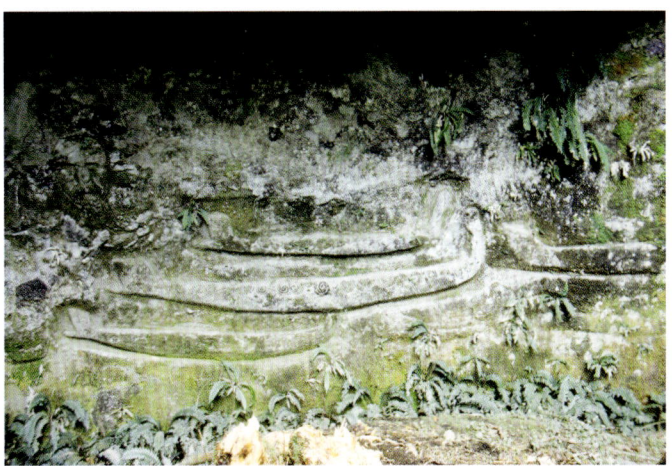
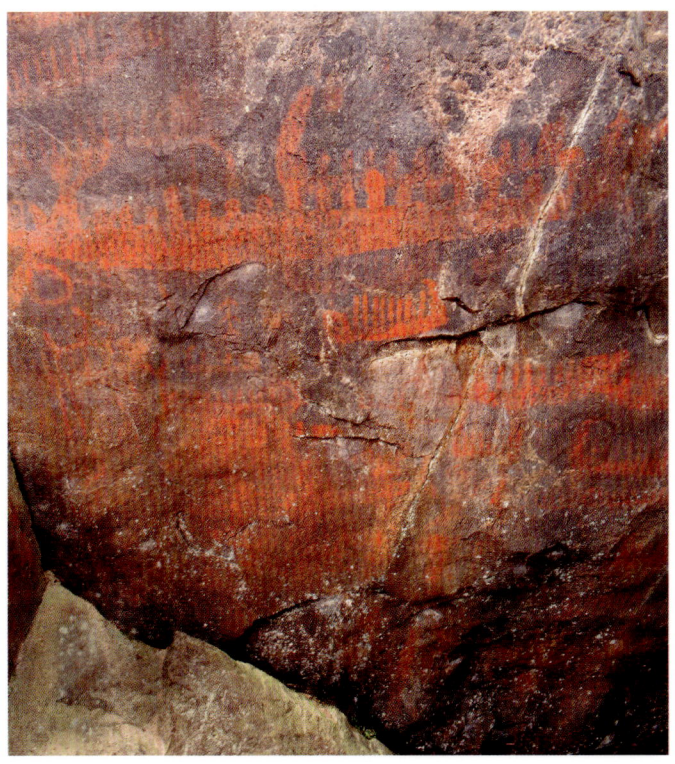

## Mahinga kai and media

Making Māori rock art was a purposeful activity: often the artists would have had to bring some of the materials and tools required for its creation with them.[11] In the South Island, Māori lived across their expansive landscape: wintering in coastal kāinga, where they survived on the bounty of the sea (seals, fish and shellfish), hunting birds in summer on the eastern and central plains, and traversing mountains to collect pounamu and other stones from the inland hills, West Coast, Fiordland and western Southland rivers and beaches. The most bountiful areas became mahinga kai, or landscapes to return to during summer hunts, and it was likely during expeditions to these places that people embellished their rocky environments, including the overhangs in which they also camped. Some of these sites were progressively decorated over many seasons, and perhaps centuries, by the Waitaha and then later Ngāti Māmoe and Ngāi Tahu people, who migrated from the North Island and eventually all became intertwined.[12] That some of the decorated shelters were used as camps is supported by evidence of hearths, bones and the detritus of everyday life found in the occupation layers of some decorated rock-shelter floors.[13] For many shelters, however, such evidence has been lost by over a century of stock trampling and erosion.

Images appear to have been applied as both dry drawings and wet paintings, using charcoal or soot for black pigment, and kōkōwai mixed with animal fat and vegetable gum for red pigment.[14] White markings were created by lightly scraping the weathered outer surface of limestone overhangs, a technique that also provided a light background for drawing. Relief work, rare in the South Island, is found in half of the North Island sites; there are currently only a few known examples of deeply carved rock.[15]

The importance of toi whenua as a deliberate art is evident in the creation and carrying of pigments and tools and the effort required to engrave often hard rock, and the illustration of the abundance and ancestry of the artists' world.

## Themes and styles

The themes of Māori rock art offer a glimpse into an ecosystem that no longer exists, within a cosmology that has survived. Animals were a repeated theme in South Island rock art: insects, dogs, fish, seals and birds, including the

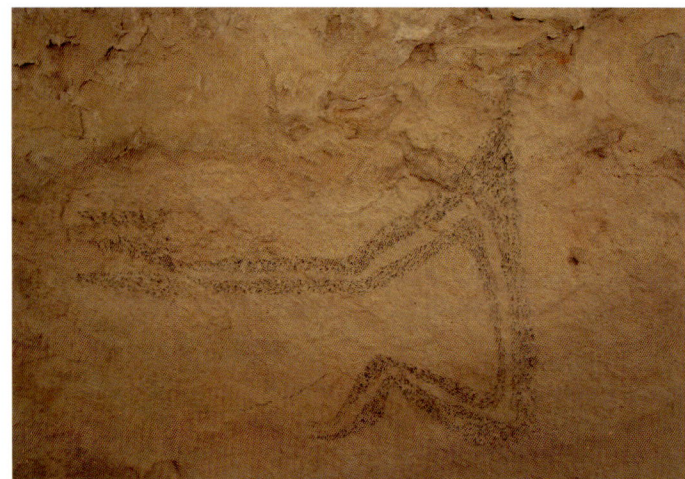
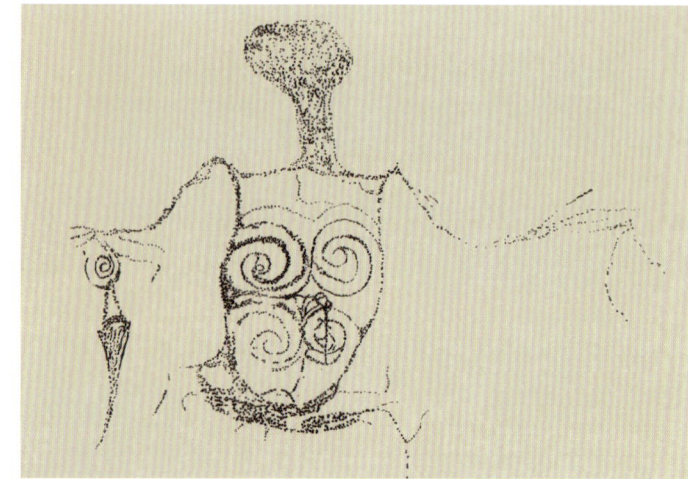

Top left: This profile tiki drawn on the ceiling of a rock shelter at Waipati, in Waitaki, features a large hand with three fingers, a digital arrangement typical of wood-carved figures.
photograph Matthew Hill, Ngāi Tahu Māori Rock Art Trust

Top right: A 'dot-for-dot' reproduction of the tiki from Maerewhenua shown on page 130 more clearly illustrates the entire figure.
illustration by Brian Allingham, Ngāi Tahu Māori Rock Art Trust

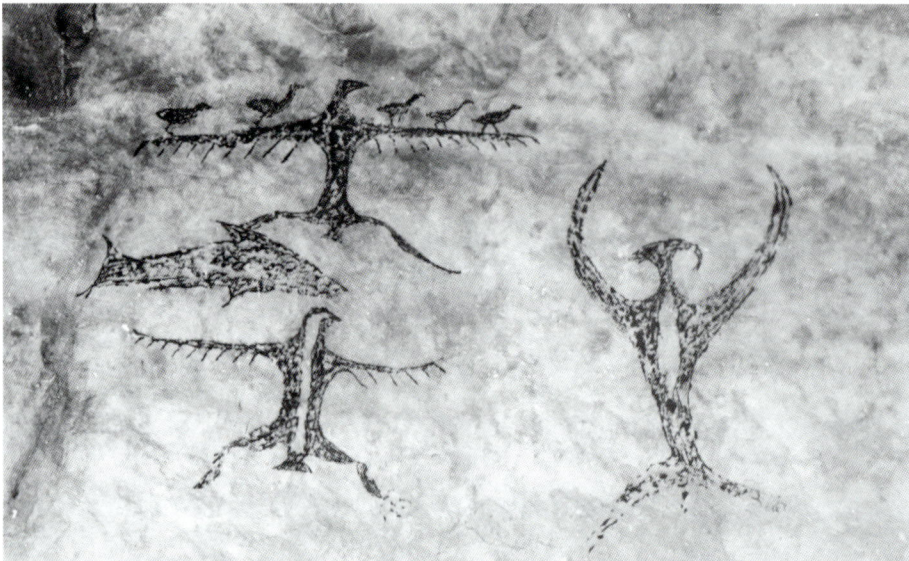

Two eagles, one with other birds on its wings, and a fish, from Te Manunui site, Maungati, inland from Timaru.
photograph by Hugh McCully, provided by Tūhura Otago Museum

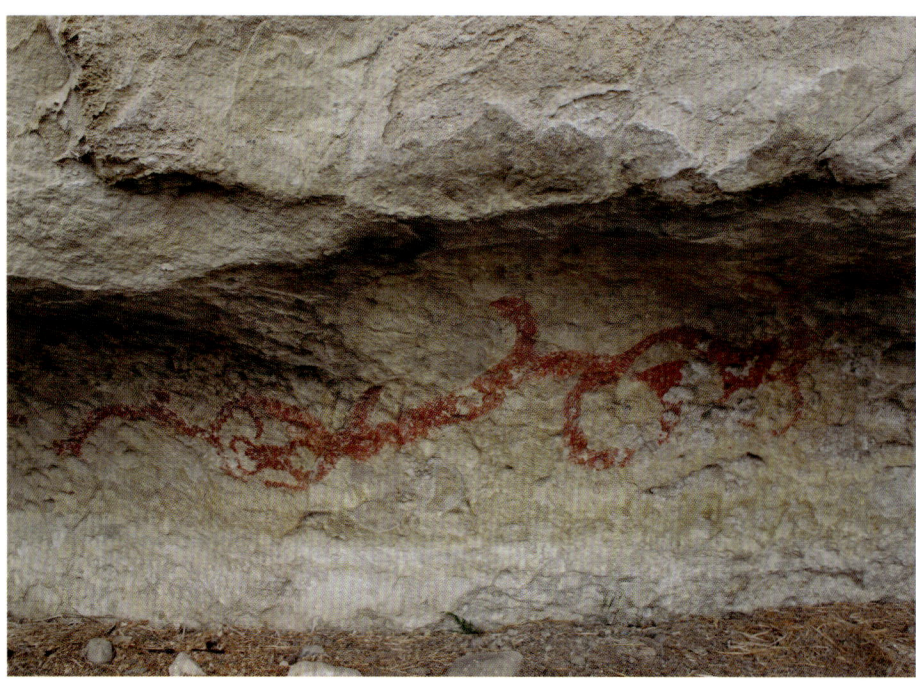

Detail of a long creature, perhaps a taniwha, at Takiroa, Waitaki. The intention to paint the site must have been planned, as the kōkōwai pigment had to be deliberately taken to the site and prepared into a paint.
photograph Yann Pierre Montelle/Brian Allingham, Ngāi Tahu Māori Rock Art Trust

now-extinct moa and perhaps the giant eagle; introduced species such as the horse; and taniwha and other wondrous supernatural creatures. Pictures of objects and abstract patterns and line work were other recurring motifs, but tiki are the most often represented subjects. In the North Island, waka – the vessels that connected and sustained communities – were a dominant theme, as were koru and tiki faces.[16] Although there is some similarity between North and South Island figures, there is also great variability between islands in the frequency of certain thematic concerns.[17]

The recurrence of the same stylised figures in sites across the South Island has led to a suggestion that they were produced by people in close artistic communication with each other. Humans were shown with bent legs and stick-figure or two-dimensional bodies, either outlined or infilled with the same pigment or white limestone. Occasionally there would be a combination of all these techniques: a figure might have a solid-colour body, the head outlined, and lines for arms and legs.[18] Bodies were either in profile or full-frontal. It is very rare for facial features to be depicted on human figures in South Island rock art. However faces, sometimes represented only by eyes, sometimes with nostrils and mouths, are widely depicted in North Island examples. As in whakairo rākau, some figures were shown with between two and seven fingers or toes, such as the footprint motifs from northern Taranaki. This indicates a shared perception of the human form across the two art practices rather than a sharing of technique, since tiki carvings were never common in South Island Māori art.[19]

Similarities to whakairo rākau and kōwhaiwhai are more common in rock art in the North Island, where these other art forms are more prevalent. The koru appears in over half of the known North Island rock art sites, but in only a few examples of South Island rock drawings. In the North Island, examples vary in complexity from single-line spirals to outlined koru, to double spirals. The spirals sometimes appear on the same elements in drawings of waka as they would in painting or carving on actual waka taua.[20] In a rare South Island example, at a site at Maerewhenua, Waitaki Valley, a human figure has four koru outlined on his torso – two on each side of the body; the koru on one side are a mirror image of the koru on the other. Reflection as a compositional device was also used in kōwhaiwhai. Other rectilinear and curvilinear patterns appear in South Island rock art, but in the absence of dates, we can only speculate as to whether they were in use concurrently or successively. Patterns include parallel or crossed lines and circular forms, and chevrons – a characteristic of early carving and body adornment – sometimes feature along the sides of bodies.[21] Subtle asymmetry appears in rock drawings of fish, lizards and dogs, which curve at one end despite being largely symmetrical down one axis.[22] Again, these similarities cannot be considered conclusive proof that carvings and paintings on wood and rock were directly influencing each other. However, they do at the very least appear to use compositional devices that derive from the same creative genesis.

In figurative rock art, human and non-human forms are largely the same, with subtle differences to indicate whether they are people, animals or fish:[23] those with tails, pointed ears, and arched bodies were most probably kurī; and some bird drawings are so naturalistic that they can be identified, such as species of moa, and raptors such as Haast's eagle and harrier hawks. Haast's eagle was the largest species of eagle in the world, with a 3m wingspan and weighing up to 14kg; it became extinct around the same time as the moa, about 500 years ago.[24] So-called 'birdmen', which appear to some viewers to combine the full-frontal bodies of people with in-profile bird heads and splayed wings, might otherwise be illustrations of raptors flying overhead or about to launch from a perch. Species of sea creatures are difficult to specifically identify, since these drawings could resemble either dolphins, sharks or other fish. There is, though, a clear similarity in form between the profile view of these drawings and the marine animals carved on a serpentine stone disc pendant found at Okains Bay on Banks Peninsula (Canterbury Museum, E148 79). To modern eyes, the human and non-human figurative drawings and paintings have little to differentiate them – a characteristic of rock art that suggests the makers used a standard formalism and recognised interconnection, either physically or spiritually, between humans and animals.

The figures, patterns and other motifs of rock art occasionally stretched along lengthy rock-shelter walls.[25] Rock artists were inventive image composers who worked within, and possibly outside of conventions normally associated with other Māori art forms. Although rock art does not depict landscapes, it does sometimes seem to illustrate

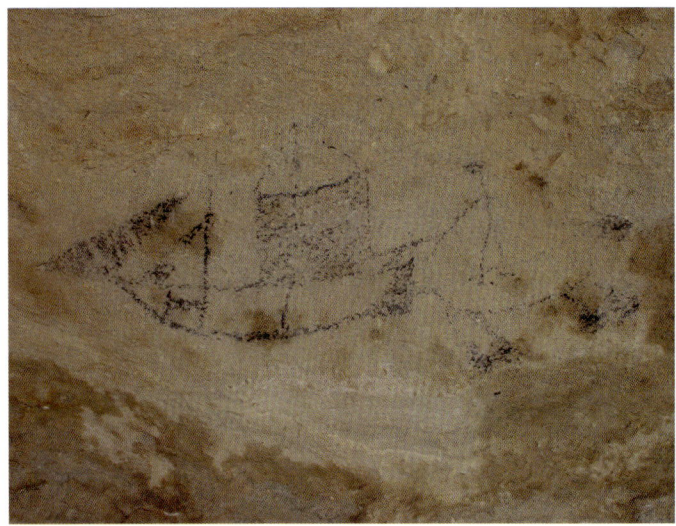

Rock artists depicted life and scenes from the wider world. A rigged ship and horse are images drawn in a small shelter at the Takiroa site.
photograph by Yann Pierre Montelle/Brian Allingham, Ngāi Tahu Māori Rock Art Trust

events – such as a shark eating a fish at the Takiroa site at Duntroon; people apparently hunting at the Ahuriri site in North Otago; and the depiction of European sailing ships.[26] A few rare examples show people holding clubs or sticks, but since the detail of these objects is limited they are located in a timeless continuum, rather than being indicative of a particular period. While South Island rock artists may have illustrated 'time' in a way that distinguished their art from that of the tohunga whakairo, both share a compositional similarity in that neither uses perspective.

This does not mean that rock art was not spatially complex: some images are so long that they are unable to be seen from a single vantage point. The taniwha drawn in black on a rock ceiling in Opihi, South Canterbury, is over 5m long and cannot be viewed all at once, even when the observer is lying on their back.[27] One pattern drawn at the Takiroa site is around 4m in length. These works suggest a conception of art that involved moving with the work in order to make – and perhaps also to appreciate – its significance, and a regard for subject matter and site that was beyond human scale. Whether these large works sought to appropriate these expansive landscapes into the human world, or to demonstrate that the artistic practice was larger than the human condition itself, is yet to be resolved.

The incursion of Pākehā culture into Aotearoa was documented on rock through the depiction of sailing ships, horses – and words. Local Te Aitanga a Hauiti people attributed drawings of boats and a ship among other Māori rock images in an Ūawa cave to Tupaia, the Tahitian priest who arrived with Cook in 1769 and who liked to nap in the cave with local Māori.[28] The words 'KOTAINUI' – in apparent reference to the great migratory vessel *Tainui* – are carved into rock with an image of a waka near Tokoroa, in the Waikato region; and the names of South Canterbury Māori who may have been supporters of the late-nineteenth-century Māori spiritual and political leader Hipa Te Maihāroa were painted on the shelter walls at Opihi. Te Maihāroa's practice of lifting the tapu on sites to demonstrate the mana of his mission and make them safe for ordinary use has led O'Regan to speculate that the names were those of local people who were either involved with him or felt able to use these places following the removal of tapu.[29] The incorporation of text as an identifying and, therefore, enhancing element was an important contemporaneous development in moko and in carved and painted whare whakairo design, too, and its use in rock art is considered a natural progression of the practice rather than vandalism, idle scrawling or evidence of its decline.

While most known rock-art sites are shallow caves or rock overhangs, where artists and their work were sheltered, other less accessible or more exposed sites have also been decorated.[30] At a few sites, rock art was drawn onto the surfaces of extremely narrow crevices. Many North Island petroglyphs are engraved on free-standing boulders, some on open beach fronts; in South Canterbury and around Lake Taupō, rock art has even been found on cliff faces 6–10m above the ground or lake surface. Some sheltered caves featuring rock art would not have been habitable – one site in the Maerewhenua River valley in North Otago, for example, has a steeply sloping floor.[31] In other instances, rock art in habitable shelters extends from the inside of the caves to their openings, which indicates that it may have continued outside shelters before it was erased by weather or erosion. Indeed, traces of South Island rock art have generally been found in almost all areas where there is a suitable smooth surface.

In some instances, rather than retouching damaged or fading images, Māori who were reoccupying a site would draw over the top of them. Archaeologist Atholl Anderson has noted that, 'since the newer figures were frequently in red, the colour of tapu, this might signify an hiatus in ancestral continuity requiring new settlers to protect themselves from the ritual danger of earlier drawings and ancestors and also to establish their own rights to the land'.[32] According to Anderson's theory, these changes may have represented a form of whakanoa, in which the original tapu was removed and made noa in order to be supplanted with another person's or group's tapu and mana. In North Otago some later designs appear to have been purposefully integrated with earlier work, creating an accumulation of meaning and perhaps also tapu.[33] Elsewhere in the region, artists wrote greetings in te reo, perhaps directed to ancestors of a place, using the roman font style popularised by early printed versions of the Māori Bible.[34] Nevertheless, the tapu of these sites was overwhelming for some nineteenth-century South Island Māori travellers, who avoided sheltering in the marked places.[35]

We do not know for certain why rock art was made. There are few surviving ancestral narratives about its meaning and purpose, and the major research projects written before the 1980s are somewhat dated in their interpretation. As O'Regan notes, 'this has resulted in a dichotomy of essentialist assertions as to the character of Māori rock art that remains unresolved and constrains consideration of how it may or may not relate to the beliefs Māori had of places'.[36] In 1868, surveyor Walter Mantell proposed that rock images were painted by moa hunters.[37] However, archaeological investigations have shown that very few rock-art sites were directly associated with moa hunting; they were instead probably used by people securing other types of food and resources and moving across their landscape.[38] Moa are also not a common theme in the drawings.

Theo Schoon, the New Zealand artist of Dutch descent who undertook a government-sponsored survey of Māori rock art between 1946 and 1948, described the caves as New Zealand's first 'art galleries'.[39] He argued that there was no simple, everyday interpretation for the drawings – naturalistic or stylised. He speculated that figures such as the taniwha were metaphors for the spirit world and death; and that groups of human figures may have represented whakapapa. The drawings he studied inspired Schoon's own art practice and that of his friend Gordon Walters (see 'Māori art as a cultural property', page 505), who visited Schoon's South Island expedition in 1946. They also provoked a very public dismissal of the mana of rock art by the director of the Canterbury Museum, Roger Duff, who believed the practice to be idle doodling – an idea that has since been discredited.[40] When artist Tony Fomison surveyed rock art sites in 1959 for the South Canterbury Historic Places Trust, he found something even more concerning: evidence of the extent to which Schoon had 'touched up' some of the images with crayon, sometimes conflating overlaying images as one – thus further confounding their interpretation.[41] Work since then, primarily led by archaeologists, has focused on the relationship of rock art and its artists to the landscape – but the meaning and purpose of the imagery in rock art remains elusive.[42]

## Rock art revisited

The decline in rock art practice and recent rise in interest in its conservation can be charted against the trials, tribulations and triumphs experienced by Māori since Pākehā arrival. The diminishment of customary harvesting grounds and practices due to reduced access in the wake of land purchases by Pākehā and the consequential dramatic alteration of ecosystems – through land clearances and the introduction of predatory species – were factors in the decline of rock art, certainly in the South Island, and possibly also in the North. The art itself has not weathered the vicissitudes of time well: rain, floods, 'collectors' (such as James Elmore, who chiselled off rock drawings around the Aoraki region in 1916),[43] vandals, grazing sheep and cattle, and other damaging activities have all taken their toll on the images.

From the 1840s, Ngāi Tahu were forced to occupy 'native reserves' – small areas of unproductive land that made them dependant on Pākehā for food and employment. It was not until 1996, almost 150 years after they engaged in the first of several attempts to solicit redress for their situation, that Ngāi Tahu signed a deed of settlement with the Crown. It included a formal apology to the iwi, along with $170 million in compensation, and the right to legally effect their kaitiakitanga through vesting Ngāi Tahu with the ownership of pounamu and the right to protect and manage some parts of their original cultural landscapes.[44] Today, Ngāi Tahu is undergoing a major cultural revival. Although rock art is no longer an active practice, the South Island Māori Rock Art Project has been a Ngāi Tahu tribal initiative to maintain the ahi kā (continuous customary occupancy) of these sites through their documentation and protection, and has added 300 more sites to the record since 1990.[45] The project is currently managed by the Ngāi Tahu Rock Art

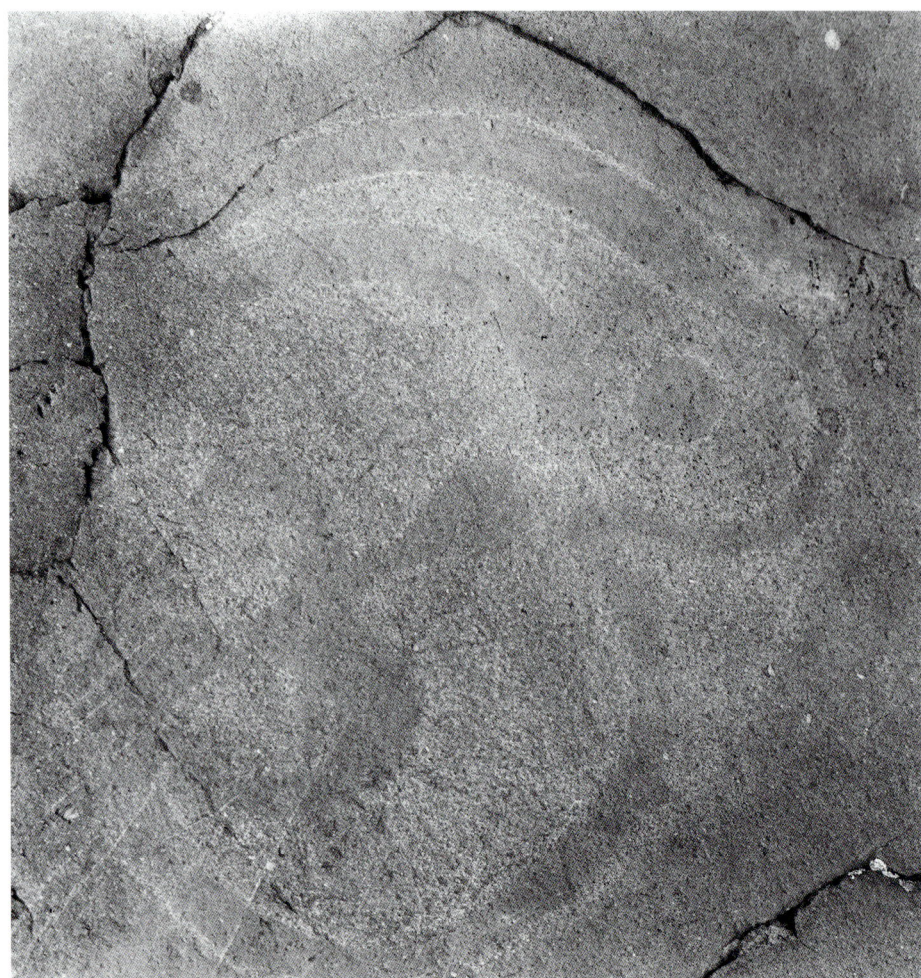

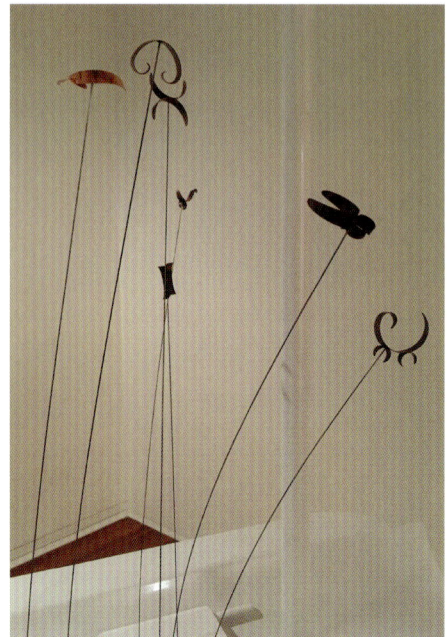

Top left: This black pigment work from Shepherds Creek, Waitaki, has been widely interpreted as a kiwi chick still in its egg.
photograph by Wal Ambrose

Top right: **Areta Wilkinson, *Star Whata: Space Odyssey 2021*, as installed at the Dunedin Public Art Gallery in 2022**
mixed media, 2500 x 1900 x 1300mm, photograph by Studio La Gonda

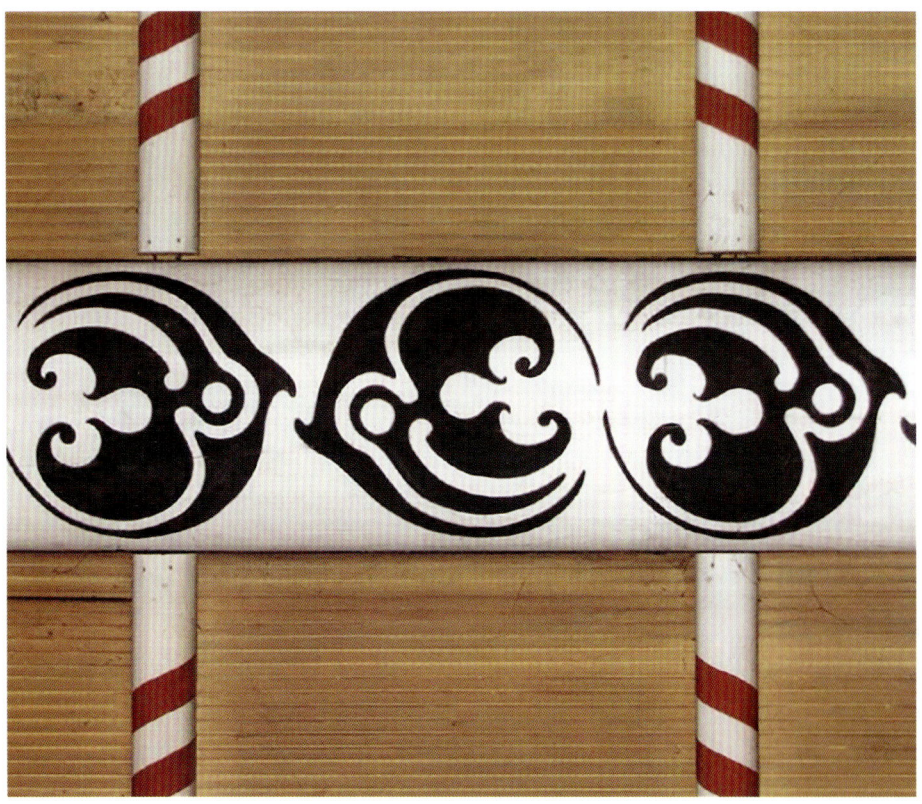

The kiwi embryo drawing from the Shepherds Creek site inspired the kōwhaiwhai paintings on the heke of Te Whatu Manawa Māoritanga o Rehua wharenui, opened in 1960 at Rehua Marae, Christchurch.
photograph by Gerard O'Regan

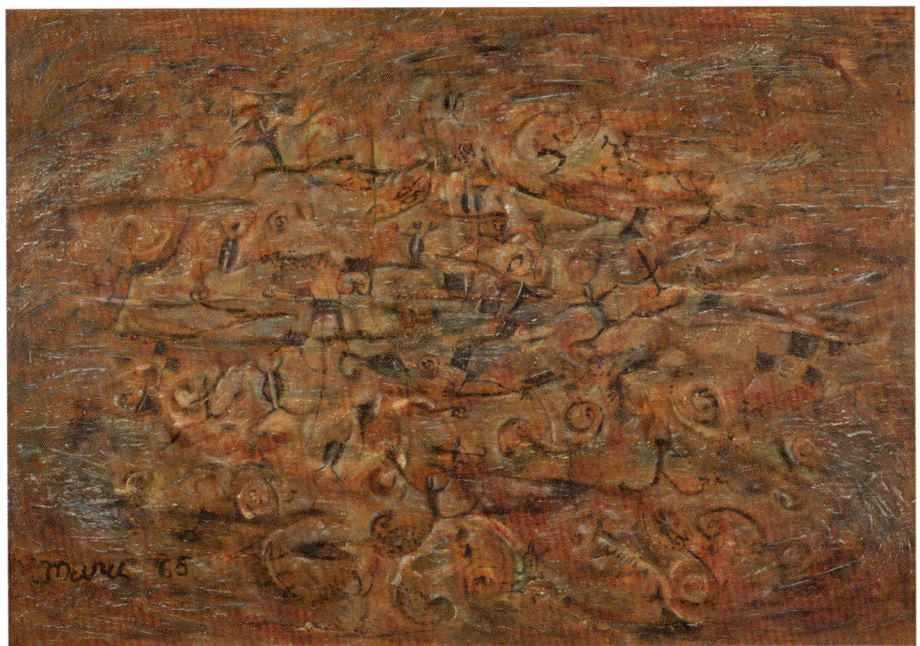

Inspired by South Island Māori rock art, Selwyn Muru's 1965 painting *Kohatu* was shown at both the Christchurch and Hamilton contemporary Māori art exhibitions in 1966. It was the first painting by a modern Māori artist to be acquired for the national art collection.
**Selwyn Muru,** *Kohatu,* **1965**
oil on hardboard, 795 x 1203mm, Te Papa Tongarewa Museum of New Zealand, 1965-0020-1, purchased 1965

Trust, which also operates the Te Ana rock art venture and its research, education and visitor centre in Timaru. Embracing Schoon's words, the Te Ana website proudly describes the Ngāi Tahu rock art caves as 'the original art galleries of Aotearoa'.[46]

O'Regan observes that for Ngāi Tahu, 'Rock-art represents a visual art heritage for a people who have not maintained the Māori wood carving traditions for which the North Island tribes are renowned'.[47] Rock-art images have pervaded other aspects of Ngāi Tahu art and inspired generations of artists who have incorporated them into the costumes of Dunedin's Ārai Te Uru kapa haka group and the moko of some iwi members.[48] A kiwi embryo image from Shepherds Creek was the inspiration for the kōwhaiwhai rafter paintings in Te Whatu Manawa Māoritanga o Rehua wharenui opened in 1960 at Rehua Marae and later at the Aoraki wharenui at Ngā Hau e Whā national marae, both in Christchurch. The image was originally painted by an artist leaning down from a ledge, and was documented in the late 1950s before the Waitaki Valley was flooded for the Benmore hydroelectric dam project. It has also been used in Ngāi Tahu graphic design to symbolise regeneration.[49] Areta Wilkinson's (Ngāi Tahu) 2022 installation *Star Whata: Space Odyssey 2021* at the Dunedin Public Art Gallery reimagined South Island rock art figures as three-dimensional forms, thus bringing them into a whakapapa that includes contemporary Māori art. These are modern-day accumulations of rock art meaning, recovered and, some might argue, secularised in the same way that whakairo rākau has found new locations, purposes and meanings for the needs of the times.[50]

### Conclusion

Although the meanings and purposes of individual rock art illustrations may remain enigmatic and elusive, its larger purpose of making sense of the land is becoming much more evident. This was an art brought from Polynesia that enabled place associations and personification to occur in specific localities, yet was adaptable enough to change as people moved between islands. In Aotearoa, the spiritual world melded with that of the mortal, with supernatural creatures mingling with hunters and the hunted, using techniques that sit beside those of the tohunga whakairo, tohunga tā moko and kōwhaiwhai painter. Rock artists laid down their illustrations like moko on the whenua, living not just on the land but in it, taking occupancy and possession of even the most remote and inaccessible places. Understanding rock art unlocks the cultural history of the landscapes it is set in, and its documentation and regeneration in new media is an important activity for the reclamation of Māori identity.

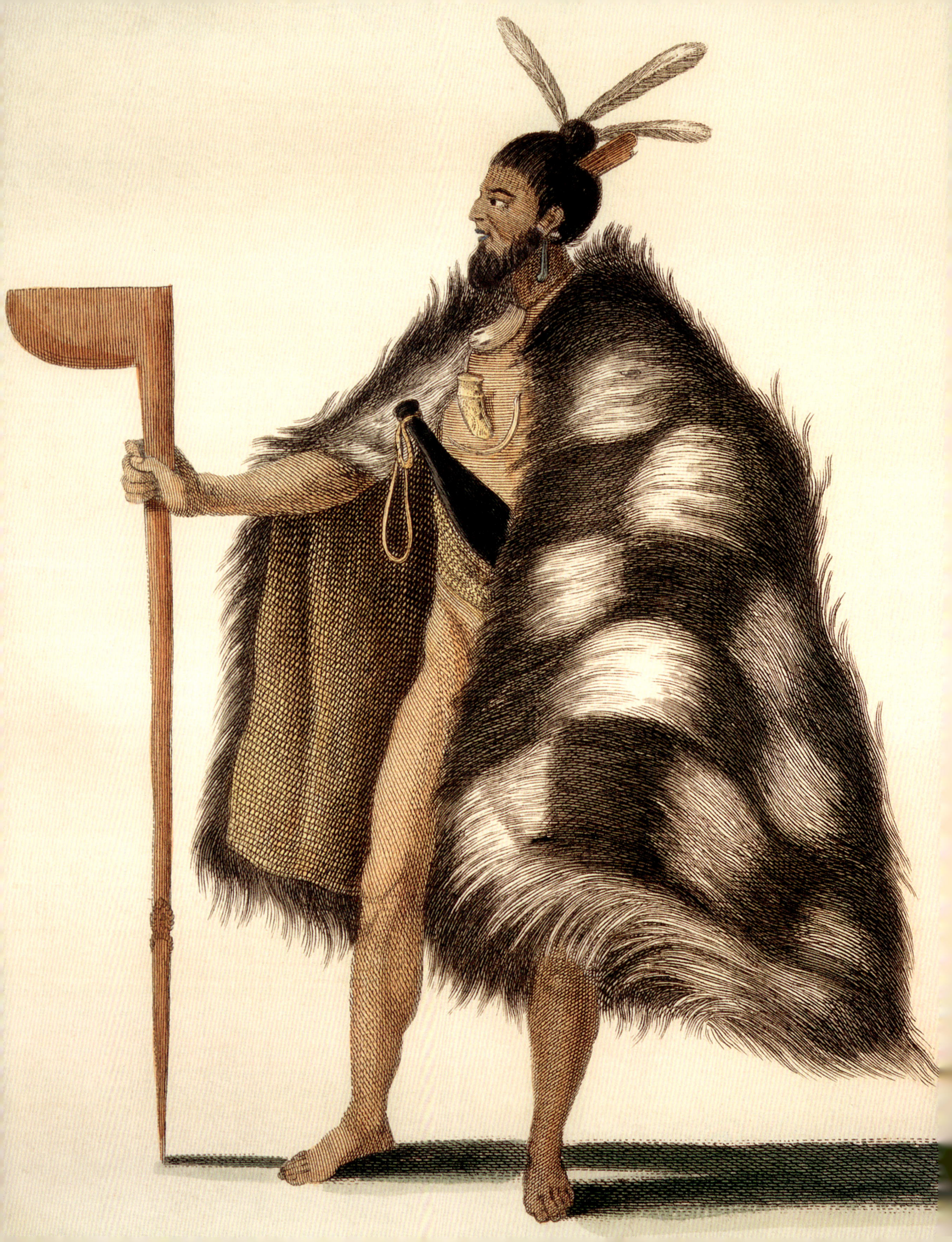

# 6 NGĀ TAONGA O WHARAWHARA
## BODY ADORNMENT
### NGARINO ELLIS

*Kia hei taku ate i te tau o tana tiki,*
*Kia tia whakaripa i te kotore huia*
*Kia kahu purua i te neko pakipaki*
*Ka pai au te hoki ki te koko i Whangaroa!*

*Let my heart be hung about the string of his hei tiki*
*And my head adorned on both sides with huia plumes*
*Let me be dressed luxuriously in a bordered cloak*
*That I may look well as I return to the bay at Whangaroa!*

—Sung by an important woman who lived at Whangaroa in the Lake Rotoehu area, when she would receive a visitor from Ahuriri (Napier)[1]

This image gives some idea of what was expected in terms of formal attire in the late eighteenth century. This man's status as a rangatira is reinforced by his dress: a wooden heru (comb) and three feathers in his topknot, a rei puta (whale-tooth adornment) and whalebone kōauau (flute) suspended around his neck, a greenstone kapeu (ear adornment) and piece of rolled tapa in his ear, mere pounamu in his tātua (belt), wooden tewhatewha (staff) in his hand, and a magnificent kahu kurī (dogskin cloak) around his shoulders, held together with a bone aurei (cloak pin).

**Sydney Parkinson, *A New Zealand warrior in his proper dress & compleatly armed according to their manner*, engraved by Thomas Chambers, 1784**

engraving, hand-coloured, 227 x 184mm, Alexander Turnbull Library, PUBL-0037-15, from Sydney Parkinson, *A journal of a voyage to the South Seas, in his Majesty's ship, 'The Endeavour'*. Faithfully transcribed from the papers of the late Sydney Parkinson. London; Printed for Charles Dilly, in the Poultry, and James Phillips, in the George-Yard, 1784

A feather worn in the septum, a live bird slowly dying in the ear, a whalebone comb to dress the head … Māori used body adornment in many ways to communicate their political, social and economic status. Personal adornment here includes physical objects worn on the body (including in piercings), and associated practices such as moko (designs inked on the skin), tangihaehae (laceration of the skin in mourning), and mata whakarewa (skin painting). Some of these methods of body decoration are still practised today; others are known now only through oral histories and early Pākehā written accounts, perhaps waiting to be re-practised once more.

The first Europeans to visit Aotearoa were avid collectors of adornments, as they were visibly and distinctively Māori, and their size made them easily portable. A provisional report from 2021 has identified a phenomenal 3446 adornments and the containers they were kept in (waka huia and papahou) in eighty-eight museums globally.[2] Many physical detachable adornments are special as named taonga tuku iho (ancestral treasures) iho that have been handed down through whānau, connecting ancestors with present-day generations. They are made from natural materials, notably whalebone and pounamu, which have great mana in their own right. Adornments become works of art through their aesthetic qualities and the highly developed skills involved in their making, as well as the kōrero tuku iho that are attached to them. Rākai (adornment) is worn today to celebrate Māori identity, and to symbolise the retention of different forms of mātauranga through the making and remaking of art forms.

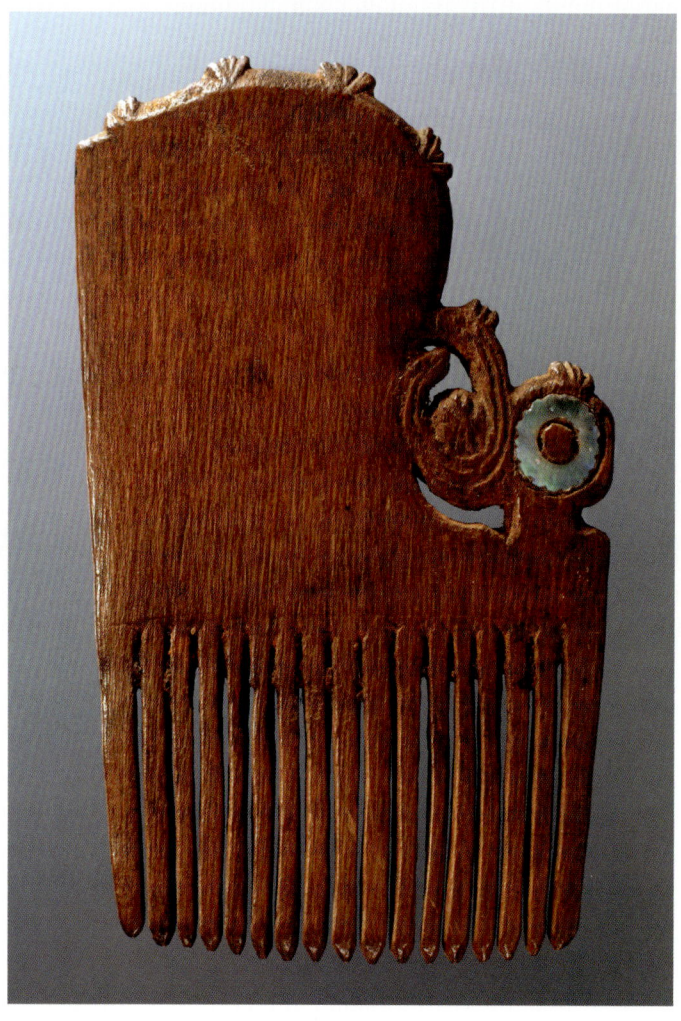

These two heru (combs) were collected by Johann Reinhold Forster, a naturalist, and his son Georg, an artist, who travelled on Captain James Cook's second voyage. The milky whalebone comb is a smaller version of a larger adornment called a titireia, which would have been worn by chiefly persons such as Paikea. The wooden one-piece heru is remarkable for the series of notches on its upper edge, and the manaia with a pāua-inlaid eye along one side. The ornamentation makes this of higher value than simpler examples. Both heru would have been tapu, as they were worn to decorate the tikitiki (topknot) on the most sacred part of the Māori body, the head.
bone, 155 x 75mm, Inv. Oz 293; wood, pāua shell, 101 x 62mm, Inv. Oz 292; National Museum of Australia

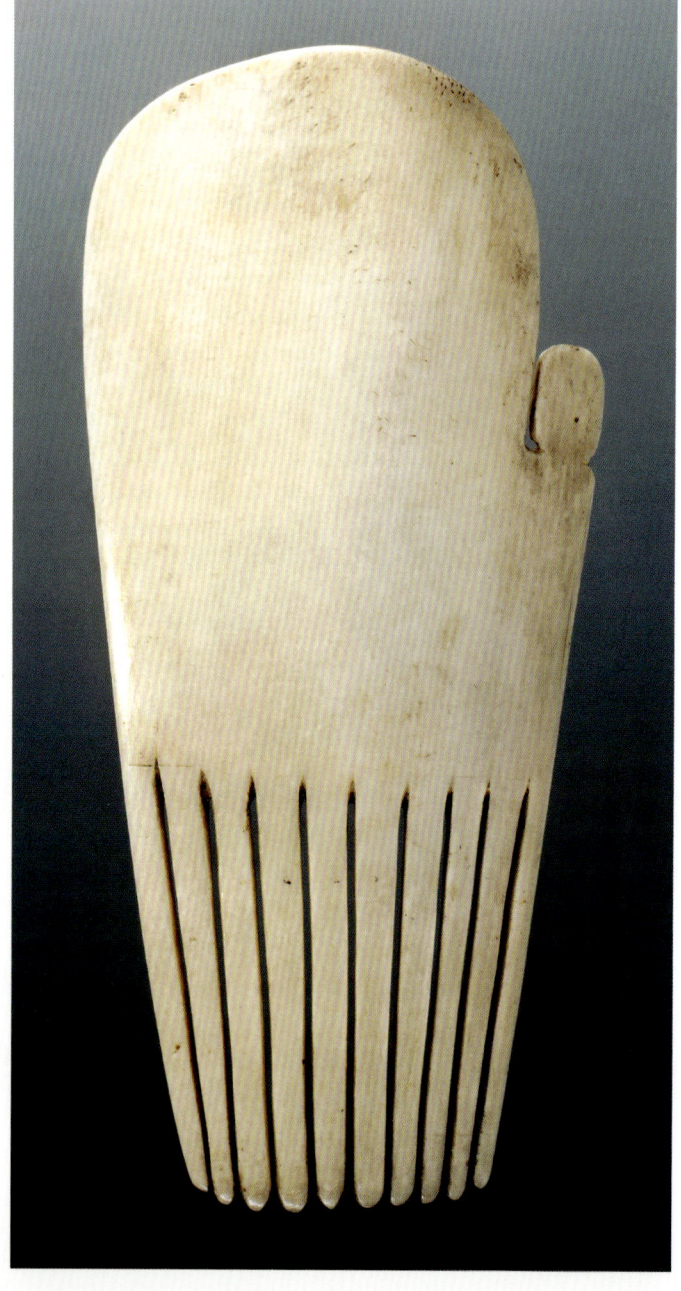

### Celestial and ancestral origins

Oral histories record a plethora of adornment forms and practices, as well as information about the origins of particular materials used in adornment. Tūhoe historian Rawinia Higgins recounts the story of moko: how the deity Niwareka was a tūrehu (spirit) who married Mataora, who was from Te Ao Tūroa (the realm of earth and sky – this world).[3] One day Mataora hit Niwareka in the face and she fled to her father Uetonga in the underworld of Rarohenga. Uetonga was a tohunga tā moko, and was himself a descendant of Rūaumoko: this gave him the right to perform this art. Mataora's face paint was messy from the sweat of his travels, and he asked Uetonga if he could receive a moko in order to prove his love for Niwareka. Afterwards, she did not recognise him, as his face was swollen from the process of tā moko; she knew him only by the cloak he was wearing, which she had made for him. She was finally persuaded to return to Te Ao Tūroa with him, to which he brought the knowledge of the designs for pōngiangia (spirals on the nostrils), pīhere (by the mouth), ngū (spiral on the upper nose) and tīwhana (on the forehead) – an entire art form represented by a few motifs.

Ngāi Tahu have their own version of the origins of moko. In this narrative, Tamanuiāraki, who is described as an ugly man, travelled to the place of the ancestors Tūmaunga and Tūwhenua in his efforts to become handsome and win back the affections of his wahine Rukutia, who had run away with the very handsome Tū Te Koropanga. Once he arrived, Tamanuiāraki was transformed into a rangi paruhi, a person with a full-face mataora, and won Rukuhia's affections once more.[4]

Other stories are also tribally specific: Ngāti Porou carver and moko artist Mark Kopua points to the origin of the word moko as being from the ancestor Rūaumoko's name: 'Rūaumoko was responsible for the deep uneven grooves left within the surface terrain of their primal parent, Papa-tūā-nuku. In short, they witnessed a natural form of moko.'[5] Higgins identifies other atua origins of moko, too, including one that relates how the deity Māui Tikitiki a Taranga placed moko on his dog's nose using his uhi (chisel).[6] The variety of narratives reflects a diversity across communities, and a rich and complex oral history network.

Ancestors in Hawaiki wore a number of important adornments. One of the best-known stories relates to a sacred comb worn by Paikea, one of the many sons of the ariki Uenuku. Paikea's brother by a different mother, Ruatapu, was jealous of the attention given to his tuakana (elder sibling), symbolised in his wearing of the heru: he sought to acquire it for himself and, by extension, the mana and tapu – the recognition from his father – that he craved. He tricked his brothers into going fishing with him; but first he sabotaged their waka and, when they were out of sight of land, he caused the waka to sink, drowning all his siblings except his tuakana. Paikea called on the paikea, a form of whale, to help him: he sat on the paikea's back (or some say transformed himself into the whale) and fled to Aotearoa, where he became an important ancestor for people on the East Coast. This is a distinctly Ngāti Porou narrative, and carvings of him typically include a whale and the comb.

The oral record identifies a person called a wharawhara who was 'an ancient expert in the art of personal decoration, including tattooing' – today, we might call them a stylist in that they were responsible for dressing a person, presumably high-born, in order to send specific messages about their political mana. The term 'Wharawhara' also appears in other mōteatea. One Ngāti Porou oriori (lullaby) describes, 'Nau te mau mai i nga taonga o Wharawhara' ('You are bedecked with the ornaments of Wharawhara'),[7] and a Te Arawa lament for Te Rangihīroa refers to 'the pricks of Wharawhara'.[8] This named person might be a deity of moko, or indeed of adornment.

Adornment was often conceived of as a metaphor for a person and their death. In the Te Arawa lament for Te Kuruotemārama, a single plume is a metaphor for the feather's 'withdrawal' – in this case referring to their death.[9] Similarly, in the Ngāti Porou lament for Tāneuarangi, the composer, Hone Rongomaitu, writes 'ngaro noa te puhipuhi' ('lost will be the plumes')[10] and later 'pae noa ki te ngutuawa, e/Te Kura a Mahina' ('washed ashore at the river's mouth/like the plume of Mahina').[11] The Ngāti Maniapoto lament for Te Hiakai cries for 'taku ate hoki ra, taku piki kotuku' ('you were my heart, my kōtuku plume').[12]

'Moko', Moana Maniapoto (Ngāti Tūwharetoa, Tūhourangi, Ngāti Pikiao), 2003

Tenei matou te hunga moko e tu nei i roto i tenei ao
Hurihuri ao tangata

*Chorus:*
I wear my pride upon my skin
My pride has always been within
I wear my strength upon my face
Comes from another time and place
Bet you didn't know that every line has a message for me
Did you know that

The word tattoo describes the marking of patterns by
Inserting coloured dyes under a smooth skin
The word moko represents a traditional custom in which
Spirals unique to Maori are carved deeply below the skin's
Surface to produce a groove scar – did you know that

Because the head the most sacred part of the body was touched
blood spilt the whole ceremony was tapu
The tip of a birdbone chisel dipped into sooty black pigment
Tapped by a beater to the sound of songs created to soothe
The painful process of creating moko so don't use that word tattoo

Every spiral has a name every line on the face don't use that word tattoo

*Chorus*

The classic Maori moko has the male bearing complex spirals on
Both cheeks both sides of the nose
Lines spread between the eyes to the temple the nose to the chin
Over nineteen names have been identified for different parts of the pattern
Women received kauae or chin moko
some copied their mothers or grandmothers

others allowed the artist to express their creativity
The moko indicated genealogy, rank, accomplishment
It represented masculinity, beauty, warriorhood, identity
So don't use that word tattoo

*Chorus*

The moko reflected the carvings and rafter patterns inside the whare tipuna
but some were made so distinctive they were like an autograph
a beautiful signature written all over the face
In 1815 Te Pehi Kupe drew his own moko without the aid of a mirror
every line firmly in his mind and then he drew the moko
Of his brother and his son

Did you know that

The moko reflected the Maori way of life
everything was connected, religion, war, lovemaking and death
For this generation, the kauae and moko were only seen in paintings
but now those images have come to life
Netana Whakaari said in 1921
You can lose your most valuable property through misfortune in various ways
you may be robbed of all your prized possessions
but of your moko you cannot be deprived
It will be your ornament and your companion until your last day
so don't use that word tattoo

*Chorus*

Korero ki nga tamariki tenei kaupapa ta moko he taonga
Tuku iho ki nga tipuna

Gordon Toi, *Mataora*, n.d.
photograph by Patricia Steur

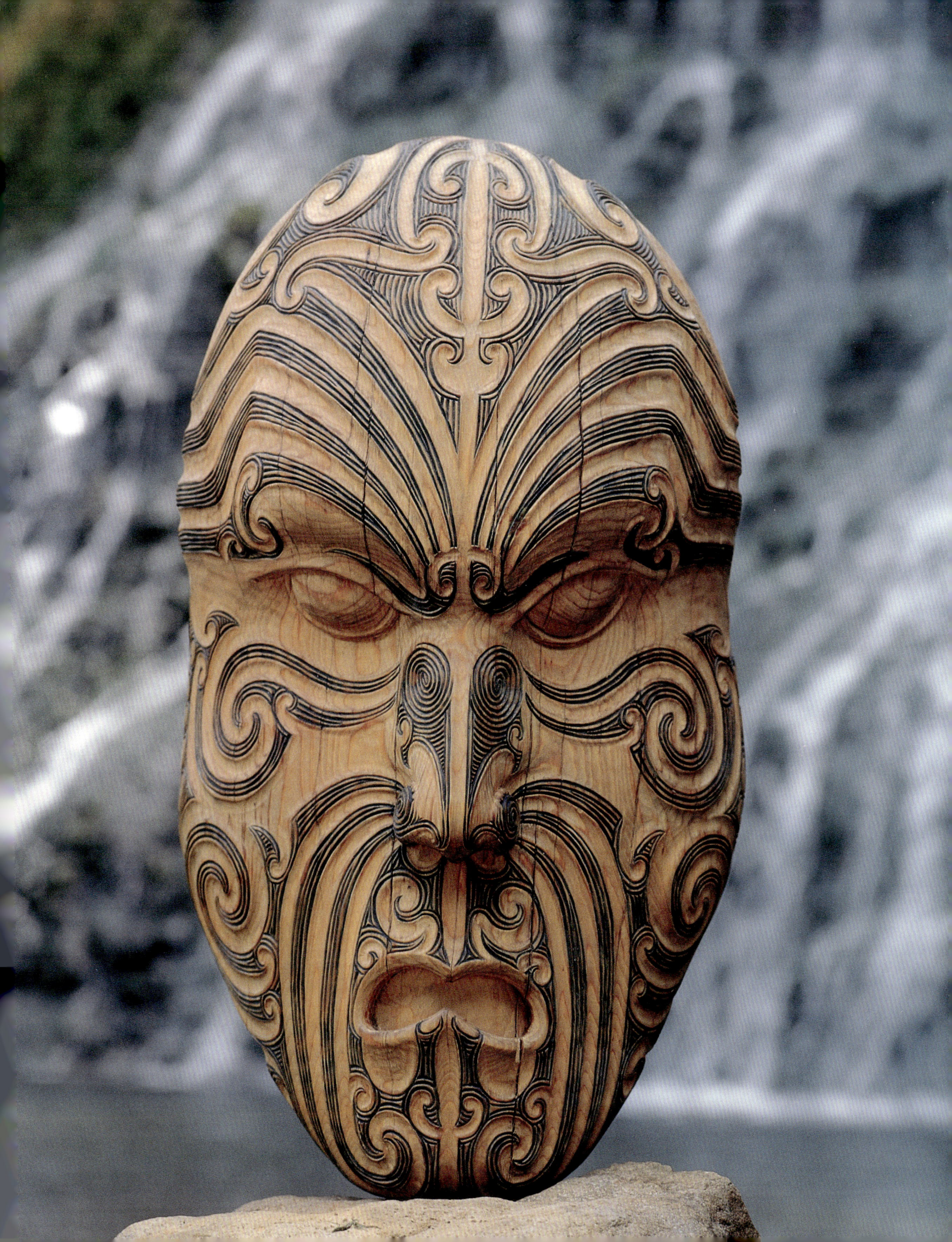

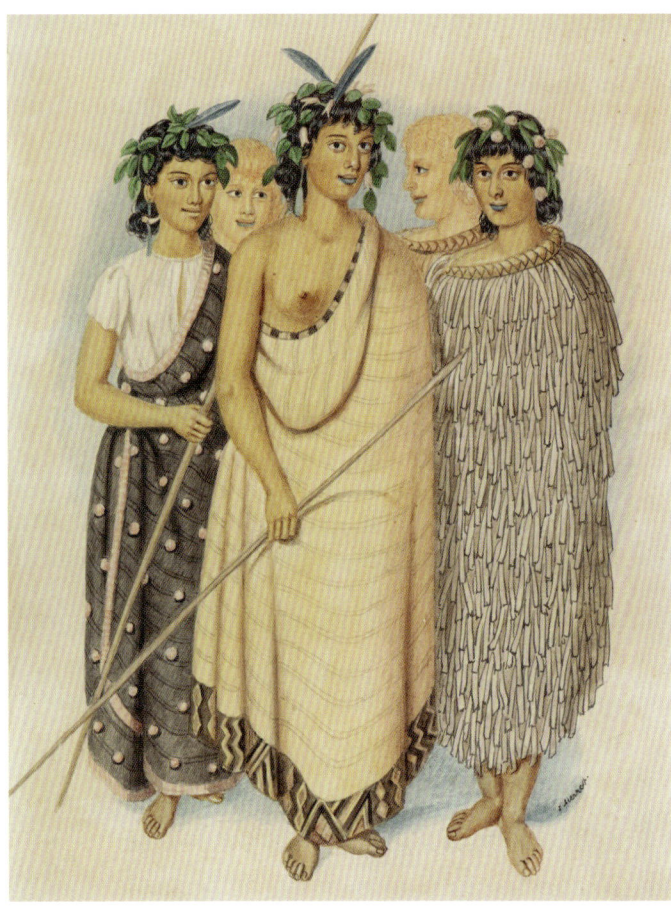

Joseph Merrett drew Māori around the country when not working as a surveyor, although he was initially based in Auckland in the 1840s. His work caught the attention of Governor George Grey, who became his patron for three years (1845–1847); those works are now in the British Museum ('The New Zealand Pictorial Scrap Book'). Though drawn smiling, these women wear a range of headdresses usually made for tangihanga; the one of the far left is a pare kawakawa, while the other two women at the front wear headdresses with delicate pink blooms, suggesting a happier moment.

**Joseph Jenner Merrett,** *Group of Maori Women,* **1850**
watercolour, pen and ink on paper, 241 x 183mm, Hocken Collections Uare Taoka o Hākena, University of Otago, 4,326 f

Opposite: Natural materials were celebrated in necklace form. From left: human teeth, sharks' teeth and notched pāua shell. By the eighteenth century, mako teeth would be worn only singly, as earrings.
British Museum, Oc1895,-.156 EOC8615 193783001

## Pacific antecedents of Māori adornment

We can track how early Pacific culture evolved into Māori culture over the centuries by examining the changes in styles, uses and materials of adornment. Personal adornment was important throughout the Pacific. Materials carried meaning in themselves, due to their social and economic value. Some were locally sourced, but others – such as animal materials – were traded throughout the Pacific. Red feathers from birds from Fiji were sent to artists in Tonga, who traded them on to makers in Sāmoa.[13] The teeth of sperm whales were particularly sought after, and were worn as body adornment to designate the high status of the wearer. Sisi (necklaces of sperm whale teeth) were made in Fiji from whale teeth sourced through trade exchange from Tonga, which only added to the social and economic value of the ornament.[14]

Artists made adornments from raw materials such as teeth and bones from dolphins, seals, sharks, birds and dogs – and, sometimes, human bones – as well as shell, tortoiseshell and seeds. Adornments were worn for a variety of reasons and occasions. They enhanced the beauty of the wearer, signalled their affiliations and marked key moments in their lives. A number of forms of adornment that were popular across the Pacific were either not brought to Aotearoa or were made only during the earliest period of settlement: only a small number have been found in archaeological excavations to date.

In Hawai'i and the Cook Islands, people wore elaborate headdresses to signify their social and political status. The earliest Māori ancestors brought these values with them in the red feather headdresses they wore; but, according to some narratives, when they saw the pōhutukawa in full bloom on the coast on their arrival, they had confidence that they could acquire raw materials to make more. Yet there are few mentions of pare (headdresses) in oral narratives. Today the word 'pare' refers to a wreath or garland worn by women at tangihanga, such as pare kawakawa (made from green kawakawa leaves, *Macropiper excelsum*) or from other materials such as waewaekoukou (climbing clubmoss, *Lycopodium volubile*).[15] Some headdresses made from feathers between the 1700s and the mid-1800s are now in museum collections. In the British Museum there is a nineteenth-century Māori headdress consisting of small, tied bunches of black and white feathers, the bases of which have been

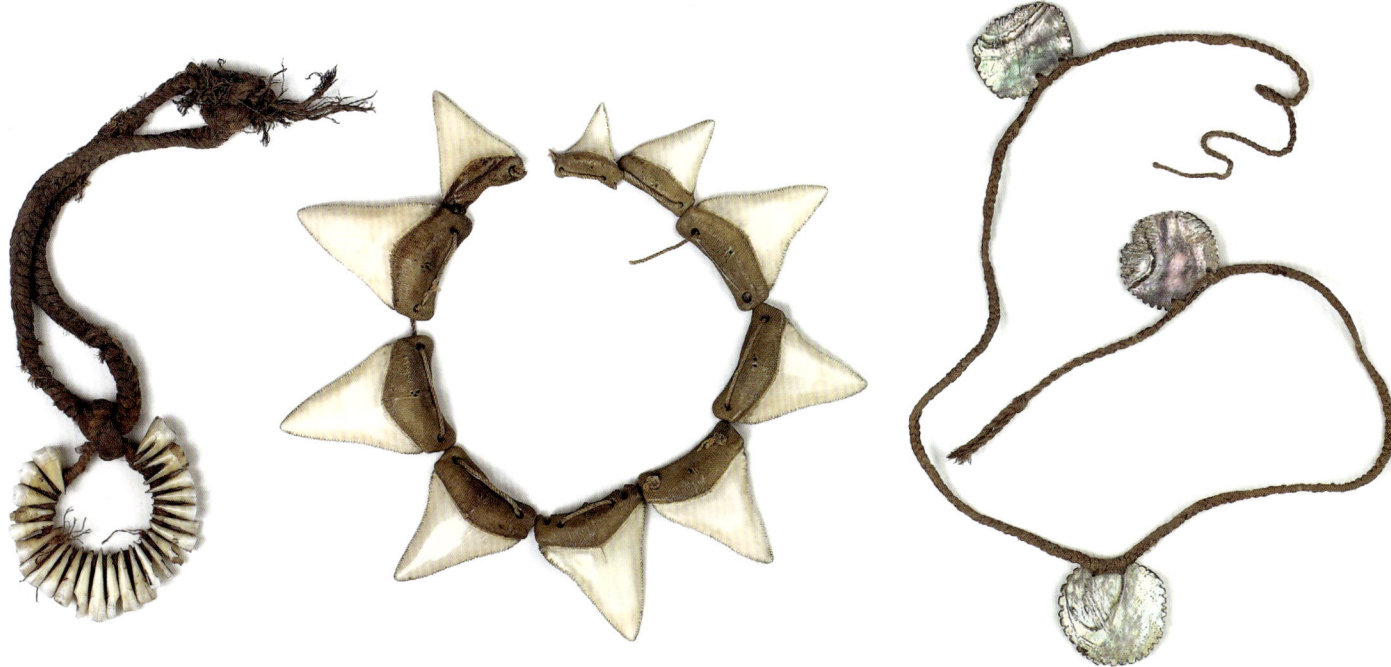

braided together to form a length which would have been worn around the head (Oc1854,1229.125). It may have been similar to another headdress in the British Museum that adorns a carving from the 1850s, possibly from the East Coast (Oc1894,0716.6).

Kōuma (breastplates) were made in Aotearoa for the first few hundred years, but for a different purpose than those used in the Pacific – for adornment, rather than protection in war – and from different materials (serpentine stone rather than shell).

These changes took place at a different rate in different regions as groups moved around the country, searching for a better lifestyle and resources. Through these periods of change, regionally specific forms of adornment began to emerge. Designs such as the koropepe (spiral-shaped adornment), pekapeka (adornment shaped like two bats) and marakihau (sea monster design) were popular in Te Tai Tokerau, and have been found only in that region. Ngāi Tahu rangatira and historian Teone Taare Tikao (1850–1927) pointed out that in the South Island there were different versions of adornments in each region – Murihiku, Canterbury, Nelson and Westland – often influenced and driven by the availability of local materials.[16] In the settlement of Rāpaki near Lyttelton, artists made shark-tooth ear ornaments called mako taniwha (tooth of a mako shark) and tautarika (tau or tautau, ornament; tarika, ear).[17]

### Early forms and styles of body adornment

Oral histories are replete with stories about body adornment – waiata, oriori and mōteatea record a wide range of terms for different forms and practices. In mōteatea these include hei tīpona for neck adornments,[18] whakateitei for personal treasures,[19] te tuhi māreikura for anointing the skin[20] and puhi ki te kakara for the placement of scented plumes on the body.[21]

Ornaments made between 900 and 1500CE often show stylistic traits that are from the Pacific making them easily recognisable. For example, a kōuma might have notches cut around the edges, similar to those made elsewhere in the Pacific: this decoration may have had a mnemonic function, where each notch represented a generation on a whakapapa. Later, carvers replicated this motif on tokotoko (orator's staffs which are still used today by speakers in their whaikōrero to delineate time). The V-shaped chevron was another early motif that artists used on different art forms, particularly the rei niho (whale-tooth ornament). One example from Okains Bay, Banks Peninsula depicts an elongated face with a series of notched chevrons along either edge. This rākai represents an example of another stylistic trait of Pacific art forms – the preference for depicting animals over humans.

Some rākai developed the face form into a full figure, often presented as a 'dancing figure', with arms raised above the head and legs splayed outwards. This style closely

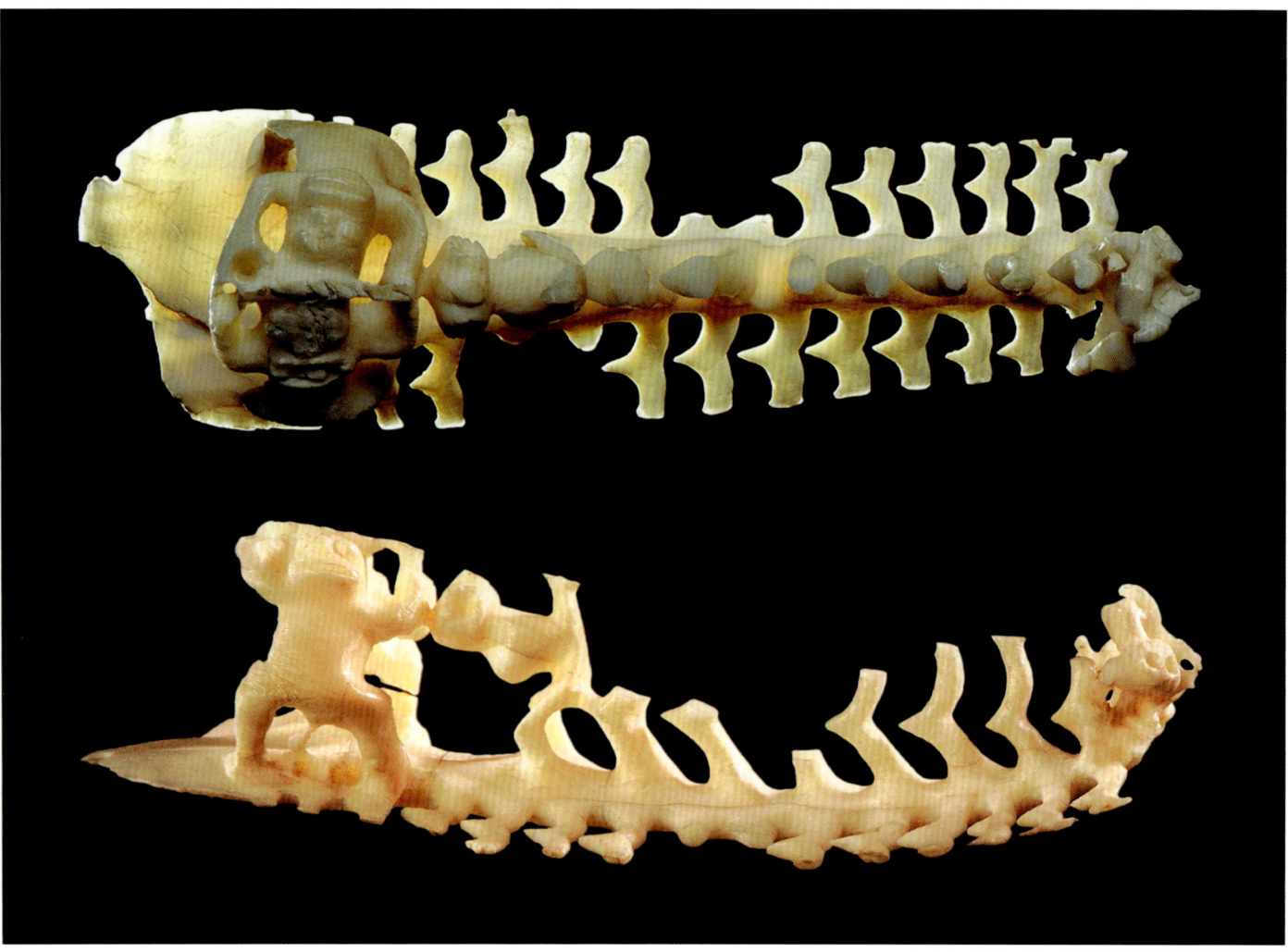

resembled Pacific models, in particular a carving remnant from Tahiti that is now in the Museum of Archaeology and Anthropology at the University of Cambridge (D 1914.34), which also depicts human figures with upraised arms. A palm-sized rei niho unearthed after a storm at Whangamumu in Northland, now in Auckland War Memorial Museum (1935.192), epitomises characteristics of early adornment. The artist has shaped the tooth into a series of parallel chevrons on the upper and lower ridge; on one end two human figures in dancing pose stand back to back with their hands joined. This imagery would have taken skill to complete, as the ivory is soft and delicate. The level of ornamentation on this rākai increases its status from a simple adornment to one that may have been worn by someone of importance.

Not all early forms of adornment persisted over time in Aotearoa. Kōuma were not made past 1700, despite their important role in the Pacific where they had a dual function: to deflect weapons in times of war, and to identify important people. In Tonga, for instance, tufuga (skilled experts) made large breastplates to deflect arrows and smaller, sometimes composite versions as the mark of a person of high status.[22] In New Zealand, artists made kōuma from a single piece of whalebone or stone such as serpentine to cover the chest, with several suspension holes drilled along the top, and notching around the edge.

Kōuma could act as a mnemonic device, recalling ancestral narratives for the wearer. A breastplate from Okains Bay features two fish on one side of the stone taonga: one fish is decorated with cross-hatching and the other with parallel incised lines. The disc has ornamental notching around the edge, and three suspension holes have been drilled on the upper edge.[23] Significantly, the fish are portrayed with a dorsal fin, and may be bonito – a species common in Te Moananui a Kiwa but which does not frequent the cooler waters around New Zealand. This kōuma represents one way

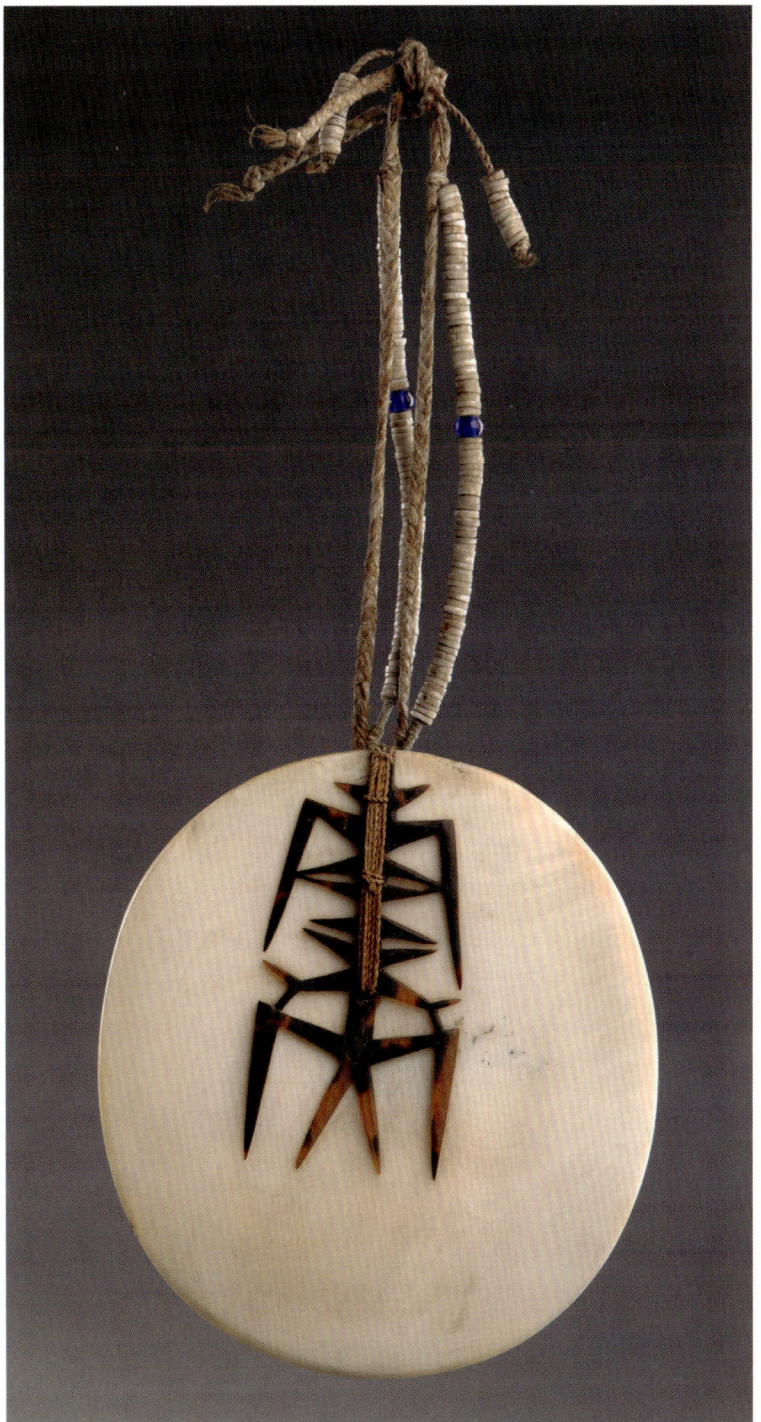
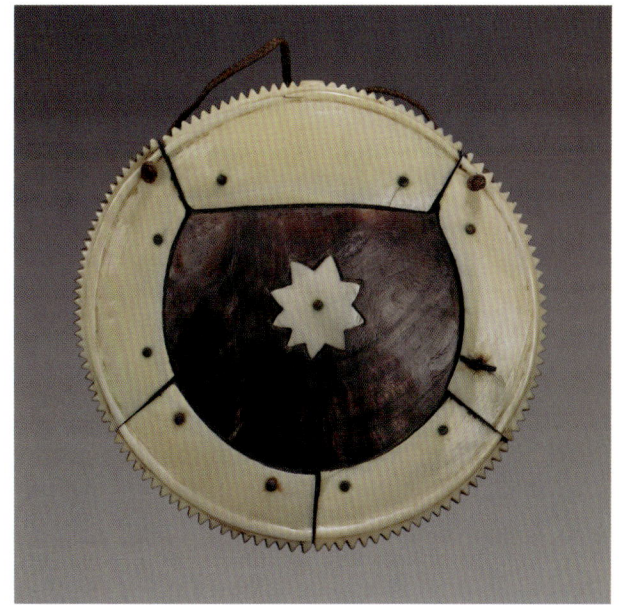
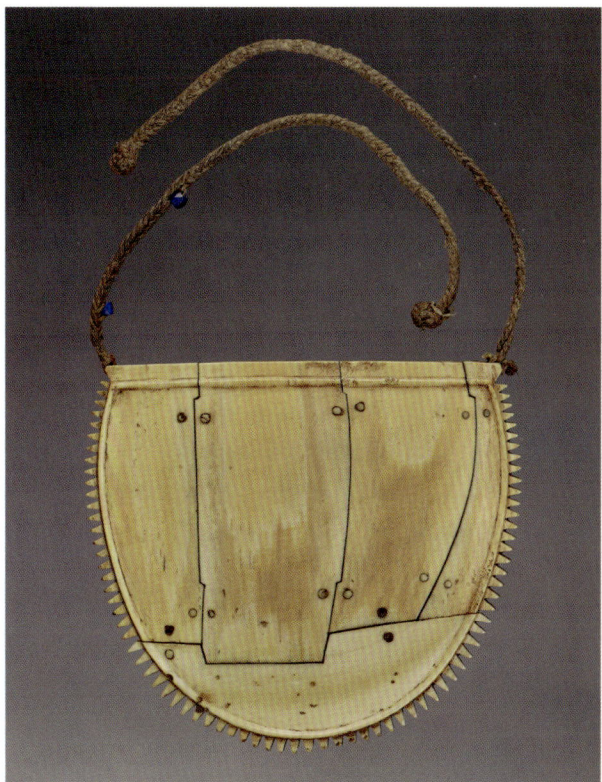

Left: Pacific breastplate from the Santa Cruz islands, made from tridacna shell and plant fibre cord, c.1870.
Te Papa Tongarewa Museum of New Zealand, FE000734, gift of Alexander Turnbull, 1913

Top right: Civavonovono (breastplate) from Fiji, made from pearl shell, sperm whale ivory, tapa and plant fibre. Other examples with a dark inner and pale outer whalebone are in Te Papa (OL002088), the Fiji Museum and Auckland Museum (13336).
British Museum, Oc1931,0714.33

Bottom right: The relationship between Fijian and Tongan breastplates is clear. Both used plates of whalebone to make a composite adornment, with a serrated edge.
British Museum, Oc,+.2395

Opposite: This early rei niho was made from a whale's tooth, and features many of the important early Māori stylistic traits, including chevrons and two figures in a 'standing' stance. This one comes from Whangamumu, eastern Bay of Islands.
Tāmaki Paenga Hira Auckland War Memorial Museum, 1935.192

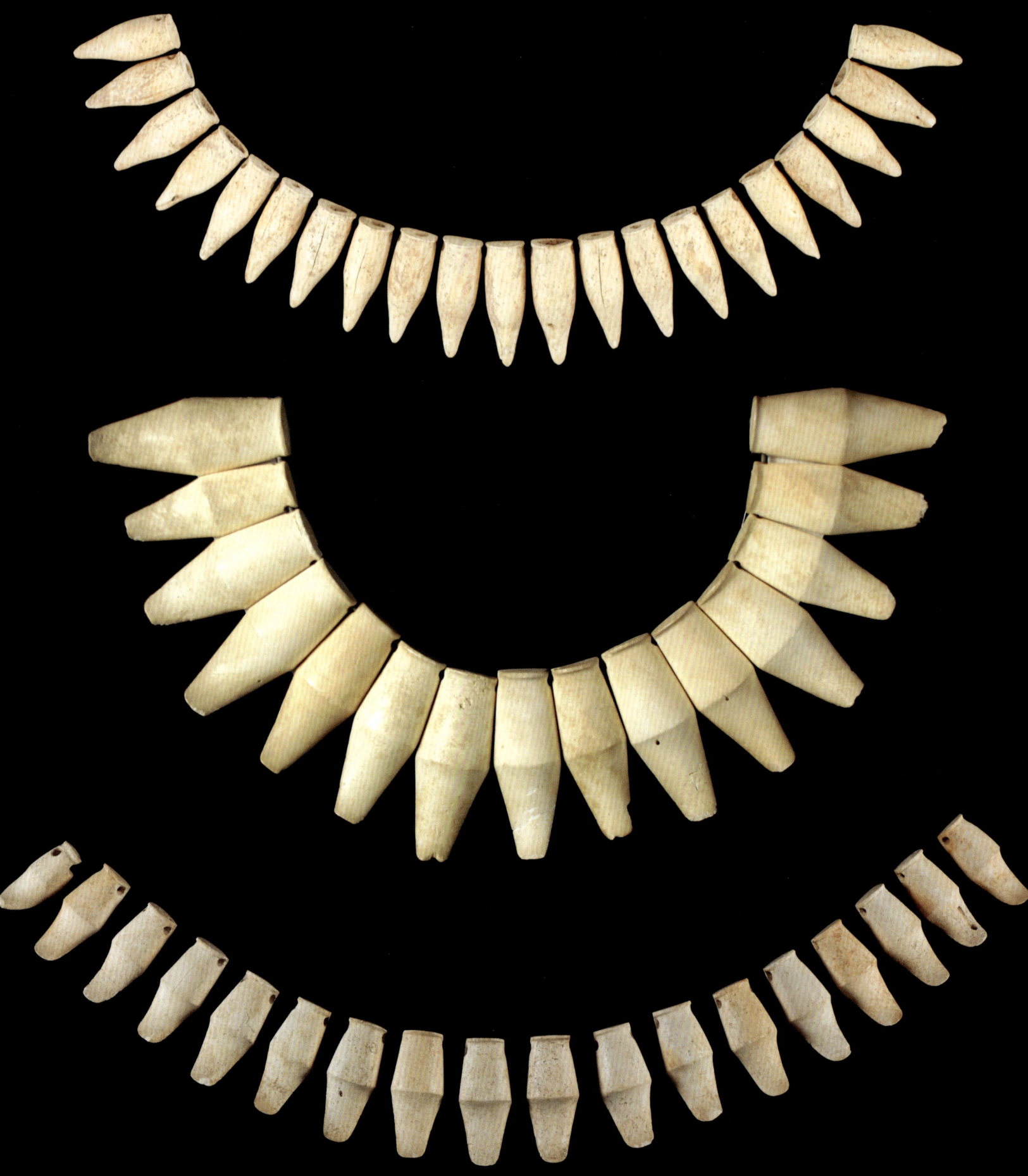

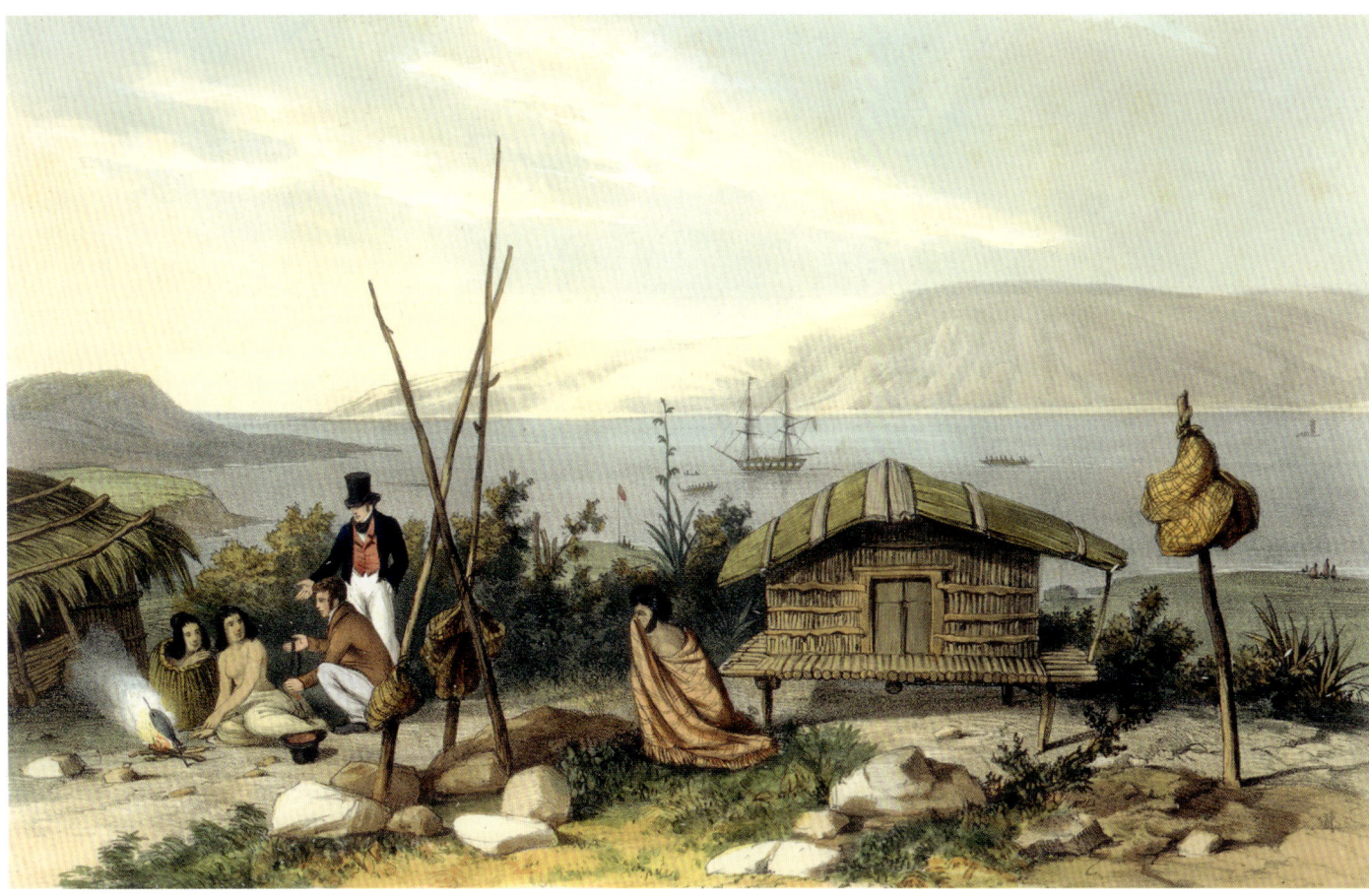

in which ancestral knowledge and history were recorded, and may very well have been a form of nostalgia for the artist at a time when their physical world was so new and unfamiliar.

## Materials used in adornment

Artists used materials that they sourced locally, or traded for other resources. The most popular materials used pre-1500CE were bones and teeth, which were materials that Pacific artists also frequently used. These held a high political and economic value, as the materials were sometimes difficult to acquire. Whalebone, for instance, was prized across the Pacific because whales were not hunted and killed; only if one beached itself could a community acquire the bones and teeth for adornment and other art forms, or to trade. Artists made necklaces of moa bones carved into a spool shape called whatu porotaka and strung on whiri to hang around the neck. They also experimented with materials that they found locally or traded within Aotearoa, such as basalt, obsidian and chert from around the Coromandel Peninsula, and pounamu from the South Island. Artists sometimes replicated whale-tooth forms in stone

The use of black ribbon for adornment was popular from the early nineteenth century. In this image the artist Augustus Earle and his friend, 'Mr Shand', are shown offering ribbons to two young women who are cooking a fish over a fire.
**Augustus Earle, *Village of Parkuni, River Hokianga*, published 1838**
lithograph, hand-coloured, 235 x 368mm, Alexander Turnbull Library, PUBL-0015-04, from Augustus Earle, *Sketches illustrative of the Native Inhabitants and Islands of New Zealand ...*, lithographed and published under the auspices of the New Zealand Association by Robert Martin & Co, London, 1838

Opposite top: Up until around 1500, adornment continued to be Pacific in style. These 'reels' were strung together to make a single necklace, a style which would soon change to focus on a single adornment strung on whiri. This whale-tooth necklace from Te Pokohiwi o Kupe (Wairau Bar) dates to c.1300.
Canterbury Museum, E142.159. The Museum acknowledges the customary takiwā rights of Te Rūnanga a Rangitāne o Wairau

Opposite middle: This magnificent necklace is made from moa bones shaped to resemble whales' teeth. It comes from Southland and dates from the early settlement of the region by Murihiku Māori, when moa were still readily available.
Southland Museum & Art Gallery Niho o te Taniwha, B81.161

Opposite bottom: Moa bone/imitation whale-tooth necklace from Te Pokohiwi o Kupe (Wairau Bar).
Canterbury Museum, E142.160. The Museum acknowledges the customary takiwā rights of Te Rūnanga a Rangitāne o Wairau

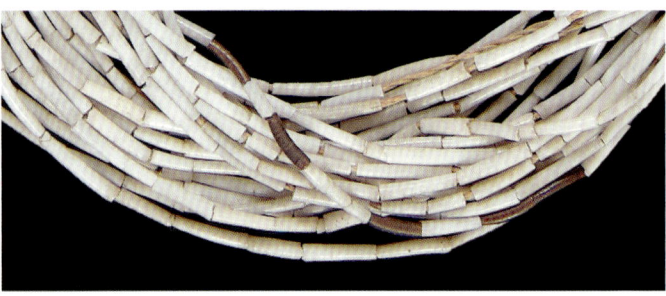

Dentalium (tusk shell) necklaces are very rare in museum collections, possibly as they were often buried with their owners upon death. The shell is hollowed out and hundreds strung on a single whiri, several strands of which are then lightly twisted and the ends brought together into a single, short whiri to make the completed adornment. Very fragile, these adornments are a clear link to adornments still made in the Pacific.
Pitt Rivers Museum, University of Oxford, 1886.1.1574

because the design was so highly sought after and the usual materials could be difficult to acquire.

Niho (teeth) sourced from a range of animals (dogs, seals, dolphins and porpoises, sharks and humans) were fashioned into ornaments to be worn in the ear or around the neck, depending largely on their weight. Dog teeth were the rarest, and thus the most precious. Several necklaces of dog teeth have been found in Te Pokohiwi, the Wairau Bar excavations in Marlborough. This site, which dates to c.1280CE, has revealed over 2000 objects and provides a fascinating snapshot of the earliest days of Pacific settlement in New Zealand. Many of the objects were made by artists in Aotearoa using the same techniques as their contemporaries in the eastern Pacific, particularly in the Marquesas Islands – Te Henua 'Enana (North Marquesas) and Te Fenua 'Enata (South Marquesas). This suggests that our ancestors left from a central dispersion point: some went south to New Zealand, and others east to the Marquesas.

Human teeth were used to embellish carvings to make them appear more realistic.[24] A number of ornaments in the British Museum are made from human teeth: in one example, the artist has drilled holes in the tops of twenty-five teeth and attached them to a harakeke whiri (Q1981.OC.1359, 26.8cm). These were likely to have been the teeth of the artist's parents or grandparents, making this a form of memorial to them.

Adornments made from shell are rare in museum collections, perhaps because the material was very delicate and fragile, and they were very labour-intensive to make. Only a few examples have survived; they are thought to date to the eighteenth century. Artists in the central and eastern Pacific created multiple-strand necklaces – notably in Hawai'i, where human hair was braided into many lengths that were pushed through a hole drilled at the top of a lei niho palāoa (whale-tooth necklace) and fastened with a loop and toggle (which in themselves were precious). The value of shells was not only aesthetic: some cultures in the Pacific used them as a form of currency; larger shells were fashioned into breastplates, and fisherpeople used them to make trolling lures. Māori ancestors brought these shell lures with them to Aotearoa: a lure discovered in the Coromandel is made from black-lipped pearl shell – a material that is not found in the colder waters of the southern Pacific. Over time, Māori began making hangaroa (shell necklaces and anklets) from the new types of shell they found here.

NGĀ TAONGA O WHARAWHARA — BODY ADORNMENT

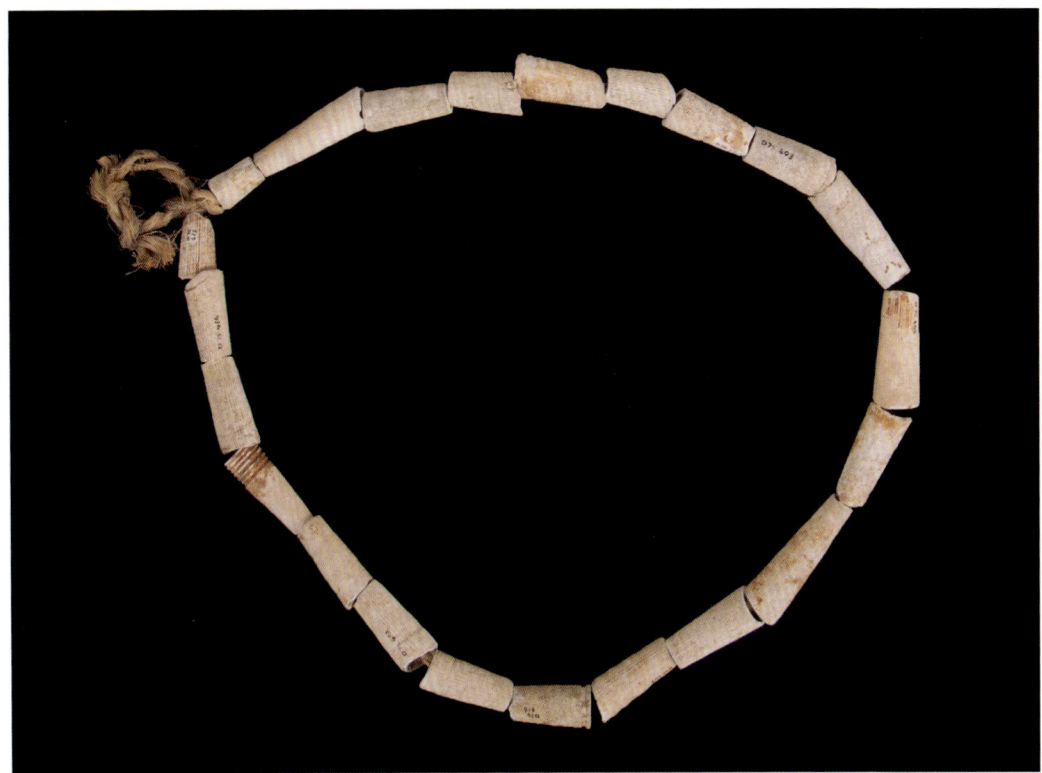

This variation of the dentalium shell necklace uses tusk shells threaded onto harakeke string.
Tūhura Otago Museum, D75.396, Harwood, Otago Peninsula

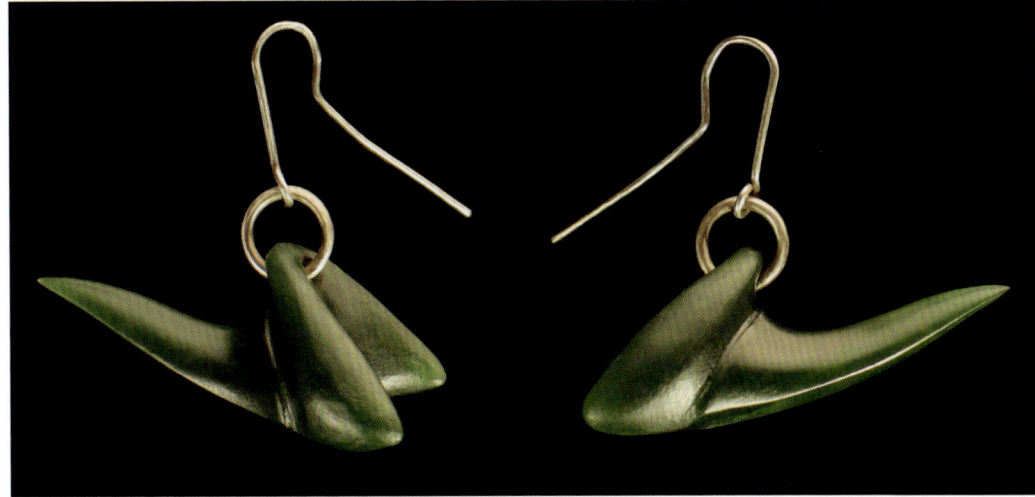

Mako teeth retain their importance as adornments for both Māori men and women today.
**Stacy Gordine, *Mako Pounamu Earrings*, n.d.**
Āhua Māori Art Gallery, Te Puia, Rotorua

Reinhold Forster collected three dentalium (tusk shell) necklaces on Cook's second voyage in the early 1770s, which he later deposited in Pitt Rivers Museum (1886.1.1568, 1886.1.1569, 1886.1.1574). The shells have been laboriously shaped into even lengths, then strung together – one is pure white with a small section of brown beads, another necklace uses alternating brown and white shells, while a third has multiple strands of white shells gathered together at each end.[25] Such styles of necklace are very rare in collections. The degree of expertise required to create shell necklaces points to the wearer being someone of significance; the fact that these Pitt Rivers examples were traded with Forster some time in 1773 or 1774 is another indication that these hangaroa were highly prized adornments.

On occasion, communities would undertake an expedition to source specific materials such as pounamu. The level of difficulty in acquiring the raw material affected its value. Some villages specialised in working greenstone into adornment – archaeologists have found around twenty-two hei tiki and almost eighteen tonnes of pounamu in a kāinga at Whareakeake near Long Beach on the coast northeast of Dunedin.[26] Pounamu was traded in both its

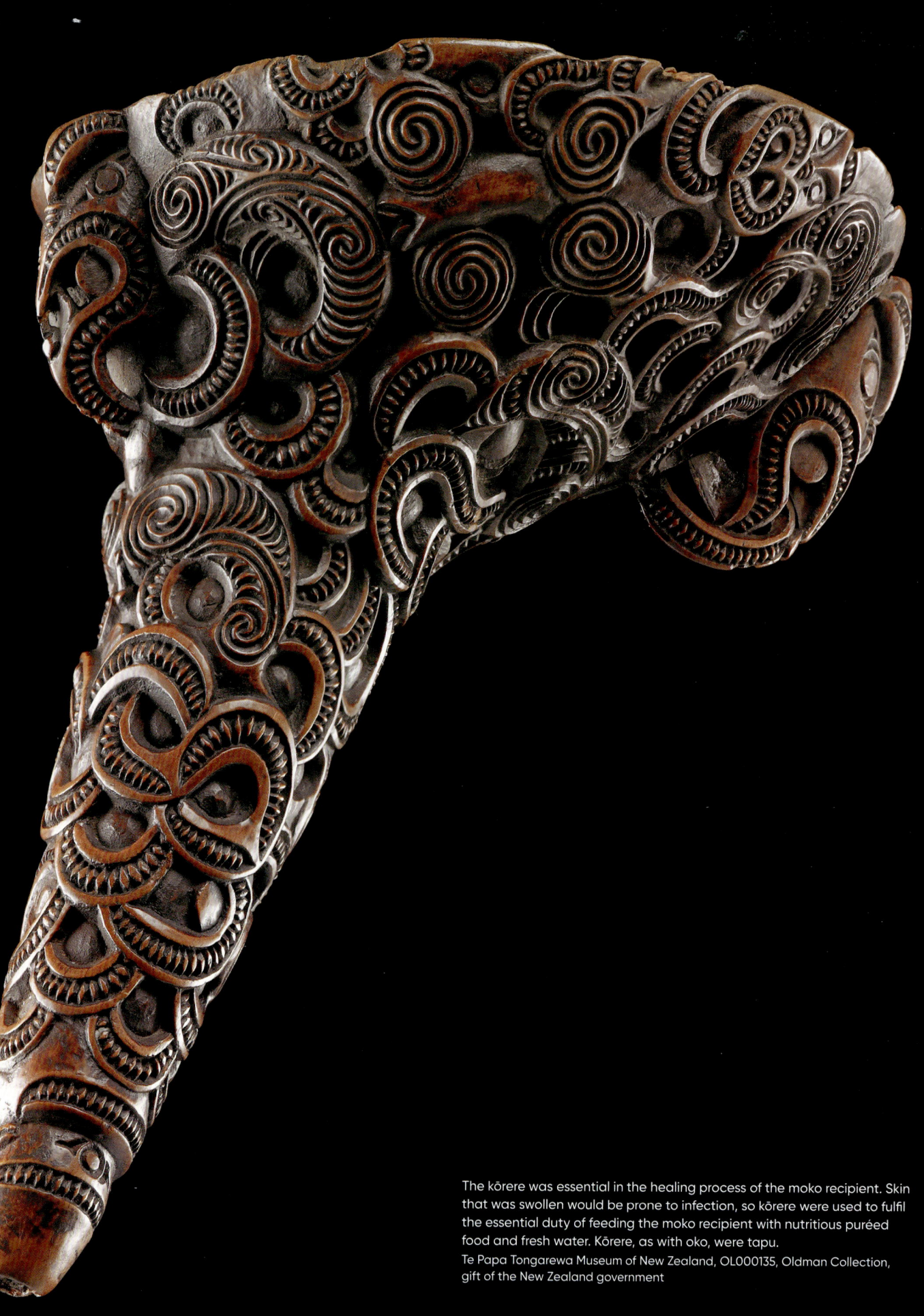

The kōrere was essential in the healing process of the moko recipient. Skin that was swollen would be prone to infection, so kōrere were used to fulfil the essential duty of feeding the moko recipient with nutritious puréed food and fresh water. Kōrere, as with oko, were tapu.
Te Papa Tongarewa Museum of New Zealand, OL000135, Oldman Collection, gift of the New Zealand government

worked and natural forms, and would have been sourced from Fiordland and the West Coast. It was exchanged for food such as kūmara and taro, and for fine whāriki and kākahu. In 1846, when Thomas Brunner and Charles Heaphy explored the West Coast with their guide Kehu (Ngāti Tūmatakōkiri), they met people working pounamu into mere and hei tiki which would be exchanged with people from the North Island.

By the 1870s several large-scale lapidaries had been established in Dunedin, relatively close to local pounamu resources. Not all workers were willing, or paid, however; between 1879 and 1881, 130 Māori political prisoners in the city were forced to make pendants and mere[27] from greenstone that the New Zealand government had supplied.[28] The prisoners were farmers and ploughmen from Parihaka pā who had been sentenced to two years' hard labour for their passive resistance to confiscation of their land and homes by the colonial government.[29] The pounamu works were destined for sale in the Pākehā community rather than exchange between Māori – pounamu was seen purely for its economic value.

### Tā moko

Moko is the permanent inking of curvilinear designs into the skin. This style emerged from the tatau art form from the Pacific, which covered and spiritually protected the ancestors when they travelled to Aotearoa. Tatau signifies rank and status. Tufuga (artists) tapped pigments into the skin in geometric and freehand designs. The areas of the body covered depended on gender and status. The extent of tatau on the body varied: men in Sāmoa and Tonga wore tatau from their lower back down to their knees; and women in Fiji wore veiqia (permanent marking) across their face, arms and chest. In Aotearoa, the tatau technique and designs evolved into incised and curvilinear designs called moko, but the values and significance of tatau were retained.

The moko kit consisted of a range of uhi grafted onto a wooden haft, a wooden mallet, a range of pigments, and an oko (a mortar for grinding and mixing pigments). The pigments came from a number of sources: charcoal from certain woods; āwheto – vegetable caterpillar (*Cordyceps robertsii*), a type of fungus that was dried and roasted; and the faeces of dogs that had been fed special foods. All aspects of the moko process were considered highly tapu, as it involved the shedding of blood and, often, working on the head, which is regarded as the most sacred part of the body. Great care was taken at all stages of the physical and spiritual moko process, and once it was completed, the recipient would remain in a state of tapu until the skin had healed. Intricately carved kōrere (broth feeders) were used during the healing process to provide nourishment to the recipient whose face was swollen from the tā moko. The entire process often took place outside the main settlement in a whare specially constructed for this purpose and taken down once the work was completed. Pigments were stored in highly ornate oko, which were buried when not in use because they were highly tapu.

The tohunga tā moko was usually male, but sometimes female. They were trained specialists who often worked as wood carvers as well – both art forms required similar skills and knowledge of chisels and designs. They worked on commission, travelling to different communities to place their work on those who could afford it. Some artists were so famous they were captured during war raids, when the victors would take them back home and put them to work. Rangi, a tohunga tā moko enslaved by Ngāpuhi in 1820, is one example: his moko skills enabled him to become wealthy, and move out of enslavement.[30] Until the introduction of a cash economy in the early nineteenth century, moko would be traded for taonga and other items of value that reflected the skill involved. George Grey observed: 'When the work is finished then the treasures are given as payment. The work of these men was highly paid. These are the payments. A greenstone eardrop, a hei tiki, a kaitaka cloak, a whalebone club or greenstone club perhaps, perhaps a hoeroa, or taiaha.'[31]

Moko marked a rite of passage or an important event in a person's life, such as reaching puberty or taking part in a decisive battle, as well as recording a person's whakapapa. Women typically wore facial moko on their lips, on and around the mouth, and on their forehead; for men it often covered the entire face. In addition, an individual might choose to have work on their chest, arms, stomach, back, buttocks, thighs and calves. Men wore the pūhoro (elongated spiral) design on their thighs and buttocks to celebrate accomplishment as a warrior, or as the mark of a chief. Artists would often paint the pūhoro on the prow of a waka taua – the design symbolised speed, and it united the warriors with their waka. Sydney Parkinson recorded women

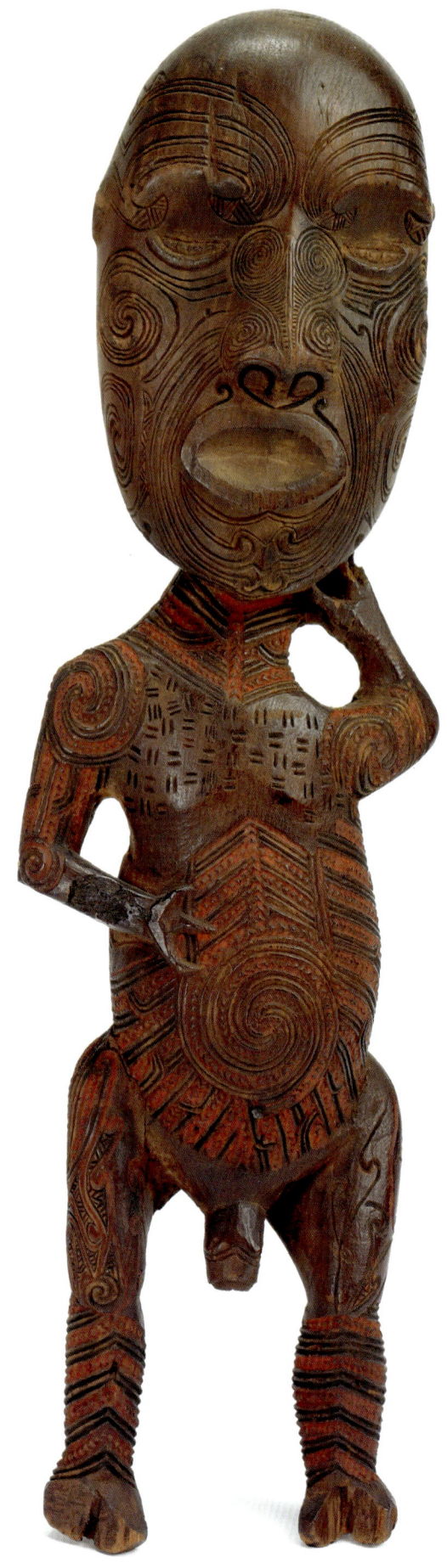

in Doubtless Bay in the Far North wearing the pūhoro design on the foreheads and necks, and on their thighs.[32]

The social and political status and military experience and skill of the recipient often dictated the moko design. A man who had demonstrated prowess in battle might be rewarded with a more extensive moko, and an individual might receive a mataora (full-face design) to mark out their high status. As a signifier of mana, the full-face moko was also carved on female figures in at least two forms. A carver from the Whanganui region in the 1840s depicted two women with full-face moko on the grip of two model hoe that are now in the British Museum (1848.3-13.1, 1848.3-13.2). Female figures were a popular choice of decoration on hoe in the nineteenth century, either on the grip or on the blade.

Around the same time, two carvers from the Bay of Plenty area depicted the Madonna figure with full-face moko – no doubt to identify her clearly as a person of mana and tapu (Auckland Museum 13895, Te Papa ME011429). This variety shows that moko was idiosyncratic; it was not generic across the country, and it changed over time. Artists often selected the moko designs, resulting in a similar style across a wide geographic region; at other times the individual's rangatira might choose a design that they liked to be given to the recipient.

The primary motifs used in moko were the koru and the double spiral. The buttocks and thigh designs were fairly similar, with double spirals on the buttocks and pūhoro on the thighs. Women's moko kauae (moko on the chin) were symmetrical, while the mataora on men was asymmetrical: a double haehae (parallel incised line) was placed down the centre of the face, and each side was different. Sometimes negative space itself was the design. The meanings were highly sacred and were only taught orally, and only some named designs have been passed through the generations.

One rare moko practice, moko kurī, consisted of parallel lines across the chest or face. Early carvings record this design as evidence of the transferal of skills from skin to wood. A carved figure in the British Museum made in the

This unusual small wooden carving includes moko kurī on the chest of the figure. An East Coast provenance is probable, due to the alternating red and black pigment highlights on the carving. It is likely the artist had seen this style of moko, had been told about it, or had even practised this style himself. The carving was originally collected by Americans, and later deposited in the British Museum.
British Museum, Oc. 1641

NGĀ TAONGA O WHARAWHARA — BODY ADORNMENT

1820s on the East Coast shows extensive moko kurī across the chest (Oc. 1641). These patterns would become synonymous with the wearer, to the extent that in the early nineteenth century rangatira signing land deeds and other documents would be recognised from the design that they placed on the document.[33]

Ngāti Rangiwewehi chief Te Rangikāheke drew two remarkable illustrations of moko in the 1850s for the governor, Sir George Grey.[34] The first picture depicts half a man's face with full-face moko, with each part of the design clearly named; a second drawing shows an expanse of a pūhoro design, which he describes as for the thighs. Te Rangikāheke created these drawings in his role as cultural advisor to Grey: they were meant as recordings, particularly at a time when moko was becoming less widely practised.

Other people were also recording this information. Ngāti Kahungunu leader Rēnata Kawepō received his moko when Ngāpuhi released him as a prisoner of war. He later drew two portraits, one of a man, and one of a woman; Kawepō has presented the facial moko as a flattened design, and their gender is discernible only by the type of moko they wear.[35] It is unclear who the drawings depict, but it is likely that their contemporaries could have identified them by the designs in their moko. This way of presenting a person – drawing a portrait through moko only – is distinctive to Māori from this period.

Drawings by colonial soldier-artist Horatio Robley (1840–1930) are another important resource for research into moko, as they represent a snapshot of moko worn by Ngāiterangi people in the mid-1860s. Some of his drawings record unique moko designs, particularly on women. In *Woman of the Ngaiterangi Tribe, Bay of Plenty* (1864, Alexander Turnbull Library A-080-002) he records a woman in a kāinga, wearing a cloak and with short hair (perhaps as a sign of mourning). Her moko is uncommon: she has darkened lips and a curious kauae on her chin, and the space between nose and lips is fully patterned. Even more unusual are the four short lines on either side of her forehead, beginning at the top of her nose and arching out above the eyebrows. This forehead design is called tīwhana and is typically placed on a man's forehead, extending all the way up to the temples – probably to mimic ferocity. This shortened tīwhana style may have been specific to Ngāiterangi women – Robley drew another woman in the same year with a similar design on her forehead (National Library of Australia 790071); he must have thought this unusual as he titled it *Ngaiterangi woman with curious tattooing*.

Moko underwent many changes in the nineteenth century, largely as a result of missionaries and others actively encouraging Māori to set aside this practice that they considered heathen – and, later, a symbol of Māori resistance to Pākehā values. Some men grew beards to cover their moko, instead of plucking the hairs out meticulously with mussel shells. Yet the practice remained strong and continued to evolve in many communities.

From the earliest engagements with Pākehā, Māori traded toi moko.[36] These were not the traditional toi moko that were preserved as part of tangi; rather, they were the heads of enemies. These were derided, and trading them off was another way of diminishing their mana. This practice was especially popular in tribal rohe where toi moko could readily be swapped for muskets. Ngāpuhi were particularly active traders of toi moko both in New Zealand and in Sydney, and many of those were on-sold to buyers in Britain. The trade became so profitable that prisoners of war would be chosen and killed for their moko; and, in some cases, prisoners would be forced to receive moko and then be killed. The trade in toi moko was eventually banned in 1835 but the practice continued in some areas, more for their macabre value than in exchange for muskets. There are at least two examples of thigh skin with pūhoro being traded overseas, too: Robley notes seeing one in a leather shop in London in 1894,[37] and the American Museum of Natural History bought an example in 1907.[38]

By the 1850s social pressure on Māori to conform to Pākehā notions of beauty affected the uptake of moko. There was a resurgence in the art form in times of political turmoil in the 1860s and 1870s but, in general, men stopped taking the moko; in fact, it was the women who kept it alive. With the introduction of the Tohunga Suppression Act 1907, tohunga tā moko were banned from performing their art. There was still demand for it, however, and so they practised it in communities and homes away from the prying eyes of police and other Pākehā.

Historian and writer Michael King and photographer Marti Friedlander documented women who had received moko kauae in the 1930s and 1940s. The resulting book, *Moko: Maori Tattooing in the 20th Century*, was part of a renaissance of moko that has heralded a new generation of Māori who are keen to revive this and other aspects of Māori culture.[39] In the 1970s gangs were emerging, with large numbers of Māori members, and these gangs often promoted the inking of Māori designs onto their skin as a badge of honour – despite some Māori not being comfortable with the warrior connotations often intended by this practice. Other Māori, though, were keen to shift public focus away from this scene and focus instead on wearing moko as a sign of Māori identity and an assertion of tino rangatiratanga (Māori sovereignty) – this was the time of the 1975 Māori land march, and later the promotion of the first kōhanga reo (Māori language nests).

There are many reasons for taking the moko these days. For most people it is to pay homage to their whakapapa and to make a clear statement of their commitment to live proudly as Māori. Moko practitioners acknowledge the keen interest in moko shown by non-Māori, and they have devised a way of thinking about moko that they call kiri tuhi, which looks identical to moko and speaks of the wearer's own family lineage and pride. Moko is alive and well.

### Tangihaehae

Tangihaehae (cutting of the skin in mourning) was another form of permanent body marking, performed by women as a physical sign of grief. The practice involved making incisions in the skin with sharp flakes of obsidian, then rubbing ash into the cuts to make permanent marks as an enduring reminder of the person or event. Tangihaehae was performed during the tangihanga or later, during the hahunga ceremony, which involved uplifting the bones, scraping them and performing other rituals, and moving them to their final resting place. The depth of the incisions sometimes reflected the depth of a person's grief, and might even lead to their own death, 'so intense was the passion of the one left behind'.[40]

The term 'tangihaehae' was recorded several times in the nineteenth century in conjunction with death rituals: in 1891 Edward Tregear described 'haehae' as 'to cut repeatedly', and 'He tangi haehae' as a wailing, accompanied with cutting of the skin'.[41] Teone Tikao (Ngāi Tahu) explained that tangihaehae was when 'parties would gash themselves and let the blood run', and noted that 'All these customs came from *Hawaiki*.'[42]

Ancestral mōteatea record this visceral practice and its significance for posterity. A Ngāti Tūwharetoa lament for Te Kohika, composed by Tikina with words and explanation by Te Tāite Te Tomo (?1872–1939), refers to 'aku kāpara puni' or 'incised lines of black',[43] and says that elders checked that this was performed properly, although in this case Tikina had not, and was required to complete it to his satisfaction. Another lament, this time for Peehi Tu-korehu of Ngāti Maniapoto, makes reference to 'haea mai ra ki te mira tuatini' or 'score the flesh in grief with shark's teeth' (line 15).[44] This pōwhiri chant was recorded in the 1970s at a kawe mate (a ceremony to bring forth the spirit of the departed):[45]

> Homai he mata, kia haehae au
> Aue! kia kotia i te kiri
> I awhi ai taua, i nawa
> Aue hi! Aue hi! Aue ha!
>
> Give me a blade of obsidian, to slash myself
> To cut the skin
> You often embraced me.
> Alas! (hiss)

There are very few images that record the practice of tangihaehae. Drawings by Jules Lejeune (1804–1851), who was in Aotearoa in 1822–1825, show two women with tangihaehae: a girl with cuts on her upper chest and face, and a slightly older woman with extensive tangihaehae over her upper arms, chest and breast.[46] This practice continued even after many communities had adopted Christianity: Robley drew three women mourning over a dead warrior, cutting their skin to mark their grief.[47] This is a remarkable moment – the 'person' they are keening over is represented by a taiaha, most likely that belonging to (and named after) the deceased person. Often when a chief died in battle it was impossible to bring home his actual body, and so sometimes his head might be removed and returned to his people; or, as is the case here, their weapon, or sometimes an item of personal adornment, such as a hei tiki, would 'stand in' for them. Robley drew tangihaehae again in 1864: he described the scene of 'Tangi at Matapihi' where those present continued to 'tangihai' for three or four days before the burial.[48] The early missionaries considered the practice of tangihaehae abhorrent: they wrote of their concern about it, and cited it

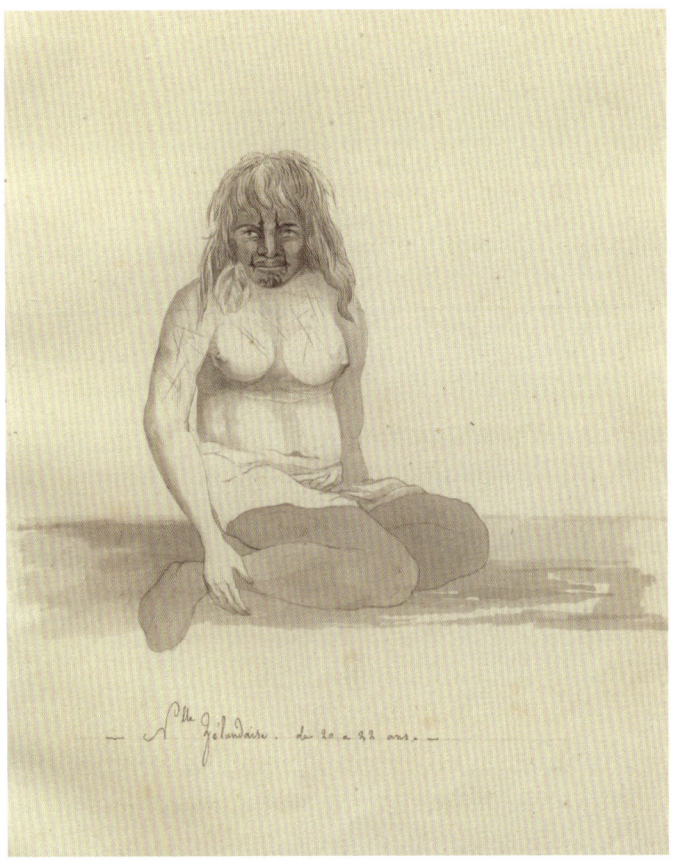

Tangihaehae was practised usually by women as an act of mourning, where they would cut the skin (sometimes deeply) as a public display of their grief. These incisions would often leave marks on the skin, as observed by a number of Europeans in the early nineteenth century.
**Unknown artist (Jules Lejeune?), *Nlle Zélandaise de 20 à 22 ans*, 1824**
pen and wash drawing, Ministère de la Défense, Service historique de la Défense, France, SH 356:2 Folio 126

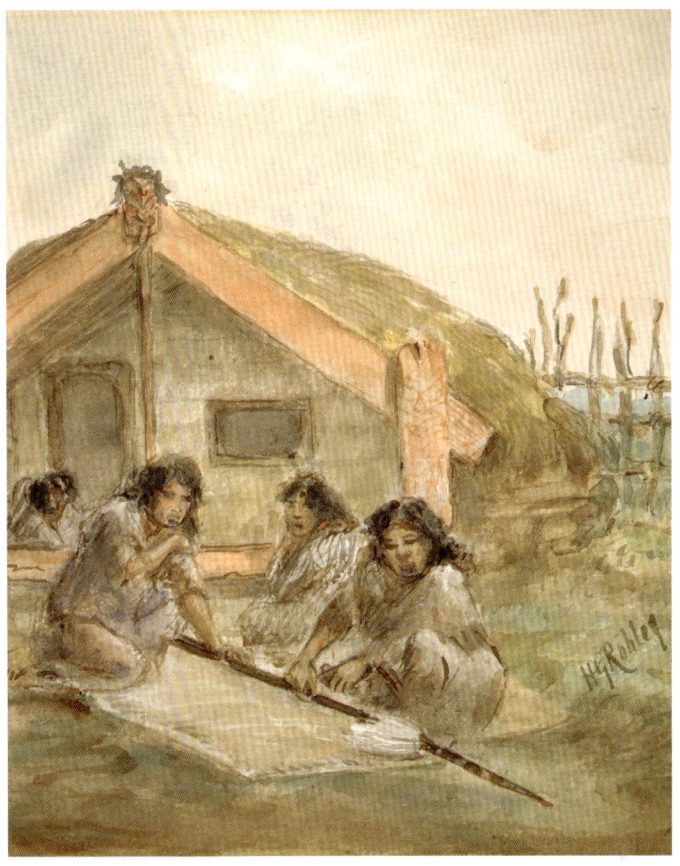

Horatio Robley recorded several women from Ngāi Te Rangi in the act of tangihaehae as they grieve over a relative killed in battle in 1864. As his body was not able to be returned to the pā, his taiaha stands in for him. Such weapons would often be named, and sometimes be used to dispatch the owner at their request if they were unable to escape from their enemy.
**Horatio Gordon Robley, *Women cutting themselves on arms for tears of blood. Mourning over the spear of a Ngaiterangi warrior killed 21 June '64*, 1864**
ink and watercolour sketch, 230 x 203mm, Alexander Turnbull Library, A-080-015

as one reason why their presence in Māori communities was an ongoing necessity.

Tangihaehae may have been revived during the New Zealand Wars, as were other practices such as moko. Some whānau today still mark the deaths of loved ones by taking a specially designed moko, unifying in their grief with the use of the same design.

### Mata whakarewa – skin painting

Māori went to extraordinary lengths to express notions of power, status and position through the marking of the body. As well as piercing and incising the skin with chisels, people embellished themselves with pigments from the earth, rivers and creeks, and from shrubs, trees and flowers. The visual impact was stunning, from all accounts. These practices continued the long history of skin painting in the Pacific, from the Papua New Guinea highlanders to the Hawaiians in the north and the people of Rapanui Easter Island in the east. As peoples migrated across Te Moananui a Kiwa, they took these painting traditions from island to island, and experimented with pigments, colours, patterns and symbols. The colour red signified tapu and mana across the Pacific: Tongans traded with Fijians for red kula feathers,[49] and weavers in Hawai'i used hundreds of red feathers from the 'i'iwi (scarlet Hawaiian honeycreeper) to make 'ahu 'ula (red feather capes) to be worn by high chiefs and kings.

There are a range of terms for painting the skin. Tīkao calls it 'pani';[50] others use the term 'mata whakarewa', for example 'I tiaria mai to mata whakarewa' in 'Lament for Te Rangihiroa' from Tūhourangi, Te Arawa[51] – 'mata

160 | 161

whakarewa' is described as 'besmeared' in the explanatory note. Whakataukī and tribal stories record accounts of mata whakarewa: the wife of Whatihua of Ngāti Awa recognised that her husband had been unfaithful because of the red ochre on his clothes from his red-painted lover.[52]

Early Pākehā visitors to New Zealand often remarked on skin painting because it was so foreign to them:[53] they recorded details about the manufacture of pigments and their application, often disparagingly (they obviously had short memories and had forgotten the extravagantly rouged and powdered faces of their fashionable kin in Europe). The earliest written records of mata whakarewa were on the first *Endeavour* voyage (1768–1771) when the surgeon William Monkhouse described a warrior at Tūranganui (Gisborne) whose 'face [was] smeared in bright red paint (or *kura*, a sign of tapu'.[54] These were men prepared for battle, and battle they did with Cook's crew.[55] Further south on the same voyage, Joseph Banks recorded a group of men whose faces were either fully or partially painted with a 'red colour in oil'.[56] Some of this ochre must have been so heavily applied that it transferred onto their tū.[57] Accounts later in the voyage from the East Coast and Te Tai Tokerau recorded similar skin painting. It must have been a popular pastime in Northland in the 1760s, as French voyager Jean François Marie de Surville recorded black pigment being used 'as a cosmetic for the face and hair',[58] and a range of designs in Doubtless Bay.

From all accounts, mata whakarewa was widely and regularly practised for different occasions and purposes, including to beautify the body, for camouflage, to celebrate important events, to emphasise the ferocity of warriors in preparation for war (such as in haka), as part of hahunga ceremonies where ancestral bones were prepared for final interment, to ward off insects and provide protection from the cold, to increase suppleness, and in preparation for moko. Men and women, young and old applied pigment: no training was necessary; rather, the application was governed by tribal and aesthetic preferences.

Pigments were made from various earth and river deposits. These were ground into powder on a large sandstone slab of around 60 x 30cm, using an autoru – a smaller, round stone. When these stone slabs were used to grind kōkōwai they became highly tapu by extension. Tohunga would guard them closely, and they were often buried or hidden when they were not in use. The autoru were also very valuable and highly sought after, and people made special expeditions to find them and bring them back. After the pigment material had been ground, it was mixed in a pāua shell with shark or bird oil and hungahunga (flax fibre) to a paint-like consistency. The prepared pigment was valuable and would be stored in a hue (gourd) until needed. Pigments used for moko were treated with the same reverence, and those that were especially precious were handed down from generation to generation.

Different colours of pigment came from different sources: blue was from pukepoto, parakawahia (blue earth) or tūtaewhetū (phosphate) clay; black pigment came from charcoal (ngārahu, ngārehu) and was used for fine moko work; and white was from taioma clay. For red pigment – the most precious – sources varied across the country. In Hawke's Bay there were four types of pigment available: taupō (a reddish-brown earth or clay), tareha, kōkōwai and karamea. Within each there could be a variety of shades: in kōkōwai, for example, the tonal palette could range from bright yellow through to hot orange, bright red or deep burgundy.

There are many different patterns recorded for mata whakarewa. Sometimes the pigment was poured directly onto the body, and at other times a design would be carefully applied with the fingers or leaves or flower buds. The face and body were first cleaned by wiping the skin with uku (white clay) using sea sponges; then the body was scented with sweet oils such as those from the taramea, toatoa, kōpuru, kāretu (a scented moss) or mokimoki (fragrant fern).

Herbert Williams lists a range of designs under tuhi ('adornment of a surface by pattern or colour ornamenting the face'), including tuhi kōhuru (diagonal lines of red), tuhi māreikura, tuhi maraekura, tuhi matakura (horizontal lines of blue tūtaewhetū), tuhi kōkihi (with the red juice of berries of a plant found in damp places) and tuhi kōnekeneke (a pattern of dots).[59]

Other designs display experimentation and innovation, including: whole face painted in red, yellow (Ngāi Tahu, 1844) or black; face half-red and half-black; red spots on the cheeks, black dot in the middle of the face (1850s); red 'beard'

Pōria were made in the eighteenth century to secure pet birds. Over time, decorative pōria were re-made in different materials, including pounamu. Note the range of styles among these kākā pōria in Te Papa Tongarewa, made from pounamu and bone.
Te Papa Tongarewa Museum of New Zealand, clockwise from top left: ME000072; ME005148/2; ME011970; ME011569; ME012855; ME001659; WE000150

NGĀ TAONGA O WHARAWHARA — BODY ADORNMENT

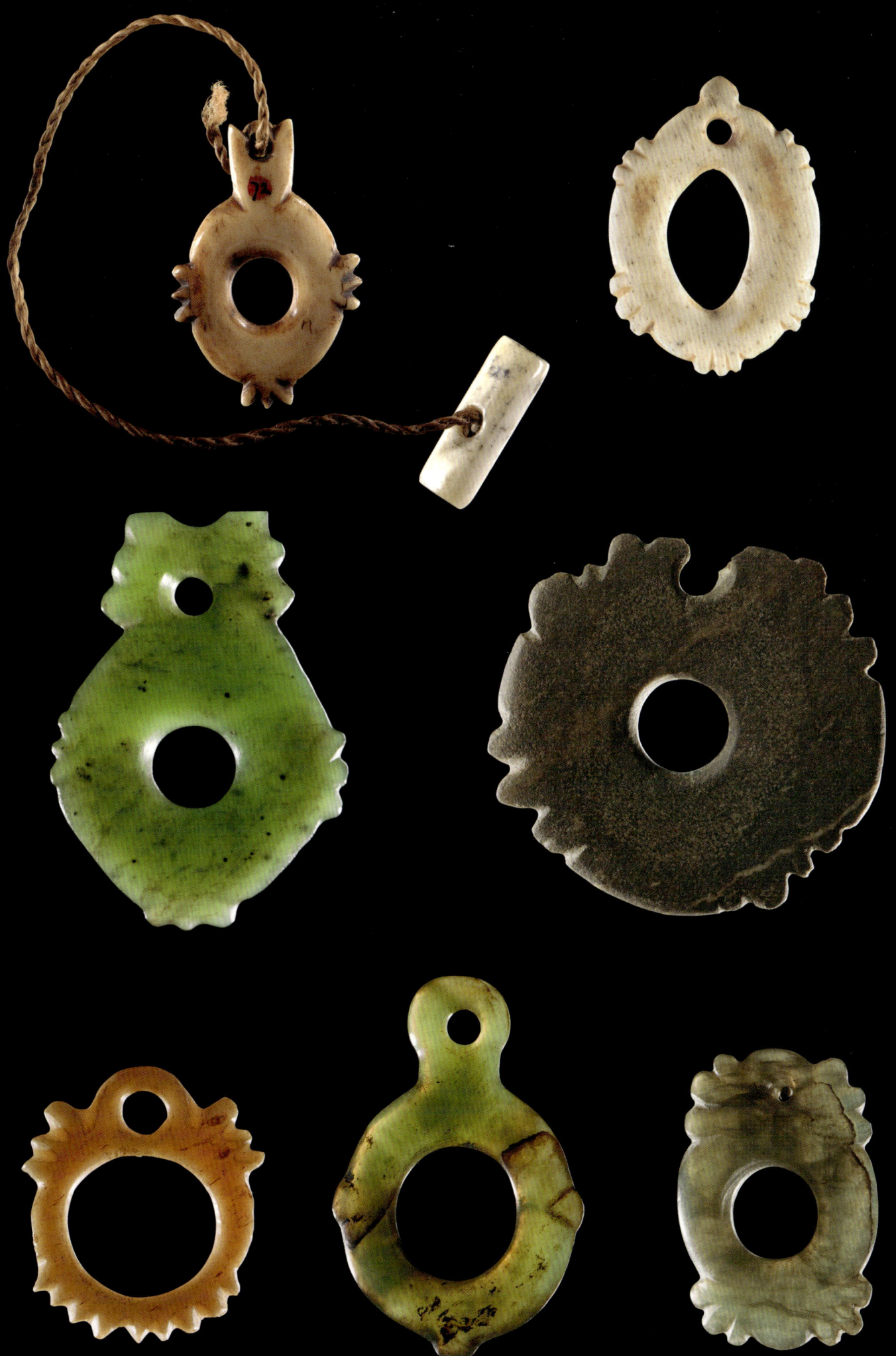

(Waiapu, 1834); alternate red and blue stripes on the face (Coromandel, 1770s); red face with blue bands round the eyes and nose; blue with a red smudge above each eyebrow (Waiapu, 1834); red face with yellow forehead, nose and chin; red face with yellow nose and chin (Cook, 1770s); crescents on the forehead, cheeks and chin (Wellington, 1844); and beauty spots on the nose, cheeks and chin (blue for girls, black for boys). For some chiefs, their entire head and body would be covered in red to signal their status and power, as was witnessed in the Coromandel in the 1770s and 1840s. The continuation of this practice through the introduction of Christianity underscores its enduring importance as a visual manifestation of tapu and mana.

Like moko, skin painting went out of fashion in many areas around the 1850s and was worn only occasionally, especially in relation to war as the mark of a warrior. In 1943 Ngāti Porou women marked their faces with pigment when they performed haka to celebrate the life of Lieutenant Moananui-a-Kiwa Ngarimu, a local man who had been awarded the Victoria Cross for valour in battle in World War Two. Few women wore moko kauae in Te Tairāwhiti by this time, and therefore painting the women's faces may have been as an assertion of their pride in being Ngāti Porou.

Skin painting made a return as part of the reclamation of Māori cultural practices from the 1980s, and it is now regularly seen in kapa haka competitions where groups compete to be the most traditional – or the most outrageous. Men paint their torso black as a symbol of ferocity, with red on the thighs to emphasise their leg movements. And with a growing number of kapa haka performers taking pūhoro, the mata whakarewa further highlights the incised patterns on their skin. Hapū members will sometimes decorate their skin for important political occasions, such as welcoming visitors from the Waitangi Tribunal or the government onto the marae.

## Hei – neck adornments

Māori made a range of neck ornaments that were strung on a kaui tiki (a cord made of fibre from tōī leaves) and attached with a poro (toggle) made of wood or poro toroa (albatross bone).[60] Traditions in adornment changed over time: early forms such as koūma disappeared after 1800, and koropepe, marakihau and kākā pōria (leg-ring adornments) were abandoned some time before the 1850s, though they have recently made a comeback. The hei matau (fishhook-shaped ornament) is based on the matau and may have originated as a favoured fishhook simply worn around the neck, but the hei tiki emerged only once artists had learnt how to drill into pounamu in the 1700s. Pekapeka ornaments, with their double bat form, were usually made from pounamu, though some rare examples are made from bone from a human skull, including one from Ruapekapeka pā, in Northland, that is now in Otago Museum (D.24.1209). Many pekapeka are now in museum collections, where Māori researchers and artists can study the works of their ancestors to learn the different forms and techniques, and to find inspiration.

Rei puta are a unique form, made from a whale's tooth shaped into a curved adornment. Artists in the South Island carved a whole face at one end of the rei puta, with eyes, nose and mouth, with a single puta (hole) drilled at the top for suspension at the other end. In the North Island artists carved rei puta with only the eyes, and a couple of incised lines for a nose. Cook observed that rei puta seemed to be the most highly prized ornaments in the communities he visited. He collected examples made from a whale tooth that had been shaped with some facial features at one end and suspension holes at the other. Rangatira wore rei puta as a symbol of their mana, and were reluctant to part with them – hence the scant numbers in museums: there are only four in the British Museum, out of its collection of over 2000 taonga; and there may well be only thirty or so in collections worldwide. Given the lack of surviving examples, it is likely that the rei puta was popular only in communities where whale teeth were readily available.

Hei tiki neck ornaments are shaped from a piece of pounamu and depict a single human figure. They relate to contemporaneous carved forms,[61] and to similar forms of the tiki elsewhere in the Pacific – from kiʻi and tiʻi in Hawaiʻi to tiki in the Marquesas. Examples of hei tiki from before 1800 are rare. This is not necessarily an indication that they were rare historically, however; it could just be that few examples have been handed down through the generations or, given that many were buried with their owners, it may be that they have not been retrieved since. Archaeologists have found few pounamu ornaments in excavations,[62] and those that they have found – twenty at Whareakeake, north of Dunedin, three at Ōruarangi (site of a former pā on the Waihou River, south of Thames) and one at Pā Bay (on Banks Peninsula) – may date to a later period.[63] According to Te Rangi Hīroa and

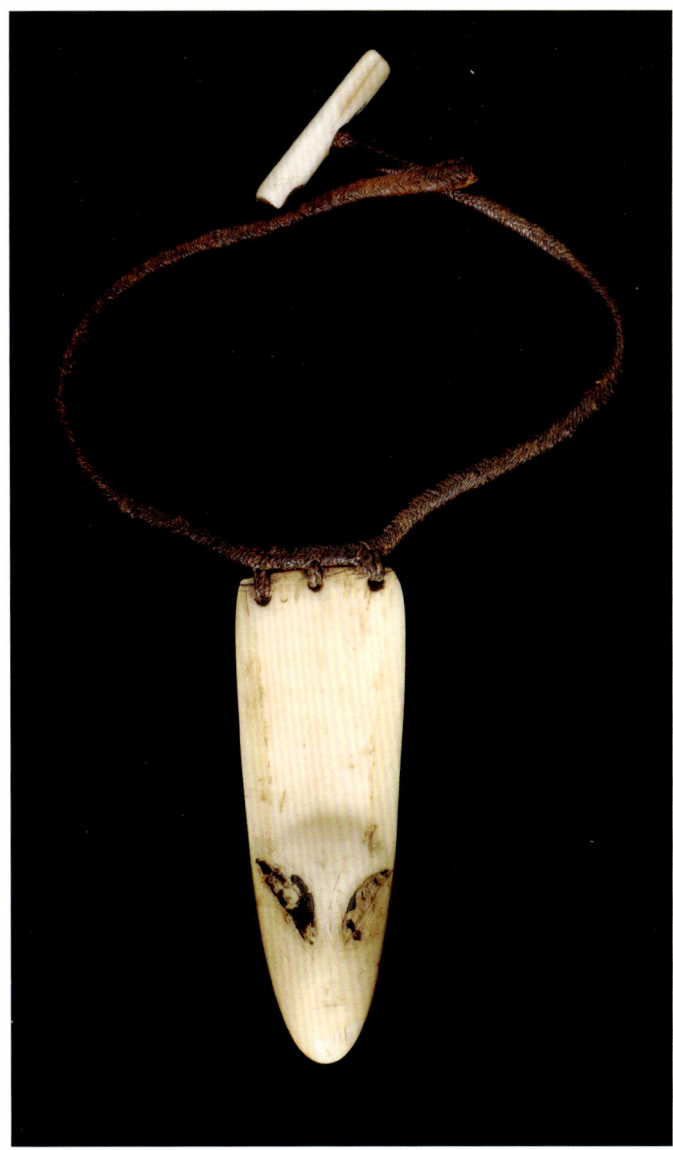 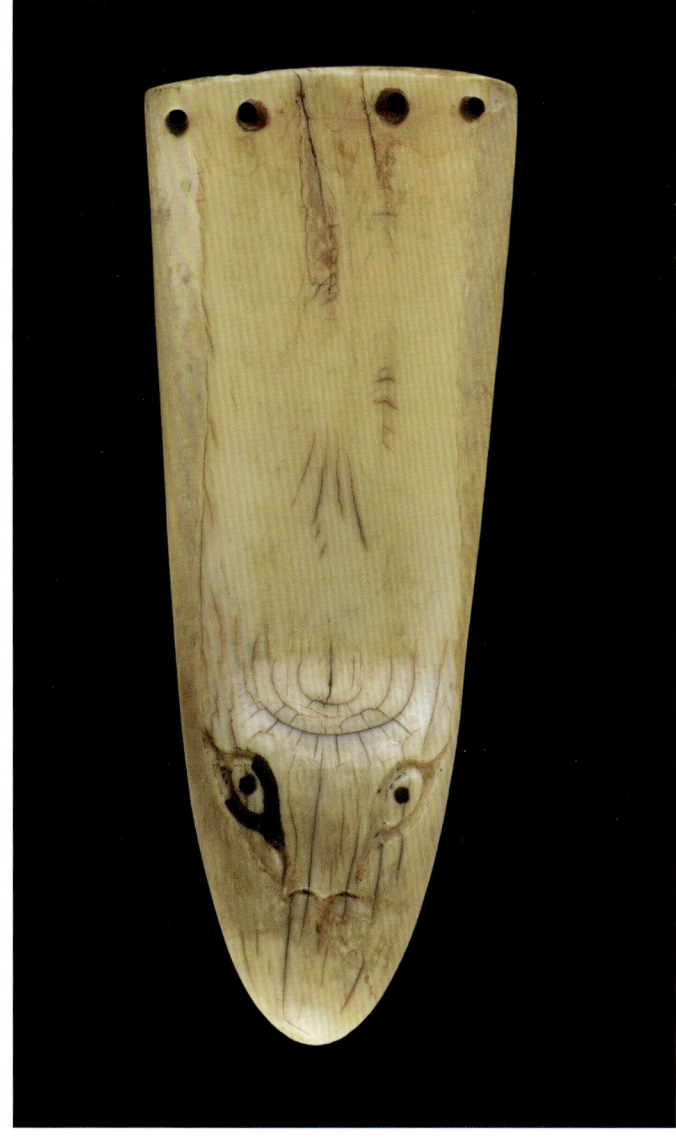

Henry Skinner,[64] the earliest examples of hei tiki were made from human bone or whalebone, as this material was easier to carve and less valuable to experiment with. A hei tiki made from bone from a human skull held in the British Museum (NZ156, 12.5cm) is of unknown provenance, but it is likely to be from Taranaki in the early nineteenth century – possibly made from the skull of an enemy in order to avenge the death of another person.

There were two types of hei tiki. The earlier form was in general more delicate: the head was free from the body, with one hand on the chest and another on the legs; both legs were vertical, with details of ears, elbows and knees; there were no ribs. The hei tiki form had small eyes, a thick neck, and a head-to-body ratio of 30:70 – very similar to figures on pou – and were, in general, 5–12cm tall. Later, artists produced a

Left: The rei puta was considered by Captain James Cook as the most prestigious of adornments, as he witnessed them being worn only by chiefs. How true this observation was is unclear. Currently only thirty-six from the eighteenth and nineteenth centuries have survived. This rei puta in the British Museum comes from the Bay of Islands, was collected by Cook, and is possibly the one worn in the drawing of the Ngare Raumati rangatira's son Te Kuku.
British Museum, Oc,NZ.159

Right: A rei puta from the North Island, recognisable by the four perforations at the top for the whiri, the gentle shaping of the eyes and minimal haehae (lines) for the mouth.
British Museum, Oc,LMS.155

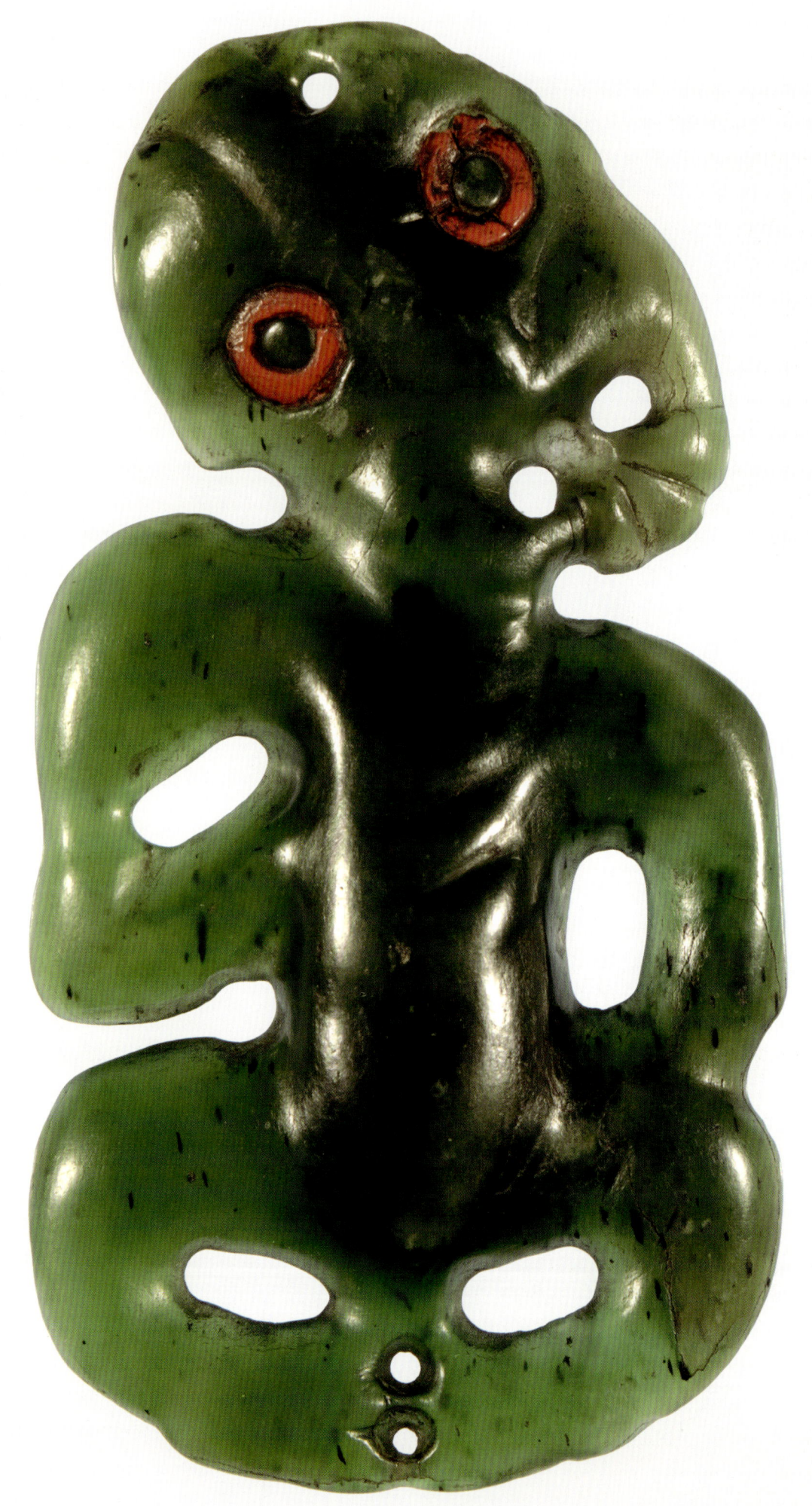

heavier type of hei tiki that was less elaborate and so required less work to produce. The head of this later form was much larger, with a head-to-body ratio of 40:60; both hands were placed on the legs, which invariably turned inwards.[65]

Hei tiki became increasingly popular over the nineteenth century and, as a result, from 1820 artists began transforming greenstone adzes into hei tiki. With the introduction of metal, toki pounamu no longer served a practical purpose, and artists began experimenting by fashioning hei tiki out of toki. Hei tiki remained a popular collector's item because of their distinctiveness. This is attested to by the sheer number of hei tiki in museum collections today, far outweighing all other forms: the British Museum for instance has fifty hei tiki compared to relatively few other types of hei (four rei puta, eight hei matau and ten kapeu – a greenstone ear ornament with a curved end).

The symbolism of hei tiki for Māori has been the subject of much debate. Based on oral accounts and mōteatea, hei tiki sometimes served as a memento of special ancestors: they were removed from the tūpāpaku after burial and kept in a safe place, and brought out again when another whānau member passed away. The hei tiki Mihi Rawhiti, for instance, was shared between two different family groups, both descended from Maru Tuahu of Taranaki. When one wearer died they would be buried with the hei tiki; then when the body was exhumed, the taonga would be passed to the other whānau, and so on.[66] Hei tiki were often named after important ancestors, whose lives were relived in their descendants' memories when the hei tiki was brought out and worn. Hei tiki were sometimes seen as a symbol of Hineteiwaiwa, atua of childbirth: a woman's in-laws might give her a hei tiki if she was pregnant, or if she was having trouble getting pregnant. These multiple meanings enhanced the mana and value of the hei tiki, particularly named ones.

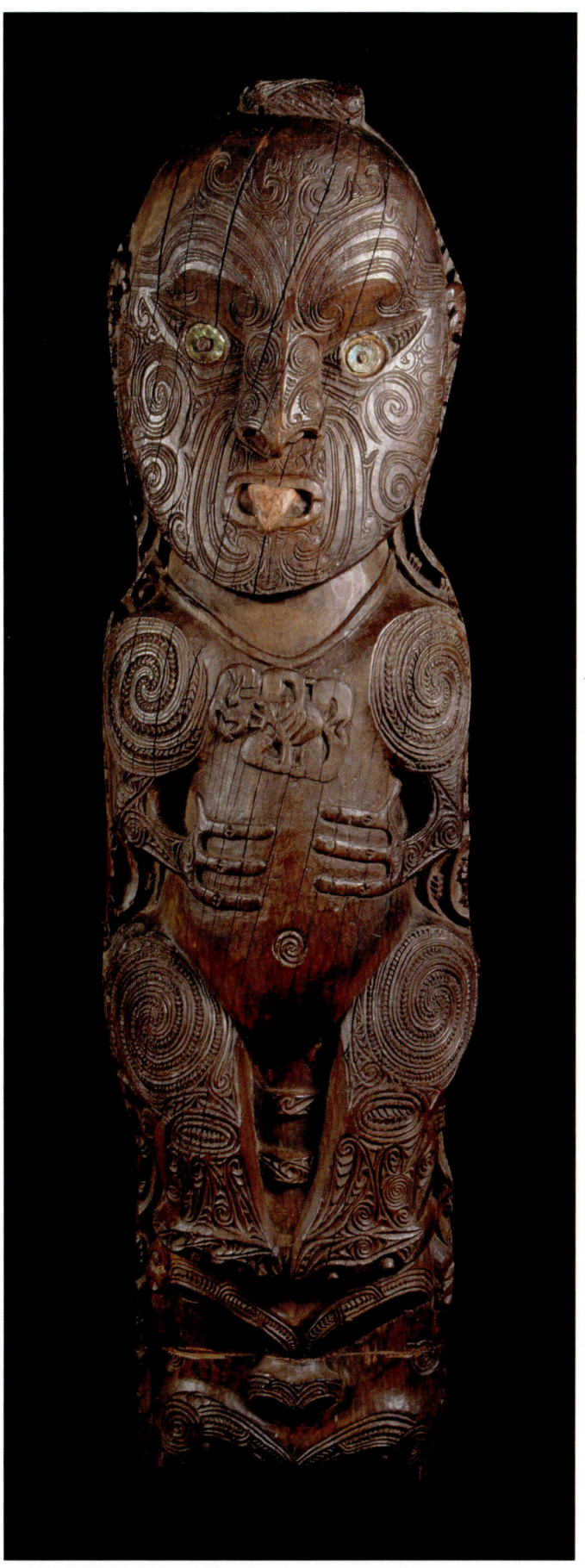

An important source of information about the practice of adornment is whakairo in which ancestors are depicted wearing adornments in their hair or ears and around their neck. In this nineteenth-century example, a koruru wears a hei tiki around his neck.
National Museum of Ireland, AE:1898.349

Opposite: Hei tiki have remained a core symbol of te ao Māori through the generations. Hundreds now reside in museums around the world, revealing a myriad of different styles.
Museum of Archaeology and Anthropology, University of Cambridge, Z 6466

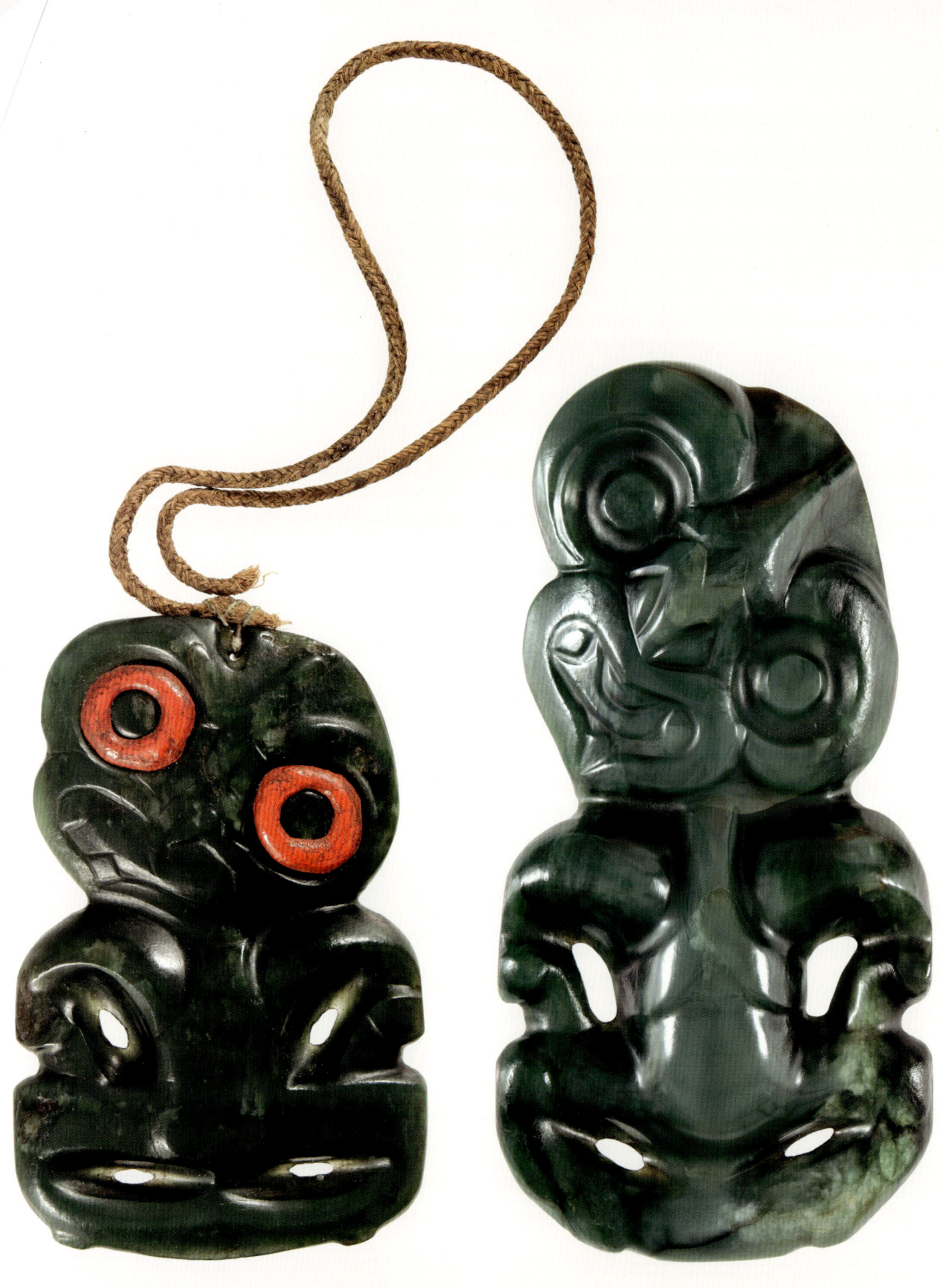

Left: Hei tiki pounamu with eyes made of sealing wax.
Museum of Archaeology and Anthropology, University of Cambridge, 1922.48

Right: Large hei tiki pounamu, probably made from an adze blade.
Museum of Archaeology and Anthropology, University of Cambridge, E 1913.5

Opposite: Hei tiki made by a Ngāti Hau artist in the nineteenth century.
Museo delle Civiltà, 459, photograph by Serena Francone

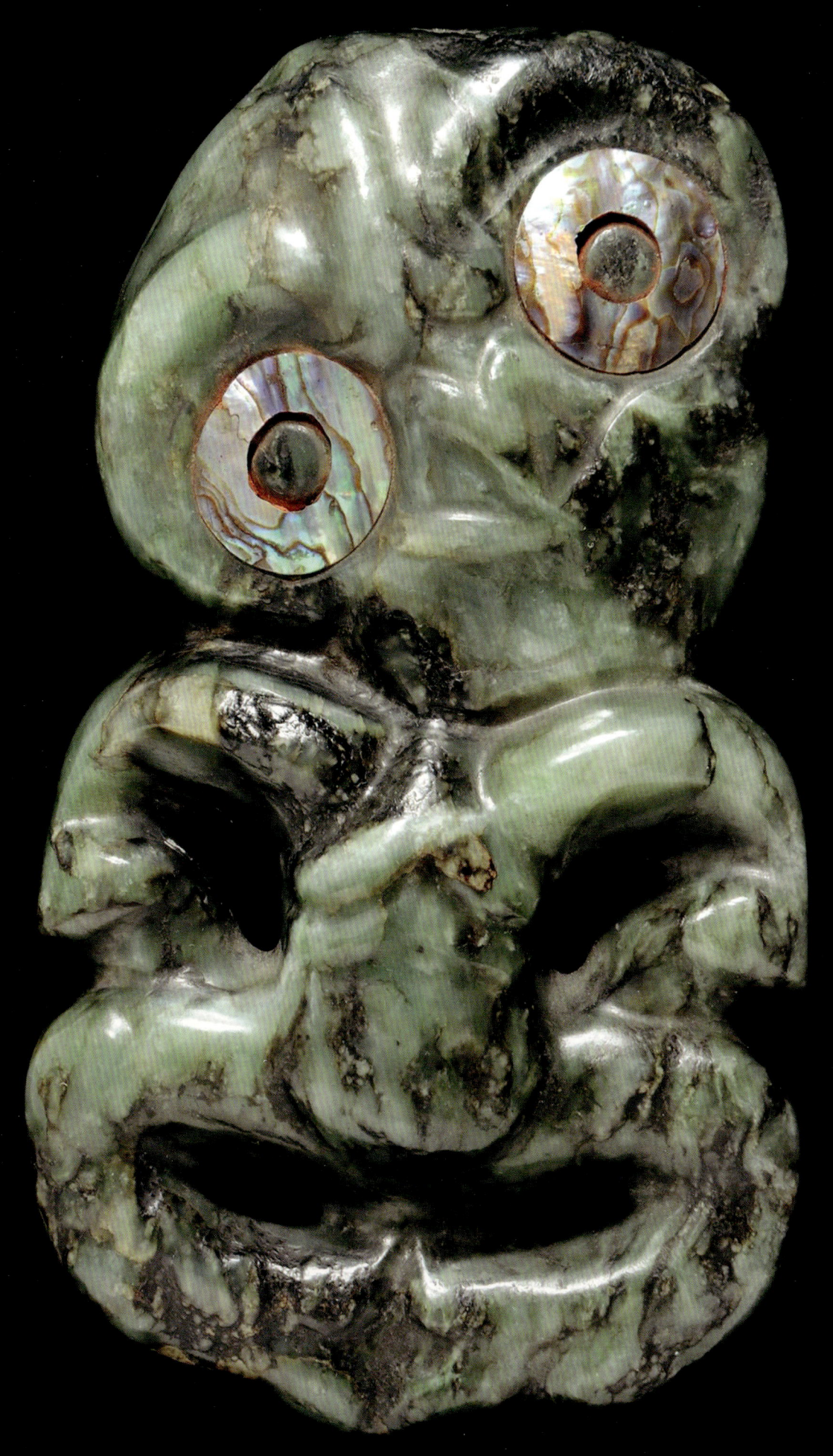

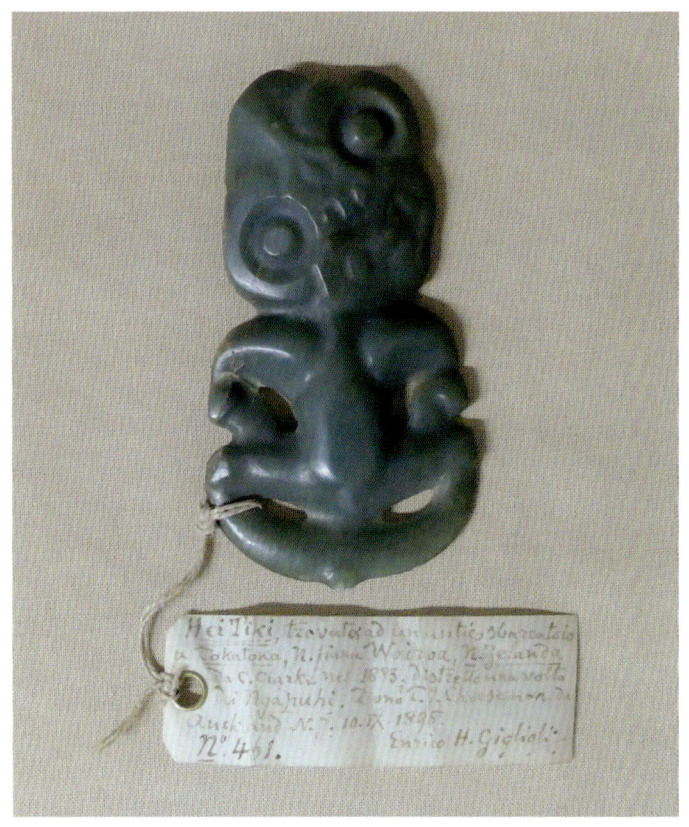
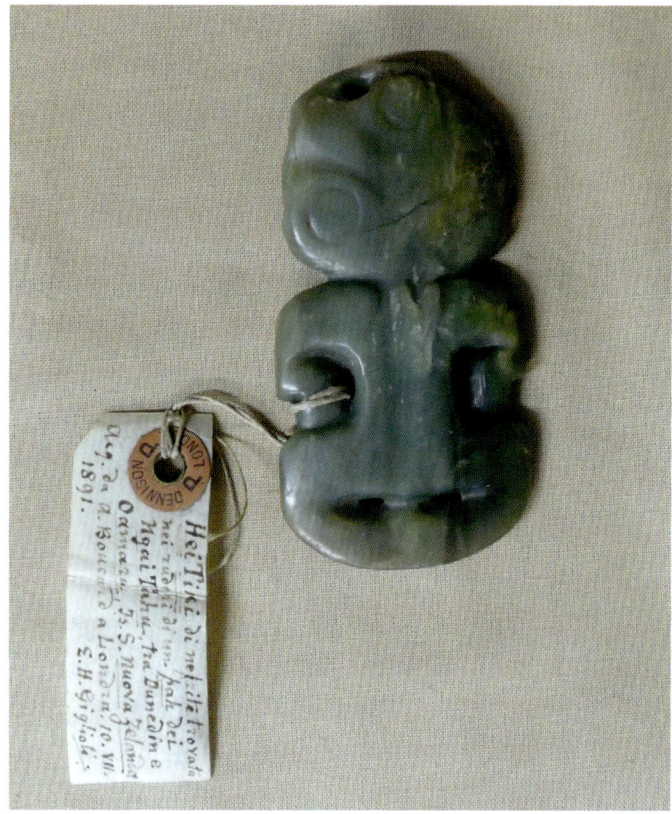

Enrico Giglioli wrote on the label of this hei tiki (now in Rome) that it had been 'found' in an 'ancient landing' at Tokatoka, on the Northern Wairoa River. Whether or not this was an urupā (burial site) is unclear, though we know that this style of collecting taonga Māori was still popular in the late nineteenth century. Giglioli also noted the hei tiki was 'dei Ngapuhi' ('of' Ngapuhi), and had been gifted by Thomas Cheeseman, curator/director of Auckland Museum, in 1895.
Museo delle Civiltà, 461, photograph by Serena Francone

Enrico Giglioli noted that this hei tiki was from a 'pah dei Ngai Tahu', also noting Ōamaru. He acquired the taonga in London in 1891 from someone named Boucard. More research by an Italian-speaking taonga researcher able to access local archival records will no doubt reveal more details about this collection.
Museo delle Civiltà, 460g, photograph by Serena Francone

Named hei tiki sometimes acted as peacemakers. The female hei tiki Te Maungārongo (now in Te Papa Tongarewa, ME013454) is a prime example.[67] Her whakapapa begins in the 1820s when she was worn by Te Rangipurewa, a Ngāti Rarua tohunga from Waiharakeke (Blenheim) in the South Island. When Te Rauparaha arrived in the área, he took a local woman for his retinue as a political alliance, much to the distress of her whānau. Te Rangipurewa intervened and presented Te Rauparaha with his own hei tiki, Te Maungārongo, and the woman was returned home. By the 1860s Te Maungārongo was in the North Island, in the hands of the Ringatū prophet Te Kooti Arikirangi. Here again Te Maungārongo was presented as a gesture of peace when Te Kooti sent the hei tiki to King Tāwhiao, leader of the Kīngitanga movement. However, her journey was diverted, and we next find her with Ngāti Maniapoto. The hei tiki was gifted to Ropata Kaihau (Ngāti Te Ata, associated with the Kīngitanga) who gifted her to William Searancke, the resident magistrate in the Waikato region, who passed her on to the governor, Sir George Bowen. The hei tiki was later bought by A. Eady of Auckland, who loaned her to Auckland Museum, but after Eady's death the Dominion Museum (now Te Papa) purchased the taonga in 1977. Te Maungārongo's complex biography reflects the changing political and social relationships of the nineteenth century, and ultimately weaves all her kaitiaki together into one multi-faceted history. This is the power of taonga.

Unfortunately, the whakapapa of most of the hei tiki in museum collections today was not recorded at the time of collection, or has since been lost. On the other hand, there are hei tiki recorded in mōteatea who have not yet been recovered in their physical form. In *Ngā Mōteatea*, Apirana Ngata's collection of waiata, one oriori (song 75, composed by Whakaawe of Ngāti Tūwharetoa) includes a reference to a hei tiki named Whakatere-kohukohu (line 14). According to George Grey, this 'was taken by Hongi Hika, and remained with his family until the time when peace was made after Hone Heke's war and Heke then presented it to the Governor'.[68]

Hei tiki, both historic and contemporary, are still important sources of cultural pride. Whānau hold them in high regard and associate them with the ancestors who have worn them. Contemporary artists experiment with making hei tiki from a range of materials, but the medium in no way detracts from the potency of the form as an icon of Māori culture. Te Ātiawa carver Rangi Kipa, for instance, practices with making hei tiki in Corian, a plastic compound, in a riot of colours; and George Nuku (Ngāti Kahungunu) explores Perspex as a material for his adornment carvings.

In comparison to hei tiki, relatively little is known about hei matau. The form is associated with the sea and fishing, and people believe they were worn by navigators, waka captains and master fishers. The matau shape derives from Pacific fishhook forms, and relates in oral history to the narrative of Māui fishing up the North Island using a matau he fashioned from his grandmother's jawbone.

There were many different styles of hei matau. Simple examples use a classic U-shape that curls inwards;[69] some had notching around the edges, which may represent generations in a whakapapa;[70] others resembled an animal figure. It seems the form allowed a great deal of artistic licence in different communities. A much more complex example is in the British Museum. The Tītore adornment is an innovative form where the hei tiki concept has been overlaid on a hei matau.[71] Revolutionary in its inception, it suggests real risk-taking by the artist who created it in the eighteenth century.

Māori also wore ornaments to fasten their cloaks together. The term 'aurei' comes from 'au' or thatch needle, and 'rei' which means whale ivory. Artists also made them from other materials, such as pāua, pounamu, human teeth and seal teeth. Pounamu and parāoa aurei were very precious and had great social value, as they signified that the person was someone with much mana. Wearers would tie two or three aurei together and use them to pin the edges of the kākahu so the aurei hung down on the right-hand side. This cluster of aurei would rattle when the person wearing it moved, drawing attention to them.[72]

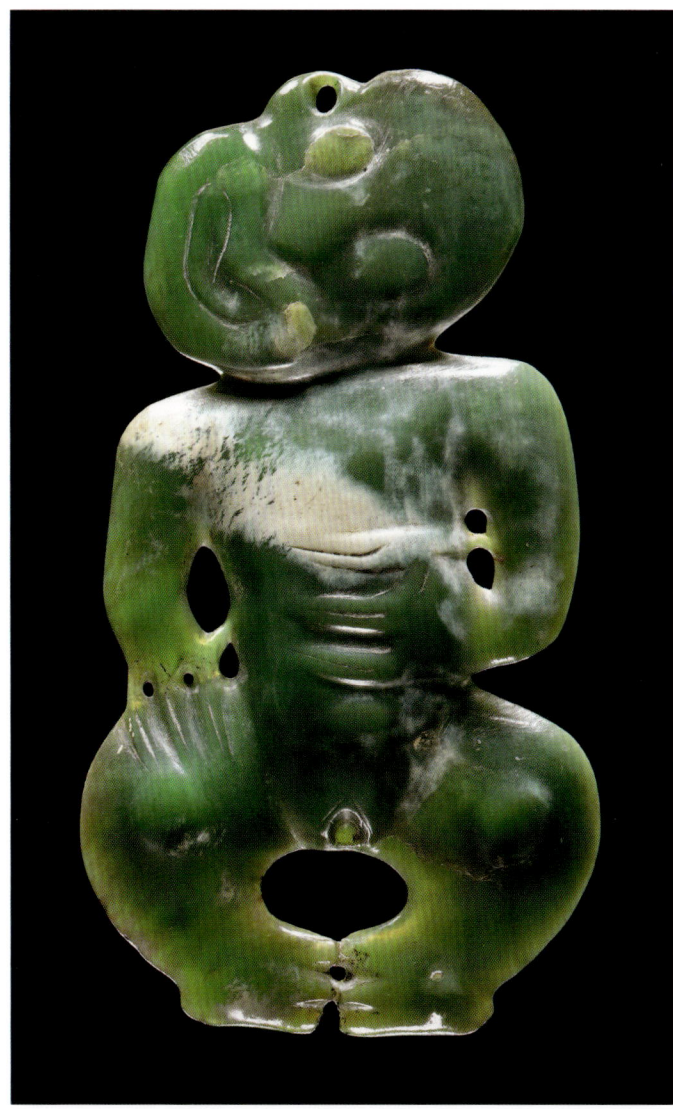

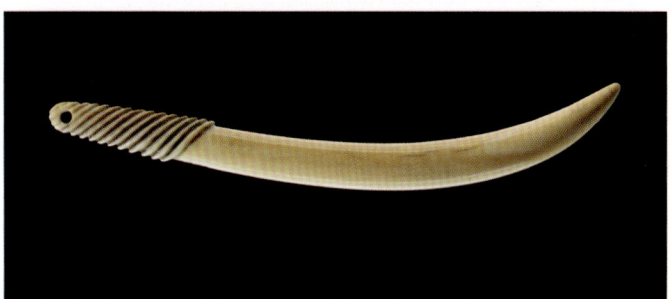

Top: Te Maungārongo ('Lasting Peace') hei tiki (Ngāti Toa, Ngāti Rārua, Rongowhakaata, Ngāti Maniapoto, Ngāti Te Ata, 1600–1820).
Te Papa Tongarewa Museum of New Zealand, ME013454, purchased 1977

Bottom: Aurei were integral to the display of kākahu, as they were clustered to pin together the edges of the cloak. Usually made of bone, they were delicately shaped and worn in such a way as to rattle when the wearer walked.
Te Papa Tongarewa Museum of New Zealand, ME001780/1, Augustus Hamilton Collection, purchased 1914

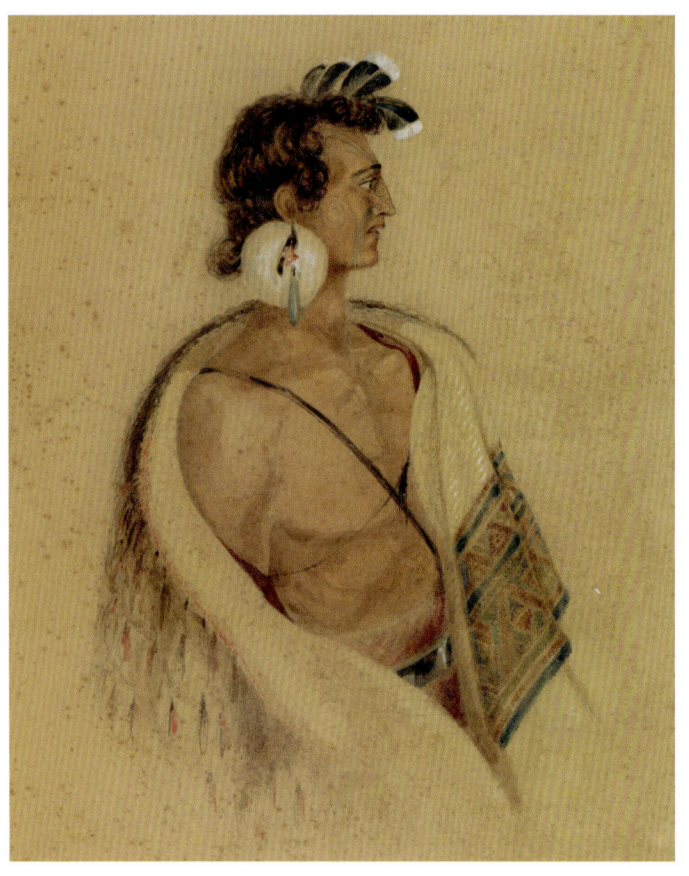

## Mau taringa – ear ornaments

Mau taringa or ear ornaments were very popular with Māori. Young people would pierce their ears with a needle made of mānuka, then thread muka fibre through the slit. They took great delight in poking a range of objects and materials through this slit and suspending things from it. The simplest were variations on the kuru pounamu (greenstone ornament), such as the kuru mahora (straight stone pendant) and kuru papa (a flattened form of the kapeu);[73] as well as the kākā pōria, the pau (long pendant),[74] and the mōtoi (earring made of pounamu or shark tooth).[75]

Mau taringa were also made from soft materials. In the early years of settlement, when aute was still available, ear ornaments such as kope or turuki were made from tapa: Cook described these, and Parkinson drew them. Kahu raurēkau were an ear ornament made from strips of a 'thin, film-like white tissue stripped from leaves of the *Coprosma grandifolia*', poked through the ear.[76] These ornaments were ephemeral and were not as well documented as others.

The pōhoi was an ear ornament that consisted of a bunch of feathers – often the downy feathers of the albatross, pōhoi toroa – gathered together in a ball and worn in the ear. The high economic and social value of the material guaranteed the wearer would be treated with respect. There are several portraits from the 1840s that show Ngāti Toa rangatira Te Rangihaeata wearing his pōhoi toroa, suggesting that this was his signature ornament.

Parts of birds were sometimes attached to the ears as ornaments. Missionary William Yate wrote an account of extraordinary sights he witnessed in 1834, where whole birds were used: 'I have frequently seen dead birds with the head squeezed through the hole made in a person's ear, where it has remained until it rotted off; and I have seen live birds served in the same way, and allowed to hang there and flap their wings and struggle till they were dead.'[77] The sheer performance value of this alone would have been quite breathtaking.

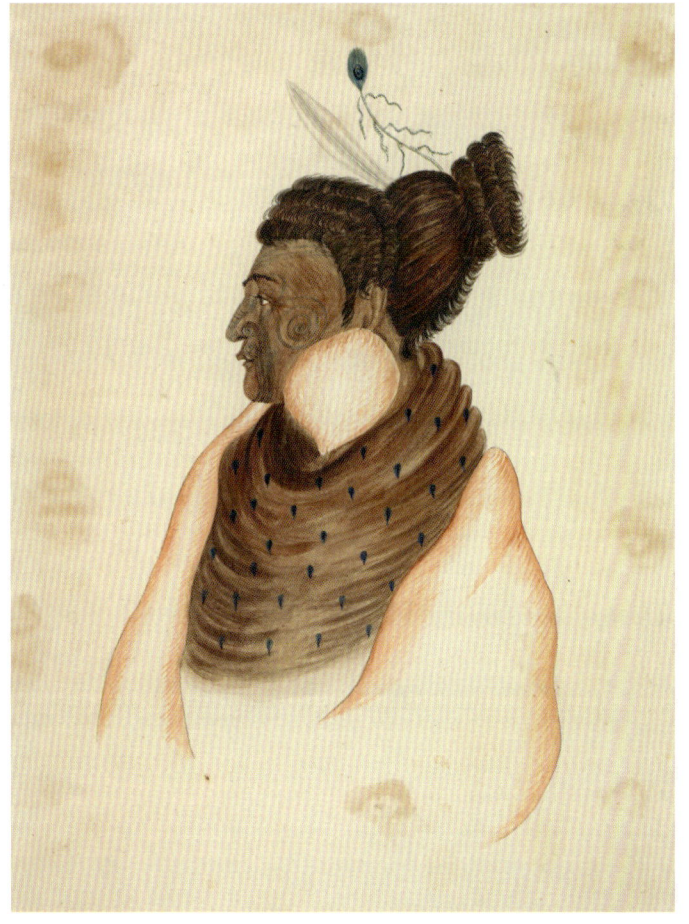

Top: Ngāti Toa chief Te Rangihaeata was often drawn with his pōhoi toroa, a downy albatross ear ornament. These were the symbol of someone with immense mana, and thus befitted this wearer.
**Charles Heaphy, *Rangiaeata*, 1840**
watercolour, 280 x 178mm, Alexander Turnbull Library, C-025-022

Bottom: **Isaac Coates, *Rangihaeata, Rauparaha's fighting general*, 1843**
watercolour and gum Arabic, 257 x 192mm, Alexander Turnbull Library, A-286-014

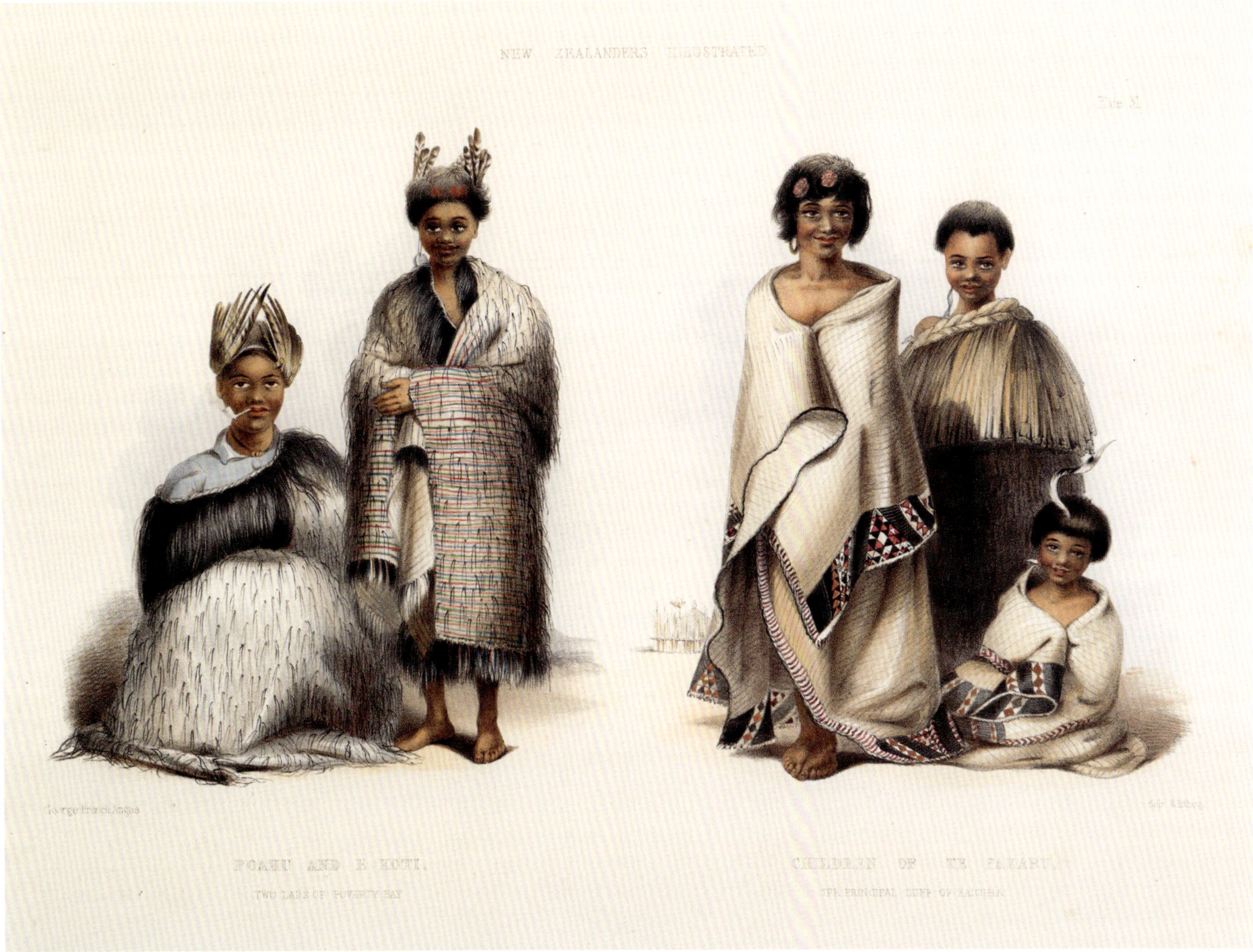

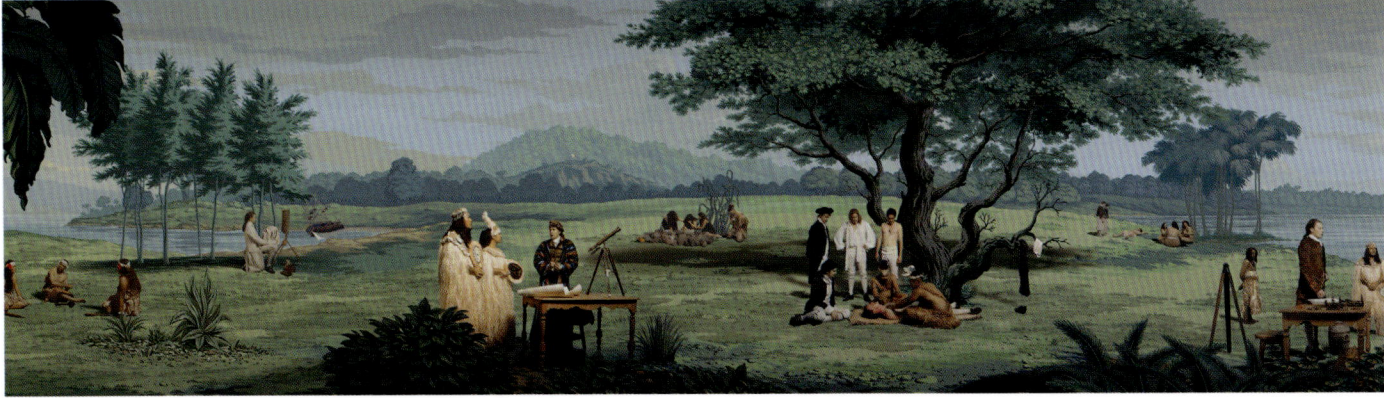

Top: Poahu (far left) adorns his head with a whole bird wing over each ear. His friend Koti has several long bird feathers on either side of his hair, and has red sections of hair on the front of his head, possibly from kōkōwai or some other pigment.

**George French Angas,** *Poahu and E Koti. Two Lads of Poverty Bay. Children of Te Pakaru, The Principal Chief of Kaioha,* c.1847

hand-coloured lithograph, 225 x 400mm, Auckland Art Gallery Toi o Tāmaki, 2009/16/13/1, purchased 2009

Bottom: **Lisa Reihana,** *in Pursuit of Venus [infected],* 2015–2017

single-channel video, UltraHD, colour, 7.1 sound, 1hrs 4min, Auckland Art Gallery Toi o Tāmaki, 2014/24, gift of the Patrons of the Auckland Art Gallery, 2014

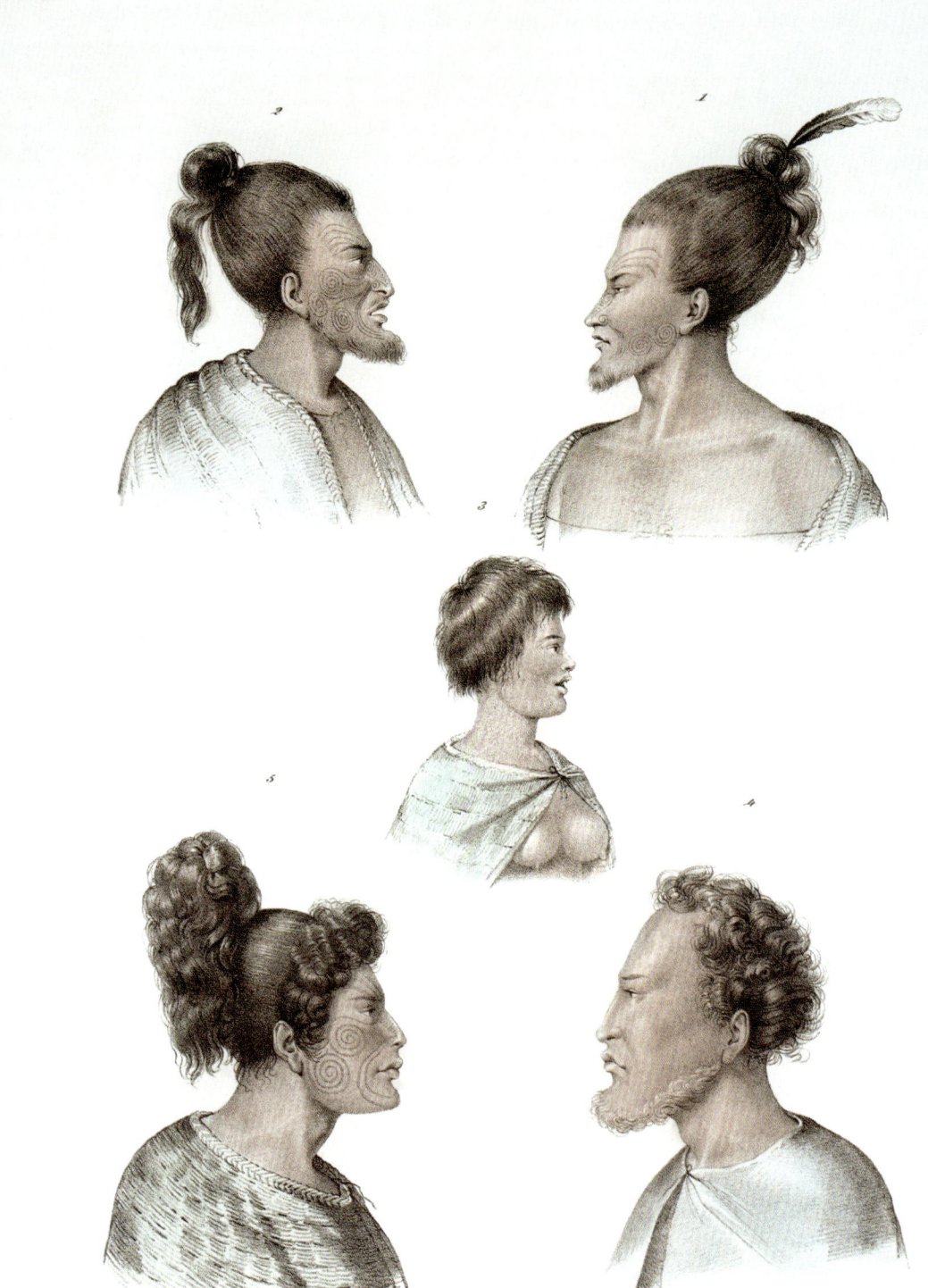

NEU-SEELAND.
1. Häuptling von Houa-Houa. 2.3. Mann und Frau aus Houa-Houa.
4.5. Eingeborne von Tirauiti.

Māori relished the materials introduced by Europeans to make ear ornaments. Joseph Banks described people in the 1760s wearing iron nails through their ears as a way of carrying them[78] – though it is more likely they were worn as a badge of distinction, to show that the wearer had been in contact with Pākehā and were able to acquire such a treasure. Accounts in the early nineteenth century mentioned Māori placing other introduced objects in their ears such as 'gun-swivels, coins, small bottles, buttons, buckles'.[79]

### He rākai mo te mahunga – adornments for the head

There were many ways of decorating the head. Māori wore feathers in their hair, through their ears, in their beard and through the nose. This might be done to beautify the wearer or to signal a person's status, especially if they wore a precious and rare huia feather. Te Rangikāheke described how 'chiefly females' who had just received their moko wore feathers to mark the occasion: 'they arise, and albatross skin is placed in the ear, and They are decorated with feathers on the head; they are dressed in kaitaka cloaks and when ready taken to eat'.[80] Parkinson drew a range of feather headdresses on six men who each wore white feathers and red or brown wooden heru placed carefully in their tikitiki (topknot). Angas also recorded a variety of adornments, including a delightful pen-and-wash showing two young people, one of whom has whole bird wings covering their ears.[81]

The head is considered the most sacred part of the body, so it was appropriate that the head was dressed in a way that reflected the mana and tapu of the wearer: the more important the person, the more valuable the type and number of feathers (such as toroa) and the heru (combs made from parāoa or whalebone were the most prized). Men and women sometimes placed feathers through a piercing in the septum (the cartilage between the nostrils): the feathers projected across the cheeks and were considered by some European visitors as a 'truly grotesque sight'.[82] Wearers favoured the long tailfeathers of kererū, kākā and kōtuku (white heron). Women would sometimes dip whole bird skins in berry oil and wear them as adornment around their head.

Māori wore their hair in a number of different styles. Sometimes women would cut their hair as an outward sign of grief, as French traveller Julien Crozet witnessed in the Bay of Islands.[83] Sydney Parkinson observed people using a shark's tooth to cut and shave the hair, and noted that 'some of them had their hair most curiously brought up to their crowns, rolled around, and knotted'; and at Palliser Bay he saw Māori with their hair in two bunches on the crown, one of which was plaited. Banks described seeing hair in a bunch on either side, arranged so that the bunch pointed forward, 'presenting a disagreeable appearance'. He noted that the women he saw rarely decorated their hair;[84] this is in line with Hirini Moko Mead's assertion that it was men who spent the most time preparing themselves for presentation.[85]

Tīkao describes hairstyles in Canterbury in the nineteenth century: 'The hair was combed and then the comb was inserted into the koukou (topknot – a bunch of hair is a puti). Women wore their hair mahora (spread out) hanging down or in whiri or whiriwhiri (one or two plaits respectively).'[86] Feathers were sometimes tucked into a pare or tīpare (headband) worn on the head, and Elsdon Best describes hair ties that were made from strips of tapa or from the inner bark of the ribbonwood, and the leaves of *Celmisia* (alpine daisy).[87]

Heru served several purposes as a head adornment: they added height, and signalled the wearer's rank and status – particularly when they were made from whalebone or featured intricate carved designs. They often held mana in their own right because of their association with the head, and with named persons. In the case of Paikea, a dispute over a sacred heru caused the migration from the Pacific (see page 145). The role of heru elsewhere in the Pacific was primarily decorative. Some, such as selu in Sāmoa, were made in one piece; others, such as helu in Tonga, were composite. Both single and composite forms were brought to Aotearoa, and evolved further into two shapes: quadrangular and curvilinear.

At least 300 early heru have survived, probably because the head was so tapu, so the disposal of items associated with the head would be done with great care. Half of these have been recovered from a pā at Kauri Point, where Ngāiterangi ancestors deliberately deposited 187 heru that had been

---

These images of four Tai Rāwhiti men and a woman from Ūawa in 1826–27 record a range of hairstyles popular in the area, challenging the idea that topknots were the norm. The woman at the centre has a short 'bowl cut' also popular in other locations – the hair was often cut during tangihanga.
**Louis Auguste de Sainson, *Neu Seeland. Hauptling von Houa-Houa; 2, 3. Mann und Frau aus Houa-Houa; 4, 5. Eingeborne von Terauiti*. De Sainson pinx., J Benz del., lith de J Brodtmann. [Plate] 24, 1826–1836**
hand-coloured lithograph, 342 x 254mm, Alexander Turnbull Library, A-191-041

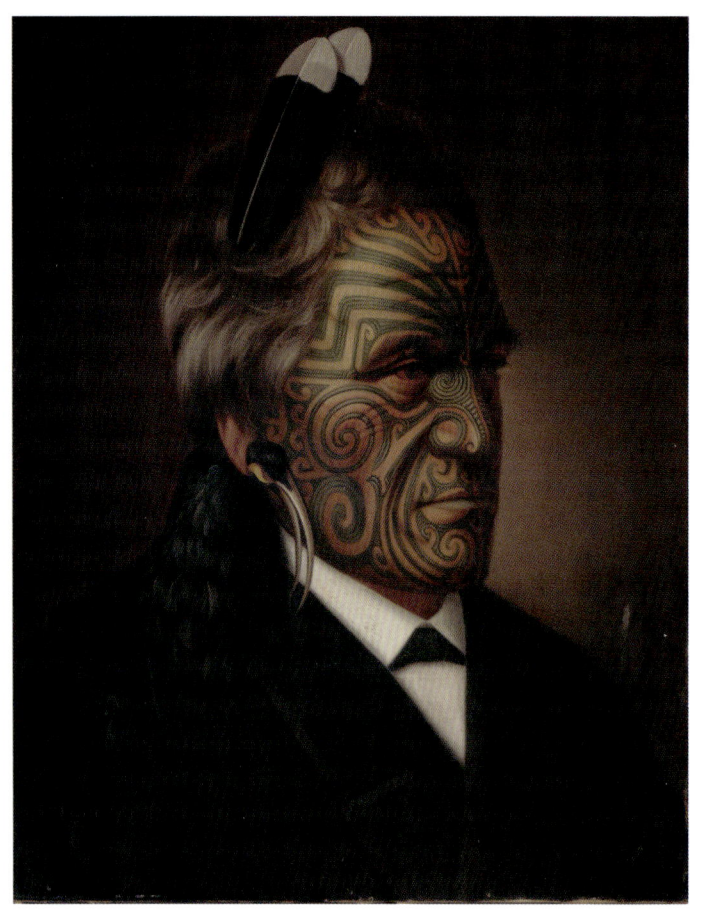
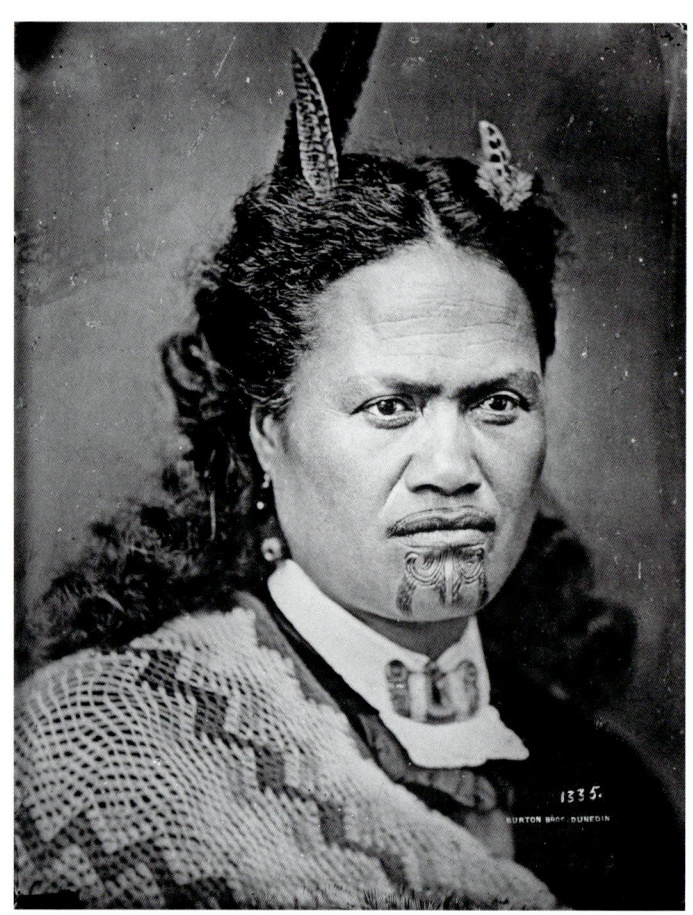
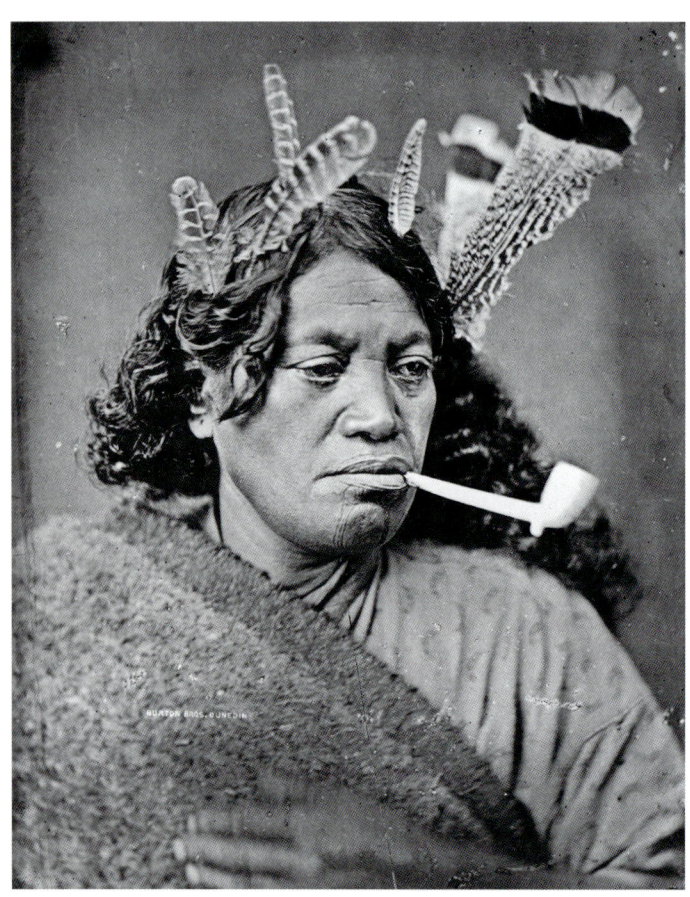
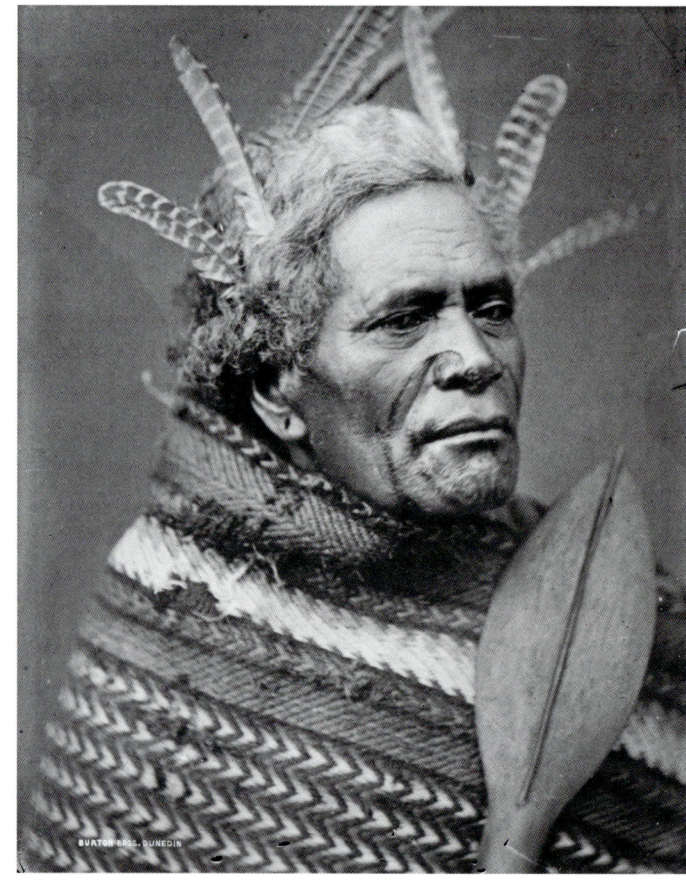

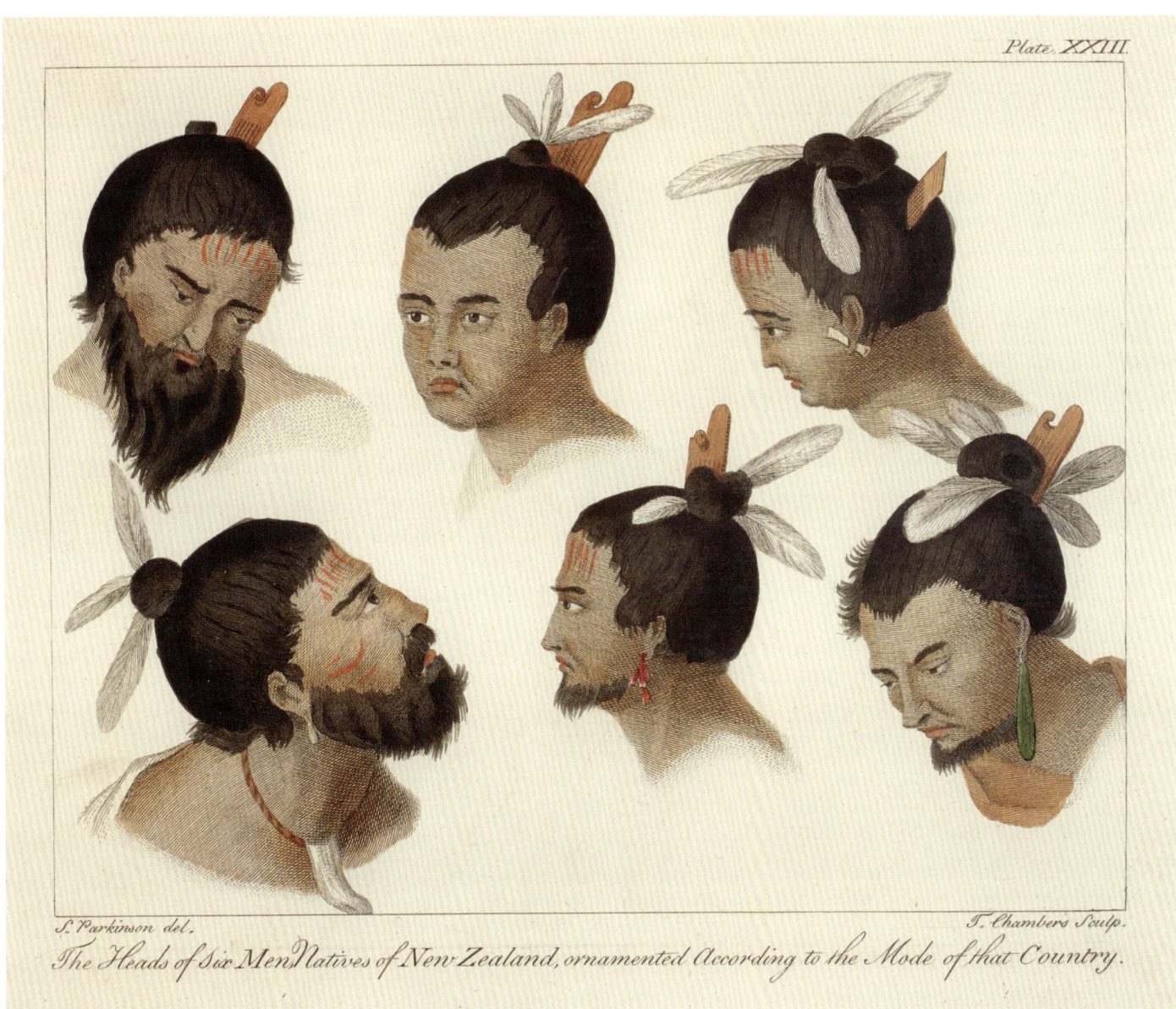

Opposite top left: Ngāi Te Rangi rangatira Tomika Te Mutu is depicted here with a whole huia suspended through a slit in his ear. Gottfried Lindauer painted Tomika several times, always based on earlier photographs (Tomika had died in 1867), none of which showed him with the huia adornment. This suggests either Lindauer had access to a photograph since lost, or was constructing this portrait based on what adornments he thought would best represent the rangatira. Huia would become extinct by the early twentieth century.

**Gottfried Lindauer, *Tomika Te Mutu, chief of the Ngaiterangi tribe, Bay of Plenty, New Zealand*, c.1880**

oil on canvas, 508 x 406mm, National Library of Australia, nla.obj-134310327

Opposite bottom left: This woman from the 1870s shows real flair in the way in which she presents herself for the camera, with no less than six feathers of various types placed to give her height and distinction.

American Photographic Company (Auckland), Te Papa Tongarewa Museum of New Zealand, C.010185, purchased 1943

Opposite top right: Māori continued to wear feathers in the hair into the early twentieth century, as these studio photographs demonstrate. Māori used feathers in different ways in their dress, from being attached to kākahu to placed in the beard and hair. This photograph and the ones below capture a range of uses which add agency to the sitters, who were often unnamed.

American Photographic Company (Auckland), Te Papa Tongarewa Museum of New Zealand, C.010171, purchased 1943

Opposite bottom right: This man photographed in the 1880s follows a similar style of placing feathers so they splayed across the head.

Burton Brothers, Te Papa Tongarewa Museum of New Zealand, C.018029

**Above: Sydney Parkinson, *The heads of six men, natives of New Zealand, ornamented according to the mode of that Country*, 1784**

Te Papa Tongarewa Museum of New Zealand, RB000268/116a, gift of Charles Rooking Carter, from Sydney Parkinson, *A journal of a voyage to the South Seas, in his Majesty's ship, 'The Endeavour'*. Faithfully transcribed from the papers of the late Sydney Parkinson. London; Printed for Charles Dilly, in the Poultry, and James Phillips, in the George-Yard, 1784

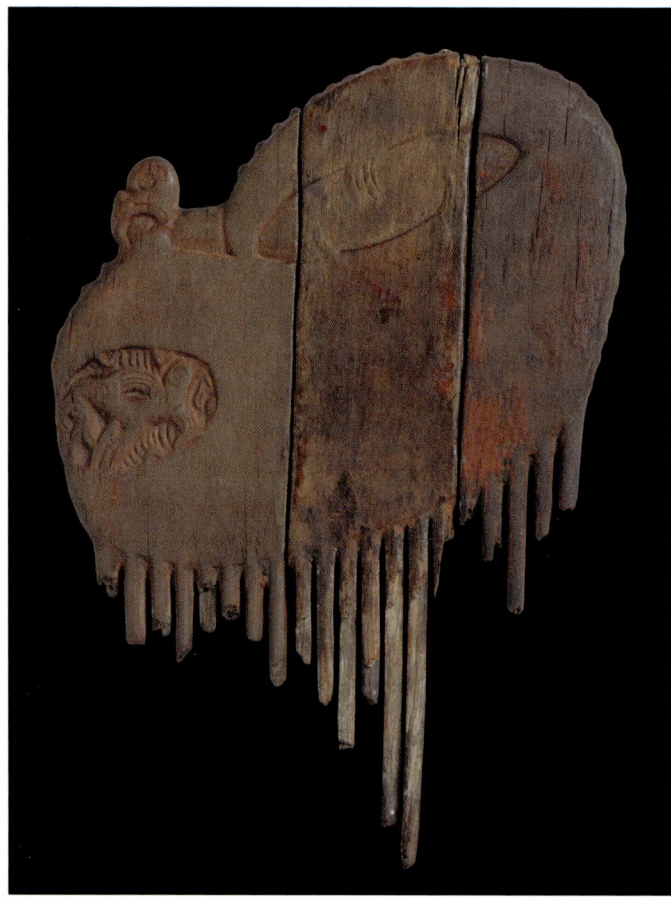

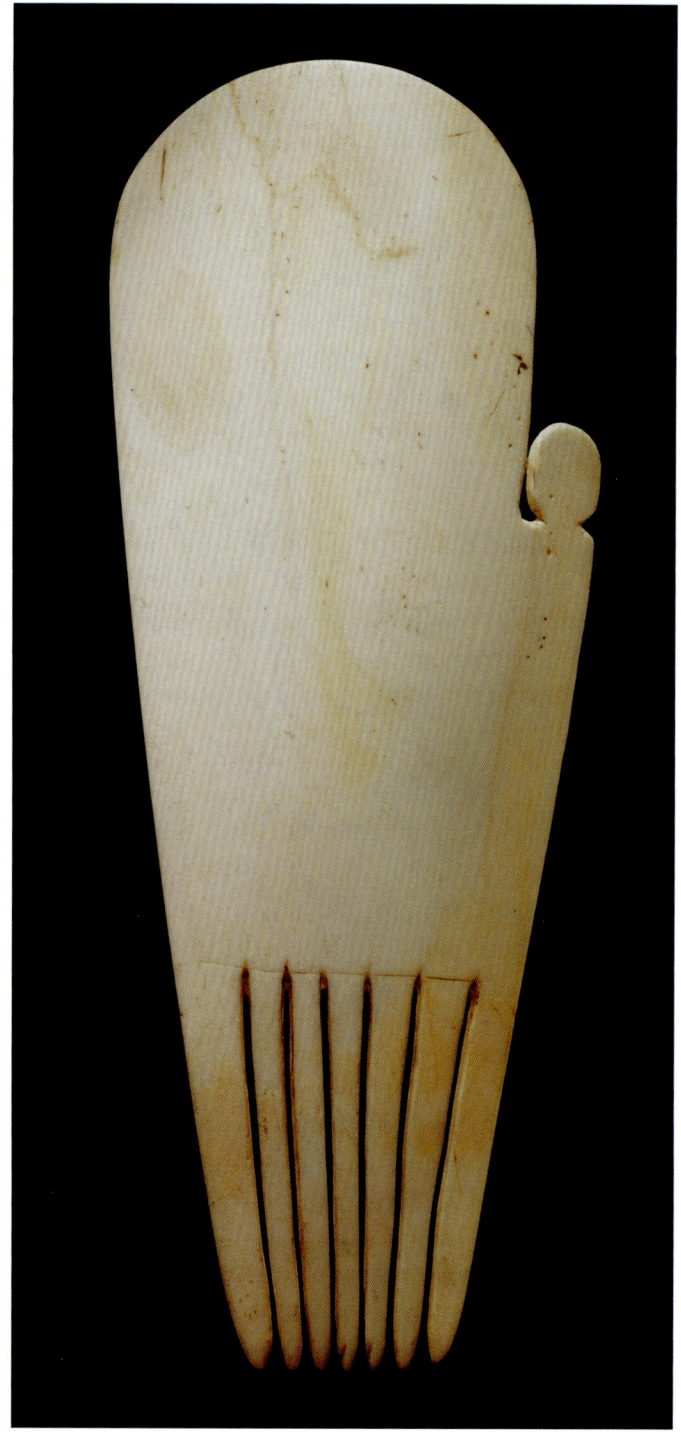

ritually broken in a nearby wetland.⁸⁸ Most of these early combs were made from wood; the few made from parāoa were probably reserved for chiefly people. Some were made from a single piece of material, others were composite, and they were on average 7–8cm high, although some were up to 15cm.

The heru deposited at the Kauri Point site enable us to track shifts in the evolution of the style of heru from Pacific to Māori.⁸⁹ Mead's research has shown that the heru chart a change in form from geometric to curvilinear, at which point they also become more decorative.⁹⁰ Heru went out of fashion around the 1830s or 1840s as the missionary preference for short hair for men became widely accepted, although they endured as important taonga that were passed down through generations. Today, as increasing numbers of Māori men choose to wear their hair long and twisted into a tikitiki, they join women in celebrating their hair by wearing heru.

## Waka huia, papahou and powaka whakairo – containers for adornments

Prized adornments were kept safe and secure in a range of lidded containers. The most popular waka huia were

Right: Heru iwi (whalebone comb).
Te Papa Tongarewa Museum of New Zealand, ME005242

Left: Heru from Kauri Point reveal changes over time to their style. This example provides a link between earlier styles, where animal imagery was popular, to a later fashion which prioritised the manaia as the only decoration.
Waikato Museum Te Whare Taonga o Waikato, 1973/50/405, gift of F. W. Shawcross

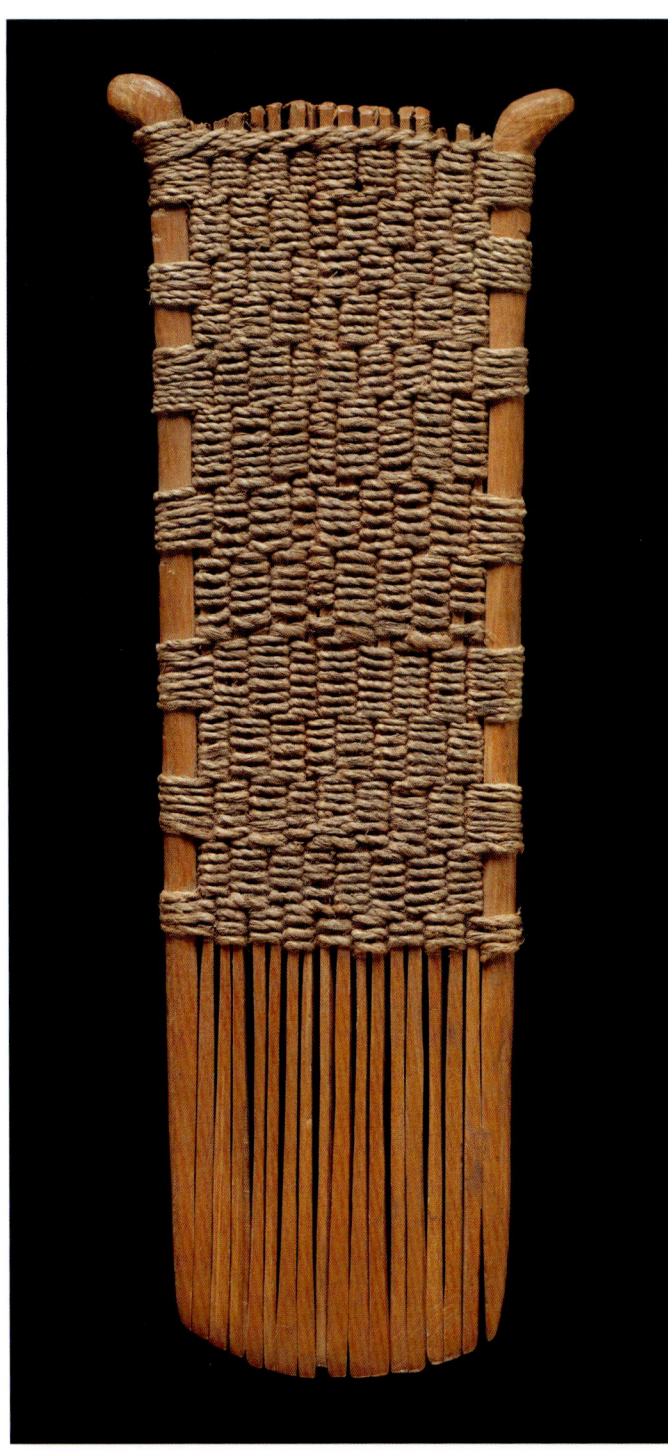

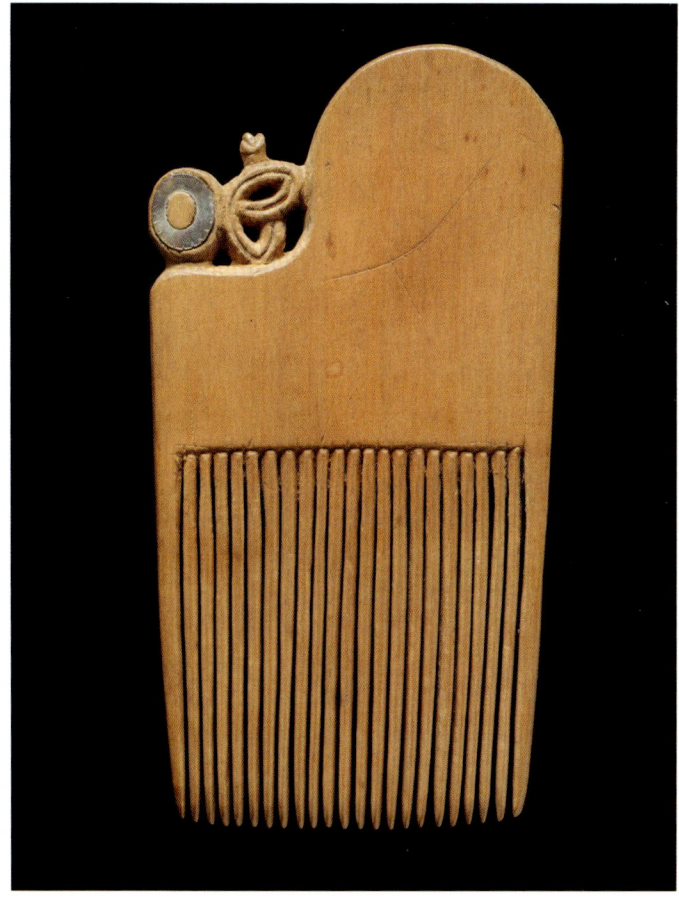

Left: Composite wooden and fibre heru were worn through the eighteenth century, but were set aside in the nineteenth century when single-piece heru became more prevalent. Similar examples were seen by Europeans in the 1760s.
Te Papa Tongarewa Museum of New Zealand, ME000663, Augustus Hamilton Collection, purchased 1914

Right: This one-piece wooden heru is beautiful in its simplicity, featuring a manaia face with pāua inlay in the eye.
Te Papa Tongarewa Museum of New Zealand, ME007851, gift of The Imperial Institute, 1955

rectangular in shape and measured between 30 and 60cm long,[91] while papahou were oval and shallower, flatter and wider. The word papahou indicates their use: papa is box, and hou is feathers, especially the tail feathers of the huia.[92] Roger Neich identified a third type that he called powaka whakairo; he described them as 'square, cubical or rectangular, deep-sided, with sharp edges and a flat bottom'.[93] His study identified 439 containers in museum collections, most of which date to between 1750 and 1850, in the United States (211), Australia (25) and New Zealand (203). They were, it seems, highly collectable and tradeable.

Artists made containers from either mānuka or kauri and then carved them ornately. They were often deeply personal treasures in themselves, made by rangatira for their own use: most received some training in carving as part of their formal education, and those with exceptional skill or passion for it might spend their adult lives working on carving projects. Waka huia were designed to be suspended from the ceiling of the whare, and were therefore often decorated only on the bottom. Many waka huia feature intricate compositions, with human figures in myriad sexual positions. While the majority

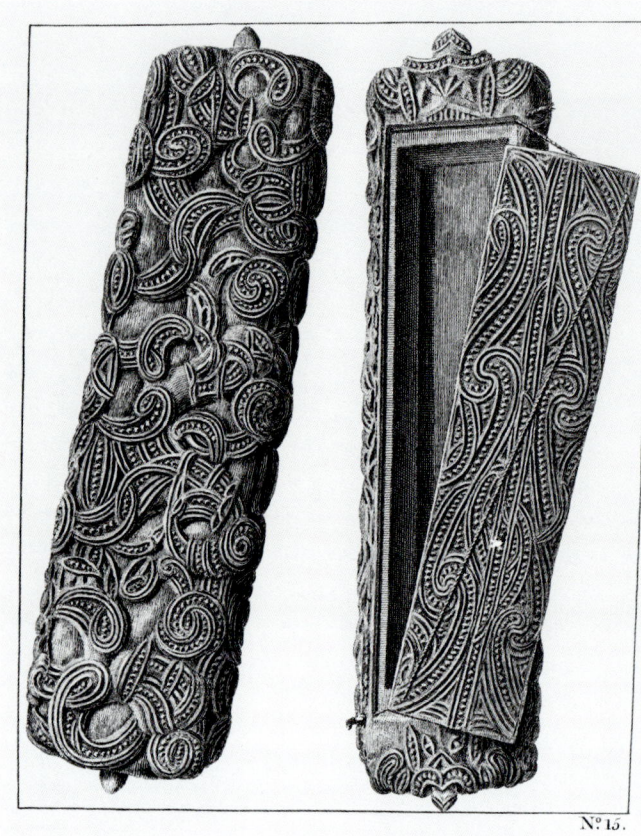

This papahou features human figures across the base in a complex composition, and a neatly fitted lid with variations of rauru spirals. As the top was often not seen, many papahou and waka huia have modest designs carved on that face.
**Richard Ralph and John Frederick Miller, *A chest of New Zealand as a specimen of the carving of that country*, 1769–1773**
engraving, 205 x 165mm, Alexander Turnbull Library, C-051-029, from John Hawkesworth, *An account of the voyages ...* (Plate 15), Strahan, London, 1773

showed heterosexual activity, there were also those showing takatāpui (LGBTQIA+ people), as well as groups of three or more; Ngahuia Te Awekotuku has seen one in the Museum für Völkerkunde in Dresden that features multiple men.[94] These waka huia would be a real celebration of tribal lineage as well as a reflection of sexual adventurousness, and they show how gender and sexuality were considered a normal part of everyday life.

### Significance of Māori adornment

Personal adornment has always been a source of pride and treated with care – as evidenced by the sheer number of taonga that have been passed down through generations, particularly those like hei tiki that are made from durable materials such as pounamu. Leading whānau held important taonga: the very fact that they held the taonga imparted title to lands and social privileges.[95] Sometimes adornments were buried then later retrieved; this reinforced their significance to whānau and hapū, and it ensured they were treated as an oha (treasured keepsake). Mākereti (Maggie) Papakura notes that 'All greenstones, whether weapons or ornaments, are a source of wealth, and may be given in utu, which is payment for insult, in dowry, or as a kōpaki for the dead.'[96] Examples include Te Paki's hei tiki Te Pirau Kakai Matua, which was acquired by Governor Grey;[97] and of course Tītore's hei tiki/hei matau (see page 171).[98]

The practice of adornment can be 'read' as delivering a number of messages from the wearer to the audience. As Christopher Steiner writes of adornment: 'The surface of the body as the common frontier of society becomes the symbolic stage upon which the drama of socialisation is enacted, and bodily adornment becomes the language through which it is expressed.'[99] Māori 'layered' their bodies with adornments, as if they were a stage, using a variety of materials to create objects with real meaning for the viewers. Each of these might be named, and might have a whakapapa linking the adornment to important figures and events through history.

By wearing adornments at important events, a person was sending a message about their own, and the group's, social and political status. Much of this knowledge has been forgotten through colonisation, but by piecing together oral narratives, early writings, colonial photographs and paintings, and taonga, we have a sense of a complex world that could be navigated through the display of the body using both permanent and ephemeral markings, and dressed with layers of adornments.

Adornments themselves acted as mnemonic devices that reinforced the knowledge of the ancestors to be remembered. This might be conveyed in the forms themselves: stories about Māui would be recounted in relation to hei matau, those associated with Hineteiwaiwa in relation to hei tiki, and the stories about Paikea and his father's sacred comb would be discussed. Information about ancestors would also be remembered in relation to the materials used: Tinirau's search for his pet whale Tutunui (see page 43) would be retold in relation to adornments made from whalebone, for example. Certain adornment practices would be a cue to the retrieval of certain stories: moko would bring to mind the ancestors Mataora and Niwareka; the wearing of headdresses would elicit stories of the earliest Pacific ancestors. Adornments also acted as mnemonic devices for core Māori values – for

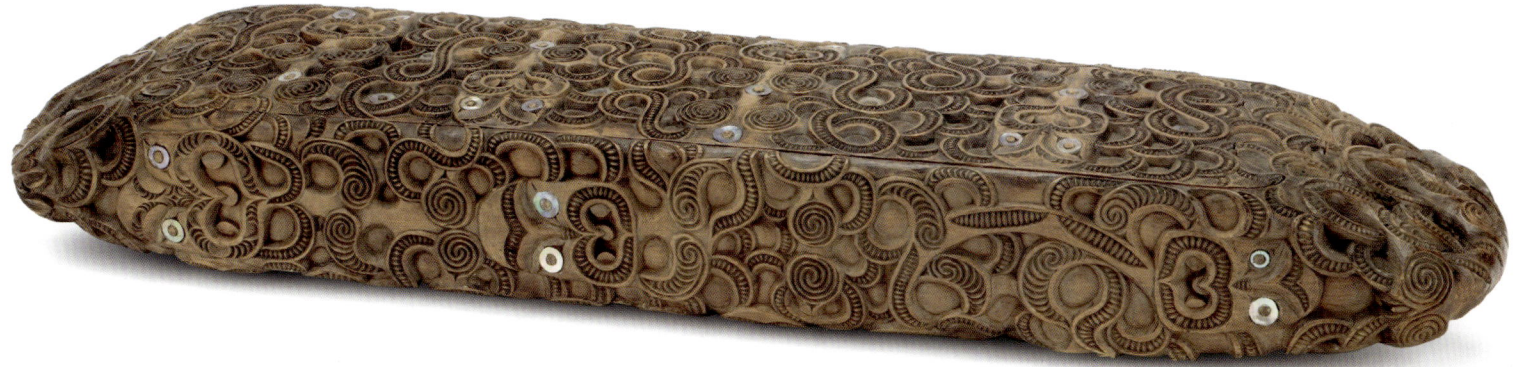

Papahou. The surface decoration is a true celebration of the serpentine style, with extensive piko-o-rauru spirals, and would have been created by a skilled chief/artist.
British Museum, Oc.7215.a

instance, the importance of the concepts of tuakana/teina (elder/junior) and mana (Paikea and Ruatapu); treating a partner with respect (Mataora and Niwareka); and not stealing (Tinirau and Tutunui).

In this way adornments can be regarded as portals to other worlds, to the ancestors, to the land. These ideas have been retained through the generations; and, if anything, they have become stronger in the past fifty years as artists have sought out older examples of adornments now resident in museums in Aotearoa and overseas. In this way knowledge has been recovered – such as the technologies of making and materials – and continues to cycle back and forth through time and space. Exhibitions that position ancestral and contemporary adornment side by side reinforce this connection, and the ways in which rākai can spark new ideas and innovations.

### Into the future

The art of personal adornment is alive and well today. This is seen most obviously in kapa haka competitions such as Te Matatini, where such practices are an important part of a team's performance, and a real celebration of the unique identity of the rōpū (performing group). And the range is stunning: almost all groups dress up their members with temporary moko painted on their skins, hei kakī (necklaces) around their necks, feathers in their hair (to emphasise the turning of the head) and red and black pigment applied, to scintillating visual effect. Together with the kākahu, poi and weapons, the rōpū come ready to instil in their audiences the ihi (power, authority, essential force), wehi (fearsomeness) and wana (inspire fear, awe; sublimity)[100] they feel.

Māori artists today are researching adornment collections in museums to recuperate forms, materials and techniques. Ngāi Tahu jeweller Areta Wilkinson (see page 182) and photographer Fiona Pardington (Kāi Tahu, Kāti Māmoe, Ngāti Kahungunu, Clan Cameron) have travelled to dialogue with taonga in collections overseas to investigate tribal heirlooms and reinvigorate the kōrero surrounding them through the making of new work. Other contemporary Māori jewellers such as Nichola Te Kiri (Ngāi Tūhoe) and Tania Tupu (Ngāti Porou) enjoy popularity due to a broader range of adornments, the use of strong Māori designs (such as mangōpare and koru) and a lower price point, enabling a wider audience to buy their adornments, and signalling their Māori identity clearly and magnificently.

# ARETA WILKINSON
DEIDRE BROWN

The relationship between tikanga Māori and contemporary body ornaments has been a central concern in the practice of Ngāi Tahu jeweller Areta Wilkinson. Between 2010 and 2018, she produced series of works exploring how contemporary jewellery practice could be informed by whakapapa, whenua and kāinga to become taonga tuku iho. This investigation led her to interview and mentor other community members, engage with local and international museum collections of Te Waipounamu (South Island) ornaments (including those from the Wairau Bar, and disseminate her findings through marae and gallery exhibitions and her 2014 PhD thesis, 'Jewellery as Pepeha'.[1]

Wilkinson, in collaboration with photographer Mark Adams, produced series of photogram works of the silhouettes of moa bones, stone tools, pendants and other taonga tuku iho currently held in museums: the images were generated by placing these objects on light-sensitive photographic paper. The process was an act of maumahara or remembering of cultural materials and treasured objects held in museums, including taonga taken from communities by collectors; and knowledges, technologies and practices that have not been passed down. Creating new objects to fill these voids was a way of remediating extinction, appropriation and other forms of cultural loss. The work, which formed part of Wilkinson's PhD in Fine Arts, was first shown in 2014 at Ngāi Tahu's Koukourārata Marae since, as she puts it: 'It was part of the philosophy or tikanga behind the work that this knowledge belongs and returns to iwi';[2] the work was then taken to a wider audience in exhibitions at museums and galleries in Christchurch, Lower Hutt and Auckland.

Wilkinson's practice extends beyond the formal aspects of producing and abstracting the āhua (shapes) of ancient taonga. She has been reproducing the tools used to manufacture these taonga through three-dimensional printing, and using them in her own practice. The tools include a drill head, scraper, file, hammerstone, grindstone and cutters, based on tools from Te Waipounamu that are currently stored in the Museum of Archaeology and Anthropology at the University of Cambridge.[3] For her *Moa-Hunter Fashions* installation at Christchurch Art Gallery Te Puna Waiwhetū (2018), Wilkinson used the 3D-printed tools to craft pendants inspired by taonga, from clay that she sourced in Canterbury; and some she painted using kōkōwai: her tools and materials thus locate her work within Ngāi Tahu whakapapa, whenua and mana. She created other body ornaments in gold and silver using hammer- and anvil-stones from the Waimakariri and Rakahuri rivers, so that they bore the marks of the geology of the whenua through their manufacture.[4] The installation spoke to the cyclical nature of Māori time in which artists can orientate themselves and their work towards their ancestors through old and new making practices, materials and landscapes.

As a jeweller, Wilkinson acknowledges that her 'contemporary art form enjoys cross-cultural alliances and is the synthesis of international silver- and metalsmithing traditions conjoined with Māori concepts'.[5] Through their making, these adornments have begun their journey to become taonga tuku iho and to reinforce the identity of their tangata whenua wearers as people of the land.

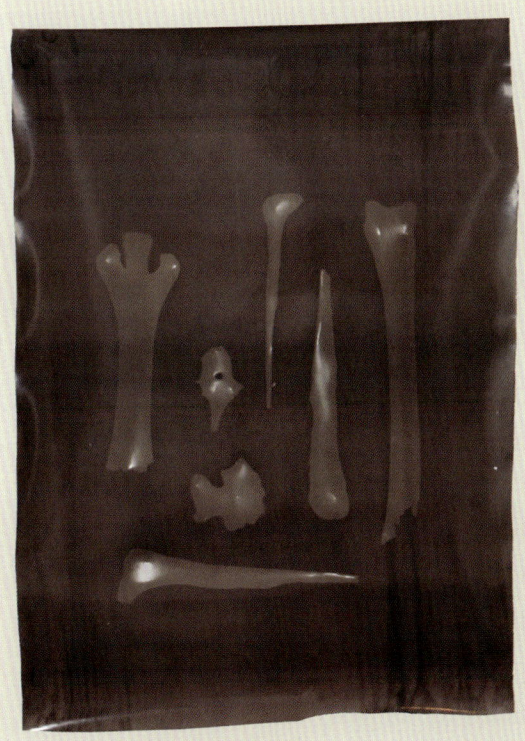
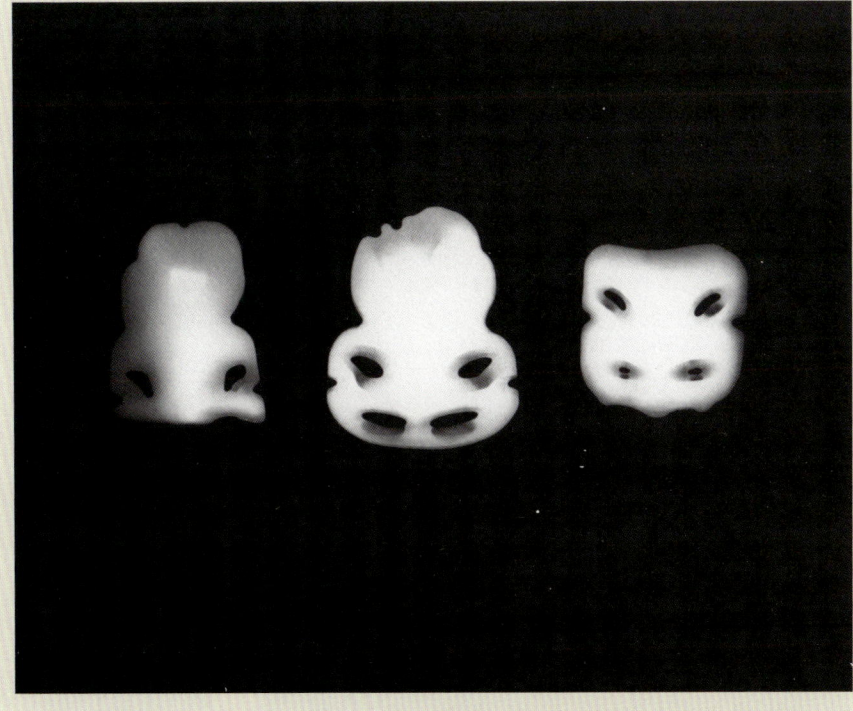
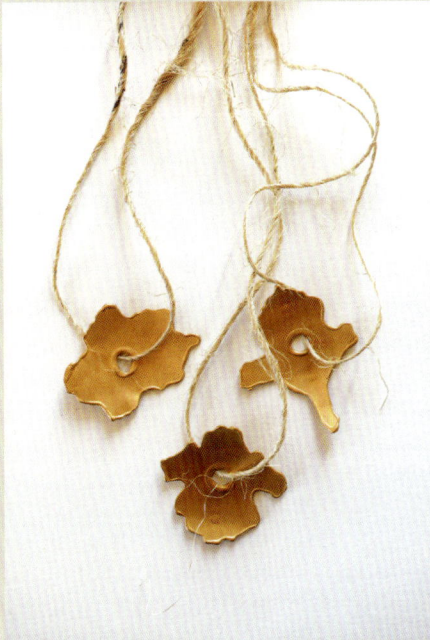
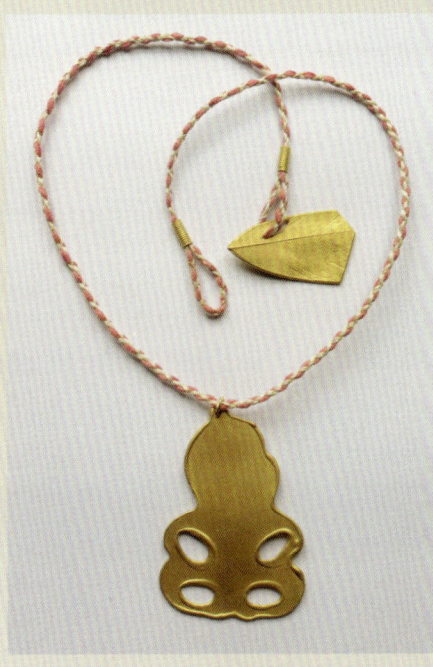

**Top left: Areta Wilkinson and Mark Adams, *5.10.2017*, 2017**
Leeds City Museum, LEEDM C2010.668-674

**Top right: Areta Wilkinson and Mark Adams, *1.11.2011*, 2011**
silver bromide photogram, Ak:1986.1046.1 Stony Bay Beach, E149.259 Onawe, E167.426 Onawe, from the collections of Akaroa Museum and Canterbury Museum, photograph by Studio La Gonda

**Bottom left: Areta Wilkinson, *Vertebra I, II, III*, Moa Hunter Fashions series, 2018**
Ōtākou 24-karat gold and mixed sizes of flax bailing twine, photograph by Studio La Gonda

**Bottom right: Areta Wilkinson, *Hine-Āhua and Huiarei (toggle)*, 2013**
24-karat gold (Tai Poutini West Coast), muka flax fibre, legal ribbon, photograph by Studio La Gonda

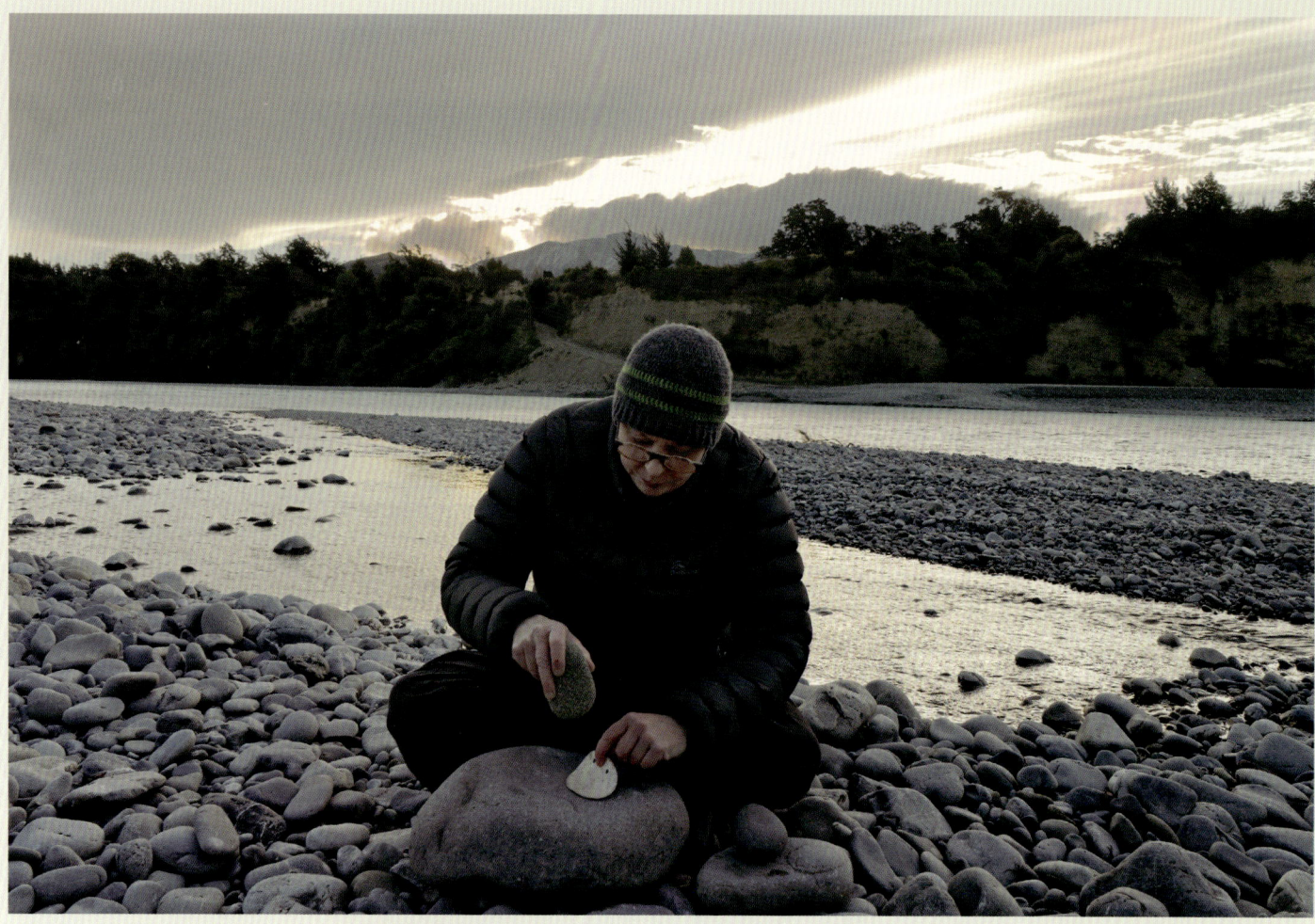

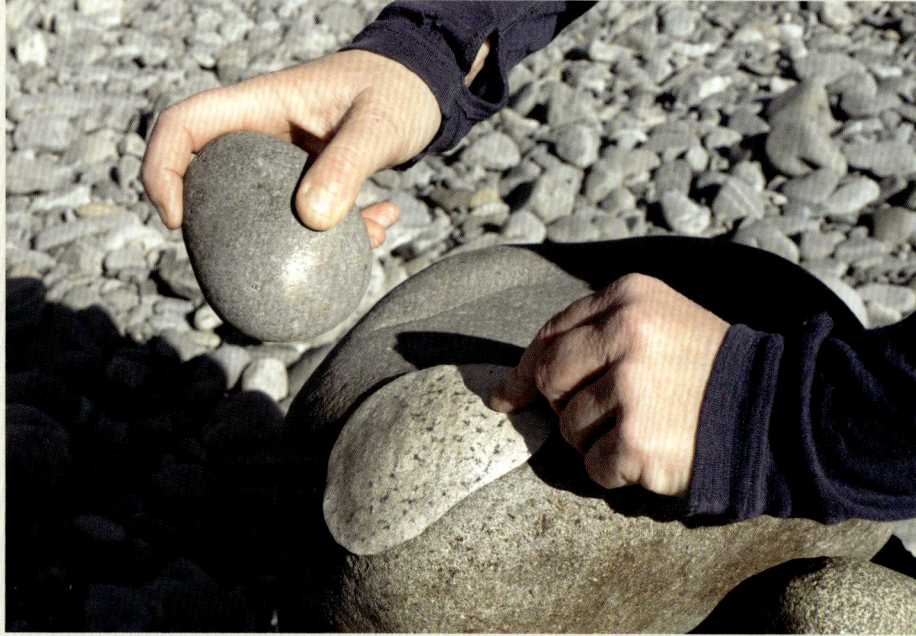

Areta Wilkinson making *Whakapapa I* for the 'Moa Hunter Fashions' series at the Waimakariri River, 2018.
photograph by Studio La Gonda

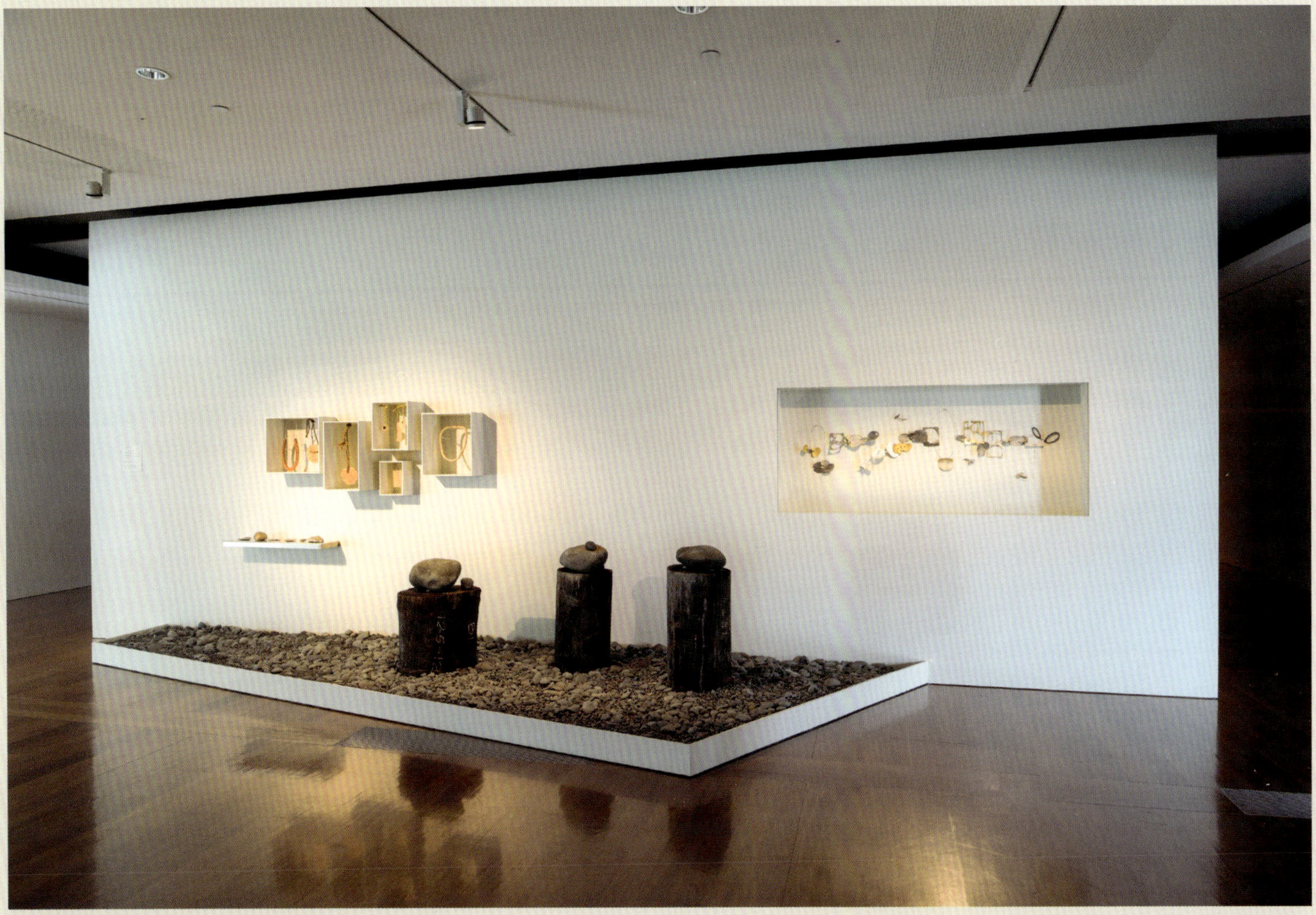

Above: **Areta Wilkinson, *Moa Hunter Fashions*** as installed at Christchurch Art Gallery Te Puna Waiwhetū, 2018
photograph by John Collie

Right: **Areta Wilkinson and Mark Adams, *Whakapapa V*, 2018**
binder jetting, stainless steel/bronze (420SS/BR), mild steel, photograph by Sam Hartnett

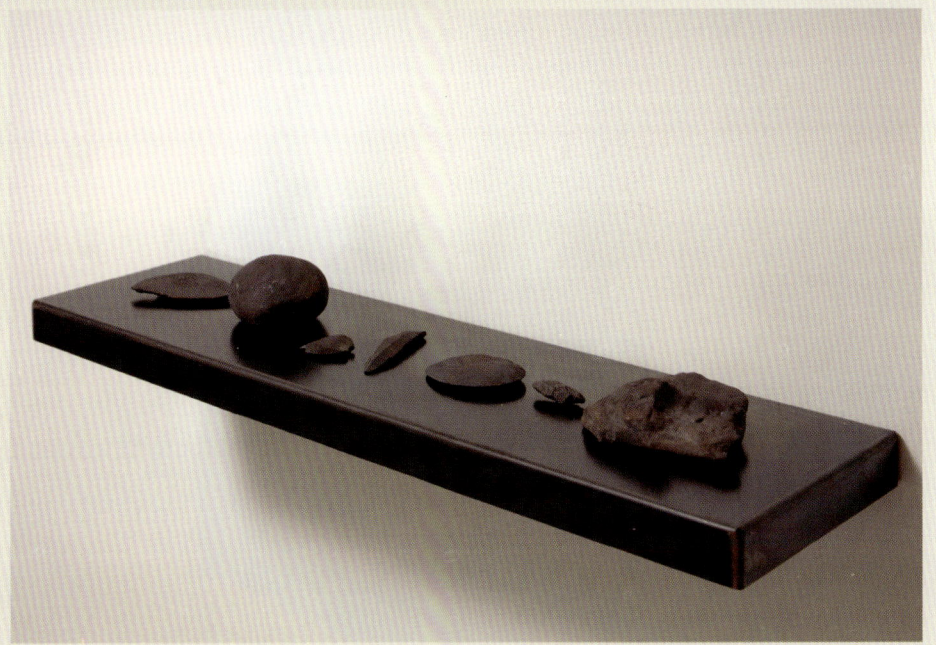

# POUNAMU
## NGARINO ELLIS

Māori artists have always favoured pounamu for two qualities: its strength and its aesthetic beauty. The earliest excavations of pounamu date to 1280CE at Wairau Bar in Marlborough, where archaeologists found pounamu adzes and chisels. By 1500 Māori were making adornments from pounamu, though this practice may possibly have been limited to the South Island, where pounamu was in ready supply. By 1700 Ngāi Tahu were firmly in control of the land where these sources were – Te Tai Poutini and Ōtākou (Westland and Otago) – and within a century the use of pounamu in Māori art was widespread. Trading routes spread throughout the country, to and from the centre of pounamu trading at Kaiapohia (Kaiapoi), as the material was exchanged for whāriki, cloaks, canoes and taramea (scented oils) from iwi in the North Island.

From the 1850s several factors, including a falling Māori population due to disease and a breakdown in tribal organisation, affected the making, circulation and function of new adornments.

Pounamu played an important role in peacemaking between groups. The concept of tatau pounamu (enduring peace; literally 'greenstone door') is a metaphor for entering into a space in which peace is made through the gifting of pounamu and/or political marriages. These negotiations are often delicate and it is important that they are approached with the utmost diplomacy to avoid breaking the pathway to peace.[1] In one instance, Ngāpuhi gave the mere pounamu Hinenuiotepāua to Ngāti Pāoa as a symbol of peace between the tribes. Horatio Robley described another episode where Tūhoe and Waikare leaders called for peace with Ngāti Kahungunu rangatira Ngā Rangimataea, announcing, 'Let us raise a *tatau pounamu* that peace may never be broken.'[2] The tatau pounamu – and enduring peace – was established by naming two different hill sites as husband and wife.

In the twenty-first century pounamu is no less significant or valued, as evidenced in the theft of taonga pounamu in 2019 – a Ngāti Porou mere from Auckland Museum in March (returned 2022), and a large piece of pounamu from a grave in Rotorua in June. The audacity of these thefts is remarkable given that such acts break tapu and can have serious consequences for those involved.

*He iti, ahakoa he pounamu –*
*Though small, it is precious.*

**Four hei matau**
Clockwise, from top left: Tūhura Otago Museum, D28.525, Long Beach, Otago; Te Papa Tongarewa Museum of New Zealand, ME002967, gift of Alexander Turnbull, 1913; Tūhura Otago Museum, D40.51, St Clair, Dunedin; Te Papa Tongarewa Museum of New Zealand, ME000608, Augustus Hamilton Collection, purchased 1914

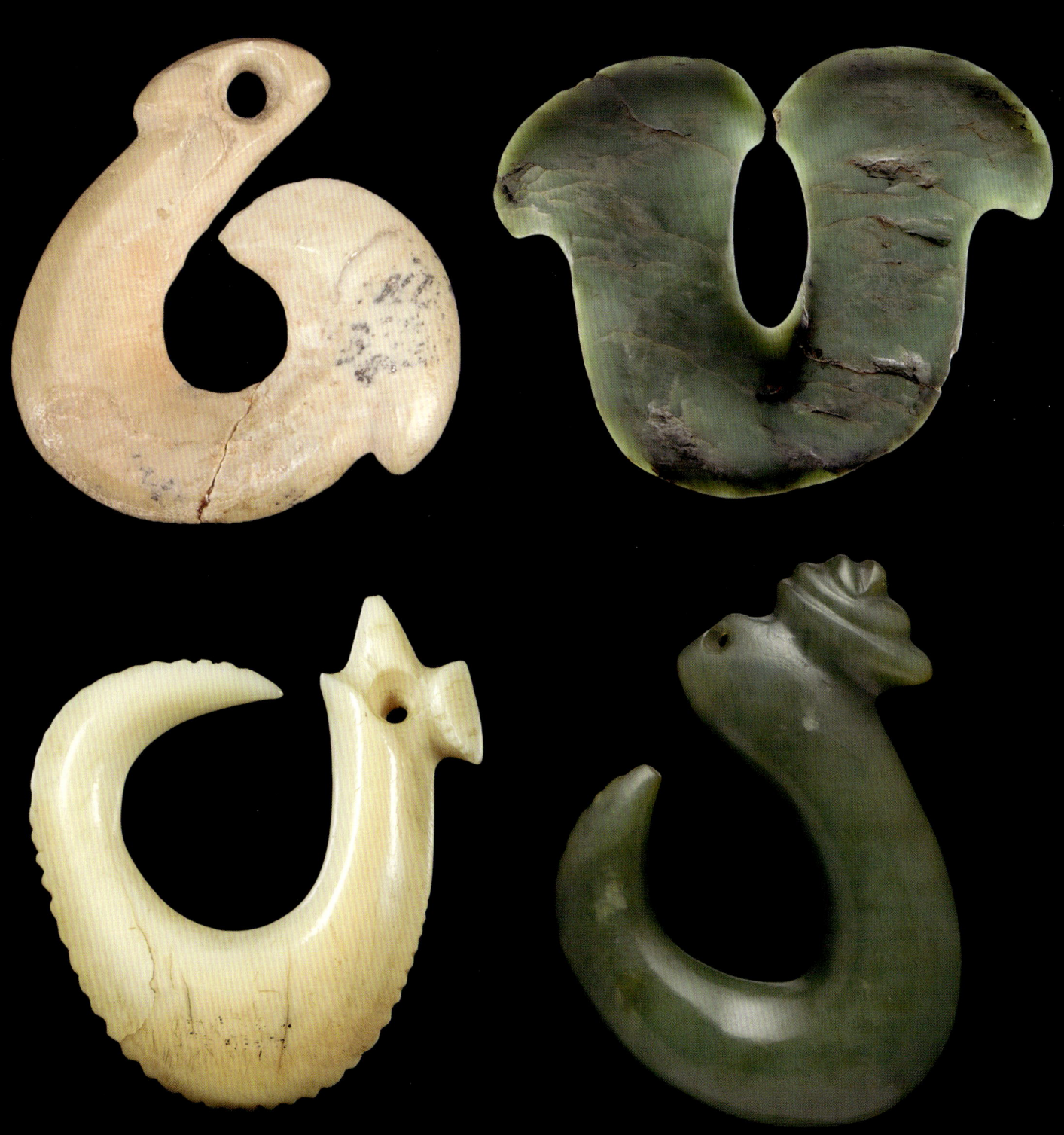

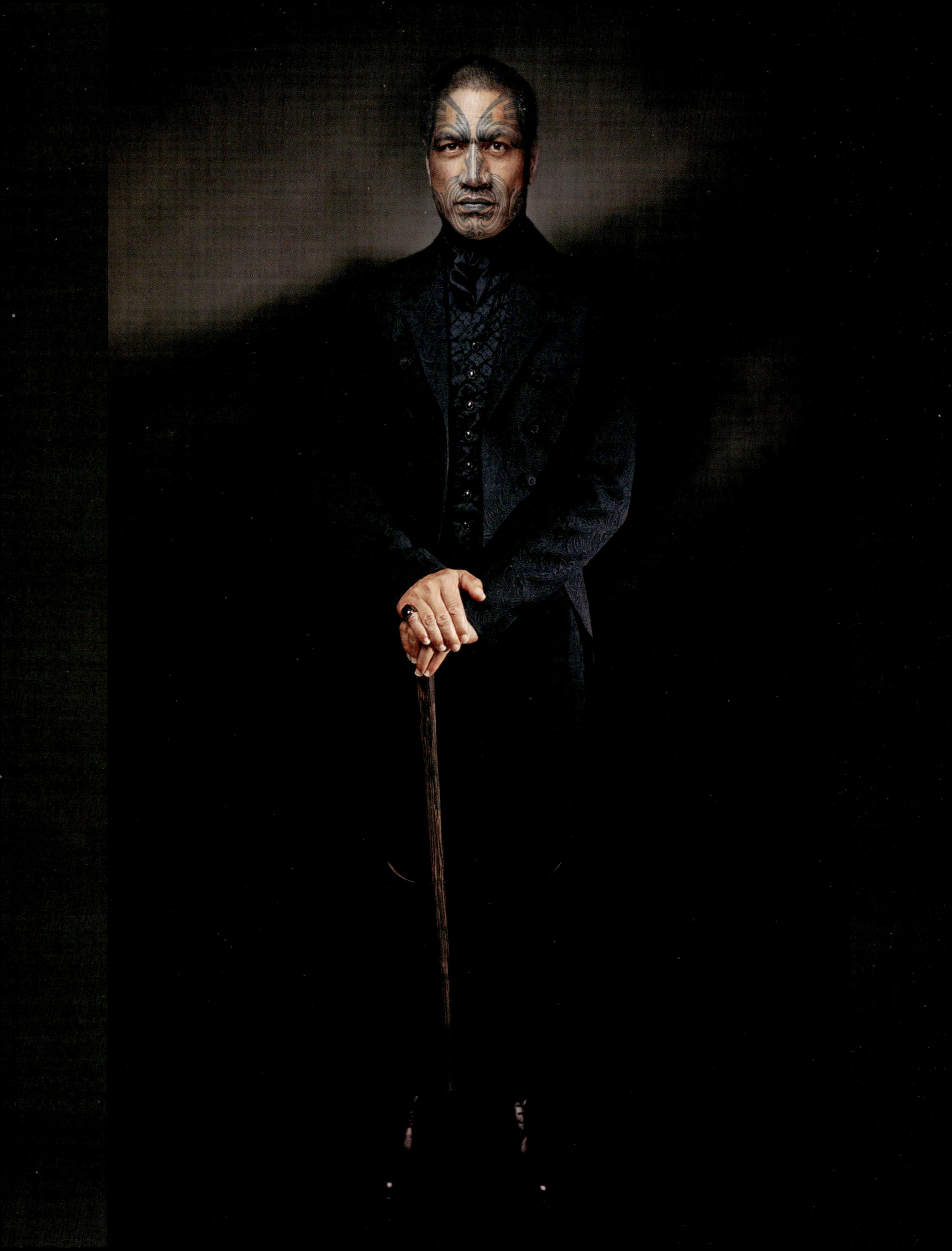

# 7 MANA WĀHINE, MANA TĀNE, MANA TAKATĀPUI
## DEPICTING GENDER IN MĀORI ART
### NGARINO ELLIS

*Kia whakatōmuri te haere whakamua.*

*I walk backwards into the future with my eyes fixed on the past.*

Gender and sexuality were repeatedly depicted across different Māori art forms such as carving and moko. The introduction of heteropatriarchy by Europeans, especially by Christian missionaries, diminished these identities by reducing and minimising their role, which in turn suppressed the use and acceptance of imagery of women and takatāpui (gay, lesbian, bisexual, transgender, intersex or part of the rainbow community) in art.

In many ancestral accounts the roles and values associated with men and women are clearly outlined through their deeds. The stories of Māui's feats are an example of this: his actions were the epitome of masculinity, with the emphasis on his strength (in bringing down the sun) and cleverness (in tricking his grandmother Mahuika into giving him her fingernails as the source of fire). Yet on closer inspection Māui gained much of his knowledge and skills from his grandmothers: Murirangawhenua gave him her jawbone to beat the sun to slow it down, and he also fashioned a matau from it to fish up Te Ika a Māui. Art forms from the pre-1850 period, in particular, tell us much about the roles of women and takatāpui: artists from these earlier communities took on roles as wood carvers and moko artists that were typically the prerogative of men. Pre-1850 art depicted all gender and sexual identities in communities, and provides an important source of information about gay, lesbian and transgender peoples.

### Presenting gender identities through art

Throughout Māori history, men, women and takatāpui[1] have held complementary roles in communities: men traditionally worked with hard materials such as wood, bone and stone, while women used soft materials such as fibre in their artworks; takatāpui could work with either. These gender roles differed across tribes, and influenced the production and consumption of works of art. For instance, Te Aitanga a Hauiti (Ngāti Porou) ariki Hinematioro commissioned a pātaka and a meeting house,[2] and her name is associated with a small whare that once stood in Ūawa (Tolaga Bay), parts of which are now in German and New Zealand museum collections. Ngāti Toa leader and political strategist Te Rangitopeora possessed an impressive collection of greenstone ornaments that were symbols of her mana and the role she played in her iwi's acquisition of greenstone fields in the South Island; the Bohemian artist Gottfried Lindauer depicted her with several of them in his portrait of her.[3]

Gender identities influenced gender roles. Those who were born female would, for instance, be expected to undertake

---

Lisa Reihana's second suite of portraits for her *Digital Marae* series showcased those who were often sidelined within narratives of Māori art and history.

**Lisa Reihana,** *Dandy*, **2007**
colour photograph, type C print, 2000 x 1200mm, Te Papa Tongarewa Museum of New Zealand, 0.037193, purchased 2010

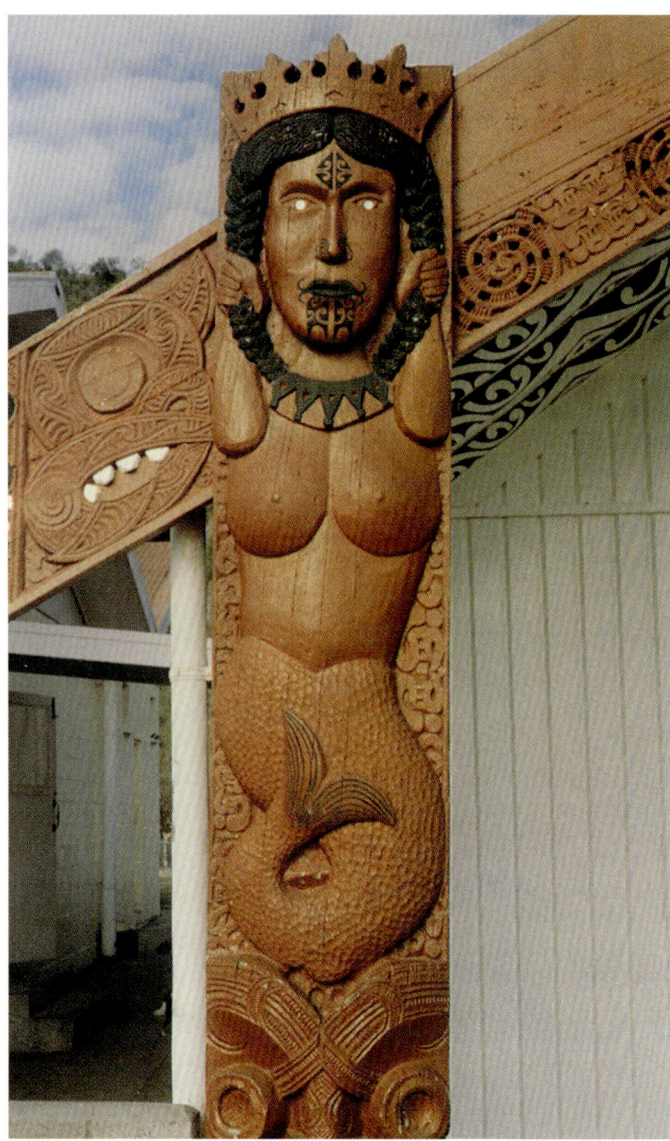

Riini Hetaraka (Ngāti Awa, Whakatōhea, Te Whānau-ā-Apanui, Ngāti Manawa, Rongowhakaata, Ngāti Porou) carved Muriwai (Toroa's sister) on the left amo of the wharenui Wairaka for his Ngāti Hokopū hapū in 1898. He was only twenty-eight at the time. The carver's great-granddaughter Te Arani Barrett describes how Muriwai's crown here refers to concerns about increasing governmental encroachment in the area.
photograph by Roger Neich

specific responsibilities. Weavers were almost exclusively female: young women would sit in the whare pora with their female relatives and learn the art until they were confident and skilled enough to make their own kākahu. Likewise, chiefly young men learnt about carving as part of their training in the whare wānanga, and when they were older some would become carvers. There were at least 200 carvers active during the nineteenth century – the high number suggests that non-chiefly men were also carving by this time, and it reflects an increase in carving projects.

Stories of women who are as strong as men (or stronger) are recorded in art forms – such as the story of Wairaka, who was the daughter of Toroa, captain of the *Mātaatua*. When the crew were having difficulty making landing, Wairaka stated the now famous words 'Kia whakatāne ake au i ahau!' – 'Let me play the part of a man!' (since shortened to Whakatāne).[4] The meeting house Wairaka at Te Whare o Toroa Marae in Whakatāne (first opened in the 1890s) depicts Wairaka on the left amo, with her hair plaited, and with legs represented as a fish tail. She is represented as a contemporary figure in order to appeal to present generations, even though she lived at least 500 years before the house was built. Artists recorded the centrality of women in tribal narratives – their mana wāhine – in their work, although this has changed over the past 150 years.

### Gender and moko

The ability to move outside a gender role as artists extended to moko and carving, and there are oral accounts of women practising both art forms in pre-nineteenth century Aotearoa. Moko was typically an art form practised by men because of the immense tapu involved in shedding blood as well as in touching the head. Yet there are at least two records by Europeans of wāhine tā moko. In the 1830s French explorer Jules Dumont d'Urville recorded seeing an enslaved woman moko artist who incised an extensive moko design across the entire back of a chief's wife in Te Tai Tokerau.[5] She was one of hundreds of prisoners of war taken from other districts in the 1820s by Ngāpuhi. Another enslaved moko artist was Rangi, as drawn by Augustus Earle.[6]

Other accounts in the nineteenth century record women placing moko on their own skin, such as a woman in the Bay of Islands who incised the name of a visiting French ship, *La Coquille*, on her arm in the 1820s,[7] and a Ngāti

Porou woman who incised the name of her late husband on her arm in the 1850s.[8] Te Hikapuhi Poihipi Clayton (Ngāti Pikiao, 1860–1934) was a weaver who placed moko on women around where she lived at Owhata on Lake Rotorua around the turn of the twentieth century; and Hukuhuku Tamati (Waikato-Tainui) practised moko around her tribal territory.[9] Some women were risk-takers who took non-traditional forms of moko, such as the young women Sydney Parkinson recorded in the 1760s from Ngāti Kahu in Te Tai Tokerau, who wore pūhoro designs on their neck and forehead (instead of more typically on the thighs); and the women he recorded with pūhoro on their thighs (a style usually reserved for men).[10] An oriori composed for Tuteremoana of Ngāi Tara (people now known as Muaūpoko, from the Wellington area) refers to Hinekorito, whom Hoari Te Whatahoro translates as 'Hine-the-maid-with-the-tattooed buttocks'.[11] This tribal range suggests that the style may have been more widespread than previously recorded.

The moko practice was part of a wider sociocultural landscape in which the body was used to display a person's allegiances and to express a commitment – certainly by the late nineteenth century – to Māori ways of living. It was Māori women, after all, who kept taking the moko kauae at the turn of the twentieth century, after their husbands, brothers and sons were rejecting the practice. By wanting to keep wearing the moko, they were making a political statement to maintain their ways of life despite peer and societal pressure to succumb to Pākehā ideals of beauty. Many of our grandmothers born at the turn of the twentieth century no longer felt the pressure or the desire to take the moko, despite the kauae being on the faces of their mothers, aunties and grandmothers.

Increasing numbers of women today practise tā moko. Artists such as Christine Harvey (Moriori), Henriata Nicholas (Te Arawa) and Anikaaro Harawira-Havili (Te Aupōuri, Te Rarawa, Ngāpuhi) have all faced challenges on account of their gender: undertaking work while pregnant; not being taught because they are women; the contradictions between tribal upbringing and taking up the chisel. All these potential setbacks have not put these women – or others – off. If anything, these challenges have been a catalyst for the women to work harder, experiment with different designs and styles, and to keep learning. Harvey became interested in moko while attending a women's carving workshop run by Te Rangikaihoro Nicholas (Henriata's brother); and Henriata herself was trained in the traditional Hawaiian art of kakau (hand-tapping) by Keone Nunes, who has revived the ancient art, and has led the way for women to take up uhi once again. Harawira-Havili learnt tā moko from Derek Lardelli (now Sir Derek, Ngāti Porou, Rongowhakaata, Ngāti Konohi [Ngai Te Riwai], Ngāti Kaipoho [Ngai Te Aweawe]), one of the pre-eminent tohunga tā moko working today. Another woman carver and tā moko artist, Paitangi Ostick (Ngāti Wai, Ngāpuhi), has faced challenges to her practice with many men disapproving of the fact that she works in tā moko, but her response is 'Hei aha. Kia ora' (So be it. That is all).[12] As increasing numbers of wāhine Māori desire to wear the kauae and commission a female moko artist to do this, the future of women tohunga tā moko seems bright.

### Wāhine tohunga whakairo rākau – women carvers

The records of women who were tohunga whakairo rākau are equally scant. Carving was considered the prerogative of men, certainly before the early twentieth century – Roger Neich counted 231 men active in the nineteenth century alone.[13] Yet there were occasional women carvers. A Ngāti Kahungunu story tells of their ancestor – and sister of their eponymous ancestor – named Iranui who lived on the Mahia Peninsula on the lower East Coast. Iranui was at least familiar with carving techniques – she may have learnt this from her husband Hīngāngāroa or from her brother Kahungunu, both of whom were expert waka builders.[14] And a woman named Pakira from Mangamuka was carving further north in Te Tai Tokerau at around the same time. Despite Neich's count, there are surprisingly no records at this stage of women carving in the nineteenth century.

In the 1930s two women are known to have carved meeting houses: Hēni (Jane) Tōpia (Te Whakatōhea, Te Rarawa, 1898–1964) was trained by Pine Taiapa when he was based in Rotorua, and she later carved the meeting house Rangikurukuru (opened 1936) in Bradleys Landing on the Kaipara in southwestern Te Tai Tokerau. Taiapa said that he did not mind teaching women or even Pākehā, so long as they had a desire to learn: 'Although it was often assumed that women were not permitted to undertake carving, this was not so. Maori tradition clearly indicated that where women were responsible for an outstanding achievement generally attributed to men, they were permitted to undertake such men's work as carving'. He noted that, 'The most outstanding pupil was a Maori girl from Tuakau, who became the first Maori woman to attempt the carving course.'[15] The identity of this latter carver is unknown.

Around the same time two women leaders carved parts of meeting houses as an expression of their leadership. Te Puea Hērangi carved at Tūrangawaewae in the early 1930s, and Whina Cooper (Te Rarawa, 1895–1994) carved two taniwha for a whare whakairo in her home settlement of Panguru in Te Tai Tokerau. In each case it was not a matter of going against tradition (of only men being allowed to carve); rather, it was the need to engage with a kaupapa of completing a project to their personal standard, which would ultimately enhance the mana of the community.

## The impact of Christianity on depictions of gender in art

When the first Europeans arrived in the 1760s, they brought with them entrenched heteropatriarchal values that placed men in leading roles. The visitors sought out only Māori men in their engagements and transactions, and expected Māori women to operate as their European counterparts did – that is, only in the domestic sphere. From the early nineteenth century mission schools promoted a gender binary of male/female, separating out boys' and girls' education: boys were sent outside to learn manual work, while girls learnt needlework, cooking and other domestic skills – a system that remained ingrained in New Zealand schools for many generations to come.[16] The church introduced another layer of leadership in communities by installing 'native teachers' and catechists – all of them Māori men – whose presence insidiously undermined existing hierarchies of leadership, particularly those of women. As translators of European culture and ideas of gender for Māori, missionary-appointed 'native teachers' invariably promoted the primacy of men and their role in a community.

As Pākehā interviewed Māori men about Māori history a century later, typically women's stories were subsumed into the exploits of men, resulting in women's centrality within whakapapa being subsequently forgotten. We can chart this occurring in the changes to naming practices of meeting houses. Around the country, most of the whare whakairo that were built after 1870 were named after eponymous male ancestors: Mātaatua, Kahungunu, Rangitihi, Tamatekapua.

Some tribes, however, reflected their own particular leadership structure in house naming – notably Ngāti Porou on the East Coast, where at least 90 percent of the meeting houses are named after women.

Missionaries endeavoured to shift ideas of sexuality that were enshrined and celebrated in Māori culture, in carvings that they targeted for purchase or destruction. Thomas Kendall, a missionary active in the Bay of Islands from 1814 to 1821, was discomfited by explicit sexual imagery: 'Like almost every one of the early nineteenth-century commentators, he was embarrassed by these nude and grotesque figures, often carved with prominent genitals and profusely decorating the storehouses and more elaborate dwellings.' Kendall purchased enough examples of these whakairo to fill three shipments, of which one consignment was sadly lost at sea.[17]

Carvings were deliberately censored to remove any overt reference to intimacy between partners (whether heterosexual or takatāpui) or, indeed, images of genitals. There are numerous examples in museum collections[18] – as Clive Aspin and Jessica Hutchings lament: 'Museums in New Zealand are full of examples of emasculated male figures with scars that now replace penises.'[19] One example is in the Museum der Kulturen Basel, where one pou has clearly had his penis cut out (VI241). There is a hypocrisy at play here: on the one hand, missionaries and other collectors sought out these carvings for this kind of imagery; on the other hand, they did not want depictions of genitalia sitting on the mantelpiece.

Inside Christian churches, female atua were rejected in favour of a focus on a single male God and his son. One of the most clear-cut examples where we can see carvers grappling with cross-cultural ideas of religion is in carvings of the Madonna and Child. When communities were planning to build a church there was often a delicate series of negotiations between the missionary who was ostensibly in charge of the project and the local rangatira – the one who was actually in charge. Māori were keen to include various art forms within the space to reinforce the mana of the building, but this was often met by a refusal to include it on the part of the missionary – see, for example, the trouble that Raharuki Rukupō had to go through over the reconstruction of the church at Manutuke in the 1840s.[20]

Two examples of carvings of the Madonna and Child have survived: one, now in Auckland Museum, was carved for the Catholic Church in the 1840s (22, 13895, 86); a second example was carved half a century later, in 1890, and is now in Te Papa Tongarewa (ME011429). It is possible that both were carved by Patoromu Tamatea, a renowned waka builder. His style changed between the 1840s (when the earlier carving was made) and the 1890s, by which time he had shifted his focus from creating waka to making kumete (large presentation bowls) for European settlers. This may explain the stylistic differences between the two whakairo, particularly in the shape of the head, the pose, the rendering of the legs and hands, and the overall composition. Another explanation is that they were made by two different carvers.

Portrayal of the Madonna and Child is a well-known motif in European and ecclesiastical art, and such works often reinforce Mary's role in church history with the use of materials such as gold, and their placement in a church, usually at the front. In Aotearoa New Zealand, in the two Māori Madonna and Child carvings the artist has honoured Mary with a full-face moko typically given only to men (with rare exceptions). Perhaps for this single design feature, the Auckland carving was rejected by the local settler priest, who was shocked that the Madonna had been depicted in the very manner (carving) that the church had sought to set aside. A small carving from the Bay of Islands from the 1830s similarly has a mataora on the face of a female figure.

### Conceptualising gender in waka huia

We can chart changing understandings of gender and sexuality by examining waka huia and papahou. Waka huia were typically made by male rangatira, and were kept in a private space inside the whare, suspended from the rafters. Perhaps because of this location, carvers frequently depicted a celebration of sexuality on the waka huia, with complex combinations of male, female and takatāpui activity. Figures are shown engaging with one another, sometimes 'hidden' in complicated surface decoration, perhaps disguised by the carver who played around with different compositions intertwining with surface designs such as spirals and mata kupenga. Waka huia may also feature sexual escapades involving more than one partner – and more than one orifice. In many cases the genitals have subsequently been removed or otherwise damaged in an effort to hide imagery of this nature. Ngahuia Te Awekotuku has seen a waka huia in Dresden that celebrates takatāpui, with multiple male figures engaging in penetrative sex,[21] and on other examples there are three or more participants, celebrating heterosexual and takatāpui relationships. Given these waka huia and papahou were initially intended to be very personal and intimate treasures, it is not surprising that they were sometimes bold and perhaps just a little inspirational (or even aspirational).

Through the late nineteenth century carvers continued to depict sexual encounters in their art, but they adapted existing carved forms and extended the narratives that were depicted. The kumete was an example of this adaptation – a presentation bowl that was similar in form to the more familiar waka huia or papahou, but much larger in scale, with a less abstract human figure composition. The supporting figures were typically male and literally 'held' the container. On a kumete from the 1850s (now in Te Papa's collection, see page 58), Patoromu Tamatea carved a number of figures: two are lying on their backs on the lid, with their heads in the middle and their legs bent up (one with their legs open). Two figures support the bowl on either side: both are clearly absorbed in the delights in front of them. Two smaller figures are facing outwards between the standing figures: their hands are covering their genitals as if to leave to the viewer's imagination who the figures may be.

### Gendered carving in architecture

Through carving, artists could depict the full range of relationships in Māori communities. On the amo of pātaka, a male and female couple would typically be depicted in the act of procreation. Fertility was essential to the continuation of the hapū and the future of the community. The sexuality of a carved figure was usually made explicit with enlarged genitals, to highlight the figure's fertility. On Te Ātiawa pātaka epa made in the sixteenth and seventeenth centuries, carvers depicted female genitals very clearly. Some carvers added breasts to reinforce the identity of the figure; in carvings from the East Coast from at least the 1760s this was a favoured style. The carving from the ariki Hinematioro's house (now in Auckland Museum), shows her breasts clearly on the plain body; and inside Te Hau ki Tūranga (opened 1845) there are a number of poupou that depict women with breasts. Inside Porourangi whare whakairo (opened 1888) women are shown breastfeeding their babies, affirming their role as nurturer.

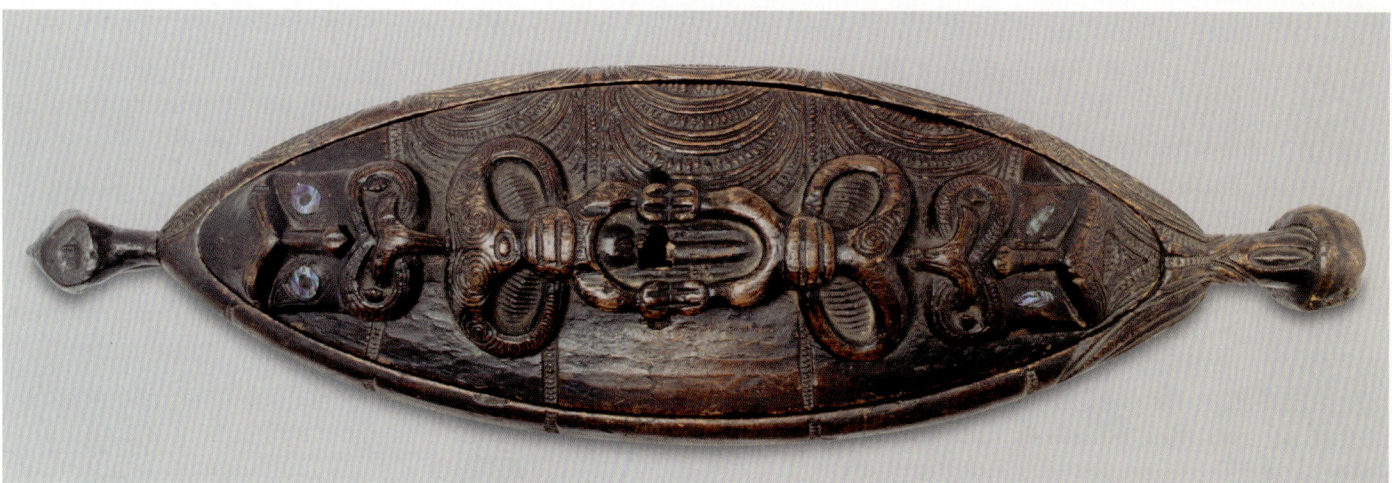

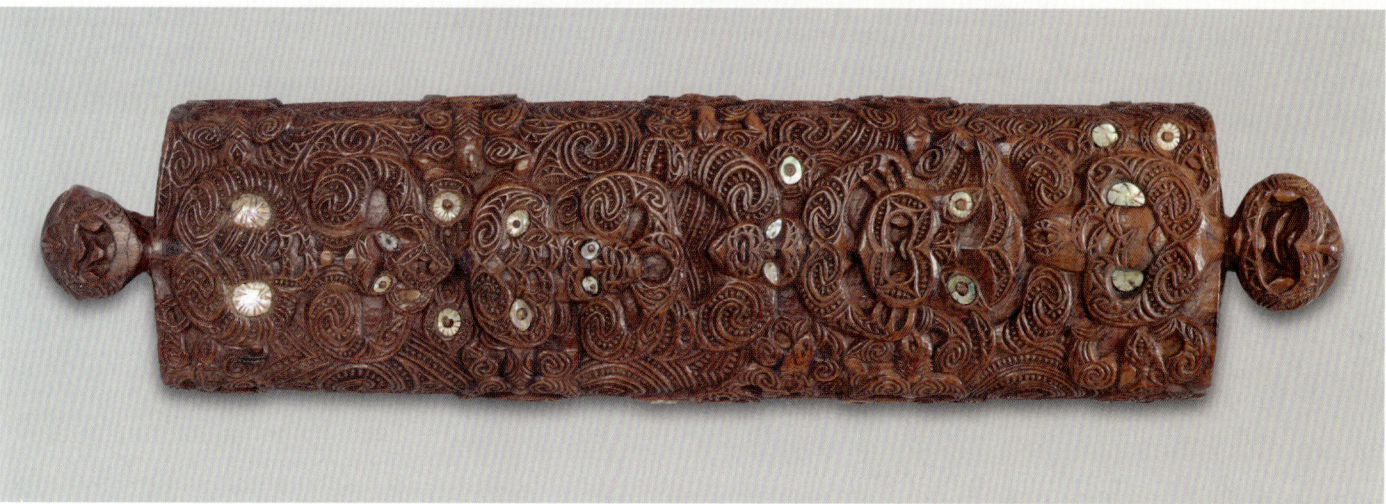

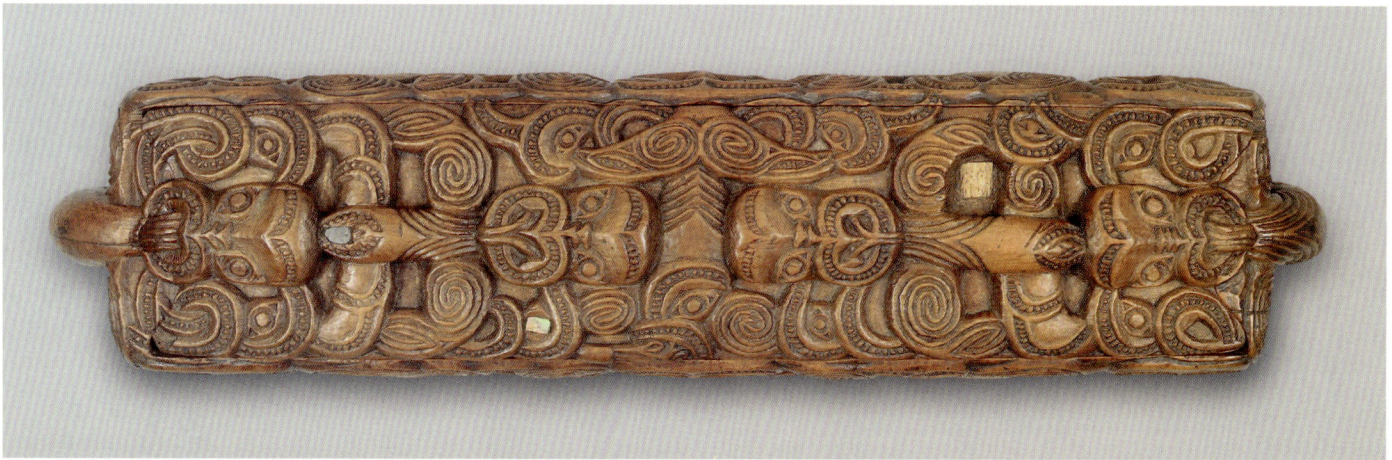

Top: Lid of a waka huia showing the removal of genitalia some time after its creation, perhaps by someone offended by the sexual imagery.
Museum of Archaeology and Anthropology, University of Cambridge, E 1909.107 / Z 660

Middle: The composition on the base of this papahou in the Metropolitan Museum of Art, New York is complex, with faces doubling as the heads of figures as well as genitalia (or covers over them).
Metropolitan Museum of Art, New York, 1978.412.755a, b, The Michael C. Rockefeller Memorial Collection, bequest of Nelson A. Rockefeller, 1960

Bottom: Papahou were popular in Te Tai Tokerau and Taranaki areas. This example from the Bay of Islands features fourteen figures across all sides, many of whom are involved in different types of sexual activity.
British Museum, Oc1964,05.1.a; EOC23100 00782938001

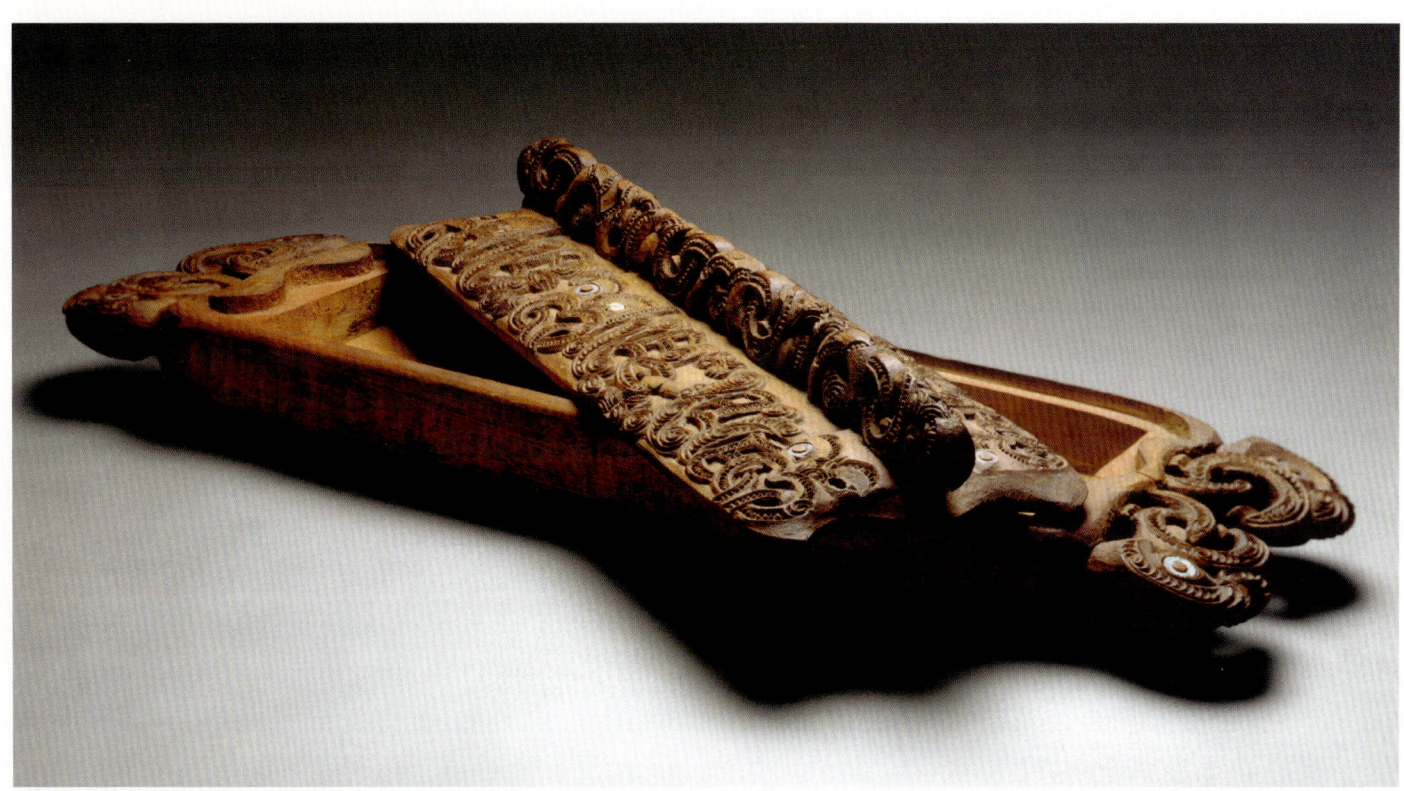

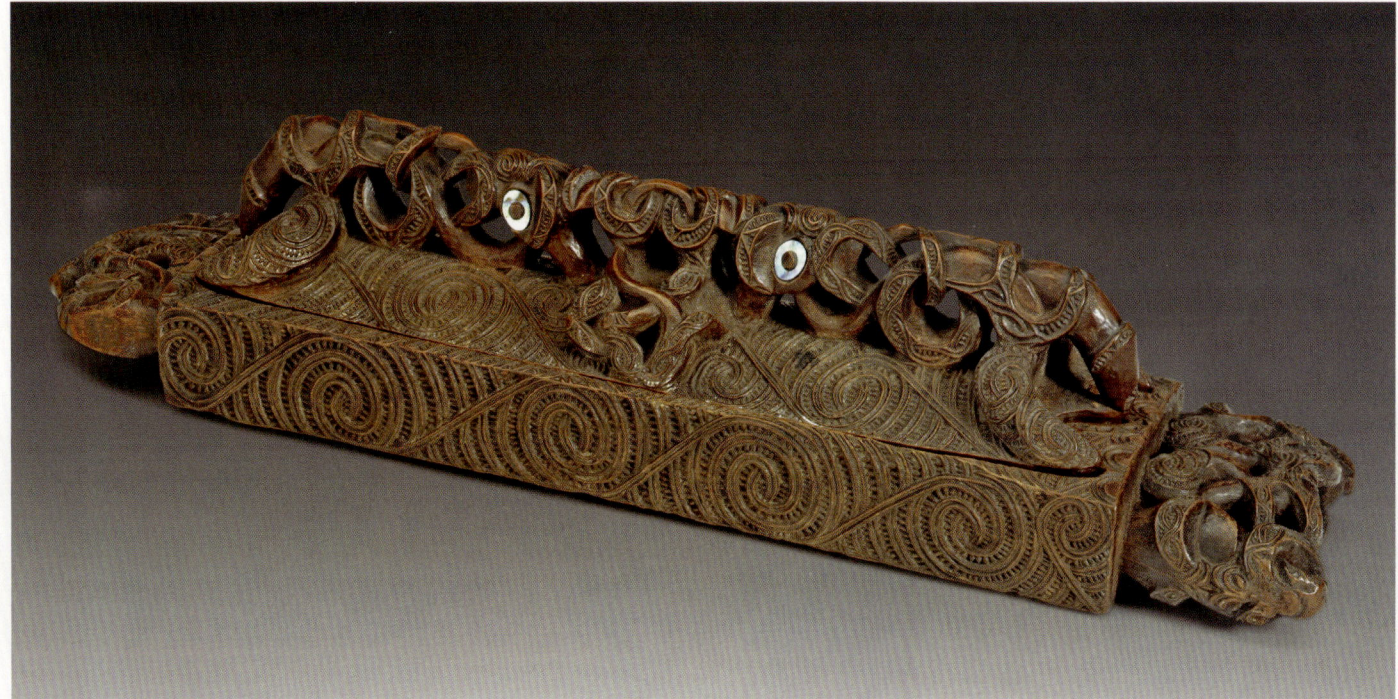

Top: Figures in flagrante delicto on the lid of a papahou donated to the Peabody Essex Museum in 1807.
Peabody Essex Museum, Salem Massachusetts, E5505

Bottom: Along the raised length of this papahou, two male figures are clearly identified through their ure (penises).
British Museum, Oc1926,0313.30.b

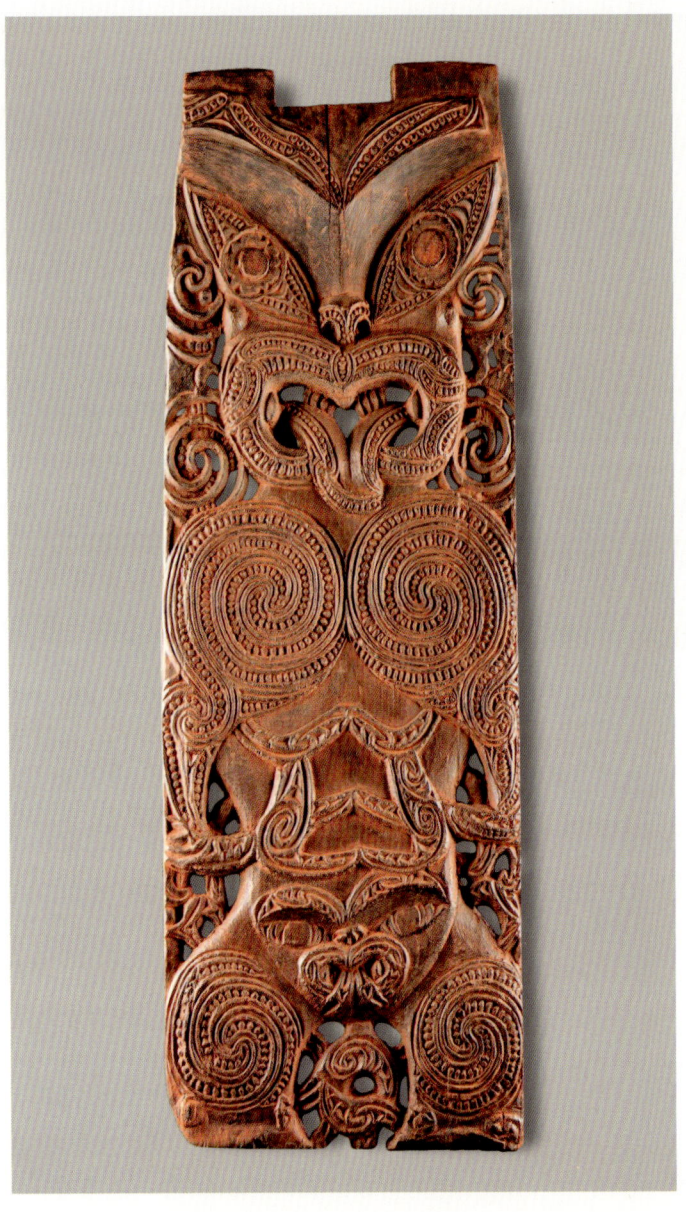

Poupou from the early eighteenth century, gifted to Joseph Banks on the first voyage of James Cook (1768–1771) by Te Aitanga a Hauiti. Now at the Museum of the University of Tübingen, Germany.
Museum of the University of Tübingen, Germany, AOI-Es-A608

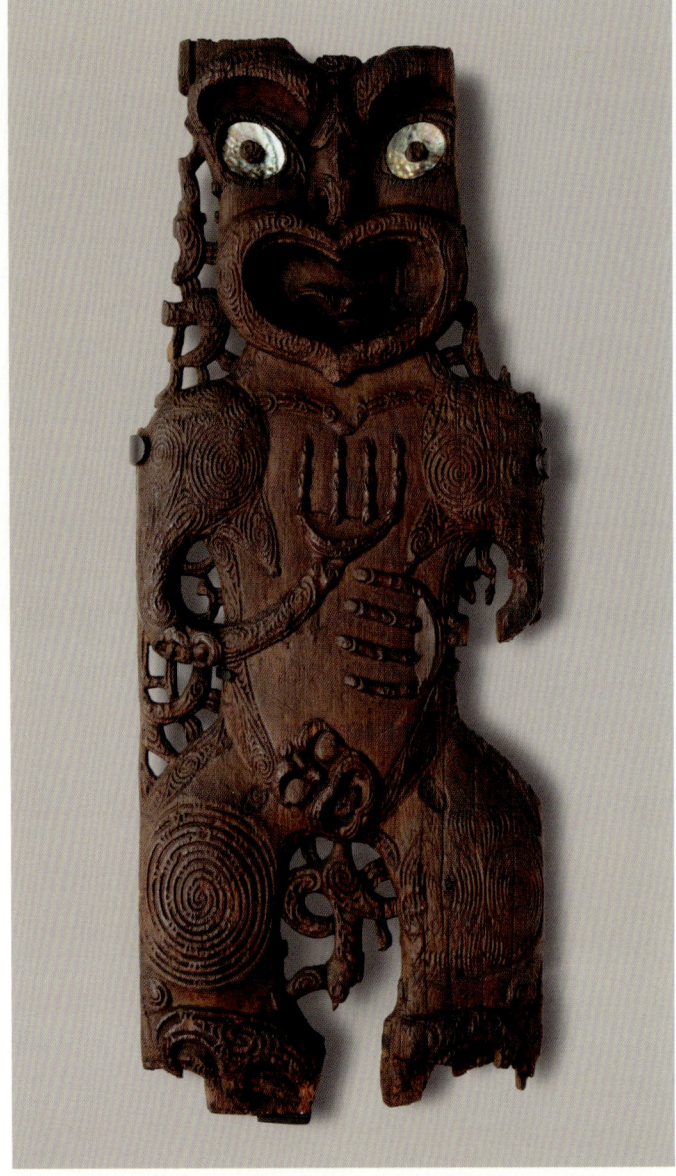

Poupou named Hinematioro, possibly from the same house as the poupou on the left but collected from a nearby site some time later, and currently in Auckland Museum. Stylistically they are quite different, with the one on the left more akin to Rongowhakaata carving, and the one in Auckland Museum similar to carvings from the Iwirākau School at Waiapu.
Tāmaki Paenga Hira Auckland War Memorial Museum, 288, 13671, 5017

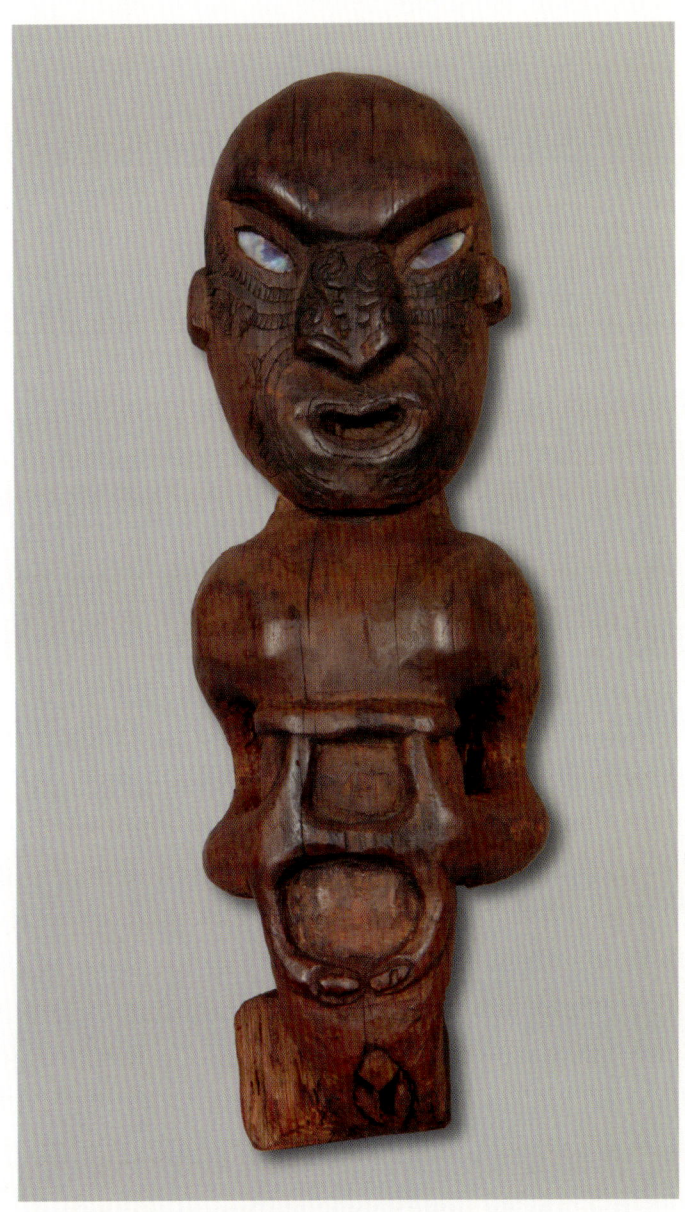

This unusual tekoteko carving depicts a woman showing breasts and genitalia yet with a face with extensive moko usually restricted to men. Collected from the Bay of Islands in 1840 by the US Exploring Expedition led by Charles Wilkes, this is one of over 4000 treasures collected from around the Pacific, thirty-four of them Māori. The original paper label reads 'God's peg, New Zealand from over the door of a native house at the Bay of Islands.'
Smithsonian Institution, 66A00050

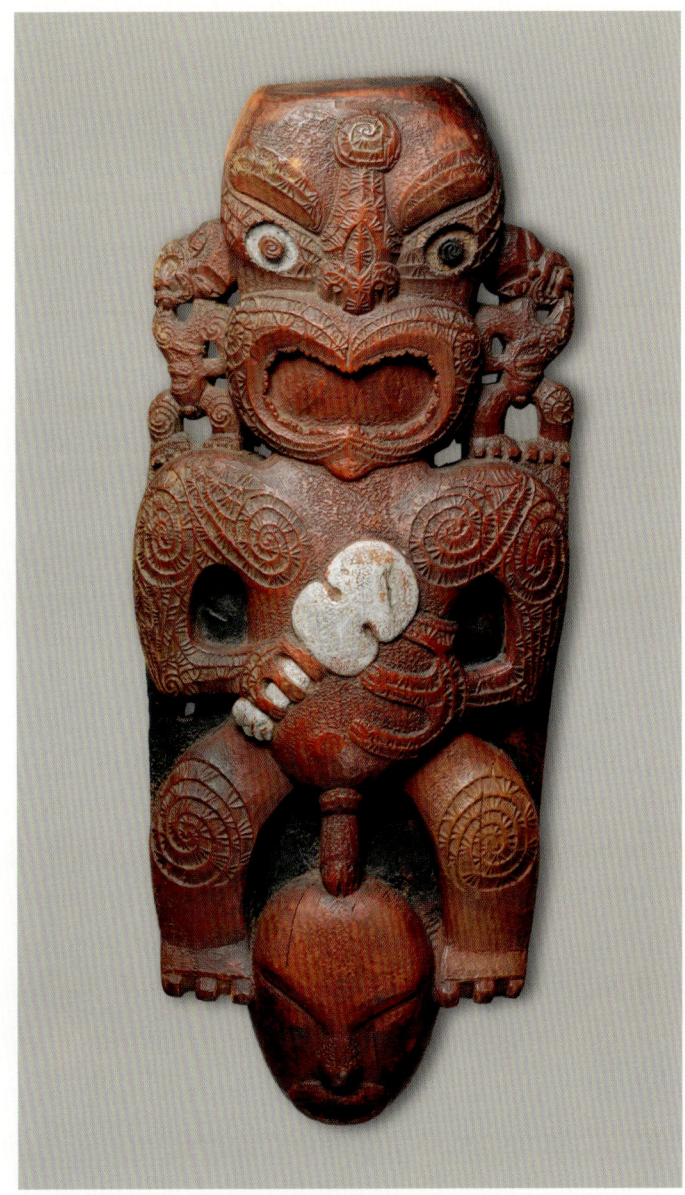

In the 1820s this Te Arawa artist depicted an ancestor whose ure rests on the head of the figure below.
Metropolitan Museum of Art, New York, 1979.206.1437, The Michael C. Rockefeller Memorial Collection, bequest of Nelson A. Rockefeller, 1979

One strategy that carvers used to address increasing community prudishness in depicting genitals was to place small figures over this part of the human anatomy – a practice that grew in popularity in the late 1800s. This double-figure composition was used in pre-European carvings, too, such as on the right-hand maihi of the eighteenth-century Te Whānau a Apanui pātaka Te Tairuku Potaka (previously in Auckland Museum, 22063), where the genital region of one figure is concealed by the head and body of a smaller figure. By the 1840s Rukupō was using this judicious positioning of smaller figures on carvings throughout Te Hau ki Tūranga and, later, Te Mana o Tūranga (1883).

Carvers depicted female figures on pare in recognition of their role in the whakanoa ceremony (making a space free from tapu). These carvings were placed above the doorway of a whare, signalling the transition between the world outside and the realm of Tūmatauenga, inside to the world of Rongomātāne. It was crucial to demarcate this important boundary, and pare were visual reminders of this shift. Women played an important ceremonial role at the opening of the house, in which a puhi (high-ranking young woman) would be chosen to go forward and free the building from a state of tapu. Pare were replete with female imagery to recognise these roles: in his survey of 200 pare in 2006, Robert Jahnke identified only one male ancestor.[22] Women's sexuality was made explicit on pare carvings across the country – sometimes the central figure was shown with a smaller figure with its face turned upwards and its mouth open, immediately below her vagina.

### Ngā toi o takatāpui

Whakairo was an important place for recording and celebrating same-sex relationships. The term takatāpui first appears in the second edition of William Williams's *Dictionary of Maori Language* in 1852, and by the third edition in 1871 it was defined as 'intimate partner of the same sex'.[23]

Several waka huia and papahou from Te Arawa depicted couples of the same sex (including one example by a carver from Te Arawa who had been enslaved by Ngāpuhi and was living in Northland). Three of these couples were male–male:[24] according to Neich this may represent siblings (in the case of the gateway Pūkākī at Rotorua) or a political alliance. Others suggest that the figures represent takatāpui couples. A watercolour by T. J. Grant depicts a carved pou from Ōhinemutu.[25] There are three tiers to the pou: at the top is a large single male figure, and on the second and third tiers are couples embracing – these figures are all male, facing each other with one arm around the other's waist, and one on the thigh – possibly celebrating takatāpui relationships.

Te Awekotuku has unpacked the renowned Te Arawa story about Hinemoa and Tūtānekai: she suggests they were both takatāpui, and she describes how Tūtānekai 'enjoyed a particular relationship with a special male friend, his "hoa takatāpui"',[26] and how Hinemoa, meanwhile, had a close physical relationship with her female cousin Wai. This interpretation gives new meaning to an ancient kōauau named Te Murirangaranga. The kōauau is an instrument that is played at ceremonial occasions or for healing. This particular example was used by Tūtānekai who, according to Te Awekotuku's understanding, sat passively waiting for his paramour Hinemoa, who took matters into her own hands and swam to him. This goes against the commonly told story that he enticed her; in this version the woman takes control of the story.

Same-sex relationships among Māori were forced into hiding in the nineteenth century because of European taboos that ostracised these takatāpui relationships. LGBTQI+ activist Elizabeth Kerekere (Te Aitanga a Māhaki, Te Whānau a Kai, Ngāti Oneone) argues that whakapapa was 'mediated by colonial and racist forms of homophobia, biphobia and transphobia'.[27] By the end of the 1800s takatāpui could no longer see their own sexuality reflected in the art in their own communities, and this, together with the promotion of heterosexuality as the only option for sexual orientation, led to a one-dimensional understanding of gender, making it increasingly difficult for takatāpui to live their lives openly. This would not change for several decades.[28]

### The impact of colonisation on Māori art

European notions of gender hierarchy impacted on Māori art during the nineteenth century. As early as 1814 ideas of male/outside and female/inside were being taught to Māori who attended missionary schools. With the quick uptake of Christianity by Māori, these values were soon having an effect in the kāinga. One example of this is in the making of tukutuku panels in wharenui. In the 1860s and 1870s, men were the leaders of this art form. Karauria Kauri, for instance, led the tukutuku project for the wharenui Porourangi at Waiomatatini on the East Coast. Indeed, one of his students on this house was Apirana Ngata. Ironically, by the time Ngata was teaching tukutuku at the School of Maori Arts and Crafts in the late 1920s, all of his students were women. Hundreds of women learnt the art form, and their legacy continues today with their students leading tukutuku projects. This shift from male to female practitioners may be a reflection of Ngata's desire to have a balanced number of men and women artists working on wharenui projects that he led, with women in charge of the woven components. There are still men who are experts in tukutuku today, though, such as Con Te Rata Jones (Te Whānau a Apanui, Whakatōhea), who led the woven work for Te Tumu Herenga Waka whare at Victoria University of Wellington (opened 1986).

During the late nineteenth century women artists felt the responsibility to work outside the home in the cash economy, and this left them with little time to practise the arts their grandmothers had practised. Financially many could no longer afford the time to spend gathering materials and creating cloaks, and there was social pressure to conform to domestic arts rather than moko or weaving. The number of commissioned works for women artists decreased as the role of kākahu within the political and economic sphere changed. Carvers increasingly chose to depict only male figures in carvings in the wharenui, and female figures were relegated to subsidiary roles in the placement of ancestors in the meeting house.

### Into the future

The depiction of gender and sexuality was an essential part of the visual landscape, in artworks that recorded and celebrated the names and exploits of certain ancestors and their role in the community. In the nineteenth century these values were censored and censured, and carvings and other art forms were doctored or otherwise damaged to appease European ideas of propriety. It is ironic how Pākehā 'gentleman' collectors would have this 'work' done to their carved treasures, yet were quite unfazed about gazing at photographs of often pre-pubescent Māori girls wearing only a piupiu. From the 1980s there was increased research and awareness of older whakairo that depicted the lives of women and takatāpui, and Māori artists began to reclaim such knowledge in their work.

Paintings from the 1980s by Robyn Kahukiwa (Ngāti Porou, Te Aitanga a Hauiti, Ngāti Konohi, Te Whānau a Ruataupare) stimulated renewed interest in mana wāhine and mana takatāpui. Her work unequivocally celebrated women from Māori history, with her brightly coloured paintings full of symbolism. They provided powerful role models to girls and young women at a time when Māori social statistics were grave. Ancestors such as Mahuika and Hinenuitepō were seen as positive energies and full of life, and their stories offered robust affirmations about being female, and the vital role women have played in the oral histories of Māori as a people.

While textiles have remained an important platform for women's artistic practice, wāhine have used other art forms to articulate their mana wāhine. A commissioned work by Lonnie Hutchinson (Kāi Tahu, Samoan), *Hoa Kōhine (Girlfriend)* (2018), is a cut-out panel made of aluminium cut like lace filigree, attached to the exterior wall of the Christchurch Art Gallery Te Puna o Waiwhetū. Commissioned as part of the 125th suffrage celebrations, *Hoa Kōhine* affirms the importance of women's friendships, visualised here as an exploration of textile practices of Māori weavers (and particularly tāniko designs) and of Pākehā settler women (with their lace curtains). The monumentality of her work, and the work of others such as Mataaho Collective (four Māori women artists) challenges ongoing expectations of Māori women's art as solely that of weavers. The art practice of wāhine and takatāpui today is as varied as the ancestral and tribal stories that are being recovered from oral histories, and articulates their realities that will ensure that Māori art once again reflects and embodies everyone in their whānau, hapū and iwi.

# MEN AND WEAVING
## NGARINO ELLIS

In pre-contact Maori communities, almost everyone would have been familiar with fibre and its many uses. Women were usually the main weavers in the community, but men also used fibre to make items such as hīnaki (nets), taura (rope or cord) and functional kete, to hold food from the sea or the gardens.

Te Tuhi Pihopa (Ngāti Whare) was one of very few men recorded as being weavers before the late 1900s. His creativity extended to kitemaking, building and carving,[1] including the wharenui Hinenuitepō at Waikotikoti Marae at Te Whāiti on the edge of Te Urewera. He was a friend and informant to Elsdon Best,[2] who wrote down Pihopa's knowledge of Tūhoe tribal whakatauakī, waiata and karakia in 1895–1896.[3] Pihopa made four uhi (moko chisels) for Best, who wrote a detailed account about moko published in the *Journal of the Polynesian Society* in 1904.[4]

Men made kahu kurī using precious fur from kurī, stitching strips of kurī fur onto the closely woven kaupapa that women had made. They used the same tuitui technique that they used for tukutuku panels, with one man sitting on either side of the cloak, which was held up vertically between them.

Since the late nineteenth century, more men have become weavers, and a number of them have become well known in Aotearoa New Zealand, including Eddie Maxwell (Ngāti Rangiwewehi, Te Arawa, Ngāti Whare, Ngāti Pūkeko, Ngāti Awa), Karl Leonard (Ngāti Rangiwewehi, Ngāti Ngāraranui, Ngāti Pahipoto, Ngāti Raukawa) and Te Atiwei Ririnui (Ngāiterangi, Ngāti Ranginui, Ngāpuhi, Ngāi Tahu). Some men were surrounded by generations of men and women weavers in their whānau, and this influenced their work as artists. James Schuster, for instance, is the son of renowned weaver and teacher Emily Schuster, and has taught tukutuku at events such as the 2017 Māori Weavers Hui at Lake Rotoiti.

Karl Rangikawhiti Leonard comes from a well-known whānau of carvers, including his father, his paternal uncle Pakake Leonard and, especially, his maternal uncle Te Kaka Niao Ngaheu, who taught him how to carve. Ngaheu himself was trained by the great carver Eramiha Kapua. Karl was influenced by his paternal grandmother Ranginui Parewahawaha Leonard, who was herself a well-known weaver who continued making kete and whāriki until she was 100 years old.[5] Leonard has paved the way for other men to become acknowledged for their weaving skills, and although controversial at the time, his expertise and leadership were recognised in 2011 when he was the first man to be nominated to the committee of Te Roopu Raranga Whatu o Aotearoa, the national collective of Māori weavers. As he maintains: 'Male or female is not an issue for me. The issue is the future of weaving and its sustainability as an innovative art form and cultural icon.'

Cori Buster Marsters (Te Arawa, Ngāti Whakaue, Te Whakatōhea, Cook Islands) is another male weaver who was inspired by women in his whānau: he learnt weaving from his kuia when he was just ten. He enrolled in a carving course at the New Zealand Arts and Crafts Institute and graduated in 2013. He went on to study weaving at Te Wānanga o Aotearoa, and in 2016 he won a Te Waka Toi award for his work as an emerging artist.

Marsters has been researching textile forms that have not been made for at least 100 years. Mostly it was women who wore the pōtae tauā – a hat made from seaweed and, sometimes, kuta (*Schoenoplectus lacustris*, a sedge or bulrush) in times of mourning; some early European voyagers such as Cook saw them, but few others; and they are mentioned in oral histories. Marsters has been researching examples in museums and interviewing families in order to learn more about pōtae tauā by making some examples.

The poi tāniko is an art form that celebrates both mana tāne and mana wāhine. Male warriors originally used these poi as a way of strengthening their wrists before using one-handed weapons such as the patu (cleaver). Poi tāniko were presumably made by women, as they were the dominant textile artists, and were not made after the late 1800s. More recently, male weavers have been revitalising this art form: Leonard made his first set of four poi tāniko in 2005, with titles such as *Matariki* and *Autahi*, and in 2020 Marsters wove poi tāniko he named *Te Pō-i-roa* for an exhibition at the Poi Room, Auckland; they were later purchased by Te Papa (ME024642). Leonard has also been investigating these forms in his works, including *Ngā Pumanawa e Waru – the Eight Attributes of Te Arawa* (2009), also now in Te Papa (ME024025). In rejuvenating this art form, both Marsters and Leonard can bring together mana tāne (through the poi's original use) and mana wāhine (with the weaving).

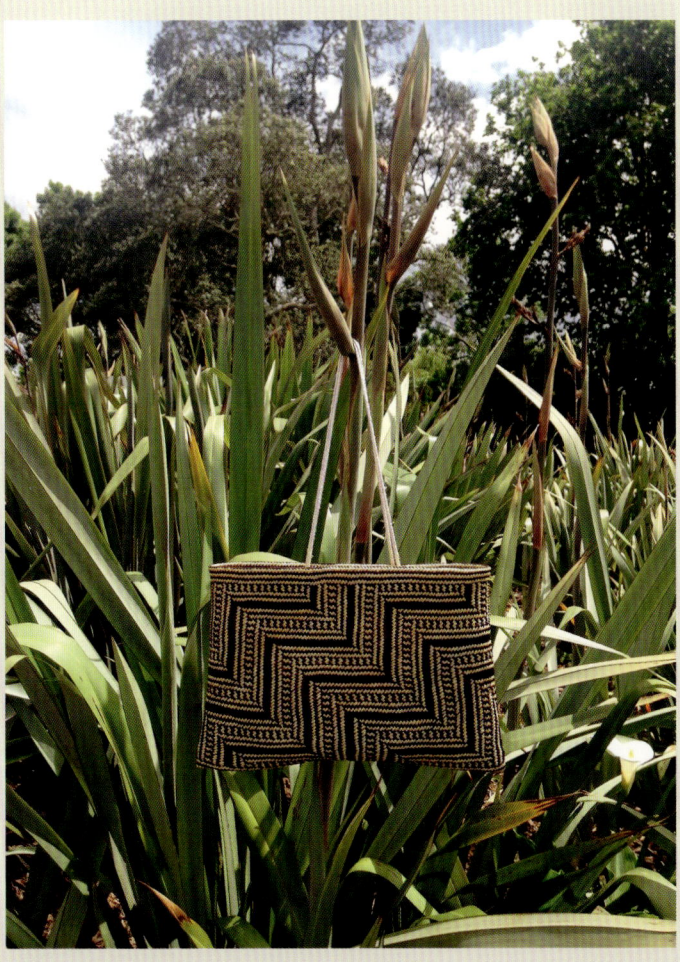

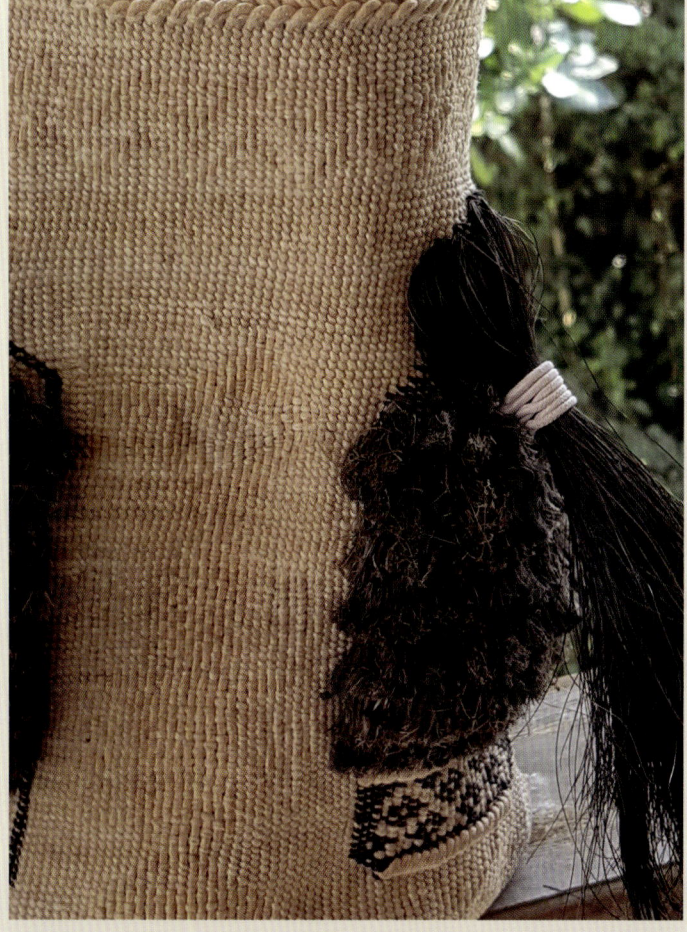

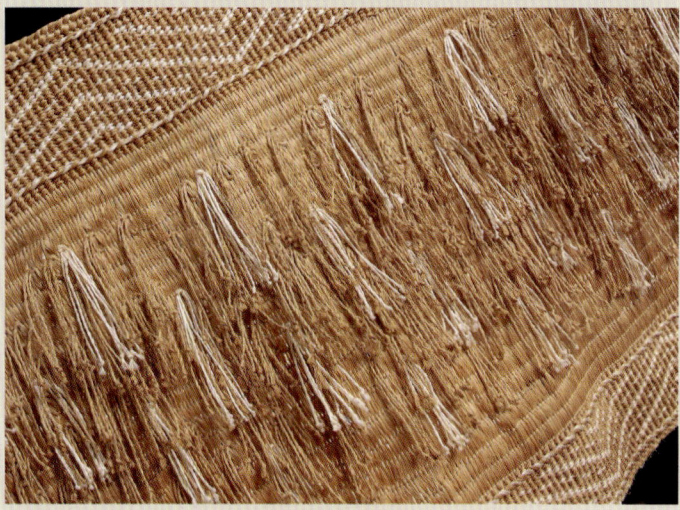

**Top left: Te Atiwei Ririnui,** *Poutama*, **2015**
private collection

**Top right: Karl Rangikawhiti Leonard,** *Mississippi, te awa kai kete – Mississippi, the basket eating river*, **2014**
muka, wax cotton, dyes – tutu (mordent), paru (peat), horse hair (black and white), *Toi Māori Exhibition*, Whiria, Wellington

**Bottom: Karl Rangikawhiti Leonard,** *Rāpaki named Rongomai* **(detail), 2006**
muka, Te Papa Tongarewa Museum of New Zealand, ME024024, purchased 2010

# PART 2
# TE KETE TUAURI

We can imagine tikanga Māori as a kete tuatea containing customs, values, beliefs and whakapapa that are readily to hand, informing the meaningful use of new materials in art, guiding creative responses to unfamiliar circumstances and embedding cultural values in innovative practice. Never was tikanga needed more than when Māori experienced the uncertainties brought by Pākehā arrival, which we characterise as Te Kete Tuauri, the basket of the unknown.

Pākehā people and culture arrived at kāinga Māori at different times and with different effects, starting with the sometimes difficult sea and shoreline encounters between Māori and European explorers in the seventeenth and eighteenth centuries that preceded the more influential social, spiritual and economic engagements that took place at harbour and mission settlements in the nineteenth century (see chapters 8 and 9). As discussed in all of the chapters in this section, these relationships resulted in an increasing influx of Pākehā tools, materials, values and concepts that would alter many Māori arts (chapter 11) – some, such as whakairo rākau, moko and fibre arts, to the point of near extinction – and an outward dispersal of thousands of taonga Māori to museums and private collectors around the world (chapter 13). Tikanga prevailed in the continuation of utu between Māori groups and leaders and involving the exchange of taonga Māori (chapter 10). Every transaction and the consequential layering of stories that accompanied these treasures through time and across regions elevated the treasures' mana. The continued practice of utu strengthened relationships between hapū and iwi and elevated the regard for those arts associated with ancestors, such as making weapons, whare, waka, hei tiki and cloaks, by providing such objects with significance beyond their original functions.

The greatest challenges to Māori art were brought by permanent Pākehā settlement and the consequential collision of British Crown authority with tino rangatiratanga. Whenua was alienated through sale, confiscation and compulsory acquisition, leaving Māori communities without an economic base to sustain customary practice and practitioners, or a resource base from which to harvest customary materials – a situation exacerbated by forest clearances and wetland drainage for Pākehā agriculture. Yet it was from one of the most socially disruptive phases of colonisation – the New Zealand Wars, beginning in Northland in the 1840s and extending across much of the North Island over the rest of the century – that the greatest acts of Māori artistic survival emerged (chapter 12). These were the arts of the Mōrehu, the drawings, paintings, flags and buildings of the Kīngitanga, Pai Mārire, Ringatū, Maungapōhatu, Parihaka and Māori Parliament movements that illustrated a resolute determination to maintain tino rangatiratanga. Many of the leaders of Mōrehu movements were Christian converts who saw themselves as being part of a whakapapa of prophet-like rangatira who would lead their people to salvation. With limited customary resources to hand, Mōrehu artists appropriated European iconography, materials and formalisms into Māori practice with immediate and often dramatic results. If colonisation was the challenge presented by Pākehā, then Mōrehu arts were the wero (challenge) returned. Although early nineteenth century hapū and iwi were not yet a homogeneous society, as is illustrated by the great diversity of artistic responses to colonisation, they were united by tikanga, and this would be the driver for their coalescence into pan-tribal groups and, eventually, a single Indigenous entity: Māori.

Isaack Gilsemans's view of Abel Tasman's anchorage at Wainui Bay, 1642. He has labelled specific aspects of the engraving: A Dutch ships; B canoes from the shore; C small boat being attacked by Māori; D detail of the waka and people; E Dutch ships under sail; F sloop which retrieved the small boat.

**Isaack Gilsemans, *A view of the Murderers' Bay, as you are at anchor here in 15 fathom*, 1642**

photolithograph, 290 x 435mm, Alexander Turnbull Library, PUBL-0086-021, from *Abel Janszoon Tasman's Journal*, Friedrich Muller & Co, Amsterdam, 1898

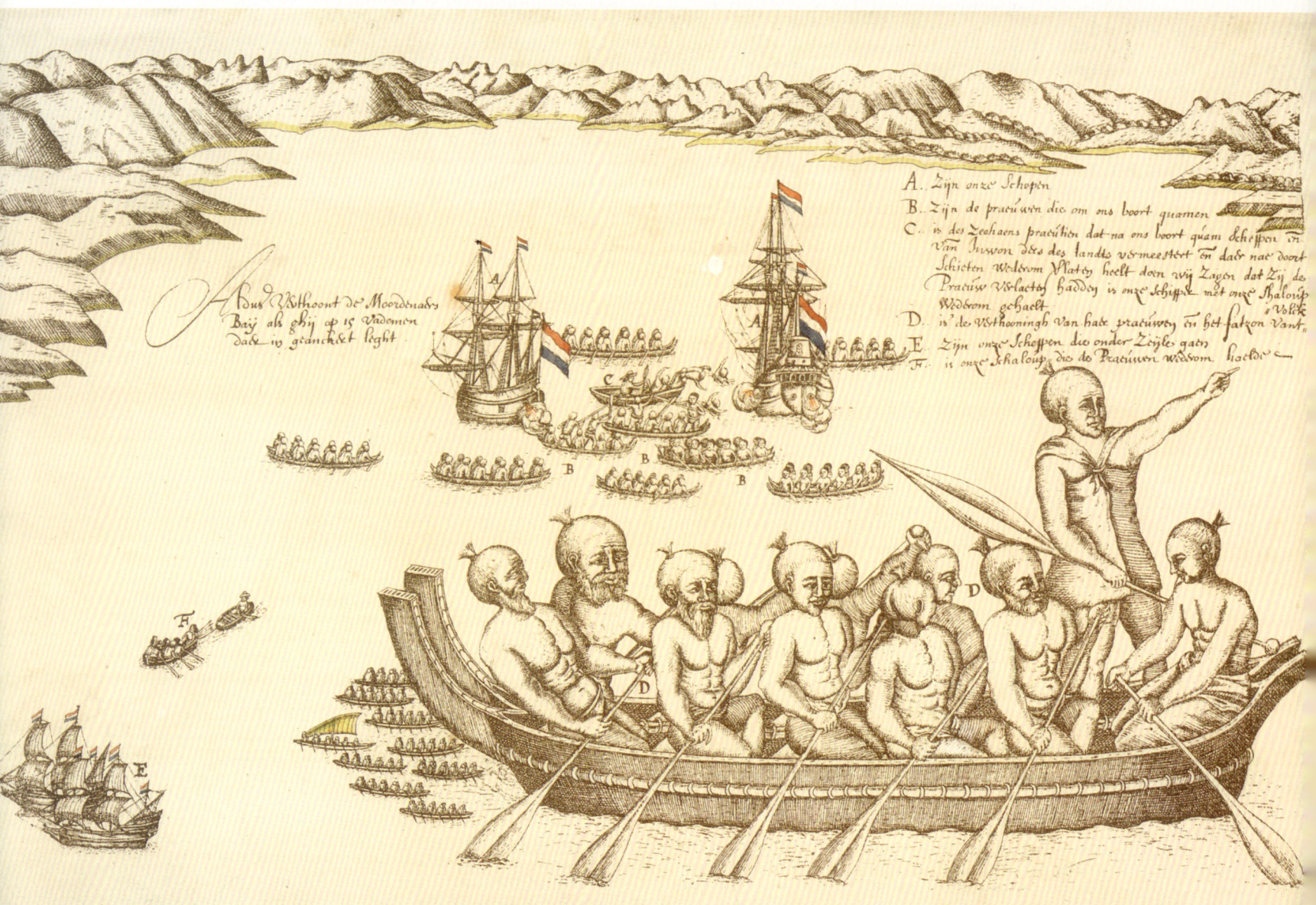

# 8 TAONGA, MĀORI AND MUSEUMS
## NGARINO ELLIS

*Ka kino tō pounamu, he kino pounamu onamata.*
*Your greenstone is awesome and its quality is ancient.*[1]

In December 2017 at Mōhua, Golden Bay, at the top of the South Island, a group of Māori and Pākehā gathered for events over several days to mark what they called First Encounter 375.[2] Doug Huria, spokesman for the local Ngāti Tūmatakōkiri, initiated the event to commemorate the 375th anniversary of the arrival of two Dutch ships into Mōhua on an expedition commanded by Abel Tasman (1602/03–1659?).[3] Visitors travelled from the Netherlands for the occasion, and the Dutch ambassador Rob Zaagman was there to represent Tasman. The day celebrated the connection of the Dutch with Māori, as well as acknowledging the violence that characterised that first engagement.

The only visual record of the dramatic moments of encounter are by Isaack Gilsemans, artist on Tasman's expedition. It presents six moments that took place over a two-day period (18–19 December 1642) in a single composition, with captions identifying each scene: 'A' shows the Dutch ships at anchor near the shore on 18 December, and 'B' depicts two waka hourua – double-hulled canoes of a type that was still virtually unknown when Cook arrived some 120 years later – loaded with Māori who had paddled out to assess the intentions of the foreign visitors. They sounded a warning on a pūtātara (conch-shell trumpet), to which the Dutch replied with their own trumpet, and the Māori scouting party then returned to shore. No doubt Ngāti Tūmatakōkiri would have held a hui on shore that night to consider the best approach. Who were these people who looked so different, whose ships were so much larger and with such tall masts? Did they come in peace? Did their trumpet in reply mean they were ready for war? Ngāti Tūmatakōkiri decided to send out another waka hourua, this time with thirteen people on board, to get closer and ascertain the strangers' intentions.

The next day they launched this second waka, which was greeted with offers to trade. Māori performed a haka: this was meant as a challenge calling on the visitors to state their purpose; the Dutch misinterpreted it as a sign of welcome. Tasman took this as a positive sign and, in discussion with his men, ordered his ships to sail closer. Perhaps Tasman should have been taking more notice of what was happening outside his boat, as seven other waka full of men soon arrived in a show of Ngāti Tūmatakōkiri prowess and military might. Their men shouted across to each other and held up their hoe, obviously preparing for direct contact, and as a show of their mana. Tasman on the *Heemskerck* became nervous and sent a cockboat to the other ship, the *Zeehaen*, to warn them; however, on the way back – as Gilsemans depicts in the centre of his drawing, at the point marked 'C' – Ngāti Tūmatakōkiri rammed the small boat, knocking the quartermaster overboard, killing three Dutch sailors with patu and hoe, and 'mortally wound[ing] a fifth'.[4] As historian Anne Salmond puts it, 'The surprise was complete.'[5] The local men then 'took one dead body into their canoe, threw another overboard and set the cockboat adrift'.[6]

The Dutch recovered the cockboat and prepared to leave, but Ngāti Tūmatakōkiri were determined to assert their sovereignty, and dispatched a further waka out towards Tasman's convoy. Gilsemans depicted one man – presumably the rangatira – standing upright, waving a piece of white cloth. Yet the Dutch also wanted to make a statement of intent and fired their cannons, hitting the chief. The waka turned and quickly retreated to shore. After another meeting of the council, the Dutch soon departed, having realised that there was no hope of a safe and peaceful landing.

This chapter takes as its point of departure the concept put forward by Ngāti Apa filmmaker Barry Barclay, who provoked us to think about the idea of a camera being 'ashore', and what was being witnessed from this angle.[7] The stories of these interactions between Māori and Europeans are often represented in the making and circulation of taonga – as recorded in the oral histories and in the taonga themselves. This book aims to facilitate the process of weaving taonga held in museums back into our histories, into the communities in which and for which they were made, by writing about them and reproducing images of them.

## Māori–British encounters, Aotearoa New Zealand, 1769–1800

The three voyages of Captain James Cook (1768–1771, 1772–1775, 1776–1780) established New Zealand as part of the English imagination, and later the British Empire. The Māori response to first contact with Europeans differed according to the level of direct engagement with the English and, soon after, the French – though it is likely that most major Māori settlements would have discussed their visits, given the active trade, the warring and the communication pathways that occurred across the country at the time. On each voyage relationships were forged, maintained and in some cases broken, and objects and ideas were exchanged; all of this had an impact on the art of the period.

European collecting of taonga Māori began with the arrival of Cook in 1769: he and others on the expedition, such as Joseph Banks, acquired a total of 242 objects across the three voyages to New Zealand,[8] including kākahu, carvings, weapons and personal adornments. Each object represented a moment of encounter and the forging of a relationship that, in some cases, carried on to subsequent voyages. The journals of those on board the British ships reveal the wonder felt by those who went ashore, as well as their suspicion and nervousness about these engagements. There are few Māori accounts that have been passed down, though more research into oral accounts may shed light on those transactions.

The journal entries give different perspectives on the people the Europeans met and the treasures they collected, the motivations behind some of the exchanges of taonga, and observations on various art forms. The Europeans were captivated by moko, for instance: Banks described the practice in detail in different parts of the country, and Herman Spöring and Sydney Parkinson drew it in various forms.

It has been difficult to identify the exact sites at which the 242 taonga were exchanged: often those who collected them made only general comments and did not specify exactly what was collected and where. Sometimes, as with the rare painted waka huia now in the British Museum (NZ113), the taonga had been traded across communities: the lid of the waka huia has been painted in a style from Poverty Bay on the East Coast; the carving on the base comes from Whanganui on the west coast of the North Island; and the taonga was collected at Tōtaranui Queen Charlotte Sound in the South Island. Such taonga had rich lives even before they moved into European hands.

Each time Cook returned to England there was much fanfare and delight. Objects that he collected were judiciously apportioned to important sponsors and others who had a vested interest in the voyages. The Museum of Archaeology and Anthropology (MAA) at the University of Cambridge was one of the most important repositories from the first voyage: thirty-six taonga at MAA come from this period.[9] One of the most generous donors was the Earl of Sandwich, First Lord of the Admiralty, who received gifts to acknowledge and enhance relationships: Banks gave him several taonga that were eventually deposited at MAA in 1914. Banks may also have given a collection of taonga to his friend and fellow naturalist Thomas Pennant, and these works were gifted to MAA in 1912.[10] Sir Ashton Lever was the recipient of most of his friend Cook's 'official' material from his second and third voyages.[11] He displayed these taonga in the Holophusicon – his private museum in a newly purchased house in Leicester Square, London; the museum opened in 1784, and was a wild success based on visitor numbers. Sadly, Lever's passion for purchasing objects stretched him financially, and he was forced to divest himself of his collection by lottery in 1786. He died two years later.

Many taonga were housed in natural history collections: Europeans considered Pacific peoples as part of the natural universe, and their cultural treasures were collected in the same way as flora and fauna. William Hodges, the artist on Cook's second voyage, often depicted Māori within the natural landscape, intimately linked to and of the land. Europeans were interested in the commercial possibilities of natural materials (stone, fibre, wood), too, so examples of these materials in their raw and worked state were also held and displayed in natural history museums and botanical collections.

The materials that the Europeans traded for these taonga, such as iron and lead, were highly sought after by Māori, who transformed the objects they had acquired by gift or trade from Cook and his men into forms that they treasured as symbols of their encounters and relationships with the British. Te Horeta was a young boy when Cook arrived at his home in Te Whanganui-a-Hei (Mercury Bay) in the Coromandel in November 1769, and was among a group of children who were invited on board the *Endeavour*, where he was given an iron nail that he later fashioned into an adze that he used to 'carve wood boxes to hold huia-feathers'.[12] Te Whakatatare o te Rangi of Te Aitanga a Hauiti on the East Coast was presented with a number of gifts, including a 'lump of lead' that he fashioned into an adze head lashed to a wooden handle.[13] In both cases, the material was transformed into something that was greatly valued by Māori. Historically, toki were named after important people or events, and those that were bound to a highly embellished wooden handle were considered toki poutangata – a ceremonial adze and a symbol of chieftainship. This naming and special treatment, when applied to metal adzes hafted onto traditional carved handles, would only have increased their value and prestige. This suggests a date for the metal adzes to the early 1770s. If they were actually used to carve, this would pre-date by fifty or sixty years the first known use of a metal adze by Raharuhi Rukupō on Te Hau ki Tūranga in the 1840s. These connections were important in a world that revolved around rank and hierarchy, which was built not only on genealogy but also accomplishment.

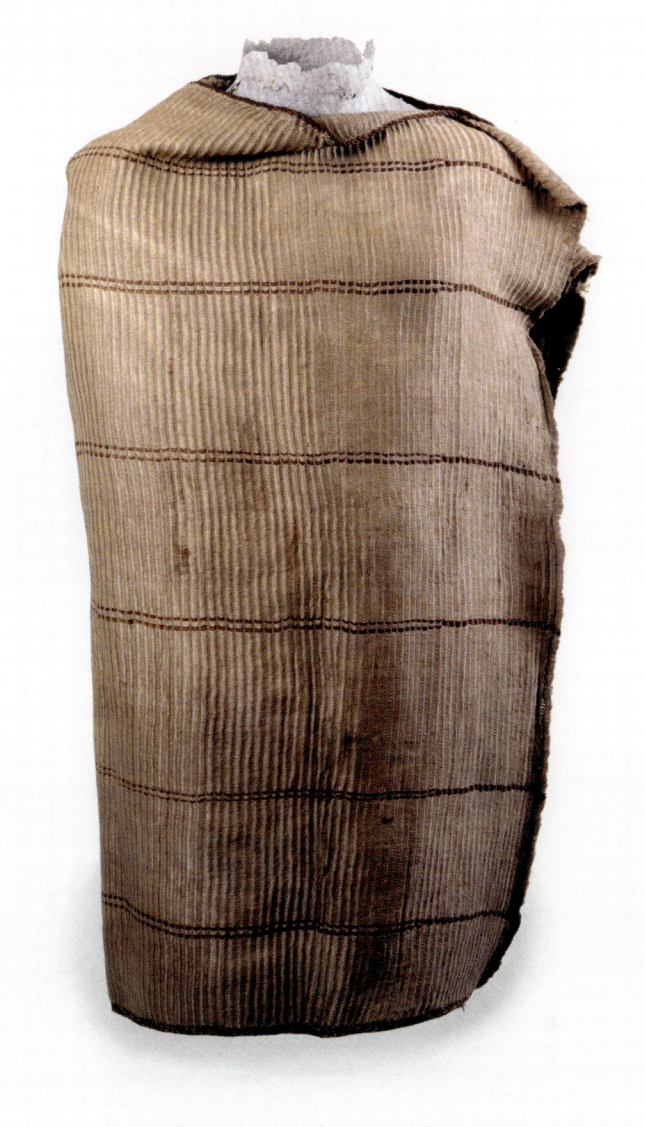

Kaitaka mai muka collected in the 1760s. These are very rare in museum collections: another example is in Te Papa Tongarewa (ME014494). James Cook collected hundreds of taonga when he visited Aotearoa between 1769 and 1780, and gifted these to patrons and friends upon his return to England. This cloak is in the Georg-August University, Göttingen, Germany, and is one of hundreds of taonga collected on Cook's voyages resident there.
Georg-August University, Göttingen, Inv. Oz 317, photograph by Harry Haase

### Māori–French encounters, Aotearoa, 1769–1800

Cook was, of course, not the only explorer from Europe: the French arrived in Aotearoa in the same year as Cook's first visit and travelled around the country, engaging with communities, making observations and collecting taonga. Jean François Marie de Surville sailed around North Cape on the *St Jean Baptiste* on 17 December 1769, then spent two weeks with Ngāti Kahu people at Tokerau (which he renamed Baie de Lauriston; Cook had recorded it as Doubtless Bay). His compatriot Marc-Joseph Marion du Fresne travelled around Te Tai Tokerau from April to July 1772. Salmond sums up the agendas of those two voyages: 'Discovery and exploration were important themes in the intellectual life of this period, for the French Enlightenment thinkers used accounts of other societies to question their own, and to investigate the nature of society itself.'[14]

Tokerau in 1769 was a busy settlement with abundant kaimoana, which Ngāti Kahu traded with the French. Accounts from de Surville's visit present a vision of a self-sufficient and prosperous kāinga, with this abundance displayed through the people's bodies, architecture and waka. The waka had carved tauihu and taurapa; and men and women alike wore moko incised on their buttocks and legs, and on the stomach as well for some women. Some wore moko on only half the face, others on three-quarters, in a style similar to those that Parkinson drew in the Bay of Islands that same year. Many were painted with red pigment, presumably kōkōwai; and they wore a range of neck ornaments including hei tiki with pāua inlay, and kuru (long pounamu drops) in their ears.[15] Jean Pottier de l'Horme, one of Marion du Fresne's lieutenants, noted 'bones in their ears, of fish teeth in the form of snakes' tongues, both sides of which are very finely serrated'.[16] The chief wore a dogskin cloak with 'the hair on the outside for ceremonial purposes but to protect themselves from the cold they turn it to the inside';[17] First Lieutenant Guillaume Labé noted several people wearing such cloaks.[18] One chief exchanged his kahu kurī for a set of jacket and breeches from the captain, though whether this was considered a trade or to follow tikanga (a gift for a gift) is unclear. Labé later traded a 'six-foot length of heavy cloth' for two mere pounamu and a hei tiki.[19]

These three treasures are now part of some 500 taonga from Aotearoa spread across fourteen museums in France. The largest collection is in the Musée du Quai Branly in Paris, which now houses collections from other museums as well. The Musée des Antiquités, just outside Paris, received many of the taonga that were brought back to France in the eighteenth century, and this material passed to the Musée d'Ethnographie du Trocadéro in Paris when it opened as the first anthropology museum in France in 1878. When this latter museum closed in 1935, the taonga were transferred to the Musée de l'Homme, part of the national Natural History Museum, which opened two years later. Most of this collection was moved to the Musée du Quai Branly when it opened in 2006. Some of this Māori collection dates to the eighteenth century: noted nineteenth-century collector Dominique-Vivant Brunet-Denon also acquired a few taonga, including a pūtōrino, hei tiki and waka huia, which are all now in the Musée du Quai Branly.

| European voyagers to Aotearoa in the eighteenth century | |
|---|---|
| October 1769–March 1770 | James Cook (Great Britain) |
| December 1769 | Jean François Marie de Surville (France) |
| April–July 1772 | Marc-Joseph Marion du Fresne (France) |
| May–June, October–December 1772; March–April, Oct–Nov 1773 | Cook |
| May and Nov–Dec 1773 | Tobias Furneaux (part of Cook expedition; Great Britain) |
| February 1777 | Cook |
| November 1791 | George Vancouver (Great Britain) |
| February 1793 | Alessandro Malaspina (Italy) |

### Māori collections in the United States

By the late eighteenth century other European nations, especially the Spanish and the Portuguese, had been voyaging around the world for 300 years. After the defeat of Napoléon in France in 1815, the British Royal Navy focused its energies on supporting the Crown's ambition for exploration and the expansion of empire, especially where there might be financial or strategic opportunities. Taonga were originally collected on these expeditions on an ad hoc basis, but gradually the focus changed to assembling an overall view of the culture – and this was reflected in the types of museums being built where such collections would be deposited.[20]

Some of the earliest collections of taonga came from American whalers and sealers based in the Bay of Islands during the heyday of these industries in Aotearoa. Both whaling and sealing began in New Zealand waters in 1791,

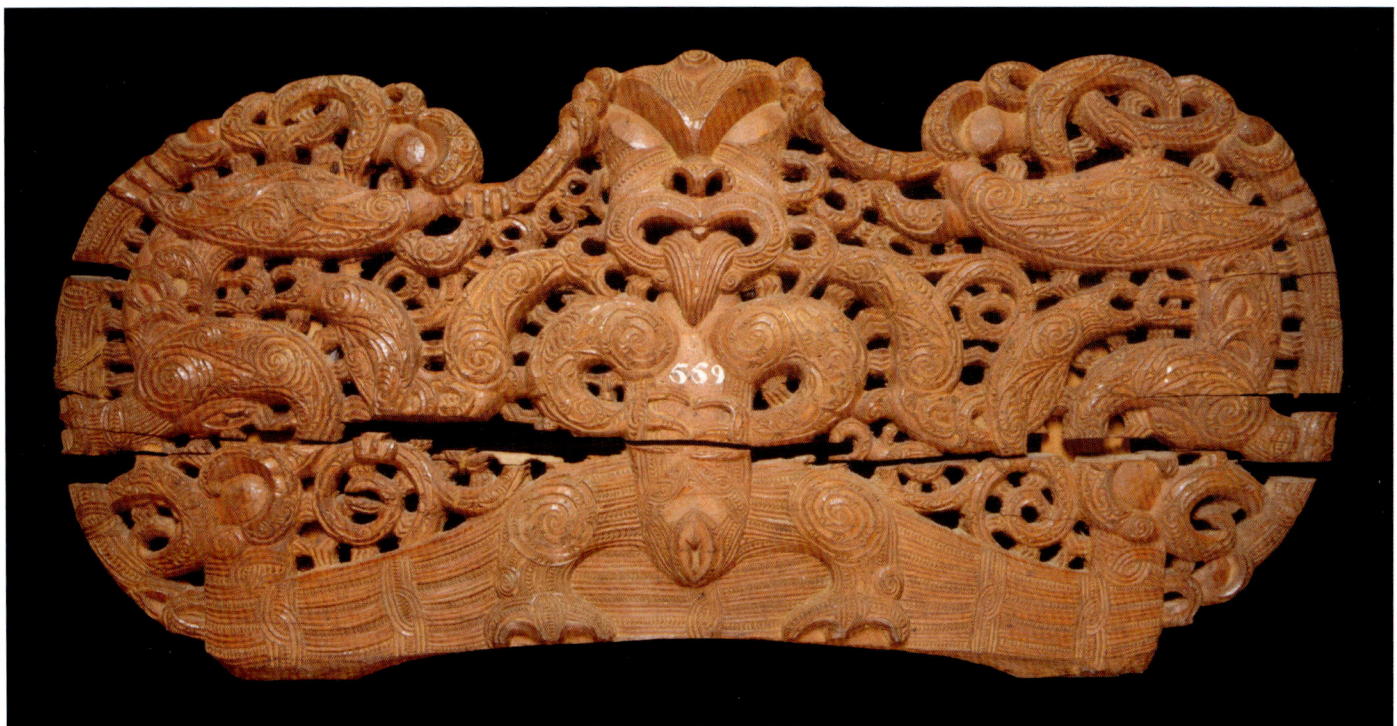

Pare collected by Captain William Richardson in the Bay of Islands, 1807, then donated to what became the Peabody Essex Museum, Salem, Massachusetts. The pare is of kauri and may be from the Bay of Plenty.
Peabody Essex Museum, Salem Massachusetts, E5505, E5501, gift of Captain William Richardson, 1807

and when the seamen left, they took taonga back with them to North America, some of which were deposited in museums.

Jennifer Wagelie, in her PhD dissertation on the collection history and display of Māori taonga in the United States, identified two taonga in the Peabody Essex Museum in Salem, Massachusetts that had been acquired from whalers: a cleaver deposited in 1821 by Captain Josiah Gwinn (who was in New Zealand 1803–1806 and 1807–1809), and a model canoe from Mana Island in 1838, donated by Captain James Neil.[21]

The earliest taonga to be placed in an American museum date to 1802, when Daniel Ward, a trader with China, donated three taonga to the East India Marine Society (EIMS, founded in 1799): a hei tiki, a matau and a kākā pōria;[22] another trader with China, John Fitzpatrick Jeffrie, donated a cleaver to the EIMS museum the following year. By 1812 the EIMS museum had received two large trader collections: in 1807 Captain William Richardson donated nineteen taonga, including, most notably, a māripi (a tool for cutting human flesh), a waka huia and a pare. Apart from the pare, which measures 1m across, the other treasures were all small and portable. Deidre Brown has described how these are significant as they provide us with a snapshot of art being produced in and around the Bay of Islands;[23] she notes that the pare is particularly interesting as, stylistically, the work may have come from the Bay of Plenty and may therefore be the work of Ngāti Awa carvers (who may have been brought to the North as enslaved people).

William Putnam Richardson's Māori collection consists of two kurukuru (long greenstone adornments), hei tiki, toki pounamu, mere pounamu, three tewhatewha (staffs), two taiaha, two tao (spears), two hoe (including a stunning, fully painted example), a kōauau, a nguru (sound instrument played through the nostrils) and a kaitaka. Apparently, Richardson and his crew were not seeking textiles, or were not offered any in trade or exchange. Textiles certainly had been offered in encounters with earlier European voyagers – Cook was offered a number of fibre artworks during his visits, and he brought back seven kākahu from the East Coast from his first voyage.[24] As such, the Putnam Richardson collection could be considered a gendered collection that offers little to researchers of a Bay of Islands style of weaving; weapons and paddles held greater appeal for the men on board.

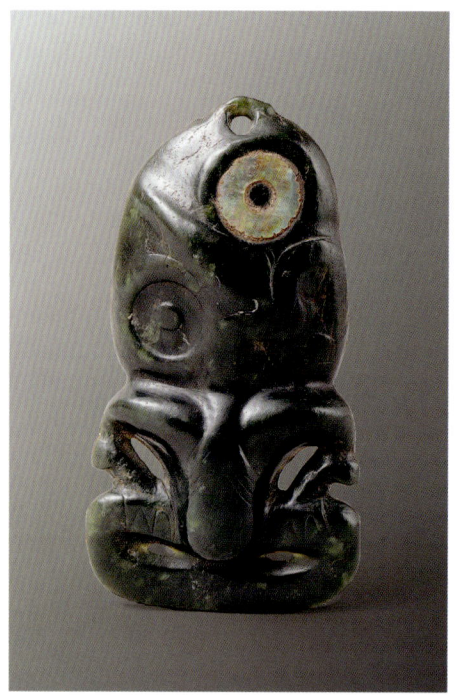 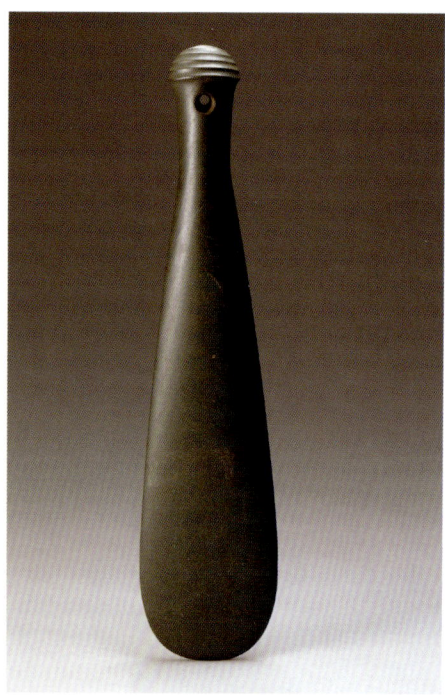 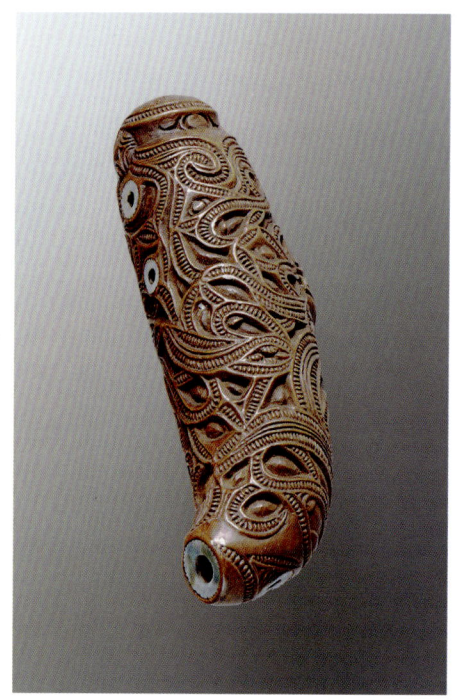

Hei tiki, patu ōnewa and nguru collected by Captain William Putnam Richardson.
Peabody Essex Museum, Salem Massachusetts, from left to right: E5528, gift of Captain William P. Richardson, 1807, photograph by Jeffrey R. Dykes; E5536, gift of William Putnam Richardson, 1812; E5520, gift of Captain William Richardson, 1807, photograph by Jeffrey R. Dykes

Whalers' collections of taonga are relatively unknown in American and Russian museums. Indeed, Māori collections in non-English-speaking countries are still relatively unknown, as researchers into these collections are predominantly English-speaking, although more recent research is starting to shed light on these collections.[25] For instance, Elena Gover has outlined the Oceanic works now in the Museum of Ethnography in St Petersburg, collected by Russian explorer and anthropologist Nikolai Miklouho-Maclay (1846–1888);[26] and more recently (2020), the Russian Special Expert Commission has identified forty-two taonga collected in 1820 by Fabian Gottlieb von Bellingshausen (1778–1852) in Tōtaranui Queen Charlotte Sound.

### Collecting portraits of Māori

The artists on early voyages to Aotearoa, both official and amateur, made portraits of Māori that provide us with much insight into the sitters. Initially, from the 1760s to around 1800, artists were fascinated by the differences in their subjects: some gave a careful reproduction of moko – such as Sydney Parkinson, who drew a faithful rendition of the intricate designs of the pūhoro that he saw on the forehead, face, neck and thighs of people he observed. Hairstyles were carefully rendered in some images, and clothing and other adornment detailed. Only rarely were the sitters named, though the location and the date were often recorded.

Given that the European artists lacked training in anatomy, it is perhaps unsurprising that they often represented Māori in a generic style in their drawings. George French Angas (1822–1886) in 1844, for instance, repeatedly portrayed both men and women as doe-eyed and soft-cheeked, with curly hair framing their faces; and with the same body types of the same weight and height. Joseph Jenner Merrett (1816–1854) created a specific type of portrait that he used across his drawings: his figures had large eyes, and their body types were covered by large kākahu. Merrett travelled between Sydney and Aotearoa from the late 1830s until his death, and visited the Bay of Islands, Auckland, the Waikato, Taranaki and Whanganui; Governor Grey was his patron from 1845 to 1847.[27] Often artists did not have long 'in the field' to draw their subject, and with very little Māori language they did not have the ability to build a relationship beyond the initial request for them to sit.

French anatomist Pierre-Marie Alexandre Dumoutier (1797–1871) made a series of remarkable – and unsettling – plaster life-casts of Māori in 1837, while on Jules Sébastien César Dumont d'Urville's third voyage to the Pacific in 1837.

Fiona Pardington has reimaged fifty of Dumoutier's life-casts, located in basements and storage facilities in France.[28] The process of having a life-cast taken is very invasive, as it involves covering the sitter's upoko (head) in plaster of Paris while they breathe through straws placed in the nostrils. It is surprising that these men would have agreed to undertake such a process due to the nature of personal tapu, especially of the head. Dumoutier must have had immense powers of persuasion: the fact that these men agreed to lie down and have wet plaster smoothed all over their head by a person who was not their equal or higher in rank is testament to the utmost diplomacy.

The life-casts provide a snapshot of the community: the sitter's physiognomy reveals what these men actually looked like. Indeed, the life-casts can be compared to moko signatures of the same period, where Kāi Tahu drew self-portraits in pen but details such as the high cheekbones (as seen on Matoua) were omitted in preference to depicting the moko. For many Māori, seeing such an image of a person's head with their eyes closed is deeply disturbing, akin to seeing a tūpāpaku – a deceased person – and they are not easy images to view. Pardington's groundbreaking practice here retrieves her ancestors from French basements and returns them to their descendants.

The ways in which visitors to Aotearoa depicted Māori changed between 1770 and 1840 as more Europeans spent longer periods of time in New Zealand. Some artists chose to create before-and-after images depicting Māori in their natural environment and again after they had entered, say, a mission world, when they would be shown wearing European clothes and conforming to European ideals of beauty, such as short hair for men. In the image of Tuai from the mid-1820s, for instance, French artist Antoine Chazal (1793–1854) presents a double portrait of the Ngare Raumati chief:[29] on the left, Tuai is dressed as befits a fashionable European man of the moment, in a black coat and cotton shirt with tall collar and wide cravat; the caption reads 'King of Savages'. Facing him is another visage: a Tuai who wears a kākahu with stippled hukahuka; this Tuai is known simply as 'Savage'. In both images his hair is the same, tied up in a ponytail rather than the tikitiki that would have been his everyday hairstyle. As the 'King', his hair has been arranged to mimic the sideburns that were popular in London at the time. In comparing this with other images of Tuai, we can see that Chazal has included

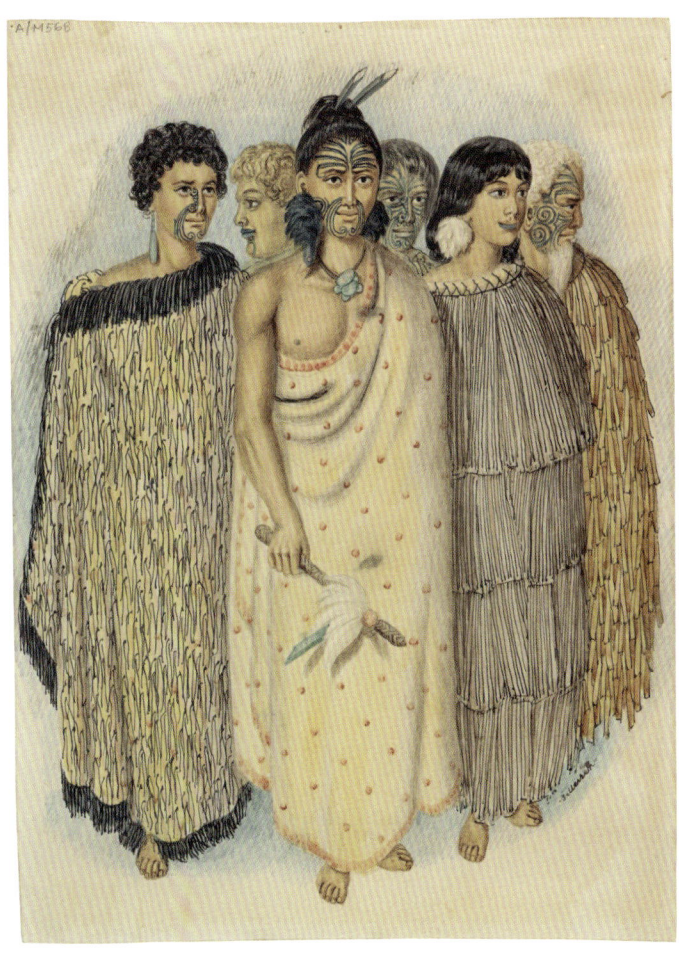

Artist and surveyor Joseph Merrett created images of Māori in the Bay of Islands, Auckland and Waikato in the late 1830s–1840s.
**Joseph Jenner Merrett, *Group of Maoris*, c.1850**
watercolour, pen and ink on paper, 238 x 178mm, Hocken Collections Uare Taoka o Hākena, University of Otago, 4,326 b

Tuai's prominent nose as a key feature. In both portraits, he looks calm and 'civilised'. These are the two faces of Māori, the before and after, the noble savage and the gentleman. The agenda of the artist is political here: although Tuai is named 'King', it is a misnomer – to Chazal (and his European viewers) Tuai will always be a 'savage', despite his clothes and hairstyle.

## Collecting of taonga Māori in the nineteenth century

While private collectors such as James Hector and Thomas Hocken were seeking out taonga for their own interests, as well as to promote industry in exhibitions, taonga were also moving out of Māori communities through warfare. During and immediately after the New Zealand Wars,[30] taonga were looted from the battlefield by Māori and Crown soldiers alike, who sought out small and portable treasures such as hei tiki.[31]

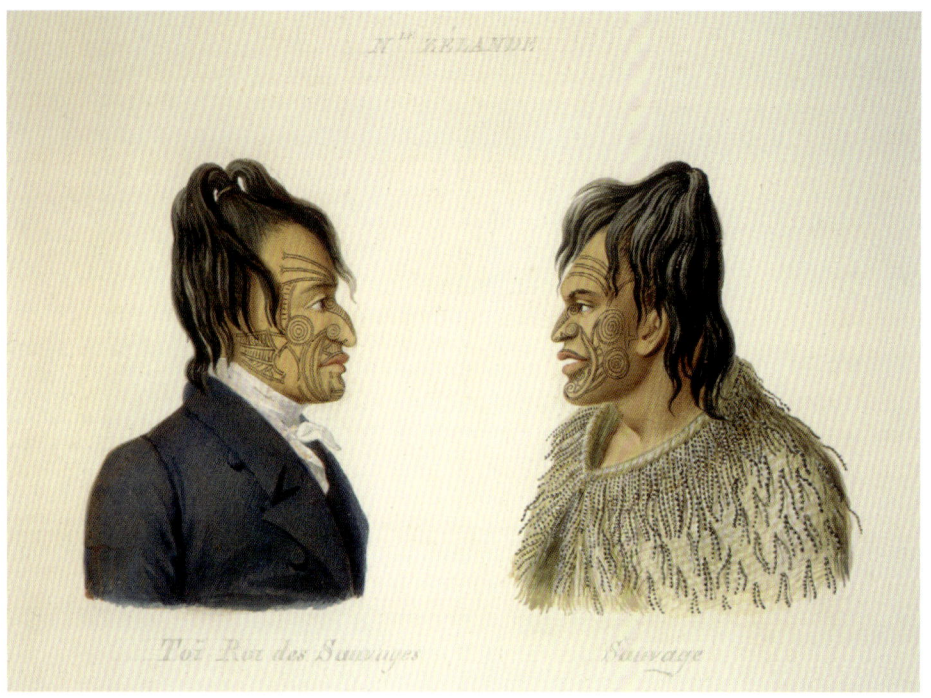

Double portrait of Tuai by Antoine Chazal from 1825–1826, copied from 1824 drawings by Jules-Louis Lejeune. On the left, Tuai is shown in European dress titled 'Toi, Roi des Sauvages' (Toi, King of Savages), while on the right in his kākahu he is simply 'Sauvage' – Savage.
**Antoine Chazal [after Jules Lejeune], *Nle Zelande. Toi, Roi des sauvages. Sauvage* [1825-1826]**
pencil, ink and watercolour, 246 x 375mm, Alexander Turnbull Library, C-082-102. From watercolours, proof engravings and aquatints by Antoine Chazal and others after drawings by Jules Lejeune and others for Duperrey's *Voyage autour du monde …*, Paris, 1822–1825

Larger wooden structures such as whare, pātaka and waka taua were burnt or otherwise destroyed or dismantled, and sometimes carvings and other taonga were removed. A letter from Ropoama Rakei to Governor George Grey on 8 September 1865 described how all the houses at the settlement of Te Papoaka on the Central Plateau were burnt.[32] The intent in such cases was to destroy the identity and break the spirit of the local community.

After the wars had ended in 1872, a second wave of taonga were alienated from whānau who sold them, often while they were in a position of financial disadvantage, having been forced off their ancestral lands through land confiscation.[33] Between 1860 and 1890, 1.3 million hectares of land was confiscated by the Crown, and Māori land ownership reduced to 40 percent: whānau and hapū lost access to urupā where their ancestors resided; to their homes and the carved and woven taonga housed in them; and to the resources that were integral to making their art.

Some colonial government officials and employees moonlighted as collectors for museums, and invariably sought out taonga for their own private collections as well. In 1873 Samuel Locke, a land purchase officer and magistrate based in Gisborne, negotiated with Hēnare Pōtae, a Ngāti Porou chief of Tokomaru Bay, to sell him carvings that he was having made for a new wharenui for £290. Locke was working in this instance on behalf of Julius von Haast, director of the Canterbury Museum,[34] where the carvings were to be shipped. Part of the sale included the employment of two Ngāti Porou carvers, Hone Taahu and Tāmati Ngākaho, who were to reside in Christchurch in order to complete the carvings, paint kōwhaiwhai panels and install the house – to be named Hau Te Ana Nui o Tangaroa – in the museum. Locke had been looking to purchase a meeting house for several years, most probably for Canterbury Museum, even before Haast was appointed as director in 1868 (the museum opened in 1870). In 1863, according to Leo Fowler, Locke had offered to buy the Rongowhakaata meeting house Te Hau ki Tūranga but the chief and carver Raharuhi Rukupō turned him down.[35] Two years later a government representative arrived at Ōrākaiapu pā under orders from the minister of Native Affairs, James Richmond, to confiscate the house as part of a wider land confiscation.[36] The house was loaded onto a steamer despite iwi protests, and taken directly to the Colonial Museum in Wellington, where Richmond was acting director at the time.

Gilbert Mair was a civil servant who was well known for his interest in collecting taonga. Born in 1843 in Northland, Mair became fluent in te reo Māori and volunteered as a soldier aged twenty-three. Paul Tapsell describes Mair's activities as 'collecting in the field':[37] it took place during his active military service and in his various roles as a civil servant across the country after 1872. Paula Savage says of

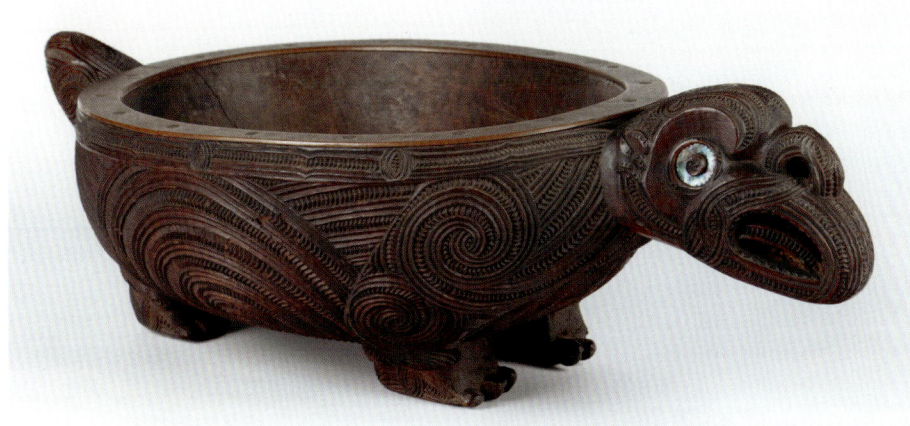

A rare example of a kumete kurī or dog-shaped bowl. Gilbert Mair collected this kumete, and donated it to Auckland War Memorial Museum, who then loaned it to Otago Museum – such complex trajectories away from Māori communities and to distant museums are commonplace for taonga.
Tāmaki Paenga Hira Auckland War Memorial Museum, 1983.165

Mair's collecting: 'he was a keen and not always completely ethical collector of Māori artefacts who ... assisted in the purchase and removal of many valuable Te Arawa carvings from the Rotorua district'.[38] In addition to his personal collecting (which numbered 247 taonga), he also acquired taonga for other major collectors of the day – Alexander Turnbull, Sir Walter Buller, as well as the Auckland and Dominion museums. Some taonga were very rare, and consequently valuable, such as the tewhatewha parāoa (whalebone staff) 'dug up' from Pukehinahina (Gate Pā) in 1875 that eventually came into his possession. He often recorded information associated with the taonga he acquired – aided no doubt by the fact that he could speak the language of those he gathered them from. These notes have proved invaluable in tracing the whakapapa of the taonga, and have ultimately enabled their reunion with the descendants of their original kaitiaki. Tapsell is one of those descendants. He surmises: 'As [Mair] constantly moved and shifted between two worlds, taonga moved alongside him and he knowingly relocated them from iwi custodianship to a museum context. Some taonga also entered into other types of relationships as he gave them to his Pākehā friends.'[39]

At other times Māori were forced to sell their taonga just to survive. On Rēkohu Chatham Islands in the 1890s, schoolmaster Joseph Walter Williams acquired at least eighty-two treasures that were later given to the British Museum. Roger Neich describes Williams as 'a persistent and rather unscrupulous fossicker ... well aware of breaking the law':[40] he stripped trees of ancient ancestral dendroglyphs and took other taonga, often at dawn to avoid being caught. In a letter he describes how he approached a group at Manukau settlement, who had: 'two bone fish and two ornaments called Reis ... The Moriori from who I obtained them was very loth to part with them, there being no other bone articles'.[41] It is clear that Williams deliberately took advantage of his position of power and influence in the community as the teacher to feed his collecting desires.

### Exhibiting taonga Māori in museums in New Zealand in the nineteenth century

The increasing numbers of taonga being taken to Europe by the 1810s spurred the creation of museums to house them, and an unprecedented fifty new museums were built between 1800 and 1850 in England.[42] Settlers who arrived in New Zealand from Britain were well aware of this, and they set about establishing learned societies and institutes where they could extend their investigations into this culture they were encountering.

The first museum in New Zealand was founded by the Nelson Institute in September 1842, and was aimed at '"diffusing scientific and literary information" to settlers'. The Wellington Institute followed in 1851, with Governor George Grey as founding president to add gravitas. These early public institutes spurred the formation of larger, more formal museums: in Auckland (1852), Christchurch (Canterbury Museum, 1861), Wellington (Colonial Museum, 1865) and Dunedin (Otago Museum, 1868).[43]

Grey was a collector of taonga in his own right, and shipped some of his collection back to England, undoubtedly to promote his work and the success of the colony.[44] He was

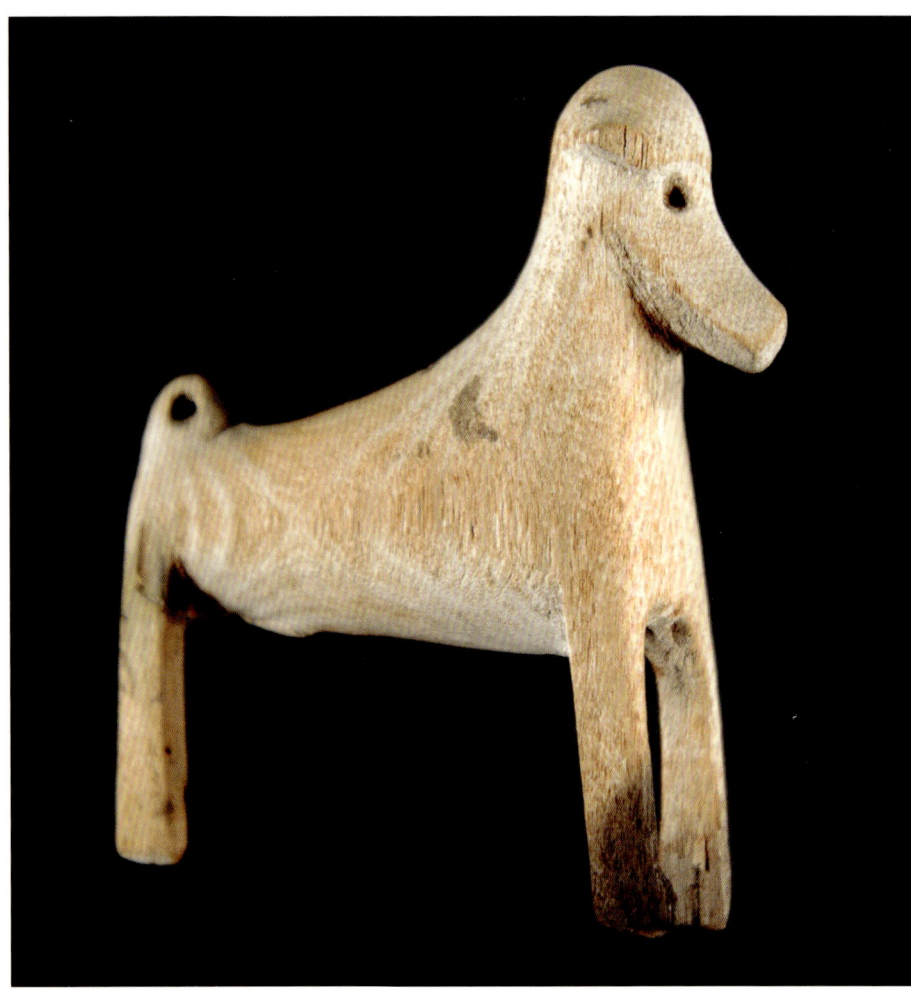

This extremely rare whakapakoko (figurine) of a kurī was found in Moncks Cave. Made of wood, and sized to fit in the hand, it may have been a child's toy (due to the size) or an amulet or adornment (note the tail).
Canterbury Museum, 19XX.1.1740. The Museum acknowledges the customary takiwā rights of Te Ngāi Tūāhuriri Rūnanga and Te Hapū o Ngāti Wheke

familiar with the study of ethnology, and he drew on this to promote his government policies. This was a common strategy for colonial administrators in Indigenous countries: they sought scientific evidence to support their legislative policies, particularly those associated with the acquisition of land. By promoting a 'scientific' scale of civilisation based on racial hierarchies – with monkeys at one end and Europeans as the paragons of civilisation at the other – Grey ensured the assertion of settler culture at the expense of Māori survival. Māori were considered to be in need of care and protection – services that could only be provided through government policy.

In New Zealand this scale of racial hierarchy was based partly on archaeological excavations. In the nineteenth century these took the form of digging and fossicking by amateurs who removed not only taonga but also human remains and associated funerary objects. Some sites were damaged irrevocably. The entrance to Moncks Cave at Ōhikaparuparu (Sumner) had been sealed by a landslide; when roadworkers uncovered it in 1889 a formal excavation was instigated, but it was too late to stop fossicking by locals. The taonga that remained – including a small wooden dog figurine, a painted hoe and an ama – were rare and unusual, and we can only wonder what else was taken.

The science of anthropology also promoted a racial hierarchy. Arrivals from England and Scotland established philosophical institutes to invigorate the intellectual culture of their communities and provide an environment where discussion of the history and culture of Māori could take place. Members included influential colonial administrators, museum staff and private collectors. James Hector (1834–1907) arrived from Scotland in 1862 to survey the geology of Otago, and soon became involved in various scientific bodies around the country: he managed the influential New Zealand Institute from its inception in 1865 until 1903; he organised the museum sector and submitted works for the 1865 New Zealand Exhibition in Dunedin; and he was the first director of the Geological Survey and Colonial Museum, Wellington from 1865 to his retirement in 1903.[45] Doctor Thomas Hocken came to New Zealand from England and set up in general practice in Dunedin in 1862. He was interested in the country's natural history and was concerned that it was being lost in the devastation of the goldfield workings. He was also a passionate collector, and from the late 1870s he turned his attention to taonga Māori. Hocken gifted his important collection to the public through the University of Otago, in what became the Hocken Library Uare Taoka o Hākena.

Many of these men, such as Hocken and Augustus Hamilton, undertook a number of roles in colonial New Zealand, and worked together on particular projects that they anticipated would promote the colony and its success. One of these endeavours was the New Zealand Exhibition (also known as the South Seas Exhibition) in Dunedin in 1865. This was based on a model set by the very popular 1851 Great Exhibition of the Works of Industry of All Nations (the Great Exhibition), held at Crystal Palace, London, where countries were invited to display their 'industrial manufactures';[46] the New Zealand contribution included 'Maori carvings, Maori-made products (such as flax *kete*), samples of flour ground in Maori mills and various woods sent by a Maori exhibitor'.[47] These showcased the diverse range of activities in the colony, and reinforced the 'progress' that was colonisation. The Crystal Palace exhibition took place only eleven years after the signing of Te Tiriti o Waitangi, at the start of a prosperous decade for many iwi who established a range of commercial ventures. Twenty-six such exhibitions were held in New Zealand between 1865 and 1925, and they proved very popular with audiences.[48] Often they were organised by museum staff working collaboratively with collectors and colonial administrators. Museums sent out envoys to source taonga, and relied on them as their collectors on the ground. Those with Māori language competency were particularly useful as they could access communities on a different level and assess the degree of willingness Māori might have to part with their treasures; or find out where the burial caves were to raid.

The degree to which Māori had agency in these exhibitions is debatable. The most notable Māori involvement was the 1906 New Zealand International Exhibition in Christchurch, but even then Māori were consultants, makers and performers rather than being involved in the shaping of *how* they were portrayed: this was driven by tourism operators who promoted an idea of Māori as still living in pā, wearing kākahu and carrying weapons, who spent their time singing waiata and performing haka. Conal McCarthy argues that Māori involvement 'complicates' the commonly held belief that these fairs 'served the interests of imperialism through the subjugation of native peoples'.[49] He cites examples such as the chief Haimona Te Aoterangi, who offered for his personal patu parāoa (whalebone cleaver) named Paiaterangi to go to Philadelphia for the Centennial International Exhibition held there in 1876. Yet Māori often had no input into the structural nature of the New Zealand contributions, no say over what was sent in general, or how it was displayed. This mirrored the situation in museums, where there were no Māori on the permanent curatorial or research staff – a situation that did not change until well into the twentieth century.

### International buyers of taonga Māori

By the 1880s and 1890s museums internationally had become interested in expanding their collections to include material from colonial nations such as New Zealand. Some museums were able to send staff to New Zealand to purchase – or attempt to purchase – carvings in particular, especially whare, waka and pātaka. Others organised purchases or swaps through lengthy negotiations by mail. At other times, taonga were brokered through Europe-based dealers who could tap into a strong complex of curators, directors and private collectors. The Ngāti Porou meeting house Ruatepupuke, for instance, came through the merchant house or 'emporium' of Heinrich Umlauff, based in Hamburg, in 1902; the house was later purchased by the Field Museum in Chicago, where he remains today. Two years later Umlauff also purchased another house, Rauru, partly carved by Ānaha Te Rāhui, Tene Waitere and Neke Kapua,[50] and sold it on to the Museum für Völkerkunde in Hamburg in 1910, where he remains on display.[51] The same carvers created Te Wharepuni-a-Māui for the 1906 Exhibition, before it was brokered through an unknown German dealer and later purchased by the Linden Museum, Stuttgart.

The wheeling and dealing in taonga by non-owners, both in New Zealand and overseas, is best demonstrated in the case of the Ngāti Kahungunu wharenui now called Te Whare o Heretaunga.[52] The house was originally commissioned by Karaitiana Takamoana in the 1870s from Iwirākau carvers from Ngāti Porou, including Hoani Ngatai, but the rangatira

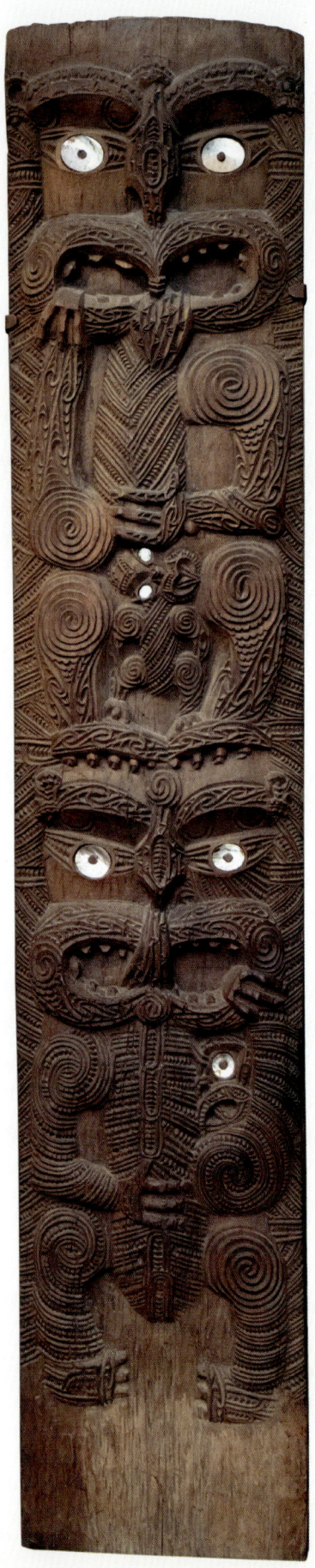 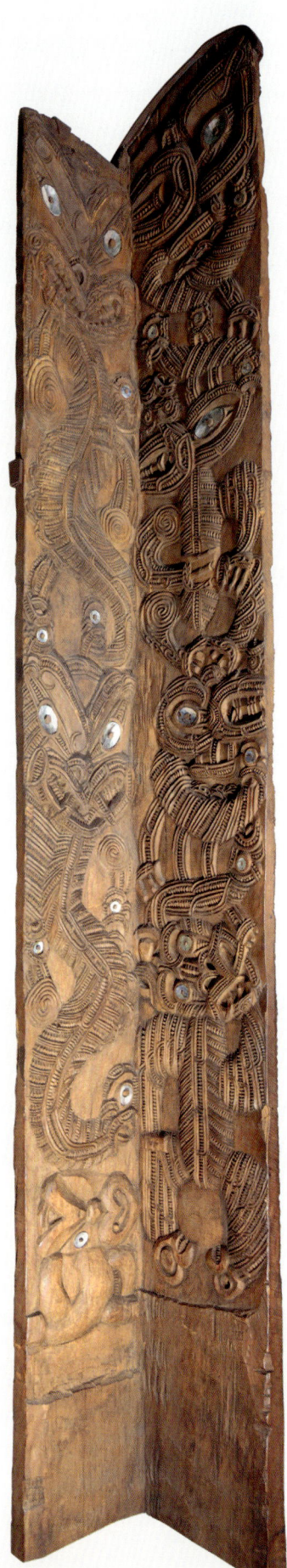 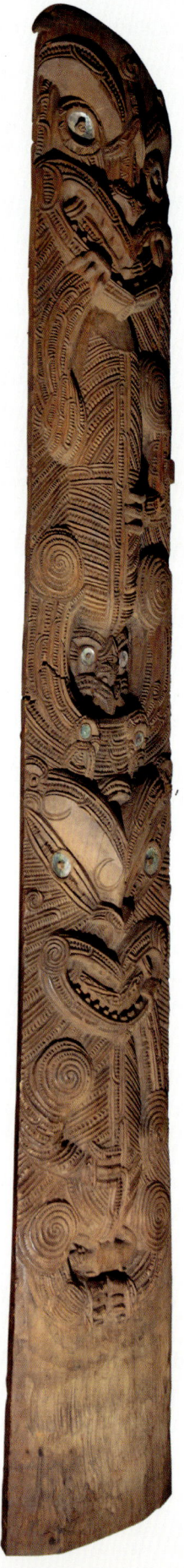

died in 1876 before the house was completed. With the New Zealand and South Seas Exhibition in Dunedin on the horizon for 1889–1890, Augustus Hamilton of the Hawke's Bay Philosophical Institute in Napier organised for most of the carvings to be shipped to Dunedin to be displayed in the exhibition.[53] When the exhibition closed, the carvings were offered for sale and were purchased on behalf of Dr Thomas Hocken, who subsequently gifted them to the Otago Museum.[54]

When Henry Devenish Skinner was appointed as curator at the Otago Museum in 1918, he began contacting museums overseas in order to increase the international collection; by the time he retired as director he had increased the museum's collection by over 100,000 objects. One of Skinner's methodologies was to swap what he considered to be 'duplicates' (a frequent museum practice) for overseas objects. The duplicates in this case were distinctive carvings from Te Whare o Heretaunga. Ultimately these carvings were dispersed to more than ten museums. At no time did Skinner contact the original owners; nor did he consider the ways in which separating out individual carvings from a meeting house might offend Māori, who conceptualised a wharenui as a living ancestor. A descendant of Takamoana, Rose Mohi, has been leading the call for the return of the carvings, and has been visiting many of them in person overseas.[55] She has identified sixty-six carvings that are either from Te Whare o Heretaunga or were likely made for the house. These are an important part of the application for settlement of grievances against the Crown by the people of Heretaunga Tamatea. The claimant group, He Toa Takitini, signed a deed of settlement on 26 September 2015 in which the Crown agreed to 'protect and restore' the house.[56]

Douglas Cole, in his book on collecting of Indigenous treasures in the Pacific Northwest, writes of the intense competition that arose between private and public collectors, which placed pressure on communities that were already reeling from land loss, reduced and demoralised population bases, and forced assimilation through education.[57] It is ironic that at a time when Māori were being expected to assimilate into the now majority Pākehā culture, divulge ancestral knowledge to Pākehā scribes and 'donate' taonga tuku iho to museums and private collectors, they were also expected to 'play Māori' in world fairs and exhibitions that promoted these assimilationist policies and the successful colonisation of land and people.[58]

Māori were not always the victims of unscrupulous dealers and collectors. At times they asserted agency over the taonga, and sold them for financial or other types of gain, such as the early Māori traders who approached European ships, from Tasman's convoy onwards, to barter and trade; Ngāti Tarāwhai carvers from the 1860s who made works specifically for sale, such as the kumete carved by Te Rāhui 'most probably made for sale or presentation to outsiders';[59] or Ngāi Tahu who sold 'curios' at the New Zealand International Exhibition in Christchurch in 1882.[60] As McCarthy argues, 'There was greater room for Māori agency in retail businesses than in the tightly circumscribed sphere of the museum.'[61]

### Into the future

By the end of the nineteenth century, thousands of taonga Māori had been moved into museums overseas, where they remain. The impetus for their collection – that Māori and their art would soon disappear – has not come to fruition; if anything, the huge physical distances between Māori and the taonga have compelled increasing numbers of Māori to visit them, to reconnect. Provenance research into the collections and those who gathered them continues to reveal a complex Māori world in which taonga were circulated and, in turn, demonstrates at times avarice and greed on the part of the Pākehā and European collectors and dealers. Ultimately, taonga in museums are themselves transforming as those working in museums overseas reconnect with Māori communities for a common goal of mana taonga – resurrecting and reinvigorating the mana of taonga and people.

Left: Poupou, Te Whare o Heretaunga, Pākōwhai, Hawke's Bay.
Tūhura Otago Museum, D31.1355, with kind permission of Rose Mohi

Middle and right: Amo, Te Whare o Heretaunga, Pākōwhai, Hawke's Bay.
Tūhura Otago Museum, D88.40, with kind permission of Rose Mohi

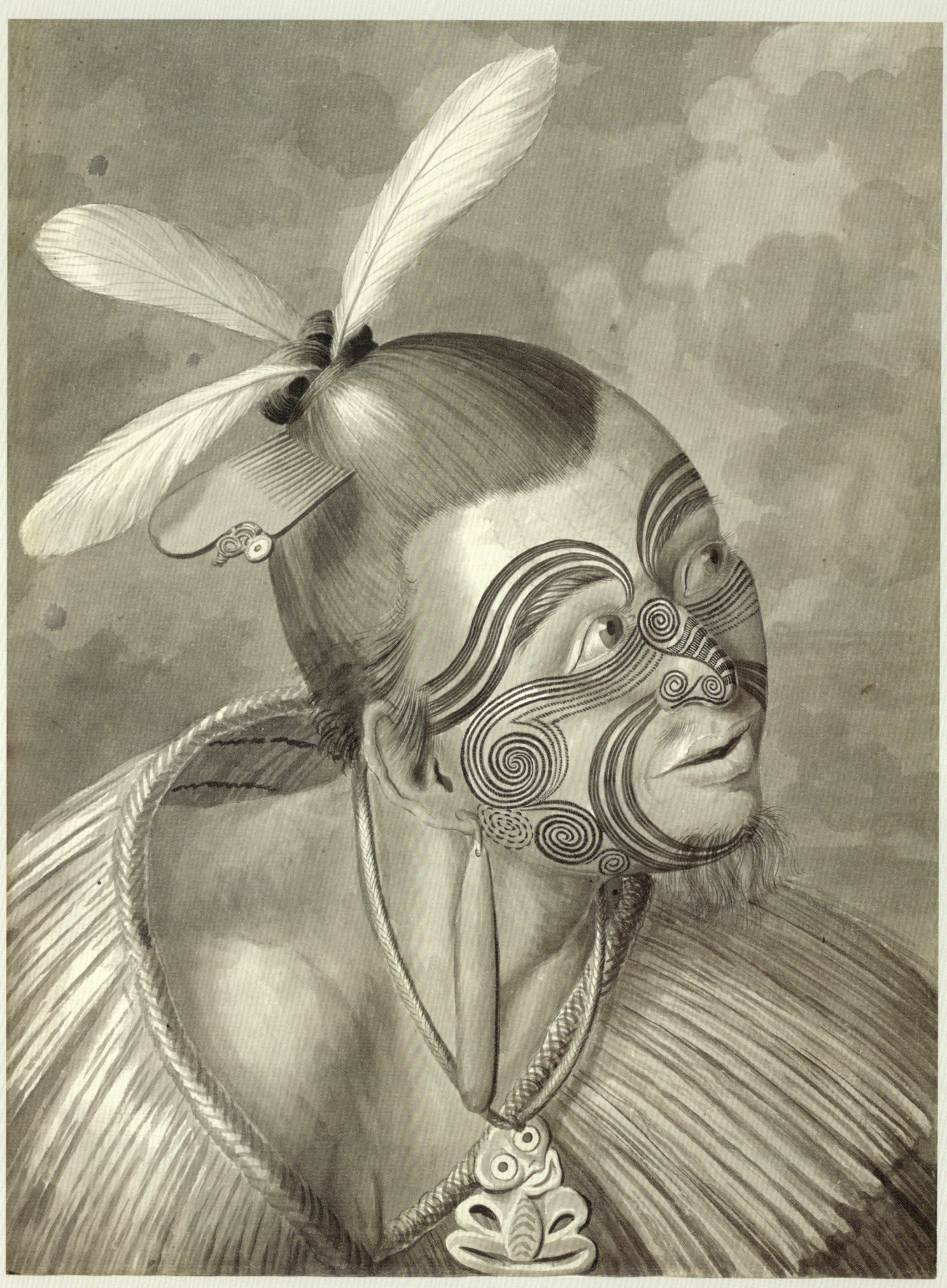

# TĀNGATA MAMAE: THE TRAGIC STORY OF TE MARO, RANGINUI AND TE KUKU

NGARINO ELLIS

Te Maro, a Ngāti Oneone rangatira, was shot by the coxswain on James Cook's first voyage at Tūranganui a Kiwa (Gisborne) in October 1769. Cook, William Monkhouse, Joseph Banks and others inspected Te Maro as he lay dead on the riverbank (Monkhouse and Banks later described his body in detail in their journals). They then placed nails and beads on his body, perhaps as a form of apology, and retreated. Desperate for freshwater and food, the English landed again the next day and were greeted by a group of around 100 armed men. A disastrous attempt to settle tensions through trade ended with yet another death when Banks shot a man in the back (Monkhouse had also fired at the same man). The other Māori retreated, but when they returned to try and retrieve their whanaunga, three more were killed or wounded: surprisingly, Tahitian navigator Tupaia was among the shooters. Tupaia had joined Cook's expedition at Ra'iātea in July 1769 and was instrumental in liaising with Māori they met – when he was allowed to. He died in November 1770 on the way to England. When Cook arrived in Aotearoa on his second voyage, Māori expected to see their hoa (friend) again, and they wept when they heard he had died.

The drawing overleaf shows Ranginui, a Ngāti Kahu chief of Tokerau (Doubtless Bay). Jean Pottier de l'Horme was a lieutenant on Jean François Marie de Surville's voyage aboard the *St Jean Baptiste* (1769–1770); the drawing is included in de l'Horme's journal, though the name of the artist is unknown. Ranginui was kidnapped by de Surville on 30 December 1769. The previous day there had been a storm, and a yawl (a sailing dinghy) had come adrift from the *St Jean Baptiste* and beached onshore. The crew saw Māori inspecting the yawl and sent out a search party to retrieve it; they landed and found drag marks but no sign of the yawl. They followed the tracks to a large kāinga, where Ranginui, the chief, came forward with green leaves of peace. The French, however, proceeded to 'arrest' him and tied him up with ropes; they then burnt a waka full of nets and took another back to their longboat. Wishing to punish those Māori even further, they burnt down around thirty whare nearby. Back at the longboat, several Ngāti Kahu warriors moved to rescue Ranginui but were driven off. De Surville then ordered another village to be burnt. Some of the French on board were keen to take more prisoners; others, including l'Horme, felt sorry for Ranginui. L'Horme recounted the incident in his journal:

> I was touched with the greatest compassion when this poor wretched man came on board. Recognising me, and not knowing what his fate would be, he flung himself at my knees, tears in his eyes. He said some incomprehensible things to me but indicated by signs that he was the one who had brought fish to me at a time when … I … had [not] a single thing to eat. This man appeared to be begging for mercy or begging me to ask it for him. I did my best to console him and explained to him that we had no wish whatsoever to harm him. It was useless; he kept on crying, especially when he saw irons put on his ankles to keep him prisoner.[1]

That night the French set sail for Peru, with Ranginui on board. He died without ever setting foot on land again, on 24 March 1770, of scurvy. Ironically – or perhaps as utu – de Surville himself drowned two weeks later.[2]

This is the only known drawing of Ranginui. He is shown facing away from the artist, his face and upper torso partially turned back towards the viewer – a composition that the same artist used in other portraits, such as one of Te Kauri of Te Hikutū. He is without the tātua kōtara (woven band of harakeke) or the kākahu that he would have worn to signify his rank. Ranginui holds a mere pounamu and has three feathers in his tikitiki. On one leg he has pūhoro (thigh moko) and raperape (buttock moko), and an unusual design on his calf that is not recorded elsewhere – though this might be either a mistake or a style of the period that was not continued. After Ranginui was kidnapped, his whānau commissioned a toki named Whakarau ('taken captive') in memory of this event; the toki has been passed down through the generations and is still in the area.[3]

Te Maro (Ngāti Oneone) as drawn by Sydney Parkinson on James Cook's first voyage.
**Sydney Parkinson, *Portrait of a New Zealand Man*, 1796**
British Library, Add. 23920, f.55, Bridgeman Images

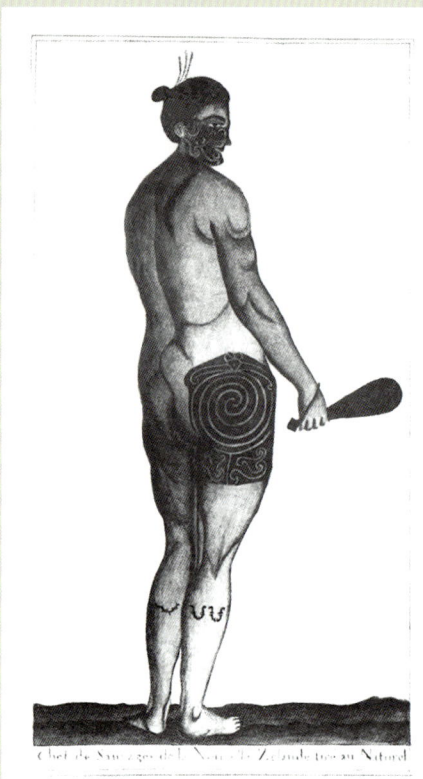

Ngāti Kahu chief Ranginui, as drawn by Jean François Marie de Surville's artist in December 1769. Ranginui was kidnapped by the French, and died of scurvy on 24 March 1770 on their ship *St Jean Baptiste*.
Milligan, *Journal of the Polynesian Society*, 1958, from the journal kept by Jean Pottier de l'Horme, second officer of the *St Jean Baptiste*

Opposite: Te Kuku (Ngare Raumati), the son of a chief from the Rakaumangamanga area of the eastern Bay of Islands. The initial sketch by Sydney Parkinson c.December 1769 has been later worked up to a finished pen and wash drawing.
**Sydney Parkinson, *Portrait of Otegoowgoow [Otegoonoon]* ... circa December 1769**
British Library, BL3284317, Bridgeman Images

The drawing opposite comes from Pēwhairangi (the Bay of Islands) and depicts a man named Te Kuku (Sydney Parkinson records his name as 'Otegoowgoow'). While we might see a sedate young man dressed to signal his status, in reality he was nursing a wound to his thigh that he had received on Motuarohia on the afternoon of 30 November 1769.

The reception that Cook and his men met with in the area vacillated between trading and warfare. European accounts place 600 people on the island's beach when a party from the *Endeavour* landed in three boats, in search of food and fresh water. They were met with a haka, a sign that they should be wary, and when three men then moved towards the boats Cook shot at the rangatira, while Joseph Banks and others fired at the ope (group) who were defending their whenua. Sensing possible defeat, Māori retreated. Tribal historian Patu Hohepa (Te Mahurehure, Ngāpuhi, Te Ātiawa, 1936–2003) explains the event: 'Cook was not to know that his actions had incited Ngāpuhi warriors, all six hundred of them, because they thought Cook and his men had hurried to Motuarohia to capture the island while all were gathered around the *Endeavour*.'[14]

Remarkably, Cook still wanted to trade. He found a group sheltering in a cave and tried to engage with them. The chief there was more concerned about his brother who had been shot, but Cook reassured him that he would survive. Both brothers met Cook again later, on 4 December in Waipao Bay, by which time Te Kuku's wounds were healing.

Parkinson's portrait is crucial for both Māori and Pākehā. For Māori, we can see symbols of chieftainship being displayed: the pūhoro half-face moko, the unusual lines on the forehead, the tikitiki with the heru iwi (whalebone comb) increasing his height, the kuru pounamu (greenstone adornment) with niho tangata (human teeth) through the ear, the rei puta around the neck, and the kaitaka around his shoulders. For Pākehā, the physical distance between Britain and Aotearoa was clear in the physical difference between this man and those from Britain.

These three drawings are problematic. On the face of it, they are portraits of ancestors whose names have been recorded, albeit in English and French approximations. Art history enables a deeper reading of these images, where we can piece together the journal entries from the European side with the whakapapa of those Māori depicted. By reframing the circumstances in which these drawings were made we gain a more complex and nuanced understanding of who these men were and the tenuous interactions between the artist and the sitters. They remain tāngata mamae – men of pain – as these drawings record moments of encounter in which European imperial powers asserted their dominance over Māori communities.

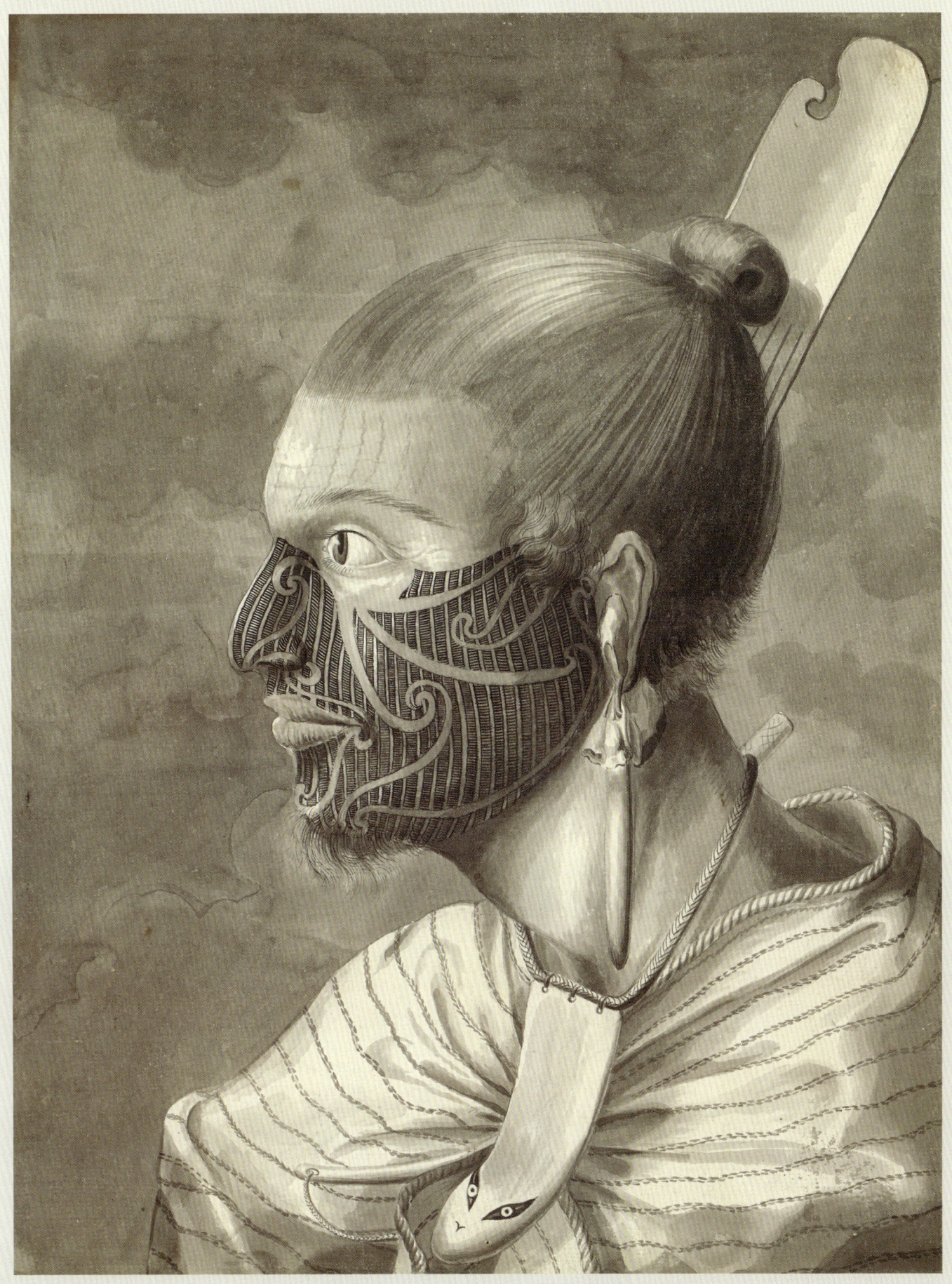

# JOSEPH BANKS AND THE FORTY BRASS PATU REPLICAS
NGARINO ELLIS

The lengths to which Pākehā sought to facilitate trade as a way to forge relationships are exemplified in forty brass replicas of patu commissioned by the naturalist Joseph Banks. He was a young, impressionable and wealthy man in his mid-twenties who had travelled to Newfoundland, Canada in 1764 and was excited at the chance to be with Captain James Cook on his first voyage to the Pacific. Across the region Banks traded for botanical and cultural specimens as part of his role as Cook's liaison with any people they met.

When Banks returned to England in 1771, he decided that he would commission new works that would be used to trade on the next voyage. He contacted Eleanor Gyles's brass foundry on Fleet Street, London in March 1772, and paid for patu to be made from brass (instead of greenstone), knowing that these were universally revered by different iwi. Each patu measured 36.5cm long, and had Banks's name, family crest and the year engraved on the blade so the recipient would have no doubt as to who the donor was.

Surprisingly, this was not the first time that Pacific treasures were remade from metal. On that same first voyage, Cook had brought with him a replica Tahitian adze (possibly made from iron) which he had been given by the First Secretary to the Admiralty, Philip Stevens. Jeremy Coote, who has researched these taonga, suggests that this 'must have been copied from one collected during Samuel Wallis's visit to Tahiti in the *Dolphin* in June 1767'.[1]

Jenny Newell describes the brass patu as 'a quintessentially cross-cultural object. It crosses the boundaries of Māori and British culture, creating a single object that belongs to both'.[2] While the form was a patu, highly valued in Māori communities for its physical and symbolic mana, it was made from brass, a material unfamiliar to Māori, and consequently had high social and political value because it symbolised a relationship between the Māori owner and Pākehā. As Nicholas Thomas notes, the brass patu 'was not an exotic object, but an improved version of a familiar one'.[3]

Banks did not travel on Cook's second voyage, as his request for a large space for his assistants and materials could not be accommodated; he eventually withdrew from the mission and travelled to Iceland instead.[4] However, the brass patu did make their way to the Pacific – for Cook's third (and fatal) voyage, as Banks gave several of them to Charles Clerke, whom he had befriended on the first voyage and who was a second lieutenant on the second voyage.[5] Clerke was promoted to captain for the third voyage, of the second ship, *Discovery*, and on 23 February 1777 he gifted a brass patu to a chief at Queen Charlotte Sound in exchange for a group of Māori weapons. By this time the brass patu had been further engraved, with details about the voyage, its mission and ships involved.[6]

In 2007 Coote identified six brass patu, mostly in English museum collections: two in the Pitt Rivers Museum (one acquired by the museum's founder in 1874 [1884.12.280], and another purchased in Bristol in 1908 [1932.86.1]), Oxford; one in the British Museum (Oc1936.0206.1), a donation from collector Harry Beasley; one in the Museum of London (O.2543) acquired by Thomas Layton; and one in the Tamátslikt Cultural Institute of the Confederated Tribes of the Umatilla Indian Reservation in Oregon, which had been robbed from a tribal grave (1865–1895) but later repatriated (in 2005); and one in a private collection.[7]

In sum, of the forty brass patu made, only one so far has remained in an Indigenous community as intended. It seems possible, then, that some of the patu never left Britain, or maybe were brought back, as objects to be regifted.[8] Coote notes that since his 2008 article no more examples have come to light in public or private collections, but 'There must be more out there…'[9] More research may reveal more of what happened, and where those other thirty-four patu are today.

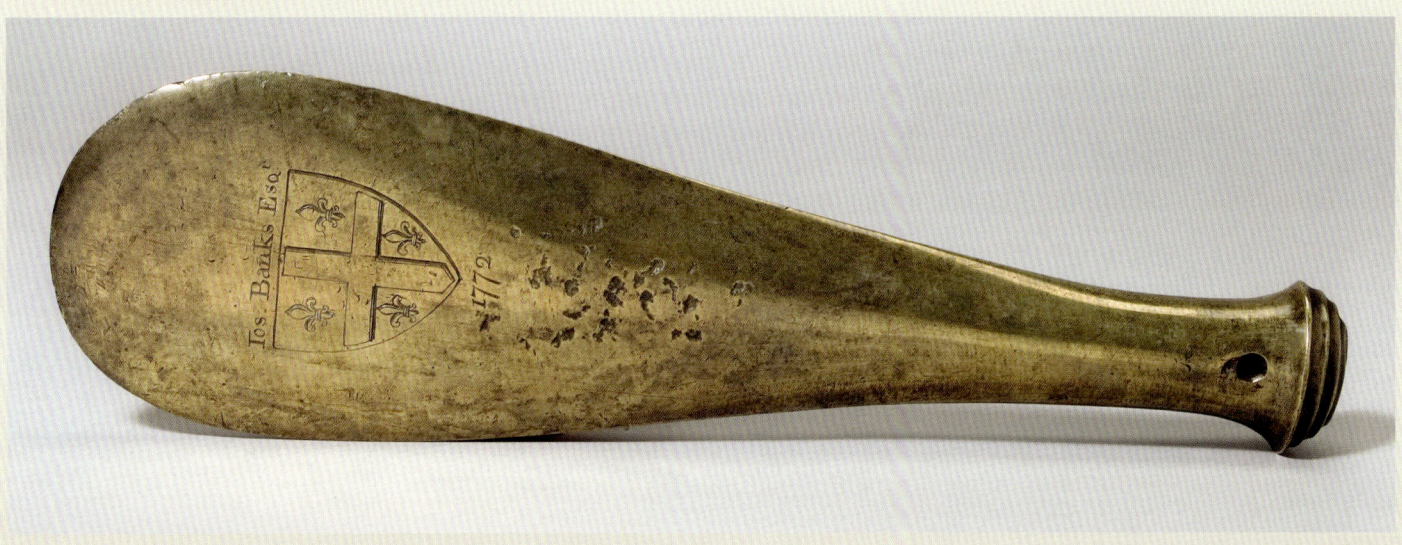

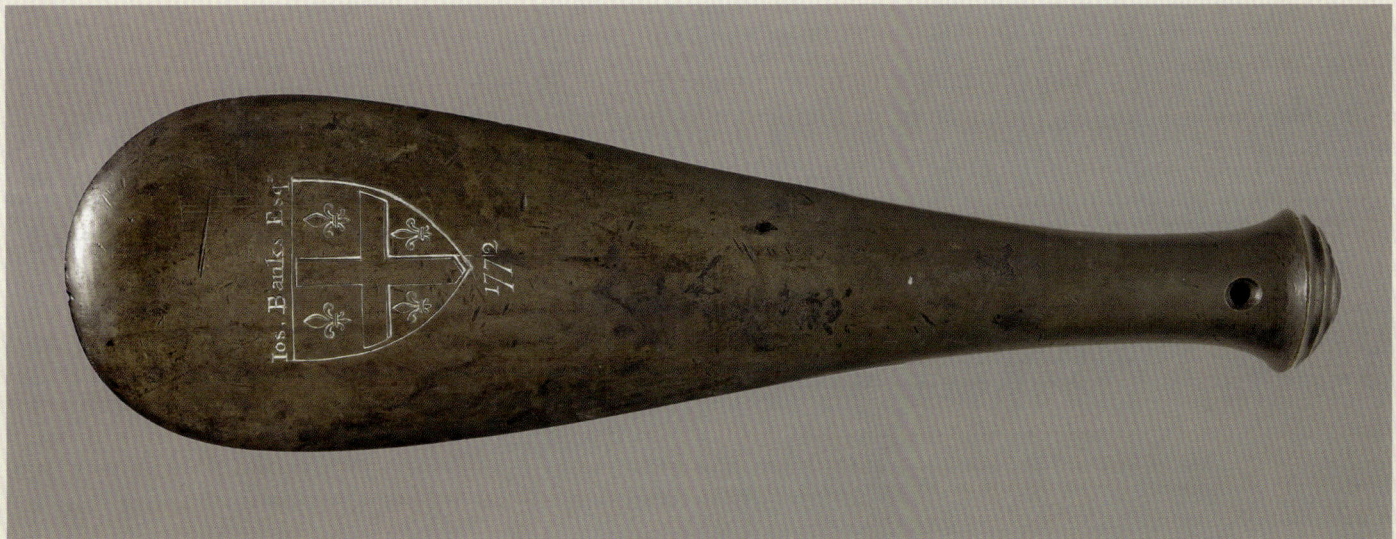

Top: Naturalist Joseph Banks commissioned forty patu to be made from brass to trade on his next voyage to the Pacific, which did not eventuate. Nonetheless, several were taken on Cook's third voyage and gifted, including to a chief in Queen Charlotte Sound in 1777. Six examples remain, mostly in English museums.
Pitt Rivers Museum, University of Oxford, 1932.86.1

Bottom: Brass patu replica manufactured by the workshop of Mrs Eleanor Gyles, London, commissioned by Sir Joseph Banks, 1772.
British Museum, Oc1936, 0206.1 EOC18187
01462411001

# TUPAIA
## NGARINO ELLIS

On Captain James Cook's first voyage to the Pacific, a Polynesian named Tupaia joined the crew at Ra'iātea in the Society Islands (now called French Polynesia). A high priest and navigator, Tupaia had a tumultuous past: he was an elite member of society on Ra'iātea, but when people from neighbouring Bora Bora attacked he fled to Paparā on Tahiti. He soon became the confidant of the leader Amo, and lover of Amo's wife Purea, which led to his rise in status to 'high priest of all Tahiti'.[1] It is at this point that Tupaia first met Europeans, when Captain Samuel Wallis of the British Admiralty arrived on the *Dolphin* in June 1767.

This encounter was fraught with tension one minute and active trading the next, prompting the English to leave quickly. Tupaia's diplomatic skills came in use soon after when his community at Paparā was invaded, and he changed allegiances to the new chiefs Vehiatua and Tutaha. This is how Cook found him when he arrived in April 1769. Cook and his crew stayed in Tahiti for three months, during which time Tupaia became confident in English, liaised with the locals and assisted with requests from those on the ship, such as Joseph Banks, who was keen to acquire botanical specimens. Banks later lobbied Cook to 'keep' Tupaia as a specimen of the Pacific.

Tupaia drew several illustrations while on board Cook's vessel. Banks described him in 1812 as an artist: 'Tupaia the Indian who came with me from Otaheite Learned to draw in a way not quite unintelligible. The genius for Caricature which all wild people possess Led him to Caricature me & he drew me with a nail in my hand delivering to an Indian who sold me a Lobster ...'.[2] Anne Salmond notes that in Tahiti men of Tupaia's social and political status were trained, as were Māori, 'in painting and dyeing bark-cloth' – which would explain his confidence in using watercolours on paper. Salmond describes how men like Tupaia from the elite arioi (religious) class would make tapa capes embellished with figurative painted designs, the motifs probably derived from local tattooing, which has distinct figurative designs of plants and people.[3]

Tupaia's drawings include a map and a drawing of a moment of exchange. The fact that these were attributed to one of the Europeans on board reflects how Europeans assumed ownership over the images that came from the voyages, especially maps. Tupaia and a young boy, Taiata, sailed with Cook when they left Tahiti in July 1769, and he helped them navigate to the islands of Huahine and his own Ra'iātea. Tupaia's advice to sail west to find more islands was ignored by Cook, who was intent on following the secret instructions from the Admiralty to 'find the southern continent'. By the time the ships arrived in Aotearoa in October 1769 Tupaia was depressed and withdrawn.

Cook's first landing, at Tūranganui a Kiwa (Gisborne), did not include Tupaia and ended disastrously. Further up the East Coast, Māori traders on waka saw Tupaia on board and a conversation started. He soon earned formal recognition from Māori, who bestowed gifts of kākahu and other treasures on him. By the time he came on shore hundreds had gathered to hear him – the Tahitian reo (language) Ma'ohi was similar enough to Māori for him to be understood. His presence on board Cook's ship did not always guarantee smooth interactions with Māori: on several occasions Māori were killed due to cross-cultural misunderstandings, and Tupaia was probably not given the deference due to his arioi rank by all the English. Tupaia unfortunately died of scurvy on his way to England in November 1770, two days after Taiata.

Tupaia was highly revered by Māori, who wept when Cook returned on his second voyage without Tupaia, in 1773.[4] As Salmond notes, at Ūawa, where Tupaia visited in October 1769: 'Long after this visit, he was remembered – children in the bay were named after him, the cave where he had often slept was called Tupaia's Cave, and the well that Cook's men had dug around a spring at Opoutama ("Cook's Cove") was called Te Wai Keri a Tepaea (the well dug by Tupaia).'[5]

Tupaia's presence on Cook's ships was an important influence on the relationships that were initially forged with hapū. Those on shore saw someone who looked and spoke like them, and he was treated with respect because of his origins in Ra'iātea in the Pacific, the place of their ancestors. He helped bridge cultural gaps where he could, mediating and negotiating on both sides. Recent research has restored him to the important place that he deserves in the history of early European contact with Aotearoa.

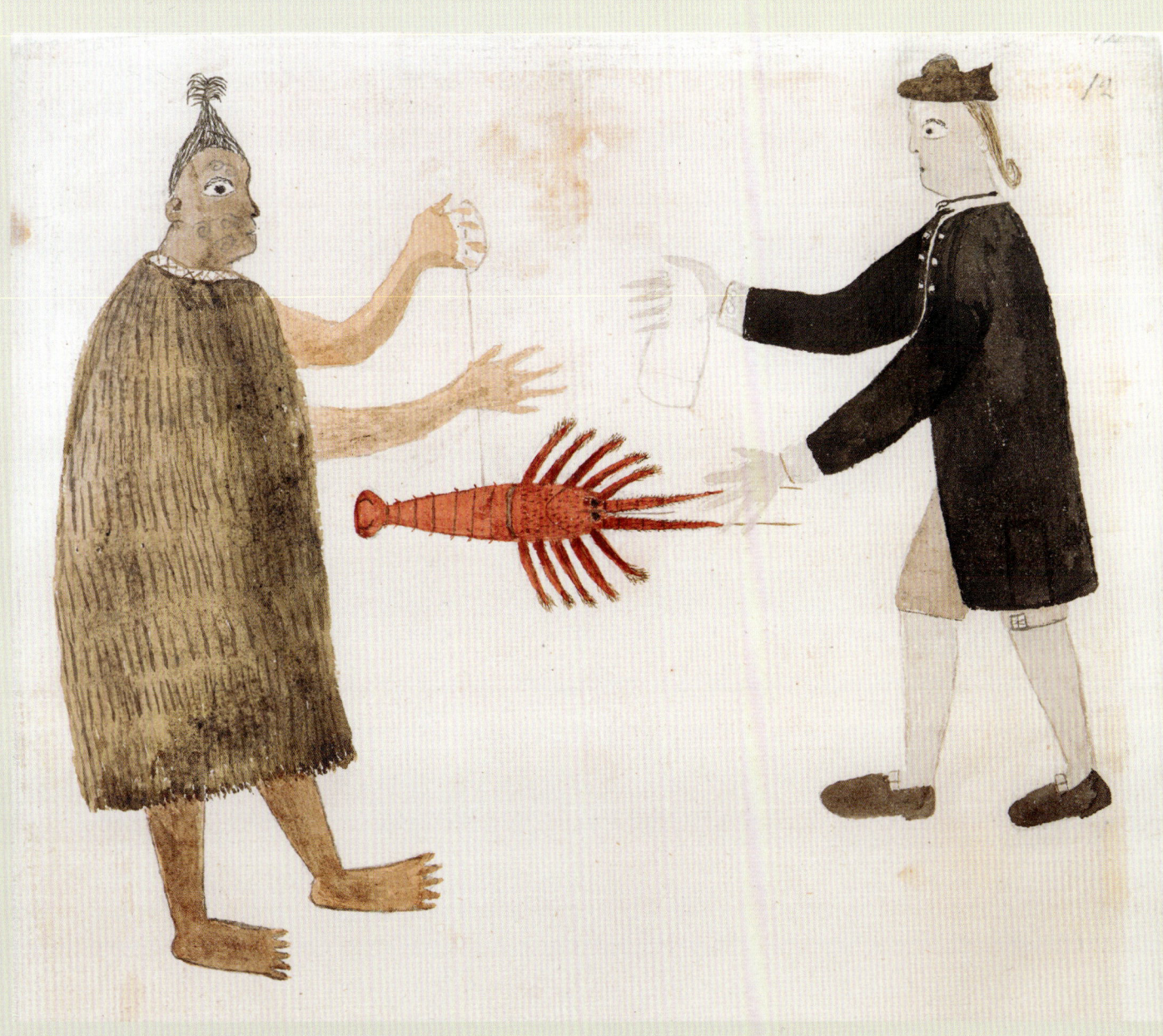

The most well-known drawing by Tupaia, 'A Maori man and Joseph Banks exchanging a crayfish for a piece of cloth', c.1769, Ūawa Tolaga Bay, East Coast.
British Library, BL3283459 MS 15508 [Drawing no.12], Bridgeman Images

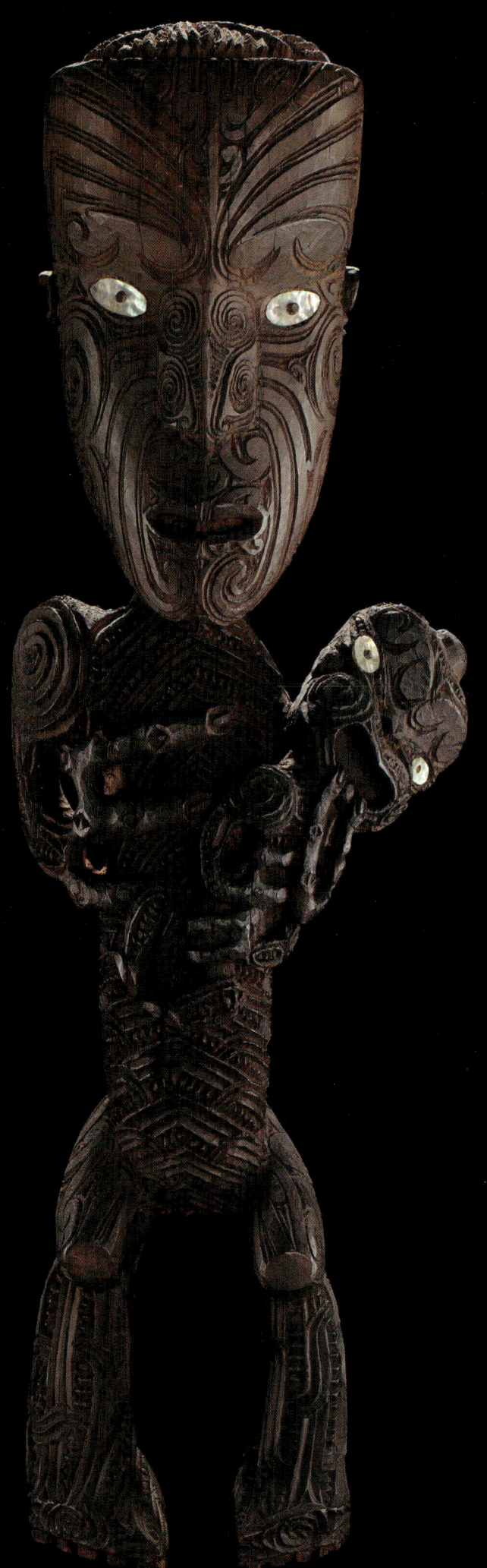

Ariki tapairu, a Māori Madonna and child sculpture.
Tāmaki Paenga Hira Auckland War Memorial Museum, 22, 13895, 86

# 9 MĀORI ART AND THE CHRISTIAN MISSIONS
## DEIDRE BROWN

*E toru ngā mea*
*Ngā mea nunui*
*E kī ana*
*Te Paipera*
*Tūmanako*
*Whakapono*
*Ko te mea nui,*
*Ko te aroha.*

*There are three things*
*Three great things*
*As stated in the Bible*
*Hope*
*Faith*
*And the greatest thing,*
*Charity.*

—Popular waiata based on I Koriniti (Corinthians) 13:13

Missionary engagement with Māori may have been brief, but the consequences were lasting and pervasive: they influenced the spirituality of Māori and of Pākehā, and the artistic cultures of Aotearoa, Britain, France and the Vatican City. Wairuatanga (Māori spirituality) had inspired the concepts and practices of Māori art for many centuries by the time the first missionaries arrived in 1814, and as large numbers of Māori started converting to the new religion, innovations – and problems – arose in artistic production.

There is no evidence that Christian teachings contributed to a 'fatal impact' on Māori art across the country through orchestrated suppression. Many missionaries were simply not that influential, or organised, or even of a single mind. What is apparent is that there are distinct local experiences, at hapū and parish level, where effects on art were determined by whether or not individual missionaries were invited into the conceptual worlds of Māori artists. The various degrees of mission and Māori engagement unfolded in the independent creation of spaces such as waka chapels and Māori-embellished churches, and the giving and receiving of taonga Māori, some of which found their way into patron and mission collections. Christian ministry also presented an alternative to the spiritual leadership of tohunga, who were the traditional knowledge-holders of the expert art practices of whakairo rākau and moko, and this was a factor in the secularisation of carving and a decline in tā moko during this period.

The encounter with wairuatanga also influenced the missionaries themselves, who were representatives of organisations grappling with integrating biblical understandings of creation, migration and time with other cultures, geologies and animals and plants – live and fossil – 'discovered' through the age of exploration. While Enlightenment-based understandings of Māori art proposed by early missionaries often missed the point of Māori art's purpose, the missions' collecting habits and exhibition practices in Europe influenced perspectives on Māori art, culture and rights there for years to come.

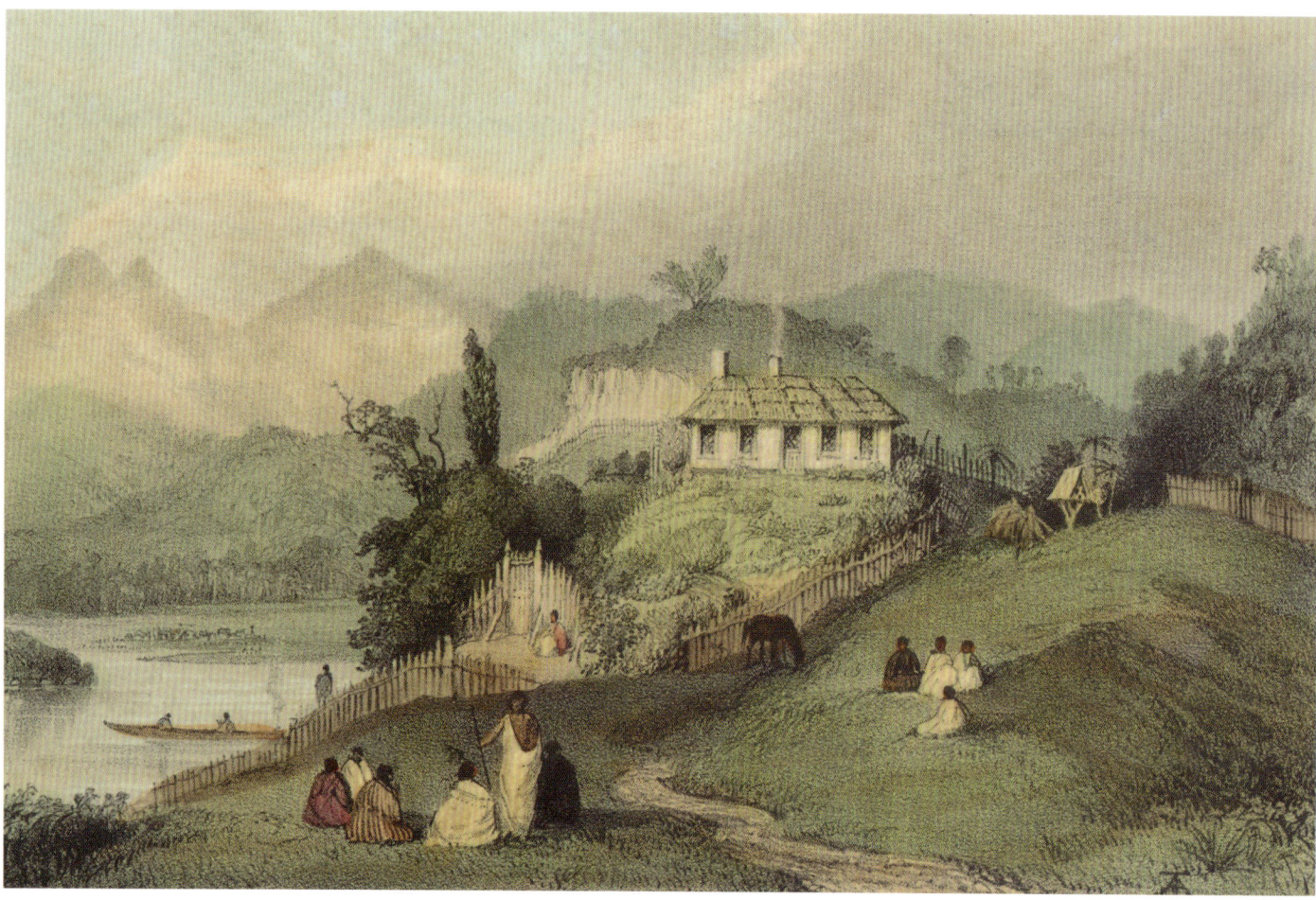

Even before the arrival of the first missionaries, some Māori had encountered Christian worship while working on ships and while visiting Sydney and Britain. Yet it was a desire to enhance hapū economies by engaging with those of the West through Pākehā intermediaries, rather than spiritual curiosity, that led Māori to invite the earliest missionaries to live in their communities.

The first to settle were the lay preachers of the London- and Sydney-based Church Missionary Society (CMS) in 1814, followed by the London-based Wesleyan Methodist Missionary Society (WMS) in 1822, and then the Catholic Society of Mary from France in 1838. The initial mission stations were built within or beside kāinga in the Bay of Islands and Hokianga regions of Northland, and then in other parts of the country as the missions expanded. The architectural synergies, exchanges of tools and negotiation of values that arose as a consequence of living in a shared space were some of the reasons why the missions' influence on Māori art practice was more immediate than their success in conversion. Although fifteen years elapsed before the first Māori conversion to Christianity, by 1850 there were over fifty mission stations across the North and South islands and the church and its teachings were becoming an important part of Māori life.

### The waka chapel

Aotearoa's first space of Christian worship was one very much framed within a Māori artistic tradition that expressed the wairuatanga of Māori creation stories. On Saturday 24 December 1814 at his kāinga at Rangihoua Bay, Ngāpuhi rangatira Ruatara carefully prepared an outdoor chapel-like space with the most suitable objects available to accommodate the first CMS mission sermon, delivered by the Reverend Samuel Marsden the following day (Christmas) to a gathering of 400 Māori from around the Bay.[1] Ruatara had recently returned from living with Marsden at Parramatta in Sydney, where Marsden was Anglican chaplain for New South Wales.

Even though the message of Marsden's sermon was lost on the Māori congregation, the aesthetics of its presentation

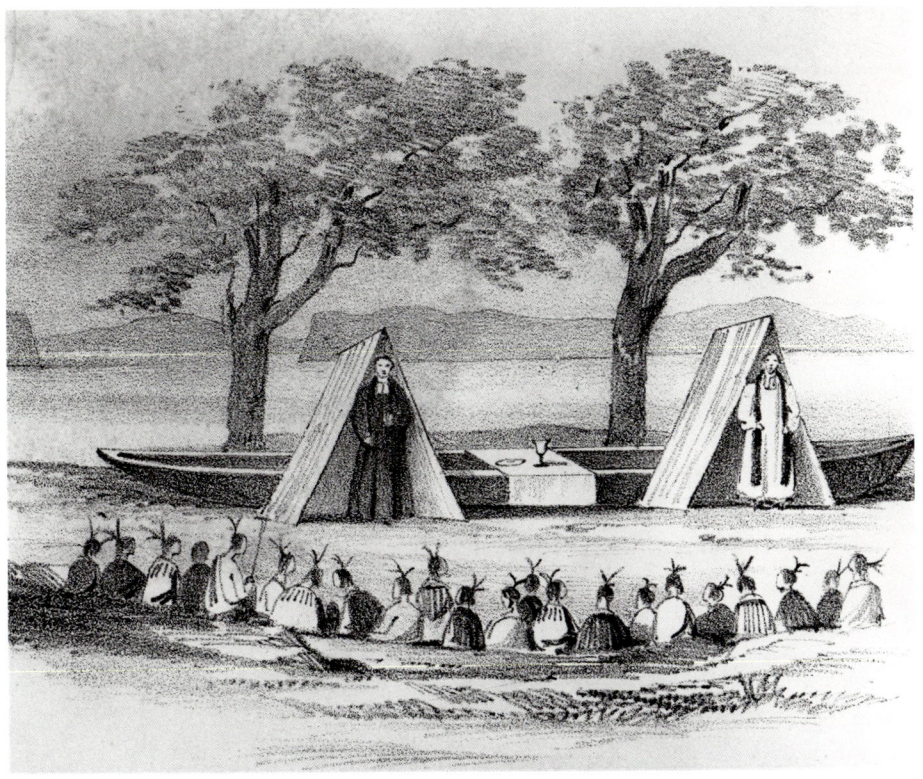

Waka were sometimes used to form improvised outdoor chapels. Rangatira Ruatara used waka components to make a pulpit, lectern and pews for the first Christian service at Te Puna, Northland, in December 1814. George Selwyn, the first Anglican bishop of New Zealand, drew this scene of a waka used as an altar for Holy Communion at Orona, Taupō.
**George Augustus Selwyn, *Natives assembled to celebrate the Lord's Supper at Orona, Taupo, New Zealand*, c.1845**
lithograph, 75 x 91mm, Alexander Turnbull Library, PUBL-0180-1845-084

Opposite: Early missionaries integrated themselves into Māori life by building mission stations within or beside Māori communities. This image shows a raupō-clad missionary's home at Pepepe on the Waikato River in 1844.
**George French Angas, *Pepepe Church missionary station on the Waikato River, New Zealand*, 1847**
lithograph, 191 x 280mm, National Library of Australia, nla.obj-135643978

must have been powerful. Ruatara had enclosed an area of around 2000m² with a fence, defining it immediately as being different, possibly a wāhi tapu, in relation to the surrounding landscapes, which had been modified for pā and cultivation. This was in keeping with the Christian idea of consecrated ground. He created a raised pulpit and lectern, both draped in black cloth, at the centre of the enclosure, using waka components. Exactly which waka parts he used is a matter of speculation, but it is tempting to think of Marsden delivering his sermon over the most obvious self-supporting element, a tauihu, carved with the figure of the paramount Māori atua Tāne, with arms stretched back like the outspread wings on an Anglican eagle lectern. Ruatara's people placed upturned waka hulls on either side of the pulpit as pews for the missionaries and erected a flagpole on one of the two neighbouring pā, from which Ruatara flew a Union Jack, to Marsden's delight. However, this was really Ruatara's moment, and after translating the Christmas sermon bringing them tidings of great joy, he likely delivered the speech Māori had come to hear, about the challenges and opportunities in hosting the first Christian mission, which was also the first permanent Pākehā settlement in the country.[2] No Māori attending, not even Ruatara, could have foreseen that the mass migration of Europeans to Aotearoa would result in Māori becoming a minority within their own country in less than fifty years; nor the struggle that Māori would have to endure to maintain art, language, customs and lives.

Waka were later used to create improvised outdoor mission chapels in other parts of the country, too. At Orona on the shores of Lake Taupō, Anglican missionaries turned a waka into an altar for an open-air communion service in 1842, reflecting the portable tabernacle and 'tent of meeting' narrative of the Bible, which was reinforced by pitching actual tents as shelters for those delivering the service.[3] The entire installation was replete with representational objects that sought to make sense of the translocation of Christianity to Aotearoa. This assemblage anticipated the major issues that would have a profound effect on nineteenth century Māori art – and, indeed, life: the relationship between Christianity and wairuatanga; cultural appropriation; and the need to retain tino rangatiratanga.

## Christianity and custom

The early Protestant and Catholic missions regarded Māori adoption of Pākehā values and virtues as a non-negotiable condition of their conversion to Christianity. How that message influenced Māori art varied according to the position of the clergyman: this led to inconsistent teachings, as

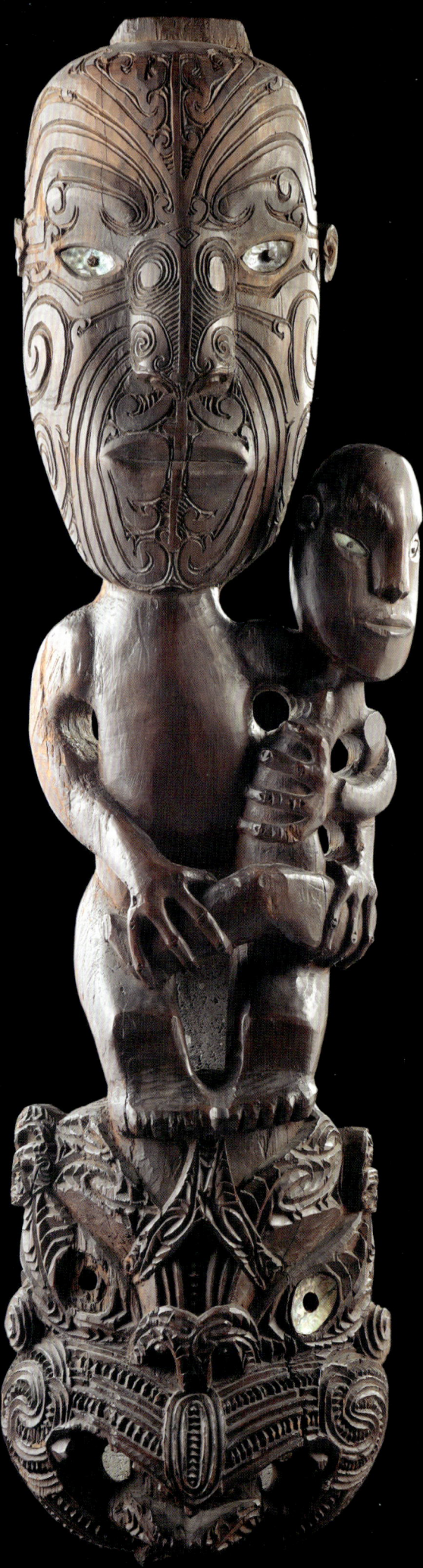

Tekoteko featuring Madonna and child carved in the mid-nineteenth century. Another similar tekoteko is in Auckland Museum, possibly carved by Patoromu Tamatea (Te Arawa) c.1845.
Te Papa Tongarewa Museum of New Zealand, ME011429

individual missionaries had different perspectives on the meanings and practices of Māori art.

Some hapū and iwi found inventive ways to reconcile customary and Christian belief systems in their art and architecture. Tohunga whakairo made at least two Māori Madonna and Child tekoteko-style sculptures. While the identities of these artists are yet to be recovered, they were clearly motivated by a desire to articulate their beliefs in a way that connected them and their ancestors to the Catholic Church. Intriguingly, surviving examples currently in Tāmaki Paenga Hira Auckland War Memorial Museum and Te Papa Tongarewa Museum of New Zealand both show the Virgin Mary with a full moko kanohi, a facial embellishment usually reserved for men. Was the figure a hybridised abstraction of both parents, Mary and God? Or did it illustrate the tikanga of some Waikato-Tainui and Ngāti Kahungunu hapū where high-born women wore this type of moko?[4] If the Te Papa example is a tekoteko, then the position of Mary above a head illustrates a whakapapa descent line, in keeping with the many generations described in the Bible, and the gender principal that man is born from woman as described in I Koriniti (Corinthians) 11:12 and Hopa (Job) 14:1. According to Gilbert Mair, a former owner, the Madonna and Child tekoteko in Auckland Museum was carved in 1845 for a Catholic chapel in the Bay of Plenty, but the priest there rejected the carving. The Catholic Church was active at the time in the settlements of Ōpōtiki, Tauranga and Maketu.[5] Assuming Mair's story was an accurate reflection of these events, this was possibly the chapel at Maketu built by the chief Te Pukuatua in the hope of attracting a resident Catholic missionary. The whare karakia, or prayer house, did receive a visit by Anglican and Catholic missionaries in 1845. One of them observed a chapel service 'full of Natives with their guns and pipes and food' – all noa items. This suggests the chapel was a building free from tapu, in which artistic experimentation could occur, leading to the creation of taonga like the Madonna and Child.[6]

The positions that early Catholic and Protestant missions held on Māori figurative wood and stone carving were complex, changeable and diverse, even between ministers of the same church. Illustrated arguments for and against hei tiki and wood-carved tiki as 'false idols' played out across the pages of the CMS *Missionary Register* as early as 1816.[7] During a visit in 1841 to Te Ngae CMS mission station on the shores of Lake Rotorua, the Catholic bishop Jean Baptiste François Pompallier engaged the resident missionary Thomas Chapman in what must have been a wide-ranging nine-hour debate about 'Images' that would likely have involved discussion of tiki, given Chapman's known disdain for figurative whakairo rākau and the wairuatanga it embodied.[8] In contrast, the Catholic chapel opened at the nearby Ōtūmoetai Catholic mission station in Tauranga in 1847 was renowned for the elaborate whakairo rākau on the sanctuary canopy and the Māori-carved clay fonts; and an 1865 watercolour of the chapel by Horatio Robley shows the sanctuary adorned with various tukutuku and kōwhaiwhai panels.[9]

Attitudes towards Indigenous art practices and taonga changed within the Catholic Church after the reforms of the Second Vatican Council (1962–1965). In 1986, the Madonna and Child tekoteko from the Auckland Museum collection was prominently displayed, beneath a canopy designed by the architect Rewi Thompson (Ngāti Porou, Ngāti Raukawa, 1953–2016), in a ceremony at Auckland Domain where Māori welcomed Pope John Paul II to Aotearoa New Zealand. The scholar Mānuka Hēnare, who was an executive officer for the Catholic Church at the time, expressed the view that, 'the Madonna and Child tekoteko are part of a wider cultural expression. They mediate between people and their new notion and insight about God, and represent an attempt to mediate, not just Māori-to-Māori, but also Māori-to-Pākehā.'[10] This perspective expressed the Catholic Church's recent objective of being a religion within cultures rather than one to Westernise cultures in preparation for spiritual conversion – a shift that is reflected in the church's appreciation of the meaning of Māori art beyond what it represents.[11]

As the nineteenth century progressed, Christian values were altering people's attitudes to appropriate dress, housing and funeral practices and this, in turn, was affecting Māori art and architecture. As Māori turned to clergy of Pākehā, Māori and Pacific backgrounds for spiritual guidance, the spiritual leadership of tohunga, for centuries the kaitiaki of Māori art and other customary practices, was gradually undermined – in Aotearoa and elsewhere in the Pacific.[12] While the missions were dependent on the protection offered by rangatira, whose authority they respected, tohunga were the guardians of spiritual and moral values that missionaries wanted to replace through spiritual conversion.

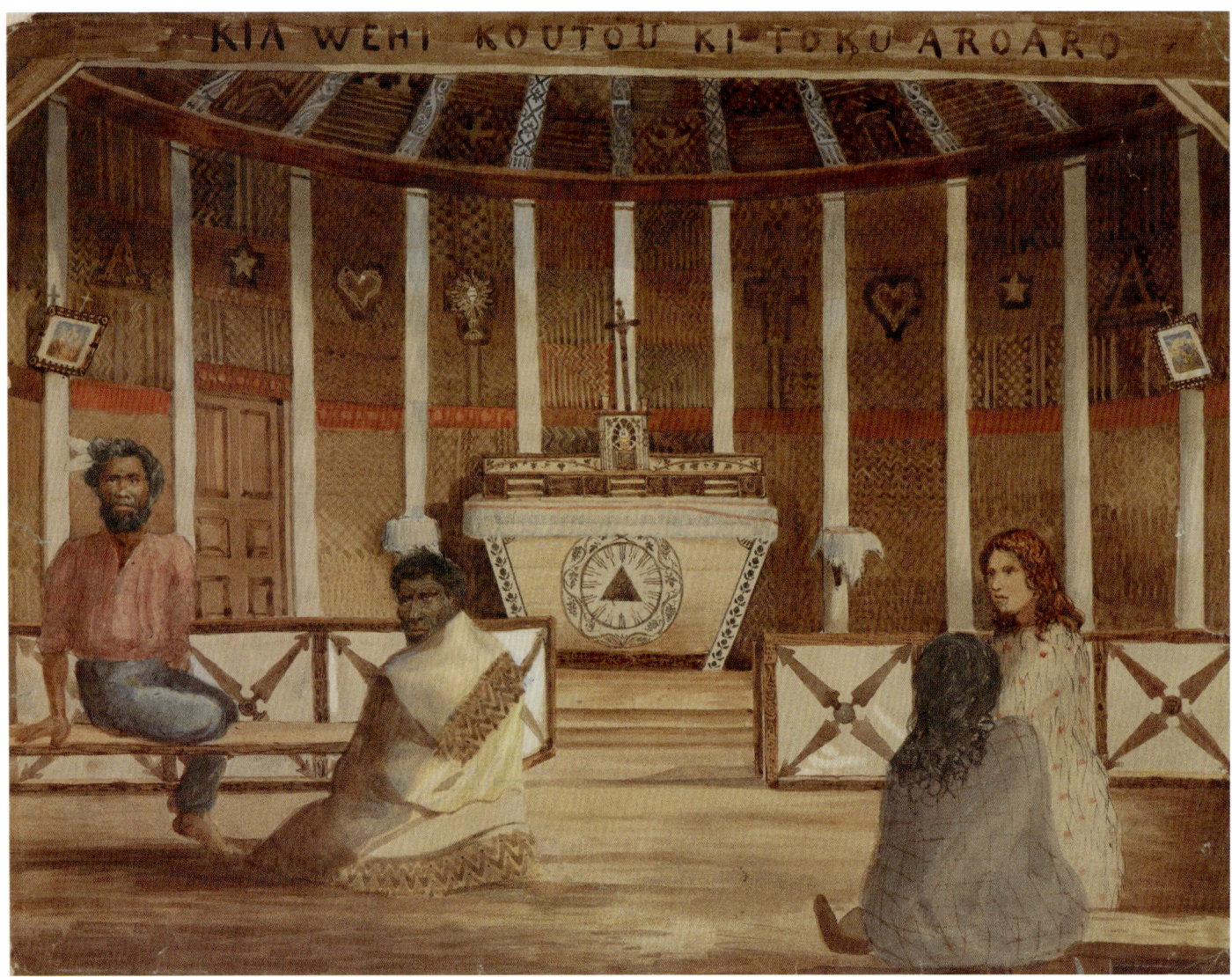

Changes in Māori values during the mission period most affected the embodied arts of moko, personal dress and wharepuni. Depending on the degree of contact they had with Pākehā, including missionaries, traders and settlers, Māori changed their manner of dress: they replaced kākahu with blankets and eventually adopted European dress as their daily attire. The missionaries contributed to this change by emphasising the association between Christian morality and the covering of breasts, genitals, torso, arms, legs and sometimes hair, as well as the differentiation of gender roles through clothing. And missionaries and Pākehā traders took advantage of the situation to offer cloth and clothing for sale and exchange.[13] Māori women, in particular, must have found that restrictive clothing such as long skirts and tight shirts constrained their social participation and depreciated their contribution as knowledge-keepers, practitioners and teachers of whatu and other fibre arts. Mission wives no doubt played an active role in instigating these changes in Māori women's arts, appearance, parenting and social roles, given their leadership of sewing circles and their 'training' of young Māori women as domestic servants in mission stations.[14] Māori women kept making clothes, but they were Pākehā in form, production and materiality. The legacy of this can be seen in the high numbers of Māori and Pacific women who have found piecework employment as seamstresses and as outworkers or factory machinists from the late nineteenth century to the present day.

The Christianisation of Māori gender values is similarly evident in the objectives of Māori Christian boarding schools and Māori participation in the New Zealand Women's Christian Temperance Union in the late nineteenth and early twentieth centuries, which brought ideas about morality and virtuous

MĀORI ART AND THE CHRISTIAN MISSIONS

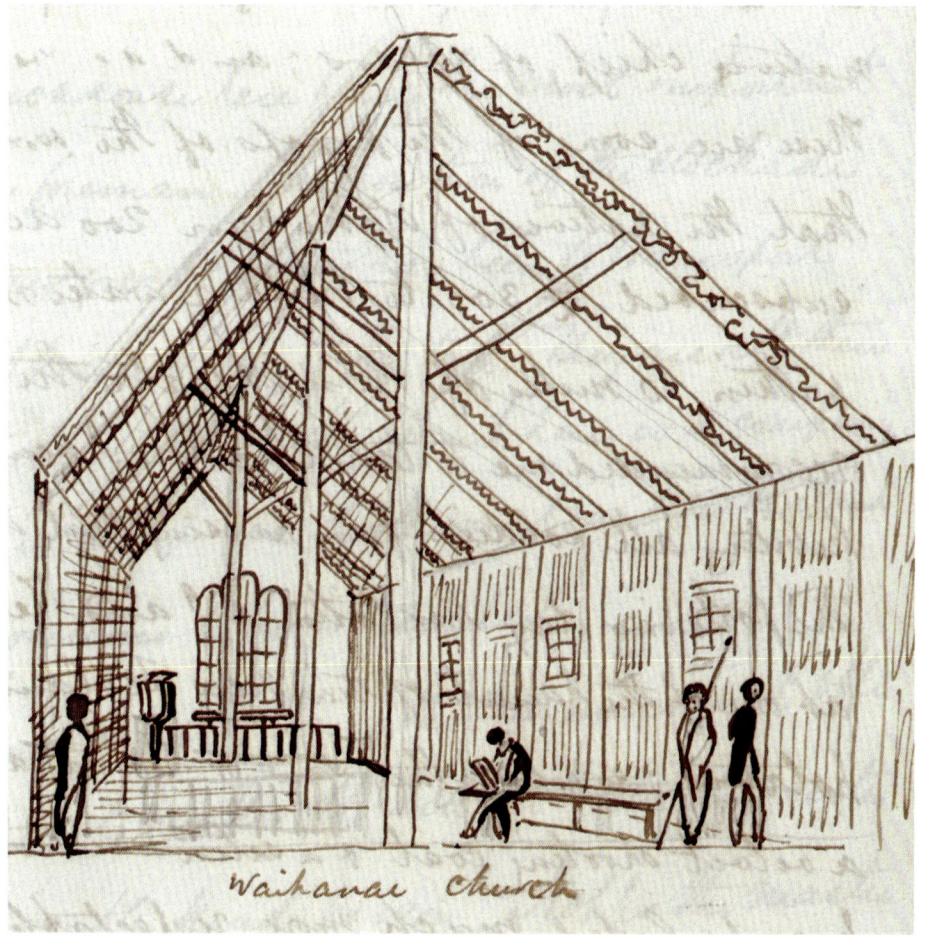

Interior of the Waikanae church, built under the leadership of the Ngāti Toa rangatira Te Rauparaha and the Reverend Octavius Hadfield in 1843.
**Thomas Bernard Collinson, *Huts and Waikanae Church*, 1847 (detail)**
ink sketch, 200 x 90mm, Alexander Turnbull Library, MS-Papers-1038-1-17

Opposite: Horatio Robley's 1865 watercolour of the Ōtūmoetai Catholic chapel, Tauranga, reveals a sanctuary that was richly adorned with tukutuku and kōwhaiwhai.
**Major General Horatio Robley, *Roman Catholic chapel Otumoetai*, 1865**
watercolour, 196 x 252mm, Te Papa Tongarewa Museum of New Zealand, 1992-0035-1705, purchased 1905

living into the whare as 'home'. These organisations were founded on the same humanitarian principals as the missions, but focused on the role of girls, boys and women as moral guardians.[15] The female and male Māori leaders who emerged from Māori boarding schools and moral improvement collectives challenged the mana of tohunga, after the decline of the missions, and of rangatira, by accelerating the secularisation of whatu, raranga, whakairo rākau and whare construction in arts revival movements, among other initiatives.

The standardisation of Māori funerary practices, particularly the requirement of burial, instigated by the adoption of Christianity brought consequential changes to whakairo rākau in some districts. Previously, whakairo mate (mortuary carvings and structures associated with high-born Māori) took the form of posts, platforms, modified waka and boards that marked the site of a body under decomposition, and waka kōiwi (caskets for cleaned bones) that were placed in remote locations, such as caves or other places distant from kāinga. Waka kōiwi were often elaborately decorated taonga, in keeping with their function of commemorating the mana of the departed and in recognition of the tapu of death.

If the sheer volume of surviving examples is any indication of the original quantities produced, then waka kōiwi deposited in caves were one of the major outputs of the Northland carving tradition before Christian conversion. The waka kōiwi were mostly in the form of female tiki and occasionally reptile figures, with hollowed compartments in their torso for bones that make them appear hapū, or pregnant – an observation that naturally leads to speculation that they are manifestations of Hinenuitepō, the female atua of birth and death.[16] In Whangaroa, Northland, where cave burial with and without waka kōiwi was common in the towering cliffs surrounding the harbour, placenames allude to stories associated with Hinenuitepō and her lover – and murderer – Māui and their fecundity. These cave burials, placenames and ancestral stories create a personified landscape in which the deceased can be interpreted as the children of Hinenuitepō, deposited within her body. Kohuru Te Whata, from Tautoro, Kaikohe and Hokianga, is remembered in

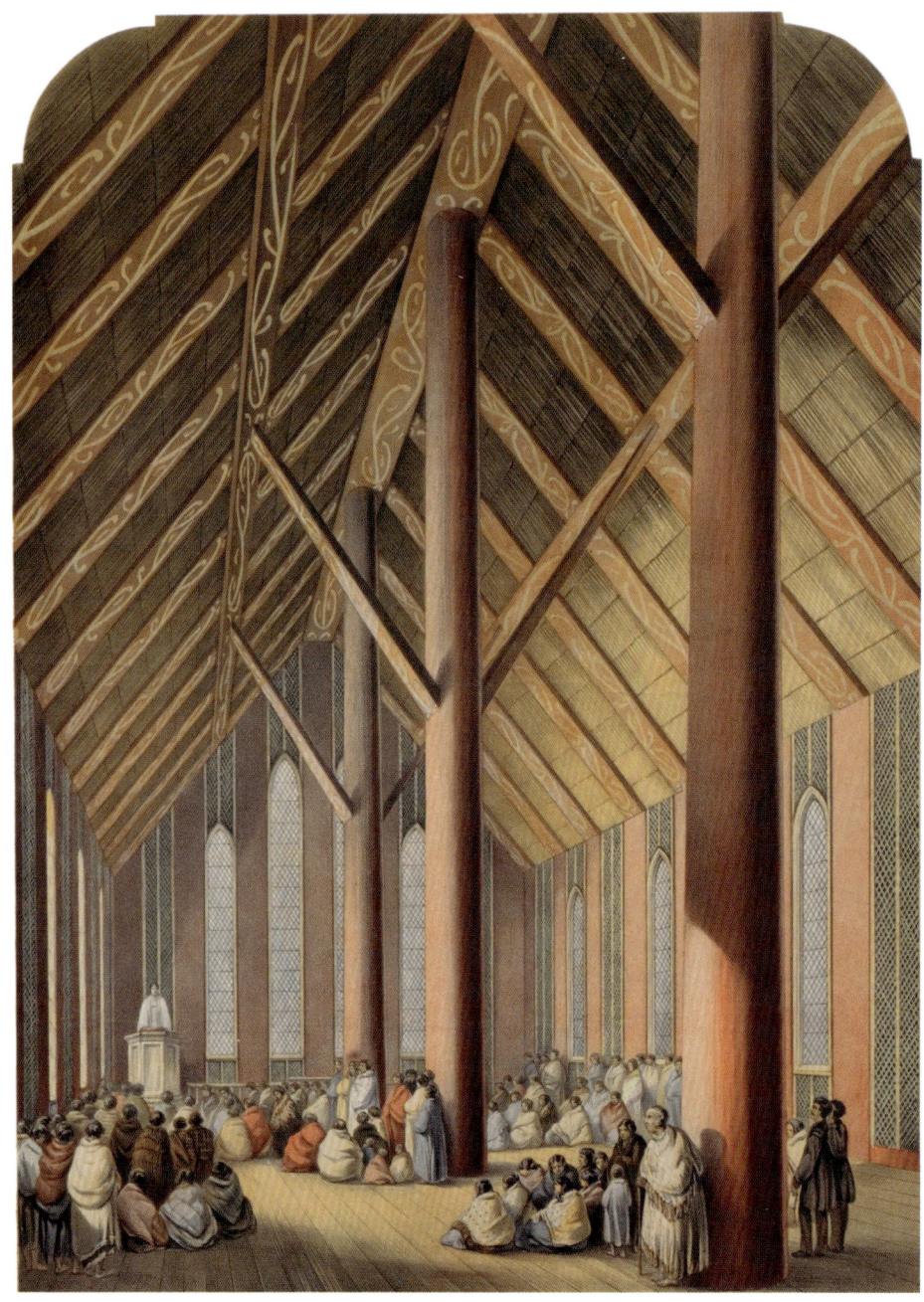

Interior of the Rangiātea church, built under the leadership of the Ngāti Toa rangatira Te Rauparaha and the Reverend Samuel Williams between 1848 and 1851.
**Charles Barraud, *Interior of Rangiatea Church at Otaki*, c.1852**
chromolithograph, Auckland Art Gallery Toi o Tāmaki, 1993/24, purchased 1993

Ngāpuhi ancestral narratives as the most highly regarded carver of waka kōiwi, as well as of pātaka carvings.[17]

From the late 1830s – when Māori began to bury their dead in cemeteries in response to missionary teachings – until the early twentieth century, Pākehā collectors took to looting burial caves in the Whangaroa and Hokianga districts: they removed waka kōiwi and other taonga surreptitiously or, if Māori became aware of their activities, in the face of great community opposition.[18] The human remains were either dumped in situ or removed to sell as anatomical specimens to amateur scientists of medical museums.[19] The decline in demand for waka kōiwi, pātaka and, eventually, waka contributed to the loss of carving knowledge in the North.

Ironically, it was waka kōiwi that Auckland Museum acquired from collectors that became the inspiration for the School of Maori Arts and Crafts (re)invention of a northern 'style' of tiki figure during the 1930s, based on the head shapes and surface decorations of the caskets. The style was perpetuated through the school's whare whakairo commissions, and influenced generations of tohunga whakairo to the present day.[20] The school emerged from the

MĀORI ART AND THE CHRISTIAN MISSIONS

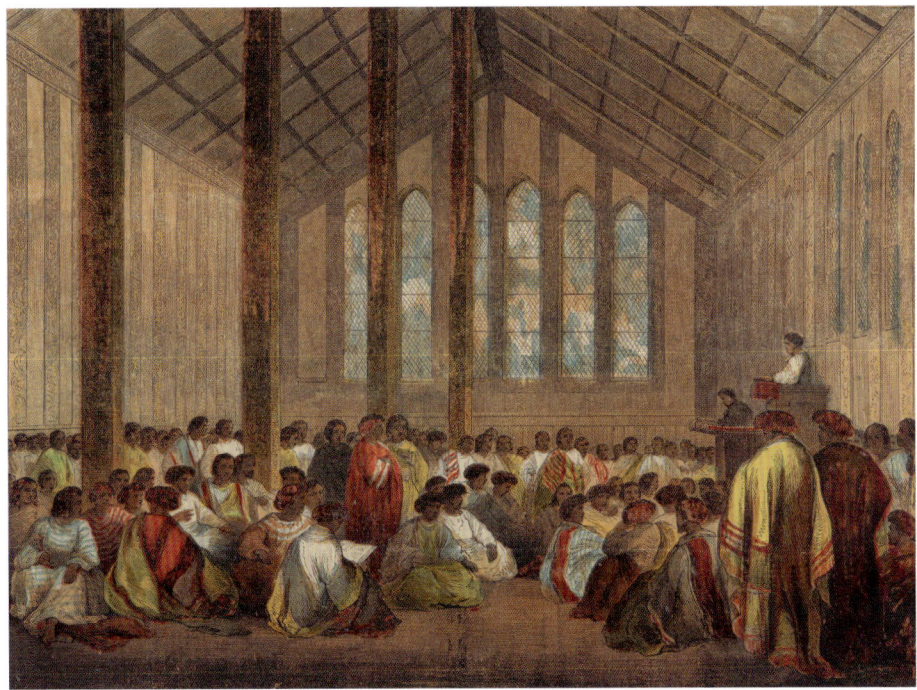

Interior of the Manutuke church, built under the leadership of the Rongowhakaata rangatira Raharuhi Rukupō and the Reverend William Williams between 1849 and 1863.
**Artist unknown, *Native Christian church at Turanga, New Zealand*, 1852**
coloured wood engraving, 282 x 370mm, Alexander Turnbull Library, B-051-017

same Māori moral conservatism as that associated with the temperance movement and church boarding schools that had continued to secularise Māori art – making waka kōiwi, which had been highly tapu only decades before, available as a precedent for study and modification.

## Māori architecture and Christianity

Christianity's most enduring influence on Māori art was in the field of architecture. It went beyond chapels and churches, and affected the way in which a number of Māori building types, including the wharenui, were conceptualised, constructed and embellished. Although they spoke to different and sometimes conflicting kaupapa, all of these buildings were united through their expression of wairuatanga as a spiritual, political and social binding force.

Rangatira, rather than missionaries, often led these architectural innovations, since they generally occurred on building projects where missions had been established under the patronage of rangatira and inside or beside their communities. Early nineteenth-century missionaries would establish their presence in an area by building a complex of mission buildings in collaboration with the local Māori community.[21] As the missionaries found acceptance within these communities, usually through strengthening their alliances with rangatira, the mission station model evolved to include Māori planning ideas: generally they comprised a whare karakia, a wharepuni and a whare mihinare (mission house) to accommodate the missionary's family, with a marae (open-air speaking forum) in between. Participation on these projects exposed rangatira and their builders and artisans to new art and architectural ideas. The most important of these was the large internal spatial volumes of churches and the height of their ceilings when compared to that of the wharepuni: this allowed people to congregate in large numbers, and it changed Māori architecture from being a place of accommodation to a space for debate and the exchange of ideas.

On the east coast of the North Island this innovation was timely, as Christanity, Te Tiriti o Waitangi and Pākehā land purchasers had all arrived around 1840. Rongowhakaata were early originators of the whare whakairo with the construction of Te Hau ki Tūranga in the early 1840s. The innovative architecture of that project allowed their community to assemble inside a larger style of building, elaborated with the whakairo rākau, kōwhaiwhai and kākaho work normally associated with pātaka and wharepuni rangatira.

The influence was mutual: Māori innovations were also occurring within mission churches. Māori artisans, under the supervision of missionaries and the chiefs who supported them, built three CMS churches, at Waikanae, Ōtaki and Manutuke. While the church exteriors remained formally European, the interiors illustrated the complex cultural agreements that had taken place before construction, through surface embellishments of kōwhaiwhai and, occasionally, whakairo rākau. The total concept of a large, elaborately built structure that had prestige in the European world and mana in te ao Māori enhanced the standing of the host community and their rangatira within the wider region.

As in other parts of Polynesia, 'competitive' church building and the patronage of missions by Māori chiefs may have been a continuation of the contest for mana that sometimes occurred between neighbouring and rival groups.[22] After helping to build the missionary Octavius Hadfield's CMS church at Waikanae in 1843, with its Gothic Revival exterior and Māori-decorated interior, Ngāti Toa leader Te Rauparaha declared that he would build a 'still finer one in his pa' at Ōtaki.[23] In collaboration with resident missionary Samuel Williams, Te Rauparaha supervised the construction of the Rangiātea church between 1848 and 1851.[24] At 12 metres high, and drawing on the multitribal talents available through Te Rauparaha's extensive relational networks, the building was a display of mana on an unprecedented physical and organisational scale. In order to assemble the estimated one thousand men needed to build the church, Te Rauparaha called on expert tohunga whakairo and builders from Te Arawa to assist Ngāti Toa and the local Ngāti Raukawa people. Working together, they followed customary construction methods, such as using dovetail joints instead of Pākehā nails.[25] Like the Māori Madonna and Child, Māori art within the building sought to elaborate ideas from the Christian world in Indigenous terms. Sequential patterns within the kōwhaiwhai of the tāhuhu, heke and kaho (underpurlins) may have indicated the repeating generations as described in the Māori-language Bible, and the purapura whetū pattern woven into the tukutuku panels may have represented Te Rauparaha's desire that there would be as many Christian converts as stars in the night sky.[26] The building's name recalled Māori understandings of the world, as it referred to the Rangiātea of ancestral stories that was the great departure point in Hawaiki for Polynesian migrants to Aotearoa. Yet unlike other Māori buildings of mana in their communities, neither Rangiātea nor the Waikanae church contained any whakairo rākau. Whether or not the inclusion of whakairo rākau was a consideration in the design is not clear, but some CMS missionaries were resistant to ancestral illustrations.

The limits of tolerance of Māori art in Protestant churches were tested at another, contemporaneous church further north in 1849. When Rongowhakaata rebuilt their church at Manutuke that had been destroyed in a storm, they decided to include sixty carved wall panels so that it would appear more elaborate than the Rangiātea church.[27] The design of the Manutuke church was writ large in other ways, too: it was planned to be 27m long, 13.5m wide, 4.5m tall at the side walls and 8.5m to the top of the gable – making it marginally larger than Rangiātea – and constructed from locally sourced tōtara brought to the site by men from five different iwi.[28] The tohunga whakairo included Raharuhi Rukupō, who had also been responsible for the Te Hau ki Tūranga house, another building that was situated between two worlds. The inclusion of interior tiki carvings was not so well received: local CMS missionary William Williams insisted they be abandoned as he was concerned they promoted non-Christian spirituality.[29] In an attempt to ameliorate an increasingly tense situation, one of the carvers, Te Waka Kurei, proposed to replace the tiki images with manaia – a compromise that satisfied Williams, who commented that 'neither man, beast nor creeping thing' would be depicted in the revised tiki design.[30] He was mistaken, though, as the manaia were, in fact, character figures variously regarded as spiritual guardians or profile views of tiki. Unaware of this, Williams was delighted with the new panels, and wrote, 'the character of native carving remains, but there is nothing to be objected to in the device … we shall have a more elaborate piece of workmanship than has been attempted by the natives before'.[31] Manaia were also cleverly disguised on the church's kōwhaiwhai-painted heke in an innovative design now known as pītau a manaia.[32] Even under the close supervision of clergy, tohunga whakairo were determined to ensure that their ancestors would not be divorced from the wairuatanga imbued in Māori churches; to exclude them was unthinkable.

The events at Manutuke emphasise the importance of mana in large-scale projects. Mana, as revealed through Māori art and architecture, is more than just prestige and status – it is also a demonstration of relational networks that can be mobilised to realise complex projects and ensure that innovation is tikanga-led. Some missionaries, while they did not always understand Māori motivations and customs, and their tolerance for innovation was limited, believed that Christian environments were enriched by

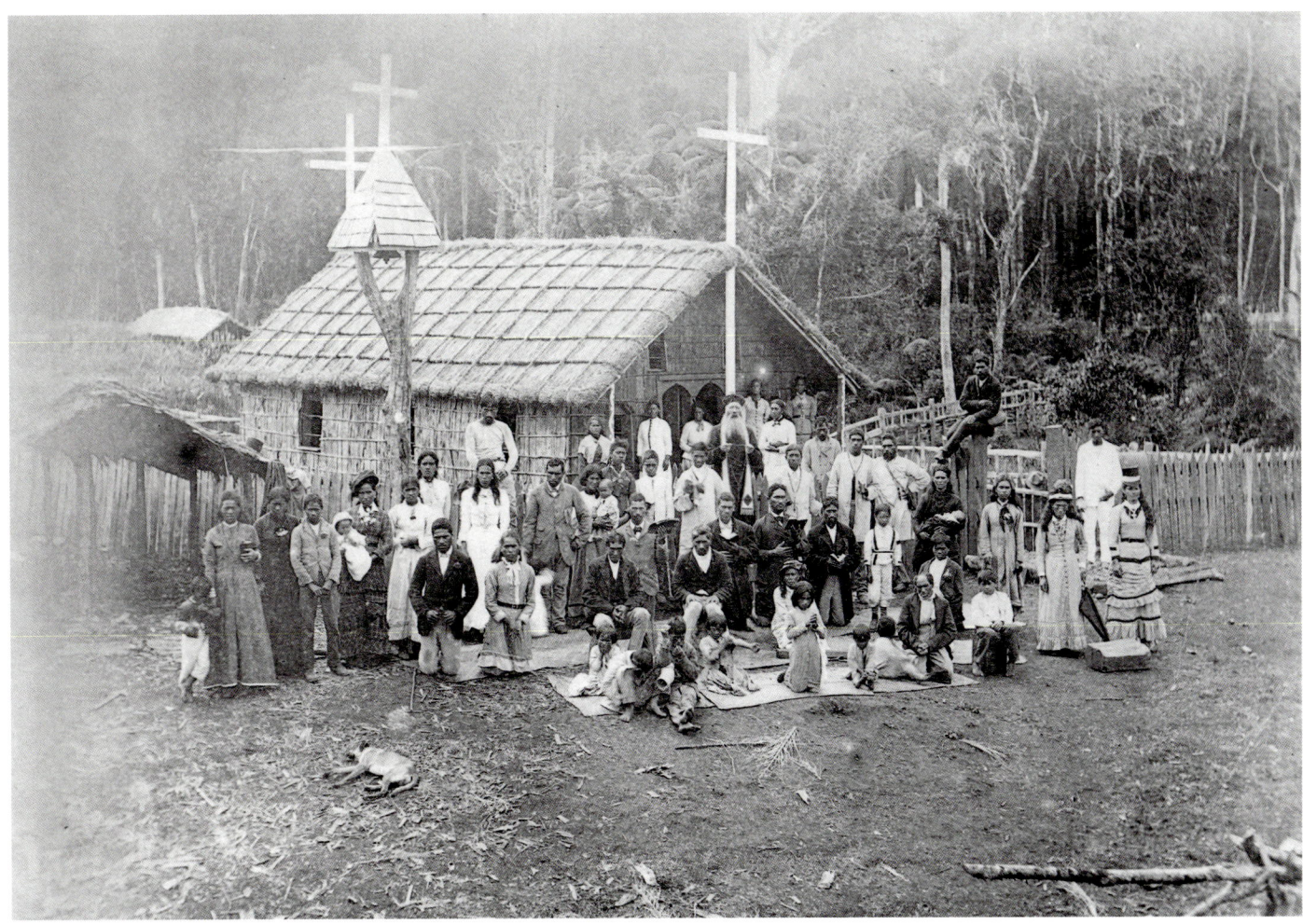

Many Māori communities used familiar customary building techniques to construct their chapels. At Opanaki (now known as Kaihū) in the south Hokianga, the Māori Catholic congregation erected a carefully constructed whare raupō for their chapel, with thatching removed to make window-like openings, and the front porch accommodating a pair of lancet windows.
photographer unknown, Alexander Turnbull Library, PA1-o-423-06-1

the inclusion of Māori art. At the opening of the Manutuke church in April 1863, Williams declared that, while from the outside the church was a plain European-style building, 'within it is elaborately carved and presents a specimen of native art which is nowhere else to be seen'.[33] His words reflect a sentiment expressed in Britain at the time, that taonga Māori could be appreciated as an art tradition.

This open-mindedness towards the inclusion of Māori art in Anglican chapels did not last. The exciting fusion of Gothic Revival exteriors and Māori interiors under the co-supervision of Māori leaders and Anglican missionaries ended with the construction of the Manutuke church. The change was due to the influence of the inaugural Anglican bishop of New Zealand, George Augustus Selwyn, who arrived in Aotearoa in 1842. Unlike the evangelical missionaries, Selwyn believed in a uniformity in church design that would reflect a uniformity in belief, regardless of country and culture – a doctrine that largely excluded Indigenous embellishment.[34]

This was not to say that Selwyn was completely opposed to Māori artists and builders working on Anglican Church projects. Before he left Britain he asked the Cambridge Camden Society – a Gothic Revival architecture group – to provide him with a Norman-style parish church model that Māori builders could replicate across the country, as 'its rudeness and massiveness, and the grotesque character of its sculpture, will probably render it easier to be understood and appreciated by them'.[35] He also requested full-scale models of Norman capitals, moulding sections and ornamented pier, door and window arches for tohunga whakairo to copy 'in the stone of their own country', since 'the ingenuity of the natives in carving is well known'.[36] Perhaps it was through the Māori collection the CMS was building in London that Selwyn and the Camden Society had become acquainted with whakairo rākau and pounamu hei tiki, although the project was clearly doomed before it began, as Māori never carved stone in this way.

Despite the inclinations of the bishop, and a period of division within the early New Zealand Catholic Church, many Māori communities still constructed their own churches as generally modest but well-built thatched whare that were sometimes replaced with simple Pākehā-style buildings. By the turn of the century, as Māori found their own identity and voice within the Anglican, Catholic and Methodist churches, whakairo rākau, kōwhaiwhai and tukutuku were (re)introduced to church buildings, particularly in predominantly Māori communities where Christian faith had become an inextricable part of wairuatanga.

### Collecting taonga

Rejecting art that suggested a reconciliation of tikanga Māori with Christianity was one strategy for missionaries to maintain their religious orthodoxy. Collecting it was another. Missionaries may have collected more taonga Māori than the European explorers and traders who preceded them, and as a permanent population within or beside Māori communities, they made more effort to document the meanings of those taonga, even if their accounts were coloured by their Christian beliefs.

Māori had their reasons for giving taonga to missionaries. Exchanges imbued a new worth into formerly utilitarian objects such as stone adzes, bone fishhooks and woven garments, once prized because of the value of the working materials and labour expended in their creation, but now rendered largely obsolete for Māori with the arrival of European iron in the form of blades, barbs and hooks, and blankets. The CMS and Catholic churches actively exchanged iron and blankets as a conversion tactic, to create material 'wants' and rewards that would make Māori dependent on them; they accepted taonga and provisions in return, although the WMS missionaries were not permitted to collect.[37]

The missionaries themselves collected the taonga as exotic gifts for the patrons in Britain who supported them, and to stock mission museums that they had set up with artefacts illustrating life before and after conversion. The rapid growth of Pākehā settlements in the Bay of Islands, where Māori were also increasingly exchanging taonga for foreign currency, eventually elevated the 'price' of taonga beyond the reach of missionaries.[38] In 1837 the Anglican missionary Philip Hansen King wrote to a patron in England begging his forgiveness: he explained that he had not been able to acquire any taonga in the district during the two years he had been resident there, as Pākehā 'had made all kinds of curiosities scarce not only to buy nor to be procured'.[39] Somewhat apologetically, King instead offered a small consignment of body adornments, waka huia, matau, a muka fishing line and a patu that he had obtained in exchange for trade goods during a six-month sojourn at Te Papa Mission Station in Tauranga, Bay of Plenty, where the market for taonga was not as vigorous.

Pākehā fascination with taonga went beyond an aesthetic interest. Missionaries also acquired or commissioned samples of muka and twined muka in the form of fishing lines and ropes to send to British patrons who were considering commercial flax harvesting and processing enterprises.[40] Maintaining these patrons' speculative interest in New Zealand ensured their continued fiscal investment in the mission.

Māori attempted to explain the meaning of these taonga to the missionaries who received them, and the many and varied ways these narratives were understood by the missionaries and their circle of associates permeated Pākehā writing about taonga Māori for the next century. Often the kōrero were simplified into accompanying descriptions of a taonga's function; any explanation of their spiritual purpose was likely dismissed by the majority of missionaries, apart from Thomas Kendall.

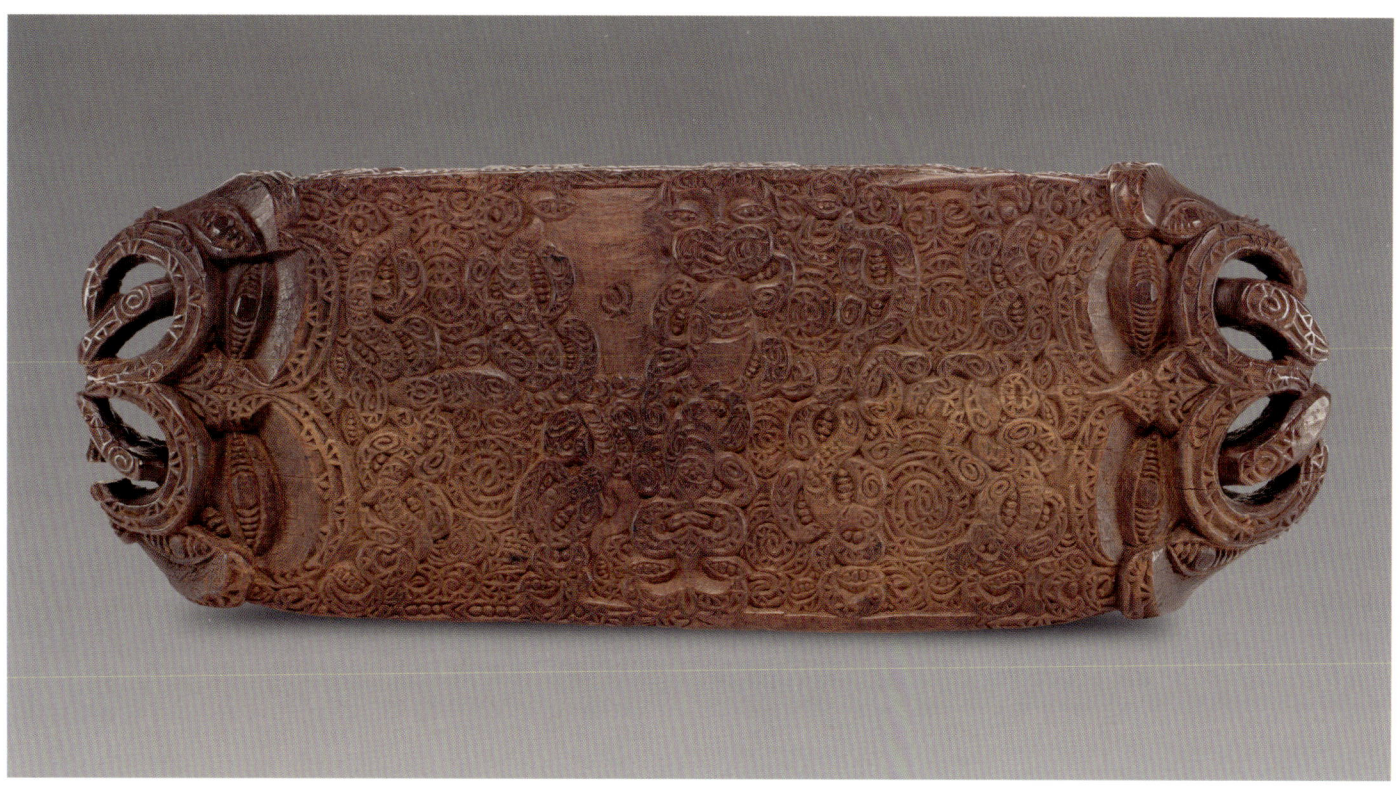

This papahou from Northland was presented to the Reverend Basil Woodd, an influential revivalist who, among his many roles, was an honorary life governor of the Church Missionary Society in London and patron of the New Zealand missionary Thomas Kendall.
Tāmaki Paenga Hira Auckland War Memorial Museum, 1962.64

Kendall was one of the first three CMS missionaries to arrive at Rangihoua Bay, where they established Aotearoa New Zealand's first Christian mission in 1814 at Ruatara's invitation. After seven stressful years without any conversions, Kendall decided that understanding the Māori metaphysical world through art would assist him with his mission. That approach instantly put him at odds with Samuel Marsden's strategy of creating material 'wants' while extinguishing Indigenous spirituality. After gaining the confidence of the Rangihoua tohunga Te Rākau, Kendall had a short – but scandalous – affair with Te Rākau's daughter Tungaroa in the early 1820s. Te Rākau and Tungaroa were likely his principal informants on Māori art and culture.[41]

Kendall's struggle to make sense of what he could see and what he was told about taonga Māori is evident in his writings and drawings of taonga. He sent these records to patrons and the CMS in Britain between 1815 and 1823, along with substantial collections of often large exemplars, including pare, paepae, kūwaha tauihu and taurapa. While some of these whakairo rākau arrived in London, and were later exhibited in the 1867 Paris International Exhibition,[42] some were lost at sea and others never made it to their destination. The bulk of them were dispersed by the CMS itself.[43] Kendall's annotated drawing of the front porch wall carvings of a pātaka, with its dominant tiki figure identified as the Ngāpuhi ancestor Nukutawhiti, has been used – most notably by historian Judith Binney – as a Rosetta Stone-type instrument to interpret the purpose and meaning of the taonga he sent to Britain; however, his writings are where the influence of Māori knowledge was most present.[44]

If we strip away layers of Enlightenment and Christian thinking – and a redundant Pythagorean influence derived from a 1797 *Encyclopedia Britannica* edition in his possession – we can see from Kendall's writings that his informants revealed to him a complex compositional system that remains evident to this day in contemporary whakairo rākau. Pare, paepae and tauihu were transitional spatial markers that, when physically crossed over, also shifted people between noa to tapu spiritual states. These changing states are represented in different combinations of tiki, manaia and ngārara (reptile) figurative compositions. Kendall attempted to identify key motifs on the figures that

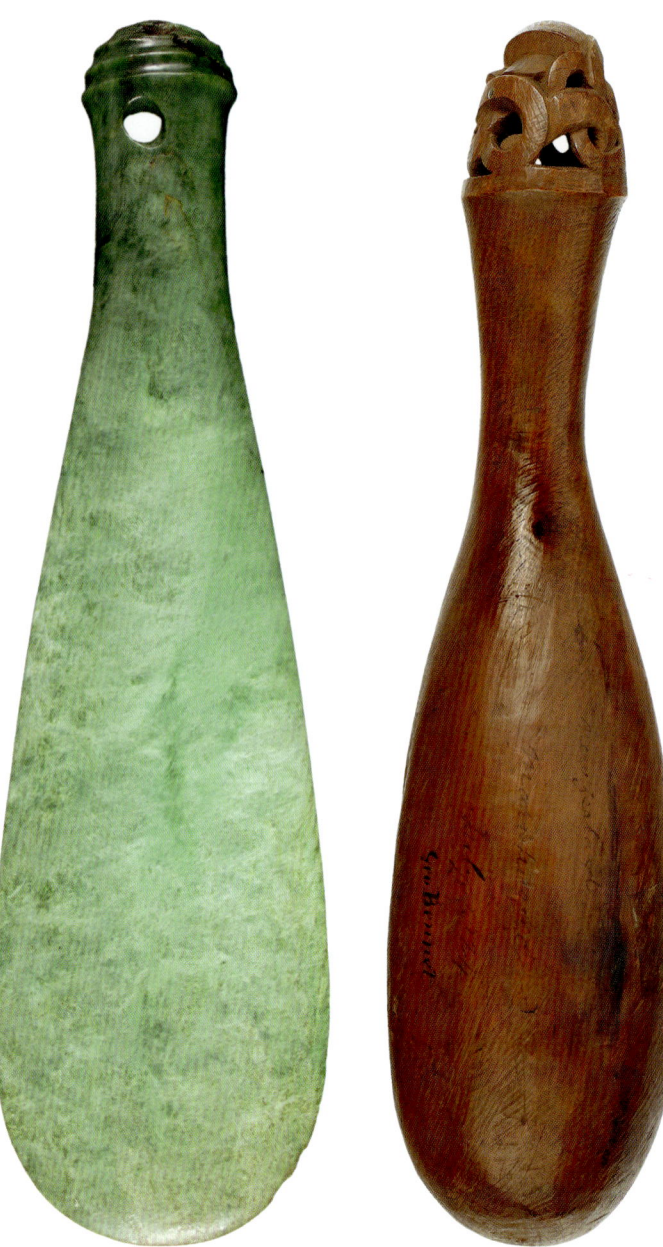

Left: Mere pounamu associated with Hongi Hika and given to Mary Marsden, daughter of Samuel Marsden, in 1830.
Tāmaki Paenga Hira Auckland War Memorial Museum, 2012.1.1

Right: Patu aruhe (fernroot beater) acquired by the Reverend George Bennet of the London Missionary Society through trade with Ngāti Pou on board the *Endeavour*, which anchored in Whangaroa in July 1824.
British Museum, Oc,LMS.153 EOC13137 16454001

he believed represented Māori philosophical and spiritual concepts, such as the horn- or moon-like manaia mouth, hand positions and numbers of fingers, and 'Trinities' of figures, but in the end it proved impossible to ascribe the singular meanings he most desperately sought for individual elements. What he had been unable to see was that Māori culture is relational, and that meaning resides in the relationship between entities, not in the entities themselves.[45]

This type of object-based thinking and missionary observances pervaded much of the Māori art historical scholarship that followed, including the late nineteenth- and early twentieth-century writings of ethnologists published in influential scholarly serials such as the *Transactions and Proceedings of the New Zealand Institute* (1869–1934) and *Journal of the Polynesian Society* (published from 1892). It was not until the 1920s that bilingual Māori scholars, embedded in their communities and educated at university, were able to revisit these assumptions and return tikanga-based meanings to published discussions of customary Māori arts.

Occasionally, very important taonga Māori with great spiritual and social mana found their way into missionary hands. The relinquishing of these taonga to the missionaries was not, initially at least, a sign of the iconoclasm inspired by changing spiritual or cultural allegiances experienced elsewhere in the Pacific.[46] Since Māori were slow to convert, these early taonga exchanges of high-cultural-value items were most likely koha that recognised the mana of the missionary recipients and attempted to bring them into an obligatory relationship with Māori to facilitate trade with the missions for iron and later (through missionaries such as Thomas Kendall) for muskets. Although Hongi Hika never converted to Christianity, his respect for Marsden was demonstrated in the gifting of a mere pounamu to Marsden's daughter Mary in 1830 (the embodiment represented by the word play between 'mere' and 'Mary' is thought to be the reason why he chose her as the recipient of this taonga). A small section of a feather collar belonging to Ngāpuhi leader Hone Heke (see page 252) appears to have been ritually divided and given to missionaries at the Waimate Mission Station in 1844. It may have been a conciliatory gift or offering to appease the governor of New Zealand after Heke had cut down a flagpole flying the Union Jack in Kororāreka.[47]

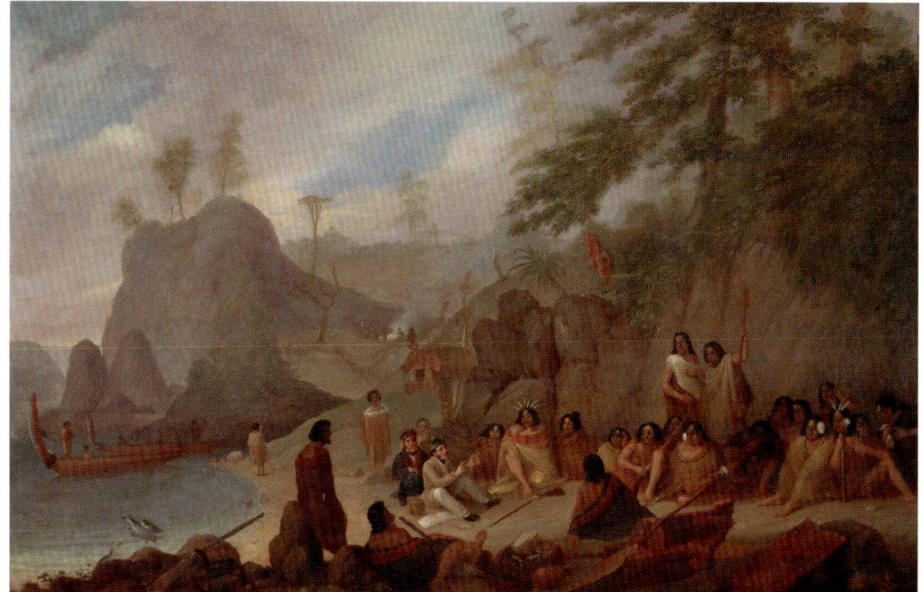

Here Augustus Earle 'constructs' (to use Leonard Bell's term) a meeting he had had with Hongi Hika (1772–1828), arguably the most powerful chief in Northland at the time. What you do not see is the wound which Hongi received whilst on a taua (war expedition) to Whangaroa, an injury which would take his life only a few months later. Earle uses all the key tropes of the period to bring the composition together: Hongi is in the centre of the scene, further emphasised with the five white feathers in his hair; Earle is wearing a bright green beret and is pointing to Hongi.
**Augustus Earle, *Meeting of the artist and Hongi at the Bay of Islands, November 1827*, 1827**
oil on canvas, 578 x 898mm, Alexander Turnbull Library, G-707

### Taonga Māori in European mission museums

While taonga Māori were important agents for bringing Pākehā into the early nineteenth-century Māori world, the contemporaneous exhibition and interpretation of taonga Māori in the United Kingdom was contributing to British ideas about Māori culture and spirituality. In displaying the objects they were receiving from their missions and supporters, the CMS, WMS and London Missionary Society (LMS) were providing some of the first public exhibitions of taonga Māori outside of Aotearoa. These institutions were three of a number of small museums in London that attracted audiences with their displays of taxidermied animals and Indigenous objects, largely from Africa, but also from China, India, Asia and the Pacific from the 1820s until the early twentieth century.[48]

Only the CMS had an active collecting strategy in New Zealand. Although the LMS did not have a mission to New Zealand – a decision made by Marsden, who was the Pacific agent for both the LMS and CMS – it maintained an impressive collection of small taonga Māori.[49] Marsden himself may have supplied the LMS with taonga sent from the CMS missions (perhaps diverted on their way to the CMS museum in Salisbury Street, London), or received from Māori he encountered either in Sydney or during one of his seven visits to New Zealand. Alternatively, LMS missionaries and patrons may have given Māori items to the museum, as was the case with a patu aruhe (fernroot beater) from Whangaroa deposited by the Reverend George Bennet, who had likely obtained it while desperately bartering for his life when he was held captive by Ngāti Pou on board the ship *Endeavour* in July 1824.[50] The WMS also had a small collection of taonga Māori, although it is not clear whether these were displayed at its museum in Bishopsgate, opened in 1838.

Unlike museums of today, the curatorial focus of the London-based mission museums was not the conservation and interpretation of artefacts: their role was to demonstrate to the visiting public and mission patrons that Christian influence was instigating spiritual and moral changes in Indigenous communities – changes that could only continue to be made with ongoing financial support, as zealously argued in the LMS museum's 1826 catalogue:

> The most valuable and impressive objects in this Collection are the numerous, and (in some instances) *horrible*, IDOLS, which have been imported from the South Sea Islands, from India, China and Africa; and among these, those especially which were actually given up by their former worshippers, *from a full conviction of the folly and sin of idolatry* – a conviction derived from the ministry of the Gospel by missionaries.[51]

Exhibits sometimes juxtaposed Indigenous work made at missions such as handwriting samples and needlework, with Indigenous art that illustrated local belief systems and practices that were at odds with contemporaneous Protestant teachings on, for example, tattooing and idolatry.[52] Mission exhibitions promoted the idea that Māori were redeemable

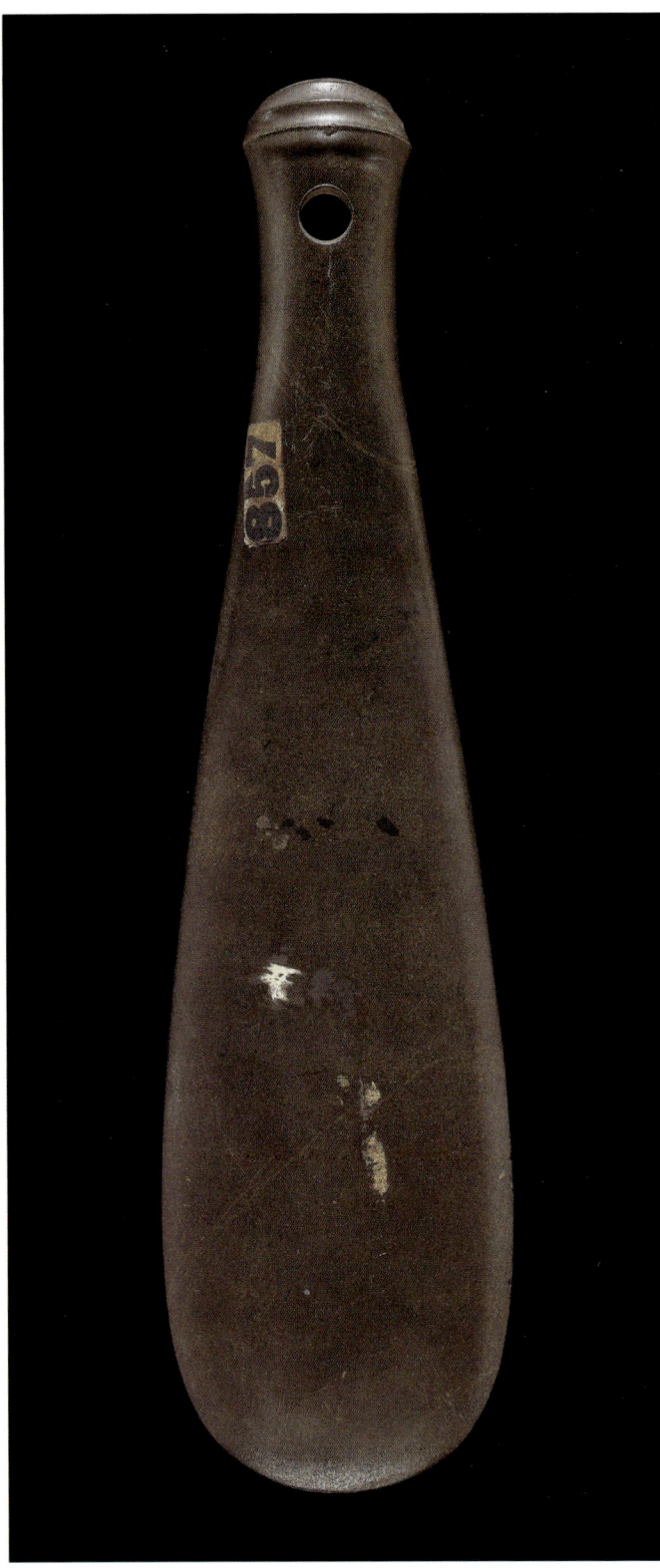

This patu ōnewa was one of over 50 taonga Māori exhibited in the 1867 Paris Exposition Universelle. It became part of the London Mission Society collection before 1860 and was transferred to the British Museum when the society's museum closed in 1910. In 1984, it joined other taonga Māori in the *Te Maori* exhibition, touring North America and briefly returning to Aotearoa New Zealand in 1987, before being sent back to the British Museum.
British Museum, Oc1910,-.289

through conversion, by including items that demonstrated skilful labour – which was in keeping with the evangelistic position that diligent work was a virtue. That so few Indigenous Australian items were sent to the CMS and LMS museums is perhaps indicative of Marsden's view that their disinterest in material 'wants' was evidence that they could not be compelled to work towards spiritual 'salvation'.[53] Marsden had interpreted the willingness of Māori to abandon stone technologies in favour of iron as a desire to assimilate Christian values into the Māori work ethic, although his embedded missionaries would soon realise that the reasons for technological appropriations were far more complex.[54]

These mission collections were representative of missionary ideas about Indigenous arts and industries that influenced early colonial policy. Many early and mid-nineteenth-century British parliamentarians and British Colonial Office officials were themselves Quakers or evangelical Anglicans, who relied on mission reports and opinions to inform their understandings of Indigenous communities; notably the British MP Thomas Fowell Buxton who, as chair of the 1837 Aborigines Select Committee, promoted humanitarian principles that were later reflected in Te Tiriti o Waitangi. Buxton, who became a leading figure in the anti-slavery campaign, had first been introduced to the problems of encounter between Indigenous peoples and British settlers through the lobbying of John Philip, director of the LMS at the Cape Colony, a decade before.[55] CMS submissions dominated the reports on Māori provided to Buxton's commission.[56] In lieu of the presence of Maori people (apart from occasional high-profile visitors such as Hongi Hika), taonga Māori in mission museums and the stories that missionaries wrapped around them must have contributed to the image of 'native New Zealanders' in British popular imagination and in the minds of those involved in early nineteenth-century foreign and, after 1840, colonial policy.

Taonga themselves became international travelling emissaries for the missions. The CMS, LMS and WMS exhibited Māori and other Indigenous cultural items from their collections at the Exposition universelle d'art et d'industrie (the International Exposition) of 1867, held in Paris on the Champ de Mars in a pavilion dedicated to mission work.[57] The objective of the missionary displays was to garner public support by highlighting the missions' 'success' in introducing European cultural values to other societies – which they presented as communities of skilful labourers living in environments that offered materials ripe for exploitation. Whether this was the only message received by audiences is another matter. The exhibition of Japanese art elsewhere in the Exposition universelle inspired a widespread fascination for Japonisme in French popular culture and impressionist and post-impressionist art. It seems likely that exposure to the arts of other parts of the world would have stimulated a degree of intellectual, if not artistic, curiosity among a cross-section of the visiting public.

Over 1500 objects were exhibited in the Exposition universelle from a number of missionary organisations working around the world. The sheer volume of Indigenous art on display was unprecedented in Europe. The catalogue provided a snapshot of the range of these collections, although each collection was not represented in its entirety at the Exposition.[58] The number of taonga Māori on show was modest compared to other Indigenous exhibits. This reflects both the distance to the metropole and the regional interests of the organisations involved: the LMS exhibited at least twenty-six taonga Māori, the CMS sixteen, the WMS nine, and the Paris Evangelical Mission Society exhibited three. The Catholic Church reputedly withdrew from the Exposition universelle when it learnt that the Protestants had been granted permission to participate: this left the Protestant churches free to promote their missionary work to the eleven million largely Catholic visitors to the seven-month event.[59]

The taonga Māori the missions presented at the Exposition included kaitaka, flax ropes, toki, patu, matau, kōrere, body adornments, poupou, waka components, model waka, flutes, waka huia and papahou, and possibly whakapākoko rākau – the last provocatively described as 'l'usage des adoreteurs du diable' or 'used to worship the devil'.[60] Mission values were reflected in the catalogue: two WMS catalogue entries emphasised the careful crafting of some of the whakairo rākau,[61] in keeping with the Protestant work ethic; and one CMS entry suggested that the demise of stone tools[62] and the decline in pre-industrial technologies was an inevitable consequence of colonisation. If that interpretation was too subtle for audiences, evidence of the direct message of Christian 'salvation' to Indigenous people was demonstrated through the inclusion of mission and other religious texts in the language of the missionaries and that of the communities they were living in.

The number of taonga Māori held in British missionary museums has yet to be fully established, and the task has been made more complex by the divestment of collections as each museum closed. The dispersal of the LMS, CMS and WMS museum collections coincides with the decline of the New Zealand missions, public disinterest in mission museums, competition from other British public museums with stronger collections, and the expense of maintaining collections to meet the rising curatorial standards of the time.[63] From the late nineteenth century, parts of the LMS Museum collection were transferred to the British Museum, where almost all of the Māori items mentioned in 1826 and 1860 LMS inventories and in the 1867 Exposition universelle catalogue can be accounted for in the present collection. The surviving LMS Māori collection consists mainly of stone and bone utilitarian and prestige taonga. Many of the wooden pieces display surface embellishments associated with Northland carving; others incorporate materials that demonstrate a Pākehā influence, such as a well-worn and therefore very old hei tiki with red wax eyes (Oc,LMS.138) and a fishhook with a refashioned barb made from an iron nail (Oc1935,0411.13).

Many of the types of taonga that were sent from the mission stations in Northland and Tauranga to the CMS museum in London were exhibited in the Exposition universelle of 1867, and may therefore have been on public display when in Britain.[64] A now rare photographic portfolio of six CMS exhibits shows a taurapa, tauihu, model waka taua, tekoteko-like figure, kūwaha pātaka embellished with taratara ā Kae surface carving, and wheku-style poupou.[65] The last two taonga Māori follow stylistic conventions typically associated with iwi in the central and eastern North Island, and were acquired by Thomas Kendall in 1823 from Bay of Islands Māori, who had either commissioned carvers from elsewhere or seized the carvings during battle.

By the beginning of the twentieth century, the CMS museum collection had been greatly reduced: the only known inventory of the CMS Māori collection, written in 1903, lists just one patu ōnewa, an uhi pounamu (greenstone chisel), a patu aruhe, and a 'chief's staff' – written underneath the ominously struck-through words 'two chiefs' staffs' with the same registration number.[66] The 'chief's staff' is one of a number of the deaccession entries in the inventory for artefacts from around the world, and the date of the

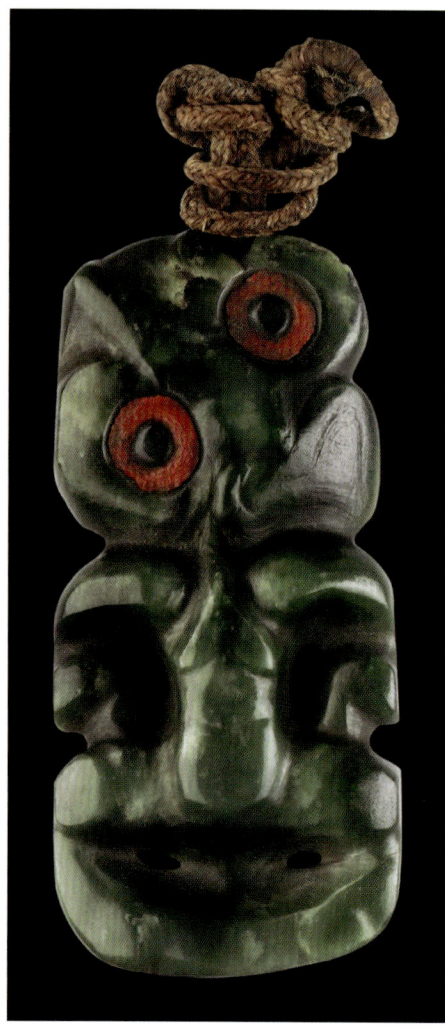
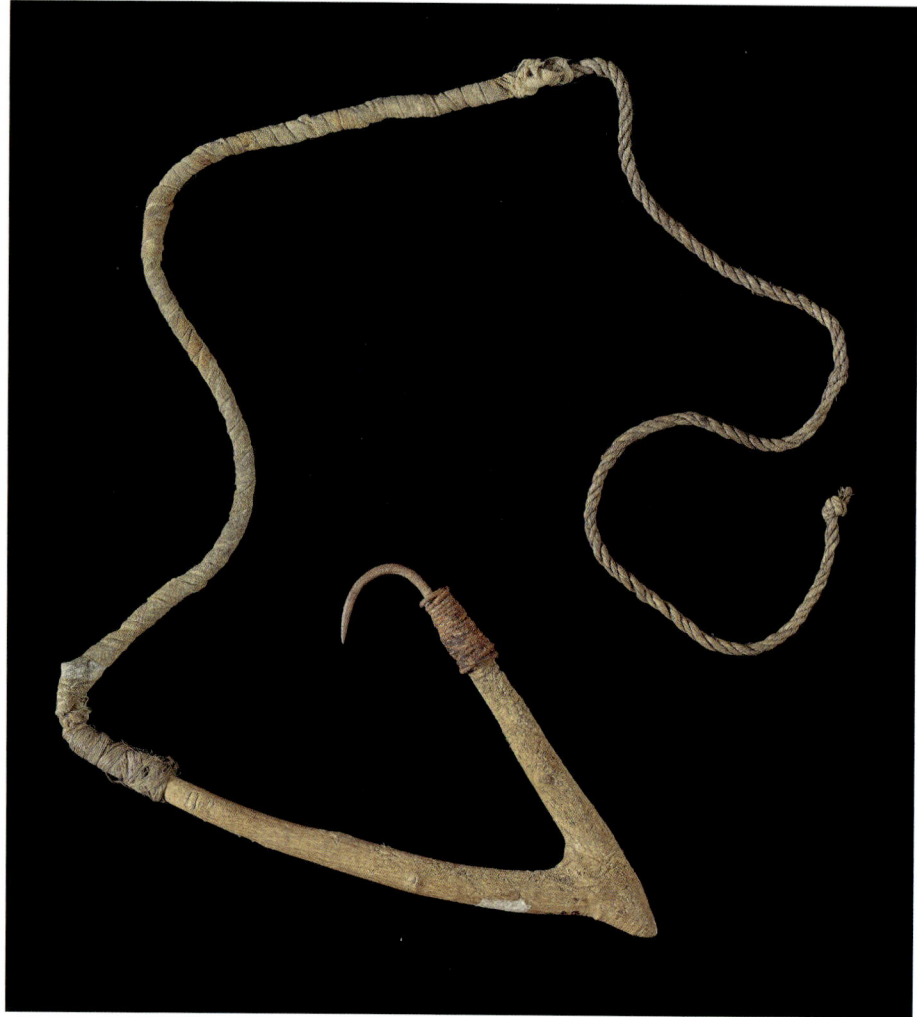

Left: Hei tiki with irises inlaid with red wax. Although the London Missionary Society did not have a mission in Aotearoa New Zealand, this hei tiki became part of its collection and is now in the British Museum.
British Museum, Oc,LMS.138

Right: Matau with a barb made from an iron nail, part of the London Missionary Society taonga Māori collection now in the British Museum.
British Museum, Oc1935,0411.13

inventory coincides with the CMS's withdrawal of funding to the foundering New Zealand mission.[67] The Māori collection had been slowly dispersed over a number of decades up to that point – items 'borrowed' to serve as visual aids in fundraising lectures were possibly not always returned, and patrons and collectors were permitted to remove or possibly purchase taonga for their own collections, especially as interest in the museum declined.[68]

The London-based collector (and New Zealand Wars veteran) Horatio Robley appears to have had access to the CMS collection: he sold a pare, paepae, poupou kūwaha, tauihu and two taurapa acquired in the Bay of Islands by Kendall in 1823 to the prolific London-based antiquities dealer William Oldman in 1910.[69] Oldman sold the paepae, poupou, kūwaha and tauihu to Berlin's Völkerkundemuseum in 1911, and they remain in Europe today (Museum Rietberg, Zürich, RPO 12; Ethnologisches Museum, Berlin, VI 31789, VI 31790, VI 31791 and VI 31792). The pare and taurapa he kept for his own collection. Unlike other Indigenous items with known provenance which he offered for sale in his catalogues, Oldman appears to have chosen to not disclose the mission associations of these taonga to their new owners. He sold most of his personal collection, including these three taonga, to the New Zealand government for £44,000 in 1948. These objects are now distributed among the country's four major museums: Auckland, Te Papa, Canterbury and Otago.

The fate of taonga Māori from the WMS collection in London is as unclear as their origins. From the 1850s, the sale of Indigenous arts at church bazaars in Auckland, London and possibly Sydney was an important source of income for Fiji-based WMS missionaries, who needed funds to pay for their children's upbringing and education in New Zealand and Britain.[70] These fundraising events, where items from many different cultures may have been for sale, are another possible point of acquisition and dispersal for the WMS Māori collection if the collection had not already been eroded through the covetous desires of mission officials and patrons, as occurred at the CMS museum.

In contrast to the early rise – and demise – of the British missionary museums and dispersal of their taonga Māori holdings, the Vatican ethnological museum in Rome was founded much later, and still maintains a small but wide-ranging collection of taonga Māori. Catholic missionaries in the Pacific and other parts of the world in the nineteenth century sent objects to the Vatican, where they were accessioned into the Museo Borgiano. In 1887 the Vatican displayed objects from this collection in the Esposizione Missionaria Vaticana (Missionary Exposition). At a time when public interest in mission work was flagging in Europe, Pope Pius XI revived Catholic support for the church's work outside of Europe – where missions were rebuilding themselves after the disruptions of World War One – by convening the largest exhibition of Indigenous art ever staged, the 1925 Vatican Missionary Exposition.[71] Visited by over one million people, the exhibition comprised 40,000 objects sent to the Vatican from missions and the faithful, and included missionary publications and other documents alongside the Indigenous art.[72] Few, if any taonga Māori were displayed.[73] The success of the event led Pius XI to establish the Pontificio Museo Missionario-Ethnologico in 1927, with the objective of demonstrating that the 'dawn of faith among the infidel of today can be compared to the dawn of faith which ... illuminated pagan Rome' – a lofty ambition that made the Protestant 'before and after conversion' curatorial strategy appear modest and unaspiring by comparison.[74] This objective shifted with the sweeping transformations inspired by the Second Vatican Council (1962–1965): the museum now aims to demonstrate the diversity of belief.[75]

As early as 1859, visitors to the British mission museums were beginning to relate to Pacific objects, likely including taonga Māori, as 'art'. A review that year of the newly reorganised LMS museum in Bloomfield Street, Finsbury, London, published in the *Illustrated London News*, singled out the Pacific collections as an aesthetic highlight:

> The contents of this museum are not only valuable in consequence of their interest as specimens of peculiar phases of art-workmanship.... The idols of wood and stone, which form a conspicuous feature of the collection, are curious examples of the dawn and progress of art ... Some of the carved work on paddles, etc, by the savage inhabitants of the South Sea Islands are, in some instances, remarkable for both design and execution. The examples of woven and other fabrics are well worthy of examination.[76]

Embedded in the review are some of the fundamental assumptions that were beginning to shape a broader European response to Pacific art, and to Māori art in particular; these assumptions would persist for the next century. They included the theory that art existed within a developmental model, with Indigenous art situated somewhere towards the beginning, where it spoke of the 'savagery' of its makers and the comparative cultural 'advancement' of its viewers. The viewers, however, did not regard the art as primitive – despite the curators' intentions – but praised it for being well conceived and skillfully made. These qualities were highly topical in Britain: the 1851 Great Exhibition and 1862 International Exhibition showcased examples of whatu and raranga as flax industries with the potential for industrial commercialisation,[77] at a time when the Anglican Church's Ecclesiological Society was promoting the craftsmanship of the Gothic Revival almost as an antidote to industrialisation.

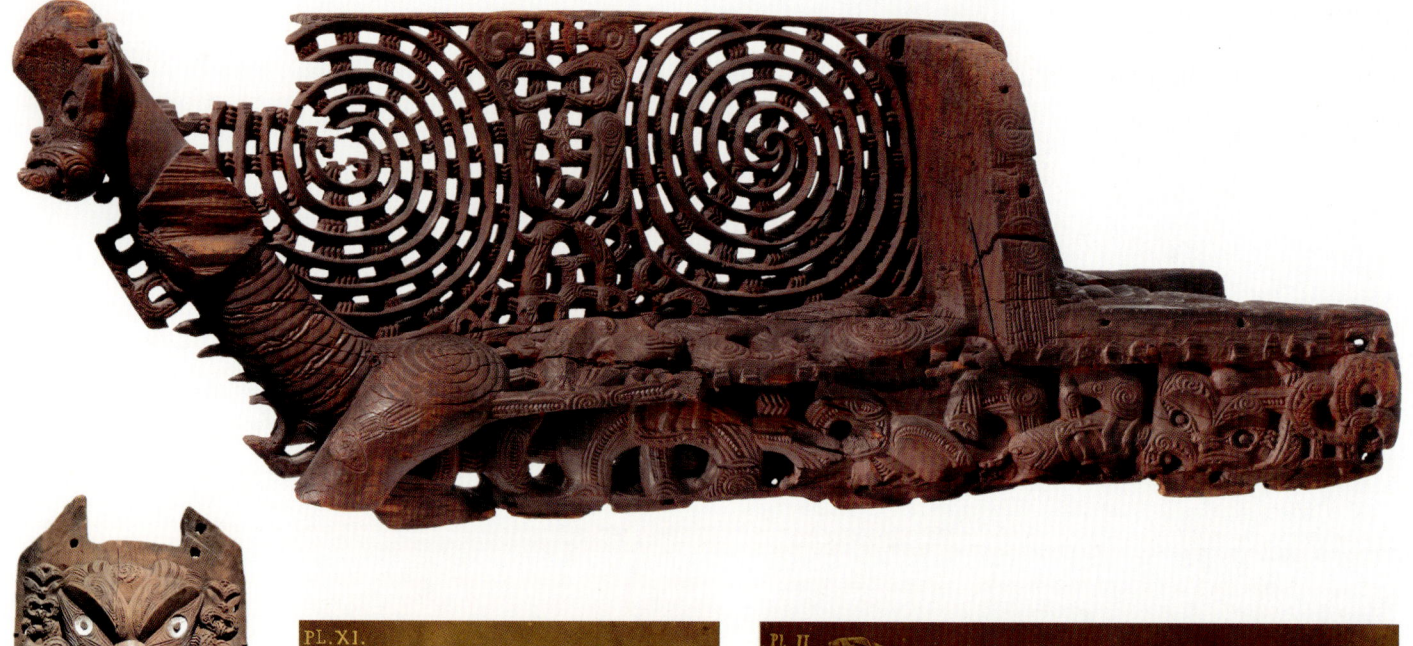

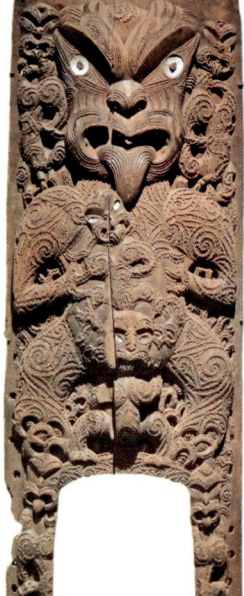
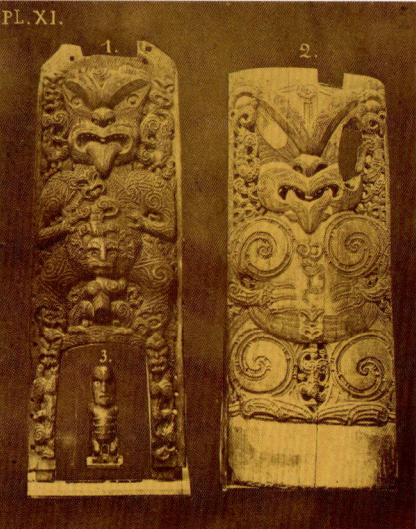
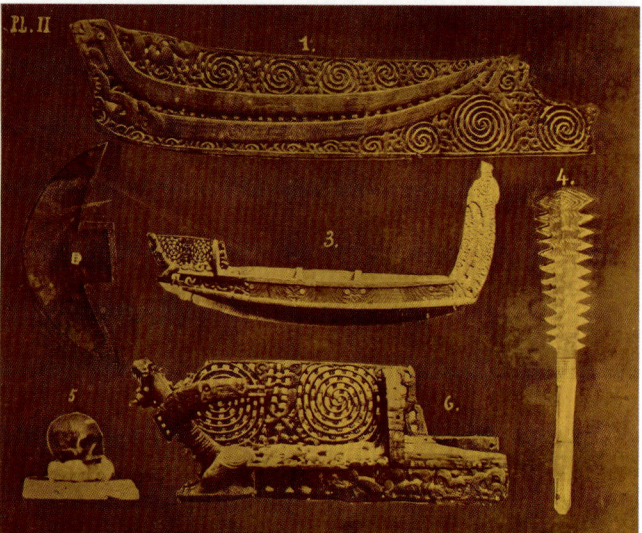

Top and bottom left: Several taonga Māori from the Church Missionary Society museum collection are in public institutions today. A tauihu (top) and kūwaha pātaka (bottom left) were among seven taonga from the CMS collection that found their way into the possession of London-based collectors Horatio Robley and then William Oldman before they were sold to Berlin's Völkerkundemuseum in 1911. The tauihu then became part of the collection of Arthur Speyer in Niederwalluf, Germany, in 1939, before it was finally deposited in Zürich's Museum Rietberg.
Museum Rietberg, inv. no. RPO 12, purchased with funds from Eduard von der Heydt, photograph by Rainer Wolfsberger; Ethnologisches Museum, Berlin, VI 31789, purchased from William Ockelford Oldman, 1911, photograph by Heinz-Günther Malenz, CC BY-NC-SA 4.0

Bottom middle and bottom right: Only one set of images, published as an album, survives as a visual record of the mission exhibits in the 1867 Paris Exposition Universelle, and of those just six taonga Māori, all from the Church Missionary Society collection, were photographed. Plate II (bottom right) shows a taurapa (1), model waka taua (3) and tauihu (6). Plate XI (bottom middle) illustrates a kūwaha pātaka (1), poupou (2) and tekoteko-like figure (3). The tauihu and kūwaha pātaka illustrated here are the ones which are now in Zürich's Museum Rietberg and Berlin's Ethnologisches Museum (top and bottom left).
Getty Research Institute, Los Angeles, 93.R.102

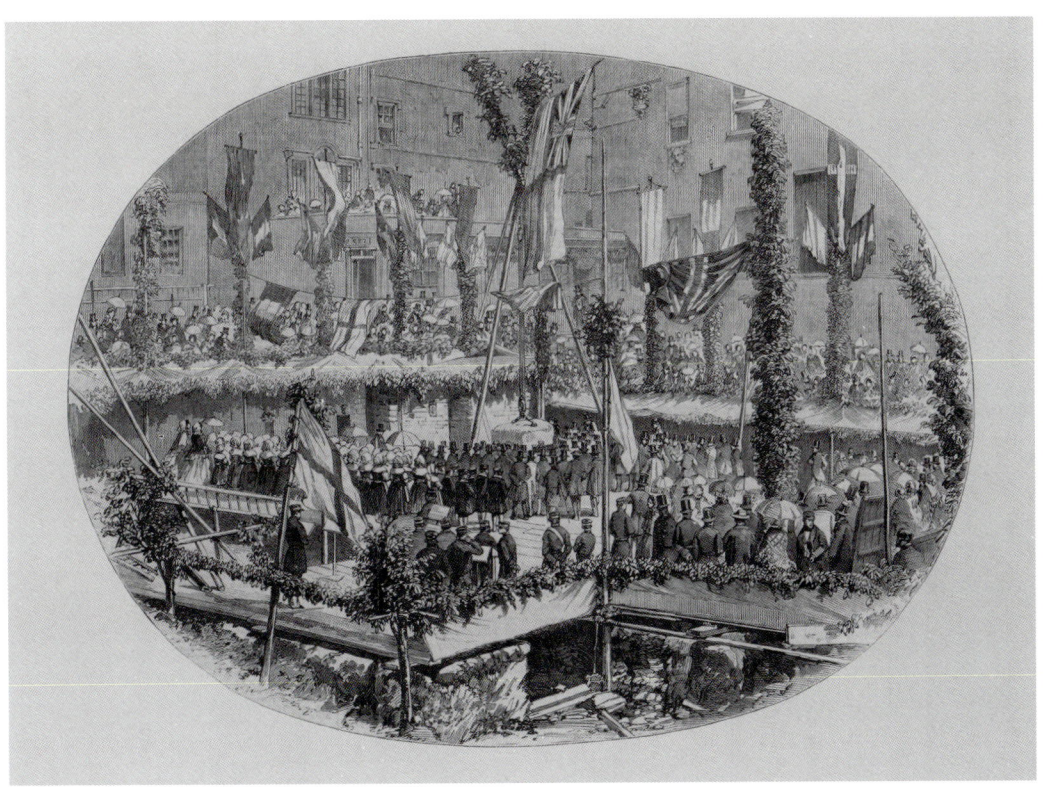

Interior of the London Missionary Society museum on Bloomfield Street, London, as published in the *Illustrated London News*, 25 June 1859.

## Conclusion

By the mid-nineteenth century the mission influence on Māori art and life had begun to wane. One of the many reasons for this was the rise of Māori spiritual leaders, some of whom were associated with churches, and others who preached a form of worship that combined Christian and Māori belief systems, practised in innovatively designed buildings. There had nevertheless been influential moments and places in which missionaries had a profound effect on Māori artistic practice, when the Christian world had either collided with or been absorbed into Māori wairuatanga.

In the Bay of Islands and other parts of the North Island, some missionaries preached inside the precincts of waka chapels, where atua and God were represented in altars, pulpits and pews made from tauihu and hulls. Other missionaries were brought into the confidence of tohunga and provided with kōrero about taonga that simultaneously fascinated and confounded them, as demonstrated in the writing of the aspiring historian of Māori art Thomas Kendall. Further south, missionaries found themselves, or chose to operate, on the outside of tikanga-derived life: they presented their aesthetic and moral values in opposition to those of Māori by rejecting figurative work such as the Māori Madonna and Child and the Manutuke church tiki carvings.

As Māori were integrating biblical time and the Christian calendar into their annual and cyclical understandings of time, Anglo-Protestant and French Catholic mission museums were employing their natural and artificial curiosities to curate stories of art and industry that suggested Indigenous people were relinquishing their past to head into a shared, but not necessarily equal future with other Christians. Within the mission museums, Māori art represented a wairuatanga at odds with Christian values and beliefs. In Aotearoa New Zealand, the diminishing role of tohunga became increasingly apparent in the secularisation of Māori art, which would only increase as Māori leaders emerged out of Christian and Christian-inspired institutions and organisations.

# HONGI HIKA'S SELF-PORTRAITS
DEIDRE BROWN

Hongi Hika's 1814 self-portrait wood sculpture was the Church Missionary Society's most admired Indigenous exhibit in its popular museum in London.[1] Three contemporary museums in different parts of the world claim to have this self-portrait in their collections. How can we identify the real one?

The original was made by Hongi during an 1814 stay at Reverend Samuel Marsden's house in Parramatta, New South Wales. Fascinated by Hongi's moko kanohi, Marsden asked him to 'either give me his Head, or make one like it of wood'.[2] Losing one's head as a battle trophy was a real danger for rangatira, and this may have been a motivating factor for Hongi to take the unprecedented option of carving a self-portrait from the top of a post, using a 12cm-long toki-like blade that he fashioned from a piece of hoop iron. Self-portraiture is highly unusual in whakairo rākau. Marsden remarked on the exactness of the moko kanohi and general likeness of the face to Hongi's own in the letter he sent with the bust to the CMS in London, with the caveat that Hongi was not able to represent the fullness of his face due to the slenderness of the post.[3]

Aside from a single report about its popularity as a foundational exhibit in the CMS museum, and an image published on the front cover of the CMS *Missionary Papers* of 1816 a year later, Hongi's self-portrait was never mentioned again in CMS letters or inventories. By the mid-nineteenth century, the self-portrait may have already been gifted to an esteemed CMS patron, or perhaps was never returned from a fundraising tour, which was the fate of much of the CMS collections. Today, however, busts fitting its description are in the collections of Tāmaki Paenga Hira Auckland War Memorial Museum, the Chau Chak Wing Museum of the University of Sydney and Brighton Hove Museum in the United Kingdom. None have provenance that directly connects them with the CMS museum.

The earliest date associated with the Auckland Museum example is its discovery in 1967 in a Welsh house by a collector, Reginald Longden, but his estate has no further documentation related to this find. The inked inscription on the bust, 'Carved by Honghi [unreadable] New Zealand 1814', has been attributed to the missionary Thomas Kendall, who travelled to Sydney with Hongi in 1814; however, the handwriting does not match that of Kendall, Marsden or the CMS secretary Josiah Pratt, who received the self-portrait in London. Furthermore, the inscription must have been made much later, since these missionaries never used this spelling of Hongi's name with a 'gh'; indeed, this spelling was not common until the mid-1830s,[4] three decades after the bust was carved. What the self-portrait does have is a flattened, elongated face, which fits with Marsden's description of a carving constrained by the dimensions of the original post.

The Brighton bust was donated to the museum in 1957 by Lilian Bately of Portslade, who had no known personal or family connection to New Zealand or the CMS, although a potential link is that she and her husband attended church in the Diocese of Chichester, and the third Earl of Chichester had been patron of the CMS.[5] The carving in the Chau Chak Wing Museum has the earliest documentation of the three, in a transfer record from the University of Sydney's Nicholson Museum in December 1896. The Chau Chak Wing and Brighton heads more closely resemble the *Missionary Papers* cover drawing of the Hongi bust than does the Auckland example. Was one of these carvings the inspiration for the cover? If not, were they both copies based on a drawing of the carving that is now in Auckland? As a popular exotic exhibit, the Hongi bust may have inspired imitations, or been duplicated, even triplicated, for fundraising tours.

These are not unique objects, however. Any or all of the three may be outcomes of a practice that offers an alternative explanation for this multiplicity of carved heads. A carved head very similar in execution to the three under discussion was acquired through trade at Whangaroa, Northland, in 1824.

With investigations of historical records exhausted and visual analysis inconclusive, wood identification remains the only unexplored option for proving which, if any, of these three heads was made from Australian timber. A preliminary examination of the Chau Chak Wing bust by an Australian wood specialist using non-invasive magnification suggested that it was 'probably' made from *Eucalyptus tereticornis* (forest red gum), an Australian hardwood used in buildings and fencing in early colonial Sydney.[6] Microscopic analysis of minute samples from each of the three heads is the only way of identifying the wood species of the different busts with a greater degree of certainty.

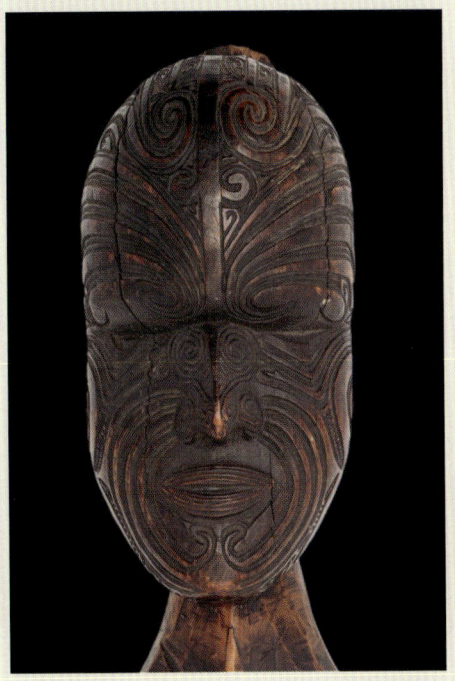 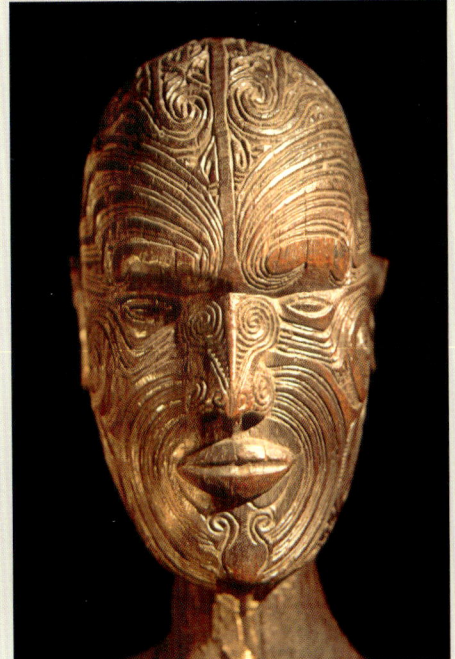 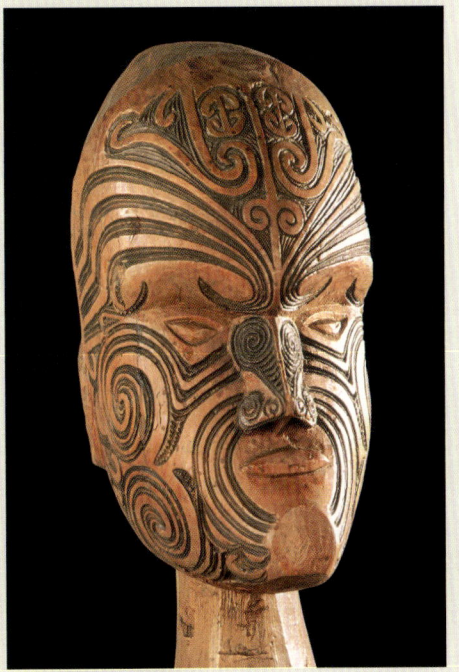

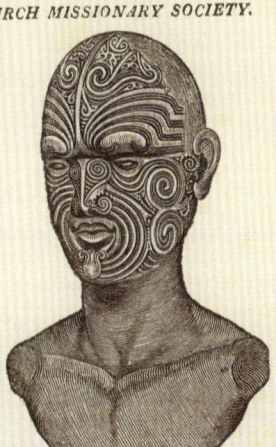

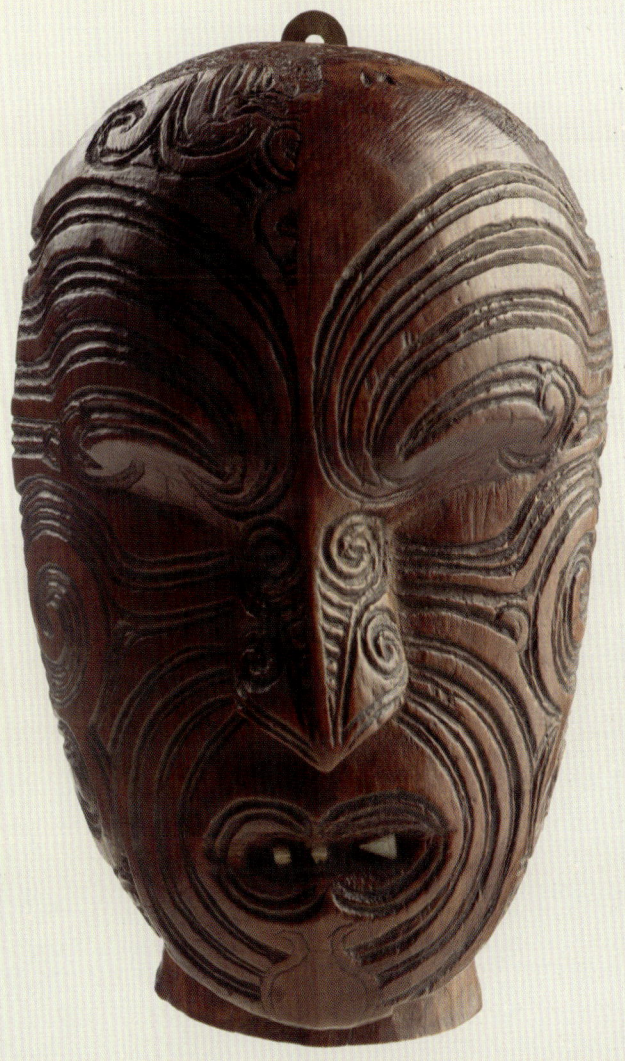

**Top:** Proposed Hongi Hika self-portraits, from left to right, Chau Chak Wing Museum of the University of Sydney, Brighton Hove Museum and Auckland Museum.
Chau Chak Wing Museum, The University of Sydney, ETI.570; Brighton Hove Museum, WA50599; Tāmaki Paenga Hira Auckland War Memorial Museum, 1971.131

**Bottom left:** Hongi Hika bust as illustrated in the Church Missionary Society's *Missionary Papers* of 1816.
Alexander Turnbull Library, PUBL-0031-1816-01

**Bottom right:** Upoko whakairo (carved head) exchanged between Ngāti Pou and George Bennet on board the *Endeavour* in Whangaroa.
Te Papa Tongarewa Museum of New Zealand, OL000628/1, Oldman Collection, gift of the New Zealand government, 1992

# HONE HEKE'S 'COLLAR'
DEIDRE BROWN

A small, square section of a fine feather-down garment that belonged to Ngāpuhi leader Hone Heke represents both the cross-fertilisation of cultural ideas and the tensions that developed between Pākehā and Māori soon after the signing of Te Tiriti o Waitangi. The backing fabric and thread are of European manufacture, but the technique of securing the feathers to the backing fabric is wholly Māori, and the stitches that secure each bundle of down to the kaupapa are so fine that they are visible only with a microscope.

The relationship between Heke and the Crown, however, was unravelling by the time the taonga came into William Nihil's possession around 1844, when the paths of the two men appear to have crossed at the Waimate Mission Station. Twenty-year-old Nihil was training for Holy Orders here when Heke and supporters arrived on 15 September in an unsuccessful attempt to placate Governor Robert FitzRoy, who was on the brink of initiating the first of the Northern Wars after Heke cut down the flagstaff flying the Union Jack at Kororāreka in protest at the rapidly dwindling rights of Māori post-annexation.[1] Twenty muskets were presented in recompense; Heke and the chiefs dictated separate letters of apology; and, possibly at some point during proceedings, Heke's beautiful garment created out of an imaginative amalgamation of Māori and Pākehā technologies was cut, perhaps as a form of penance (Heke was Christian) or as a ritual division of mana. Nihil may well have taken this piece with him to New Caledonia, where he worked in the Melanesian Mission until he died. The taonga was donated to the University of Cambridge Museum of Archaeology and Anthropology in 1901 by William Still, the newly installed bishop of Norwich, who may have come into possession of the piece through his association with the Melanesian Mission.[2]

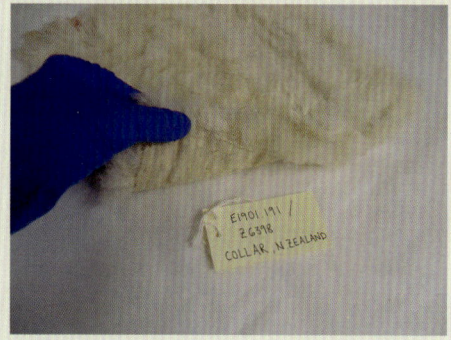

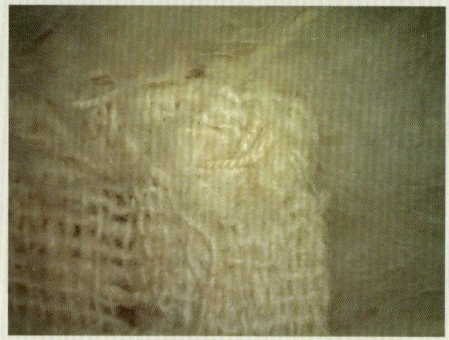

Top: The Hone Heke 'collar', as it is described by its present keepers, the Museum of Archaeology and Anthropology, University of Cambridge.
Museum of Archaeology and Anthropology, University of Cambridge, E 1901.191

Bottom: Kat Szabo's investigation of the fabric using a Dino-lite AM 4815ZT microscope.
photographs by Kat Szarbo and Deidre Brown

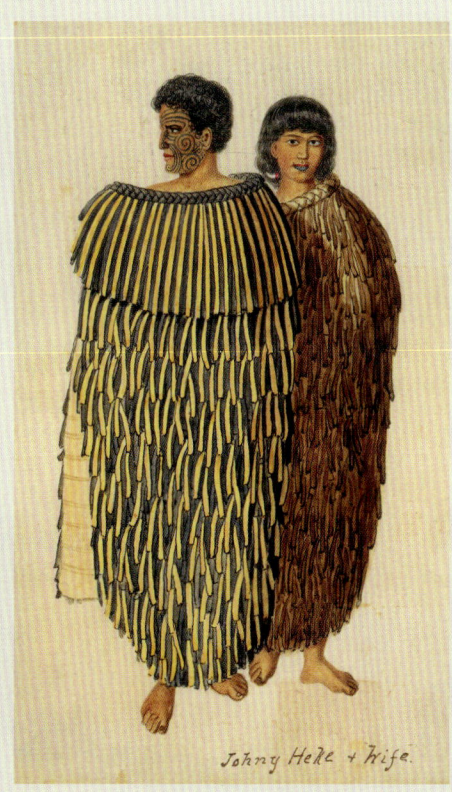

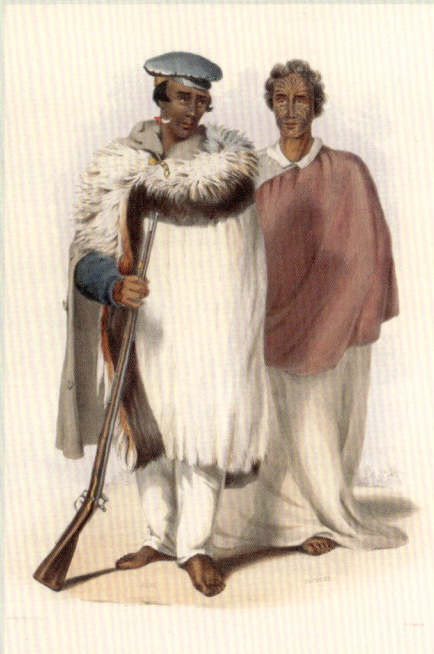

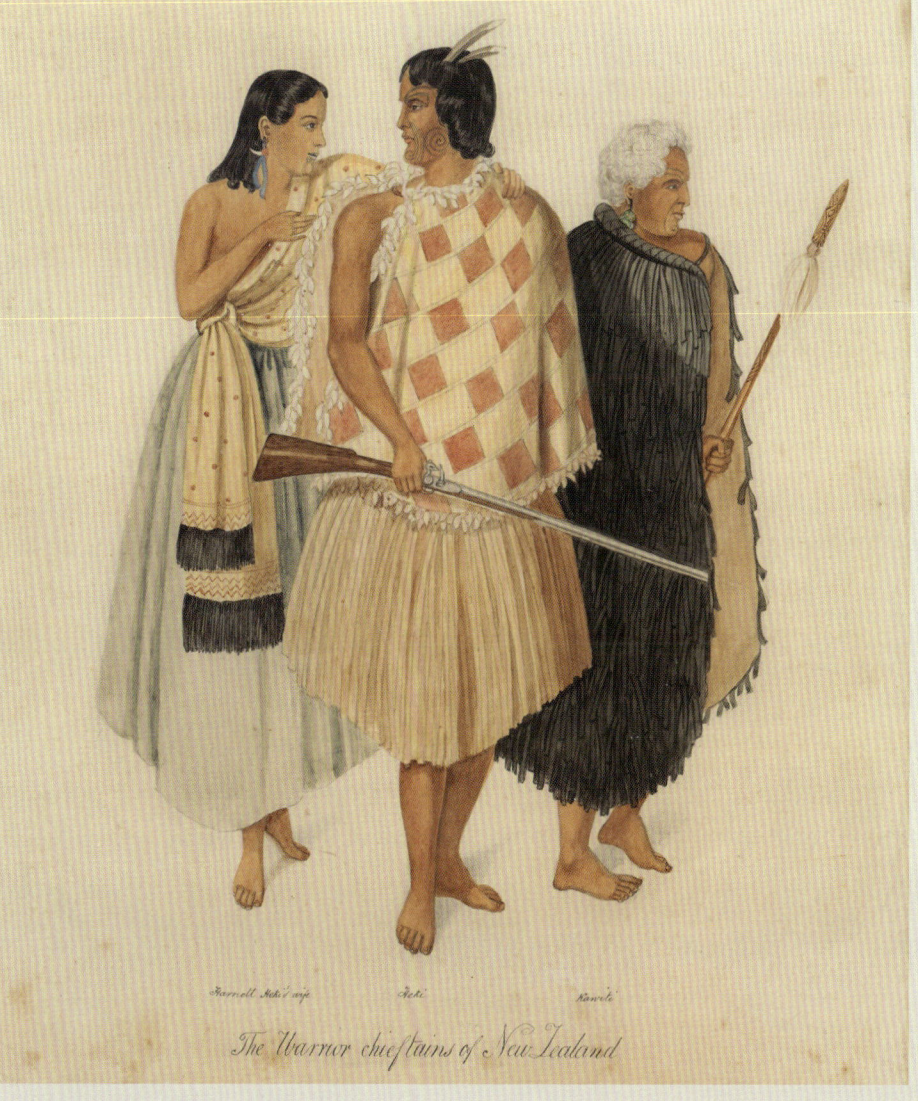

Hone Heke was a connoisseur of fine cloaks, as demonstrated in these historical images.

Top left: **Joseph Jenner Merrett, *Johny Heke & wife*, c.1845**

watercolour on cream wove paper, 230 x 177mm, Alexander Turnbull Library, E-309-q-2-033

Bottom left: **George French Angas, *Honi [Hone] Heke and Patuone*, 1847**

lithograph, 550 x 376mm, National Library of Australia, nla.obj-135649240

Right: **Joseph Jenner Merrett, *The warrior chieftains of New Zealand*, 1846**

watercolour, 558 x 460mm, Alexander Turnbull Library, C-012-019

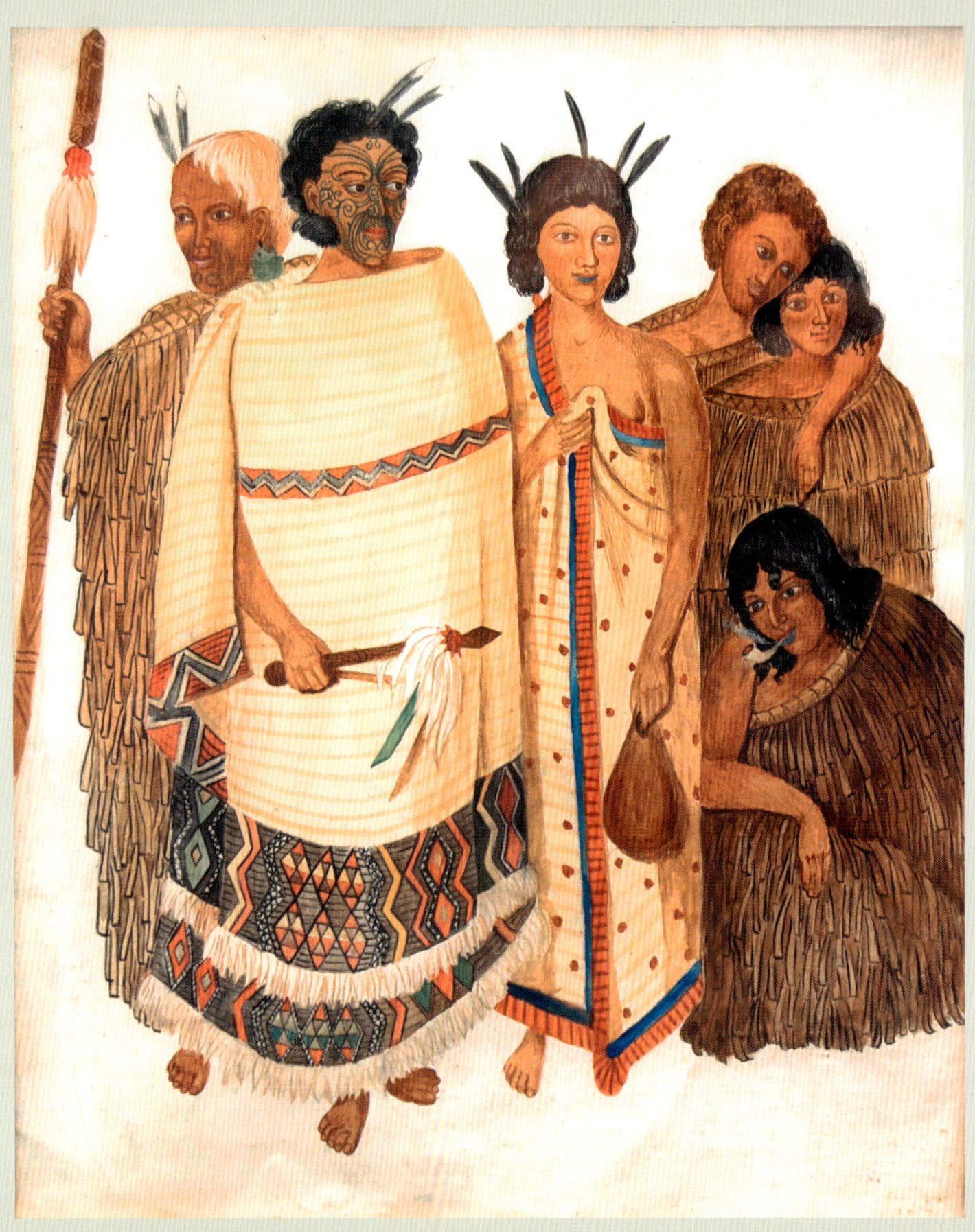

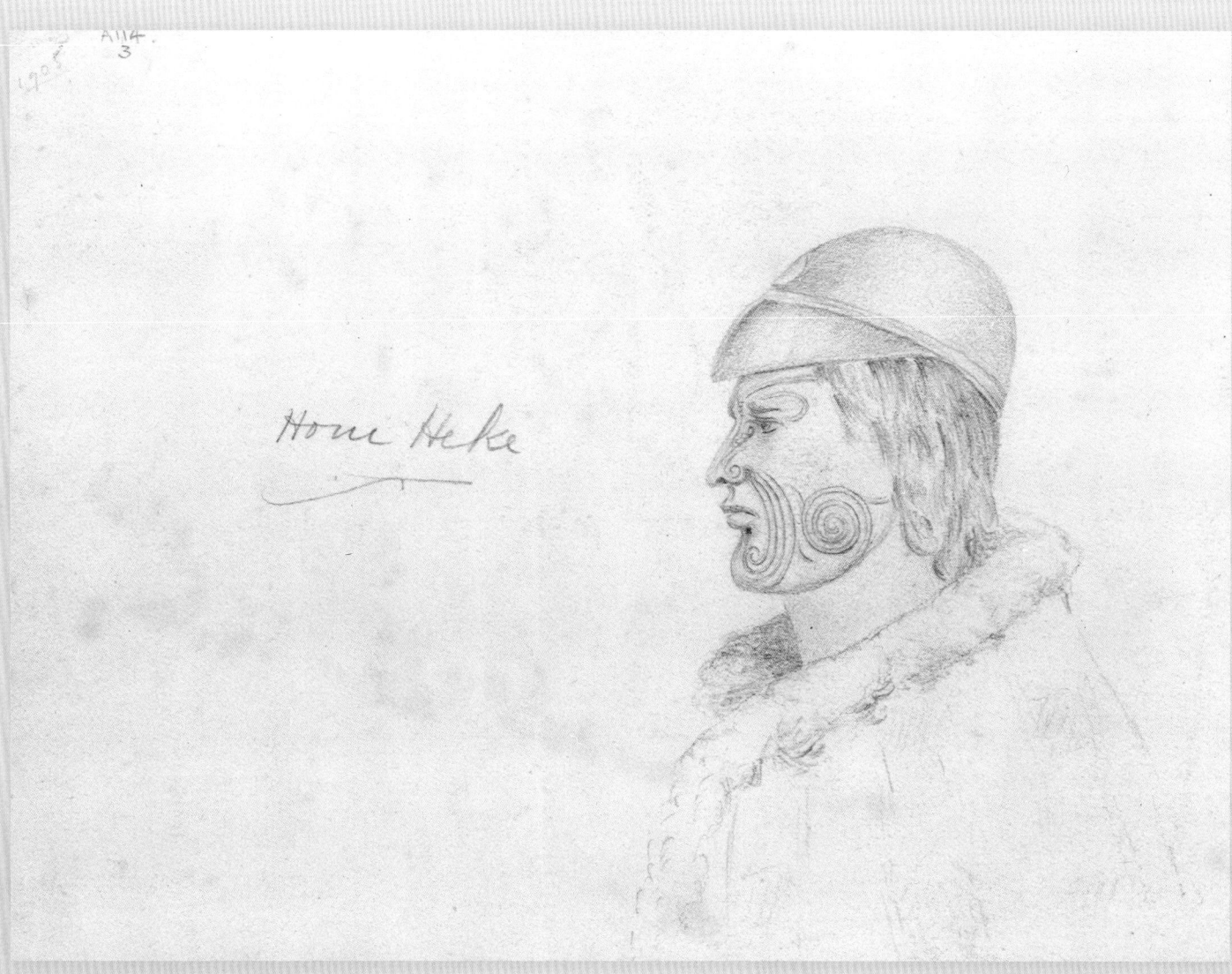

**John Alexander Gilfillan**, *copying Joseph Jenner Merrett, Honi [Hone] Heke*, **1847**

pencil, 114 x 101mm, Alexander Turnbull Library, A-114-003

Opposite: **Joseph Jenner Merrett,** *Hone Heke and his Wife Harriet with Four Attendants*, **1845**

watercolour, 227 x 222mm, Fletcher Trust Collection

## HE TIKANGA HŌU? FIGURATIVE ART IN RANGITUKIA IN 1838

NGARINO ELLIS

The arrival of Christianity meant different things to different iwi, and each denomination took a distinctive approach to converting Māori. CMS missionaries William Williams and William Yate were the first missionaries to arrive on the East Coast, at Hicks Bay in 1834. Knowledge about the new religion was already circulating, introduced by Māori traders and travellers. The missionaries were touring with several Ngāti Porou men whom they had rescued from a life of servitude as Ngāpuhi prisoners of war: the men had been taken north after a series of military raids by Hongi Hika and Pōmare, Tītore and Te Wera between 1818 and 1823. The triumphant return of the prisoners undoubtedly influenced the reception of Williams and Yate – and, ultimately, of Christianity.

The Māori evangelist Piripi Taumata a Kura was the most influential of the returnees: he was able to convince the local people of the importance of Christianity, and to build a chapel in which to worship. Though he was not a chief when he was taken north, he was certainly treated as one on his return because of the knowledge he brought – of religion, and of the Pākehā and their way of life and culture. The impact he made has been recorded in oral histories, as well as the names of the first native teachers, who were seen as 'missionaries in fact if not in name'.[1] The haka 'Tihei Taruke' composed by the Reverend Mohi Tūrei for the opening of St John's Church in Rangitukia in 1856 includes:

Rangitukia ra te pariha i tukua atu
   ai nga kai-whakaako tokowha:
Ruka ki Reporua
Hohepa ki Te Paripari
Kawhia ki Whangakareao
Apakura ki Whangapirita, e.

Rangitukia is the parish from which four
   evangelists were sent:
Ruka to Reporua,
Hohepa to Paripari,
Kawhia to Whangakareao,
Apakura to Whangapirita.[2]

The first chapels to be built on the East Coast were initiated by Taumata a Kura and the local rangatira, Uenuku, at Whakawhitirā pā (where Taumata a Kura was from); and by the rangatira Kakatarau and Enoka Rukuata at Rangitukia, a pā further out towards the coast. Taumata a Kura had seen chapels while being held a prisoner of war in the North.

The first chapel was built in Whakawhitirā between December 1838, when Henry Williams visited, and early April 1839, when his brother William Williams and Richard Taylor travelled to the coast. The building was made from adzed timber joined with timber nails, covered with sheets of bark 'sewn together with flax string', and the roof thatched with raupō. The chapel was separated from the pā by a palisaded fence with pou whakarae (carved posts) rising high every few metres. Taumata a Kura modelled the chapel on one they had seen in Paihia in 1827–1828. The Whakawhitirā chapel was replaced the following year, in May 1840, by a larger building with capacity for 1000 worshippers: it was distinctively Māori, with red-and-white-painted kōwhaiwhai on all the internal beams and the pulpit. Kōwhaiwhai was only just coming to the attention of European artists elsewhere, who compared its designs to moko. Its inclusion in the chapel at Whakawhitirā may have been the first time it was used in architecture on the East Coast.

In May 1840, William Williams visited the East Coast and saw a chapel at Rangitukia pā that Hemi Kiko, one of the native teachers, had built, working alongside Kakatarau and Enoka Rukuata (one of the returnees from the North). This chapel was rebuilt by November 1841, when missionary William Colenso described seeing a new building in the community. During those intervening months there had been a shift in political power, and Hone Rangikatia, a recently appointed native teacher who was active at Rangitukia, had been instrumental in rebuilding the chapel. Rangikatia was a rangatira in his own right, and had trained as a carpenter and cabinetmaker while he was in the North. The style of the chapel at Rangitukia was based on a thatched whare, with walls and roof of raupō and toetoe, attached to a tōtara framework. Inside there were several poutokomanawa that held up the tāhuhu, with whāriki mats covering the floor.

Rangitukia II was striking for three major features: the kōwhaiwhai, the figurative carving and the mural painting. Kōwhaiwhai was not included in either of the original chapels at Whakawhitirā or Rangitukia, but by 1840 it was a feature in both the rebuilt chapels: this reflects a level of confidence on the part of the builders in using traditional modes of decoration. The carving on the poutokomanawa in Rangitukia II depicted the biblical story in Numbers 21:9 where Moses follows God's direction to make a snake and mount it on a pole – a reference to the uplifting of the people through Christianity. The story was carved naturalistically on the poutokomanawa to ensure that it would be seen by all because of its central location in the chapel. This style of carving had no known precedent in the area: this single occurrence is an example of the innovation of the artists. Figurative carving was not repeated in

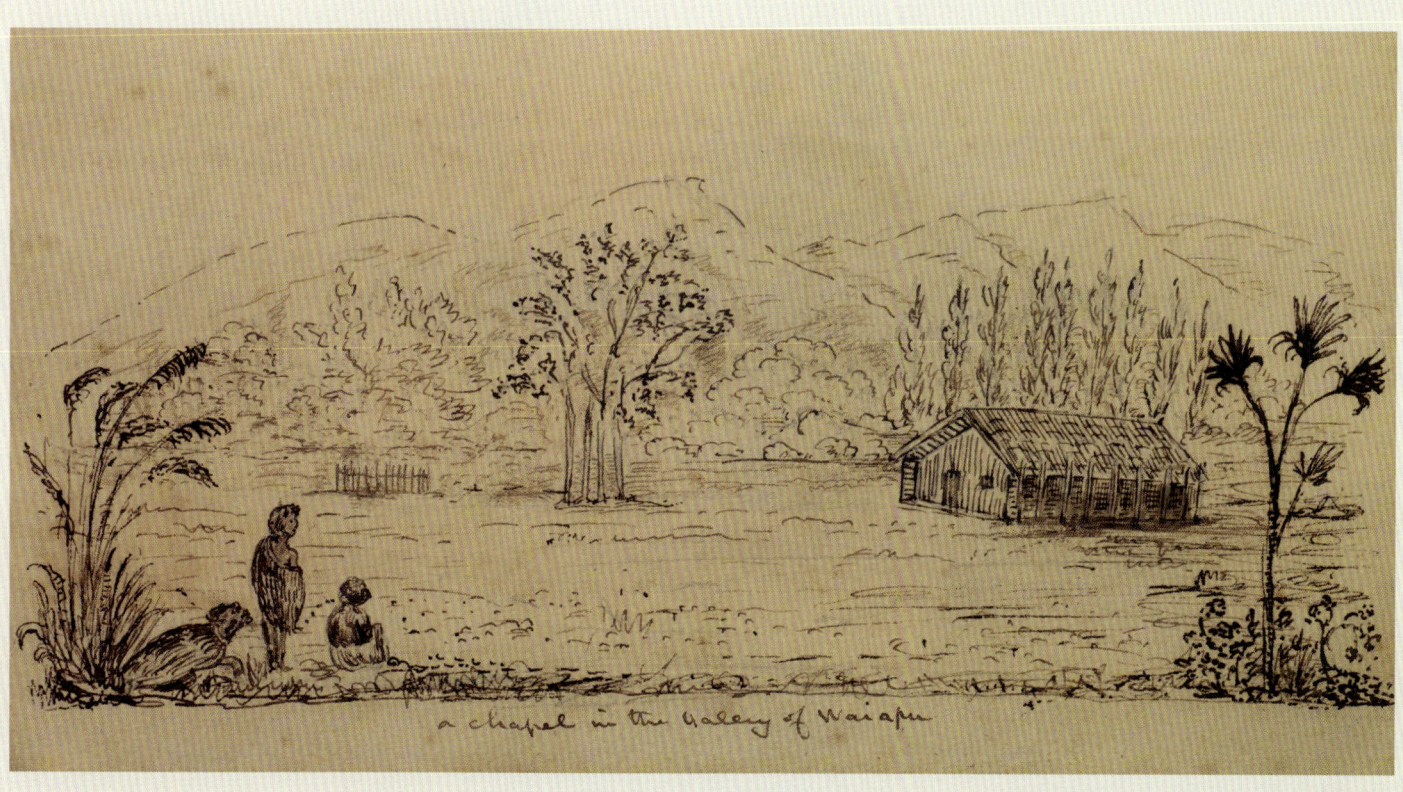

any other chapel elsewhere, although naturalistic carvings appeared in meeting houses from the 1860s onwards.

A third novel element in Rangitukia II was a painted mural representing William Williams in the act of preaching. This appears to be the first instance of figurative painting on the East Coast, and the depiction of a living person in the mural pre-dates this feature being used in other architectural forms by thirty years or more. Williams, though, was not impressed by this feature: he called it 'most hideous' and asked that the work be removed. It is not known whether it was changed; the church was rebuilt in the 1850s, and it was burnt down by Hauhau in 1865.

With these chapels, hapū were declaring their interest in Christianity, but they were also making clear their determination to worship on their terms. These Māori chapels were replaced by much larger churches built around the country from the 1840s, including the renowned Rangiātea at Ōtaki. These religious buildings were a public statement of iwi political autonomy in the face of increasing encroachment by non-Māori. The kōwhaiwhai and other elements were visible markers of culture, and highlighted the importance of the continuation of mana Māori across all forms of spirituality.

No drawing exists of the Rangitukia church – it may have looked like this one, which was drawn a year later, location unspecified except that it was in the Waiapu area, on the East Coast.
**Rev. Richard Taylor,** *A chapel in the valley of Waiapu*, **1839**
Tāmaki Paenga Hira Auckland War Memorial Museum, MS-302-30 neg.no. C229

256 | 257

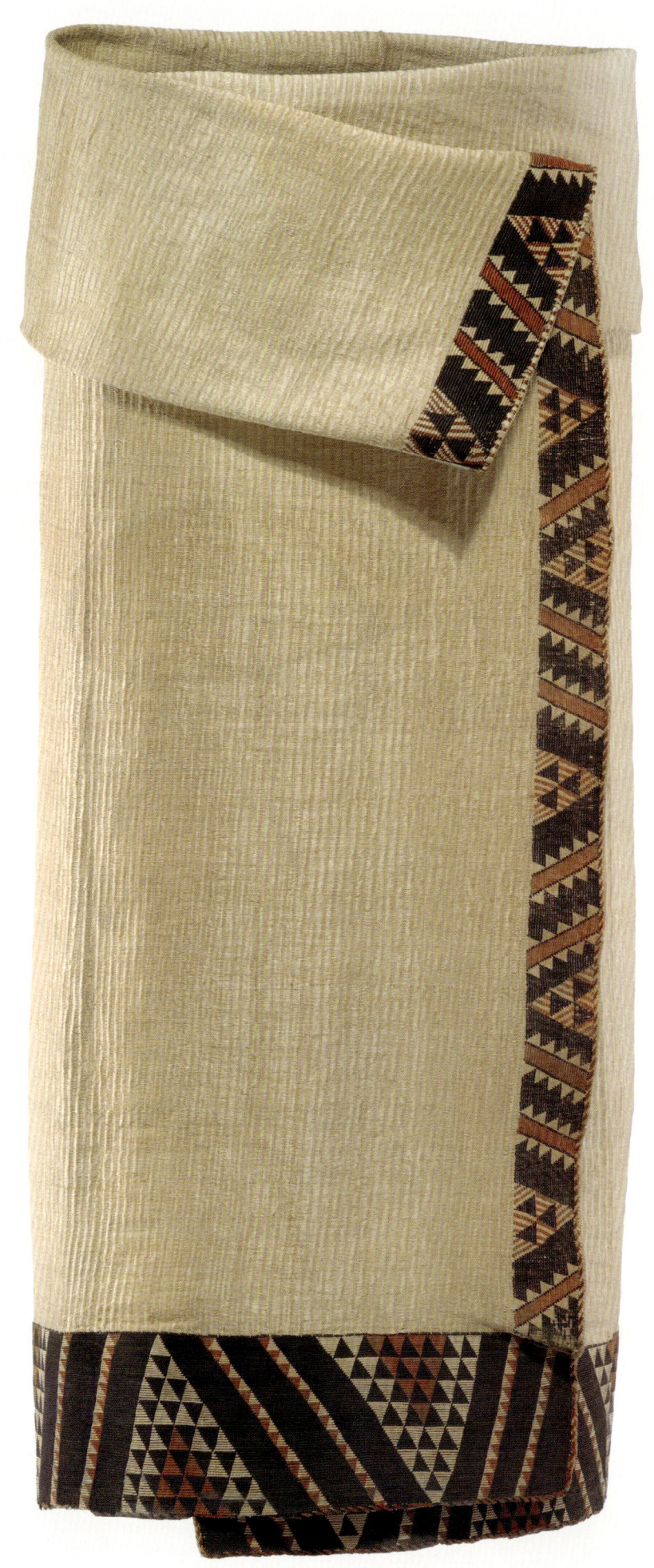

# 10 THE ART OF UTU
## DEIDRE BROWN

*He whakahohou rongo wāhine, he tatau pounamu.*

*A peace secured by a woman is as a greenstone doorway – durable and lasting.*

For Māori, art has been the mediator between life and death, peace and war. Māori social relationships and consequential co-management of resources and land boundaries depend on the maintenance of balance, sometimes through utu (reciprocal actions), such as the exchange of taonga. Taonga could be given as koha in the form of a present, offering, feast, donation or contribution to maintain social relationships in situations ranging from takawaenga (arranged marriages) that united groups to rongopai (the settlement of disputes). Disputes were also sometimes settled through muru (plundering another group's treasures), taua (war) and whakanoa (tapu removal through the desecration of objects and people). By these reciprocal actions, mana and tapu were either enhanced, maintained or lost.

Rangatira, as the promoters and defenders of group mana and tapu, introduced their weapons, whare, waka, hei tiki and cloaks into these social transactions to emphasise the sincerity of their utu, and the taonga themselves accumulated mana and tapu as they were exchanged.

Paepaeroa belonging to Te Ātiawa rangatira Ruhia Pōrutu, thrown over Pākehā boy Thomas McKenzie as protection in 1840.
Te Papa Tongarewa Museum of New Zealand, DE000107/1

Many of these taonga were given personal names and took on lives of their own as they passed between kaitiaki, were displayed at important exchange ceremonies and became the subject of waiata. In the nineteenth century, even as newly introduced weapons, architecture, adornments and clothing effectively stifled the production of these chiefly taonga, they maintained their status as utu and were used to strengthen inter-hapū, inter-iwi and cross-cultural relationships.

As with other aspects of Māori culture, there were male and female dimensions to the exchange of taonga as utu: taonga associated with female makers and leaders were often used to divert aggression or form new alliances; and taonga presented by men were sometimes weapons used in the conflicts they had settled. This distinction was critical in the settlement of differences. As Ngāti Porou leader Matutaera Nihoniho, who fought in the New Zealand Wars, explained:

Ki te houia e te tane te rongo o te whawhai, e kore e mau, ka kiia tera he rongo tama-tane, he atua, he taitahae. Engari ka riro ma te wahine e hohou te rongo, ka kiia tera he rongo tama-wahine, ka mau te rongo, he rongo taketake.

If a peace is concluded in time of war by men, it will not be a firm or lasting one. It is termed a male peace, and stands for treachery, deceit, trouble. But if women assume the function of making peace, that is known as a female peace, and it will be a firm, durable one.[1]

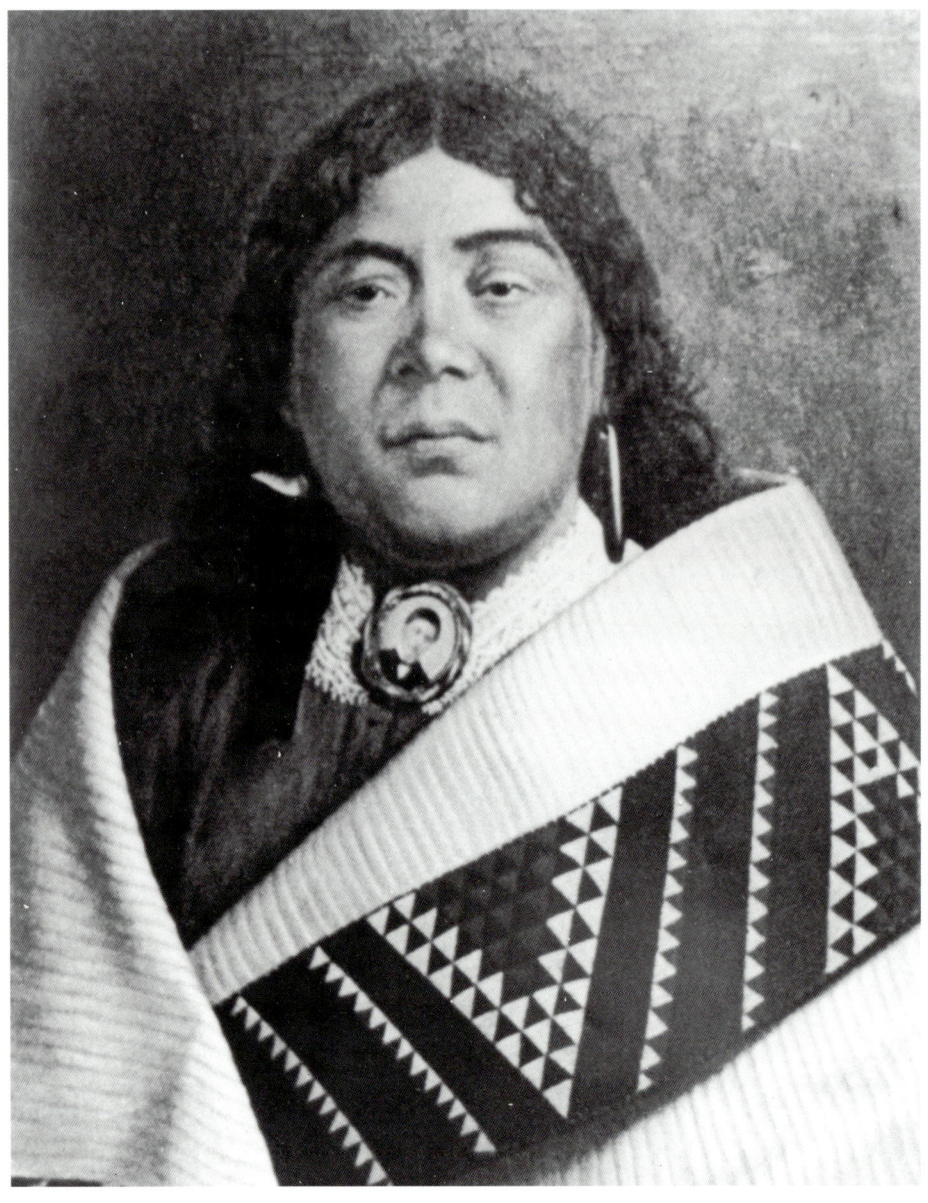

Ruhia Pōrutu, daughter-in-law of Te Rira Pōrutu, paramount chief of Te Ātiawa at Thorndon, wearing her paepaeroa. The cloak is worn upside down to show the bottom tāniko border.
Alexander Turnbull Library, PAColl-5345-1

Pounamu is identified as the female element of utu exchanged between male leaders in the famous whakataukī, 'He whakahohou rongo wāhine, he tatau pounamu' (A peace secured by a woman is as a greenstone doorway – durable and lasting).[2] Women and pounamu both feature prominently in narratives passed down about the art of utu.

### Te taonga o rongo – taonga utu and women

Women participated in the art of utu as makers, receivers of gifts, and partners of equally ranked men in strategic marriages between groups. If we were to liken the fabric of Māori social relationships to a kākahu, then women were the wefts that kept the warps of relationships together.

Cloaks have always been highly valued for their protective properties, so it is not surprising that they were used in utu transactions. Tightly woven kaitaka were an effective armour against taiaha and patu blows to the body during battle, and they could prevent an assault if the owner of the garment was a person of mana. In 1840, Te Ātiawa rangatira Ruhia Pōrutu threw her paepaeroa over a Pākehā boy, Thomas McKenzie, to save his life after he had taken shelter in a house that local Māori were building, without realising his actions had broken the tapu. Pōrutu and McKenzie became lifelong friends, and when McKenzie died, her paepaeroa was draped over him once more when it was placed on his funeral casket in 1911.[3] When a rangatira removed their cloak – and, thereby, their protection and mana – and placed it in front of another

THE ART OF UTU

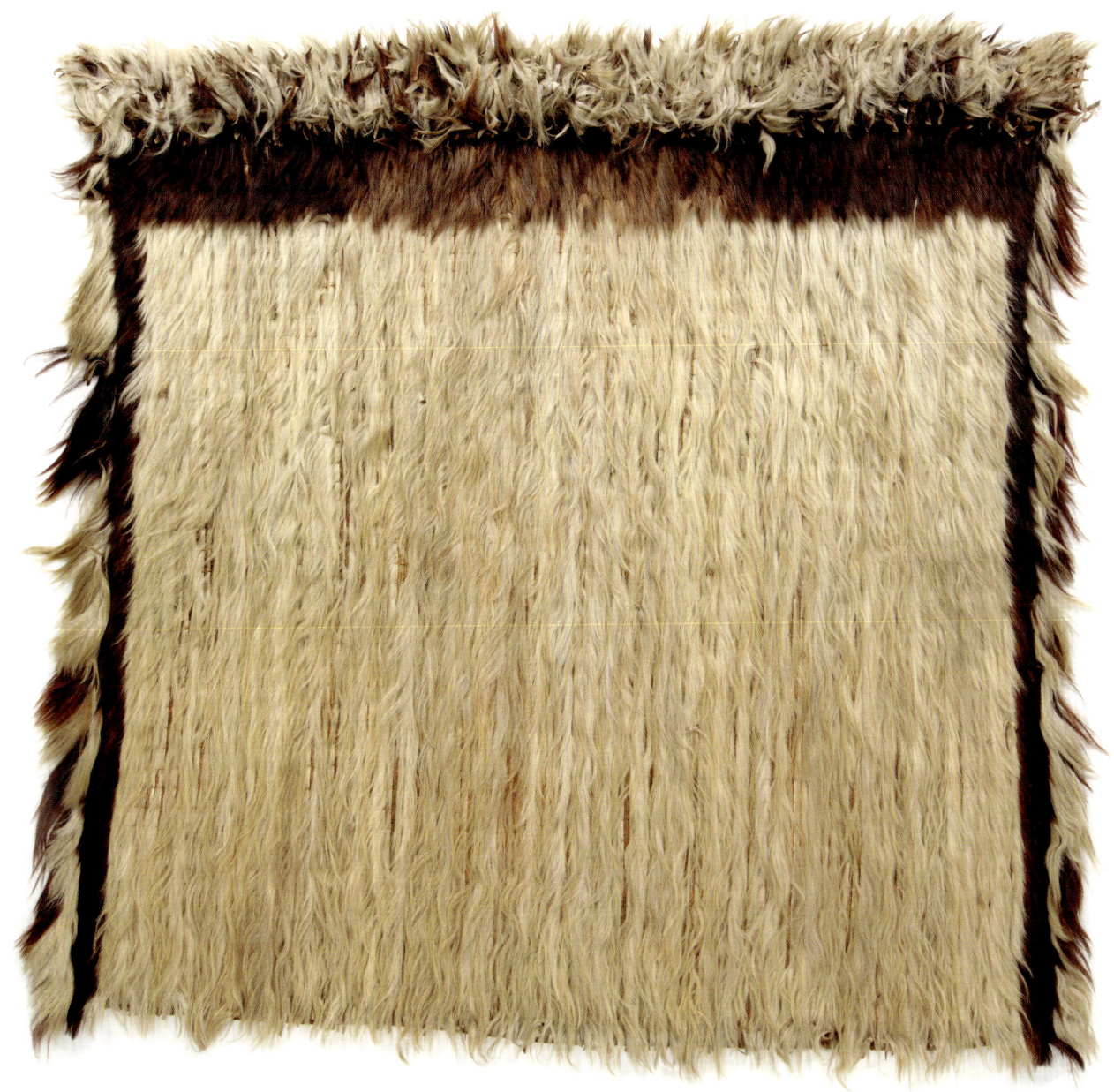

leader, they were demonstrating their peaceful intentions and, sometimes, humility. Te Pahi laid down his kaitaka when he met the governor of New South Wales, Philip Gidley King, at Parramatta in 1805; and Hongi Hika and Waikato laid down their cloaks before King George IV at Carlton House in London in 1820. Cloaks were embedded with the mana of the wearer, and this mana could be transferred – making these prized garments ideal as exchange items in utu transactions.

Because of their scale and complexity, cloaks, like waka and whare, were often made by collectives. The names of individual makers have been passed down where their identity is integral to the mana and tapu of the taonga. Parerautuu was the weaver of the celebrated kahu kurī Te Kahumamae o Parerautuu, her 'cloak of pain', which

Te Kahumamae o Parerautuu, Parerautuu's 'cloak of pain'. This cloak has a muka foundation over which strips of dog skin have been sewn. The cloak is predominantly white, with a brown border along the top and sides, and a fringe of short white and brown strips.
Tāmaki Paenga Hira Auckland War Memorial Museum, 812, 481

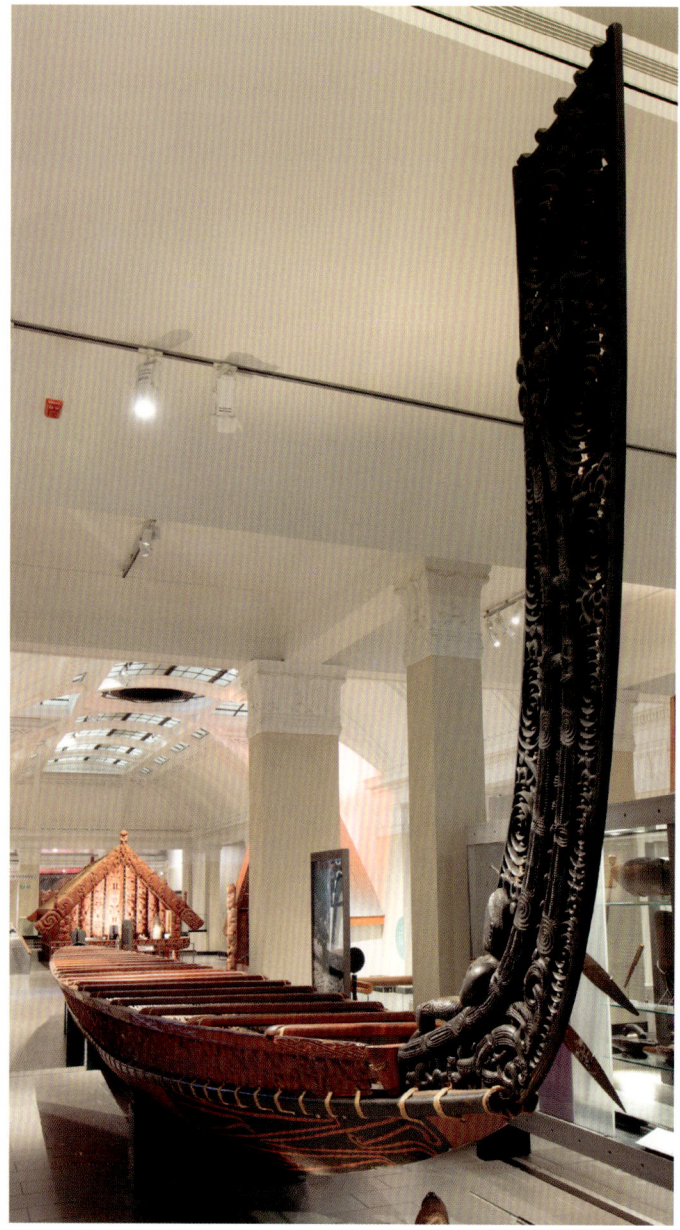

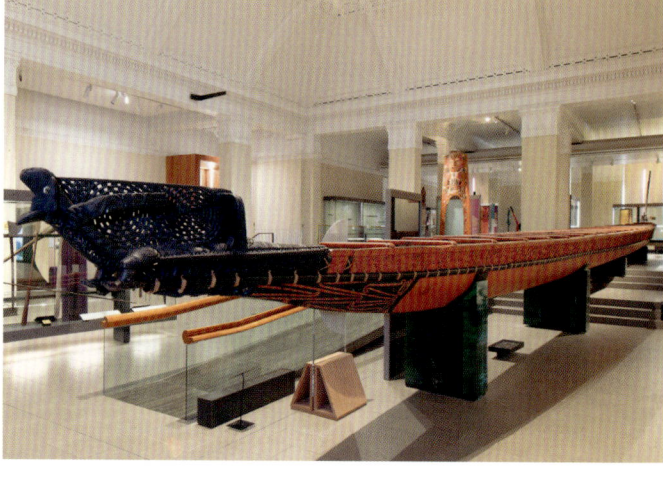

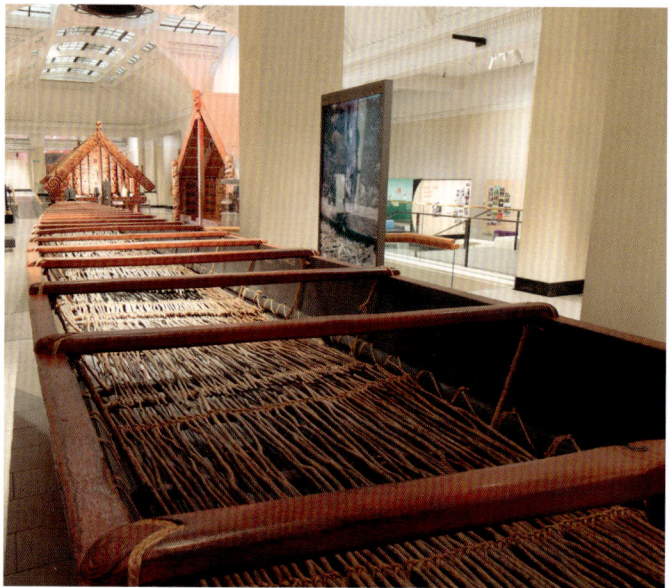

Te Waaka Perohuka exchanged a cloak known as Karamaene for the hull of the waka taua *Te Toki a Tāpiri*, shown here.
Tāmaki Paenga Hira Auckland War Memorial Museum, 150;290

she constructed from the pelts of dogs that had belonged to several Ngāti Rangitihi rangatira who had been killed by Tūhoe in the 1821 battle of Pukekaikahu. As a descendant of both Ngāti Rangitihi and Tūhoe, Parerautūtu's grief must have been unbearable. Parerautūtu went to meet with the Waikato leader Tukorehu to try to persuade him to take up her cause for utu. She sat silently on his marae for several days without speaking or eating, wearing Te Kahumamae. He acknowledged her cause by relieving her of the cloak of pain and placing it on his own shoulders.[4] Tūhoe returned the remains of Ngāti Rangitihi warriors a short time later and peace was eventually achieved between the two groups through strategic marriages.

Te Kahumamae o Parerautūtu was passed down to Tukorehu's grandson, Rewi Maniapoto, who presented it to Ihakara Tukumaru of Ngāti Raukawa to celebrate the birth of his daughter. Ihakara gifted the cloak to Ngāti Tūwharetoa rangatira Poihipi Tukairangi in 1866; the cloak passed to Gilbert Mair nine years later and then into the collections of Tāmaki Paenga Hira Auckland War Memorial Museum.[5] Te Kahumamae o Parerautūtu was repatriated to Parerautūtu's descendants in 1993.

Production was closely associated with gender – male for waka, female for cloaks. The exchange of these taonga would have reinforced the complementarity of men and women's roles in Māori society. Kākahu and waka were

THE ART OF UTU

present in utu transaction stories from the earliest times. Turi gave his father-in-law Toto a kahu kurī in exchange for the waka *Aotea* so that he could bring a founding Polynesian population from Hawaiki to Aotearoa: the cloak was of such mana and importance that even the names of the dogs whose pelts the garment was made from are still remembered today.[6] Rongawhakaata rangatira Te Waaka Perohuka exchanged the cloak Karamaene for the hull of the celebrated waka taua *Te Toki a Tāpiri*, which was originally made for Te Waaka Tarakau of Ngāti Kahungunu by the carvers Tamati Parangi and Paratene Te Pohoi in 1836 and is currently the centrepiece of Auckland Museum's Māori exhibition space.[7] Unfortunately, though, there is no published record of the person or people who were responsible for Karamaene's manufacture. In at least one instance, a cloak was used to settle a dispute concerning waka. When Rongowhakaata attacked Maramatawhana pā on the Ūawa River in retribution over the failure to return the borrowed waka *Te Wherowhero*, the dispute was settled only when the local chief Tawaputa offered his cloak called Ruataraongaonga as utu.[8] In all of these exchange stories, cloaks assume the mana of their owners and eventually assume their own identity as emissaries of goodwill.

Women also received important taonga within utu contexts. The Ngāti Awa wharenui Hotunui (see page 52), now in Auckland Museum, was originally a gift from Apanui Te Hamaiwaho to his daughter Mereana Mokomoko on the occasion of her wedding, but not before she was called on to use her personal mana to avert tragedy during the fraught construction process. While the wharenui was being built in 1878, a number of the male builders became seriously unwell and died soon after eating food cooked in a fire made by local women from woodchips off the house. This was a violation of both the tapu of the house and carving practice, and the illness was described by some as a mate ruahine (sickness caused by women).

Mokomoko restored balance to the situation by using her own mana – which was considered equivalent to her father's – and consuming kūmara cooked in another fire made from Hotunui's woodchips. Later, she and two other women participated in the whai kawa ceremony: this involved crossing the paepae of Hotunui to remove the tapu from the house and enable its daily use. Mokomoko was thus central to the reason for the construction of Hotunui, as well as the remedy to the violation of tapu and the ritual to lift the tapu of the house.

Perhaps unsettled by the deaths that had occurred during construction, the house builders refused any further customary koha for their services beyond the food and gifts given during the project. Mokomoko's father-in-law Wirope Hotereni Taipari felt that utu had not yet been realised. A thoroughly contemporary resolution was reached when Mokomoko presented £1000 to the builders as a cash payment on behalf of Taipari – a form of remuneration that at this time would have sat outside of traditional gifting protocols and therefore did not invoke tapu.[9]

One exchange, of mere pounamu for cloaks as part of a dispute settlement, illustrates how types of taonga could have specific purposes in rebalancing relationships. The transaction took place between Te Arawa and Ngāiterangi, and it served to end twenty generations of conflict over the Ngāiterangi's occupation of Maketu. Powerful and important taonga were required after such a long period of warfare: in this case the leading rangatira of each group exchanged korowai, mere pounamu and offspring in marriage. At least one of the mere pounamu had been actively used in the battles and was therefore intimately associated with the mauri and wairua of its victims: the exchange of weapons such as these was tantamount to 'returning' these fallen warriors to their people and closing the (pounamu) door on animosity. Amity was then initiated through the exchange of the leaders' korowai, and marriages between their children. Marriage ensured that the whakapapa of the groups could never be untangled and it also provided access rights to previously disputed territory. When the rangatira died, the korowai they had received were buried with them to ensure that the peace between Te Arawa and Ngāiterangi could never be retracted. Only the mere pounamu that originally belonged to Te Arawa was interred with the Ngāiterangi leader, permanently ending war; the Ngāiterangi mere pounamu was passed down through generations of Te Arawa until it was deposited in Rotorua Museum.[10]

What these exchanges illustrate is that utu transactions were complex and potentially gendered, and certain taonga were employed to perform certain roles in permanently resolving disputes and relationships. This was not just a case of ending 'past' disputes in order to move 'forward' into the future, as might be expected in a linear chronology. The outcome was a peace situated in a continuous cycle of time. Taonga associated with war and charged with the

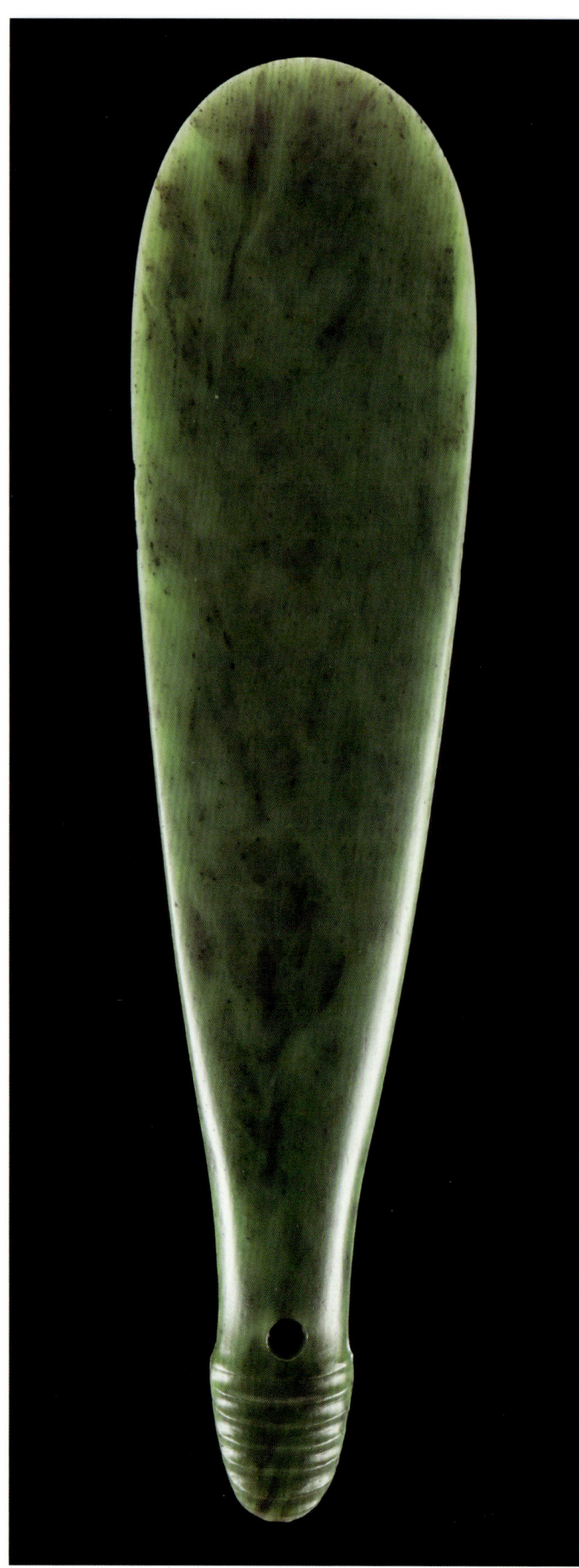

wairua and mauri of deceased ancestors were exchanged to settle the spirits of those ancestors. The living and generations to come thus became engaged in an enduring peace.

### Te tatau pounamu o Te Rauparaha – Te Rauparaha's greenstone door

Peace between iwi, made to settle conflicts, often involved the exchange of taonga such as weapons and waka taua used to transport fighting parties. These taonga were also important agents in the transference of mana between succeeding rangatira. Taonga pounamu ensured an enduring peace and, with stone resources carefully controlled by Ngāi Tahu, they became an insignia of rangatiratanga. Many Māori leaders coveted pounamu, none more so than Te Rauparaha.

The acquisition of pounamu was a recurring theme in Te Rauparaha's leadership of Ngāti Toa. He had been educated in close combat fighting at a time before iron and muskets began to replace pounamu tools and weapons. He associated pounamu with the practical and symbolic instruments of leadership, and therefore with his own mana and identity as a rangatira. While he was still a child, he became weapons-bearer to his uncle Hape-ki-tūārangi of Ngāti Raukawa, and carried his taiaha and patu into battle.[11] When Hape-ki-tūārangi passed away, his mana and leadership position within Ngāti Raukawa were ceremonially passed to Te Rauparaha by his marriage to his uncle's widow Te Akau, and his inheritance of the late chief's celebrated mere pounamu Amokura.[12]

Engagements with the South Island Ngāi Tahu iwi between 1827 and 1828 enabled Te Rauparaha to acquire more taonga. Te Rauparaha and his forces, armed with muskets, attacked those groups in the northern South Island who had made an unsuccessful attempt to overthrow Ngāti Toa on Kapiti Island in 1824.[13] Once again, taonga were used as instruments of utu: a number of the waka taua Te Rauparaha used in these battles were ones the same enemy had abandoned during the Kapiti incident.[14] The enemy thus suffered the double humiliation of defeat by their own taonga. Te Rauparaha took his celebrated taiaha Kimihia, named after his grandfather, to a subsequent battle at Kaikōura.[15]

Te Rauparaha and a reduced entourage travelled from Kaikōura to Kaiapoi, where there were known to be quantities of pounamu.[16] A number of Ngāti Toa entered Kaiapoi pā to trade for pounamu, while Te Rauparaha remained outside the

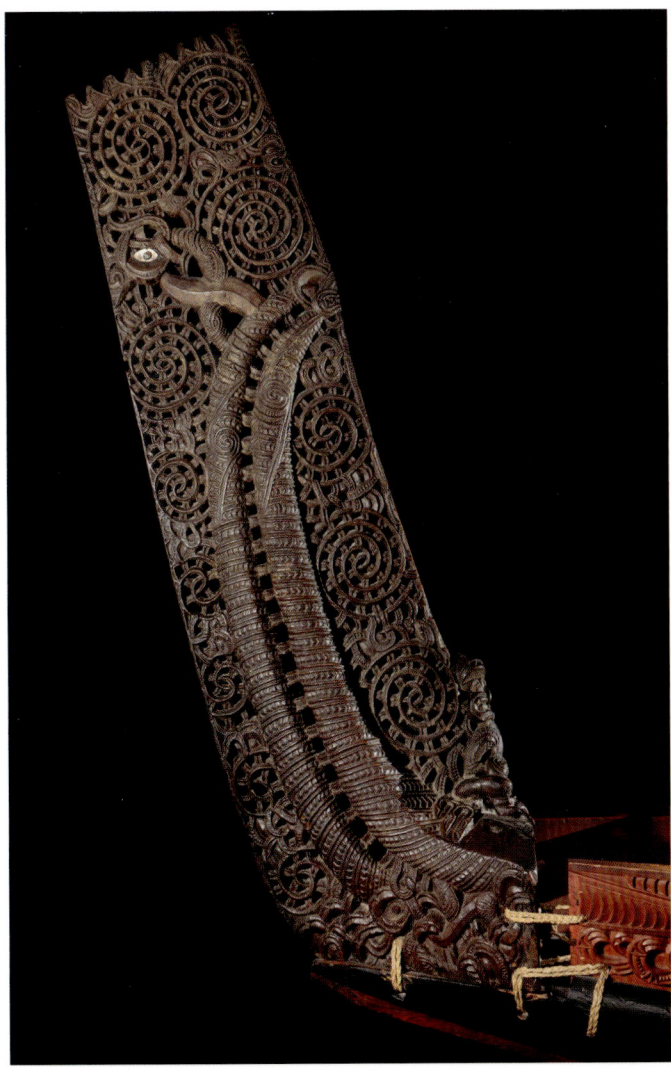

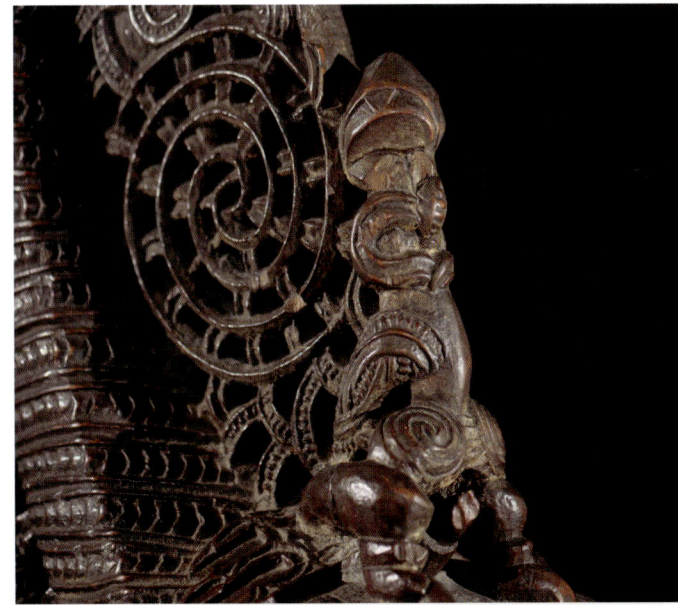

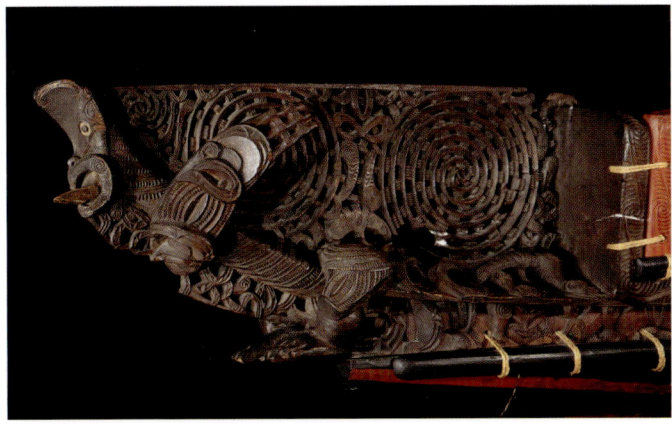

palisades, where he traded muskets for pounamu, giving the mere pounamu Te Kāoreore to a younger relative who was going into the pā.[17] The name Te Kāoreore has ancient origins and has been given to more than one mere pounamu: the first was made by Tamaahua, who arrived at Wairau on the migratory *Kurahaupō* waka and took a pounamu block to Taranaki, where he crafted this mere pounamu, as well as a toki known as Tamapinaki and a pendant called Parakore.[18]

Aware of Ngāti Toa's earlier attacks further north, Ngāi Tahu were particularly careful in their dealings with Te Rauparaha's party. However, a conflict arose inside the pā, with accounts differing as to the cause, and several Ngāti Toa were killed.[19] Te Rauparaha and his forces returned to the area in the summer of 1831/1832 and took Kaiapoi pā and Ōnawe pā in Akaroa.[20] Within two years, however, they had reached a stalemate with Ngāi Tahu, who by that stage had accumulated enough muskets to repel them.[21]

Te Rauparaha's waka taua *Waikahua* was exchanged for the Ngāi Tahu mere pounamu Tuhiwai in 1843 to cement the peace between Ngāti Toa and Ngāi Tahu. The tauihu and tauarapa of *Waikahua* are shown here.
Tūhura Otago Museum, D34.147, D34.148, Kapiti Coast

Opposite: Te Rauparaha was given the mere pounamu Amokura, shown here, after the death of its owner, Hape-ki-tūārangi, to demonstrate the inheritance of his mana.
Te Papa Tongarewa Museum of New Zealand, ME011850, gift of Roger Chorlton, 1968

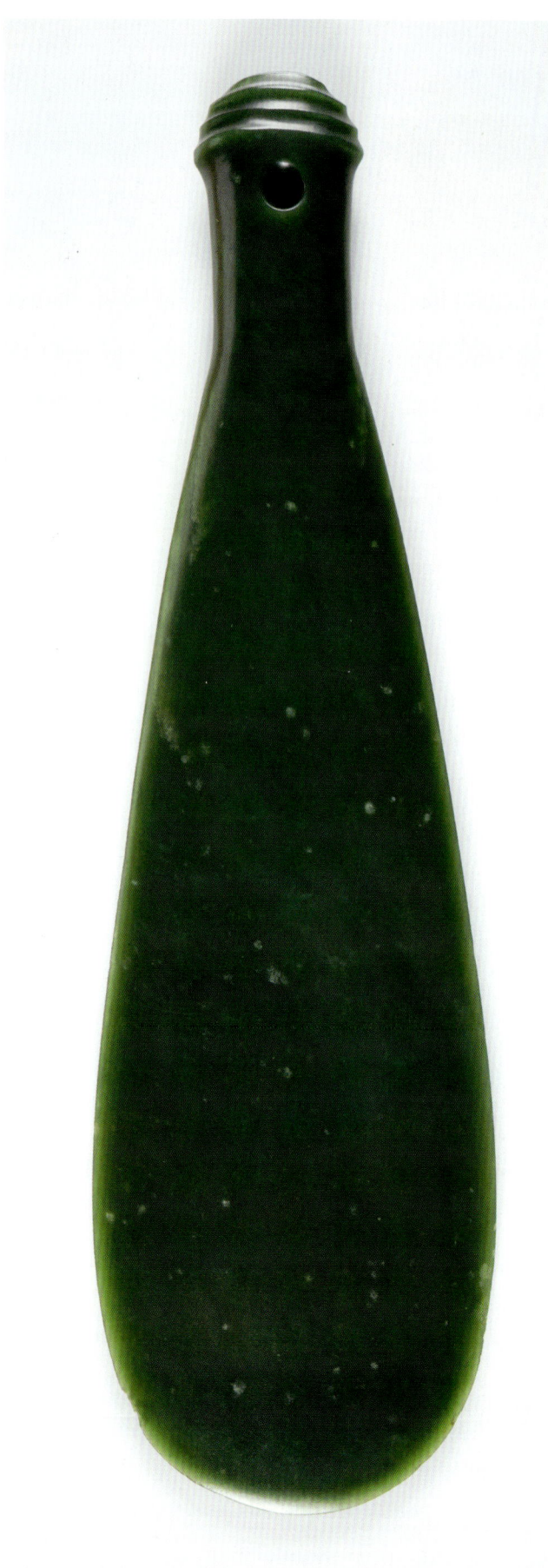

Taonga played an important role in establishing peace during the years that followed. In 1834, Ngāi Tahu rangatira Ihu offered Paewhenua (described at this time as a mere pounamu), Te Kāoreore (which had stayed in Ngāi Tahu possession after the attack on Kaiapoi pā) and other taonga to Te Rauparaha at Karauripē (Cloudy Bay), to persuade Te Rauparaha not to send a war party to Ōtākou and Murihiku.[22] Although Te Rauparaha did not accept what must have been, for him, a tempting utu, he did not proceed with his plans.

To end any further animosity between their tribes, Te Mātenga Taiaroa of Ngāi Tahu exchanged a mere pounamu known as Tuhiwai for Te Rauparaha's waka taua *Waikahua*.[23] *Waikahua* was one of four waka – the others are *Ahikākāriki*, *Parinuiowhiti* and *Waikatohu* – commissioned by Te Rauparaha in 1828 and carved from timber felled on Te Rangihaeata's lands. The taurapa and tauihu of *Waikahua* are currently on display at Otago Museum.[24]

Tuhiwai was acclaimed for its formal qualities and high standard of manufacture. The mere pounamu possessed remarkable powers of divination while under the guardianship of Te Rauparaha, who would perform the ritual of tuhiwai (striking water) with the taonga to gain matakite (foresight) for future strategic decisions.[25] Tuhiwai was said to move of its own volition, and it had the ability to change colour: it grew lighter to signal upcoming good fortune, and darker when difficult times lay ahead or one of Te Rauparaha's descendants passed away.[26] The Wineera whānau became the kaitiaki of Tuhiwai and presented the taonga to the Dominion Museum in 1963.[27]

Constructing a linear 'history' for taonga like Tuhiwai, Paewhenua and Te Kāoreore is difficult, as Ngāti Toa and Ngāi Tahu narratives can appear at odds with one another. Like human whakapapa, the sequential events related to Māori art do not necessarily progress in a linear fashion and can attach themselves to other taonga. Further complexity arises when more than one taonga is given the same name.

The mere pounamu Tuhiwai.
Te Papa Tongarewa Museum of New Zealand, ME010922, gift of the Wineera family, 1963

**Opposite:** Mere pounamu given by Tītore to Captain Frederick Sadler of HMS *Buffalo* in 1834.
British Museum, Oc1896,-.929

THE ART OF UTU

Any attempt to identify the 'authentic' story of taonga used in utu transactions somewhat misses the point of understanding the trajectories of these treasures within hapū and iwi. For Te Rauparaha, the acquisition and exchange of taonga marked important turning points in Ngāti Toa history, and a binding peace symbolised by the strength of te tatau pounamu, the metaphorical greenstone door.

### Tītore's utu

Enterprising rangatira in the early 1800s sometimes sought to enhance their community's mana and resources by giving taonga to visiting European and American trading vessels, in order to create ongoing reciprocal relationships. Through these utu transactions, the leaders planned to establish their communities as preferred suppliers for timber and provisions such as potatoes (which helped prevent scurvy on board ship) in return for iron and, later, muskets. Tītore, a Ngāti Rēhia rangatira, seized on such an opportunity when the British naval storeship HMS *Buffalo* arrived at Kororāreka in the Bay of Islands in 1833 to acquire timber for masts and booms.[28] He directed the *Buffalo* to Whangaroa Harbour and its abundant kauri forests; there he organised a large party of men to work alongside the crew for six months, felling trees and dressing the timber, for which they received 200 muskets with ammunition, as well as blankets, fishhooks, tobacco, iron pots and forks.[29] When the *Buffalo* departed on 26 June 1834, Tītore and his people presented the crew with kaitaka, mere pounamu and other customary weapons, and presented the ship's captain, Frederick Sadler, with personal gifts designed to oblige him to return, as well as other presents for delivery to King William IV in Britain.

Sadler's family kept his gifts from Tītore until July 1896, when his granddaughter Belle Sadler offered nine for sale to the British Museum. The museum purchased four: a mere pounamu; a unique split or double-headed pounamu hei tiki with a bone toggle; a kōauau made of human bone; and a whalebone aurei.[30] A sketch by Belle Sadler shows that the remaining taonga were another pounamu hei tiki, a taiaha, and three non-Māori items – a 'polished wooden stick or club carved at either end' (likely a Fijian bowai or pole club), and two long objects that are possibly Fijian i-ula tavatava throwing sticks.[31]

One measure of a rangatira's mana was their social and economic networks, which in Tītore's case extended well

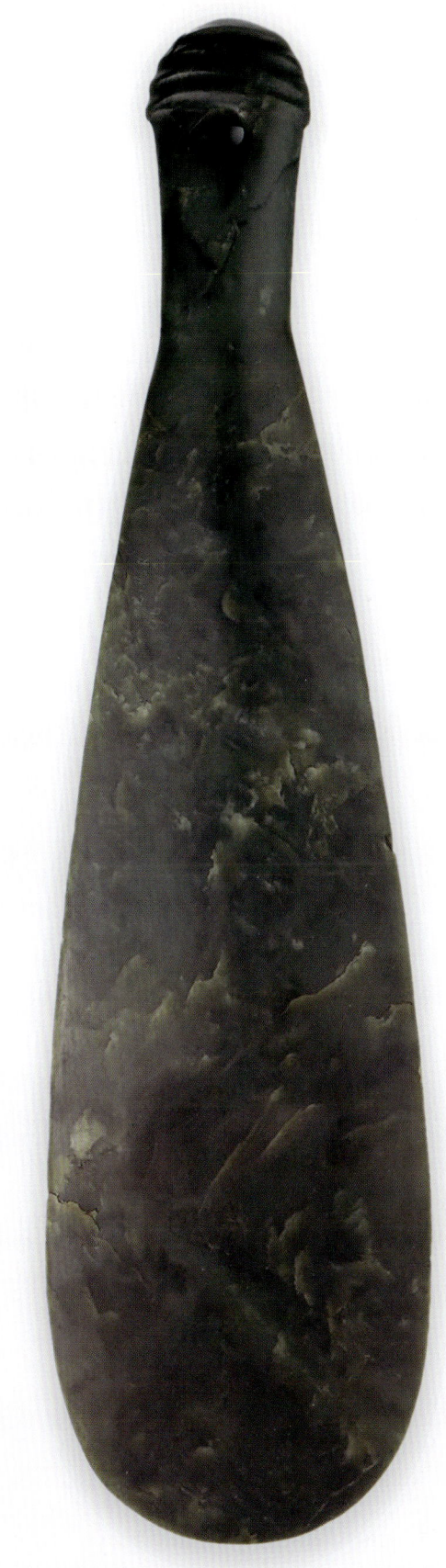

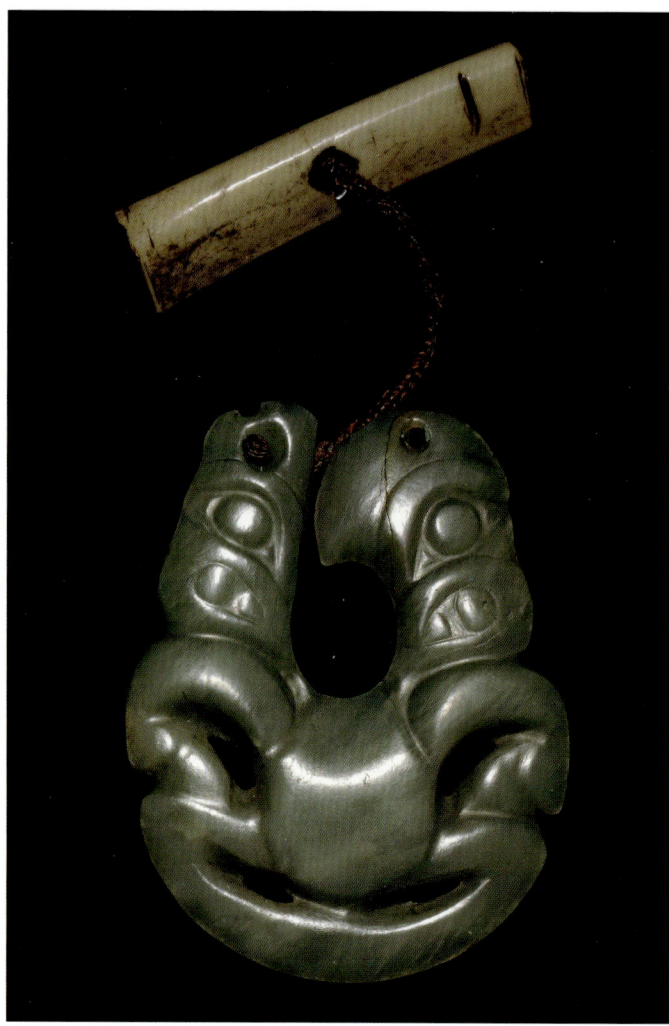

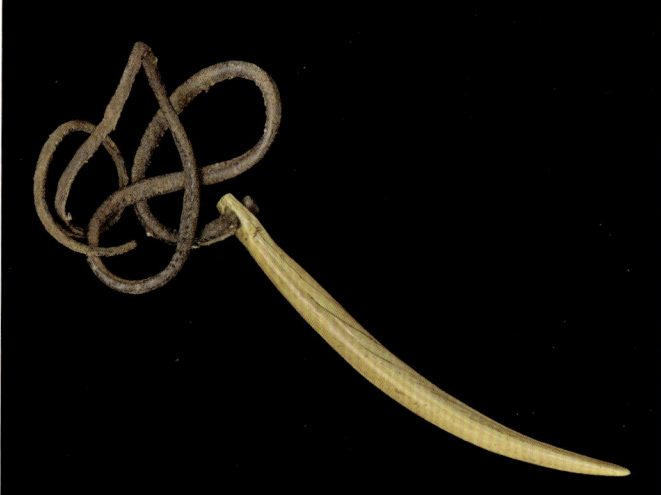

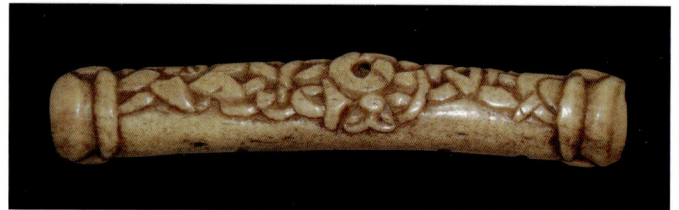

Gifts given by Tītore to Captain Frederick Sadler of HMS *Buffalo* in 1834; clockwise from top left: hei tiki, whale ivory aurei, kōauau made from human bone.
British Museum, Oc1896,-.925.b EOC9500 00818565001; Oc1896,-.930 EOC9503 162090001; Oc1896,-.931

beyond the shores of Aotearoa – an attribute he clearly wanted to demonstrate to his British trading partner.[32] The exchange networks required for pounamu sourced in South Island West Coast rivers to arrive in Northland would have meant any object made from it was highly valuable. Tītore, together with the rangatira Patuone from the Hokianga, gave Sadler a gift for King William comprised of two kaitaka and two mere, one of which Tītore called Puwaro – its naming was an indication of its considerable mana.[33] Tītore added, in a transcribed letter to the king, that he would be happy to supply the British navy with timber to build battleships to fight the French, whom Tītore and other northern rangatira saw as a potential enemy.[34]

Tītore and Patuone's gifts were taken to the British Admiralty soon after the *Buffalo* arrived in Portsmouth on 20 November 1834, along with instructions from Sadler about 'the motives of these chiefs in sending the presents and the New Zealand custom of a return being made'.[35] The current whereabouts of the kaitaka and mere is not known, but the king did send suits of armour back to Aotearoa for the rangatira. Tītore's armour became a taonga tuku iho in its own right and was exchanged through a chain of chiefs including Te Wherowhero (Waikato), Taonui Hīkaka I (Ngāti Maniapoto), Te Heuheu (Tūwharetoa), Aperahama Ruke (from Taupō) and Hori Kingi Te Anaua (Whanganui),

Opposite: Tītore's suit of armour, as seen at Paripari, Northland, 1844.
**George French Angas, *Suit of armour*, c.1860s**
pencil, 283 x 232mm, National Library of Australia, PIC Solander Box A17 #R6586

THE ART OF UTU

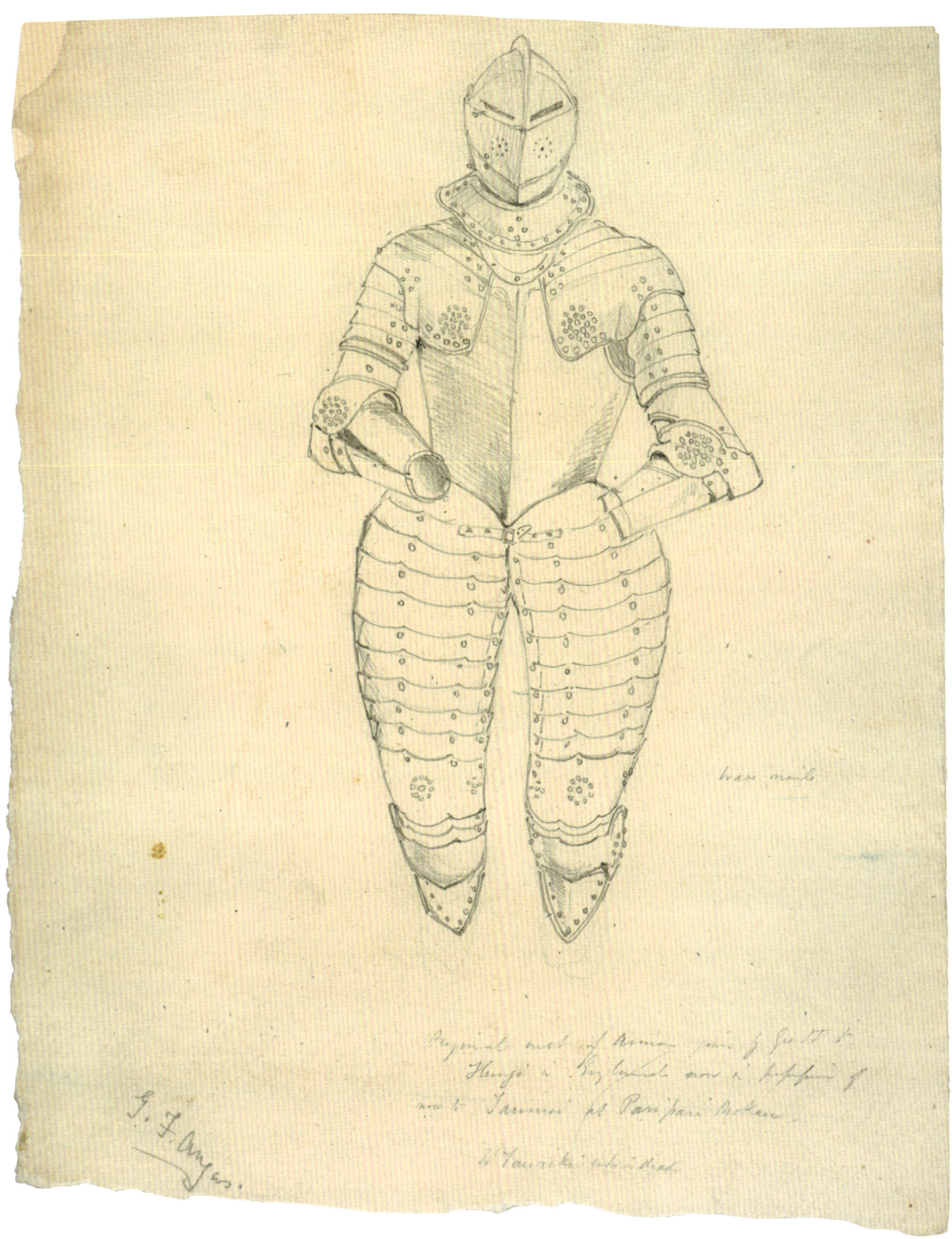

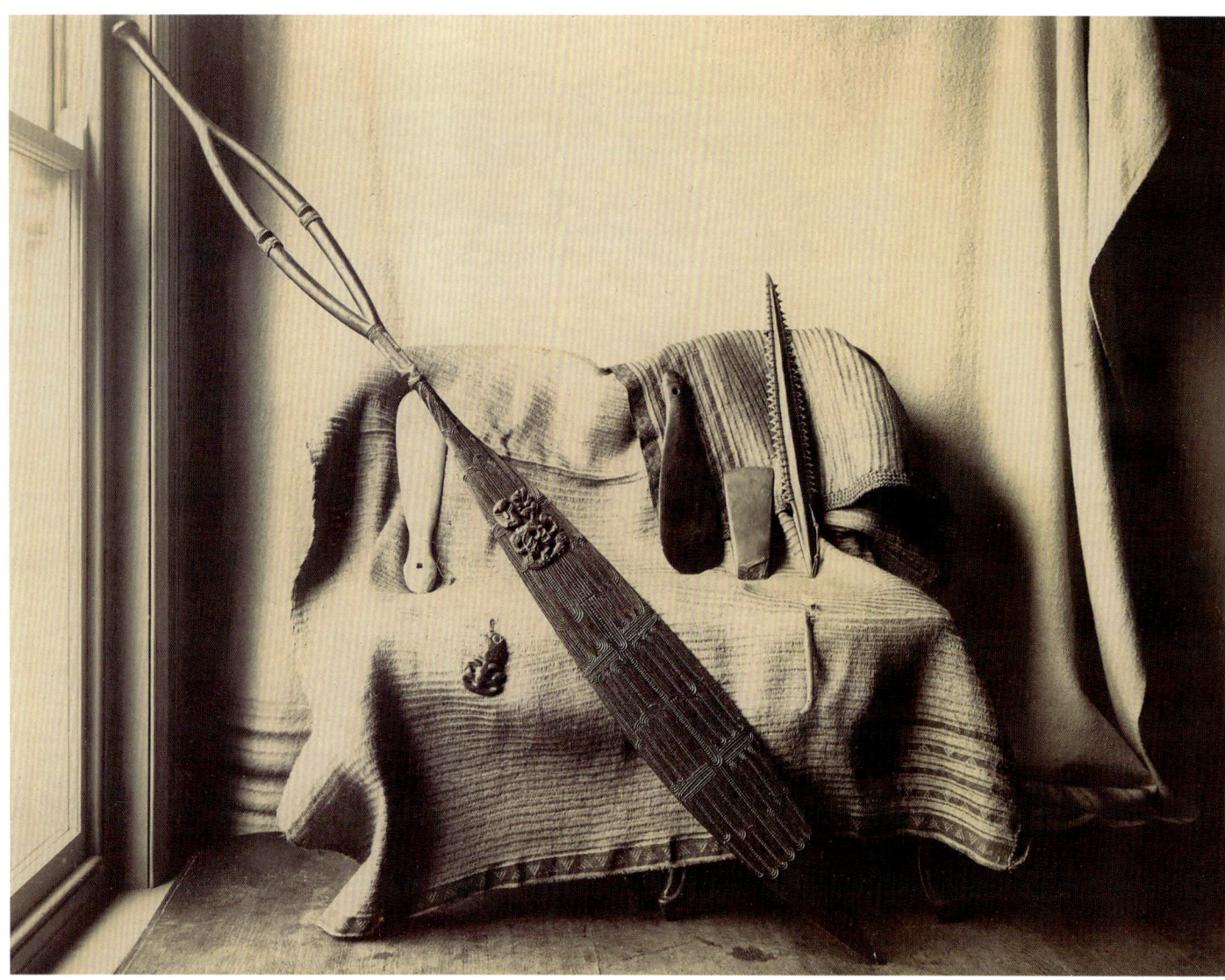

This photograph of the taonga presented to Joseph Chegwyn of HMS *Buffalo* in 1837 was commissioned by his son in 1896, who offered the collection for sale to the British Museum and various London dealers. The hoe is now in the Dresden Staatliches Museum für Völkerkunde and the kapeu in the Museo Nazionale Preistorico ed Etnografico Luigi Pigorini in Rome. The hei tiki was last seen in the Augustus Pitt-Rivers 'second collection' and was sold to an unknown buyer in the 1950s. The ethnographic dealer William Webster offered the two patu parāoa and toki for sale in his 1896 catalogue; their current whereabouts, along with that of the mere pounamu, kaitaka and shark-tooth knife, is yet to be determined.
British Museum, Oc,B3.18

until Hōri Pukehika and Māui Pōmare deposited it in the Dominion Museum in 1908.[36]

When the HMS *Buffalo* returned briefly to the Bay of Islands in September 1837, a posthumous gift from Tītore (who had succumbed to tuberculosis three months before) was presented to the ship's senior master, Joseph Chegwyn.[37] The presentation comprised a mere pounamu, a patu parāoa, a pounamu toki, a pounamu hei tiki pendant, a kapeu pounamu, a finely made kaitaka with tāniko border, a unique split-handled hoe made by a captive chief, and a shark-tooth knife, possibly of Hawaiian rather than Māori origin. The breadth of this and Tītore's earlier collection of gifts demonstrates that rangatira were collectors of objects from their ever-expanding sphere of influence, and they deployed these treasures to enhance their mana and that of their people through exchange. Tītore's posthumous gift has value in both worlds, and his dying wish that it be presented to the *Buffalo* demonstrates his belief that he was already in a binding relationship with the Royal Navy and, by extension, the Crown.[38]

## Conclusion

Taonga associated with utu had a greater purpose, status and meaning beyond their symbolic exchange within larger social and political encounters. They accumulated a whakapapa of guardianship as they were passed down through a sequence of utu transactions, as each kaitiaki and exchange imbued them with additional kōrero. The stories passed on with a taonga increased their mana and tapu.[39] It required effort and resources to safely house such taonga and to transmit their histories in the interval between exchange events, which could sometimes last for many generations, and this only increased the regard in which they were held.

These taonga were given carefully considered names that represented their intended or actual purpose (such as Tuhiwai), or the wairua of a deceased leader (Kimihia). The taonga became 'actors' alongside human, animal and supernatural participants involved in the events that required rebalancing.[40] A taonga's mana and tapu were enhanced through effective use in utu events and living up to their name (such as Tuhiwai) in realising the objectives of particular utu events. Taonga with a long and successful history of maintaining agreements were used in progressively more complex transactions. Their original utility – as weapons, buildings, clothing or watercraft – was superseded by their accumulated transaction value, so they could effectively settle major disputes, such as the inter-iwi wars between Ngāti Toa and Ngāi Tahu. They did not symbolise an agreement: they *were* the agreement.

The use of taonga in utu transactions between Māori groups declined during the twentieth century as the factors that caused an imbalance in relationships changed. Principal among them was land rights, which became a fixed rather than a fluid concept when the Native Land Court imposed collective and individual land titles from the 1860s onwards.[41] Strategic marriages became less popular, muru was branded as theft rather than restitution, and large inter-group feasting hākari were scaled back as resources became scarce. As hapū collectivised politically into iwi and a consolidated 'Māori' social identity emerged, attention turned towards negotiations with Pākehā and the government as a means to retaining remaining resources in the face of colonisation. Māori made a number of attempts to settle disputes and form alliances with influential Pākehā by drawing them into utu arrangements: this is why Gilbert Mair received Te Kahumamae o Parerautūtu, and a number of British monarchs, governors and politicians received taonga with long transaction whakapapa. Some of these taonga were donated or sold to collectors and museums by the recipients or their descendants who were unaware of the practices of kaitiaki and utu. The recognition of the mana of these taonga now relies on their rediscovery and their spiritual, if not actual, reclamation by descendant groups – as has been the case with Te Kahumamae o Parerautūtu. Their mana, tapu and whakapapa endure.

# THE MĀTAATUA WHARENUI
JONATHAN MANE-WHEOKI

The Mātaatua whare was intended 'to mend the breaks in the tatau pounamu between Ngāti Awa and Tūhoe' that had been breached during the Te Kooti campaign,[1] or, as Captain George Preece, resident magistrate of Ōpōtiki, put it, 'to reconcile the tribes Ngāti Awa and Urewera, between whom there existed much ill-feeling in consequence of murders perpetrated by the latter tribe during the war'.[2] The iconographical schema, said to have been devised by Wepiha Apanui, to celebrate the ancestors of Ngāti Awa and its allies, is set out in Preece's 'History of the Carved House "Mata[a]tua"', and published in the *Appendices to the Journal of the House of Representatives* in 1879.[3]

At one stage Mātaatua was also proffered as a symbol of reconciliation not only among iwi of the region but between those iwi and the Crown. In a letter written by Tiopira on Wepiha Apanui and Patara Toihau's behalf, and dated 4 October 1873,[4] 'The desire of the people above mentioned [Apanui, Tamarangi, Rangitukehu and Kaperiere] ... that this house should be for Queen Victoria' was conveyed to the Native Minister, Donald McLean. This stated intention has been interpreted by later writers as a completed action. There is no evidence to show that Mātaatua was presented to either the queen or the minister at the time of his visit to Whakatāne in March 1875. Of the two letters published in the *Bay of Plenty Times* in March 1874, the first, written by Tiopira on behalf of Wepiha Apanui and Patara Toihau, and addressed to McLean, is conciliatory in tone and the offer seems genuine and sincere.

But what did Ngāti Awa intend by this gesture? Had there been some prior informal (and unrecorded) exchange between Ngāti Awa and McLean to ascertain whether such a gift would be acceptable before the offer was put in writing? Was it understood that if the gift were accepted the whare might be dismantled and re-erected elsewhere on another site, perhaps even in England, as the queen or her representatives determined? Or had Ngāti Awa intended the whare to remain in Whakatāne as a queen's house in name only, as a symbol of their 'loyalty and goodwill'?

In his reply (the second letter published in the *Bay of Plenty Times*), H. T. Clarke, the under-secretary for the Native Department, stated: 'you have heard Mr McLean's words in answer to that letter ... Their [the chiefs'] desire to present the house to the Queen is commendable, and the Government appreciates your expressions of loyalty and goodwill. With respect to the house, let the offer you have made suffice.'[5] Subsequent negotiations between Ngāti Awa and the government over the whare indicate that it had not been presented to Queen Victoria, and that Ngāti Awa had retained ownership. Thus, when the under-secretary wrote, 'let the offer you have made suffice', he meant that the generosity of Ngāti Awa's offer of the whare as a gift to the queen was so convincing as a demonstration of their loyalty and goodwill to the Crown that there was no necessity to carry it through. As a symbol of reconciliation, the collaborative effort which saw the whare completed was wholly effective.

*Note: This text is an extract from Jonathan Mane-Wheoki's 1993 report to the Waitangi Tribunal for the Ngāti Awa (Wai 46) Claim. In response to his report, the Mātaatua wharenui was repatriated from Otago Museum to Whakatāne in 1996: the wharenui was finally returned after being dismantled and removed by the Crown in 1879. Mātaatua was restored and reopened as a Ngāti Awa cultural centre in 2011.*

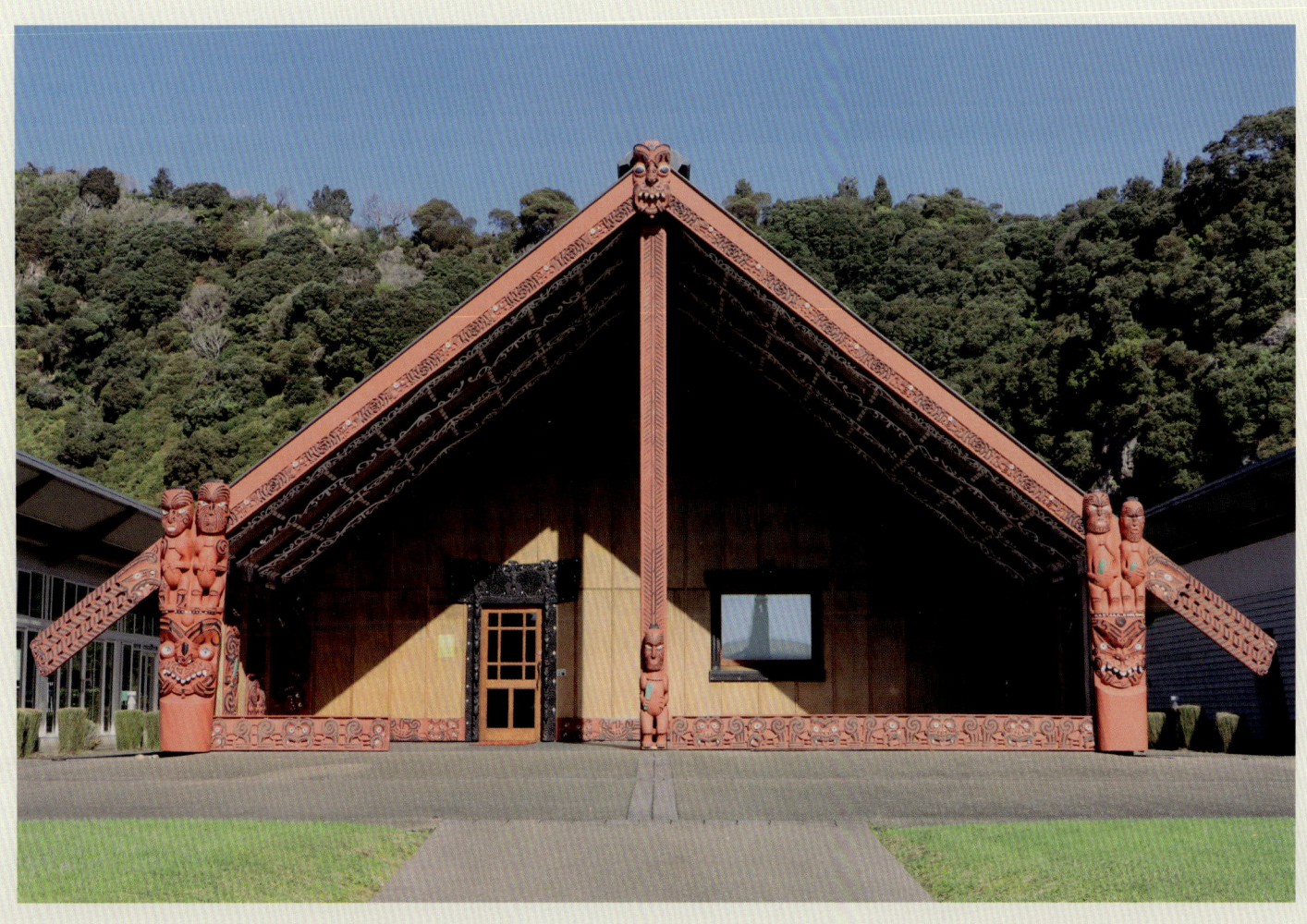

**Mātaatua, Te Mānuka Tūtahi Marae, Whakatāne.**
photograph courtesy Te Mānuka Tūtahi Marae

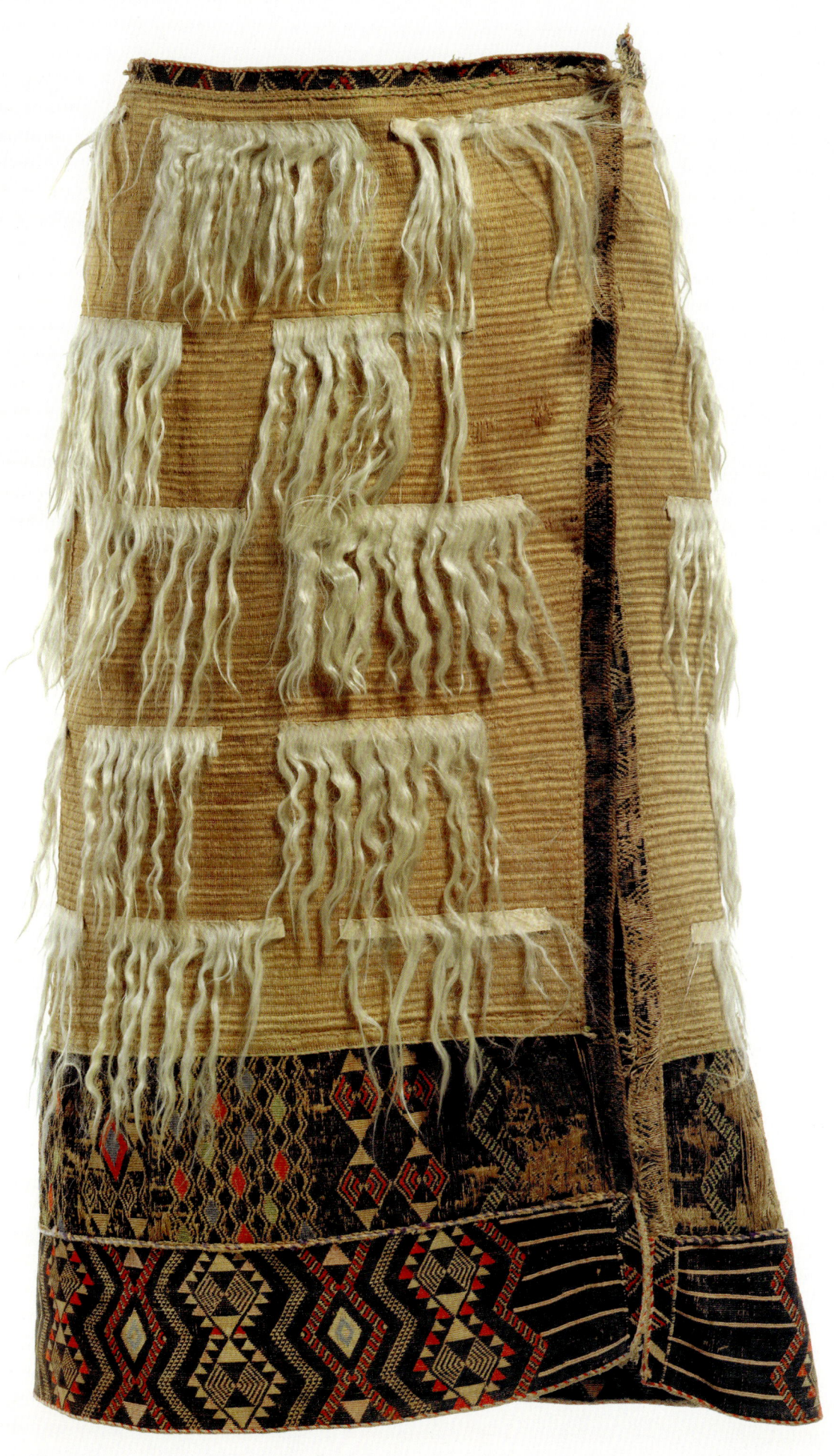

# 11 TRANSFORMING CULTURES AND TRADITIONS
## NEW MATERIALS, IDEAS AND TECHNOLOGIES
### NGARINO ELLIS

*Mate atu he tētē kura, ara mai anō he tētē kura.*
*As one fern frond dies, another takes its place.*

The arrival of Europeans brought opportunities for Māori. For artists there were new materials and technologies, as well as a fresh audience for their work; for patrons the newcomers represented a chance to extend their ambition to support larger and more complex taonga; and for communities there was the potential for trade and to forge relationships that could bring economic, political and social benefits. The whakataukī above reflects the importance in Māori culture of the need for constant renewal, and for the ongoing shifts in practice, form and meaning of Māori art and culture that characterise the nineteenth century in particular.

This chapter focuses on transformations of art practices, forms, materials and technologies, particularly in the nineteenth century, after the arrival of Europeans. What art forms were set aside, and which ones thrived? What materials did not grow in this new place, and how did Māori innovate using unfamiliar media? Throughout this period, it becomes clear how artists were active agents of change, mediating between worlds, artistic, political, economic and social.

### Translating one form into another

Over the course of the nineteenth century Māori art underwent radical transformations in a number of different forms. Beginning in the 1830s the three major carved forms – whare rangatira, pātaka and waka taua – were reconfigured and replaced by two new forms – the decorated church and the whare whakairo. The artists and patrons who led this shift were reshaping the visible manifestation of culture within art forms. Each of the earlier types represented the mana of rangatira and their community, but rapidly changing political, cultural and economic dynamics demanded artistic adaptation. Aspects of the chief's houses, pātaka and waka taua were retained but reorganised. The architecture of the chief's house was enlarged and the range of carving was extended, including into the interior. The symbolism of pātaka carvings, particularly on the maihi, amo and the kūwaha, was retained and reconfigured into new sites in the whare whakairo and the church. The concept of a single log that united all physical and spiritual aspects of a waka was applied to the tāhuhu of the whare whakairo. Such changes enabled artists to reflect the ongoing cultural shifts within their communities, and to build on existing forms that they knew were artistically, socially and culturally acceptable.

Kahu koati, made in the late nighteenth century. Weavers began using goat hair in kaitaka to simulate kurī fur, which historically was used as a prestige medium to signify the mana of the wearer. Kaitaka were rarely being made by this time, with weavers focusing more on kahu huruhuru and korowai in particular. These kahu koati can be dated to post-1867, when goats were introduced to New Zealand, though James Cook introduced some in 1773.
Te Papa Tongarewa Museum of New Zealand, ME001154, Henry Hill Collection, purchased 1905

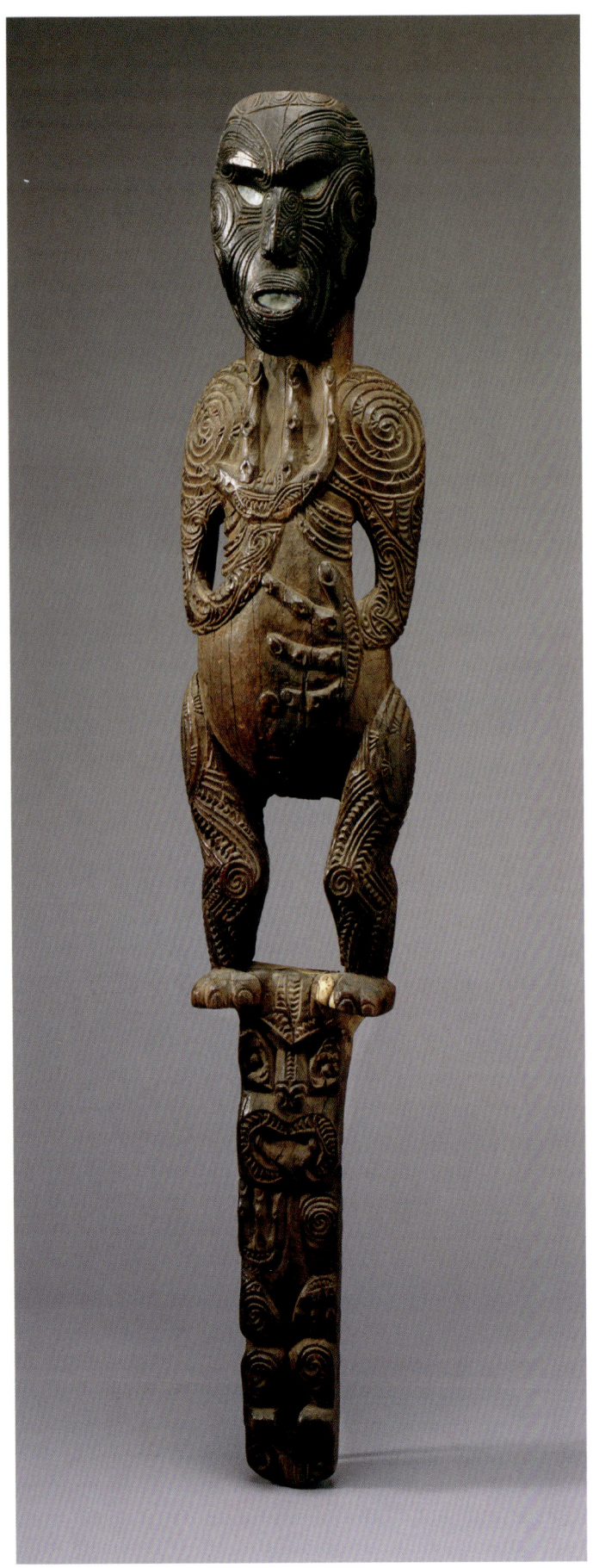

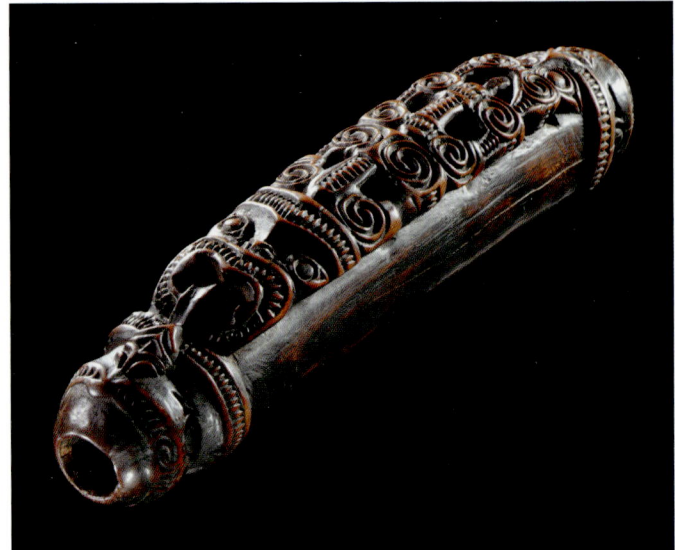

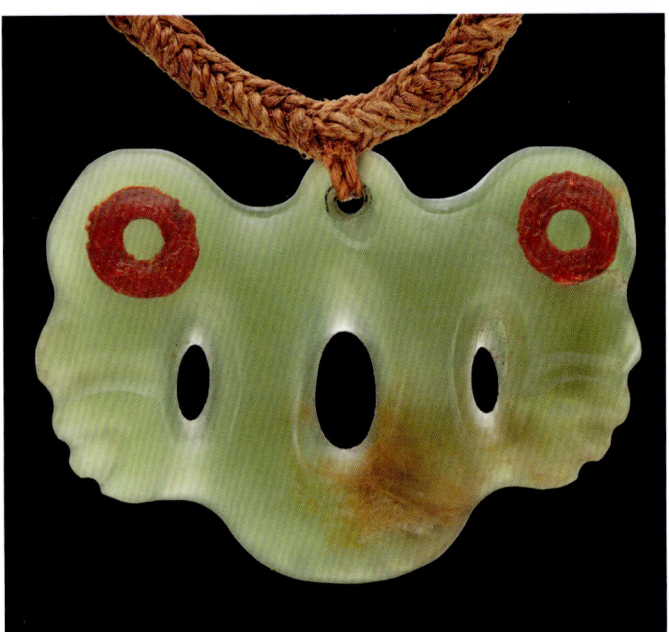

Top: Kōauau (sound instrument).
Te Papa Tongarewa Museum of New Zealand, ME007664

Bottom: Pekapeka named Te Waitarewa made from pounamu and red sealing wax, hung on a red-pigmented cord made from harakeke with a bone toggle.
Te Papa Tongarewa Museum of New Zealand, ME024109

Carving collected by Baron Carl von Hügel, 1834. Von Hügel spent two weeks in the Bay of Islands in March 1834, and a further five days in Whangaroa, further north, tramping inland to fulfil his passion for botany.
Museum of Archaeology and Anthropology, University of Cambridge, D 1897.76

Carvers extended their role as artists within the building process: they broadened their skills to become architect and general planner for the whare whakairo and the embellished church. They liaised with teams brought in to complete the project: for the church this might include a local native teacher (in the 1830s and 1840s) as well as the resident missionary. Tukutuku and kōwhaiwhai took on a new prominence in the whare whakairo, and sometimes in the church, too, whereas earlier, carvers had used art forms judiciously as a form of ornamentation on the porch of some chief's houses.

According to travelling European artists Joel Polack on the East Coast and Richard Taylor in the Bay of Plenty, by the 1830s Māori artists were transferring kōwhaiwhai from hoe and, less frequently, waka huia into chief's houses.[1] By the 1860s, almost all new wharenui incorporated some form of kōwhaiwhai. Tukutuku had previously been relatively unknown in whare rangatira, but it became an essential design element in wharenui from the 1860s, as the desire to represent a plethora of kōrero and tūpuna in the house drove innovation. Tukutuku artists depicted tūpuna in their panels around the interior walls of Porourangi meeting house (opened 1888), and in text woven as part of the tukutuku panels on the front porch wall of Hikurangi meeting house in northern Hawke's Bay in the 1880s.

Patrons commissioned ambitious projects that it was sometimes difficult to persuade their communities to accept. Te Kooti, for instance, commissioned houses that were very large and that drew on a range of imagery. In some, the exterior resembled that of a traditional heavily carved whare, but inside the design shifted towards ancestors and narratives painted on panels, and these were more of a challenge for people to recognise and accept because they were not carved. Sometimes it was contentious that there were portraits of living people – this practice was not widespread, though it did exist in some areas.

While artists were reconfiguring some art forms, others stopped being made altogether (though they have recently been resurrected). Taonga pūoro were one example of this. Sound instruments such as the kōauau (sound instrument played with the lips) and nguru (sound instrument played with the mouth or nose) were exquisitely and intricately carved and were obviously much loved, based on the wear and tear on examples now in museum collections (mostly from before 1850). These were not 'musical instruments', as they are often described; they were sound instruments that served a number of purposes, some of which have been passed down. Made from wood, bone and pounamu, they were used as part of healing.[2] By the mid-nineteenth century many of these were no longer being made, in conjunction with the passing of the whare wānanga.

Since the late twentieth century there has been a revival of interest in taonga pūoro. In particular, Hirini Melbourne (Ngāi Tūhoe, Ngāti Kahungunu, 1949–2003), Richard Nunns and Brian Flintoff spent decades researching and examining these ancestral taonga – a real challenge within museum practice – as well as composing and performing with them. They have held wānanga to share their knowledge and worked together to bring back the sounds of the pūoro across spaces.

Māori fashion constantly changed, but this became more pronounced in the nineteenth century with new materials that resulted in different forms of textiles and modes of wearing them. There are many accounts from the early nineteenth century of Māori adapting European dress according to their individual sense of style – this could be quite outrageous, showing real flair and confidence in their sense of identity. Photographic portraits commissioned by Māori show many wearing European formal clothing but with a cloak draped over their shoulders, a hei tiki around their neck or other traditional dressings to signal the importance of the sitter.

Dress cloaks were worn only on special occasions. By the 1850s most Māori were wearing European clothing, certainly in towns. Clothing such as the rāpaki and the maro were set aside in favour of the long skirts and trousers that were fashionable in Pākehā settlements. Rāpaki were reconfigured as piupiu, with the kaupapa base shifting to become a narrow whiri at the waistband by the end of the nineteenth century. The fact that rāpaki were considered ordinary worker garments and of little worth can be seen from the dearth of examples of these in museum collections, as few were considered worth collecting: there are only five rāpaki and six maro in Te Papa Tongarewa Museum of New Zealand, compared to 228 piupiu.

Other art forms lay dormant until the late twentieth century. This included the pekapeka – an adornment specific to North Auckland and Waikato that represents two pekapeka back to back – and the kākā pōria adornment. Few examples

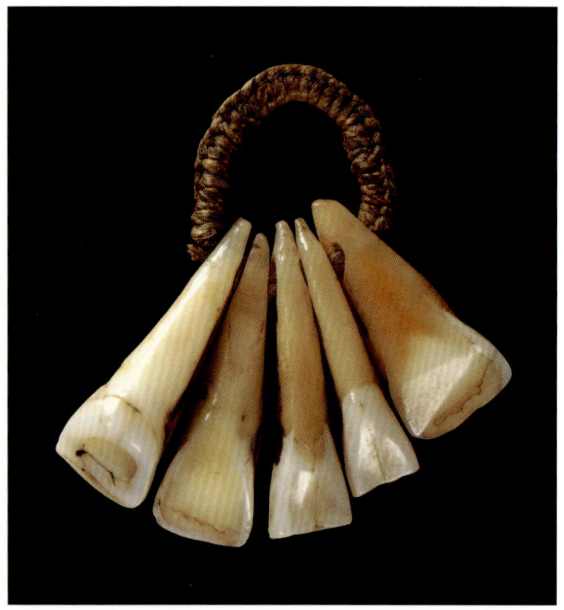

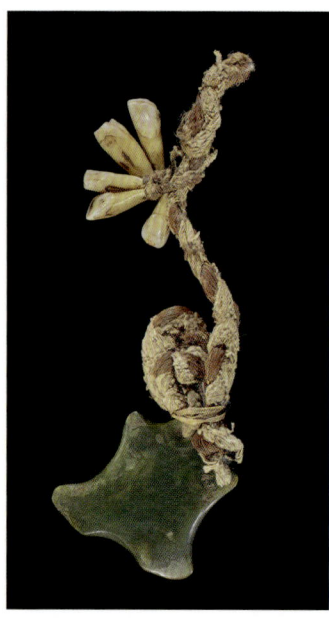

Left: This group of five human teeth have been drilled through the root and threaded through a short woven cord. It is unclear what their purpose was, though stringing the teeth of one's parents and grandparents to wear suspended in the ear was done by some Māori in this period. They were collected by Georg Forster, who described these as 'a form of rosary for prayer'. Forster describes trading for such ornaments in Queen Charlotte Sound on 1 June 1773: 'They considered these in no way as priceless as stated in the description in Captain Cook's previous voyage; instead they sold them gladly in exchange for iron tools or other trifles.'
Georg-August University, Göttingen, Inv. Oz 296, 297

Right: Another person strung five human teeth along with a small piece of worn kawakawa-type greenstone. It is likely a deeply personal memento of loved ones.
British Museum, Oc1981, Q.1378

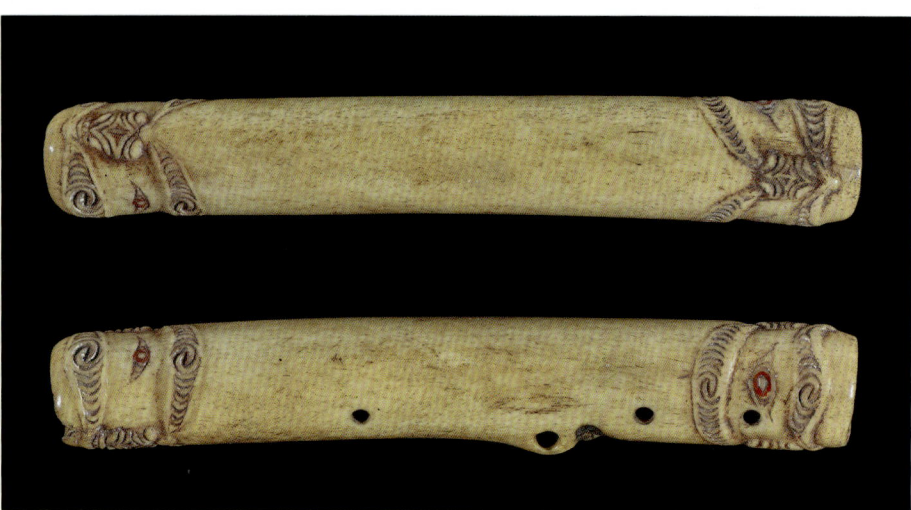

Early nineteenth-century kōauau wheua (sound instruments made from human bone).
British Museum, Oc.1716

of these forms can be dated later than mid-nineteenth century. Ariki no longer wore downy feathers in their ears either.

## How new materials transformed Māori art

Trading was integral in forging and maintaining relationships between Māori and Pākehā. New materials and technologies spurred the emergence of novel art forms. Europeans were fascinated at the speed and creativity with which Māori transfigured introduced materials, as Julien Crozet noted in 1771 in the Bay of Islands:[3]

> They brought large quantities of fish, for which we gave them glass trinkets and pieces of iron in exchange. In these early days they were content with old nails two or three inches long, but later on they became more particular and in exchange for their fish demanded nails four or five inches in length. Their object in asking for the nails was to make small wood chisels of them. As soon as they had obtained a piece of iron, they took it to one of the sailors and by signs engaged him to sharpen it on the millstone; they always took care to reserve some fish wherewith to pay the sailor for his trouble.

The value of developing relationships in order to acquire new materials from Europeans was essential, particularly until the 1840s. Māori artists transformed these materials into Indigenous objects, including taonga, through use and incorporation into and onto Māori art forms. Māori were seen wearing coins as earrings and even a teaspoon on one occasion, and a biscuit on another. Displaying

TRANSFORMING CULTURES AND TRADITIONS – NEW MATERIALS, IDEAS AND TECHNOLOGIES

Top left: Te Rauparaha, uncle of Te Rangihaeata, also wore a pōhoi toroa.
**Isaac Coates, *Rauparaha. Chief Capiti. &c. &c. Principal chief of all New Zealand*, 1843**
watercolour and gum Arabic, 257 x 192mm, Alexander Turnbull Library, A-286-012

Top right: The artist Isaac Coates drew a number of Ngāti Toa chiefs and their relatives, who often dressed themselves in the most wonderful styles of dress, especially the hairstyles. This is Pipi Kutia, who was the stepdaughter and wife of Te Rauparaha.
**Isaac Coates, *Cootia. Rauparaha's head wife*, 1843?**
watercolour and gum Arabic, 257 x 192mm, Alexander Turnbull Library, A-286-013

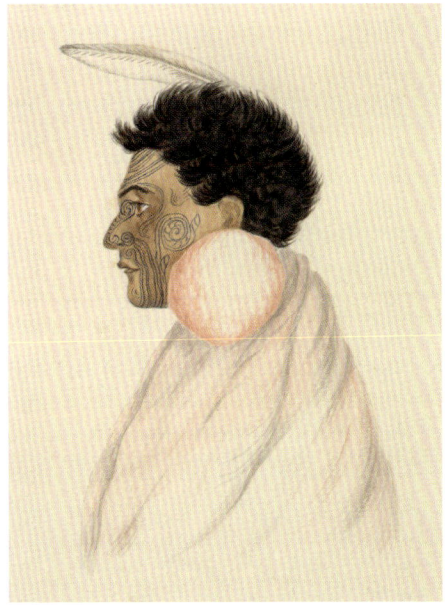
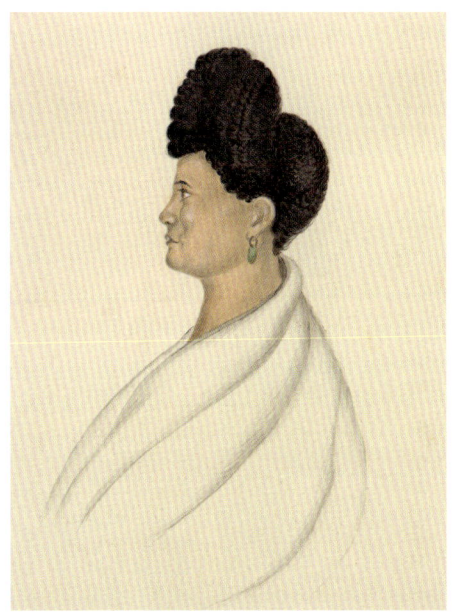
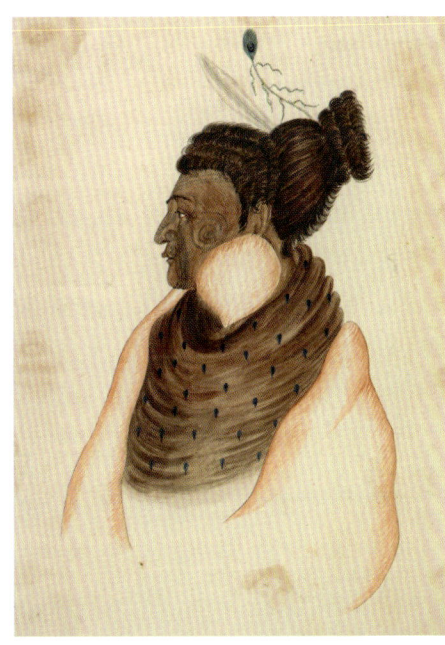
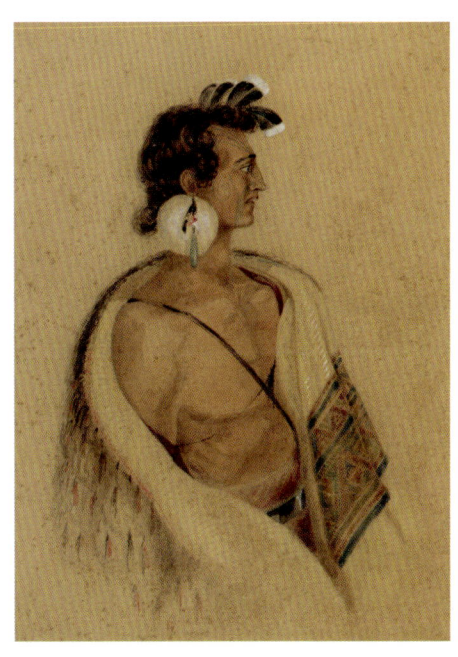

Bottom left: **Isaac Coates, *Rangihaeata, Rauparaha's fighting general*, 1843**
watercolour and gum Arabic, 257 x 192mm, Alexander Turnbull Library, A-286-014

Bottom right: Ngāti Toa chief Te Rangihaeata was often drawn with his pōhoi toroa, a downy albatross ear ornament. These were the symbol of someone with immense mana, and thus befitted this wearer.
**Charles Heaphy, *Rangiaeata*, 1840**
watercolour, 280 x 178mm, Alexander Turnbull Library, C-025-022

these European goods so visibly signalled a person's status in relation to Europeans.

Conversely, some materials became scarce, eventually leading to the disappearance of certain art forms. Kurī were a 'luxury' resource, so precious that every part of the body was used: the meat as a prestige food, the jawbone made into fish-hooks, the teeth into ornaments, and of course the fur transformed into a range of at least ten different types of kahu kurī, including awarua, with alternating black and white stripes, and the unusual kahu waero, with only dog-tail fur attachments. White fur was the most highly sought after, and white kurī slept on special mats in order to protect the colour of their fur. This white fur would also be used, alongside red kākā feathers, on the taura of a taiaha in order to heighten its mana.

By the mid-1830s kurī were becoming very rare, and this increased the value of their skins and fur. Once kurī started breeding with European dogs, weavers were reluctant to use the resulting material, which was seen as inferior. Artists discovered that goat hair was visually similar to the highly valued kurī hair, and they began using it in their textile work, resulting in the kahu koati (goat-hair cloak), which emerged some time around 1870. The only two examples of kahu koati in Te Papa date from this period (ME010765, ME001154).

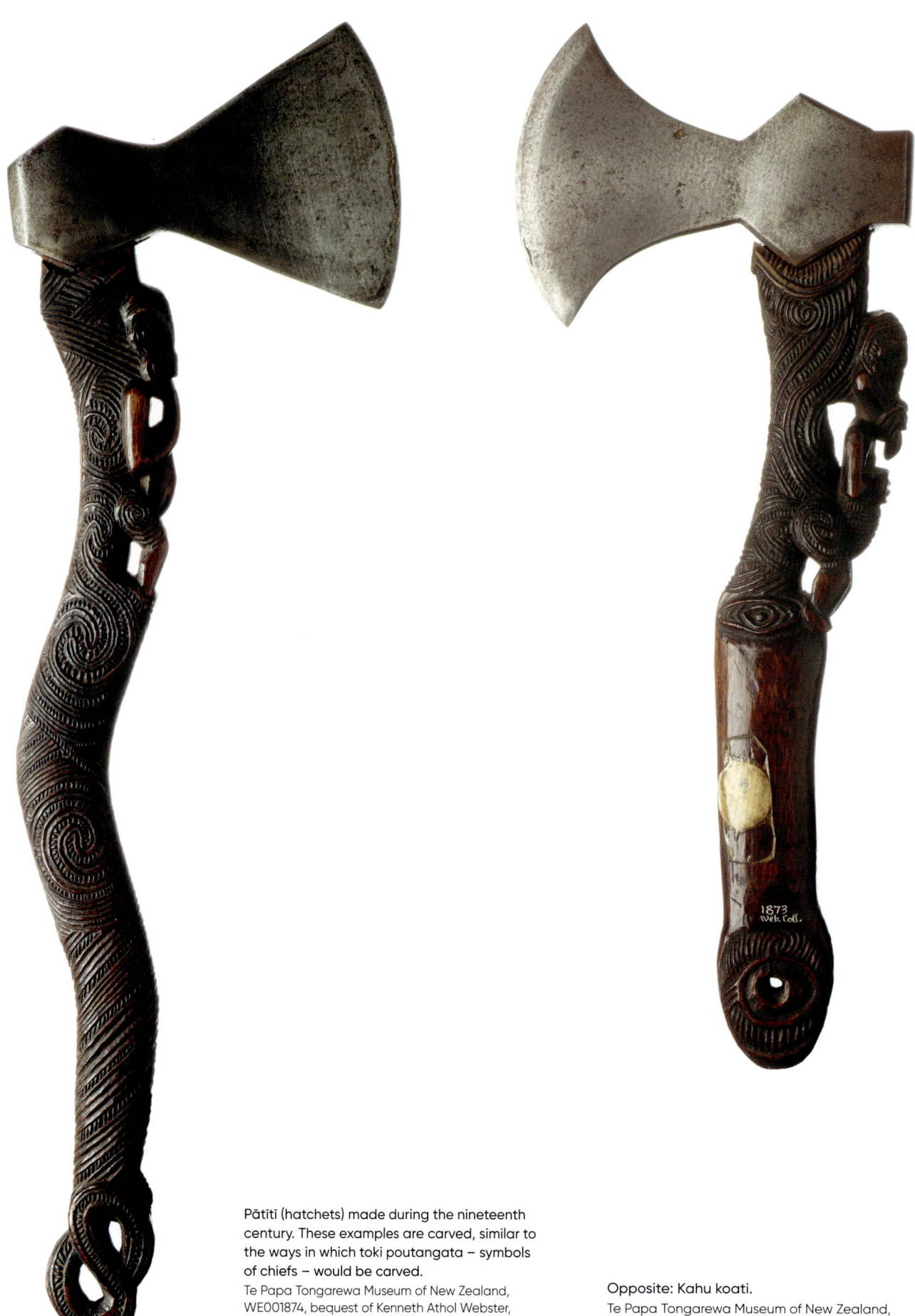

**Pātītī (hatchets) made during the nineteenth century.** These examples are carved, similar to the ways in which toki poutangata – symbols of chiefs – would be carved.
Te Papa Tongarewa Museum of New Zealand, WE001874, bequest of Kenneth Athol Webster, 1971 (left); WE001873 (right)

**Opposite: Kahu koati.**
Te Papa Tongarewa Museum of New Zealand, ME010765, purchased 1947

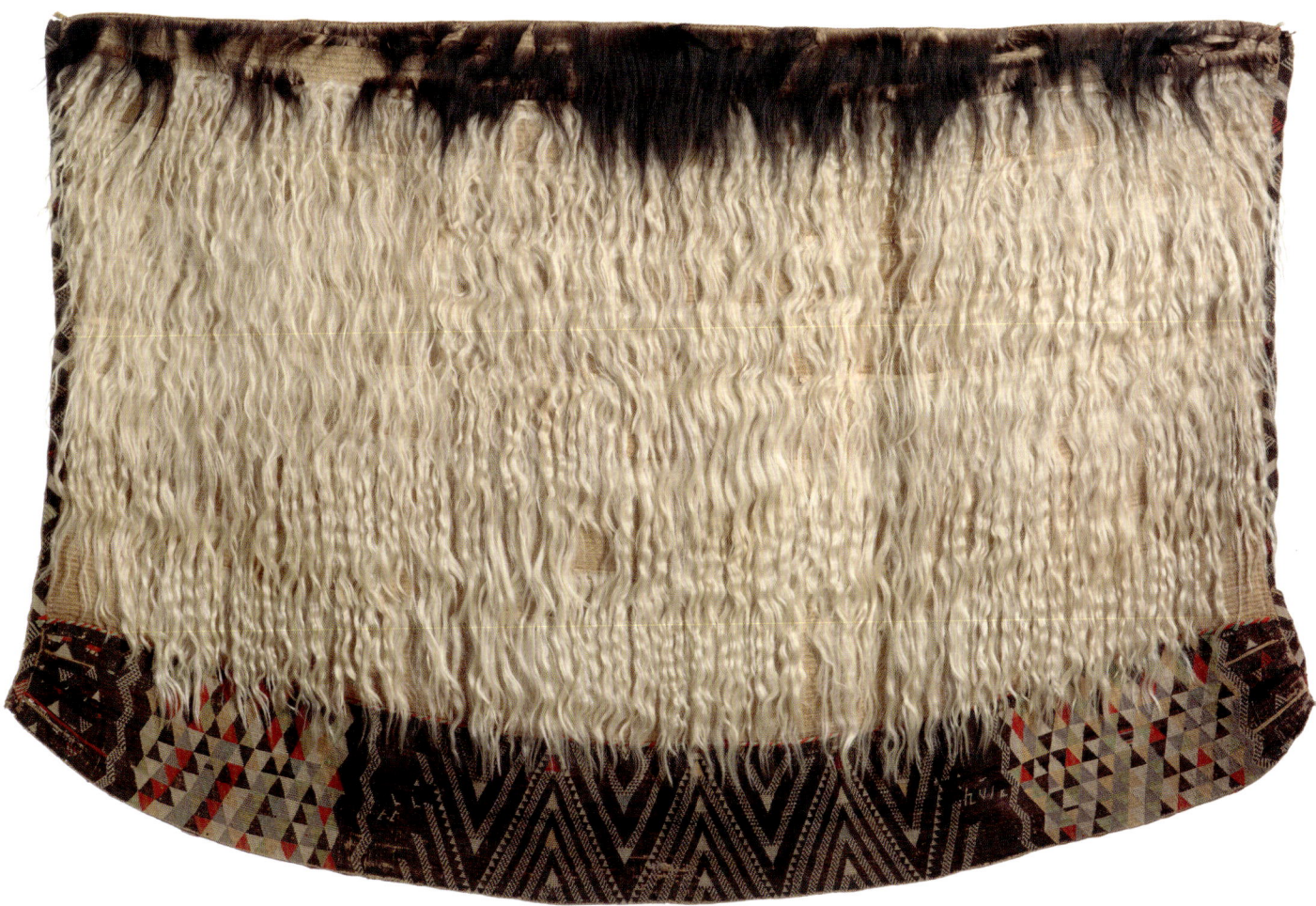

A kaitaka huaki in the British Museum (Oc1995.Q.8) represents innovation with materials. The huaki style of cloak was rare by the 1870s, as it had been replaced by the korowai and kahu huruhuru type of cloak. The difficulty in making huaki, and their rarity, suggests that they may have been made as special commissions. Historian Judith Binney has noted that the raw materials for cloaks – in this case dog skins – were sometimes sent to Sydney to be 'turned into chiefs' cloaks in New Zealand'.[4] What happened to the skins, or the cloaks? Were they then sold to collectors? Evidently traditional materials became a commodity that was traded across the Tasman, at least. Pounamu was also exported to be made into adornments that were then imported into Aotearoa New Zealand for sale. It is unlikely Māori were driving these initiatives, as the ritual value of kurī fur and greenstone required them to be imbued with values such as mana and tapu, and to be created according to tikanga that was not, in general, shared outside Māori communities.

Māori weavers welcomed wool as a fibre from the moment they set eyes on it. They sourced it wherever they could – including by unravelling European woollen garments – and wove it into kākahu. They found red wool especially attractive because of the high social status conveyed by the colour. Sometimes they alternated red wool with other colours to highlight special features in the kaupapa, as seen in a kaitaka paepaeroa from Te Papa (ME0013460). Later, weavers made woollen ngore and attached them to the cloak base: these cloaks were known as korowai ngore.

### The impact of literacy on Māori art

Māori artists incorporated text into their art from some of the earliest periods of contact.[5] The earliest opportunity to formally learn to read and write was at the CMS mission school at Rangihoua in the Bay of Islands, led by Thomas Kendall in 1816–1818, and missionaries taught these skills informally in their communities. The first attempt to compile

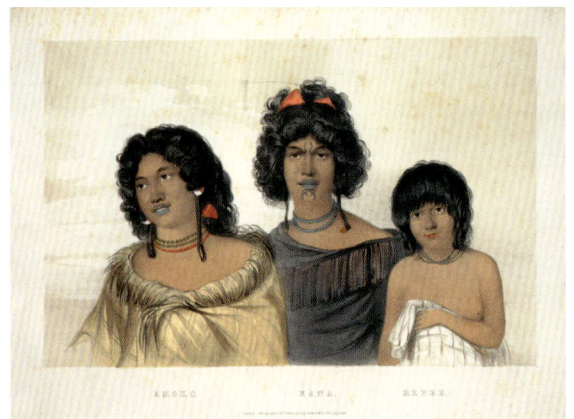

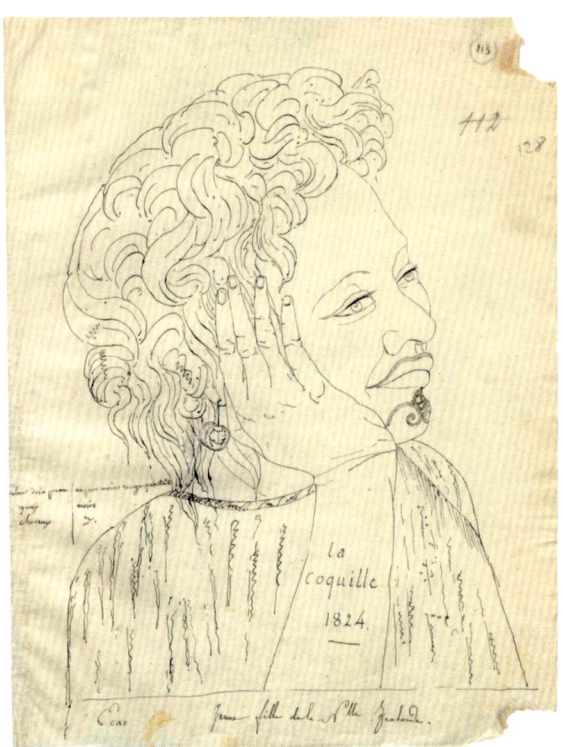

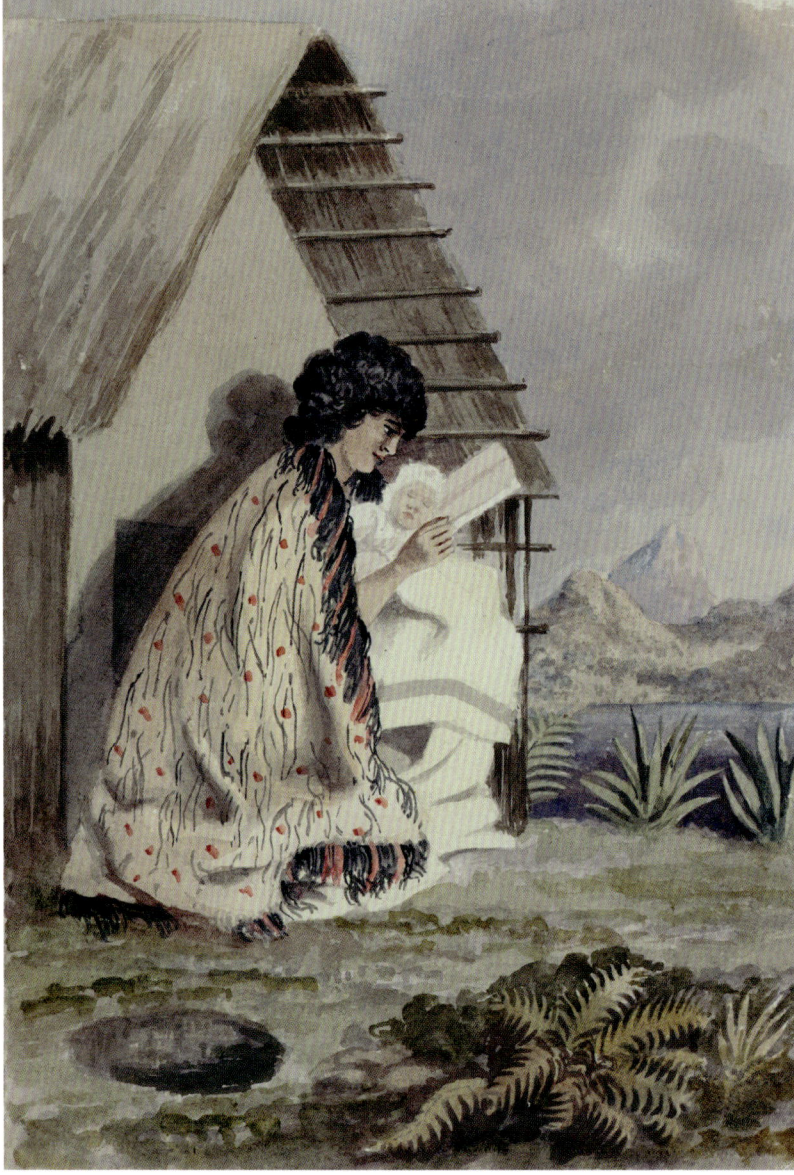

Top left: Augustus Earle described how Amoko and Eana were about twenty-five years of age, while the young girl on the far right, aged around thirteen, was Amoko's enslaved attendant.

**Augustus Earle, *Amoko, Eana, Hepee*, 1838**

hand-coloured lithograph, 260 x 395mm, Alexander Turnbull Library, PUBL-0015-010-a. From *Sketches illustrative of the Native Inhabitants and Islands of New Zealand from original drawings by Augustus Earle Esq, Draughtsman of H. M. S. 'Beagle'*, lithographed and published under the auspices of the New Zealand Association by Robert Martin & Co., London, 1838

Bottom left: This remarkable drawing depicts a young woman who has incised the name of a visiting French ship on her forearm as a memento of their visit. This is one of the first known recordings of text being used in moko.

**Jules Lejeune, *Ecao. Jeune fille de la Nouvelle Zélande*, 1824**

Bibliotheque Marine, Service historique de la Défense, Château de Vincennes, Paris

Right: The woman pictured here is possibly named Ewaka/Waka. This album was given by Mrs Eliza Hobson to her daughter Eliza (Lady Rendel), whose family gave it to the British Library in 1940. It is an important image as it records a Māori woman reading a book to her child, reflecting the transformation of the transmission of mātauranga from wholly through oral methods, to text, to oral word. It is an intimate portrait of māmā and pēpi, and reinforces the role of women as educational as well as physical nurturers.

**Joseph Jenner Merrett, *Woman and child, from The Hobson Album*, c.1842**

watercolour on cream wove paper, 170 x 120mm, Alexander Turnbull Library, A-275-002

Opposite: By the latter part of the nineteenth century Māori were incising names of loved ones onto their arms, chests and backs, in often very large lettering in roman font.

**Frank James Denton, *Portrait of an unidentified Maori woman, Wanganui region*, c.1900s**

negatives of Wanganui and district taken by Alfred Martin, Frank Denton and Mark Lampe (Tesla Studios), Alexander Turnbull Library, 1/2-070308-G

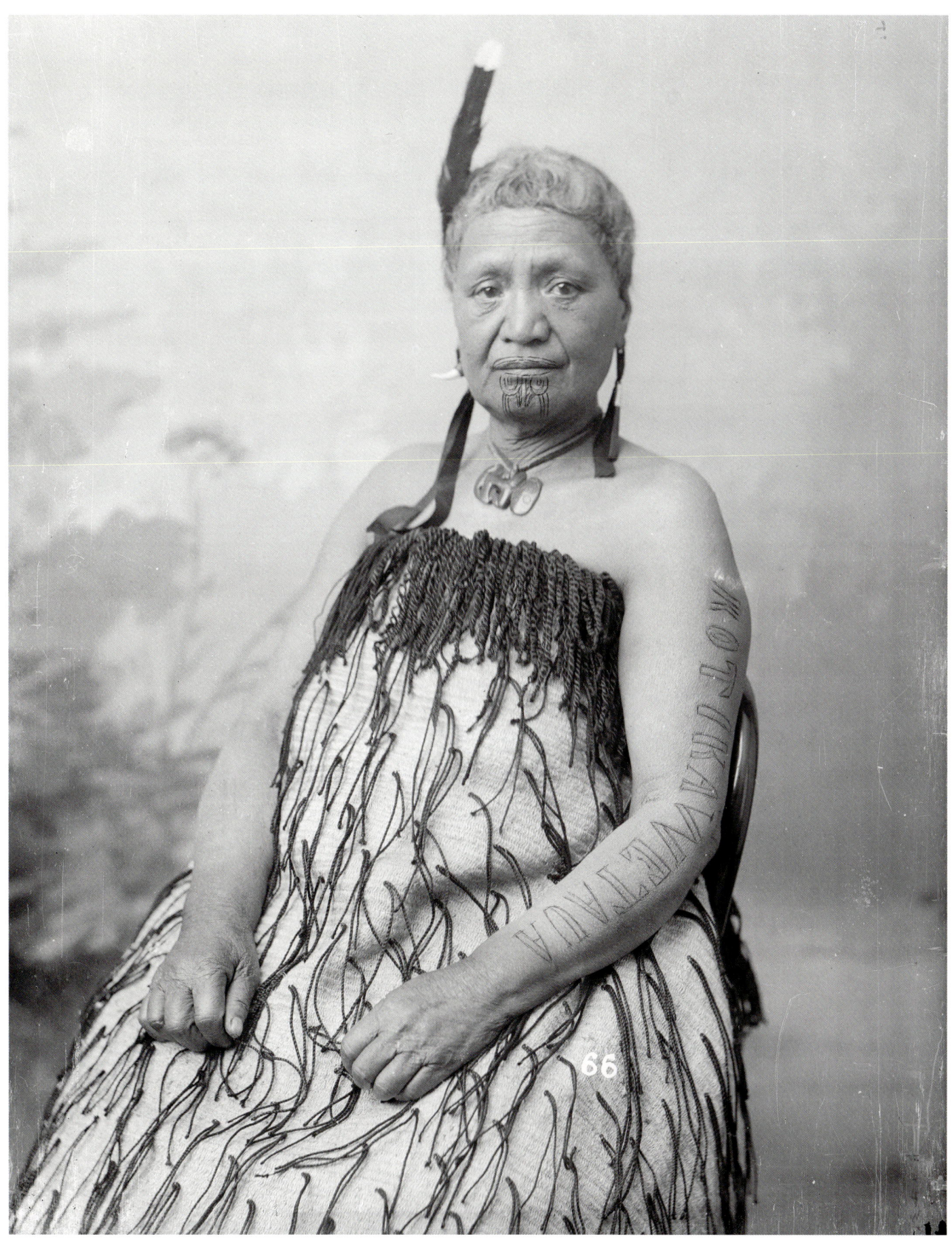

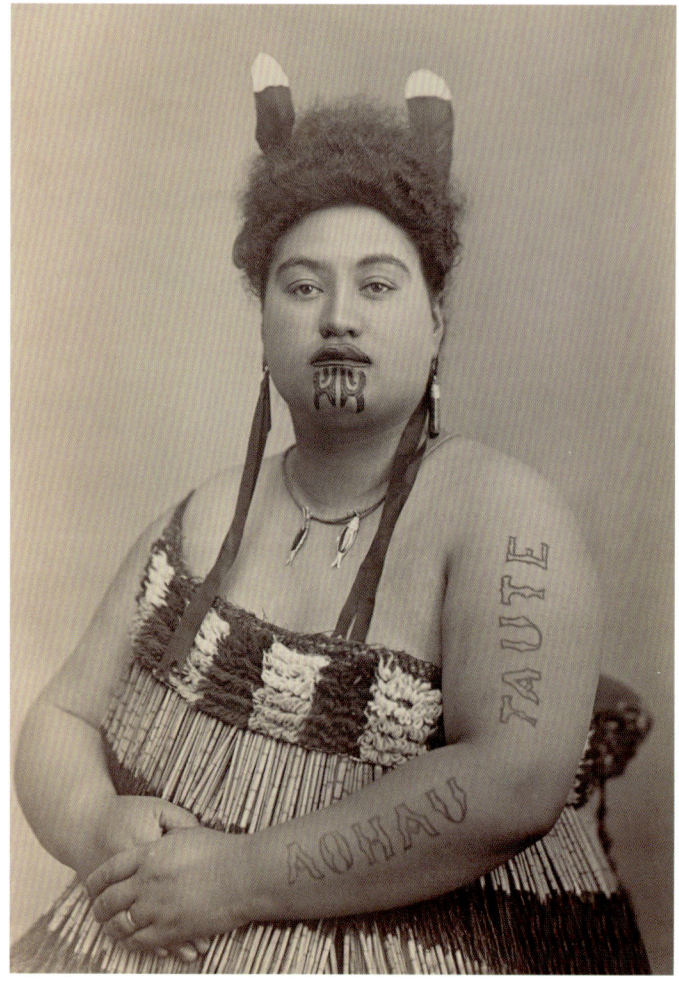 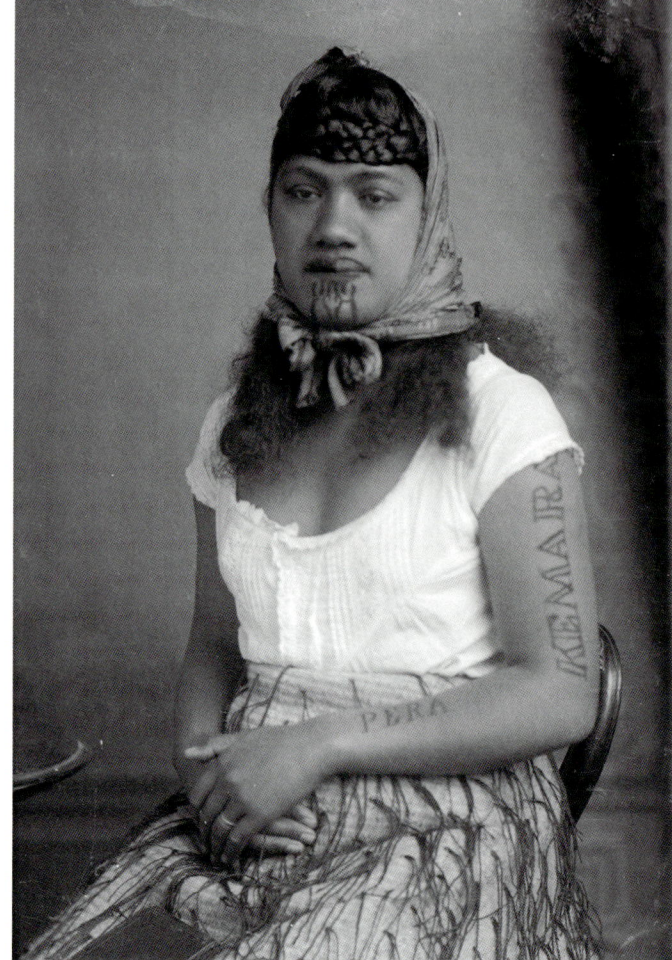

a dictionary was a lexicon that the chiefs Hongi Hika and Waikato worked on with Professor Samuel Lee at Cambridge University while they were in England in 1820. The literacy project was given a boost when a printing press and CMS printer William Colenso arrived in December 1834. By 1837 the demand had grown for books – particularly religious ones: Colenso printed 5000 copies of the New Testament in Māori, and then 27,000 copies of the Book of Common Prayer, and the Catholic missionaries printed 6000 copies of the 648-page *Ko te ako me te karakia o te hahi Katorika Romana* (The teachings and prayers of the Roman Catholic Church) in 1842.

Some of the first examples of Māori use of text and the pen are drawings made by Māori early in the eighteenth century. On New Zealand's first land deed, recording the sale of land by Hongi Hika to the CMS in 1814, the chiefs have 'signed' the document – a legally binding form – with their own moko. This practice continued until the 1850s, mainly in Te Tai Tokerau and in the South Island,

Left: Portrait of Pikau Teimana of Putāruru, wearing a piupiu, huia feathers in her hair and adornments in her ear and around her neck. The words 'Aohau Taute' are incised on her left arm, possibly made with needles rather than uhi, which by the time the photograph was taken (c.1910) were the more popular tools for moko.
unknown photographer, 'Pikau Teimana', c.1910, Alexander Turnbull Library, PAColl-3861-44-01

Right: Carte-de-visite portrait of Irini Kemara, a young Māori woman with the words 'Pera' and 'Kemara' tattooed on her left arm. She is wearing a korowai around her waist.
Samuel Carnell, 'Irini Kemara', July 1888, Alexander Turnbull Library, 1/4-022019-G

Opposite: On the right arm of Te Aho o Te Rangi Wharepu is written in ink 'ERANA.' He was a carver and moko artist himself, as well as a chief of Ngāti Mahuta of Waikato.
**Charles F Goldie, *The Calm Close of Valour's Various Day*, 1906**
oil on canvas, 1270 x 1016mm, Auckland Art Gallery Toi o Tāmaki, 1952/16/2, bequest of Emily and Alfred Nathan, 1955

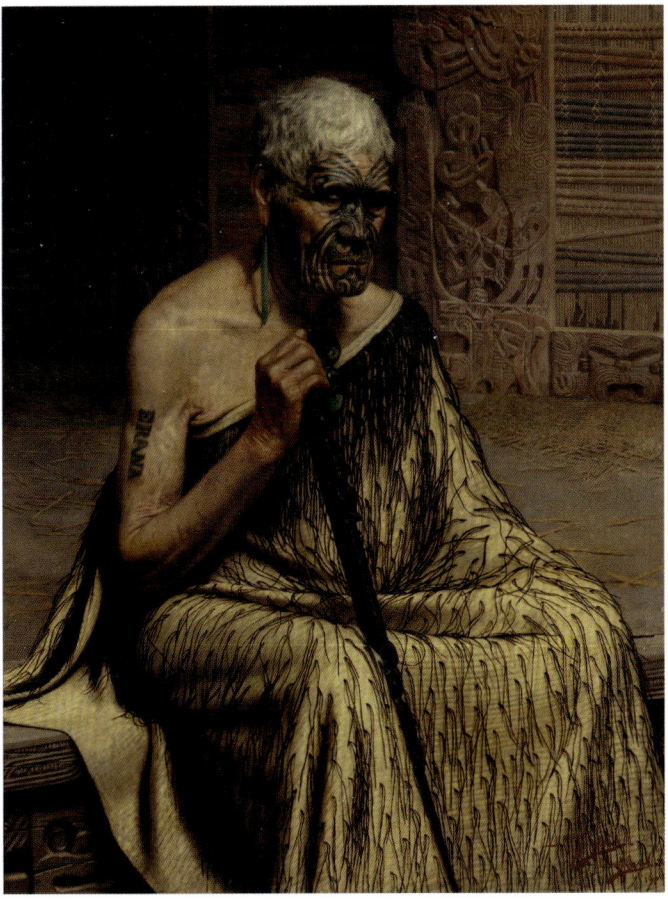

to ensure the agreement was binding under European legal requirements. Māori may have regarded the document as tapu because of the presence of the moko on the parchment. On the 1840 Te Tiriti o Waitangi, forty-four of the 544 signatures were derived from moko, using spirals (double and single) and parallel lines joined at one end – the latter probably sourced from the tapawaha (lines around the edge of the mouth) – and Te Hakeke (Ngāti Apa) signed with a mangōpare-type design. Descendants of Pōmare (Ngāti Manu), Kawiti (Ngāti Hine) and Tirarau (Te Parawhau), who attended a hui at Kawiti Marae, Waiomio in 2011, spoke of how they believed their ancestors' moko represented 'sky, water and Papatuanuku'.[6] They explained that 'Tirarau's [signature] is Te Taki-o-Autahi (the Southern Cross), Pomare's is Nga Wai Ata Rere (the meeting/confluence of three rivers), and Kawiti's koru represents Te Whanautanga o Te Ao (the birth of the world).'[7] As evidence of the veneration that they gave these marks, the whānau called them tohu – a word that can be translated on one level as marks, but on a deeper level as signs that stand in for the ancestors, as if they were still here – rather than being just a mark on paper.

These tohu foretold great change for the chiefs and their communities, in unforeseen directions, following the signing of Te Tiriti. A letter to King William IV (1831) and He Whakaputanga o te Rangatiratanga o Nu Tirene/Declaration of Independence of the United Tribes of New Zealand (1835) had already signalled Māori determination to assert their sovereignty. Only two chiefs signed all three documents: the brothers Te Wharerahi and Rewa (Ngāi Tawake, Ngāti Tautahi, Te Patu Keha and Te Uriongongo). Both were well-known figures around the Bay of Islands and regularly took part in Hongi's taua around the North Island. Rewa was known as a peacemaker and, probably because of this, he took over the leadership from Hongi when he died in 1828.[8] Te Wharerahi, the elder brother, had strong alliances in the Bay of Islands, as his wife Tari was the sister of the chiefs Eruera Maihi Patuone and Tāmati Wāka Nene. The brothers later signed Te Tiriti.

Māori also started incising lettering into the skin. Moko was a widespread practice throughout New Zealand, with mainly curvilinear designs, but by the 1820s other designs were introduced. The earliest example of this was made by a young girl from the Bay of Islands, who in April 1824 carved on her arm the name of the French ship *La Coquille* that she had just visited. René Lesson, a naturalist aboard the ship, saw several women in the bay who 'had tattooed on their arms, the way European sailors do, the name of our ship and the year we put it there. There will at least be some living medallions to mark our passage'.[9] By this account, this girl and her friends were experimenting with a style of 'tattoo' (rather than moko) that they had seen around them: by marking her skin in this way the girl is memorialising the event, as well as marking herself out as someone who has been on the ship.

This moko practice of inscribing text on skin re-emerged in the late twentieth century, when Māori began marking their skin with the names of their partner, children or other whānau members on their arms, upper chest and back. Designer Johnson Witehira calls these markings 'kupu tā tangata' – 'tattooed text', and he points in particular to those of Turanui of Whanganui, who has the word 'RAMAIPAHA' inscribed across his chest, and Koha Hipango, also of Whanganui, who has 'RAHAPA' and 'WARI' down her right arm.[10] From a design perspective, he says, there may be regional and tribal stylistic variations based on the style of

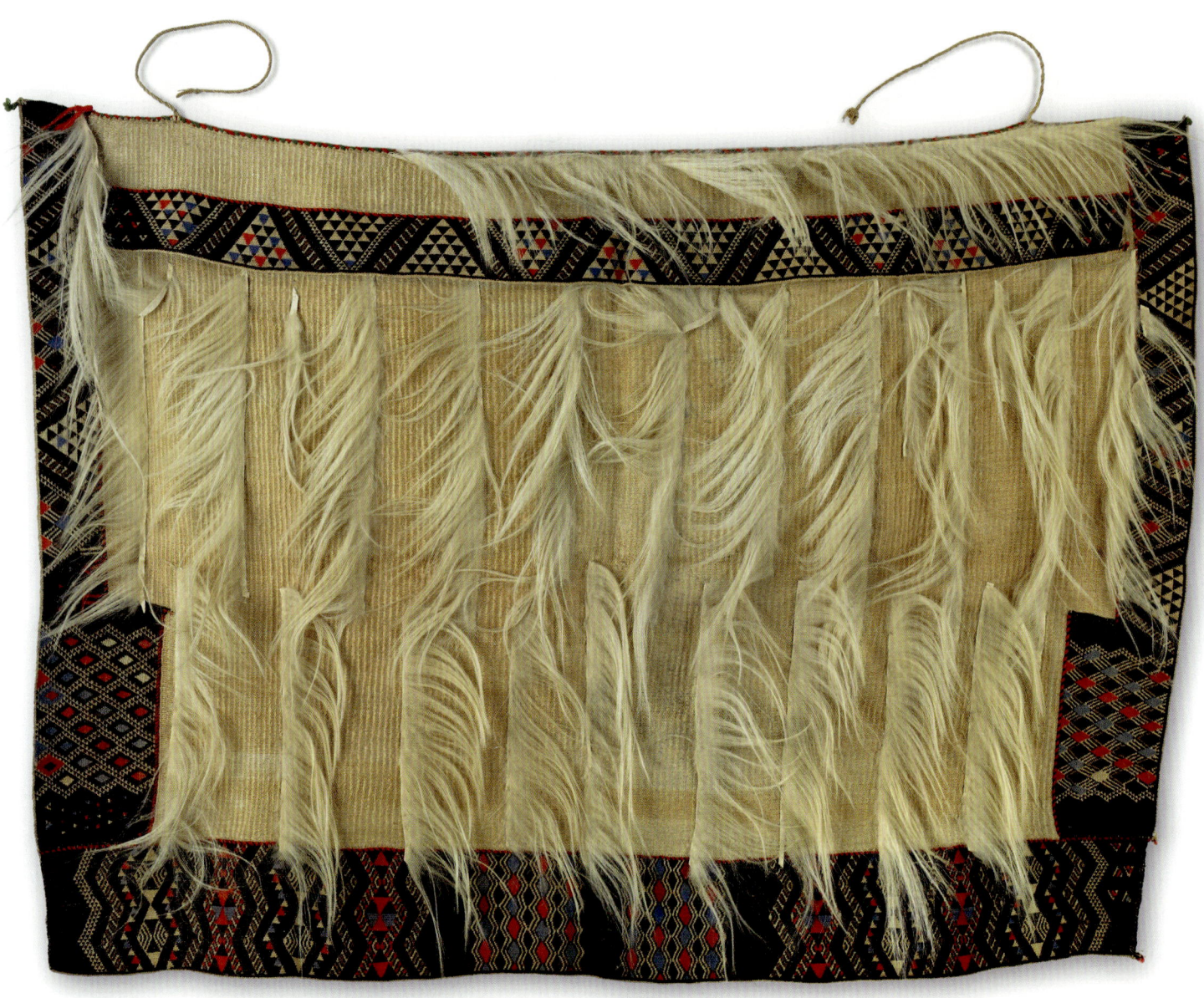

Remarkable kaitaka huaki with tāniko borders on all sides and strips of dog skin. The weaver has made the tāniko in traditional black, brown and undyed fibre, along with red, blue and yellow wool. The initials 'TA' are incorporated into the tāniko border on the left side, just above its wide part, possibly referring to the name of the weaver. Two bands of vertical dog-skin strips with straight hair are attached to the kaupapa; the skin has been cured and precisely cut into strips, which have been sewn into vertical lines with cotton.
British Museum, Oc.1995.Q.8

the text; another interpretation is that different moko artists were involved.

In Māori architecture, lettering came to be used in tukutuku and in carving. The artist Karauria Kauri pioneered the practice when he placed the names of tūpuna in tukutuku around the walls of the wharenui Porourangi (1888). This was even more unusual in that it was the male ancestors who were depicted in the tukutuku panels in Porourangi, and the female ancestors who were represented in the carved poupou. This may relate to the fact that Ngāti Porou women often held positions of leadership, and almost all their meeting houses are named after female ancestors.

In carvings in the wharenui Te Hau ki Tūranga (1845), Raharuhi Rukupō carved the names of the ancestors he depicted on the poupou – though these names appear to have been removed when the house was moved into the Colonial Museum in the 1860s. Apanui Te Hamaiwaho chose to use lettering to identify the carvings of ancestors in Ngāti Awa wharenui Hotunui (1878, now in Auckland Museum); and Ngāti Kahungunu carvers placed the names of the ancestors depicted on the large pou on the ancestors' chests, such as on Te Kauru o Te Rangi. This practice also occurred in the South Island, as Atholl Anderson records:

> The posts and doors of the meeting house at Tuahiwi [north of Kaiapoi] were covered in Maori writing by 1849 and some Ngai Tahu, as had Ngati Mamoe before them, went back to the rock shelters to add their pictures to the Waitaha drawings – and with their pictures of sailing ships and horses they sometimes left their names and greetings to the ancestors, all in neat missionary script.[11]

In this lettering practice, tohunga whakairo were acknowledging the changes that were occurring in the way in which knowledge was being transmitted through the generations, shifting from oral to written. The role of the kaikōrero in interpreting the carving also changed, because now everyone could see who the carving depicted.

By the mid-nineteenth century the traditional whare wānanga – that ancient institution brought to Aotearoa by Pacific ancestors to preserve knowledge and traditions – was changing. The transmission of tapu knowledge was increasingly shifting from an oral to a written system. In the 1850s the Ngāti Kahungunu tohunga Te Mātorohanga (1836–1865?) dictated the stories of genealogy, creation, how Aotearoa was discovered and settled and much more to Hoani Te Whatahoro and Aporo Te Kumeroa, who had been taught to read and write in mission schools.[12] These manuscripts were soon marginalised as printed histories written by Pākehā authors – with all of their prejudices and misunderstandings – became widely available. Books soon replaced the fluid oral narration of history, and within a generation almost all the whare wānanga had closed down.

Māori weavers also used text in their artworks. They began incorporating text in traditional kākahu, as seen in a number of cloaks in museum collections. A nineteenth-century korowai in Te Papa's collection has letters in wool woven into the kaupapa. It is not known what the letters represent: perhaps they are mnemonics for concepts, or people's initials. Another cloak made slightly later has the letters 'MA' and 'KU' included in the tāniko border: these could refer to the maker (Makurata Paitini) or, more cheekily, to the Māori word 'māku' or 'it is mine'.

There are numerous other examples in museum collections where weavers have added text or lettering to kākahu. The largest kākahu in Auckland Museum measures a phenomenal 3m wide. The weaver has embroidered in serif font the text 'NOMAERATATAI' in bright red wool just above the tāniko on the lower edge of the cloak. The 'E' has lost its wool, and this makes interpretation of the word difficult: perhaps 'Maeratatai' was the name of the weaver, making the translation 'By Maeratatai'. There are also several examples in the British Museum of kaitaka from the nineteenth century where weavers have incorporated text, including a kaitaka from the early nineteenth century with a name embroidered in blue wool, now illegible (1938.7-7.1); and a pre-1850 kaitaka where the weaver has added the name 'Eliza' on one corner (1938.10-1.78) – possibly the 'E' of 'E. L. Bateson', who was given the cloak in 1850 by J. A. Lister, and maybe added after the change of owner to personalise the gift;[13] and a kaitaka with 'TA' in the tāniko border on the left-hand side.

There are undoubtedly many more cloaks in collections that include text as a way for weavers to assert their agency over the work by literally 'signing' it, especially if the cloak was made on commission. Some weavers included a secret signature in the textile by adding surprising details in discreet sections of the work. With more knowledge about

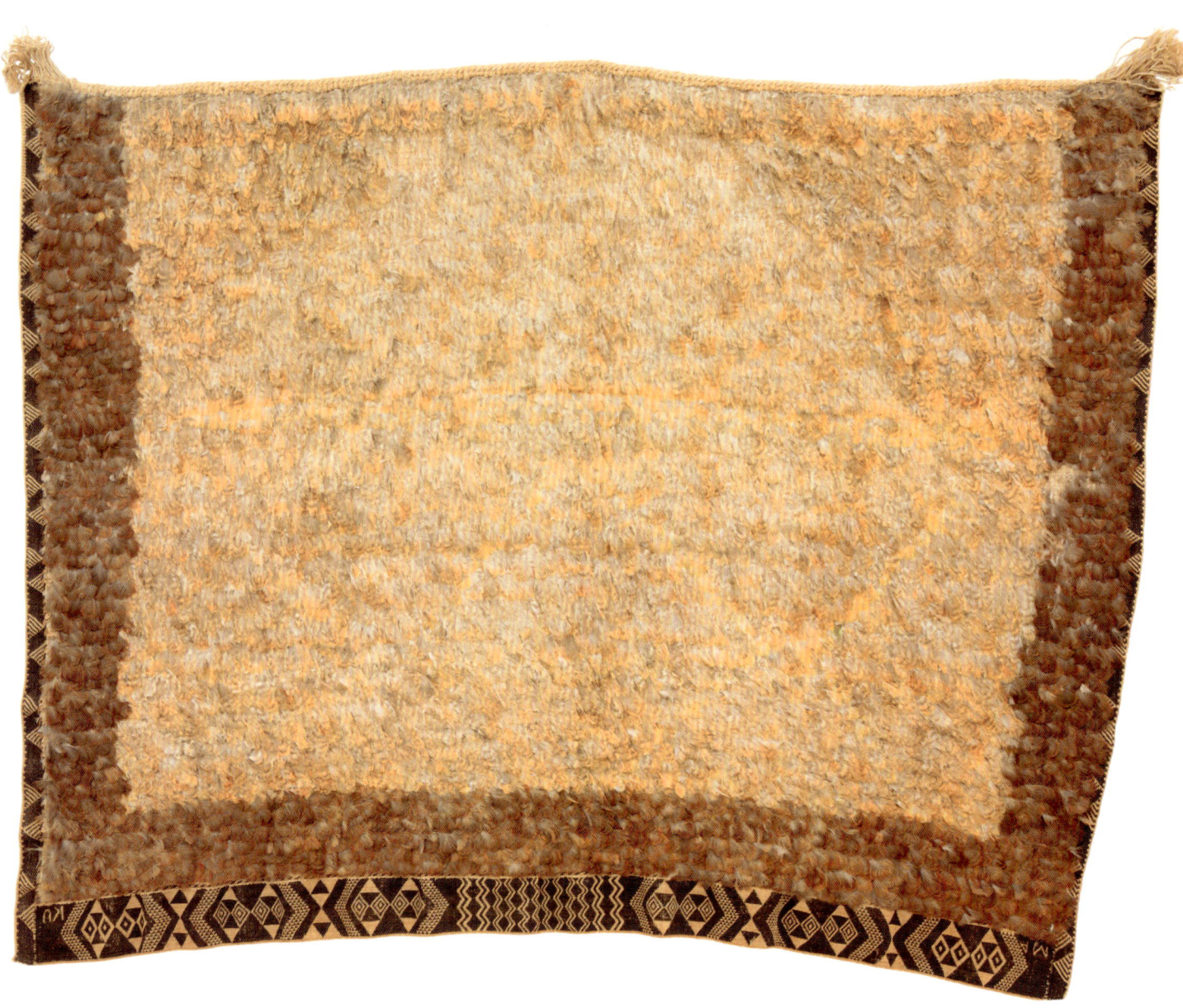

Kahu kura woven by Makurata Paitini (Tūhoe), with MA/KU included in the tāniko on the lower edge.
Tāmaki Paenga Hira Auckland War Memorial Museum, AM5975

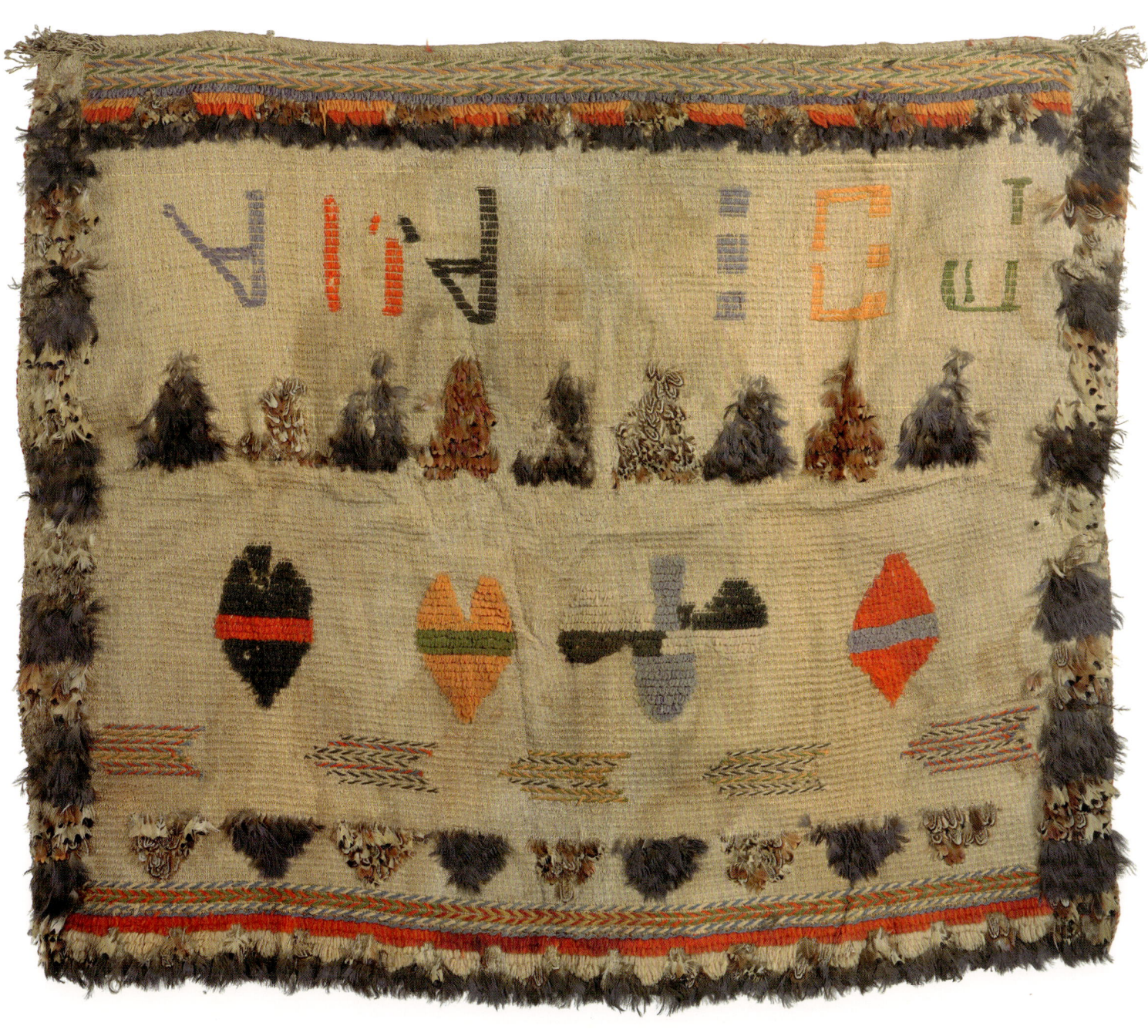

The maker of this remarkable kākahu has decorated the kaupapa with feathers and used brightly coloured wool for lettering and playing-card motifs. The cloak was found in the flooded basement of the New Zealand High Commission, London in 1984. No other information about its provenance is known.
Te Papa Tongarewa Museum of New Zealand, ME015747

what is in museum collections, especially overseas, more cloaks with text will be revealed, and perhaps be tracked back to the artist and the community they originated from.

## Changing traditions in South Island art

While Māori adapted and changed their art forms over generations, it was during the nineteenth century that the most dramatic changes occurred. Māori responses to contact with Europeans and North Americans varied in different settlements. Often the changes were prompted by the level of interest the newcomers showed in the extraction of natural resources such as gold and timber on the one hand, and their desire for political control over the land on the other. These activities often ran in tandem. The creation of new art projects reflected these changing dynamics, both within kāinga and externally, because art was often only made during periods of relative peace, when artists, who were often chiefs in their own right, had the time and energy to be creative and to reflect on current values and ideas through artistic expression. Indeed, in some kāinga, art thrived throughout the nineteenth century in periods immediately after warfare, as communities sought to mend relations, and to bring into balance various close social and political relationships. The emergence of the whare whakairo in the 1870s is a case in point.

A study of art from the South Island gives a snapshot of some of these concerns in the nineteenth century. Atholl Anderson lists the various commercial and trading interests that were active in the South Island over this period. They include: sealers (1790s–1827), those involved in the flax trade (1813–1840s), whalers (from 1839), and passing ships that called in to Foveaux Strait, between the South Island and Rakiura Stewart Island.[14] The whalers were the largest group – a phenomenal 271 whaling ships visited New Zealand waters between 1833 and 1839. Members of each of these groups intermarried with local women, and this gave them access to ancestral land and resources. They introduced foods, goods and technologies which, by 1840, had started to affect the ways in which kāinga operated. Many people moved to be closer to new economic ventures, or began producing crops such as potatoes or rearing pigs to sell, so they could purchase whaleboats and other European items.

Artists continued to articulate and imbue their works with central Māori concepts, despite being surrounded by increasing numbers of Europeans and their culture. Key values associated with art continued. Anderson notes that throughout the nineteenth century, 'traditional social practices and ideology were hardly troubled by alien influences. The rules of tapu were plain and were applied comprehensively and decisively.'[15] One example is a series of taua muru in 1825 that centred on the tapu associated with a cloak. A woman named Murihaka, while she was looking after the chief Tamaiharanui's house, tried on his kahu kurī, thereby compromising his personal tapu and mana. This episode, which was witnessed by others, led to at least five kāinga being attacked: more than eighty people were killed and others injured in an event that has since been called the Kaihuānga ('eat relations') feud. Such events reinforce how important concepts such as mana and tapu were within communities at this time, and the steps that hapū would take to protect and enforce these values.

In the south, art forms began to incorporate European materials and technologies. This occurred over a relatively short period. By 1827 waka were being fitted with oars and square sails (and soon were replaced completely by whaleboats); two-roomed thatched cottages were replacing whare in some areas. Like their northern counterparts, South Island chiefs would wear European-style clothing when around Pākehā, but would often revert to customary clothing when at home.

In the South Island many art traditions were no longer practised by 1850. Selected women wore full-face moko, such as the wives of Karetai and Pokeni in 1840. The practice of tangihaehae (see page 160) was active in Akaroa (east of Christchurch) the same year: one commentator wrote, '[we] saw a woman crouching over her husband's corpse as two female relatives scored her face, breasts and belly with vertical slashes from shells, pouring into the cuts a dark liquid to perpetuate the sign of widowhood'.[16] Tangihaehae was also practised further south in Ōtākou, a small settlement on the Otago harbour, as revealed in the plaster cast made of the chief Heroua in 1840 that shows tangihaehae across his cheeks. In other areas, clothing and ornaments were 'indigenised' – such as European-style shoes made from whītau (scotched flax),[17] and kahu kurī made from European dog fur and held together with aurei made from pigs' tusks.[18] Architecture evolved with different functions, such as needing to provide a closed building for large-scale meetings:

large whare rangatira were used for women's activities such as weaving during the day, and men's kōrerorero (speeches) at night; and by 1840 the architecture of these whare was set aside altogether in favour of buildings modelled on cottages at whaling stations.[19]

The institution of kai haukai (tribute) was active in the South Island. These distributions were based on the dominant/subservient hapū dynamic, but also the tuakana/teina (older/younger sibling) concept. As Anderson describes it, 'Distribution of commodities served to reinforce the social order more generally.'[20] As with tahuaroa described earlier, the kai haukai event would consist of speeches and hākari across several days, and the exchange of taonga and other 'luxury goods' such as 'kotuku feathers ... mats and canoes'.[21] These kai haukai were 'severely disrupted' by the coming of Pākehā, and the focus shifted in many hapū to the acquisition of European goods, materials and tools – as potatoes replaced kūmara, so too did metal replace pounamu.

### Conclusion

By the start of the 1840s Aotearoa New Zealand was a very different place than it had been 200 years before. The Pākehā population was increasing exponentially, and hapū were under no illusions as to the implications of this for them. Rangatira and ariki were still the dominant political force among Māori, but other types of leaders began to emerge and to challenge their people for allegiance. Frustration at a lack of accountability by Pākehā and general lawlessness among their people had made Māori listen when the idea of a treaty was raised. European materials and technologies introduced during the early decades of the nineteenth century reinvigorated traditions and forced others to be set aside. The political world impacted on whānau, hapū and iwi as the settler government sought to balance illegal land grabs and the settlers' desire for land as well as, most importantly, the formal expansion of the British Empire. The creation and circulation of newly made taonga among Māori became ever more important as relationships between Māori and Pākehā pivoted on this exchange. Unprecedented rates of change would forever impact on the cultural landscape.

# MOKO SIGNATURES AND TINO RANGATIRATANGA
## NGARINO ELLIS

During the early nineteenth century the individual mana of a rangatira was often made public through the creation of artworks, either by themselves or by others. These are now considered taonga tuku iho, as they signify relationships between individuals and/or hapū. From 1815 rangatira began putting pen to paper for several different purposes, and they used their moko as a form of signature and self-portrait.

Land deeds and formal letters often required signatures to make them legally binding. The earliest land grant in Aotearoa was confirmed in 1815 when Ngāpuhi chief Te Uri o Kanae signed a sale deed with his moko. This practice soon spread to other parts of the North – initially to sites where the missionaries were settling and, later, to other deeds and letters. A letter to King William IV dated 5 October 1831, for instance, was signed and sent by thirteen chiefs from the North to ask the monarch to stop his people from making illicit purchases of Māori land. As Ngāpuhi historian Mānuka Hēnare notes: 'The placing of the *tohu* on paper was considered an invitation to a relationship between the leader and his people.'[1]

Eleven of the thirteen who signed the letter in 1831 sought a further confirmation of their rangatiratanga in 1835 when they and twenty-two other rangatira formed the United Tribes of Nu Tirene: they adopted a flag called Te Kara and signed He Whakaputanga o te Rangatiratanga o Nu Tirene/Declaration of Independence of the United Tribes. They were not only from Te Tai Tokerau; they included Te Wherowhero (Waikato-Tainui) and Te Hāpuku (Ngāti Kahungunu). In this document, rangatira chose to sign with their moko to signal their solidarity in the face of an increasingly unstable political landscape.

Of course, this practice spread nationwide when the sheets of Te Tiriti o Waitangi began circulating throughout the country in 1840: rangatira could see how other chiefs were signing using their moko, and many followed suit. Often they chose one design from their moko to place in pen and ink; constraints of space prevented any elaboration.[2]

That same year another important document was signed using moko. Now known as the Wentworth Indenture, this was a land deed for the prospective purchase of the entire South Island and Stewart Island by William Wentworth and John Jones from eight Ngāi Tahu chiefs. On the second page of the deed, seven rangatira signed with their moko: John Towack (Hone Tūhawaiki), Kaikoraira, 'Jackey White' (Karetai), 'Tohowack', Tuckawa (Tukawa), Tyroa (Te Mātenga Taiaroa), and 'Bogener'. Four of the men drew their entire moko kanohi, one drew almost his full-face moko (except for his left upper cheek – but this may have been left blank in real life), and the remaining two chiefs drew only their foreheads. The indenture is a taonga as it is a snapshot of the practice and styles of moko for Ngāi Tahu in 1840, which is important information for artists practising today – especially those who are Ngāi Tahu.[3]

Hēnare writes about the significance of this practice: 'The *moko* mark was considered something holy and binding, because it was taken from the skin of the head, believed to be the most sacred part of a leader's body.'[4] The documents are now considered tapu as they carry the mana and kōrero of those who signed. This signing practice was relatively short-lived, however, reflecting the quick uptake of literacy by Māori, and a desire to sign using text. Despite this, Ngāi Tahu chief Tūhawaiki used his moko and text signatures interchangeably: in doing so he was making an important political statement of his knowledge – and his mana. Today these documents remind us of the quickly changing landscape that rangatira were facing, and the importance of their moko to their chiefly identity.

Portraiture and self-portraiture are art practices that reveal not just the appearance of the subject but also how to conceptualise who they are politically, socially and culturally. It was no different for Māori. From 1815 rangatira began drawing themselves with pen on paper at the request of European missionaries and traders. Examples are now rare, but those we have give a remarkable insight into how Māori conceptualised themselves at this time. What stands out with these drawings is that their moko subsumes their physiognomy – the physical traits of the face such as a long nose or wide cheekbones. Moko becomes first and foremost the indicator of identity – one that is instantly recognised and remembered by others. Ngāti Toa chief Te Pehi Kupe, when he was in England in 1824, could draw not only his own moko but also those of his father and brother. Likewise, Rēnata Kawepō could draw those of a woman (most likely his mother or sister) and of a man (not Kawepō himself).[5] Portraits of whānau members with moko prompted feelings of homesickness and loneliness – Te Pēehi wept when he had drawn his father and brother. These drawings are not just pen on paper; they are considered *as* the person. Just as ancestors depicted in carvings are greeted with hongi (pressing noses in greeting) and spoken to as if present, this tikanga is extended to drawings – and, later, to photographs. All reproductions of them depict an ancestor, a loved one, recognisable primarily from their moko.

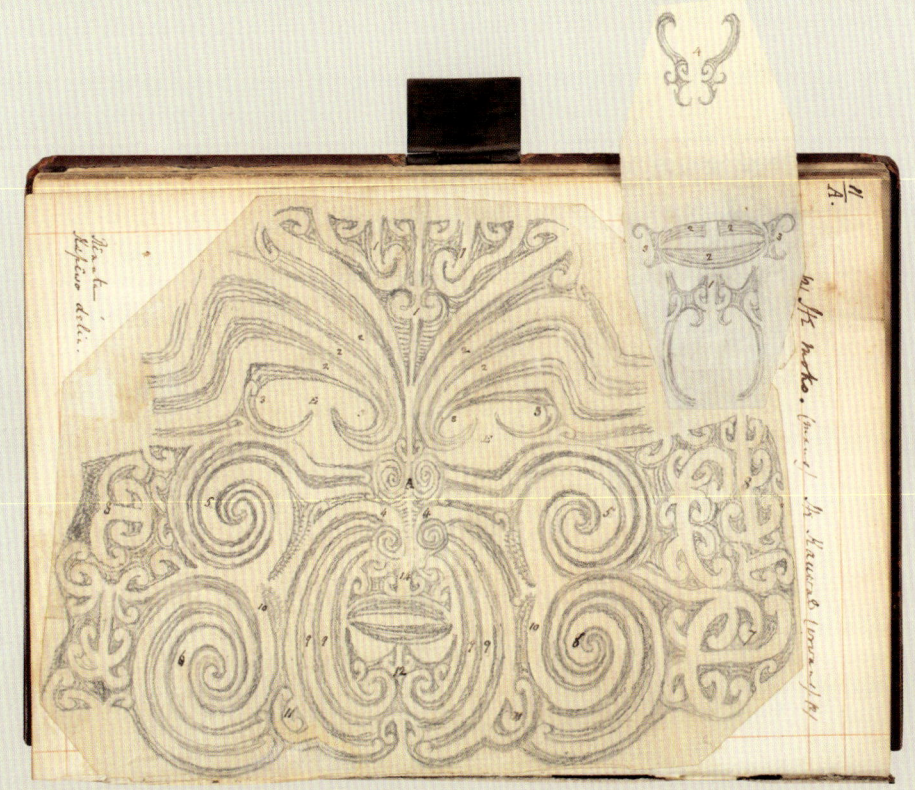

Drawings of moko by Māori in the early nineteenth century. Rēnata Kawepō drew the moko of a woman, possibly his mother or sister, in the 1840s.
State Library of New South Wales, SAFE/DLMS 36, 997463, bequeathed by Sir William Dixson, 1952

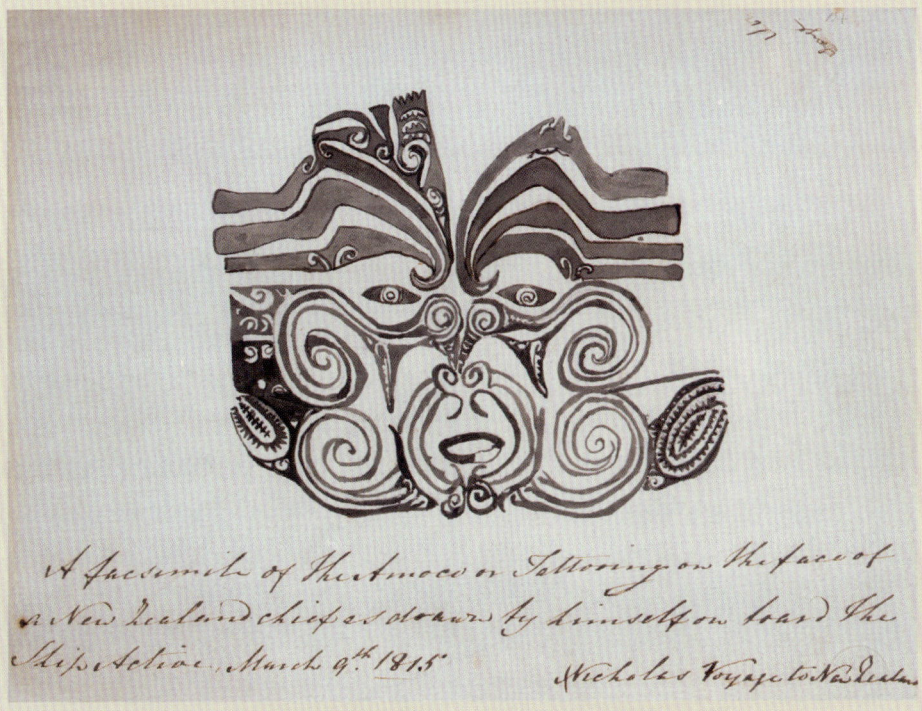

Te Morenga's self-portrait, drawn when he was on board the *Active*, 9 March 1815. This is not the original but one copied from a drawing made by Te Morenga. Juniper Ellis suggests that this drawing may have been done by the engraver of John Liddiard Nicholas's *Narrative of a Voyage to New Zealand* (1817).
Alexander Turnbull Library, A-080-061

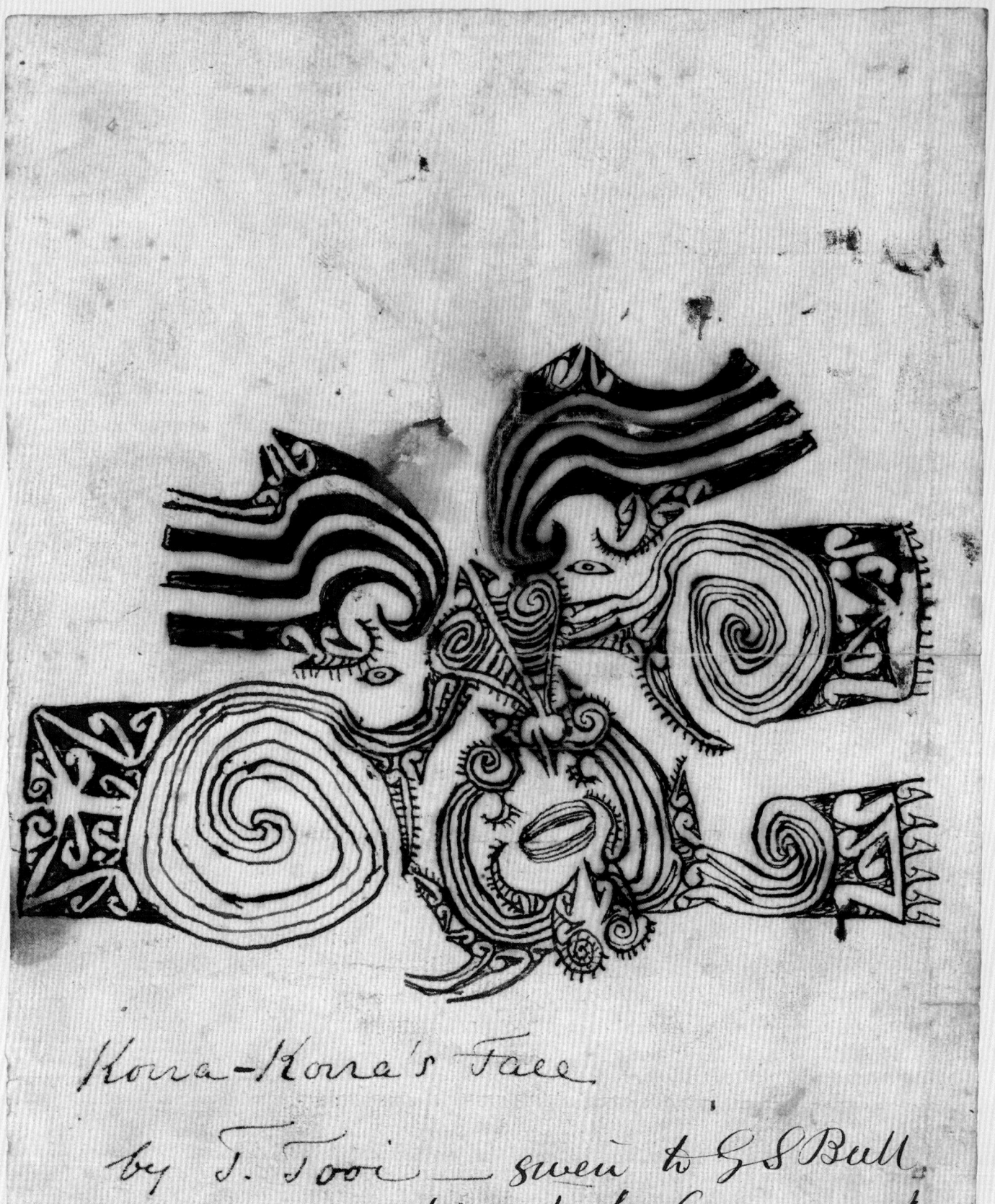

Korra-Korra's Face

by T. Tooi — given to G S Bull
and by him to W Greenwood

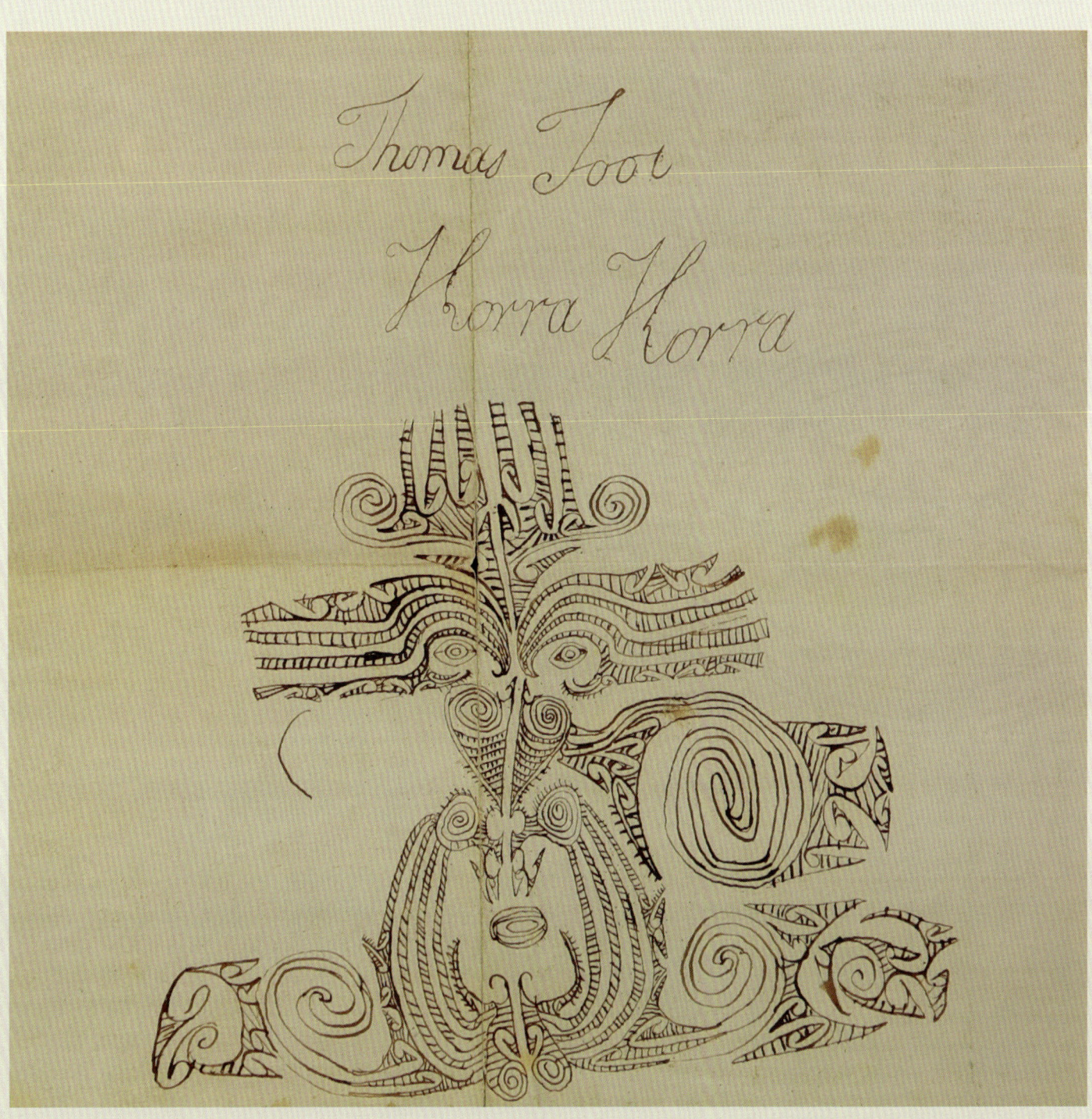

Two portraits drawn by Ngare Raumati chief Tuai in London of his elder brother Korokoro in 1818. In the image on the left he clearly writes who the portrait is destined for – G. S. Bull.
Cadbury Research Library Special Collections, University of Birmingham, CMS/ACC14 C2

# EARLY MĀORI DRAWINGS
## DEIDRE BROWN

Māori adopted pen, pencil and chalk drawing as a means of expression from the late eighteenth century onwards. Some of the earliest drawings were made at the behest of Pākehā for the purpose of cross-cultural communication; others were Māori artists' responses to issues that were affecting Māori. The artists ranged from the unskilled novice to those who had learnt to write and draw on slates in mission schools. People and supernatural creatures animated these drawings, as they had done in rock art and whakairo rākau, in addition to new themes of ancestral and cultural landscapes.

A drawing made in 1793 by Tuki Tahua is likely the earliest Māori drawing. Tuki and his friend Huru were abducted from Tokerau (Doubtless Bay) by Pākehā sailors and taken to the Australian-governed territory of Norfolk Island for six months, where Tuki was to learn English and identify, for the benefit of colonial officials, resources in his homeland. At one point Tuki's captors handed him a piece of chalk and asked him to draw a map of Aotearoa with 'resources' and 'flax industries' marked on it – as best as they could explain those terms.[1] The confident map that he drew on the floor indicates that during his six-month stay he had already come to terms with holding a drawing implement and had shifted his own understanding of moving through the landscape to thinking of it as something to look down on, possibly as the result of seeing nautical charts for navigation.

The map is egocentric – the northern region that Tuki was most familiar with is drawn the largest, and the rest of the country is increasingly smaller and less defined. The South Island is an amorphous form labelled 'Pounamu' and featuring a large circle – because Tuki knew that was the source of the stone. The annotations made on the map by one of his hosts indicate that Tuki had never been to the South Island, but had been told about it by a respected chief, since this was the place where 'stones for hatchets' came from. Indeed, all of the annotations that record Tuki's verbal comments indicate that he related to the natural and physical landscape through whakapapa – demonstrated by his association of human endeavour with each place. Tuki showed in his drawing how the pounamu travelled from the south to the north – a journey of over 1500 kilometers – through a trading trail that becomes more defined as it enters his tribal region. Regardless of what his hosts might have wanted it to be, Tuki's map is an expression of a Māori cultural landscape.

By the nineteenth century Māori were becoming more conversant with cartography, through their participation in land surveys and maritime navigation. Instead of being a constraint, for some Māori artists knowledge of these conventions inspired interesting ways of articulating cultural and landscape knowledge. One 1855 drawing shows a nākahi, a sort of cross between a biblical serpent of Eden and a taniwha, flying above settlements in the Hokianga and Whangārei districts – it was possibly protecting these places against a structure depicted on the right, described as the 'house of evil on the water coming hither'. The 'house' has been interpreted as a ship, and it may represent the introduction of some disease epidemic to the Māori community, since these were known to have arrived by ship. The illustration shows how the supernatural can be recorded with cartographic-style representations of localities. What is interesting is that the map was hand-copied many times and displayed in Māori houses as a talisman to ward off disease.[2]

A drawing made by 'Aporo', a member of the Pai Mārire movement, also features a taniwha. A soldier took the sketch from Aporo's body after he died in an 1867 battle with government troops who had invaded the Bay of Plenty. He has used the edges of the page as a continuous horizon line, and a mixture of perspective and elevation for the depiction of one of the movement's niu (a flagpole and divination structure). The supernatural is present in the figure of the taniwha, who is interacting with the subjects shown on the page. This was one of many drawings made by Pai Mārire followers that documented – perhaps for the purpose of redistribution and instruction – the spiritual practices associated with niu poles and their flags (see page 324).

Anthropologist Merata Kawharu describes ancestral landscapes as 'part of a network of places and areas that were created or used by gods, mythological heroes, ancestors and their descendants … replete with stories about groups acquiring and then defending, often vigorously, their political association with regions'.[3] Māori familiarity with Pākehā cartography as travellers, survey assistants – and as people under pressure to sell or lose their land to colonists – would have informed their understanding of the power of the drawn line as an instrument of access and land division. Perhaps it was with this knowledge that many decided to pick up chalks, pens and pencils to document, define and defend their communities and ancestral landscapes.

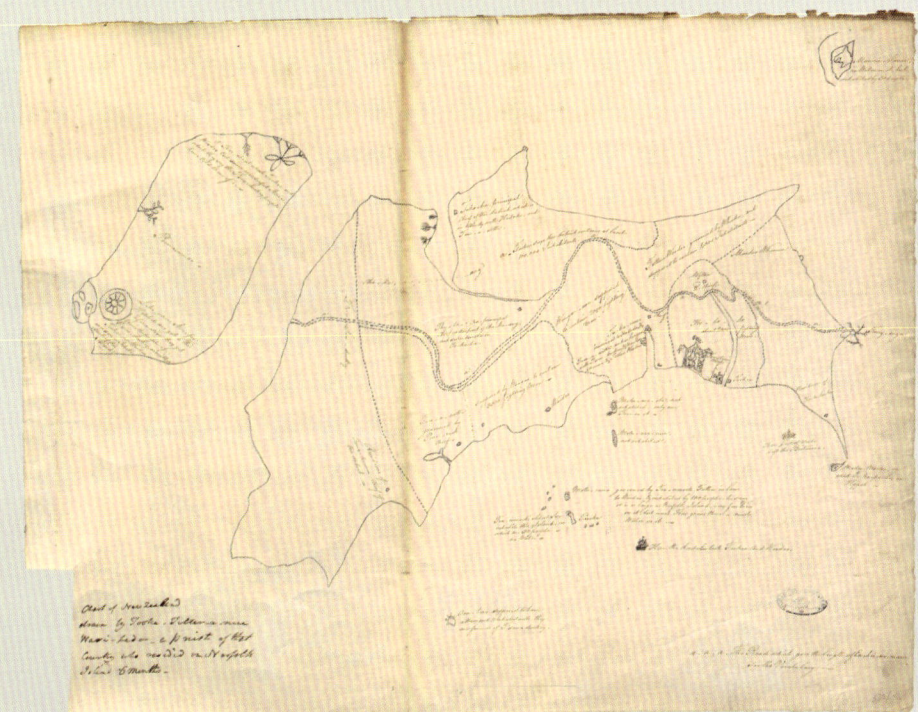

Map drawn by Tuki Tahua of his 'universe', to use Judith Binney's term. Unfortunately, this is an engraving after Tuki's own sketch, and has to be understood as having had an intervening hand in the representation.
Alexander Turnbull Library, MapColl-830ap/[1793] (1798)/Acc.42785

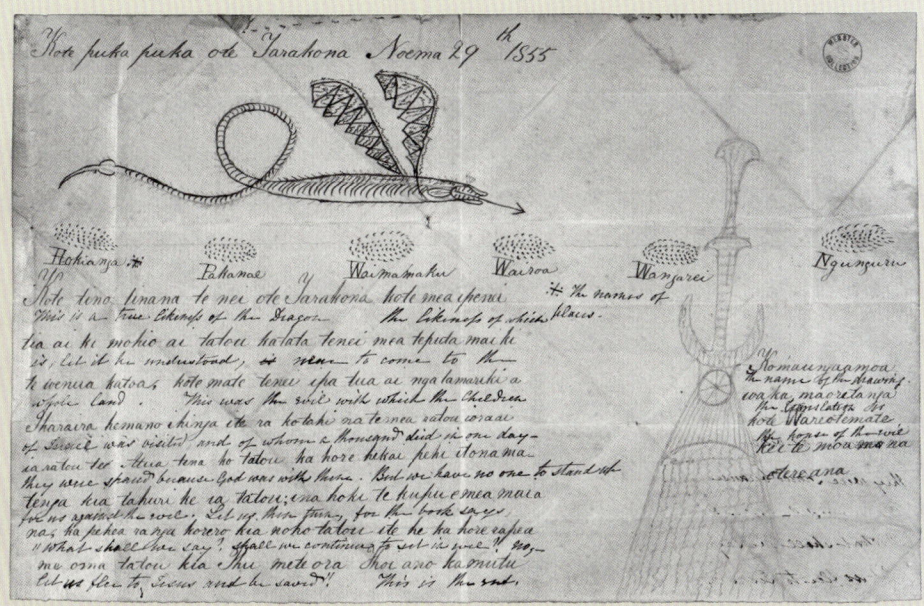

Unknown artist, nākahi drawing, 1855, from a manuscript called 'Ko te Pukapuka o te Tarakona' (The Book of the Dragon), c.1855, collected by the missionary Richard Davis, who sent it to the Church Missionary Society in 1856.
Alexander Turnbull Library, MS-Papers-1009-2/79

# THE SECOND AGE OF IRON
## DEIDRE BROWN

'Kia tu koe to toki Uropi, ka hari tou ngakau: When thou art served with European axes, thy heart will rejoice.'[1] So said Hongi Hika in 1820, as one of the last Māori chiefs to become wealthy through trading goods with Europeans for iron. His words shed light on the centrality of iron to Māori life in the early decades of the nineteenth century.

Iron was introduced to Māori communities in 1769 through trade with James Cook's first voyage. As Māori continued to acquire it, the trade in iron redefined Māori trade routes, influenced the value of stone technologies and transformed Māori architecture and whakairo rākau.

Te Hikutū rangatira Te Pahi established an iron trading station at Te Puna in the Bay of Islands in around 1805. At the station, Māori traded pork, potatoes, fresh water and timber with visiting whaling, sealing and trading vessels for nails, axes, adzes, hoop iron and cauldrons.[2] Māori either bartered with ship smiths to have these iron objects forged into blades, or they used splitting and grinding techniques adapted from stone-tool making to create sharp-edged implements. Around the country, axe heads were turned into weapons and nails and harpoon heads into fishhooks. Many of the examples that survive today are hafted onto elaborately carved wooden and whalebone handles, which is an indication that they had ceremonial and spiritual as well as practical usages. Gouges, drills, chisels and axes were used for tree felling, timber dressing, bush-cutting and making utilitarian and decorative wooden objects, buildings and boats. These iron utensils appear to have performed no better than pounamu, obsidian or shell tools, as Māori struggled to keep them sharp. But their advantage was their accessibility through the sheer volumes available for trade, when compared to stone resources.[3]

Māori were fascinated with every aspect of forged-iron tool production. John Nicholas, who travelled on the *Active* from Sydney to the Bay of Islands in 1814, noted that:

None of the [European] artisans who accompanied us to New Zealand attracted so much attention amongst the natives as the smith. To watch his various labours, they would seat themselves for hours together in his forge; looking at each other occasionally with significant amazement, whenever any part of his operations appeared more intricate than usual ... On these operations they made several remarks among each other; and at first their senses were astonished at the malleability of iron in its ignited state. They always took care to keep at a secure distance from the sparks that were struck out by the hammering, of which they seemed extremely apprehensive.[4]

Māori had no forged iron or fired ceramics tradition, so the transformation of a hard element into a pliable substance that could then be returned to solid as a different useful shape must have been a fascinating, if not close to spiritual, experience for them. In the Māui cycle of Māori oral histories, the fingernails and toenails of Māui's grandmother, the great deity Mahuika, were made of fire. The

The profusion of pātaka with extensive whakairo rākau in the early nineteenth century may have been an outcome of the large quantity of metal tools circulating in the north at that time.
**Augustus Earle, *A tabood store-house at Range-hue [i.e. Rangihoua] Bay of Islands, New Zealand*, 1827**
watercolour, 203 x 343mm, National Library of Australia, nla.obj-134504017

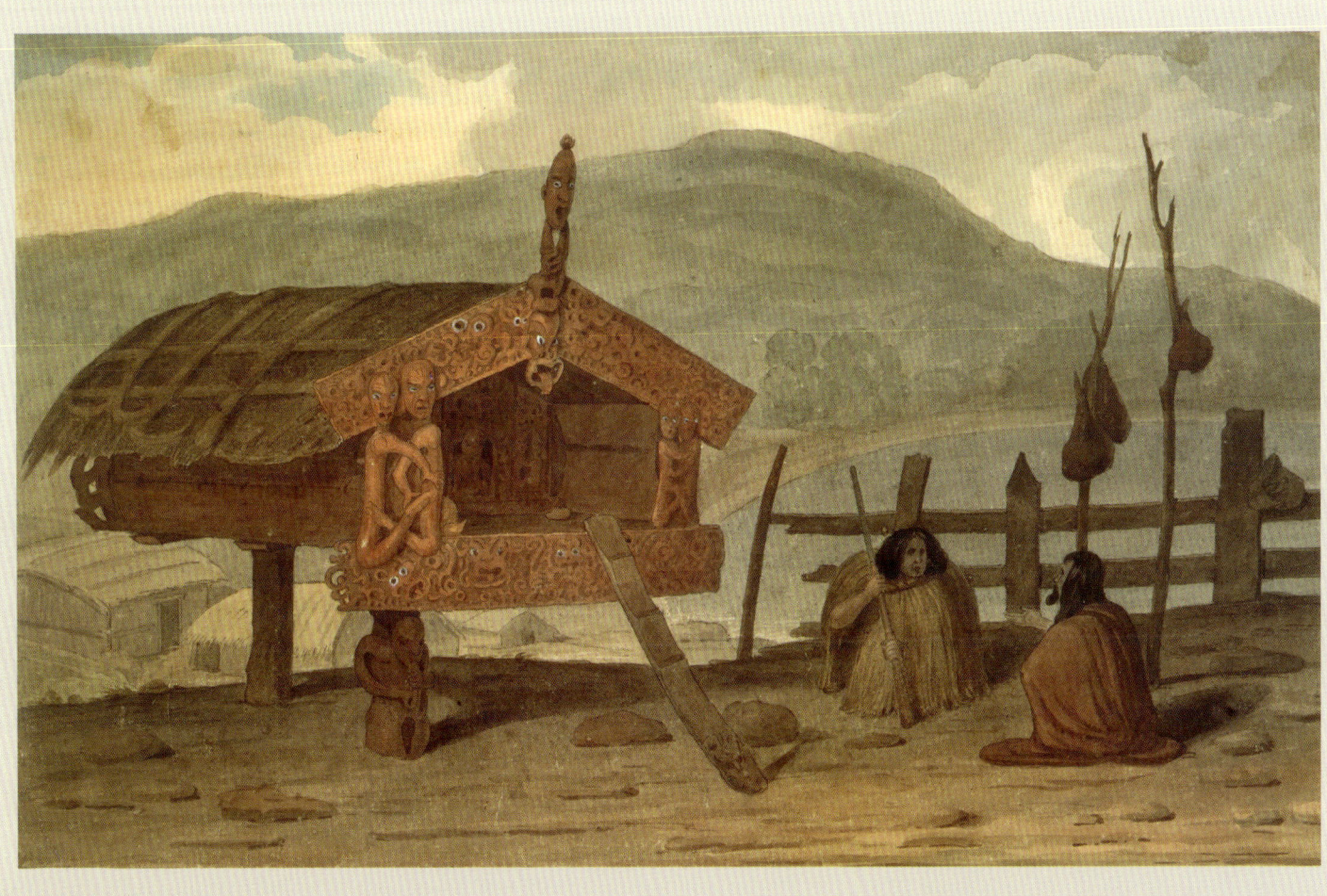

ancient associations of fire made it a tapu commodity that was to be treated with respect – if not avoided – when it was used in unfamiliar circumstances.

Iron transformed the manufacture of utilitarian and artisan objects within communities. The large number of pounamu tools acquired (rather than archaeologically recovered) by nineteenth-century European museums and collectors represents the scale of their divestment by Māori keen to extract any value from these recently obsolete objects. We can only speculate as to how the availability of iron tools might have increased the scale of production of everyday wooden implements such as bird snares, digging sticks and weaving pegs, and how this, in turn, may have affected ecologies, agriculture and textile production – until these implements were themselves made redundant by Pākehā equivalents. At the other end of the production spectrum, Pākehā visitors to the Bay of Islands commented on the number of pātaka that featured a profusion of ornate figurative woodcarvings not seen elsewhere in Aotearoa. This suggests both an enhanced tool kit and a bountiful economy able to support a productive artisan class.[5]

Iron axe-heads were a formidable addition to Māori weaponry when attached to often exquisitely shaped and carved handles. Māori used short-handled pātītī (hatchets) as weapons in close combat: the ancestral figures carved on the handles were like those on the handles of chiefly toki pounamu. The long-handled toki kakauroa provided Māori fighters with the reach required to overcome Pākehā fixed bayonets during the New Zealand Wars.[6] The handles of these weapons were sometimes decorated in the same fashion as customary tewhatewha. A celebrated toki kakauroa named Ringakaha (strong arm) includes one of twelve adze heads that the Church Missionary Society traded with Ngāti Torehina for the land on which the CMS built the mission station at Rangihoua, Northland, in 1814. Te Warihi Kokowai carved the handle, including three straight manawa (strength) lines near the blade to represent the prophecies of the Māori religious leader Te Atua Wera.[7] Ringakaha was taken into battles against government troops at Ruapekapeka, Ōhaeawai and Waikare in 1845 and Kororāreka in 1846, and the taonga is regarded as representing the rights of Māori to defend their lands.[8] In this instance, iron has been the catalyst for a radical fusion of worldviews: it has served to upend the relationships of provider and recipient, coloniser and colonised, by becoming a counter-colonial instrument. The appropriation of iron came to symbolise local resilience and resistance rather than assimilation.

Pātītī with iron heads.
Te Papa Tongarewa Museum of New Zealand, OL000013.S, Oldman Collection, gift of the New Zealand government, 1992; WE001872, bequest of Kenneth Athol Webster, 1971

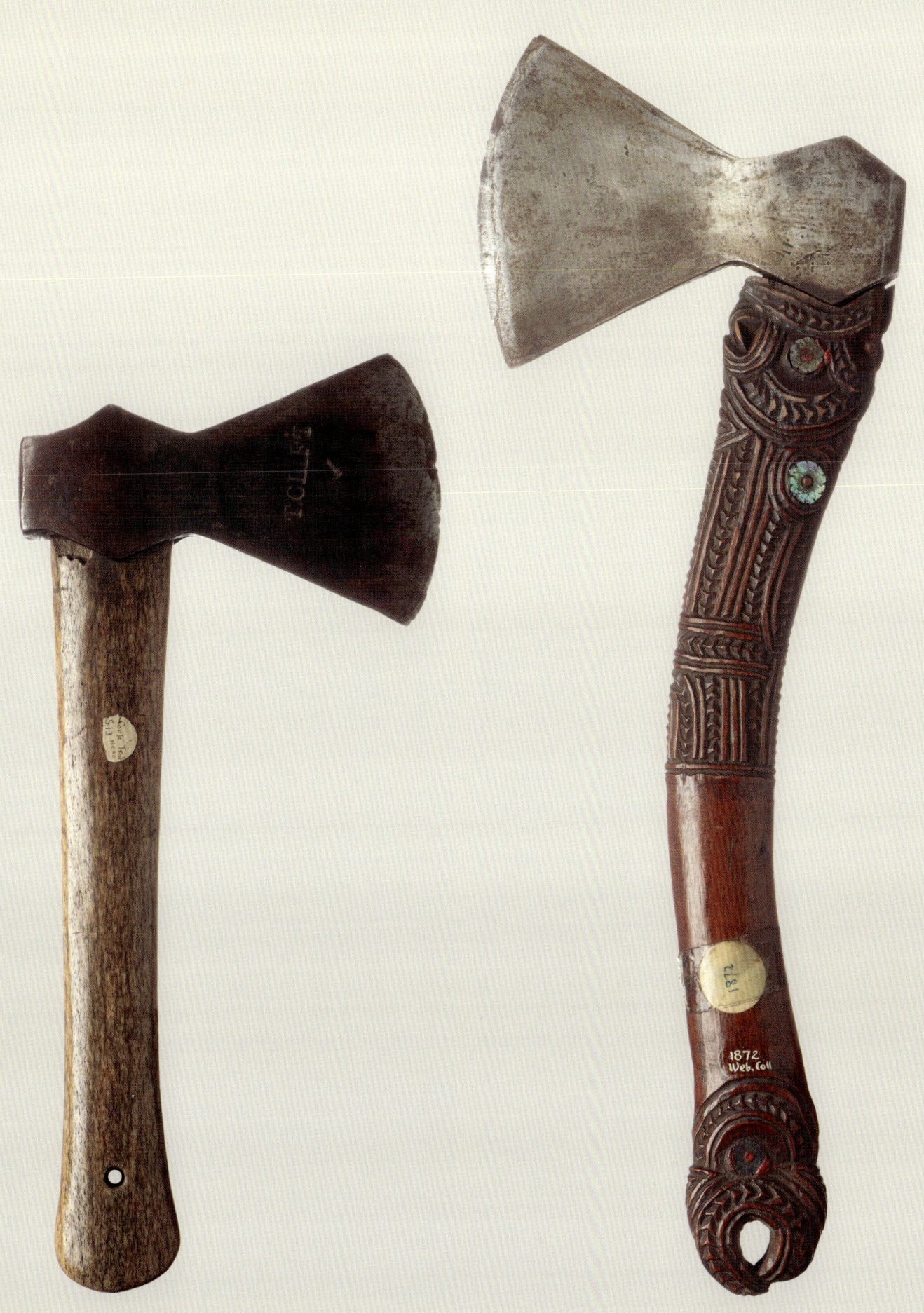

300 | 301

Village at Parihaka, with Taranaki behind.
Josiah Martin, c.1880, Auckland Libraries Heritage Collections 1596-539

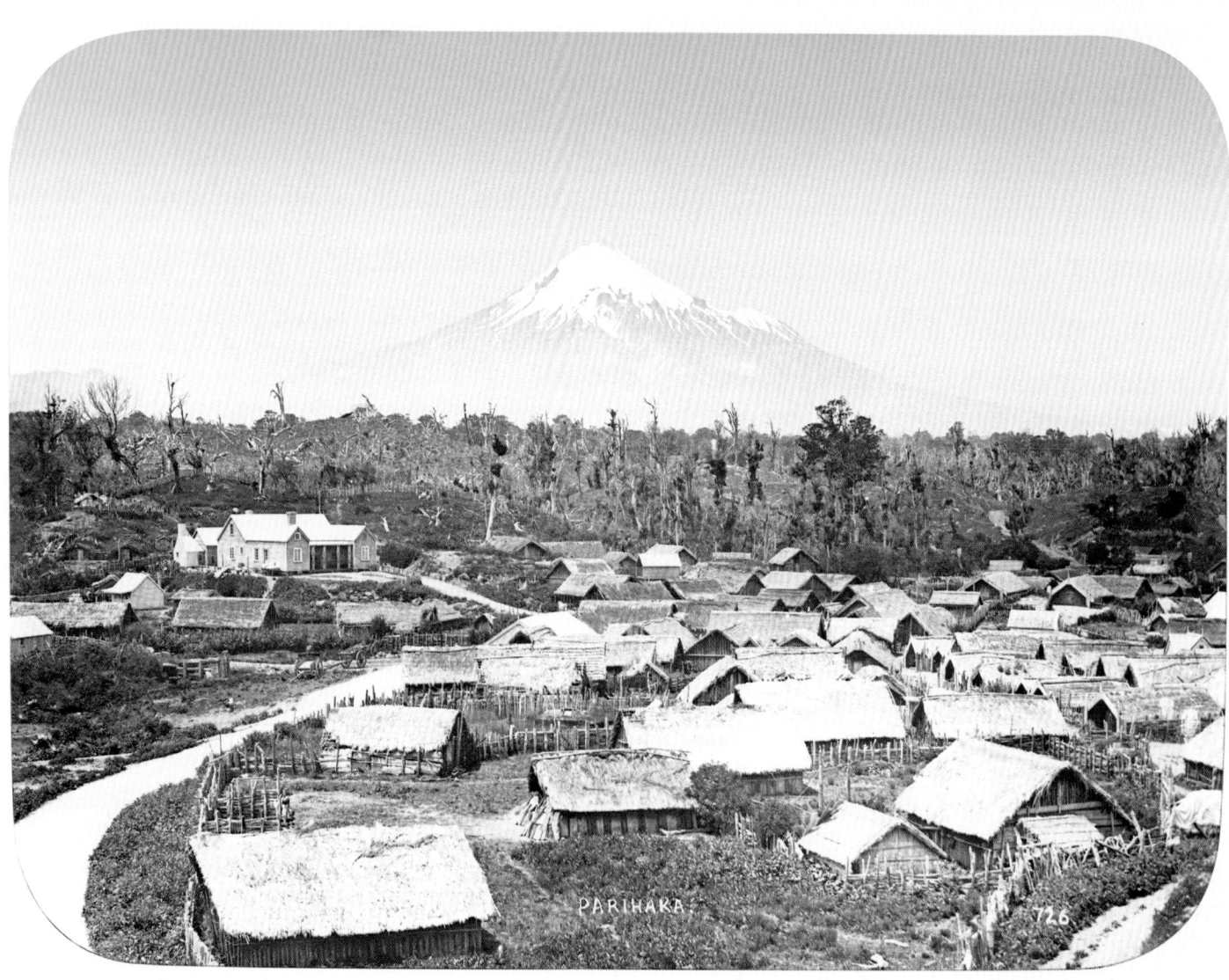

# 12 NGĀ TOI MŌREHU
## THE ARTS OF SURVIVAL
### DEIDRE BROWN

*Kotahi te kōhao o te ngira e kuhuna ai te miro mā, te miro pango, te miro whero. I muri, kia mau ki te aroha, ki te ture, ki te whakapono.*

*Through the eye of the needle pass the white threads, the black threads, and the red threads. Afterwards, looking to the past as you progress, hold firmly to your love, the law, and your faith.*

—Whakataukī about Māori unity given by Pōtatau Te Wherowhero on the occasion of his coronation as first Māori king in 1858

As missionary influence waned, the mana of a new kind of Māori religio-political leader grew, who supplanted and sometimes challenged the artistic, spiritual and political roles of tohunga and rangatira. The second half of the nineteenth century was a tumultuous time for Māori, who struggled to hold on to ancestral lands in the face of mass European immigration. At the same time, they were fighting to maintain their self-determining authority, as conflicts with the settler-dominated government spread through the country.

Even before the signing of Te Tiriti o Waitangi in 1840, Māori in areas with growing Pākehā populations were concerned about how the transfer of land to missionaries and settlers might affect future generations' ability to maintain their ahi kā and access hapū harvesting grounds and resources.[1] Architecture, both Māori and Pākehā, came to symbolise Indigenous land rights and community. Five years after the signing of Te Tiriti, the government was at war with Ngāpuhi. The conflict had the effect of uniting hapū who were outraged by the removal of the capital to Auckland, government authoritarianism, and the complicity of the Anglican Church in military actions against them.[2] As the wars spread to other North Island regions, the notion of a 'Māori' culture, united by ethnicity but diverse in its art practices, began to emerge.

Art embodies struggle in times of great upheaval. Unity as Māori, rather than as a network of hapū and iwi, offered hope to many, and the various collective and leadership models proposed by Māori leaders created opportunities for other types of architecture and associated arts to develop. It was during this period of war, political reorganisation and faith that Māori architecture took on innovative functions, symbolised a contemporary identity, and represented resistance to Pākehā encroachment on land and rangatiratanga. As the number of Pākehā settlers increased, so too did the pressure on Māori to surrender land for towns, farms and transportation routes. Kāinga, and especially marae, became bastions of Māori lifeways, language and art, as Pākehā settlers and the government acquired the land around them by sale, confiscation in the aftermath of the wars, and compulsory purchase through the Public Works Lands Act 1864. Māori designers of the buildings on these vulnerable sites increasingly appropriated Pākehā tools, materials, construction techniques, aesthetics and functional concepts to suit their own, often counter-colonial programmes and needs. This led to imaginative solutions for the representation of tikanga, which was now redefined as a benchmark of cultural stability in an age of social, political and spiritual upheaval. The roles of rangatira and tohunga as leaders in the commissioning and creation of art changed as different types of leaders, practitioners and knowledge-keepers assumed roles within movements that united iwi.

Some of these leaders envisaged a future in which Crown and Māori could be partners in the spirit of the Treaty. Buildings associated with pan-iwi Māori authority were constructed as early as the 1850s, when some tribes sought unity under the Māori king, and this architectural movement spread across war-affected tribal rohe of the North Island in the late nineteenth and early twentieth century. Two parliamentary organisations – the Kauhanganui, which supported the Māori king as the singular head of a Māori nation; and the Paremata Māori, which offered a Westminster-style binational government under the authority of the British monarch – operated within specially designed buildings. Māori parliamentary buildings responded to a growing sense of Indigeneity with a shared culture and outlook that was distinct from that of the Pākehā community, by providing forums for the consolidation of Māori identity, sovereignty and self-determination.

Other leaders, such as Te Kooti Arikirangi Te Tūruki, assumed the spiritual and artistic mantle of tohunga and the mana of rangatira to direct wharenui design towards objectives that embraced custom within a contemporary context. Te Kooti supported his inter-iwi community through a network of wharenui in the eastern North Island; and to the west, at Te Whiti o Rongomai and Tohu Kākahi's Parihaka pā, a large, multi-iwi community was occupying confiscated lands in thatched whare, an architecture that represented the distinct lifeways of Māori. The systematic destruction of Parihaka's buildings by colonial forces after they invaded the settlement in 1881 was one of the closing government actions of the New Zealand Wars: it could be considered a symbolic demonstration of colonial denial of Māori rights to land and self-governance. Te Whiti and Tohu's subsequent reconstruction of Parihaka in the colonial style might also be regarded as the ultimate act of counter-colonisation, heralding an alternative path through these difficult times that would be followed by a generation of charismatic leaders.

## Ngā Pou o te Kīngitanga pātaka and the Kauhanganui Māori parliaments

A model of nationhood that Wiremu Tamihana Tarapīpipi Te Waharoa (Ngāti Hauā) presented during his consultation hui to search for a suitable Māori king inspired Kauhanganui pātaka, wharenui and parliament houses. In these meetings, he would perform a simple architectural act to demonstrate his concept of a workable dual sovereignty. He would plant two branches in the ground – one representing a Māori king and the other the governor of New Zealand – and balance a third branch across the posts which, he explained, was the 'ridgepole of the house', representing the law of God and of Queen Victoria.[3]

Tamihana's ridgepole supported by two posts may have been the inspiration for the eight pātaka known collectively as Ngā Pou o te Kīngitanga (the pillars of the Kīngitanga). The pātaka, which were commissioned and built at a time when rangatiratanga was still strong but was under threat from Pākehā land encroachment, were dedicated to the search for a suitable Māori monarch between 1853 and 1856. This represented an unprecedented display of inter-iwi unity through the western, central and lower North Island.[4] The commissioners were some of the most important paramount leaders of large Māori regions: they included Iwikau Te Heuheu, Tareha Te Moananui, Paora Te Pōtangaroa, Tamihana Te Rauparaha, Te Whiwhi, Tūroa and Wī Tako Ngātata (also known as Wī Tako).[5] Each rangatira was a potential candidate for the Māori kingship, yet in declining the role they continued to demonstrate their support for the kaupapa of the union by building Ngā Pou o te Kīngitanga. Iwikau's relative Horonuku Te Heuheu and his carving team produced a number of Ngā Pou o te Kīngitanga, including the southernmost pātaka, Nuku Tewhatewha, completed in 1856 on the site of Te Mako pā, Te Taitai (also known today as Taitā), and now on permanent display at the Dowse Art Museum in Lower Hutt.[6] Wī Tako (Te Ātiawa) commissioned this pātaka, which was reputed to have cost £3000. It was situated next to his expansive seventeen-room house, also called Te Mako – one of a number of impressive colonial-style homes built by wealthier rangatira to demonstrate their contemporary mana by adopting the trappings of contemporary European 'gentlemen'.[7] Originally from Taranaki, Wī Tako had a difficult relationship with both the mana whenua and the Pākehā settlers of the district

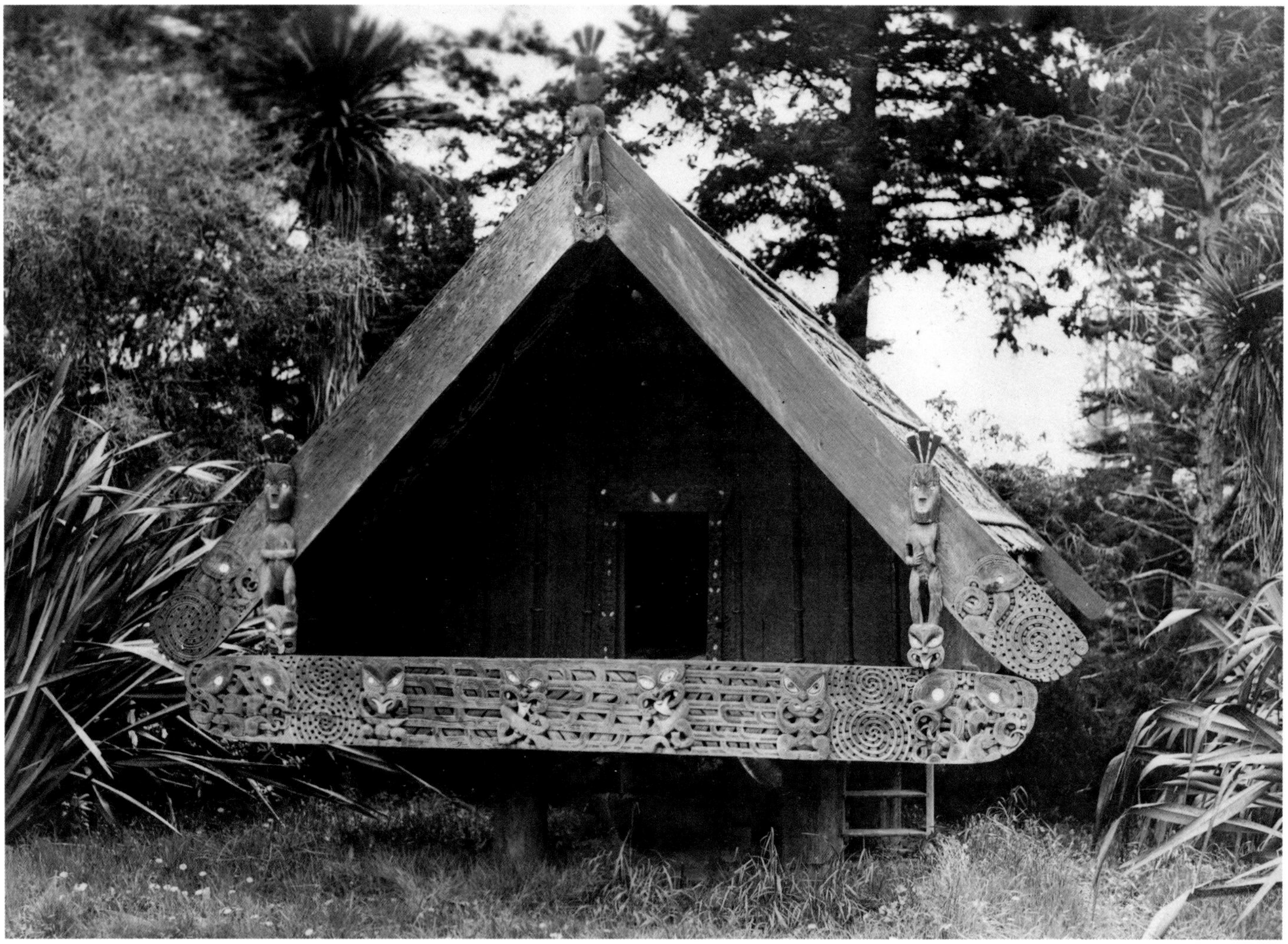

Nuku Tewhatewha at Brancepeth Station, Wainuioru, c.1920, the last of three outdoor locations in which this Ngā Pou o te Kīngitanga pātaka was situated before it was transferred to the Dowse Art Museum in Lower Hutt in 1982.
Alexander Turnbull Library, 1/1-000641-F

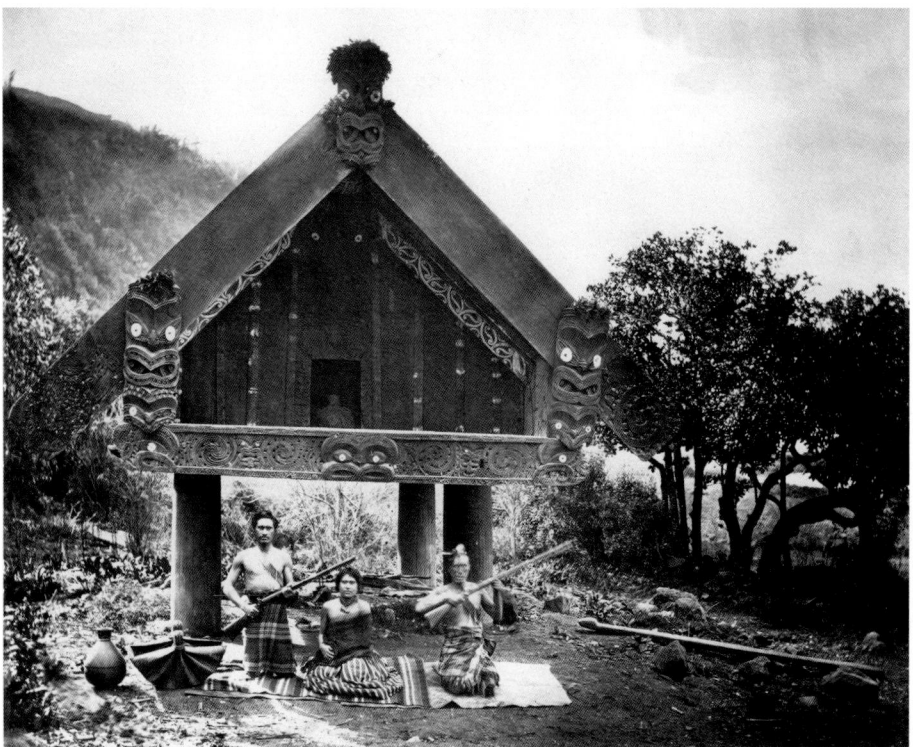

Hīnana ki uta, Hīnana ki tai (Search the Land and the Sea) had been built at Waihi, Lake Taupō in 1855, and was named after the pan-tribal meeting at neighbouring Pūkawa the following year. The local Ngāti Tūwharetoa ariki Iwikau Te Heuheu may have presented the pātaka at this hui; Iwikau's nephew Horonuku (Te Heuheu Tūkino IV) carved both Hīnana and Nuku Tewhatewha, as well as others.
Daniel Louis Mundy, between 1863 and 1872, Alexander Turnbull Library, 1/2-082343-F

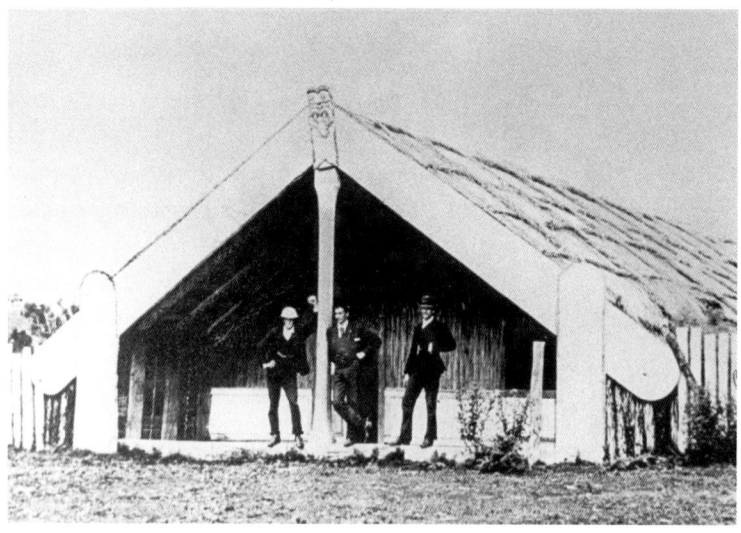

Kauhanganui parliament house at Maungakawa, shortly after its opening in 1891.
Alexander Turnbull Library, PAColl-0940-1

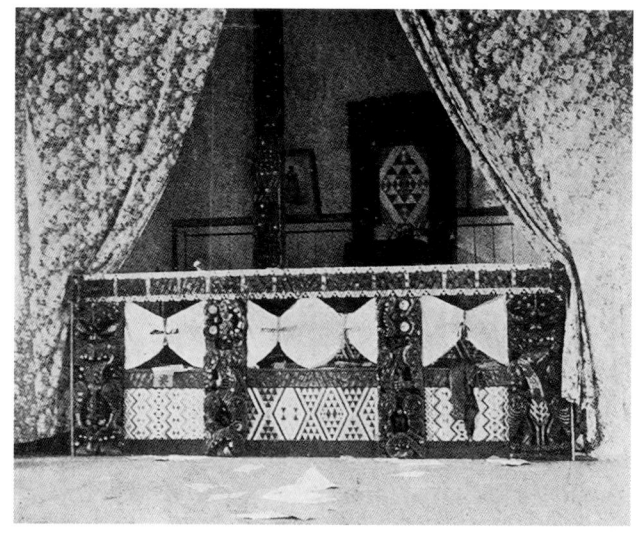

The Māori king's throne in Kauhanganui parliament house, Maungakawa, in 1905.
L. M. Eastgate, *Auckland Weekly News*, 14 September 1905, Auckland Libraries Heritage Collections, AWNS-19050914-16-1

he had moved to, and his support for the nascent Kīngitanga movement – symbolised by Nuku Tewhatewha – in many ways expressed the frustration he was experiencing in obtaining title for Māori land.[8]

Aesthetically, the pātaka is firmly situated in the customary world. It is adorned with figurative paepae, amo, tekoteko and maihi, and a kūwaha carving depicting Wī Tako's wife Te Hamene and their daughter Merania; its porch is supported by kōwhaiwhai-painted heke and lined with kākaho, and the roof is thatched.[9] In 1861, Wī Tako leased his Te Mako land to a Pākehā settler, William Beetham, and with it the care of the pātaka passed into Beetham's family for the next 121 years, after which it was gifted to the city of Lower Hutt.[10] The symbolic meaning of Nuku Tewhatewha and the other Pou o te Kīngitanga far outweighed any functional purpose they may have had as storehouses: they were customary representations of chiefly mana, authority and, in a colonial age, resistance.

A network of innovative wharenui also supported the establishment and development of the Kīngitanga. The idea of a Māori king had originally been mooted at a hui in April 1854, attended by one thousand Māori; the hui was held in the recently opened Taiporohenui wharenui at Manawapou in South Taranaki. This was likely the largest meeting house ever built at the time, at 36m long and 9–10m wide, and with two doors.[11] It is not clear if it featured whakairo rākau or kōwhaiwhai – there are no images of this building or descriptions of its appearance – but it inspired the construction of a number of smaller wharenui in districts that supported the Kīngitanga and, collectively, these buildings demonstrated the unity of the movement.[12] Te Kirima of Ōtaki and Te Puku Mahi of Waikanae were wharenui in the southernmost outposts of the Kīngitanga.[13] Kaumātua dedicated the Hikurangi wharenui in Taumarunui to the movement by depositing a scroll outlining the principles of the Kīngitanga within the structure of the house, following the long-standing Māori and Polynesian custom of transferring mana to structures through the integration of tapu materials.[14] By architectural acts such as this and by strategic naming, tribal buildings became connected within a larger political system: the wide distribution of Kīngitanga wharenui and pātaka demonstrated the reach of the Māori king's mana across the central and lower North Island.

Kīngitanga architecture was the physical manifestation of a powerful paramount leadership that operated beyond customary tribal structures and distinct from the authority of the Crown. Yet from the time of his selection in 1858, the first Māori king, Pōtatau Te Wherowhero, struggled to unite all iwi. While many hapū in the central North Island gave him their allegiance, others in the south, east and north did not support his election, as they saw themselves as cultural and political entities distinct from each other.[15] When Pōtatau died in June 1860, his son Tūkāroto Matutaera Pōtatau Te Wherowhero, also known as Tāwhiao, succeeded him in a reign that spanned the Kīngitanga's involvement in the New Zealand Wars and their aftermath, during which time the government confiscated over 1.2 million hectares of Māori land. Although he did not achieve the unity that Tamihana had envisioned, after two years of war, twenty years in exile, and an unsuccessful attempt in 1884 to gain an audience with Queen Victoria, Tāwhiao eventually realised Tamihana's ambition of founding a separate Māori political system – the Kauhanganui – accommodated within its own parliamentary architecture.[16]

The first Kauhanganui parliament house was built at Maungakawa, north of present-day Cambridge, and opened in 1891.[17] Although all tribes were invited to appoint their own representatives, only those associated with the Kīngitanga responded. They created a parliament based on the Westminster system, comprised of an upper house for the manukura (nobles) and a lower house for the matariki (commoners). The building to accommodate the parliament was, however, thoroughly Māori. A single remaining photograph of the exterior shows a wharenui with thatched roof and walls, tekoteko and porch embellishments that included kōwhaiwhai-painted porch rafters and possibly tukutuku. It was large, and could accommodate hui of up to 500 people. A photograph of the interior shows an elaborate throne installation for the Māori king, comprised of whakairo rākau, tāniko (or possibly tukutuku) and sumptuous Pākehā fabrics. The opulence of the throne and the use of carvings as framing devices and fibre as panelling was part of an emerging practice of reinterpreting wharenui interior poupou and tukutuku configurations as high-culture Victorian-inspired dadoes and framed furniture. Both traditions conveyed mana and authority. Fire destroyed the parliament and its throne in 1908.[18]

Tupu Taingakawa, the leader of the Kauhanganui, exercised his mana as a contender for the role of king by building a Kauhanganui parliament house at Rukumoana pā, south of Morrinsville, between 1916 and 1917, complete with a two-roomed Pākehā-style chamber and an Italian-made bronze statue of the third Māori king, Mahuta Tāwhiao Pōtatau Te Wherowhero, who passed away in 1912.[19] The smaller 'throne room' housed the Māori king's throne.[20]

However, Taingakawa faced formidable competition from Te Puea Hērangi, a close relative of the late king and a supporter of his son, Te Rata.[21] In response, Te Puea built an alternative Kauhanganui parliament building, Tūrangawaewae House, in Ngāruawāhia, opened on 18 March 1919.

Planning for the project had begun as early as 1909, when Mahuta donated £600 towards the building. He believed it would become more than just a political forum: it would represent a triumphant homecoming to the seat of the Māori king's power, Ngāruawāhia, after decades of exile caused by the New Zealand Wars. However, the project stalled after the local authority declined the first application for building consent, and with the intervention of World War One. Te Puea raised £1800 for construction by levying £1 from each member of the Waikato-Tainui, Hauraki, Taranaki, Maniapoto and Rangitīkei tribes; the budget shortfall was made up by the host iwi, Ngāti Rereahu, who also donated the timber to build the parliament.[22] The spirit of competitive building that had driven the development of large Māori church buildings in the previous century was now manifest in the competition between Kauhanganui parliament buildings.

John Warren, a Pākehā architect from the Hamilton-based practice Warren and Blechynden, designed Tūrangawaewae House in the Arts and Crafts style using Pākehā construction techniques and materials, including stucco walls and a tiled roof. The only Māori elements were two kōwhaiwhai-painted doors, and carvings made in the Waikato-Tainui style by Te Motu Heta around the entrance porch and two gabled bays at the front of the building. This was possibly the first Māori building to be designed by a Pākehā architect. It illustrates the considerations and tensions that are inherent in the design of community spaces by non-community experts – in this case expressed through the 'application' of Māori art as aesthetic rather than integral and/or structural elements. Like the Maungakawa Kauhanganui, Tūrangawaewae House incorporated a throne room – with a stage for the king's chair and for Taingakawa's stool and another advisor's seat. It also had a space for the rest of the assembly to sit – apparently on the floor, as the seating arrangement reflected a hierarchy of mana.[23] Even though Te Rata was installed as Māori king, the building was hardly used as it had no marae, and its reputation as the Kīngitanga's ancestral home was eclipsed in the following decade by Te Puea's Tūrangawaewae Marae and settlement nearby.[24]

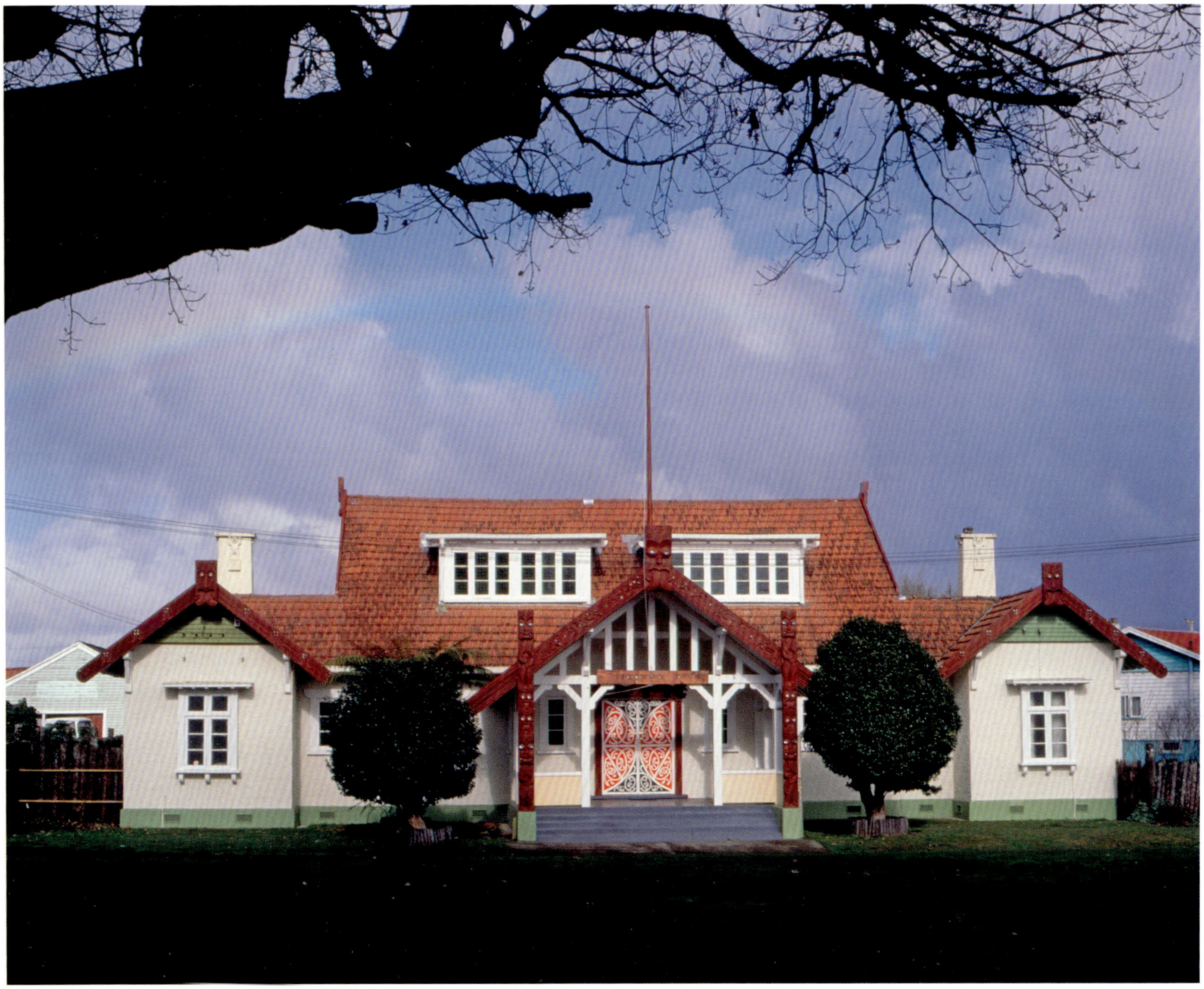

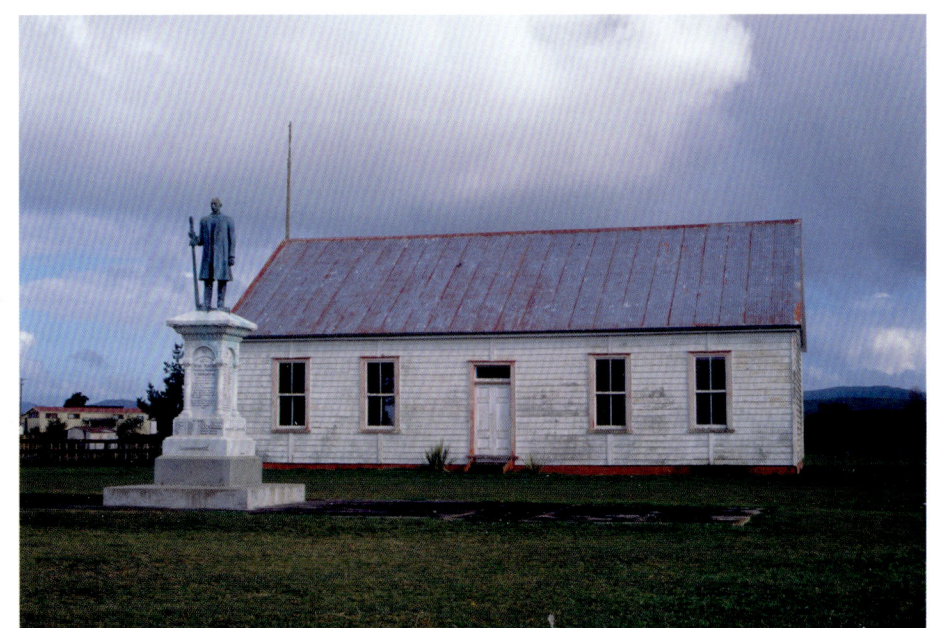

Tūrangawaewae House, designed by the architect John Warren, was commissioned as a Kauhanganui parliament building by Te Puea Hērangi.
Logan Photographs Collection, Architecture Archive, Special Collections, Waipapa Taumata Rau University of Auckland, photograph by Lynne Logan

Kauhanganui parliament at Rukumoana pā, with statue of the Māori King Mahuta in the foreground.
Logan Photographs Collection, Architecture Archive, Special Collections, Waipapa Taumata Rau University of Auckland, photograph by Lynne Logan

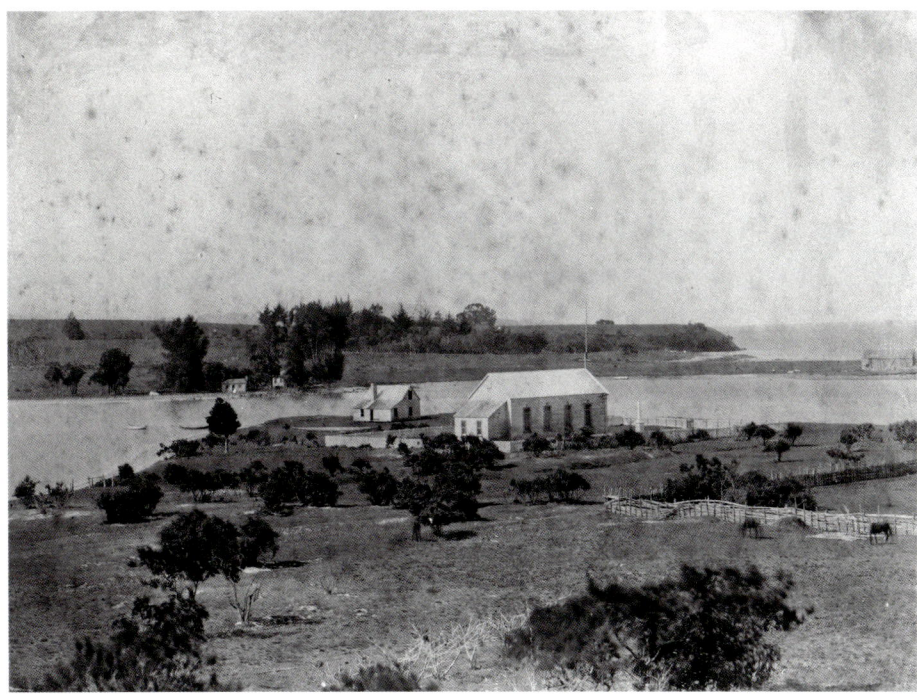

Te Tii Marae, Waitangi, with the recently completed Te Tiriti o Waitangi building in the foreground, 1880.
Josiah Martin, 1880, Alexander Turnbull Library, PAColl-8454

The Maungakawa, Rukumoana and Ngāruawāhia Kauhanganui, constructed between the 1880s and 1920, were three Māori parliamentary buildings that expressed the same kaupapa through very different, contemporary means. The Maungakawa wharenui was one of a lineage of Kīngitanga large wharenui that were built from the mid-1850s, beginning with the Taiporohenui house, and continuing to the present day. Rukumoana was an uncarved weatherboard hall made parliamentary through classical accoutrements; aesthetically it was upstaged by the architect-designed Kauhanganui parliament constructed in suburban Ngāruawāhia that was, in terms of its architectural precedents, literally a world away from Ngā Pou o te Kīngitanga pātaka. Architecture, in all these instances, was a means to an end. The success of the buildings is evident in their enablement of the Kauhanganui to remain topical and contested, and survive to the present day as a governing body of the Waikato-Tainui confederation. These buildings and associated architectural arts were precedents for those built during the re-establishment of the Kīngitanga at Ngāruawāhia in the twentieth century.

### Paremata Māori

The Kīngitanga was not alone in attempting to unify Māori and defend political and land rights through pan-tribal parliaments. The Paremata Māori was a collective term for a number of Māori political organisations with democratically elected representatives and leaders that emerged during the nineteenth century. These parliaments were established in response to the inadequacies of the 1867 Maori Representation Act, which provided only four Māori constituency seats in the New Zealand Parliament. The Paremata Māori sought instead to improve on the work of the 1870s repudiation movement, a Hawke's Bay initiative that aimed to reclaim alienated land by lobbying Pākehā legal and parliamentary representatives.[25]

The Kotahitanga movement evolved in northern Aotearoa New Zealand with the objective of promoting Te Tiriti as a mandate for Māori self-determination and influencing the government's policy on Māori, while adopting the same parliamentary processes as the New Zealand General Assembly. By 1898 tens of thousands of Māori in the north and east of the North Island had signalled their allegiance to the Kotahitanga.[26] Pre-existing wharenui accommodated Kotahitanga meetings at the Bay of Islands (1892), Pakirikiri (1894), Rotorua (1895, 1900 and 1901) and Waiomatatini (1902), while other congresses sat in purpose-built parliaments that were designed in the Pākehā style within the uniquely Māori contexts of marae and pā.[27] The wharenui Te Tiriti o Waitangi – the second of that name to be built at Waitangi

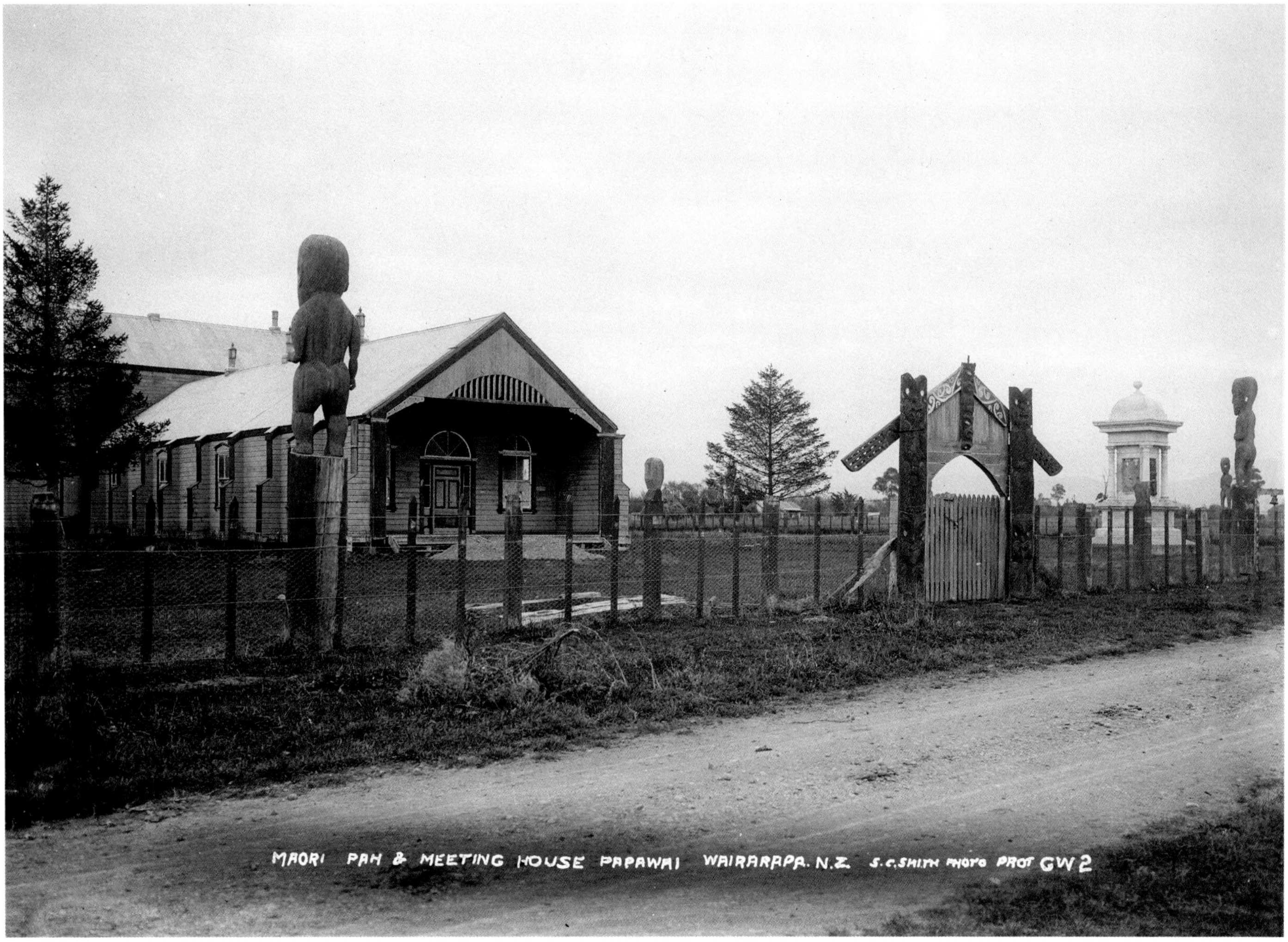

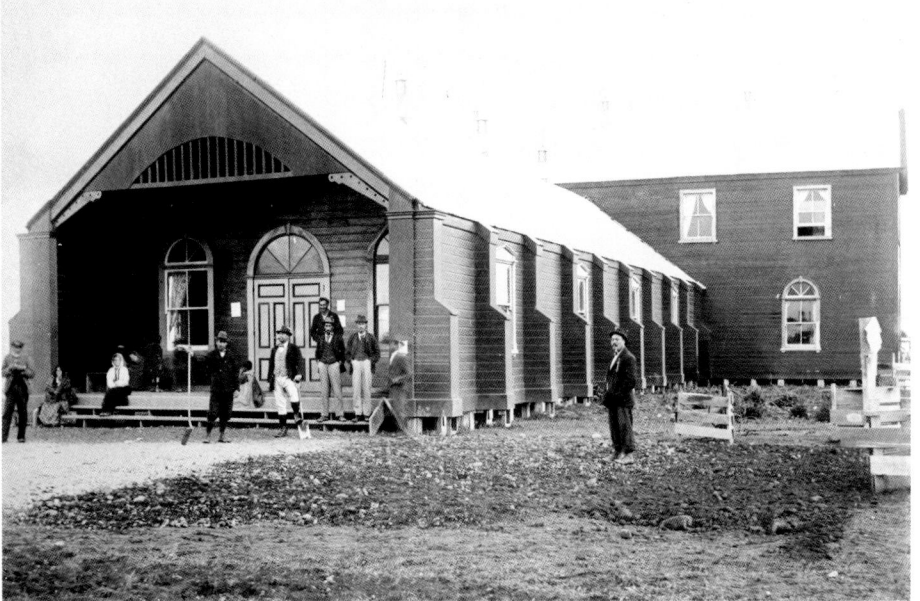

Papawai pā, Wairarapa, a stronghold of the Kotahitanga movement.
Sydney Charles Smith, 1920s, Alexander Turnbull Library, 1/2-048471-G

The distinctive Te Waipounamu meeting, dining and sleeping house at Papawai pā, Wairarapa.
Alexander Turnbull Library, PAColl-1892-78

– was a purpose-built, hall-like parliament house with an iron roof and weatherboard cladding, opened in 1880. It was funded by northern Māori after the government refused a request to build a forum for explaining policies to Māori,[28] and it hosted inter-iwi parliaments in 1884, 1890 and 1899. The third eponymous hall-style wharenui on the same site is still an important forum where views on government policies are debated every Waitangi Day.[29]

By the beginning of the twentieth century, the will to find common political ground had initiated influential tribal confederations, even though old rivalries were inhibiting a complete Māori unity. This was reflected in an architectural 'middle ground', composed of largely unembellished buildings that could be built quickly using the technologies and formalisms of the day. They eschewed local decorative traditions that might associate these parliamentary forums with a particular hapū or iwi instead of a larger inter-iwi movement. The ancestral world had not been completely abandoned: pātaka represented a continuity of mana from the ariki to the Kīngitanga. In the eastern North Island, these connections were maintained in Ringatū wharenui built as part of an ambitious programme to unite Māori spiritually and politically.

### Ringatū architecture

Te Kooti Arikirangi Te Tūruki, founder of the Ringatū Church, was actively involved in the reconceptualisation of wharenui as Indigenous spaces of worship and political activity. He may have been one of Raharuhi Rukupō's apprentices, which would explain his familiarity with the arts, practices and intellectual traditions of tohunga whakairo. Te Kooti was engaged in a guerrilla-style resistance campaign against the colonial government that led to his ten-year exile in the autonomous Māori region known as Te Rohe Pōtae (also known as the King Country) and his establishment of the Ringatū Church. After he was pardoned in 1883, he became a travelling spiritual leader. He and his followers were responsible for ingenious innovations in wharenui aesthetics and construction that were based in tikanga and addressed the challenges that faced Māori after the New Zealand Wars of the 1860s and 1870s. There are over forty meeting houses associated with Te Kooti and his church, built mainly on the East Coast between 1869 and 1908.[30]

What distinguished Ringatū wharenui from others was their size – an innovation that arose from their unique programmes of use. At between 18 and 24m in length and between 3 and 7m in height, the scale of some Ringatū wharenui was larger than many earlier Māori buildings, and comparable to contemporaneous mission churches and later Māori parliament buildings.[31] In many Ringatū communities, services of worship modelled on those of the Anglican Church took place inside wharenui, as did discussions about the challenges of colonisation. These gatherings necessitated larger interior spaces, to accommodate congregations who were also communities, and who used the same space for hui and as wharepuni when hosting visitors.[32] Ringatū spiritual ideas were influencing the function of wharenui embellishments, too – such as at Ōtoko Marae, northeast of Whanganui, where followers claimed that their prayers and speeches were being transmitted heavenward to God through the kōwhaiwhai, tāhuhu and maihi of the Tauakira meeting house.[33]

Yet, tapu prevailed. After problems arose at their opening ceremonies, neither Tāne Whirinaki nor Rongopai was regarded as safe for daily life, and both wharenui were used only for worship.[34] Despite their design innovations, many Ringatū buildings were still constructed using Māori technologies, including tōtara framing systems, earth floors and raupō cladding.[35] While the Ringatū wharenui embodied a Māori worldview in which spirituality and politics were inseparable, their formalism was derived directly from other Māori buildings of mana, such as earlier wharenui and the wharepuni and pātaka that preceded them. Many of these buildings still personified the tribal ancestor, the community's identity, and chiefly mana and tapu.[36] Ringatū wharenui and the tikanga they represented offered a powerful alternative to Protestant and Catholic churches. These wharenui became places of spiritual observance for communities in need of stability after the New Zealand Wars.

A group of travelling tohunga whakairo from the Mātaatua tribal confederation in the Bay of Plenty assisted Te Kooti in realising strategic partnerships by building some of the earliest Ringatū wharenui. They carved pou for new and existing meeting houses that illustrated ancestors whose whakapapa connected Te Kooti to the host communities. This breakthrough concept – of

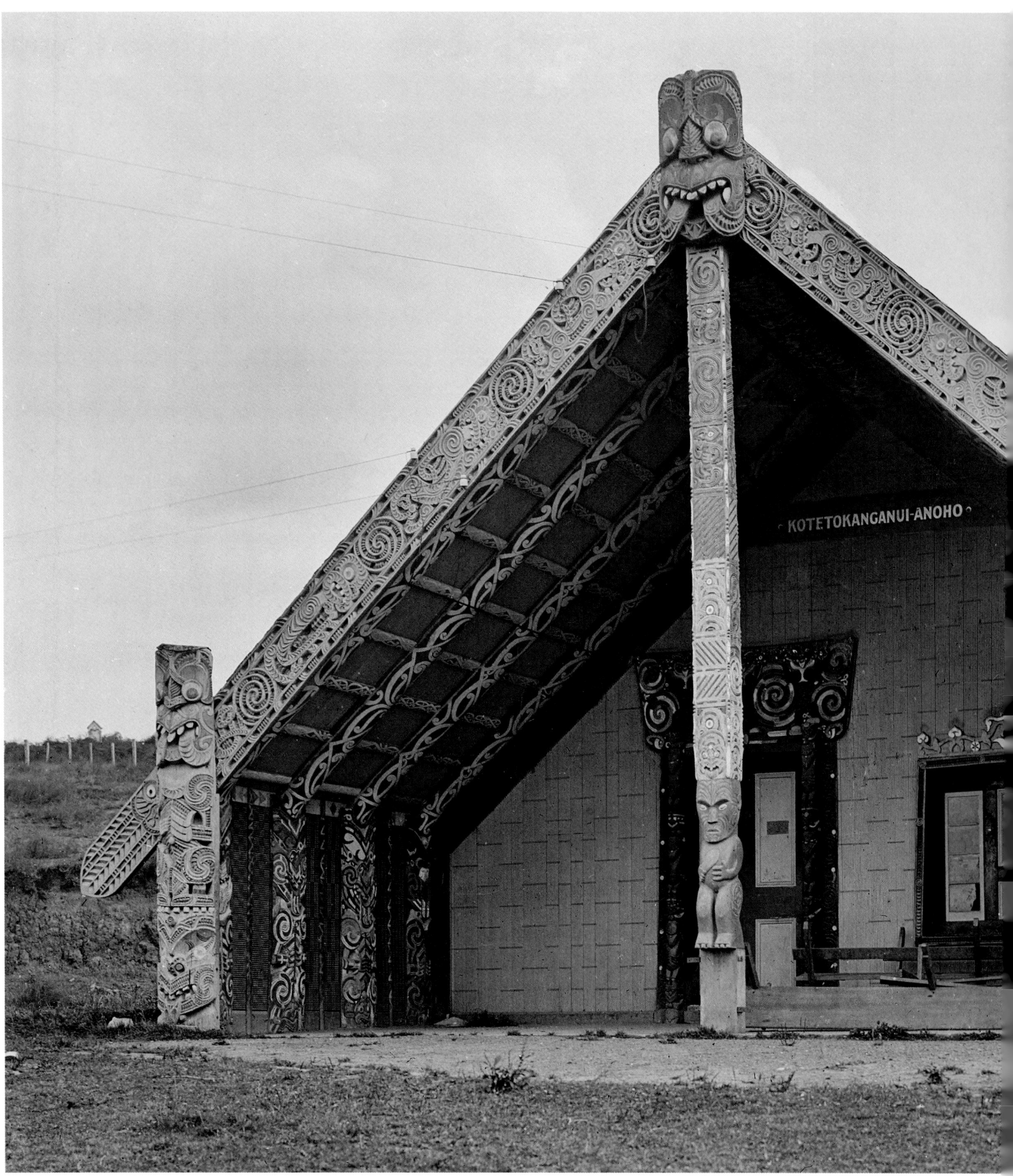

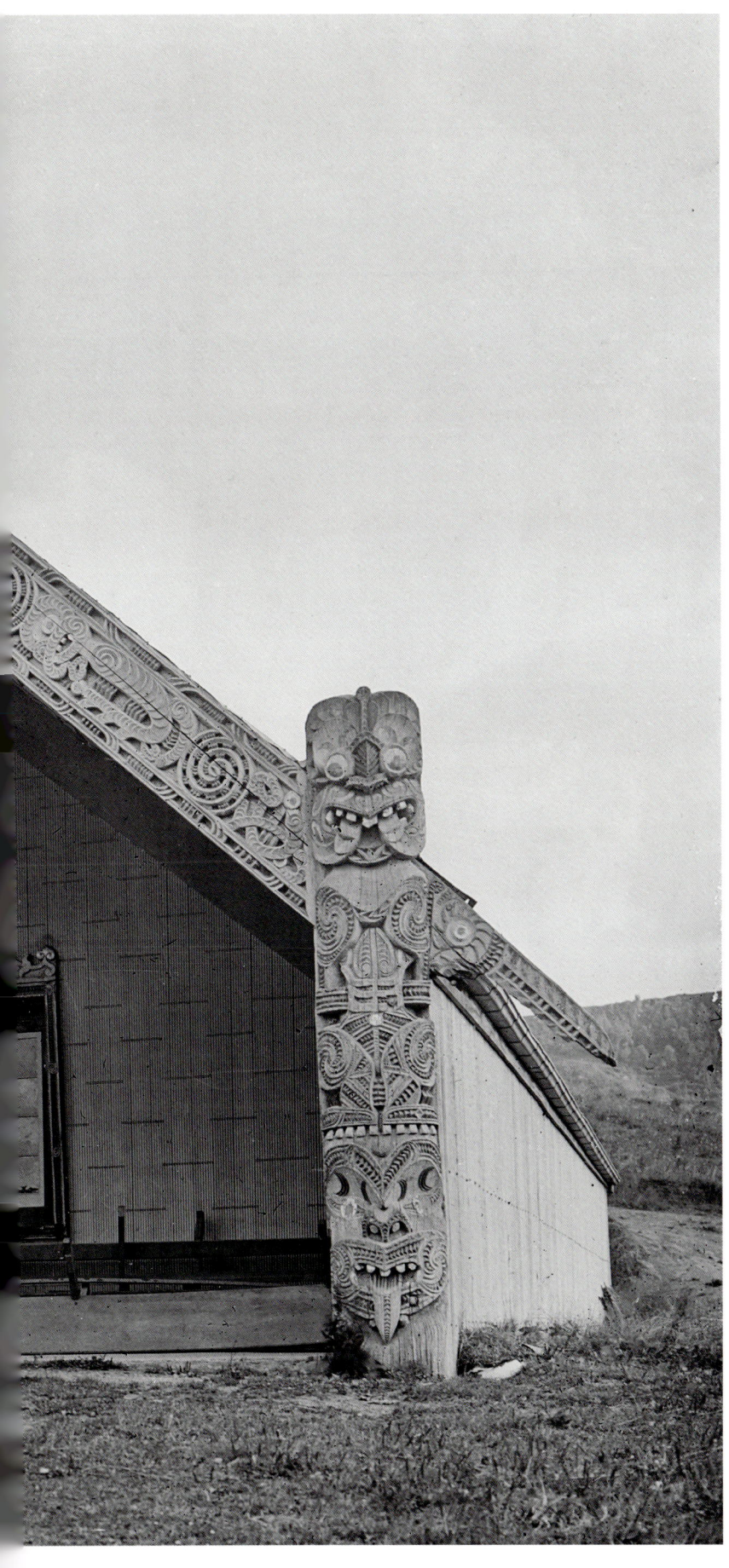

embodying pan-iwi connections in wharenui – extended ideas about whakapapa relationships that had been explored in buildings such as Te Hau ki Tūranga, and firmly established the wharenui as a physical and metaphysical gathering space. Te Tokanganui a Noho wharenui was an early example of this innovation, completed in 1873 and renovated between 1881 and 1882 under Te Kooti's supervision.[37] The building's novel use of whakairo rākau, commercial paints and figurative paintings influenced the design of other Ringatū buildings in the eastern North Island over the next three decades.

Te Tokanganui a Noho had to be spectacular. Te Kooti's fortunes and those of his followers were dependent on its reception when he presented the wharenui to the groups who provided him refuge from 1873 to 1883. After accepting King Tāwhiao's condition that he cease fighting, Te Kooti had sought asylum in Te Kūiti, a Māori settlement within the Rohe Pōtae. Te Kooti used his supervision of this wharenui project, which had been started by Ngāti Hauā as a house for Tāwhiao's use, to illustrate his recognition of the king's mana.[38] He increased the number of named ancestral poupou whakairo from eighteen to twenty-eight, as well as others on the front and back walls and central columns. The poupou acknowledged all exiled groups living together at Te Kūiti. The idea of carving ancestor names on the bodies of the tiki was possibly derived from the engraving of Ngāti Kahungunu and Rongowhakaata ancestor names on the poupou in Te Hau ki Tūranga.[39] Strength through unity must have been an important consideration in this ancestral matrix. The figures of Māhinaarangi and Tūrongo were included on the poutokomanawa – the most structurally and therefore most symbolically important wharenui members, whose marriage had once united Tāwhiao's Waikato people and Te Kooti's East Coast iwi.[40] Ancestors from the Maniapoto, Porourangi, Tūhoe and Tūwharetoa iwi and the culture heroes of Māui and Paikea were also depicted in the poupou whakairo, ensuring that the wharenui's community was bound into a powerful whakapapa that had its origins in the foundations of Māori culture and the creation narratives.

Te Tokanganui a Noho was one of the first wharenui to include polychromatic painted carvings. The building project was begun by Ngāti Hauā, and in September 1873, Te Kooti Arikirangi Te Tūruki assumed supervision of the last of the wharenui's carvings. Almost a decade later, Te Kooti renovated the house and rededicated it to Ngāti Maniapoto, who were the tangata whenua of Te Kūiti, where the house is sited. The image of the exterior of the house was taken in 1917 by Albert Percy Godber.
Alexander Turnbull Library, APG-0485-1/2-G

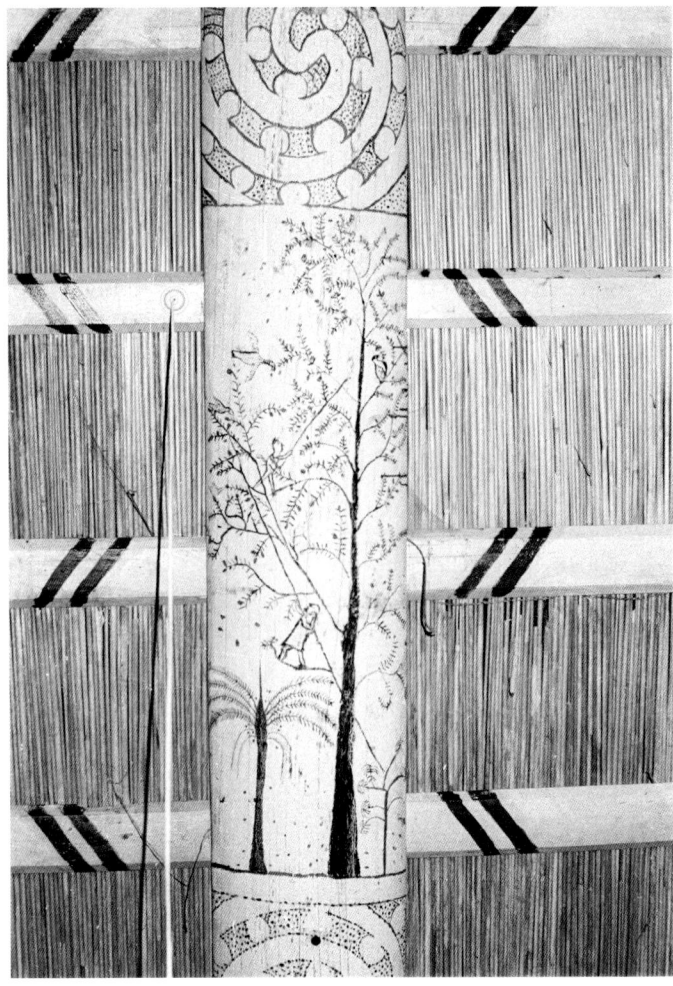
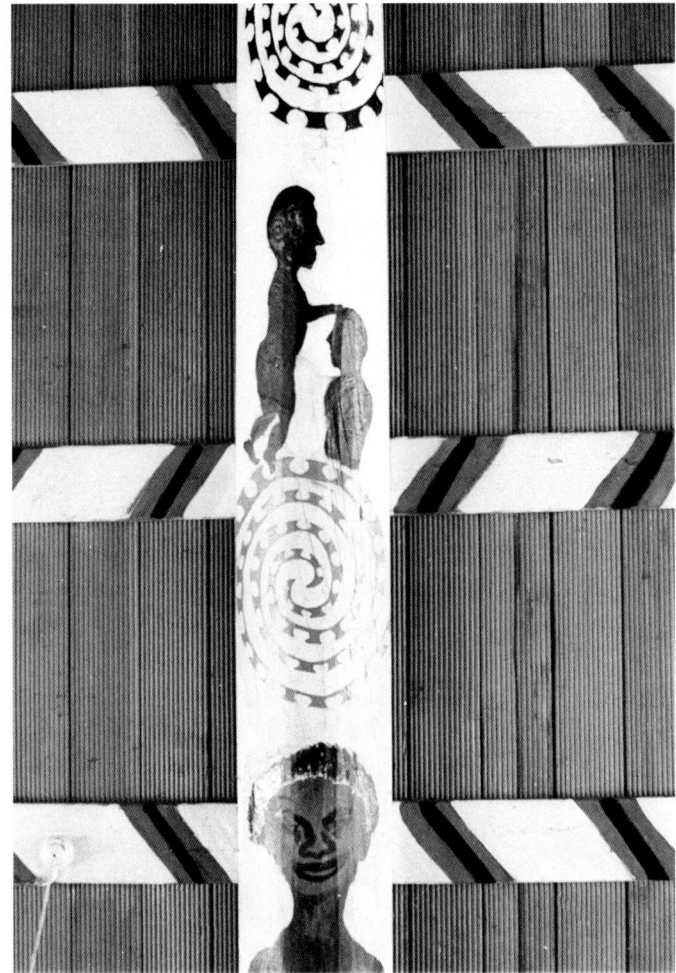

The workmanship was equally impressive. Many of the tohunga whakairo who participated in the renovation were not refugees, but Māori who chose to cross into the Rohe Pōtae to demonstrate their support for Te Kooti through their artistic practice.[41] The celebrated Ngāti Kahungunu tohunga whakairo Wiremu Kaimoana was one of those working alongside the Mātaatua carvers, and their collaboration produced work that went on to become closely identified with an emerging Ringatū 'style', comprised of a traditional carving formalism and an emerging painting custom.[42] Mātaatua craftsmen also worked on the Ruataupare wharenui in their own territory, at Te Teko, under the direction of Te Kooti, who funded the project in recognition of Ngāti Awa's support during the wars.[43] As at Te Tokanganui a Noho, Te Kooti conceived of the building as the expression of a whakapapa that related the local people to his own and, therefore, to his mission through its incorporation of Ngāti Porou ancestor carvings and the naming of the wharenui after a common ancestor.[44] And as at Te Tokanganui a Noho, the carvings at Ruataupare were polychromatic, with details on figures highlighted in black, red, green and blue.[45]

The practice of polychromatic painting had been popularised by the Mātaatua carvers. It had spread beyond the confederation's influence through its association with the Ringatū Church, whose followers chose paints purchased from Pākehā merchants over Māori pigments, since they were ready to use and available in many colours.[46] With this spectrum of colours at their disposal, Ringatū communities developed their own signature palette, such as the Whakatōhea and Ngāti Porou tohunga whakairo who painted the Tāne Whirinaki wharenui carvings in black, white and pink.[47] Te Kooti assigned meanings to colours, sometimes based on biblical interpretations, but they were not recorded in writing.[48]

Figurative painting was another painting technique that was pioneered in Te Tokanganui a Noho and is now synonymous with the Ringatū style. This practice involved

NGĀ TOI MŌREHU – THE ARTS OF SURVIVAL

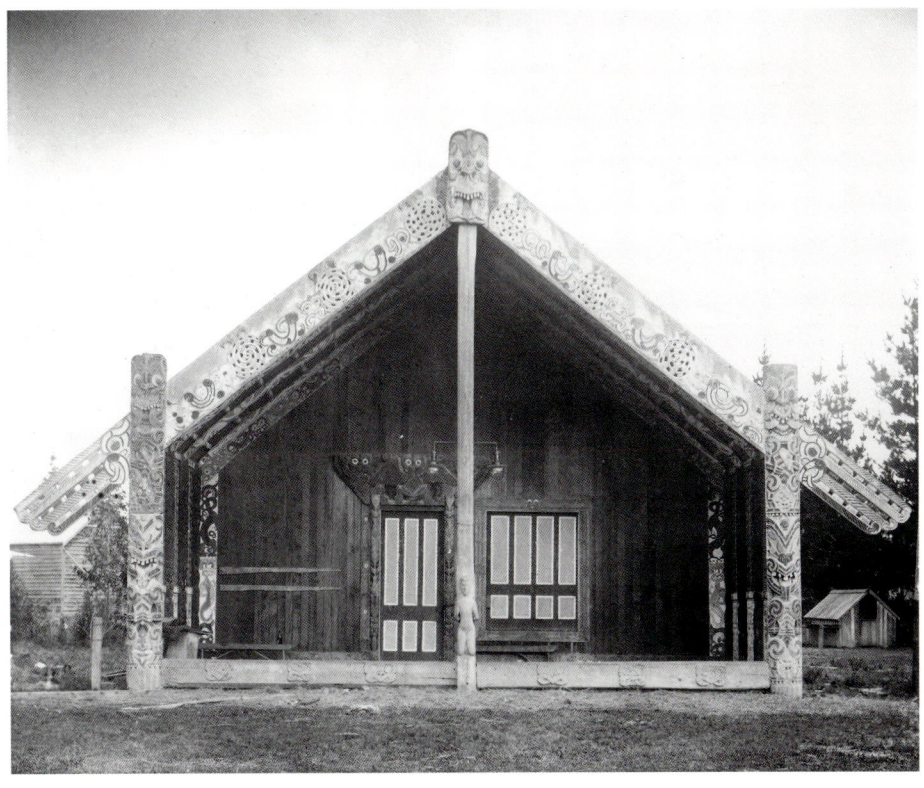

Top: Exterior of Tākitimu meeting house, which stood at Kehemene (Gethsemene), Martinborough, showing the carvings and paintings decorating the porch.
Alexander Turnbull Library, PAColl-5554

Bottom: Interior of Tākitimu meeting house.
private collection

Opposite left: Bird-hunting scene on a rafter in the Te Whai a te Motu wharenui, opened at Ruatāhuna in 1891.
Department of Anthropology Photographic Archive, Waipapa Taumata Rau University of Auckland, 372573, photograph by Sydney Moko Mead

Opposite right: Baptism scene on rafters in the Tama ki Hikurangi wharenui, built at Te Houhi.
Department of Anthropology Photographic Archive, Waipapa Taumata Rau University of Auckland, 374234, photograph by Sydney Moko Mead

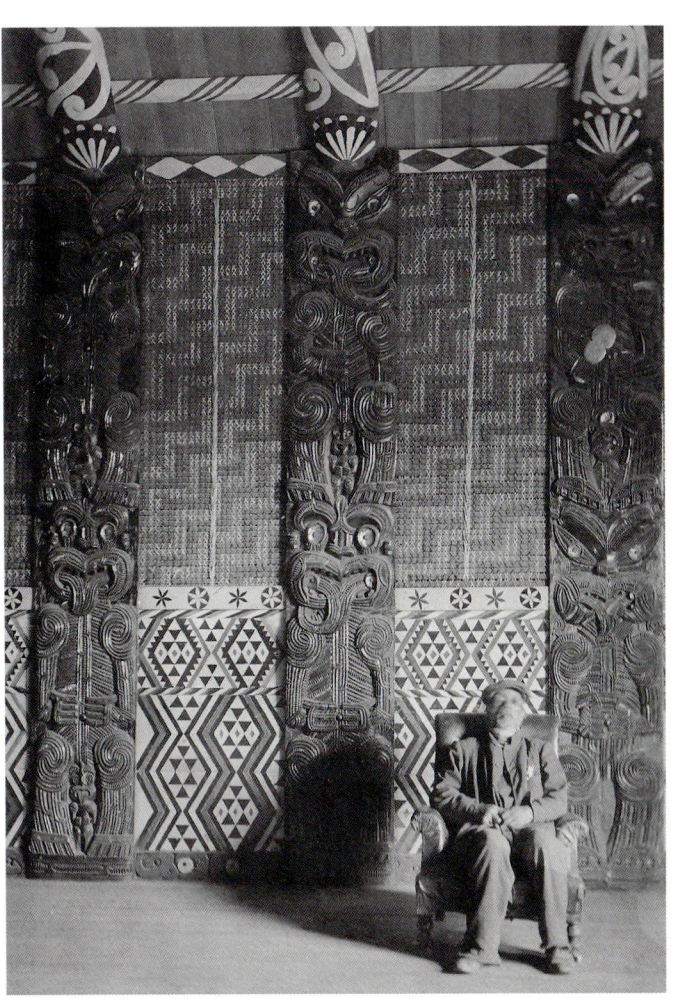

painting wharenui elements to resemble stylised carvings, and as naturalistic murals,[49] again using paints purchased from Pākehā. It was influenced by kōwhaiwhai painting as well as naturalistic representation, which Māori had become accustomed to through printed illustrative materials such as newspapers, Bibles, posters and books and, as time went on, photography.[50] Stylised figurative painting developed as a response to time constraints, particularly in communities that were preparing a house in anticipation of an event – such as a visit from Te Kooti – or that did not have the resources to commission tohunga whakairo.[51] Te Kooti likely decided to use stylised figurative paintings in order to complete the construction of Te Tokanganui a Noho, as he joined the project in its later stages.[52] At least two of the painted figures in this wharenui were based on carved manaia, and a third one was a hybrid figure that combined elements of a stylised marakihau with a naturalistic mermaid design.[53] The convenience of the technique – and the influence of Te Tokanganui a Noho – inspired the use of stylised figurative painting in other Ringatū buildings such as Pākira, Rongopai and Tākitimu.[54]

Naturalistic figurative painting depicted a Ringatū world in which recent events, challenges and Pākehā influences were made explicable through action scenes, portraiture

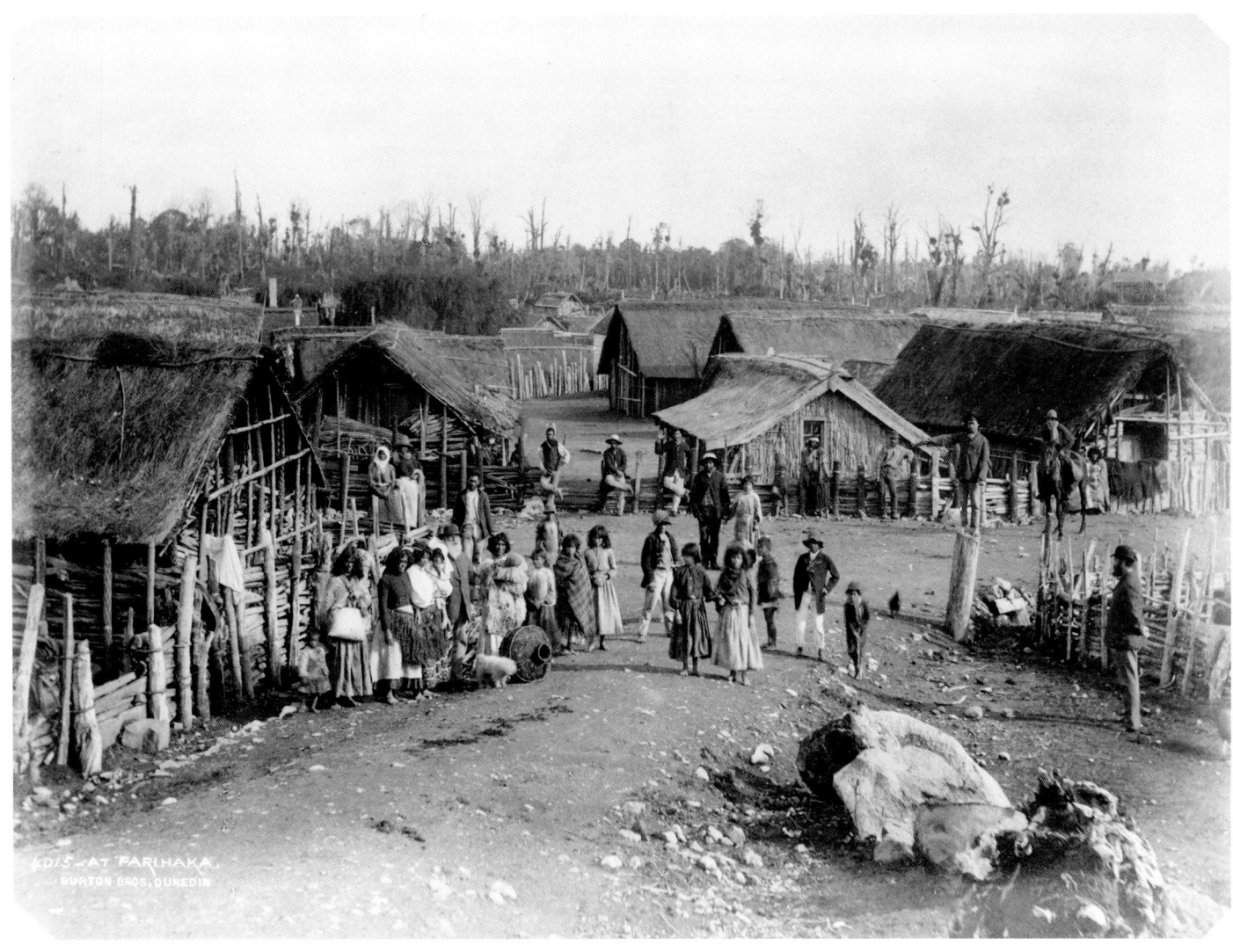

Whare at Parihaka in 1885. Note how densely settled the village was and the diversity of whare design, including buildings with entries on their long or short sides.
Burton Brothers, 1880s, Alexander Turnbull Library, 1/4-002570-F

and images of flora and fauna. Te Tokanganui a Noho was probably the earliest Ringatū building to feature such paintings, with illustrations of Māori playing cricket and soccer; this preoccupation with Pākehā sports was also evident in the boxing and horse-racing scenes in Rongopai at Waituhi. Customary practices were painted in this style, too, such as the bird-hunting scenes on the rafters in Te Whai a te Motu and Tama ki Hikurangi.[55] Poignant themes painted in Tama ki Hikurangi wharenui included a bayoneting scene that is believed to be based on Te Kooti's attack on Mohaka, and a Christian blessing – possibly a baptism.[56] These naturalistic figurative scenes located Ringatū life in the present and, more unusually for Māori art, within the lived experience of the painters. People are located in moments of time in identifiable places, instead of the timeless and locationless contexts of customary figurative art.

Naturalistic figurative art did not represent a break with a perceived 'past', or with tikanga: new and enduring temporal and spatial concepts might be present in the same scene. This shows the role that art plays in representing and explaining community perspectives on the continuing relevance of mana, whakapapa and wairuatanga. On the back wall of Rongopai, Wi Pere, the local MP for the Eastern Maori electorate, was depicted wearing a moko kanohi that he never had in life. The moko was probably added to demonstrate that he had inherited considerable mana from his mother, Riria Mauranui of Te Aitanga a Māhaki and Rongowhakaata, who appears in the same portrait.[57] A Tama ki Hikurangi portrait of a man wearing clerical clothing and a full facial moko has been interpreted as Māori authority within Christianity.[58]

NGĀ TOI MŌREHU – THE ARTS OF SURVIVAL

On another painted panel on the back wall of Rongopai, the pre-Pākehā ancestress Hakirirangi is depicted wearing a white Victorian dress and holding a rose – suggesting that the mana and values she embodied were just as relevant in the contemporary age as they were in earlier times.

The introduction of commercial paints led to a reconsideration of compositional techniques. Wi Pere's head and legs are in profile, while his body is facing the front. This is an aspective view in composition that was sometimes used in customary whakairo rākau. Hakirirangi's obliquely turned torso, on the other hand, was an innovation in that it is neither frontal nor profile. Riria Mauranui's positioning as a smaller figure in the Wi Pere portrait is ambiguous: she could be a guardian figure, like the manaia often shown next to larger tiki in whakairo rākau; or this could be the first known example of a Māori figure shown in perspective.[59]

Ringatū portrait artists were clearly making groundbreaking decisions about the representation and meaning of time and space, as Māori art moved from abstraction to naturalism – unaware that on the other side of the world, European modernists were transitioning from naturalism to abstraction, prompted by an awareness of Indigenous compositional techniques. These Māori painters were more than just artists attempting to meet a pressing deadline, or ad hoc and untrained decorators pitching in when there were no available tohunga. They were members of the community who were intellectually engaged, using new media as an opportunity to express topical themes for current and future generations.

### Parihaka

In 1866, Te Ātiawa leaders Te Whiti o Rongomai and Tohu Kākahi reoccupied confiscated Taranaki lands and set about reestablishing a thriving Māori urban centre at Parihaka. The settlement grew to a population of over 2000 Māori, including many who had been dispossessed through land confiscations and forced land sales.[60] Both men had attended Johann Riemenschneider's Lutheran mission school at Warea, and both had become active members of Pai Mārire during the Taranaki conflicts in the mid-1860s.[61] Their purpose in establishing Parihaka was to create a self-sufficient community that was insulated from the after-effects of war, poverty and land confiscation. Many Māori were attracted to Te Whiti and Tohu's social philosophies, and the population of Parihaka quickly grew, with arrivals from other parts of Taranaki and representatives of supporting iwi and the Kīngitanga.[62] Parihaka, with its thatched whare, offered shelter and hope after the chaos of armed conflict.

For two years, from 1878, the Parihaka community exercised passive resistance to government attempts to survey their land for Pākehā settlement, by removing survey pegs, ploughing up settler fields and building fences across roads.[63] In mid-1880 the method of protest changed, after the Armed Constabulary tore down Parihaka's fences in a government attempt to destroy the settlement by driving a road through its centre.[64] The people rebuilt the fences and placed branches across the roadworks to stall further construction. Yet, despite the fact that Parihaka was referred to as a pā and was within 8km of two military redoubts, it remained unfortified – in keeping with the passivism of its leaders.[65]

On 5 November 1881 the Armed Constabulary, under the leadership of Native Minister John Bryce, stormed Parihaka with over 2000 men. The residents deliberately offered no physical resistance. The constabulary evicted around 1500 non-Taranaki people and destroyed their Parihaka whare and wharenui so they could not return; they assaulted many of the remaining 600 residents and pillaged their homes.[66] Te Whiti and Tohu were arrested and detained for two years without trial in various locations throughout the country.[67] While they were imprisoned in the South Island, the two men were taken to the Mosgiel Woollen Mill and the Dunedin railway yards in order to show them that Māori separatism was a hopeless cause when compared to the benefits of Pākehā technology.[68] On their release, however, Te Whiti and Tohu chose not to submit to Pākehā authority; instead they embraced the Industrial Age technologies they had seen by further developing Parihaka with street lighting, macadam roads and many Victorian-style residential and communal buildings.[69] To this day, the Parihaka story is an affirming narrative of Māori self-determination and the power of passive resistance.

Before the 1881 invasion, Parihaka was likely the most densely settled kāinga in the country: residents had built around 250 thatched wharepuni and wharenui in whānau- and hapū-related clusters.[70] Photographs of the village taken around this time, while thatched whare were still the dominant archetype, reveal the diversity of whare construction techniques that Māori were using across the country. Since all of the builders would have had access to the same range of materials available at Parihaka and its surrounds, the demands on the environment must have been heavy, given the unusually large population. The architectural diversity of the neighbourhood represented the unique convocation of the different groups who were living there, supporting Te Whiti and Tohu and the wider objective of demonstrating resistance to Pākehā encroachment on Māori land.

The technique of building thatched whare had been adapted from earlier Polynesian architecture, and had undergone at least six centuries of development before Pākehā arrived. Survival was not possible without knowledge of whare construction. Within kāinga, these collectives of buildings symbolised the familial, spiritual and social cohesiveness of hapū members, and their authority over the whenua they occupied. As with the art of kākahu making, whare construction was an essential skill, and some practitioners were more skilled than others in terms of their knowledge of gathering and processing plant materials, and in the virtuosity with which they could assemble these materials into an integrated system of load-bearing, weathertight and carefully bundled, stacked and joined architectural elements.

Photographs of Parihaka's whare are a unique resource that offers a window on the rich diversity of domestic dwelling styles that were still practised in the late nineteenth century. Raupō thatched whare at the settlement were slightly lower in height than those with walls of ponga logs. This may indicate they had different functions, or it may be an outcome of distinct iwi or hapū methods of building. Whare built in the late eighteenth and early nineteenth century were generally sunken or low to the ground in order to retain the heat from a central fire, vented through one or more apertures in the front wall. The images of Parihaka raupō whare show that some were made additionally watertight and airtight with the application of mud daub on outer walls, a technique observed on earlier Taranaki buildings.[71] The adoption of layers of warmer Victorian-era clothing and woollen blankets as cloaks and bed coverings is thought to have removed the necessity for dwellings to be sunken below ground. It may also have meant that wharepuni could be built with higher ceilings, leaving room to stand upright in the interior.[72] Long, lightweight ponga logs were embedded vertically into the ground to create walls that may have been lined internally with raupō.[73] Unlike the wharenui at Parihaka, the wharepuni did not have gable-end porches, although some buildings with entrances on their long sides did have veranda-like eave extensions.

The significance of the whare at Parihaka as a symbol of Māori land occupation was not lost on the Armed Constabulary. Immediately after the 1881 invasion of the settlement, they destroyed many of the buildings as a way of suppressing Māori occupation and aspirations for the site. Some of the buildings were pulled down with ropes and others were burnt.[74] The destruction of thatched whare was more than an attempt to clear the settlement; it represented a battle of ideologies, stemming from long-simmering tensions over race, class and the rule of government. For Parihaka's residents and for Pākehā, whare had come to represent a Māori identity based on tikanga values – those aspects of life that Māori needed to uphold in order to survive as Māori, and that the government increasingly regarded as inhibiting Pākehā interests. Although the struggle had been described, in reports to government at the time, as a contest between the 'ways of the past' and a colonised future, Parihaka's resistance had always been concerned with continuing tradition.

The Māori lifeways that gave the thatched whare purpose were at risk from increasing government control. After the occupation, whare and the lifestyles associated with their use were blamed for exacerbating the spread of disease, with no causal evidence.[75] Such opinions echoed those of other influential Pākehā such as James Pope who, in his 1884 book *Health for the Maori*, advocated abandoning thatched whare in favour of adopting Pākehā housing and hygiene practices. The book become a compulsory text in state-run native schools.[76] Similar repression of modes of living had incited rebellion, not just in other parts of the British Empire, but in Britain itself. Much of the rhetoric about hygiene, lethargy and lack of ambition that the government used to criticise Parihaka's residents, their buildings and built infrastructure echoed criticisms that the British government aimed at its own working class, accusing them of being responsible for their own socioeconomic and housing situation. Some of these workers rose up in response and created the Chartist movement, which demanded universal male suffrage: they argued that an imbalance of power had created class division

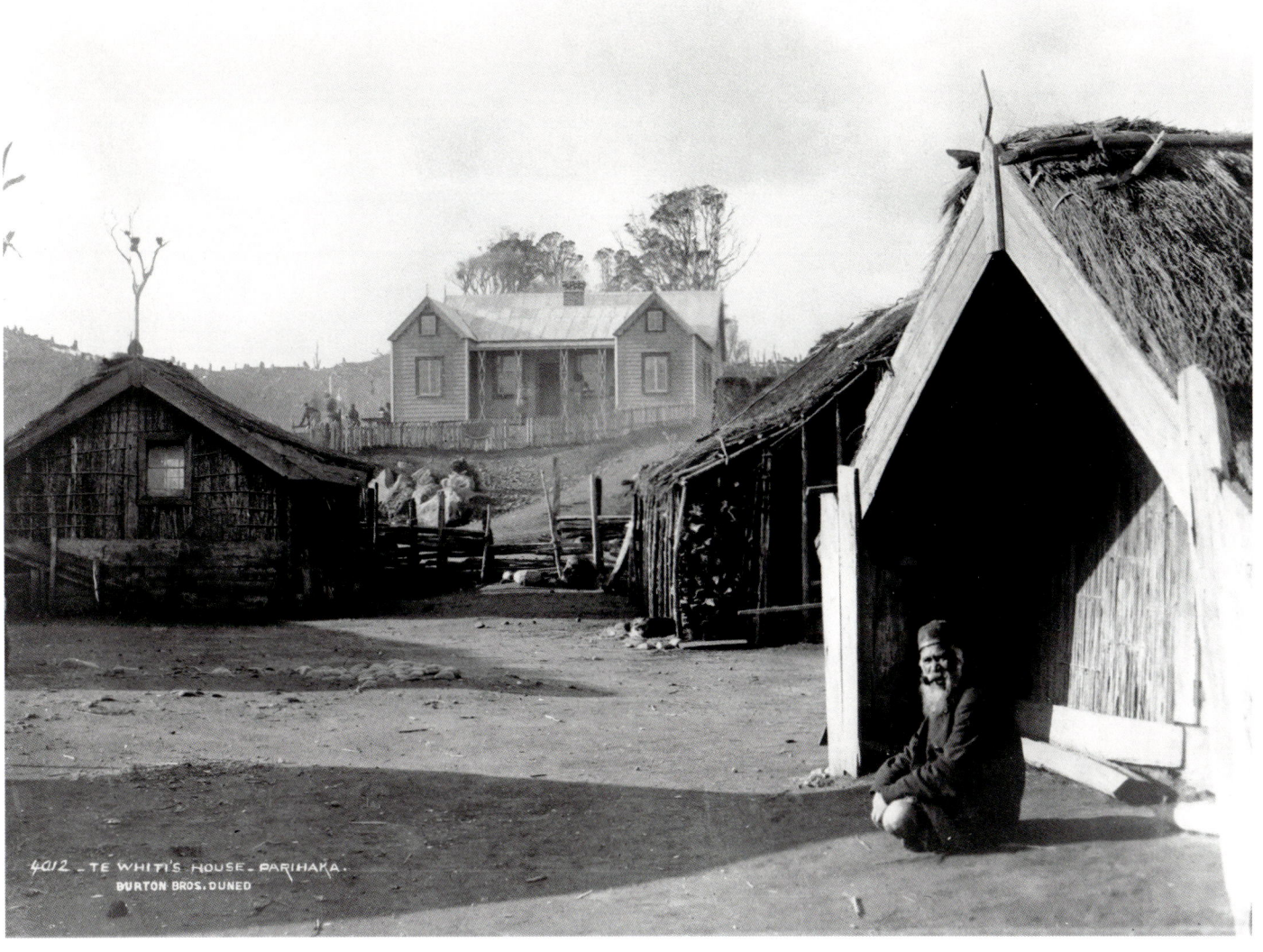

Te Whiti o Rongomai's residence Miti Mai Te Arero is the double-bay villa shown in the centre of this image of Parihaka.
Burton Brothers, c.1890, Alexander Turnbull Library, PAColl-6001-48

and an inequitable distribution of wealth. Politicians in New Zealand would have been well aware of these recent political debates in Britain. The transferral of ideas concerning 'appropriate' ways of living and building from the working classes of Britain to Māori, singled out through the Parihaka example, was as much a class-based method of sociopolitical suppression as it was a cultural one.

That the destruction of Parihaka's whare was ideologically motivated is also apparent in the curious exception of Parihaka's two Pākehā-style buildings from the demolition programme, despite their important functions in the community. Te Whiti's impressive Victorian-style residence Miti Mai Te Arero and the community bank Nuku Tewhatewha were constructed in 1881 by Parihaka's 'ploughmen' after their release from prison and before the settlement was invaded.[77] Miti Mai Te Arero was a weatherboard villa with a front veranda flanked by two enclosed gabled rooms. Its name, which can be translated as 'the tongue lashes out at me', was a reference to the negative effects of Pākehā settlement.[78] Nuku Tewhatewha (four elevated platforms) was one of a number of Māori banking initiatives established within Māori communities during the late nineteenth century in an attempt to curb Māori debt to Pākehā.[79] The building was pātaka-like and raised 1m off the ground, with weatherboard cladding, fretwork gables and finials.

As was the case with the Paremata Māori, the appropriation of Pākehā building techniques was regarded as a modernising, rather than assimilatory activity. The most important pan-iwi buildings in Parihaka were left standing while iwi, hapū and whānau structures were demolished. When Te Whiti and Tohu returned in 1883, they reoccupied

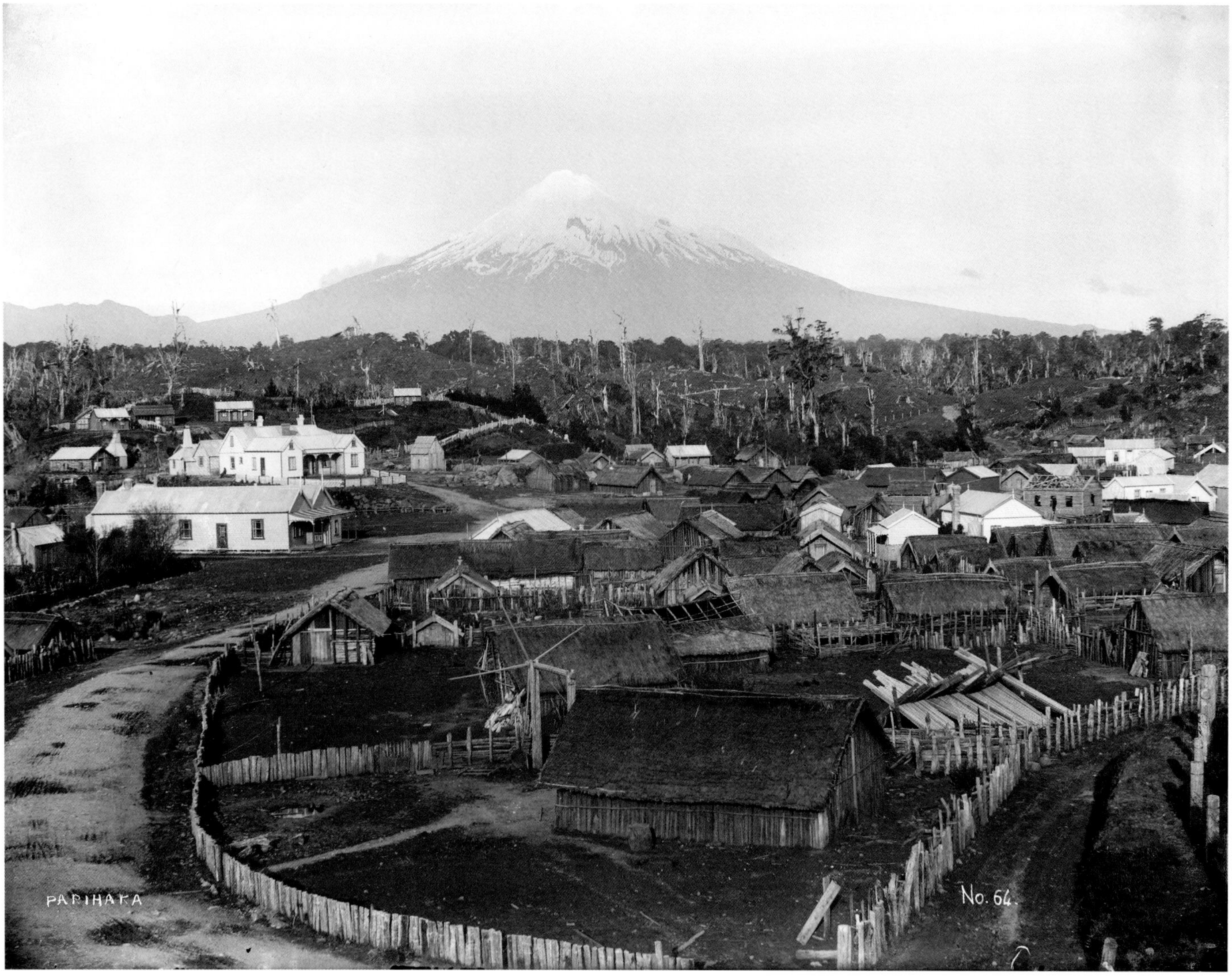

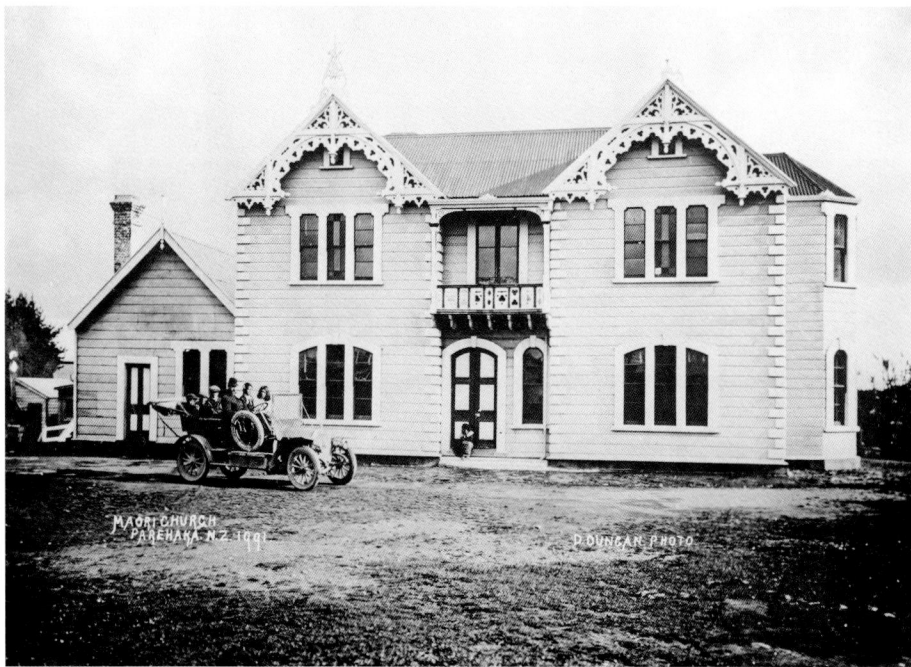

The progressive replacement of whare with Victorian-style buildings can be seen in this image of Parihaka from 1889. The dining hall Te Niho o te Ātiawa is the large weatherboard building next to Miti Mai Te Arero.
William Andrews Collis, c.1890, Alexander Turnbull Library, ATL 1/1-012106-G

Tohu Kākahi's house at Parihaka, Rangi Kapuia, was an impressive double-storey Victorian-style building constructed by Emmanuel (Mahuhera) Dix.
David Duncan, c.1910s, Alexander Turnbull Library, 1/2-001270-G

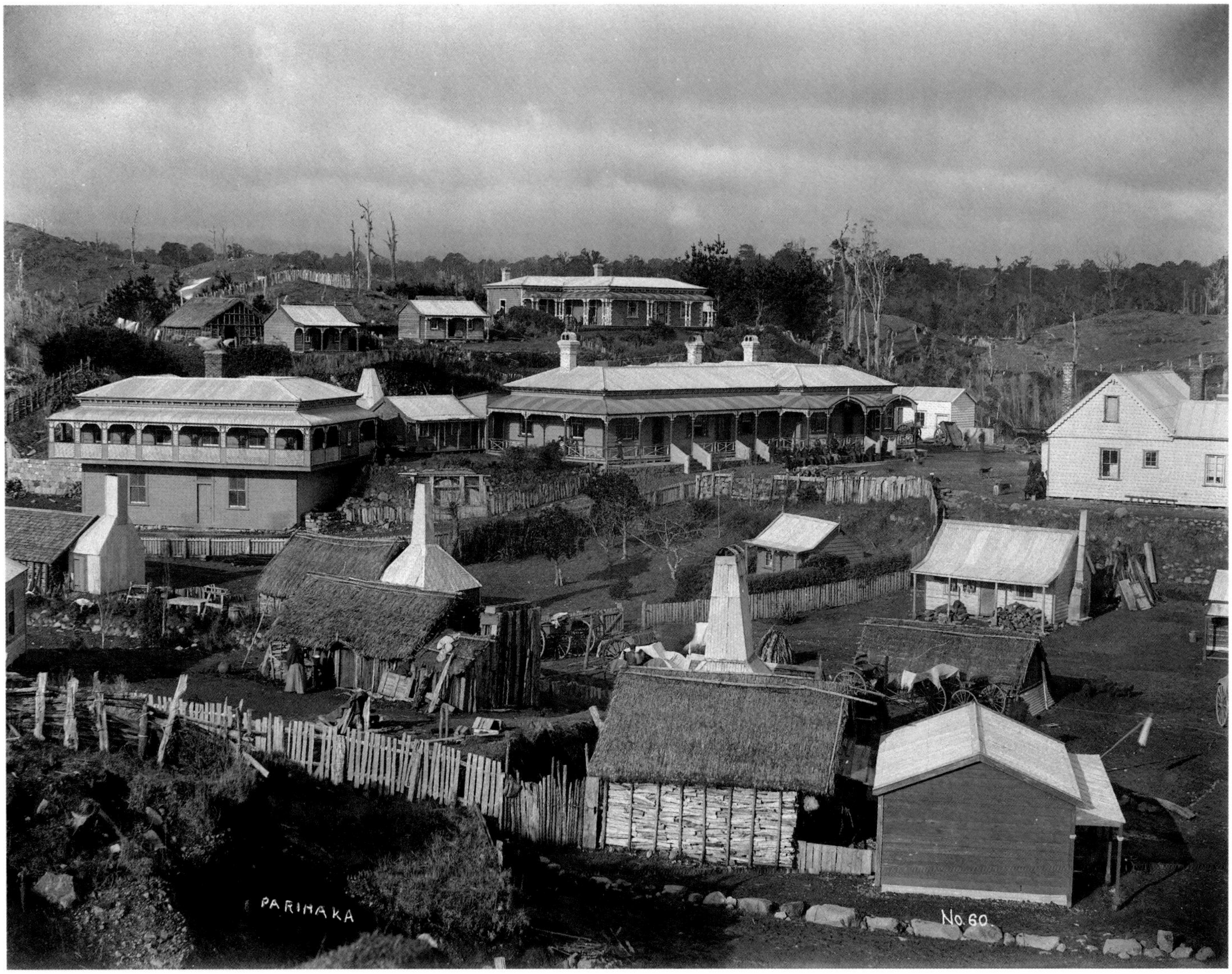

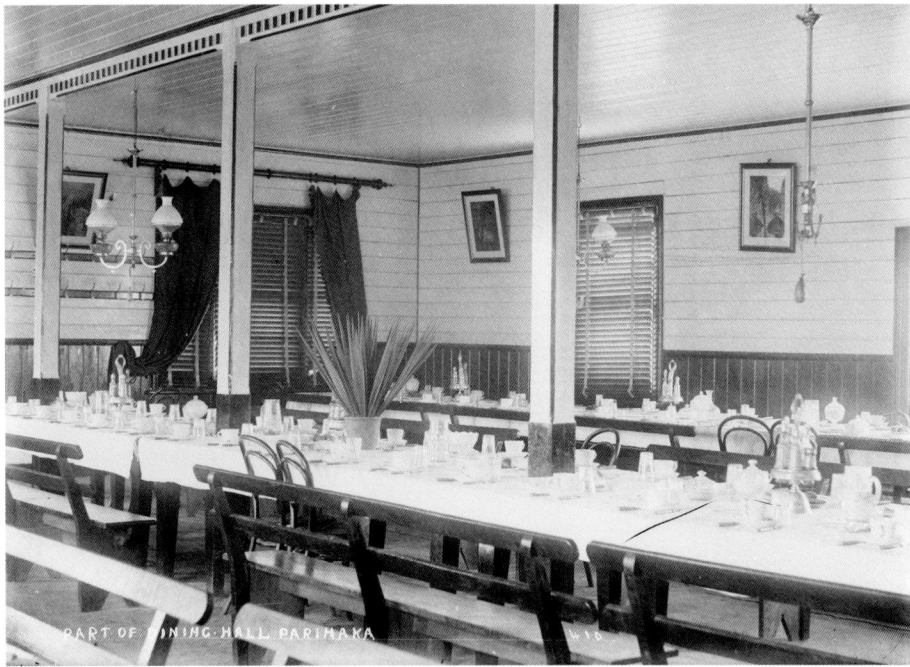

A large complex of community and residential buildings developed behind Te Whiti's house towards the end of the nineteenth century.
William Andrews Collis, n.d., Alexander Turnbull Library, 1/1-011758-G

While Te Niho o te Ātiawa's interior was similar in style to Victorian teahouses of the age, its long communal dining tables enabled Māori communal feasting.
William Andrew Collis, Alexander Turnbull Library, 1/1-012042-G

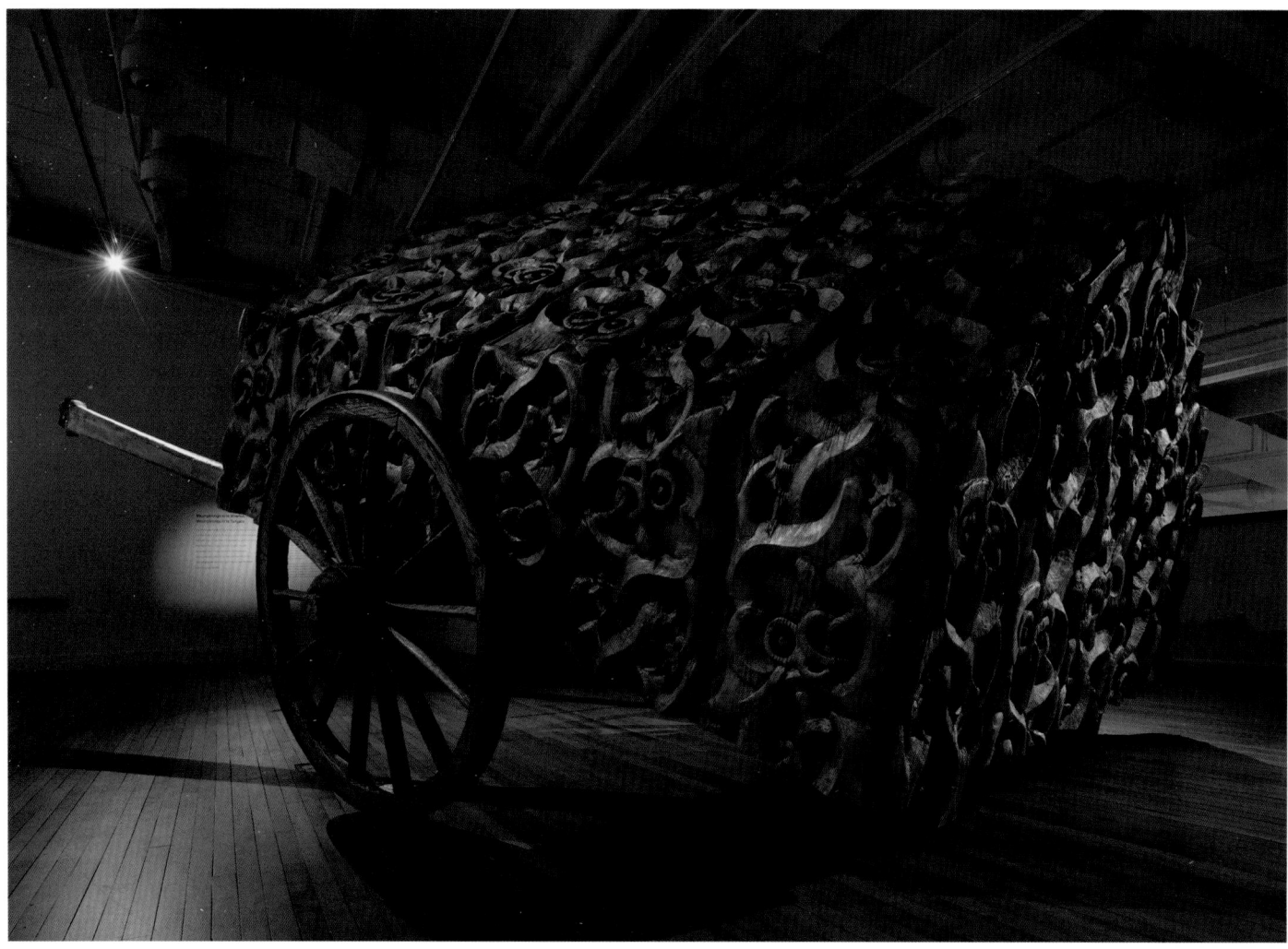

Brett Graham's 2020 sculpture *Maungārongo ki te Whenua Maungārongo ki te Tangata* recognises the strength and determination of the nineteenth-century Māori leaders Te Whiti o Rongomai, Tohu Kākahi and Riwha Tītokowaru who resisted colonisation in the Taranaki region. The pātaka form is closely associated with Māori lifeways and mana, and the intricate carvings on this sculpture are in the Taranaki style. The carriage beneath the pātaka alludes to the complexities of peace and the New Zealand Wars. When Pākehā surveyors and soldiers encroached on their lands, Te Whiti, Tohu and Tītokowaru sent them wagons of provisions as a gesture of manaakitanga to remind them they were guests on Māori land.

**Brett Graham, *Maungārongo ki te Whenua Maungārongo ki te Tangata*, 2020**

wood, synthetic polymer paint and graphite, 3200 x 8000 x 3200mm approx., photograph by Neil Pardington

these buildings, and they instigated a radical transformation of Parihaka architecture.[80]

Over the next twenty-five years, Parihaka metamorphosed from a large kāinga Māori to a Māori town. The change was internally driven, and it led to the progressive replacement of thatched whare with Victorian buildings – mostly cottages, with some exceptional grand residences and community facilities. While Te Whiti took inspiration from Pākehā culture, Tohu was less impressed and was more conservative in his village reforms. Over this time of reinvention, the founding kaupapa of Parihaka remained Māori self-determination and mana whenua. The architectural changes showed the influence of new aspirational values that, while they were articulated through buildings that were manifestly Pākehā in appearance, remained resolutely Māori in function and purpose.

By 1885, Parihaka had been rebuilt, with European-style houses facing paved roads, and with services such as gas and electric street-lighting that even the country's capital, Wellington, did not have.[81] The division of the settlement into two adjoining but distinct villages, following Te Whiti and Tohu's estrangement around 1888, did not inhibit change. By the end of the decade Tohu also had his own two-storey colonial-style residence, Rangi Kapuia, built by Emmanuel (Mahuera) Dix, which was considerably larger than Te Whiti's house.[82] Spade and heart emblems cut into the veranda balustrade and the gable fretwork may have been an allusion to Tohu's earlier affiliation to Pai Mārire, which used these symbols on its flags (see page 326).

Perhaps not to be outdone, Te Whiti developed the area behind Miti Mai Te Arero into a sprawling complex of Victorian buildings that housed meeting spaces and visitor accommodation. These and other changes were funded by Taare (Charles) Waitara, a Hutt Valley landowner who was Te Whiti's son-in-law.[83] A wharekai called Te Niho o te Ātiawa built on Te Whiti's marae in 1889 was one of the first permanent Māori dining halls in the country. In many respects it resembled a Victorian colonial teahouse, complete with veranda – except for the inclusion of long communal dining tables.[84] In the spirit of manaakitanga, the building could seat over 100 people and was intended to host visitors from iwi who had contributed funds to the rebuilding of Parihaka.[85]

Almost all of Parihaka's thatched whare had been replaced with iron-roofed colonial-style weatherboard residences at the end of the century. The settlement's Pākehā-style residences each had at least three bedrooms, a kitchen and stained-glass fanlight windows, and some of the larger houses had hot and cold running water in bathrooms, although toilet facilities were at a remove from the settlement.[86] Communal living had not been extinguished with the destruction that followed the 1881 invasion: each hapū had its own wharepuni to accommodate visiting relatives.[87] Some of these were weatherboard; others – particularly those belonging to older residents – were single-room thatched whare clad in raupō and ponga.[88] Maintenance was carried out by a group of Māori tradesmen who had learnt their skills from Pākehā employed earlier in the settlement's redevelopment.[89]

After Te Whiti and Tohu passed away in 1907, the impetus to continue developing Parihaka slowed considerably. The community continued, but in a smaller group of residences and revitalised community buildings.

## Conclusion

The search for unity inspired innovation in Māori architecture and associated arts. During and after the New Zealand Wars, many communities redirected their energies and resources towards survival and cohesiveness by fostering creative practices and appropriating materials and ideas. Architecture and art played a pivotal role in the struggle to maintain self-determination. Ngā Pou o te Kīngitanga pātaka and Ringatū whakairo rākau and figurative painting illustrated the relevance of tikanga and Māori ways of understanding time and space in overcoming the challenges of colonisation and colliding worldviews.

Community congregation was imperative for iwi unity. Gatherings were accommodated in the large Parihaka whare, Ringatū wharenui and Māori parliaments, which were designed to stand in defiance of settler land encroachment and Crown aggression. As in other parts of the Pacific, the authority of tohunga as spiritual, artistic and architectural knowledge-keepers and practitioners was under threat. This was due to a complex set of factors that included the rise of Christianity and of Māori religious leaders such as Te Kooti, Te Whiti and Tohu, the appropriation of Pākehā materials and technologies, the secularisation of Māori leadership and the decline of the hapū in favour of iwi and pan-iwi confederations. At the dawn of the twentieth century, new moral codes – particularly those associated with hygiene and sobriety – were influencing Māori life and would soon have a profound effect on Māori arts and leadership.

# MĀORI FLAGS AND BANNERS
DEIDRE BROWN

Māori flags and banners have been an important symbol of Māori identity since the nineteenth century – whether they were connecting to Ranginui by flying in the wind, or displayed as pictorial histories in buildings. In 1834, northern Māori adopted their own New Zealand flag from a choice of three prepared by Henry Williams. The flag they selected became known as Te Kara, the flag of the United Tribes. It featured a Saint George's Cross with, in the upper-left quarter, the Southern Cross on a blue background inside a smaller Saint George's Cross.[1] Northern Māori still regard Te Kara as a symbol of self-determination from an age that pre-dated Te Tiriti o Waitangi.

The Kīngitanga readily adopted flags as an expression of sovereignty. When Te Wherowhero accepted the role of Māori king at Rangiriri on 23 April 1857, flags were hoisted that bore the words 'Kingi' and 'Niu Tireni' (New Zealand). From this time on, every leader of the Kīngitanga has had their own highly tapu flag, which is buried with them when they pass away. A number of other Kīngitanga flags were in use during the nineteenth century, some with the words 'Ingiki Potatau' (King Pōtatau), and others using shared symbols such as stars, crosses and a triple-diamond arrangement that represented the three main islands of Aotearoa New Zealand. Hēni Te Kiri Karamū (Ngāti Uenukukōpako and Ngāti Hinepare), also known as Hēni Pore (Jane Foley), is remembered as the designer and maker of the Kīngitanga's 'Aotearoa' red silk flag that belonged to the rangatira and Kīngitanga adherent Wī Koka of the Koheriki hapū.[2] As a child, Te Kiri Karamū had attended a number of mission schools, where she likely developed her skills as an expert seamstress and embroiderer.[3]

Inspired by the Kīngitanga, the Māori religio-political movements that began to appear around the country from the mid-nineteenth century adopted flags of their own. Pai Mārire, a religion that originated in the Taranaki region in 1862, created flags for a number of occasions. Many were displayed on niu (poles) from which the hau (angel's) messages were transmitted from the skies to followers below. Kenana (a transliteration of Canaan) was the personal flag of the movement's leader Te Ua Haumēne and featured a playing-card-derived trefoil device that represented the Trinity.[4] Some flags alluded to Pai Mārire's allegiance with the Kīngitanga. Flags with the words 'Ingipotatau', meaning the 'Kingship of Pōtatau', and 'Ingimene' ('King of Men'), and a cross and three diamonds, appear in a drawing of the 'Pūtahi' niu pole within a Pai Mārire manuscript known as 'Ua Rongopai'.[5]

Pai Mārire followers showed their support for the Kīngitanga during the Waikato conflicts in the New Zealand Wars by flying the Kīngitanga flags Maui – a flag associated with unity – and Pōtatau from a Hawke's Bay niu.[6] They used red and white flags as indicators of peaceful and warlike intent respectively. White flags were often seen flying from the niu during religious services: they were called Rura because they were associated with the teachings of Rura (ruler), the angel Gabriel. Some white flags were emblazoned with red lettering or symbols, such as stars and crescent moons.[7]

Top: Te Kara, the United Tribes flag, as illustrated in 1845. The original 1834 flag design had a black rather than white border around the smaller Saint George's Cross.
***United Tribes Ensign*, 1834–1845**
ink and watercolour sketch, 125 x 190mm, Alexander Turnbull Library, MS-Papers-0009-09-01

Bottom left: The middle flag in this March 1861 sketch of the 'Tainui' flagpole at Puke Karaka, an Ōtaki Catholic community, belongs to the Māori king and was a black pennant with white border, red cross and three diamonds. Above it is the flag of Wī Tako Ngātata, rangatira of the local Te Ātiawa tribe, and the flag beneath is the French tricolore, alluding to the origins of French Catholic missionaries who came to Ōtaki.
**Charles George Hewson, *Sketch of flags at Pukekaraka community*, 1861**
ink sketch on paper, 125 x 200mm, Alexander Turnbull Library, MS-Papers-0032-0339-05

Bottom right: Jane Foley (Hēni Pore), also known as Hēni Te Kiri Karamū, who risked her own life to give water to the wounded during the battle of Gate Pā, Tauranga, on 29 April 1864. She is pictured standing next to a flag adorned with a cross, three stars, a crescent moon and the word 'AOTEAROA'.
Puke Ariki, New Plymouth, PHO2012-0016

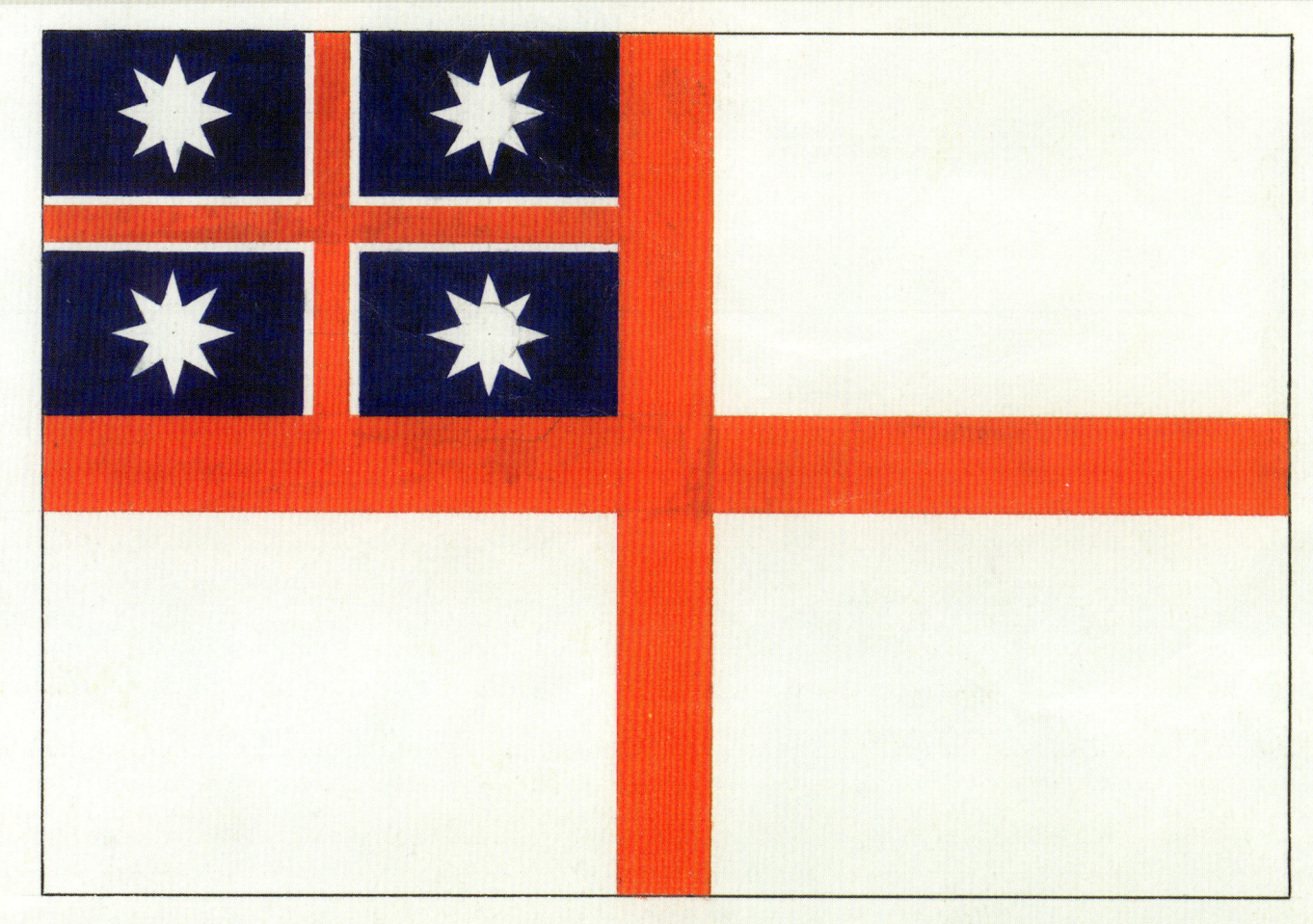

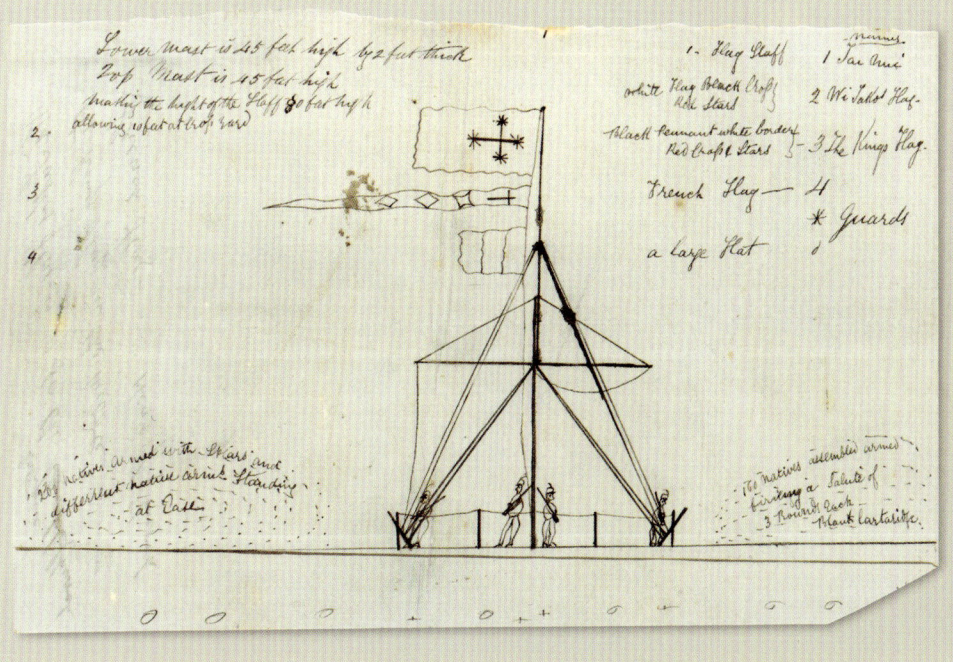

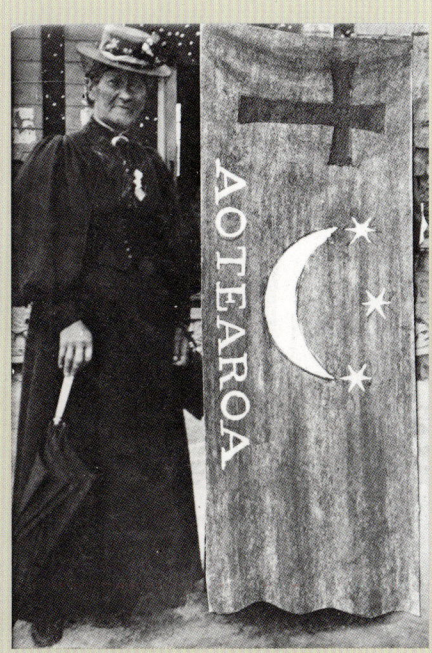

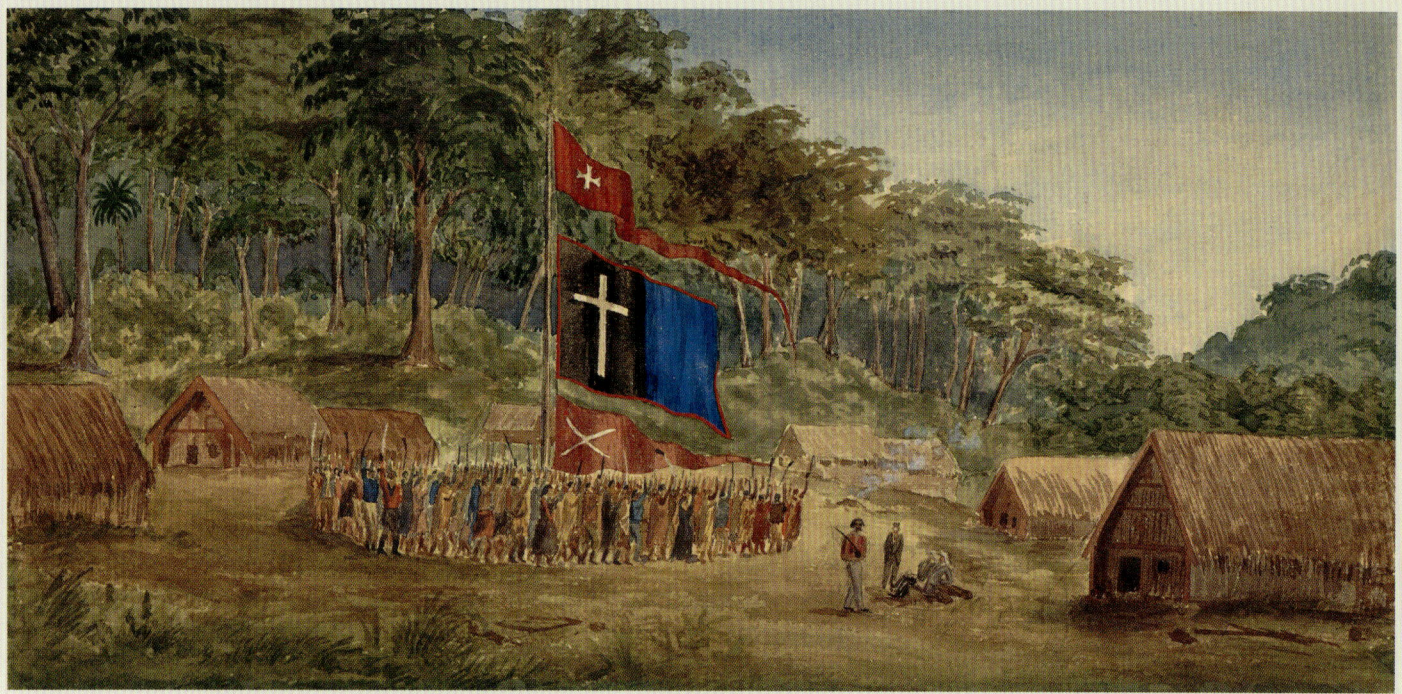

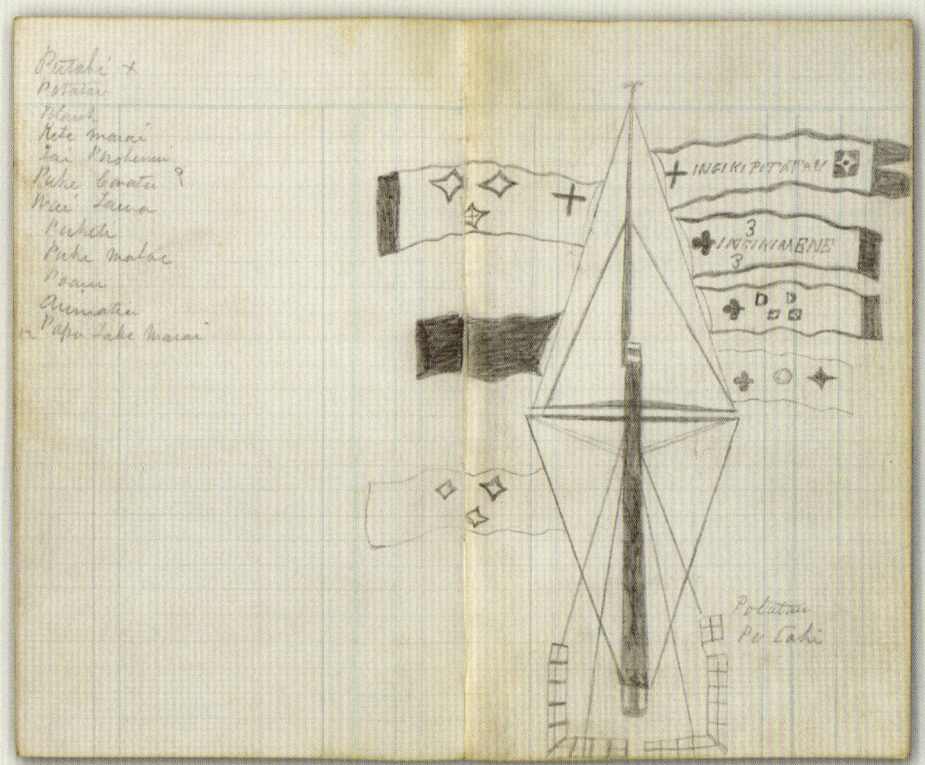

Above: Pai Mārire flags flying from a niu pole at Tataroa, 27 January 1865. This niu ceremony was conducted to decide the fate of the soldier who would later paint this image, Lieutenant Herbert Meade, here shown tied up beside his translator Hemepo. Both men were released.
**Herbert George Phillip Meade, *Pai Marire karakia, held by the Te Hau fanatics at Tataroa, New Zealand, to determine the fate of their prisoners*, 1865**
watercolour on sheet, 188 x 388mm, Alexander Turnbull Library, B-139-014

Left: Kīngitanga- and Pai Mārire-inspired flags flying from the Putahi niu pole as illustrated in the 'Ua Rongopai' manuscript.
Auckland Libraries Heritage Collections, GNZMMS1

Opposite top: Te Wepu (the whip), Te Kooti Arikirangi Te Tūruki's best-known flag.
**Gilbert Mair, *Te Kooti's flag, Te Wepu*, 1921?**
ink drawing, 83 x 203mm, Alexander Turnbull Library, A-173-031

Opposite bottom: Paratene Matchitt's *Te Wepu Assemblage* of 1986 is a contemporary response to the iconography and meanings of Ringatū flags.
**Paratene Matchitt, *Te Wepu Assemblage*, 1986**
painted particle board and other woods, mixed media, 2440 x 3500 x 150mm, Waipapa Taumata Rau University of Auckland Art Collection

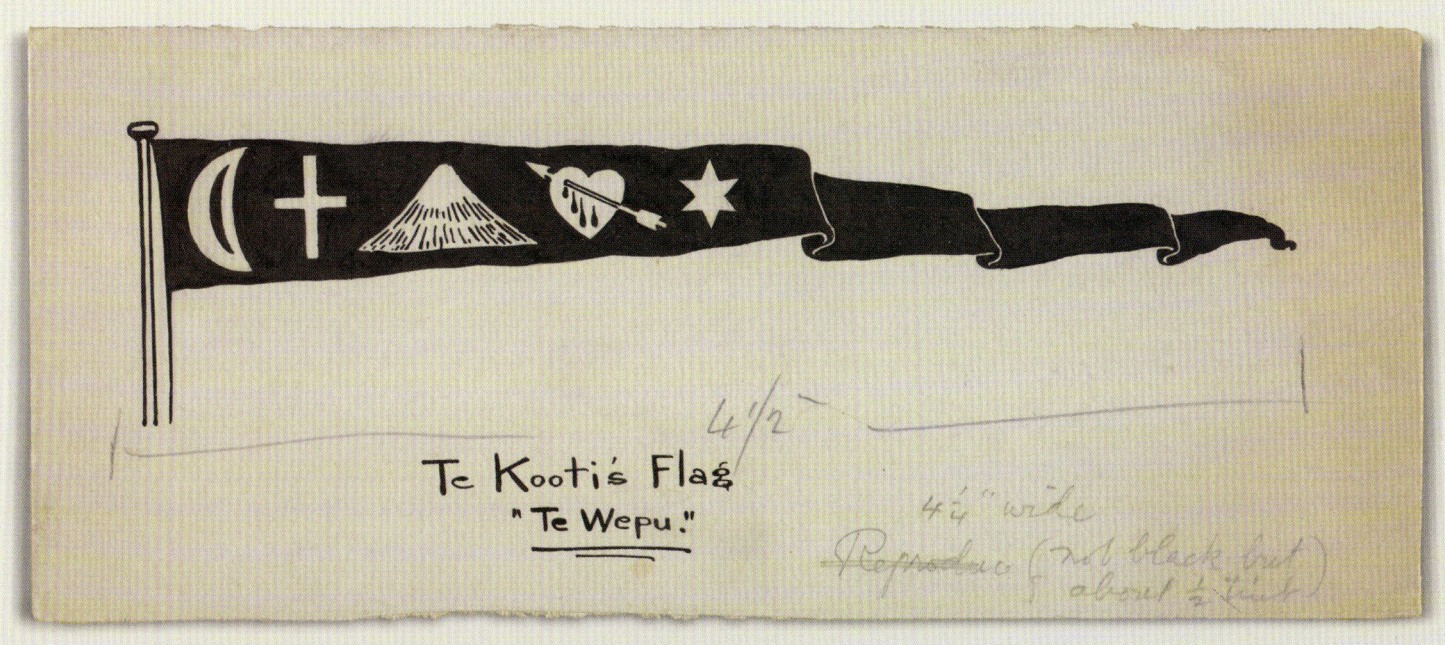

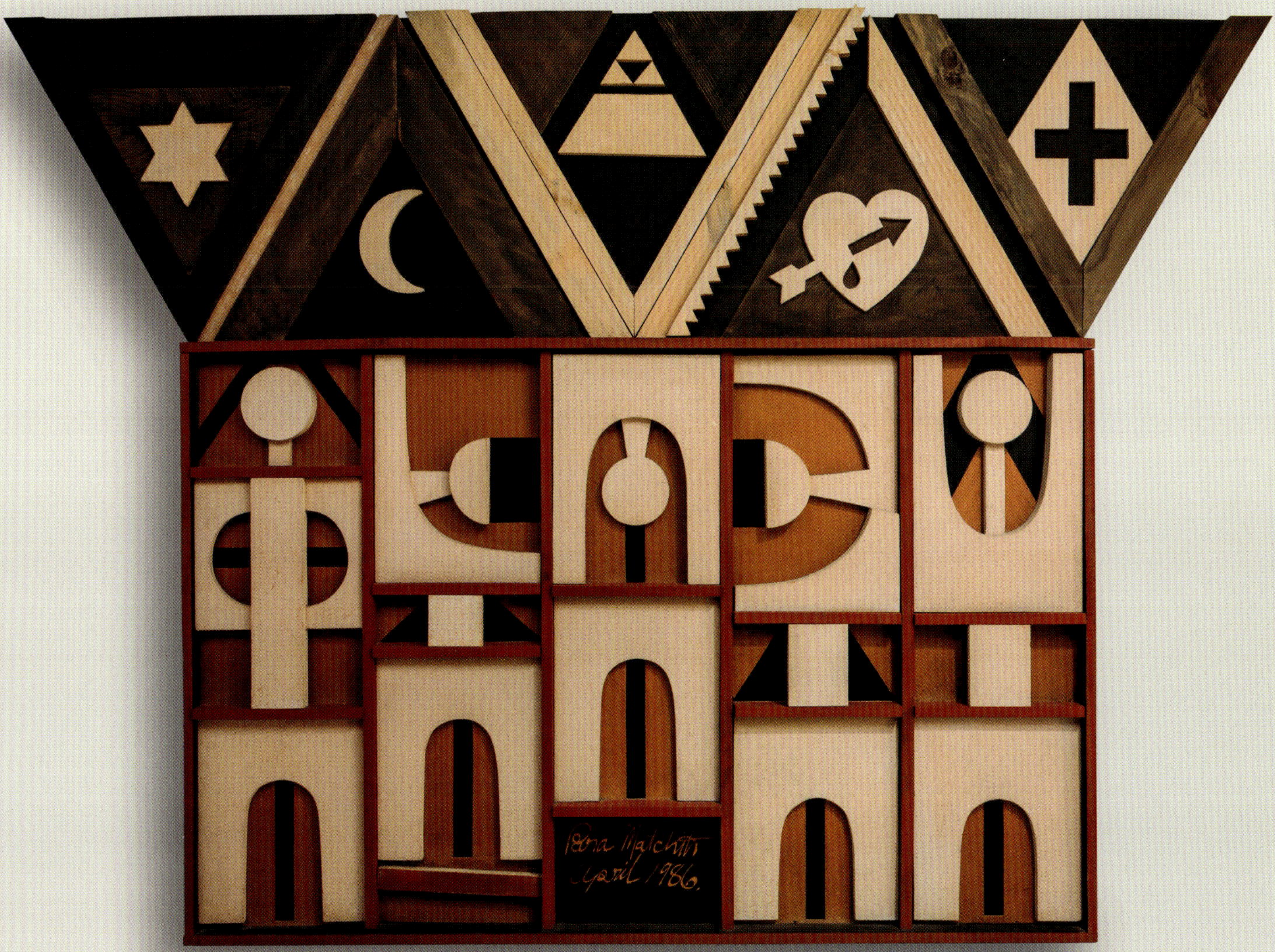

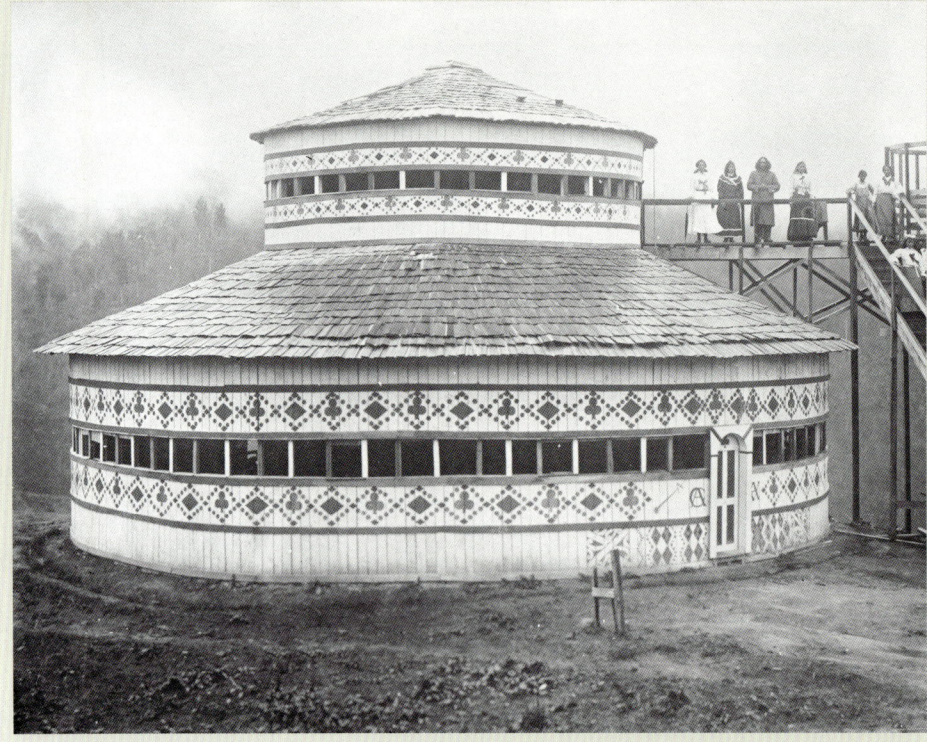

The diamond and club iconography encircling the Hīona building, constructed in 1907, linked its Maungapōhatu community to the mana and lineage of earlier Māori movements, such as Ringatū. The community's leader, Rua Kēnana, can be seen here standing with some of his wives and kin on the gangway.
George Bourne, c.1908, Alexander Turnbull Library, APG-1679-1/2-G

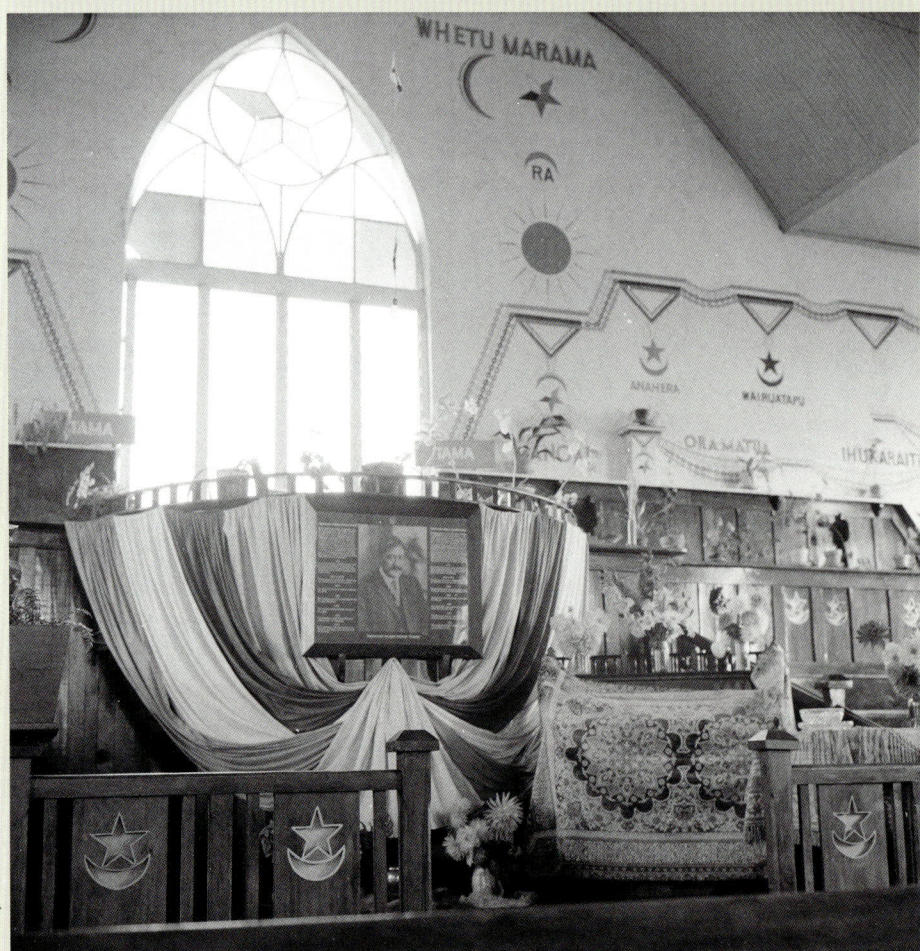

Altar of the Temepara showing whetū marama (star and moon symbols) on the walls, altar rails and balustrades, Rātana Pā.
Ans Westra, Alexander Turnbull Library, AWM-0766-F, copyright Ans Westra

**Overleaf:** Tino Rangatiratanga flag by Hiraina Marsden, Jan Smith and Linda Munn, 1990.

Prayers under the red 'Riki' flag – which probably represented Te Ariki Mikaera, the archangel Michael – always preceded fighting.[8] Other Pai Mārire flags included red half-moons, a five-pointed star and spade designs.[9] The flag emblems were most likely painted or sewn on by women.[10]

Te Kooti adopted flags during his te whai a te motu (pursuit through the island) when he was chased across the North Island by government forces during the latter stages of the New Zealand Wars. The most famous of his flags is Te Wepu (the whip), a red silk pennant 52 feet (16m) long – reputedly a foot for each week of the year – and 4 feet (1.2m) at the widest end – perhaps for each week of the month – tapering to a point. The flag featured a white crescent moon, a cross, Mount Taranaki, a heart shot through with an arrow, and a six-pointed star. Although the flag was originally made by Catholic nuns from Napier for Ngāti Kahungunu, who lost it to Te Kooti in 1868, the symbolism has been read as relevant to Te Kooti's cause in a number of ways. Gilbert Mair captured the flag and deposited it in the Dominion Museum. Later, when it was no longer to be found in the museum, Mair claimed it had been cut up a few years after he deposited it and used as cleaning cloths; and historian James Cowan wrote that he had seen a shortened flag of this description in the museum in the early twentieth century.[11] There are others who believe that the flag was secretly returned to the community.[12] A year after Te Wepu was captured, Te Kooti flew two other white flags, at the battle of Te Pōrere pā. One of these flags bore a similar crescent moon, cross and letters – in this case 'W' and 'I', likely to refer to Wairua (spirit) or Wairua Tapu (Holy Spirit):[13] it is now in Te Papa.[14] The self-determination and struggle that these and other Te Kooti flags represent have been a source of inspiration for contemporary Māori artists, especially Paratene Matchitt, Brett Graham and Shane Cotton.

By the twentieth century, stars, crescent moons and playing-card symbols on flags had become so closely identified with self-determination initiatives that they began to appear on the buildings, clothing and banners of Māori religio-political movements. Rua Kēnana's Hīona council chamber – built at Maungapōhatu in 1907 and based on descriptions of Solomon's Temple on the Temple Mount in Jerusalem and on a lithograph of the Dome of the Rock – was adorned with yellow diamond and blue club symbols.[15] Te Ua Haumēne's Kenana flag included a trefoil, and the use of the trefoil on Hīona may have been a play on words, relating to Rua Kēnana's name as well as a connection back to Te Ua. The Rātana Church developed other celestial symbols into the whetū marama (star–moon) motif that was applied to the belltowers of its Temepara (opened at Rātana pā, near Whanganui, in 1928), the walls of its other churches and secular buildings, clerical robes and pictorial history banners. Each point of the star represents an identity in the Rātana godhead, while the moon represents the māramatanga, or enlightenment, offered by the church.

The use of symbols to allude to a whakapapa of powerful leaders and to communicate solidarity between communities offered an alternative means of expression to the figurative whakairo rākau of whare whakairo, which were not widely made outside of the East Coast and the central North Island before the 1930s. Flags and flagpoles were also signs of settlement and belonging. Māori leaders had used them to assert their authority over Māori land much as the settlers had – an action that was not lost on the government, which began to issue British flags and, later, the New Zealand Red Ensign to rangatira and iwi who had been their allies during the New Zealand Wars. In 1990, the sesquicentennial of the signing of Te Tiriti o Waitangi, Hiraina Marsden, Jan Smith and Linda Munn designed the Tino Rangatiratanga flag, which quickly became identified with contemporary Māori self-determination initiatives such as the Foreshore and Seabed protests of the early 2000s. However, it was not until Waitangi Day 2010, and after many years of public lobbying, that the government finally agreed to allow the Tino Rangatiratanga flag to be flown alongside the New Zealand flag on government buildings.

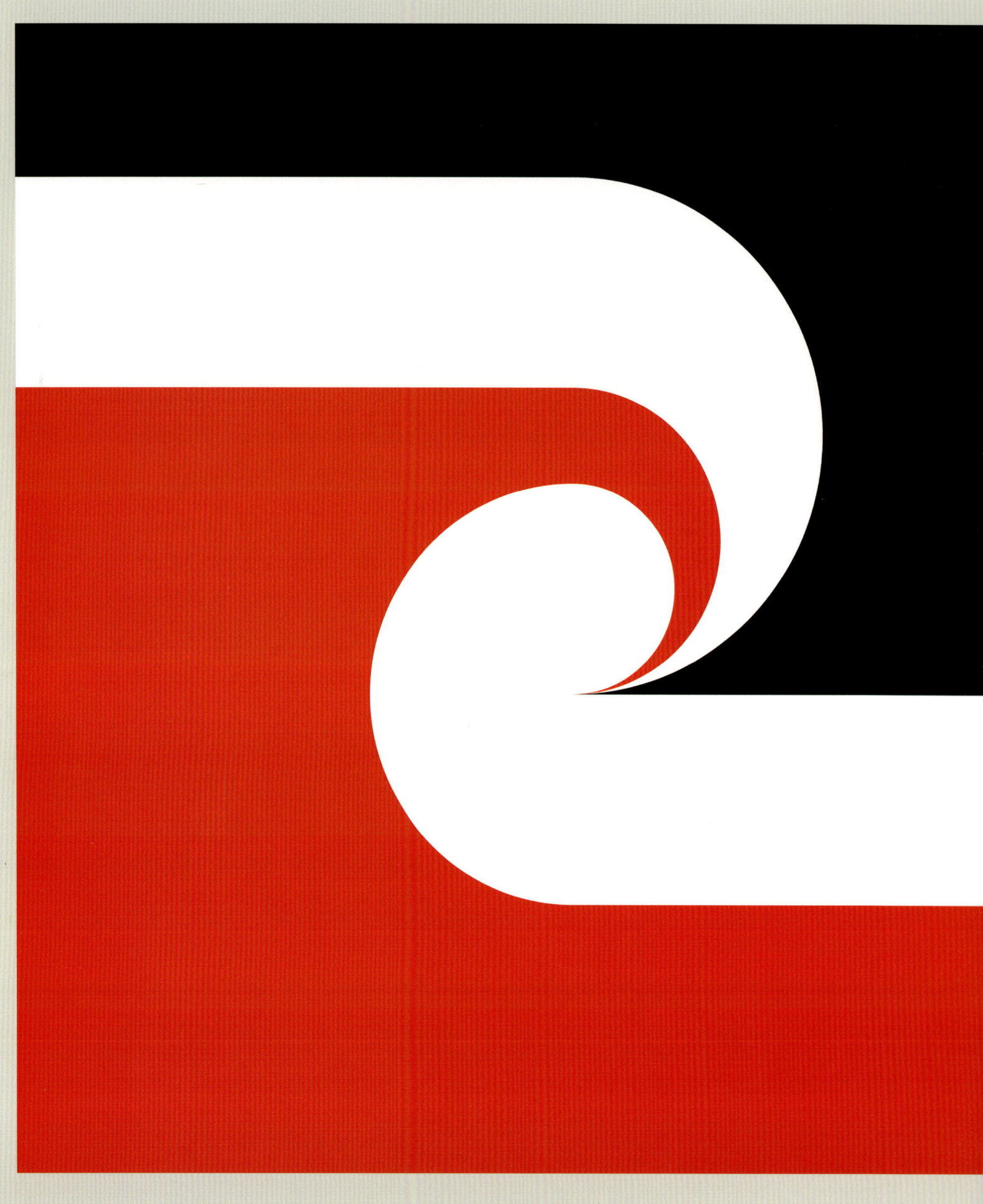

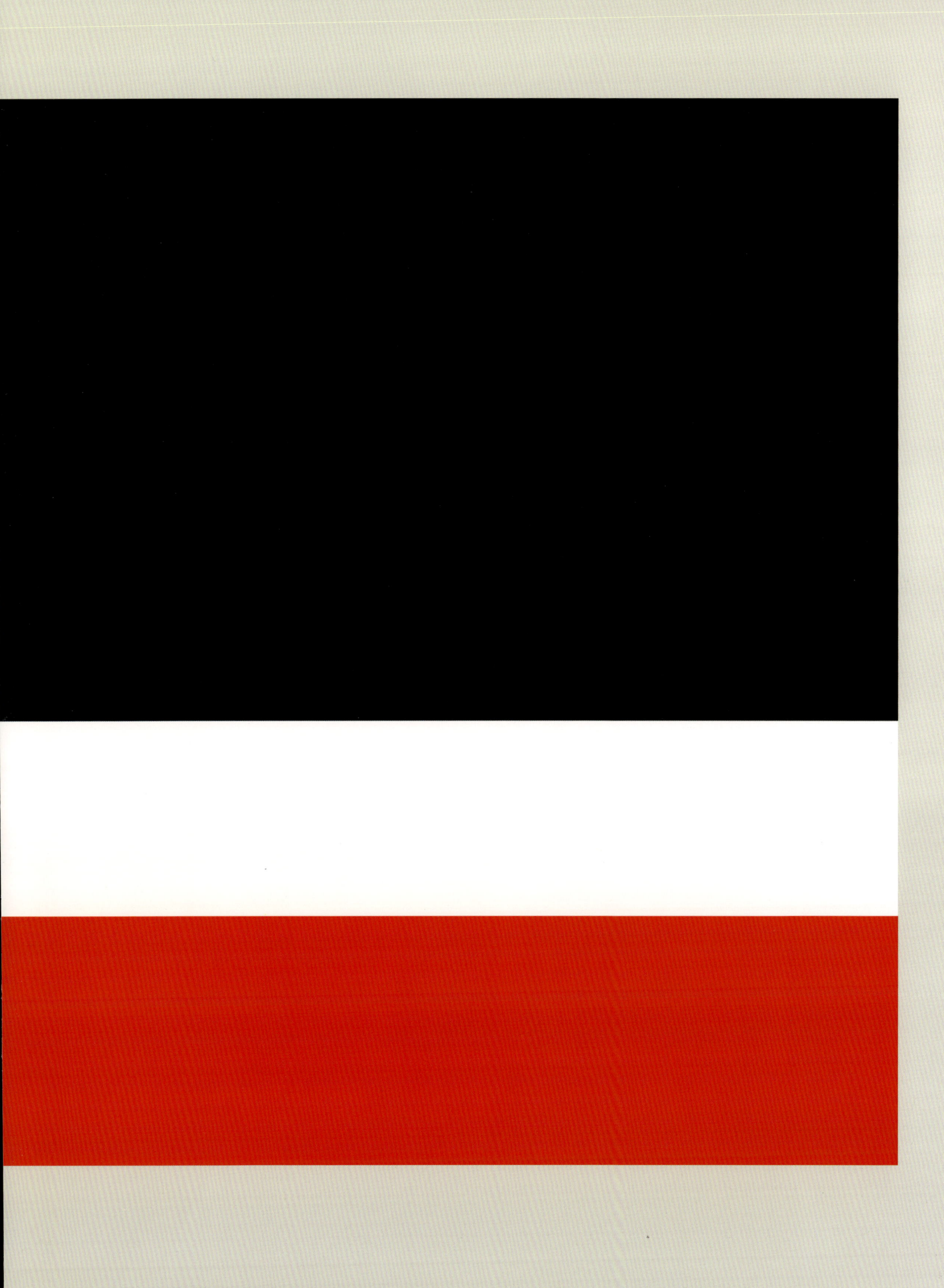

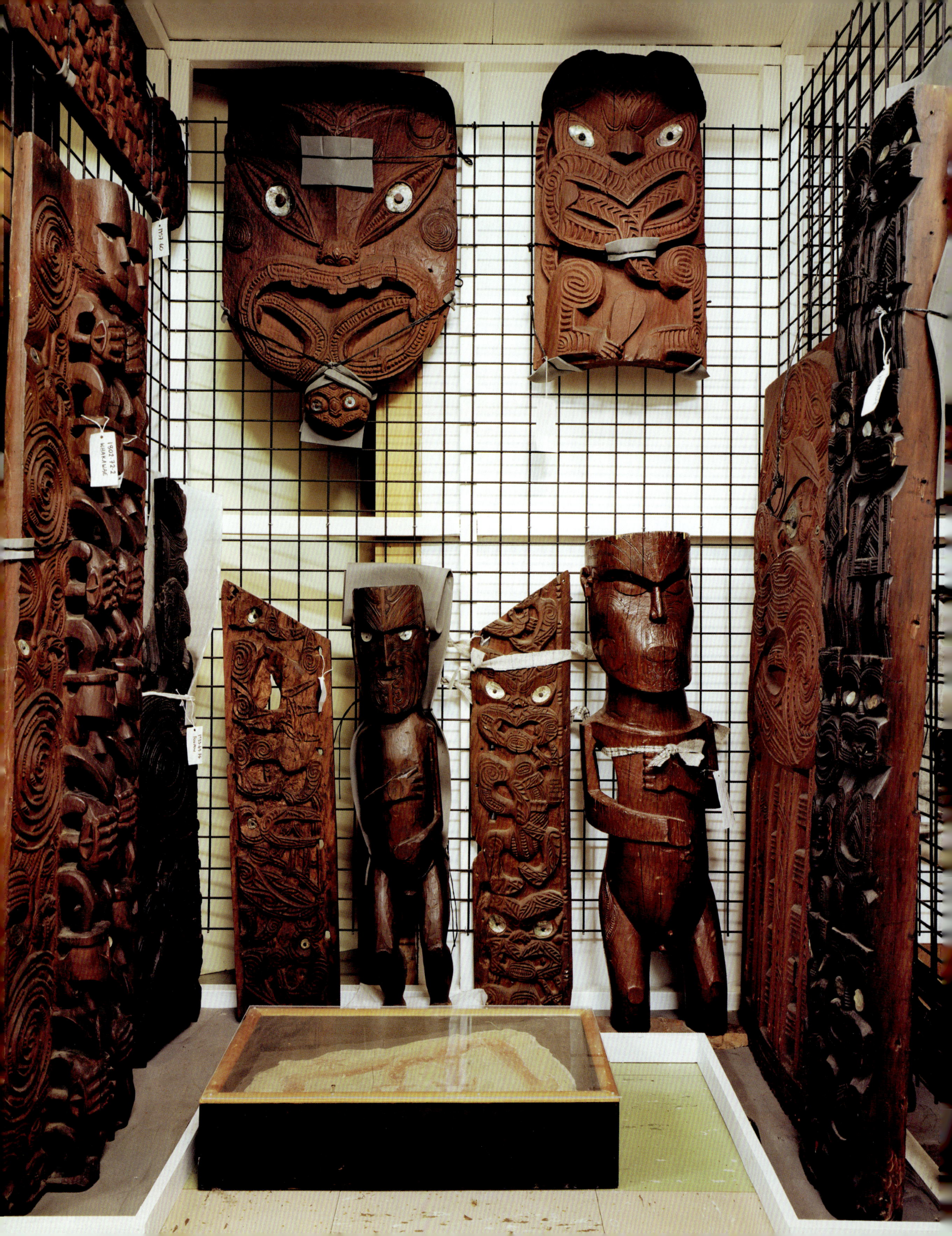

# 13 KA WHAWHAI TONU MĀTOU
## TAONGA AND MUSEUMS SINCE 1900
### NGARINO ELLIS

*Ko tō rourou, ko taku rourou, ka ora te iwi.*

*With your food basket, and my food basket, the people will be well.*

By 1900, thousands of taonga had been removed from Māori communities into public institutions, both in Aotearoa New Zealand and overseas. The ramifications of this were numerous. A direct correlation could be seen in the dismal statistics for Māori at this time: Māori were a minority demographic in their own lands. Their political status on a national level within the government structure was minimal at best. In addition, forced relocation of many hapū away from their ancestral lands meant no access to spiritual sites of significance, including urupā, no access to physical materials necessary in their art making (timber, fibre, pigments), no access to earlier models/templates for the artists to draw inspiration from. Despite this, ka whawhai tonu mātou – Māori endured. Museums became crucial repositories of private collections, long ago removed from Māori, together with their own acquisitions. The challenge then became how to display these collections, and for whom.

Neil Pardington, *Taonga Māori Store #2, Whanganui Regional Museum* 2006
Lambda / C-print, dimensions variable

### A Māori museum?

Since the time when taonga were removed from their whānau and hapū, there have been calls for their return. Raharuhi Rukupō petitioned the government in vain for the return of the whare whakairo Te Hau ki Tūranga in the 1860s. He explained that he had not given consent for the removal of the whare, and that in any event he had no power to grant any removal as the house was communally owned. Māori members of the House of Representatives were concerned enough at the turn of the century to lobby for legislation to stem the mass removal of taonga Māori out of New Zealand.

The Maori Antiquities Act was passed in 1901 after lobbying by Augustus Hamilton (who in 1903 became director of the Colonial Museum); it was presented in Parliament by James Carroll (Ngāti Kahungunu, 1857–1926), member for Eastern Maori and native minister. In effect, the legislation supported the museum's constant and by now difficult search for taonga Māori for its collection.[1] Carroll called on whānau to place their taonga, along with their stories, in the proposed museum 'as a constant reminder to the coming generations of the capabilities and taste of the Maori race'.[2] The Act made it illegal to export taonga ('Maori antiquities') without first offering them to the governor or his agent.

Certainly, there was concern that gifts of ancestral treasures to overseas-based dignitaries would be lost to New Zealand forever. In 1901, when the Duke and Duchess of York visited New Zealand, iwi had competed to present memorable and important taonga to the royal couple. These would eventually include a model waka; whāriki; kākahu decorated with feathers of weka, kererū and kākā, as well as dogskin; mere pounamu; hei tiki; hoeroa; taiaha; and a toki pounamu from Te Pokiha Taranui.[3] As Walter Buller commented: 'I fear HRH the Duke of York will bring away many things that are irreplaceable.'[4] Despite the passing of the Act, some taonga were still able to be exported legally: Elizabeth Pishief notes the furore surrounding the sale of the wharenui Rauru by Charles Edwin Nelson to a German dealer in 1904.[5] The Act was amended in 1908 to address this loophole, and to introduce a £100 fine.

Some queried whether a museum dedicated to Māori would be prudent. Hamilton approached Carroll, who was keen to expand the Colonial Museum as 'a repository of all kinds of Maori relics, which would thus find a place of safe custody', a place where 'several prominent Maoris were keen to deposit historical "jewels", battleaxes and so forth'.[6] Hamilton and the ethnologist Stephenson Percy Smith envisaged a 'National Maori Museum' that would be managed by a board of governors composed of Māori and Pākehā. As part of this plan, there would need to be 'Government purchasing officers' appointed to identify and facilitate the acquisition of Māori art. Names suggested were a run-sheet for the major Pākehā writers about Māori art at the time: Gilbert Mair (Auckland), Smith (New Plymouth), land purchase officer William Goffe (Whanganui) and surveyor Edward Tregear (Wellington).

Māori supported the idea of a national Māori museum, probably because they were also concerned at the numbers of taonga leaving the country. Ngāti Kahungunu leader Tamahau Mahupuku (1837/42–1904) contacted Carroll to offer his support, along with that of his people from Ngāti Hikawera and Ngāti Moe. To reinforce their lobbying, they presented their whare whakairo Tākitimu to the government. Mahupuku continued:

> Under this gift you have the right to take, remove, or transfer it from its present site at Kehemane, Nga-waka-a-kupe, Wairarapa, with its carved timbers, its laced worked sides, and all its furniture, together with the likenesses of the old chiefs which are contained within the said carved house – namely, Wereta te Kawekairangi, Hoera Whakatahakiterangi, Ngairo Takatakaputea, Heremaia Tamakitematangi, and Wiremu Hikawera Mahupuku, whose names are to be found in the deeds ceding lands to the Queen in former days.[7]

Unfortunately, the house burnt down before it could be moved.

Māori everywhere were becoming increasingly wary of selling taonga, and purchasers found it difficult to source the types of taonga they deemed worthy and 'authentic' – that is, those that were 'untainted' by the use of European motifs, materials or techniques. One agent sent from Berlin to acquire taonga lamented how difficult it was to source and purchase Māori 'objects' for the sum he had been sent with. The tide was turning.

Collectors still sought out material from dealers of taonga Māori, both Māori and Pākehā, both in New Zealand and overseas, especially England. British-based collectors of Pacific material in the early twentieth century included Harry Beasley, Alfred Fuller, James Hooper, James Edge-Partington, William Oldman, Kenneth Webster and William Downing Webster.[8] Roger Neich notes that collectors based in Europe 'had their own traditions of field and private artefact collecting [with] only limited overlap and interchange between these separate theatres of collecting'.[9]

William Oldman's activities were characteristic of dealers in the early twentieth century. He became interested in collecting in his twenties, and in 1927 he set up a private museum in Clapham Park, London. He built up his collection over the next twenty years, sourcing work through private correspondence with museums and other collectors in Britain, the United States and Europe. In 1948 he sold his entire Oceanic collection to the New Zealand government for £44,000 (the equivalent of NZ$2.1 million in 2024). He passed away the following year.

### Māori patronage 1900–1950

Apirana Ngata and Te Puea Hērangi were major patrons of Māori arts in the first half of the twentieth century. As tribal leaders, they understood the importance of Māori visual and performing arts to the wellbeing of whānau, hapū and iwi. They were aware that much of the older visual culture had either been destroyed or was now located in museums. In just two generations the knowledge of tribal carving had been almost lost; carvers from Ngata's School of Maori Arts and Crafts had to visit museums in order to study early examples of tribal styles.

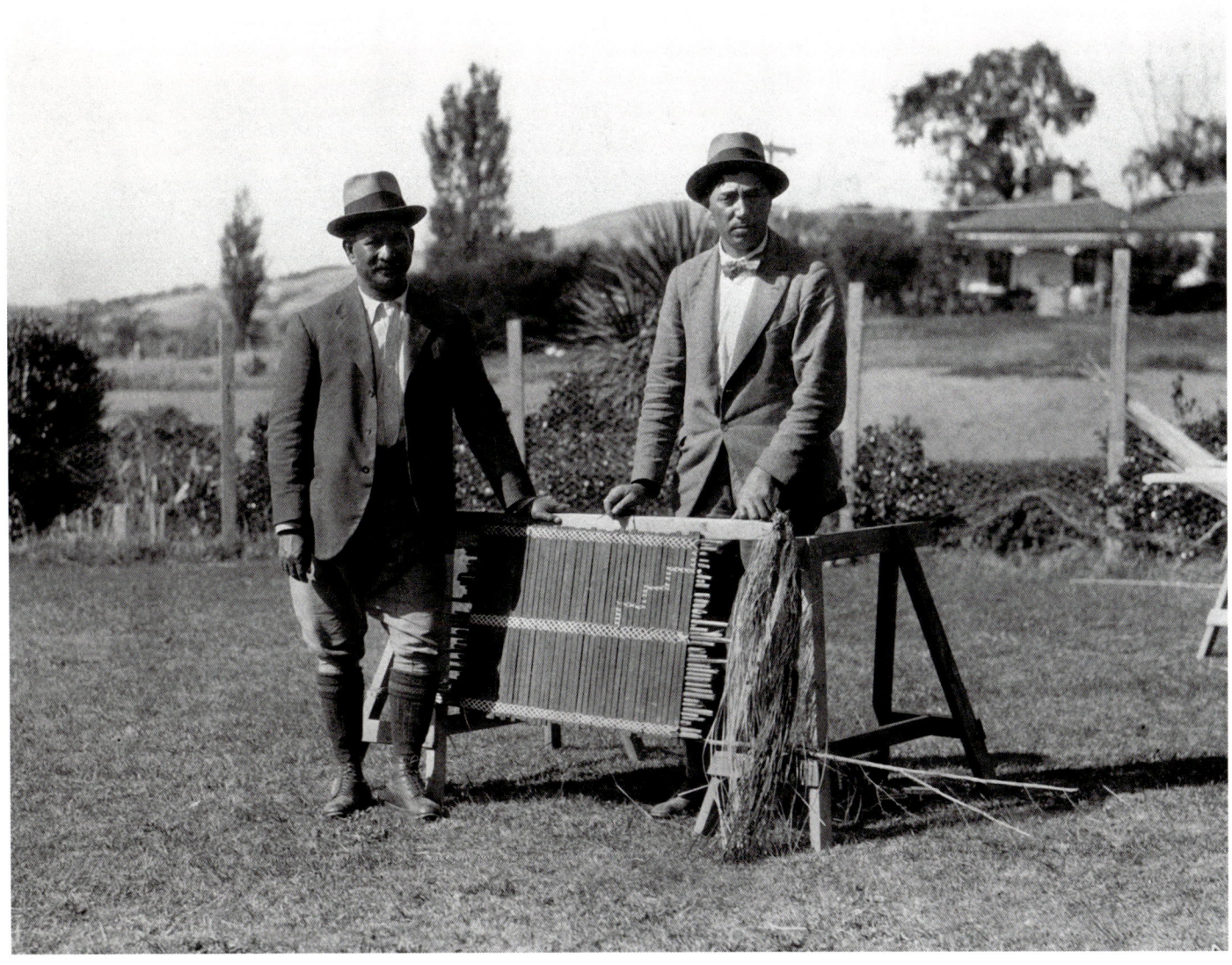

Museums in the 1940s employed ethnologists as curators. These were people who were familiar with the collections. They regularly visited communities to collect information and observe art, and they published their findings in journals such as the *Journal of the Polynesian Society* (1892–) and *Records of the Dominion Museum* (1942–1975). William Phillipps joined the Dominion Museum staff as an ethnologist in 1915, and began working with Māori in documenting their meeting houses. He contacted Ngata for recommendations on which East Coast whare whakairo to study, and for introductions to experts in the community who were knowledgeable about the houses. Phillipps published several important studies of tribal meeting houses from around the country before his retirement in 1958. Today these are still regarded highly as a 'line in the sand' of what *was* there.

James Ingram McDonald, 'Apirana Ngata and Peter Buck Alongside a Tukutuku panel at Waiomatatini'. Ngata had been pulled out of his schooling at Te Aute College to be trained in the arts of tukutuku and work under the direction of Karauria Kauri in the house Porourangi at Waiomatatini in the 1870s. Ngata would later build his homestead next door to the marae. This photo was taken in 1923 when he led an expedition around the East Coast in order to record tribal traditions such as net-making.
Alexander Turnbull Library, 1/2-007887-F

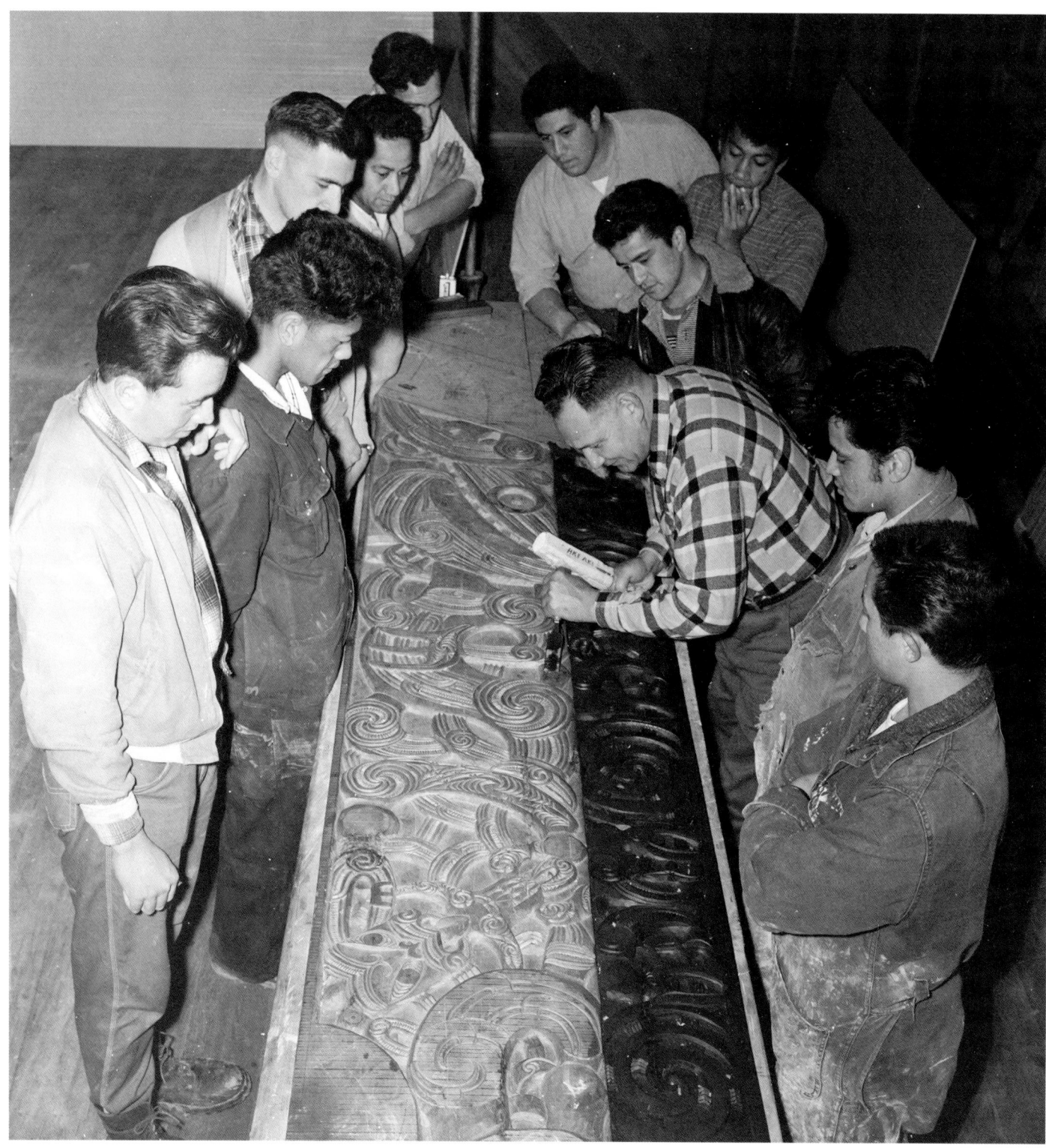

Young Māori men watching a carving demonstration at the Dominion Museum, Buckle Street, Wellington, 5 October 1959, photographed for the *Evening Post*.
Alexander Turnbull Library, EP/1959/3355-F

Events in 1940 provide an interesting survey of the state of Māori art and agency at the time. The government pitched the centennial of the signing of Te Tiriti o Waitangi as a momentous occasion – something to be celebrated – and to this end it commissioned a meeting house (described as a whare rūnanga) to be built at Waitangi, on the site of the first signing. This was to be a pan-tribal meeting house, a showcase of different carving styles, to promote the rhetoric of the government that assimilation was working successfully, as exemplified in the building and decoration of the house.[10]

Iwi economic and political strength could be measured by the style and size of the meeting house that they commissioned. Deidre Brown argues that the whare rūnanga must be considered as part of Ngata's 'wider counter-colonial programme'.[11] He worked tirelessly to use the process of building and decorating the house to weave together different iwi, mimicking the process used in ohu (working party) projects in the 1870s.

From 1940 until 1960, ideas of tradition and conservatism were considered, negotiated and eventually reconceptualised. Many of the wharenui that had anchored hapū communities since the 1870s were renovated or replaced as a direct reflection of a renewed sense of iwi identity and purpose. Conal McCarthy points to a shift in identity after World War Two – not only among Māori, but also Pākehā, many of whom no longer felt 'British'; instead, they identified much more strongly with this country.[12] Meanwhile, Māori returned soldiers were no longer content with their inequitable compensation package and began to demand their rights as New Zealand citizens.

### Māori involvement in museums

By the mid-1950s, museums were seeking to establish more formal Māori involvement in their institutions. In 1954 Gisborne Museum established a 'Maori museum committee' to discuss the return of the Ngāti Porou meeting house Hau Te Ana Nui o Tangaroa from Canterbury Museum. Gisborne Museum staff visited tribal committees along the East Coast and Māori associate members were appointed to the committee. Sadly, when the carvings in Christchurch were inspected, they were found to be 'not in a sufficient state of repair' and the decision was made not to purchase the house.[13] In 1959 Leo Fowler wrote to express his concern at the state of Māori collections in museums:

> a museum such as the Maori Wing financed, administered and supported by the Maori people of a district is much more than a mere collection of casually acquired relics. It is, and will become even more, a central point of Maori culture and Maori history for the whole East Coast. It is in fact the modern *whare wananga* the repository of all those outward, tangible and visible things which are the material basis of what has come to be summed up in the word *Maoritanga*. The old time pattern of community living, centred around the marae, tends to become dissipated with every passing and changing year. The prized relics of tribe and hapu become more and more restricted to the keeping and to the possession of family groups and individuals. The opportunity of sharing these things, of restoring them to their proper place in communal culture, becomes distressingly restricted.[14]

Fowler warned of what might happen if such a site was not available:

> Too often they are buried away in safe-deposit boxes in a bank or lawyer's office, even worse they are lost, sold or otherwise pass out of the possession of their former owners. Other and more highly prized more *tapu* objects, entrusted to the keeping of one or two elders are secretly hidden away and all too often the hiders take their knowledge with them to *Reinga* rather than leave them to less hallowed keeping. When such things are lost, or even with-held, something very precious and important is lost or with-held with them. These relics, and especially the history which so often surrounds them, are the very *mauri*, the *pou manawa* of Maori tradition, of tribal cultural heritage and of all that is summed up in the word *Maoritanga*.[15]

This knowledge – mātauranga – about the past as a source of inspiration for the future prompted teacher and anthropologist Maharaia Winiata to endorse, as he put it, 'the current attempt to organise instruction work within ... Academies of Maori Arts and Crafts' in 1957.[16] Winiata was lobbying for educational institutions like the School of Maori Arts and Crafts to be rolled out to other tribal areas. He noted that 'Maori Adult Education classes' had been established at the University of New Zealand (UoNZ) by Henare Toka (Ngāti

Whātua) and Mere Toka (Ngāti Ruanui) in 1956, and another at Judea, Tauranga for Ngāti Ranginui people. As Winiata wrote: 'The incentive for learning and also for attendance was the personal pride derived from participation in the construction of a building that belonged to the tribe. Another aspect of the work was the lectures and discussions in tribal history and genealogies from which designs for the carving were conceived.'[17] Tuition at the Auckland Academy of Maori Arts and Crafts (at UoNZ) was largely practical, but it also involved visits to wharenui and the Auckland Museum. In 1940 Ngata had called for museum collections to be used as a source of inspiration, and he later established a workshop at the Dominion Museum specifically for this purpose.

This idea of contemporary artists engaging with collections set a pathway of practice that continues today with artists such as Areta Wilkinson, Rangi Kipa and Lisa Reihana. These artists of today draw inspiration from taonga that reside in museum collections, not only in New Zealand but also overseas, and they bring home ideas about materials, techniques and forms, many of which had fallen by the wayside through the process of colonisation.

Museums in the mid-twentieth century were still very staid spaces with a colonial focus, where Māori collections were designed to appeal to a primarily Pākehā audience who depended on museums to reinforce ideas about 'traditional' Māori. At the opening of the Maori Court at Wanganui Museum in 1968 – an event attended by over 2000 people – Minister of Maori Affairs Ralph Hanan spoke about how Māori saw spaces such as this as part of a Pākehā culture that had overseen the dislocation of taonga from their rightful owners, and he 'appealed to members of the public to return traditional Maori treasures to recognised Maori families, tribal leaders, a tribal trust board, a museum, or some other accepted place of guardianship, for safe keeping'.[18] Museum research on meeting houses in communities supported the fact that many of them were in a state of disrepair and in need of support. Some groups dismantled their whare and stored the carvings locally, or else gave them to their local museum for safekeeping.

## Te hokinga mai – the return home

But what did Māori think? The 1960s represents a turning point: Māori began publicly calling for sovereignty over their land as well as control over education, employment, housing and health. The collection and retention of taonga was seen as a potent example of how the Crown's actions had directly contributed to the alienation of cultural heritage for Māori. Māori staff were scarce in museums: even though most ethnologists were sympathetic to Māori perspectives, it was non-Māori who were invariably in charge of collections, directing museums and setting policies in relation to taonga Māori.

The Treaty of Waitangi Act 1975 established the Waitangi Tribunal, a permanent commission of inquiry to investigate historic breaches of Te Tiriti o Waitangi. The Tribunal consists of Māori and non-Māori historians and judges who are assigned different claims to examine. This may take many years from the point of submission of original documents through to hearings and finally government settlement or redress. The Waitangi Tribunal provided Māori with a platform from which to collectively lobby for settlement or redress based on the effects of breaches of Te Tiriti on their communities.[19] One of the main criticisms of the Tribunal is that it has, as yet, no binding powers; it can only make recommendations.

Many recent tribal claims have included redress specifically in relation to the treatment and alienation of taonga.[20] This is based on Article 2 of Te Tiriti o Waitangi, which was intended to protect 'o ratou taonga katoa', translated in the English version as 'all their treasures'. However, as Sir Hugh Kawharu (Ngāti Whātua , 1927–2006) explains, in Māori understandings, '"taonga" refers to all dimensions of a tribal group's estate, material and non-material heirlooms and wāhi tapu (sacred places), ancestral lore and whakapapa (genealogies), etc'.[21] This includes tangible and intangible heritage, the physical taonga and the kōrero, tapu and mana that surround them.

The Te Roroa Wai 38 claim lodged in the Waitangi Tribunal (1992) focused on ancestral remains.[22] The tribe sought the return of kōiwi and associated funerary taonga such as waka tūpāpaku that had been illegally removed from a community urupā in the late nineteenth century, and later sold to institutions such as the Auckland Museum.[23] Some of the kōiwi and waka tūpāpaku were returned to the iwi in 1988, before Te Roroa Claims Settlement Act was passed in 2008. This law recognised that the taonga of Te Roroa, which should have been protected by the government under Article 2 of Te Tiriti o Waitangi, had been looted, and it formalised

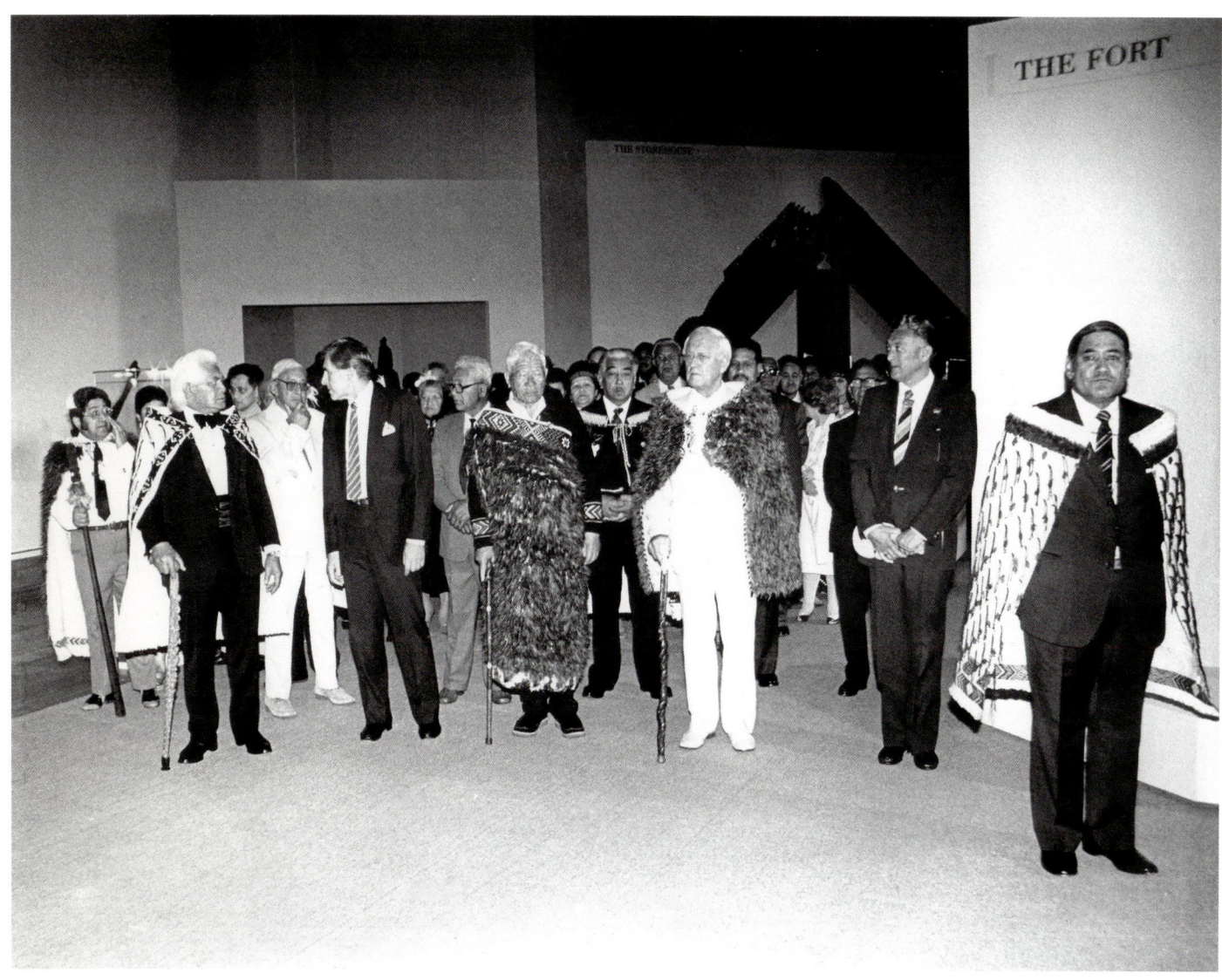

The pōwhiri for the *Te Maori* exhibition at the Metropolitan Museum of Art, New York, in 1984 reinforced the importance of tikanga in all aspects of exhibition making. Pictured are (from left) Ruka Broughton (behind glass), Sonny Waru, Kara Puketapu, Archbishop Paul Reeves, Archdeacon Kingi Ihaka, Henare Tuwhangai (partly obscured), Bruce Gregory and the Honorable Mr Koro Wetere, minister of Maori affairs.
New Zealand Ministry for Foreign Affairs and Trade

the Crown's apology to the iwi. The Act also acknowledged that Auckland Museum retained several kōiwi and taonga that should rightly be returned to Te Roroa.[24]

Several reports from the Waitangi Tribunal have found that the Crown acted illegally in relation to Māori art, and have recommended the return of ancestral remains (Wai 38) and meeting houses (Wai 46, Wai 814). For these communities, repatriation was a cornerstone of their Tribunal applications: Ngāti Awa sought the return of the wharenui Mātaatua from Otago Museum (Wai 46, 1999), and Rongowhakaata the return of Te Hau ki Tūranga from Te Papa Tongarewa (Wai 814, 2004). In both cases, the Crown formally apologised to iwi for the illegal removal of the houses from their communities.[25] Jonathan Mane-Wheoki's report on Mātaatua for the claim was pivotal: in it he outlined the vexed history of the whare and the ongoing culpability of the Crown through its agent, the

New Zealand government, in acting wrongly as owner of the house.[26] Mātaatua was relocated back to his tūrangawaewae at Whakatāne and was formally reopened in 2011. Te Rūnanga o Ngāti Awa have set up a tourism venture offering a cultural experience that showcases the house and educates the public about his history. On the recommendation of the Waitangi Tribunal report, the iwi is working with Te Papa Tongarewa to consider options for Te Hau ki Tūranga. The exhibition *Ko Rongowhakaata* at Te Papa (2017–2020), as part of Te Papa's ongoing iwi exhibition series, showcased the iwi's history and aspirations.

The return of taonga to source communities today is a far cry from the circumstances in which they originally entered the museum. Leonie Pihama (Te Ātiawa, Ngāti Māhanga, Ngā Māhanga ā Tairi) argues that the issue is one of historical trauma: whereas, to museums and other institutions, these taonga might be just a registration number in an accession register, for whānau, hapū and iwi they represent histories of land confiscation, murder, and long-term dispossession and alienation of land and culture. Repatriation represents more than just a shifting of locations – it is an acceptance of the history, and a determination to make amends by returning the taonga to descendants.

### Te Maori: Maori Art from New Zealand Collections exhibition (1984–1987)

The recent repatriations of taonga have come as the result of decades of advocacy led by Māori seeking to reconnect with their ancestral treasures. Maori art history can be characterised by a series of what Robert Jahnke has termed 'turning points' – events or people that have changed the direction of history. *Te Maori*: *Maori Art from New Zealand Collections* (1984–1987) was one such turning point. This international exhibition was a catalyst for many changes within the GLAM (galleries, libraries, archives and museums) sector, throughout all aspects of museum practice. Co-curated by Tā Hirini Moko Mead (Ngāti Awa, Ngāti Tūwharetoa, Tūhourangi) and Bernie Kernot, *Te Maori* represents one of the first instances of Māori being involved in an exhibition about taonga as curator, rather than as consultant. Mead and Kernot worked together in the Māori Studies Department at Victoria University of Wellington, where they researched and taught on many aspects of Māori art. The exhibition consisted of over 170 taonga, covering mainly personal adornment, weaponry, waka and whare carvings, many of them dating back to the 1500s.

Each taonga was carefully selected and permission was sought from their kaitiaki for them to travel. This was new, as it acknowledged Māori as the owners despite the taonga's location in a museum; by following this tikanga it also acknowledged that Māori had a different understanding of how taonga needed to be handled. These practices went on to influence later exhibitions.

Four venues were chosen for the exhibition in the United States: the Metropolitan Museum of Art, New York (1984); St Louis Art Museum, St Louis (1985); de Young Memorial Museum, San Francisco (1985); and the Field Museum, Chicago (1986). The exhibition then travelled to each of the main cities in New Zealand, reframed as *Te Hokinga Mai* (the return), until it closed in September 1987. The venues were major art galleries (rather than museums); this was significant, as it reflected a change in perspective on the aesthetic value of the works. Previously Māori and Indigenous art was regarded as 'ethnographic' and was exhibited exclusively in 'ethnographic' spaces – that is, in museums. The art gallery space was usually reserved for pre-1900 works that were considered to be 'art', which was presumptively defined as works produced in Europe. Kernot and Mead's insistence on art galleries – and the Met, no less – as the most appropriate spaces made art gallery curators worldwide, but most importantly in New Zealand, reconsider their own understandings of taonga Māori as art.

*Te Maori* was a catalyst for change: it prompted museums to reconsider Māori involvement in all aspects of museum practice. The exhibition had Mead as Māori co-curator and Māori docents who guided the public in the exhibition space. Each opening at a different venue was heralded with a pōwhiri involving huge groups, many of whom had arrived from Aotearoa New Zealand to warm the taonga – and the exhibition. *Te Maori* set a new standard, too, in how Māori engaged with collections and museums in active, meaningful and long-term ways. Museums felt pressure to hire more Māori staff, and into positions of authority, where they would have a direct impact on exhibition-making that would reflect current aspirations and understandings of history. They would also influence the overall understanding of the importance of taonga as living ancestors and as a crucial aspect of contemporary Māori identity.

## Repatriation in the 1990s

> Freedom. Repatriation.
> I'm in a country I've never seen, somewhere else
>     I've never been, the misery
> I'll be leaving all my friends behind
> Stranger amongst strangers
>
> —'Repatriation', Herbs, 1987, from the album *Sensitive to a Smile*

There were huge changes in the museum sector in the 1990s. Globally art galleries and, especially, museums finally began responding to calls from Indigenous peoples and other 'source communities' to re-engage with their treasures. In Canada, the 'Task Force Report on Museums and First Peoples' (1992) made this explicit with its mission statement: 'to develop an ethical framework and strategies for Aboriginal Nations to represent their history and culture in concert with cultural institutions';[27] and in the United States the Native American Graves Protection and Repatriation Act 1990 (NAGPRA) required federal institutions, including museums, to return 'cultural items' such as human remains and sacred objects to Native American and Native Hawaiian tribes.[28] Both called on museums to actively engage with Indigenous groups on all levels, from governance to collections to front-of-house to education programmes. They represented a shift in focus from objects to people. This mirrored rethinking in other disciplines such as art history, anthropology and history.

The emergence of the concept of 'new museology' has brought shifts of power – albeit at a glacial pace in some institutions – as museum staff have sought to reach out to social and cultural groups and Indigenous communities. Reconnection is recognised as a two-way process: Indigenous groups can now re-engage with their treasures (often still on museum premises), while their presence enables non-Indigenous museum staff to learn first hand about the ongoing importance of taonga for whānau, hapū and iwi. This shift in attitude extends right across the spectrum from directors to curators, collections managers, conservators, volunteers and docents. It has resulted in better care and display of Indigenous treasures and this, in turn, has given communities a renewed sense of identity and strength.

Some museums have explored using new technologies to effect 'e-repatriation' or 'virtual repatriation'[29] as an alternative to actual repatriation of taonga. The goal now is often to work with communities on several different levels. This might be creating a digital database of all related material, not just taonga but also archival material, sound tapes and even field notes. Innovative databases such as Mukurtu content management system have sought to enable communities to create their own databases based on their specific cultural and historical terminology and frameworks. In this way Indigenous communities retain control over their own cultural material, enabling access to non-members on their own terms, for example for research projects. E-repatriation could mean the creation of a 'digital surrogate' – a 3D model of the original. The possibilities are endless.

## New roles for Māori in museums

Māori are employed in a number of roles in museums today. Museums, galleries, libraries and archives are theoretically guided by the principles of Te Tiriti o Waitangi, through which they are to recognise and accept mana whenua and their tikanga. One of the guiding principles of Archives New Zealand, for instance, is to 'encourage the spirit of partnership and goodwill envisaged by the Treaty of Waitangi'. The board of governance of most public institutions will include at least one iwi representative. A number of kaihautū (museum directors) are Māori, including Arapata Hakiwai (Te Papa Tongarewa Museum of New Zealand), Karl Chitham (Dowse Art Museum) and Larissa McMillan (Wairau Māori Art Gallery). Many museums, art galleries and archives have Māori advisory boards to guide and create policy and practice in their institutions, such as Haerewa at Auckland Art Gallery and Ōhākī o Ngā Tīpuna at Canterbury Museum. There are specific positions for care of Māori collections, such as those held by Nigel Borell (Tāmaki Paenga Hira Auckland War Memorial Museum), Nathan Pohio (Auckland Art Gallery Toi o Tāmaki), Āwhina Twomey (Whanganui Regional Museum) and Gerard O'Regan (Otago Museum). Other Māori hold different curator roles, including Megan Tamati-Quennell (curator modern and contemporary Māori and Indigenous art, Te Papa Tongarewa), and Taarati Taiaroa (assistant curator, contemporary Māori art, Govett-Brewster Art Gallery). Notably, many have art history or fine arts degrees, and/or have taught in art history programmes.

Kāhui Kaitiaki, a Facebook group, offers support for the over 200 Māori working in museums. They run regular workshops and hui (in person and via Zui/Zoom) to 'network and

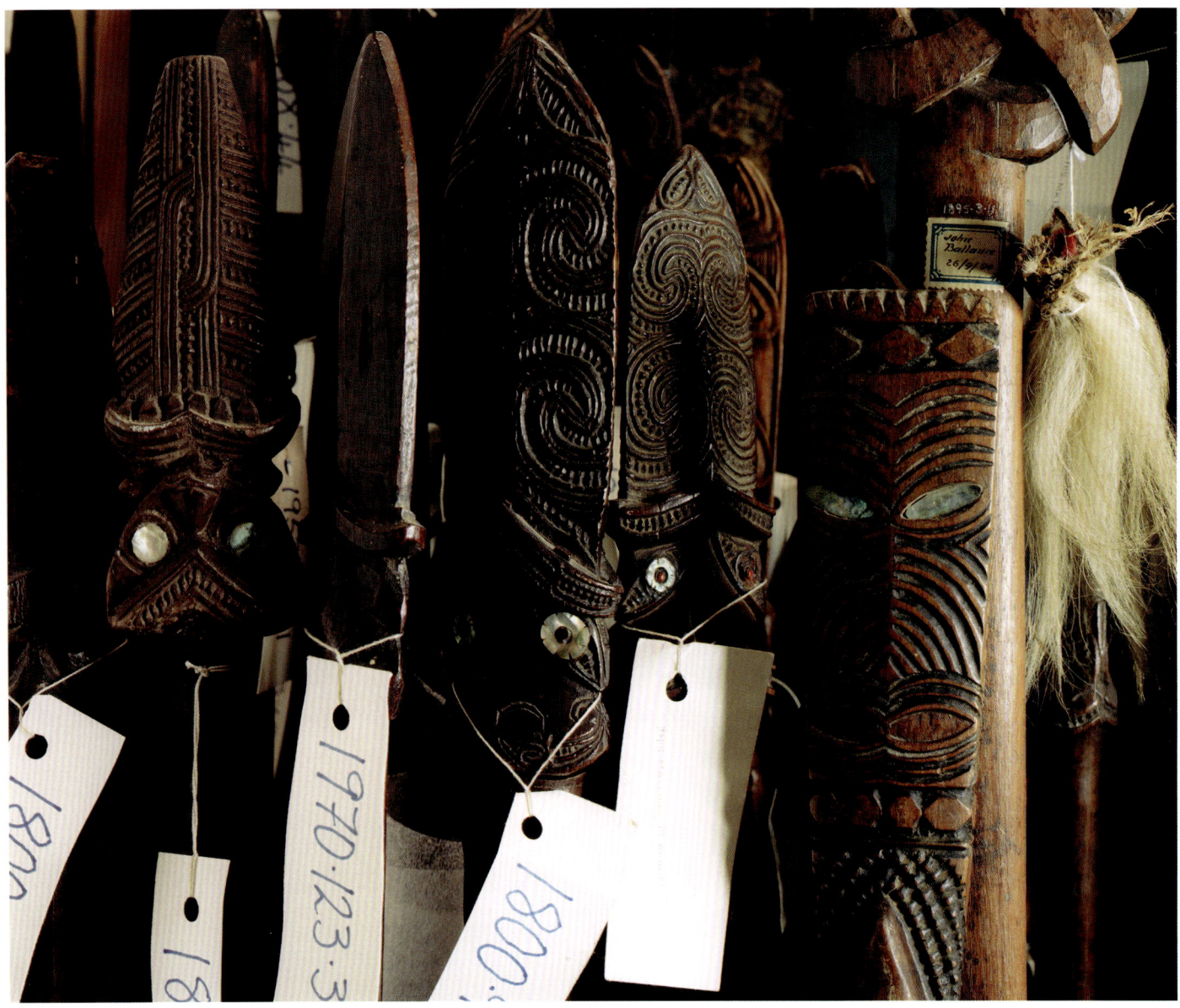

Neil Pardington, *Taonga Māori Store #3, Whanganui Regional Museum* 2006
Lambda / C-print, dimensions variable

share ... to fill our kete with insights, tools and resources to improve our shared well-being',[30] such as on repatriation – both national (2020) and international (2021). Te Paetangi, the professional development arm of Museums Aotearoa, offers courses for people working in the GLAM sector, with some course units focused on Māori. And four tertiary providers – Waipapa Taumata Rau University of Auckland, Massey University, Te Herenga Waka Victoria University of Wellington, and Canterbury University – offer studies focused on museums to postgraduate level; at Auckland and Victoria, Māori teach some of these courses (Ngarino Ellis, Awhina Tamarapa).

### Conclusion

Arapata Hakiwai, curator of Te Papa Tongarewa, has recently assessed the size and extent of Māori collections overseas, and the numbers are staggering: in total, there are 18,000 taonga in over 160 museums.[31] There is yet to be a single comprehensive inventory – a few collections are online and others are published (most notably those of the British Museum). These collections are particularly rich in relation to pre-1900 taonga. There are types of taonga overseas that are not only no longer made, but the knowledge of them has not been transmitted through the generations. The skills and techniques used in the creation of many of these taonga have also been 'lost' to artists for many generations.

Linda Tuhiwai Smith has described treasures belonging to her iwi, which are dispersed around many museums, as 'bits and pieces all over the place', and she has called for their return home.[32] For many tribes with huge numbers of their cultural treasures in museums near and far, the idea of 'taonga mokemoke' (lonely treasures) is partly assuaged in Aotearoa as more Māori are employed in the museum sector. There is pressure on museums to open their collections to whānau, hapū and iwi as one strategy to address ongoing historical intergenerational trauma from the New Zealand Wars and subsequent acts that resulted in the removal of taonga from communities.

Overseas, of course, is another story: there is still so little information circulated from museums about their collections. While we may hope for legislation similar to NAGPRA in the United States, even that has met with roadblocks, with museums pleading lack of funding and resources to create formal inventories of Indigenous materials. Increasingly, though, institutions have been disseminating information about taonga in their care through a number of strategies: by inviting Māori artists and conservators to visit their collections; publishing papers and books about the collection, or aspects of it; and curating exhibitions based on or including taonga, such as *Māori: Art and Culture* (British Museum, London, 1998); *Oceania* (Royal Academy, London, 2018; Musée du Quai Branly, Paris, 2019); *Māori Markings: Tā Moko* (National Gallery of Australia, Canberra, 2019); and *Pasifika Styles* (Museum of Archaeology and Anthropology, Cambridge University, 2008). This is decolonisation of museums in action. These exhibitions are typically co-curated with Māori: *Across Time, Place and People: Whakawhanaungatanga: Connecting Taonga Māori* at the Linden Museum, Stuttgart (2022–2024) was a partnership between the Curator Oceania Ulrich Menter, and a small group from New Zealand: Ngarino Ellis, Awhina Tamarapa (Ngāti Kahungunu, Ngāti Ruanui, Ngāti Pikiao), Dougal Austin (Kāti Māmoe, Kāi Tahu, Waitaha) and Justine Treadwell (Pākehā).

Some institutions, such as the Museum für Völkerkunde (Hamburg) and the Field Museum (Chicago), have reached out to tribal communities and descendants to forge meaningful engagements based on the meeting houses located there. Other international museums are creating Pacific/Māori advisory boards. Melbourne Museum, for example, in tandem with the renovation of its Pasifika Gallery, convened a Pasifika Advisory Board of representatives who are artists, performers, writers, academics and architects, who have been rethinking the gallery in relation to Pacific concepts. Ngāti Rānana (London tribe) – Māori based in Britain – have a good working relationship with the British Museum, British Library and other European institutions that hold Māori collections. For the opening of *Whakawhanaungatanga* in Stuttgart they sent a small delegation to support the pōwhiri in December 2022.

The relationship between Māori and museums remains ambiguous. While some museums have made the effort to reach out to whānau, hapū and iwi, at museums overseas this often hinges on the initiative of individual museum workers rather than a value that is integral to the institution. The project to return Māori ancestral remains has brokered a certain leverage with many museums and has opened the doors to dialogue. The digital landscape, while it is not ideal, can and should be used more by both sides. Information about collections must be made more accessible.

Some Māori are concerned at who is undertaking research, and call for this to be driven by Māori only. The task of some research projects is often seen as so large, and – at least at present – there are too few Māori in positions to facilitate the circulation of information about taonga in the care of their institution. Placing collections online, especially with good photographs of taonga (particularly of the back, where information about the making of the work is often evident) and with associated records (as the National Museum of Natural History in Washington DC has done) can be an initial step towards engagement. Positioning taonga in displays and photographs aestheticises them, and important knowledge that might be revealed by back, bottom and top views is lost. The tendrils of reconnection can be powerful, and can enhance our sense of mana motuhake (self-determination), to use Hakiwai's phrase.[33]

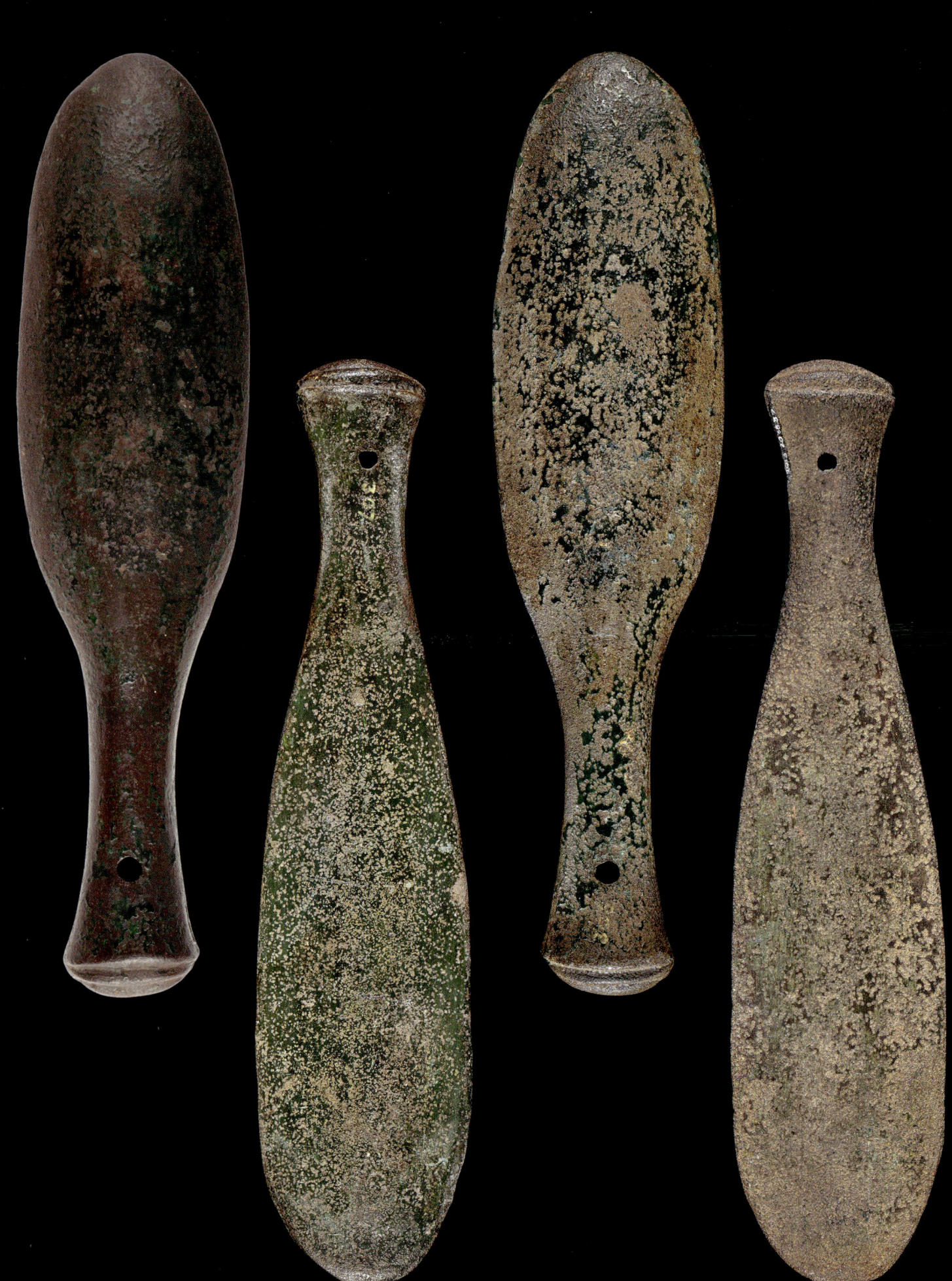

# TRICK OR TAONGA: THE MYSTERIOUS CASE OF THE GREEN-PAINTED PATU PORA

DEIDRE BROWN

When is a taonga not a taonga? This is the conundrum presented by a patu pora (iron cleaver, ME007684), that is currently in the collection of Te Papa Tongarewa Museum of New Zealand. Collector William Webster had bequeathed the patu to Te Papa's forerunner, the Dominion Museum, in 1971; he had obtained it from another collector, Harry Beasley, some time before 1954.

Researchers have been eager to find some context for this intriguing object. Recent histories have associated it with other Māori weapons made of iron,[1] in particular a patu pora that Whangaroa leader Te Puhi beat out of an iron bar some time before 1815.[2] Historian James Belich even went so far as to say that, 'if museums were to choose one object to symbolise the Māori response to contact, Te Puhi's patu might be it'.[3] But this was never Te Puhi's patu. A closer inspection reveals that it was cast in a mould rather than forged, and it is covered in flecks of green paint. Further investigation of the patu's acquisition history takes us back to 1909, when Beasley purchased it from the London-based exotic animal and curio dealer Albert Jamrach, two years after he collected three similar patu pora from the same dealer.[4] Of the earlier purchase, Beasley wrote:

> two are from the same mould, and are 15¾in. [400mm] long, and weigh 5lb. 5oz [2.4kg] ... The third is from a different mould, measures 14⅞in. [377mm] in length, and weighs 9½lb [4.3kg]. In use it would be a most unserviceable weapon, the balance being bad, while its great weight would retard its utility. All three mere [patu pora] have at one time been painted green in imitation of jade.[5]

Beasley was correct in assuming that these patu never saw combat because of their extraordinary weight. It was highly likely that Jamrach also knew the items were inauthentic in manufacture and purpose: his father Charles Jamrach revealed in an interview in 1891 that these were not the first fakes of this nature to enter his store, and that they were:

> A testimony to the guile of the wily Maori in an axe made of iron only, but painted and got up to exactly resemble greenstone. The reason of the disguise becomes apparent when it is explained that for the genuine greenstone article of this pattern a collector will gladly pay a hundred pounds, while the metal imitation is worth its weight as old iron and no more.[6]

Albert Jamrach, to his credit, sold the iron patu now in Te Papa to Beasley for an honest sum of 13 shillings.[7] Beasley's widow Irene donated two of his other iron patu purchases to the British Museum in 1944, and a third was donated to the museum by the London School of Economics in 2013.[8] A comparison of their weights and profiles reveals that two of the British Museum patu (Oc1944,02.821 and 2013.2038.37) were made from one distinctly shaped mould, while the third (Oc1944,02.822), together with the Te Papa example (WE1822), are made from a different mould.

Were these patu made by the same 'wily' person? If so, and if they were made by Māori, should we treasure these objects in the same way as we now value the early souvenirs made by enterprising tohunga whakairo who were forging a living in the changing socioeconomic climate of late-nineteenth-century Aotearoa? Or should we regard them as fakes?

**Patu pora.**
From left to right: Te Papa Tongarewa Museum of New Zealand, WE001822, bequest of Kenneth Athol Webster, 1971; British Museum, Oc1944,02.821 EOC19893; Oc1944,02.822 EOC80740; 20132038.37 EOC133659

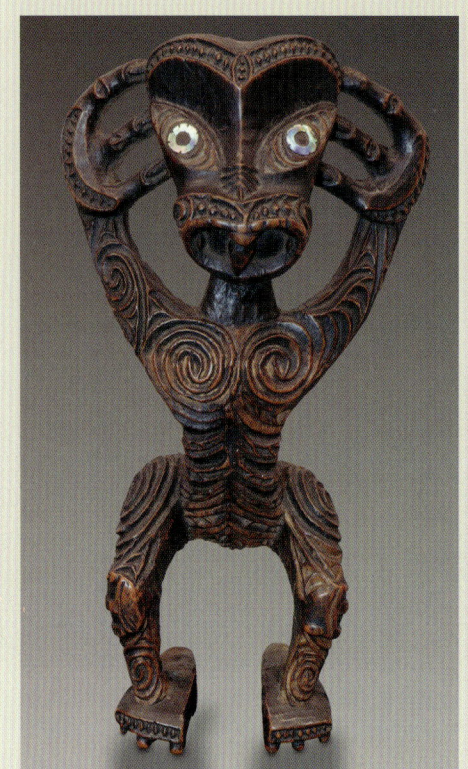
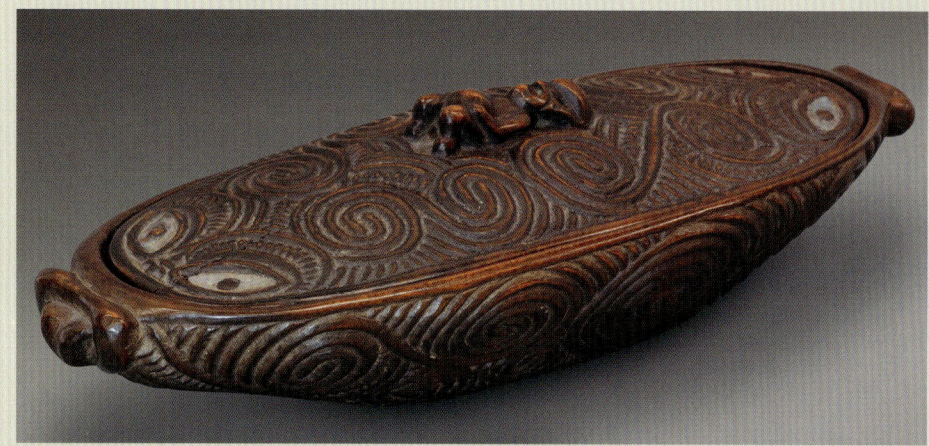
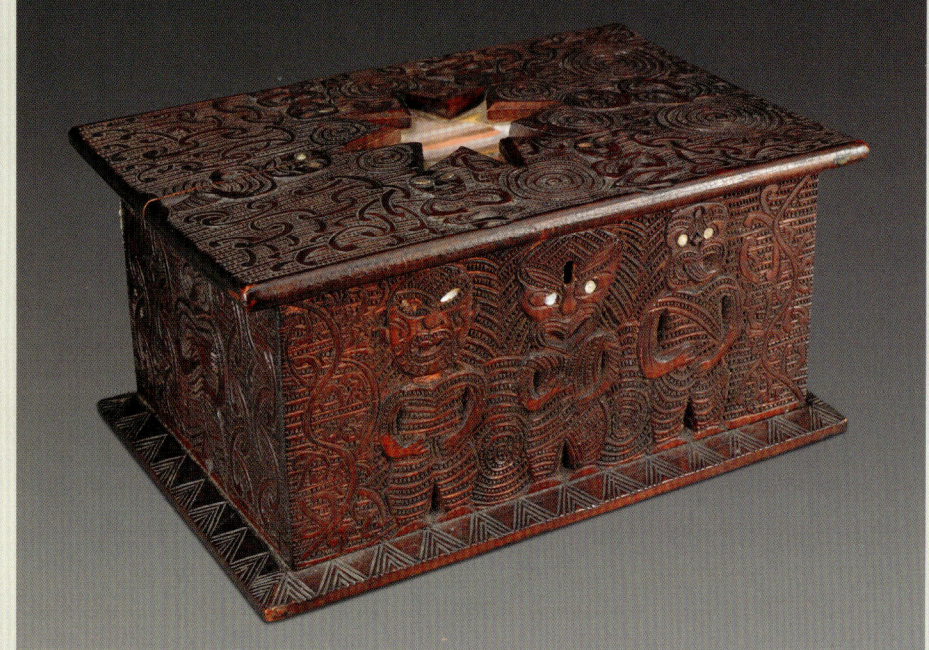
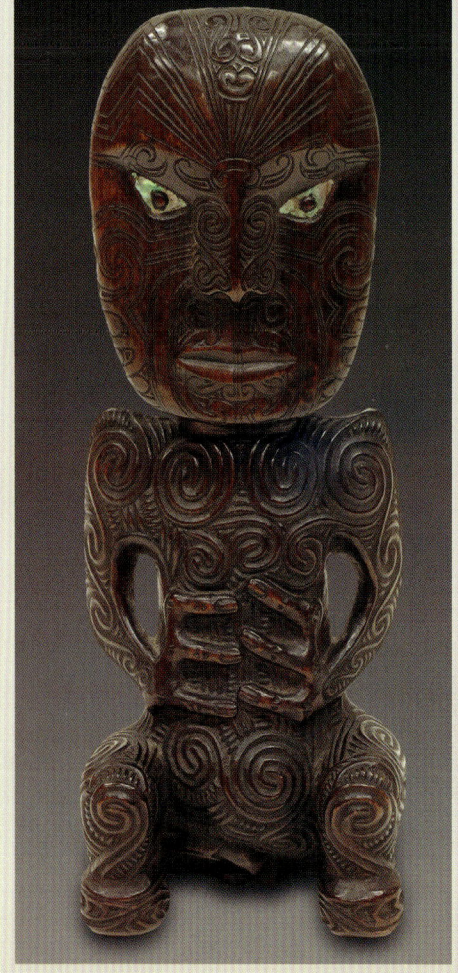
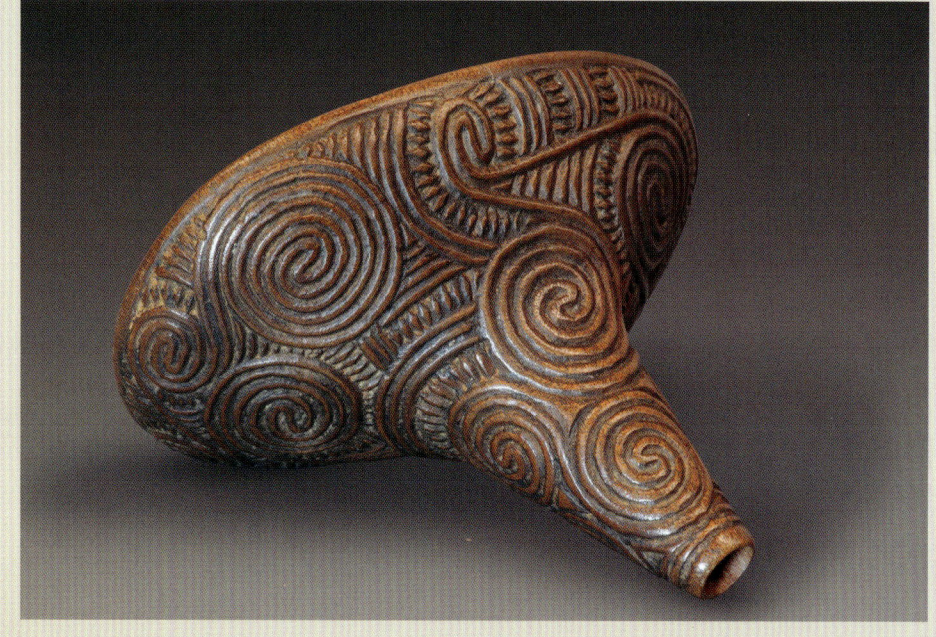

# FAKES IN THE COLLECTION
NGARINO ELLIS

The demand for taonga sometimes exceeded supply in the early twentieth century, and this prompted some people to begin faking treasures for financial gain.

James Edward Little (1876–1953) was ostensibly an English furniture restorer, which fitted in well with his sideline activities as a curio collector and dealer. Little was based in Bath: he never visited Aotearoa, but his appetite for Māori treasures was whetted when he was in his twenties, after a chance meeting in 1900. London-based antique dealer J. B. Russell was staying in the same boarding house as Little; he visited Little's antique shop asking for 'native curios'. Little began seeking out 'curios' by placing ads in newspapers that were read by some of the well-known Pacific art collectors of the day: William Oldman, Harry Beasley and Alfred W. F. Fuller. He soon set up a mail-order business; the only contact that occurred was through written correspondence.

With a shortage of taonga available to him, Little started copying existing works, as well as making completely new works. This was a more difficult enterprise, and one that, according to Henry Skinner, he was not so successful at.[1] Little also began faking toi moko. He replicated older materials using timber from old sailing ships. Initially he offered both fake and authentic works to clients, but he progressed to selling only his forgeries once he realised that most of his clients had no idea of what Māori art looked like. Like other forgers, he became adept at creating a fictitious provenance for each object.

Little was also stealing taonga from museums, but he was not very good at this either, and he was caught several times. At one point Fuller realised he was being swindled by being offered a stolen item, and Little was arrested and charged with theft. The police evidence was Fuller's coat, on which they found flecks of paint of the same shade as the stolen waka huia.

Fortunately for Little, the curator at the museum the objects were stolen from could not confirm whether the waka huia was from their collection, so he was released. Fuller then warned as many people as possible about Little's practices. Oldman had also been caught out by Little in 1910[2] and he, too, warned others.

Two years later, in 1939, Little was again caught stealing from a museum. This time he was easily identified as he had been the only visitor in three days, so he was easily remembered and identified, despite having left a false name in the visitor's book. Over the next few years, Little was in and out of jail on theft charges; eventually he died a pauper in 1953. Many of his works were later purchased by Skinner for his collection in Taranaki; and there are several items in the Field Museum, that were purchased by Fuller, who was a patron of the museum.[3] Little's fakes still turn up at auctions.[4]

Faked works by James Edward Little. The 'sewing box' (right, middle) made by James Edward Little, pictured in an auction catalogue for Bonham's New York, 2014, when it sold for US$3500 including premium. The catalogue stated clearly that it was 'carved by notorious forger James Edward Little with almost every design element of Māori art known'.
Clockwise from top left: Puke Ariki, New Plymouth, A94.707; A76.811; Bonhams New York, Art of the South Seas, 9 February 2014, Lot 172; Puke Ariki, New Plymouth, A94.700; A94.703

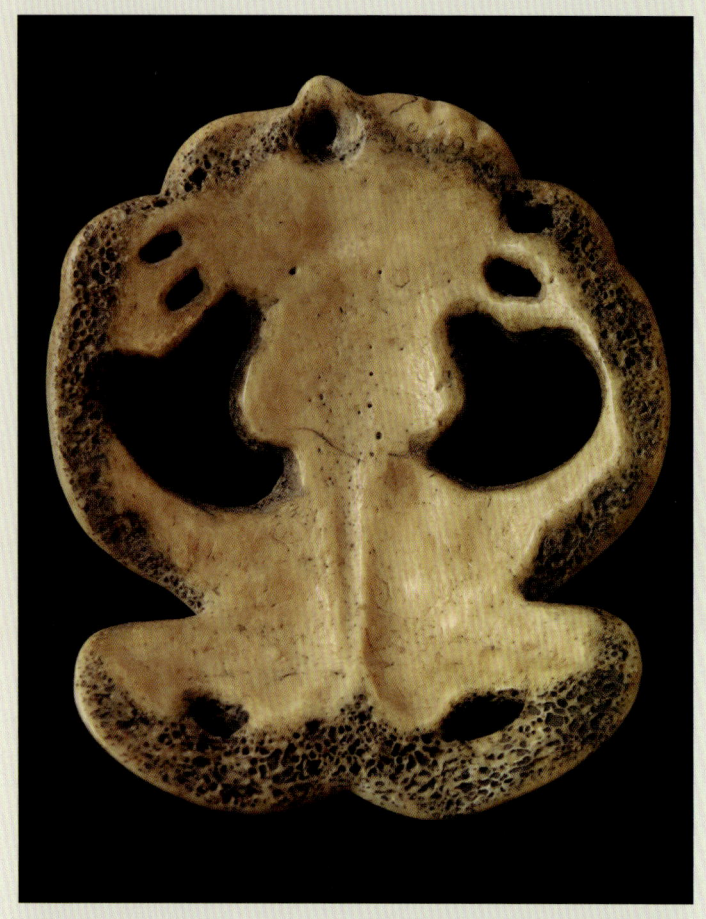
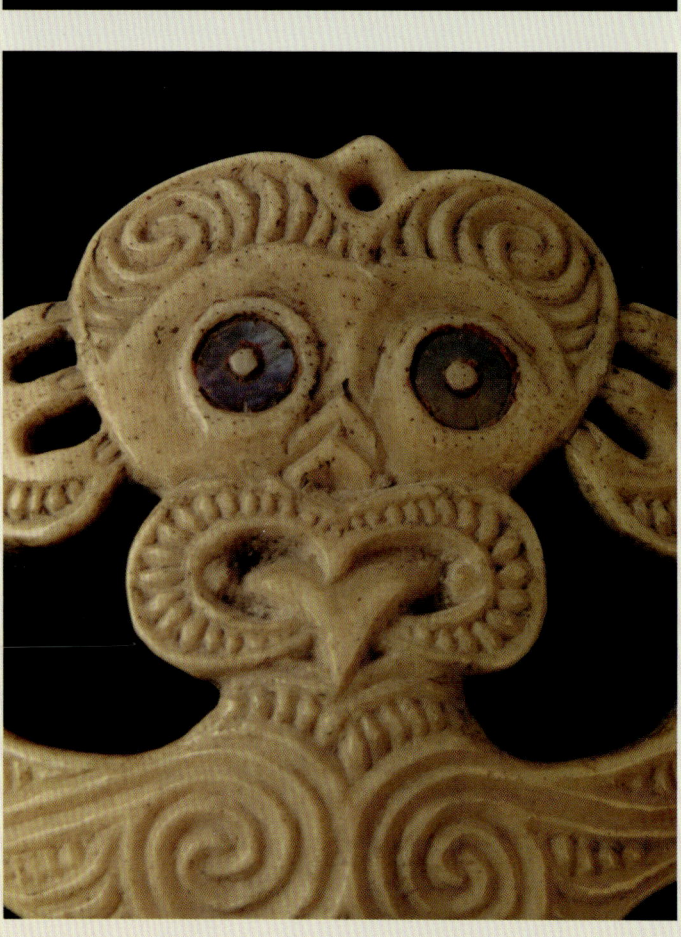
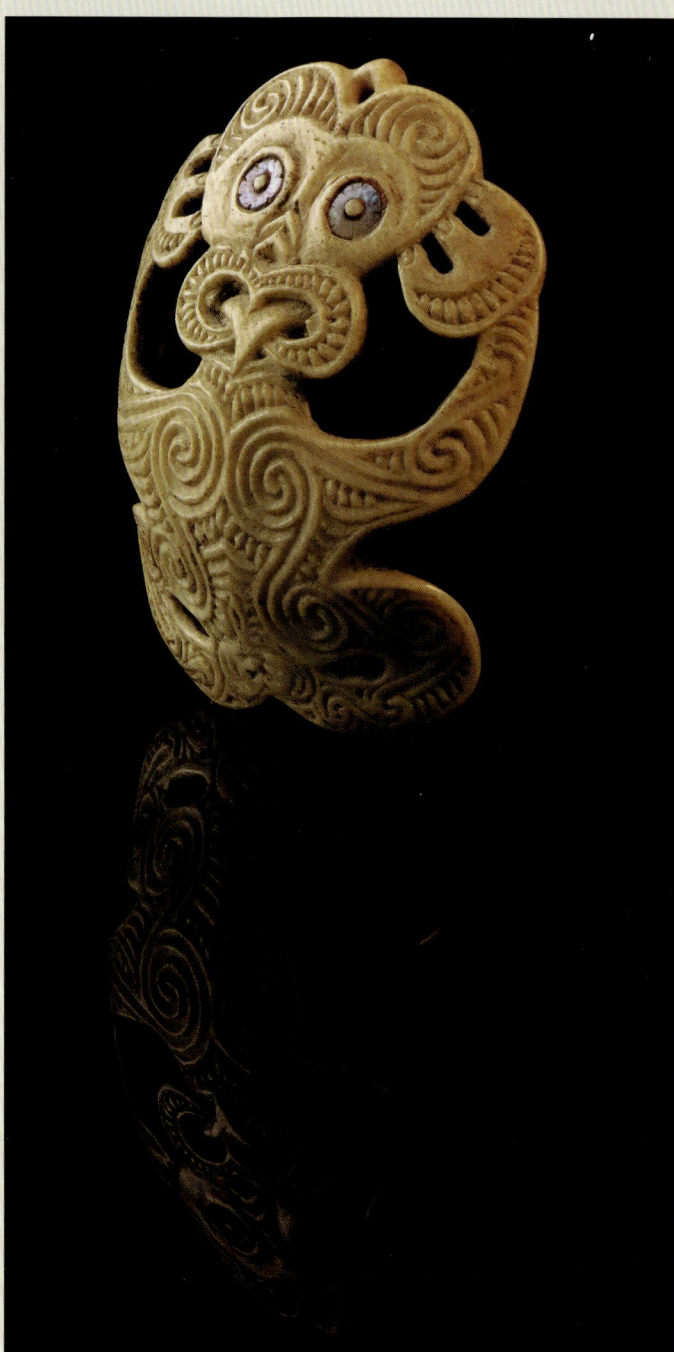

James Frank Robieson was born and raised in New Zealand and learnt about Māori art while working at the Rotorua branch of the New Zealand Tourist and Publicity Department. Rotorua was one of the primary tourism hubs in the country, and it was home to an active group of carvers working mostly on commission for this market. Robieson was trained by two of the masters, Ānaha Te Rāhui and Tene Waitere – and he soon put his learning into practice.

Robieson began collecting taonga as a young man,[5] and had gone on 'foraging' expeditions near his home in Dunedin. He met and began learning from the Devlin family, who had set up a greenstone business in 1890 through which they sold taonga to a wide market, including to Māori whose own taonga had been stolen or otherwise taken from them.

After World War One Robieson moved to England. He took with him large quantities of raw materials, including moa bone and shell, that he fashioned into works that he sold through auction houses and elsewhere. He sold at least twenty-one objects to Pitt Rivers Museum in 1930 – a fact that was not revealed until 1965. Robieson's scam was exposed in the mid-1960s by London-based dealer Kenneth Webster, who warned his dealer and collector friends about the fakes. With the resulting sharp decline in business, Robieson returned to New Zealand, where he died in 1966.

Today when we look at the forged works of Little and Robieson it seems obvious that they are fakes, yet many are still sold at auction and through other means.[6] Indeed, at times a provenance that includes their names might almost have notoriety value, as with the work of twentieth century New Zealand forger Carl Sim, who painted works in the style of colonial artist Charles F. Goldie.

A 'carved bone neck ornament tiki, in Māori style' identified in the auction catalogue as 'possibly made by James Frank Robieson', which sold at Woolley & Wallis's Salisbury salerooms on 11 February 2014 for £700.
Woolley & Wallis

# COLLECTING THE ANCESTORS
NGARINO ELLIS

Over the past twenty years there have been major changes in how Māori human remains and associated funerary taonga are stored in museums, and an increase in their return to their homeland.

Members of hapū and iwi would ritually preserve the head of a person who had died. These heads, called toi moko or upoko tuhi, would be kept in an urupā and brought out during the tangihanga of relatives, to remember others who had passed away and whom they would meet again in Te Rarohenga (the afterworld) or in Hawaiki. This was sometimes the only part of a fallen warrior that would be returned home with his war party. Today Māori use photographs to continue this practice.

If an enemy was killed, often his head would be removed and taken back to the victor's pā, where they would heap insults on him.[1] Ngāti Rangitihi tell the story of Tionga, who was killed by a Tūhoe raiding party; they took his body back to their kāinga at Maungapōhatu where it was 'used like a scarecrow overlooking a *mahingakai* (cultivation)'.[2] This act prompted Tionga's granddaughter Parerautututu to weave a kahu kurī (later named after her), and take it to neighbouring Tainui to ask them for help to retrieve Tionga's head. The rangatira Tukorehu arranged for this to happen and, in return, Parerautututu gave him the cloak.

The trading of toi moko[3] made during times of war was almost certainly practised in pre-contact Māori communities. However, this trade took on another dimension with the arrival of James Cook on the *Endeavour*, when Joseph Banks acquired a preserved head in March 1770 at Queen Charlotte Sound. An elderly chief paddled out to the *Endeavour*, and Banks spied six or seven toi moko in the canoe. He asked the chief if he would part with them. The chief was reluctant, but he finally agreed to exchange one head for 'a pair of old drawers of very white linen' that were offered. After he had taken the clothing, he was still hesitant to pass over the toi moko, but his hand was forced when Banks pointed a musket at him. Te Awekotuku sums up the moment: 'And so the trade began, with a white man's recycled underwear.'[4]

The trade in toi moko soon expanded as Europeans arrived in increasing numbers. Many of them were keen to acquire evidence of a marked cultural difference, and often a toi moko was top of the list. By the early nineteenth century there was increased warfare in some areas, and Māori preserved the heads of enemies to take home; later these were traded for muskets. Dealing in toi moko was outlawed in the late 1830s but despite this, the 'sale' of upoko tuhi continued, both from source (Māori) but also, from the late nineteenth century, by ethnographic collectors.

Horatio Robley is probably the most notorious perpetrator. An artist and soldier who served in the British army in the New Zealand Wars, Robley 'collected' between thirty-five and forty toi moko; this is corroborated by notorious photographs of him with his 'collection'. Robley offered his collection to the New Zealand government in 1908 for £1000 but the offer was declined; instead, the American Museum of Natural History in New York purchased them for £1250.[5]

Even though many of the toi moko collected in the early nineteenth century were taken as the heads of enemies, they are regarded by Māori today as ancestors. Most are still 'unprovenanced', as often they were taken from one community to another hundreds of kilometres away. One of the earliest advocates for the return home of ancestral remains was MP Māui Pōmare (Ngāti Mutunga, Ngāti Toa, 1876–1930): through his lobbying, the first thirty-seven ancestors were returned home.[6] The singer Dalvanius Prime (Waikato-Tainui, Ngāpuhi, Ngāti Ruanui, Tūwharetoa, Ngā Rauru, Pakakohi, Ngāi Tahu, 1948–2002) took over the cause, and founded the Mokomokai Education Trust to facilitate the process.

Māori sought to have toi moko removed from public display. Elizabeth Ellis (Ngāpuhi, Ngāti Porou) undertook a study in the 1970s and 1980s to document toi moko in museums in England and Scotland; when she visited each museum, she asked that the toi moko be removed from display – which most agreed to. A lack of understanding of the tapu nature of toi moko is best exemplified by an incident that Ellis recounts, where a tray of 'heads' was presented to her in the tearoom in a Glasgow museum – much to her horror.[7] Toi moko are tapu, and this state can be broken with the presence of cooked food, which is considered noa. Most people working with Māori collections in international museums today have a better understanding of Māori art and culture, partly thanks to the number of Māori who are now able to visit their ancestors.

Te Papa Tongarewa Museum of New Zealand hosts the national repository for the repatriation of all toi moko to Aotearoa New Zealand. The Karanga Aotearoa repatriation programme, under the management of Te Herekiekie Herewini (Ngāti Tūwharetoa, Ngāti Whakaue, Ngāti Apa, Ngā Rauru Kītahi, Whanganui, Ngāpuhi and Ngāti Porou), employs a repatriation researcher and a repatriation coordinator to identify kōiwi tangata (Māori skeletal remains) and kōimi tangata (Moriori skeletal remains) in national and international collections and begin negotiations for the return home of the ancestors. They are supported by a repatriation advisory panel of iwi representatives. To date the team has facilitated the return of 420 ancestors from Australia, Europe and the United States, and a further 600 are still waiting overseas to come home.

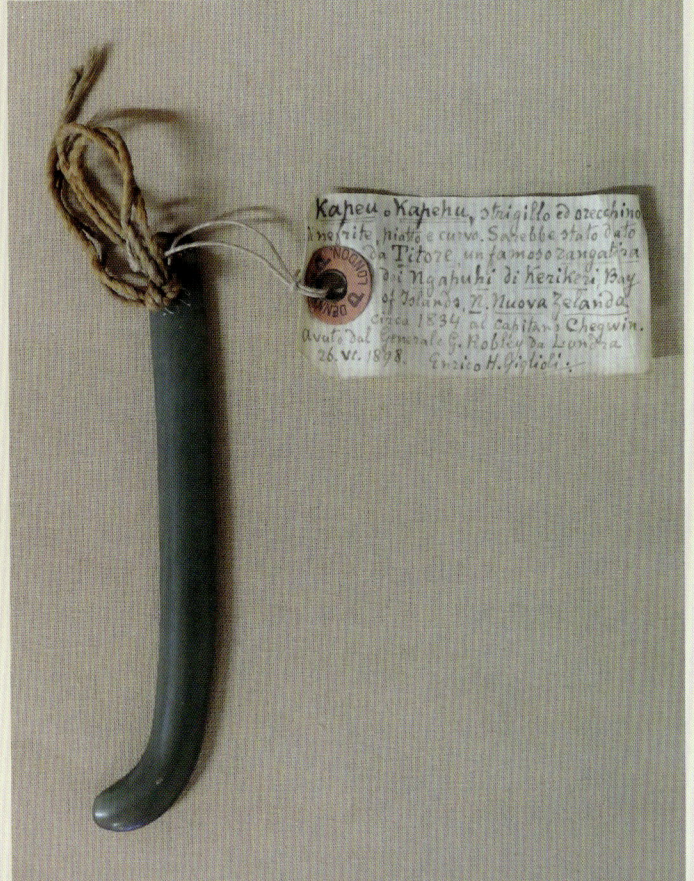
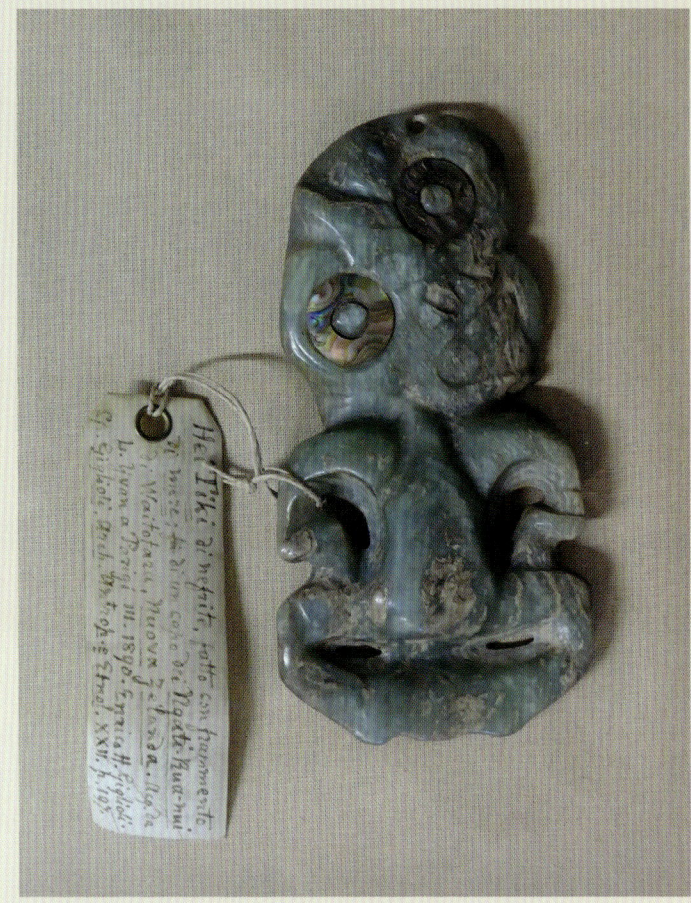
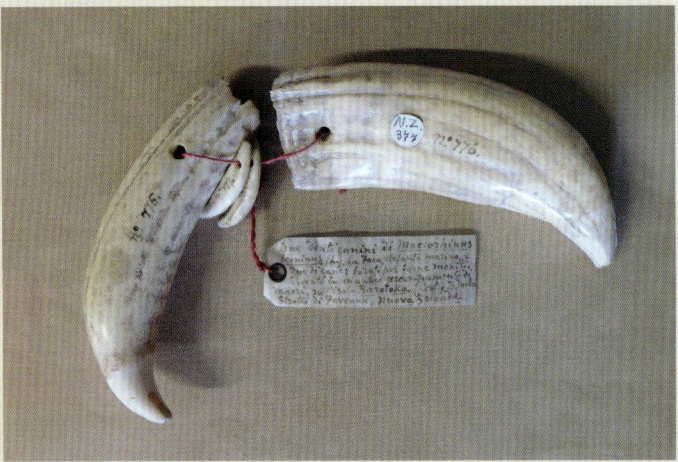
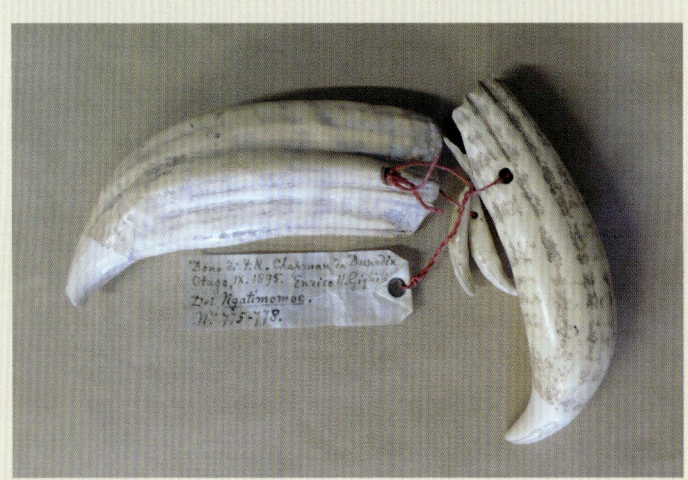

Top left and right: Florentine museum director Enrico Giglioli left his huge taonga Māori collection to the Pigorini National Museum of Prehistory and Ethnography in Rome when he died. He wrote detailed provenances for almost all the forty-six adornments, including this kapeu (top left) which belonged to Ngāpuhi chief Titore. This hei tiki comes from Ngāti Ruanui.
Museo delle Civilta, Rome, 450, 463, photograph by Serena Francone

Bottom left and right: These unworked whale's teeth were collected in the Kāti Māmoe settlement at Tamatea (Dusky Sound), and were acquired by Giglioli from someone called Heymann, one of his many sources.
Museo delle Civiltà, Rome, 775–778, photograph by Serena Francone

# ENRICO GIGLIOLI AND THE TAONGA COLLECTION IN THE PIGORINI NATIONAL MUSEUM OF PREHISTORY AND ETHNOGRAPHY, ROME

NGARINO ELLIS

The circulation of taonga out of Māori communities and into private and public collections was extensive in the nineteenth century. Arapata Hakiwai has recently estimated that more than 16,000 taonga are located in 180 museums overseas.[1] The benefits for Māori, especially artists, of being able to reconnect with these taonga cannot be underestimated. The circumstances in which taonga left their communities were often not recorded, and their subsequent circulation reflects a complex network of Pākehā and, later, European dealers and collectors.

One of the most fascinating accounts involves zoologist Enrico Hillyer Giglioli (1845–1909) and a collection of taonga that is now in the Pigorini National Museum of Prehistory and Ethnography in Rome. Born in London to an Italian father and an English mother, Giglioli spent his first twenty years travelling between England and Italy for his education. At twenty, he was invited to travel with the Italian navy's first circumnavigation of the globe, on board the corvette *Magenta* in 1865–1868. His interest in collecting began while he was on this voyage. Back in Italy, he taught zoology in Florence and eventually became director of the Royal Zoological Museum,[2] a position he held until he died.

From 1877 Giglioli began corresponding with Thomas Cheeseman, the first director of the Auckland Institute and Museum, and this led to several exchanges of items between the two institutions between 1885 and 1899. From Florence came boxes of birds, reptiles and fish, while Cheeseman sent fifteen toi moko , some 'stone work' (presumably adzes) and photographs of Māori. Giglioli was particularly keen to acquire Māori stone implements that he could study closely for an article he was writing. At one point, Giglioli became so desperate for specimens that he suggested he could obtain a knighthood for Cheeseman; this was no empty offer, as he had already negotiated a knighthood for Julius von Haast (of the Canterbury Museum) in exchange for a collection of moa skeletons.[3] He eventually dispatched the Galileian Silver Medal of Merit from the Florence Faculty of Sciences,[4] conferred on Cheeseman via a letter in 1888.[5]

Giglioli maintained a personal collection, as did many other museum staff at the time. He meticulously collected information at the point when he acquired an item – such as the name of the object, and the name and iwi affiliation of the donor or vendor. This was rare for the period, and is invaluable to researchers today.

Giglioli's collection of adornments in Rome gives us a glimpse into the world of the gentleman collectors at the turn of the twentieth century. He acquired forty-six Māori adornments that he catalogued as having come from at least twenty-two iwi, including Ngāpuhi (eight), Kāti Māmoe (five) and Te Arawa (four). He recorded the names of specific people (often unusual in collection notes): for example, a bone aurei acquired by Captain Cook in Queen Charlotte Sound in February 1777 (reg #437), a kapeu belonging to Tītore of Ngāpuhi (reg #450), and a classic whakakai (simple greenstone ornament) that once belonged to Te Whiti o Rongomai (reg #448). He purchased the forty-six adornments from thirteen different people. Many of these were major dealers of the period, from whom he acquired multiple taonga between 1888 and 1909: they included Walter Buller (a lawyer and collector who was renowned in New Zealand for his research on birds), Francis Dart Fenton (a Native Land Court judge) and Horatio Robley. Curiously, when Giglioli died he left his private collection to the Pigorini Museum rather than to the Royal Zoological Museum, of which he was director.[6]

We know comparatively little about collections in non-English-speaking countries, including these Italian collections, and more research needs to be undertaken. Curators and collection staff from museums in Europe meet biannually at the Pacific Arts Association – Europe conference to discuss collections and debate current topics. They are keen to engage with Te Papa Tongarewa in relation to toi moko and their return home. At this stage, though, it is unlikely that taonga Māori from Europe will be repatriated any time soon.

In 2002, eighteen museums signed the Declaration on the Importance and Value of Universal Museums, in which they emphasised the importance of museums holding encyclopedic 'universal' collections – so that a visitor to any museum around the globe could enjoy collections from the Pacific. In effect, this was a clear statement against repatriating those artworks that Māori communities are keen to bring home. Such museums now look to other strategies to enable Māori to reconnect with taonga such as e-repatriation and extending open invitations to meet with Māori . All parties need to initiate these conversations and ensure they are meaningful, reciprocal and ongoing.

For now, Māori collections in countries such as Italy remain relatively unknown. This presents a challenge for European museums who are reaching out to whānau, hapū and iwi to share what is in their institutions. We look forward to hearing from them.

# PART 3
# TE KETE ARONUI

The social, political and physical turmoil of the nineteenth century had prompted a strong Māori artistic response that was manifested in the creation of new arts, occasionally at the cost of the old. From the twentieth century to the early twenty-first, Māori artists have sought to rediscover, revive and replenish their culture through an ever-expanding range of media, venues and kaupapa. Te Kete Aronui, the basket of pursuit, could be characterised as a survival kit equipped with the tikanga-based arts knowledge needed to begin to repair the damage done by colonisation to hapū and iwi, and to seek different artistic modes and relationships in other parts of the world and with other Indigenous peoples.

The twentieth century began with the rise of charismatic Māori leaders Te Puea Hērangi, Apirana Ngata and Tahupōtiki Wiremu Rātana, who spearheaded inspiring and sometimes competing art and architectural missions that sought to reform Māori society and reclaim whenua (chapter 14). These were grassroots, rural-based initiatives that gained national prominence through modern means such as the media, long-distance land and sea transport, and political activity. Within the space of a few decades, Māori art and architecture had become polarised. It was now divided between the revival of customary practice promoted by Te Puea and Ngata in the Waikato and eastern North Island regions respectively and the distinctive Mōrehu-based creative responses that Rātana and other Māori churches and political organisations were using elsewhere.

Education would determine the future direction of Māori arts. The intergenerational training associated with customary practice ensured that these arts remained alive in rural and, increasingly, urban Māori communities after World War Two (chapters 15 and 17). Urbanisation had a dislocating effect on generations of Māori, and this has been a recurring theme in the work of artists trained in tertiary institutions (chapter 16). The terms 'Māori modernism' and 'Māori postmodernism' are used throughout these chapters to acknowledge Jonathan Mane-Wheoki's lifelong practice of doing so in order to firmly place art that Māori have consciously made in these idioms into the canons of modernism and postmodernism.

The point at which Māori art left communities to be exhibited as art objects in museums and galleries was a pivotal and polarising development. The 1984 *Te Maori* exhibition, which opened to critical acclaim in New York before touring the United States and returning to tour Aotearoa, aestheticised Māori art and introduced tikanga to curatorial practice. The engagement with museums and art galleries has not been easy. Māori have continuously agitated to have Māori art shown on Māori terms in institutions, and their contemporary art accepted as Māori art by critics – and sometimes by their own communities (chapters 17–19).

Diaspora and global mobility have transported Māori art practice around the world in recent decades (chapter 18). Ngāti Rānana, the UK-based Māori group, have surrounded taonga Māori languishing in European museums with tikanga and tiaki (care). Some of these institutions have taken notice and provided a platform for contemporary Māori artists to show their work, although the associated breakthrough to important art galleries has taken more time and effort. In Australia, where up to 20 percent of the Māori population now resides, visual and performance arts have provided social cohesion and identity and have taken on new meanings as 'migrant' art in community galleries, alongside that of other diasporic groups. Indeed, the movement and translocation of people and ideas since the late twentieth century has created opportunities for Māori artists to participate in international Indigenous art residencies and exhibitions, and this fosters a spirit of connectedness between Māori and other Indigenous peoples of the land (chapter 19). Equipped with contemporary kete filled with cameras, paintbrushes, chisels, feathers and fibre, Māori artists are completing the journey begun by their Austronesian ancestors by circumnavigating the planet and finding other creative places and spaces.

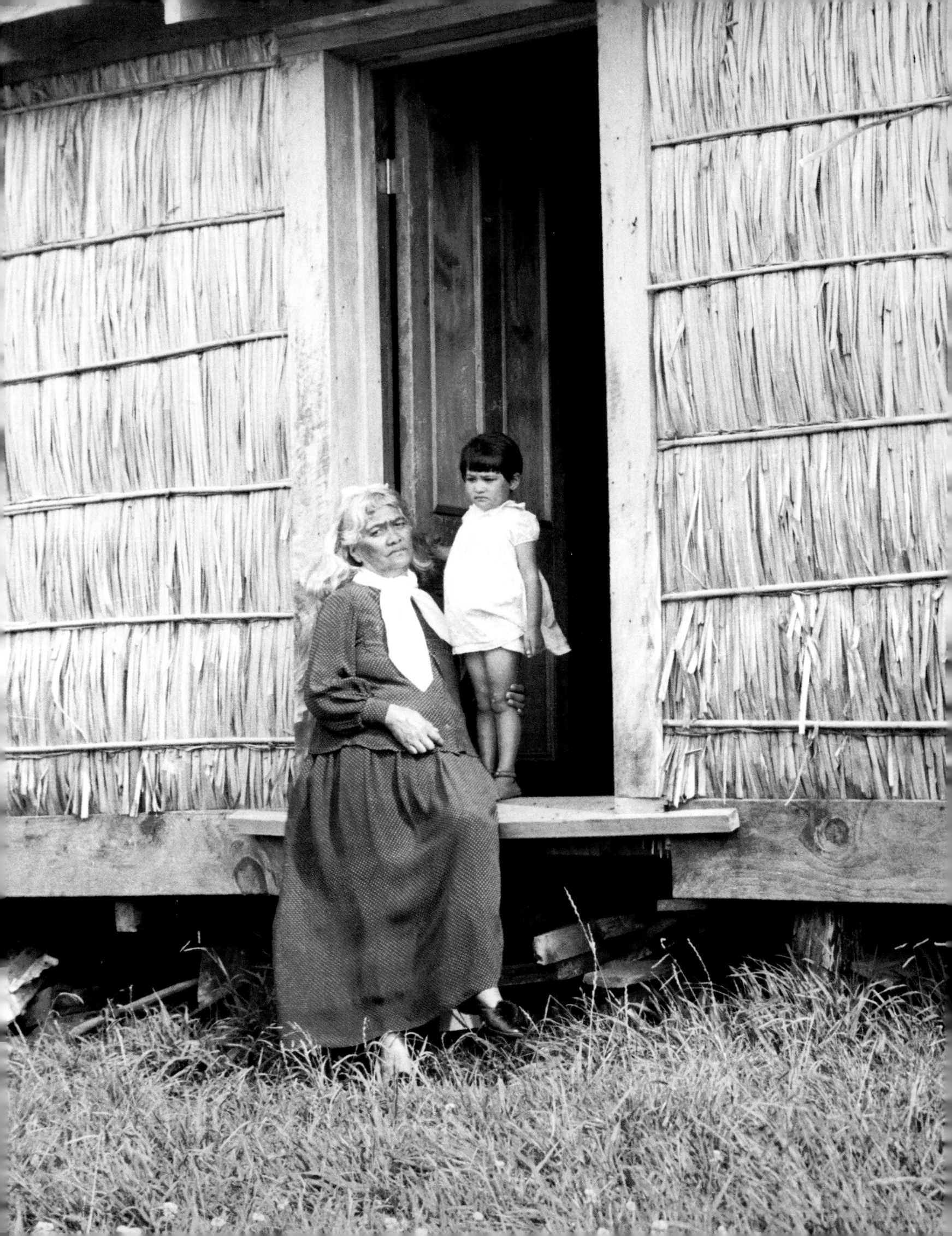

# 14 THE ART OF SOCIAL REFORM
## TE PUEA, NGATA AND RĀTANA
### DEIDRE BROWN

*Ka mahi au, ka inoi au, ka moe au, ka mahi anō.*
*I work, I pray, I sleep, and then I work again.*

—Te Puea Hērangi's whakatauākī

The Māori leaders Te Kirihaehae Te Puea Hērangi, Apirana Turupa Ngata and Tahupōtiki Wiremu Rātana looked to art and architecture as instruments and practices that could create a cohesive Māori identity and support communities. Social reform was at the heart of their projects, which began in earnest around the time when many Māori communities had been destabilised through land loss and the 1918 influenza epidemic.

They each took a different approach to addressing Māori self-determination and wellbeing. Te Puea was one of only a few Māori women in the twentieth century – along with Whina Cooper, Meriana Tōpia (Te Whakatōhea and Te Rarawa, 1862–1960) and her daughter Hēni Tōpia – who designed and commissioned whare whakairo. Building on the momentum of her 1929 Māhinaarangi project, Te Puea established a carving school at the community she founded at Tūrangawaewae for the purpose of redeveloping the Kīngitanga marae. She invented a 'hybrid' housing model that was affordable and designed to meet the needs of her people.

Te Puea Hērangi and a child sitting on the doorstep of her house, Ngāruawāhia, 1939.
Werner Kissling, 1939, British Museum, Oc,F.N.4017 EPF111434, with permission of David Lockwood, Dr Kissling's executor

Ngata envisaged a future for marae, and their whare whakairo and wharekai, as the social and economic hubs of tribal land-development schemes that would put Māori lands into production through farming. Since there were few remaining practitioners of customary Māori architectural arts, he instigated an architectural renaissance through the establishment of the School of Maori Arts and Crafts, to train tohunga whakairo and makers of tukutuku, kōwhaiwhai and kākaho linings.

Rātana, while he shared many of Te Puea and Ngata's social objectives, challenged their means of realisation. His leadership was based in the Māori religio-political tradition and rejected tribalism and customary aesthetics, as demonstrated in his Romanesque churches and Spanish Mission-style community centres. Although a large number of Māori were attracted to Rātana's spiritual and later political mission, it was the customary art and architecture promoted by Te Puea and Ngata that has been perpetuated in Māori communities because of the ubiquity of marae, where their students can pass on their customary knowledge to the next generation.

### Te Puea Hērangi

Te Puea was one of the most influential iwi-based social reformists after World War One and – unusually for a Māori woman – established her own architectural movement. In her role as a leader within the Kīngitanga, she led its return to Ngāruawāhia in 1921. This was a triumph for the movement, which had been forced off this land after the 1863

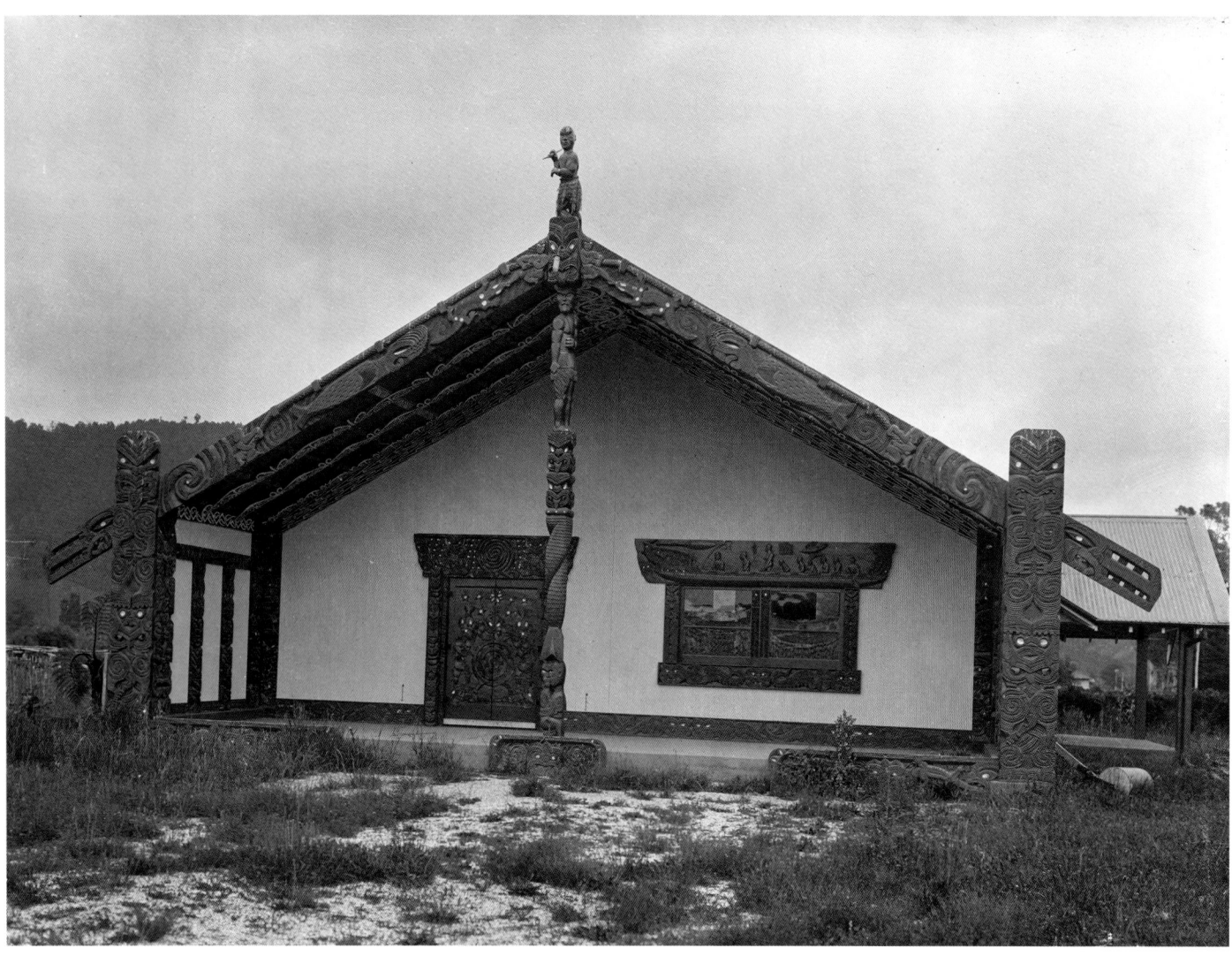

Māhinaarangi, Tūrangawaewae Marae, after completion and before her 1929 opening.
Alexander Turnbull Library, APG-0953-1/2-G

Opposite: Māhinaarangi's front window showing Waikato taniwha and *Tainui* migratory waka.
Alexander Turnbull Library, APG-0952-1/2-G

invasion of the Waikato by government troops. On a less-than-promising 4 hectare lot by the Waikato River she supervised the construction of Tūrangawaewae Marae and several of its notable buildings, with the assistance of iwi members who had been left dispossessed by land confiscations, or without whānau after the devastating 1918 influenza epidemic.[1]

The first months were challenging for Te Puea and her workers, who slept on site in tents or shelters made from sacks draped over mānuka frames while they cleared and drained the land.[2] By the end of the first year, they had constructed about a dozen mānuka- and ponga-framed houses for older workers, with raupō walls, nīkau-thatched roofs, earth floors and sackcloth internal partitions. Despite the best efforts of its Pākehā neighbours to have the settlement deemed unsanitary, Tūrangawaewae passed a Health Department inspection.[3] Te Puea was well aware of the relationship between Māori housing and health, even as the science connecting the two had yet to be fully understood. Māori living conditions and lifeways had (somewhat erroneously) been blamed for the high Māori mortality rate from infectious diseases. She would have heard this viewpoint expressed many times while accompanying the successful 1911 Western Maori parliamentary election campaign of Māui Pōmare, a Māori health officer who had been responsible for burning nearly 2000 uninhabited whare.[4]

THE ART OF SOCIAL REFORM – TE PUEA, NGATA AND RĀTANA

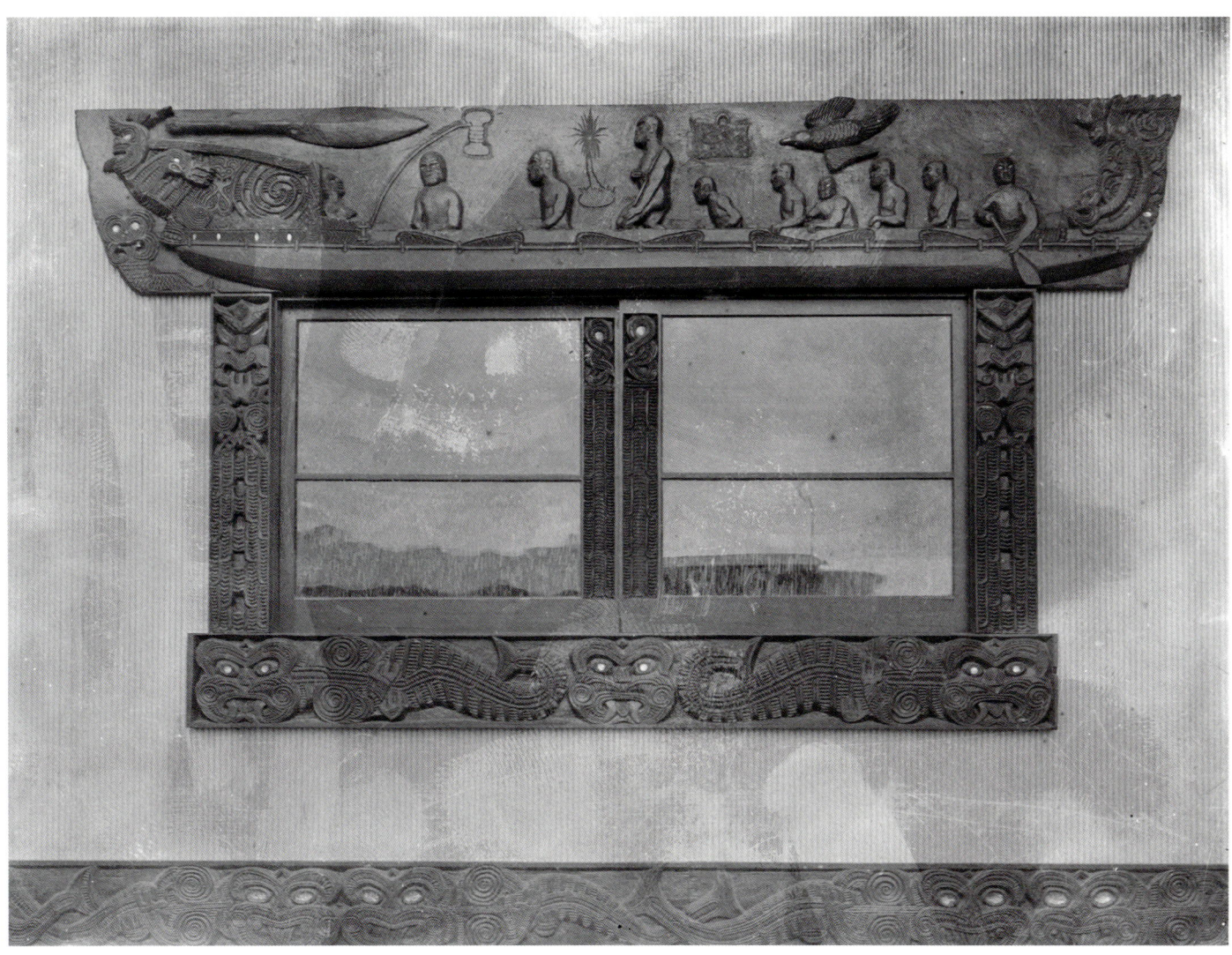

By the late 1920s Tūrangawaewae was a thriving village with a number of residences, each with its own garden,[5] as well as a sports field, billiards room and tennis courts. Visitors entered the marae through a formal northern gateway, and a southern entrance gave locals easy access to Ngāruawāhia township. The construction of recreational facilities, township access, private gardens and paths suggests that Te Puea may have been influenced by Pākehā-style town planning or by large-scale kāinga such as Parihaka and Pāpāwai pā in the design for Tūrangawaewae Marae.[6]

### Māhinaarangi

The community grew stronger in the 1920s. Te Puea raised money for architectural projects by levying Kīngitanga members and touring with her own Te Pou o Mangatawhiri (T.P.M.) concert party – a group of young people who performed waiata and haka. The T.P.M. also contributed to maintaining waiata, and to the modernisation of customary Māori performance costume, based on the contemporary flapper style of dress, with shorter piupiu and tāniko headbands.[7] The funds they raised were used to build the Kimikimi dining and assembly hall (opened in 1922) and Pare Waikato whare whakairo (opened in 1927).[8] Te Puea supervised this latter project, including the carvers – Bill Muru, Pero Muru, Tom Porter and Piri Poutapu – and the women who were seconded to the project to lay the flooring as opening day loomed.[9]

At the opening, kaumātua resolved to build a second carved house at Tūrangawaewae. Te Puea envisaged this project as a Māori hospital staffed with Māori nurses where Māori patients could receive treatment in a familiar environment and overcome their fear of Pākehā medical practices.[10] Although this objective was dashed on its opening, the building went on to become a flagship

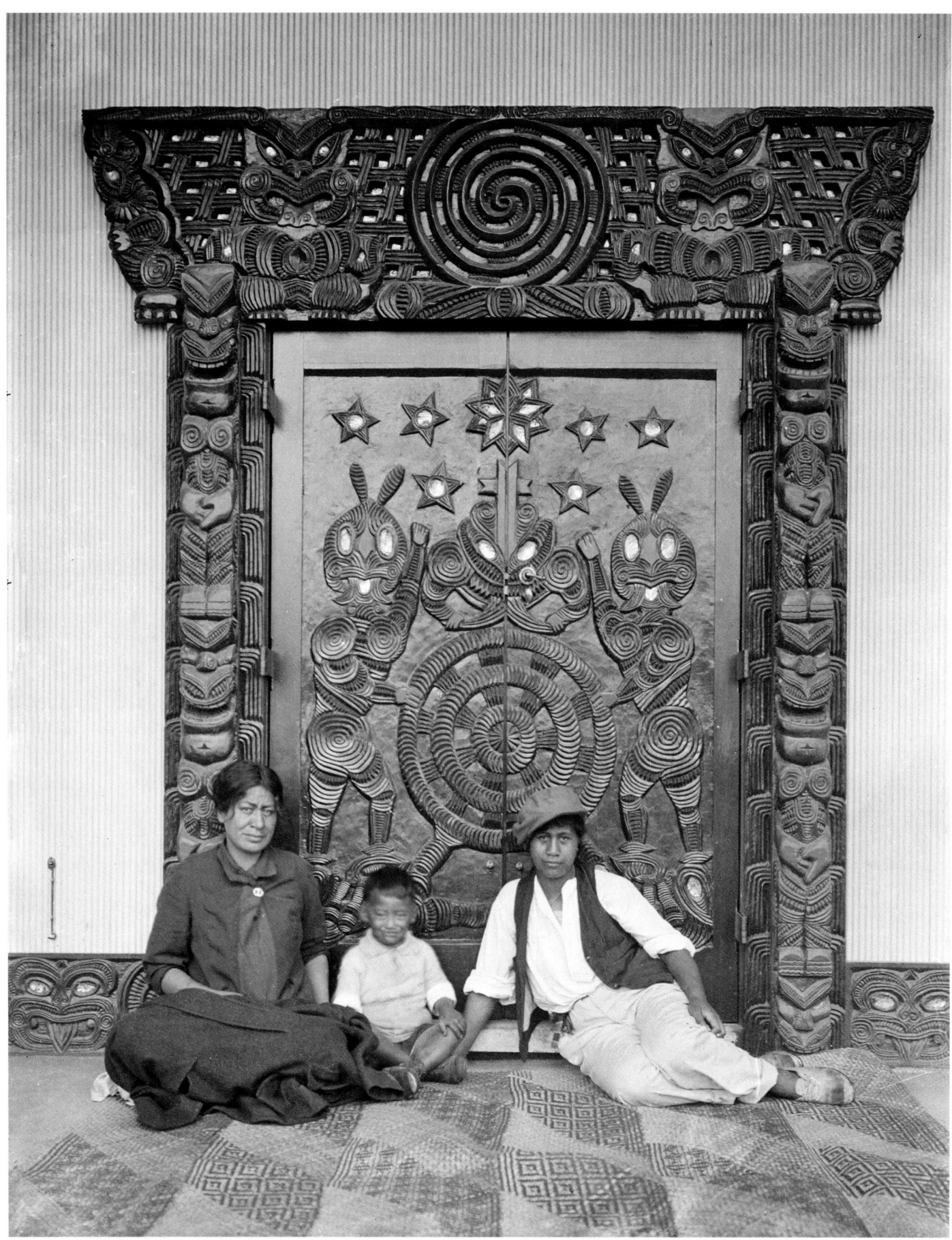

project for one of the world's most important Indigenous building revivals.

To raise funds for the project, Te Puea took the T.P.M. concert party on tour over 1927 and 1928 to the East Coast, home to the comparatively wealthy Ngāti Porou.[11] She wrote to Ngata outlining the purpose of her visit, and Ngata responded by inviting her and the T.P.M. to spend Christmas 1927 on his home marae at Waiomatatini.[12] This occasion must have been a meeting of minds. Not only did Ngata persuade Te Puea to name the yet-to-be-built project Māhinaarangi, after the ancestress whose union with Tūrongo had united her East Coast people with the Waikato tribes, she also agreed to engage the services of Ngata's School of Maori Arts and Crafts in order to solicit Ngāti Porou's interest in the tour.[13]

After the school was commissioned, Prime Minister Gordon Coates offered state assistance to Te Puea, including a £1000 grant and timber from the Frankton Railway Timber Mill.[14] Te Puea allowed Ngata to appoint many of the specialist craftsmen, as she believed 'he thoroughly understands Maori art and architecture, so that relieves me of a fair amount of responsibility'.[15] He commissioned the school's builder, Richard Wills, to produce plans for Māhinaarangi and supervise the local labourers, and arranged for eight tohunga whakairo from Te Arawa to prepare the interior carvings at the school in Rotorua.[16] The Arawa carvers were Sonny Brees, Wi Hau, Rotohiko Haupapa, Henare Haupapa, Iharaira (Te Whakarewarewa) and Tuhaka Te Kapua. They directed Waikato men selected to be carving trainees, including Joe Hoera, Waka Kereama, George Muru, Wiremu Muru and Piri Poutapu, who worked on external whakairo rākau.[17]

The Waikato style of carving had not been used since the New Zealand Wars.[18] Determined to depict local themes in their work, the Tūrangawaewae carvers carved Waikato taniwha on the maihi and poutāhū and a naturalistic illustration of the Tainui canoe on the porch window lintel.[19] The Kīngitanga coat of arms, Te Paki o Matariki, appeared on the carved front doors.

Local women made important contributions to the project, under the direction of Ngata and his wife Arihia.

The door of Māhinaarangi with the Kīngitanga coat of arms, Te Paki o Matariki.
Alexander Turnbull Library, APG-0951-1/2-G

They completed the tukutuku panels and painted kōwhaiwhai patterns on the rafters; this last they carried out in situ while lying on a platform, which was a departure from the custom of not allowing women inside whare under construction.[20] The kōwhaiwhai patterns concealed the modern joints of the unusual composite ridgepole.[21]

Te Puea wanted Māhinaarangi to look like a whare whakairo, rather than a hospital, so that Māori patients would feel more comfortable about being inside the building and using its services.[22] She made a concession to modern healthcare and building requirements by permitting the inclusion of opening windows and side porches with fire exits. Windows that opened were positioned on the wall between the carved internal poupou to admit fresh air and light, to assist with patient recuperation.[23] Load-bearing columns placed on either side of the ridgepole created a clear central aisle to allow passage between two rows of beds.[24] Western materials were used for the cladding, including weatherboards, fluted linings that simulated kākaho stems for the porch, and an iron roof.[25] From the front – the principal elevation of formal approaches to wharenui – Māhinaarangi appeared as a grand whare whakairo, yet this building had pushed the limits of custom, as the opening ceremony would demonstrate.

Māhinaarangi was opened on 18 March 1929 at an event that also officially recognised the transferral of the Māori king's mana from Waahi to Tūrangawaewae Marae – and, thus, the return of the Kīngitanga to Ngāruawāhia.[26] Two rituals were performed to remove Māhinaarangi's tapu. A series of ominous mistakes in the first multitribal ceremony, which was performed a day before the official opening, led to the hasty arrangement of a second Waikato ritual for the next day. During the first, Ngata's wife Arihia was unable to pull the veil off a tekoteko effigy of Pōtatau, despite the lack of any apparent obstruction; and the officiating tohunga Tūtānekai did not provide the tekoteko with a name.[27] After the second opening ceremony, two disastrous events struck Ngata and Te Puea.[28] Ngata's wife and their eldest son, Makarini, died of dysentery they had contracted during the ceremony. He and many Ngāti Porou elders blamed their deaths on the mistakes made during the first ritual.[29] Then Te Puea was informed that Māhinaarangi did not fit the criteria necessary to operate as a private hospital.[30] She was disappointed, but instead she made Māhinaarangi the focal

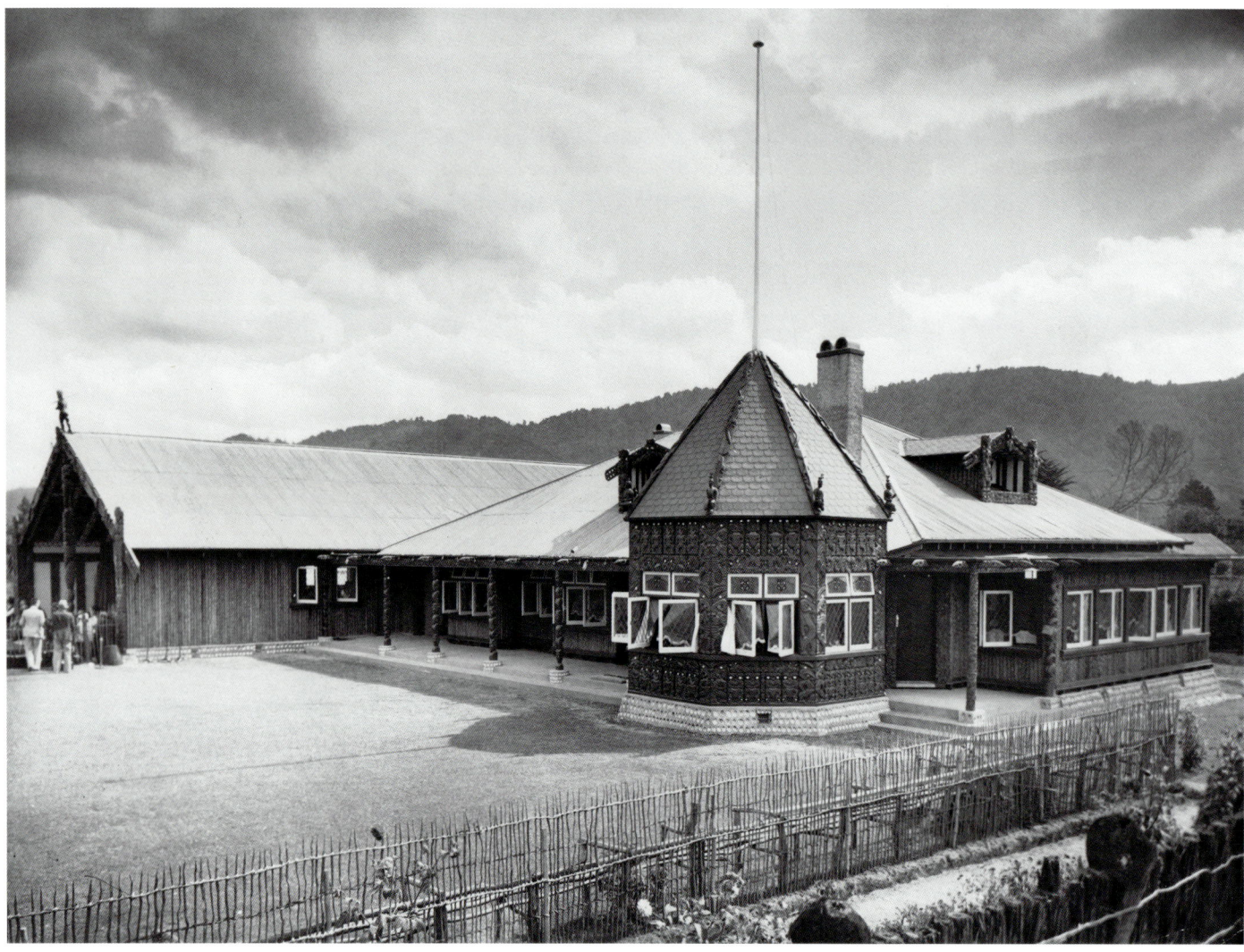

point of the marae; she turned it into a reception hall and museum and fitted it out with fine Western-style furniture.[31] Although Māhinaarangi was never used as a Māori hospital, and despite personal rifts, the project had led to new relationships for the Kīngitanga with Ngāti Porou and the government, and the rebirth of Waikato whakairo rākau.

### The Tūrangawaewae carving school

After the Māhinaarangi project, Te Puea established the Tūrangawaewae carving school – also known as the Tainui carving school and the Tūrangawaewae Maori Adult Education carving school – to support her marae improvement programme.[32] Like Ngata, she believed that the marae and the social and cultural cohesion it engendered were central to Māori self-determination.[33] The Māori king's annual 'poukai' tour of Kīngitanga marae had helped to maintain unity between hapū through the most difficult of times, so she was determined to ensure that every marae had a wharenui and a permanent wharekai to host these visits. Her dedication led to the completion of at least fifteen Kīngitanga marae buildings.[34] The Tūrangawaewae carving school produced whakairo rākau for Kīngitanga buildings, trained local men to be tohunga whakairo, and continued the recovery of the Waikato style of carving. In 1929, Te Puea sent Piri Poutapu and Waka Kereama to be trained in the School of Maori Arts and Crafts.[35] Poutapu returned to Ngāruawāhia to run the Tūrangawaewae carving school under Te Puea's direction and to work on new buildings and renovation projects at Kāwhia, Mangatāwhiri, Rukumoana, Tauranganui, Tūrangawaewae, Whatawhata and Waihi.[36]

Te Puea chose Poutapu for training after seeing the panels he carved for Māhinaarangi. Initially he was reluctant to leave his wife Ngāmako in Waikato to attend the Rotorua-based school: he told Te Puea that there were better-qualified men

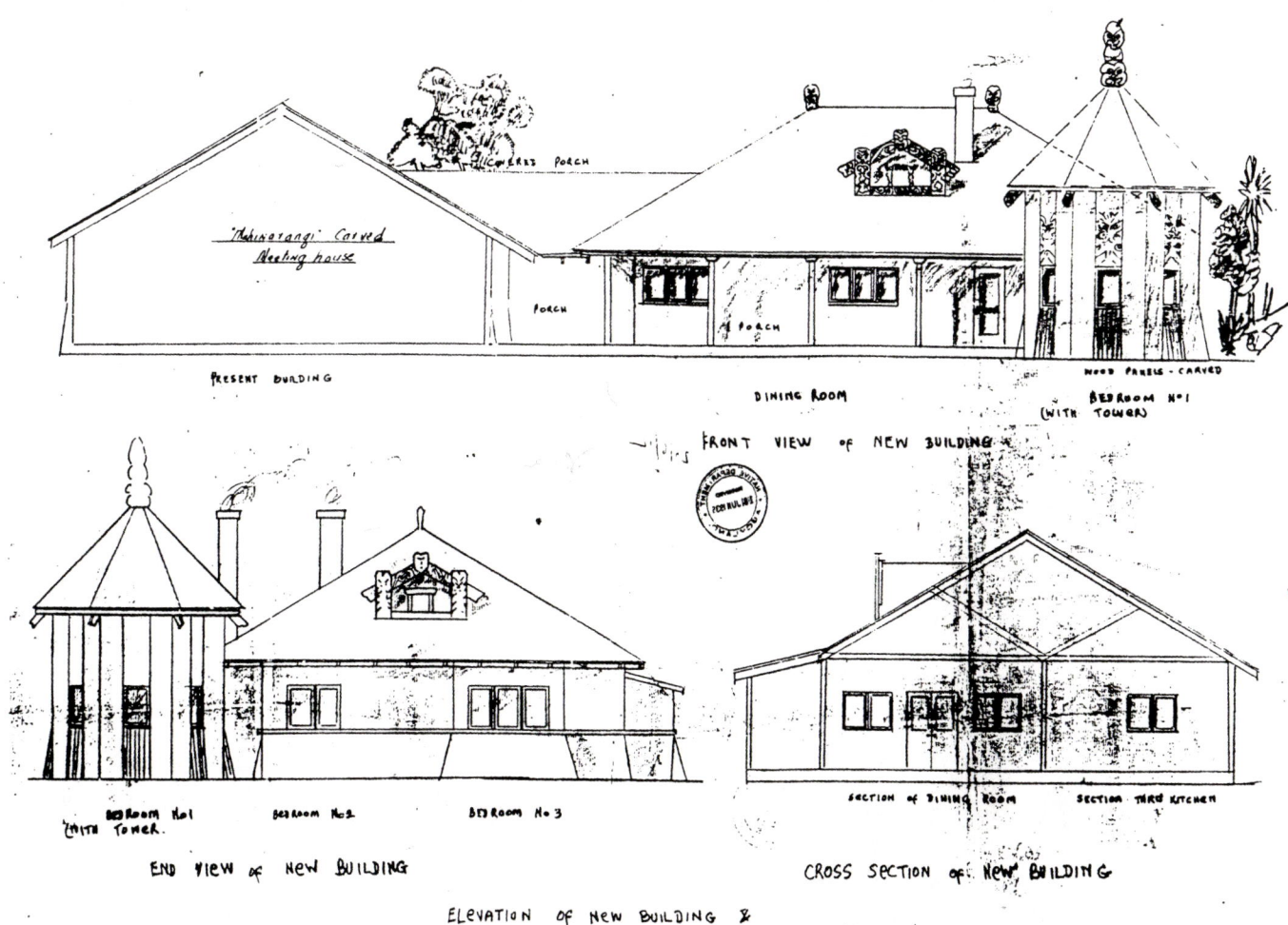

Elevations and plan of Tūrongo.
Archives New Zealand, MA 1/17/4/1

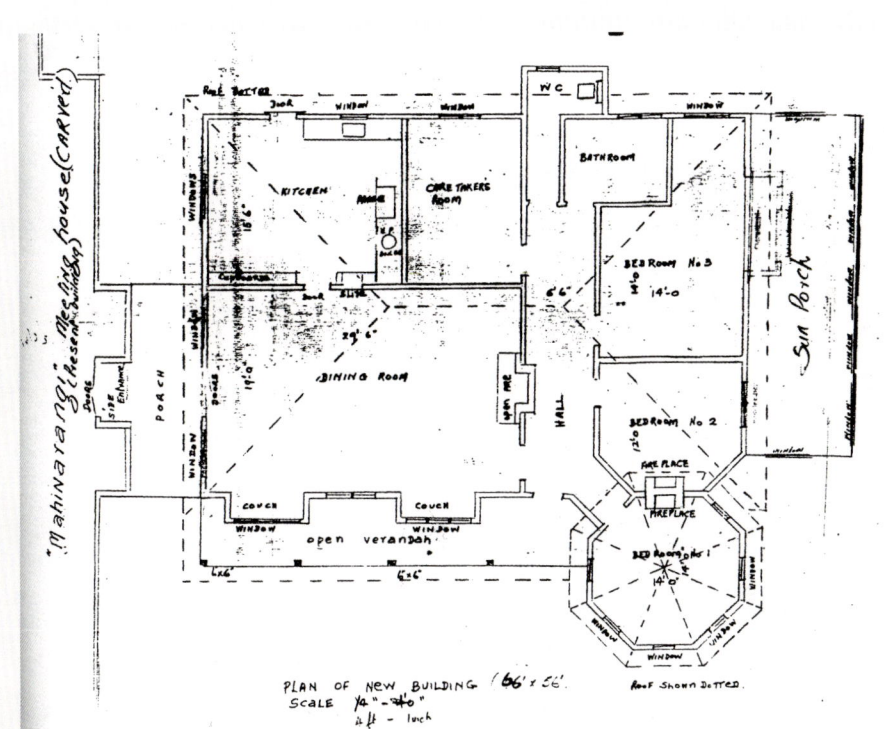

Opposite: Tūrongo at Ngāruawāhia, taken around 1931 by an unidentified photographer.
Alexander Turnbull Library, PAColl-9376

364 | 365

'of standing' who were more suited to carving. However, Te Puea told him that he had no choice, and she added, 'I say that goes and don't you answer me back.' 'So I shut my mouth from that day up to this day,' Poutapu later recalled. 'I had to do what I was told.'[37] Te Puea appears to have removed both men from the school around 1932 to work on Kīngitanga projects, despite Ngata's belief that Poutapu had mastered only shallow work and had much more to learn about deeper, more intensive carving.[38]

There were still many issues around the contemporary practice of whakairo rākau to be worked through on Poutapu's return to Tūrangawaewae. Some men refused to be taught by him, possibly because of his relative youth (he would have been about twenty-seven). Nevertheless, he taught those who were willing to learn and maintained the tapu rituals he had observed older, wānanga-trained tutors using at the School of Maori Arts and Crafts.[39] These rituals included the appropriate disposal of woodchips, spatial division of gender-related building tasks, and recitation of karakia. Unlike other graduates of the school, such as the Taiapa brothers, Poutapu refused to be paid for his work: such a transaction would be considered noa because it involved money, and would violate the tapu of his practice.[40] He was very conscious of his ancestral and tribal background, and he tried to reflect his heritage in his carving. For instance, he encouraged the continued use of the Waikato River taniwha motif in the Tūrangawaewae school's work, and he recovered other local motifs by studying carvings in museums, and George French Angas's 1844 Waikato architectural illustrations.[41] His most outstanding students were Īnia Te Iwiata (later known as Īnia Te Wiata when he became an internationally renowned opera singer), who joined the school in 1933, and Te Puea's nephew Tāmati Hērangi, who started around 1937.[42] Like Poutapu, Hērangi took a scholarly approach to his work and he, too, studied Angas's illustrations in the Alexander Turnbull Library in Wellington. While he was in Wellington, the Dominion Museum taxidermist Charles Lindsay showed Hērangi how to make plaster casts of existing carvings; these casts could be used to manufacture concrete carvings, which were popular with some iwi in the 1940s.[43] In 1945, Hērangi became head of the school after Poutapu had a disagreement with Te Puea and left.[44]

Tūrongo House, opened on Tūrangawaewae Marae in 1938, was the Tūrangawaewae carving school's most important early project. Four years earlier Te Puea had decided to build the house next to Māhinaarangi as a residence for Korokī, the fifth Māori king – a plan that would remove him from Rātana's influence in Waahi and would provide accommodation for special visitors.[45] The house would be, in Te Puea words, 'more Maori than Pakeha' in appearance and elaborately decorated, as befitted the mana of a Māori monarch.[46]

The Tūrangawaewae school began making whakairo rākau and tukutuku for Tūrongo under Poutapu's supervision in October 1935. The carvers included Te Iwiata, Pihi Muru, Paraone Rauwhero, Te Waharoa Tamehana, Turi Tahapeehi and Whata Tupaea.[47] The building was replete with Kīngitanga-specific imagery: Te Iwiata used a photograph of Tāwhiao, sent from Sydney by Te Puea's friend Eric Ramsden, as a model for a carving of the king; Te Heuheu was shown greeting Tāwhiao on a carved panel fixed above a fireplace inside Tūrongo; and Tāwhiao's moko was carved onto one of the veranda pillars.[48] The dining-room carvings were executed in a number of tribal styles in order to capitalise on relationships between the Kīngitanga and other Māori visitors.[49] There was no Ringatū-style polychromy – all of the carvings were stained black.

Te Puea declined Ngata's offer of the services of Ngāti Porou carvers and tukutuku experts for this project. She privately admitted that she did not want to be indebted to Ngata, particularly as he had implied that she had been responsible for his wife's death.[50] Nevertheless, Ngata brought a Ngāti Porou carved panel to Tūrangawaewae for the Tūrangawaewae school's carvers to copy. He was disappointed with the result, however, and this provoked the carvers to make an improved version of the panel. They presented this copy to Ngata on his next visit, without telling him it was a new version. When Ngata was about to leave with what he thought was the original carving, Poutapu demanded his work back. Ngata was amused when he realised his mistake and the mana of the carvers was restored. This carving was installed on the tower.[51]

Tūrongo contained a formal dining room lavishly decorated with whakairo rākau and tukutuku, a sitting room, kitchen, caretaker's room, two bedrooms and a sunporch. The house was linked to the side of Māhinaarangi by a covered walkway that was seen as an architectural metaphor for Māhinaarangi and Tūrongo's life partnership.[52] A 14m long veranda ran along Tūrongo's front elevation; at

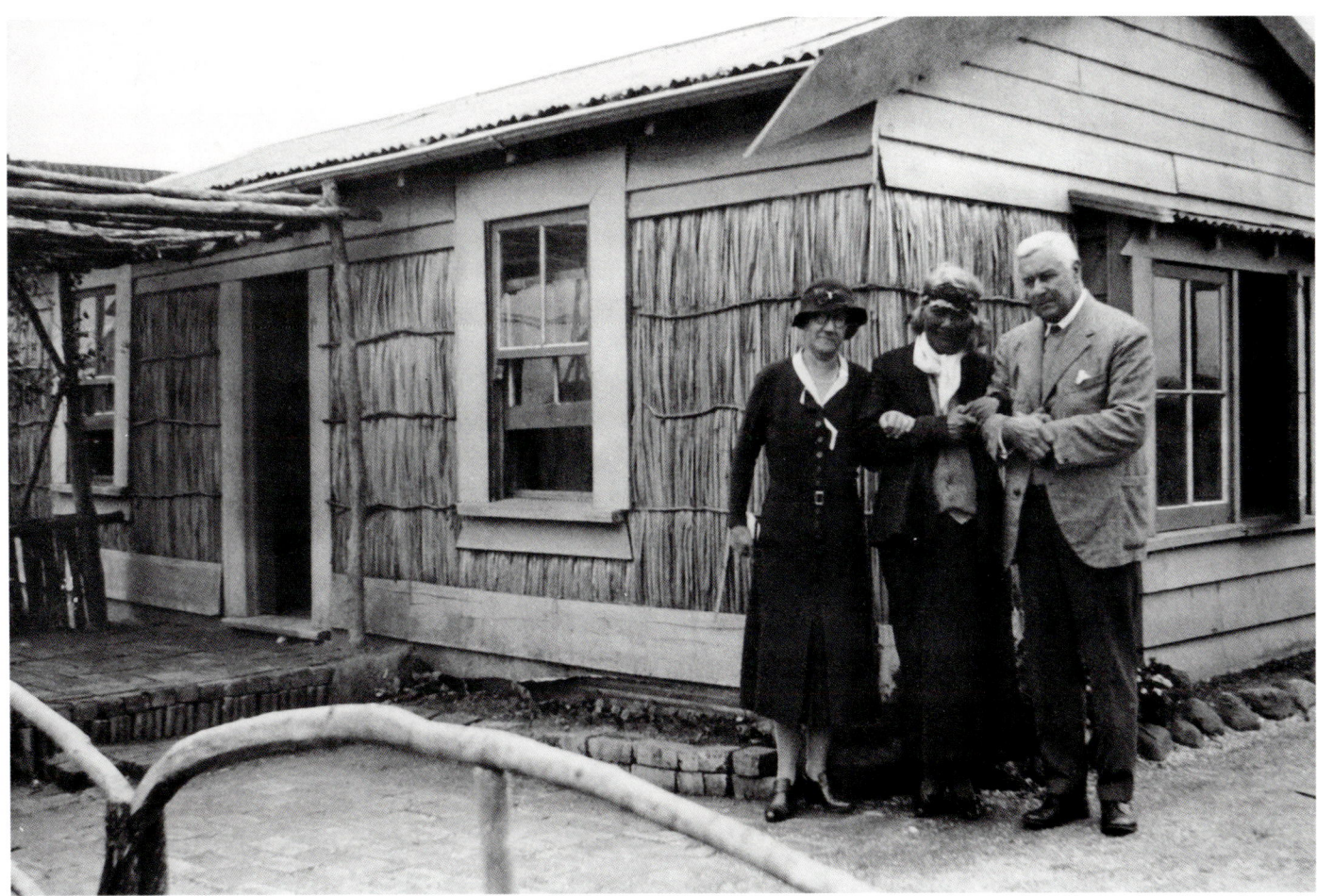

Te Puea Hērangi and two others outside a Land Development Scheme house clad in a combination of raupō and weatherboard.
Alexander Turnbull Library, 1/2-059950-F

one end of the veranda was an octagonal-plan lantern tower containing a bedroom: the design of the tower was inspired by a pentagonal-plan tower that Te Puea had seen on a villa in Hamilton East.[53] On top of each corner of the tower was a carved figure: seven of these represented the captains of Māori migratory waka, and the eighth represented Kupe the explorer.[54] The roof of Tūrongo featured two pātaka-like dormer windows named Hīnana ki Uta (look to the land), like the Pou o te Kīngitanga pātaka built at Pūkawa, and Hīnana ki Tai (look to the sea), representing Māori and Pākehā united under their kings.[55] Other innovations included inlaying pāua shells in the concrete base of the tower, and cladding part of the exterior in undressed ponga trunks.[56]

Before the opening ceremony, Governor-General Viscount Galway invested Te Puea with the insignia of Commander of the British Empire on the porch of Tūrongo – a small step towards reconciliation after the government's 1863 invasion of the Waikato, land confiscations and the 1918 imprisonment of Tainui men who had refused to be conscripted. After the investiture, she found a group of carvers sitting behind Tūrongo; threw her insignia to them and declared, 'It is yours. You boys have earned it!'[57] Once Te Puea and the viceregal deputation had left Tūrangawaewae, Korokī told the workers that he could not live permanently in Tūrongo: he said that 'during its construction and right up to this moment it seemed to me that if it was to be mine, then I was drinking the sweat and blood of you all'.[58] Te Puea was dismayed, but she accepted his decision.[59]

### Māori housing, 1932–1934

By the beginning of the twentieth century, Māori were becoming familiar with the Pākehā notion of the 'house' as a grouping of living, dining, cooking and sleeping spaces under one roof. The Pākehā-style house was by no means commonplace in Māori communities as it was expensive to build, supported nuclear rather than whānau family

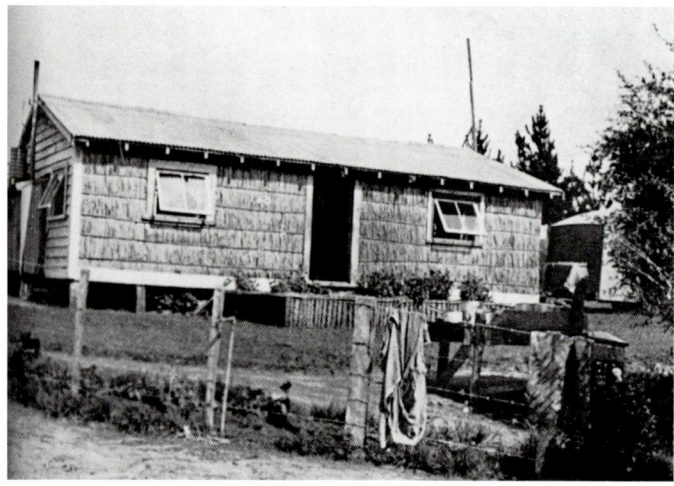

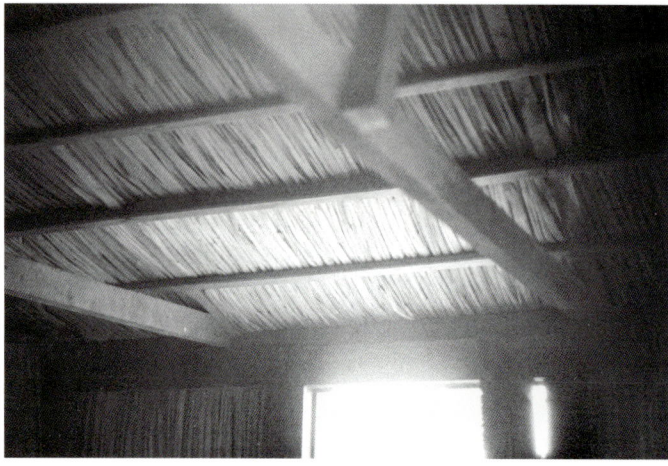

Top: Hybrid raupō and weatherboard house, most likely Te Puea's at Ngāruawāhia.
from I. L. G. Sutherland, *Maori People Today*, Massey University, 1973

Bottom: Thatch ceiling and wall linings of Te Puea's house at Ngāruawāhia. The timber roof structure is a combination of Māori and Pākehā construction techniques, and is possibly the outcome of building with Māori and Pākehā materials and/or a transition period in Māori building techniques and knowledges.
Werner Kissling, 1939, British Museum, Oc,F.N.4021 EPF111438, with permission of David Lockwood, Dr Kissling's executor

Opposite: Apirana Ngata leading the haka during the opening of the whare rūnanga at Waitangi in 1940.
Alexander Turnbull Library, MNZ-2746-1/2-F

life and provided inadequate separation of tapu and noa activities. Te Puea, who was always looking for ways to improve the wellbeing of her people at a domestic level, developed a 'hybrid' bungalow-style house that combined Māori and Pākehā design elements in spatial planning and structure. She built a small number of four-roomed dwellings that contained living, cooking, eating and (presumably) shared sleeping activities, with separate outdoor ablution facilities.[60] In keeping with her philosophy that familiarity was the greatest attractor for Māori, the houses were clad in either raupō thatch or a combination of thatch and weatherboard; they were raised above ground on piles, with wooden floors and an iron roof. Photographs of the interior of these buildings show a structure that was based on – but not completely the same as – Western light timber frame construction. Thatch lowered the construction cost to about one quarter of that for a weatherboard home, and provided a weatherproofing system that was more familiar to Māori builders.[61]

## Ngata and the School of Maori Arts and Crafts

Like Te Puea, Ngata employed art and architecture to consolidate iwi presence on their whenua, strengthen relationships between constituent hapū and improve wellbeing – in his case, across the North Island, where most Māori lived. His principal concern was the revival of the customary Māori art practices of whare whakairo construction, whakairo rākau, kōwhaiwhai, tukutuku and plain kākaho linings that, by the beginning of the twentieth century, were on the brink of being lost. The decline in interest in learning these practices was due to the development of new forms of architectural and artistic expression influenced by Pākehā culture, and a shift in the Māori economy away from a koha system of labour that respected tapu to a money-based economy, which was inherently noa.[62] Ngata, through his political and Māori leadership roles, established the School of Maori Arts and Crafts at Rotorua in 1927 to counter the loss of customary culture by reviving interest in whare whakairo construction.[63]

In addition to Māhinaarangi, its first marae-based project, the school was responsible for the completion of more than forty building projects – including whare whakairo, whare kai, exhibition houses, churches and chapels – in the course of its existence. Tohunga whakairo as well as tukutuku,

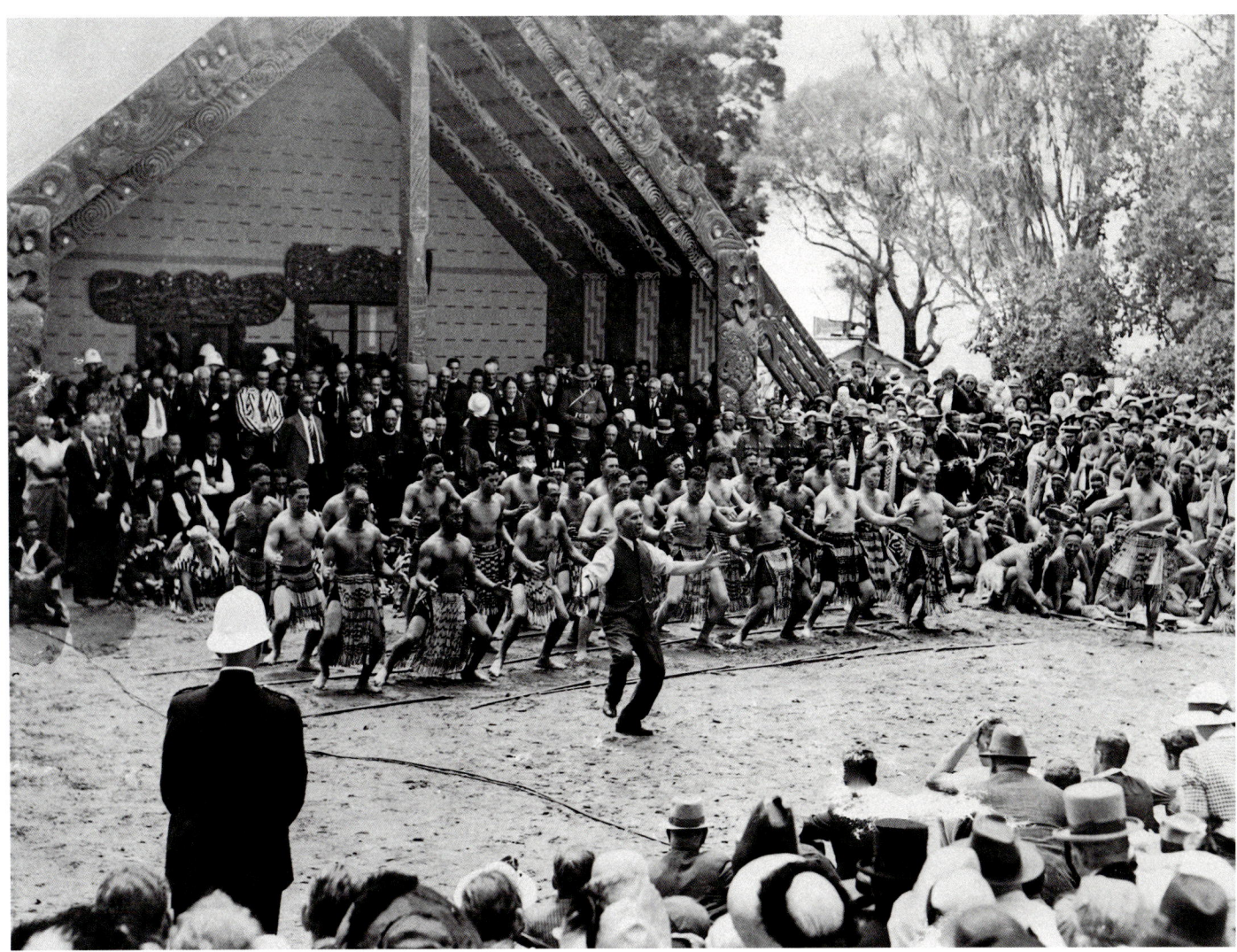

kōwhaiwhai and kākaho specialists were trained at the school and on site within communities.[64] With Māori social cohesion under threat from the individualisation of Māori land title, Ngata's land-development programme had the survival of marae culture at its heart. The development of whare whakairo architecture on marae had created a unified identity for East Coast iwi in the nineteenth century, and Ngata believed that building whare whakairo on all marae (or at least those associated with his land-development programme) would unite all iwi across the country in the twentieth century.[65] At the same time he instigated other Māori 'renaissance' initiatives, such as recording ancestral waiata and developing whaikōrero and kapa haka competitions.

While he was seeking to commission whakairo rākau for his residence at Waiomatatini in 1916, Ngata discovered that there was only one surviving carver, Hone Ngatoto, still working on the East Coast – an area once renowned for its continuous whakapapa of artistic tradition from ancient times.[66] Ngata's close friend Te Rangi Hīroa (Peter Buck) reported four years later that tukutuku was a similarly endangered practice that was being produced only in the tourist regions of Whanganui, East Coast and Rotorua.[67] The impending demise of these arts prompted Ngata to lobby the government for a partly state-assisted School of Maori Arts and Crafts. Although he was not the director of the school – that role was filled by Harold Hamilton – Ngata was very much in control of its operation and goals.[68] He decided which commissions the school would undertake, what 'styles' of whakairo rākau and tukutuku would be used, and the overall design of each building.[69] The focus of the school was on the recovery and perpetuation of arts as they had been before the New Zealand Wars – an objective that was deliberately dehistoricising through its avoidance of the innovative developments that had occurred at

Pāpāwai, Parihaka and Maungapōhatu. The school chose not to continue with the Ringatū arts of polychromatic and figurative painting, since Ngata associated them with the pain, conflict and loss of the New Zealand Wars.[70]

The school negotiated a delicate balance between the tapu protocols and processes of the whare wānanga on the one hand, and the scholarly analysis and copying of work in a workshop-cum-studio setting on the other. Local Te Arawa carvers – including Rotohiko Haupapa and Tamatekapua Te Raihi, whose practice had survived in Rotorua due to European patronage – were the school's first instructors;[71] they were joined in 1929 by Poutapu and Kereama, as well as brothers Pineāmine (Pine) and Hone Taiapa from Ngata's own Ngāti Porou tribe.[72] The situation inside the workshop was tense: Haupapa was reluctant to pass on his skills, which had a commercial value, to the trainees; Pine Taiapa found the preoccupation of his tutors with the production of small objects frustrating; and Ngata did not like the slow, chisel-dependent Te Arawa style. Eventually these issues were resolved when the Te Arawa carvers left in 1930 and Eramiha Kapua, a Ngāti Tarāwhai expert in the use of long-handled steel adzes, became the head tutor. The trainees travelled to Auckland to visit the museum, where they photographed, studied and copied its extensive whakairo rākau collection.[73] At the same time, Ngata was researching, identifying and grouping existing tribal work that he knew of into 'schools' or iwi 'styles', based on northwestern and eastern divisions, which the trainees 'learned' by meticulous reproduction. Through this process of artistic recovery, the school was able to reconstitute both the Waikato and the northern styles of whakairo rākau (the latter had been largely dormant since the Musket Wars a century before).[74]

Ngata was not keen on spontaneous innovation: he believed that only when the tribal styles had been mastered could the carver be allowed the freedom to create designs. In his opinion, it was six years before the initial group of trainees had reached this level of competency.[75] This strategy of reclaiming culture through precedent studies sat very much within the revivalist tradition of art- and building-making that Ngata would have been familiar with through his Anglican upbringing at Waiomatatini and his classical studies at Te Aute College, all of which would have brought him into contact with the Gothic Revival and possibly neoclassicism. The Arts and Crafts movement, with its focus on skilled manual making, had been an active presence in Pākehā decorative and architectural practice since the late nineteenth century, and the school's naming capitalised on this. Furthermore, an impetus to 'preserve' the Māori artistic tradition had been present in government and public thought and had led to the Maori Antiquities Act in 1901 – a cause that was championed by Harold Hamilton's father Augustus Hamilton, who became director of the Colonial Museum two years after the passing of the Act. Augustus Hamilton's serialised compendium of Māori design, *The Art Workmanship of the Maori Race in New Zealand*, published between 1896 and 1900, could be considered a local version of Owen Jones's 1856 *Grammar of Ornament*, an influential book on global design used by early Arts and Crafts designers such as William Morris and, later, by Prairie School architects such as Frank Lloyd Wright. The intersection of revivalism, craft and Māori cultural revitalisation created the conditions in which the School of Maori Arts and Crafts would carry out its own Māori artistic revival.

The Taiapa brothers eventually became the school's head tohunga whakairo: they trained an ever-changing group of students at the school and on site in communities that commissioned the school to build their whare whakairo and wharekai. The Taiapa brothers were versatile carvers who, unlike earlier practitioners, could work in a number of different tribal styles depending on the project.[76] About four to five hundred women and schoolgirls undertook the school's tukutuku programme begun in 1933 under the instruction of a few paid experts,[77] despite a widespread belief that women had not been the principal makers of tukutuku in the past.[78] The involvement of women had the potential to engage the participation of a representative cross-section of the community into a project, which was in keeping with Ngata's philosophy of mobilising ohu or Māori 'working bees' to ensure the delivery of building and farming projects. The school's programme did not extend to maintaining the arts of whatu or raranga whāriki, both of which were in serious decline until their revival in the 1950s by the Maori Women's Welfare League.

Ngata had reconceptualised the whare whakairo as a community facility that could accommodate all manner of contemporary social functions, especially dances, which would attract the interest of rangatahi in marae activities. Footwear meant floors had to be resilient surfaces, so mats

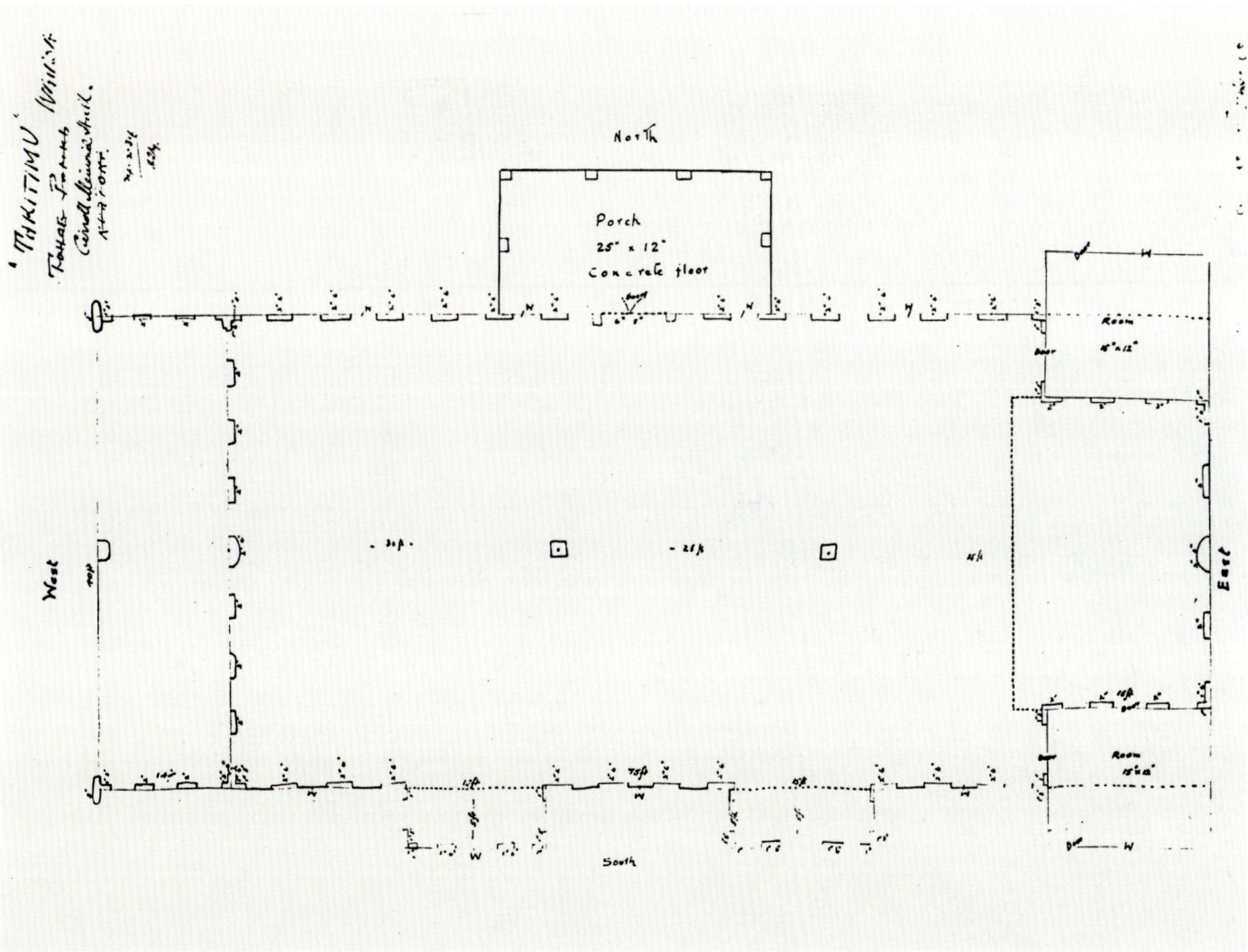

Richard Wills's plan for Tākitimu whare whakairo, built at Wairoa and opened in 1938. As can be seen in the title block, the plan was adapted from the drawings for the Tūhoe Pōtiki whare whakairo for Ruatoki, which was never built.
Archives New Zealand, MA 51/14/139

were redundant. On many marae, though, tikanga prevailed, and people still removed their shoes so as not to bring tapu from the marae and dirt from outside into the interior. Others who were involved in the management of the school were likewise faced with decisions about whether to suspend or maintain tikanga. Kapua retained practices from the whare wānanga concerning design memorisation, safe woodchip disposal, gender separation and karakia recitation.[79] His workshop, however, was divided, with one side reserved for experienced tohunga who observed tapu and the other for students who did not practise these observances.[80] He remained sceptical of the school's capacity to be a whare wānanga; he believed it was safer for the students to work in a more secularised environment than to expose them to the risk of transgressing poorly understood tikanga.[81]

These applied elements of whakairo rākau, tukutuku, kōwhaiwhai and kākaho linings for porches, interiors and façades were being attached to otherwise Western-style light timber and metal frame structures. This accelerated a trend of progressively abandoning traditional Māori building systems, in which these elements would have once been important weatherproofing elements and load-bearing, tensile or bracing members. Their decoration, connections and structural purpose had previously been conceived of in terms of a Māori physical world derived from metaphysical principles.

By the twentieth century, building regulations based on Western science required construction methods and materials to mitigate hazards such as fire and earthquake, and to prevent the spread of disease. Widespread deforestation, wetland

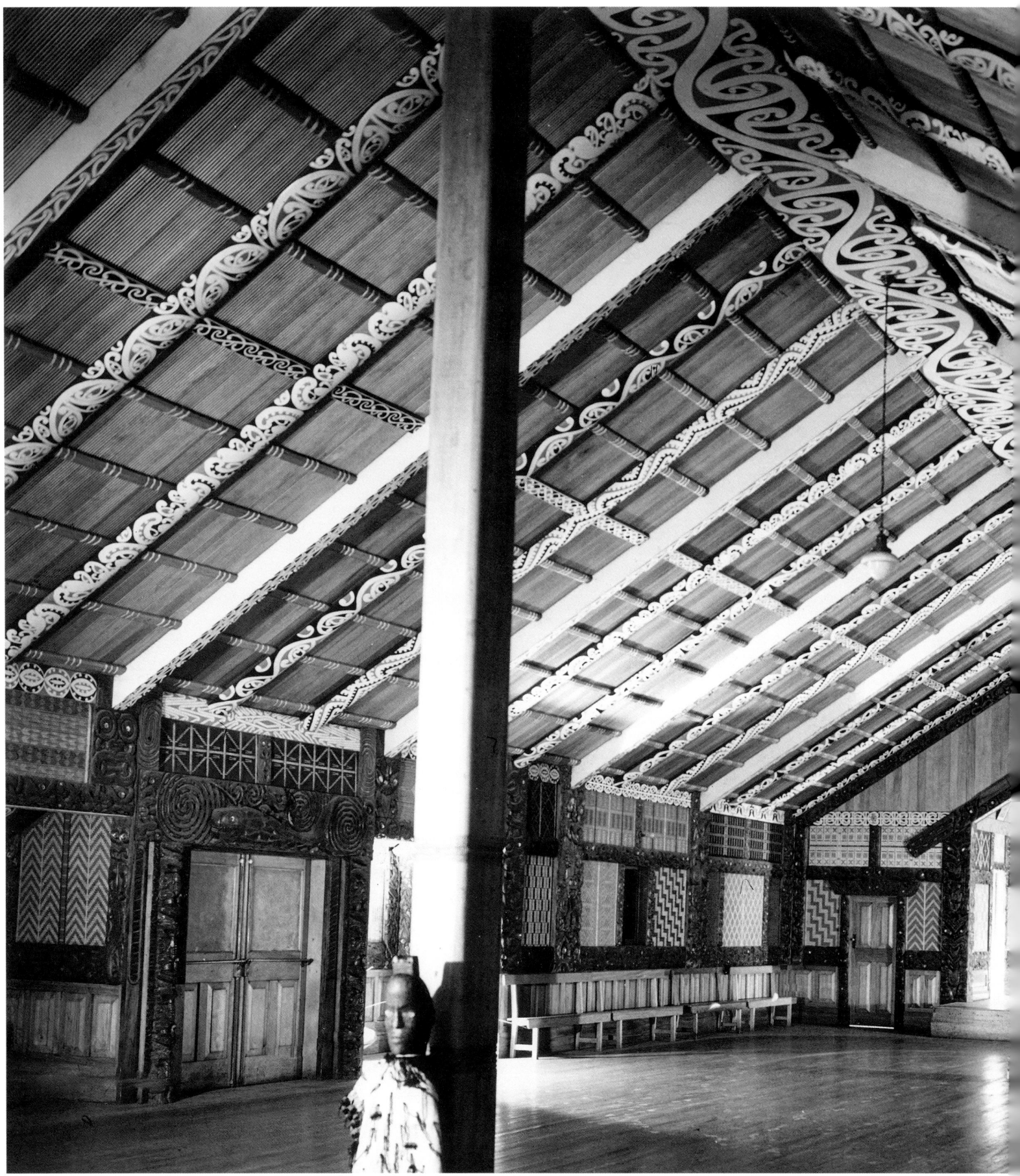

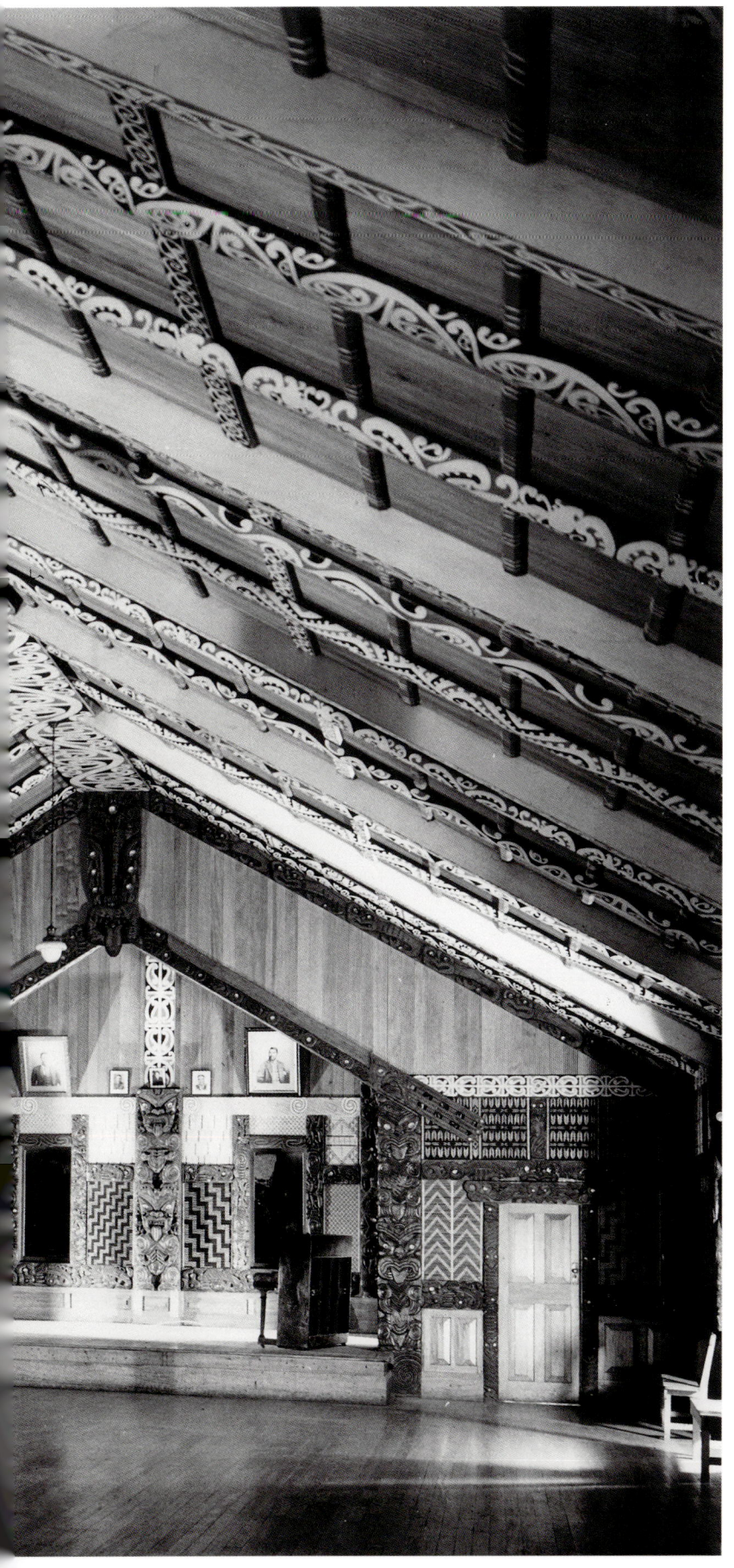

drainage and land loss meant that many nineteenth-century Māori building materials were no longer available to Māori, and those that were available were not permitted under building regulations. Non-flammable cladding materials such as weatherboard, iron and tiles and permanent foundations were now required under fire and building regulations. The school's Te Poho o Rāwiri (opened at Kaitī in 1930), Te Ikaroa a Māui (Waitara, 1936), Raukawa (Ōtaki, 1936), Tākitimu (Wairoa, 1938) and Whitirēia (Whāngārā, 1939) whare whakairo projects had concrete foundations, floors and lower walls; and a number of the school's projects had rigid metal frameworks, in compliance with earthquake regulations.[82] Side porches provided the alternative fire exit demanded by the fire regulations, and windows that opened gave improved ventilation. Glazing and electric lighting allowed light to penetrate the whare whakairo, which meant functions could go on into the evenings – although this met with some resistance from Ngata who, in 1929, complained that the regulations 'have done enough mischief by compelling rows of windows where there were none and letting light into places it had no business to pry into'.[83]

The revitalisation of marae participation was as important as the revival of art and architecture for Ngata and the school. His land-development scheme relied on Māori, particularly young adults, remaining in their communities to work as farmers on large, community-owned farming enterprises. Marae had to move with the times in order to make community life more appealing. Contemporary Māori preferred to sit on chairs and so speakers and performers needed a raised stage to be seen. Stages were incorporated into many of the school's projects, such as Te Poho o Rāwiri, Ruatepupuke III (Tokomaru Bay, 1934) and Tākitimu whare whakairo, and Rongomaitapui (Te Araroa, 1938), Taihoa (Wairoa, 1938) and Tawhiorangi (Ruatōria, 1938) wharekai.[84] Since the school modelled these stages and the proscenium arches on mahau (meeting house porches), Ngata described this innovation as

Te Poho o Rāwiri wharenui opened at Kaitī on 11 March 1930. The whakairo rākau, tukutuku, kōwhaiwhai paintings and kākaho linings continue to the inside and cover the contemporary constructional system. Seating along the walls and matai timber floors were included to allow for modern dances, which would attract the attention of the community's youth. The inclusion of a stage allowed speakers to be seen by audiences seated on chairs and its meeting house porch-like form enabled tikanga normally conducted on the external mahau, such as tangihanga, to be brought into this internal space.
William Hall Raine, Te Papa Tongarewa Museum of New Zealand, B.013096

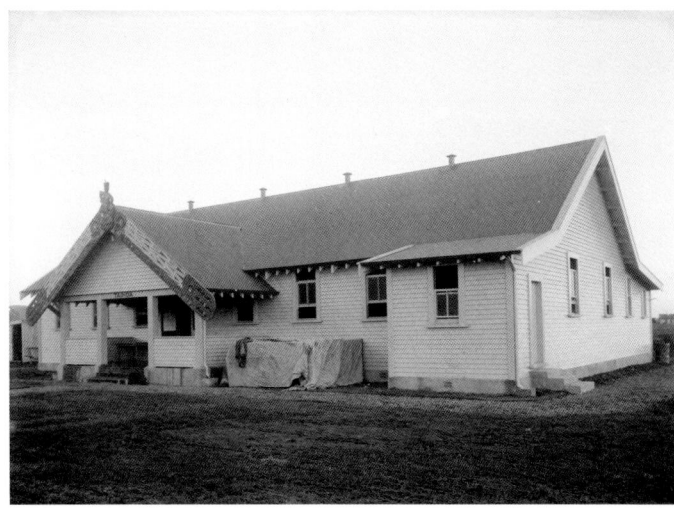

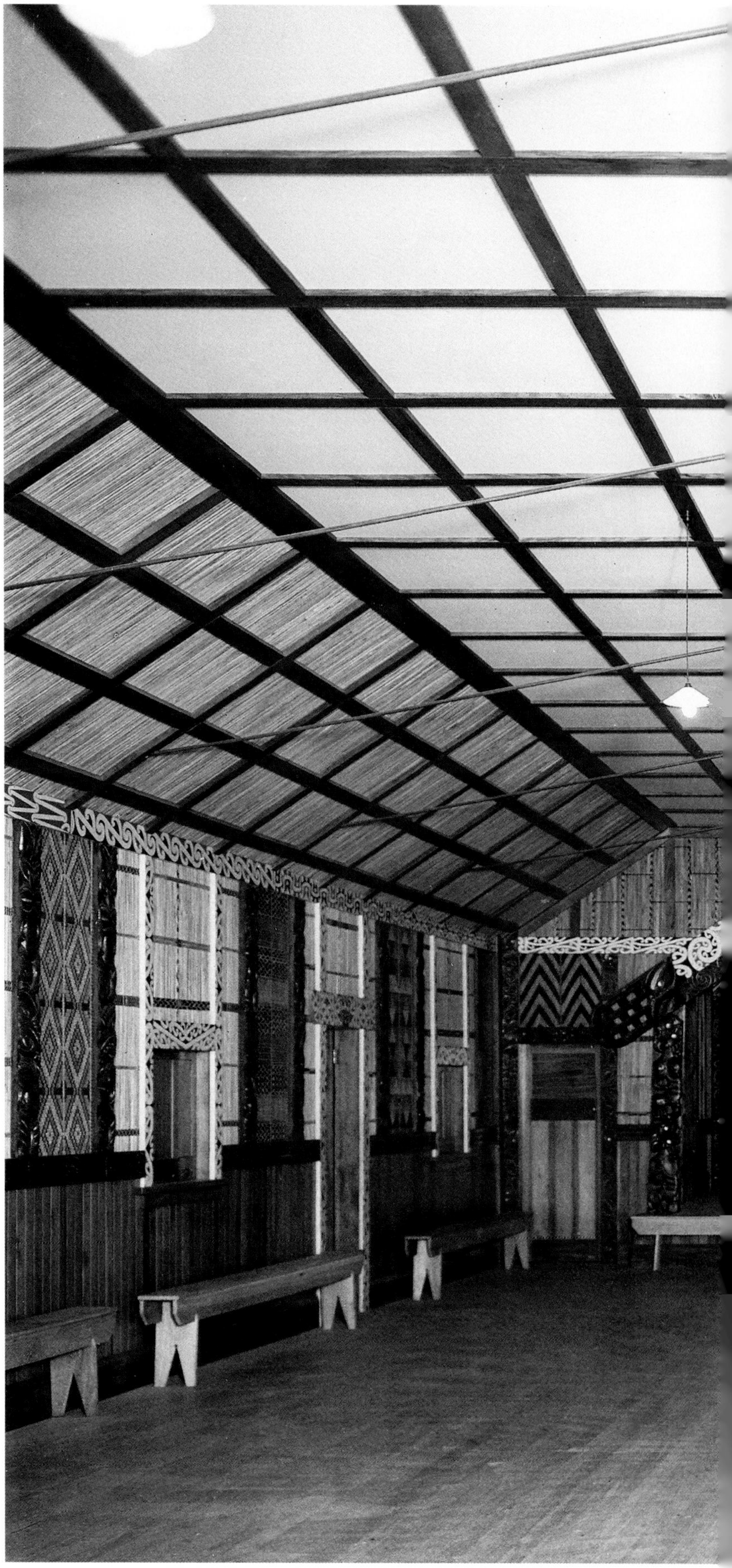

Interior and exterior of the Taihoa Marae wharekai opened in 1938 at Wairoa.
Alexander Turnbull Library, 1/2-051504-G; William Hall Raine, c.1930–1940, Te Papa Tongarewa Museum of New Zealand, B.012844

a 'house within a house – as the front of a Maori house with the audience seated on the marae or plaza before it'.[85] Metal structural framing enabled the main body of the school's marae buildings to be largely cleared of internal columns. Like a Pākehā community or dance hall, seating could be placed along the walls and wooden floors laid so that dances and other social functions could be held there.[86]

Ngata promoted permanent wharekai as essential, tapu-free companion buildings to whare whakairo, and they were fitted with Pākehā-style commercial kitchens and long tables.[87] Wharekai were not subject to tikanga and Ngata considered them an ideal place to display the work of novice carvers and tukutuku makers, and to accommodate the activities of children and young people when they were not being used for dining. A useful outdoor space, which Ngata regarded as a secondary informal marae, was formed between the whare whakairo and wharekai, enabling the continuation of discussion. The rise of wharekai, however, was a contributing factor in the decline of food storage and preparation architecture such as pātaka, whata, rua and kāuta, and in changes to Māori feasting habits and foods.

The precedents for many of the school's carved, stitched and painted elements were in the collections of the Auckland Institute and Museum and the Dominion Museum. Raharuhi Rukupō's masterpiece Te Hau ki Tūranga, the precedent for the overall proportions and decorative systems of a whare whakairo, stood in the Dominion Museum. The school

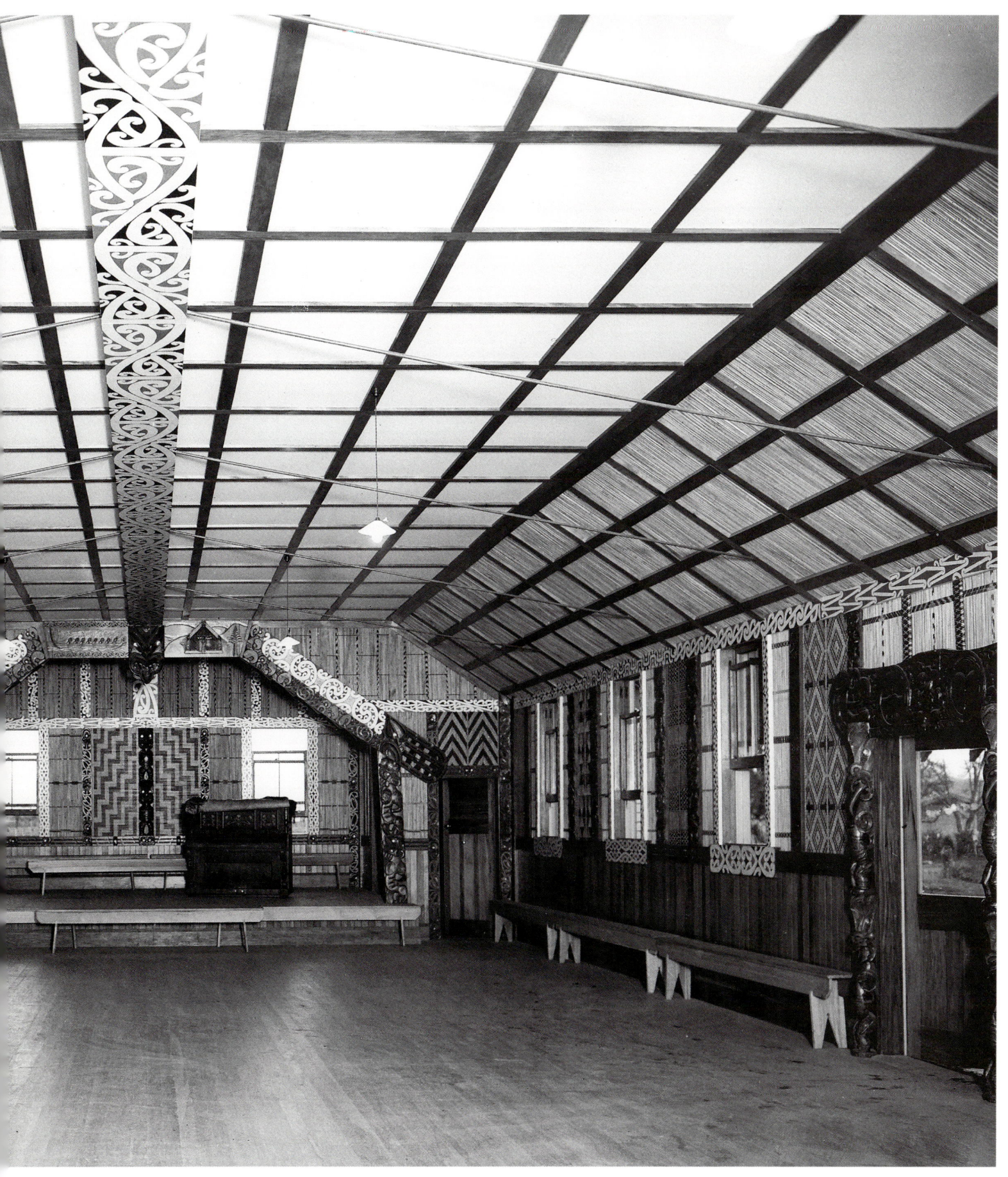

initially engaged with Te Hau ki Tūranga during the 1935 renovation, when staff and students replaced the tukutuku panels and extended the length of the house with additional poupou.[88] Ngata was a great admirer of the building – he described it as 'the finest flowering of Maori art' and claimed it as the prototype for the school's later projects, such as Te Ikaroa a Māui and Whitirēia.[89] He believed that whakairo rākau was at its stylistic peak at the time of the construction of Te Hau ki Tūranga, unadulterated by the changes to Māori artistic practice that occurred in the aftermath – and as a result – of the New Zealand Wars.[90] It was, therefore, a prototype that represented an age of unification before conflict.[91]

Despite an increase in demand for services, bolstered by funding for Te Tiriti o Waitangi centennial building projects, the school closed in 1937 – the same year that Harold Hamilton passed away.[92] By the time the last project was finished, the school had assisted in the construction and renovation of around twenty-one whare whakairo, two exhibition whare whakairo, ten wharekai, two assembly halls and six chapels or churches.[93] The objective of training a new generation of Māori artists was realised: many men and women had been trained in their own communities by experts who continued to find their own private commissions.[94] Most importantly, whare whakairo and their marae had been revitalised as forums for community cohesiveness, where te reo Māori was spoken and tikanga observed, even if the land-development projects they were associated with were not always successful. Because their makers had been trained to pass on their skills to the next generation, the whare whakairo became an enduring typology, setting the aesthetic and functional benchmark for all subsequent Māori buildings across the country for many decades to come.

### Tahupōtiki Wiremu Rātana

Not everyone agreed with Te Puea and Ngata's vision of a future for Māori arts and architecture as more secularised, iterative practices. Tahupōtiki Wiremu Rātana (Ngāti Apa, Ngā Rauru, 1873–1939), a leader from the Whanganui region, promoted advances in innovative Māori architectural design and challenged the marae-based leadership championed by Te Puea and Ngata – all the way to Parliament.

Rātana was initially a faith healer whose religio-political overtones attracted around 40,000 Māori followers – about one third of the Māori population – to the church he founded in 1925.[95] A core group of 400 established a settlement on Rātana's farm that became known as Rātana Pā, a name that recalled similar large-scale, multi-iwi 'pā' at Parihaka and Pāpāwai. The settlement was serviced by shops, a recreation complex and a school, as well as an extraordinarily large wharekai and seven dormitory-like wharepuni.[96]

In 1927, the movement's most important and influential building opened: the 1000-seat Temepara (temple). Like Hīona, the Temepara promoted the concept that Māori were akin to the Hebrews in bondage by referencing biblical temple architecture, although its form was based on Romanesque Revival cathedral buildings. Rātana's Temepara was a large, single-gable concrete structure with two domed belltowers on either side of its front face, buttresses (that performed no structural purpose), lancet windows and a barrel-vaulted interior. It is thought that the twin belltowers were based on a Japanese precedent, most likely the Roman Catholic Urakami Cathedral in Nagasaki, which opened the year after Rātana visited Japan in 1924 and was destroyed twenty-one years later in the atomic bombing.[97] The towers were named Ārepa and Ōmeka (Alpha and Omega), as the personification of Rātana's two sons and in recognition of the 'beginning' and 'end' of Rātana's spiritual mission. Painted around the inside walls of the Temepara were chains connected to te whetū mārama (the movement's star and moon symbol), representing the church's godhead of the Christian Trinity, ngā Anahera Pono (the faithful angels) and Te Māngai (Rātana's identity as the 'mouthpiece' of God).

The Temepara had a powerful formalism that inspired the construction and decoration of Rātana whare whakamoemiti (houses of praise) built elsewhere in the years after Rātana's death. Four were built in Northland. Te Rito o te Temepara Matua Hāhi Rātana was opened at Mangamuka in 1947 and Ngā Tapuwae o te Māngai in Te Kao in 1952. Both were originally weatherboard buildings that were much smaller than the Temepara and with simplified windows and towers. The design of Te Kao was based on a sketch made of the Temepara, and Te Kao's builders, Wiremu Peters and Paki Murupaenga, used the design again as the inspiration for Te Reo Pōwhiri whare whakamoemiti at Te Hāpua, opened in 1954.[98] Shortly afterwards, work began on another, Takutai Moana te Rohe at Ahipara, which was built in concrete and not completed until 1965.[99] A fifth church, at Raetihi in the

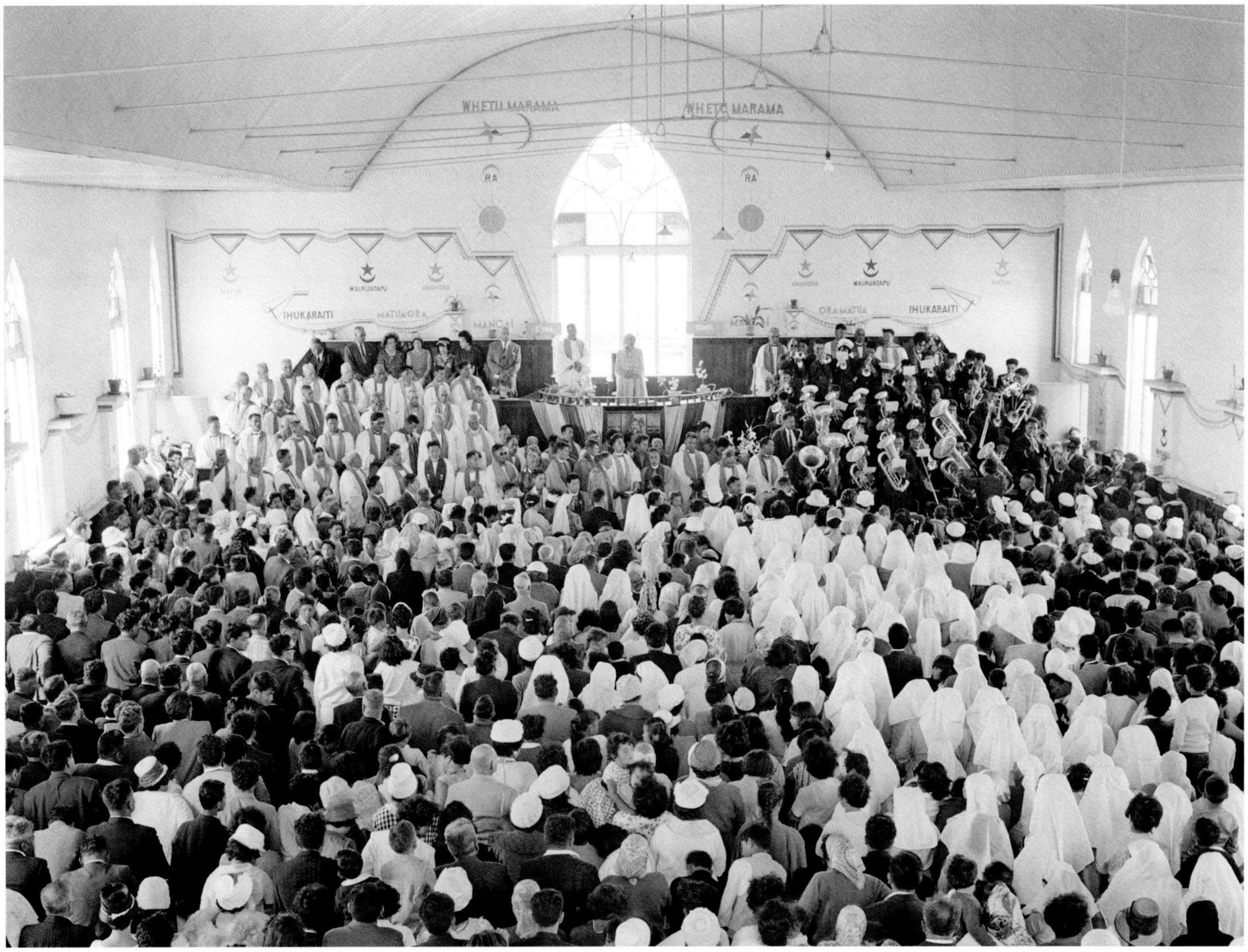

**Temepara interior, Rātana Pā, opened 1927.**
Ans Westra, 1963, copyright Ans Westra

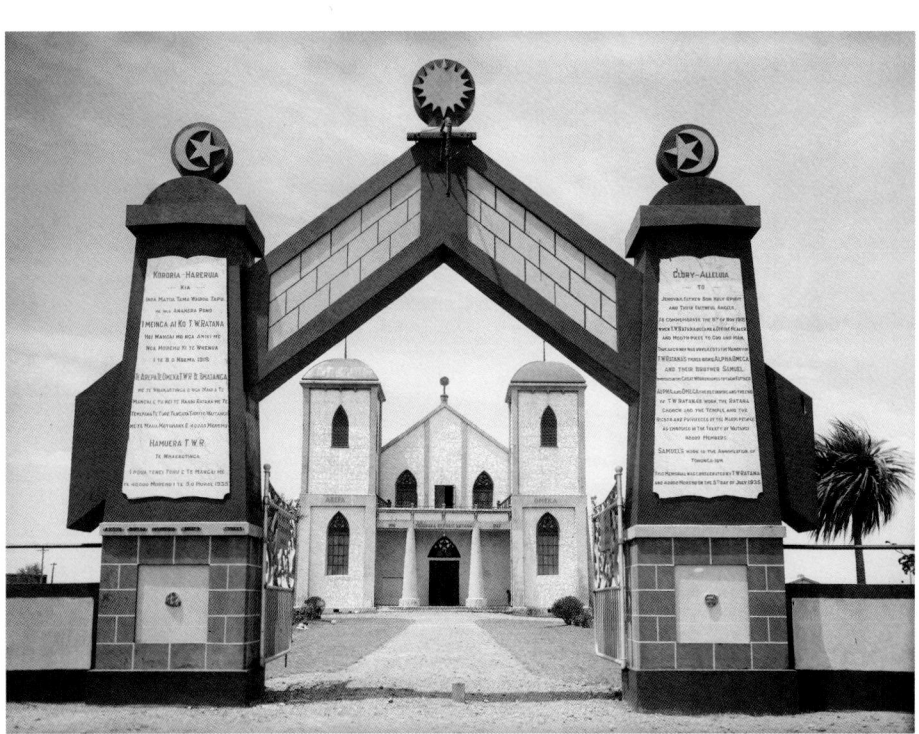

**Temepara, Rātana Pā.**
William Hall Raine, c.1930–1950, Te Papa Tongarewa
Museum of New Zealand, B.013035

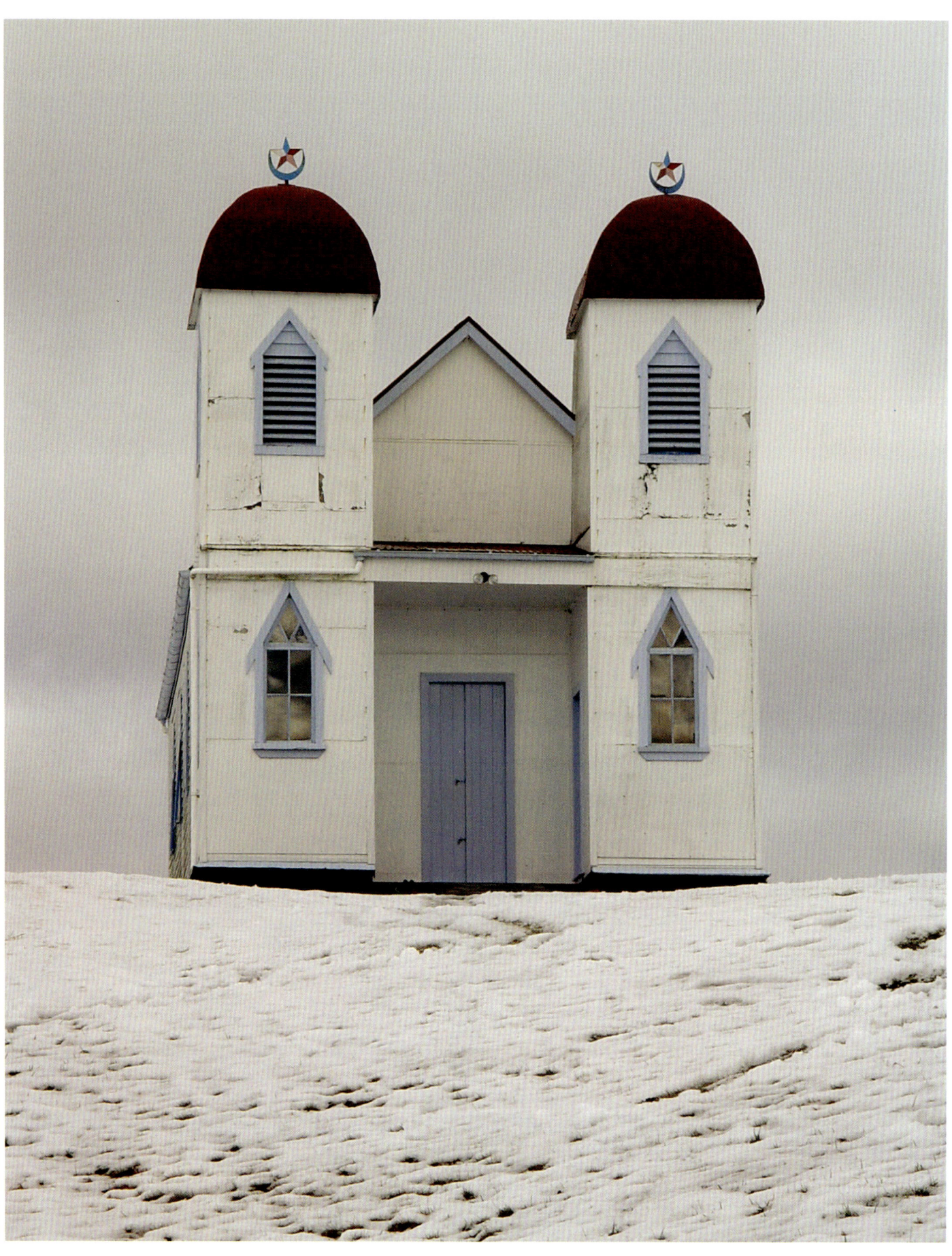

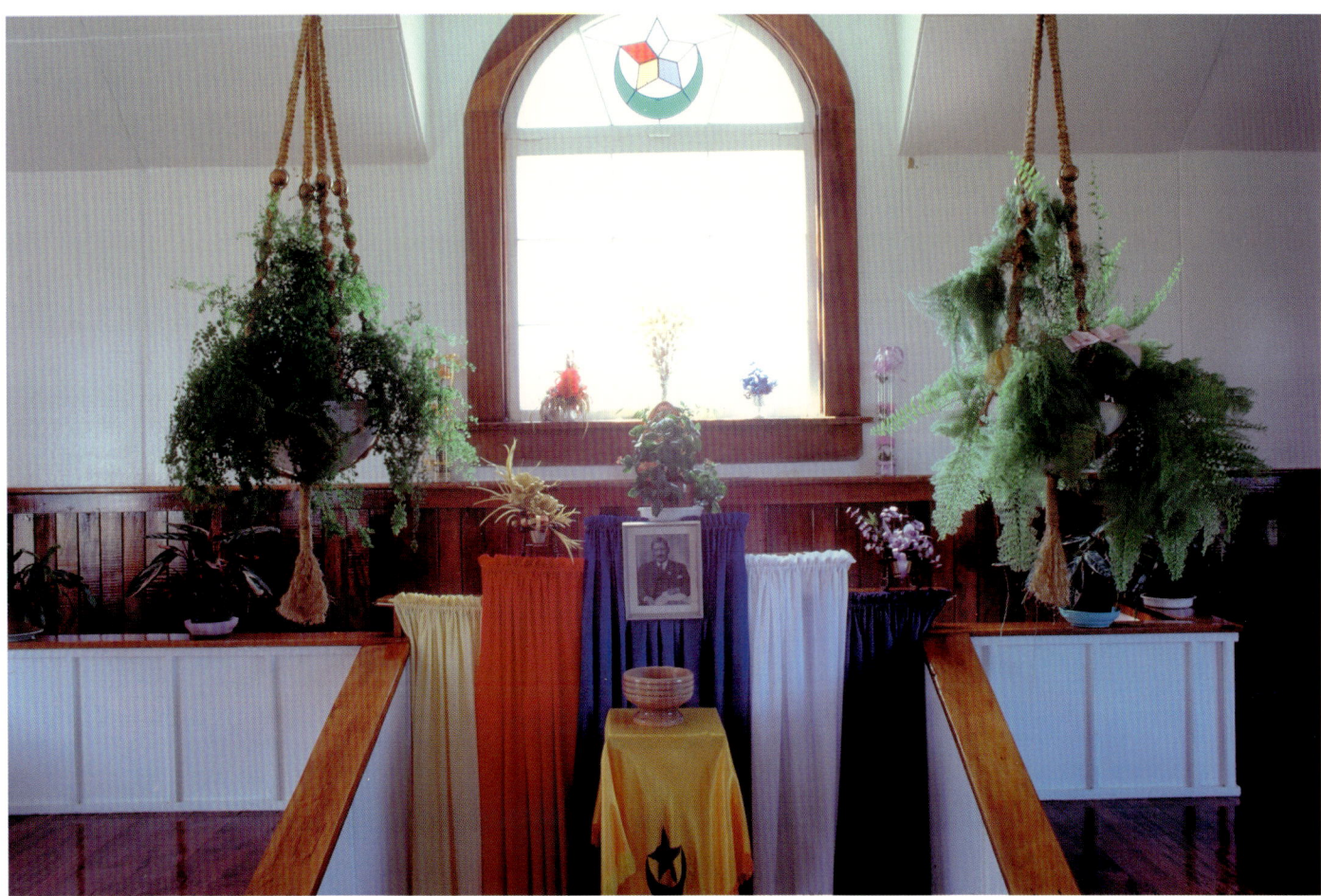

Rātana whare whakamoemiti at Te Kao.
Robin Morrison, Tāmaki Paenga Hira Auckland War Memorial Museum, PH-NEG-RMS-rSOP70-481

central North Island, was made to resemble the Temepara with the addition of two belltowers in 1957.¹⁰⁰

There have been many other buildings used as Rātana churches across the North and South islands. Although some of these are wharenui, the only carved building at Rātana Pā was the Whare Māori, a single-gable building that was decorated in the 1920s with whakairo rākau gifted by Ngāti Tūwharetoa from Te Ika a Māui meeting house built at Tūrangarere, near Taihape, in the nineteenth century.¹⁰¹ The Whare Māori became the repository for the crutches, spectacles and wheelchairs left over from Rātana's faith-healing sessions as well as tapu taonga, including mere pounamu, taiaha and tewhatewha, that Rātana encouraged his followers to relinquish. When these taonga were placed under Rātana's mana, they became safe through whakanoa – a form of tapu removal that Māori leaders sometimes used to demonstrate that their mana was greater than that of a previous rangatira or tohunga. The whakairo rākau of the Whare Māori were considered part of this past, and the building has sometimes been treated with trepidation and

Opposite: Rātana whare whakamoemiti at Raetihi.
photograph by Grant Bulley

Overleaf: Rātana whare whakamoemiti (branch churches).
Clockwise from top left: Ahipara, Te Kao, Mangamuka, Te Hāpua.
photographs by Grant Bulley

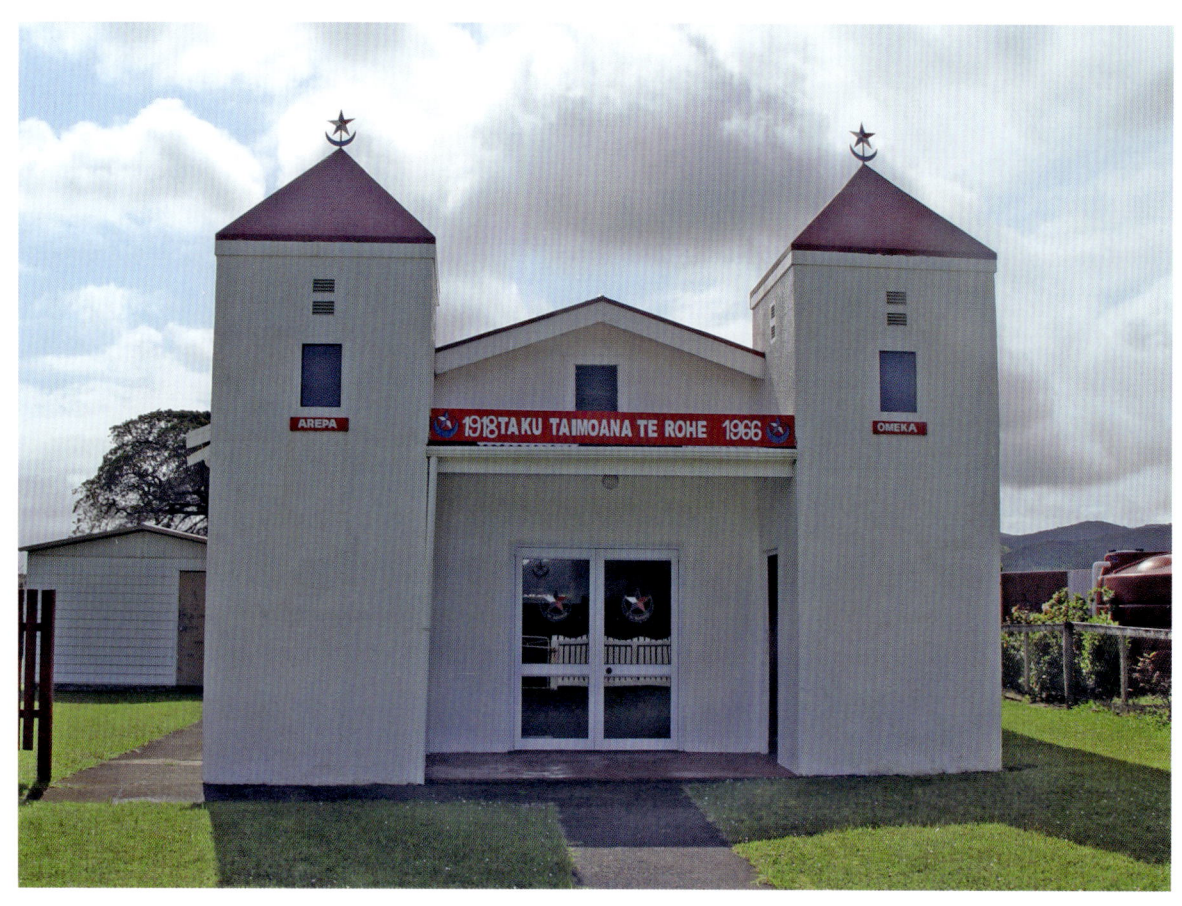

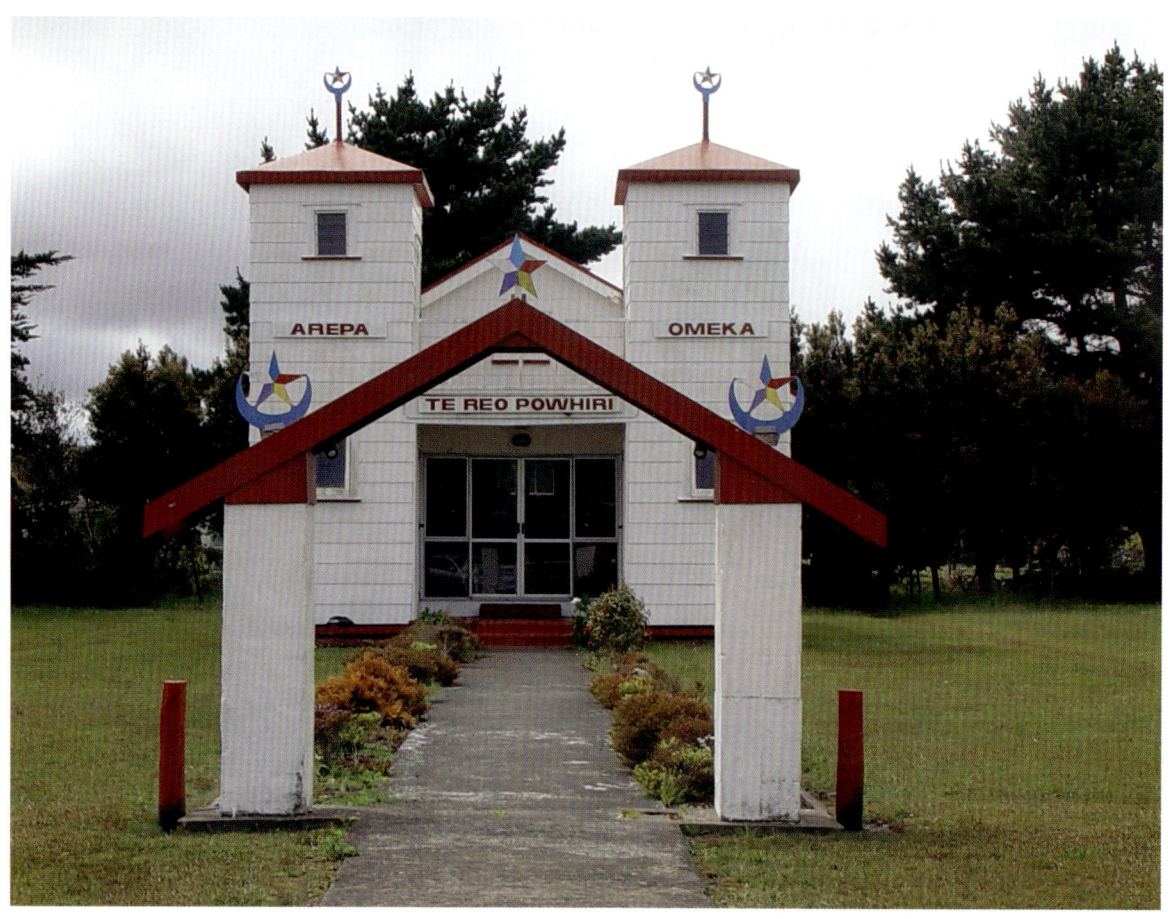

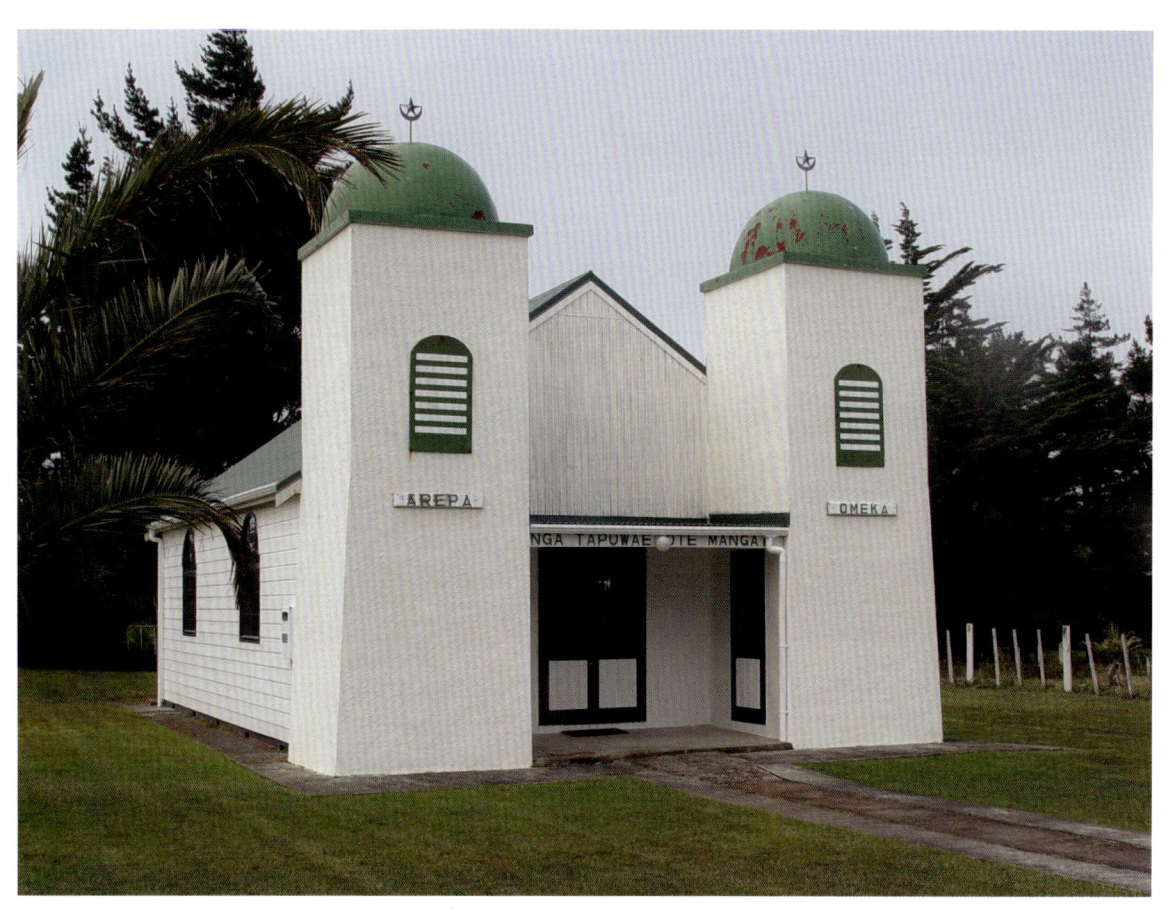

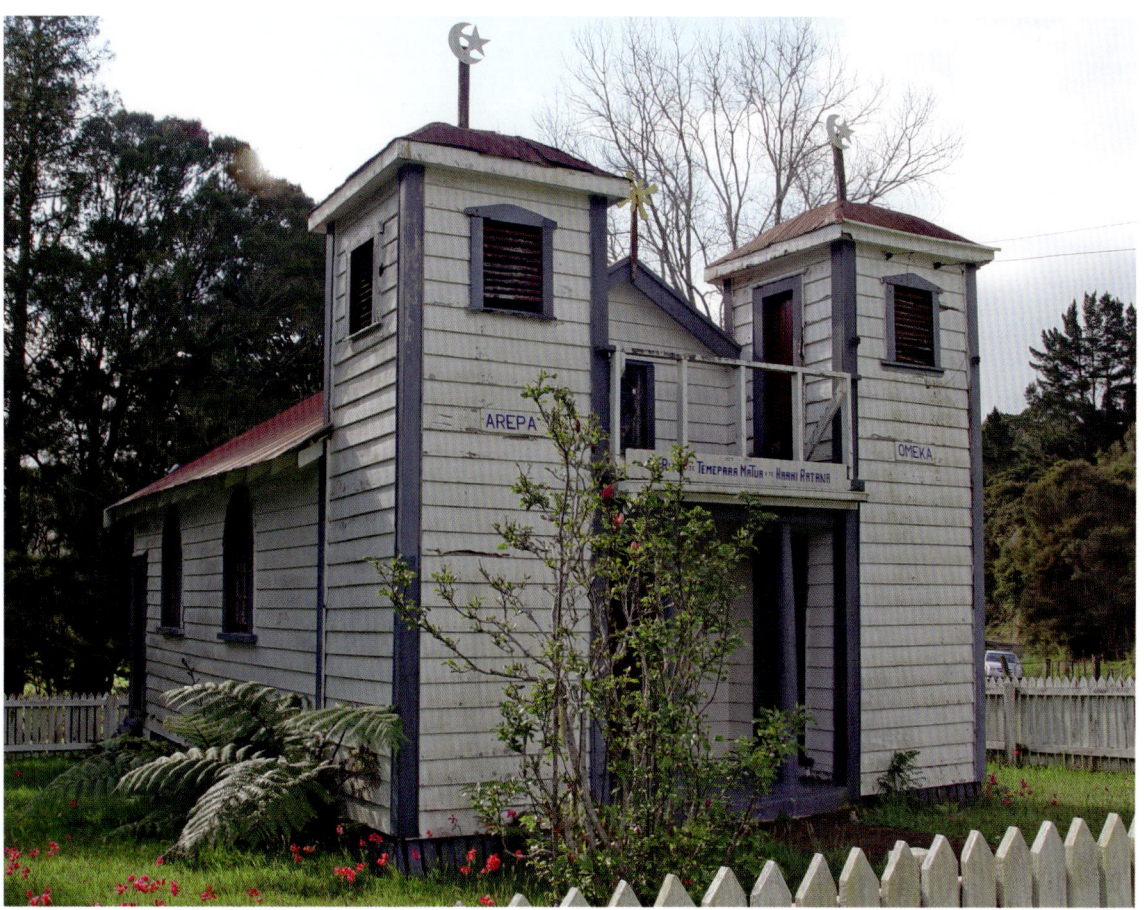

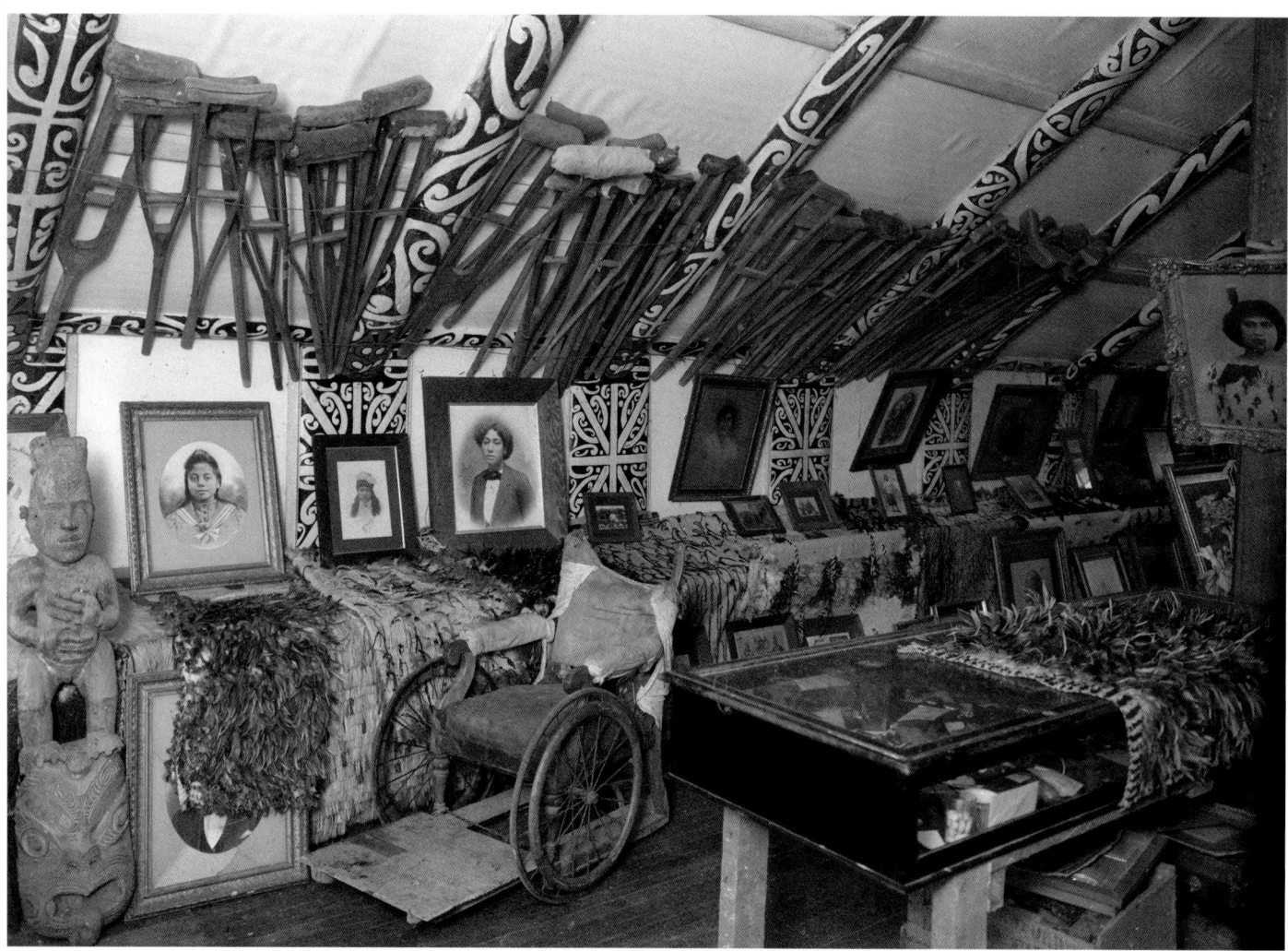

suspicion by followers as a consequence, although these feelings were not necessarily transferred to other whare whakairo in followers' own communities.

Rātana's relationship to marae architecture and its arts seems to have been ambivalent. He occasionally refused to observe tikanga on marae, which put further strain on his relationships with other leaders of the time, including Te Puea and Ngata, who came to regard him as a threat to their own movements for social reform. In 1924, after Rātana and his entourage visited the Mātaatua whare whakairo at the British Empire Exhibition in London, his press secretary Pita Moko released a statement to the *New Zealand Times* in which he declared: 'Our party is disgusted with the Maori Hut [Mātaatua] at Wembley, because it is only half Maori workmanship. The carvings are a poor example of Maori art. In comparison with the Burma exhibits the Maori Hut suggests to the public that we are low down in the scale of native races.'[102]

From the beginning of his mission, Rātana had immersed himself in James Pope's book *Health for the Maori*, which advocated the abandonment of tapu and the replacement of thatched houses with Western construction as measures to improve Māori health.[103] Rātana's mission followed these recommendations, and he would probably have had little regard for Te Puea's hybrid houses or Ngata's School of Maori Arts and Crafts projects.

Rātana's vision for the future was pan-tribal. His followers were required to relinquish their iwi affiliations on joining the movement, which automatically excluded them from participating in Ngata's land-development and School of Maori Arts and Crafts programmes. With no convergence of opinion on the social, religious and political future of Māori, there were no grounds for a shared Māori art and architectural vision. This divergence was manifest in the political opposition between Rātana and Ngata, and in 1936 the Rātana Party formed an alliance with the Labour Party,

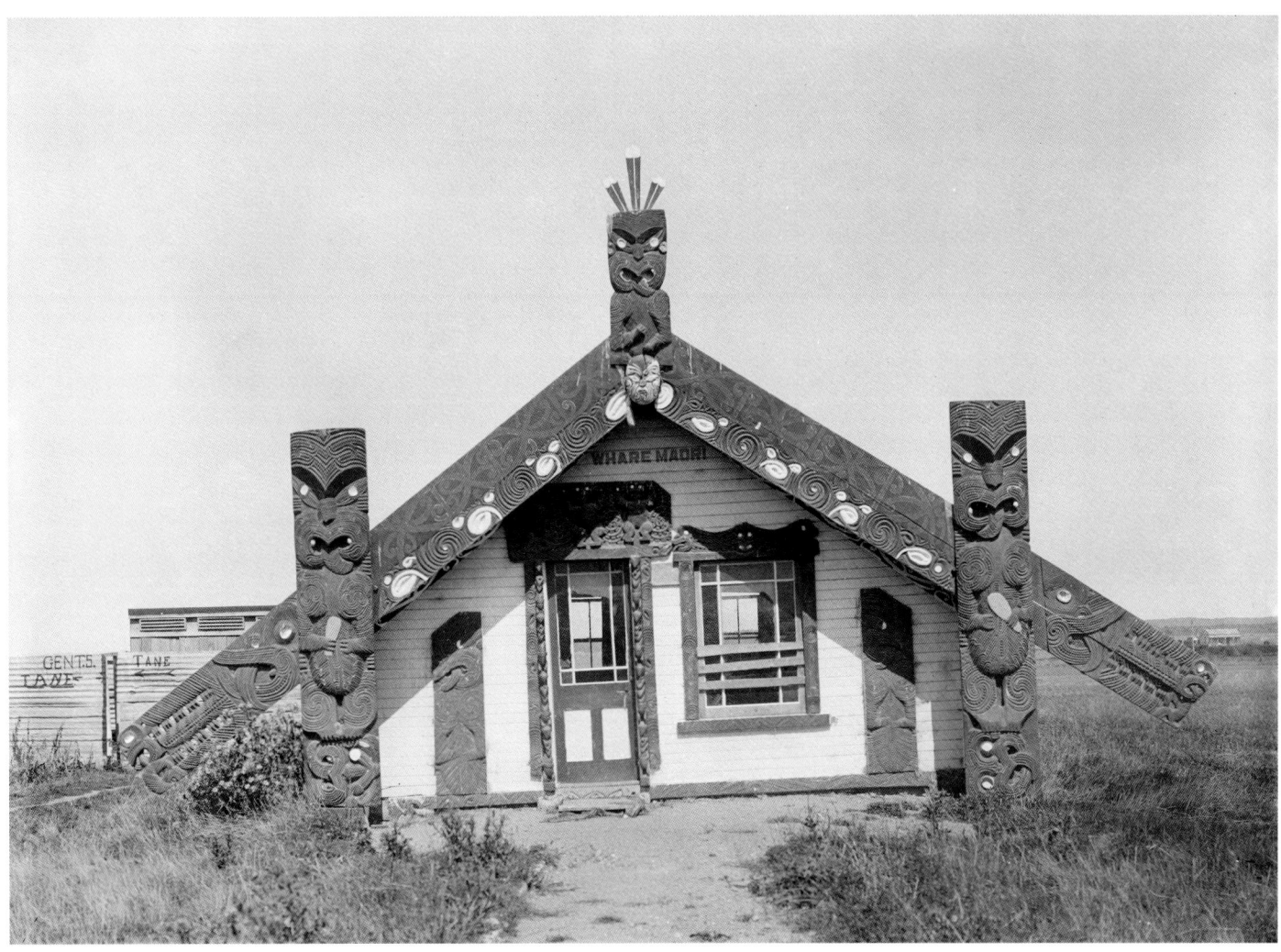

Whare Māori exterior, Rātana Pā, shortly after the whakairo rākau gifted by Ngāti Tūwharetoa were installed.
Alexander Turnbull Library, APG-1936-1/2-G

capturing all four Māori seats in the New Zealand Parliament within seven years, including Ngata's.

Having succeeded in converting many Māori around the country to his faith, with the exception of Ngata's people on the East Coast, Rātana turned his attention to the Māori king and his followers. He established a secular building at Matamata, within Waikato territory. This was the multi-purpose hall at Ōmeka Pā, opened in 1937 as a centre for his movement's political activities, a place to attract Kīngitanga supporters, and a centre for organising Waikato land claims.[104] Behind the hall's Spanish Mission-style weatherboard façade was a post office, billiards room, shop, storeroom, recreation area, projection room and large-scale dining room and dormitory.[105] Seven of the Māori migratory waka were painted on the front façade of the Ōmeka hall – pre-dating by one year the carved captains on Te Puea's Tūrongo House. Within two years of its opening, after a disagreement with local elders,

Opposite: Interior of Whare Māori, Rātana Pā, showing crutches and a wheelchair left over from Rātana's faith-healing sessions as well as taonga relinquished by followers.
William Hall Raine, c.1930–1950, Te Papa Tongarewa Museum of New Zealand, B.013004

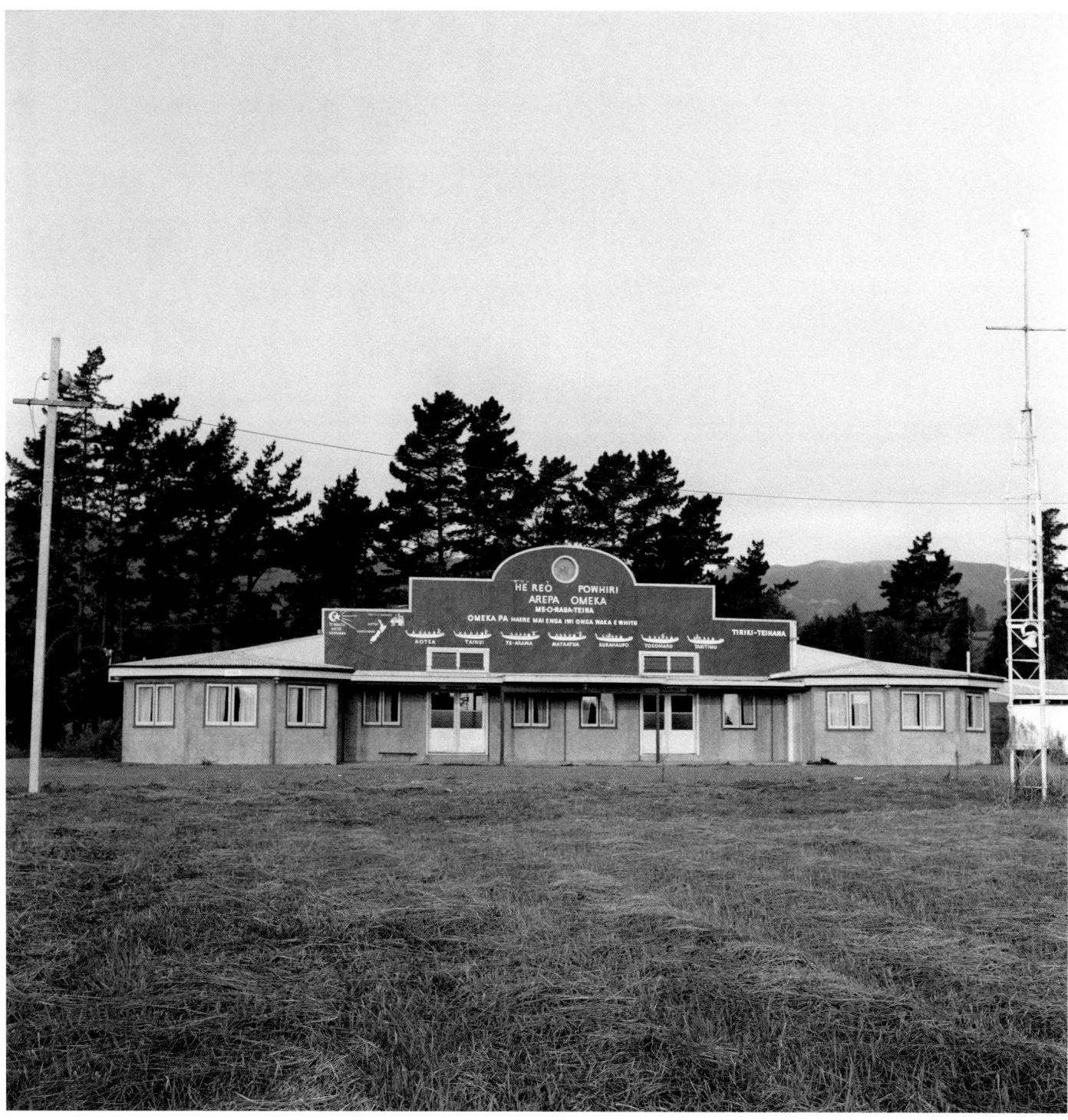

Ōmeka hall, Matamata, opened in 1937.
Ans Westra, Alexander Turnbull Library, AW-0356,
copyright Ans Westra

**Opposite: An early photograph of the completed Manuao at Rātana Pā.**
William Hall Raine, c.1930–1950, Te Papa Tongarewa Museum of New Zealand, B.012977

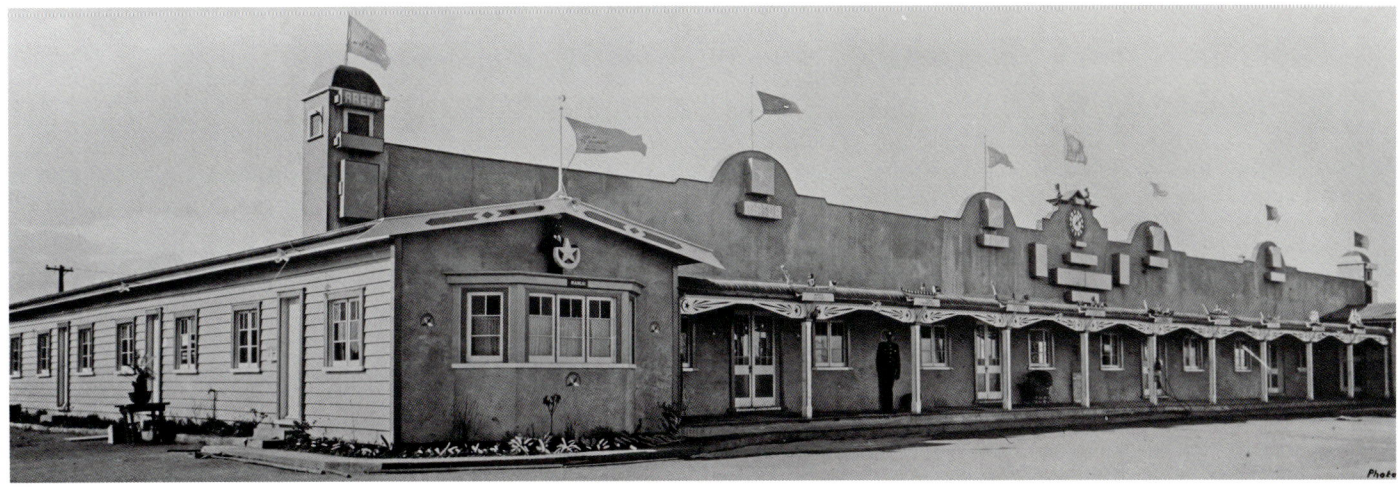

Rātana relocated his mission to Rātana Pā, although Ōmeka continued to function as a Rātana centre.[106] Back at Rātana Pā, he built a nationally focused political centre called Manuao (man-o-war), based on a similar Spanish Mission-style design and using the same builders.[107] The long façade united four existing houses, which were still used for sleeping, faith healing, cultural practice, dining and dancing, and added printing, postal, church and storage facilities.[108] Again, models of seven migratory waka – alluding to the national objectives of the movement – adorned the façade, lined up above the veranda roof; and a further two vessels – Tasman's *Heemskerck* and Cook's *Endeavour* – referred to the arrival of Pākehā and the potential of political partnership through the Labour–Rātana alliance. Illuminated pictures of Rātana, Ārepa, Ōmeka and Rātana's wife, Te Whaea, were fixed to the parapet: this was a more naturalistic personification than that used on the Temepara's belltowers or, indeed, the ancestral depictions within wharenui. The building was named after the man-o-war seen in a dream by Te Whaea that would promote and defend Rātana's religio-political mission; and it was painted green – the colour of Rātana's political persona, the Piriwiritua.[109] Although they were quite different in appearance, the two lantern towers at either end of the Manuao and Ōmeka façades echoed the Temepara's belltowers. This presented a unifying architectural language across the Rātana movement's political and religious buildings.

### Conclusion

By the mid-twentieth century, Māori art and architecture were at a crossroads. The Rātana movement had employed an innovative approach to design: it added the Romanesque Revival and the Spanish Mission styles to an oeuvre that had already embraced the Gothic Revival, continued the practice of figurative illustration, and further extended the large-scale kāinga model pioneered at Parihaka, Pāpāwai and Maungapōhatu. Te Puea and Ngata championed a different approach based on iwi and hapū cohesiveness, centred on the marae and supported by customary arts and architecture. They and their artists made important choices about the role of tikanga in the schools of art that rose in place of the whare wānanga. These two futures – one based on Rātana's spiritually infused innovation and the other on Te Puea and Ngata's more secularised traditionalism – were irreconcilable socially, politically and artistically. Despite Rātana's pre-eminence as a spiritual and political leader, and Te Puea and Ngata's localised influence in the central and eastern North Island, it was the whare whakairo that prevailed as the enduring architectural style and vehicle for the perpetuation of many (but not all) related Māori arts. Education had always been a shared objective of the arts institutions that Te Puea and Ngata founded, and the artists trained in those institutions found work across the country and passed on their knowledge, ensuring the ubiquity and the perpetuation of their practice. Concessions to building regulations meant that the work of these specialists was regarded as art, rather than architectural practice, because of its applied nature, and this would have a significant effect in how their work was received by the next generation of Māori artists and art institutions.

# TE ARAITEURU PĀ AT THE 1906 NEW ZEALAND INTERNATIONAL EXHIBITION
DEIDRE BROWN

Te Araiteuru – the Māori pā built for the 1906 New Zealand International Exhibition in Hagley Park, Christchurch – was a place where different Māori and Pākehā perspectives about the past, present and future of Māori art and society converged. The exhibition proclaimed the 'achievements' of the country to two million visitors – more than twice the national population – through social, industrial and agricultural displays, following the example of other large-scale international expositions held around this time.

Although Pākehā exerted some control over the design of the pā and procurement of the taonga in it, Māori were more than just participants in the creation and operation of Te Araiteuru. As Amiria Salmond observes, 'here the display, intended by the show's organisers as an entertaining tourist spectacle, became a fully functioning marae or meeting place under Māori control'.[1]

Together with a team of Whanganui tohunga whakairo, Hōri Pukehika led the creation of a towering waharoa that was the gateway through the outer palisades of Te Araiteuru pā. The Ngāti Tarāwhai tohunga whakairo Neke Kapua and his sons Tene and Eramiha were also commissioned to produce work for the 'outer pā', based on older whakairo rākau in the collections of the Colonial Museum in Wellington and illustrated in Augustus Hamilton's 1896 book on Māori art.[2] Relocating to Christchurch, they completed a pātaka, which was moved to the Whakarewarewa Village after the exhibition. They were also responsible for a magnificent waharoa to the inner pā (now in Te Papa Tongarewa Museum of New Zealand) that followed the design of an earlier gateway at Maketu, as illustrated by Horatio Robley. Kapua and Pukehika were among the few surviving long-handled toki experts and their work contrasted strongly with the chisel-led carving practised by younger tohunga elsewhere in the country at the time.

The inner pā was a reinterpretation of a mid-nineteenth-century kāinga and featured wharepuni (said to be of a variety of styles), a 'tohunga's house', two whare kāuta brought from the Whanganui, and the Wharepuni-a-Māui whare whakairo. The latter was leased from Thomas Donne, who had commissioned the whare from the Ngāti Tarāwhai tohunga whakairo Tene Waitere. After the exhibition it was displayed in the Government Gardens in Rotorua before being sold to Linden Museum, Stuttgart in 1911.[3]

Several waka were exhibited in Te Araiteuru. Many were from the Whanganui River, except for one long waka taua known as *Taheretikitiki* that had been sent to the exhibition by Mahuta, the third Māori king, and had originally been carved for Pāora Tūhaere of Ōrākei of the Kaipara River in 1880.[4] Kahu huruhuru and tāniko-making were demonstrated by Tiria Hōri from Ngāti Tuera.[5] While the concern that Māori were a 'dying race' because of depopulation and colonisation continued to be misreported in the press, Te Araiteuru presented a culture that was still intact through its customs, customary art and the 500 inhabitants who occupied and performed in the pā over the five and a half months of the exhibition.

Te Rangi Hīroa (who was the exhibition's medical superintendent and one of the Māori performance artists) and Apirana Ngata were active in the creation of Te Araiteuru, a project that no doubt shaped their early ideas about the future of Māori art. Indeed, the Araiteuru project could be regarded as a precedent for Ngata's School of Maori Arts and Crafts, opened twenty years later. Both men demanded an exacting adherence to older whakairo rākau, observed and copied from illustrations and museum collections, and both reimagined the wānanga system of training as a master–apprentice relationship undertaken within an increasingly capitalist economy. Ngata employed Eramiha Kapua to be the lead tohunga whakairo at the school because of his knowledge of long-handled toki carving. Furthermore, the Araiteuru pā project and the school's other projects provided an opportunity for tohunga to produce large-scale work that situated Māori art within a kāinga or community setting where Māori people, language and customs prevailed.

Hōri Pukehika using a long-handled toki to form a pou at the 1906 New Zealand International Exhibition.
Alexander Turnbull Library, 1/2-005558-F

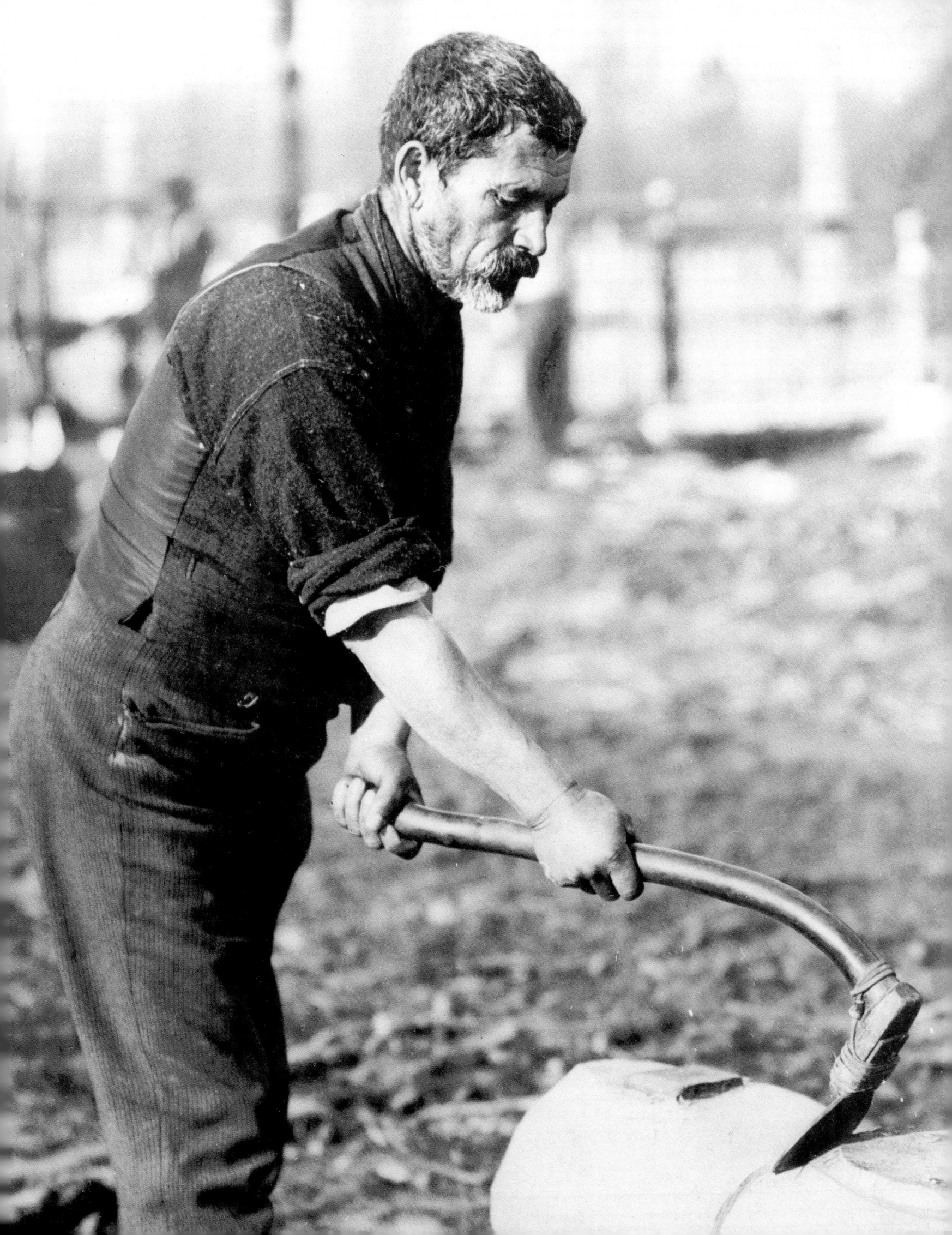

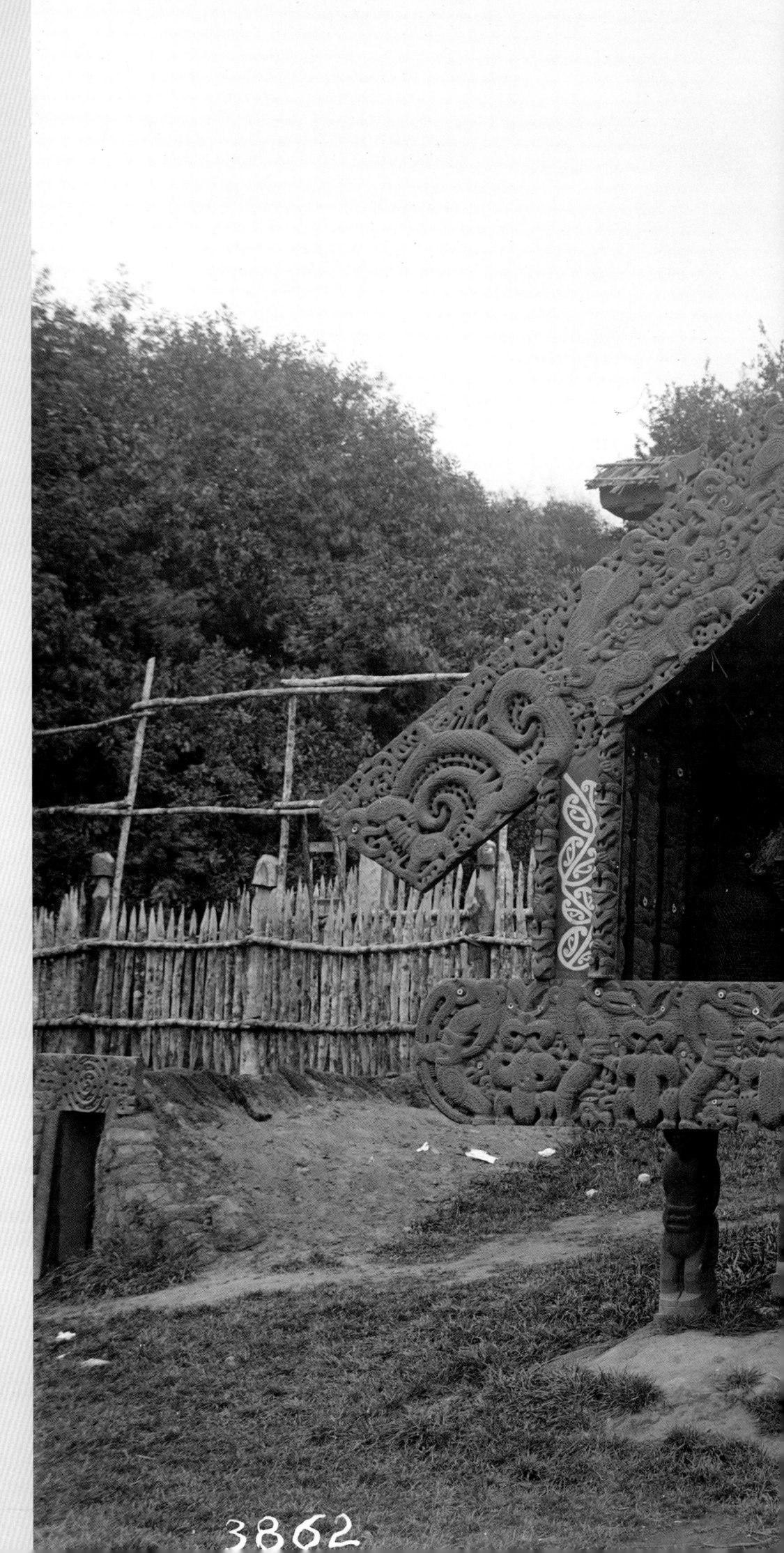

**Pātaka and waharoa at the 1906 New Zealand International Exhibition.**
James McDonald, 1906, Te Papa Tongarewa
Museum of New Zealand, MU000523/001/0079

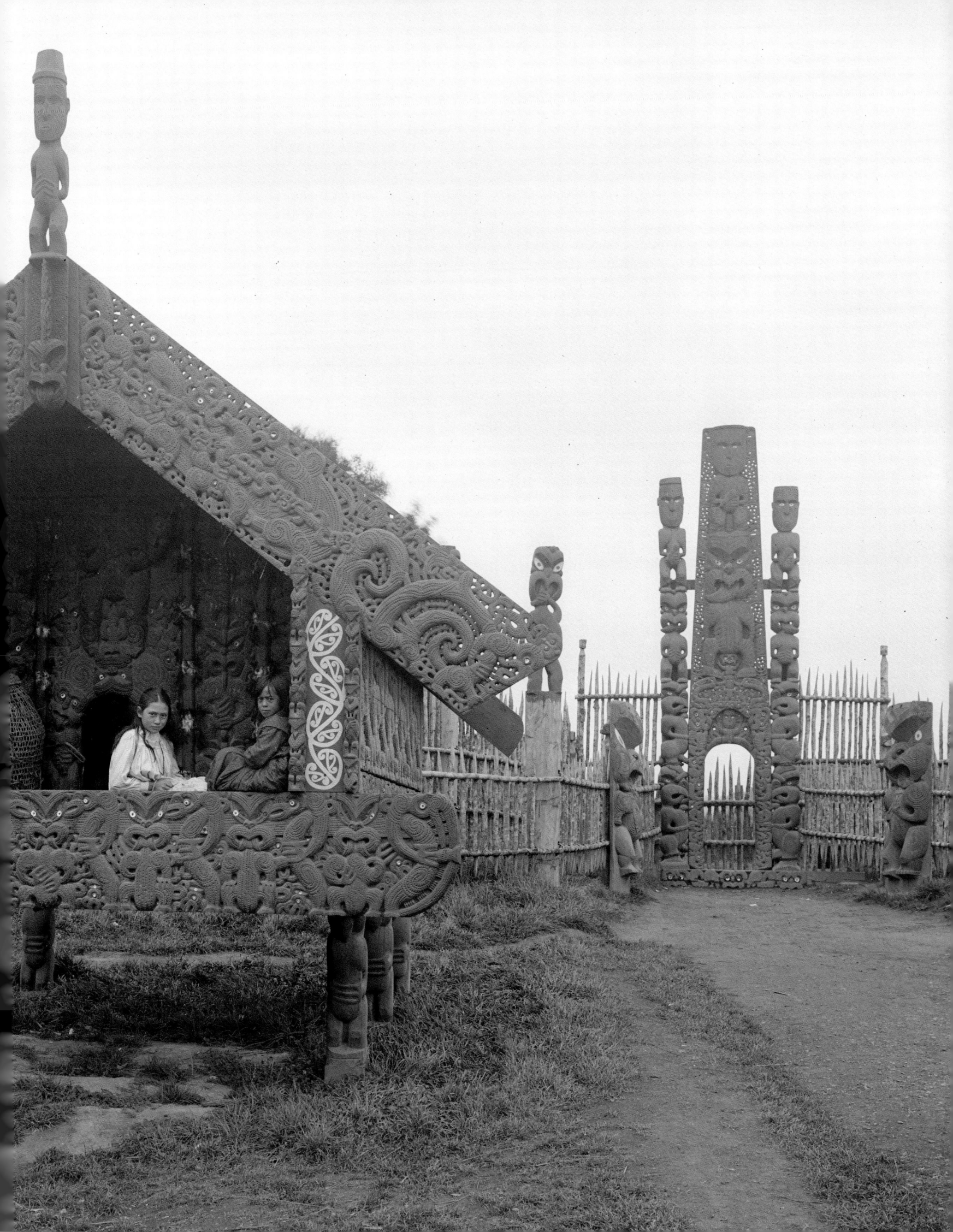

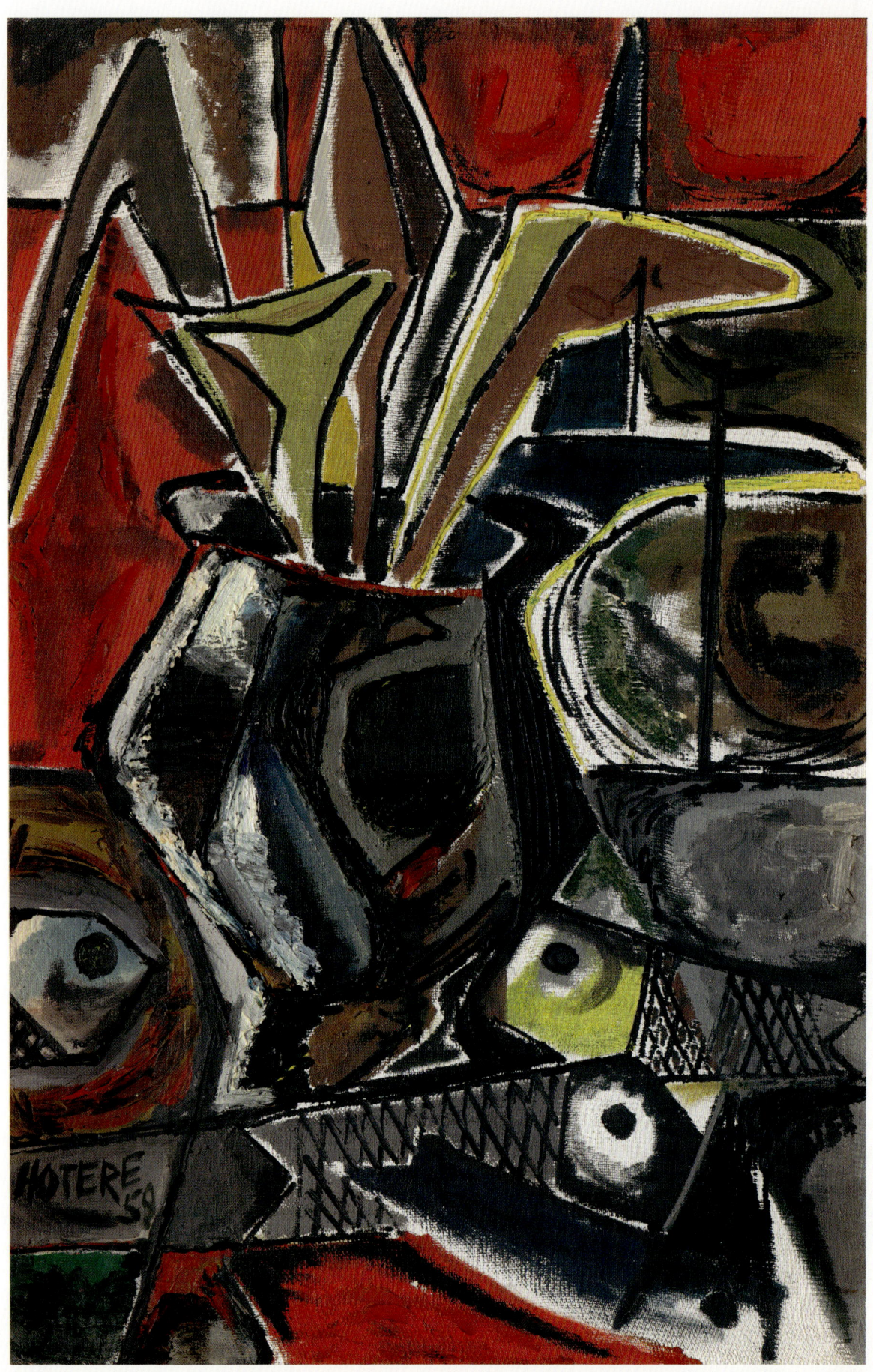

# 15 THE EMERGENCE OF CONTEMPORARY MĀORI ART 1950-1975

## JONATHAN MANE-WHEOKI

*Ka pū te ruha, ka hao te rangatahi.*

*The old net is cast aside, while the new net goes fishing.*

In the first century since the signing of Te Tiriti o Waitangi, Māori and non-Māori artists had continued to operate in two distinct practice worlds located within their own cultural spheres. Museums and the Māori tourist villages of Whakarewarewa and Ōhinemutu were largely the only places for a one-way and highly mediated artistic encounter between cultures. All this would change in the space of a generation. From the 1950s, Māori began to publicly exhibit art that engaged seriously with the styles, materials and techniques of modern Western European art, especially as they were manifested in the work of Georges Rouault, Pablo Picasso, Constantin Brâncuși, Jean Arp, Henry Moore, Barbara Hepworth and the postwar School of Paris tachistes. A desire to engage with modernism and an opportunity to nurture talent through Western art education contributed to the conditions that established a contemporary Māori art movement that straddled two artistic traditions, often struggling to be recognised by either of them. In the years since then, the contemporary Māori art movement has gathered momentum, thanks to the perseverance of the first generation of contemporary Māori artists.

**Ralph Hotere, *Still life*, 1959**
oil on board, 900 x 595mm, Te Papa Tongarewa Museum of New Zealand, 1996-0020-2, purchased 1996 with New Zealand Lottery Grants Board funds, by permission of the Hotere Foundation Trust

In 1940 the centenary of the signing of Te Tiriti was commemorated despite the fact that New Zealand was engaged in World War Two. The first event of the year was the opening, on 6 February, of the whare rūnanga at Waitangi, a magnificent expression of customary carving and weaving. A touring *National Centennial Exhibition of New Zealand Art,* launched in Dunedin two weeks later, contained no examples of Māori art, although one artist, Oriwa Haddon (Ngāti Ruanui, 1898–1958), is described in the catalogue as a 'Maori artist'. In his introduction to the catalogue the curator, Alexander McLintock, justified the exclusion of Māori art from his foundational survey of New Zealand art with this melancholy observation: 'when the first Europeans arrived in New Zealand, the country possessed in its Maori art a unique native culture which the impact of civilisation was ultimately to destroy'.[1] This perceived situation, and Pākehā perceptions of their responsibility for creating it, caused R. O. Ross, president of the Auckland Society of Arts, to remark in his 1943 annual report:

> May I be permitted to draw attention to one aspect of Arts Crafts, where practically nothing has been even attempted much less accomplished? We have in Auckland Province 60,000 Maori people who have a rich artistic culture of their own; but this Society of Arts does nothing to encourage them to develop and strengthen it. Is a renaissance, a new flowering of the Polynesian genius for sculpture and painting, so unlikely that we need do nothing about it, or is our outlook so insular, so parochial that we cannot find interest or duty outside the narrower outlook of the European arts?[2]

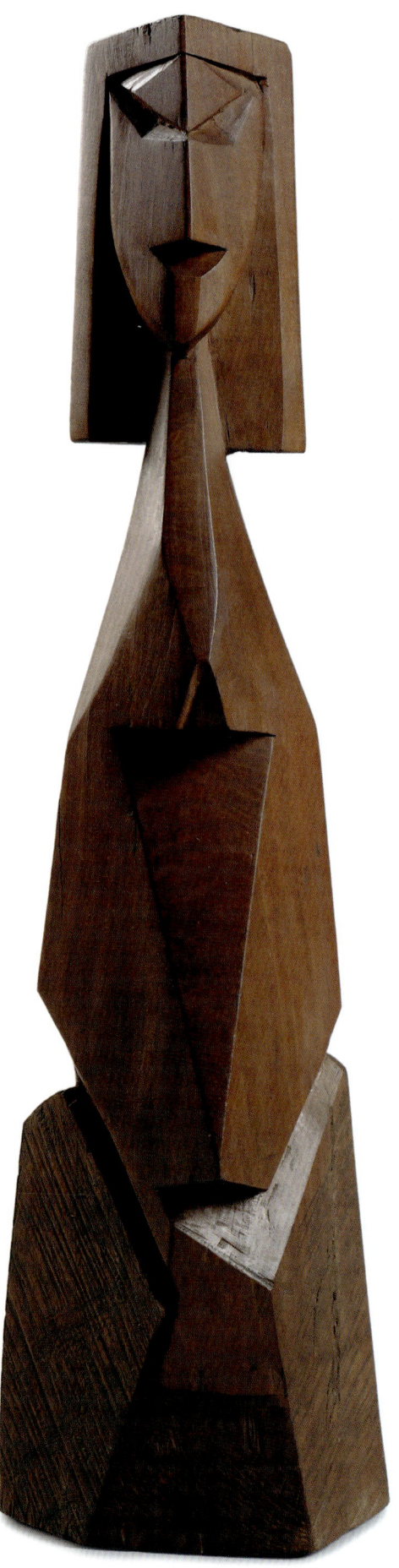

Ross seems likely to have been talking about the kind of 'Arts Crafts' commonly found in Pākehā art society exhibitions – painting, sculpture, prints, and the applied and decorative arts, all Western European art forms. Some Māori were intrigued by this type of practice in relation to their own. Apirana Ngata interpreted the Gottfried Lindauer oil-on-canvas portraits of Māori sitters at the Lindauer Gallery in Auckland in 1901 in terms of tikanga Māori: he described them as 'te ata whakairo a te tohunga Pakeha' or the 'shadow carvings of the European expert' – an analogy reiterated by other Māori visitors to the exhibition, at least one of whom looked forward to the day when Māori could paint like Lindauer.[3]

The misperception that Māori art was a dead or dying tradition persisted in Aotearoa New Zealand until well into the 1960s. Writing in the *Encyclopedia of New Zealand*, Stewart Bell Maclennan, director of the National Art Gallery, concluded that, 'No Maori artist of stature has yet arrived. The process of integration has isolated the Maori of today from the living meaning of the arts of his forefathers, and his culture must, from now on, be one with his European forefathers.'[4] Elsewhere in the *Encyclopedia*, in his 'Maori Art' entry, Jock McEwen took exception to:

> the habit of ethnologists to study Maori art as if it had come to an abrupt end on the arrival of the European settlers in New Zealand and to regard post-European work as being of little importance. It is necessary to point out, however, that the major forms of Maori art have never died out and that there is a continuous tradition from pre-European times to the present.[5]

This continuity had come from a concerted campaign of Māori artistic revitalisation and recovery, instigated by Ngata and the Maori Women's Welfare League. But even with developing, if not flourishing, Māori and Pākehā art communities, by 1940 neither seemed, or needed, to be making meaningful contact, connection or conversation with the other. Although individual Māori had taken up easel painting (Haddon, from the late 1920s and Pauline Yearbury [Ngāpuhi, 1927–1977], from the early 1940s) and photography (Ramai Rongomaitara Hayward [née Te Miha/Miller, Ngāti Kahungunu, Ngāi Tahu, 1916–2014], from the late 1930s) these were isolated examples and they did not, at this time, constitute a school or movement.

THE EMERGENCE OF CONTEMPORARY MĀORI ART 1950–1975

### The first contemporary Māori art exhibitions

By the 1950s, Māori studying fine arts at tertiary institutions were beginning to extend ideas about what Māori art was and what a Māori artist could be. In June 1957, when Muru Walters (Te Aupōuri, Te Rarawa, 1935–2024) was asked about 'modern Maori art, the carving of the present day, for example', he replied that 'to his eye, it had not yet bridged the gap between old and new; that some modern carvers seem content to repeat the old forms endlessly without considering how these apply to modern conditions'.[6] Exactly one year later, in 1958, Walters had joined four other Māori art teachers from Northland in 'the first Maori art exhibition seen in Auckland',[7] held at the Adult Education Centre. This was, in fact, the first group exhibition of contemporary Māori art anywhere. The *Auckland Star* critic observed that the show had its 'crudities':

> But throughout are the strong lines and sweeping rhythms, the gusto and the naiveté, that stamped the workmanship of the exhibitors' forebears. And a part of the new look is a play of colour, such as the old Maori did not know, and in the instance of Muru Walters, colour applied with fine perception.[8]

What this indicates is a recognition that the painters in the group – Walters, Ralph Hotere (Te Aupōuri, 1931–2013), Kāterina Mataira (Ngāti Porou, 1932–2011)[9] and Selwyn Wilson (Ngāti Manu, Ngāti Hine, 1927–2002) – were expressionists. As sculptor and carver Arnold Manaaki Wilson (Ngāi Tūhoe, Ngāti Tarāwhai, 1928–2012) recalled, 'The new Maori work done at that time was experimental, was really bringing out the forceful, the highly emotive'.[10] *Blue Faces*, one of Walters's three abstract paintings in the exhibition, is a vigorously expressive work, reminiscent of the 'primitivist' tachism of the most advanced European modernists of that time. Arnold Wilson's sculptures and carvings the critic described as being 'of exceptional interest … for he has applied the elements of ancient symbolism with modern conceptions of the timeless'.[11] Arnold Wilson's ability to straddle two traditions, more especially to engage with Western European art traditions in his own Māori terms, was pointing to new directions for Māori art.

In developing their hybrid aesthetic, the sculptors in the group had studied at first hand the carving of Henry Moore,

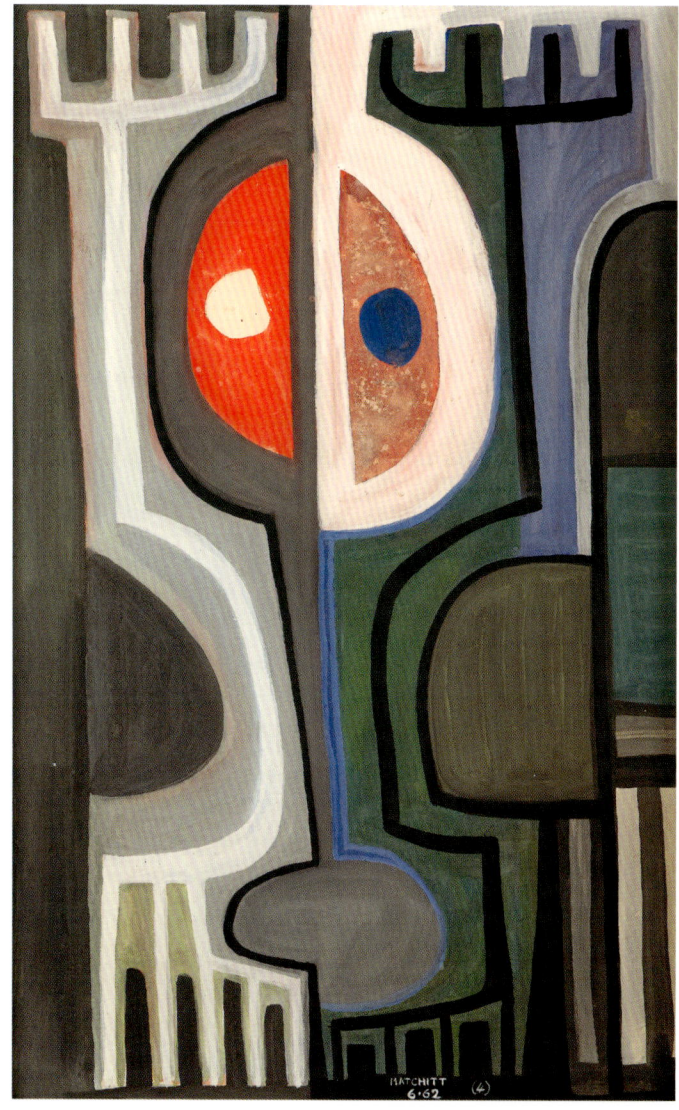

**Paratene Matchitt,** *Whiti te ra*, 1962
gouache on board, 675 x 430mm, Te Papa Tongarewa Museum of New Zealand, 2003-0019-1, purchased 2003

Opposite: **Arnold Wilson,** *Mihaia te Tuatahi*, 1965
wood (pūriri), 748 x 140 x 208mm, Te Papa Tongarewa Museum of New Zealand, 1999-0009-1, purchased 1999 with New Zealand Lottery Grants Board funds

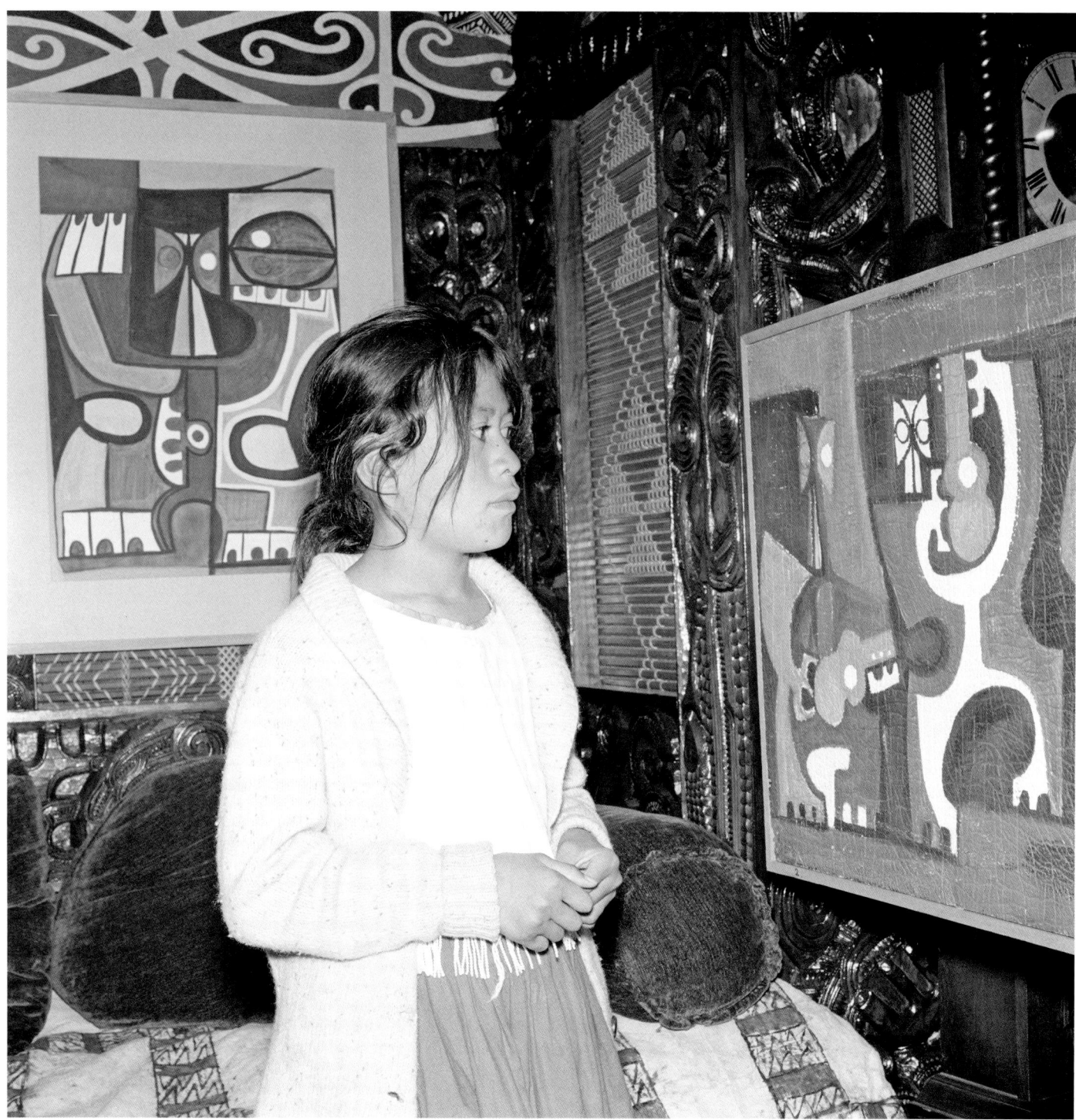

A girl looking at a painting by Paratene Matchitt in the wharenui Māhinaarangi, during the first Māori Festival of the Arts, Ngāruawāhia, 1963.

Ans Westra, 1963, Alexander Turnbull Library, AWM-0643-12-F, copyright Ans Westra

Opposite: **Buck Nin,** *The canoe prow*, **1965**

oil on board, 558 x 813mm, Te Papa Tongarewa Museum of New Zealand, 2000-0022-2, purchased 2000 with New Zealand Lottery Grants Board funds

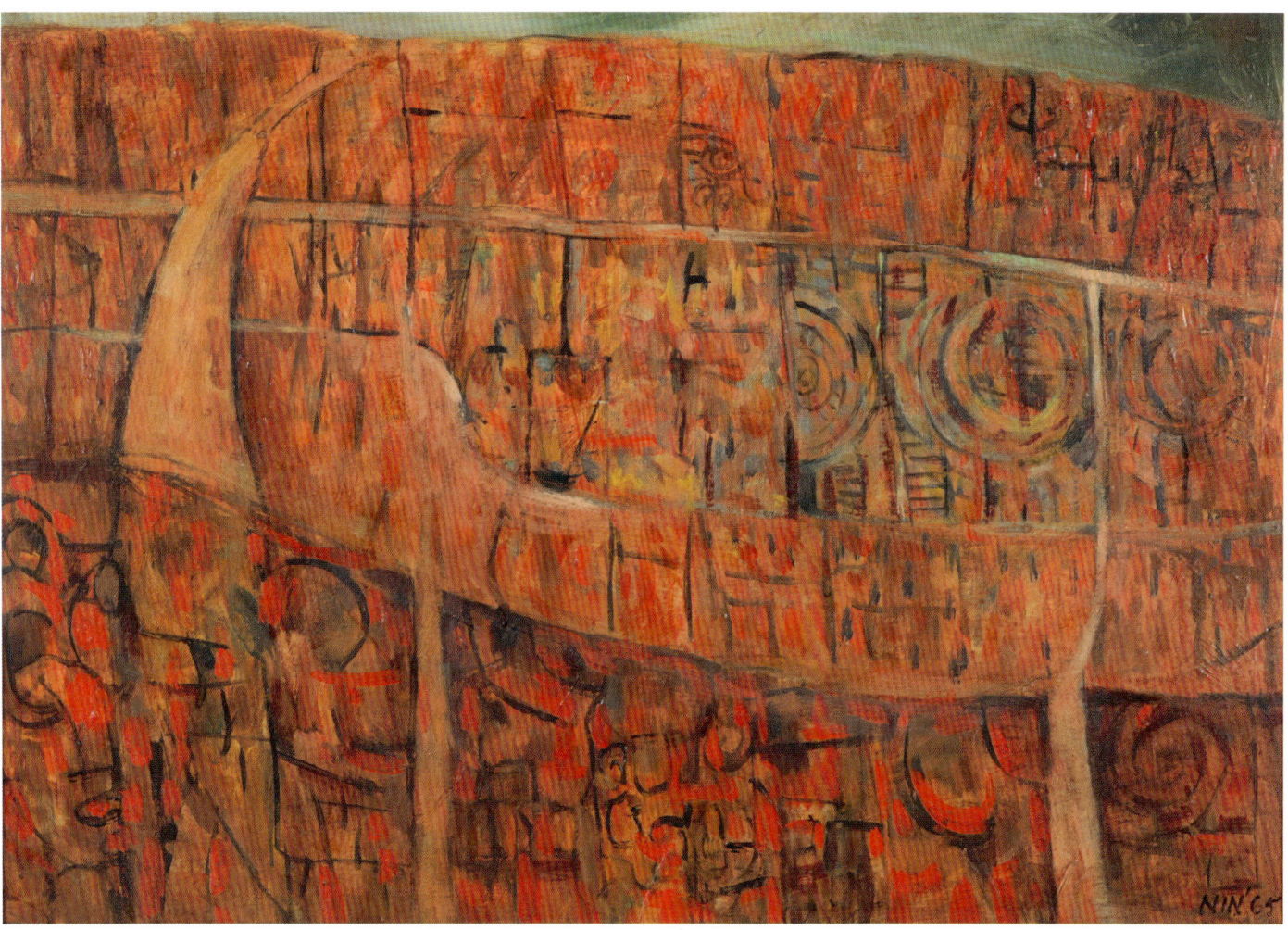

whose survey exhibition in Auckland in 1956 was hugely influential on New Zealand art;[12] and they had acquainted themselves, through illustrations in books, with the direct carving of other modernists such as Barbara Hepworth and Constantin Brâncuși. The painters in the group were inspired by the Paris School's 'primitivism' and the work of artists such as Georges Rouault and Jean Dubuffet. But of all European modernists it was Picasso whom Māori artists looked to as their model. Many years later, one artist suggested that Picasso was the founding father of modern Māori art, while another referred to him as 'our old koroua' – our elder.[13] It was the likes of that generation of Māori artists that an artist from the following generation described as putting 'Picasso in the pā'.[14]

In December 1963 a national grouping of contemporary Māori artists was represented at the first Maori Festival of the Arts held at Tūrangawaewae, Ngāruawāhia. These included Paratene Matchitt (Ngāti Porou, Te Whānau-ā-Apanui, Te Whakatōhea, 1933–2021), Selwyn Muru (Te Aupōuri, Ngāti Kurī, 1937–2024), who earlier that year had exhibited six paintings at the Auckland Society of Arts;[15] and Arnold Manaaki Wilson, now numbered 'among the most promising younger artists working in New Zealand today'.[16] In his sculptures Wilson 'endeavoured to marry European and Māori art to give "a true New Zealand art".'[17]

'This modern movement in Maori expression is barely five years old and subject to many changes in direction,' as Baden Pere (Ngāti Kahungunu, Rongowhakaata, Te Aitanga a Māhaki, 1922–2012) and Buck Nin (Ngāti Raukawa [Horowhenua/Manawatū], Ngāti Toa, 1942–1996) declared in November 1966 in their foreword to the catalogue of *New Zealand Maori Culture and the Contemporary Scene* – the first curated art show of its kind to be held in a public institution, the Canterbury Museum. They add, 'This exhibition permits only a glimpse of the new idioms and motifs which have emerged during the past five years.'[18] The exhibition suggested that a school or movement of Māori artists was emerging, and it could be found in the

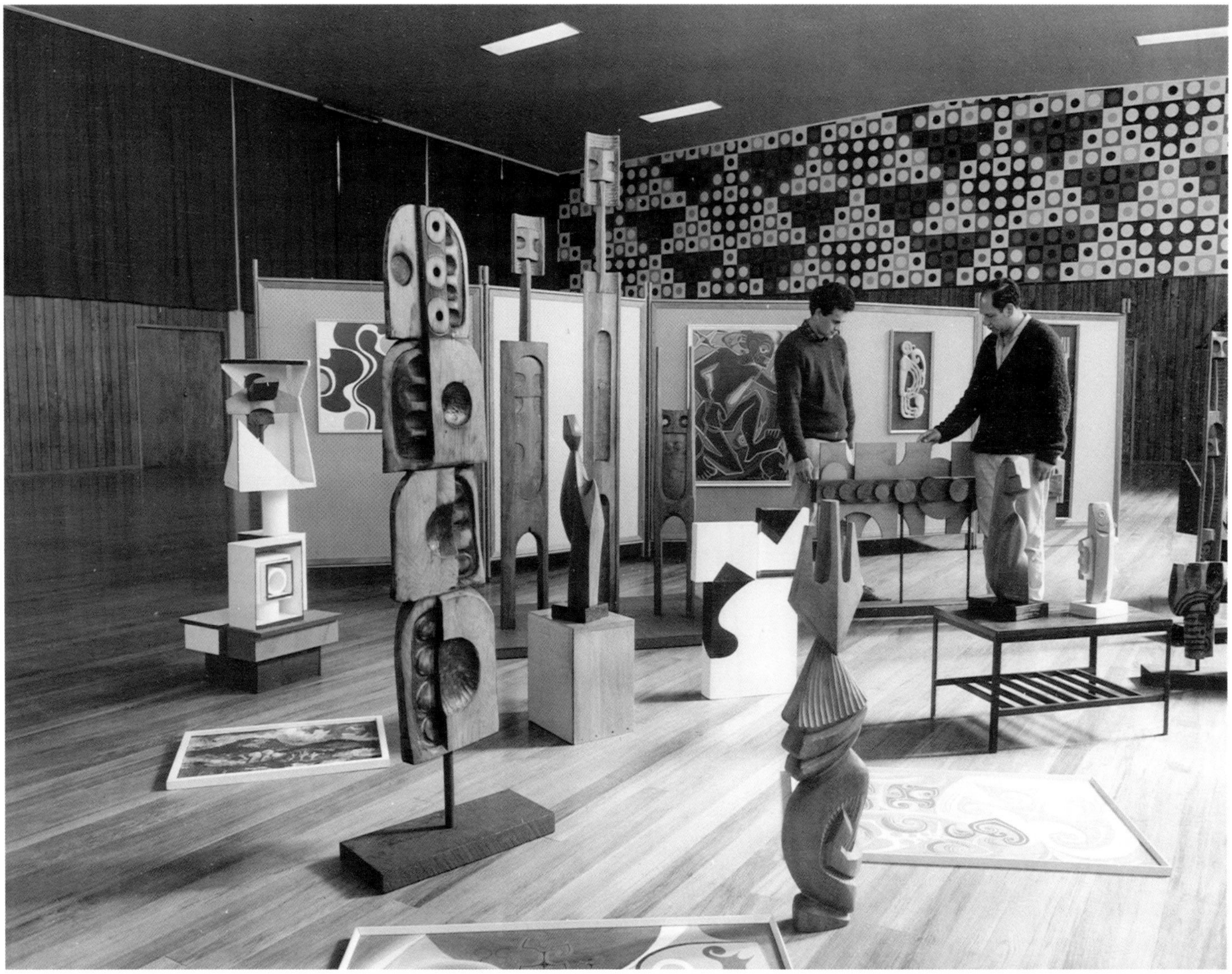

Artists Cliff Whiting (left) and Paratene Matchitt in discussion during the installation of *Contemporary Maori Painting and Sculpture* (1966), St Paul's Methodist Centre, Hamilton.
Archives New Zealand, AAQT 6539 A81942

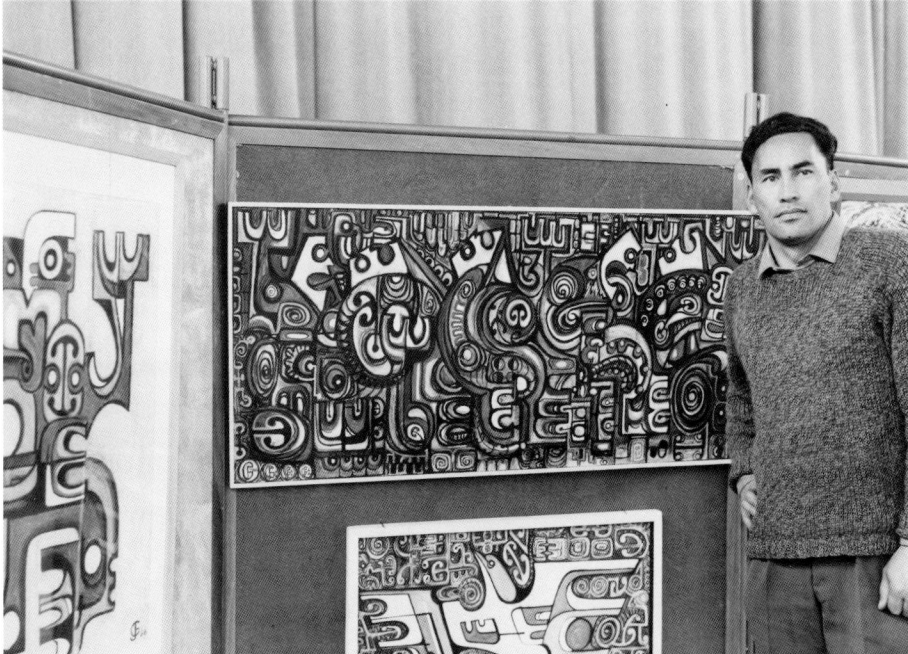

Fred Graham standing in front of his oil on board work *Whiti Te Ra* (1966) at the *Contemporary Maori Painting and Sculpture* exhibition.
Archives New Zealand, AAMK 27839 W3495/28/28a

work of Cath Brown (Ngāi Tahu, 1933–2004), Fred Graham (Ngāti Korokī Kahukura), Norman Lemon (Te Whata), Jonathan Mane-Wheoki (Ngāpuhi, Te Aupōuri, Ngāti Kurī, 1943–2014), Kāterina Mataira (Ngāti Porou, 1932–2011), Muru, Nin, Arnold Wilson and Pauline Yearbury. The exhibition encompassed paintings in the traditional European medium of oil and the synthetic medium of PVA, and sculptures carved from pear wood, jarrah, tōtara, tawa, rimu, pine, Oregon and kauri as well as cast in *ciment fondu*. Collage and assemblage techniques tentatively investigated by some of the artists harked back to the experiments and innovations of European artists in the early years of the twentieth century in response to the traditional tribal art modes of Africa. As it was, 'the contemporary works [were] set among traditional Maori artefacts which belong to the Canterbury Museum to contrast the styles in Maori art'[19] – presumably in order to gauge whether a sense of continuity with the past could be sustained, and to validate the use of 'Maori motifs presented in the forms of today'.[20] The resulting visual bilingualism and hybridisation proved difficult to locate in either culture, however. *New Zealand Maori Culture and the Contemporary Scene* went on to tour, with the support of the New Zealand government. After showing at the National Art Gallery, Wellington, a recharged and augmented version of the exhibition left New Zealand in mid-1967 to tour Australia, Western Sāmoa, Singapore, Malaysia and Japan.

In August 1966 a display of seventy examples of contemporary Māori art was one of the revelatory events of the Festival of Maori Arts held in Hamilton. Harry Dansey noted that: 'Nearly all the exhibitors make art their primary activity and are engaged in it daily – painting, carving, pottery, etching, casting, sketching. And teaching. That is perhaps the most significant aspect. These young men and women are nearly all employed as art advisors to the Education Department.'[21] The fourteen artists represented – Sandy Adsett (Ngāti Kahungunu ki Te Wairoa, Ngāti Pāhauwera), Clive Arlidge (Ngāpuhi, Ngāti Awa), John Bevan Ford (Ngāti Raukawa ki Kāpiti, 1930–2005), Fred Graham, Mere Harrison (Lodge), William (Bill) Henry, Ralph Hotere, Paratene Matchitt, Elizabeth Mountain (Ellis; Ngāpuhi, Ngāti Porou), Selwyn Muru, Freda Rankin (Kawharu; Ngāpuhi, 1934–2000), Cliff Whiting (Te Whānau-ā-Apanui, 1936–2017), Arnold Wilson and Pauline Yearbury – were soon to become prominent as Māori art educators or artists.

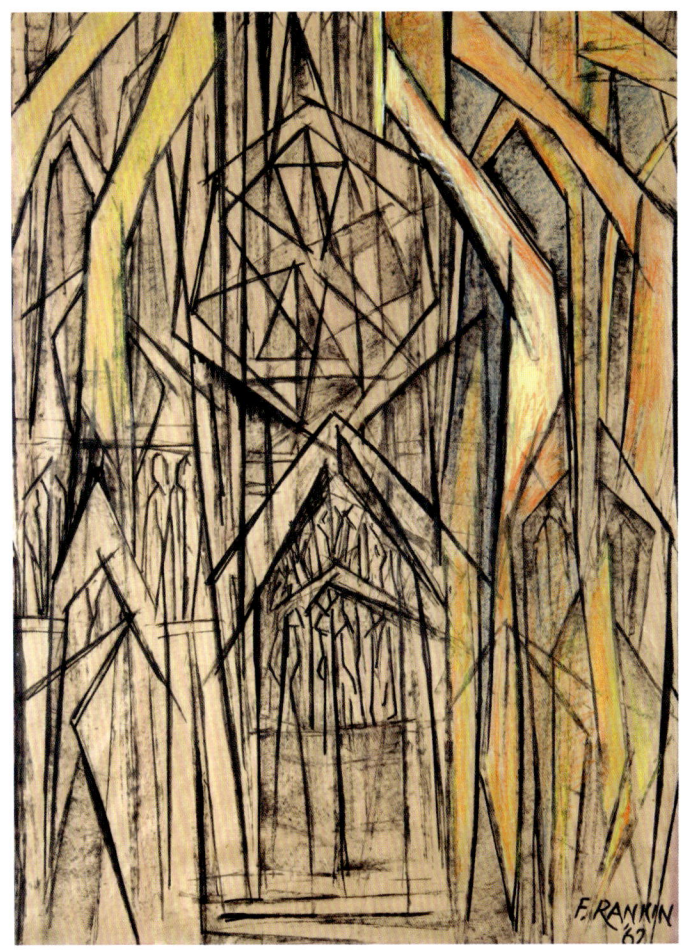

**Freda Rankin (Kawharu),** *Gothic Tracery,* **1962**
ink and pastel on paper, 770 x 550mm, private collection

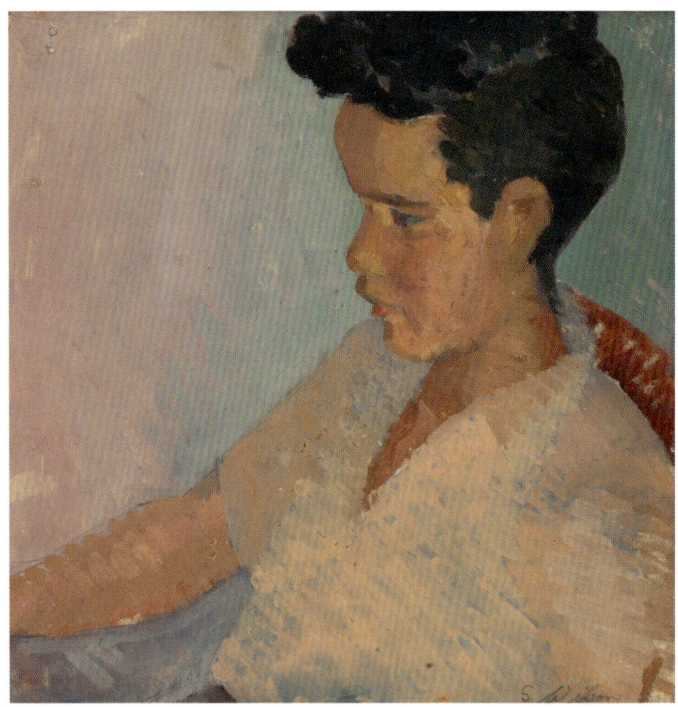

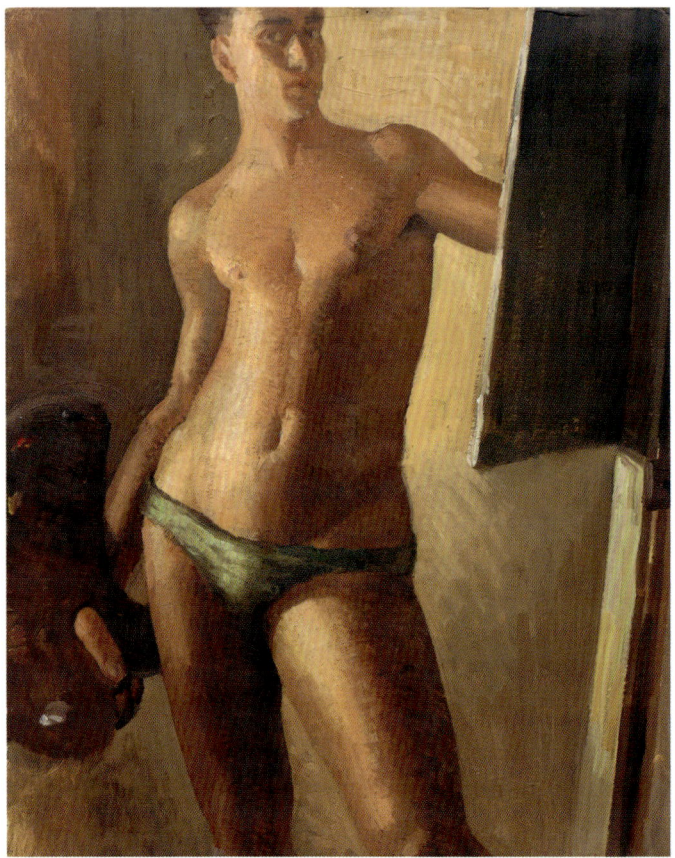

Top: **Selwyn Wilson**, *Study of a head*, **1948**
oil on board, 520 x 520mm, Auckland Art Gallery Toi o Tāmaki, 1948/4, purchased 1948

Bottom: **Selwyn Wilson**, *Figure study*, **1949**
oil on board, 707 x 583mm, Auckland Art Gallery Toi o Tāmaki, 1950/8, purchased 1950

## The 'Tovey' generation

These landmark exhibitions came towards the end of the year in which Gordon Tovey (1901–1974) had retired (in January) after twenty years as national supervisor of art and craft in the Department of Education. By this time the contemporary Māori art movement was gathering its own momentum, but the phenomenon may be viewed as embodying Tovey's vision for art education in New Zealand. His role in recruiting Māori for specialised training as art and craft teachers alongside their Pākehā counterparts was crucial. Through his scheme Māori were inducted into a range of art and craft skills, styles and concepts that they would almost certainly not otherwise have encountered. Whiting explains: 'Tovey brought young Māori potential into the art education advisory service and into in-service training – and this is where you get people like Ralph Hotere, Paratene Matchitt, Clive Arlidge, Muru Walters and myself. There were also women like Mere Kururangi and Mihiata Fairlie, who later had influence.'[22]

Tovey took up his appointment in January 1946, too early to be involved in the selection of Hirini Moko Mead for training at Auckland Teachers' College and Keriana Tuhaka (Hunter) at Wellington Teachers' College. 'As far as I am aware we were the first Māori art specialists to go through the third-year training scheme, and then to go out and work with Gordon Tovey,' Mead recalls.[23] Mead was assistant area organiser in art and craft on the East Coast from 1948 to 1951, then taught at Waimarama School in Hawke's Bay from 1957 to 1960, where he 'became very involved with Gordon Tovey' and implemented 'his ideas of teaching through the arts and drama'.[24] His experience in the classroom revealed, however, that the European art tradition could not meet the expectations of either the Māori teachers or their predominantly Māori pupils. As an itinerant art specialist whose job was to visit all Māori schools on the East Coast, Mead found that the 'kids wanted Māori art [so] I virtually had to teach myself Māori art and especially what to teach in primary schools.'[25] It was at this point that a divide began to open up between essentialist purity and modernist hybridisation in Māori art expression.

Meanwhile, Selwyn Wilson had been recruited for training. He worked as an itinerant art specialist in Northland from 1948 to 1950, then returned to Elam School of Fine Arts where he completed his Diploma in Fine Arts, majoring in

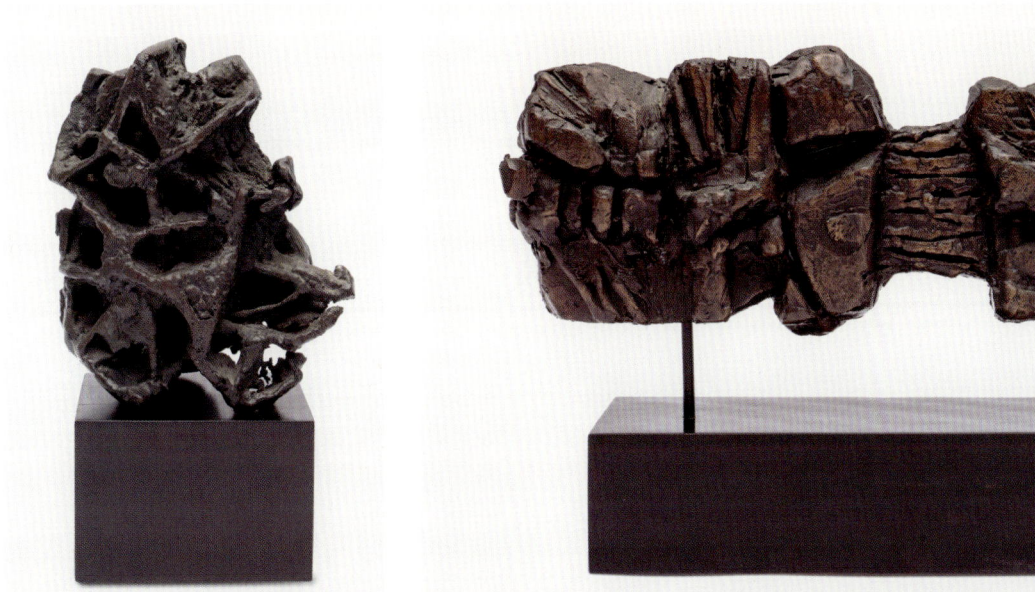

painting, in 1951.²⁶ He was clearly a talent to be watched: the Auckland Art Gallery purchased two of his works, one in 1948 and the other in 1950²⁷ – the first artworks by a Māori artist to enter a public art collection. He returned to the advisory service as the Auckland-based liaison organiser for the art and craft branch of the Department of Education.²⁸ In 1956 he did relief teaching at Northland College, Kaikohe. The following year he was awarded the Sir Apirana Ngata scholarship to study ceramics at the Central School of Art in London, but his studies were cut short by family illness. He returned to a permanent position at the college at the end of 1959, where he taught alongside Kāterina Mataira. Among his students who went on to complete university qualifications in fine arts were Buck Nin, Elizabeth Mountain (Ellis), Margaret Sampson, Mere Harrison (Lodge) and Kura Te Waru Rewiri (Ngāpuhi, Ngāti Kahu, Ngāti Rangi, Ngāti Raukawa ki Kauwhata; whom Nin also taught at Bay of Islands College). In 1970 Wilson became head of the art department at Bay of Islands College, where he taught for seventeen years.

Fred Graham and John Bevan Ford joined the advisory service in 1951, Ralph Hotere in 1952, Kāterina Mataira and Cath Brown in 1953, Mere Kururangi in 1954, Muru Walters in 1955,²⁹ Paratene Matchitt in 1957, Marilynn Webb (Ngāti Kahu, Te Roroa, 1937–2021)³⁰ and Cliff Whiting in 1958, Clive Arlidge in 1959 and Sandy Adsett in 1961. Most of these artists had completed the third-year specialist course for primary school teacher trainees at Dunedin Teachers' College. Even so, the ethos of art education was entirely Eurocentric. In

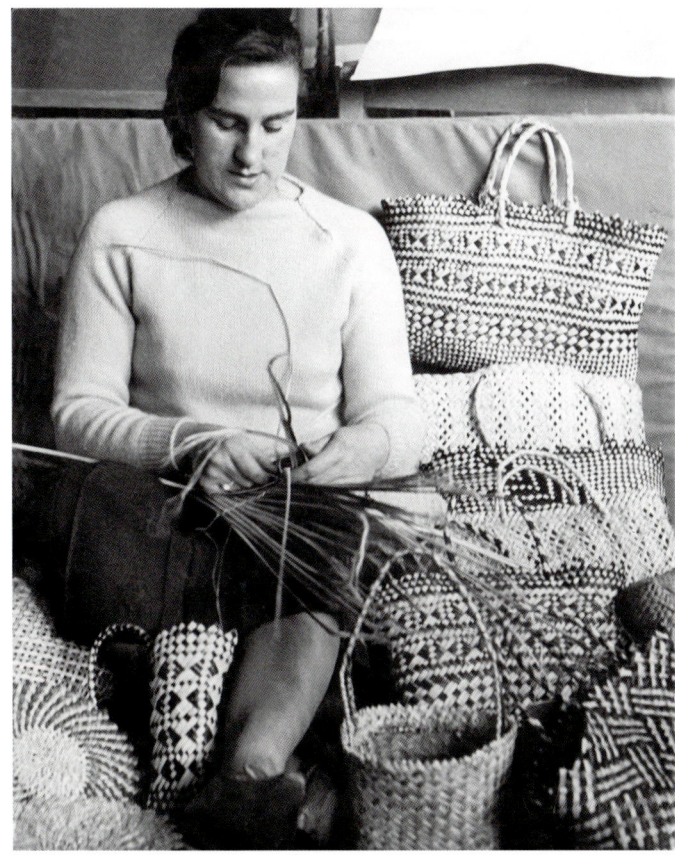

Top left: **Mere Harrison Lodge**, *Mata Whenua*, **1963**
bronze with wooden base, 400 x 300mm, Auckland Art Gallery Toi o Tāmaki, X2020/73/1, courtesy of the artist

Top right: **Mere Harrison Lodge**, *Te Toka-a-Torea*, **1963**
bronze with wooden base, 170 x 140mm, Auckland Art Gallery Toi o Tāmaki, X2020/73/2, courtesy of the artist

Bottom: Cath Brown, c.1960.
courtesy of Liz Brown

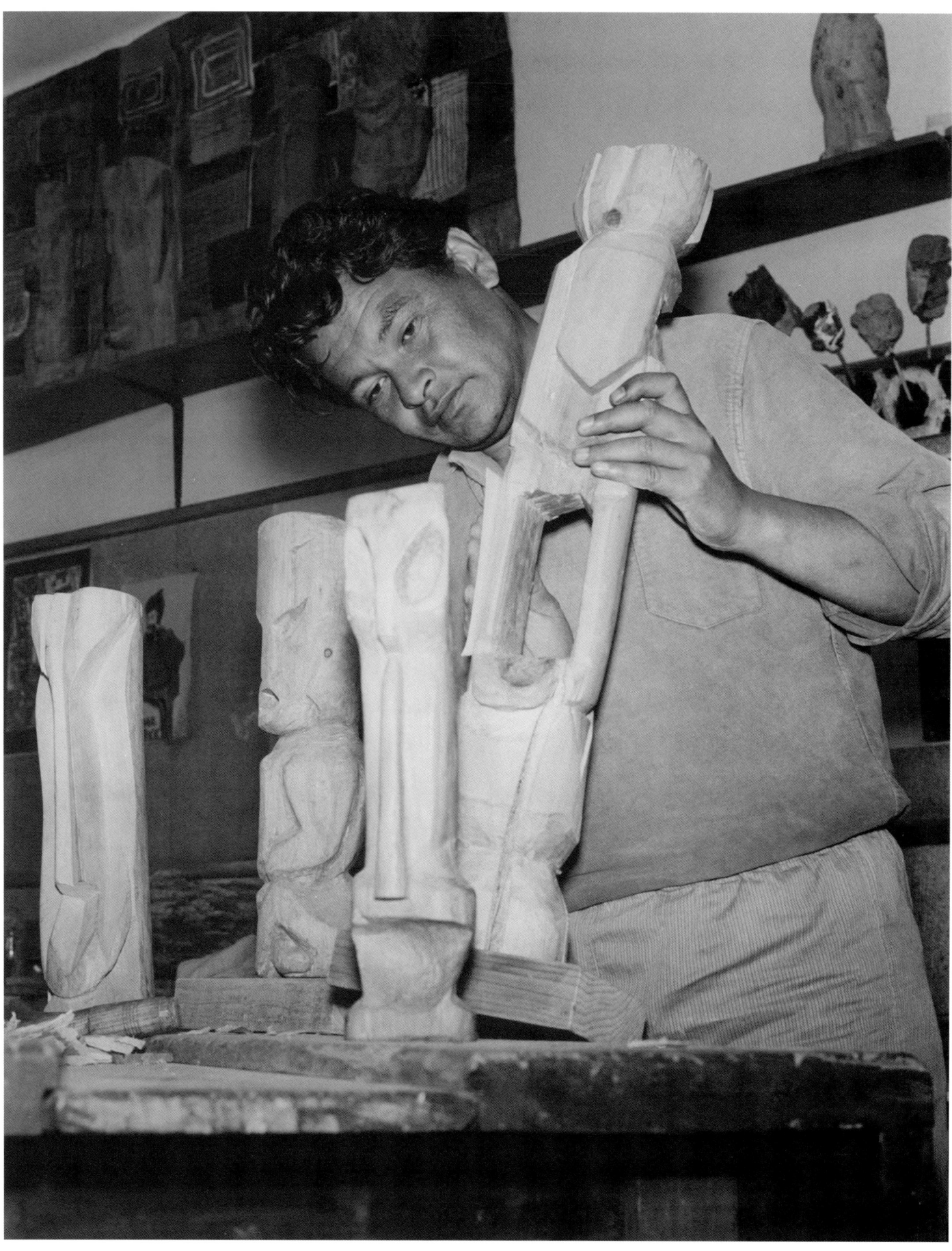

1946 Mead received 'general training in the arts, how and what to teach, all Western arts, no Māori art'.[31] Hotere's exhibition history began in 1952 with a joint show (with John Kim) at the Dunedin Public Library, of European-influenced works. Before 1964, Whiting recalls, 'I was painting, but not in terms of Maori things. In those days art was all about landscape painting.'[32]

In 1954 Arnold Wilson graduated with a Diploma in Fine Arts with Honours from Elam, the second Māori to graduate in fine arts; the first in sculpture. He was a highly accomplished realist sculptor, although this was not the type of art he was particularly known for. After a year at Auckland Teachers' College with Peter Smith, one of Tovey's most influential associates, he was appointed as an itinerant teacher at Ōkaihau and Kawakawa district high schools. When the Kawakawa school became Bay of Islands College in 1958, he settled in to a permanent position there. He later became head of the art department at Mount Albert Grammar School in Auckland.

At Kawakawa Arnold Wilson's students were predominantly Māori, and most spoke Māori. This encouraged him to inculcate in his charges a knowledge of, and pride in, their heritage of Māori carving and creation stories as a starting point for their artistic education and development, and then 'letting it happen'.[33] What happened – simplification of form, creative distortion, untrammelled expressivity – was consistent with the modernist's reverence for children's art and tribal art that Tovey shared with his teams of art advisors. From this kind of experience the contemporary Māori art movement emerged.[34] 'It all started from there,' Wilson insists, 'from Kawakawa. I don't care what anyone says.'[35]

In 1959 the Labour prime minister, Walter Nash, directed that Māori arts and crafts be incorporated into the general education curriculum.[36] With this end in view Tovey enthusiastically began planning for a national two-week in-service training hui to be held at Ruatōria, the heartland of Ngāti Porou, in March 1960. Māori and Pākehā teachers worked alongside each other at the hui,[37] learning 'the historical and local aspects of Māori art'.[38] Customary arts such as poi, action song, haka, weaving and carving were taught by experts. The acclaimed carver Pine Taiapa, a guest instructor, inducted the women into the mysteries of carving. He later insisted that 'Maori tradition clearly indicated that where women were responsible for an outstanding achievement

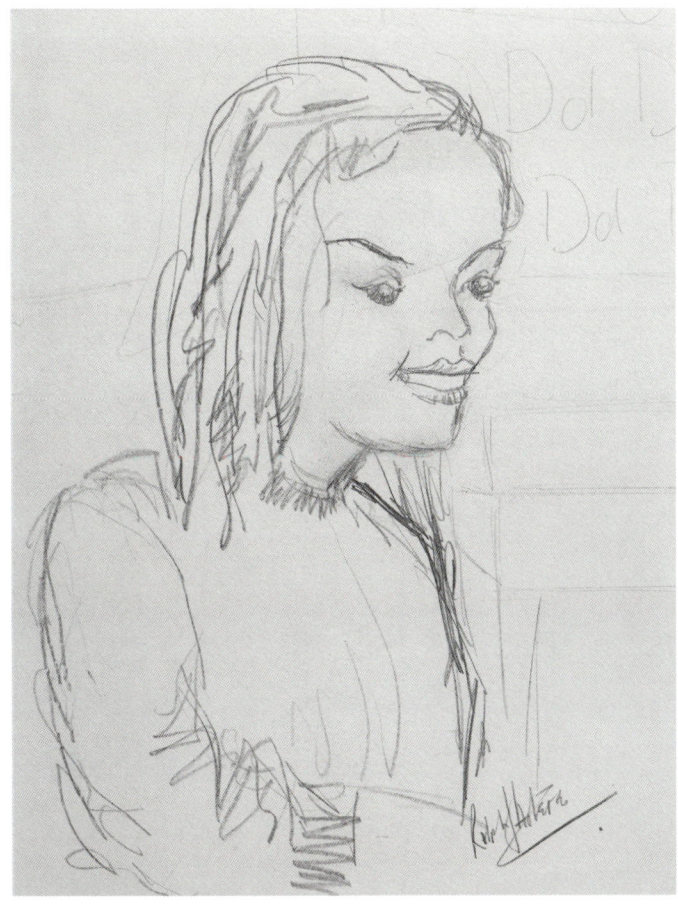

Ralph Hotere's sketch of a child was made during his time as an arts advisor for the Department of Education in Northland in the mid-1950s.
**Ralph Hotere, untitled [signed pencil sketch of a girl, Maori Schools Register of Daily Attendance, Oromahoe], 1958**
Archives New Zealand, BAAA 1006/28a, by permission of the Hotere Foundation Trust

Opposite: Arnold Wilson, 1965.
Ans Westra, Te Papa Tongarewa Museum of New Zealand, O.010537/02, purchased 1993 with New Zealand Lottery Grants Board funds, copyright Ans Westra

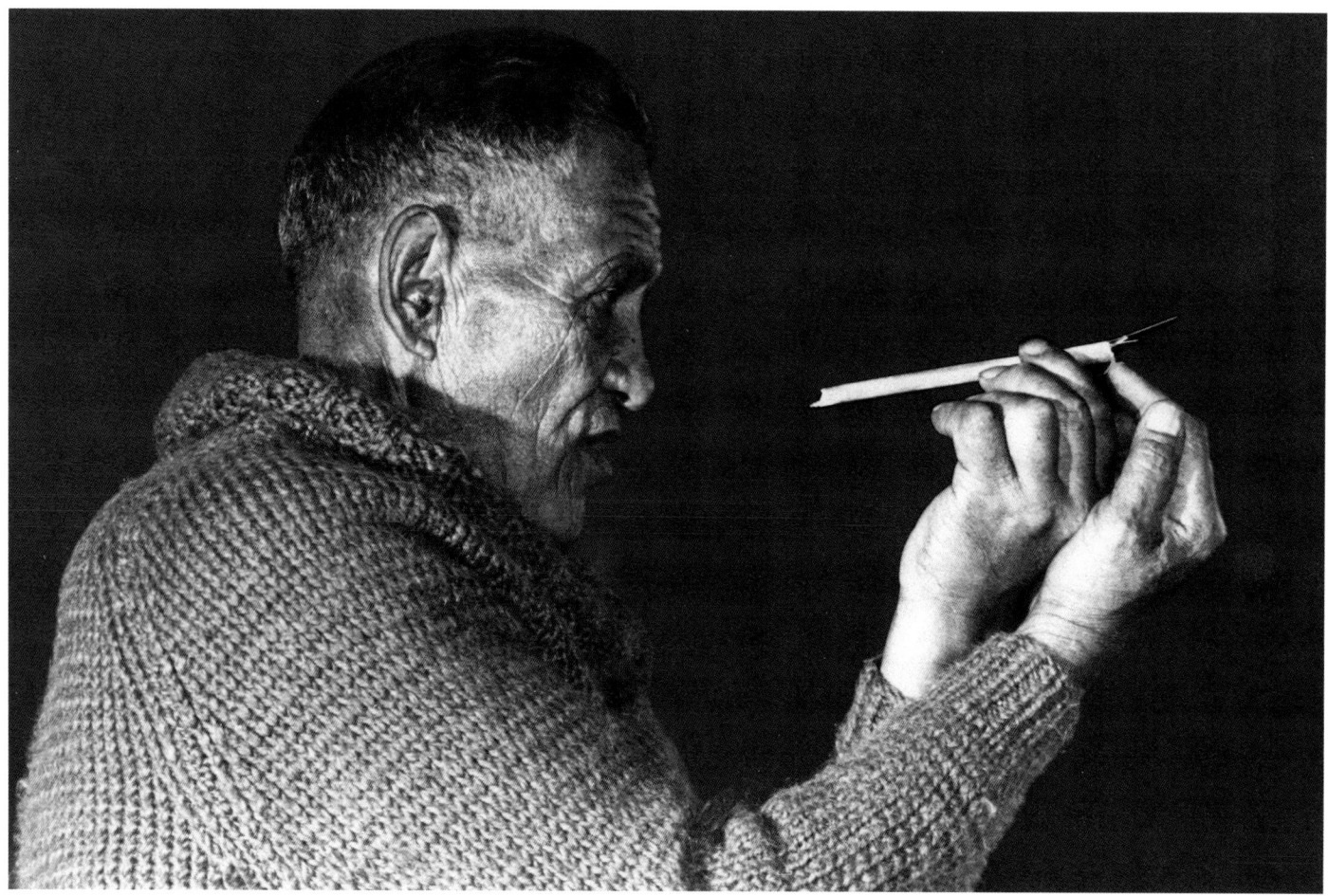

generally attributed to men, they were permitted to undertake such men's work as carving.'³⁹ The men, likewise, were expected to weave – indeed, the artists were encouraged to ignore whatever customs had previously inhibited them. The delegates were heartened by this apparent liberality of outlook.

The Māori art specialists who had converged on Ruatōria found themselves grouping naturally on the basis of shared culture, language, identity, history and – where they existed – kinship ties. For some the hui was a catalyst, a revelation: those whose connections to the Māori world had been tenuous now found themselves bonded firmly into the group. All gained confidence, strength and security from groundedness in their cultural base. Whiting remembers that 'There was a lot of emphasis placed on working together as a group';⁴⁰ 'I think that was when we developed as a group of people. Away we went.'⁴¹

One important outcome of group endeavour was the book *The Arts of the Maori*, prepared by Tovey and published by the Department of Education in 1961. The advisory Committee comprised Marewa McConnell (Ngāi Tahu, 1908–1988), Maud Isaacs (Ngāti Porou, 1927–2010), Mere Kururangi, Hirini Mead, Whare Isaacs, Pine Taiapa and Murray Gilbert (the sole Pākehā in the group). Māori arts flourished as part of the general education curriculum. Mataira was 'astounded at the high standards' achieved by schoolchildren: 'If this is happening throughout the country then I must applaud the efforts of Gordon Tovey and his associates in the Arts and Crafts Branch.'⁴²

The courses in the 'Arts of the Maori' were followed by 'Arts of the Pakeha'. The object was to encourage the kind of bicultural literacy in all New Zealanders that was already becoming apparent in contemporary Māori art. Secure in their own cultural base and birthright, Māori artists such as Muru pitched into European modernism: of traditional Māori art, he said, 'I feel the old masters have done an excellent job; therefore there's no point in trying to better what they did. But the creative avenues leading from traditional Maori art are still open for the artist to explore.'⁴³

Nin and Pere, in the catalogue to *New Zealand Maori Culture and the Contemporary Scene*, asserted that:

Patterns derived from two cultures are being created here in great diversity by these artists ... Maori motifs are here represented in the forms of today ... The works displayed indicate beyond any doubt that Maoris are at the forefront of New Zealand contemporary art. If a true New Zealand school of art emerges the rich inheritance of the Maori people, here interpreted in modern forms, may well provide a major source of inspiration for the future.[44]

From the convergence of the two cultural streams, as the Māori modernists had hoped, a distinctive New Zealand art might flow.

### Recognition and reception

The directions and reception of contemporary Māori art were many and varied. Of the five participants in 'the first Maori art exhibition' of 1958 only Hotere and Selwyn Wilson continued as practising artists for the rest of their lives. But their careers were to diverge sharply in the early 1960s. In 1961 Hotere was awarded a New Zealand Art Societies Fellowship that enabled him to study in Europe: he trained at the Central School of Art in London, and then the Karolyi Foundation in Vence, France. He returned to New Zealand four years later utterly transformed; he now painted in a manner that was informed by his exposure to constructivism, the minimalism of Ad Reinhardt, post-painterly abstraction and the American pop of Jasper Johns. Harry Dansey remarked of Hotere's highly abstract work shown in the Festival of Maori Arts in 1966 that it revealed 'no influence whatsoever of a Maori background, either in theme or execution'.[45] Two years later Hotere became the first, and for many years the only Māori to be written into the mainstream history of New Zealand art.[46]

Recognition from New Zealand's art establishment came for Arnold Wilson with his inclusion in the Auckland Art Gallery's exhibitions *Contemporary New Zealand Painting* (in 1962) and *Recent New Zealand Sculpture* (in 1968).[47] Wilson had, by this stage, reconciled the competing demands of community expectation and fine arts reception. During his time studying at Elam, he had been discouraged from pursuing the study of Māori art by the school's director, Archibald Fisher; yet each time he returned home to Ruatoki he found the community's expectations of him diametrically at odds with his art school training.[48] On one occasion he

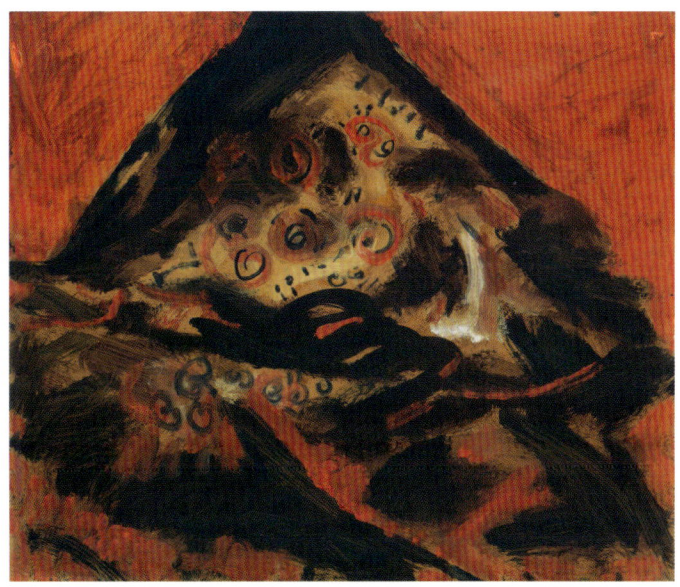

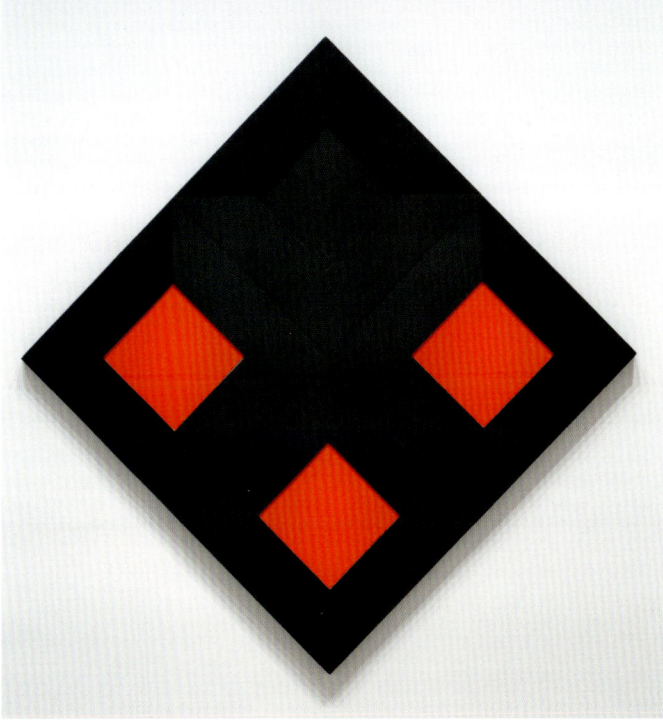

Top: **Selwyn Muru**, *Untitled Taupiri Mountain*, c.1965
oil on board, 620 x 725mm, Auckland Art Gallery Toi o Tāmaki, 2011/4, purchased 2011

Bottom: **Ralph Hotere**, *Black Painting*, 1964
acrylic on wood, 207 x 1207mm, Auckland Art Gallery Toi o Tāmaki, 1965/24/2, purchased 1965, by permission of the Hotere Foundation Trust

Opposite: Pine Taiapa at the Ruatōria hui for art advisors, 1960.
photograph by Edward Zagorski

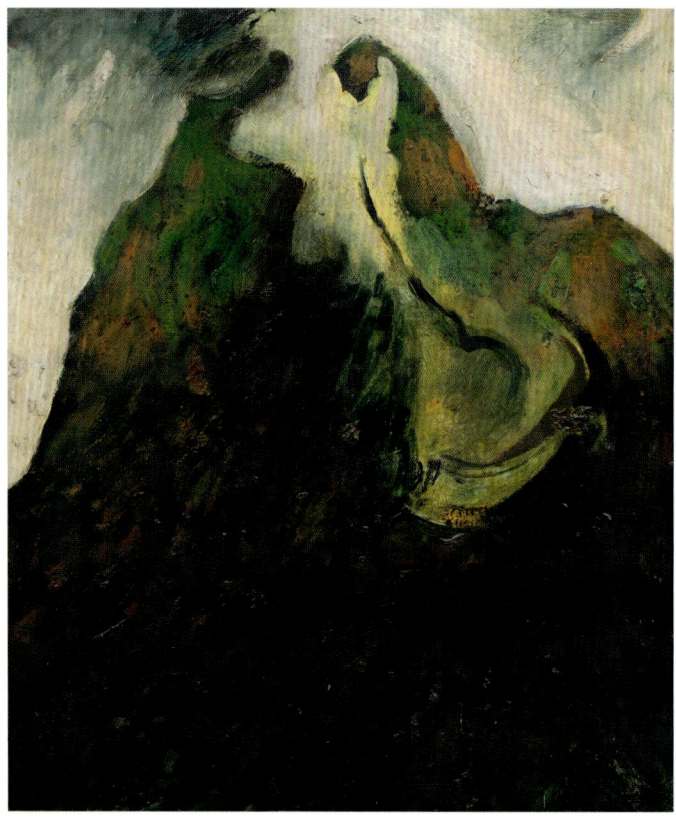

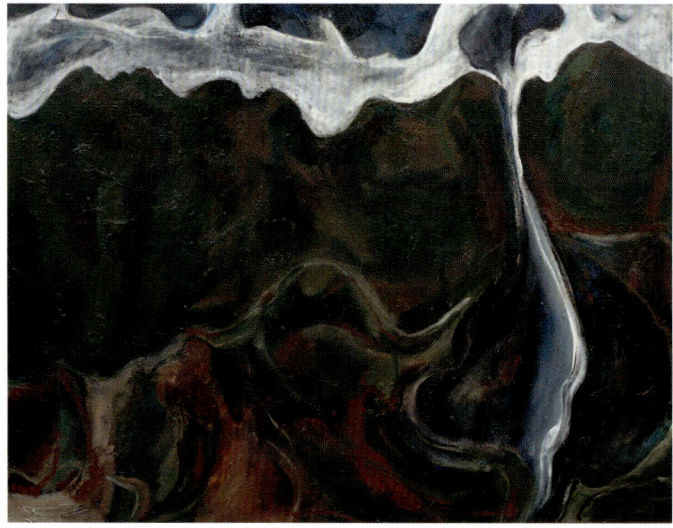

Top: **Elizabeth Mountain Ellis, *Puke Huia*, 1966**
oil on board, 724 x 623mm, Auckland Art Gallery Toi o Tāmaki, X2020/48/4, courtesy of the Mountain Ellis whānau

Bottom: **Elizabeth Mountain Ellis, *Te Rawhiti Rakaumangamanga*, 1966**
oil on board, 927 x 1220mm, Auckland Art Gallery Toi o Tāmaki, X2020/48/3, courtesy of the Mountain Ellis whānau

proudly showed drawings he had done in life class and was taken aback by his father's horrified reaction. Wilson had thought his whānau might be amused by a photographic snapshot of him posing with 'Horace', the art school's skeleton. Instead, he was promptly marched down to the river by his aunts and subjected to a ritual dunking. No wonder he decided to complete his art school training first, and then focus on the Māori dimension. 'It wasn't until after Elam that I began to relook at Māori art,' he recalled.[49]

Some Māori, inevitably, were dismayed at what they saw as the dilution or diminution of their cultural heritage. According to Arnold Wilson, 'There was a big resistance, especially from Rotorua'[50] – where the New Zealand Maori Arts and Crafts Institute had been established in 1964. Mead had also taken a line of firm resistance. Whiting recalls that:

> Two or three people said Māori art was dead; some of us had an exhibition in the 1960s and a well-known anthropologist [i.e. Mead] said, 'This is not Māori art'. In actual fact what they were really saying is that what is hung in museums and a few houses around was their idea of what Māori art should be. They were concerned about some of us altering traditional colours.[51]

Mead remained unconvinced. In the catalogue of the celebrated 1984 exhibition *Te Maori*, he wrote:

> New forms of art, borrowed from the traditions of the West, have been introduced into the Maori world. Maori artists trained in the art schools of the Pakeha are spearheading a movement to change the face of Maori art more radically than ever before. One does not know whether they innovate with love and understanding, or whether they are about to ignite new fires of destruction.[52]

Such art could create confusion in the minds of Pākehā and Māori alike. Adsett explains:

> Though I happen to be Maori, I am still using ideas that equally come through from a strong Pakeha influence. I've heard Pakeha people say my work is Maori. For Maori people it is not necessarily Maori. To them it does not have the traditional meaning behind some of the work; it does not have the base it originated from. My work is an

'in-between' art. I try to understand Western art forms. They allow me to make comparisons and open other avenues to experiment with.[53]

Even so, Adsett is adamant that it is his art which allows him to identify as Māori.[54]

Some practitioners of the more traditional arts are sympathetic to this approach. Diggeress Te Kanawa, herself an innovator, insists that: 'The old and the new can go together.'[55] Matchitt recounts the story of an incident in Hamilton where Pine Taiapa had been asked to open the exhibition that included his work. What Taiapa saw on display shocked and angered him, and he vented his ire on Matchitt. When he came to open the exhibition, however, he relented: 'The world of art is so big,' he conceded, 'there's room in it for everyone.'[56]

In 1958 Ron O'Reilly wrote: 'Not yet categorised for easy reference are artists who are Maoris and who do not want to be considered as Maori artists but simply as artists; Ralph Hotere is one …'[57] In 1976 Hotere, in a rare outburst, explained: 'I am a Maori by birth and upbringing. As far as my work is concerned this is coincidental.'[58] Otherwise he maintained an enigmatic silence, resisting being pigeonholed. This ambivalence was shared by Paratene Matchitt and Selwyn Muru. All three declined to be covered in the lavishly produced book *Mataora: The Living Face: Contemporary Maori Art*, published in 1996.

Nevertheless, many of the 'Tovey Generation'[59] Māori artists – including Hotere, Matchitt and Muru – were present at the inaugural hui of the New Zealand Maori Artists and Writers Association (now known as Ngā Puna Waihanga) at Te Kaha in 1973, and they have featured in innumerable local, national and international exhibitions of contemporary Māori and New Zealand art. Apart from Hotere, they largely found themselves marginalised and unsupported by New Zealand's Pākehā-dominated art establishment, and denied access to 'mainstream' exhibition venues. However, there was a certain ambivalence – arising from a concern to respect the integrity and ensure the continuity of Māori culture and tradition – about engaging with local manifestations of the international art world's processes of commodifying and marketing artworks. Artists are torn both ways. On the one hand, there are those who wish to maintain their strong sense of community, collectivity and whanaungatanga by bridging ability and experience gaps in 'by Māori for Māori' exhibitions. On the other hand, the urban context and the opportunities it affords to engage with the art market encourages individualism, independence, competition and – as some Māori would see it – selfishness.

The dynamic of their art – their attempts to straddle two traditions and, more especially, to engage with Western art traditions on their own Māori terms – pointed to other directions for Māori art. It was informed by a burgeoning context of dislocation, disruption and alienation wrought by a mass migration, a diaspora driven by economic necessity, of Māori from their tribal areas to the towns and cities. A number of the artists who emerged in the 1950s and 1960s continued to practise as part of the resurgence in Māori nationalism and culture that has been a feature of New Zealand politics since the enactment of Treaty of Waitangi legislation in 1975. Today it is almost impossible to consider the contemporary Māori art movement as a separate entity from the political context to which it so clearly relates.

# ORIWA HADDON (1898–1958)
DEIDRE BROWN AND JONATHAN MANE-WHEOKI

The first Māori 'tohunga ata whakairo', or shadow carver, as Ngata had described painters, was Edward Oliver Haddon, who as an artist was more widely known as Oriwa Tahupōtiki Haddon.[1] Born at Waitōtara, South Taranaki in 1898, he was the eldest son of the Māori Methodist minister Robert Tahupōtiki Haddon of Ngāti Ruanui and his wife, Huihana (Susan) Haerehau Shelford of Hokianga. He attended Wesley College at Three Kings, Auckland in 1914, but does not appear to have had any formal art training beyond what he would have received at secondary school. A man of many interests and talents, Haddon worked at various times as a Methodist minister, pharmacist and radio broadcaster.[2] From the late 1920s, he was practising as a cartoonist and illustrator for New Zealand and Australian journals, and as a muralist; the journalist Pat Lawlor – for whom he sometimes illustrated – described Haddon as 'in his day something of a genius' who 'spent many weeks painting murals … in country hotels'.[3] Along with Jack Kingi, Haddon also painted the kōwhaiwhai for the School of Maori Arts and Crafts project at St Paul's Church (opened in 1937), but there is no record of his having undertaken any other work for the school.[4]

Haddon's career as a painter began to develop as the centenary of the signing of the Te Tiriti o Waitangi approached. An important history-painting commission came in 1933, when the Taranaki Maori Trust Board asked him to paint the 1840 signing. The painting is a competent and confident work, illustrating both Māori and Pākehā as leaders actively engaged in dialogue – an image of cultural equality not seen before in New Zealand history paintings showing Māori. The following year, the painting was presented to Governor-General Lord Bledisloe, and it was hung in the Treaty House at Waitangi. Sadly it has since disappeared from there: a photograph of the original now hangs in its place in the original carved frame.[5]

The same year as he produced the Tiriti work, Haddon completed a painting to commemorate the arrival of Turi, the founding ancestor of Ngāti Ruanui and Ngāti Rauru, at Pātea. He and Charles Duncan Hay-Campbell – a professionally trained artist and at that time the Wanganui Arts and Crafts Society's president – were commissioned to create the painting.[6] Haddon was a direct descendant of Turi, and the collaboration was an association that added an Indigenous cultural authority to a work that sat well within the Western European painting paradigm. The Department of Tourist and Health Resorts also commissioned Haddon to execute a series of oil paintings for the centennial celebrations. His pen-and-ink sketch titled *Hine Kohu and Uenuku* was the only contribution by a Māori artist to the New Zealand Centennial Exhibition in Wellington in 1940.[7]

Haddon continued to paint and illustrate after he enlisted in the air force in World War Two. His painting *Maori Mythology* was included in the 1944 *New Zealand Artists in Uniform* exhibition; he regularly contributed cartoons to *Contact* – the national magazine of the Royal New Zealand Air Force; and he illustrated Andrew Grimwood's 1943 autobiography of his air force years, *Flights and Fancies*.[8] After a short stint in politics after his war service, Haddon focused on the execution of large-scale works. He produced a series of eight paintings of the history of Nelson, from Cook's arrival and including the attempted arrest of Te Rauparaha at Wairau, for Blenheim's Commercial Hotel; and he painted murals for the Returned Services' Association at Utiku, near Taihape.[9]

Haddon's painting career was cut short when he died in a car crash in 1958 at the age of fifty-nine.[10] By this time he had established himself as the first exhibiting Māori oil painter, adapting the Western European tradition of history painting to show how Māori as tūpuna (including one of his own) negotiated Te Tiriti with Pākehā and then – as in the case of Te Rauparaha – resisted Crown action against them. These were very different paintings and perspectives of Māori life than those that Pākehā would have been used to seeing in provincial and municipal New Zealand galleries, museums and public places, and they spoke to events that were still raw, contentious and difficult moments for both communities.

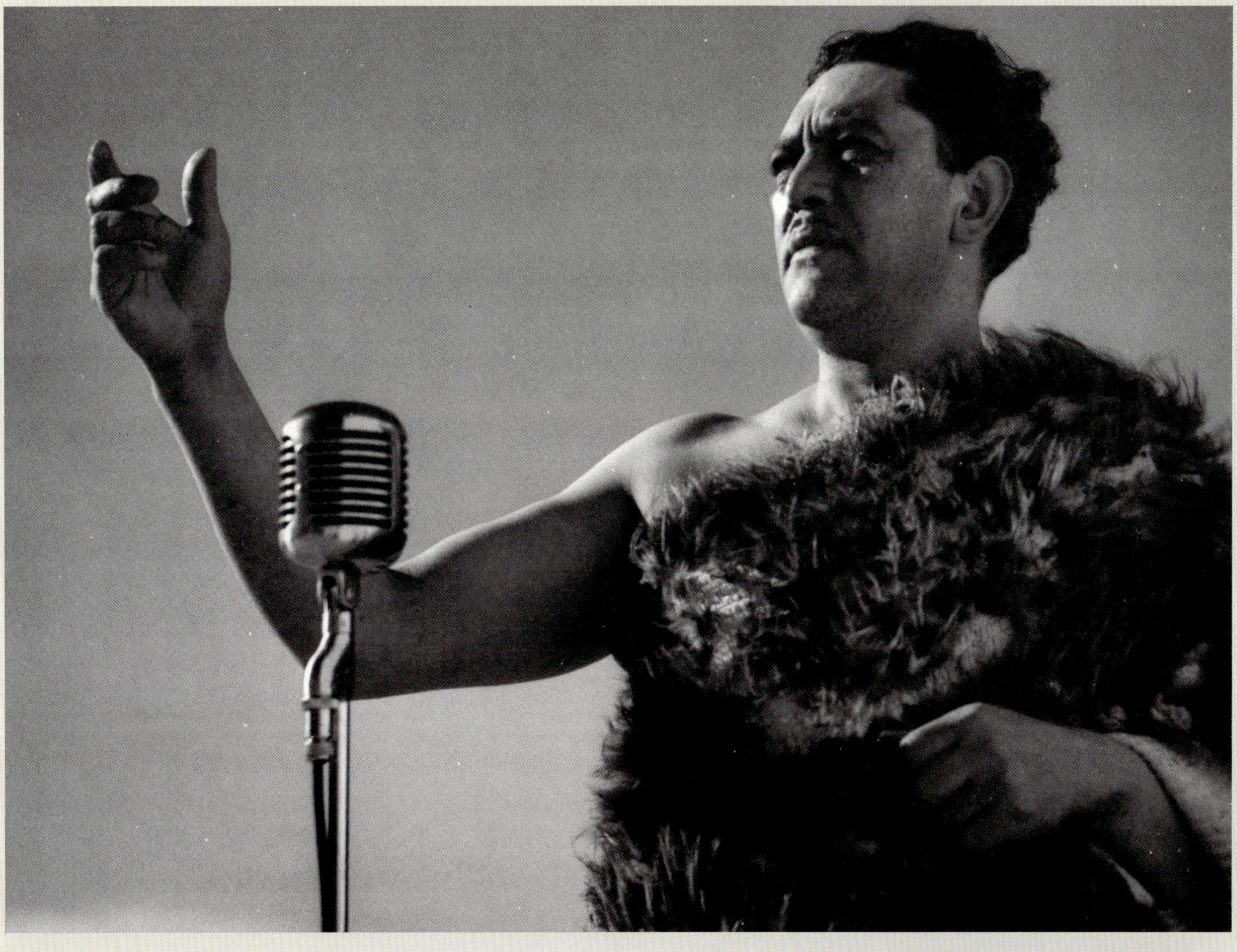

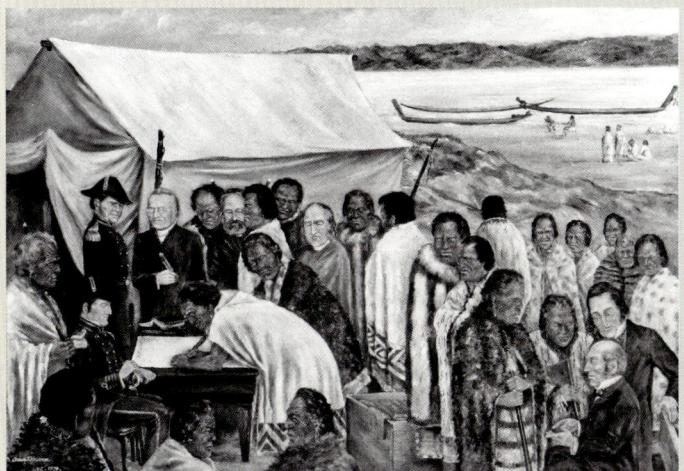

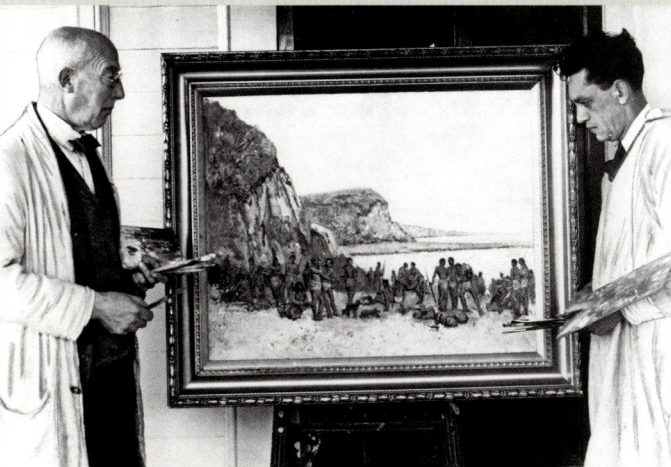

**Top:** Oriwa Haddon, 1940.
Hector Alfred Farmer William McDonald, Alexander Turnbull Library, PAColl-9832-1-11

**Bottom left: Oriwa Haddon,** *Signing of the Treaty of Waitangi,* **1934**
Archives New Zealand, AEGA 18982 PC4 1934/3067

**Bottom right:** Oriwa Haddon and Charles Duncan Hay-Campbell, 1933, with their painting depicting the arrival of Turi at Pātea.
Alexander Turnbull Library, PAColl-5671-29

# RAMAI HAYWARD (1916–2014)
DEIDRE BROWN AND JONATHAN MANE-WHEOKI

Ramai Rongomaitara Hayward (née Te Miha/Miller, 1916–2014)[1] was the first professional Māori artist and cinematographer, one of the earliest Māori studio-based photographers,[2] and possibly the first person of Māori descent to study at a Pākehā art institution. She was born in Martinborough to Roihi Te Miha (Ngāi Tahu, Ngāti Kahungunu) and Fred Mawhinney, who was Irish. She attended Queen Victoria School for Maori Girls in Auckland.[3] In 1935 she was apprenticed to Henri Harrison, a French photographer with a studio in Cuba Street, Wellington, where she learnt all aspects of studio photography.[4] She also studied with the painter Marcus King at Wellington Technical College, and joined the Ngati Poneke Young Maori Club, where Apirana Ngata was a founding member and may have tutored her in kapa haka.

She moved to Auckland and in 1937, using money from the sale of family land in the Wairarapa, established Patricia Miller Studios in Devonport on the North Shore – a commercially successful portrait photography business that grew to a staff of eight.[5] Her timing could not have been better, as the dawn of World War Two ensured good custom from New Zealand and American servicepeople from the nearby naval base, and pre-deployment wedding parties.[6] The studio had the ambience of a salon and the hospitality of a marae, she recalled, 'with its leather armchairs, Indian rugs, and log fires in winter … it became a haven for American servicemen. Coffee and cookies would be served. Someone would invariably begin playing the piano, and there would be a party atmosphere most days.'[7] One of only a handful of women professional photographers in Auckland, Hayward produced studio portraits that exuded the elegance and glamour of Hollywood photography.

It was during this time that she met the filmmaker Rudall Hayward and agreed to star as Ariana, the heroine in his remake with sound of his film *Rewi's Last Stand*. They both became celebrities on the film's release in 1940. Hayward used her considerable flair as a commercial designer to produce publicity posters for the film from linocuts.[8] Ramai and Rudall married in 1943 and in 1946 they sold the photographic studios so they could work together as filmmakers – with Ramai working on both sides of the camera – in New Zealand, the United Kingdom and, in 1957, in China.[9] During their visit to China – the first by English-speaking filmmakers since the founding of the People's Republic – she presented a kahu huruhuru from the Māori king Korokī to Mao Zedong, chairman of the Communist Party of China; Rudall filmed the presentation and included it in their documentary *Inside Red China*. The US Central Intelligence Agency later attempted – unsuccessfully – to block screening of the pro-China film by Kerridge Odeon cinemas in New Zealand.[10]

Although Ramai Hayward was steeped in the Pākehā filmmaking tradition, her back-catalogue of documentaries and films shows her ongoing desire to promote Māori achievements and raise Māori issues with a wider audience. In 1964 she collaborated with Rudall to produce a documentary, *Arts and Crafts of the Maori*, on the Māori arts and crafts advisory service, which featured Paratene Matchitt (Kawhia School), Arnold Wilson (Bay of Islands College) and Selwyn Wilson (Northland College). The film highlighted the exciting artistic possibilities arising from this

Photograph of Ramai Te Miha (later Hayward) dressed as a bride, used to advertise her photographic studio. This is the only known surviving photograph from her studio, which was the first to be established by a Māori woman.
Patricia Miller, c.1937, Ngā Taonga Sound and Vision, S219097, Hayward Collection, courtesy of the Ramai Hayward whānau and Patricia Miller Studio, Devonport, Auckland

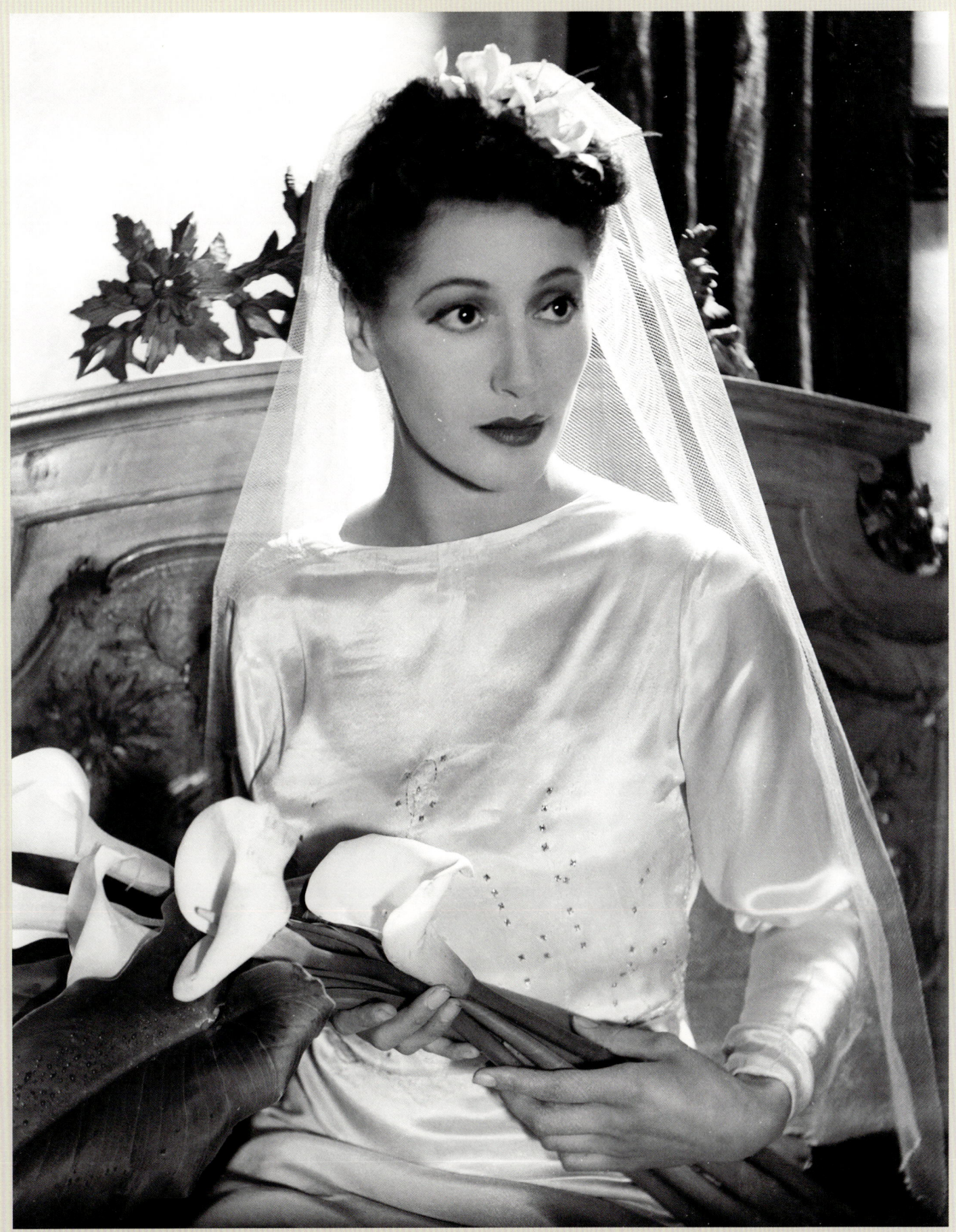

period of experimentation and the fusion of Māori and modern art traditions, as well as the accomplishments of the teachers as artists. Although the documentary was popular in Japan, it was not purchased for distribution in Britain as the buyers said, according to Hayward, that Māori was 'a dying culture'.[11]

Hayward's concern for the future of the urban Māori she was teaching at Auckland Technical Institute led her and Rudall to produce and direct *To Love a Maori* in 1972 – a feature-length film (in which she played a supporting character) about an intercultural relationship that built on themes popularised in John O'Shea and Roger Mirams's New Zealand film *Broken Barrier* (1952) and Stanley Kramer's *Guess Who's Coming to Dinner?* (1967). This was Rudall Hayward's last film before his death in 1974.

Ramai Hayward went on to become a kuia of Māori arts and culture. She was appointed a branch delegate of the Maori Women's Welfare League and, from 1976 to 1981, president of Nga Puna Waihanga, the national body of Māori artists and writers. She immersed herself in Māori land-rights issues, and continued to paint and exhibit well into the 1990s.[12]

Posters by Ramai Te Miha (later Hayward), for *Rewi's Last Stand* (1940).
Ngā Taonga Sound and Vision, PO03845.01

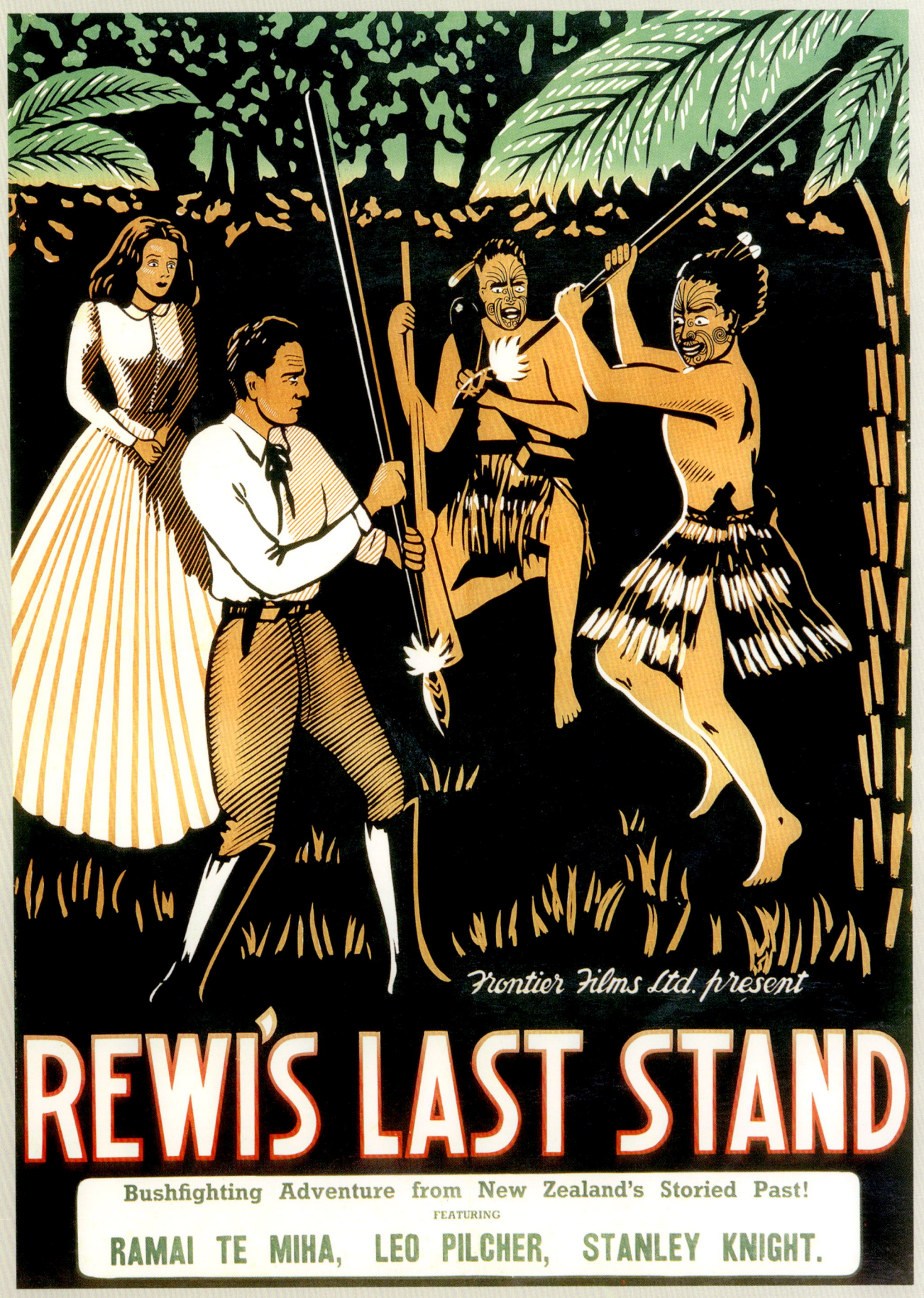

# PAULINE KAHURANGI YEARBURY (1926–1977)
DEIDRE BROWN

Pauline Kahurangi Yearbury (née Blomfield, Ngāpuhi, 1926–1977) entered the Elam School of Art in 1943 and completed her Diploma of Fine Arts in 1949.[1] She was introduced to Cubism at Elam, likely by her tutor John Weeks – a style that would have a long influence on her angular and muscular figurative paintings.[2] After graduating, she was appointed to the staff of Elam, where she became the first Māori fine arts academic. She and her husband, artist Jim Yearbury, moved to Russell in 1951, where she was commissioned to paint a number of murals on public and commercial buildings.[3] She had been introduced to muralism – an art form associated with social and political content – at Elam by the head of school, Archibald Fraser, and tutor Lois White, and like other graduates she saw opportunities to use this medium to advance regionalism in public art.[4]

One of her largest commissions, undertaken with Jim, was an epic 9m long depiction of the signing of Te Tiriti o Waitangi for the new Waitangi Hotel in 1964. In 1967 the couple opened the Colonial Gallery in Russell, where they sold their paintings, pottery, sculpture and craftwork. They became known for their collaborative incised and painted wood panels depicting atua, inspired by the work of South African artist Cecil Skotnes.[5] Yearbury considered the reinterpretation of Māori narratives through contemporary media as imperative to cultural survival. As she put it:

> I have always been interested in Maori mythology and legends – it is part of my inheritance. What was important to my ancestors is still important to me, but the way in which they did their things is no longer important. I will not sit in the yard with hammer and chisel – but using traditional myths and legends in more modern idiom is very important, otherwise our culture would become static and die. One must use legends but interpret them in the modern manner.[6]

In 1966 her work was included in the *Maori Culture and the Contemporary Scene* exhibition at Canterbury Museum, and in the Festival of Maori Arts in Hamilton; the two exhibitions were regarded as breakthrough moments for Māori modernism. The 1976 publication of her illustrated book on Māori creation and ancestral stories, *The Children of Rangi and Papa*, brought her paintings to wider public attention. She died the following year, aged fifty.

Yearbury has not had the recognition she deserves as an early Māori modernist painter, as much of the scholarship on this group has focused on the accomplishments of her contemporaries who joined the Māori arts and crafts advisory service. Together with later Elam alumnae Mere Harrison (Lodge), Rankin (Kawharu) and Elizabeth Mountain Ellis, Yearbury is a foundational Māori woman artist who, through her public and published work, introduced contemporary Māori art to a large audience.

Pauline Yearbury, *Tane Makes the First Woman*, n.d.
385 x 280mm, Russell Museum, photograph by Grace Cadogan

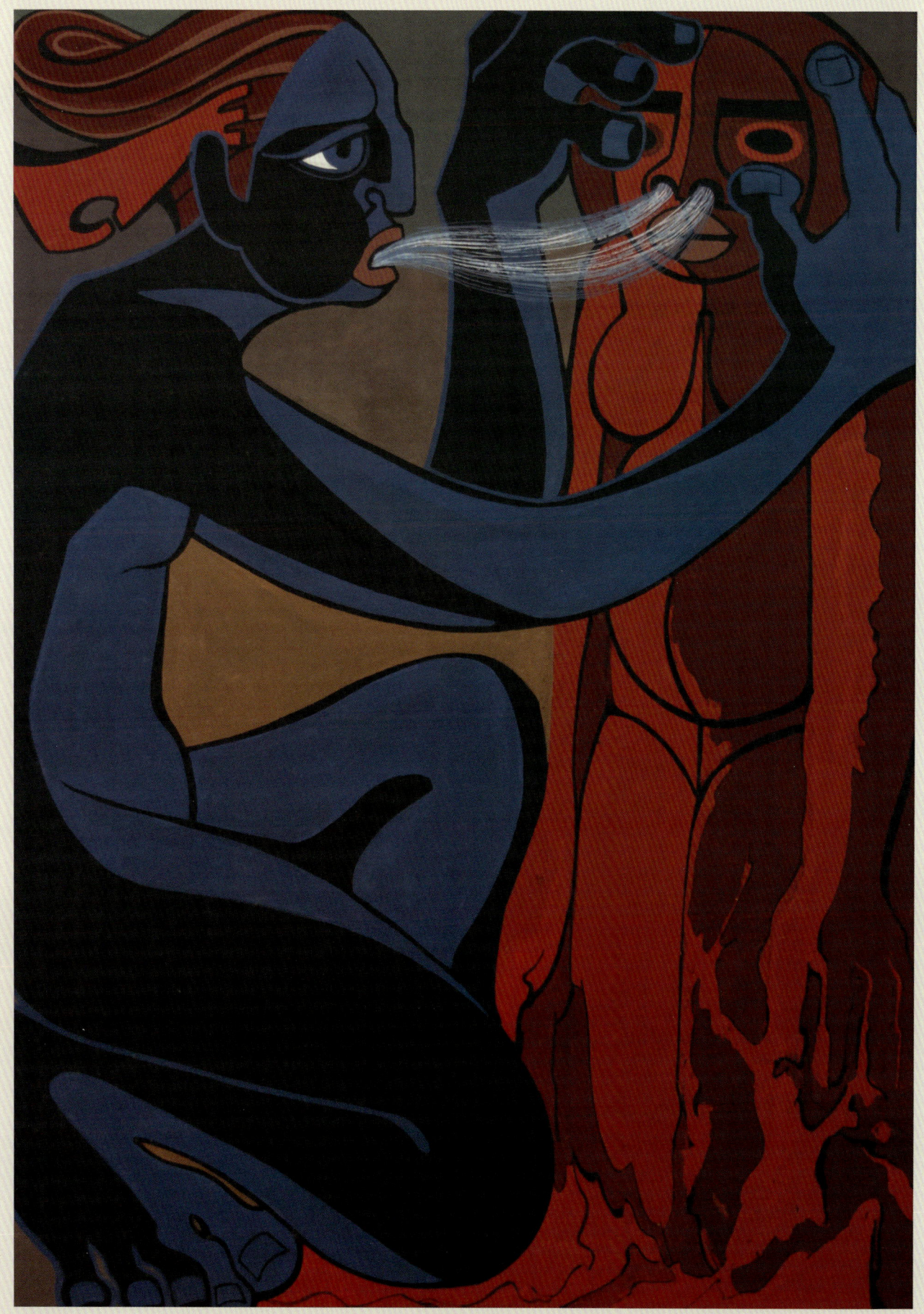

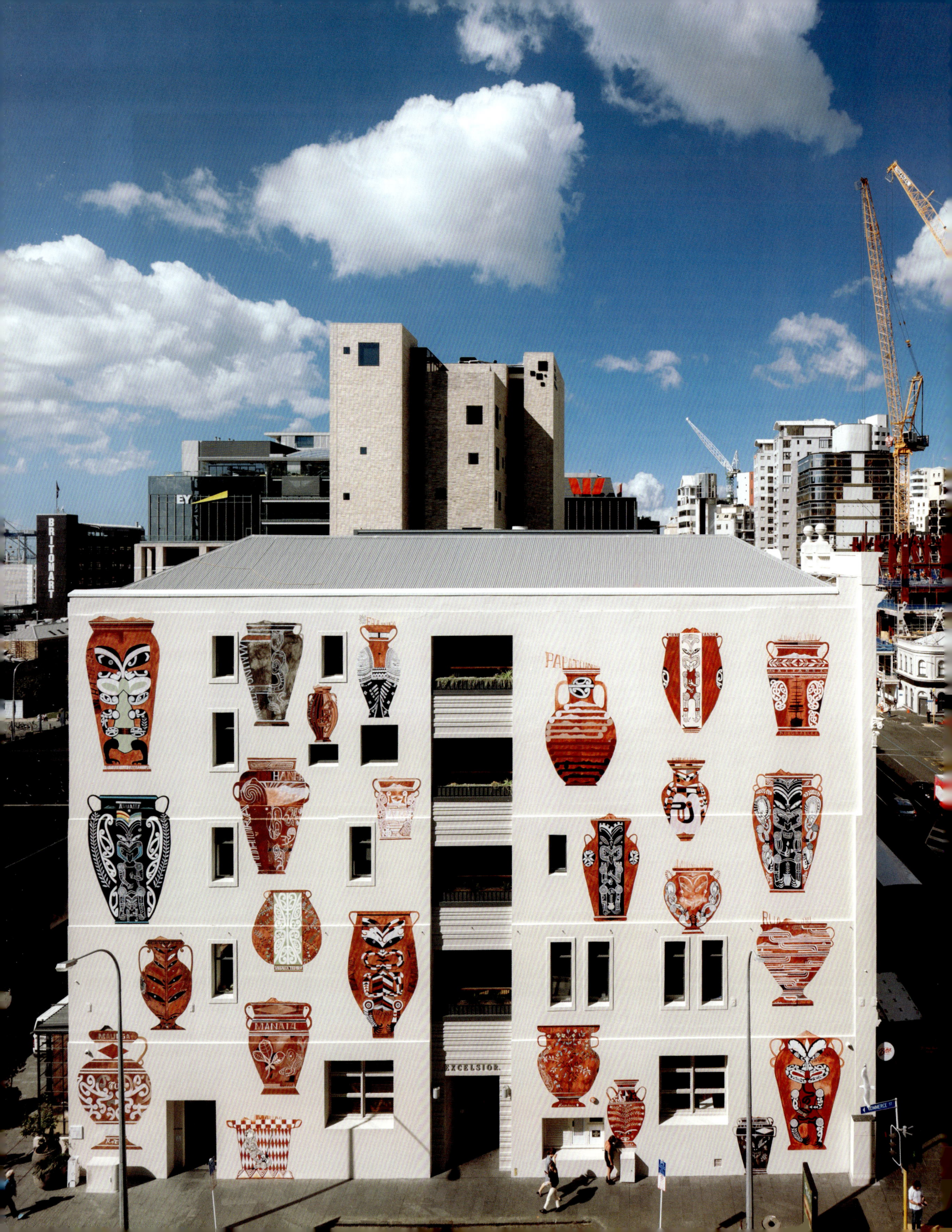

# 16 URBAN MĀORI ART AND ARCHITECTURE
## DEIDRE BROWN

*Karanga, rangatahi, whakarongo, whakarongo.*

*We're ngā tamatoa, so we must light te ahi.*

*Don't get led astray by Babylon, kia mau ki tō Māori.*

—Dean Hapeta/Te Kupu, excerpt from original lyrics for 'E Tū' by UHP, 1988

Selwyn Muru created the impressive gateway *Te Waharoa o Aotea* (1990) that welcomes manuhiri to Aotea Square, imbuing the largest outdoor public space in inner-city Auckland with a mauri that is not provided by the surrounding environment dominated by concrete and glass. The gateway is embellished with images of native and introduced animal life, Māori atua, celestial and mōrehu icons, tapa barkcloth patterns from elsewhere in Te Moananui a Kiwa, and the Campaign for Nuclear Disarmament symbol.[1] Its situation at the place where the Waihorotiu Stream (now under Queen Street) once flowed from the Aotea wetland (now Aotea Square) is a reminder that nineteenth-century Pākehā town settlement and urban growth led to the destruction of wetlands and waterways – once the hunting grounds and highways of Māori – and the progressive exclusion of Māori residents, builders and traders from central Auckland. Artworks like Muru's seek to reclaim these spaces. They are part of a Māori art and architectural movement that has sought to represent the challenges of maintaining the enduring mana of Māori on lands that have become cities.

In the fifty years after World War Two, almost half of the entire Māori population moved from rural areas to cities to seek better employment and educational opportunities.

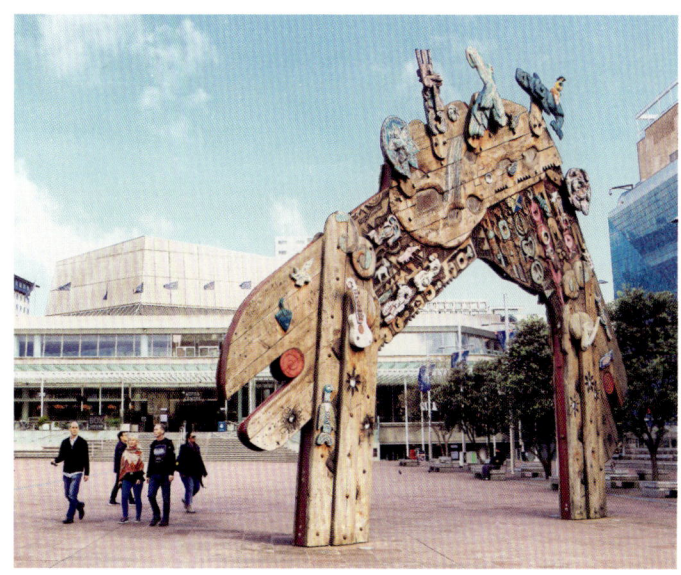

**Selwyn Muru, *Te Waharoa o Aotea*, 1990**
Auckland Council Te Kaunihera o Tāmaki Makaurau, photograph by Marlaina Key

**Opposite: Shane Cotton, *Maunga*, 2020**
photograph by David St George, courtesy of Britomart Art Foundation

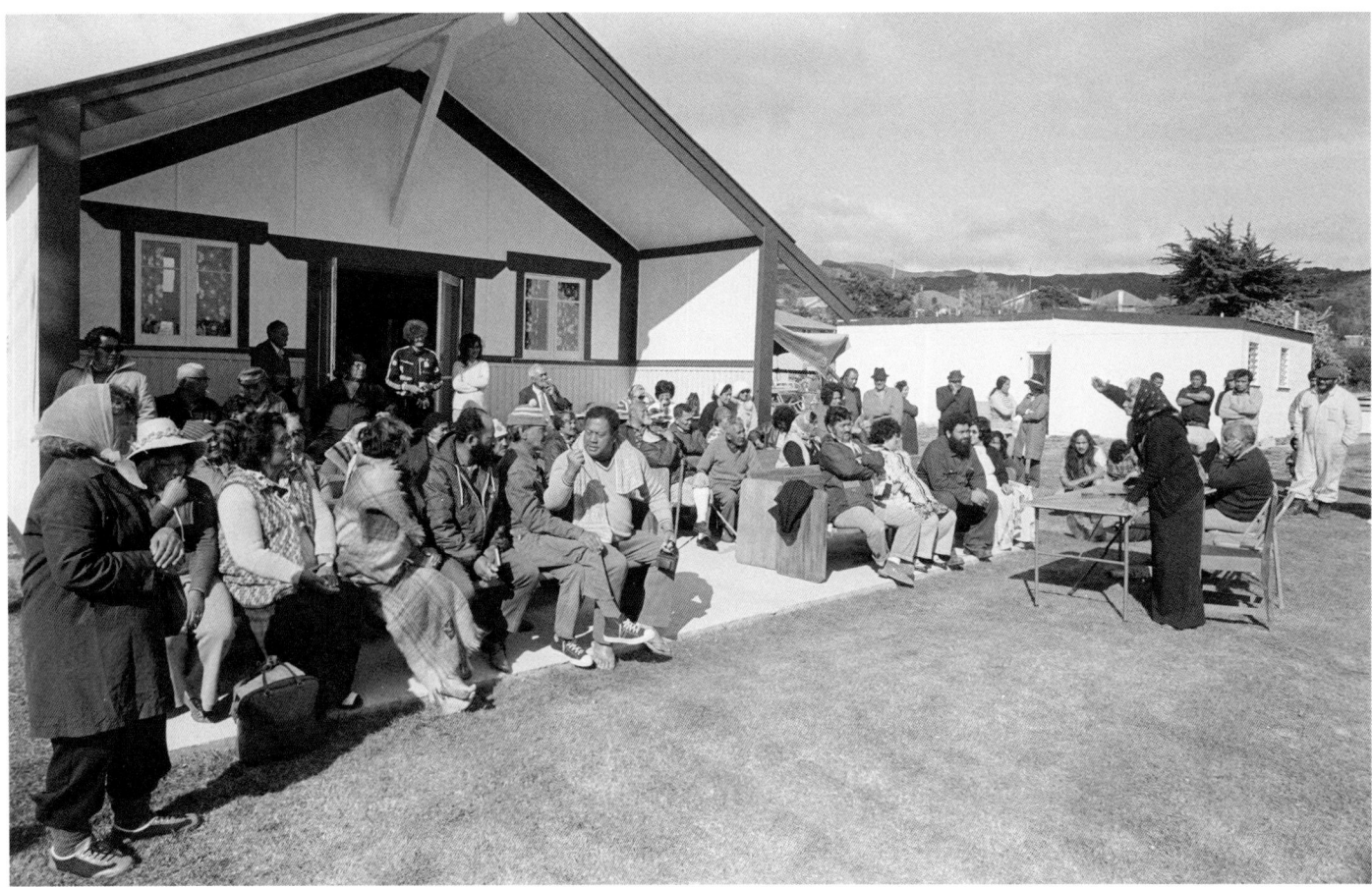

Whina Cooper (standing, right) speaking at Takapūwāhia marae, Porirua, during the hīkoi to Wellington in 1975.
Alexander Turnbull Library, EP/1975/4297/4

Their hopes were often dashed by discrimination in the job and housing markets, and this forced many into low-paid work and satellite suburbs, often with under-resourced education and health services. 'Urban Māori' were isolated in homes built for the nuclear-family model that did not allow for extended and permeable family living. Their employment and educational environments suppressed tikanga and te reo Māori. It was a situation inevitably eroded cultural values and stymied contact with whānau and tribal marae in other parts of the country. By 2013, 84 percent of the 715,000 Māori resident in Aotearoa New Zealand lived in urban areas, and one sixth of Māori did not know their iwi affiliations. A further 100,000 people self-identified as Māori in the 2011 Australian census – evidence of a belief among many Māori that life as a migrant in another country was better than as an Indigenous person in their homeland.[2]

Not surprisingly, when the Māori civil rights movement initiated a 'second Māori renaissance' of arts, architecture, tikanga and reo in the 1970s (the first renaissance was the one inspired by Apirana Ngata in the 1920s and 1930s) it did so with considerable support from urban Māori.[3] Māori direct-action groups based primarily in cities, such as Ngā Tamatoa and the Polynesian Panthers, drew strength from the struggle, achievements and consciousness-raising efforts of African American organisations associated with Martin Luther King, Malcolm X and the Black Panther Party. And they drew parallels between their own political and sociocultural objectives and calls for the recognition of Indigenous rights from the First Nations/Native American activists of the 1972 Trail of Broken Treaties caravan. Three years later, at the age of seventy-nine, Whina Cooper led a similar caravan – a Māori land-rights hīkoi (march) of about 5000 marchers from Te Hāpua in the Far North to Parliament in Wellington. They slept at sympathetic marae along the route of the hīkoi. This had the effect of bringing urban and rural communities into the fold of direct protest action, and drawing attention to the role that marae – and their arts and architecture – could play in the contemporary,

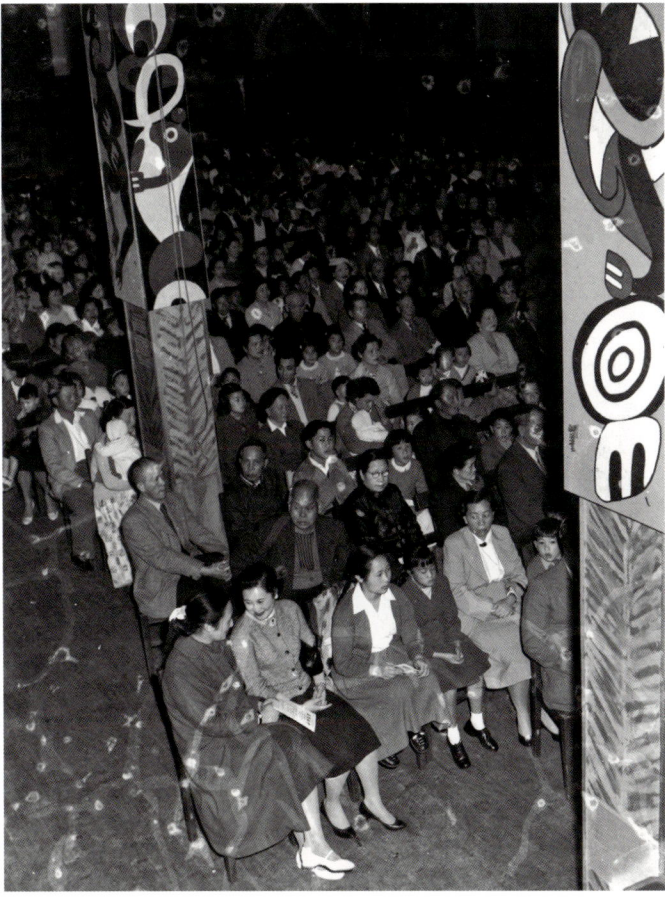

Auckland Maori Community Centre, Freeman's Bay, 1958, with its painted interior columns.
Tāmaki Paenga Hira Auckland War Memorial Museum, PH-NEG-H2021

politically engaged Māori world. Māori contemporary artists, trained or working in Western media and associated with Ngā Tamatoa, Ngā Puna Waihanga and the Māori feminist movement, expressed their messages of protest, pain and hope to an audience that extended beyond Māori communities and into galleries and public spaces.

## Māori urban architecture

Boarding houses and community centres became forums for the assembly of the Māori urban diaspora, and these were later complemented by 'urban marae'. Marae were by this stage increasingly regarded as the last bastion of Māori culture.[4] Some mid-twentieth-century Māori migrants to the major cities established pan-tribal facilities in new and existing buildings for social gatherings and for residential housing. Ngati Poneke Young Maori Club set up their clubrooms in the Hotel Cecil Buildings on Lambton Quay in 1943; the club itself had evolved from a concert party formed by young Māori women who had travelled to Wellington to work on tukutuku panels for the School of Maori Arts and Crafts Te Ikaroa a Maui wharenui project in 1936. From 1948, the Auckland Maori Community Centre operated out of a former United States army barracks beside Victoria Park, where it soon became a meeting place for rangatahi who were drawn to its dances with live music.[5] These otherwise Pākehā urban spaces were 'made Māori' through the activities of their communities and the inclusion of kōwhaiwhai and manaia-inspired paintings in their interiors.

While many Māori migrants to cities arrived as families seeking houses, over 1000 young Māori men, recruited into apprenticeships by the Department of Maori Affairs from 1959 to the 1980s, were accommodated in Māori hostels in Auckland (in Owens Road, Domett Avenue, Gillies Avenue and Dominion Road), Lower Hutt (Trentham) and Christchurch (Rehua and Te Kaihanga hostels).[6] The migration of Māori women to Auckland had started earlier, when women went to the city to carry out essential work during World War Two. A group of Māori women founded the United Maori Women's Welfare Society Incorporated in 1943 to continue the work of Māori social reformers from earlier decades. They partnered with church organisations and the Women's Christian Temperance Union to establish city hostels for single Māori women in Parnell, Mount Eden, Remuera and in Auckland city.[7] Māori hostels were not new: the first one opened near the Waipapa River on the edge of Auckland's emerging central business district in the 1840s to accommodate Māori traders from outside the city.

While none of these venues and accommodation spaces were designed on Māori principles, later urban marae acknowledged their role as resolutely Māori spaces in an otherwise colonised landscape through their names – such as Waipapa Marae at the University of Auckland and Rehua Marae in Christchurch. Most of these urban Māori spaces used painting as a medium to express their identity – a practice that arose out of a similar set of circumstances in which Ringatū figurative painting had developed. Paint was a tapu-free medium that could be deployed more easily and with less training than whakairo rākau, and one that could directly express the ideas and images relevant to its community.

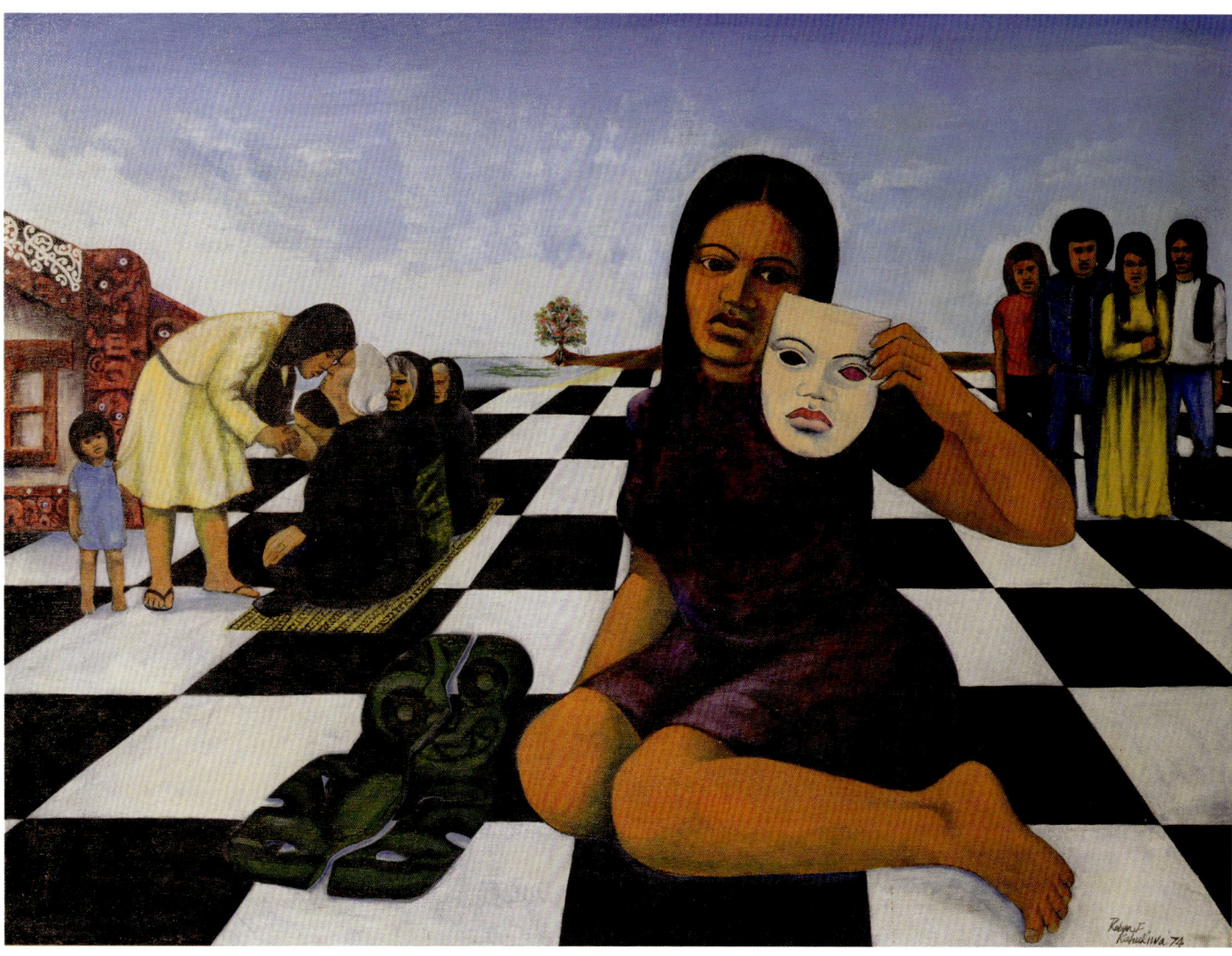

### 'My work is my patu'

The medium of paint, in particular, has been common to both Te Ao Māori and the world of Western art. From the 1970s, Māori artists who were trained in the Western tradition used paint to communicate the situation of urban Māori, and in the assertion of their tino rangatiratanga. This generation of painters included Robyn Kahukiwa, Emily Karaka (Ngāi Tai ki Tāmaki, Te Kawerau ā Maki, Ngāti Tamaoho, Te Ākitai Waiohua, Te Ahi Waru, Ngāti Mahuta, Ngāti Tahinga, Ngāti Hine, Ngāpuhi) and Kura Te Waru Rewiri. It is no coincidence that many of the Māori artists who rose to national prominence during this time were female, as New Zealand art galleries, curators, art writers and art audiences became increasingly curious about feminist art and its local manifestations in the 1970s and 1980s. These women artists were influenced by the formalism of painters such as Colin McCahon and Philip Clairmont, and by new realism (*nouveau réalisme*) and expressionism, but the content was Māori and addressed issues such as urbanisation, the 1978 police clearance of Māori land occupiers and their buildings on Takaparawhau (Bastion Point), the 1981 Springbok rugby tour, and the rights promised by Te Tiriti o Waitangi but not realised.

As a consequence of Māori internal migration, a generation of urbanised and detribalised Māori became adults during the 1970s and 1980s, and the art produced by that generation, some of whom were self-taught and others educated in art schools, reflects a search for an identity that would allow them to be Māori within a Pākehā-dominated society. Robyn Kahukiwa was born and raised in Australia and, after moving to Aotearoa New Zealand, trained as a teacher and, between 1972 and 1982, taught art at Mana College in Porirua – a Wellington commuter suburb. She became a mother figure to Porirua's Māori and Pacific

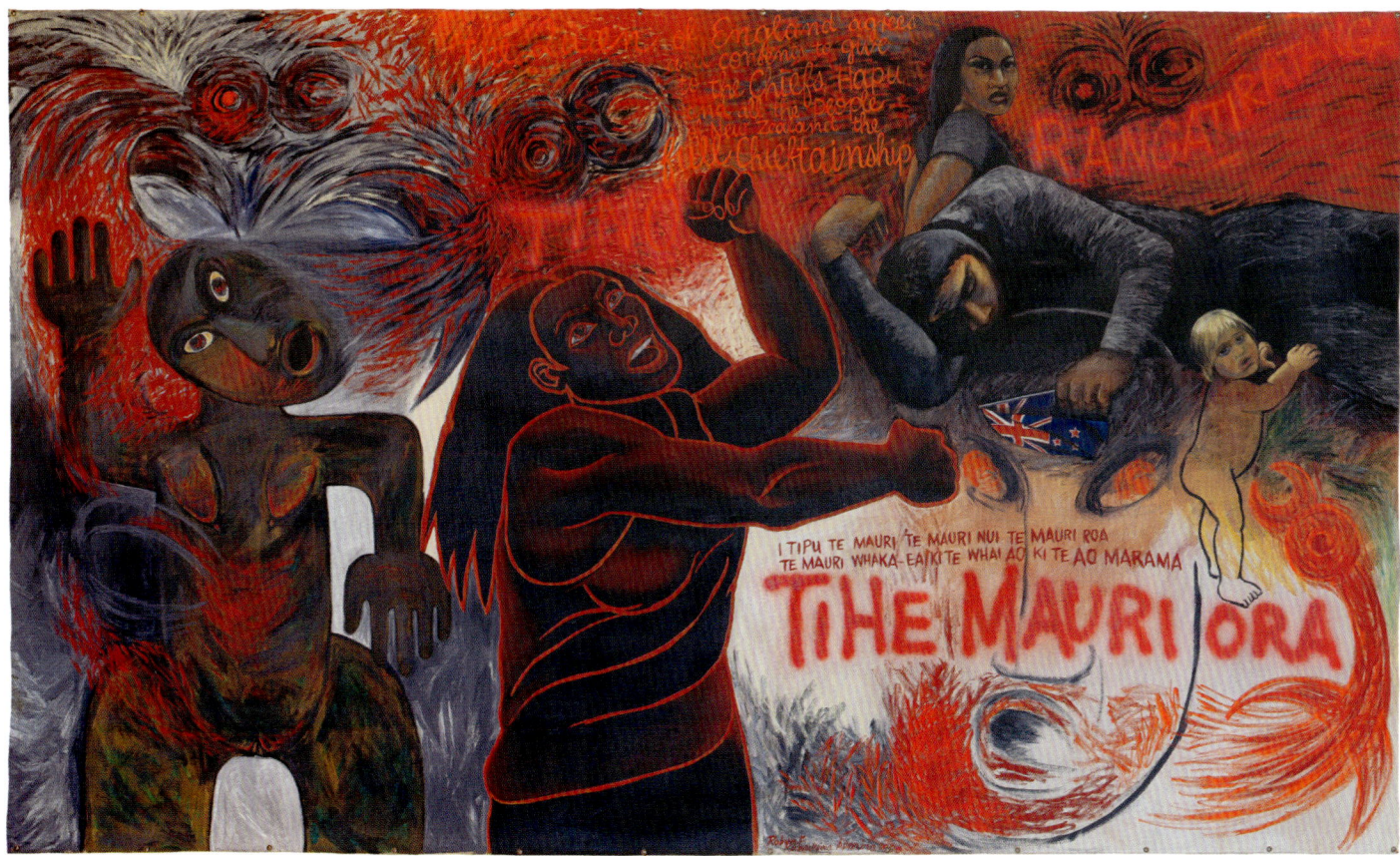

students, many of whose parents had been part of the rural Māori shift to the city.⁸ Her personal and professional awareness of the problems that faced her urbanised students made her conscious of the two sides to contemporary Māori life – one based on rural marae and the other focused on the opportunities of city living. An early painting, *The Choice* (1974), depicts the dilemma of a young Māori woman who is torn between these two seemingly irreconcilable worlds – represented by the symbolism of the white mask, the broken tiki, the chequerboard floor and the kuia and whānau of the marae on one side of the canvas, and her streetwise friends on the other. A later work, *Tihe Mauri Ora* (1990), featured a woman coming to terms with her identity through the karanga.

The directness and accessibility of the imagery Kahukiwa has used throughout her career has imparted a sincerity and clarity of message that has appealed to Māori and Pākehā audiences alike. Jonathan Mane-Wheoki has suggested that Kahukiwa's realism was influenced by that practised by new realism painters from Auckland from the 1960s, in particular McCahon; and that her work displayed commonalities with the personally themed works of Jacqueline Fahey and Robin

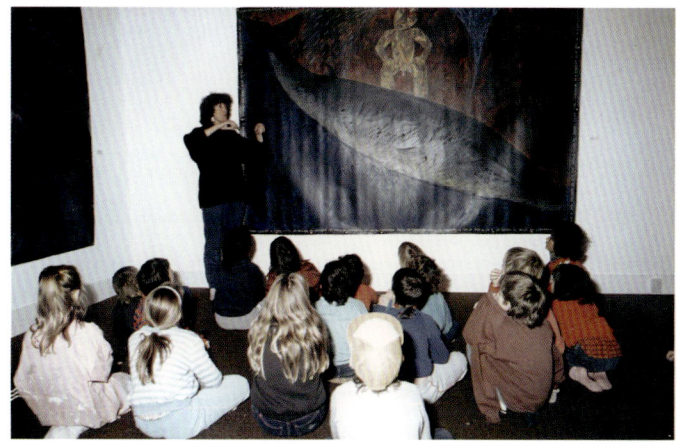

Top: **Robyn Kahukiwa, *Tihe Mauri Ora*, 1990**
oil on unstretched canvas, 2100 x 3580mm, Fletcher Trust Collection

Bottom: Robyn Kahukiwa talks about one of her paintings to new generations of art lovers.
photograph by City Gallery, Wellington

Opposite: **Robyn Kahukiwa, *The Choice*, 1974**
oil on board, 960 x 1260mm, Pātaka Art + Museum Collection, PA2016.22, photograph by Mark Tantrum

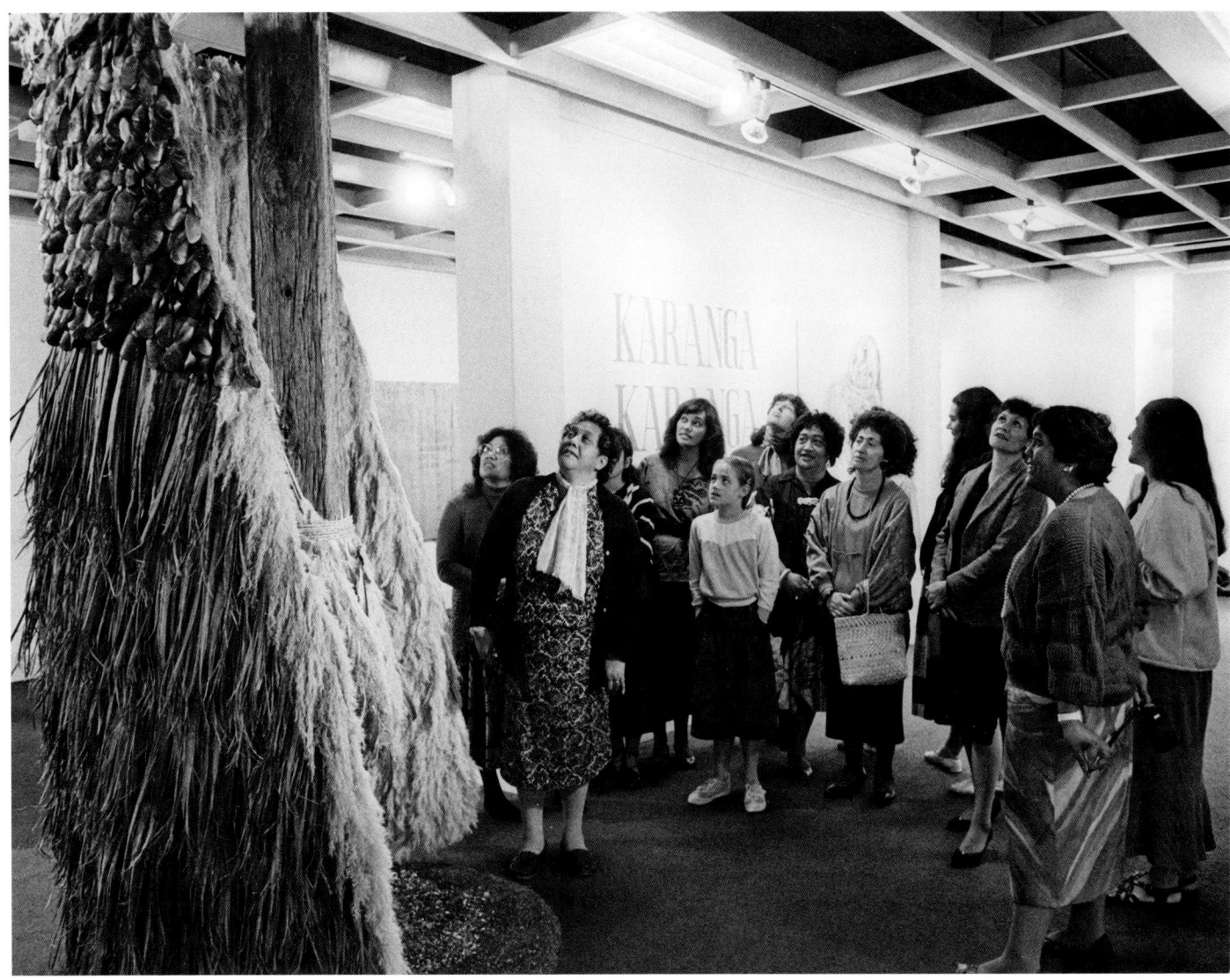

White.⁹ He writes that Kahukiwa's background and artistic life in the 1970s did not entirely overlap with that of other artists associated with Ngā Puna Waihanga, and her work was not represented in many of the Māori group art exhibitions of the time, although in 1978 it was included in the travelling exhibition *Ten Contemporary Maori Artists* and in Peter Cape's 1979 survey book, *New Zealand Painting Since 1960*.¹⁰

About this time, and inspired by carvings of women inside her ancestral Tokomaru Bay whare whakairo, Kahukiwa began to paint the great female figures from Māori ancestral stories: this led to the 1983 *Wahine Toa* touring exhibition, which marked a turning point in her career. Ancestresses such as Hinenuitepō, who had been much maligned in published English-language 'mythologies' as the goddess of death, were portrayed instead as positive role models in Kahukiwa's paintings. Although the works toured galleries around the country, the Auckland Art Gallery refused the exhibition; this infuriated some feminist commentators, who claimed that the gallery's decision was politically motivated. The paintings were reprinted as plates in a 1984 book, *Wahine Toa*, with accompanying text by Patricia Grace (Ngāti Toa, Ngāti Raukawa, Te Ātiawa).

Throughout the 1980s, political issues that had an impact on Māori – such as the Takaparawhau invasion and the 1981 Springbok rugby tour – inspired content that some people considered 'radical'. In 1987, National MP Ross Meurant identified the painter Emily Karaka as a terrorist who was attempting to overthrow the New Zealand government. Meurant had been a member of the police Armed Offenders Squad and second in command of the infamous 'Red Squad' unit that was deployed, with sometimes violent consequences, against anti-tour demonstrators who were protesting against

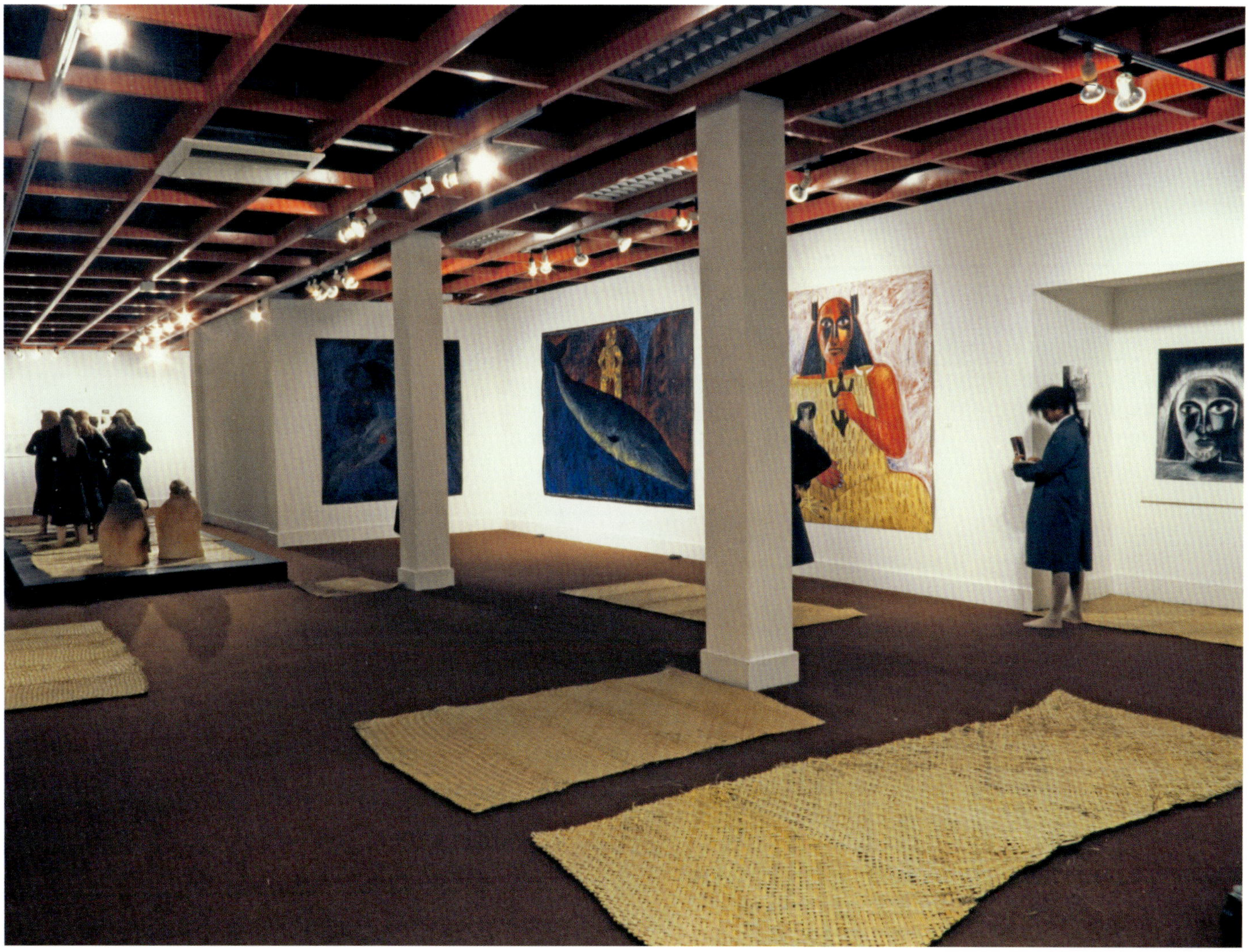

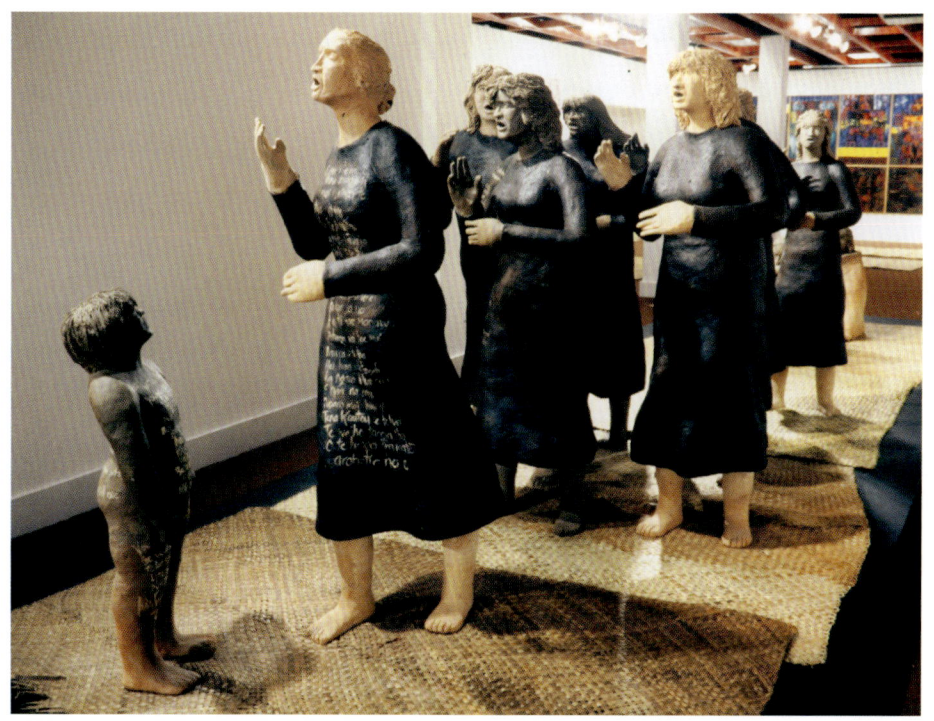

Above: The *Whakamamae* exhibition featured the work of Robyn Kahukiwa and Shona Rapira Davies, and opened at City Gallery, Wellington in 1988.
photograph by City Gallery, Wellington

Right: Shona Rapira Davies, *Nga Morehu (The Survivors)*, 1982–1988, as exhibited in the *Whakamamae* exhibition, City Gallery, Wellington. The work is now held by Te Papa Tongarewa Museum of New Zealand (1992-0001-1/A to Q).
photograph by City Gallery, Wellington

Opposite: The show *Karanga Karanga* at City Gallery, Wellington in 1986 was groundbreaking for its exhibition of the work of only wāhine Māori.
Ian Mackley, Alexander Turnbull Library, EP/1986/2098/12-F

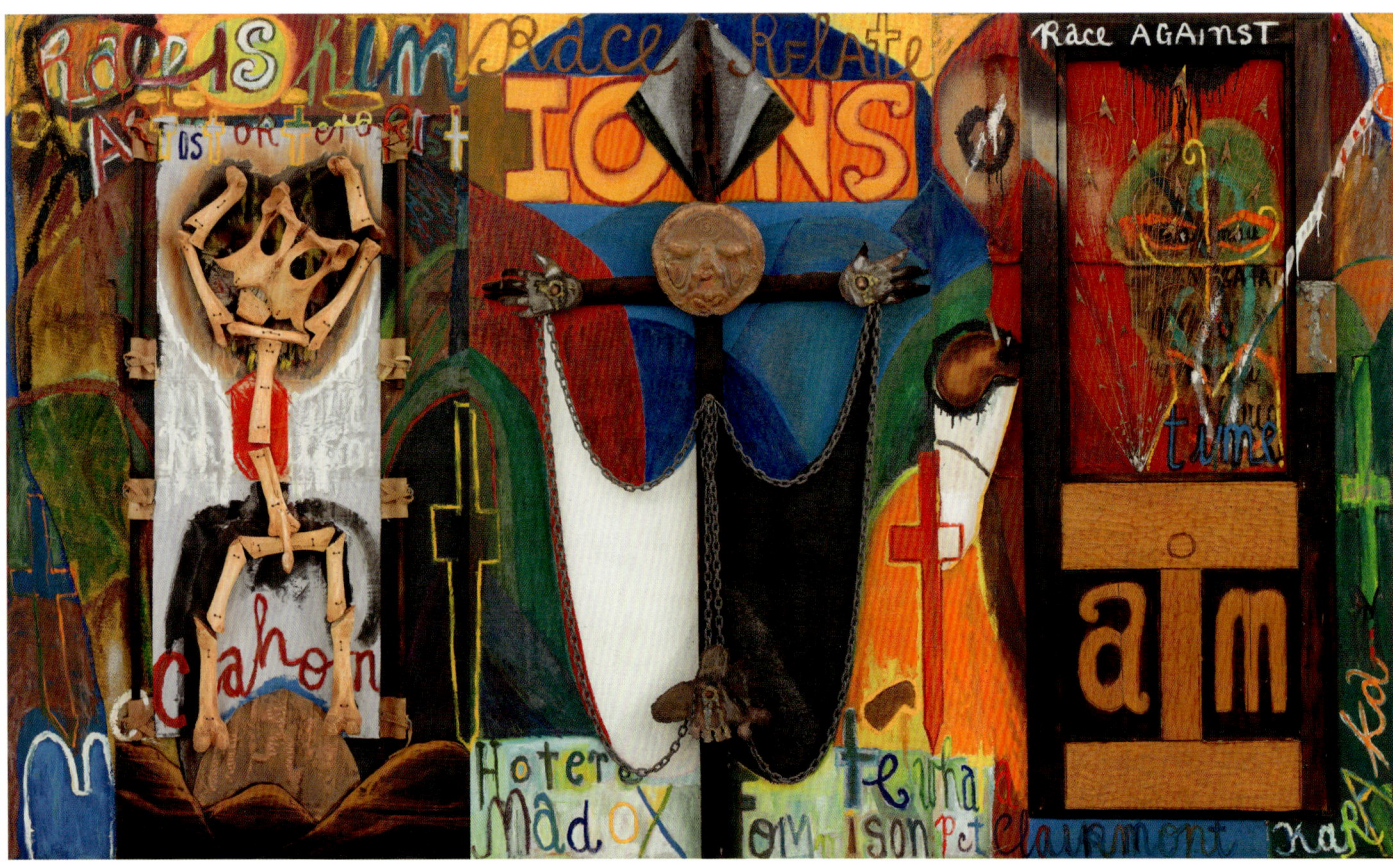

the South African rugby team's racial selection under apartheid. Karaka responded with the statement: 'I am armed with a paintbrush. If that is regarded as terrorism, then I am a terrorist. My artwork is my platform. My work is my patu.'[11] Karaka's use of brilliant and shrill colours emerged from an interest in expressionism that she shared with Philip Clairmont, who was among a group of mentors that included McCahon, Ralph Hotere, Allen Maddox and Tony Fomison. Karaka adopted a more politicised aesthetic during this time: she was inspired by protest banners and graffiti. Karaka's 1988 *Race Relations* triptych drew on religious paintings, especially those of McCahon. The work refers to McCahon's painting through its title, the use of the words 'I Am' and the inclusion of McCahon's name. For Karaka, politics and spirituality are an inextricable part of life and were therefore central to artistic practice, as was the case for other Māori artists who were addressing colonisation in their work.

Kura Te Waru Rewiri was another member of the group of politically engaged, predominantly female Māori painters who emerged in the 1970s and 1980s. She had studied fine arts at Canterbury University on the recommendation of Buck Nin (her art teacher at Bay of Islands College). At Canterbury, she was taught by the expressionist Rudolf Gopas, who had also taught Philip Clairmont. She met Karaka, who inspired her to address land issues in her work; she participated in Ngā Tamatoa's Christchurch chapter along with the artist and activist Tame Iti; and she attended the inaugural Ngā Puna Waihanga hui. Rewiri's honours thesis was a study of whakairo rākau, which was then still considered a male-only art. Carved figures featured in a number of her paintings that were exhibited from the mid-1980s, one of which, *Te Kahurangi* (1986), featured on the cover of Ngahuia Te Awekotuku's groundbreaking book of Māori feminist essays, *Mana Wahine Maori* (1991). Other paintings from this time, such as Te Tiriti o Waitangi-inspired *Nga Tohu o Te Tiriti* and *The Covenant* (1990), used the cross as a metaphorical and literal device – denoting signatures on Te Tiriti, an inability to write one's name through a lack of access to education, error and, in the centre of the triptych, the Christian cross. Daily life as a Māori woman, colonial trauma and urban Indigenous identity were important themes in Rewiri's work, as they were for Kahukiwa and Karaka.

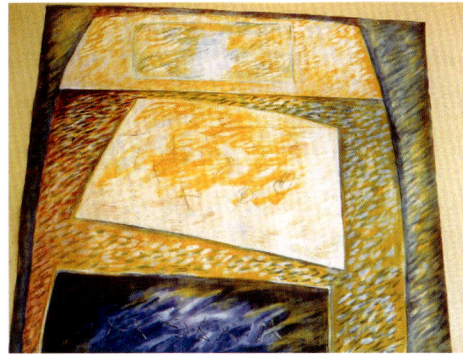 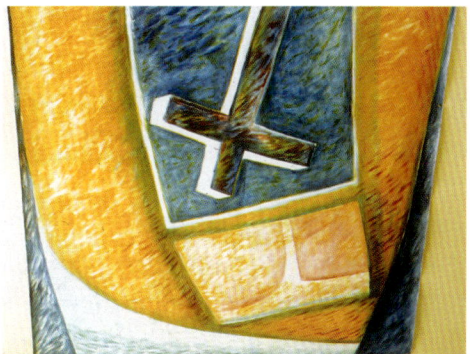 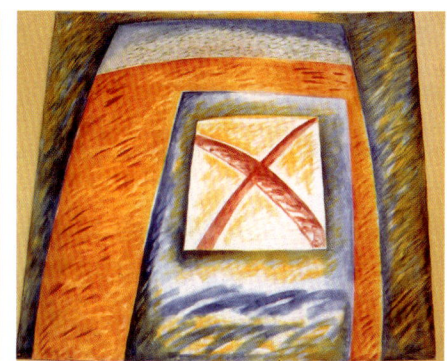

## Urban marae

Marae are strongly associated with tūrangawaewae, whether they are for communities with ancestral authority over a region, or for multitribal communities creating place attachments, such as those at Parihaka or Rātana pā. The earliest urban marae had strong iwi connections. Te Puea Marae, opened in the South Auckland suburb of Māngere in 1965, was established as a community hub for members of Waikato-Tainui iwi who were affected by the encroachment of urban sprawl from Auckland into their rohe, and also to support Māori from other tribes who had moved to the area. A pā, under the mana of the Waikato-Tainui chief Te Wherowhero, had been established there in the early 1840s as a military garrison at the request of the governor, George Grey, who feared Ngāpuhi invasion. However, it was Grey who invaded the Waikato, after he became alarmed at the assertion of Māori rights represented by Te Wherowhero's appointment as Māori king in 1858. Government troops evicted the Māori garrison from Māngere; they confiscated Māori land, imprisoned potential leaders and seized or destroyed all waka in waterways that gave access to the Manukau harbour. It was through this process that the waka taua *Te Toki a Tāpiri* was confiscated from the southern shores of the Manukau; eventually it ended up in Auckland War Memorial Museum, where it is still on display. The re-establishment of a marae in Māngere represented a reinstatement of Kīngitanga mana in the area, continuing a process of land reclamation through architecture and its associated arts that Te Puea Hērangi herself had instigated at Tūrangawaewae Marae in 1921.

Te Puea Marae was the first urban marae to have a whare whakairo. By this time, building education and the construction industry had become regulated through local body authority and national building codes, making it difficult for Māori communities to legally construct

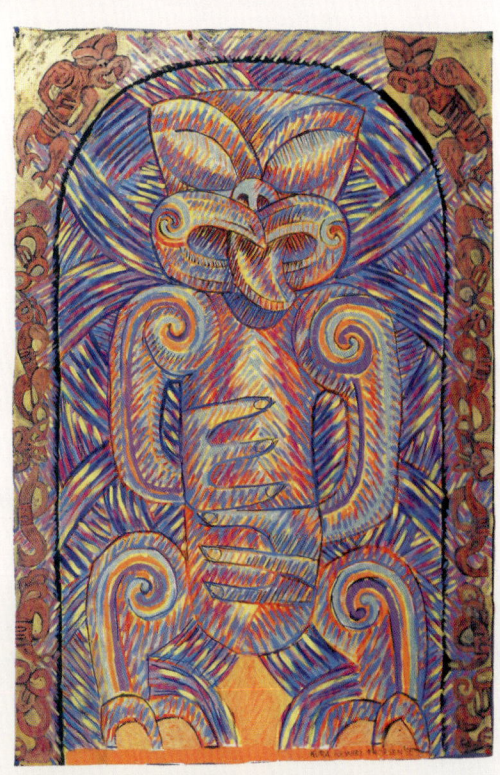

Top: **Kura Te Waru Rewiri, *The Covenant*, 1990**
acrylic on canvas, each 1750 x 1750mm, Waipapa Taumata Rau University of Auckland Art Collection

Bottom: Cover of Ngahuia Te Awekotuku's 1991 book *Mana Wahine Maori*, featuring Kura Te Waru Rewiri's *Te Kahurangi* (1986).

Opposite: **Emily Karaka, *Race Relations*, 1986**
oil paint and mixed media, 2120 x 3600mm, Sarjeant Gallery Te Whare o Rehua Whanganui, 33848, purchased 1992

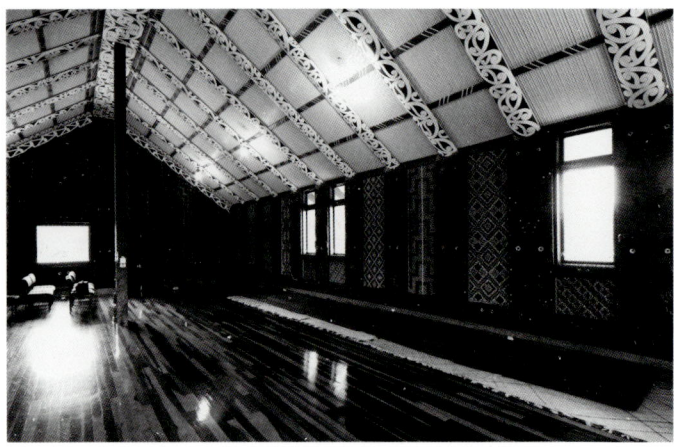

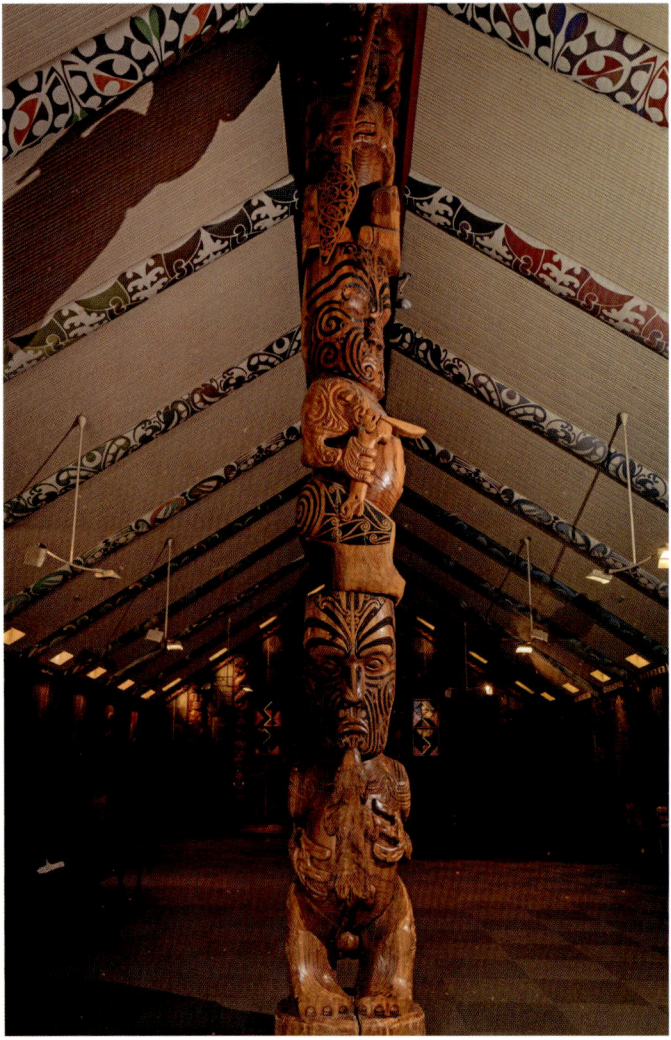

Top: Interior of the wharenui at Hoani Waititi Marae, Glen Eden, Auckland, opened in 1980.
photograph by Vincent Kar

Bottom: Interior of Tāne-nui-ā-rangi, Waipapa Marae, Waipapa Taumata Rau University of Auckland, opened in 1988.
photograph by Godfrey Boehnke

Opposite: Aoraki wharenui, Ngā Hau e Whā Marae, Christchurch.
image courtesy of Ngā Hau e Whā Marae

large buildings without engaging external, usually non-Māori specialist design and engineering consultants. As a consequence, the work of tohunga whakairo, kōwhaiwhai painters and tukutuku weavers became less a part of the integral structural scheme of marae buildings and more of an applied art, added to already completed structural shells. Earlier in the century, Ngata had written of his frustration with the way in which he was treated by the architect Cecil Wood over a proposed Māori 'decorative' scheme for Wellington Cathedral.[12] Wood's attitude reflected a wider Pākehā misunderstanding of the value of Māori creative practices. Now, the challenge was to find a way to reconcile marae architecture and its arts with the requirements of the building industry in a way that acknowledged mana Māori.

The partnership that developed between tohunga whakairo Pakaariki Harrison and New Zealand-born Croatian architect Ivan Mercep of the architectural practice JasMaD (later Jasmax) sought common ground between the increasingly distinct practices of Māori art and architecture. Harrison and Mercep met on the Whaiora Catholic marae project (1975) in Ōtara, South Auckland. They were linked through a mutual relationship with Pine Taiapa, who, as he had done for the art advisors in Ruatōria in 1960, brokered the bridging of the two worlds of practice. Taiapa had taken Mercep on a tour of East Coast marae in 1972, during which he endorsed the establishment of wharenui in the whare whakairo tradition in an urban context.[13] Mercep went on to design Hoani Waititi Marae, opened in West Auckland in 1980, for a diasporic Māori community who were mainly from Taiapa's Ngāti Porou. He worked in partnership with Harrison again on the Tāne-nui-ā-rangi whare whakairo on Waipapa Marae at the University of Auckland (1988).

Tāne-nui-ā-rangi, which can accommodate up to eighty people, was deliberately built to the same scale as late-nineteenth-century wharenui as a retort to larger urban wharenui that Harrison felt were 'oversized'. It is considered one of Harrison's most impressive whare whakairo projects. It illustrates the Māori cosmos through the depiction of major atua from the creation story on the ridgepole, with Tāne-nui-ā-rangi in prominent position as the koruru. Characters from the Tāwhaki and Māui cycles of stories on the columns bear the load of the ridgepole, and navigators and founding ancestors line the walls. The kōwhaiwhai painter John Hovell illustrated the progressive movement of light/life to darkness/

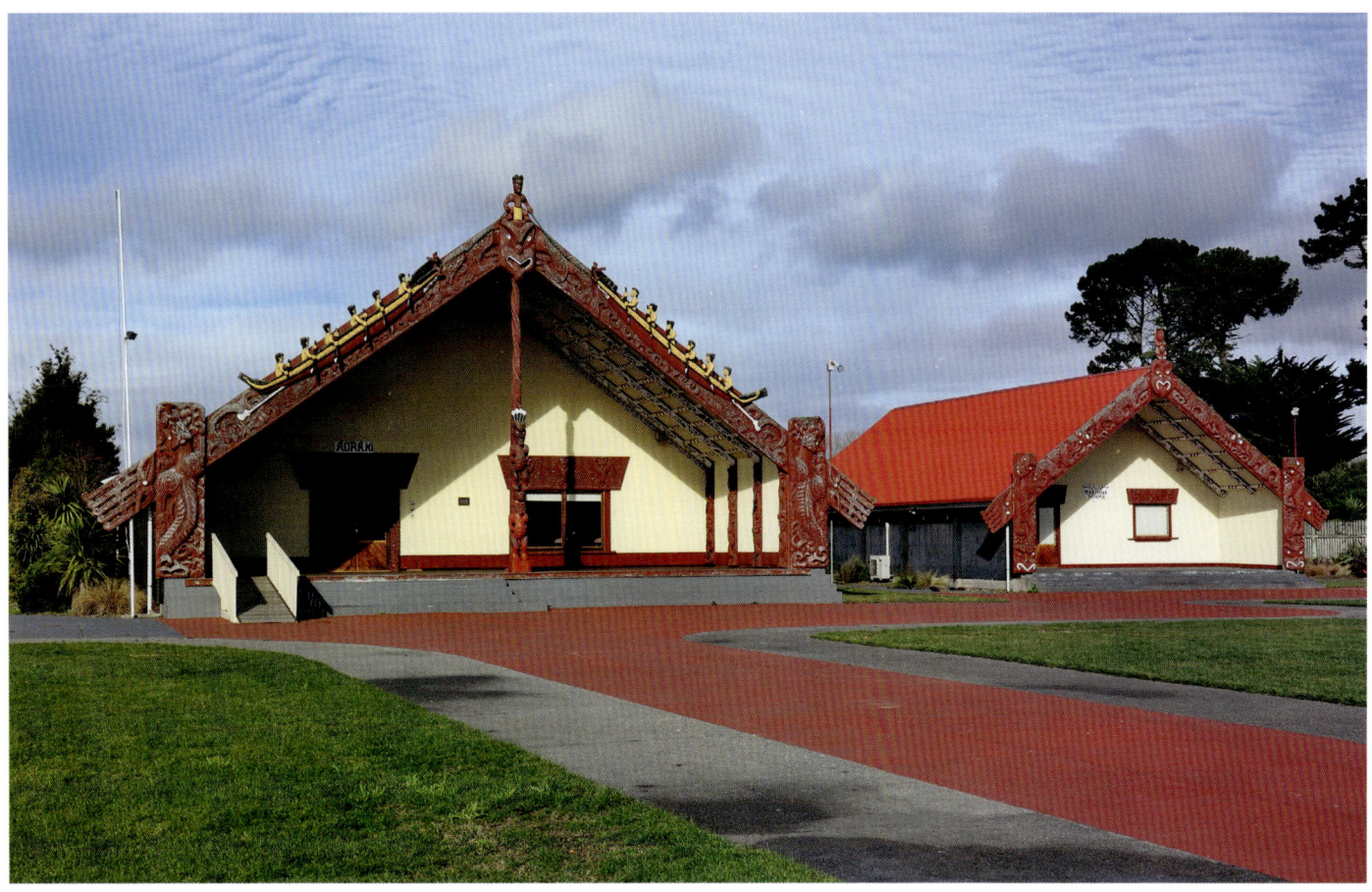

death on the rafters from the front to the back of the house.¹⁴ This working relationship – of a tohunga whakairo leading a team of specialists breathing life into the shell of a building designed by architects and built by contractors – has been the practice model followed for almost all marae building projects since then.

Tāne-nui-ā-rangi was the second of two wharenui built for marae complexes on tertiary campuses. This was the beginning of a new phase of marae construction within institutions with bicultural and, for some, self-determining mandates, such as mainstream schools, Māori language immersion schools, mental healthcare facilities and correctional facilities.¹⁵ Two more urban marae opened in 1979 and 1980 – Araiteuru Marae in Kaikorai Valley, Dunedin and Pipitea Marae in Wellington Central – to cater for the cultural needs of Māori families who were primarily connected by where they lived rather than by tribal affiliation.¹⁶ In 1990, a 'national' marae, Ngā Hau e Whā, opened in Christchurch on land gifted to the marae trust board by the city council in recognition that the mana whenua, Ngāi Tahu, had never received the permanent reserves they were promised after their sale of land to the New Zealand Company for Pākehā settlement in 1848. Ramari Brennan led the tukutuku weavers for the whare whakairo Aoraki, and the tohunga whakairo was John Rua, who trained a number of other carvers on the project. In keeping with its role as a national marae on Ngāi Tahu land, the embellishments in the whare whakairo recount the creation story of Aotearoa and its highest mountain, Aoraki, through the role of the culture hero Māui, who is the tekoteko figure on the apex of the front gable. Customary and naturalistic figures within the house represent Māori and Pākehā ancestors.¹⁷ The inclusion of a diverse group of ancestors and landscapes – illustrated in fibre, wood, paint and space, and united through the concept of a national identity – reinforced the idea that Māori were the tangata whenua wherever they were in the country, even if they did not have mana whenua status.

Although many urban marae have a customary formalism comprised of a gabled wharenui and wharekai that evoke an aesthetic connection to a wider network of marae buildings, others have adapted this form to suit contemporary contexts. Tapu Te Ranga Marae in Island Bay, Wellington was established

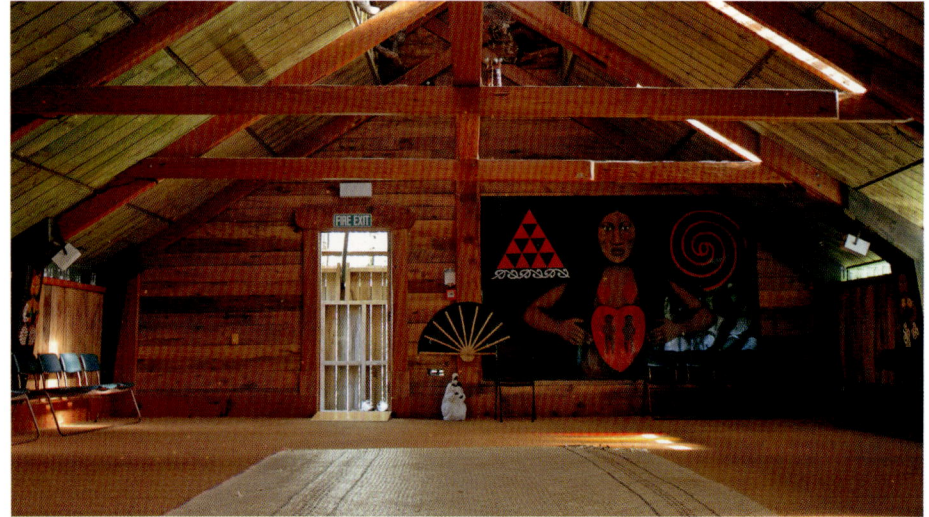

Top: Ūkaipō whare, Tapu Te Ranga Marae, Island Bay, Wellington.
photograph by Vanessa Patea

Bottom: Tapu Te Ranga Marae, Island Bay, Wellington, established in 1974.
photograph by Vanessa Patea

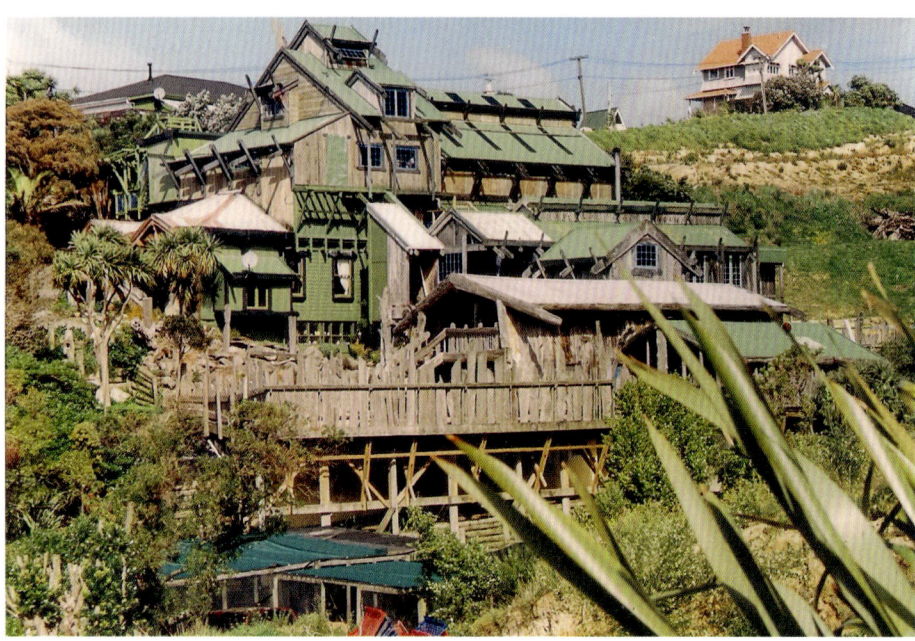

Opposite: Court hearing on Ngā Hau e Whā Marae, Christchurch, 2013.
photograph by John Kirk-Anderson, courtesy of Stuff Limited

by Bruce Stewart (Ngāti Raukawa, Te Arawa, 1936–2017) as a tūrangawaewae for the urban unemployed and homeless. In 1974 his community began building Pare Hinetai nō Waitaha – a cluster of whare on ten levels, running down a slope, that was possibly the largest wooden structure made of recycled materials in the world.[18] Stewart was guided by his knowledge of marae-based culture that bound communities together, and by Bernard Rudofsky's book *Architecture Without Architects* (1964), about self-built architecture made from locally available materials. Much of the timber was derived from car cases, and the dimensions of these determined the modularity of the building. The kaupapa was that by building the whare, the whare built the character of the builders and the community; and many elements of the whare celebrated the societal role of Māori women, especially Stewart's mother. The embellishments of whakairo and paintings were created by whānau and community members. Robyn Kahukiwa and Diane Prince (Ngāpuhi, Ngāti Whātua and Ngāti Kahu) also provided paintings for Ūkaipō, the 'female' whare within the complex.[19] Unfortunately, Pare Hinetai nō Waitaha was badly damaged by fire in 2019.

The role of the marae as a stronghold of culture was extended to that of a place of refuge and resilience at the beginning of the twenty-first century, in response to the impact on communities of a series of natural disasters and economic events. After the devastating Christchurch earthquake of 2011 that caused extensive damage to the city's buildings and infrastructure, Ngā Hau e Whā Marae

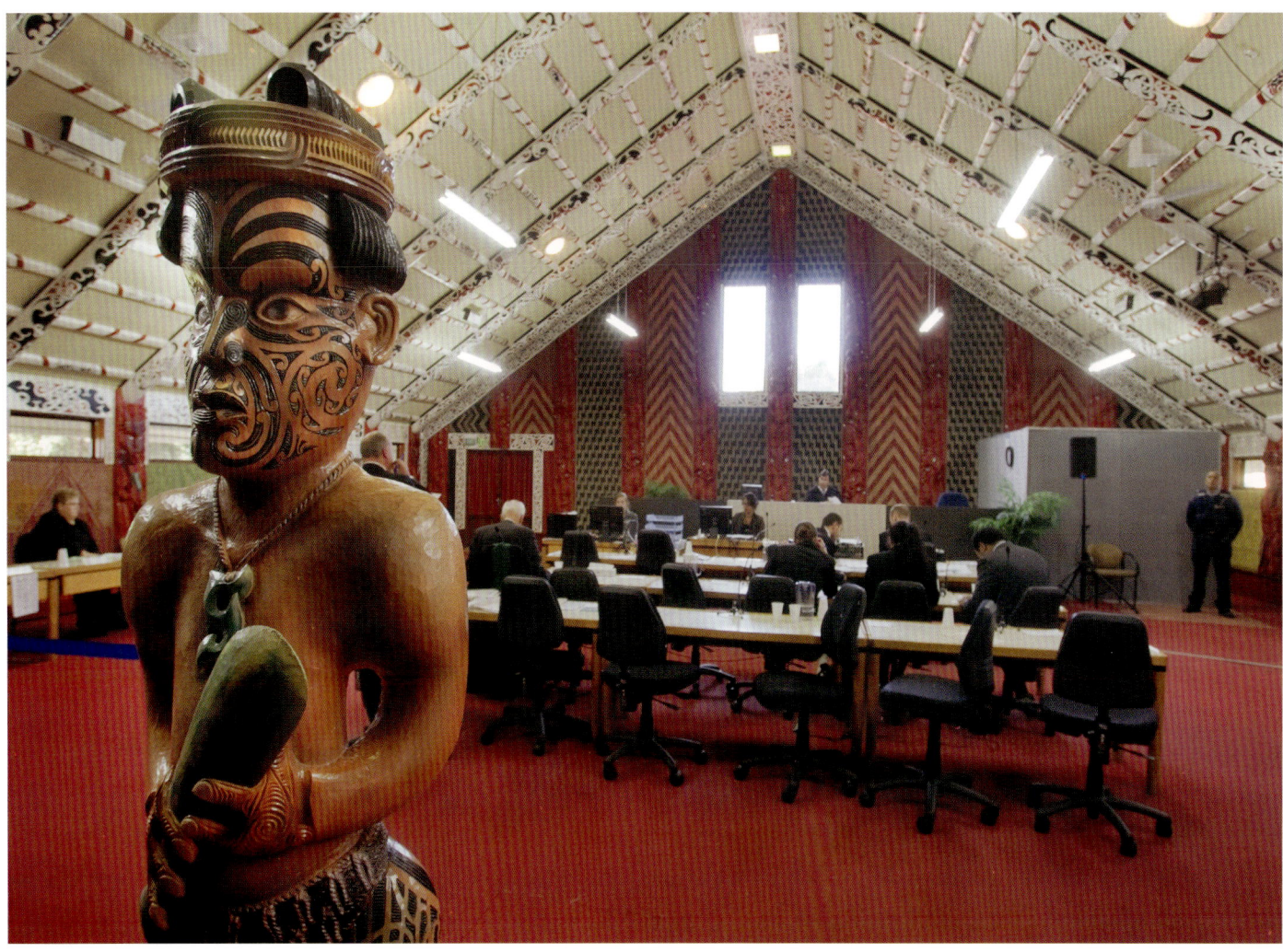

delivered services and resources to affected residents, and for a short time in 2013 it hosted the Justice Department law courts.[20] Marae around the country have become Civil Defence centres in response to flooding events. In 2016, Te Puea Marae attracted national – and international – attention when, for several months, it opened its doors to shelter and feed predominantly Māori and Pacific families and individuals who had been made homeless by the shortage of rental and freehold housing in Auckland, as local and central government and NGOs scrambled to find emergency housing alternatives. This act of generosity, and that of other marae that have provided temporary accommodation to service agencies or displaced people, reinforces the marae's function as a place of manaakitanga.

Within the Tāmaki (greater Auckland) region, there are currently at least eighteen mana whenua marae (for groups with ancestral territorial rights), twenty marae taurahere ('binding ropes', for translocated iwi) and mataawaka marae (for use by people from different groups living in the same area), and thirty-three marae associated with institutions such as secondary and tertiary education providers, churches, the armed forces, and mental health and prison services.[21] Māori groups in Sydney, Melbourne and Perth have considered building marae in those cities to accommodate the cultural needs of Māori families, some of whom have lived in Australia for generations. While there has been support for these initiatives on both sides of the Tasman, they have attracted criticism from other Māori and from some Australian Aboriginal elders who believe that marae belong on Māori, not Indigenous Aboriginal lands.[22]

Claiming space for Māori in places that have become urban has not always been easy. Building and planning legislation has sometimes been inhibitive: the inclusion of tikanga, kawa (protocol) and the right to express ideas that are different present a challenge to Pākehā ideas about urban space, architecture and art. The Te Aro Park project

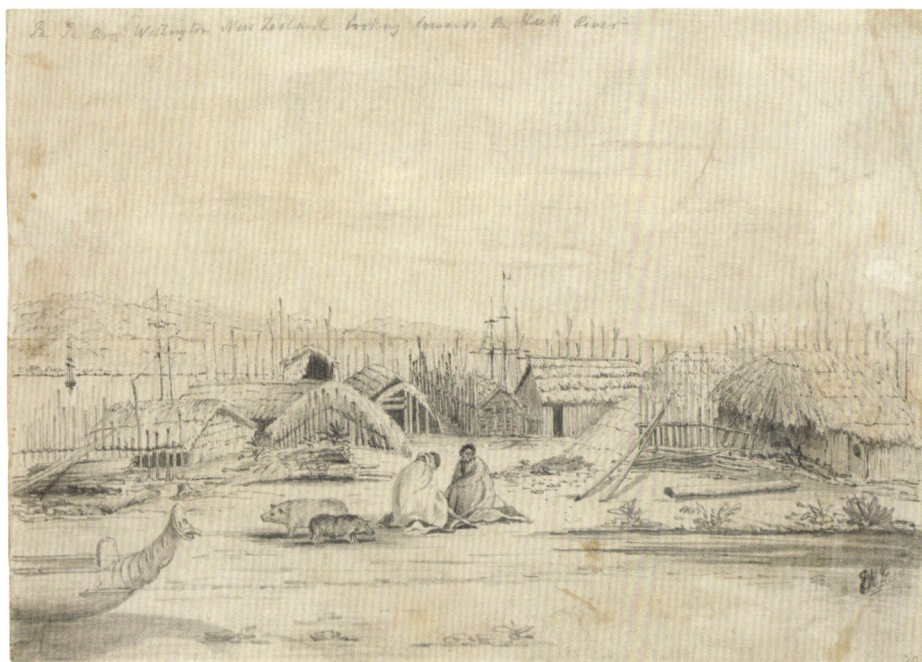

**Artist unknown (Edmund Norman?),** *Pa, Te Aro, Wellington looking towards the Hutt River*, 1840–1845
pencil, 169 x 242mm, Alexander Turnbull Library, A-049-001

Opposite: Te Aro Park sculptural park, designed and crafted by Māori ceramicist Shona Rapira Davies, with additional artwork by Kura Te Waru Rewiri, opened in 1992.
photograph by Neil Price, Wellington City Archives, 00517:6:1480-B7

in central Wellington, created in 1992 by Shona Rapira Davies (Ngāti Wai ki Aotea), is one of the country's largest artworks. Situated on a wedge of land formed by the convergence of Manners and Dixon streets, the park was originally part of Te Aro pā, built by Ngāti Mutunga in 1824 and later occupied by Ngāti Ruanui, Ngāti Haumia and Ngāti Tupaia. It was home to the region's largest Māori community, who resided on the two hectares of land within the pā and cultivated 25 hectares of surrounding land. The iwi had strongly resisted Pākehā attempts to alienate the land in the mid-1800s.[23] The pā was abandoned after a series of events that had a negative impact on the site, including an earthquake in 1855 that destroyed the adjacent wetland and diminished the eel, shellfish and flax resources that supported the community; the consequences of the Taranaki conflicts in the New Zealand Wars; and the pressures of colonisation. Most of the site was sold in 1870 and was soon engulfed by the growing Pākehā township.[24]

The Te Aro Park project reinstated the Māori presence on this land. It was built in the form of a waka taua, recalling the arrival of the ancestral navigator Kupe to the site. A tauihu at the point of the triangular park represented the male element of the Māori world, and horizontal, tāniko-like forms in the seating, water features, grassed spaces and ceramic pavers represented the female dimension. The artist was guided by tikanga in their practice and concerns:

they regarded the 30,000 handmade and painted clay tiles that covered many of the surfaces as Papatūānuku, and the firing process as Mahuika (the atua of fire).[25] Karakia were said at critical junctures in the project to protect its mauri. This was vital, as the artist faced criticism, including abuse by members of the public during installation. These were powerful Māori themes, messages and practices to be physically reinstating in central Wellington, particularly at a time before biculturalism had become a working principle for local body authorities, and when the public was not yet used to large-scale urban artworks as landscapes that people could traverse and use, rather than interventions that people navigated around and viewed.

Twenty-five years on, a more blatant statement about urbanisation by a Māori artist reignited debate on the Indigenous presence in the city. *The Lighthouse / Tū Whenua-a-Kura* by Michael Parekōwhai (Ngāti Whakarongo), completed in 2017, was commissioned by the real estate company Barfoot and Thompson for Queens Wharf, a prominent public area on the Auckland waterfront, and presented as a gift to the city. Parekōwhai's response was an immaculately crafted reconstruction of a 1950s two-storey state house. *The Lighthouse* was a shell; its hollow interior was inaccessible to the public, who were otherwise able to peer through its windows and see interior wall-mounted representations of star constellations and a mirror-finished sculpture of Captain James Cook (called

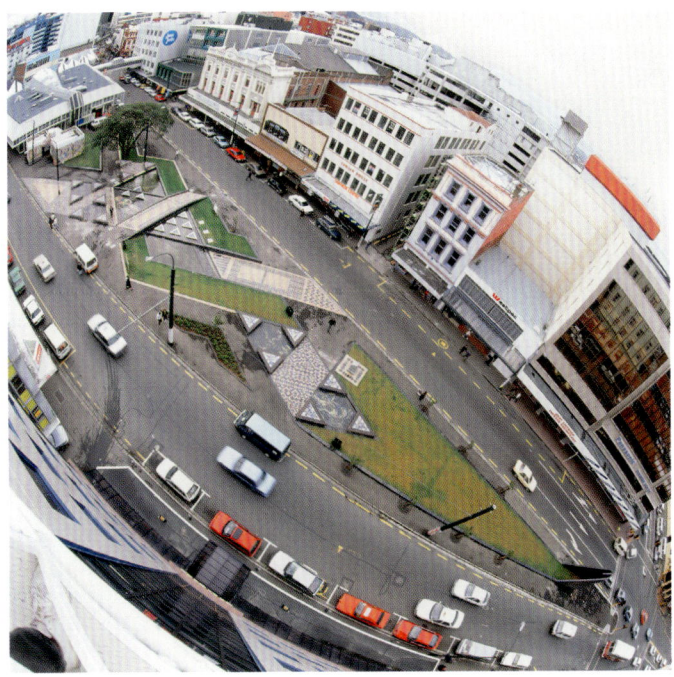

*The English Channel*) looking pensive, melancholic and anti-heroic. Auckland was, by that stage, one of the most unaffordable cities in the world and gripped by a housing shortage. The cost of the work, reported to be in excess of $1 million (with top-up funding from anonymous donors), created a public uproar and protests at its opening by public housing advocacy groups. The incongruity of recognising the role of public housing on a site surrounded by expensive waterfront apartments and superyachts left those who did not appreciate Parekōwhai's irony confused. These were all intentional outcomes. The inability for the house to be occupied was a comment on the inaccessibility of waterfront property to most. Parekōwhai's re-creation of a whole universe – one that had provided the celestial navigational aids for Polynesian navigators – within the house turned the relationship between inside and outside inside out. Chevron patterns on the exterior shutters of *The Lighthouse* recall the continuity of the use of this motif from Polynesian to early Māori art and, therefore, their shared cultural heritage: Pacific peoples make up a disproportionate number of state-house tenants. The siting of *The Lighthouse* on the waterfront acknowledged the arrival of people to Aotearoa by sea, including Cook; and it made a connection across the harbour to Ngāti Whātua at Takaparawhau, and acknowledged their successful resistance to government eviction to make way for a private housing development in 1977–1978. A confronting expression of urban identity, Parekōwhai's *The Lighthouse* asks why the artefacts associated with working-class Māori and Pacific peoples and culture should not be recognised through public art, and should not occupy sites that were now regarded as commercially 'valuable'.

The devastating Canterbury earthquake sequence of 2010 to 2016, including the 2011 Christchurch earthquake that levelled large swathes of the CBD, initiated an artistic response that revived, reclaimed, reimagined and began to reindigenise the city. Originally a wetland, Ōtautahi had been a mahinga kai for Ngāi Tahu who lived in surrounding areas, and it is this rich history that has been used to heal the landscape and its communities and to situate new buildings through site-specific Māori art. *The Lambs' Book of Life (Folder Wall)* by Darryn George (Ngāpuhi), opened shortly after the 2011 earthquake, is a large-scale work installed on the newly exposed side wall of the Christchurch Civic Offices, once the neighbouring and badly damaged St Elmo Courts building had been demolished. George's multi-storey installation continued the cultural and geometric visual language seen in his earlier paintings through the formalism of an abstracted filing cabinet drawer and files that refer to the registers and records of Christian theology and to office blocks as human filing cabinets. The work was the largest of the so-called 'gap-filler' projects – commissioned and informal art installations that created hopeful and positive spaces in the openings in the urban fabric left behind when quake-damaged buildings were removed. Lonnie Hutchinson's *Kahu Matarau* is a kahu huruhuru that measures 8m x 36m, composed of aluminium kākāpō feathers, that cloaks the carpark of Te Ōmeka Christchurch Justice and Emergency Services Precinct, opened in 2017. Another of Hutchinson's works, *Pikihuia i te Ao, i te Pō* – a glazing design on the precinct's Durham Street façade – is based on the feathers of the now-extinct huia, and is a warning to act with care. These references to taonga species and the adornments of rangatira represent the mana of the mana whenua on this site.[26]

Making te ao Māori more visible in Aotearoa's largest city has become frequent in permanent commissions. The name Tāmaki Makaurau, also known today as Auckland, can be translated as 'Tāmaki desired by many' since the region's fertile soils and double harbour made it a highly attractive place to settle in before European arrival. The 2020 five-storey-high mural *Maunga* painted by Shane Cotton

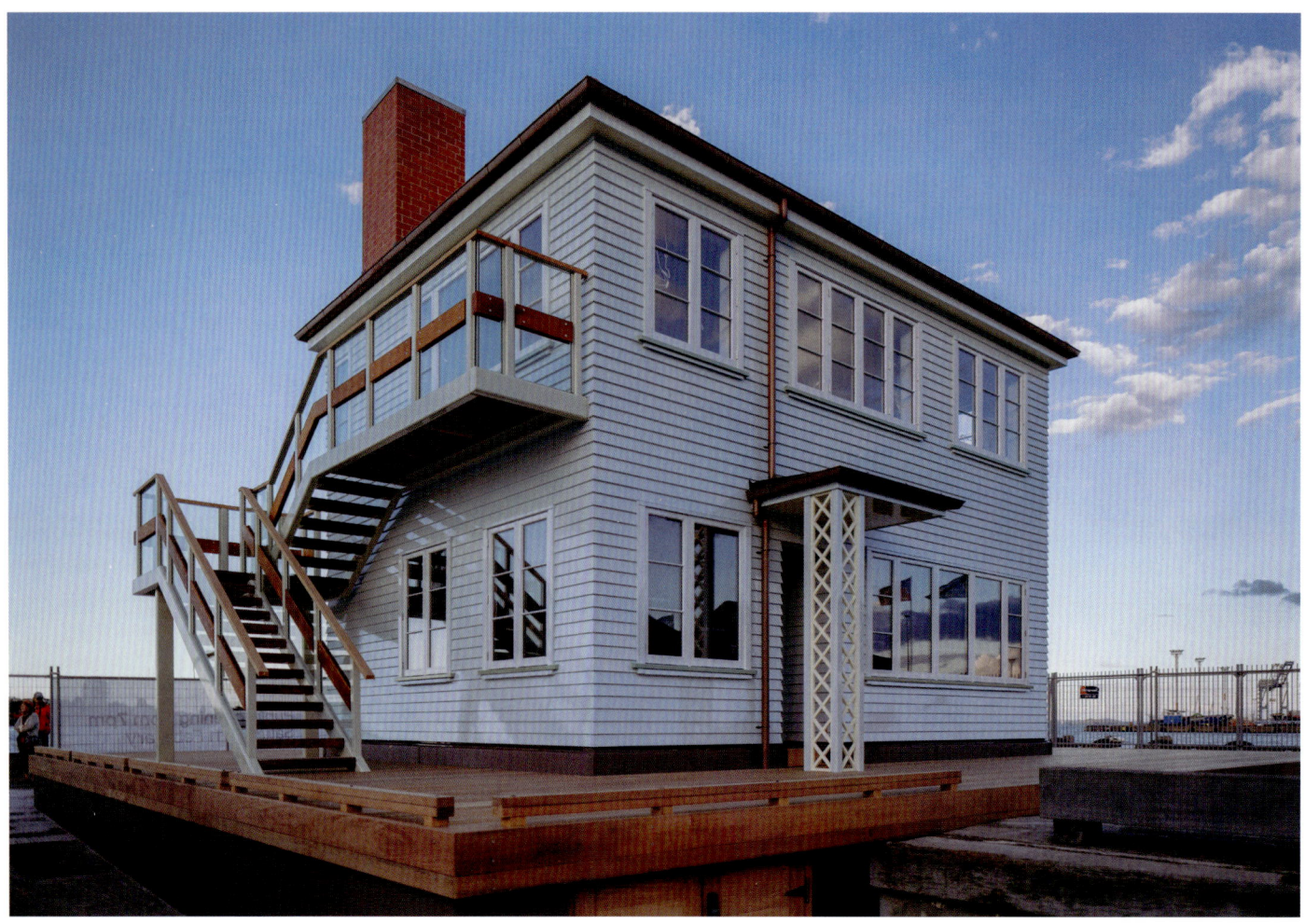

Michael Parekōwhai, *The Lighthouse / Tū Whenua-a-Kura*, 2017 including the interior installation *The English Channel*, 2015
photographs by David St George, gifted by Barfoot & Thompson Limited, courtesy of Auckland Public Art Collection

(Ngāpuhi, Ngāti Rangi, Ngāti Hine, Te Uri Taniwha) on the side the Excelsior House in the CBD's Britomart precinct was inspired by the concept of migration into the city. The wall is covered in images of pots decorated with whakairo rākau patterns and figures, landscape profiles and plant imagery, each labelled with the name of a maunga (mountain) from outside the city that Cotton either had a connection to or had visited. The pot has been a recurring theme in his painting since the 1990s, its use referring to similar imagery used in Ringatū figurative art to represent whenua. In *Maunga* the pot motif recalls the ancestral stories concerning the named maunga and also the remembered landscapes that migrants bring with them into new landscapes.[27] The mural was commissioned as a permanent artwork by the Britomart Art Foundation, which has also supported the creation of urban artworks by other Māori artists including Chris Bailey (Ngāti Porou, Ngāti Hako, Ngāti Pāoa, Te Aupōuri), Charlotte Graham (Pare Waikato, Pare Hauraki), Lyonel Grant, Lonnie Hutchinson, Chaz Doherty (Ngāi Tūhoe), Renata Blair (Ngāti Whātua) and Bernard Makoare (Ngāti Whātua, Te Uri o Hau, Te Waiariki, Te Kaitūtae) as a collective.

To the west of Britomart, Eke Panuku, the Auckland Council organisation responsible for urban regeneration in the city, has commissioned a series of artworks by mana whenua artists: Tessa Harris (Ngāi Tai ki Tāmaki), Reuben Kirkwood (Ngāi Tai ki Tāmaki), Lawrence Makoare (Ngāti Whātua Ōrākei), Lisa Reihana (Ngāi Tai ki Tāmaki), Graham Tipene (Ngāti Whātua Ōrākei) and Janine Williams (Ngāti Whātua ki Kaipara, Ngāti Pāoa) with Charles Williams (Ngāti Kahungunu, Ngāi Tūhoe, Ngāpuhi).[28] For the artists involved, the commissions have provided an opportunity to make tangible for their communities and wider public the stories and people of Tāmaki Makaurau and begin to reindigenise the city.

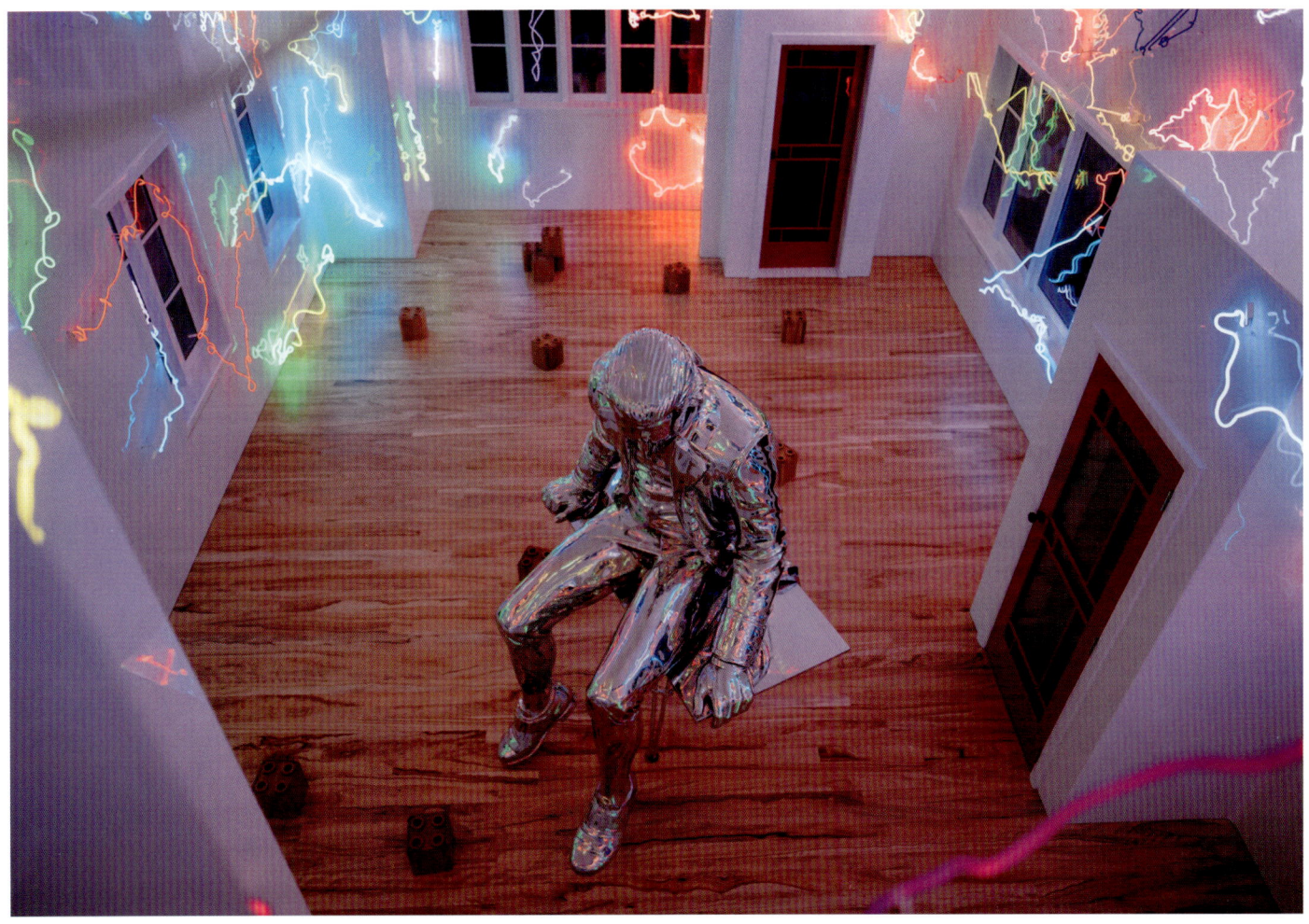

## Conclusion

Over many centuries, as Māori moved into regions previously uninhabited by humans, they prepared the land for human occupancy: they used the materials to hand to shape tools and elements of buildings, and represented their mana and kōrero in painted, woven and carved art. The imposition of Pākehā urban settlement on Māori land added complexity to the social, cultural and artistic lifeways of the mana whenua, who had tūrangawaewae through rights of descent, and of those who continued the customary practice of Māori migration by settling in the cities. The greatest challenge in these places in the 1970s and 1980s was not the environment or the negotiation of space with other hapū and iwi; it was the discrimination Māori faced from some, often influential Pākehā who sought to exclude them from the same opportunities and freedoms as they enjoyed, and to deny Māori their tikanga and reo.

As was the case at communities such as Parihaka, Maungapōhatu and Pāpāwai and Rātana pā, Māori found strength in whānau as defined by descent or by experience, and made community spaces through whakairo, weaving and painting. From a shared tradition of painting and sculpting in Māori and Western cultures, a generation of Māori artists emerged armed with paintbrush and chisel to defend their tikanga and te reo Māori and to express uniquely urban concerns. By the beginning of the twenty-first century, Māori were reoccupying, decolonising and reindigenising urban areas, making manifest the current and ancestral stories of the land on which they lived.

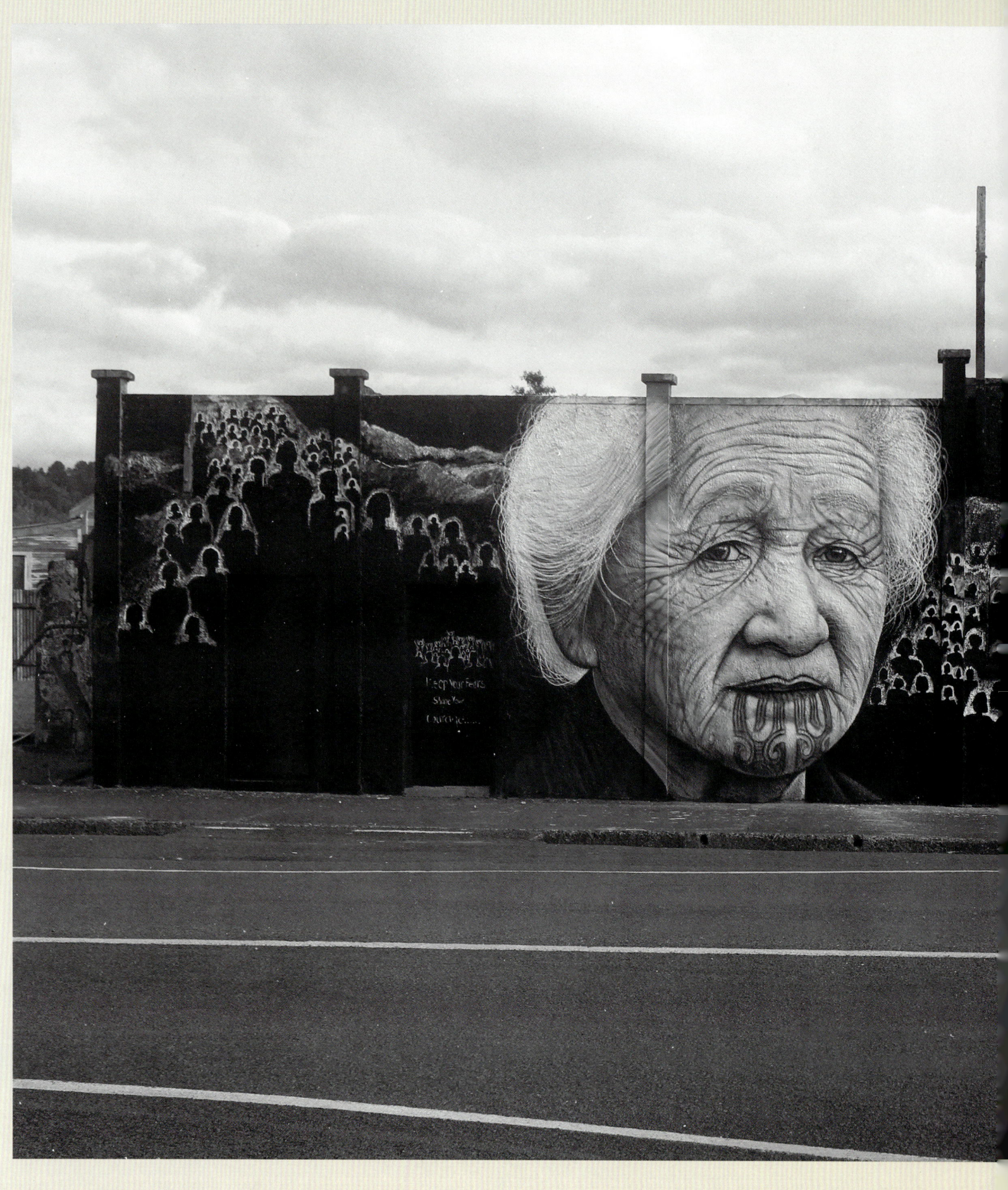

# STREET ART
## DEIDRE BROWN

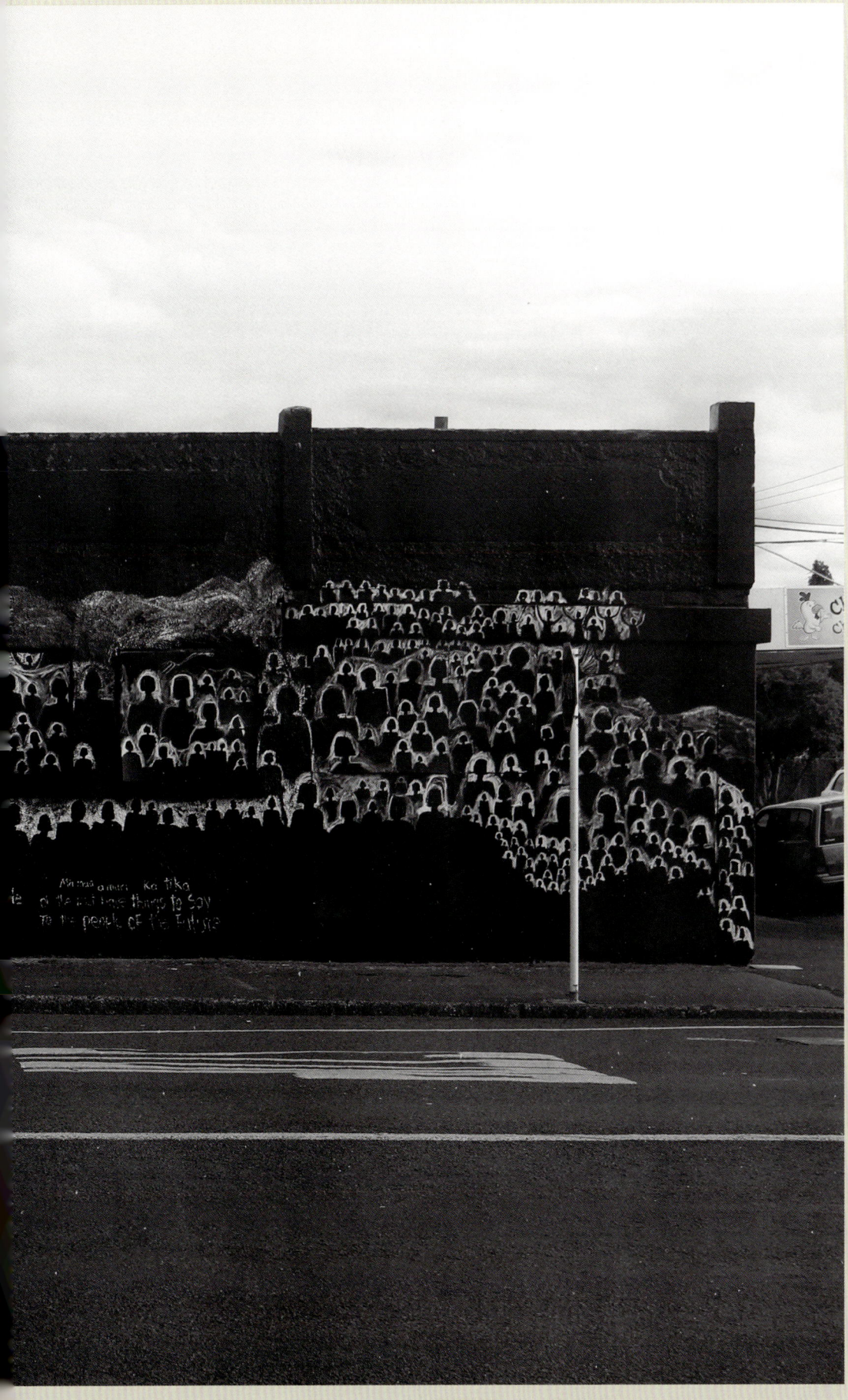

Tame Iti and Owen Dippie, *Mural of Hokimoana Tawa*, Tāneatua, 2015
photograph by ashworth

Tagging was introduced to Aotearoa New Zealand with the 1984 television broadcast of *Style Wars* (1983), a documentary about the burgeoning graffiti art, hip-hop music and breakdancing scene in New York. The inscription with spray paint and marker pens of identifying marks onto urban surfaces such as train carriages and block walls appeared both empowering and anti-authoritarian to young people struggling to find a sense of belonging in the working-class neighbourhoods of West and South Auckland and the commuter suburbs of Wellington. The association of tagging with urban African American culture particularly resonated with some Māori and Pacific youth. This co-opting of identity, which extended beyond art to clothing and language, was both an empathetic response to the African American struggle and a result of the alienation of young Polynesian people from their customs and traditional leadership through urbanisation.[1] Tagging, whether a stylised signature or a large, complex and colourful composition of letters and images, is often undertaken without permission and is therefore regarded as vandalism and considered illegal. For the taggers, however, their expressions personalise often dystopic urban landscapes and make proprietary claims to public and private spaces. Their actions take back the city.

As the art became more refined through the broadening aesthetic influence of street art, skateboarding culture and cartoons, and the first generation of taggers matured in age, some forms of tagging

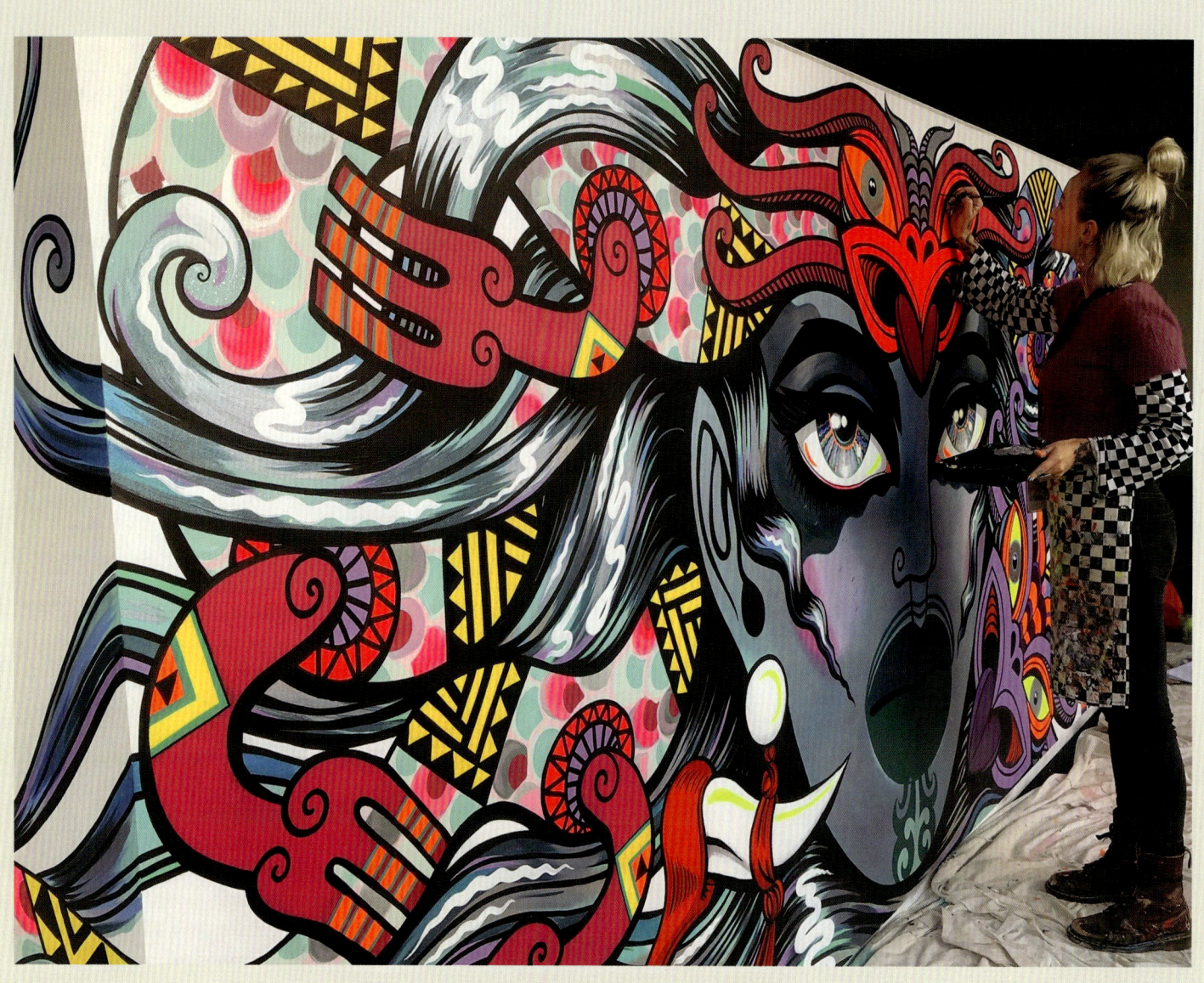

became sanctioned through institutional recognition and even civic commissions. The Dowse Art Museum in Lower Hutt curated the exhibitions *Street Crimes* in 1999 and, ten years later, *Common Ground*. Some local body authorities accepted that tagging was inevitable in some public spaces and invited talented taggers to 'bomb' or paint blank walls with colourful designs to deter ad hoc tagging.[2]

Some taggers have developed careers as street artists, creating large-scale painted or sprayed murals. Local body authorities and public agencies have been particularly receptive to the inclusion of street art made by Māori artists from all art backgrounds that indigenises public space by referencing customary art or local Māori stories or identities. Whakapapa, whenua, nature and social activism are common threads in this work, the purpose of which is to positively transform environments through raising public awareness of Māori culture. In 2015, the artist and activist Tame Iti (Tūhoe) collaborated with street artist Owen Dippie on a street portrait of the Tūhoe kuia Hokimoana Tawa against a background of the landscape and people in Tāneatua. The purpose of the mural is to welcome travellers entering the Urewera region.[3] Taupuruariki (Ariki) Brightwell (Te Whānau-a-Ruataupere, Rongowhakaata, Ngāti Kahungunu ki Heretaunga, Ngāti Mutunga, Rangitāne, Ngāti Raukawa, Te Arawa ki Tūwharetoa) is known for her large portraits of ancestresses: she painted her own ancestor Heeni Taiwaiae Te Kawhena at Alfred Cox Skatepark in Gisborne in 2018 'because she was such a definitive leader of Rongowhakaata'.[4] The mural was part of the Gisborne Girls' High School Project Ātaahua scheme, which has also commissioned street art for Gisborne from other Māori artists, including Nick Tupara (Ngāti Oneone) and Simon Lardelli (Ngāti Konohi, Rongowhakaata, Taranaki).[5] Graham Hoete (Mr G; Ngāi Te Rangi, Ngāi Ranginui, Ngāti Awa) has established an international reputation for his work, and has painted murals of basketballer Steven Adams in Oklahoma and the musician Prince in Minnesota; and street artists Janine Williams (Lady Diva; Ngāti Pāoa, Ngāti Whātua ki Kaipara) and Charles Williams (PHAT1; Ngāti Kahungunu, Ngāi Tūhoe, Ngāpuhi) have extended their mural and commissioned graffiti practices to the streets of French Polynesia, Guam and Australia.[6]

Graffiti – now a universal art language with its own conventions – and street art are more apparent and accessible practices than many other forms of Māori art that exist only in specific locations, such as art gallery and marae. For many young urban Māori, graffiti and street art form the only connection they have to large-scale artistic practice in the environments they live in.

The work of Xoë Hall (Ngāi Tahu) has a strong Indigenous and third-wave feminist presence, as is apparent in the commission for the Wakefield Street i-Site mural in Wellington.
image courtesy of WellingtonNZ

# 17 A NEW TRADITION OR OLD DISRUPTION?
## CONTEMPORARY MĀORI EXHIBITIONS 1990–2021
### DEIDRE BROWN

*Ground Control to Major Māori, Māui are you reading me? Please provide co-ordinates so we can locate. Papatūānuku on standby. Māui come in please.*

*I'm loading up my graf bomb my rap gun my big mouth waka house and girlie scenes, boy stuff and acting tuff – like you. I'm backing up the through line, DNA history time. But let them know I'm not stuck with no palette or no paintbrush, a PC rush is faster than a canvas. Yeah that's us in reel time . . .*

*I walk in I walk out
I am judged or ignored
I walk in I walk out
to shouts of praise or deft silence.
The gallery is not my marae
even when I pretend it is.
I walk in I walk out.*

—Roma Potiki (Te Rarawa, Te Aupōuri, Ngāti Rangitihi), extracts from 'Getting Brown in Hyper Town', a commissioned poem written about the works in the *Techno Māori* exhibition, 2001[1]

**Peter Robinson, *Boy Am I Scarred Eh*, 1997**
oil and oil stick on canvas, 2145 x 1745mm, Te Papa Tongarewa Museum of New Zealand, 2012-0016-5, purchased 2012

The year 1990 marked an important turning point in the reception of Māori art. Events held to observe the sesquicentennial of the signing of Te Tiriti o Waitangi included 'soul-searching' exhibitions that sought to establish what had been lost and what – if anything – had been gained for Māori in the Tiriti relationship. This opened up opportunities for established and emerging contemporary Māori artists to exhibit collectively, or with Pākehā artists in the decades that followed. By 1990, no exhibition or historical survey of 'New Zealand art' could be considered complete without the inclusion of art made by Māori. By 2001, exhibitions of Māori art in contemporary spaces made for Māori audiences were becoming a more common feature of metropolitan gallery programmes.

Māori artists who resolutely claimed to be modernists had already challenged the idea that Māori art could only be found on marae or in a museum. Contemporary Māori artists were increasingly making and showing their work in Māori communities, studios and public places – including art galleries – from the 1990s onwards. They did this at a time when the relationship between Māori and Pākehā was being re-evaluated – a discussion that would influence curatorial approaches to the questions of what 'contemporary' Māori art was and who a 'contemporary' Māori artist might be. Two types of exhibition evolved in response. The first has been described as a 'new traditionalism', in which the continuities between the work of Māori artists working in customary idioms and later generations of Māori artists were linked through curatorial selection and art historical scholarship.[2]

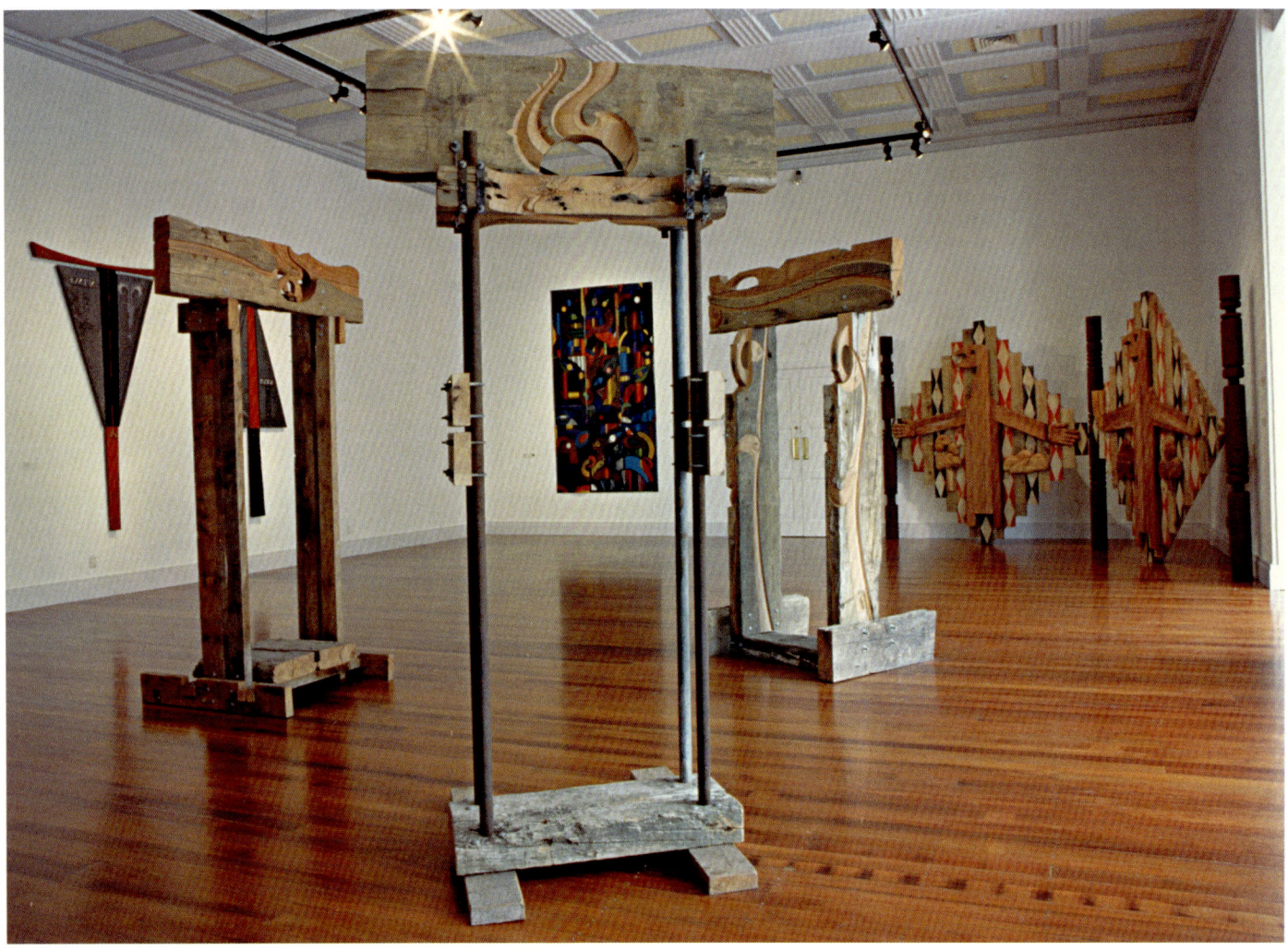

*Kohia ko Taikaka Anake* exhibition, Waitaha gallery, National Art Gallery, Wellington, 1991.
Te Papa Tongarewa Museum of New Zealand, MA_I406278

Many of these exhibitions argued for a whakapapa of Māori art in which all artists of Māori descent could be brought into Māori art's ever-evolving story. Some shows highlighted the work of artists from particular rohe or iwi and at least one made a critical distinction between Māori artists who were working with tikanga and those who were not. The second kind of exhibition suggested a rupture between Māori modernism and Māori postmodernism: it resisted the notion that Māori art could exist only when brought into the fold of a longer story of practice and identity. Ironically, work by the same artists and sometimes the same artworks were often included in both types of exhibition – a situation that illustrates the growing influence of curators, many of whom were Māori, in shaping perceptions and definitions of contemporary Māori art at the turn of the millennium.

## Whakapapa exhibitions

The *Kohia ko Taikaka Anake* exhibition held at the National Art Gallery in 1990–1991 proposed that contemporary Māori art was now a generational practice comprised of identifiable 'waves' of artists, emerging from specific circumstances that defined their practice. The exhibition showcased the work of former Māori art advisors and the politically engaged artists of the 1970s and 1980s, as well as a number of young Māori artists who had recently graduated from the schools of fine art at Canterbury and Auckland universities. Members of this generation included Shane Cotton, Jacqueline Fraser (Ngāi Tahu), Brett Graham (Ngāti Korokī Kahukura, Tainui), Michael Parekōwhai, Peter Robinson (Ngāi Tahu) and Lisa Reihana (who was not a participant in *Kohia ko Taikaka Anake*). Collectively, they have been called the 'Young Guns' and also the 'Urban Generation', because of their diverse and sometimes complex relationships with their Māori and non-Māori ancestral backgrounds.[3]

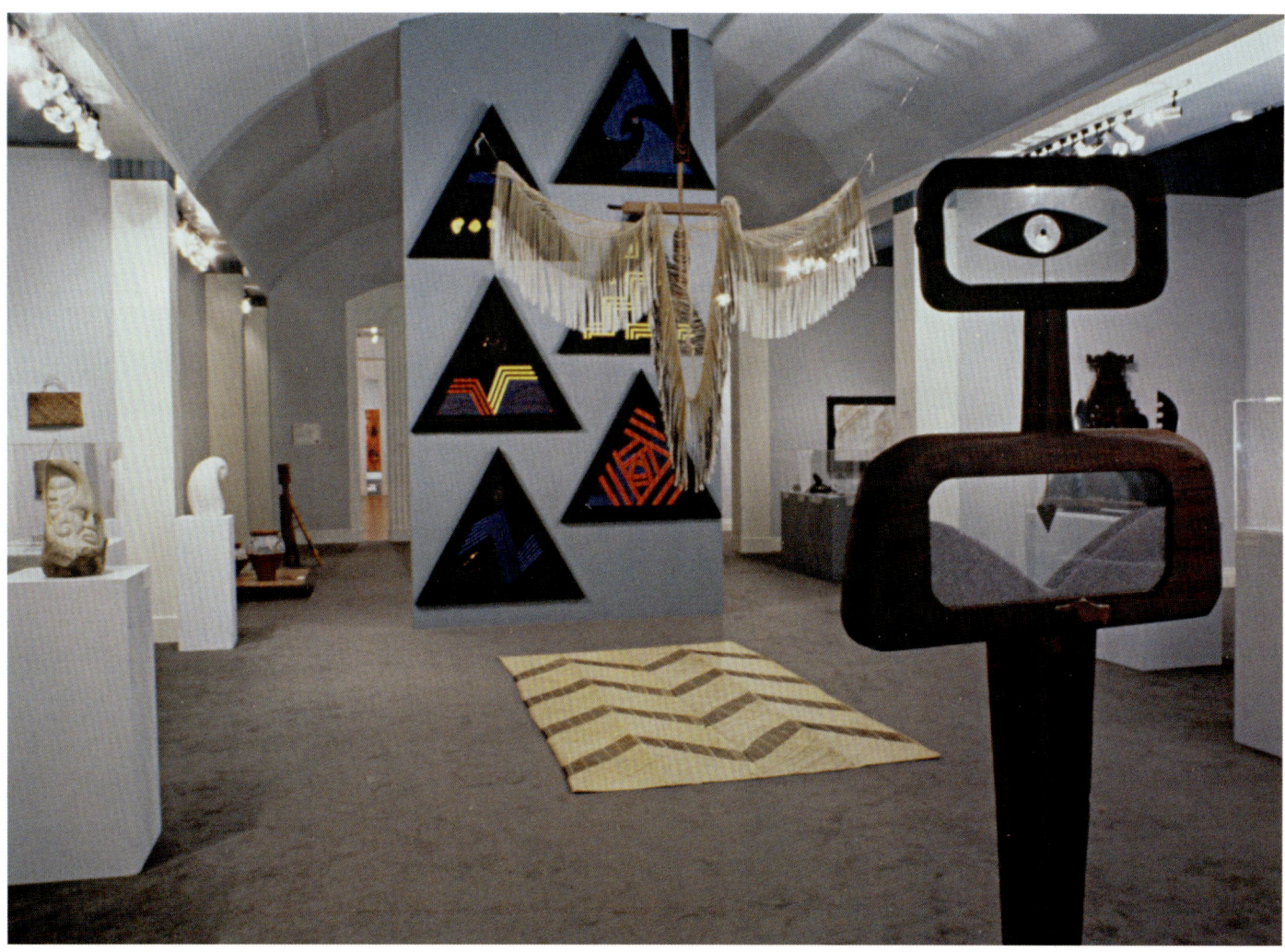

*Kohia ko Taikaka Anake* exhibition, Takitimu Gallery, National Art Gallery, Wellington, 1991.
Te Papa Tongarewa Museum of New Zealand, F.001422/05

Fraser was the most experienced artist in the generation and had been exhibiting for a number of years, since graduating from Elam School of Fine Arts at the University of Auckland in 1977. It was not until the 1990s that her work received substantial critical attention, however, due in part to art institutions and writers responding to the ideas and possibilities arising from third-wave feminism, particularly those concerned with the experiences of Indigenous women. Cotton and Robinson were part of a cohort of exceptional University of Canterbury art students – along with Chris Heaphy (Ngāi Tahu), Séraphine Pick and Tony de Lautour – who, not long after graduation, had their work included in major group exhibitions and solo shows. Their time at Canterbury coincided with the development of Māori art history as a discipline within the art school and under the leadership of Jonathan Mane-Wheoki, who actively mentored Māori students and encouraged many to embrace their identity, even if their links with Māoritanga were still developing.

Reihana graduated from Elam in 1987 and quickly established herself as an artist working at the cutting edge of digital art and conceptual filmmaking through early art animations *Wog Features* (1990) and *Tauira* (1991). She participated in the 1993 *Pu Manawa: A Celebration of Whatu, Raranga and Taniko* exhibition at Te Papa Tongarewa, curated by Megan Tamati-Quennell (Ngāi Tahu, Te Ātiawa), alongside established Māori women artists working with contemporary media such as Kura Te Waru Rewiri and Diane Prince, and the highly regarded weavers Dame Rangimārie Hetet, Puti Rare (Ngāti Kinohaku, Ngāti Maniapoto) and Diggeress Te Kanawa. Parekōwhai completed his fine arts degree in sculpture at Elam in 1990 at the height of the cultural appropriation debate on campus.

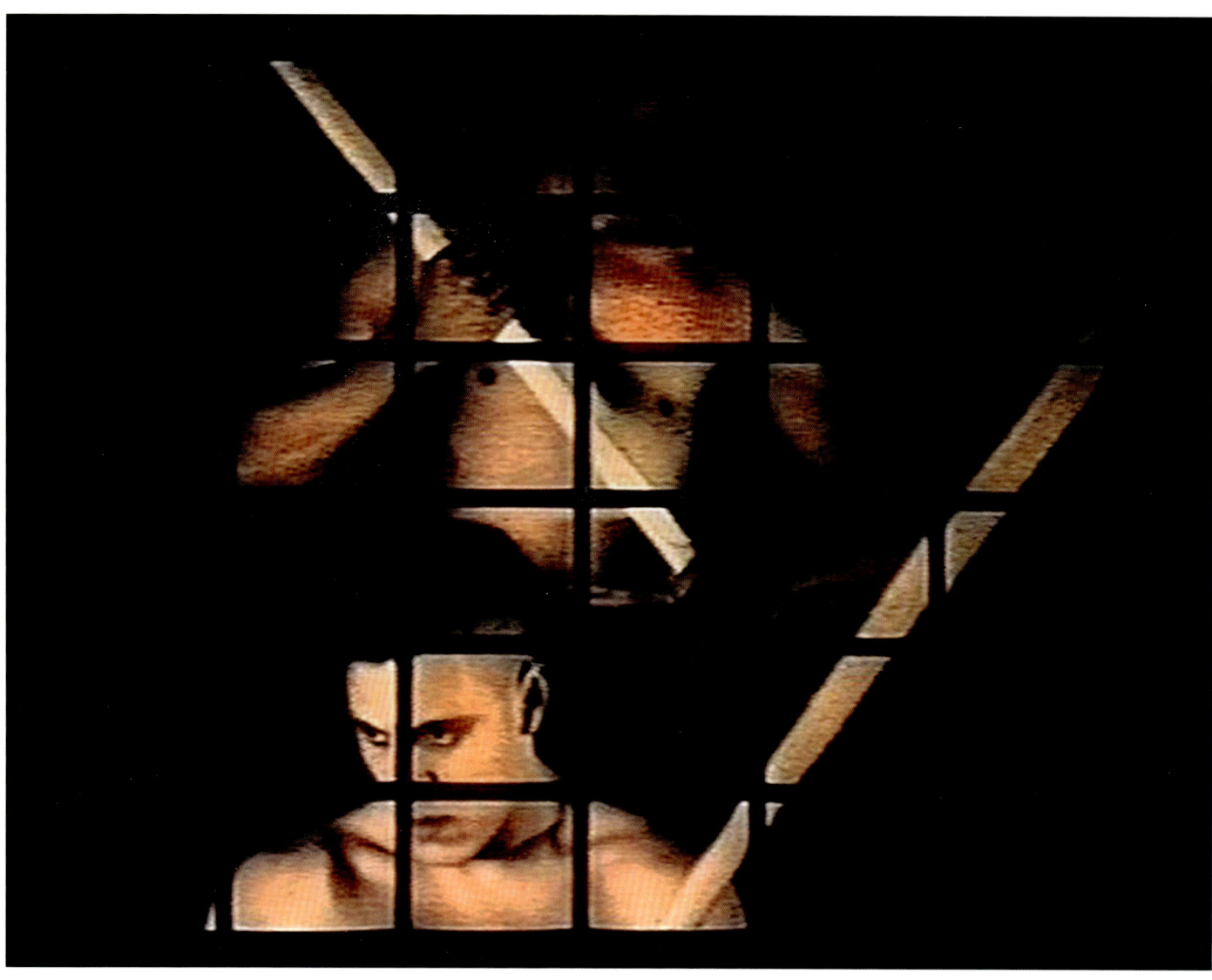

**Lisa Reihana, *Tauira*, 1991**
single-channel video, standard definition (SD), 4:3, colour, stereo sound, 5 min 24 sec, Auckland Art Gallery Toi o Tāmaki, 2005/13/2, purchased 2005

Opposite left: Shane Cotton became aware of Ringatū figurative painting through the ethnologist Roger Neich's 1993 book *Painted Histories*. Cotton employed a vocabulary of forms derived from figurative painting including the potted plant, associated in Ringatū art with land alienation through sale and confiscation.

**Shane Cotton, *Whakapiri atu te whenua*, 1993**
oil on canvas, 1772 x 1608mm, Te Papa Tongarewa Museum of New Zealand, 1993-0020-1, purchased 1993 with New Zealand Lottery Grants Board funds

Opposite right: First shown in the 1990 *Choice!* exhibition at Auckland's Artspace gallery, this painting by Michael Parekōwhai refers to Colin McCahon's epic 1954 painting *I Am*, itself a reference to Jesus's self-declaration as the son of God. Since the indefinite particle of te reo Māori is 'he' which means 'a', 'an' or 'some', the whole work is an examination of individual Pākehā and collective Māori identity.

**Michael Parekōwhai, *The Indefinite Article*, 1990**
wood and acrylic, 2489 x 6096 x 356mm, Auckland Art Gallery Toi o Tāmaki, 2009/26.1-5, Chartwell Collection, purchased with generous assistance from Jim Barr and Mary Barr, 2009

Brett Graham, son of the sculptor Fred Graham, had been raised in an environment surrounded by tikanga-based art expressed in contemporary media. His inclusion in *Kohia ko Taikaka Anake* coincided with completing his studies for a Master of Fine Arts degree at the University of Hawai'i (he had earlier graduated from Elam, where he later completed a doctorate) – an overseas experience that greatly broadened his perspective of Māori art within the context of Pacific and Indigenous arts. It also offered him the opportunity to consider the future trajectory of Māori art without constant reference back to the relationship with Pākehā – a perspective that would distinguish his practice from that of other Young Guns whose work at the time interrogated biculturalism and colonisation. His practice anticipated a shift in Māori art towards the expression of fundamentally Indigenous concerns.

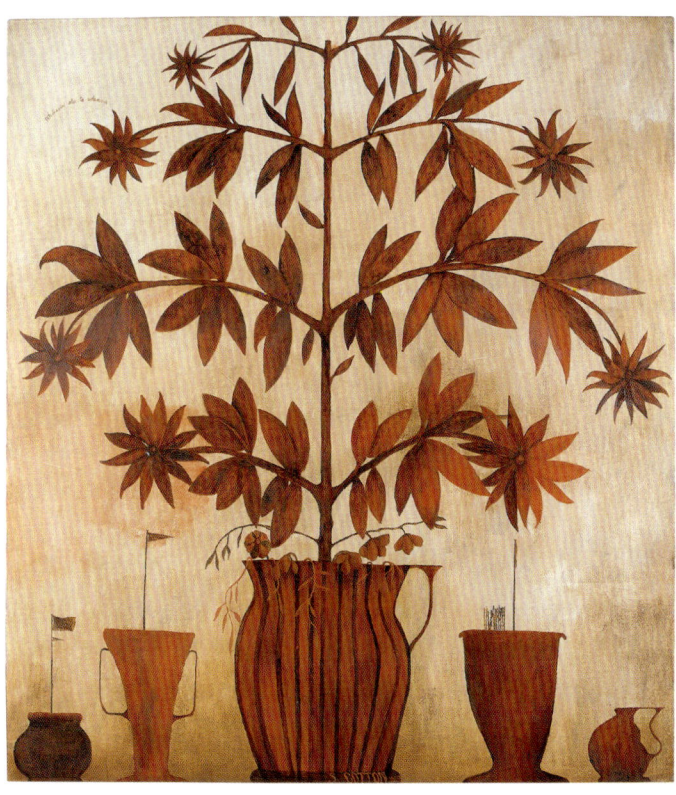
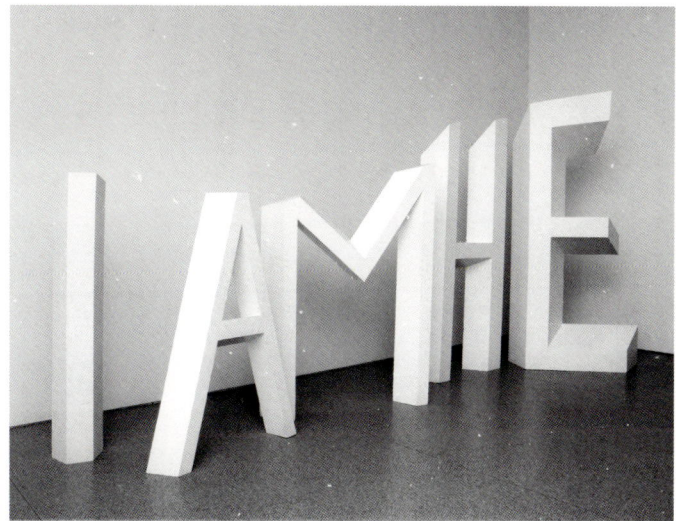

With perspectives shaped by their university training, the Young Guns belonged to the postmodern movement and used a visual language that incorporated irony, popular culture and multi-layered concepts. Compared to the politically engaged Māori artists who preceded them, their work addressed identity in a less direct, representational way – an aspect that complicated its relationship with earlier contemporary Māori art. They had the support of an emerging group of Māori (and some non-Māori) curators and art writers who were narrating this period of art for Māori and wider audiences through often provocative exhibitions, publications and seminars that either emphasised its disjuncture from, or asserted a connection to, a whakapapa of Māori art.

*Kohia ko Taikaka Anake* brought a new generation of Māori artists to public attention, presented as standing on the shoulders of more senior practitioners. The exhibition was not without its controversies, including boycotts and allegations of the exclusion of women artists from the senior group. It was organised by Ngā Puna Waihanga and Te Waka Toi, curated by Paratene Matchitt, Sandy Adsett and Tim Walker, and hosted by the National Art Gallery, whose staff were instructed to facilitate but not interfere, in an early pilot for bicultural curatorial practice.[4] Māori audience numbers at the National Gallery during the show, at just under 15 percent, were more than double the normal – a marked increase, but still only just representative of the population at large.[5] Mane-Wheoki remembered the show as having 'redefined contemporary Māori art as encompassing both traditional and non-traditional or Pākehā forms of art-making by living practitioners'.[6] This was particularly important in 1990, the sesquicentennial year of the signing of Te Tiriti o Waitangi, an anniversary observed by the curation of a number of exhibitions that attempted to capture and reconceive the state of Māori art at that time.

### Disruption

One of these was a much smaller, but just as influential exhibition called *Choice!* – a common affirmation for things and events that are good, as well as a reference to a perceived 'choice' of identity that some urban Māori faced. Curated in 1990 for Artspace gallery in Auckland by George Hubbard (Ngāti Kurī, Te Aupōuri, Te Rarawa) and Robin Craw, *Choice!* featured the work of Fraser, Parekōwhai and Reihana as well as work by Rongotai Lomas (Ngāti Hikairo), Barnard McIntyre (Ngāpuhi), Diane Prince and Darryl Thomson (Ngāti Kahungunu).[7] The exhibition challenged the idea that contemporary Māori art could so easily and unquestionably be folded into a whakapapa that included Māori modernists and customary makers, and the show supported the break from 'tradition' that Mead had suggested with his 'fires of destruction' comment (see page 405). Hubbard continued to explore and expand on this proposition as a curator for *Cross-Pollination* (Artspace, 1991),[8] *Stop Making Sense* (City

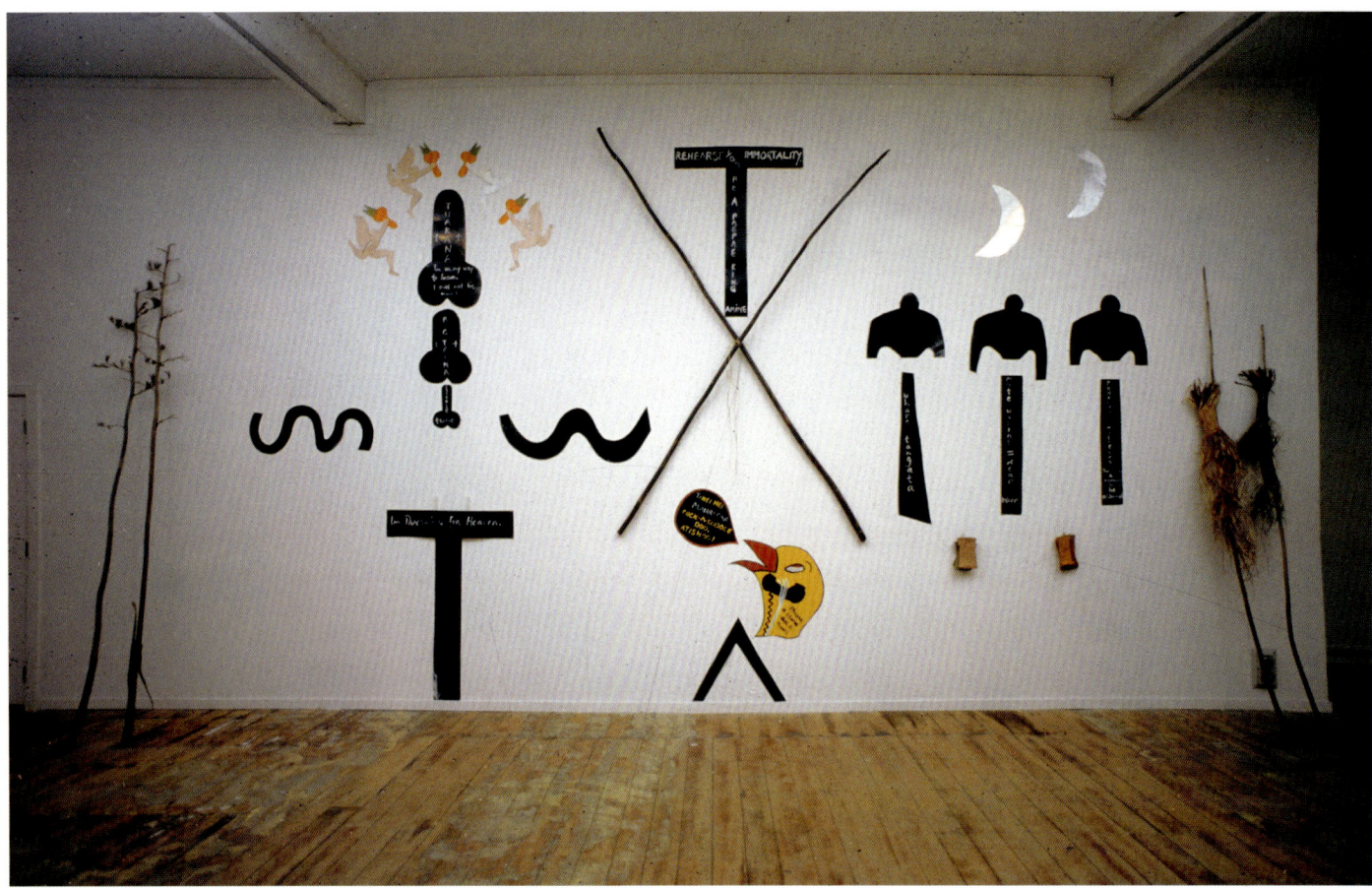

Gallery, Wellington, 1995), *Pilot Error* (Gallery 23a, Auckland, 1995) and *Korurangi: New Māori Art* (1995); this last show was a fraught collaboration with Auckland Art Gallery that Hubbard wanted to call the potentially inflammatory *Brownie Points* until the name was changed.⁹

Art historian Peter Brunt described *Choice!* and its successors as amounting to 'a critique of biculturalism'; the exhibitions suggested that 'new Māori art' was a diverse practice that was resisting historical and aesthetic associations with earlier Māori art.¹⁰ This was distinct from exhibitions such as *Kohia ko Taikaka Anake* that were a partnership between Māori and state, and that included Māori artists within a whakapapa of art in which Māori modernists – no longer outsiders – were now positioned as the patriarchal bridging generation between customary and contemporary art. The division was summed up in Brunt's account of Diane Prince's *Untitled* wall sculpture in *Choice!* as:

> [an] arrangement of cut-out shapes and objects mocking *Taikaka*'s three-tier hierarchy through various visual puns, slogans and cartoonish parodies. T-crosses with McCahon-like handwriting inscribed: 'Rehearse your immorality' and 'Be a paepae king.' Three erect penises in ascending order of size, inscribed (in translation) 'big brother', 'little brother', with the top one surrounded in mock apotheosis by a halo of headless cherubs holding chicken-heads in their hands and inscribed with the words, 'I'm on my way to heaven, I will not be moved.' A trio of cutouts alluding again to the three-part structure of *Taikaka*, the middle one reading, bitterly: 'Wahine=dead.'¹¹

The exhibition rejected the suggestion that a century and a half of Crown–Māori conflict could be so easily and neatly resolved through bicultural Crown–Māori partnerships, like that embodied by the National Gallery's foray into biculturalism. This kind of artistic rupture had occurred at least once before, and on a much greater scale, in the divergent architectural directions taken by the revivalist School of Maori Arts and Crafts and the innovative Rātana movement in the early twentieth century (see chapter 4). Whereas the school's programme succeeded, even after it had closed, through its establishment of a system of

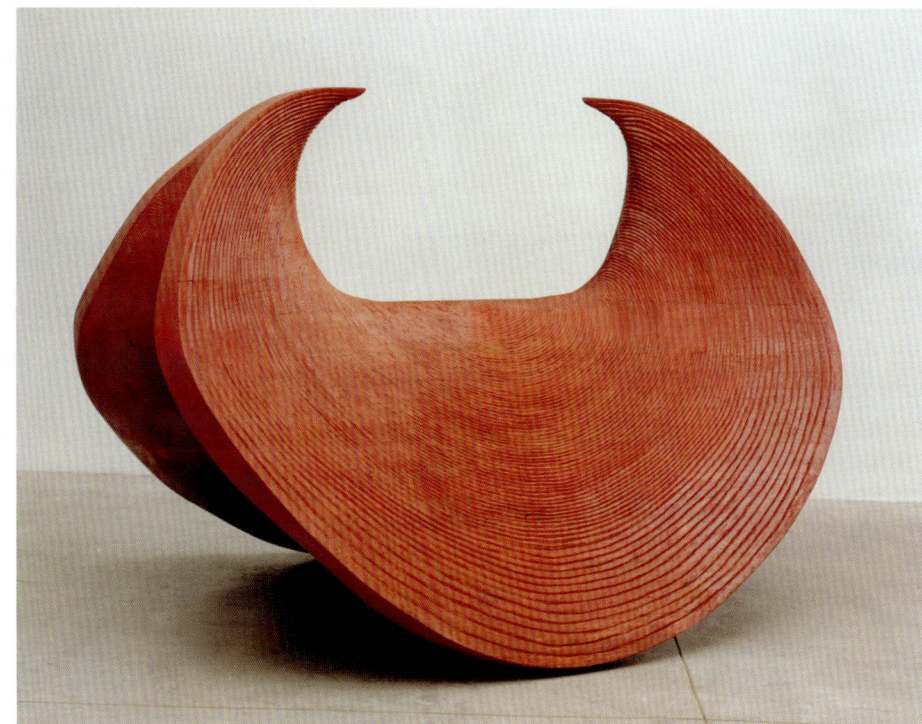

Top: In his artist's statement for Auckland Art Gallery Toi o Tāmaki's 1995 *Korurangi* exhibition (the only one in te reo Māori), Brett Graham dedicated *Kahukura* to the acclaimed Māori weaver Rangimārie Hetet, who had recently passed away. His recognition of her challenged the curatorial selection of Ralph Hotere as the 'kaumātua' figure among the exhibiting artists.

**Brett Graham, *Kahukura*, as installed in the Vanuatu Cultural Centre, Port Vila, Vanuatu, 1995**
wood, paint, 2070 x 1500 x 1500mm, Auckland Art Gallery Toi o Tāmaki

Bottom: **Robert Pouwhare, *Raupatu, Te Kaea and The Waiohou Fraud*, as installed in *Mana Tiriti: The Art of Protest and Partnership* at City Gallery, Wellington, 1990**
City Gallery, Wellington

Opposite: **Diane Prince, *Untitled*, 1990, as installed in *Choice!*, Artspace, Auckland, 1990**
Artspace Archive, Auckland Art Gallery Toi o Tāmaki

knowledge-transfer between generations, by the early 1990s experimentation in Māori art was largely confined to university and polytechnic art schools that were teaching the 'new art'. It would be many years before the impact of wānanga – Māori-context tertiary training institutions – would be apparent in the growing number of tohunga whakairo and weavers.

### Tikanga

Somewhere between the inclusivity of *Kohia ko Taikaka Anake* and the resistance of *Choice!* was the 1990 exhibition *Mana Tiriti: Art of Protest and Partnership* at City Gallery, Wellington. The Haeata Collective originally conceived of the exhibition as showcasing the work of six Māori and six Pākehā women artists; however, the gallery persuaded them to include male artists as well. Haeata selected the Pākehā artists in collaboration with Project Waitangi – an initiative to educate Pākehā about Tiriti issues. The artists in *Mana Tiriti* included Haeata (Tungia Baker [Ngāti Raukawa, Ngāti Toa, Te Āti Awa, Te Arawa, 1939–2005], Ani Crawford [Ngāti Porou], Hinemoa Hilliard [Ngāti Kahu, Ngāpuhi, 1960–2013], Robyn Kahukiwa, Roma Potiki, Irihapeti Ramsden [Ngāi Tahu, Rangitāne, 1946–2003], Rea Ropiha [Ngāti Kahungunu, Te Whānau-ā-Apanui, 1960–2021], Megan Tamati-Quennell), Robert Jahnke, Robert Pouwhare (Ngāi Tūhoe), Diane Prince,

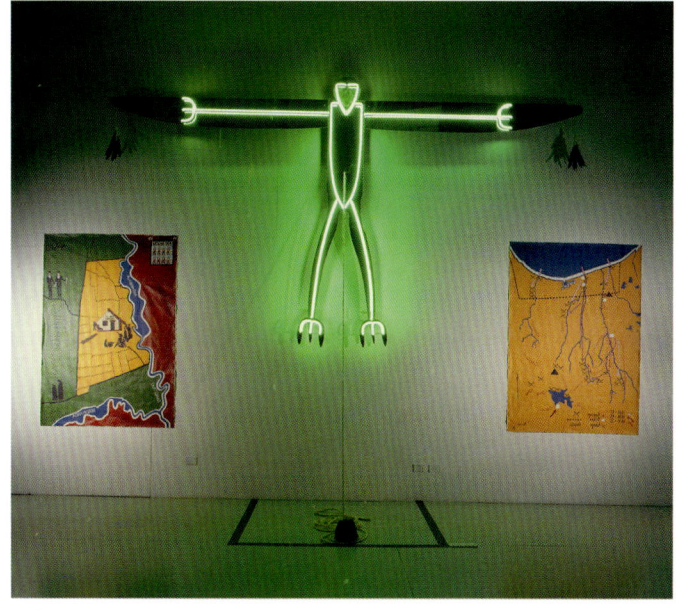

Papaarangi Reid (Te Rarawa) in collaboration with Irihapeti Ramsden, and Kura Te Waru Rewiri.

Art as a medium of cross-cultural discussion was a central curatorial concept for *Whatu Aho Rua: A Weaving Together of Traditional and Contemporary Māori Art*, curated by Rangihīroa Panoho (Ngāpuhi, Ngāti Whātua), that opened at the Tandanya National Aboriginal Cultural Institute in 1992 as part of the Adelaide Festival. Although the show included the work of Māori and Pākehā artists, it was the intergenerational

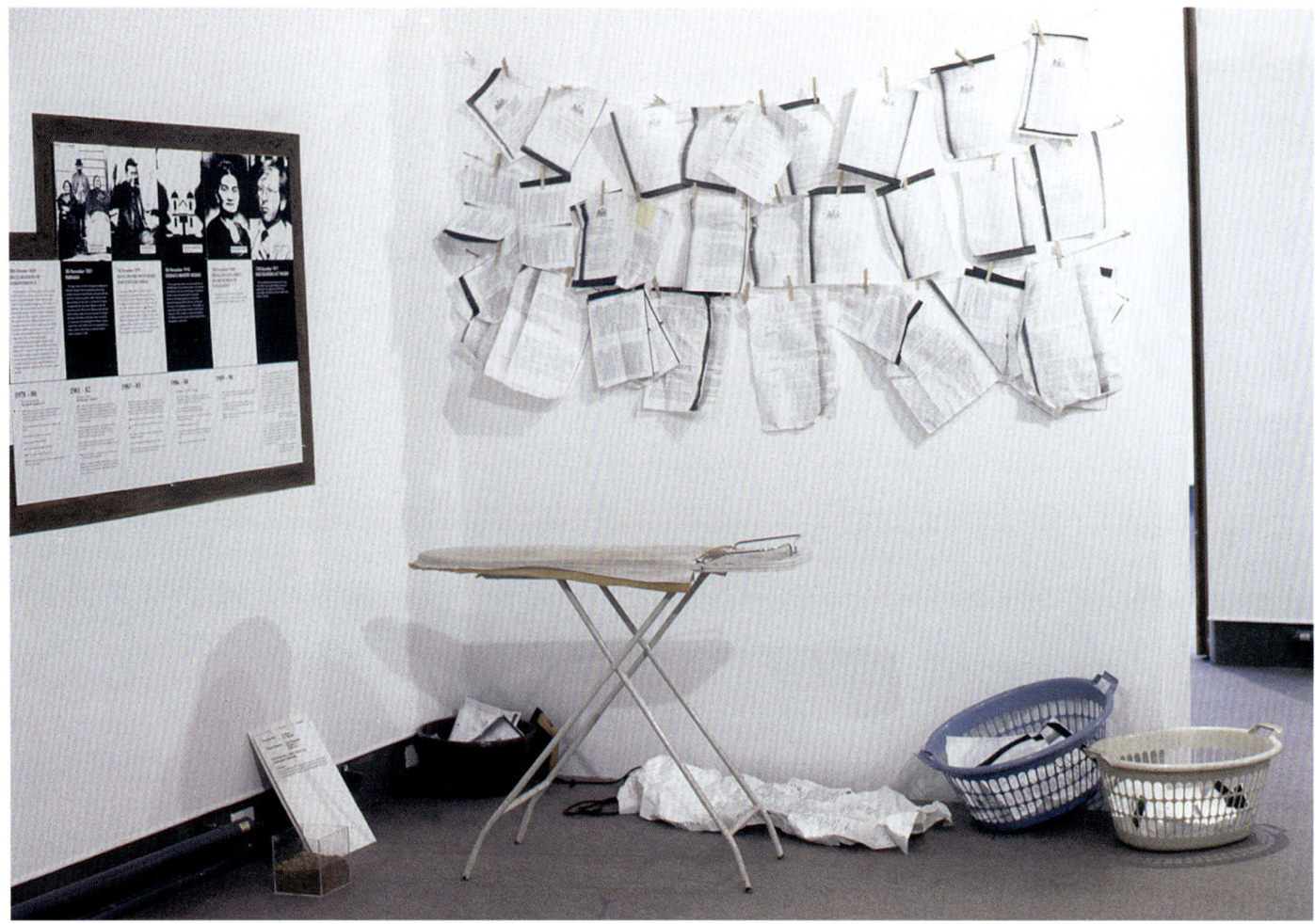

artistic relationships between customary, mōrehu and contemporary Māori artists that was the central concern of Panoho's catalogue essay, which carefully situated and sometimes critiqued more recent work relative to tikanga values and practices associated with taonga Māori.[12] So while the work of Rewiri, Kahukiwa and Selwyn Muru was celebrated for its reconceptualisation of whakairo rākau as a medium to express contemporary Māori concerns, wood sculptures made with power tools by Matt Pine (Te Āti Haunui-a-Pāpārangi, Te Āti Awa, Ngāti Tūwharetoa, 1941–2021) and Fred Graham were dismissed as being too easily and quickly manufactured. 'In some respects,' Panoho wrote, 'Māori art today can never hope to acquire the mana of old taonga because it takes time and generations of human association to gain such prestige.'[13] Panoho's essay and some of his subsequent writing has questioned whether whakapapa alone is sufficient for a Māori artist's work to be considered Māori art, or if the intentional (and appropriate) use of tikanga Māori is a better litmus test for such definitions.

### Curious questions

Conversely, *Choice!* and *Korurangi* had questioned whether works produced by Māori artists needed any visual references to Māori culture in order to be considered Māori art. The answer proposed by these exhibitions was that any art produced by an artist of Māori descent could be considered Māori art, regardless of its relationship to past precedents.

The definition divided opinion, largely down cultural lines. When asked in a 1995 radio interview about the burgeoning national and international interest in Māori art, Hubbard made the incendiary remark 'because Pākehā art is so boring'.[14] The comment brought to a head tensions about cultural identity in art that had been simmering for some time. In response, Pākehā artist Alan Pearson launched a blistering attack on the Māori exhibitors themselves by asking, 'How does a small percentage of Māori blood produce Māori artists? … Māori painting methods are wholly European and the subject matter subsists on what the

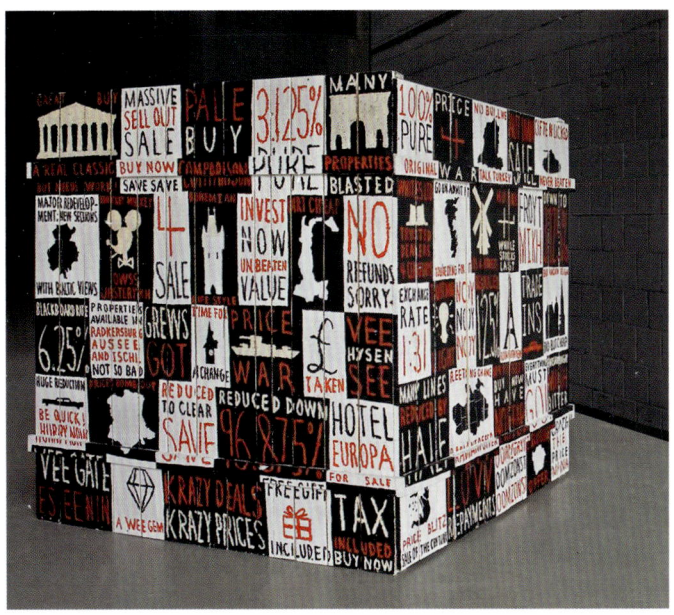
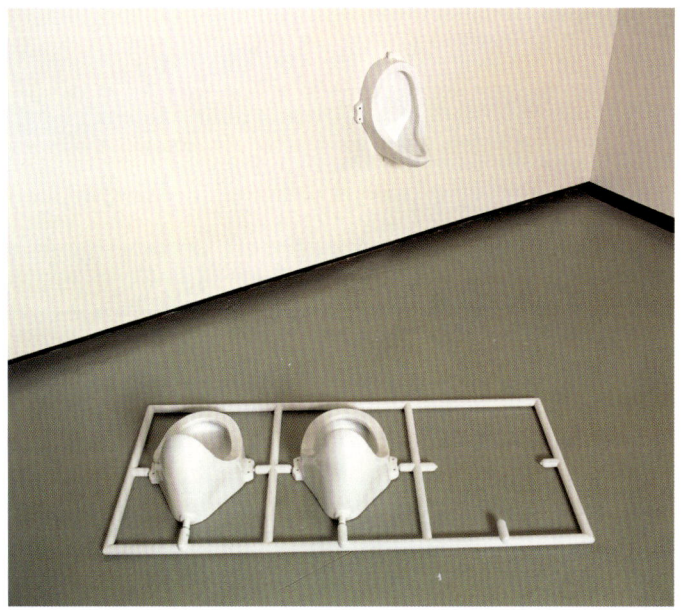

Left: The works in Peter Robinson's *Old Lines/New Stock* exhibition, held in 1994 at Christchurch's Brooke Gifford gallery, addressed the loss of Māori land and resources. This crate indicated the containment of land and its resources, while the text was an ironic protest commentary and reference to the use of text by Colin McCahon.
**Peter Robinson, *Untitled*, 1996**
wood, oil paint, crayons, lamp, 2000 x 2000 x 2000mm, private collection

Opposite: Irihapeti Ramsden and Papaarangi Reid, *150 Years of Dirty Laundry*, as installed in *Mana Tiriti* at Fisher Gallery (now Te Tuhi), Pakuranga, Auckland, 1989
image courtesy of Te Tuhi

Right: Four years after *Choice!*, Parekōwhai staged his breakthrough solo show *Kiss the Baby Goodbye*, at the Govett-Brewster gallery in New Plymouth and the Waikato Museum of Art. *Mimi*, which means 'urinate', is a replica in kitset form of Marcel Duchamp's groundbreaking 1917 *Fountain*, which had questioned whether even the most profane objects could be considered art if placed in a gallery. Parekōwhai took this concept one step further by making a urinal-shaped object, returning to (and complicating) the idea that sculpture involves an artist's labour.
**Michael Parekōwhai, *Mimi*, 1994**
wood, fibreglass, automotive paint, private collection, image courtesy of the artist and Michael Lett Gallery

Europeans have created.'[15] As the history of nineteenth-century Māori art had demonstrated, however, the tools and media of Pākehā culture had in fact been used to strengthen Māori cultural identity, in the process taking practices such as painting a long way from their origins in Europe. Intermarriage had also not interfered with the ability to claim Māori ancestry by descent from a Māori ancestor; the government itself had abandoned blood quantum as a measure of identity in 1974.[16] Mane-Wheoki wrote of the critical reception of Parekōwhai's work during the *Headlands: Thinking Through Maori Art* exhibition at the Museum of Contemporary Art, Sydney in 1992:

> Back in New Zealand the 'Press' commented how 'Contemporary Māori art has been singled out by the Australians as one of the most exciting features' … Unpalatable though it undoubtedly is to some New Zealand artists, critics and journalists, the possibility that the European and American art world may be less interested in art by Pākehā and, conversely, much more enthusiastic about the indigenous art of New Zealand has not been lost on Māori, and to some degree drives the separatist agenda of several Māori artists in support of stand-alone exhibitions (which are then attacked as racist).[17]

The 'Young Guns' shifted into the next century by positioning themselves, and being positioned by others, on a continuum of Māori identity and art practice that had been laid down for them by previous generations of Māori artists. The discussion of their practice, however, had raised important questions, particularly for the making, curation, criticism and historicisation of Māori art – such as 'What is the role of tikanga in this practice?' and 'Who should write about Māori art?'

### Snapshots and surveys

At the turn of the millennium, three of the major metropolitan galleries – Robert McDougall Art Gallery (now the

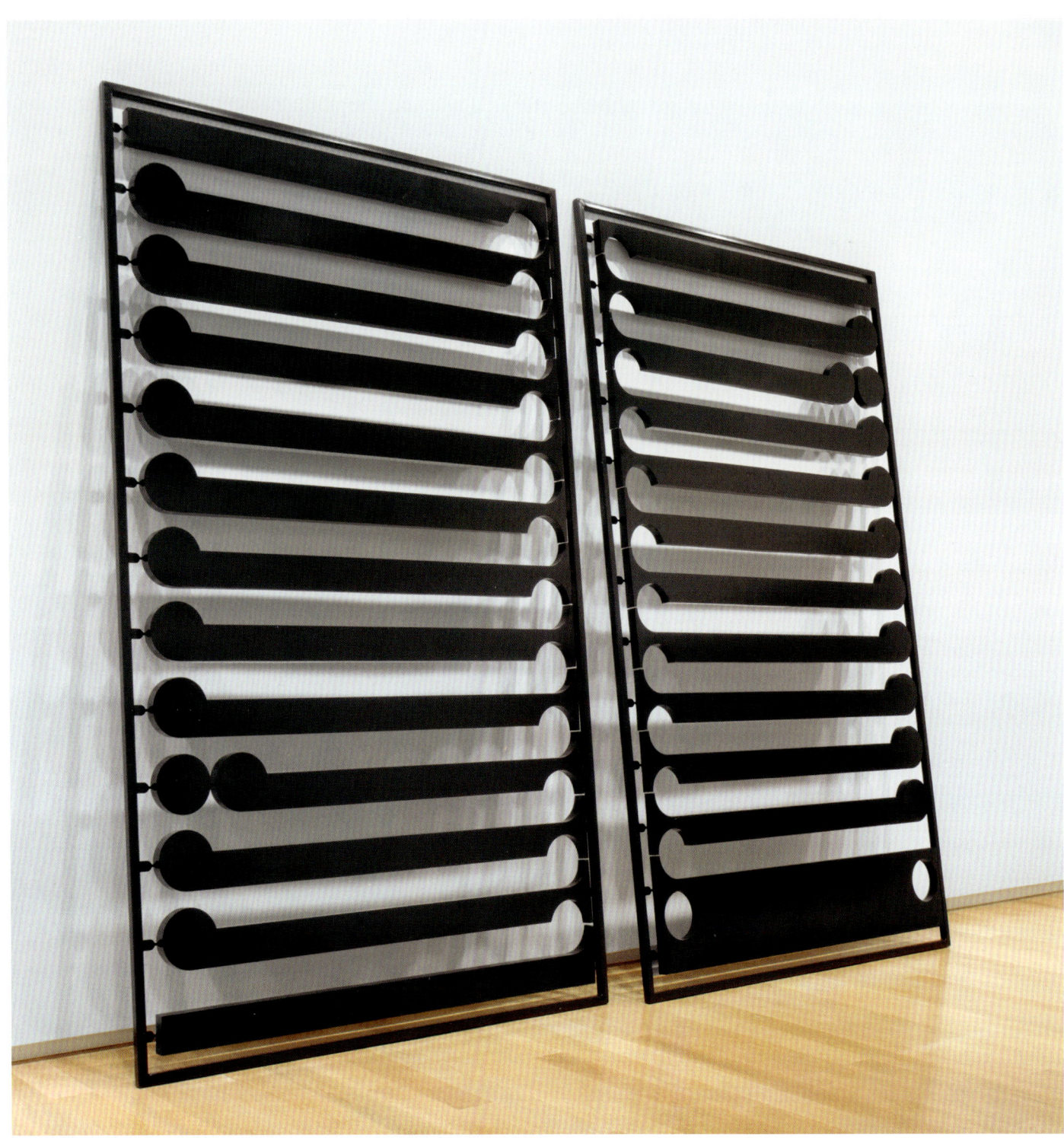

This kitset was an almost-exact copy of Gordon Walters's 1968 *Kahukura*, with the addition of an extra circle at the bottom to 'stop' recent criticism of Walters's appropriation of Māori motifs.

**Michael Parekōwhai,** *Kiss The Baby Goodbye,* **1994**
powdercoated steel, 3600 x 4600mm, Auckland Art Gallery Toi o Tāmaki, C1994/1/540.1-2, Chartwell Collection

Opposite: *Hiko! New Energies in Māori Art* exhibition, 1999. Eugene Hansen's *Some Kind of Vague Landscape* is installed across the gallery floor, Darryn George's *New Generation* painting is on the back wall of the gallery and, to its right, Olivia Haddon's digital-born work is shown on the monitor.
Christchurch Art Gallery Te Puna o Waiwhetū, courtesy of the Robert and Barbara Stewart Library and Archives

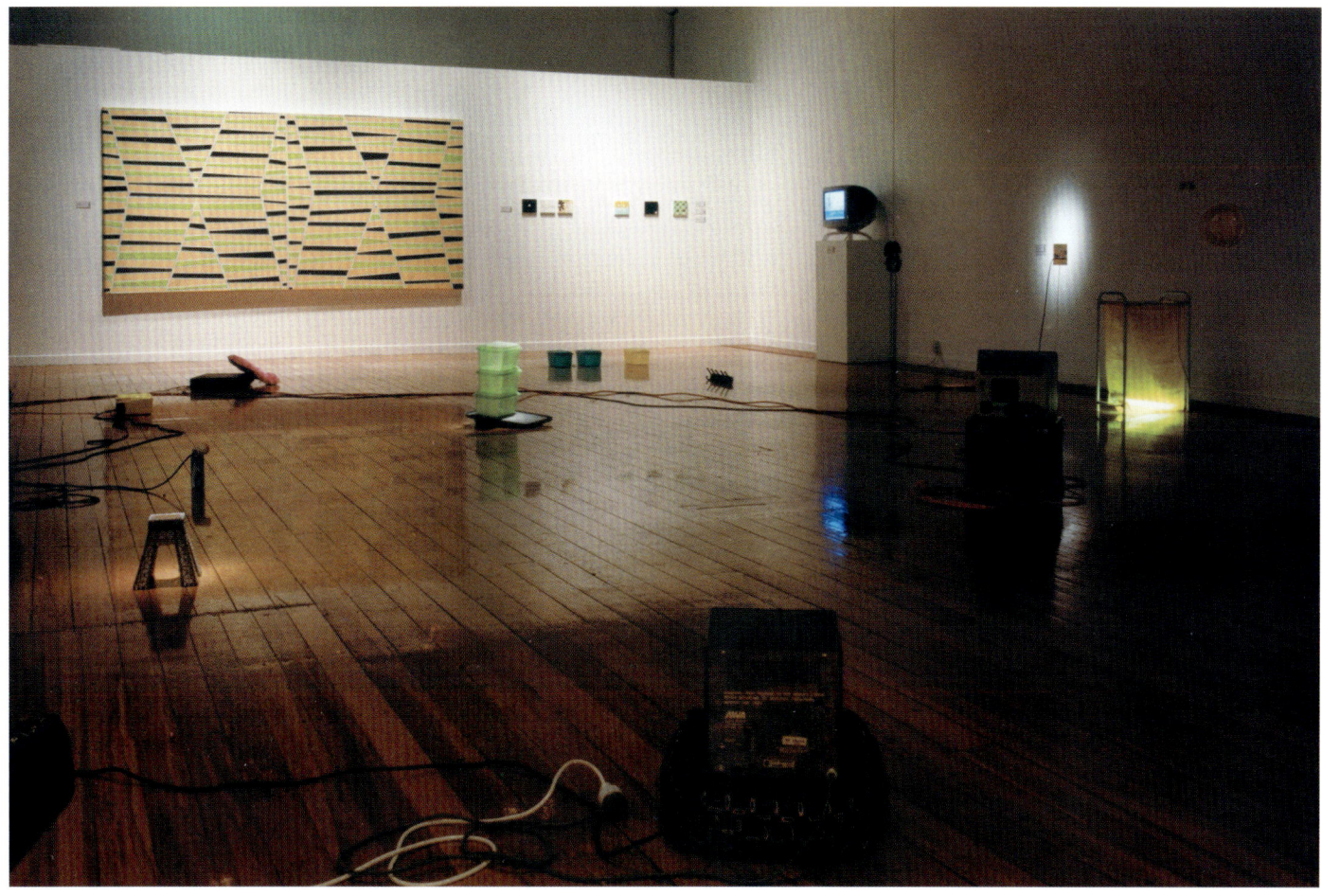

Christchurch Art Gallery); City Gallery, Wellington, with Porirua's Pātaka Art + Museum; and Auckland Art Gallery – all staged exhibitions surveying the contemporary state of Māori art. Questions from the previous decade about the definitions of Māori art after modernism had been superseded (more so than resolved), and Mead's 'fires of destruction' had been largely doused by the embedding of biculturalism in art institutions and, as Brunt put it, 'the new Māori artistic sensibility ... affirmed, institutionalised and marketed'.[18] The first two exhibitions were concerned with the influence of digital culture on Māori art and examined the role of changing media on the production of Māori art, while the third considered the continuity of Māori concepts across an increasingly diverse range of contemporary art practices. Snapshots in time, all three supported the kaupapa that Māori art was defined by whakapapa and Māori art history's role was to identify and articulate continuities of practice. As the millennium progressed, whakapapa-based exhibitions evolved into two distinct curatorial approaches: rohe and iwi surveys, assembled with the objective of inspiring mana, hope and pride in communities; and remembering, in which foundational Māori modernist exhibitions were reassembled and reconsidered.[19]

Originally conceived as a survey of emerging art at the dawn of the millennium, the 1999 show at the McDougall brought to light that digital culture was expanding not only the media in which Māori artists were working, but also the concepts they were investigating in their art, and even the standard of finish in manual production. The resulting exhibition, *Hiko! New Energies in Māori Art*, curated by Mane-Wheoki, Deidre Brown and Felicity Milburn, featured the work of seven Māori artists who had recently graduated and had not had work shown before in a major gallery – and, for some, had not considered their work within a Māori cultural paradigm. *Te Rongopai* by Olivia Haddon (Ngāti Wai, Ngāti Ruanui; great-niece of Oriwa Haddon) was likely the first 'digital-born' Māori image to be shown electronically in a gallery. The image recalled the tōtara and maple trees she had planted on a visit to the Rongopai wharenui, and was a metaphor for both the joining together of 'native'

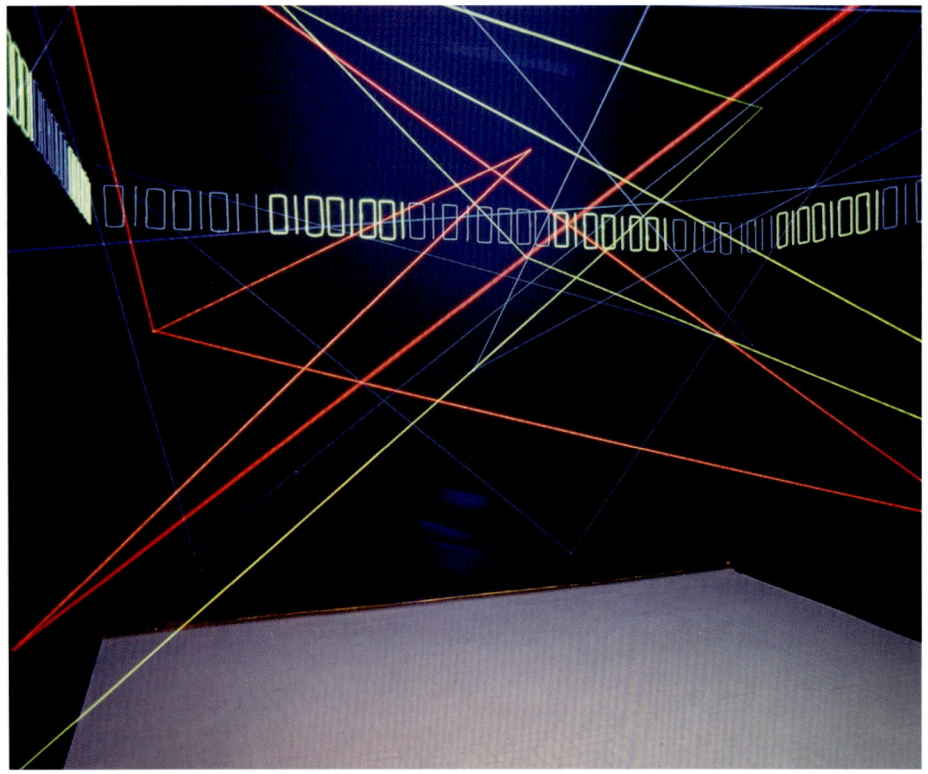

Left: Maureen Lander and John Fairclough's *Binary Strings* was a component of *Digital String Games II*, an interactive installation exhibited in 2000 at the Fisher Gallery in Pakuranga, Auckland. Here it is shown as installed in *Techno Māori: Māori Art in the Digital Age*, City Gallery, Wellington, 2001.
City Gallery, Wellington

Below: Olivia Haddon's *Te Rongopai* was likely the first 'digital-born' Māori image to be shown electronically in a gallery.
courtesy of Olivia Haddon

Opposite: *Pūrangiaho: Seeing Clearly*, Auckland Art Gallery Toi o Tāmaki, 2001. This image shows the exhibition entrance with the Māori Madonna and Child set into the gateway, and paintings by Shane Cotton beyond.
Auckland Art Gallery Toi o Tāmaki, E. H. McCormick Research Library

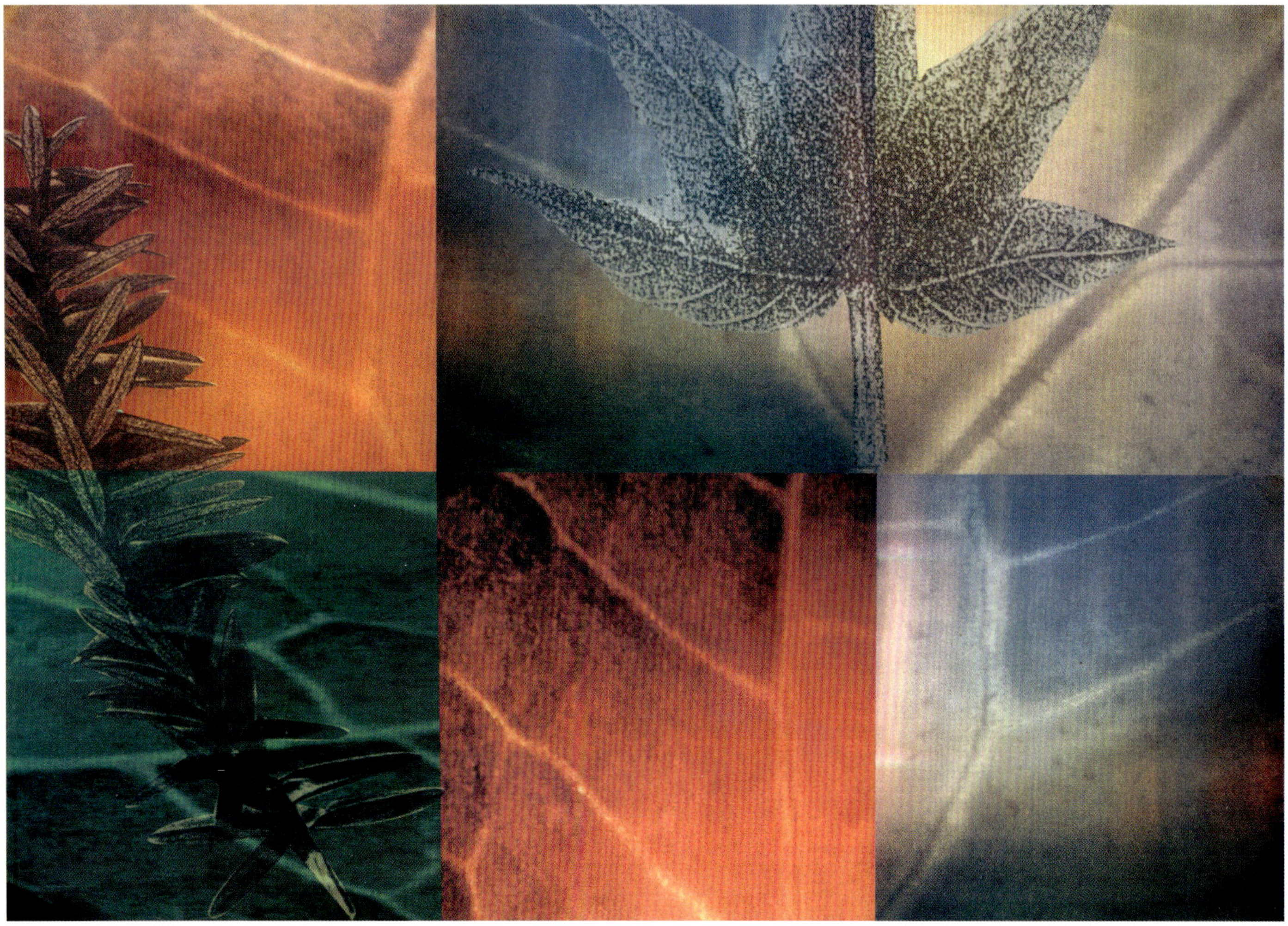

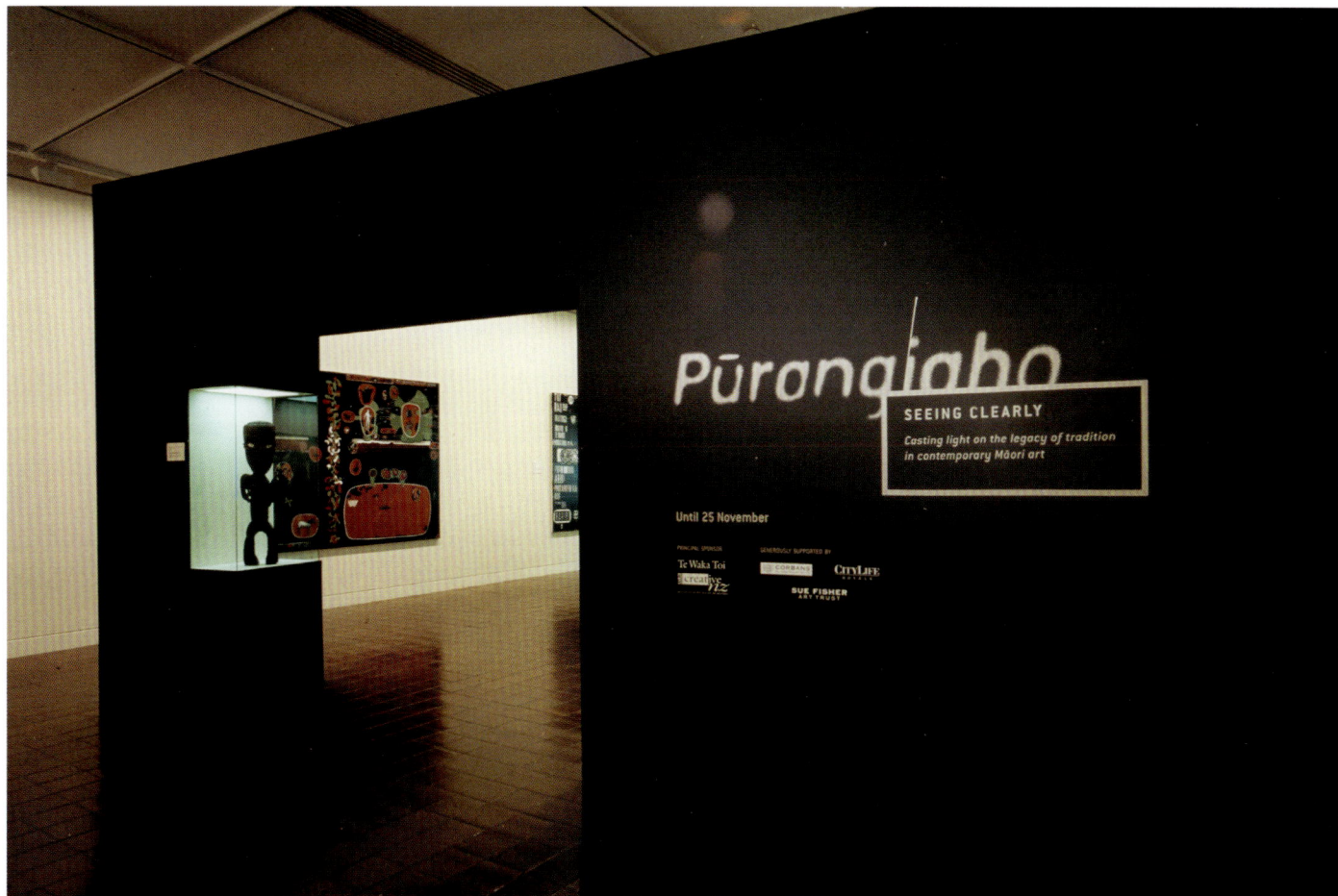

and 'exotic' cultures, and the progress of life from a green student state to an autumnal elder condition. The role of cinema in legitimating and critiquing colonisation was the subject of a floor-centred video installation by Eugene Hansen (Ngāti Maniapoto, Tainui). The work featured sound sequences from Westerns and science fiction films (in which space is the 'final frontier'), and an eclectic arrangement of televisions, video cassette recorders and cables. The array was reminiscent of a new digital landscape influencing urbanised and sometimes detribalised Māori. *Hohoko: Trading Terms* by Keri Whaitiri (Ngāi Tahu, Ngāti Kahungunu) introduced another defining element of Māori identity into the gallery – te reo – as a sound installation. It developed the theme of language encounter that had been the basis of an earlier collaborative sound work with Mike Dunn, *huri, ka huri, huri noa*, shown at the nearby Physics Room artist project space two years earlier. Other painted works by Darryn George and Kirsty Gregg (Ngāti Mahuta), while they did not specifically address Māori themes, were concerned with values associated with New Zealand morality and rugby culture, and used highly precise geometrical components that recalled Gordon Walters's use of paint. Indeed, by the late 1990s, George was already producing preparatory works on computer before committing paint to canvas as well as scaling work through pasting virtual canvases into pictures of gallery spaces. The works of the 'Hiko' or 'Digital' generation had a less earnest approach to Māori culture than that of the Young Guns, and suggested their makers were comfortable with intersectional Māori identities that could account for urbanisation, feminism and lives lived in a partly virtual world where reinvention might be possible.

Mane-Wheoki's catalogue essay connected these artists to a whakapapa of contemporary Māori art in which the 'founding' ancestors – Adsett, Graham, Hotere, Matchitt, Muru, Manos Nathan (Te Roroa, Ngāti Whātua, Ngāpuhi, 1948–2015), Wi Taepa (Ngāti Pikiao, Te Arawa, Te Āti Awa, Ngāti Te Roro o Te Rangi), Colleen Waata Urlich (Te Popoto o Ngāpuhi ki Kaipara, Ngāpuhi, Te Rarawa, 1939–2015) and Cliff Whiting – had used power tools, composite materials, fluorescent bulbs, furnaces and kilns to create their work.

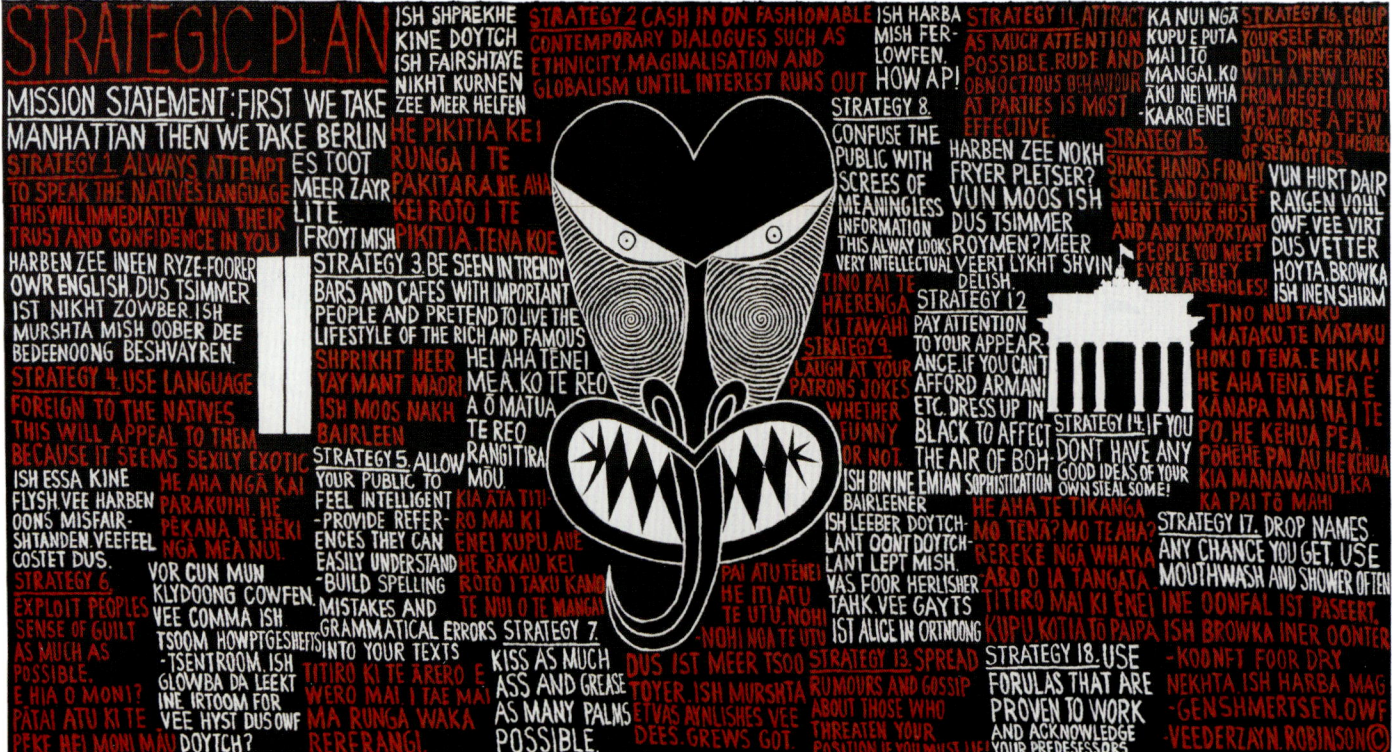

He also contextualised these machine-assisted practices within a wider twentieth-century modernising movement that had brought electricity, the telephone and email to marae, thus suggesting that technology and tikanga were not incompatible.

The 'digital turn' in Māori art was further explored in the exhibition *Techno Māori: Māori Art in the Digital Age*, concurrently shown at the City Gallery and Pātaka in 2001 and curated by Brown, Mane-Wheoki and Mark Amery. This exhibition featured work from established artists, including Maureen Lander, Rongotai Lomas and Michael Parekōwhai, and those still emerging, such as George, Haddon, Hansen, Ngahiraka Mason (Tūhoe), Nathan Pohio (Waitaha, Kāti Māmoe, Ngāi Tahu, Ngāi Tuahiwi), Rachael Rakena (Ngāi Tahu, Ngāpuhi), Natalie Robertson (Ngāti Porou) and Whaitiri, among others. A clear distinction of practice was apparent. Established artists were digital immigrants, adult witnesses to the 'computer revolution' whose work was attempting to either mediate or critique digital and manual modes of production. Lander's installation with John Fairclough was an enlarged Māori string game that immersed the visitor in a network of fluorescent cables that generated sound when touched. The work delighted in the similarities between the two communicative technologies of the internet and instructive Māori string games, while also coalescing virtual and manual arts. The emerging artists, who were generally younger (born since 1970), were digital natives who had been introduced to computers as one of a number of means of expression during their pre-tertiary education. Their work utilised digital media as tools to convey a range of conceptual concerns that were not necessarily about electronic or virtual worlds.

A much larger show than those in Christchurch, *Pūrangiaho: Seeing Clearly: Casting Light on the Legacy of Tradition in Contemporary Māori Art*, opened at Auckland Art Gallery in 2001, and unashamedly reclaimed the whakapapa principle that *Korurangi* and its precedent exhibitions had sought to shake off. In the six years between the two shows, Auckland Art Gallery had appointed a curator of Indigenous art, Ngahiraka Mason, and Mason, Ngarino Ellis and acclaimed weaver Kahutoi Te Kanawa co-curated *Pūrangiaho*. Applying an increasingly common curatorial method for Māori survey exhibitions at this time, a taonga Māori – in this instance the Māori Madonna and Child sculpture from Auckland War Memorial Museum (see page 232) – was placed at the entrance to locate the show within a whakapapa of Māori art. An outsider artwork of its time, the Māori Madonna and Child was rumoured to have been

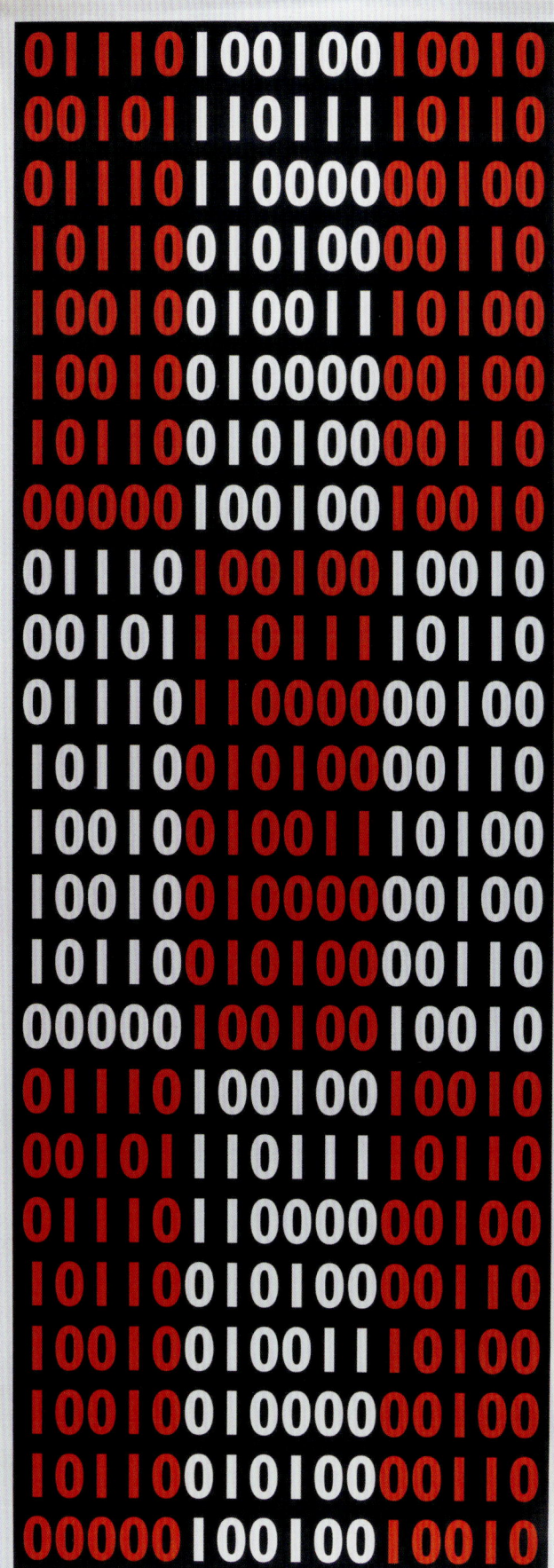

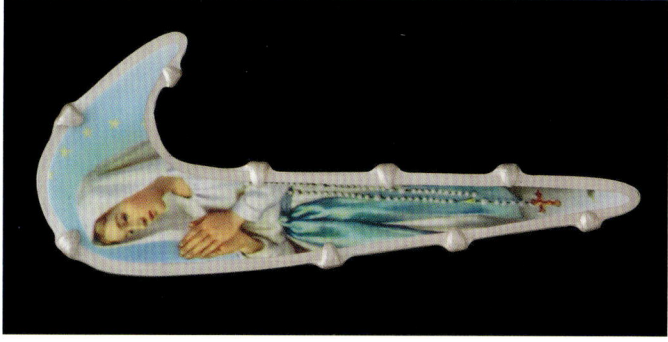

Above: **Gina Matchitt,** *Praying Madonna Nike*, 2001
laminated card, fine silver, stainless steel wire, Te Papa Tongarewa Museum of New Zealand, 2002-0001-2, purchased 2002

Left: **Peter Robinson,** *I Am I, I Am Not I*, 2001
Lambda print, 3190 x 1200mm, Auckland Art Gallery Toi o Tāmaki, 2001/21, purchased 2001

Opposite: **Peter Robinson,** *Strategic Plan*, 1998
oil and acrylic on canvas, 2500 x 5000mm, Auckland Art Gallery Toi o Tāmaki, 1999/30, gift of the patrons, 1999

rejected by the Catholic Church for representing the Holy Mother and Child in whakairo rākau. Around it were other taonga Māori, mainly fibre arts and body adornments made by customary means and incorporating materials and concepts from Pākehā culture, in association with contemporary Māori body adornments by Areta Wilkinson (see page 183) and Rangi Kipa (Taranaki, Te Ātiawa, Ngāti Maniapoto). The effect was an unambiguous statement about the long history of Māori engagement with Pākehā media for predominantly Māori purposes – an artistic relationship that pre-dated Māori modernism by over a hundred years.

From this kaupapa, *Pūrangiaho* launched forward. Various rooms within the exhibition, which filled the entire art gallery, unpacked different directions in contemporary Māori art. In the 'Up the Ante' section, Peter Robinson's *Strategic Plan* (1998) provided a cutting commentary on what an artist needs to do in order to 'make it' in the global contemporary art scene. His *I Am I, I Am Not I* (2001) print of binary code in tukutuku formation was a critique of capitalist and global popular cultures and was coupled with jeweller Gina Matchitt's (Ngāti Rangitihi, Te Arawa, Ngāti Ngahere, Whakatōhea) hei matau made of global trademarks and religious imagery. This was art about cultural identity that went beyond exploring Pākehā–Māori relationships, which would find resonance with Indigenous and non-Indigenous audiences outside of Aotearoa in years to come.

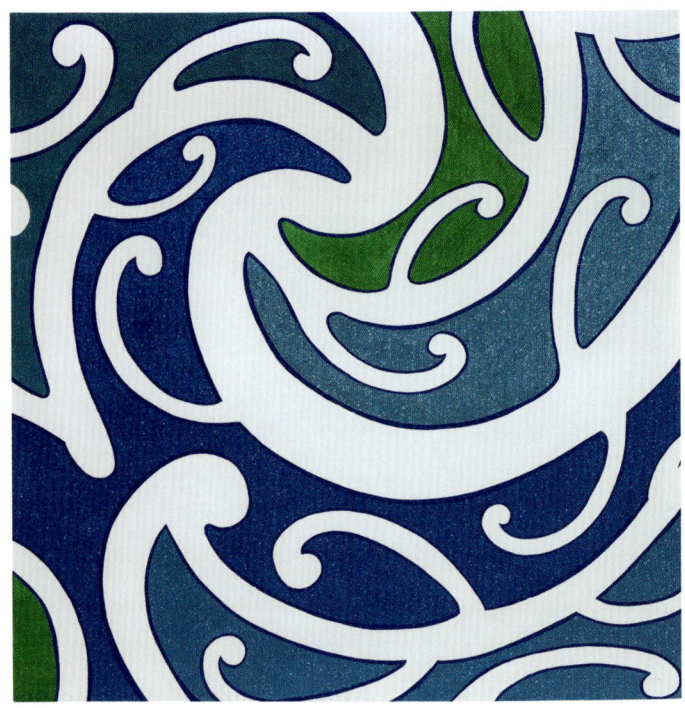

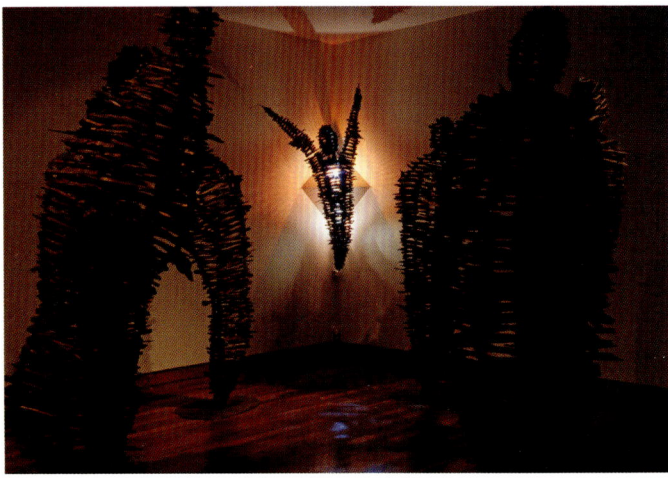

Top: **Reuben Paterson**, *The Kaiahuwhenua and his Three Sons*, 2001
glitter dust on canvas, 1720 x 1720mm, Auckland Art Gallery Toi o Tāmaki, 2001/36, purchased 2001

Bottom: **Dion Hitchens**, *Manaaki Patupaiarehe*, 2001
tōtara wood and steel, Auckland Art Gallery Toi o Tāmaki, E. H. McCormick Research Library

Two of the next generation of artists, presented as 'Te Ringa Hou: Recent Talent' in *Pūrangiaho*, embraced customary iconography and concepts rather than moving further away from them. Reuben Paterson's (Ngāti Rangitihi, Ngāi Tūhoe, Tūhourangi) glitter painting and Lonnie Hutchinson's hanging cutouts referenced kōwhaiwhai, an art that had proved to be adaptable and translatable across a variety of taonga from eighteenth-century hoe to nineteenth-century wharenui. Other Ringa Hou – Dion Hitchens (Tūhoe, Ngāti Porou), Ngataiharuru Taepa (Te Arawa, Te Ātiawa; son of the ceramicist Wi Taepa) and Saffronn Te Ratana (Tūhoe) – were of a generation comfortable in their Māoritanga and their Māori artistic practice and therefore less tentative about taking inspiration from the whakairo rākau of wharenui. Mason described Taepa's layering of concentric painted circles as 'resonances of the weatherboards used to construct meeting houses' by the School of Maori Arts and Crafts, and Te Ratana's biomorphic painting as 'an enigmatic methodology of cataloguing figures that have their origins in the carved image'.[20] The towering forest of quivering wicker figures installed by Hitchens lived up to the promise of its *Manaaki Patupaiarehe* (guardian forest figures) title.

Earlier generations within the contemporary Māori art whakapapa were distinguished in *Pūrangiaho* through their own spaces that impressed on viewers that the kaupapa of their work was far from over. Michael Parekōwhai's *Story of a New Zealand River* (an elegant grand piano with pāua-shell fleur-de-lis marquetry detailing) and *Bosom of Abraham* kōwhaiwhai lightboxes joined Shane Cotton's *Lying in the Black Land* (1998), *Eden to Ohaeawai* (2000) and *Stelliferous Biblia XVI* (2001), which includes an image of the Māori Madonna and Child, to illustrate the changes in nuance and complexity that had taken place in their work since their Young Guns years.

Lisa Reihana was given her own space for the next chapter in her *Digital Marae* project, where she installed as poupou large photographic prints of models dressed and staged as the legendary Māori ancestresses Hinepūkohurangi, Hinewai, Karangaituku, Mahuika and Marakihau, alongside an accompanying video installation of the women in action. A clear link to Pacific Sisters – a collective of Māori and Pacific artists, designers and performers Reihana had been part of in the 1990s – was apparent in the costumed and performative aspects of the installation. In another space,

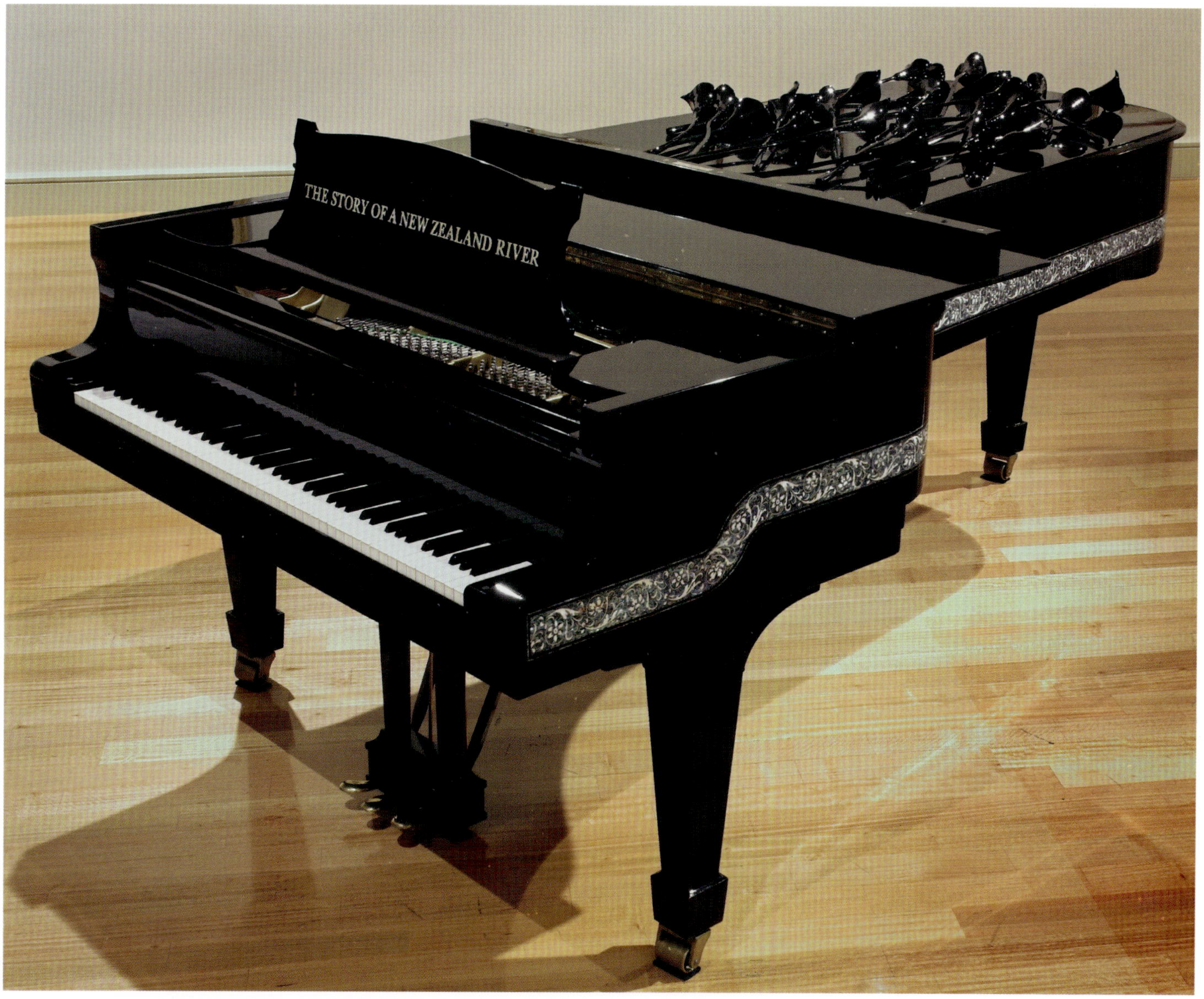

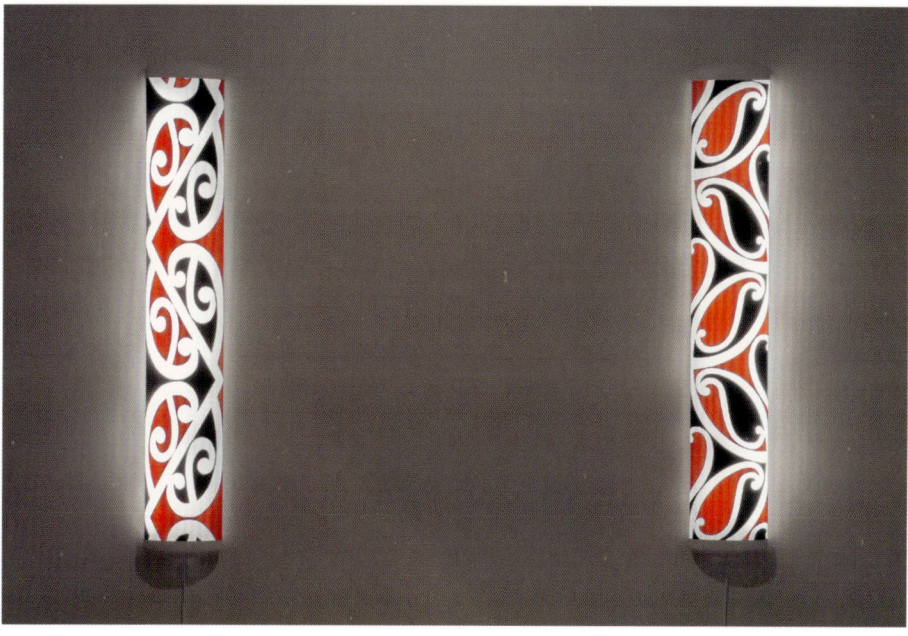

**Michael Parekōwhai, *The Story of a New Zealand River*, 2001**

pāua, capiz, lacquer and wood on a concert grand piano, 1015 x 1580 x 2725mm, Auckland Art Gallery Toi o Tāmaki, L2001/26, Auckland Triennial Collection, on loan from the Thanksgiving Foundation, 2001

**Michael Parekōwhai, *The Bosom of Abraham*, 1999**

ink on lightbox, 1300 x 220 x 80mm, Auckland Art Gallery Toi o Tāmaki, 1999/24/2, purchased 1999

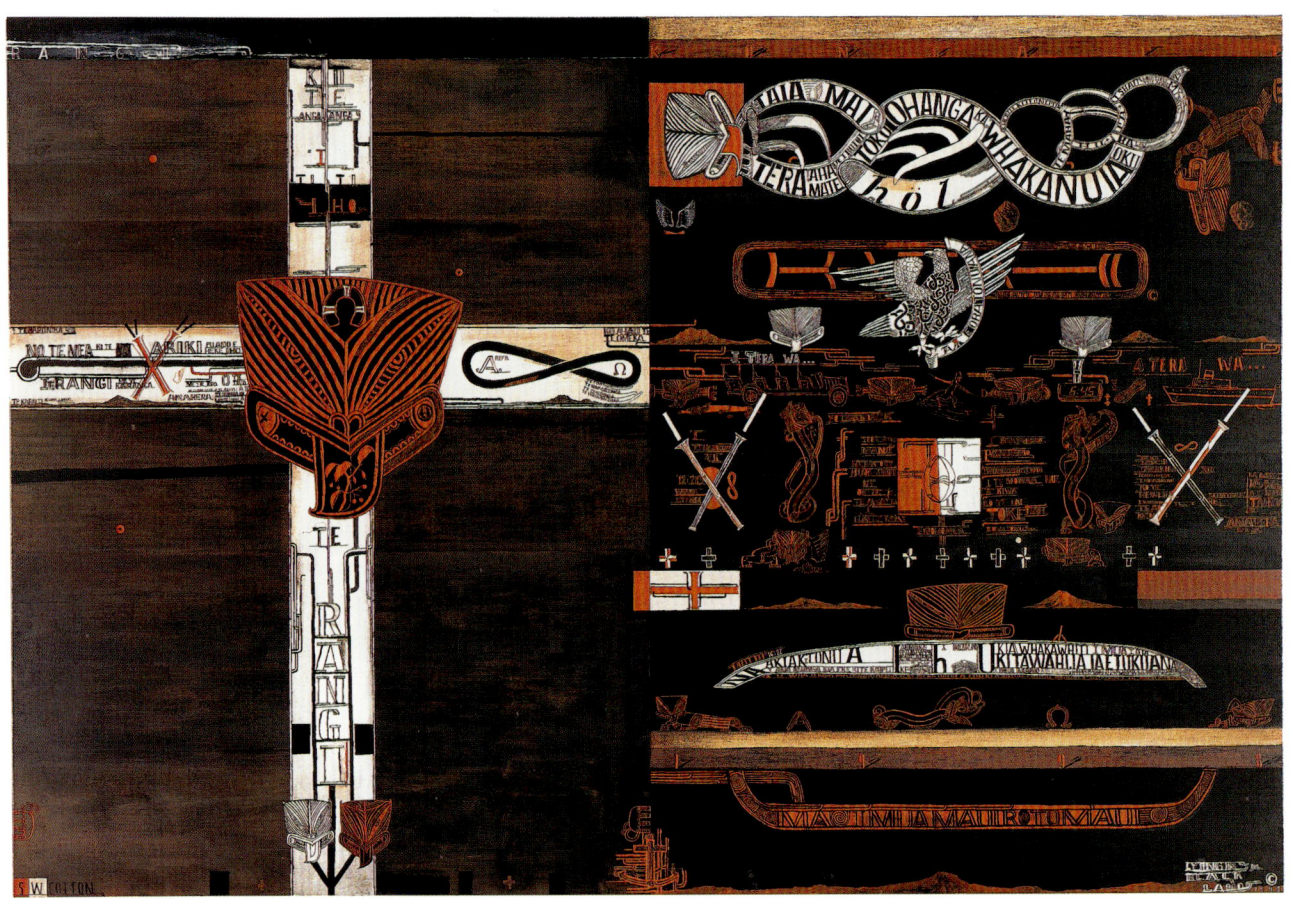

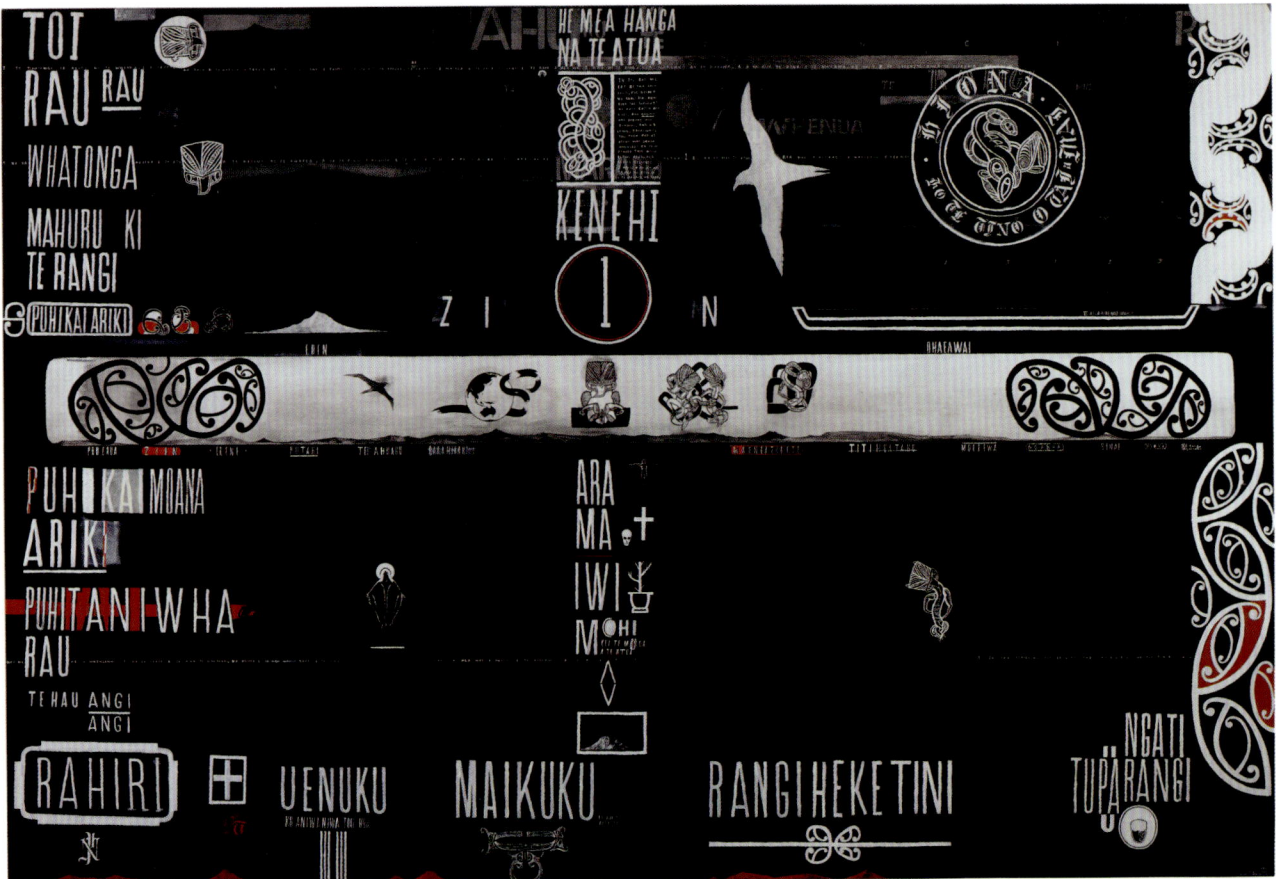

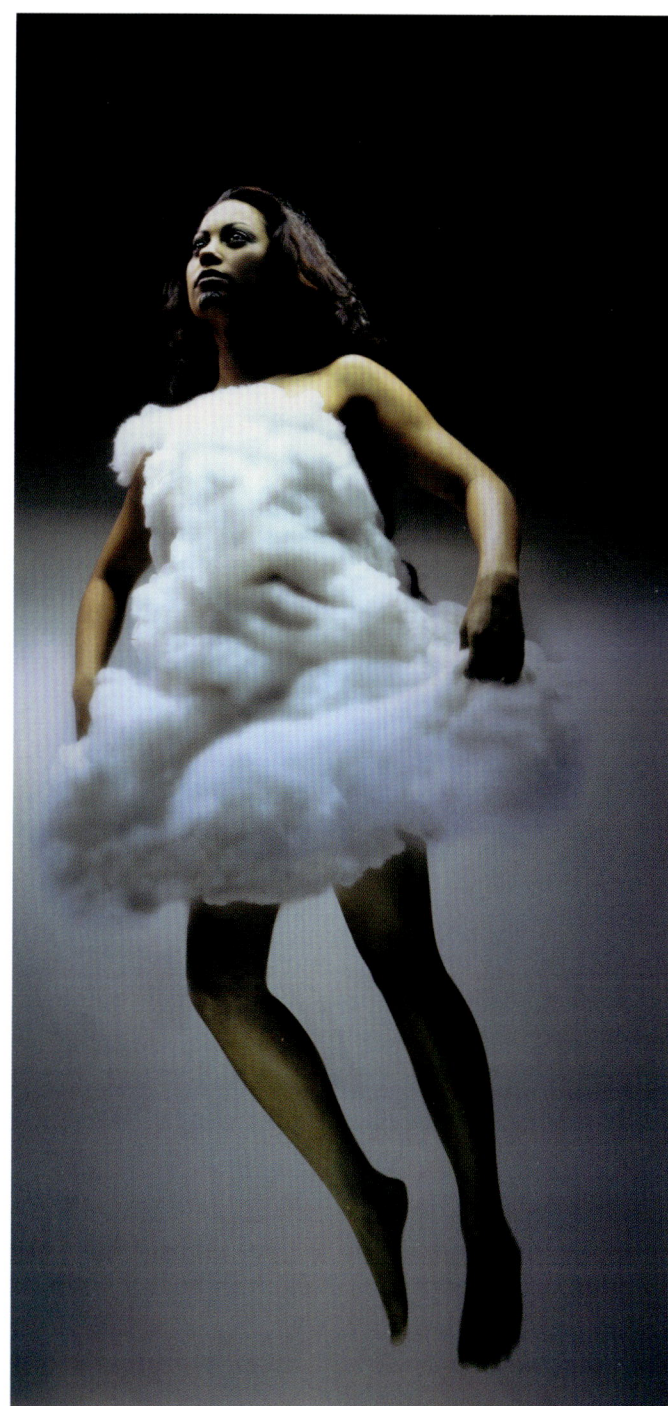
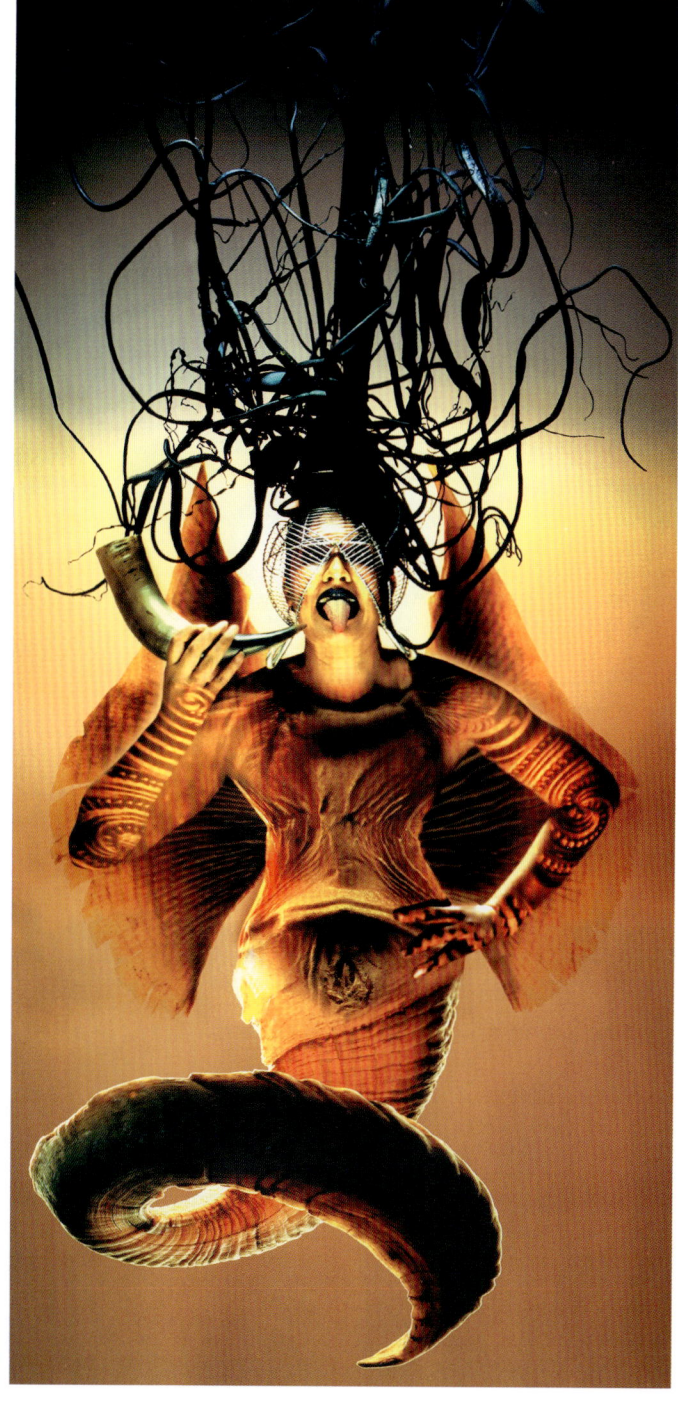

Opposite top: **Shane Cotton,** *Lying in the Black Land,* **1998**

oil on canvas, 2000 x 3000mm, private collection

Opposite bottom: **Shane Cotton,** *Eden to Ohaeawai,* **1998–2000**

oil on canvas, 2000 x 3000mm, Auckland Art Gallery Toi o Tāmaki, 2012/16, gift of the patrons, 2012

Lisa Reihana embarked on the *Digital Marae* project in 1995 as a rolling, multi-series production of digital photographs and art cinematography that, when reassembled, would be a contemporary wharenui. These portraits are the poupou of the *Digital Marae* and this series, shown at Auckland Art Gallery Toi o Tāmaki's *Pūrangiaho* exhibition, celebrated the roles of Māori ancestresses.

Left: **Lisa Reihana,** *Hinepūkohurangi,* **2001**

colour photographic print on aluminium, 1990 x 990mm, Auckland Art Gallery Toi o Tāmaki, 2002/3/1, purchased 2002

Right: **Lisa Reihana,** *Marakihau,* **2001**

C Type print, 1190 x 1990mm, Te Papa Tongarewa Museum of New Zealand, O.026797, purchased 2002

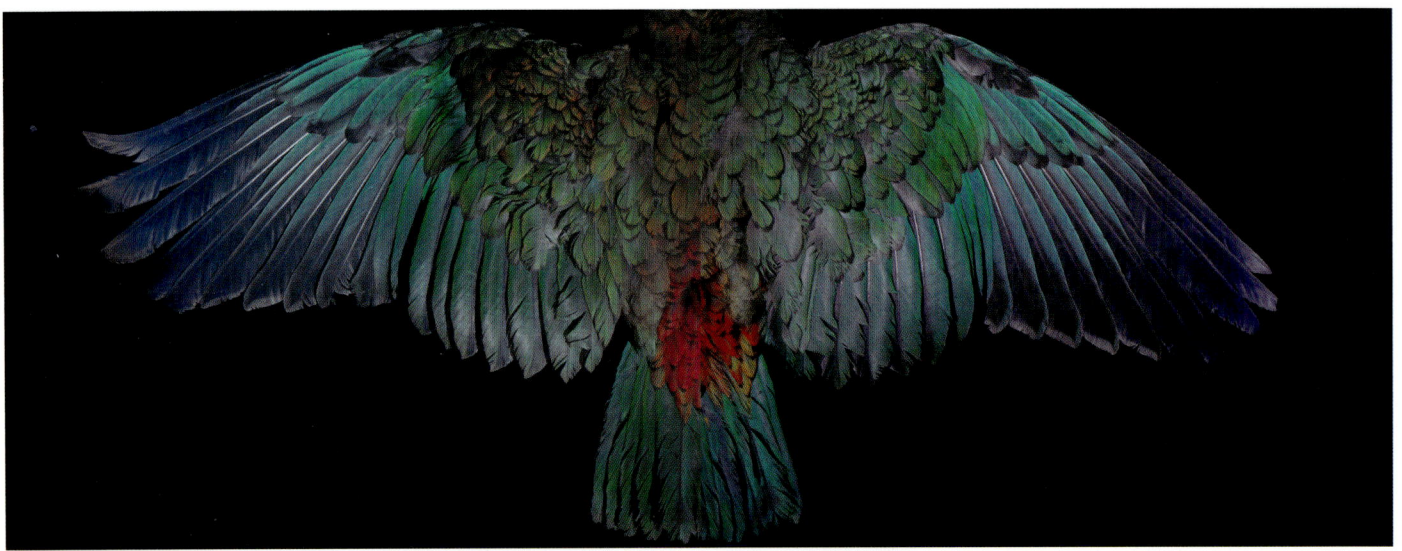

**Fiona Pardington,** *Davis Kea Wings (above),* 2015
pigment inkjet print on paper, 880 x 2360 x 65mm, Auckland Art Gallery Toi o Tāmaki, X2016/16/45.1-2, private collection

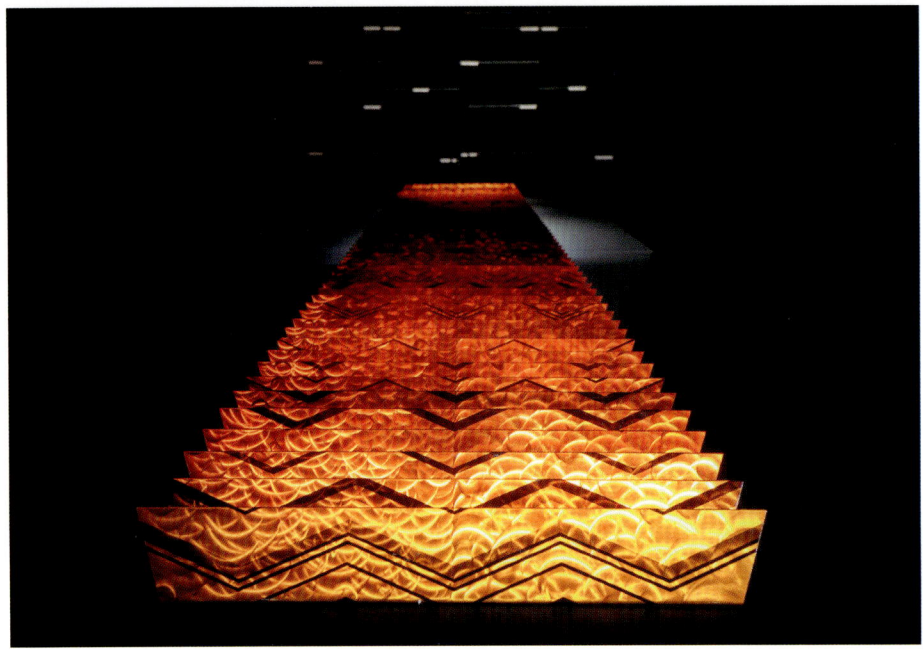

**Israel Tangaroa Birch,** *Ara-i-te-uru,* 2011
spray-lacquered stainless steel sheets, each 130 x 1200 x 1400mm, Auckland Art Gallery Toi o Tāmaki, X2020/35/1, collection of Te Manawa Museums Trust

politically engaged artists of the 1980s Robert Jahnke, Emily Karaka and Kura Te Waru Rewiri were represented by a selection of works from 1989 (Rewiri's iconic *Whenua, Wahine, Whenua*) to 2000 (Karaka's *Polynesian Potae* and *Pot of Honey*). At the end of the exhibition, John Miller's 1973 photographs from the inaugural Maori Artists and Writers Association meeting (before it became Ngā Puna Waihanga) at Te Kaha provided a window on the coalescence of the Māori art movement and, indeed, the larger Māori cultural renaissance that had supported and encouraged succeeding generations. The photographs included images of Rei Hamon, Witi Ihimaera, Hana Jackson (Te Hemara), Syd Jackson, Paratene Matchitt, Dun Mihaka, Selwyn Muru, Buck Nin, Hone Tuwhare, Ngahuia Volkering (Te Awekotuku) and Haare Williams. The curators' positioning of these kaumātua figures of postwar art and politics at the end of the exhibition was a deliberate riposte to any suggestion that there was ever a rupture between Māori modern and Māori postmodern art.

In 2020, almost twenty years after *Pūrangiaho*, Auckland Art Gallery opened *Toi Tū Toi Ora: Contemporary Māori Art*, an epic survey exhibition of contemporary Māori art that was the institution's largest ever show, at more than 300 artworks by over 100 artists. *Toi Tū Toi Ora* was curated by Mason's successor Nigel Borell (Pirirākau, Ngāi Te Rangi, Ngāti Ranginui, Te Whakatōhea), who was appointed in 2015.

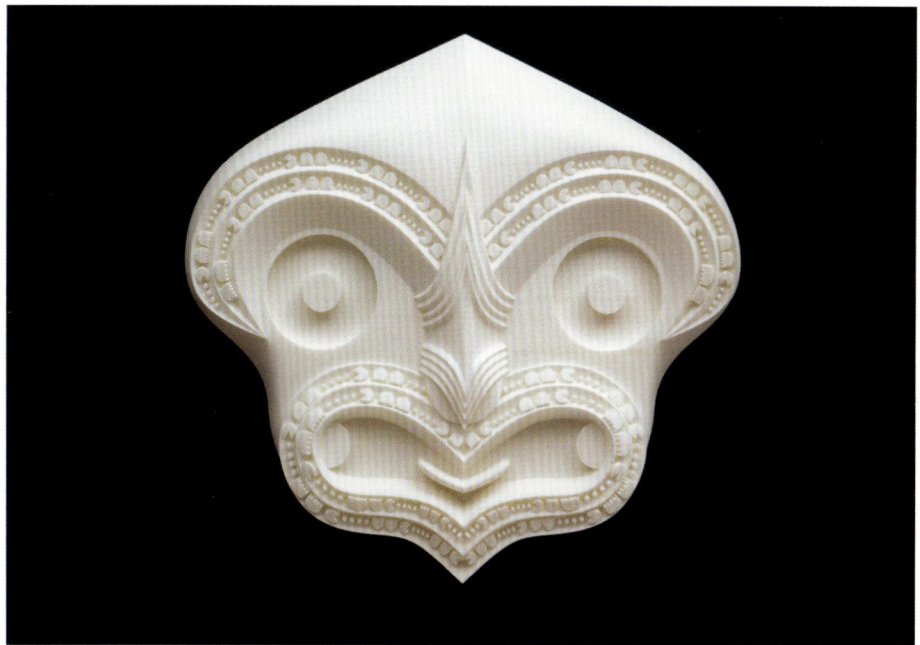

**Kereama Taepa, *Pākati Pakemana*, 2017**
3D-printed polyamide, 300 x 280 x 50mm,
Pātaka Art + Museum

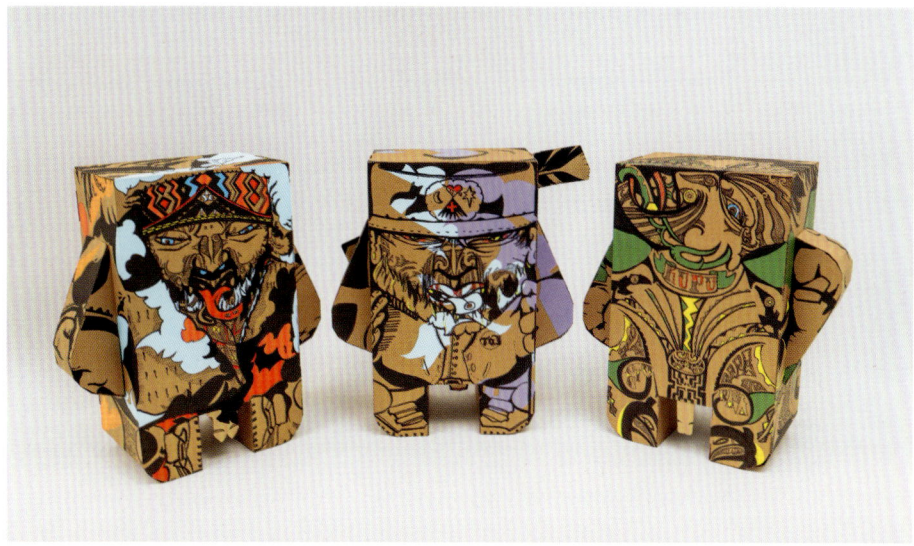

Calling on the figurative painting tradition established by the Ringatū movement and the visual language of street art, Reweti Arapere's *Poropiti Wairua, Poropiti Rongomau* and *Poropiti Toi* (all 2020) use everyday media – cardboard and marker pens – to model a whakapapa of prophetic leaders since Te Kooti. Ārapere is a graduate of the Toioho ki Apiti master's programme at Massey University and received his primary, secondary and tertiary education in te reo Māori learning environments.
**Reweti Arapere, *Poropiti Wairua, Poropiti Rongomau, Poropiti Toi*, 2020**
cardboard, 860 x 520 x 345mm (each), Auckland Art Gallery Toi o Tāmaki, X2020/85.1-3, courtesy of the artist

Borell was an artist who had worked on wharenui projects with Pakaariki Harrison, was a graduate of Massey University's Toioho ki Āpiti Māori visual arts programme and the University of Auckland Elam School of Fine Arts, and was a curator of historical, ancestral and contemporary art.

In the twenty years since *Pūrangiaho*, the whakapapa of Māori artists had grown, as had a confidence that contemporary Māori art could be exhibited and curated according kaupapa Māori and without reference to the Western art canon. The need to demonstrate a connection to innovative, older forms of practice that had once been signalled by the inclusion of taonga such as the Māori Madonna and Child in *Pūrangiaho* was no longer necessary. *Toi Tū Toi Ora* was entered through a sequence of darkened installation spaces associated with the Māori creation narrative, which not only contextualised the exhibition within a tikanga-based paradigm but also suggested that pūrākau could be expressed if not also explained through contemporary Māori art.

The exhibition began with a space dedicated to Te Kore, the great nothingness, featuring Robert Jahnke's shining, sequential neon work *Whenua Kore* (2019), a series of Ralph Hotere's *Black Paintings* from 1969, Reuben Paterson's hypnotic and sparkling video *Te Pūtahitanga ō Rehua* (2005) and a 2001 series of prints and sculptures by Peter Robinson exploring the relationship between Western and Māori knowledges (although the latter was emphasised for this

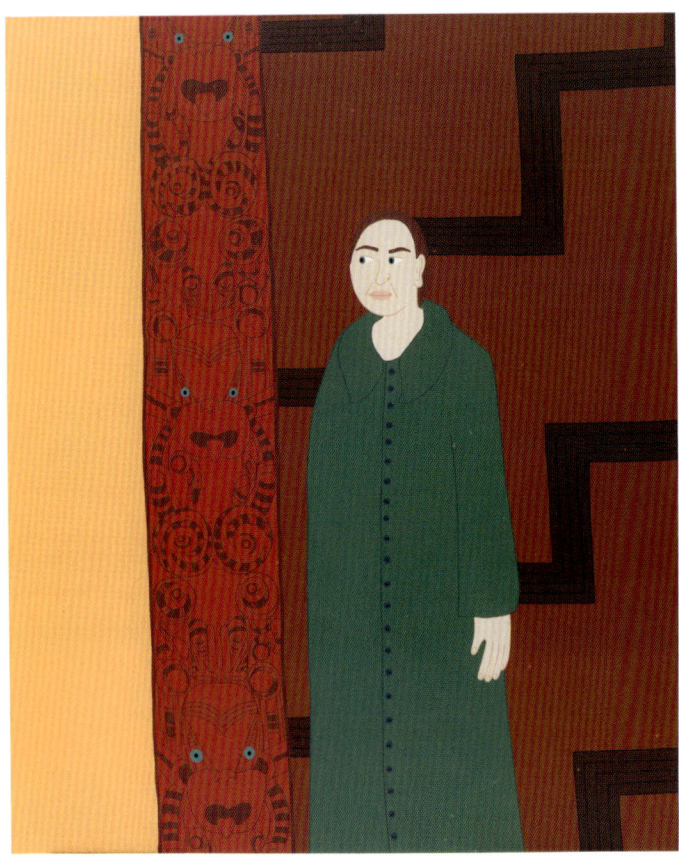

Ayesha Green, *Mum (May 1985)*, 2020
acrylic on canvas, 1700 x 1400mm, X2020/38/2,
Fletcher Trust Collection

installation). Another darkened space associated with Te Pō, the perpetual night, followed. Compared to the Te Kore exhibits, the work in this part of the exhibition was more easily related to traditions of making, as might be expected with a transition out of the ethereal world: fibre arts as exemplified by Maureen Lander's *Wai o te Marama* (2004) maro (apron) and Toi Te Rito Maihi's *Taniko* (n.d.); Darryn George's *Konae Korero #2*, a highly-abstracted heke; and, situated between Te Pō and Te Ao Mārama, Israel Tangaroa Birch's (Ngāpuhi, Ngāi Tawake, Ngāti Kahungunu, Ngāti Rākaipaaka) shimmering representations of taniwha in *Ara-i-te-uru* (2011) and Robert Jahnke's *Ripeka* series, an expression of whakapapa. The critical moment of Te Wehenga, the separation of Ranginui and Papatūānuku, was indicated with a shift towards narrative-based art in the third darkened installation area. Lisa Reihana's video installation *Ihi* (2020) used performance and digital animation to recount the separation, the creation of Te Ao Mārama and Tāne's acquisition of the three baskets of knowledge. Te Wehenga also included works associated with legendary ancestors and animals by established artists Maihi, Randal Leach (Te Aitanga a Hauiti, Ngāti Konohi) and Fiona Pardington. These themes continue in the fully illuminated installation spaces for Te Ao Mārama, where pivotal work by some of the kaumātua of contemporary Māori art, Arnold Wilson, Robyn Kahukiwa and Manos Nathan, were displayed alongside a collaborative installation by Saffronn Te Ratana, Hemi Macgregor (Ngāti Rākaipaaka, Ngāti Kahungunu, Ngāi Tūhoe) and Ngataiharuru Taepa, the emerging artists of the *Pūrangiaho* generation who were well established by the time of *Toi Tū Toi Ora*.

The rest of the exhibition thematically organised an impressive range of artworks by an extensive line-up of senior, mid-career and emerging artists. Themes included Tangaroa (deity of the sea), Te Poropiti me te Whakapātari (Prophecy and Provokation), Kōwhaiwhai, Hauora me te Oranga (Health and Wellbeing), Tikanga Ora Tikanga Toitū (Living Traditions, Enduring Traditions; including body adornments and ceramics), Wāhine, and Huri te Ao ki te Pō (Turning of Day to Night). In many ways, this larger section of the exhibition continued *Pūrangiaho*'s inclusive kaupapa in which the work of emerging artists was interspersed with that of established artists to demonstrate vitality, continuity and sometimes whanaungatanga, including dynasties of artists (Wi, Kereama and Ngataiharuru Taepa; Fred and Brett Graham; and Cliff and Gary Whiting) and generations of graduates (from Toioho ki Āpiti, Massey University; Elam School of Fine Arts, University of Auckland; and Bay of Islands College).

*Toi Tū Toi Ora* identified a large group of artists whose engagement in art was identifiably kaupapa-Māori-based, whose work across of range of media was concerned with te ao Māori, whose identity was founded on collective rather than individual practice, and whose careers were situated in communities and galleries. These aspects had been present in the early group exhibitions of the Māori modernists and collaborative work by Māori women artists like the Haeata Collective, but by 2020 were increasingly becoming the norm rather than the exception in Māori art. Collectives embracing this kaupapa include Te Ātinga, Kauwae (Māori women's collective), Toi Whakaata (Māori print collective), and Mataaho Collective, who with Maureen Lander contributed the majestic *Atapō*, a suspended double-height installation of layered textiles recounting Hine-tītama's transformational

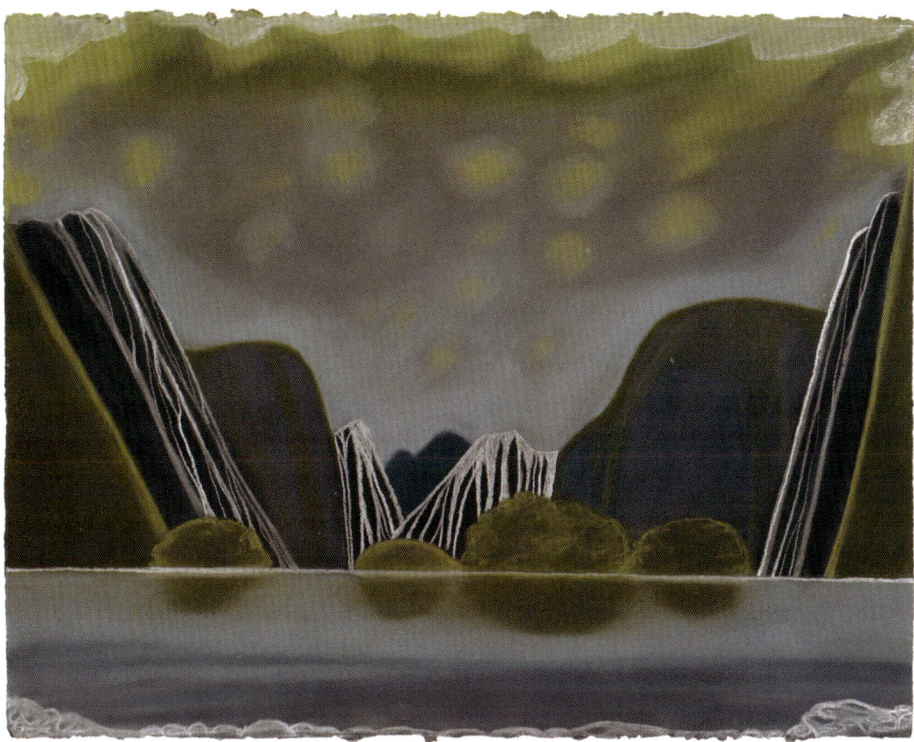

**Marilynn Webb, *Going Through Fiordland Suite No 15*, 1997**
pastel on paper, 580 x 760mm, Dunedin Public Art Gallery, 22-1997, purchased 1997 by the Dunedin Public Art Gallery Society with funds from the Westpac Trust for the 1998 Commemorative Collection

journey to become Hinenuitepō. Institutions including Massey University's Toioho ki Āpiti, Toihoukura at Tairawhiti Polytechnic, tertiary wānanga and supportive communities had provided the platforms for this art to flourish.

*Toi Tū Toi Ora* was an opportunity for kaupapa Māori artists to be shown within the larger whakapapa of contemporary Māori art and in a major gallery. By championing these artists, and bringing them to wider public attention, Borell wanted to challenge the 'ambitions of mainstream art institutions … in their own artistic agendas and positions'. He argued that some influential institutions had become overly comfortable in their promotion of work by selected Young Guns (Cotton, Parekōwhai, Reihana and Robinson), whose work continued to have strong ties to the Western tradition, but were unwilling to accommodate and perhaps unsettled by the prospect of including another generation of Māori artists, especially those working in an Indigenous canon.

An enduring legacy of *Toi Tū Toi Ora* will be the wero that Borell laid down to institutions, a challenge made more poignant by his resignation from Auckland Art Gallery immediately before the opening. The gallery's unwillingness to allow Māori control over the exhibition was widely cited as a reason in the media. The indigenisation of art institutions remains a critical and yet-to-be-realised milestone in the history of Māori art.

## Iwi exhibitions

Iwi exhibitions have been more deliberate in defining whakapapa-based perspectives of Māori art than the large Māori survey shows, and they have often embraced an even greater diversity of art forms and venues. Tribal identity had grown increasingly more important throughout the twentieth century and into the next, and was the basis for regular iwi visual and performance arts biennials, including Tūhoe's Ahurei (established in 1971) and the Ngāpuhi Festival (held since 2006). These events bring together contemporary raranga, whakairo rākau, craft, design and fine artwork by emerging, mid-career and senior practitioners, and generally do not have a curatorial strategy beyond inclusivity. More deliberate curatorial strategies have been employed by iwi wanting to foster iwi-based contemporary art or to communicate iwi distinctiveness on a national and international stage.

In 2000, Ngāi Tahu identified visual culture and identity as a focus in its twenty-five-year strategic plan for its eighteen rūnanga (the post-settlement governance entities charged with furthering the tribe's interests).[21] The iwi already had a vibrant arts community, collectivised early on through the efforts of the Ngā Puna Waihanga Southern Branch and its leader, the acclaimed weaver and former Māori arts advisor Cath Brown. Ngāi Tahu also had close links to, and many

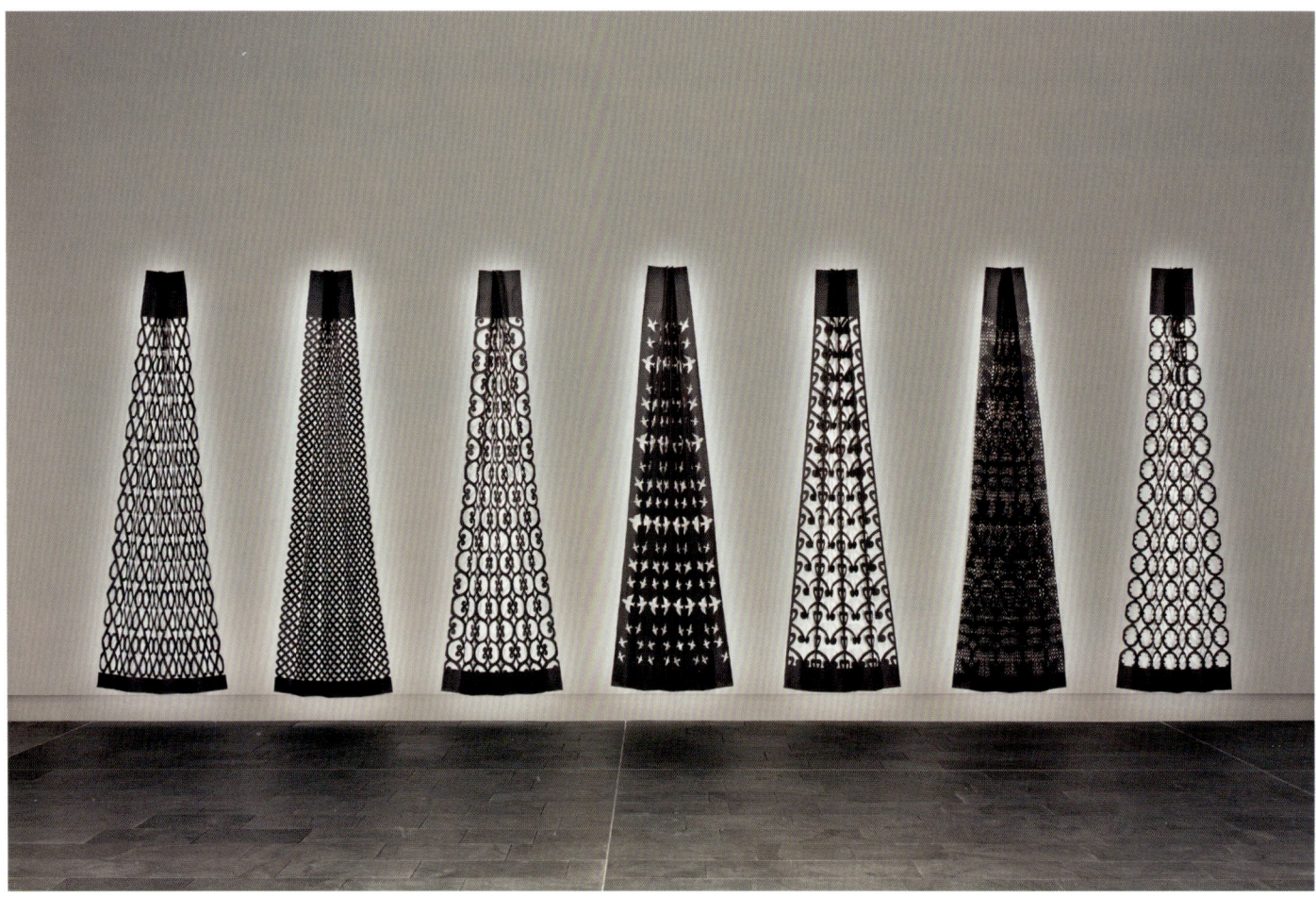

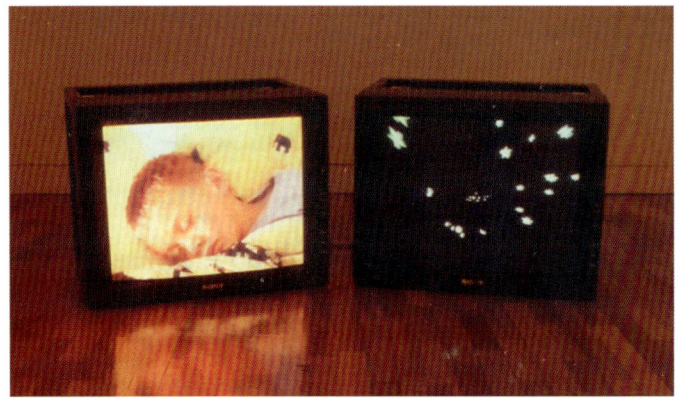

Top: Lonnie Hutchinson's 'seven sisters', representing the peaks that form the caldera wall of the volcanic crater filled by Lyttelton Harbour, as installed in *Te Puāwai o Ngāi Tahu: Twelve Contemporary Ngāi Tahu Artists*, Christchurch Art Gallery Te Puna o Waiwhetū, 2003.
**Lonnie Hutchinson, *Sista7*, 2003**
black building paper, 2500 x 1000 x 100mm, Christchurch Art Gallery Te Puna o Waiwhetū, 2003/36.a-g, purchased 2003

Bottom: **Nathan Pohio, *Sleeper*, 1999, as installed at Melbourne Art Fair, 2002**
courtesy of the artist

Opposite: **Simon Kaan, *Ka Waka Tipuraka*, 2003**
oil on board, eight panels, 1600 x 1600mm, courtesy of the artist

graduates from, the University of Canterbury School of Fine Arts, and arts and design programmes at Christchurch and Otago polytechnics. These foundations had been recognised in two earlier events curated by Te Rūnanga o Ngāi Tahu arts facilitator Moana Tipa (Ngāi Tahu, Ngāti Kahungunu). *Tino Rakatirataka* was a small exhibition of Ngāi Tahu artists held at Christchurch Polytechnic. It was followed in 1999 by *Rukutia! Rukutia!*, a much more expansive 'southern Māori' art show, installed in the lobbies of nine Christchurch hotels and the Ngāi Tahu boardroom. *Rukutia!* featured the work of fifty Māori artists who were either of Ngāi Tahu descent, were living in the South Island, or had worked in the Māori art advisory service,[22] such as Sandy Adsett, Clive Arlidge and Marilynn Webb.[23]

The first Ngāi Tahu exhibitions in art galleries took place as part of the 2000 Kāi Tahu Arts Festival in Dunedin; it included *Aukaha Kia Kaha: Strengthen the Bindings of the Earth, of the People, or the Soul*, a showing at Dunedin Public Art Gallery of work by fourteen artists working across a range of visual art forms.[24] The show was curated by Megan

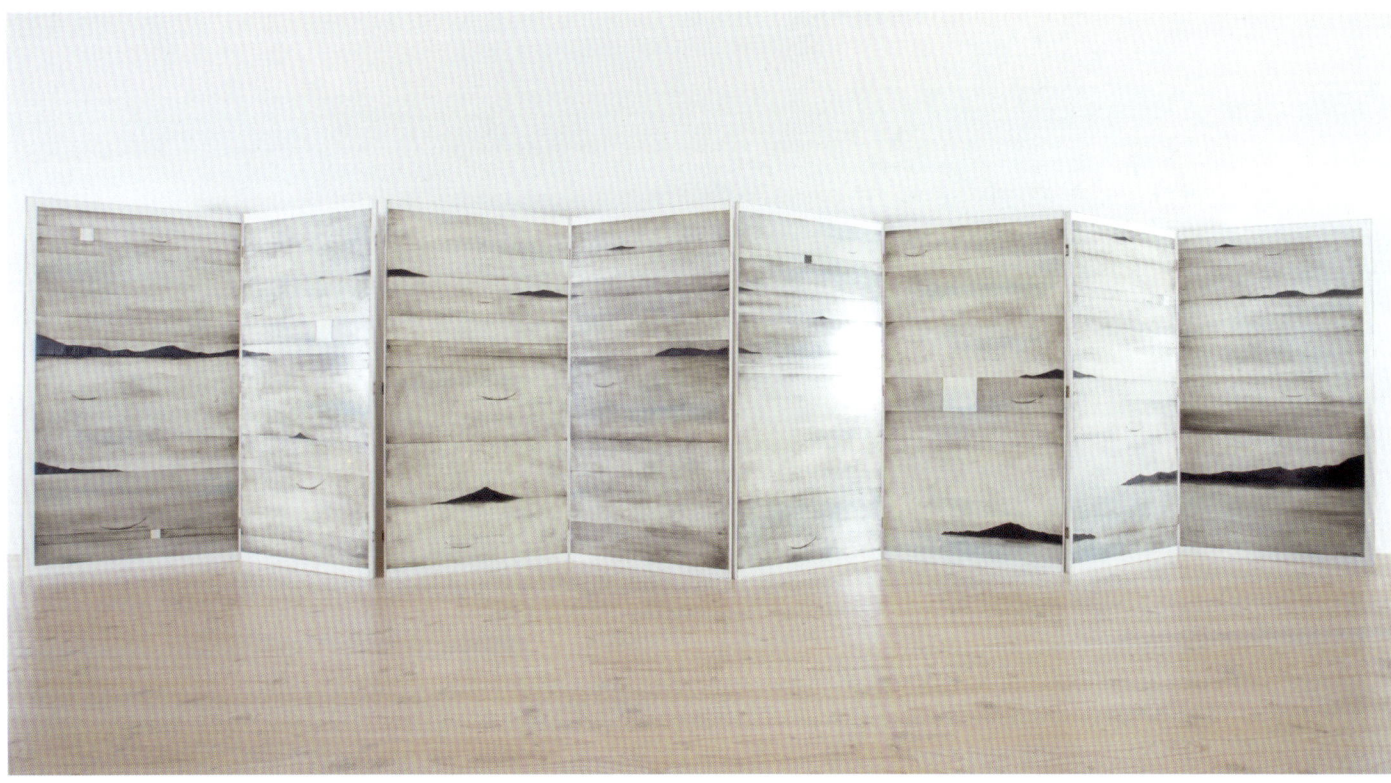

Tamati-Quennell, seconded from her position at Te Papa Tongarewa Museum of New Zealand, who described the exhibition as an attempt to:

> highlight Kāi Tahutanga through the work shown and the whakapapa relationships which bind the artists together. Interpreted as 'bringing the past forward,' *Aukaha Kia Kaha* is based on ideas about identity and uses the cultural redress aspect of the 1997 Crown Settlement Offer made to Ngāi Tahu – a contemporary and pivotal event within Kāi Tahu history – as a reference point for the show.[25]

Her description of the exhibition in the catalogue left no doubt about the importance of whakapapa and post-settlement revitalisation to Ngāi Tahu art. While many of the works closely referenced Ngāi Tahu concepts, landscapes and customary art practices, the inclusion of Robinson's infamous 1997 painting *Māori Have Rights Too!* (a companion piece to his even more controversial *Pākehā Have Rights Too!*) with stylised koru swastika must have raised eyebrows, given the kaupapa of the show. Tamati-Quennell curated a follow-on show the next year at the McDougall Contemporary Art Annex in the Christchurch Arts Centre, *Haumi e! Hui e! Taiki e!: A Ngāi Tahu Visual Arts Exhibition*, in which whānau connections bound many of the artists together even though their practices ranged from Reihana Parata and Florence Reiri's weaving through to Nathan Pohio and Rachael Rakena's video installations.[26] The show was part of the Christchurch Arts Festival under the kaitiakitanga of Ngāi Tahu's Canterbury-based rūnanga, and it followed a practice of including Māori and iwi-specific shows in larger municipal arts festivals that had begun in 1966 with the Hamilton Festival of Maori Arts.[27]

Similar expectations were associated with the opening of public art galleries. In 2003, Tamati-Quennell joined with Mane-Wheoki and Milburn to curate an inaugural exhibition for the recently opened Christchurch Art Gallery Te Puna o Waiwhetū, *Te Puāwai o Ngāi Tahu: Twelve Contemporary Ngāi Tahu Artists*. Whereas the work of senior artists such as Cath Brown and Otene Rakena had provided the matriarchal and patriarchal foundations for the previous two shows, *Te Puāwai o Ngāi Tahu* also located Ngāi Tahu arts in the ancestral past through the inclusion at the entry of a taurapa from Okains Bay, a kaitaka passed down through the Taiaroa family and held in the Canterbury Museum, and footage of whitebaiting from the New Zealand Film Archive.[28] Together, the three taonga made a connection to the site as

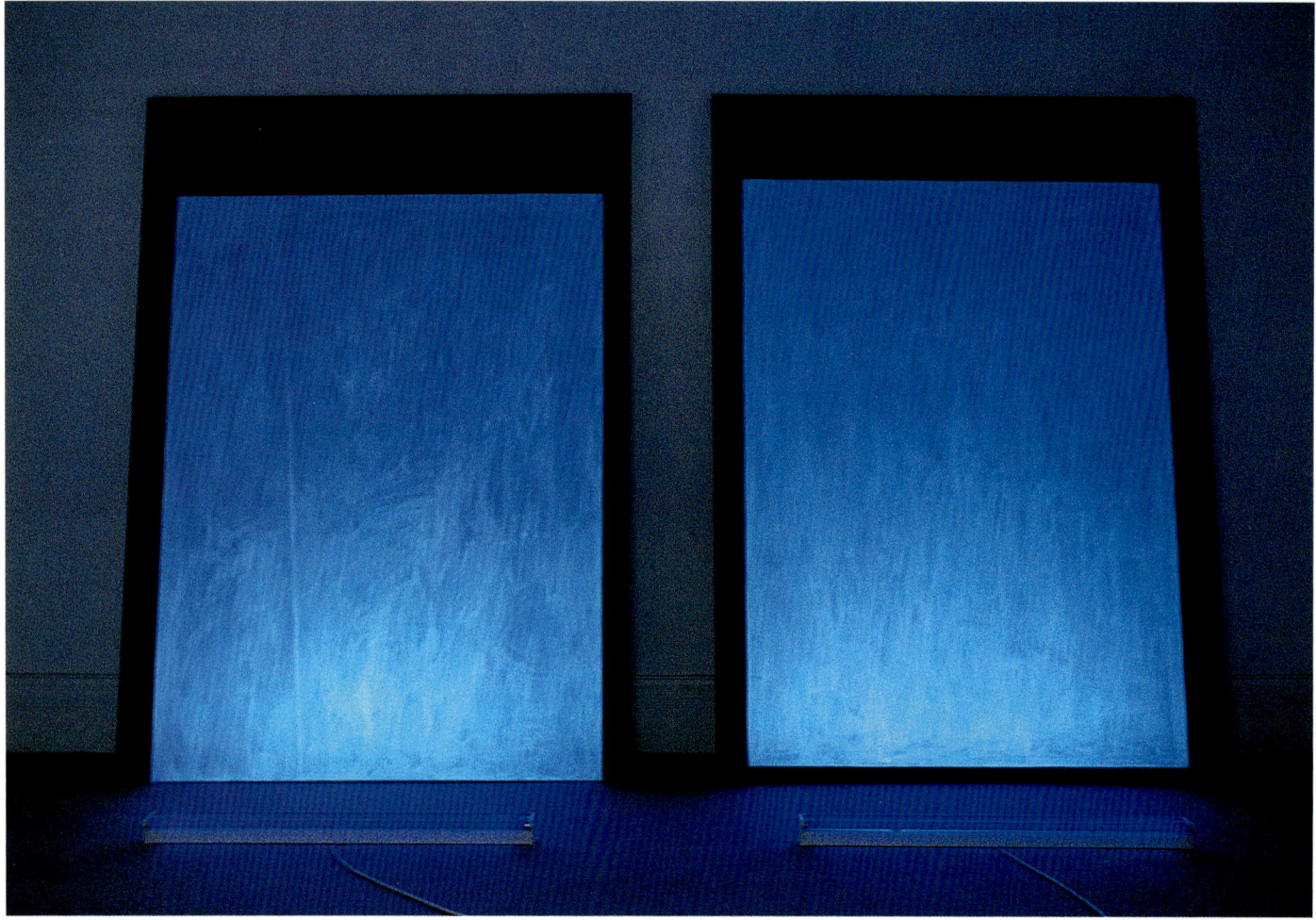

**Chris Heaphy, *Te Ika a Maui & Te Waka a Maui*, 1999**
acrylic on canvas, 2430 x 1830mm, Christchurch Art Gallery Te Puna o Waiwhetū, 2000/206.a-d, purchased with the generous assistance of the artist and Jonathan Smart Gallery, 2000

a mahinga kai and puna (a spring used for healing). These taonga set in place a water narrative that ran through many of the works to 'highlight the fluidity between old and new practice and expression and place the artists in the broader Ngāi Tahu whakapapa and definitions of Māori art', thus entangling landscape with identity and tikanga.[29]

The manifestation of Ngāi Tahutanga through contemporary art and group exhibitions has found expression outside of the South Island, too. In 2006, Simon Kaan (Ngāi Tahu) curated *Akona ki ngā Rekereke: Learning from the Knee*, which was exhibited at Burrinja Cultural Centre, Dandenong Ranges, in Melbourne.[30] Many of the artists had by this stage exhibited together as Ngāi Tahu several times, leading Kaan to claim 'a collective consciousness' on the part of the fourteen participating artists, despite their different practices.[31]

Ngāi Tahu group exhibitions stopped when the rūnanga ceased to employ arts facilitators. In 2012, in order to maintain the momentum of whanaungatanga that had accrued between 1998 and 2006, Ross Hemara, Kaan,

Areta Wilkinson and others founded the Paemanu Rōpū, a collective of Ngāi Tahu contemporary artists independent of the rūnanga. Speaking of the collective, Hemara reinforced the whakapapa connections between the current artists and their ancestral counterparts; as he explained it, 'We're visual artists who work in a contemporary manner, but we are also very aware of our whakapapa and of our relationships with the forms and practices of our weavers and carvers in particular.'[32] The collective's first exhibition was *Paemanu: Nohoaka Toi* at the Centre of Contemporary Art Te Moroki in Christchurch in 2018. The show sought to anchor Ngāi Tahu art within Ngāi Tahu whakapapa and wairua through site-specific works and sculpture and a vibrant public programme including workshops. One installation, *Takiroa, takinui, Takitāwhiti, taki hotuhotu, takinoa e!* by Nathan Pohio and Rachael Rakena situated a section of rock art, removed by a collector from Takiroa in the Waikati Valley, in a vitrine in front of a split-screen livestream from Takiroa showing the hole left behind and also the view out to the landscape from the original position. *Paemanu: Tauraka Toi – A Landing Place* opened in 2021 at Dunedin Public Art Gallery. The exhibition had an ambitious kaupapa addressing Ngāi Tahu histories of migration and occupation, tīpuna, kaihaukai (sharing and exchanging food) and relationships to tohorā and water in work by established and emerging artists.

Iwi exhibitions have been central to Te Papa Tongarewa Museum of New Zealand's bicultural partnership and participation curatorial strategy, and its promotion of Māori arts and culture. Since the museum opened in 1998, there has been an almost continuous series of iwi exhibitions, beginning with Te Ātiawa (1998–1999), followed by Te Aupōuri (1999–2001), Tūhoe (2001–2003), Whanganui (2003–2006), Ngāi Tahu (2006–2009), Waikato-Tainui (2011–2014), Ngāti Toa (2014–2017) and Rongowhakaata (2017–2022).[33] Each show relates an iwi's story over a period of ancestral and historical time through the presentation of a range of documentation and representations, including contemporary art and taonga Māori. These exhibitions are narrative-driven and heavily interpreted for the purpose of having relevance to iwi and clear messages to other audiences. In *Ko Rongowhakaata: The Story of Light and Shadow* there was an additional theme of reconciliation, based on the 2011 Deed of Settlement between the Crown and Rongowhakaata and symbolised by the Crown's planned repatriation of Rongowhakaata's prized wharenui Te Hau ki Tūranga, which has been in the museum since its removal without permission from its original site in 1867. A number of other regional museums and art galleries have also curated exhibitions concerned with the customary and contemporary taonga of their local iwi. Wrapped in a tribal narrative, Māori art is once again recontextualised, not within an ethnological or aesthetic paradigm, but as exemplars of constant and changing artistic practices that explain those moments, ideas and values that have shaped iwi identity.

### 'Remembering' exhibitions

The curators of Māori art exhibitions have been attuned not only to the layers of whakapapa laid down by successive waves of Māori artists, but also to the whakapapa of Māori-led art exhibitions themselves. Art historian and artist Taarati Taiaroa has described events commemorating earlier Māori shows as 'remembering' exhibitions, curated to maintain the memory of the foundations of contemporary Māori art.[34]

*Ngā Mahi o te Aka o Tūwhenua: New Zealand Māori Culture and the Contemporary Scene* commemorated the thirtieth anniversary of Buck Nin and Baden Pere's 1966 *New Zealand Maori Culture and the Contemporary Scene*. Nin and Pere's show had sought to make associations between taonga Māori in the museum's collections and work produced by emerging Māori modernists, in order to contextualise contemporary practice within a longer whakapapa of Māori making, while at the same time situating the taonga within an artistic rather than material-culture paradigm. Assuming that link to have been well established, the curator of *Ngā Mahi o te Aka o Tūwhenua*, Ngapine Tamihana Te Ao (Allen; Ngāti Porou, Ngāti Raukawa, 1952–2016), presented the original contemporary artists as grounding, kaumātua figures, and encouraged the audience to find the relationship between their work and that of Christchurch artists and University of Canterbury School of Fine Arts students which was also included in the show.[35] Apart from adding another generational layer to the whakapapa of Māori art, *Ngā Mahi o te Aka o Tūwhenua* sought to reinforce the position of the South Island, and Christchurch in particular, as the birthplace of the contemporary Māori art movement – at least from a curatorial perspective.

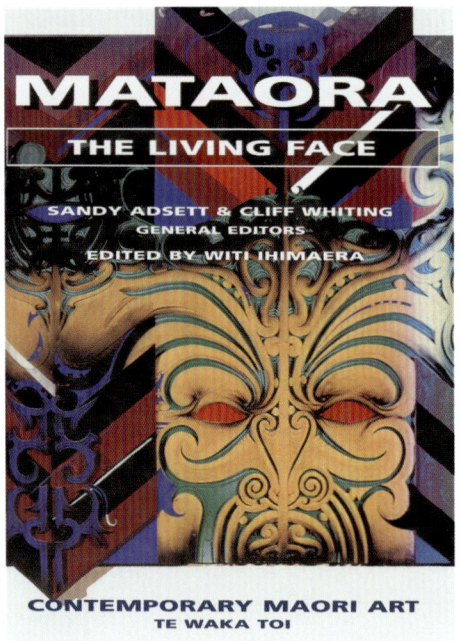 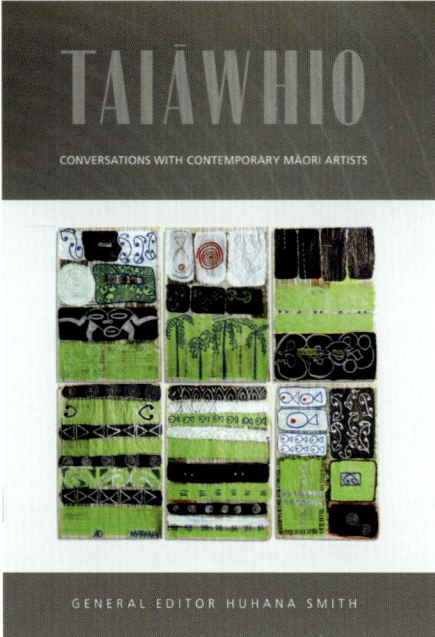 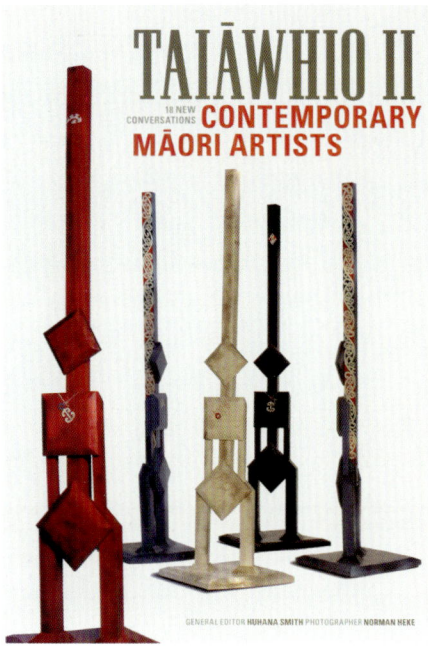

Cover of *Mataora: The Living Face: Contemporary Maori Art*, edited by Sandy Adsett, Cliff Whiting and Witi Ihimaera (David Bateman, 1996).

Cover of *Taiāwhio: Conversations with Contemporary Māori Artists* edited by Huhana Smith with Oriwa Solomon, Awhina Tamarapa, Megan Tamati-Quennell and John Walsh (Te Papa Press, 2002).

Cover of *Taiāwhio II: Contemporary Māori Artists, 18 New Conversations*, edited by Huhana Smith with Oriwa Soloman, Awhina Tamarapa and Megan Tamati-Quennell (Te Papa Press, 2007).

That claim was challenged when Fred Graham 'reconvened the class of '66' at the Waikato Museum for the fortieth anniversary of both *New Zealand Maori Culture and the Contemporary Scene* and *Contemporary Maori Painting and Sculpture,* which had originally been shown in shop windows and at St Paul's Methodist Centre as part of the 1966 Festival of Maori Arts in Hamilton.[36] Work made by artists from both shows in the years since was included in *Aukaha: 40 Years On*, a reunion exhibition that established 1966 as the year when contemporary Māori art emerged – if not forced its way – into the New Zealand arts scene. In his catalogue essay for the show, Brett Graham asserted that Hamilton was the movement's wellspring, and pointed out that *Contemporary Maori Painting and Sculpture* not only pre-dated *New Zealand Maori Culture and the Contemporary Scene*, but also included much of the same work.[37] *Aukaha: 40 Years On* was one of a number of exhibitions that have commemorated *Contemporary Maori Painting and Sculpture*, including *Contemporary Maori Art* in 1976 and *Haongia Te Taonga* in 1986. As Taiaroa observed, the reunification of artists from both shows in remembering exhibitions 'recognises and reflects a significant year for Māori art, in which a generation of Māori artists can historically be seen to be working towards the establishment of a single project – contemporary Māori art'.[38] In this sense, the curatorial project of remembering reinforces, if not also reifies, that generation of Māori artists as producers of Māori art and demonstrates the continuing currency of that work, its collective value and mana and its relationship to the ongoing practice of contemporary art by Māori.

## Compilations

Te Tiriti o Waitangi sesquicentennial and the turn of the millennium inspired several handsome published compilations of contemporary Māori art, presented in biographical format and written by Māori art historians, theorists and critics primarily for a Māori audience. *Mataora: The Living Face* (1996), edited by Witi Ihimaera (Te Aitanga a Māhaki) and artists Sandy Adsett and Cliff Whiting, featured the work of forty-one artists spanning the modernist to the Young Gun generations.[39] Each artist was profiled with a photographic portrait, between one and three images of their work and a short personal quote. The business of explaining the context of their art was left to Ihimaera and Robert Jahnke, who wrote a series of essays on a range of topics covering art history and criticism. Ralph Hotere, Paratene Matchitt and Selwyn Muru refused to be profiled.

Given that there were no comparable full-colour, large-format hardcover precedents, the book was seen as somewhat of a missed opportunity for a detailed exploration of the individual approaches of the artists profiled. That task was taken up a decade later by the Māori curatorial staff at Te Papa Tongarewa Museum of New Zealand, who produced *Taiāwhio: Conversations with Contemporary Māori Artists* in 2002 and, five years later, *Taiāwhio II: Conversations with Contemporary Māori Artists, 18 New Conversations*. Both volumes were edited by Huhana Smith (Ngāti Tukorehe, Ngāti Raukawa ki Te Tonga) and contained illustrated essays on thirty-six contemporary Māori artists by Smith, Oriwa Solomon (Ngāti Ruanui, 1951–2018), Awhina Tamarapa, Megan Tamati-Quennell and John Walsh. A notable feature was the mixed biographical and autobiographical method, which included long quotations from the artists, tied together with the writers' observations. Despite a wealth of information, no concluding section that would have drawn the stories together into a larger narrative was provided in either book.

However, while all of these books and other publications produced by Māori art historians and theorists demonstrated that there were enough Māori writers to write about Māori art, the trickier question was whether Māori should write critically, in open forums, about Māori art. Curatorial practices of inclusivity, and a desire to protect and promote Māori art and artists within a previously hostile general arts environment, have made writers reluctant to publicly comment on the variable quality of Māori art being produced and exhibited.

### Conclusion

Māori curatorship and art writing emerged as disciplines in their own right in the 1990s, and Māori curators and art writers have been influential in promoting Māori art as a continuing tradition from its Polynesian roots to its contemporary manifestations. Surveys and remembering exhibitions, and the catalogue- and review-writing around them, have been critical to this process. This is as a separate project to the perpetuation of Māori art as supported by iwi, which have their own processes for promoting visual culture as part of their identity and sociocultural strategic missions.

The story of contemporary Māori art is always open to contestation, as is apparent in the disruption versus continuity debate that was played out in metropolitan gallery spaces in the 1990s and early 2000s, when curators and writers asked 'Who is a Māori artist?', 'What is the role of tikanga in this practice?' and 'Who can write about and curate Māori art?' The answers posited by Māori artists, historians and curators were many and varied and sometimes polarised. These divisions of opinions can be likened to what occurred in the age preceding Māori modernism, when Ngata and Te Puea instigated 'traditionalised' revival initiatives to rescue artistic continuity, in contrast to Rātana's disruptive aesthetic and architectural interventions. They resurfaced during the early period of Māori modernism, when artists such as Arnold Wilson criticised customary practice for being iterative rather than innovative.

Group exhibitions, clustered around the sesquicentennial in 1990 and the new millennium, were retrospective in nature and responded to a mood of introspection and cultural awareness, from which emerged bicultural curatorial models and an inclusive whakapapa of Māori art. Importantly, these exhibitions – no matter their kaupapa – made space for contemporary Māori art in major galleries and brought interesting, rising artists to the attention of curators who then began promoting their work on the world scene. In the decades since there has been a slow but steady increase in the number of Māori curators; however, more work needs to be done to shift expressions of tino rangatiratanga off gallery walls and into gallery management.

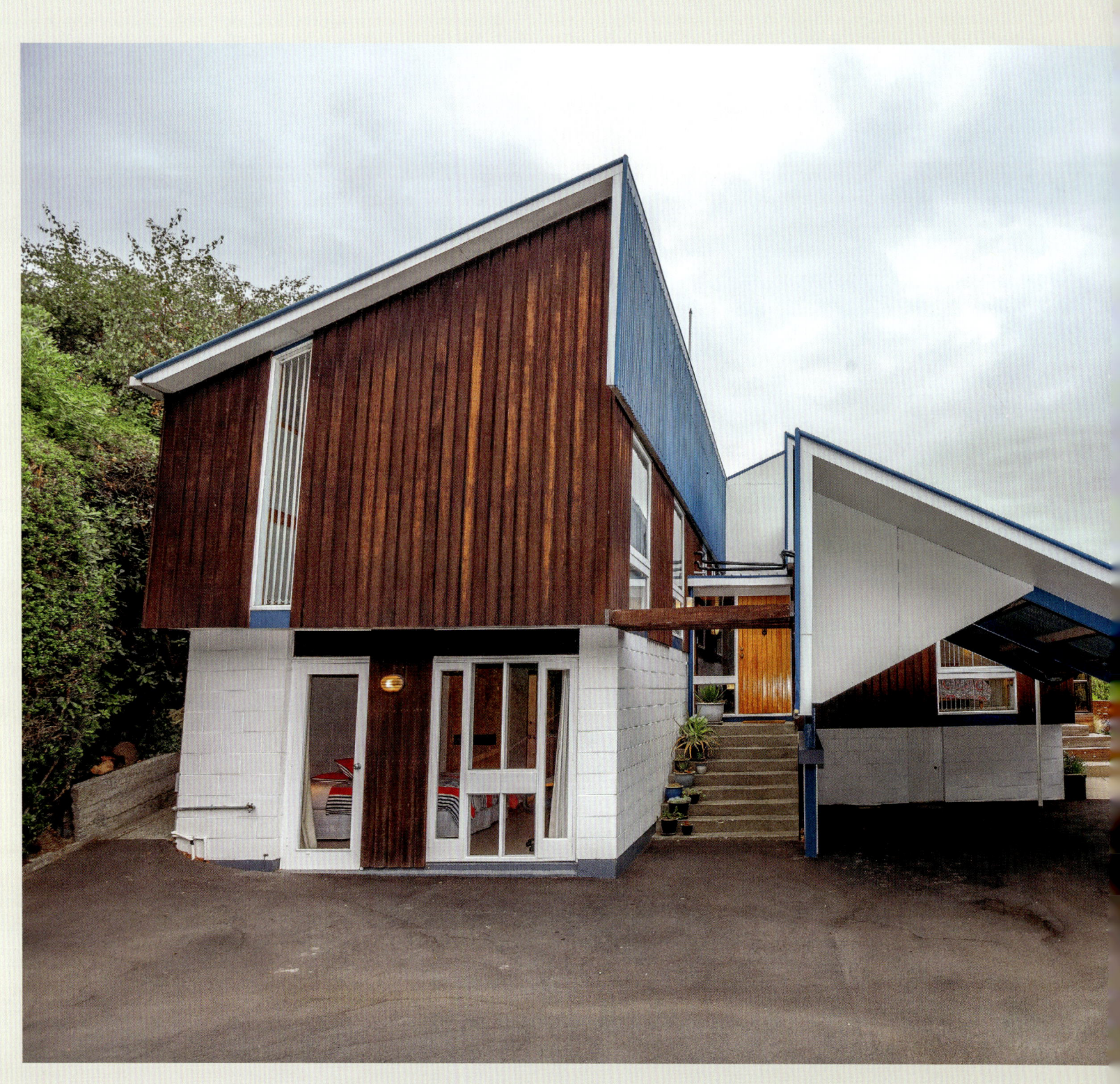

# MĀORI ARCHITECTS AND ARCHITECTURAL DESIGNERS
DEIDRE BROWN

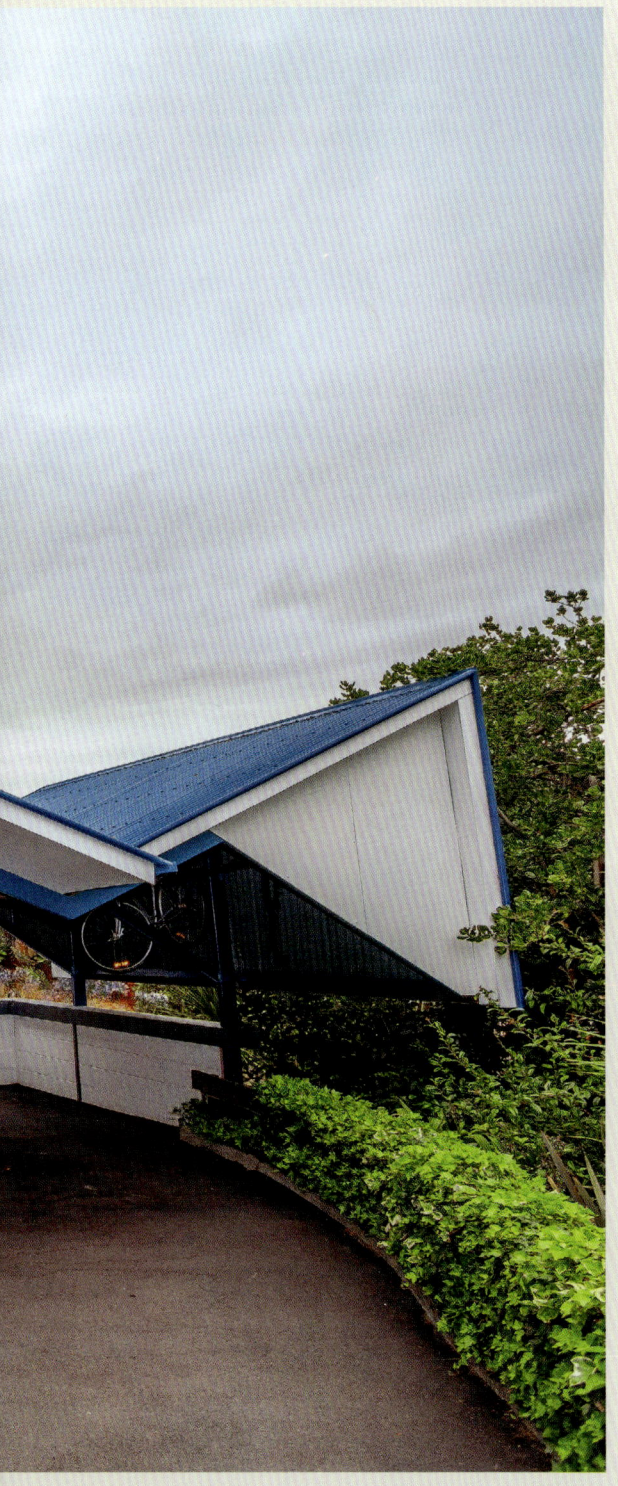

Wiremu (Bill) Royal, Dyers Pass Road house, Christchurch, c.1960.
photograph by Michelle Ward

Māori architects and architectural designers, although they are still relatively few in number, have played an important role in maintaining a Māori presence in New Zealand's building professions since World War Two and, more recently, embedding tikanga values into the design of the built environment. William Bloomfield (Ngāti Kahungunu, c.1885–1969) was likely the first Māori to study architecture: he graduated from the University of Pennsylvania School of Architecture in 1913 and practised in Auckland between 1925 and 1960. His projects included Yorkshire House (completed 1928), St Augustine's Church (1930) and Lopdell House (1930).[1]

However, it appears that Bloomfield was not the first Māori architect to work on specifically Māori buildings. That achievement belongs to the first Māori person to graduate in architecture from a New Zealand university, Wiremu (Bill) Royal (Ngāti Raukawa, 1931–2013), who began his studies at Auckland in 1950 and completed his diploma in 1960.[2] Conscious of his background and the cultural pressures to succeed in an architectural academic environment that was new to Māori, Royal once commented, 'from day one I had to succeed, because I was a guinea pig for Maoridom. I couldn't afford to let the race down.'[3] He became well versed in the late-modernist tradition early in his career at Warren and Mahoney Architects in Christchurch. In 1968 he established his own practice and worked on a variety of residential, commercial and institutional projects as well as more than sixty marae. His company, Royal Associates, continued in Christchurch, under the directorship of his son Perry.

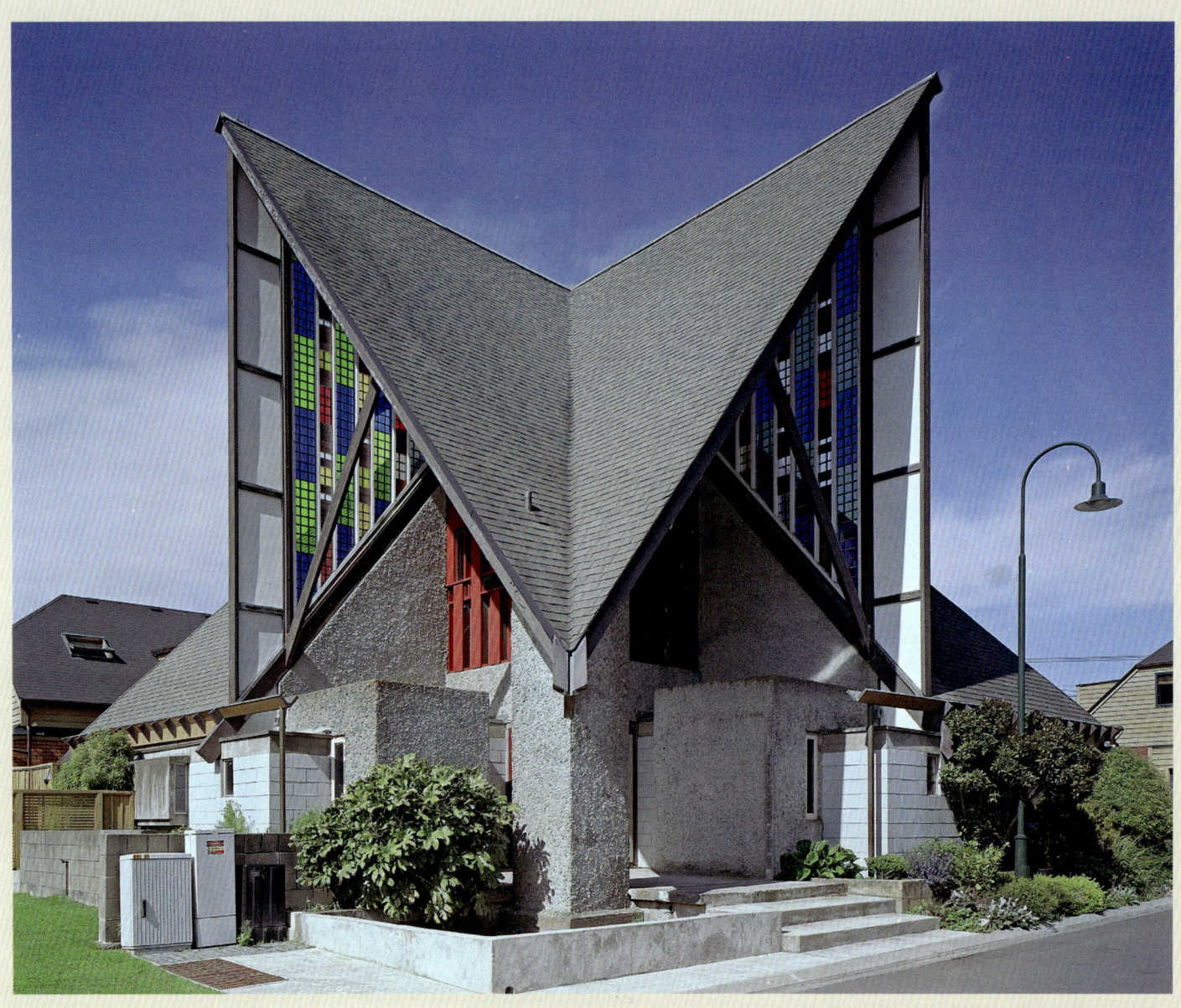

John Scott, Futuna Chapel, Karori, 1961.
photograph by Jim Simmons

**Opposite:** John Scott, Maori Battalion Memorial Community Centre, Palmerston North, 1964.
*Te Ao Hou* 47, 1964, with permission of the Maori Purposes Fund Board

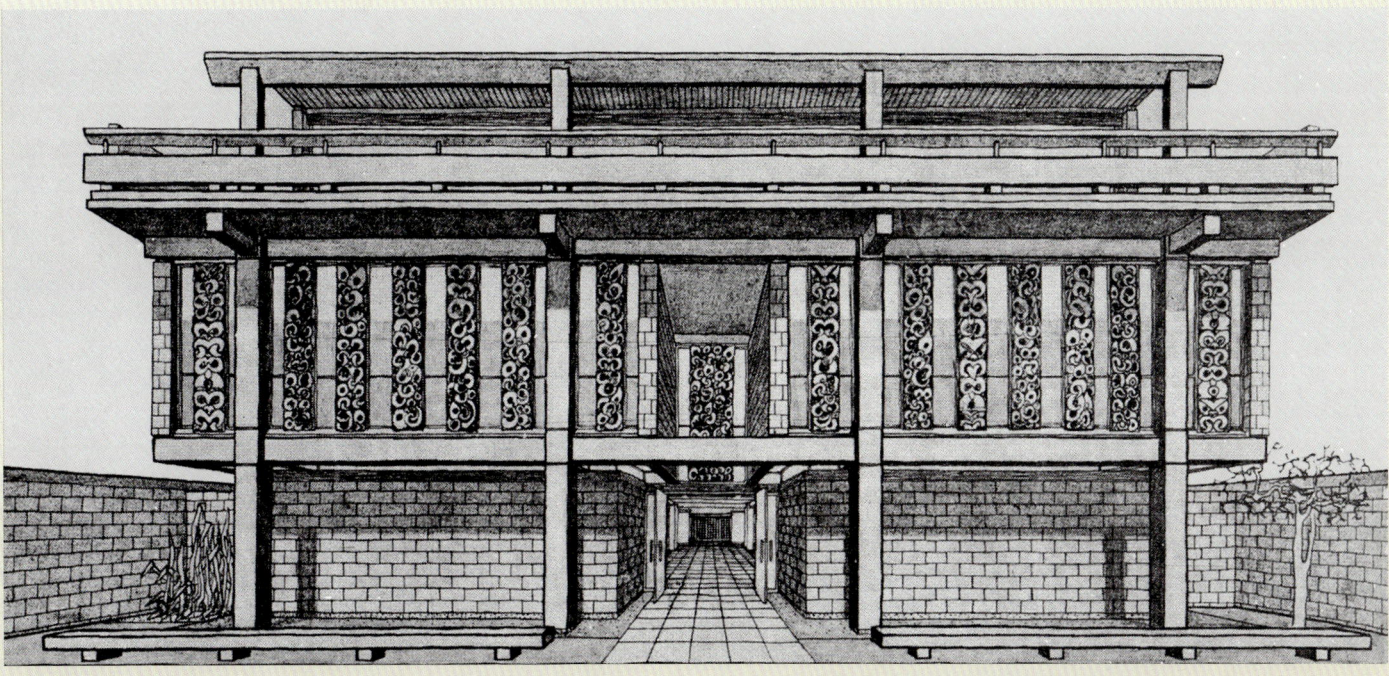

John Scott (Taranaki, Te Arawa, 1924–1992) was one of a number of designers who brought regionalist and Indigenous sensibilities into modernist architectural practice in Aotearoa New Zealand. He studied architecture at Auckland University College from 1946 to 1949 and part-time in 1950, but did not graduate. He worked with Structural Developments and very briefly with Group Architects. In 1953 he returned to his birthplace of Haumoana, near Hastings, in Hawke's Bay to start his own practice.[4]

Scott's architecture was founded on powerful Māori and non-Māori design concepts and responded to site, not just as a series of ground and climate conditions, but as a whole landscape. It was also 'up-to-the-minute' in terms of its use of modernist concepts from Europe, North America and elsewhere. The woolshed and wharenui are often cited as the local forms of building that inspired the formalism and materiality of Scott's work.[5] Hallmarks of his residential designs include Māori-style porches; strong, shed-like roof lines; and 'honest' materials such as exposed native timber and raw concrete. These localised elements were arranged so that they related to site and landscape conditions through carefully placed glazing.

An acknowledgement of the Māori sense of community and communal living is apparent in the multi-purpose living spaces in a number of Scott's designs. The kitchen is a central entry and gathering point and its importance in his schemes can be likened to the significance of wharekai and kāuta as places of tapu-free discussion and togetherness. The kitchen table – not the living room – is the main gathering space for Māori in family homes.

Scott's deep sense of spirituality was evident in the churches he designed. The strong positive reception for his St John's Chapel project in Hastings (opened in 1956) attracted the offer of the project for which he is best remembered, Futuna Chapel, Karori, Wellington (opened 1961). The chapel's overall form was influenced by Le Corbusier's Notre-Dame du Haut (1955, Ronchamp, France), and the ribbed rafters, central 'heart' column and low eaves are reminiscent of the anthropomorphism of wharenui. Likewise, Scott's Maori Battalion Memorial Community Centre (1958–1964, Palmerston North) combined a contemporary late-modernist interest in Japanese post-and-beam construction with customary exterior whakairo rākau panels carved by Kelly Kereama.[6] The resultant biculturalism of the buildings situated them within a larger and emergent Māori modernism that included the contemporaneous paintings and sculptures of Fred Graham, Paratene Matchitt, Cliff Whiting and Arnold Wilson.

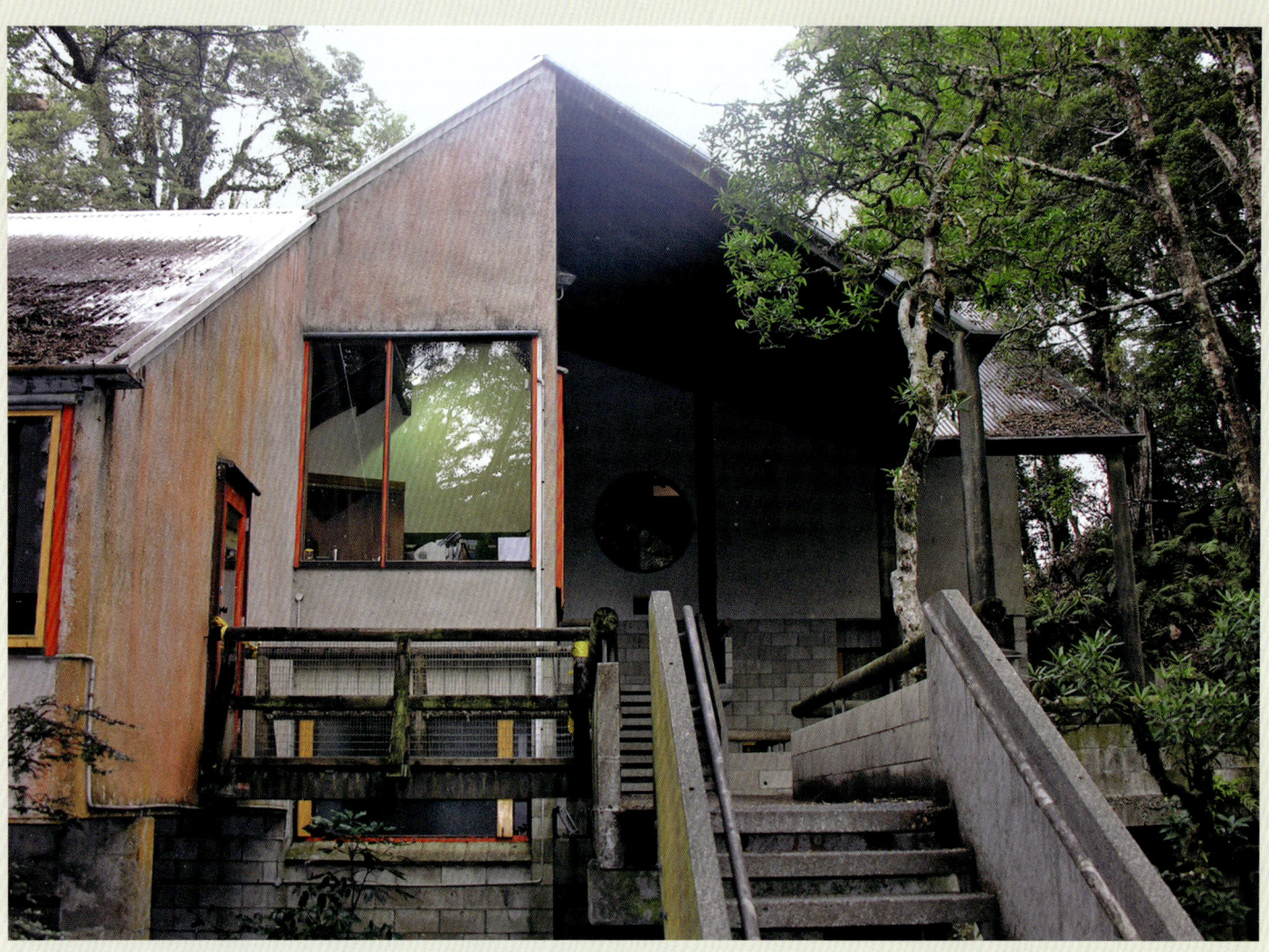

John Scott, Aniwaniwa Visitor Centre, Te Urewera National Park, 1976.
photograph by Julia Gatley, 2007

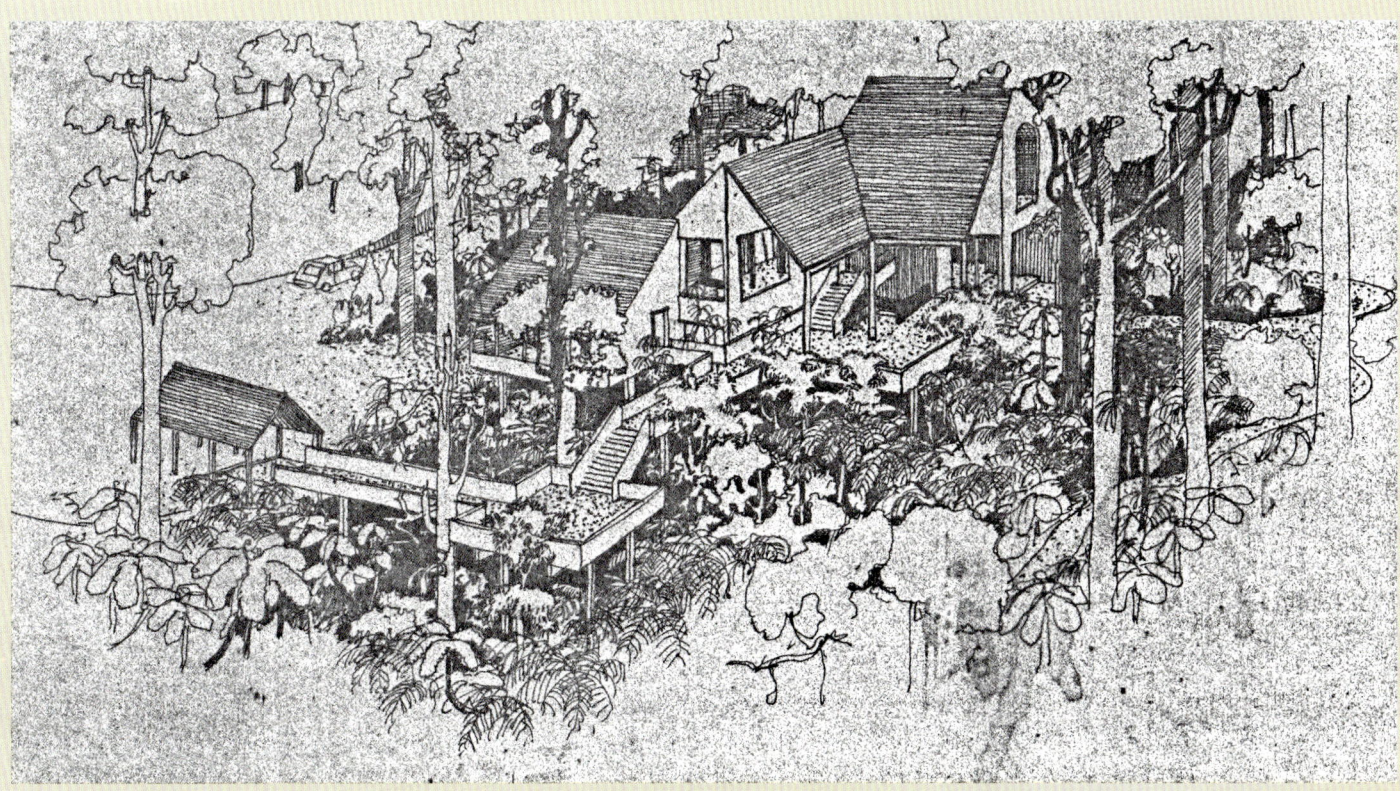

Isometric drawing of the Aniwaniwa Visitor Centre by John Scott, Te Urewera National Park, 1976.
Architecture Archive, Special Collections, Waipapa Taumata Rau University of Auckland

Biculturalism implies a partnership between cultures. This is a different concept to Indigenous self-determination, in which Indigenous people control their own destinies. This difference was brought into sharp relief by the fate of Scott's visitor centre at Aniwaniwa, built for the former Te Urewera National Park Board in 1976. The building had been widely recognised as an important example of modernism, particularly for the way its massed geometric forms responded to its natural setting. For some time, the Crown's assumption of ownership over Te Urewera National Park had been contested by the local Tūhoe tribe, and this had led to considerable tensions. In 2014 the national park was disestablished and replaced by a legal entity, Te Urewera, to be co-governed by Tūhoe and the Crown. By that stage, the Aniwaniwa Visitor Centre had been closed for seven years and had fallen into material and structural disrepair. The decision by Tūhoe and the Department of Conservation to demolish the Aniwaniwa centre in 2016 provoked protest from the New Zealand Institute of Architects and Scott's own family. The model of biculturalism that the building had pioneered – of a Māori architect commissioned to design a building for the Crown – had passed, as the Crown and Māori were seeking negotiated partnerships that supported Māori community aspirations towards self-determination.

Rewi Thompson (Ngāti Porou, Ngāti Raukawa, 1953–2016) was the best-known Māori architect to emerge after the modernist period. He believed that architecture was fundamentally concerned with land and people, and had the power to affirm identity and wellbeing. His design work expressed this philosophy, as seen in the undulating hill/cloud-like forms of the Wiri state housing precinct (1986–1989, Auckland), the Polynesian 'fish' canopies that enlivened the bland Ōtara Town Centre shopping mall (1987, Auckland), the dynamic Capital Discovery Place (1988, Wellington) and, in collaboration with Paratene Matchitt and the Pākehā architect John Gray, the City to Sea Bridge (1990–1994, Wellington) that reimagined the creation stories of Te Whanganui a Tara.

Thompson's most notable projects were his own home in Kohimarama, Auckland (1985), with its distinctive poutama tukutuku-pattern façade; and a proposal, in collaboration with Ian Athfield and the internationally acclaimed North American architect Frank Gehry, for Te Papa Tongarewa Museum of New Zealand building (their design was not the winning entry). Thompson felt that good architecture could, in his words, 'improve' the land through imagining it as more than just a surface; rather, as an active whenua comprised of rhythms, forms, scales, stories and needs. This approach is apparent in the layers of land/sky/cloud cladding on the Pūkenga Māori Studies building at Unitec Institute of Technology (1991, Auckland) and, more controversially, through excavation for the Northland Region Corrections Facility (Ngāwhā Prison) site in Northland (2005).

Thompson's whenua- and whānau-first philosophies found expression in many of his later residential projects, including his posthumous 'Everyday Home' public housing precinct in Northcote, Auckland, designed with Isthmus Group; and in his training of the next generation of architects at the Waipapa Taumata Rau University of Auckland School of Architecture and Planning.

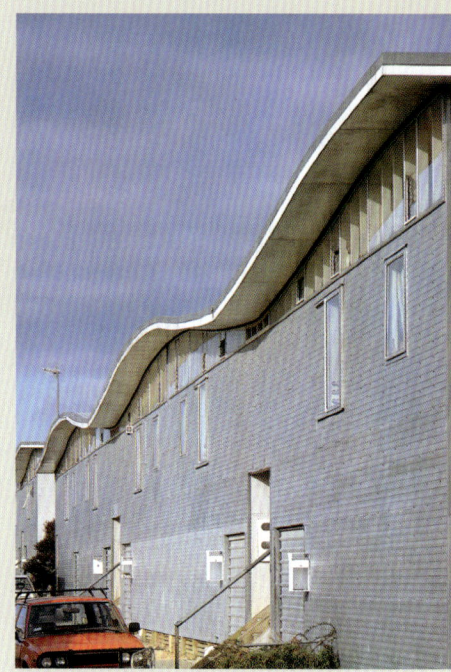

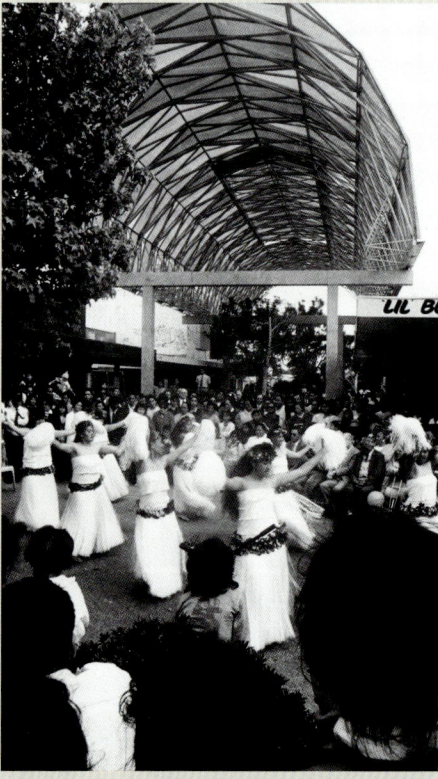

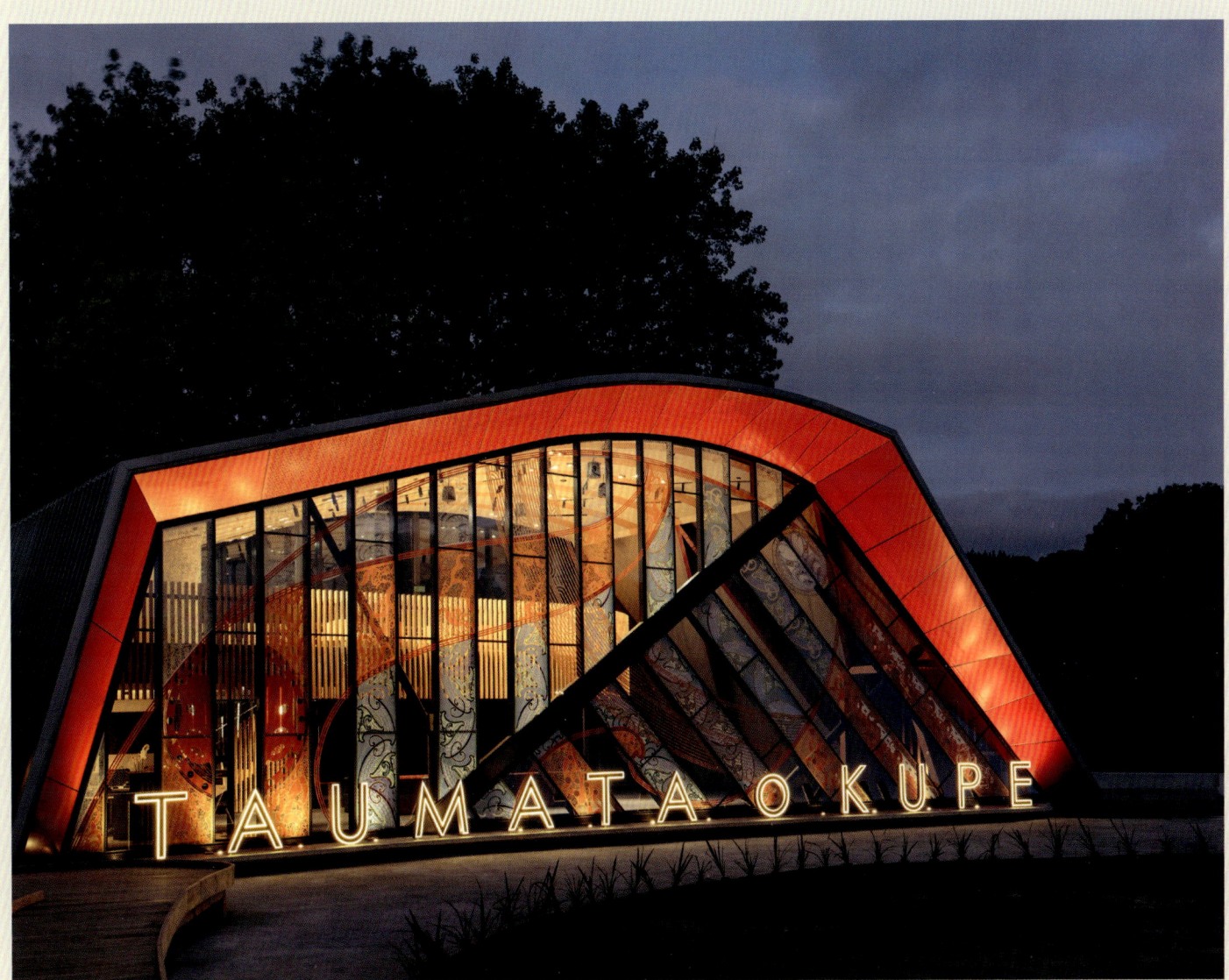

Te Taumata o Kupe, Te Mahurehure Marae by TOA Architects, Auckland, 2022.
photograph by David Straight

**Opposite:** Tere Insley, C Company Maori Battalion Memorial House, Gisborne, 2014.
photograph by Andy Spain

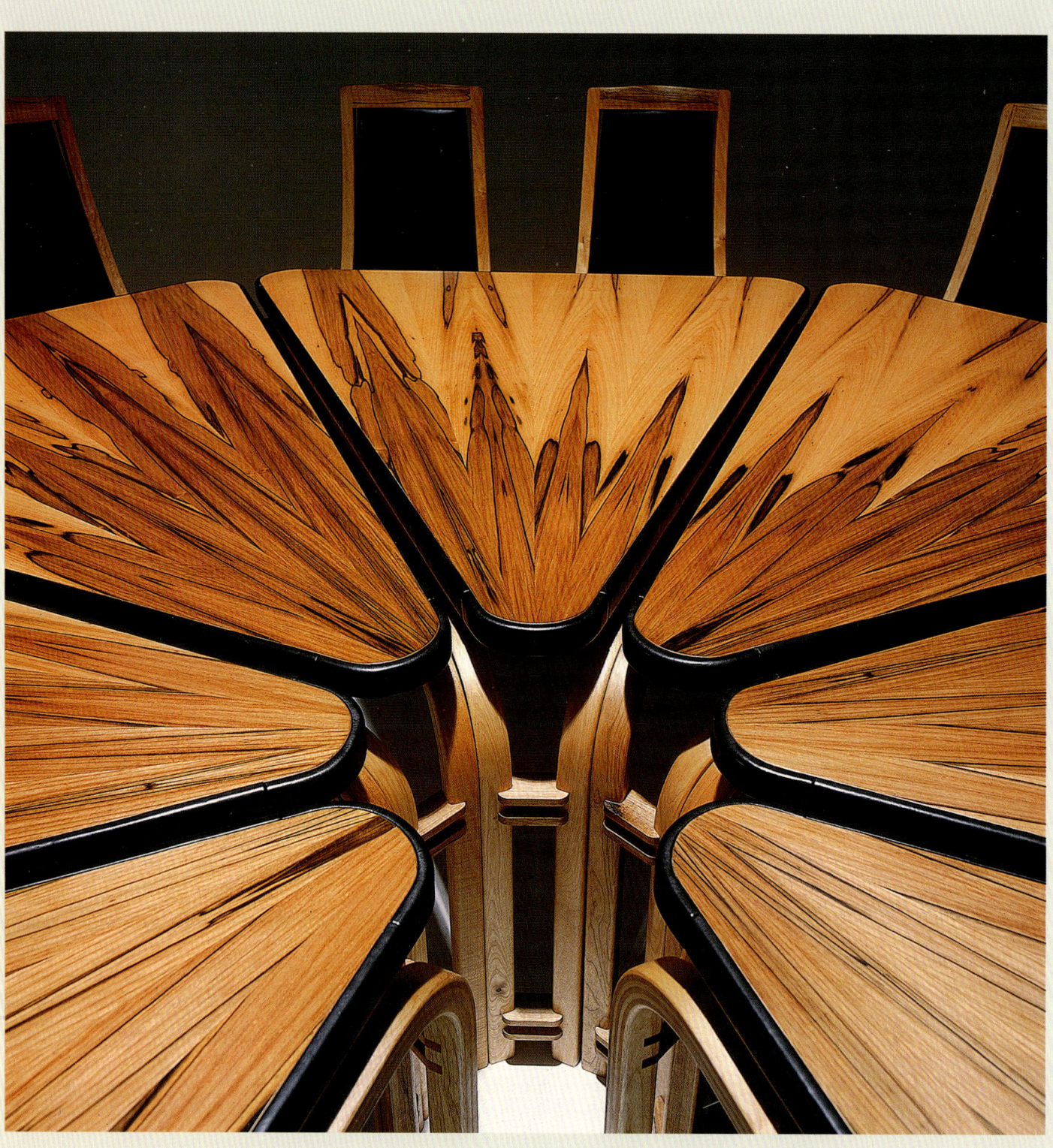

Rewi Thompson, Thompson House, Kohimarama, 1985.
photograph by Rewi Thompson

Opposite top: Rewi Thompson, Rata Vine development, Wiri, Auckland, 1987.
photograph by Rewi Thompson

Opposite bottom: The Tangaroa College Cook Islands cultural group performs at the opening of the first stage of architect Rewi Thompson's 'fish canopy' at Ōtara Town Centre, 1 November 1991.
photograph by Gerard Johnson, Auckland Libraries Heritage Collections, Footprints 03577, courtesy of Stuff Limited

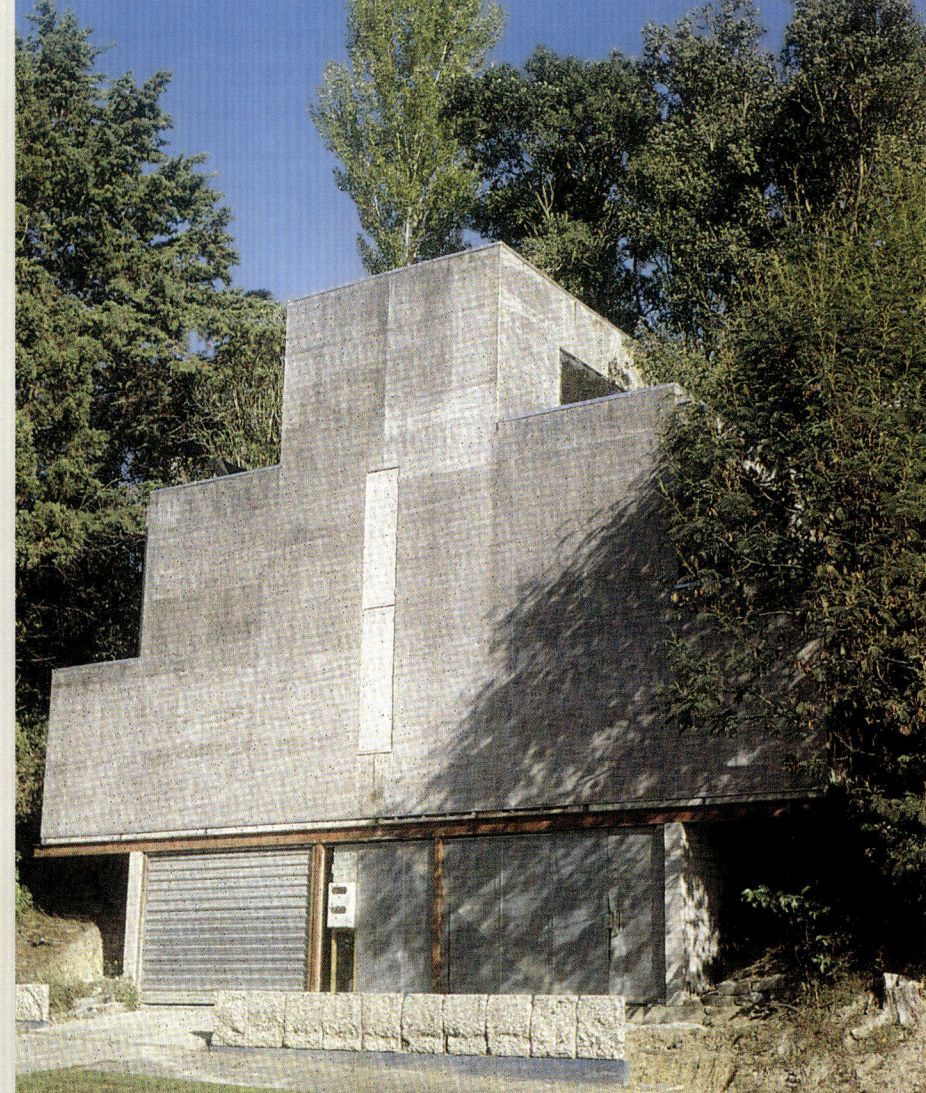

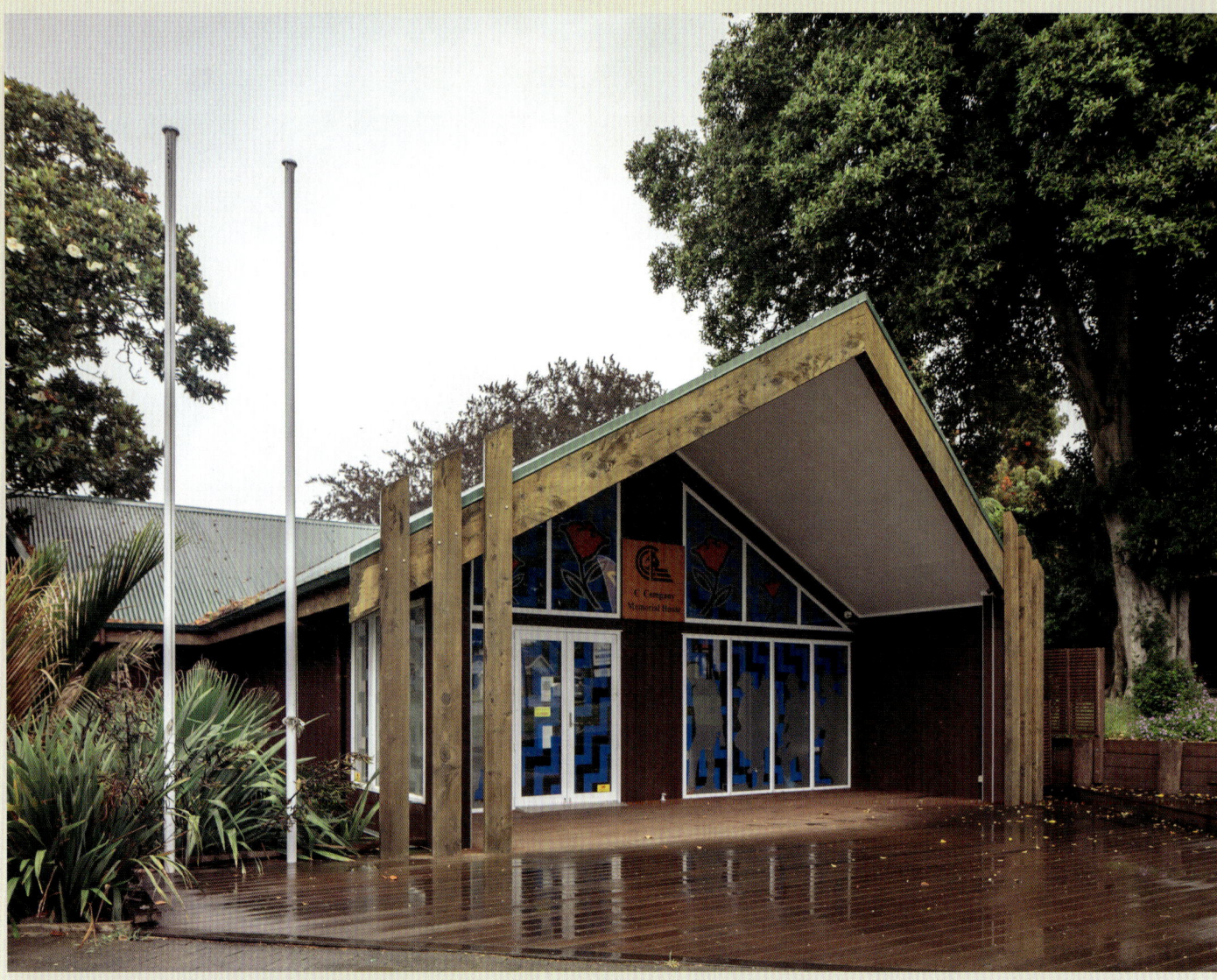

Many other Māori architects and architectural designers have since graduated from architecture schools at the University of Auckland, Victoria University of Wellington and Unitec. They include a number of prominent women architects, such as Tere Insley (Ngāti Porou, Te Whānau ā Apanui), the first Māori woman to be registered as an architect; the award-winning practitioner Louise Wright (Te Arawa, Tūwharetoa, Te Aitanga a Māhaki, Te Aitanga a Hauiti, Rongowhakaata); and Elisapeta Heta (Ngāti Wai, Waikato-Tainui), who established the Waka Maia Māori design unit within the large multi-disciplinary practice Jasmax. At least another fifty Māori women have graduated with professional qualifications in architecture, most within the last ten years.

Māori-run practices such as design-TRIBE (founded by Rau Hoskins; Ngāti Hau, Ngāpuhi), TOA Architects (established by Nicholas Dalton; Tūhoe, Te Arawa) and Matakohe Architecture and Urbanism (established by Jade Kake; Ngā Puhi, Te Whakatōhea, Te Arawa) operate simultaneously in residential, community and commercial spheres. Their new buildings are revitalising marae and other community-owned places, and housing whānau; their collaborative work on civic projects is changing the way that te ao Māori is represented and engaged with by users in towns and cities. As it is for Māori artists in survey art exhibitions, it is now becoming the norm for large-scale civic projects to include Māori architects.

# MĀORI DESIGNERS
## DEIDRE BROWN

Of all the contemporary forms of Māori art, design – comprised of graphic, gaming, clothing and furniture design – is the most accessible to Māori audiences. The first Māori designer – in the commercial sense of that term – was likely Ramai Hayward, who applied her exceptional talents to designing a series of movie posters in 1940. However, it was not until degree-based design courses were offered at polytechnics and some universities in the 1990s that trained Māori practitioners began to make an impact on New Zealand design and design education.

Contemporary design, like contemporary fine arts and architecture, is a conceptual discipline, and for many Māori practitioners the concepts of tikanga are the basis for their practice. This approach contrasts with the commercial products made between the late nineteenth and mid-twentieth centuries by non-Māori designers who appropriated and manipulated Māori design elements, in particular the tiki and koru, in order to regionally locate items ranging from stamps to crockery to fabrics.

Carin Wilson (Ngāti Awa, Ngāi Te Rangihouhiri) is the first Māori studio furniture designer and maker. Initially self-taught, Wilson was a founding member of the Canterbury Guild of Woodworkers in 1978 and four years later became president of the Crafts Council of New Zealand. At that time Māori and Pākehā craft and design practitioners found professional support in different places, with few Māori joining the Crafts Council. Wilson recalls 'asking Cliff Whiting to come and talk with my Executive at the Crafts Council about the possibility of gaining a better understanding of the work of Māori artists in our field. And at lunch time, Cliff looked completely bewildered and said to me, "Look, I just don't know how I can make any contribution to this meeting." Here we have a prominent Māori artist and he's finding it difficult to connect with other craft practitioners equally dedicated in their own way, but at that time we just hadn't been able to find a common ground.'[1]

It was not until 2008 that Wilson was able to realise this aspiration through the founding of Ngā Aho, an organisation that advocates for the needs and aspirations of Māori design and design professionals. Ngā Aho has more than 150 Māori members working in design, architecture, landscape architecture, planning and engineering design. As the director of Studio Pasifika, established in 1993, Wilson has undertaken major design commissions for companies, galleries and government ministries. Many of these projects reinterpret customary concepts and historical precedents in contemporary materials and contexts, such as the concrete walls based on raranga principles at Te Puia in Rotorua (2006) and on Tuki's map (see page 297) at the Te Rerenga Wairua Cape Reinga visitor facilities (2007).

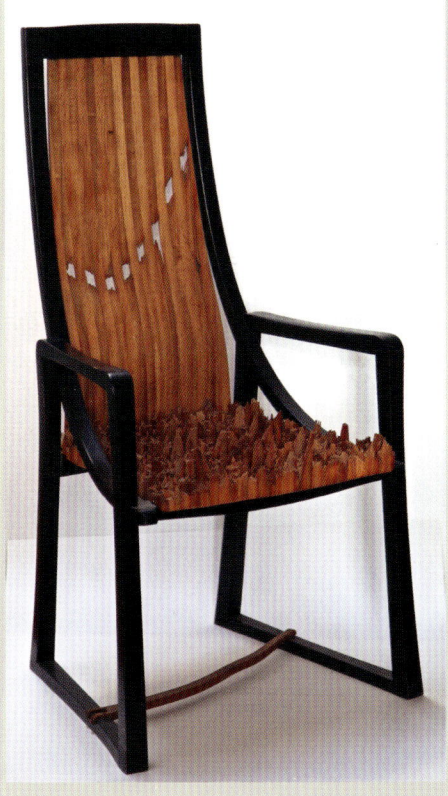

The chair recalls those made for the Queen Elizabeth II Arts Council in 1985 but with an ironic twist.
**Carin Wilson, *Royal Pain in the Arse*, 1987**
tawa, oak, blackwood, courtesy of the artist

**Opposite: Carin Wilson, *Boardroom Table and Chairs*, for the Queen Elizabeth II Arts Council, 1985**
courtesy of the artist

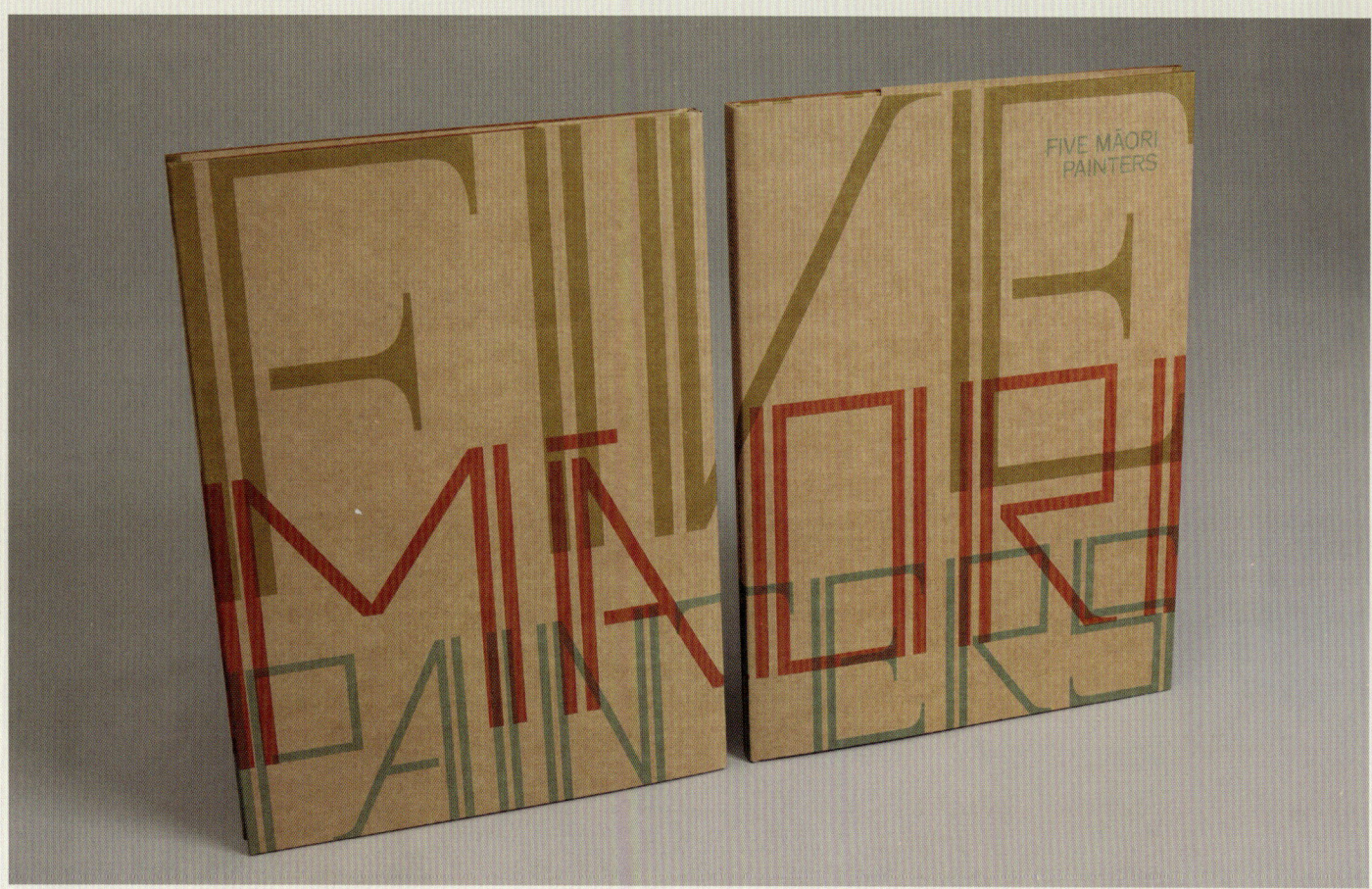

Visual communication of specific ideas is an important aspect of Māori art, and the impact of literacy has at different times either undermined or contributed to the dissemination of Māori knowledge. Neil Pardington (Kāi Tahu, Kāti Māmoe, Ngāti Kahungunu), in collaboration with Aaron McKirdy and George Clarke, invented the Parihaka typeface for the catalogue of the exhibition of the same name held at City Gallery, Wellington in 2001. The typeface extended unused work that Pardington had developed, inspired by taonga in the National Museum, for a John Bevan Ford sculpture plaque. The form of the letters was based on the font Māori used on the pou and heke in nineteenth-century wharenui, which itself was based on the roman typeface used in Māori-language bibles. Pardington and colleagues gifted the typeface to the Trustees of Parihaka pā. As art historian Cheryl Bernstein notes, 'the ongoing history of what's now known as the Parihaka font describes the way in which design is fundamentally a circular and

Above: Neil Pardington, *Five Māori Painters* typeface, 2014.
photograph by Neil Pardington

Left: Neil Pardington, Parihaka typeface, 2001.
courtesy of the artist

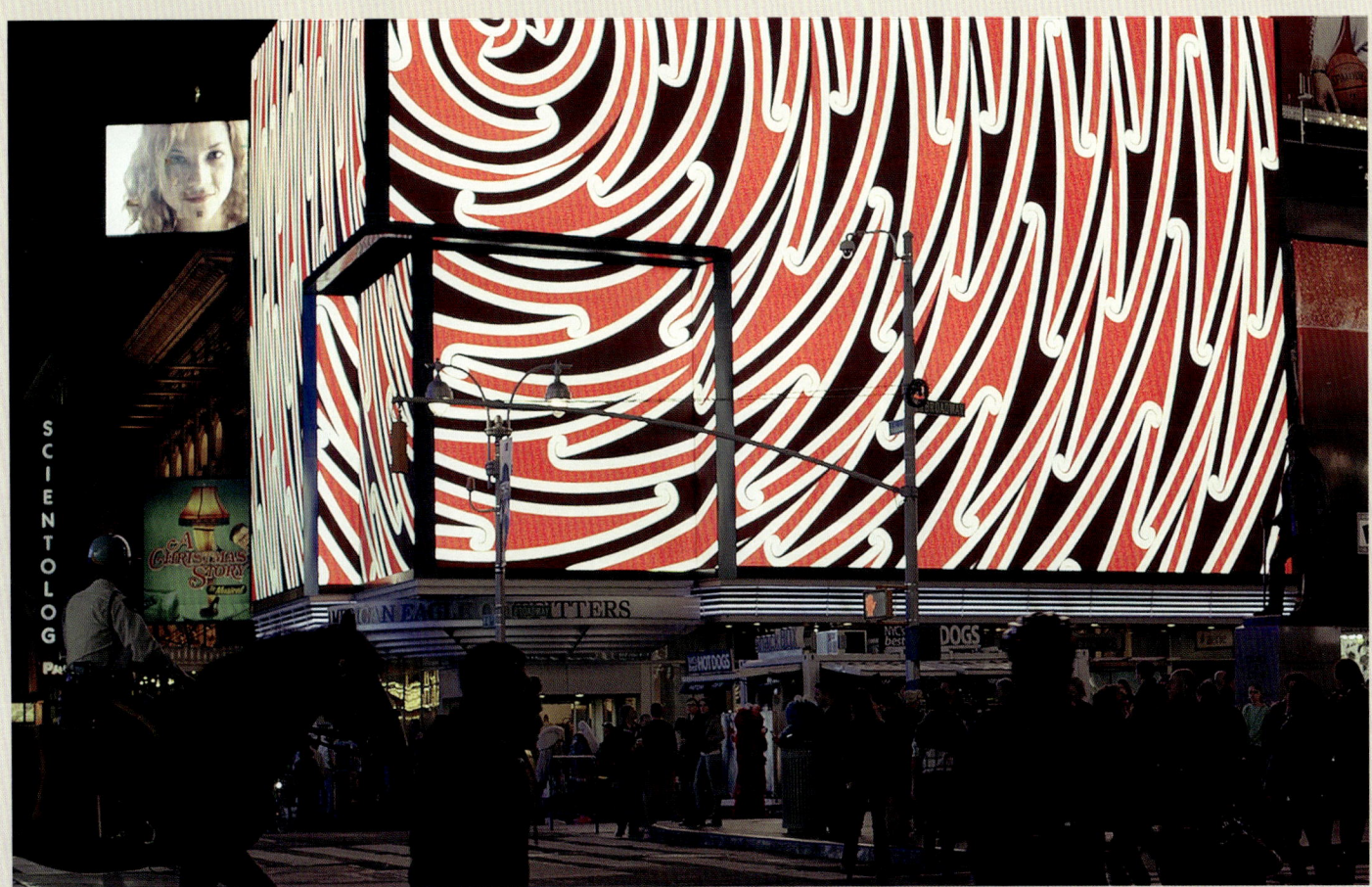

cyclic process, the passing of a baton back and forth between artists of different generations and places.'[2] Pardington revisited this source when he developed a typeface for the *Five Māori Painters* exhibition catalogue, published by Auckland Art Gallery in 2014: this was a more geometric font inspired by customary raranga, tāniko and tukutuku.[3]

Also in 2014, Johnson Witehira (Tamahaki, Ngā Puhi, Ngāti Hauā) designed the Whakarare typeface based on the whakarare whakairo rākau pattern and on text carved and painted onto whare, in order to address the question, 'Can a Māori typeface be used to reclaim the printed page in which our indigenous knowledge is captured?'[4] The resulting font is an instrument to decolonise the written word and its historical use in the subjugation of Māori. Witehira's design practice extends far beyond typography: it has appeared on billboards in Times Square in New York City, concrete sound barriers along an Auckland motorway, and in set design for musical theatre.[5]

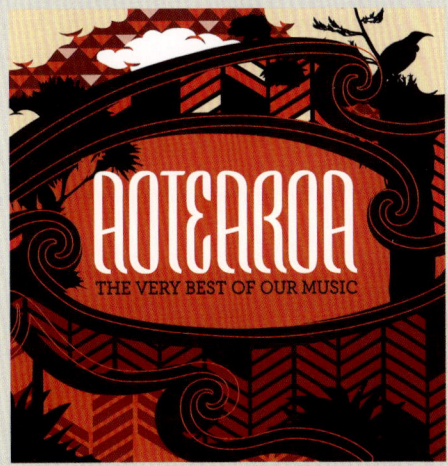

Top: Johnson Witehira, billboards in Times Square, New York, 2012.
courtesy of the artist

Middle left: Johnson Witehira, Whakarare typeface on the *Aotearoa* CD compilations, 2014.
courtesy of the artist

Middle right and bottom: Johnson Witehira, Whakarare typeface, 2014.
courtesy of the artist

## MĀORI MOVING IMAGE EXHIBITION

NGARINO ELLIS

New media feature prominently in recent group exhibitions by Māori. The field of the moving image offers artists the language with which to consider ideas about history and identity. This can be seen in the exhibition *Māori Moving Image: An Open Archive*, co-curated by Bridget Reweti (Ngāti Ranginui, Ngāiterangi) and Melanie Oliver, which opened at the Dowse Art Museum in Lower Hutt (2019) before travelling to Christchurch Art Gallery (2020).[1] *Māori Moving Image* examined art since the 1970s through the animation, film and video work of twenty artists, beginning with Robert Jahnke's experimental *Te Utu: The Battle of the Gods* (1980) through to the most recent work, Janet Lilo's, entitled ↑ [shift symbol] *SHIFT #* (2019). In addition to the works shimmering and glowing around the walls, the curators presented an archive – literally – of research materials on each of the artists included in the show. Reweti explains this:

> I think it's important to provide points of access into an artist's practice and, by learning their area of interest, provide another spark of connection. There were both national and international art theory texts sitting alongside Radio New Zealand web series and programmes from Māori Television. So while the archive holds texts about the artists' work, the influences they suggested help to further unpack the depth of their work and practice.[2]

This was not the first exhibition to focus on Māori artists working in the field of the moving image. *The Earth Looks upon Us/ Ko Papatūānuku te Matua o te Tangata* (2018), exhibited at Adam Art Gallery Te Pātaka Toi, Victoria University of Wellington, featured four Māori women artists: Ngahuia Harrison (Ngāti Wai, Ngāpuhi), Ana Iti (Te Rarawa), Nova Paul (Te Uruoroi/Te Parawhau, Ngāpuhi) and Raukura Turei (Ngāi Tai ki Tāmaki, Ngā Rauru Kītahi). All four artists have a tertiary qualification in fine arts or architecture from different institutions. In the exhibition, the artists used as a point of departure a whakataukī gifted to them by Rawinia Higgins, deputy vice-chancellor (Māori) at Victoria University of Wellington – herself a scholar on Māori women's moko. This proverb is a reminder that Papatūānuku is the parent to everyone, and the earth, as her body, needs to be understood accordingly. The works presented covered many media, including not only moving and still images, but also sculpture and painting, and the written word.[3]

The depth and quality of Māori art using the moving image is increasingly being recognised in arts prizes and awards. In 2016 Shannon Te Ao (Ngāti Tūwharetoa) won the prestigious Walters Prize for his work *Two shoots that stretch far out* (2013–2014) and *okea uruoatia (never say die)* (2015); and Lisa Reihana was a finalist that same year for *in Pursuit of Venus [infected]* (2015) and *Tai Whetuki: House of Death Redux* (2016). Te Ao had been commissioned to create the work for the Sydney Biennale at the Art Gallery of New South Wales in 2014 – the only New Zealander to be chosen.[4] Auckland Art Gallery Toi o Tāmaki, which hosts the Walters Prize, later purchased *Two shoots that stretch far out* – a thirteen-minute single-channel HD digital video in which, as Te Ao describes it:

> I recite multiple versions of a single lament to a menagerie of animals. Images of myself reciting poetry to a donkey, a wallaby and a swan propose visions of an absurd discursive space. At the core of the project was an ambition to promote discussion around alternative discursive models and newly imagined empathetic forms.[5]

Māori oral history is integral to *Two shoots*. The title comes from the whakataukī 'E kimi ana i ngā kāwai i toro ki tawhiti' (Seeking deep connections that stretch out far). In the work, Te Ao recites the English translation of a Ngāti Porou waiata composed by Matahira, who was upset when her husband took a second wife. This framing is essential to understand the work, which is populated with characters including a donkey, a swan, a rabbit and chickens, and a wallaby. By drawing on two different types of Māori oral culture – the whakataukī and the waiata – Te Ao makes the work esoteric: all is not what it seems. This prompts the viewer to think more deeply about the relatedness between Indigenous worlds – Māori and Aboriginal or, more specifically, Ngāti Tūwharetoa and Gadigal.

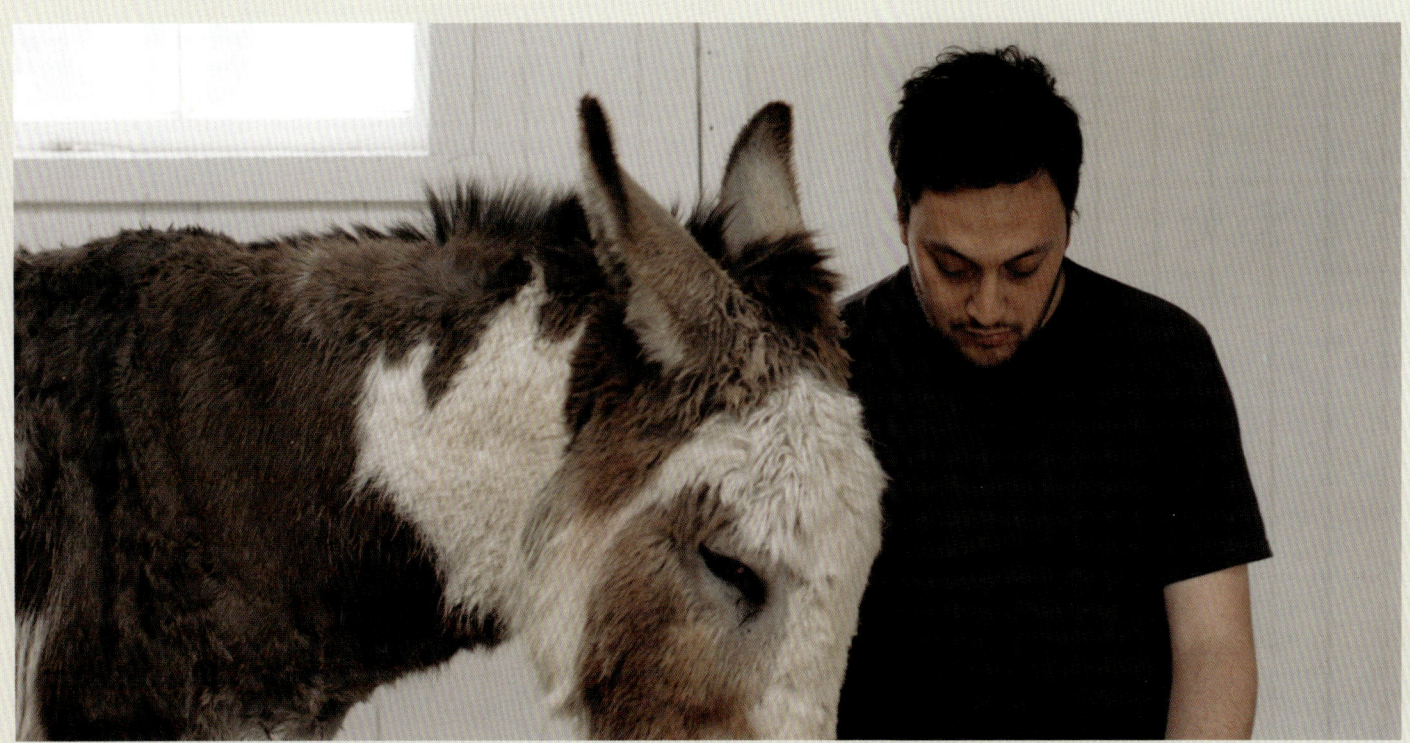

**Shannon Te Ao, film still from *two shoots that stretch far out*, 2013–2014**
courtesy of the artist

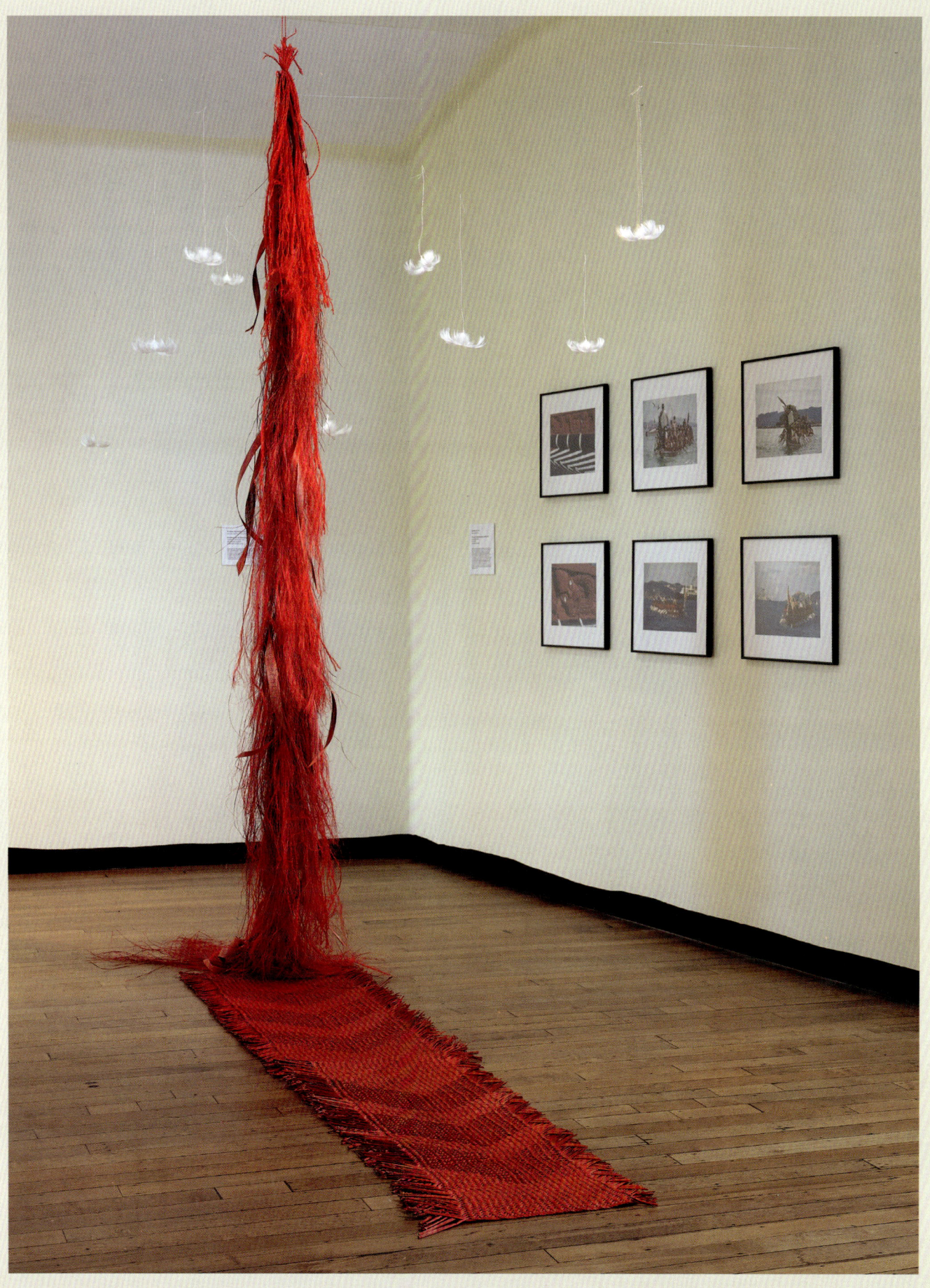

# WAIRAU MĀORI ART GALLERY: THE FIRST PUBLIC MĀORI ART GALLERY

DEIDRE BROWN

In 2022 the Wairau Māori Art Gallery, the first dedicated public Māori art gallery, opened in Whangārei as part of the new Hundertwasser Art Centre. The gallery's objective is to elevate the profile of Māori art, established Māori artists and experienced Māori curators through a programme of three Māori art exhibitions each year. The gallery is governed by a trust board of Māori artists and creators chaired by Elizabeth Ellis, which supports director Larissa McMillan (Ngāpuhi, Te Parawhau).

Wairau's opening exhibition was *Puhi Ariki*, a group show curated by Nigel Borell that traced the whakapapa of Te Taitokerau (Northland) Māori art through the work of nine artists from the first generation of northern contemporary Māori artists (Ralph Hotere and Selwyn Muru) to established (Te Hemo Ata Henare [Ngāti Kahu, Ngāti Hine, Te Whakatōhea], Emily Karaka, Maureen Lander and John Miller [Ngāpuhi, Ngaitewake ki Uta]) and more recent and emerging artists (Israel Tangaroa Birch, Nova Paul, Leilani Kake [Ngāpuhi]) practising today. Following *Puhi Ariki* was *Tohu Whakatipu*, a show curated by Karl Chitham (Ngāpuhi, Te Uriroroi) exploring the use of visual languages based on the concept of tohu, signs and wayfinding devices, as demonstrated in the work of Lonnie Hutchinson, Kaaterina Kerekere (Te Aitanga a Hauiti, Ngāi Tāmanuhiri, Rongowhakaata, Rangitāne, Ngāi Tahu) and Rangi Kipa. An exhibition of recent work by the acclaimed painter Shane Cotton and another, *Te Whanga a Reipae*, about the connections between Te Taitokerau and the Waikato-Tainui iwi of the central North Island (featuring works by Aroha and Star Gossage [Ngāti Wai, Ngāti Manuhiri, Ngāti Ruanui], Amorangi Hikuroa [Ngāpuhi, Ngāti Maniapoto, Ngāti Toro, Te Popoto], Tracy Keith [Ngāpuhi], Jeremy Leatinu'u [Ngāti Maniapoto] and Raukura Turei) have since followed. Thematised shows, like *Tohu Whakatipu* and *Te Whanga a Reipae*, built around a single concept, and solo shows are rare for Māori exhibiting in public art galleries, which have little latitude for nuanced Indigenous exhibitions. This is Wairau Māori Art Gallery's point of distinction.[1]

The inclusion of a Māori art gallery in the art centre was a requirement of the foundation representing the building's Austrian designer, Friedensreich Hundertwasser, who achieved global recognition for his organic designs and promotion of sustainable living practices. Hundertwasser owned land in Northland and periodically lived and worked in Aotearoa New Zealand, forging a co-design relationship with Ngāti Hine on the Hundertwasser toilets in Kawakawa, which became a major tourist attraction. In 1993 he created a concept design for a site occupied by Whangārei's Northland Regional Council Building to transform it into an art gallery, but the cost of the project prohibited its realisation until thirty years later (and more than twenty years after Hundertwasser's death).[2] 'Wairau' means 'One Hundred Waters' in te reo Māori and is both an acknowledgement of the importance of water in Māori culture and also a play on Hundertwasser's own name, which has the same meaning in German.

Jade Kake has noted that, 'There's an argument to be made that the architectural identity of our rohe should not be defined by and so closely associated with a European architect, albeit one with strong local ties (including with Māori communities in the North).'[3] Kake's words lay down the challenge for the next public Māori art gallery to be also Māori designed and built.

Work from the *Puhi Ariki* exhibition, Wairau Māori Art Gallery, Whangārei.

**Te Hemo Ata Henare, *Ka Nukunuku! Ka Nekeneke!*, 2022**
harakeke, muka and dye, various dimensions, courtesy of the artist

**John Miller, *The Launch of Ngātokimatawhaorua* (series), 1974**
archival digital prints, each 410 x 510mm, courtesy of the artist, photograph by Sam Hartnett

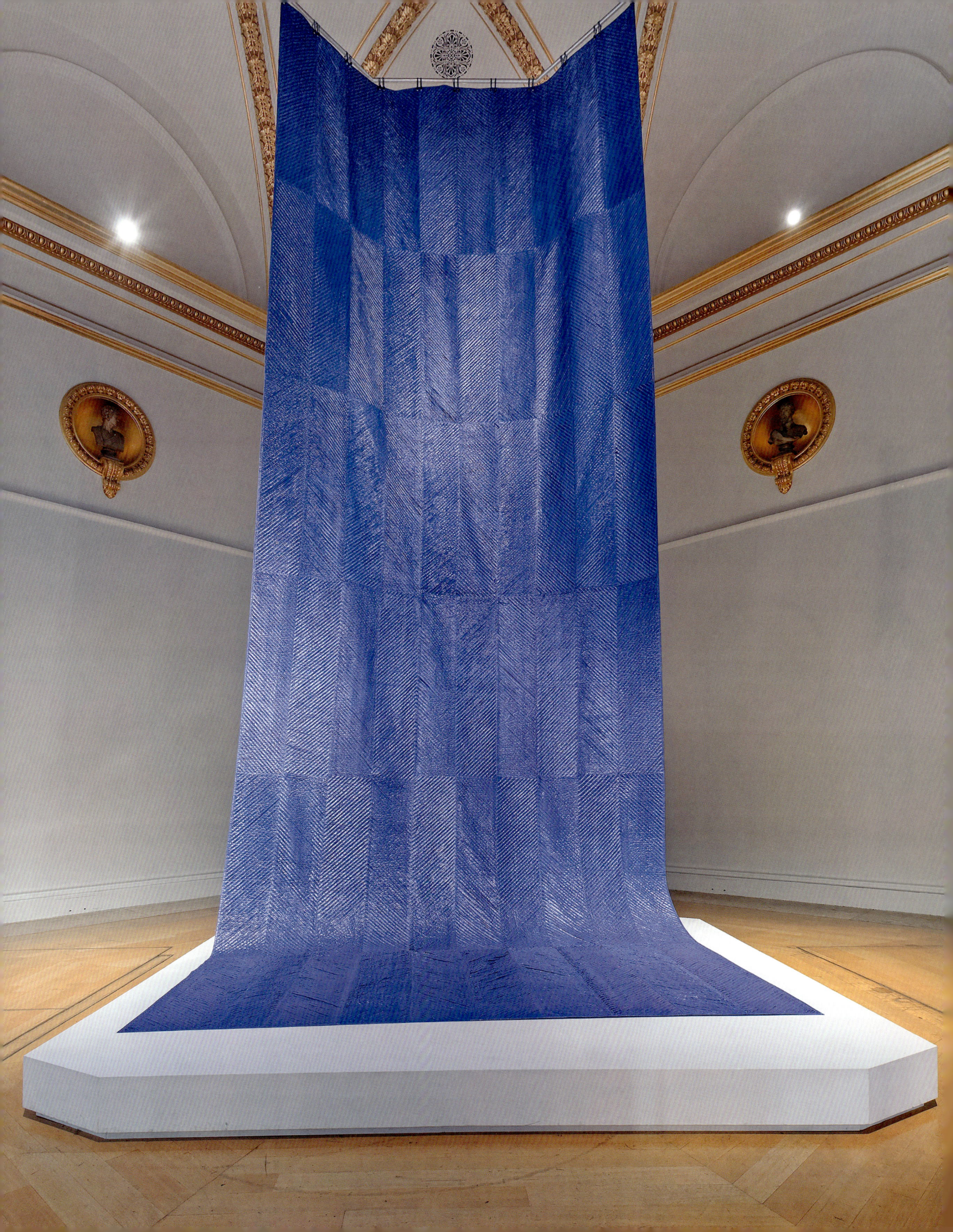

# 18 Māori Art in Western Europe and Australia
## Deidre Brown

*Inā kei te mōhio koe ko wai koe, i anga mai koe i hea, kei te mōhio koe, kei te anga atu ki hea.*

*If you know who you are and where you are from, then you will know where you are going.*

As the post-World War Two rural-to-urban drift widened out beyond the shores of Aotearoa New Zealand, a growing number of Māori were settling in Australia and the United Kingdom. This diaspora has played an active role in negotiating spaces and opportunities for the creation of art, not just for those who have migrated to, or been born in, these counties, but also for Māori based in Aotearoa who are expanding their practice into the international scene. The great wealth of taonga Māori in British and European museums, and the interests of the curators who keep them, have had a defining influence on the kinds of venues and types of opportunities available to Māori artists who exhibit in these countries. However, it has been the great size of the Māori population in Australia that has enabled Māori artists to create relationships with community-focused and community-facing art institutions in major metropolitan centres.

**Mataaho Collective, *Kiko Moana*, 2017, as installed in the *Oceania* exhibition, Royal Academy of Art, 2018**
polyethene tarpaulin, cotton thread, 4000 x 11000mm, Te Papa Tongarewa Museum of New Zealand, ME024286

### Māori art from and in Western Europe

Since the 1990s, members of the Ngāti Rānana Māori cultural group in London have developed a relationship with a network of museums in Western Europe that has laid the foundations for Māori artists based in Aotearoa to exhibit internationally. In turn, the artists have received a welcome reception from the curators of Pacific collections in European ethnological museums that are keen to reinvent the meanings and purpose of taonga obtained through means fair or foul in the age of imperial expansion and colonisation. The art they have created is intended to activate, and be activated by the collections. It is intentionally different to much of the art that is exhibited in Western European art galleries, art fairs, the Venice Biennale and *documenta* (Germany) by already established Māori artists – despite the fact that both groups of artists are often exhibited together in group art shows in New Zealand. While the museum-generated exhibition opportunities are often framed as Pacific shows, Māori and New Zealand-based Pacific contemporary artists have been the most active partners in the organisation and content of these exhibiting opportunities and associated residencies.

The desire among Māori to engage with European museum collections through research and creative interpretation coincided with a sea change in the way the museums themselves were regarding their collections. From the 1990s, European museums experienced a steady increase in requests from Indigenous peoples, mainly scholars and artists, to visit collections from their regions that were held in storage or on display. Their interest had been fuelled by the rise of Indigenous and tribal art history and curatorial studies and practice in some countries (including Aotearoa New Zealand), aided by the availability of information about collections through catalogues and online databases, as well as low-cost European airfares that made visits to multiple institutions affordable.[1] David Simmons's detailed field notes from his visits to North American (1973), British and European (1978) and Australian (1978–1990) museums have been an invaluable finding tool for Māori researchers and communities. Simmons's notes, which were in the Ethnology Department at Auckland War Memorial Museum and have recently been relocated to the Museum Library, document the accession details, registration notes, size and sometimes shape of taonga Māori in the various museums' collections (although his own attempts to attribute these taonga to specific iwi have not always been accurate).[2] From the late 1960s, museums in the northern hemisphere had become more aware of the importance of their Pacific collections through the research of anthropologists Adrienne Kaeppler and Peter Gathercole on objects gathered during Cook's voyages for the bicentennial of his first voyage. Before this time, Pacific collections had been often ignored as a subject of research in favour of those from Africa, Asia, the Middle East and the Americas, particularly as the Pacific became increasingly considered to be more 'remote' and less strategically important in post-World War Two Europe, except in France and the United Kingdom, where old colonial ties lingered.[3]

The reconnection between these collections and Pacific contemporary artistic practice can be traced back to 1992 and Jim Vivieaere's *Southern Response to Northern Possession* installation at the Übersee-Museum in Bremen, which was his response to the large number of Oceanic objects in their collection.[4] The following year, Cliff Whiting and members of Takahanga Marae in Kaikōura carved *Te Kūwaha o Wharetutu*, a large gateway commissioned for Berlin's Ethnologisches Museum. The carving was accompanied to the museum by Ngāi Tahu elders who participated in its whakatūwhera (opening), following the precedent for such events set by *Te Maori*. Tipene O'Regan, who was part of the group, later reflected on the installation in this overseas context as 'a symbol of the Ngāi Tahu renaissance', a statement that suggests the mana of iwi and their artistic heritage was not

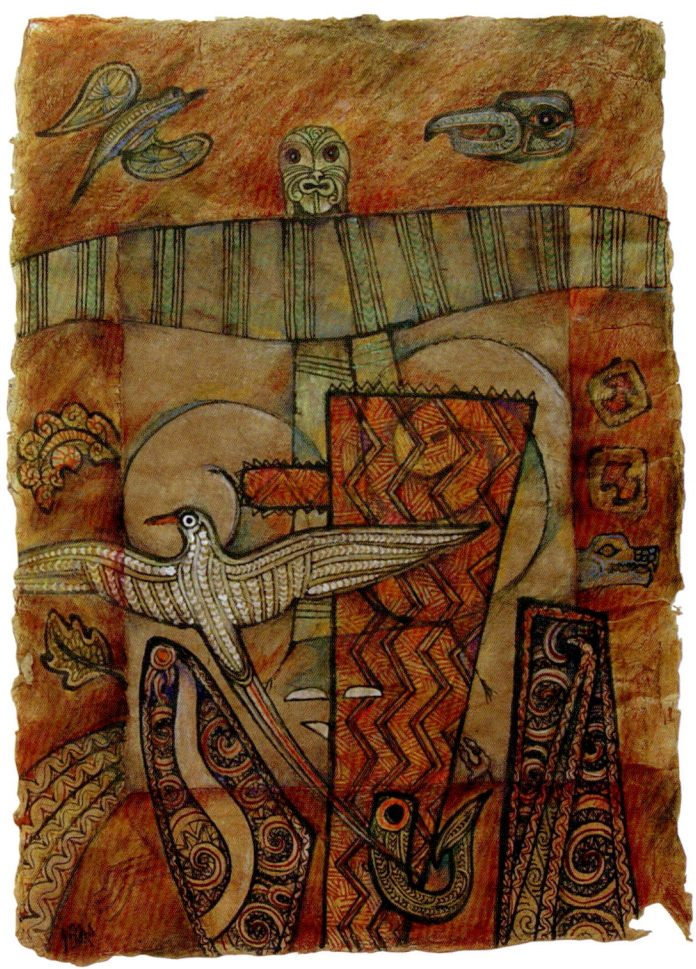

constrained by New Zealand's national borders and could be anywhere that Māori wanted it to be.[5]

The British Museum, keeper of one of the largest collections of taonga Māori outside of Aotearoa New Zealand, opened *Māori* in 1998 – the first exhibition in Europe devoted entirely to Māori art. In another first, the museum employed a Māori exhibition consultant, the painter John Bevan Ford, who was also a visiting artist. The show had been scheduled to open two years earlier at the British Museum's Museum of Mankind in Mayfair, but it was postponed when it was decided to close this branch and shift its collections to the British Museum. Despite this, an edited volume of essays to accompany the exhibition was published in 1996.[6] A highly regarded text, it included chapters on whakairo rākau (written by Roger Neich, ethnologist and curator), body adornment (Ngahuia Te Awekotuku, art historian), Māori early history (Janet Davidson, archaeologist), fibre arts (Mick Pendergrast, curator) and contemporary Māori culture (Arapata Hakiwai, curator). A second edition of the book, published in 1998, included a chapter on contemporary Māori art by the artist, scholar, curator and educator Robert Jahnke. When the exhibition did open, the arrangement of taonga on display awkwardly straddled old and new models of curatorship, with taonga described in interpretative material as being of 'the old days' and 'traditional' even though many were made during the dynamic and challenging times of the early colonial period.[7] In keeping with the precedent set by *Te Maori* and the wave of exhibitions that followed it, a Māori community – in this case Ngāti Rānana – led the opening.[8] Plans for a Pacific Gallery at the British Museum never materialised, despite the fact that Oceania was the only region (still) not represented in this way at the museum.[9]

### The arrival of the contemporary Māori artists

The partnership between Western European museums and contemporary Māori artists took a radical turn with the arrival of artist Rosanna Raymond (Sāmoa) and tohunga whakairo George Nuku (Ngāti Kahungunu and Tūwharetoa) to the United Kingdom. Raymond, a member of Pacific Sisters and cofounder of Auckland's Pasifika Festival, moved to London with her family in 1999 and became involved in recataloging Pacific barkcloths that had been transferred from the Museum of Mankind to the British Museum.[10] She also joined Ngāti Rānana and, using her experience as an artist and museum worker, began a movement to reconnect communities with their taonga in British museums. This was more than just bringing members into storerooms: it included the re-engagement of taonga with their descendant communities through site-specific object-making and performance, taking inspiration from the taonga. These interventions reflected larger shifts in social anthropology to recognise Indigenous peoples as authorities rather than subjects and their art as something more meaningful than just 'material culture'. Some institutions encouraged the 'activation' of taonga through contact with communities: they abandoned blanket rules based on inflexible conservation standards in favour of providing the opportunity for emotional and tactile connections between taonga and their descendants, and the space for this to be expressed creatively.[11] When Indigenous artists are members of these communities, their creative responses have created a feedback loop in which taonga inform the new artwork and the new artwork informs the taonga.

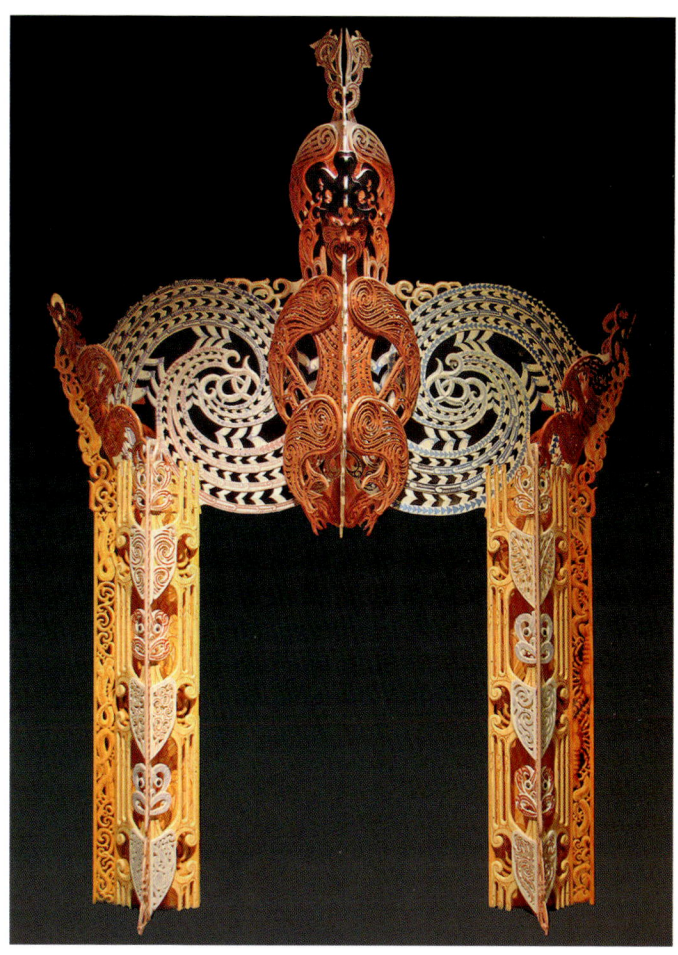

**Cliff Whiting and Takahanga Marae, Kaikōura,** *Te Kūwaha o Wharetutu*, **1993**
Ethnologisches Museum Berlin, CC BY-NC-SA 4.0

Opposite: This drawing was made during John Bevan Ford's residency at the British Museum in October 1998. In the artist's words, 'I was attracted to using the Manu Tukutuku [in the exhibition] in my work as a symbol of Māori identity, and to signify a reaching out toward all peoples.'
**John Bevan Ford,** *Untitled*, **1998**
drawing on bark fibre, 795 x 595mm, British Museum, Oc2006,Drg.95

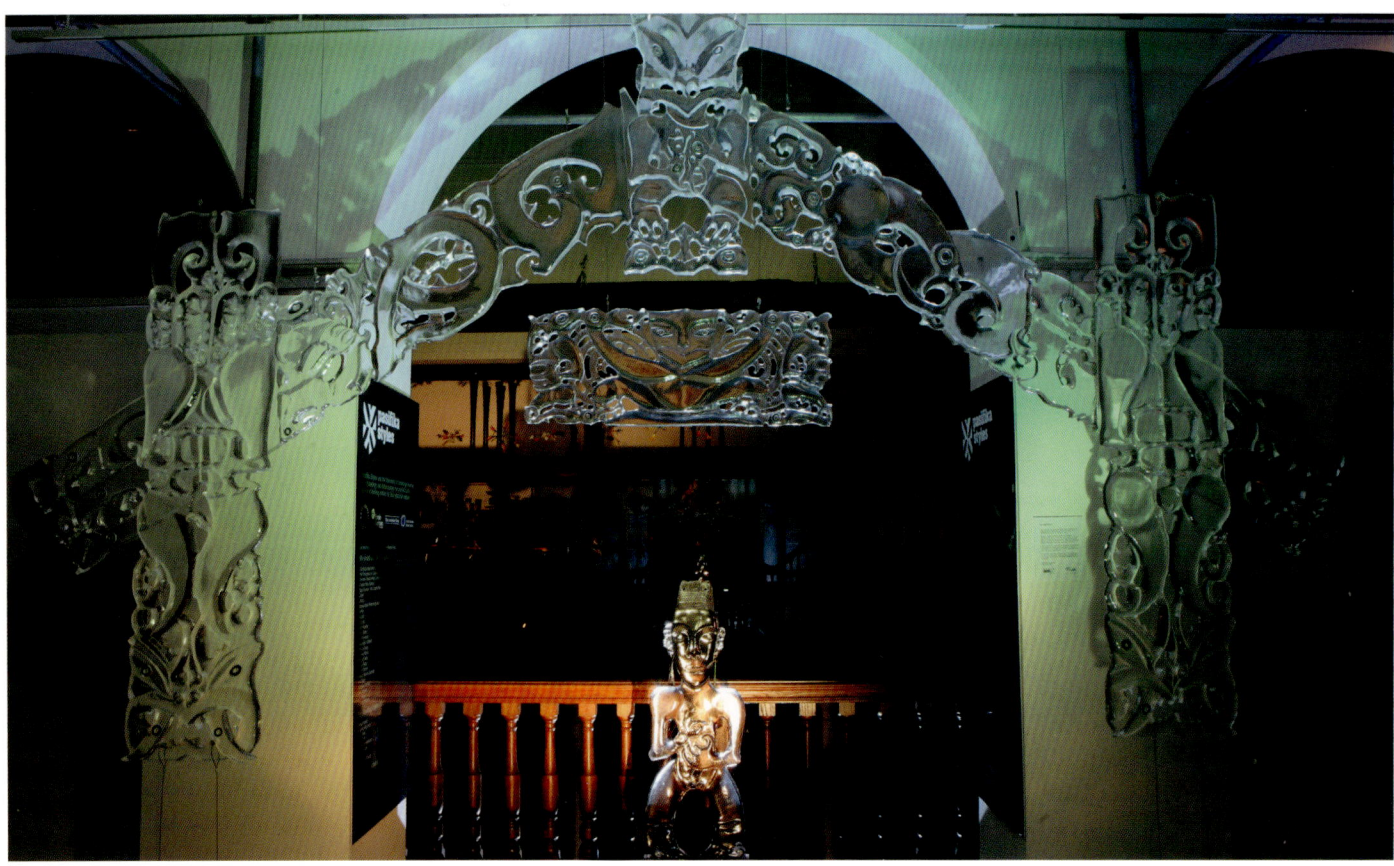

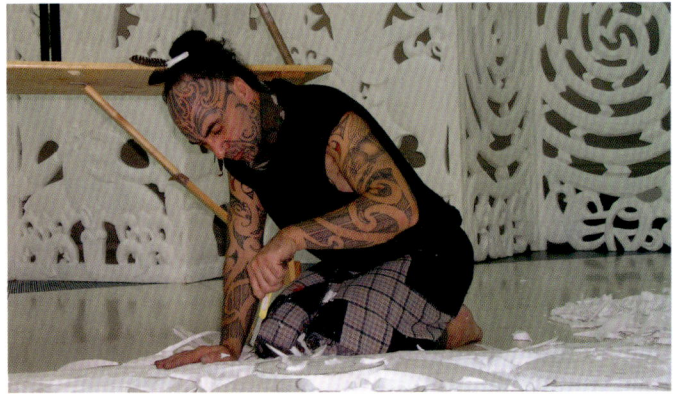

Top: George Nuku, *Outer Space Marae*, as installed in *Pasifika Styles*, Museum of Archaeology and Anthropology, University of Cambridge, 2006
photograph by Kerry Brown

Bottom: George Nuku in the Great Court of the British Museum during his residency in 2006.
British Museum, 313190001

Opposite left: This work was based around a tekoteko figure collected by Baron Carl Von Hugel in the Bay of Islands in 1834.
**Lisa Reihana, *He Tautoko*, as installed in *Pasifika Styles*, Museum of Archaeology and Anthropology, University of Cambridge, 2006**
photograph by Kerry Brown

Opposite right: *ethKnowcentrix* exhibition poster from 2009 featuring Lisa Reihana's *Dandy* (2007).
image courtesy of October Gallery

Raymond also brought Māori and other Pacific artists to the attention of museum-based curators in Britain and Europe. Nuku was an already established tohunga whakairo known for his carving of timber and synthetic materials by the time he moved to the United Kingdom in 2005. Within a year, he and Raymond had become involved in a series of large Pacific exhibitions that occurred in what the artist Bethany Matai Edmunds (Ngāti Kurī) has described as the 'new Polynesian triangle' of Cambridge, Norwich and London.[12] These shows, which all opened in 2006, were defining moments, not only for Raymond and Nuku's ongoing careers, but also for a number of Aotearoa New Zealand-based Māori artists who wanted to establish a presence in the northern hemisphere.

The 2006 exhibition *Power and Taboo: Sacred Objects from the Eastern Pacific* at the British Museum focused primarily on the period of Polynesian art production between 1760 and 1860, but it also included work by John Bevan Ford and Lyonel Grant.[13] The show, which was attended by an impressive 123,000 visitors, was heavily interpreted through the use of historic images, landscape-painting reproductions and larger-than-life portraits in

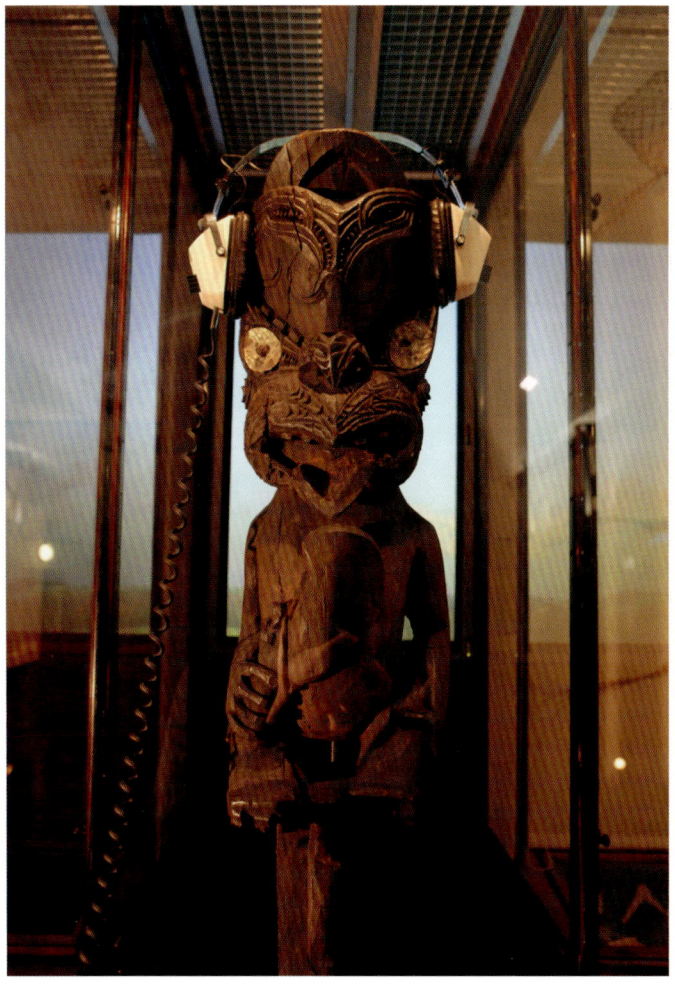
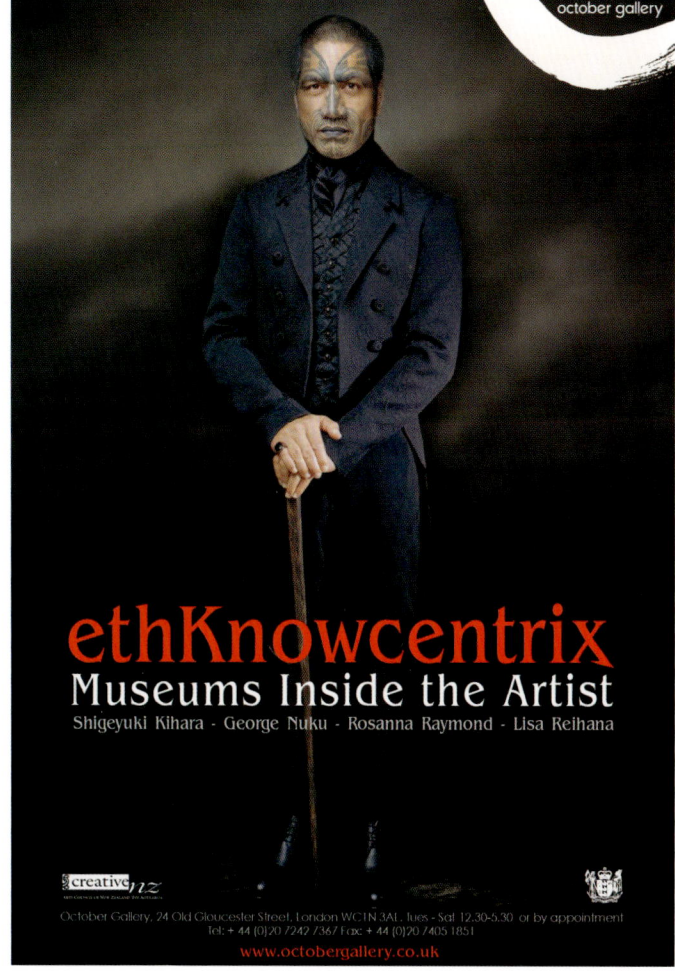

order to populate the exhibition with named people and their stories.[14] Nuku was artist-in-residence at *Pacific Encounters: Art & Divinity in Polynesia 1760–1860* – a largely eighteenth- and nineteenth-century artefact-based exhibition at the Sainsbury Centre for Visual Arts at the University of East Anglia in Norwich; after that, he became artist-in-residence at the British Museum for *Power and Taboo*.[15] He was the first (and, so far, only) Māori artist permitted to work in the museum's Great Court, where he continued carving the polystyrene whare he had begun at Norwich, which represented all of the Polynesian principal deities that featured in the exhibition.[16] Nuku's residency was very popular with visitors: it was extended from two weeks to a month, and helped raise his profile in Britain.[17]

Raymond co-curated the *Pasifika Styles* exhibition with Amiria Salmond at the Museum of Archaeology and Anthropology at the University of Cambridge. She also contributed to the show, along with more than thirty Māori, Pacific and Pākehā artists.[18] Work by Māori artists included *Outer Space Marae* – the suspended front of a wharenui carved by Nuku, with Perspex amo, maihi and tekoteko. Nuku's intention for *Outer Space Marae* was that it would shed light on the taonga in the collection that were otherwise lifeless, because of their lack of engagement with Māori and Māori environments.[19] One of the attendees at the opening – which was once again performed by members of Ngāti Rānana – was Chili Hawes, director of the October Gallery in London, who invited Raymond to curate and exhibit in the gallery's first New Zealand show, *ethKnowcentrix: Museums Inside the Artist*. The exhibition opened in 2009 and featured photographs from Lisa Reihana's *Digital Marae* and Nuku's *Outer Space Marae* – at that time regarded as the artists' most impressive works to date – as well as self-portraits by Samoan–Japanese photographer Shigeyuki Kihara.[20] Three years later, October Gallery opened *Current: Contemporary Art from New Zealand and the Pacific*, which included work by Reuben Paterson and the Australian-trained artist James Ormsby (Ngāti Maniapoto, Waikato, Te Arawa), as well as other Pacific artists.[21]

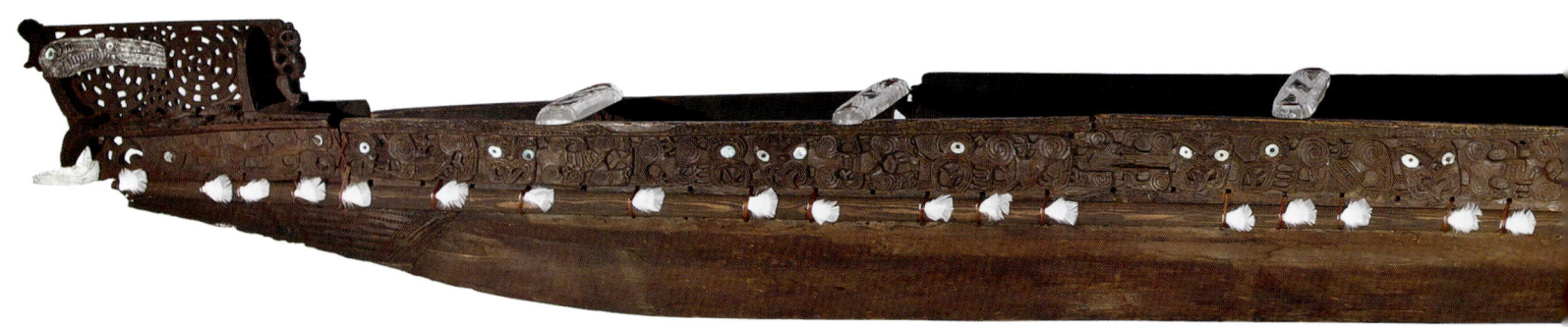

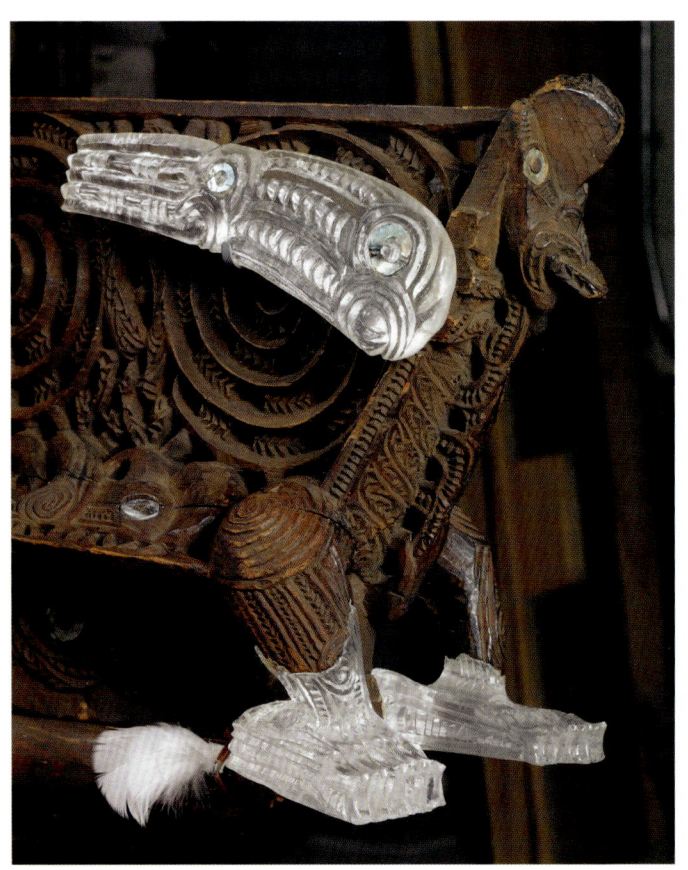

The exhibitions *Power and Taboo*, *Pacific Encounters* and *Pasifika Styles*, while they were quite different in intent, all aestheticised Māori art for British audiences, elevated the importance of Pacific collections in major institutions and created an excitement among museum staff at working collaboratively with Māori and Pacific artists and curators.[22] Nuku and Raymond seized the moment and expanded their practice and that of other Māori artists to other types of galleries, such as October, and into continental Europe.[23] The Pacific Arts Association European branch was a principal vehicle for their making contact with curators from other European countries: the association was a group comprised mostly of curators and art historians, which held its annual conference in Cambridge and Norwich in 2006.[24]

Other northern hemisphere exhibitions, residencies and commissions followed for Nuku – at the Venice Biennale (2009), Antwerp's Museum aan de Stroom (2011), the Muséum d'Histoire Naturelle de Rouen (2011), Stuttgart's Linden Museum (2012) and Vancouver's Museum of Anthropology (2013). He had a solo show at the Captain Cook Birthplace Museum in Middlesbrough and a six-month commission in

MĀORI ART IN WESTERN EUROPE AND AUSTRALIA

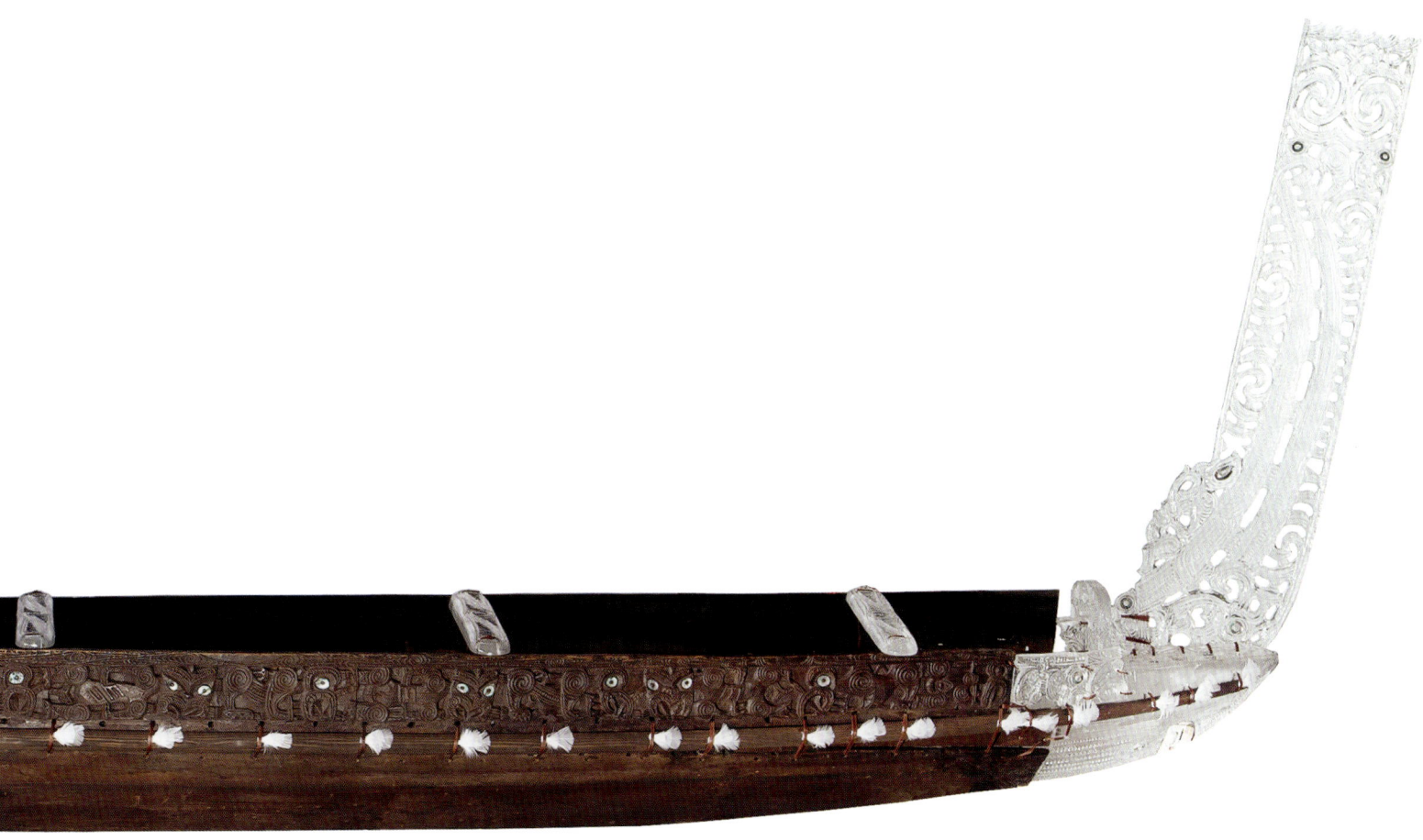

2008–2009 at the National Museum of Scotland to 'complete' the waka taua *Te Tuhono* with the addition of Perspex taurapa, and arms and feet for the existing tauihu – made with the assistance of the museum conservators. The project was challenging, as conservator Charles Stable noted, 'the curator, the artist and the conservator were out of their comfort zones, and the ethical considerations and viewpoints of other parties challenged each profession equally ... we had to continually reflect, reassess our ideas and take a flexible approach as new aspects and views about the renewal of *Te Tuhono* emerged, developed and asserted themselves.'[25] In this instance, the transparency of Perspex offered an ideal means by which to reimagine, rather than reinvent, the waka taua as a complete entity.

After this project, Nuku undertook an artist residency for the 2010–2011 *Mana Māori* exhibition at the Museum Volkenkunde in Leiden, curated by Fanny Wonu Veys: his *Outer Space Marae* was exhibited alongside Reihana's *He Tautoko* installation from that earlier exhibition. Alongside their individual successes, Nuku and Raymond had been magnets for visiting Māori artists wishing to make connections in Europe.[26]

George Nuku's Perspex additions to *Te Tuhono* waka taua were undertaken between 2008 and 2009 at the National Museum of Scotland, where the waka taua is currently kept.
National Museums Scotland, A.UC.767

'Activation' art projects undertaken by Māori artists in European museums have not always been received with the same enthusiasm back in Aotearoa New Zealand, where some would rather that the taonga be repatriated. Not surprisingly, Raymond and Nuku have defended the purposes of collections. At the 2007 Pacific Arts Association conference in Paris, Raymond said she was sure her ancestors had given their taonga to foreign collectors because they knew their descendants would eventually join them overseas.[27] Nuku has even said, 'I would rather have the ancestors stay here [in overseas museums] ... They enjoy a tremendous amount of attention, and they are the subject of continuous debate and study ... If they stay here, they are a reminder of our relationship with the empire and a reminder to be treated equally.'[28]

The call for the return of taonga Māori to Aotearoa was reawakened by *Oceania*, an exhibition of five centuries of Pacific art-making through 200 works, opened in 2018 at

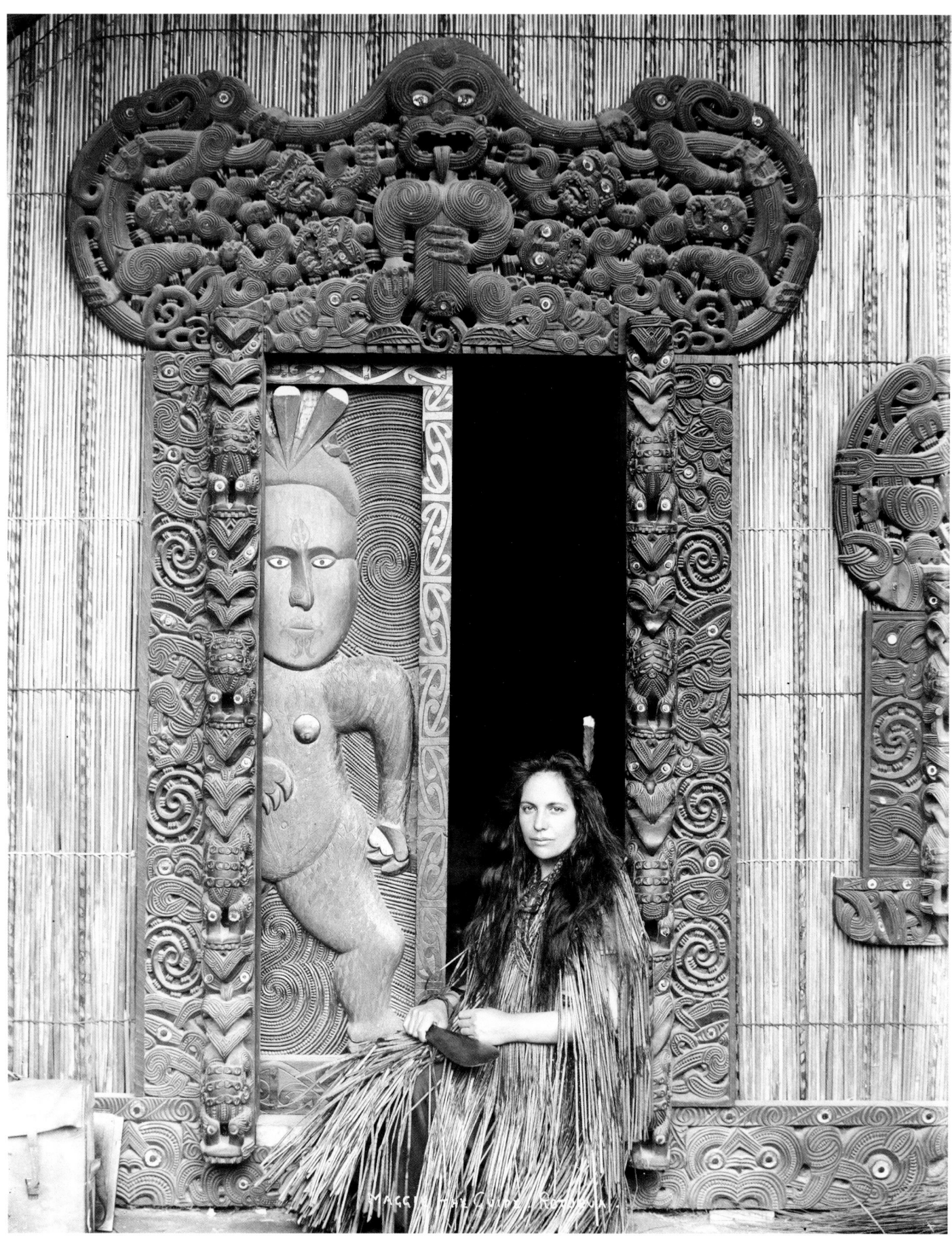

the prestigious Royal Academy of Art in London. The show highlighted the conundrum of Māori art being exhibited as art, not artefact in Europe. To 'cross over' from the museum to the art gallery, Indigenous artists are often required to demonstrate their artistic pedigree within their culture's history of art – in this case Pacific art. However, the legacy artworks used to 'contextualise' contemporary Indigenous making are borrowed from museum collections and are therefore decontextualised through their removal from communities. By being exhibited alongside contemporary Indigenous art made for exhibition, these earlier artworks are aestheticised in a way that only emphasises their ongoing and seemingly unending separation from their community contexts. The counterpoint to *Oceania* was the Pacific Encounters Gallery, which opened that same year at the Greenwich Maritime Museum: the first permanent Pacific gallery in London, Pacific Encounters questions the ethics of the British 'voyages of discovery' and the consequential activity of collecting.

Māori artists who would normally show work in the same spaces in Aotearoa New Zealand have found themselves exhibiting on two very distinct circuits in Europe: one circuit, associated with ethnological museums, includes spaces that have shown the work of Nuku, Reihana, Paterson and Maureen Lander, among others; and the other, related to the world of fine arts, is where Shane Cotton, Michael Parekōwhai and Peter Robinson have found audiences for their paintings, sculptures and installations. The Venice Biennale and *Oceania* are two of the few points of intersection, but the meaning of Māori art within these events is far from resolved. The thematic focus of some of these artists – on ancestral and contemporary cultural continuity and the disjunctures caused by European colonisation and collecting – has found a natural 'home' in museums seeking to redefine their role in an age of decolonisation and repatriation, and an ally in a diasporic Māori community making place and object attachments outside of Aotearoa New Zealand. Creating a meaningful and impactful entry into the European contemporary art exhibition circuit is more difficult, as it requires the development of workable networks with curators, gallery directors and writers who are already in high demand. European audiences have little or no knowledge of Māori issues, and the challenge is still how to bring those audiences into Māori understandings of the world, when those understandings are the conceptual foundations of the work.

## Māori art from and in Australia

In Australia, Māori art has mostly been shown in community and regional art galleries and with deference to Australian Aboriginal people as first inhabitants. Here, too, Māori are considered as part of a larger Pacific arts community. Māori art has a long presence in Australia – one that might even be considered to pre-date that of Europeans, if the harakeke and pōhutukawa planted there and the toki left behind by pre-fifteenth-century Māori on Norfolk Island may be considered evidence of art production.[29] Tuki Tahua's map that he drew in 1793 on Norfolk was the first Māori engagement with European visual media; and Hongi Hika's 1814 self-portrait carved in Parramatta is regarded as the first bust. The international exhibitions in Sydney in 1879 and in Melbourne the following year were stopping points for the Mātaatua wharenui on its journey around the world, and in 1910 Mākereti ('Guide Maggie') Papakura established a model Māori village in Sydney to support her concert party.[30] This was one of many Māori performance troupes that have performed in Australia, including popular music acts such as the Maori Hi-Five and the Maori Volcanics. These temporary excursions across the Tasman became more permanent after a series of economic downturns in New Zealand and a relaxation of the 'white Australia' policy prompted an increase in Māori migration to Australia from the 1960s onwards. In 2011, nearly 130,000 people claimed Māori ancestry in the Australian Census, and 'Australian Māori' are now estimated to comprise as much as 20 percent of the total Māori population in the world.[31]

It is the conjunction of this large Māori migrant population with the close proximity of Aotearoa to Australia that has shifted the perception of Māori art from something that exists only in museums to a vibrant gallery-based practice within an already established migrant and Indigenous arts scene. As in Europe, Māori art was first exhibited within

Mākereti Papakura was one of the earliest to write an art history of Māori, specialising in her own iwi, Te Arawa. Her writing reflects her passion for history and the culture of her people, whose lives were rapidly changing due to tourism and shifting demographics in her local community. Here she is photographed seated in the carved wooden doorway of Te Rauru meeting house at Whakarewarewa (c.1910) carved by Tene Waitere in 1898–1899. Like the sitter, the whare travelled to Europe, to the Museum für Völkerkunde, Hamburg, Germany, where he remains today.
William Andrews Collis, Alexander Turnbull Library, 1/1-006417-G

museum contexts. The ethnographic displays of the Antarctic, Pacific and New Guinea Gallery opened in Sydney in 1967 at the Australian Museum[32] – which has over 1500 taonga Māori in its collection – and they were complemented by the 1974 *Art of Oceania* and 1976 *South Seas* exhibitions at the same venue. The *Taonga Maori: Treasures of the New Zealand Maori People* exhibition opened at the Australian Museum in 1989 and toured to the Museum of Victoria in Melbourne and the Queensland Museum, Brisbane in 1989–1990: the inclusion of customary alongside contemporary Māori art in the exhibition anchored it to museum venues.[33]

It was not until 1992 that Māori art was shown in an art gallery alongside Pākehā art, when *Headlands: Thinking through New Zealand Art* opened at the Museum of Contemporary Art in Sydney. The exhibition showcased the work of Sandy Adsett, Shona Rapira Davies, Lyonel Grant, Michael Parekōwhai and Cliff Whiting alongside the weaving of Rangimārie Hetet who, at 100 years of age, was regarded as the matriarch of Māori art. The following year, the first Asia Pacific Triennial of Contemporary Art opened at the Queensland Art Gallery, and since then it has been an important international event for participating Māori artists.

The mainstay of Māori exhibiting opportunities, however, has been provided by community-focused institutions from the early 2000s, in galleries such as the Blacktown Arts Centre, Blak Dot Gallery, Campbelltown Arts Centre, Casula Powerhouse Arts Centre, Parramatta Artists Studio and Footscray Community Arts Centre. It is no coincidence that most of these galleries are located in parts of West Sydney, South Brisbane and Melbourne, where there are large Māori and other migrant populations who appreciate this work. These galleries have also provided a testing ground for the international careers of Aotearoa New Zealand-based Māori artists such as Israel Tangaroa Birch, Brett Graham, Lonnie Hutchinson, Maureen Lander, Reuben Paterson and Lisa Reihana.

Curator and fibre artist Keren Ruki (Ngāti Maniapoto) is a leading figure in the contemporary Māori art movement in Australia. She was a founder of the Pacific Wave Association, an organisation dedicated to the promotion and exhibition of Pacific art in Australia through the Pacific Wave festivals, held biennially from 1998 to 2004. Her curatorial career includes a number of Māori and Pacific group exhibitions in Sydney, such as the 2013 show *Towards the Morning Sun* at Campbelltown Arts Centre, *Stitching the Sea* at Blacktown Arts Centre in 2014, and *Pacific Spirit* at the Australian Museum in 2015. In 2004, Ruki wove the now famous kahu kurī Tuhono te Karangarua with a kaupapa made from harakeke grown at her marae and dogskin from six Australian dingoes. The combination of materials located the garment in both countries, while its purpose, as a taonga tuku iho, remained specifically Māori.[34] The skins were sourced with the assistance of the Australian Museum, where Ruki supplemented her weaving knowledge by examining kahu kurī in the institution's collections; she also examined kahu kurī at the Melbourne Museum and Auckland Museum, and undertook archival research at the Mitchell Library in Sydney. Ruki sought permission to make Tuhono te Karangarua not only from kaumātua and kuia within her descent line, but also from a local Australian Aboriginal elder – an acknowledgement of the importance of seeking Indigenous authority for any creative act, whether at home or abroad.[35]

Belongingness and cultural memory are recurring themes in Australian Māori creative practice. In an interview with the Māori curator and art historian Jo Diamond (Ngāpuhi), Ruki said of her practice:

> During my time teaching Māori weaving at [Australian] youth centres I saw how much these [Māori and Pacific] kids grew when they could identify with their roots through a bit of culture. I saw how important it was to keep our practices alive and how participating in something as simple as weaving an armband could give these young people a sense of connectedness in knowing who they were and where they were from. So the cloak is also about creating a piece that bridges their dual experience of being of Pacific heritage and living in Australia.[36]

Exploring the idea that art could be the conceptual bridge between Australia and Aotearoa New Zealand, Tuhono te Karangarua was shown in the 2007 *News from Islands* exhibition at the Campbelltown Arts Centre alongside work by New Zealand-based Māori artists Reuben Paterson and Lonnie Hutchinson, as well as other Pacific practitioners.

The reality of belongingness in a diasporic context was expressed through Ruki's production of pākē (rain capes) from high-visibility vests, which were exhibited in her 2013 installation *A Place to Stand* at the Salamanca Arts Centre in

Hobart. As a translation of tūrangawaewae, *A Place to Stand* similarly expressed the sense of translocation and reinvention associated with cross-cultural negotiation, in this case through migration, and referenced the blue-collar work that many expatriate Māori have sought in the Australian building, infrastructure and mining industries, where they have 'swapped' pākē for modern forms of protective clothing.[37]

A new generation of Māori Australian artists who have been raised (and some of them born) in Australia is emerging from esteemed Australian art schools, including the Royal Melbourne Institute of Technology and the Victorian College of the Arts.[38] These artists, who identify closely with their diasporic identity, have found kinship with other Pacific artists and are exploring the complexity of their situation through their work. They include multimedia artist Tyson Campbell (Te Rarawa, Ngāti Maniapoto), printmaker Tama tk Flavell and photographers Sean Miles (Ngāti Maniapoto) and James Taylor; Taylor's intersectional practice addresses his Māori (Te Arawa), Aboriginal Australian (Kaurna) and Pākehā ancestry.[39]

The role of cultural memory in constructing an enduring identity among the Māori diaspora is an important theme in recent work by Melbourne-based photographer Kirsten Lyttle (Waikato). Like Ruki, Lyttle was drawn to weaving kākahu with contemporary materials for her 2019 *Whakaahua* exhibition at the Blak Dot Gallery in Melbourne; however, the materials she chose were photographs of feathers from Australian birds. Since the twentieth century, the photograph has assumed the place of whakairo rākau in maintaining the presence of departed ancestors in wharenui – a change that Reihana's *Digital Marae* suggested could expand to include other marae spaces constructed through photographs. In Lyttle's work, the photograph likewise becomes material and the avatar, although in this instance the feathers belong to the birds of another land.[40]

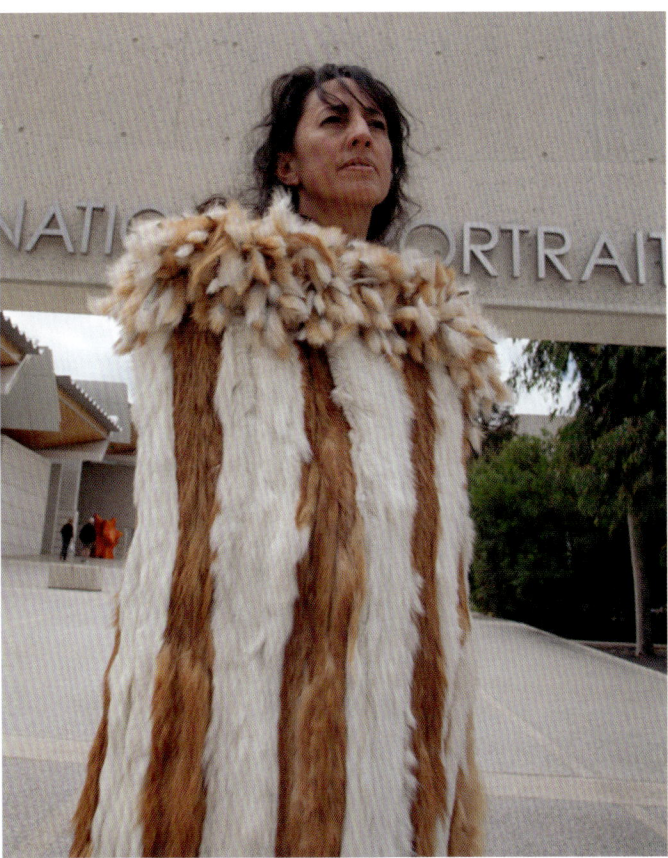

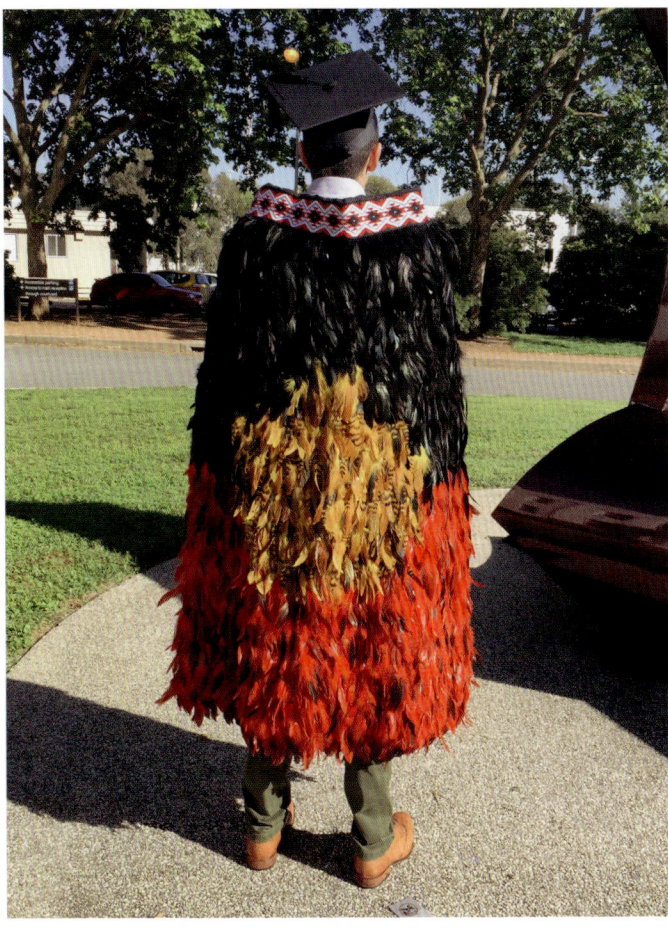

Top: **Keren Ruki**, *Tuhono te Karangarua*, 2004
muka and dingo skins, 1200 x 1000mm, photograph courtesy of Khadija von Zinnenburg Carroll, National Portrait Gallery, Canberra, Australia, 2013

Bottom: This kahu huruhuru featuring an Australian Aboriginal flag design made by Rehutai Tahana was commissioned for Tyrell Piripi Te Toko Kamira Sams's graduation from Australia National University, Canberra, in 2017. Sams is of Aboriginal (Wodiwodi) and Māori (Ngāpuhi, Te Rarawa, Te Aupōuri, Ngāti Whakaue) descent.
**Rehutai Tahana**, *Kahu huruhuru featuring the Australian Aboriginal flag*, 2017
private collection

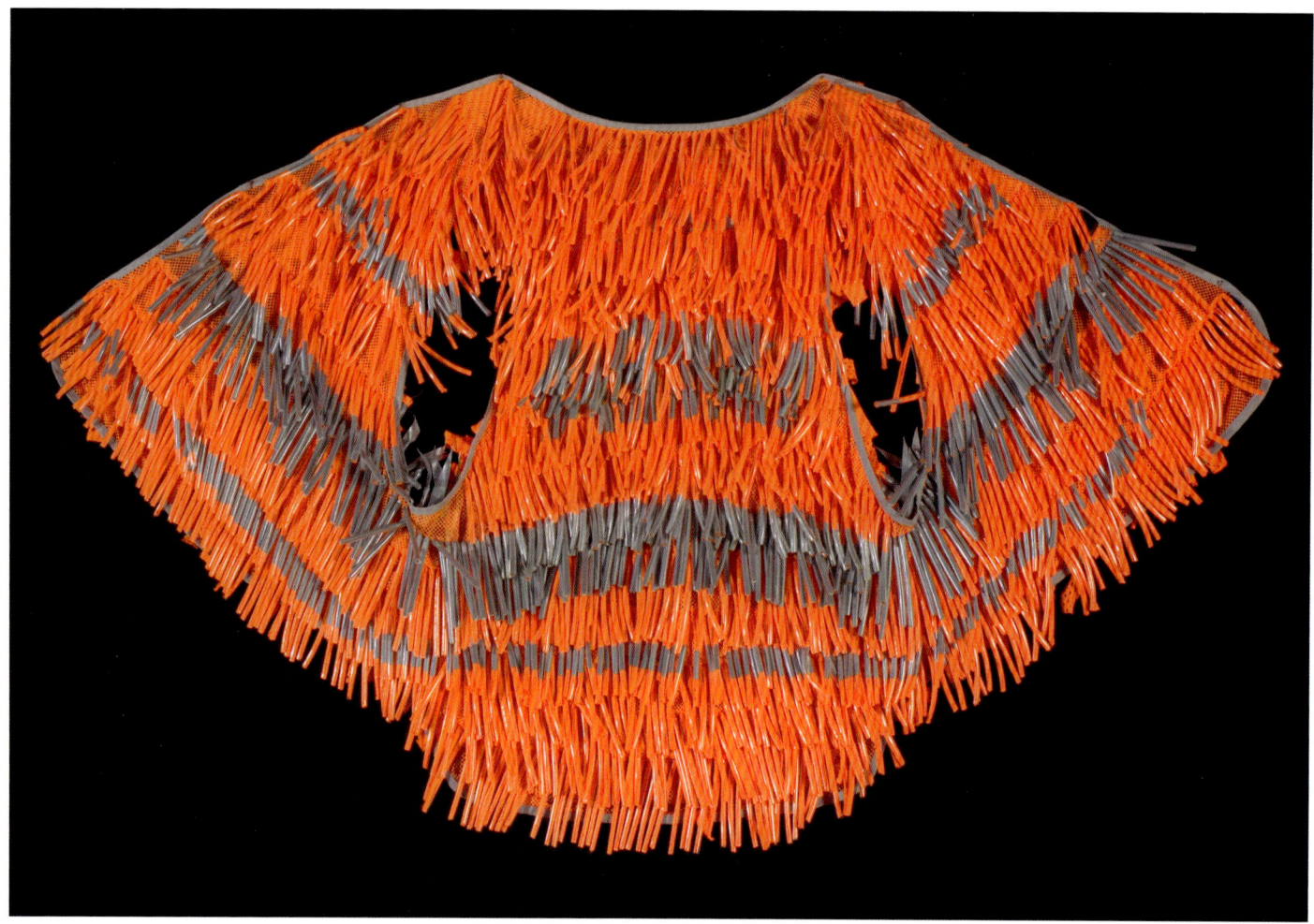

Keren Ruki, *Cultural Safety Vest*, 2007
plastic tubing, nylon, reflexive tape, 800 x 600mm, courtesy of the artist

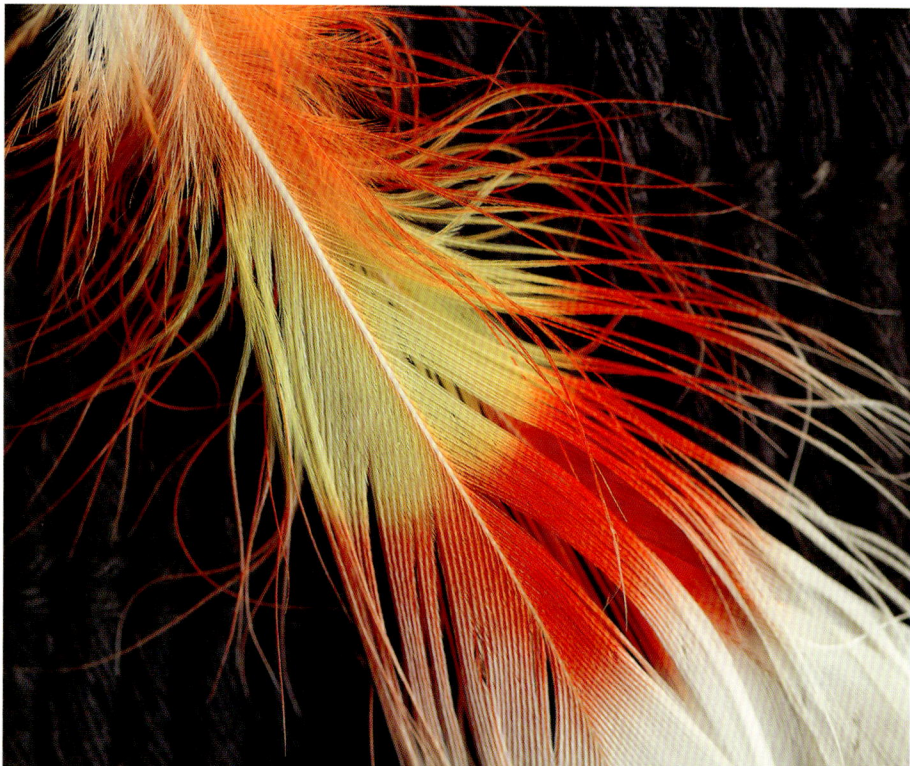

An Australian cockatoo crest feather woven into a kaupapa textile made with black macramé cord and black cotton twine.
**Kirsten Lyttle,** *Major Mitchell's Cockatoo*, 2018
archival giclée fine art print on Canson Platine Fibre Rag (310gsm) Lustre Paper, 594 x 841mm, edition 1 of 5

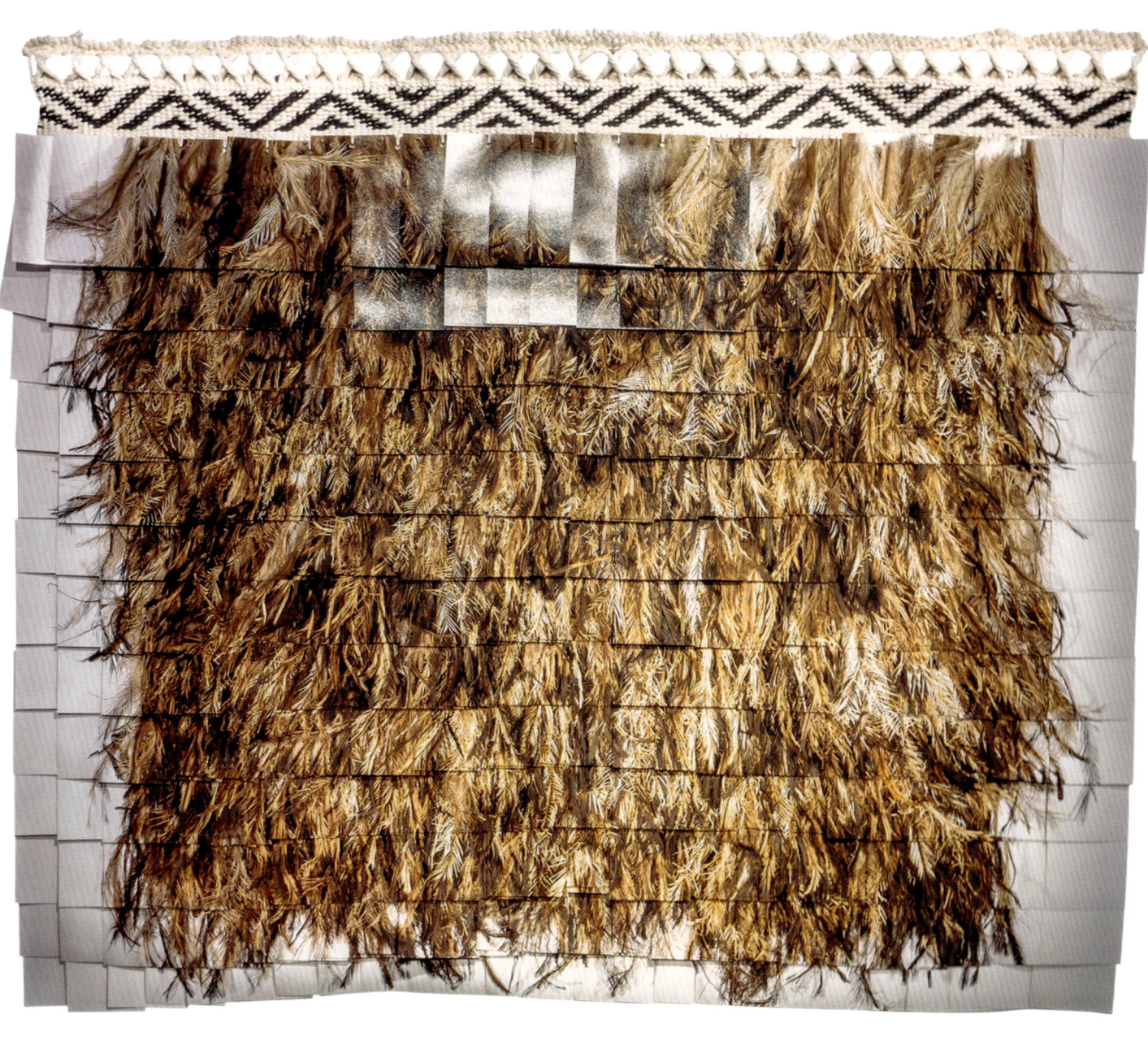

**Kirsten Lyttle,** *Gundulu/Emu Kākahu huruhuru*, **2018–2019**
macramé cord (cotton), cotton twine, digital prints on Fuji lustre paper,
1180 x 1430mm, edition 1 of 1, courtesy of the artist

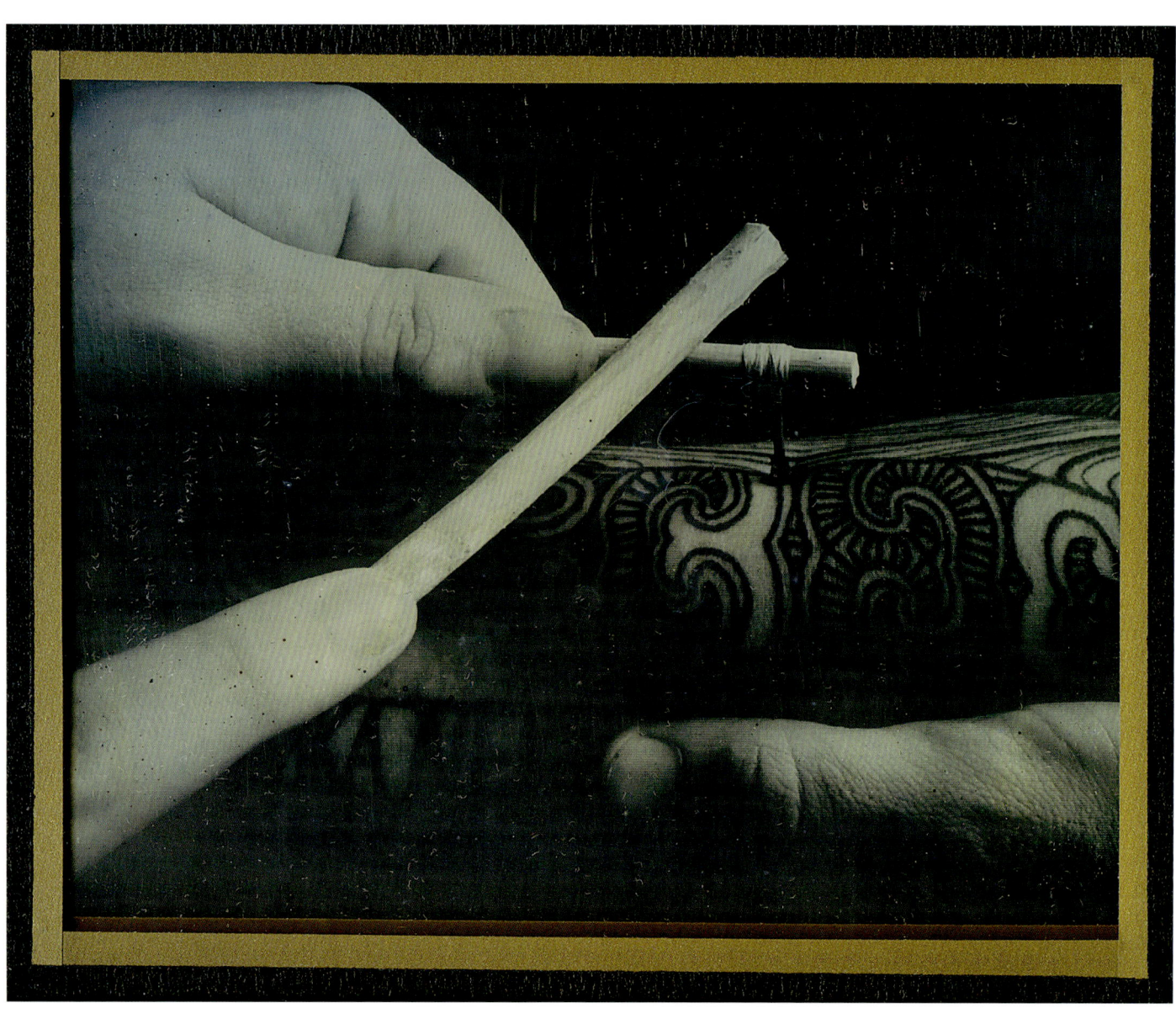

James Tylor, *Tā Moko (More Than Skin Deep)*, 2017
daguerreotype, 100 x 125mm, Museum of Contemporary Art, Sydney

Lyttle and her Māori Australian artist compatriots are increasingly attracting the interest of curators and being included in group shows in well-respected art galleries in Australia, Aotearoa New Zealand and elsewhere. Even though they have been raised away from their tribal homelands, the careers of these artists may well follow the path set by New Zealand-born Māori artists such as Shane Cotton, Michael Parekōwhai and Lisa Reihana, who articulate their Indigenous identities in an aesthetic language that speaks to an international audience.

Sydney, Melbourne and Brisbane sit beside Auckland, Wellington and Christchurch as major population and 'satellite cities' to Māori tribal centres. Since the experience of urbanisation for Māori living in Australia is little different to that in Aotearoa New Zealand, we can draw parallels between themes in work by emerging Māori artists raised and educated in Australia and in the work of Māori artists living in Aotearoa. The latter have sometimes been kaumātua figures in the Australian Māori arts scene – particularly the weavers Maureen Lander and Christina Wirihana (Te Arawa, Ngāti Maniapoto, Ngāti Pikiao, Ngāti Rangiunora, Ngāti Raukawa, Tainui) – who have shared their practice with Māori and non-Māori practitioners; and role models such as Reihana, who have developed a practice that transcends continents. Australia has also nurtured the talents of Māori in the arts who have since returned or migrated (in the case of those born in Australia) to Aotearoa New Zealand, such as curator Dion Peita (Ngāti Tipa, Ngāti Teata, Te Rarawa), curator, artist and academic Huhana Smith, art historian Jo Diamond and painters James Ormsby and Robyn Kahukiwa. With such a large and embedded Māori population, there have been recent calls to establish pan-tribal and even tribal marae in Australia, but this has been complicated by some strong feelings on both sides of the Tasman about whether Māori can claim the strength of connection required to establish a marae on Aboriginal country.[41] It would appear that there are some aspects of Māori art that are not so easily translocated.

## Conclusion

Chisels, weaving pegs and cultural memory are among the instruments of art that were brought by the first Polynesian settlers to Aotearoa. Carving, weaving and cultural memories have also accompanied their descendants who have settled in Western Europe and Australia over the past six decades. These more recent migrants have faced the same challenges as their whanaunga did when they moved to cities after World War Two – an inescapable pressure to conform to Western lifeways that they have resisted through a desire to hold on to those art forms that locate and identify them as Māori.

Museums in the UK and Europe have developed into nurturing spaces for a particular type of Māori art that often activates and is activated by taonga long removed from Aotearoa. This work has served the institutions' own needs to recontextualise their collections and missions in a post-imperial age. In Australia, where the Māori population is large, contemporary Māori art is exhibited in contemporary art galleries and includes the work of Aotearoa New Zealand-based practitioners, migrants and a generation of Māori trained in Australian art schools. Māori artists in both locations – Western Europe and Australia/the museum and the art gallery – have often found collective strength in showing beside other Pacific artists, positioning themselves not in contradistinction to Pākehā (as has been the case in Aotearoa for some decades now) but in relationship with each other, as Oceanian artists.

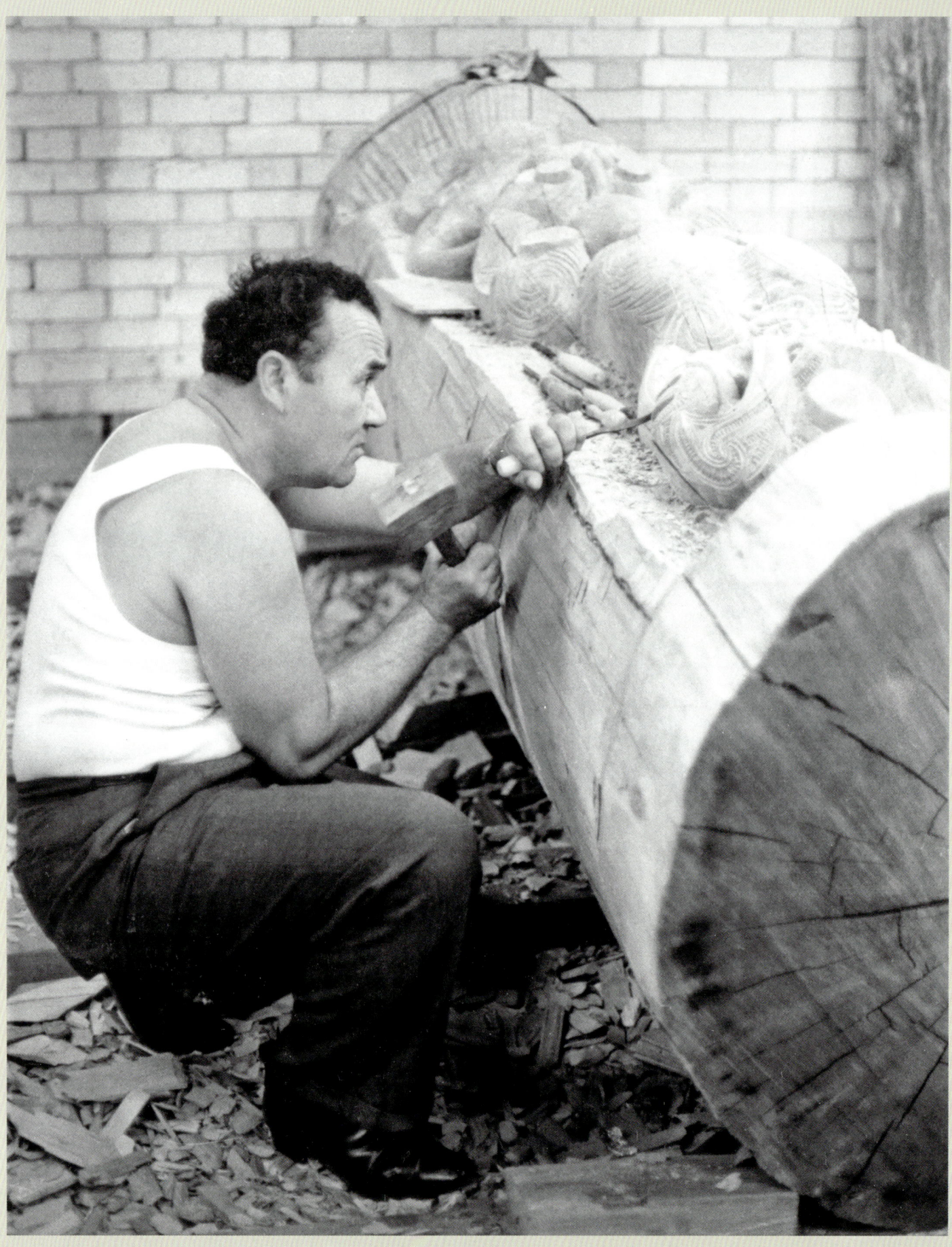

# NGĀTI RĀNANA AND HINEMIHI
## DEIDRE BROWN AND NGARINO ELLIS

In 1957, Esther Kerr, a young Ngāi Tai woman, formed a Māori performance group on the *Rangitoto*, the ship on which she was travelling to London and where she would meet her husband, Jeff Jessop. Two years later, Esther Jessop established the London Māori Club, a cultural organisation similar to the urban Māori clubs of Auckland and Wellington. The club was renamed Ngāti Rānana, the London Tribe, in 1971. Ngāti Rānana has played an important role in the kaitiakitanga of taonga Māori in European museum collections by 'keeping them warm' through curatorial and interpretative activities. Apart from a core group of members permanently domiciled in the United Kingdom, Ngāti Rānana is composed mainly of young Māori and Pākehā people on short-term working visas who regard their participation as reinforcing, redefining or decolonising their cultural identities in a place far away from home.[1]

Ngāti Rānana adopted New Zealand House, London as their regular meeting place: they assemble there under Īnia Te Wiata's impressive tōtara pouihi,

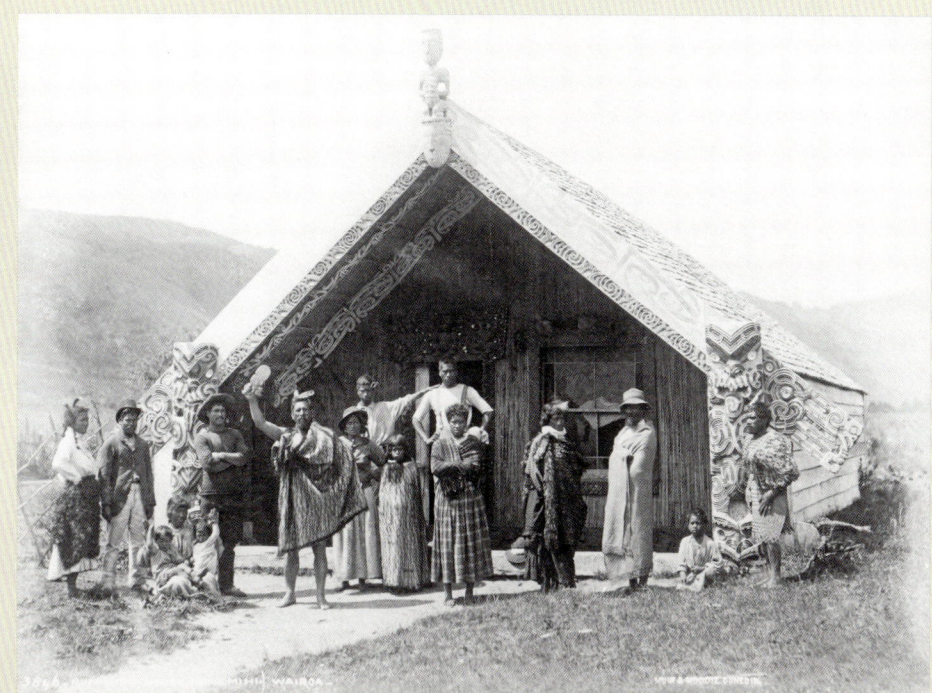

Top: Whānau in front of Hinemihi, Te Wairoa.
Burton Brothers, c.1880-1886, Alexander Turnbull Library, PA7-19-19

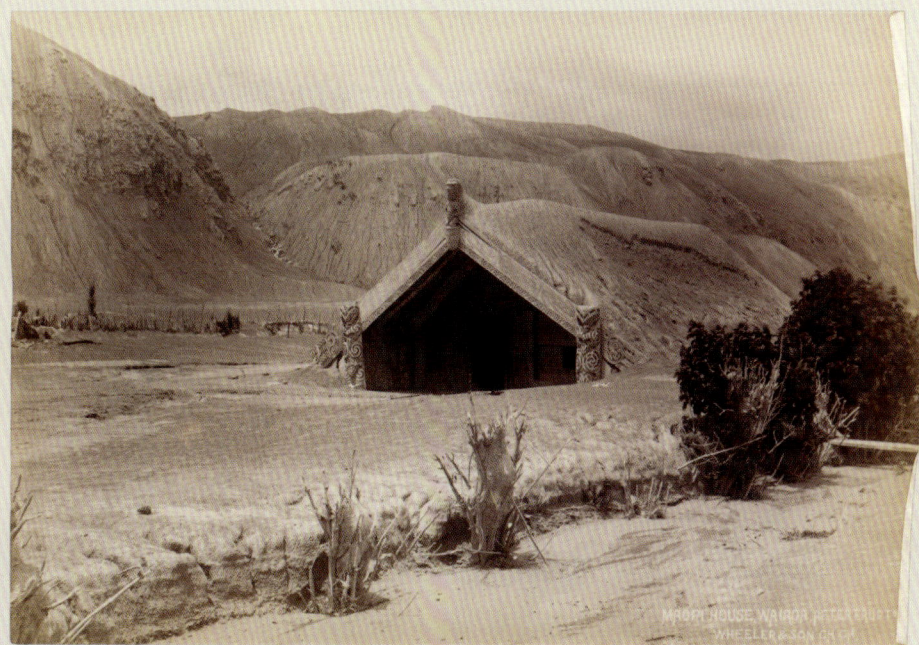

Bottom: Hinemihi meeting house at Te Wairoa, covered in mud, rocks and ash from the Tarawera eruption, 1886.
Edmund Wheeler and Son, c.1886, Alexander Turnbull Library, PAColl-2981-2

Opposite: Īnia Te Wiata carving a pouihi for the foyer of New Zealand House in Haymarket, London, photographed in the 1960s by Geoff Adams. The carving took place in the basement of the building.
Alexander Turnbull Library, Ref: 1/2-190156-F

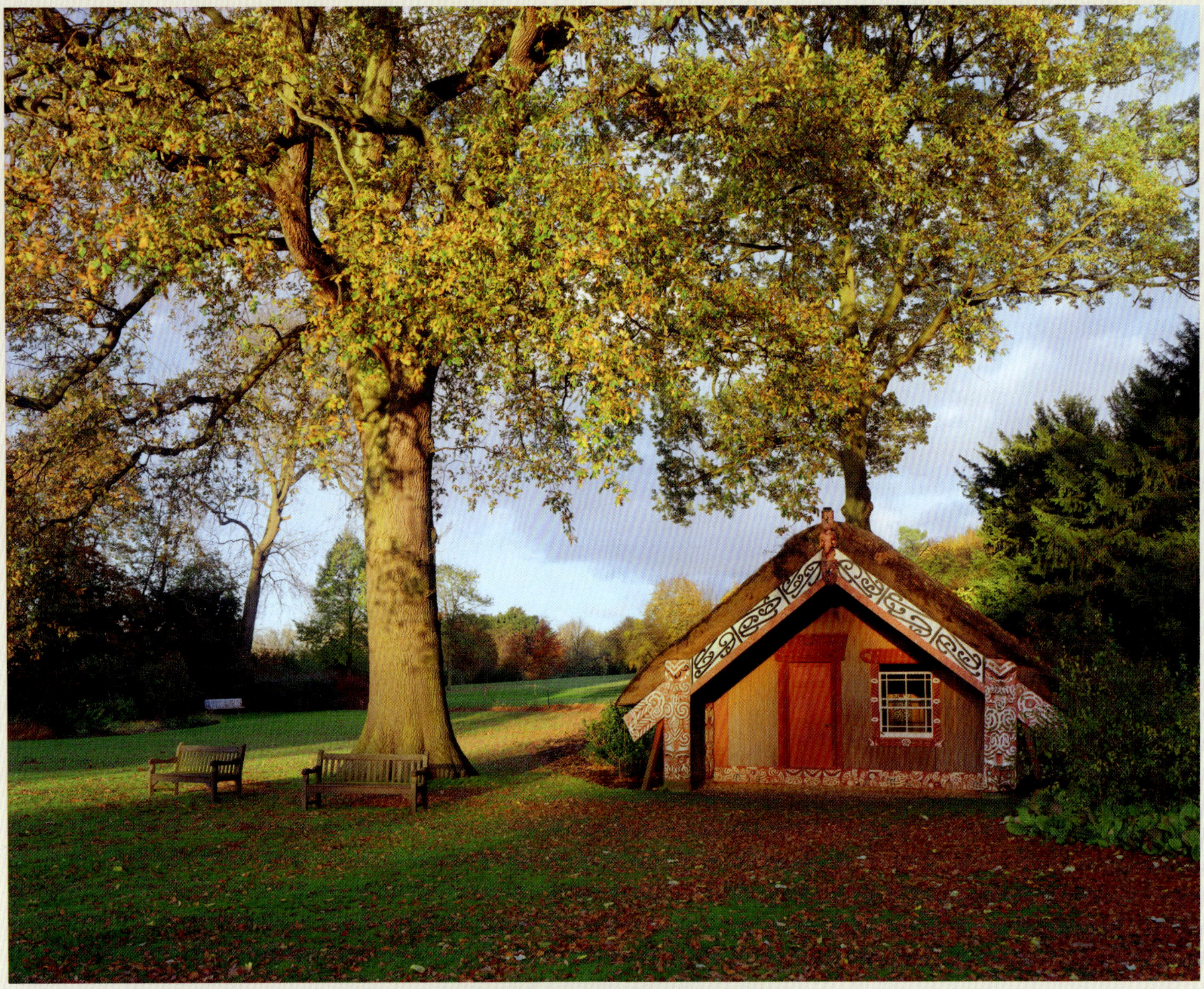

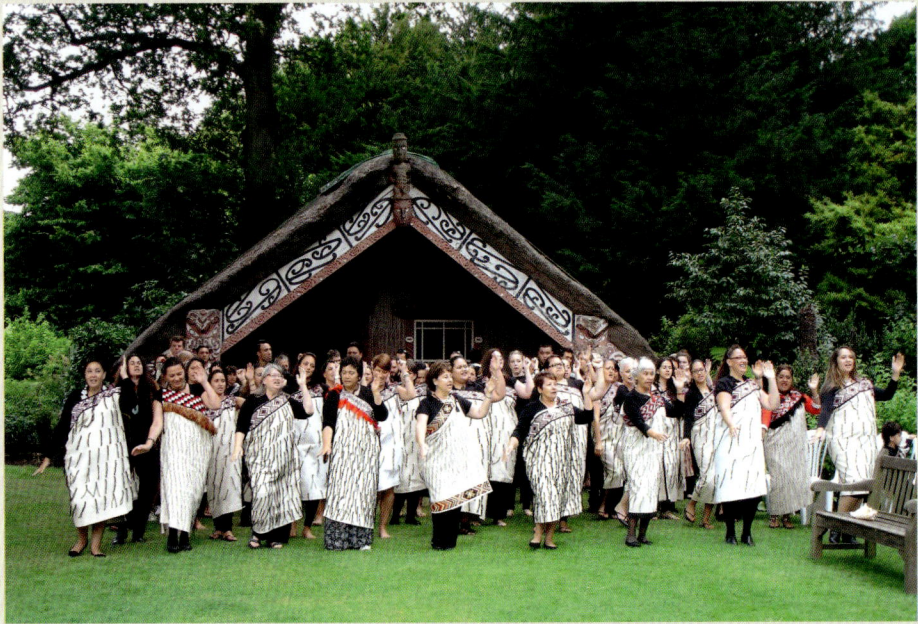

Hinemihi in Clandon Park.
photograph by Mark Adams

Ngāti Rānana performers outside Hinemihi, welcoming the New Zealand Olympic team, 2012.
photograph by Mark Adams

conceived in partnership with the building's architect as an integral part of the building's design and completed by Te Wiata in the basement of the building between 1963 and 1971.[2] Since the mid-1990s, the wharenui Hinemihi in Surrey has also been a centre for Ngāti Rānana's activities in a reciprocal relationship that enables the house to be 'kept warm' by their kaitiakitanga.

Hinemihi, like her adoptive community, is a world traveller. She was opened in 1881 at Te Wairoa, a kāinga Māori that was at the centre of a burgeoning Victorian tourist industry that included the nearby 'eighth wonder of the world', the Pink and White Terraces. Commissioned by Ngāti Hinemihi rangatira Aporo Te Wharekaniwha, Hinemihi was both a wharenui and a place of commercial entertainment for visitors, and it was from this latter role that the building became known as the 'house with the golden eyes', a reference to the gold sovereigns that were placed in the eyes of the ancestral carvings.[3] Wero Taroi and Tene Waitere, the renowned Ngāti Tarāwhai tohunga whakairo, completed her carvings. In 1886, Hinemihi reached a folkloric level of national fame as the place of refuge for a number of Māori and Pākehā who fled their damaged homes during and after the Mount Tarawera eruption.[4] Ash and mud engulfed the Pink and White Terraces and Te Wairoa, forcing many of the kāinga's surviving inhabitants to resettle elsewhere.

After six years of standing empty, the house was sold for £50 by Aporo's son Mika to departing Governor-General Sir William Onslow, who wanted a memento of his time in New Zealand. Hinemihi was then shipped to England and reassembled at Onslow's ancestral estate Clandon Park as a summer house, becoming one of five wharenui built in Aotearoa New Zealand that now stand oversees (the others are all in museums: Ruatepupuke [1881] in Chicago's Field Museum; Rauru [1900] in Hamburg's Museum für Völkerkunde; Te Wharepuni-a-Māui [1905] at the Linden Museum in Stuttgart and Te Aroha o te Iwi Māori [1963] at the Polynesian Cultural Centre, Laiʻe, Hawaiʻi.)[5] In 1917, Hinemihi was 'restored' by soldiers including members of the New Zealand (Māori) Pioneer Battalion, who were recuperating at Clandon House, which had become a military hospital. This re-engagement of Māori with Hinemihi ensured that the building remained in the hearts and minds of Māori visiting and living in the United Kingdom.

Clandon Park was gifted to the National Trust in 1956, and two years later the first of several renovations began. Over time there have been calls for the return of Hinemihi. In 1974 the minister of Maori affairs approached the National Trust to express concern at the trust's inability to care properly for the house. The Trust's response was to employ an English restorer – against the minister's advice to hire Māori carvers for this work. An unsympathetic restoration in 1978 resulted in the installation of a heavy thatched roof, which was a misinterpretation of the ash-covered roof that appears in photographs of the building taken immediately after the Tarawera eruption (the original roof was wood shingles).[6] As Māori short- and long-term migration to the United Kingdom increased from the 1980s, so did Māori engagement with Hinemihi, leading to her use, along with the surrounding grounds, as a marae for Ngāti Rānana – and another request for her return.[7] This was again turned down, but the trust agreed to allow two Māori carvers, both of whom were descendants of the original carvers, to restore carvings.[8] Since that time Jim Schuster, the great-great-grandson of Tene Waitere, has been involved in negotiations for new carvings, and for the return of Hinemihi.

In the early 2000s, Ngāti Rānana, Ngāti Hinemihi and associated academics and conservators developed an innovative participation-centred proposal to preserve Hinemihi's conservation of use rather than conservation of materials. This included installing a floor, heating, lighting, insulation and roof, with further plans for a semi-subterranean extension designed by then London-based Māori architect Anthony Hoete (Ngāti Awa).[9] At the time, the scheme seemed radical when compared to conventional conservation of wharenui, although interventions to improve warmth and comfort are now becoming more commonplace in Aotearoa New Zealand.[10] The ambitious plans for Hinemihi were suspended after she survived another tragic event – the razing of the adjacent manor house (built in 1721) by fire in 2015. Unfortunately, tukutuku panels for the whare woven in the UK under the direction of Cathy Schuster and a kahu kiwi gifted to Onslow's son at his christening in 1891 were lost in the blaze.[11] Since the fire, the National Trust has agreed in principle to repatriate Hinemihi's whakairo rākau in exchange for new whakairo rākau.

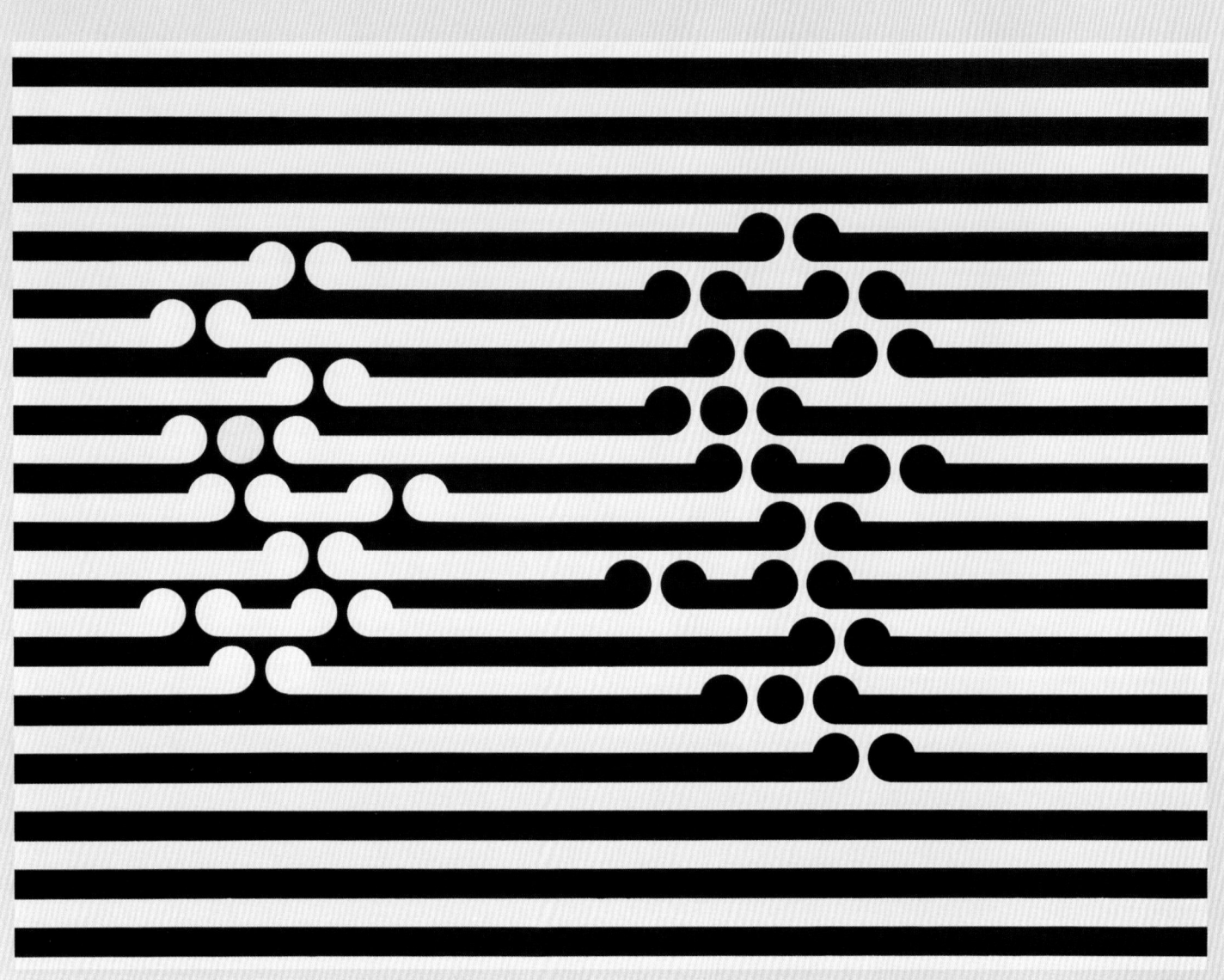

# MĀORI ART AS A CULTURAL PROPERTY
DEIDRE BROWN

Māori have, from their earliest contacts with non-Māori culture, made careful decisions about which taonga and art knowledges can and cannot be shared with non-Māori. The appropriation and commodification of Māori art without Māori consent has had costs, including the loss of control over proper care of heritage, diminished respect for tapu, replacement of original, tribally produced work with reproductions, and loss of livelihood. Whereas intellectual property bestows exclusive-use rights to individuals through copyright, trademark and patents, cultural property is a recognition of community rights to safeguard their knowledges through tikanga and/or conventional legal means.[1]

Discussions concerning the role of taonga Māori in institutional and commercial settings began in earnest after the *Te Maori* exhibition, co-curated by Hirini Moko Mead. Among its many achievements, the exhibition firmly placed Māori art within the canon of New Zealand art and, in doing so, initiated a highly charged debate between Māori art and New Zealand art scholars about the historical and contemporary misappropriation of Māori symbolism into non-Māori art.[2] The discussion ranged from the commercial use of the koru symbol as trademark devices to the symbol's use in 'high art' as emblems of a local identity in the work of Pākehā artists such as Colin McCahon, Theo Schoon and Gordon Walters. Criticisms led by the Māori art historians Rangihīroa Panoho and Ngahuia Te Awekotuku were part of a wider response to unauthorised,

**Gordon Walters, *Painting No. 1*, 1965**
PVA on hardboard, 930 x 1233 x 32mm, Auckland Art Gallery Toi o Tāmaki, 1966/4, purchased 1966

ill-considered, exploitative and potentially harmful misappropriation of customary Indigenous knowledge and resources by non-Indigenous individuals, companies and the government.

Mead's presence was influential in these and other discussions of Māori cultural property. He was the chair of the 1993 First International Conference on the Cultural and Intellectual Property Rights of Indigenous Peoples, held at his tribal home in the Bay of Plenty. The conference produced the Mātaatua Declaration on Cultural and Intellectual Property Rights of Indigenous Peoples, a seminal document that affirmed that while Indigenous knowledges (including art) can benefit all humanity, the international community must respect the rights of Indigenous people to define, protect and control the sharing of these knowledges.[3] Mead and others went on to advance the principles of the Mātaatua Declaration for his iwi by successfully arguing for the repatriation of the Mātaatua meeting house from Otago Museum in 1996 (the house was reopened in Whakatāne in 2011).

The most notable community-led response to the unauthorised appropriation and use of Māori art by non-Māori was the Wai 262 'Flora and Fauna' claim (so named because of its inclusion of bioprospecting as a concern) to the Waitangi Tribunal, filed by a consortium of Māori tribes in 1991 and reported on by the Tribunal in 2011.[4] The claim is similar in intent to the Mātaatua Declaration, but was contextualised by the Crown's guarantee to Māori, in Article 2 of the 1840 Tiriti o Waitangi, to recognise 'the unqualified exercise of their chieftainship over their lands, villages and all their treasures'.[5] After considering a number of submissions on how Māori imagery might be used commercially, for example in trademarks and artworks for sale, the Tribunal suggested a distinction between the way in which 'taonga works' and 'taonga-derived works' might be evaluated.[6] It defined taonga works as works with a kaitiaki – that is, they have a relationship with an identifiable community; for example, 'a story in a name or a song-poem … tā moko, a whare tupuna, or waka taua' associated with an iwi or hapū.[7] Taonga-derived works are works derived from Māori knowledge, in particular aesthetics and concepts, but have no kaitiaki, such as – the Tribunal argued – the Air New Zealand koru trademark and (somewhat surprisingly given the appropriation debates that surrounded them at the time the claim was lodged) the koru prints and paintings of Walters.[8] These definitions, however, fell short of recognising Māori authority over all Māori art knowledges. The Tribunal recommended the establishment of an expert commission that would provide rulings as to whether commercial use of a taonga work might be offensive or derogatory and to establish best-practice guidelines for the use, care, protection and custody of taonga works and taonga-derived works.[9]

The most influential legal protective measures to date have been in the area of trademarks, specifically through the government's Intellectual Property Office of New Zealand's Māori Trade Marks Advisory Committee and the 'Toi Iho' trademark. The Māori Trade Marks Advisory Committee was established in 2003 to prevent objectionable misappropriations and misuses of traditional cultural expressions in trademarks.[10] As the mana and associated tapu of a Māori word or image increases, so does the likelihood of offensiveness that might be caused by a noa product

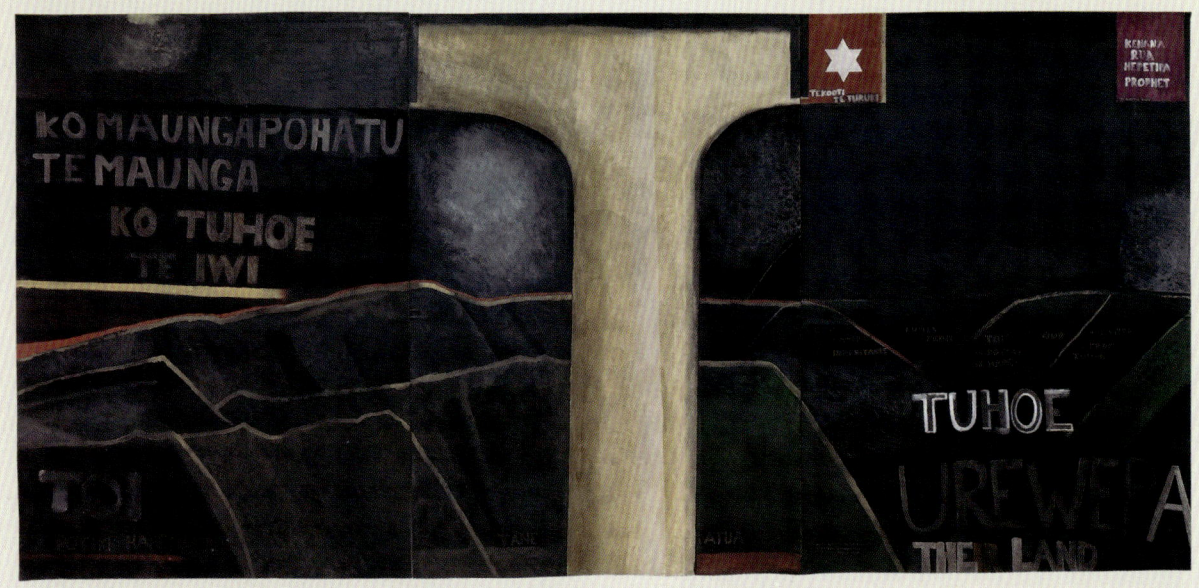

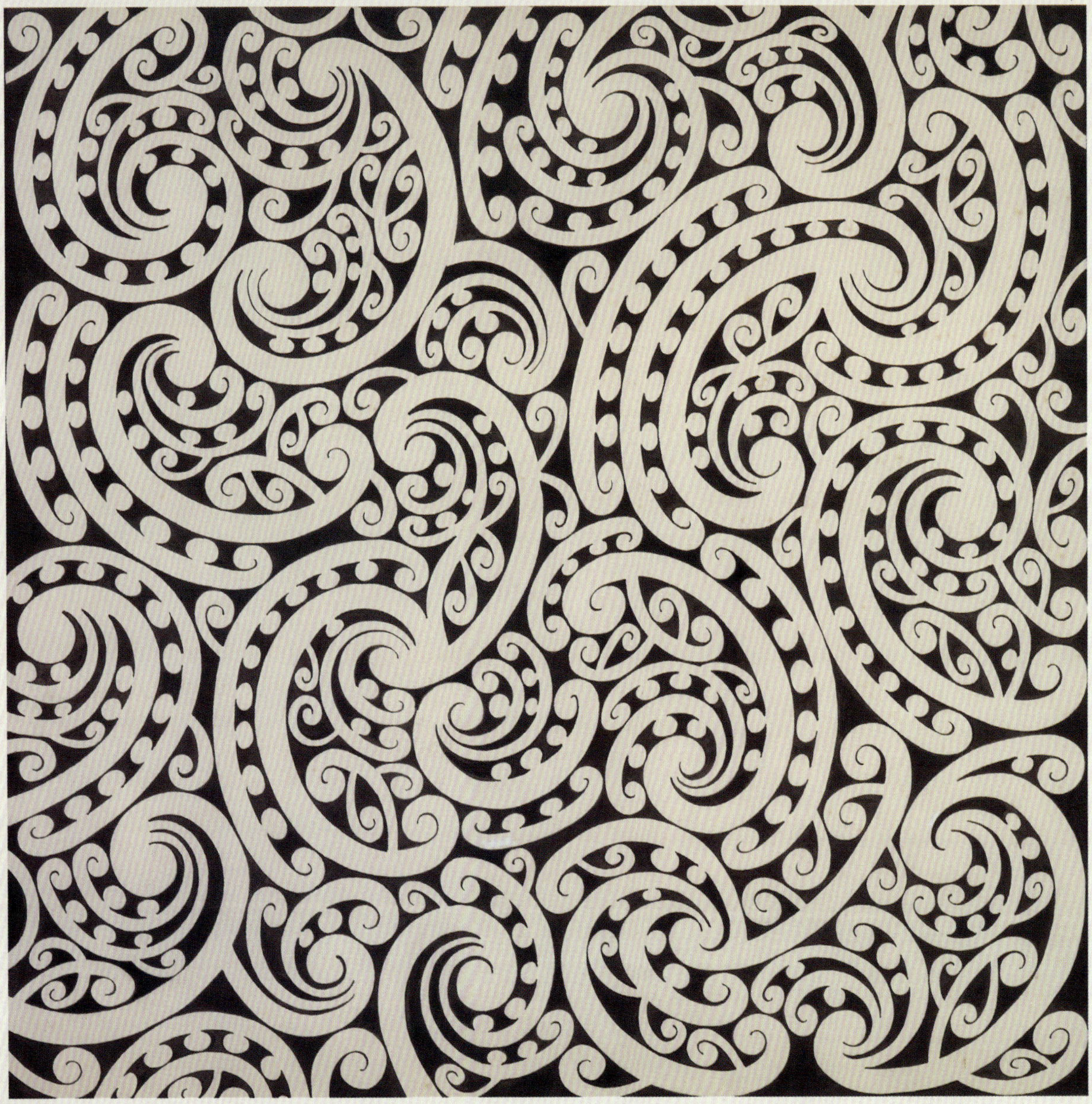

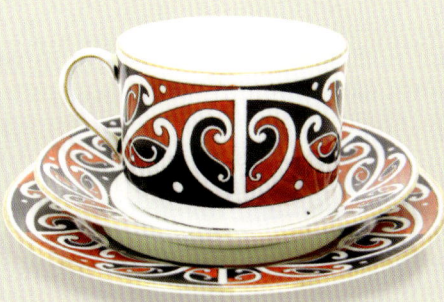 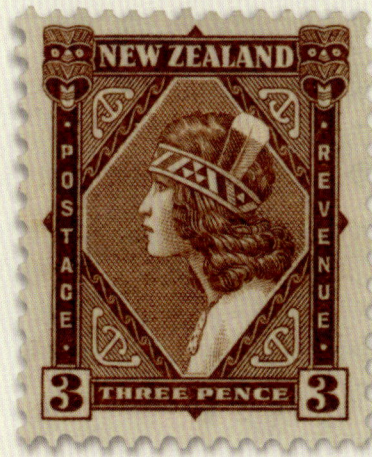 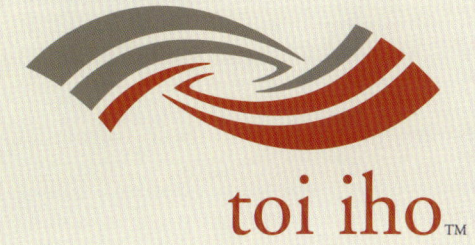

(such as food, alcohol, tobacco) bearing these words or images. Although much of the discussion about the misappropriation of Māori words and symbolism into commercial culture has revolved around the concept of appropriateness, the Trade Marks Act prohibits the registration of only marks that are offensive, with the threshold of offensiveness being much higher than that of inappropriateness.

The Toi Iho Māori Made trademark was registered as a trademark in 2002 by Creative New Zealand (CNZ), the arts funding arm of the New Zealand government. As a protective device, the original purpose of the Toi Iho trademark was to identify the quality and authenticity of a diverse range of Māori arts made by Māori for the commercial market. In June 2010, the Toi Iho trademarks and associated intellectual property rights were transferred from CNZ to the newly established entity Toi Iho Kaitiaki Incorporated, which relaunched the Toi Iho trademark. Over 100 Māori artists, working in customary arts and contemporary art, design and performance, today have the right to use the trademark.[11]

Not all Māori agree with the application of intellectual property laws to cultural property, including art and art practices, even if such a process is managed by Māori, because of the legal and commercial imperatives and the commodification of culture that underpin such measures. The rapid advance of digital and scientific technologies, in which Indigenous people are sometimes active and at other times unwilling participants, has led to the emergence of cultural and intellectual property issues for which conventional legal means may or may not be able to offer protection. As things stand today, intellectual property initiatives and education based on the dissemination of appropriate practice models are two means by which cultural properties, including Māori art, can be protected from exploitation.

Left: Royal Doulton Maori Ware, produced from 1906 to 1923.
Te Papa Tongarewa Museum of New Zealand, CG000153/1-3, bequest of Miss A. Quinney, 1959

Middle: New Zealand pictorial stamp, 1935.

Right: Toi Iho trademark, originally registered in 2002.

Opposite top: Colin McCahon's *Urewera Mural* (1975) at the Aniwaniwa Visitor Centre, November 2005.
synthetic polymer paint, each canvas 2158 x 1820mm, overall 2158 x 5460mm, collection of Department of Conservation Te Papa Atawhai and Tūhoe Te Uru Taumatua, courtesy of McCahon Research and Publication Trust

Opposite bottom: Theo Schoon, *Untitled*, c.1963
ink on paper, 560 x 607mm, Te Papa Tongarewa Museum of New Zealand, 1988-0052-1, purchased 1988 through Special Projects in the Arts Fund

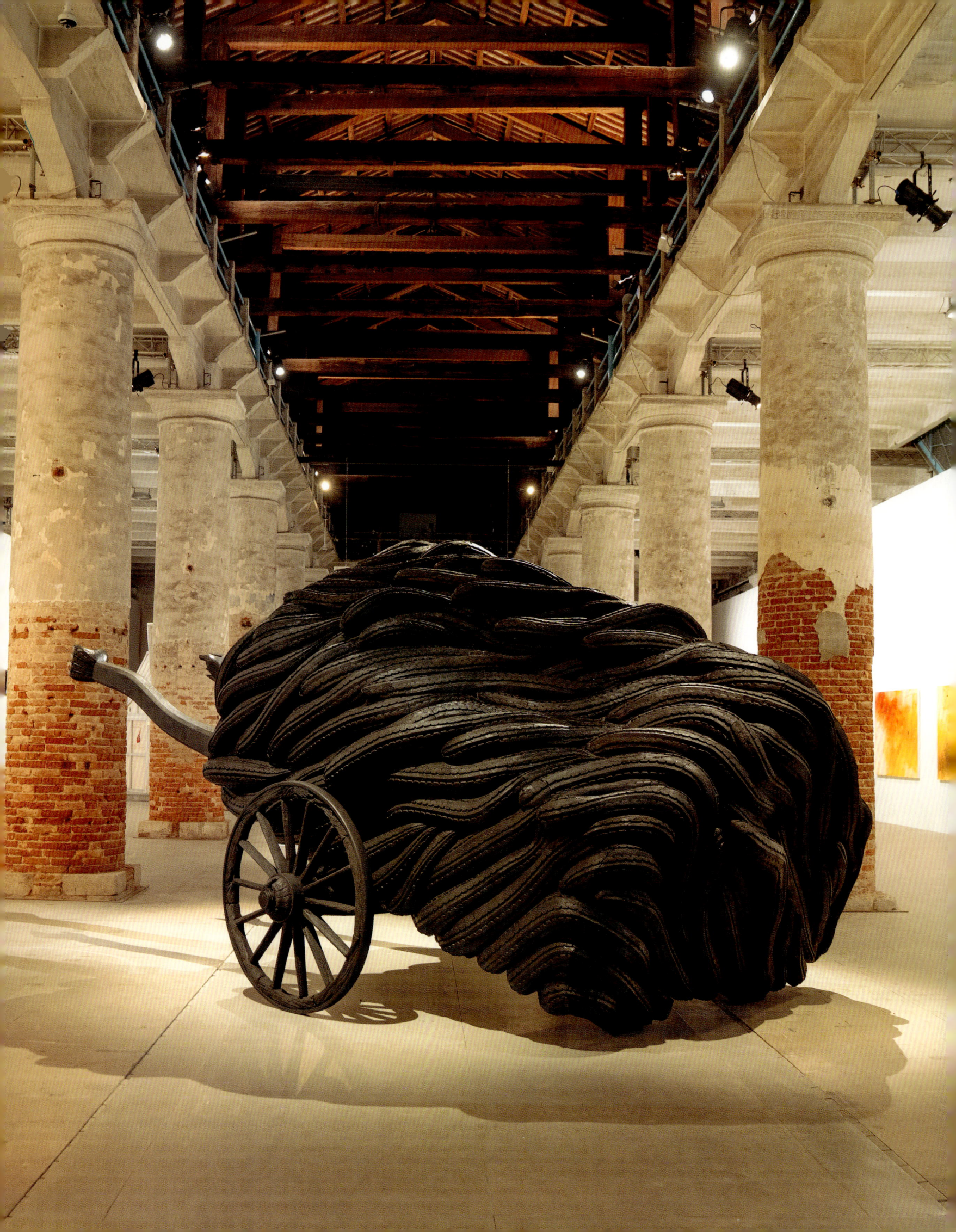

# 19 HAUMI Ē! HUI Ē! TĀIKI Ē!
## MĀORI AND INDIGENOUS ART ON THE GLOBAL STAGE
### NGARINO ELLIS

*Being Māori is a political position and a place from which to draw empowerment.*

—Ngahiraka Mason[1]

*Our tools of survival are rooted in our ability to work in collective methods and Indigenous methodologies.*

—Heather Igloliorte, Julie Nagam and Carla Taunton[2]

Māori artists have always travelled. As they moved across Te Moananui a Kiwa they took with them their tools, techniques, materials and ideas; they used these to reflect the changing dynamics of their peoples, and in doing so they constructed innovative meanings and histories embedded in new lands. These knowledges and practices played out in different ways once the ancestors arrived in Aotearoa. The excitement they felt for the unfamiliar transformed the type of art they produced: from tatau to moko, from tapa to whatu, from geometric to curvilinear. The artist had a central role within their community in articulating important social, political and economic issues for the people.

Māori artists in the twenty-first century are navigating a complex and ever-changing landscape and in this way their role as agents of change has not changed. One of the biggest shifts in the past couple of generations has been their audiences and patrons, ranging from the nannies at the pā through to curators in international art fairs and biennales. Māori artists are now engaging with their Indigenous counterparts overseas in exhibitions and art projects and are part of this global Indigenous art world.

**Brett Graham, *Wasteland*, 2023, as exhibited at the 60th Venice Biennale, 2024**
steel, found wagon wheels, macrocarpa wood, paint, photograph by Ben Stewart

### The nature of Indigenous

Most of this book has been concerned with art made here in Aotearoa, shaped by the dynamics of culture as it shifted from identities located firmly in Hawaiki, towards those located in specific communities. Today, arguably, most Māori artists – indeed most Māori – refer to themselves in relation to their tribal affiliations. But this book is entitled *Toi Te Mana: An Indigenous History of Māori Art* for a reason. While it is by, for and about Māori, we do not exist in isolation. Indian literary critic Gayatri Chakravorty Spivak calls this 'strategist essentialism'; as she explains it: 'The ways in which subordinate or marginalised social groups may temporarily put aside local difference in order to forge a sense of collective identity through which they band together in political movements.'[3] This deliberate kind of reaching out to our Indigenous cousins across the waters of Te Moananui a Kiwa recognises that we are part of a wider Indigenous network of peoples who are joined under shared histories and experiences – a 'global collective consciousness among First Peoples',[4] as Métis scholar David Garneau puts it – that includes lived responses to colonisation by European powers. Yet this is not our only connection; indeed, Indigenous peoples have so much more in common, ranging from descent from the land to approaches to family and reverence for elders.

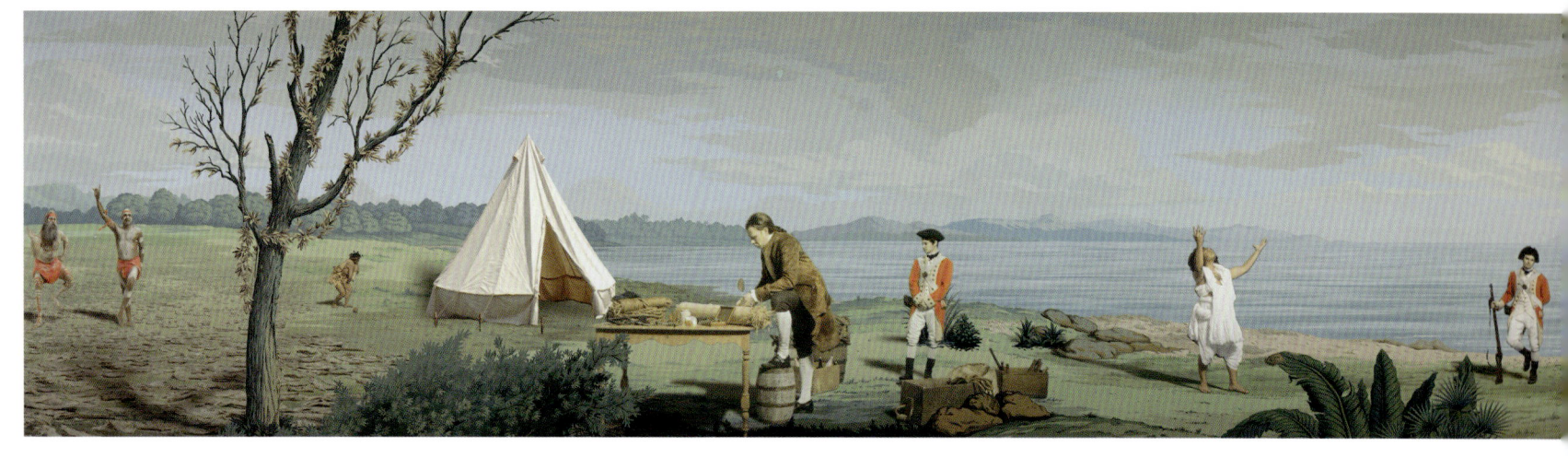
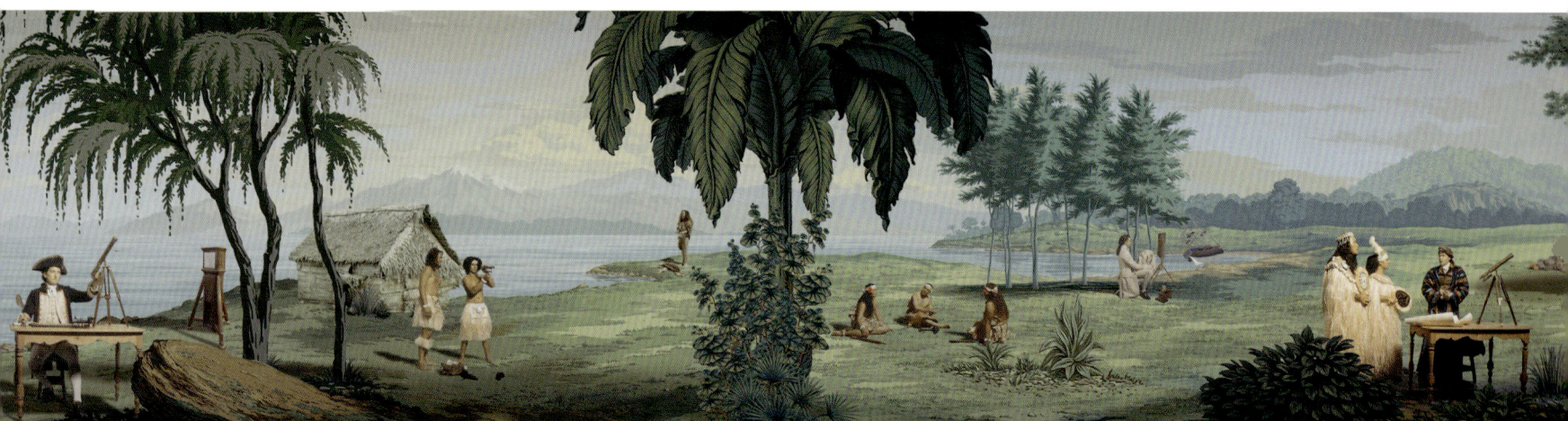
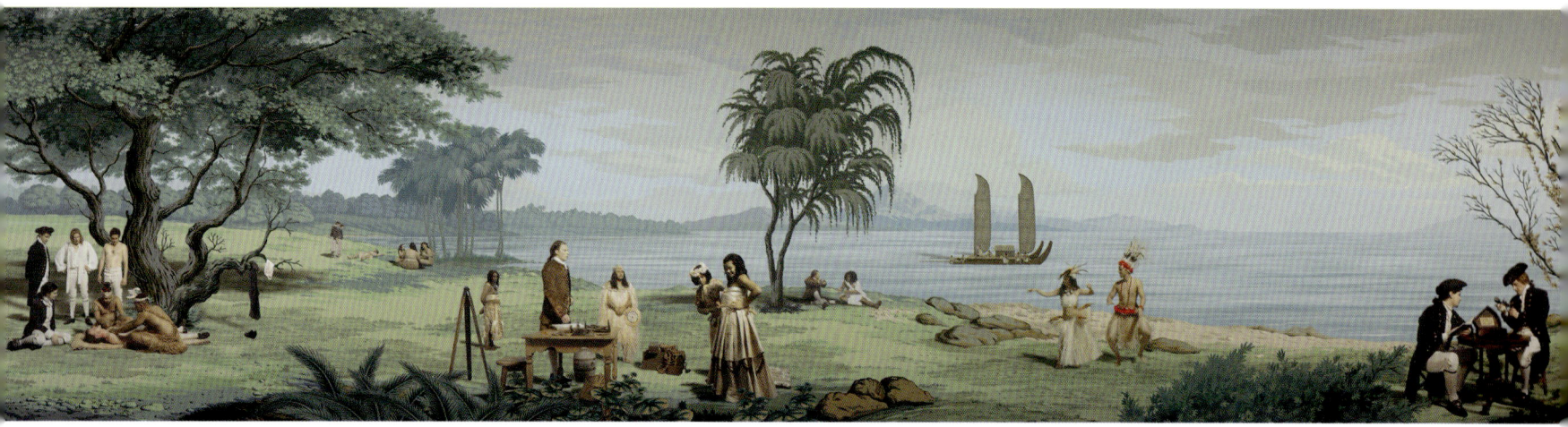
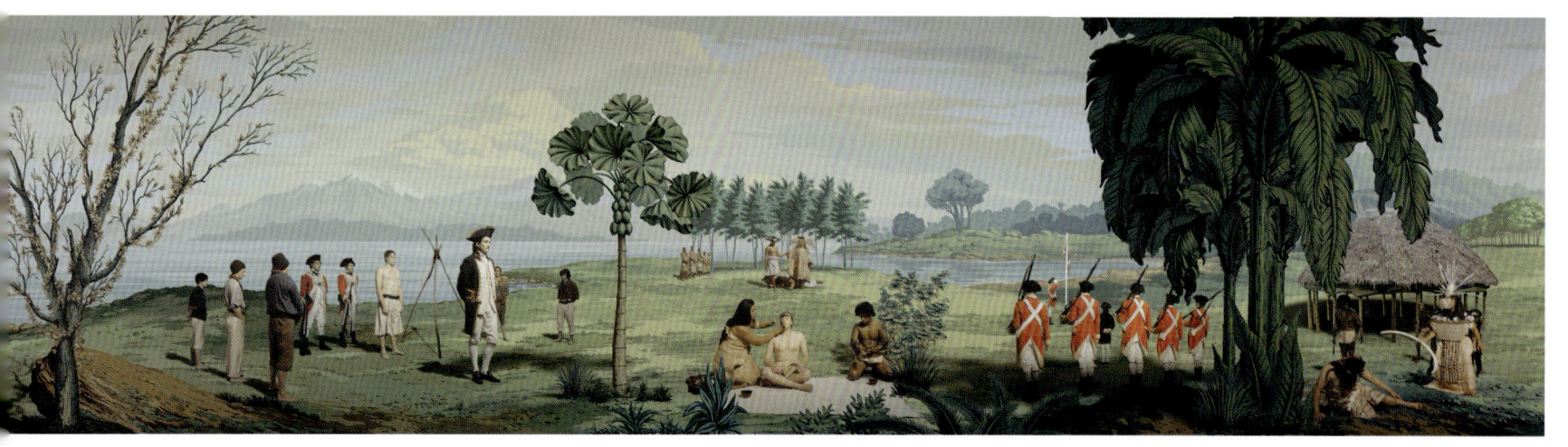

It is these shared traits that are often central to contemporary Indigenous identity. Linda Tuhiwai Smith argues that, for Indigenous peoples, 'a new agenda ... has been framed that goes beyond the decolonisation aspirations of a particular indigenous community towards development of global indigenous strategic alliances'.[5] She refers to the call from her Ngāti Porou relation Donna Awatere, who explains that 'These alliances are necessary because changes cannot occur on our own.'[6] Smith argues for an 'Indigenous Research Agenda',[7] in which self-determination is at the centre, structured with goals of survival, recovery and development. This is supported by scholar and artist Jolene Rickard of the Tuscarora nation, Turtle clan, who advocates for an 'expansion of art criticism and visual theory to include a discourse read across Indigeneity, colonization and sovereignty'.[8] Indigenous advocates globally then call for a solidarity across nations as a key positive strategy for the future.

Literary theorist Chadwick Allen (Chickasaw) has proposed the term 'trans-Indigenous' as one way in which to understand Indigenous connections. He promotes thinking about 'the mobility and multiple interactions of Indigenous peoples, cultures, histories, and texts'.[9] The idea of 'trans' anything has become popular as one strategy to acknowledge the sometimes complicated and messy world that is contemporary art. The Australian art journal *Artlink* dedicated its June 2017 issue to 'the transcultural relations of Indigenous contemporary artists'.[10] In that issue, Australian art historian Ian McLean wrote of the shift from 'post' in the 1970s and 1980s to what he terms 'trans-discourse', 'because it moves between and across its terms of reference in ways that unsettle and look beyond their conventional relationships'.[11]

Osage scholar Robert Warrior cautions about openly embracing the concept of 'transnationalism': in his experience, this can lead to 'Native critics ... [who] remain in the end more interested in what is beyond borders (Southeast Asia, Africa or the Caribbean, for instance) than the transnationalism produced by colonialisms within its borders'.[12] The distinctiveness of Indigenous experiences across tribal nations is the point of difference here. While we link hands over important political issues – note, for example, the presence of Māori and Aboriginal activists at the Dakota Access Pipeline water protectors protests of 2016–2017, and at the Mauna Kea Thirty Meter Telescope protests in Hawai'i from 2014 – we do so bringing our own histories and traumas. Artists are pivotal lobbyists here, as they come together on international residencies and exhibitions to foster conversations about art, life and culture.

The concept of sovereignty is integral, and has been configured by Indigenous writers and artists globally to help articulate a certain way of seeing. It responds to the notion of 'historical amnesia', which curator Candice Hopkins (Carcross/Tagish First Nation) describes as 'an active forgetting'.[13] Why do so many histories and artworks, even today, deliberately ignore Indigeneity? Artists globally seek to address this through their work. Cree artist Kent Monkman's *The Four Continents* and Lisa Reihana's *in Pursuit of Venus* both insert an Indigenous presence into a colonial absence; they do this, at the simplest level, by peopling the canvas with ancestors who are industrious and curious, reacting to the newcomers on their own terms.

Sovereignty is an essential component of decolonisation, which might be described as a fractious, ever-moving and complicated range of processes. This concept means different things to different people, and often it is shaped by their own personal and communal experiences of colonisation. Photographer Hulleah J. Tsinhnahjinnie (Taskigi/Diné) created the term 'visual sovereignty' to identify 'a particular type of consciousness rooted in confidence which is exhibited as a strength in cultural and visual presence'.[14] She explains that artists 'must not limit [themselves] to specific areas, as responsibility should always include innovative and peripheral vision ... including different approaches'.[15] All these concepts are familiar within the Māori art world, and help shape their approaches to creating new works as well as generating discussion about reception and circulation of artworks.

### The new contemporary Māori art

Contemporary Māori art engages with concepts of sovereignty, with transnationalism, with trans-Indigeneity. Its reception overseas continues to transform as the art does – the introduction of different technologies and materials has impacted on the forms made. Contemporary Māori art is here defined as art 'made now' – while these forms may be considered

**Lisa Reihana, *in Pursuit of Venus [infected]*, 2015–2017**
single-channel video, UltraHD, colour, 7.1 sound, 1hr 4min, Auckland Art Gallery Toi o Tāmaki, 2014/24, gift of the Patrons of the Auckland Art Gallery, 2014

under the mantle of 'traditional' or 'customary' art now, those same artists from the early nineteenth century were grappling with similar issues, in relation to the making and reception of their work, as their descendants experience today. In the past few chapters we have pinpointed a distinct shift away from arts based in the marae towards those made for exhibition in the art gallery. While these pathways were forged with different degrees of success in the 1960s, by the 1970s a new consciousness among Māori artists led them to think of themselves *as* Māori artists.

The formation of Ngā Puna Waihanga in 1973 was a turning point. This group recognised the need for contemporary Māori artists to come together to work as a collective and as a community of practice. The artists considered some of the key debates of the period, and the ongoing importance of being Māori in the gallery space. The next 'turning point' was the *Te Maori* exhibition (1984–1986) which forever transformed the galleries and museums sector in relation to their understanding of Māori art and its contemporary significance. At this time the New Zealand government funded a variety of Māori art initiatives enabling Māori artists to seek opportunities overseas, such as the Maori and South Pacific Arts Council (MASPAC) in 1978 and the creation of Te Atinga Contemporary Maori Arts Board in 1987. *Te Maori* also influenced policy, resulting in appointments of roles specifically designed for Māori, such as Rangihīroa Panoho, who was appointed to the Sarjeant Art Gallery, Whanganui in 1988.

It was at this time of increased involvement of Māori across the arts sector that galleries overseas began exhibiting Māori art as part of major exhibitions of Indigenous art, with varying degrees of success. Jonathan Mane-Wheoki wrote about the 1989 *Les Magiciens de la Terre* exhibition at the Centre Pompidou, Paris, curated by the director of the Musée National d'Afrique et d'Océanie, Jean-Hubert Martin: 'In this selection of [Indigenous] artists lie the seeds of an indigenous global consciousness in contemporary art.'[16] This exhibition was revolutionary in its inclusion of 104 non-Western European artists, chosen in no small way as a pushback against the debates surrounding the Museum of Modern Art exhibition *'Primitivism' in 20th Century Art: Affinities of the Tribal and the Modern*, which had attracted severe criticism for the ways in which African art was included under the subtitle 'primitive'. *Les Magiciens*, on the other hand, had sought to present 'a truly international exhibition', in the words of Martin.

In the 1990s curators began to include Māori artists in exhibitions not only because of their Indigeneity but also the quality of their work. An unprecedented number of Māori were graduating from the tertiary art schools: the Elam School of Fine Arts at the University of Auckland, and the University of Canterbury School of Fine Arts. Programmes were also being established in the regions, including Toioho ki Āpiti at Massey University, Palmerston North,[17] Toihoukura in Gisborne, and Toimairangi in Hastings. At the same time, Māori curators were emerging, such as George Hubbard, for whom Māori was both a badge of honour but also an unwelcome denominator. The exhibitions that Hubbard curated, specifically *Choice!* (Artspace, Auckland, 1990) and *Cross-Pollination* (Artspace, Auckland, 1991), sought to unpack identity politics that had become problematic for the current generation of Māori artists. They did not want to be pigeonholed as Māori; rather, they sought to forge their reputations on the quality of their work alone. Hirini Moko Mead criticised the style of this younger generation in a keynote presentation at the *Toioho ki Apiti* conference at Massey University, Palmerston North in 1996. Mead presented thought-provoking questions in relation to the contemporary art scene that are still relevant today, and which have, in some ways, prompted this book:

> There are Māori artists who have no grounding in their own culture and no training in Māori art now wanting to do art which they want to call Māori art? Then there are well educated Māori trained in Western art traditions entering the field of Māori art and shaking the very foundations of our art. Another category are well trained Pākehā artists entering the field and producing Māori art forms. Do they produce Māori art? And what about works that are a mixture of Western and Māori traditions, and paintings that have just a little bit of Māori art but are painted by a Māori artist?[18]

We might conceptualise the plethora of contemporary Māori art exhibitions globally as an ever-evolving spiral, with Aotearoa at the centre. Artists' reputations emanate out from here and their works snowball from one exhibition to the next: see, for instance, Brett Graham and Rachael Rakena's *U.F.O.B* (2006), which was exhibited at the Sydney Biennale then at the Venice Biennale the following year,

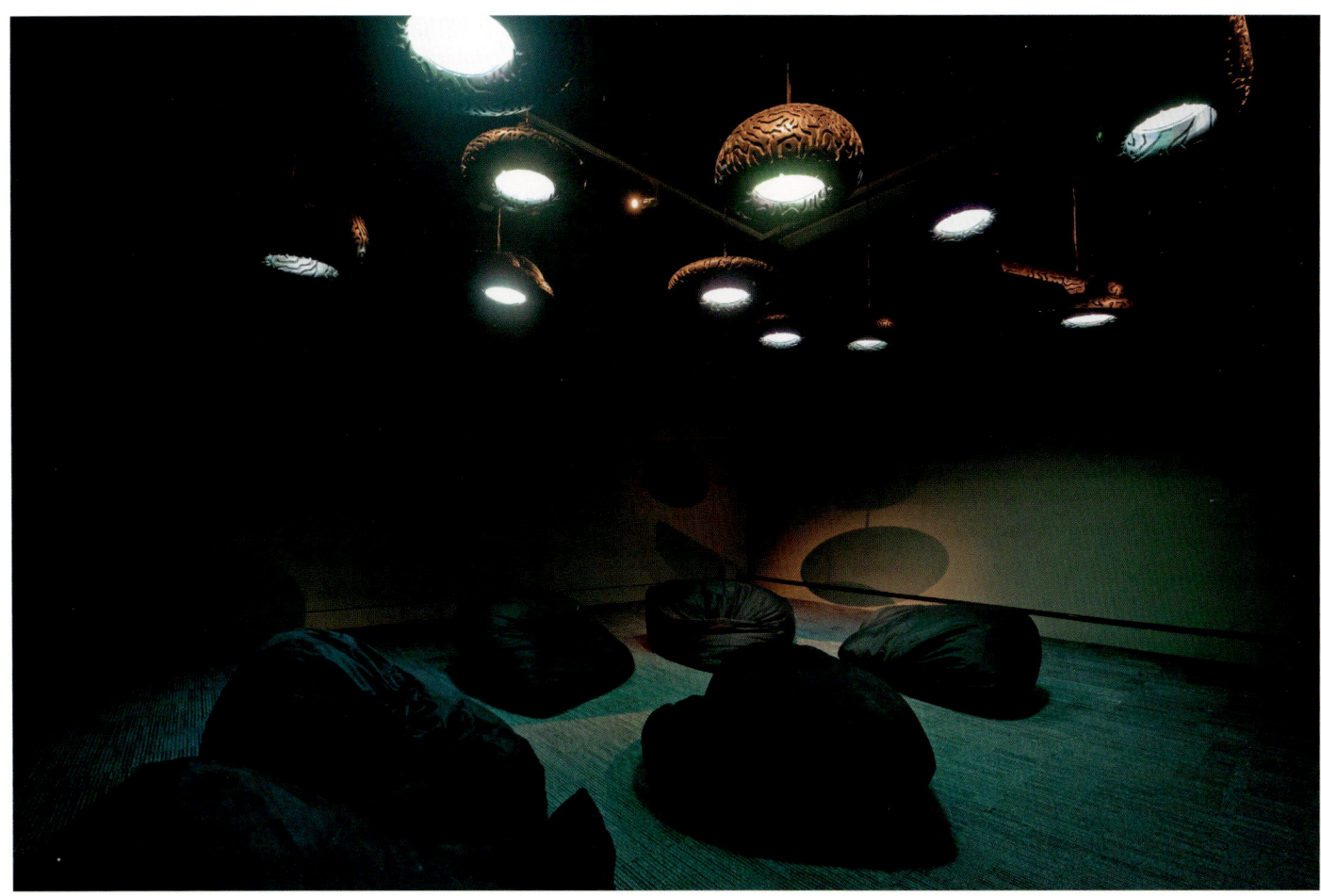

**Brett Graham and Rachael Rakena, *U.F.O.B.*, 2006**
wood, glass, video and sound installation, Dowse Art Museum,
photograph by Mark Tantrum

reconfigured as *Aniwaniwa* (and then home to Waikato Museum in 2008); and Fiona Pardington's *Nabokov's Blues: The Charmed Circle* at the Honolulu Biennial in 2017, and later exhibited at the London Art Fair (2018), Art Basel Hong Kong (2018) and at the New York Public Library. Most of these works start and/or end at home. As their works and their ideas circulate, so too does the prominence of Māori art.

### Contemporary Māori art and the market

Just as the spiral moves through time and space, so too does the art market. Increasingly Māori are being 'picked up' by dealer galleries overseas, who include them in exhibitions as well as contract them to create work: Shane Cotton, for instance, has shown his work at the Asia Society Museum (New York), Anna Schwartz Gallery (Melbourne) and Museum of Contemporary Art (Sydney); and Rangi Kipa built an entire house for a major exhibition at the Museum of Contemporary Art in Denver, while he was on the Creative New Zealand Craft/Object Art Fellowship residency in Thailand in 2006 – a truly global affair.

Māori art is also seen in major private art galleries – such as the now closed Spirit Wrestler Gallery in Vancouver, which created a strong network of Indigenous visual artists with ongoing exhibitions, as well as an exchange system where artists attended workshops in Hawai'i and Aotearoa New Zealand. In 2006 Spirit Wrestler hosted the exhibition *Manawa: Pacific Heartbeat*, and produced a high-quality catalogue of the same name, as a celebration of ten years of its existence. The gallery's close relationship with Māori began in 1999 when the painter June Northcroft Grant (Ngāti Tūhourangi, Ngāti Wahiao, Ngāti Tūwharetoa) and carver Roi Toia (Ngāti Hine, Ngāpuhi) first walked into the gallery; this moment was the catalyst for Māori involvement in the exhibition *Fusion: Tradition & Discovery* later that year, which showcased the work of ceramicists Colleen Waata Urlich and Manos Nathan, jeweller Alex Nathan (Te Roroa, Ngāpuhi,

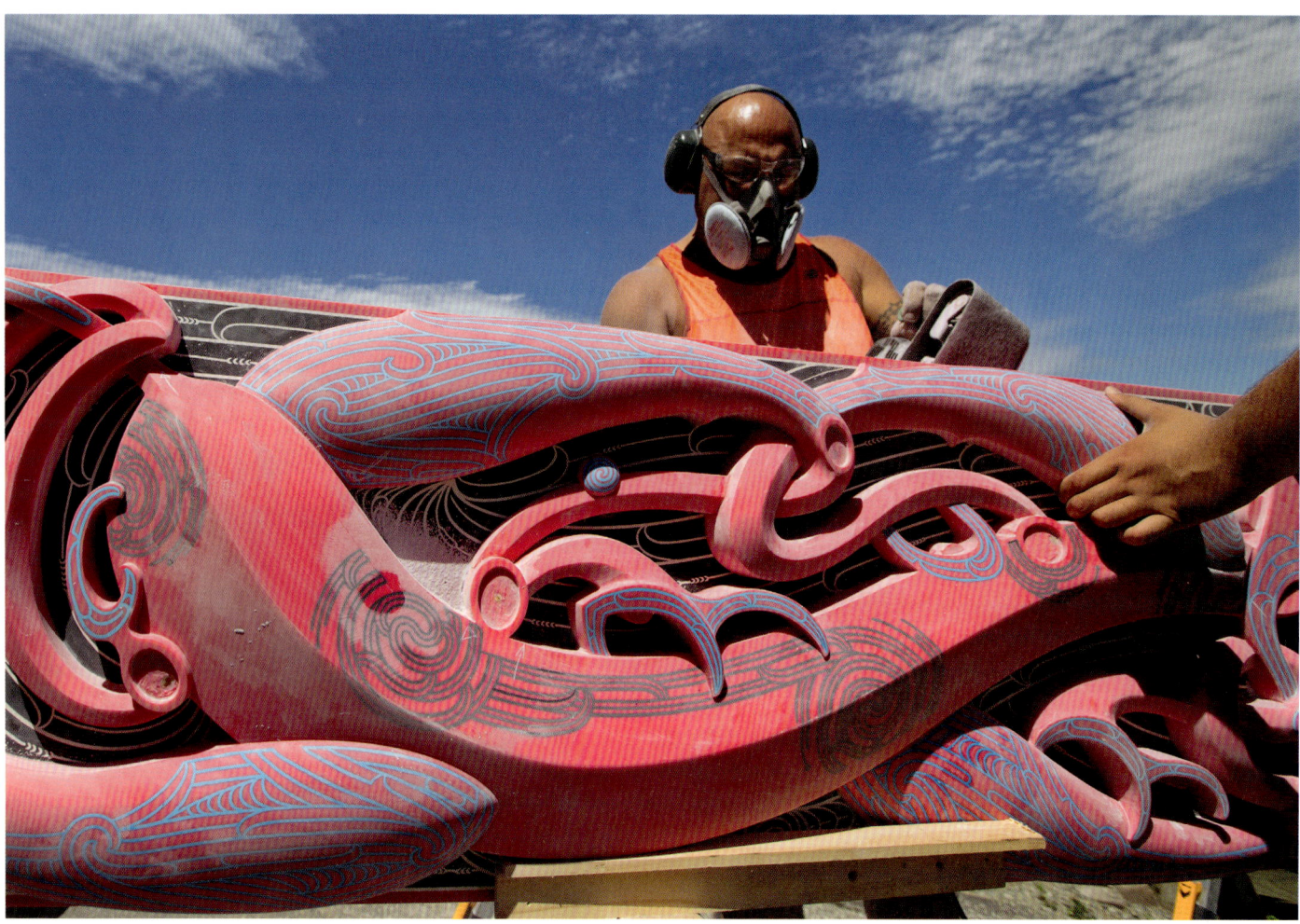

Rangi Kipa working on the Te Papa artwork, 2019.
photograph by Norm Heke

Ngāti Whātua), and Toia, alongside Native American, Northwest Coast and Inuit artists.[19]

There are few opportunities to buy Māori art online from retailers as opposed to from the artists themselves or from their dealers. The Poi Room, with Melanie-Jane Smith (Ngāti Porou) as creative director, has a strong base of Māori artists,[20] as do Kura Gallery (established 1998 in Wellington and Auckland) and Āhua Māori virtual art gallery, run by Te Puia and the New Zealand Māori Arts and Crafts Institute. Some Māori artists have their own websites, through which they reach a global audience: Bill (Ngāpuhi) and Anne Rawiri (Ngāti Whātua, Te Rarawa) sell their carving and textiles through maoriartsgallery.co.nz; weaver Veranoa Hetet (Ngāti Maniapoto, Ngāti Tūwharetoa) and carver Sam Hauwaho (Tūhoe, Te Aitanga a Hauiti) offer popular online courses in making kete, tāniko and weaving through www.hetetschoolofmaoriart.com;[21] and other artists, such as Rangi Kipa, Lisa Reihana, Natalie Robertson and Fiona Pardington, also have their own websites to share their artwork and history.

Māori art is showcased in the Māori Art Market (MAM), which is held every two years by Toi Māori, a charitable trust established in 1996 to promote Māori art. It is modelled on the very successful Indian Art Market in Santa Fe, Arizona, which attracts hundreds of artists selling to thousands of art lovers and tourists. In 2019 MAM was held in Wellington and attracted 250 artists and over 3000 visits over a three-day period. Many Māori groups associated with Toi Māori were involved, including Te Uhi a Mataora (moko experts), Te Roopu Raranga Whatu o Aotearoa (weavers) and Te Ātinga (contemporary Māori visual artists).

## Festivals, biennales and triennials

Māori art can be viewed globally across a wide spectrum of events. While for many artists internationally the pinnacle of their career might be exhibiting at the celebrated Venice

Biennale, for others the Festival of Pacific Arts and Culture (Pacific Arts Festival) offers an environment where they can practise whakawhanaungatanga and connect with their Pacific cousins. There is no one right way to 'be a Māori artist'. Mead would include those taught in wānanga such as Toihoukura (Gisborne), Toimairangi (Hastings) and Toioho ki Āpiti (Palmerston North), where students are immersed in the arts and also in te reo Māori me ōna tikanga (Māori language and protocols). Art made in these institutions is often inflected with core values that are imbued in the students as part of their studies, and many steer towards artistic forms with clear references to Te Ao Māori, such as kōwhaiwhai and carving.

For others, especially those who have studied at university, their work pushes the edges of Māori art. Often they have been exposed to a wide range of Euro-American art forms and traditions, through the artistic background of their teachers and the pedagogies of universities. To be Māori in those places is often a challenge in itself, and there are few Māori role models on the teaching staff to manaaki (support) them. The home lives of students are broad, with some being raised within whānau close to marae, while others know that they are Māori but have no further understanding of what that means. In all cases, the ways in which they negotiate their identity as Māori are often depicted in the artworks.

Opportunities for Indigenous artists from different cultures to work alongside each other are still rare. One of the most important opportunities is during the Pacific Arts Festival. Held every four years in a different Pacific nation, these ten-day festivals provide a space in which artists can come together and share their practices. The first was held in 1972 in Suva, Fiji under the umbrella theme of 'Preserving Culture'; the most recent was in 2016 in Guam, where over 2000 attendees came together for two weeks to think through the theme of 'United Voices of the Pacific'. The next festival was scheduled for June 2024 in Hawai'i,[22] with plans for several visual arts events, including an arts market, body ornamentation, carving, a fashion and wearable art show, film, floral arts, tattoo, weaving, and a Pacific Island Queen pageant for LGBTQ Pacific peoples. Creative New Zealand will fund a delegation to the festival that will include contemporary Māori and Pacific artists, and Ngā Tūmanako, winners of the 2019 Te Matatini national kapa haka festival.[23]

Other artists regularly attend the Polynesia Tatau tattoo convention, held over four days in Tahiti. The event attracts more than sixty artists who work alongside each other, learning a variety of styles and techniques, and reinforces the importance of the art form as a living tradition, linking Indigenous artists across the Pacific. Moko practitioners also attend mainstream tattoo conventions both near and far, such as the annual Auckland International Tattoo Convention, and work on commission in Australia, the United States and Britain. Many of these artists and practitioners are part of Te Uhi a Mataora, a national collective of moko artists, who meet to support one another and the art form. They maintain their links through regular wānanga and other events where they can work alongside each other and learn from each other in their practice.

Other moko practitioners are based overseas and have regular commission work. Te Rangitu Netana (Ngāpuhi, Ngāti Wai, Te Arawa) has been based in Suffolk, England since 2015, working on his whakairo rākau and moko practice. He was initially trained by his father and grandfather, and later by Samoan tatau master Sua Sulu'ape Paulo II, who taught him the hand-tapping technique that he has also used for moko. Netana then began using the uhi, which produces a unique style of moko where the skin is literally incised, leaving deep grooves on the skin's surface. In an interesting trans-Pacific twist, Keone Nunes, a Hawaiian master of hand-tapping, gifted Netana with a moko kanohi, a full-face moko. Such practices of placing different Pacific community's marks on others from outside the community is contentious: in 2001 Netana placed a design on singer Robbie Williams's shoulder, and in 2019 he was commissioned by French designer Hermès to design a scarf for them. The use of moko designs by fashion houses has historically been problematic as they have misappropriated Māori and other Indigenous designs for the sake of fashion with little interest in their sources or – just as importantly – the social and political structures that have enabled them to do so.

Some Māori artists build strong relationships with museums, and this has led to innovative work. George Nuku has been based overseas for many years (he is currently living in France with his whānau), and his art practice has often hinged on his personal relationships with people in museums, with whom he has worked on numerous commissions – over fifty to date, in New Zealand and overseas (see pages 488–91). He is known for his carving, creating not only architectural forms but also waka and adornments. His work uses distinctive materials such as Plexiglass and polystyrene that reflect his contemporary world, as well as more traditional resources such as pounamu, stone and bone. In the exhibition *Bottled Ocean 2118,* at the MTG Hawke's Bay Tai Ahuriri, Napier, he worked collaboratively with the local community and school groups to project what life might look like for the Pacific in the year 2118 and to consider how fish and other sea animals might adapt to environmental pressures, such as the accumulation of plastic.[24] Conservation issues are a global concern, and one that joins Indigenous peoples across the moana, particularly with the imminent threat of rising sea-levels and the impact on atolls such as Kiribati and Tuvalu. Artists have responded to climate change in their work, as Nuku's work demonstrates.

International biennales and triennales have provided a platform for Māori artists to showcase their work. The Venice Biennale is the world's oldest contemporary art exhibition (established 1895). Since 2001 New Zealand has sent artists to represent this country, many of them Māori, including Peter Robinson and Jacqueline Fraser with *Bi-Polar* (2001), Brett Graham and Rachael Rakena with *Aniwaniwa* (2007), Michael Parekōwhai with *On First Looking into Chapman's Homer* (2011) and Lisa Reihana with *Emissaries* (2017). Māori have been involved in other aspects of the Venice Biennales, too, as catalogue writers (Shelley Jahnke-Bishop, 2009; Cushla Parekōwhai, 2011; Megan Tamati-Quennell, 2017), project writers (Tanea Heke, 2009), designers (Neil Pardington, 2001, 2014) and attendants (Megan Tamati-Quennell, 2001; Gina Matchitt, 2013; Talei Siʻilata, 2017). Significantly, in 2024 all eight artists selected for Venice were Māori. We look forward to seeing a Māori curator of the Venice Biennale some time soon.

The Asia Pacific Triennial (APT), based at the Queensland Art Gallery and Gallery of Modern Art in Brisbane, has welcomed a number of Māori artists over the years. In the first iteration in 1993, the APT profiled seventy-six artists and over two hundred artworks, including painter Robyn Kahukiwa and sculptor Selwyn Muru, whose works were a balance between both traditional and contemporary. The ninth triennial (APT9, 2018–2019) included four Māori among the group of eighty artists and collectives: Peter Robinson, Areta Wilkinson, Lisa Reihana and James Tylor. While the first three have been regulars on the international scene, Tylor is probably not as well known here in Aotearoa.

He draws on his broad Nunga (Kaurna), Te Arawa, English, Scottish, Irish, Dutch, Iberian, Norwegian and Australian whakapapa to tease out themes of colonisation and migration. His drawn and photographic works are reminiscent of Tracey Tawhiao's (Ngāiterangi, Whakatōhea, Ngāti Tūwharetoa) drawings, and explore juxtaposing Māori designs drawn from tāniko, kōwhaiwhai and whakairo with other designs that play with form, colour and scale. In APT9, Tylor's work used a restricted palette of black, red, white and shades of light brown and olive green to form wide borders that framed mainly black-and-white photographs. Displayed together, the works offer visual stimulation and link, through these designs, with the artist's whakapapa.

Two other recent biennales have featured Māori and Pacific artists in different ways. The 4th International Casablanca Biennale in Morocco (October–December 2018), entitled *A Maternal Lens*, involved Ema Tavola (Fiji) as one of four curators, and the artist line-up included Margaret Aull (Te Rarawa, Ngāti Tūwharetoa, Fiji), Leilani Kake, Julia Mageʻau Gray (Papua, Mekeo), Kolokesa Mahina-Tuai (Tonga) and Vaimaila Urale (Sāmoa). Tongan art historian Nina Tonga[25] curated the exhibition *To Make Wrong/Right/Now* for the Honolulu Biennale (March–May 2019) at ten locations. The biennale featured forty-seven artists and art collectives, of whom twenty-five were Indigenous, including four Māori: Natalie Robertson, Janet Lilo (Niue, Ngāpuhi, Sāmoa), Jeremy Leatinuʻu (Ngāti Maniapoto, Sāmoa) and the Mataaho Collective. One of the most recent exhibitions, the 14th Gwangju Biennale in South Korea, featured Mataaho's *Takapau* (2022) as the sole Māori work. In 2024, Nigel Borell curated *Indigenous Histories* for art galleries in Sao Paulo, Brazil and Oslo, Norway. He also advised curator Adriano Pedrosa's selection of Māori art for the 60th International Art Exhibition, La Biennale di Venezia (2024). The increasing presence of Māori in these exhibitions demonstrates an acute awareness by art worlds globally of the distinctive power of Māori (and Pacific) voices, and the ways in which their perspectives and artworks make statements about the complexity of their own worlds.

### Indigenous art exhibitions

The art world is a complex beast, and one that is constantly changing. Māori artists have increased opportunities to exhibit their work outside New Zealand because of the

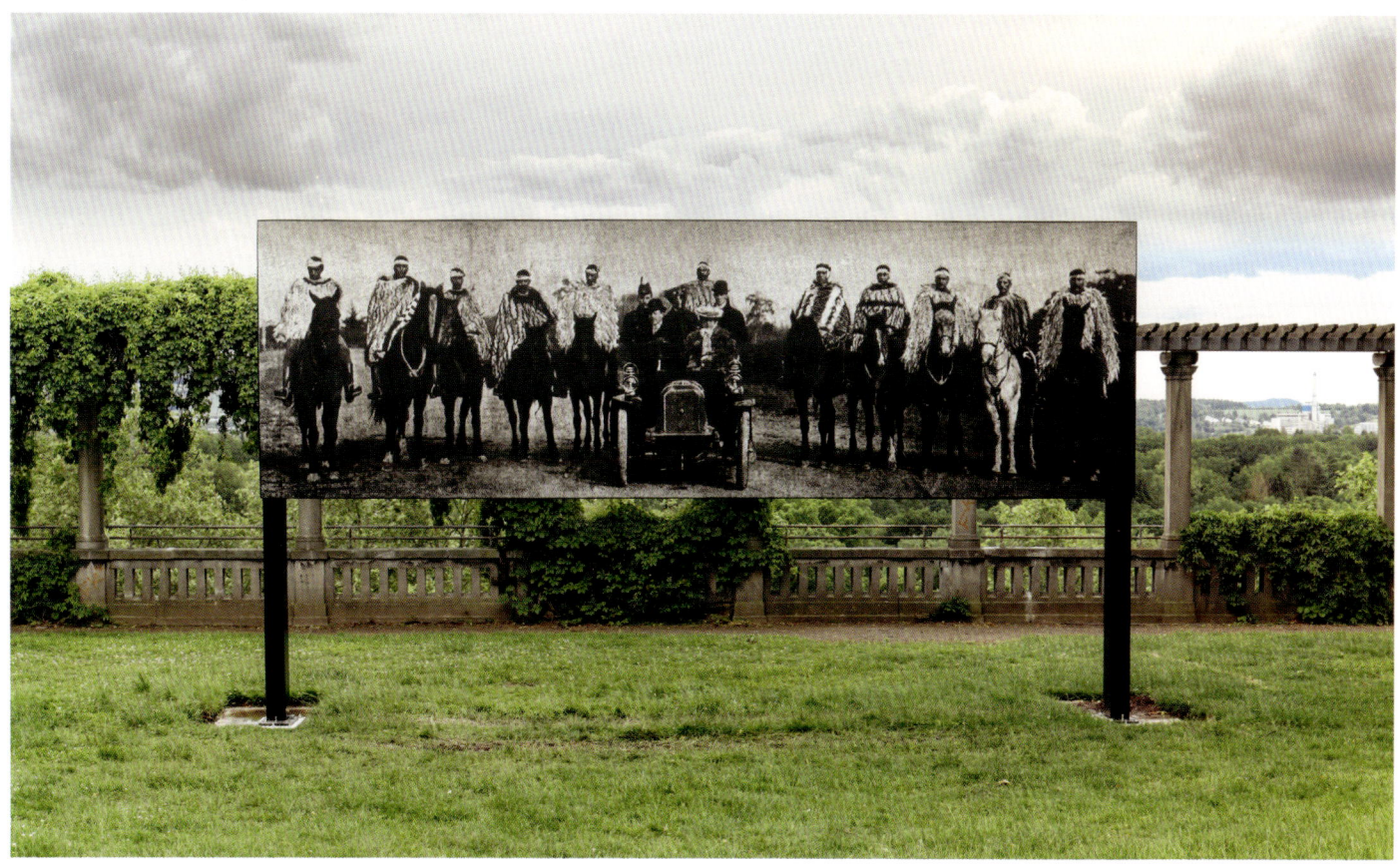

Nathan Pohio, *Raise the anchor, unfurl the sails, set course to the centre of an ever setting sun!*, 2015
commissioned by SCAPE Public Art, photograph by Liz Eve

constant travel of artists, their works and reputations. Chadwick Allen's concept of trans-Indigenous is explicit in events such as the Sydney Biennale which, in 2020, was curated by an Aboriginal Australian curator and included several Indigenous artists. The exhibition *Sakahàn: International Indigenous Art* (2013, National Gallery of Canada) was curated by Greg Hill (Kanyen'kehà:ka, Six Nations of the Grand River Territory) and Candice Hopkins along with Christine Lalonde, the NGC's non-Indigenous curator of Indigenous art. *Sakahàn* included the work of eighty artists, whom David Garneau described as 'members of this cosmopolitan cohort'.[26] This included four Māori artists who were all regulars on the global Indigenous scene: Lisa Reihana, Brett Graham, Rachael Rakena and Michael Parekōwhai. All four had been to Venice and are regular contributors to major New Zealand art exhibitions.

Some contemporary art exhibitions globally stand out from the others because of the calibre of the curators and artist involved. They have a reputation as being exclusive because of this, and previously could even be said to be excluding. But one exhibition, *documenta* in Kassel, Germany, reversed this in its 2017 iteration. Begun in 1955, *documenta* occurs every five years and lasts for 100 days. The 2017 *documenta 14* took place in the same year as the Venice Biennale and Art Basel, and that year for the first time, it was held on two sites – in Athens (8 April to 16 July) and in Kassel (10 June to 17 September). It was also the first time any New Zealand, let alone Māori, artists were involved: Ralph Hotere and Mataaho Collective in Kassel, and Nathan Pohio at both venues. Funding from Creative New Zealand enabled the curators to come to New Zealand over a two-year period, under the international delegate programme Te Manu Ka Tau, to gain an understanding of the Māori dynamic.

Nathan Pohio's *Raise the anchor, unfurl the sails, set course to the centre of an ever setting sun!* (2015) had previously been exhibited in New Zealand. The artwork, as presented in the Walters Prize exhibition (2016) and for *documenta 14*, comprises two different large-scale photographic works printed onto billboards. It captures a moment in which the British governor-general and his wife, Lord and Lady Plunket,

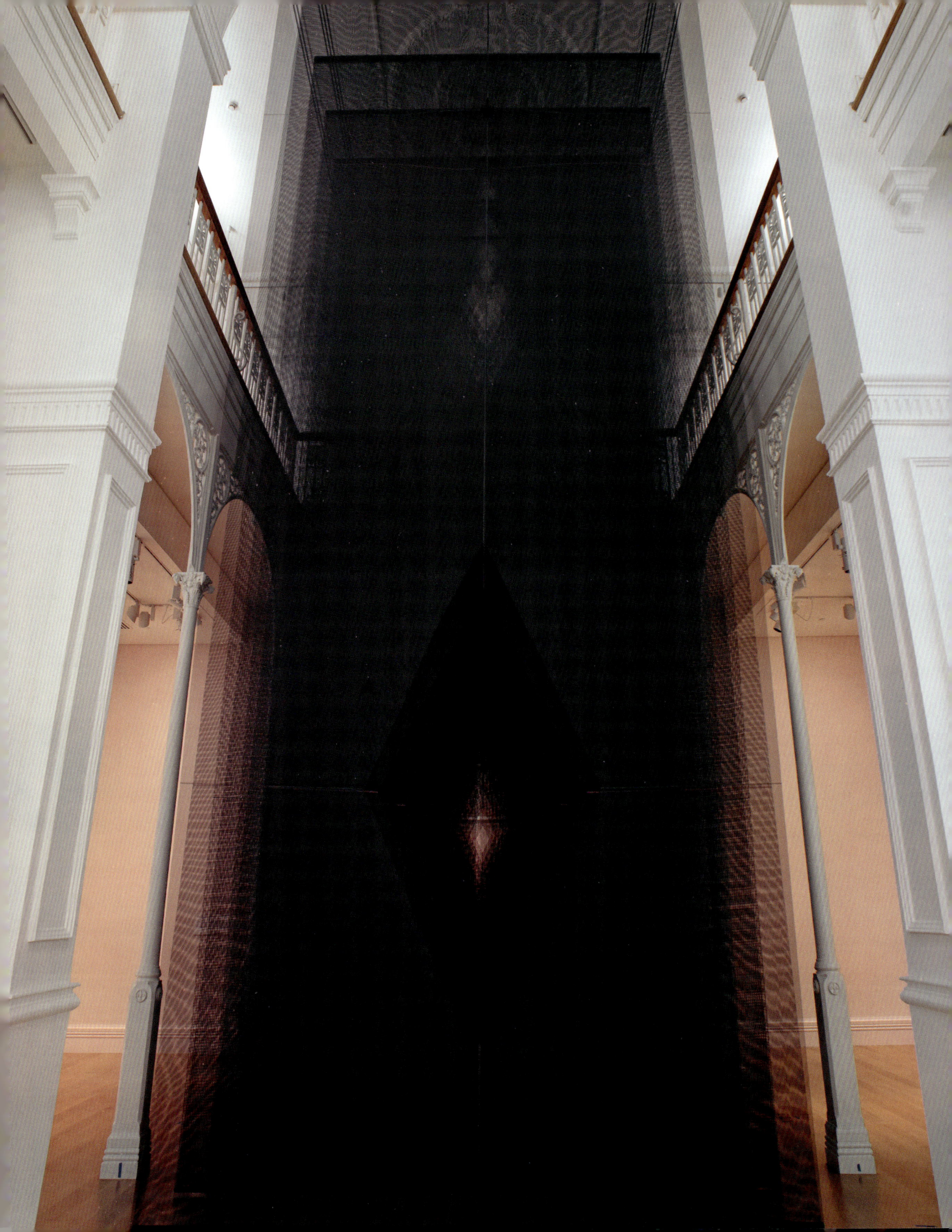

visit the settlement of Tuahiwi, a small kāinga to the north of Christchurch where Pohio lives. Māori and Pākehā alike are dressed formally, as befits the occasion of a pōwhiri. But these are not just artworks, and not just photographs: they represent the grandfathers and grandmothers of Ngāi Tuahiwi today, and operate within a Māori worldview of the practice of revering ancestors in photographs *as* the people depicted, rather than as an image of them. This is evidenced by the mihi whakatau (tribal farewell) when the works left New Zealand for Europe.[27] This cultural practice is similar to the treatment of Lindauer's Māori portraits when they travelled to Europe in 2016, and is what makes one aspect of Māori art distinctly and actively Māori.

The Mataaho Collective represents a new direction in contemporary practice. They are a shining light for Massey University, from which all four Māori women graduated: Erena Baker (Te Ātiawa ki Whakarongotai, Ngāti Toa), Sarah Hudson (Ngāti Awa, Ngāi Tūhoe), Bridget Reweti (Ngāti Ranginui, Ngāiterangi) and Terri Te Tau (Rangitāne ki Wairarapa). Their artwork was nationally recognised when they won the 2021 Walters Prize, and were appointed Arts Foundation Laureates the following year. Their work for the 2019 Honolulu Biennale, *Kiko Moana*, was the result of a wānanga process where they collaborated with weaver and researcher Maureen Lander on ideas about the taniwha. Mataaho reconfigured common blue tarpaulin to examine ideas of multiple Indigenous voices and to promote 'taniwha attributes such as protection, assistance with travel and harbingers of potential danger'.[28] Mataaho's methodology of collective practice continues the ohu style of working as a group, which was popular in the past in the making of art forms such as waka taua and whare whakairo. Other examples of Māori collectives are House of Natives Aotearoa, Paemanu – Ngāi Tahu Contemporary Visual Arts, The Roots and Kaihaukai.[29] Working as a group seems to come naturally for some Māori artists, who draw strength from working side by side with others, especially when working as Māori in an international context.

Monumentality is a crucial aspect of the work of Mataaho. In 2012 their *Te Whare Pora* (exhibited in Wellington, Masterton and Christchurch, 2013–2017) featured a large-scale textile made up of black minky blankets – a type of blanket often seen in homes and in wharenui, but transformed here to be 'a vehicle to explore customary notions of wānanga, contemporary

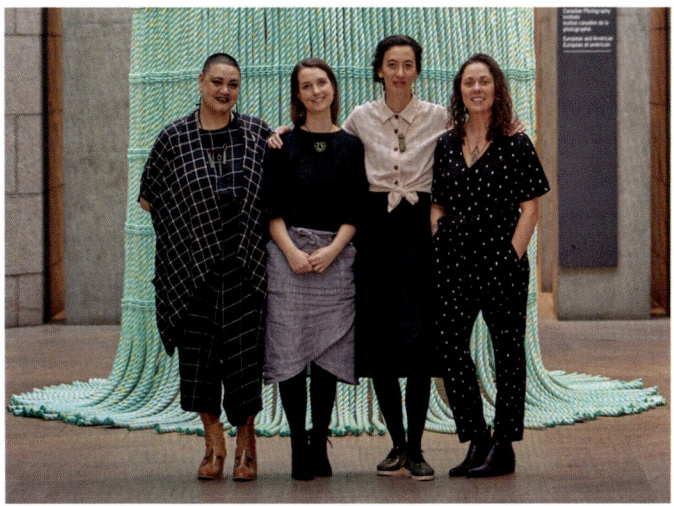

Mataaho Collective in front of *AKA*.
photo courtesy of National Gallery of Canada

**Opposite: Mataaho Collective and Maureen Lander, *Atapō*, 2020**
mixed media, commissioned by Auckland Art Gallery Toi o Tāmaki, 2019, X2020/70, photograph by Jennifer French

marae styles and women's experiences'.[30] In this way their work is similar to Cook Islands artist Ani O'Neill's *Kua Marino Te Tai* (1994) with its plaited florist ribbon, Lonnie Hutchinson's *Light My Fire* (2016), where she used large-scale patterned textile forms. Because of the size, the work becomes experiential and invokes a sense of grandeur and wonder.

It is no surprise that Ralph Hotere was chosen to be included in *documenta 14*.[31] His works transcend time and space through the simplicity of form and depth of meaning they embody. The *Malady Panels* (1971, acrylic on canvas, 1802 × 7605 millimetres) are seven works with a circle in the top two thirds, barely perceptible in the inky black background from which it emerges and recedes. The panels are part of Hotere's iconic *Black Paintings* series, in which he explored the power of the colour black, not as something bad (as European colour symbolism often suggests), but as a place of creative potential (for Māori, who come from Te Pō, the darkness, it is a place where we began). *Malady* refers to a poem by Bill Manhire that plays on the words 'malady', 'melody' and 'my lady', which inspired a series of Hotere's works from 1970. His inclusion in *documenta* demonstrates how his works continue to have relevance to new generations of artists and critics. At the 60th Venice Biennale in 2024, Mataaho won the prestigious Golden Lion award for a curated exhibition for their work *Takapau* (2022).

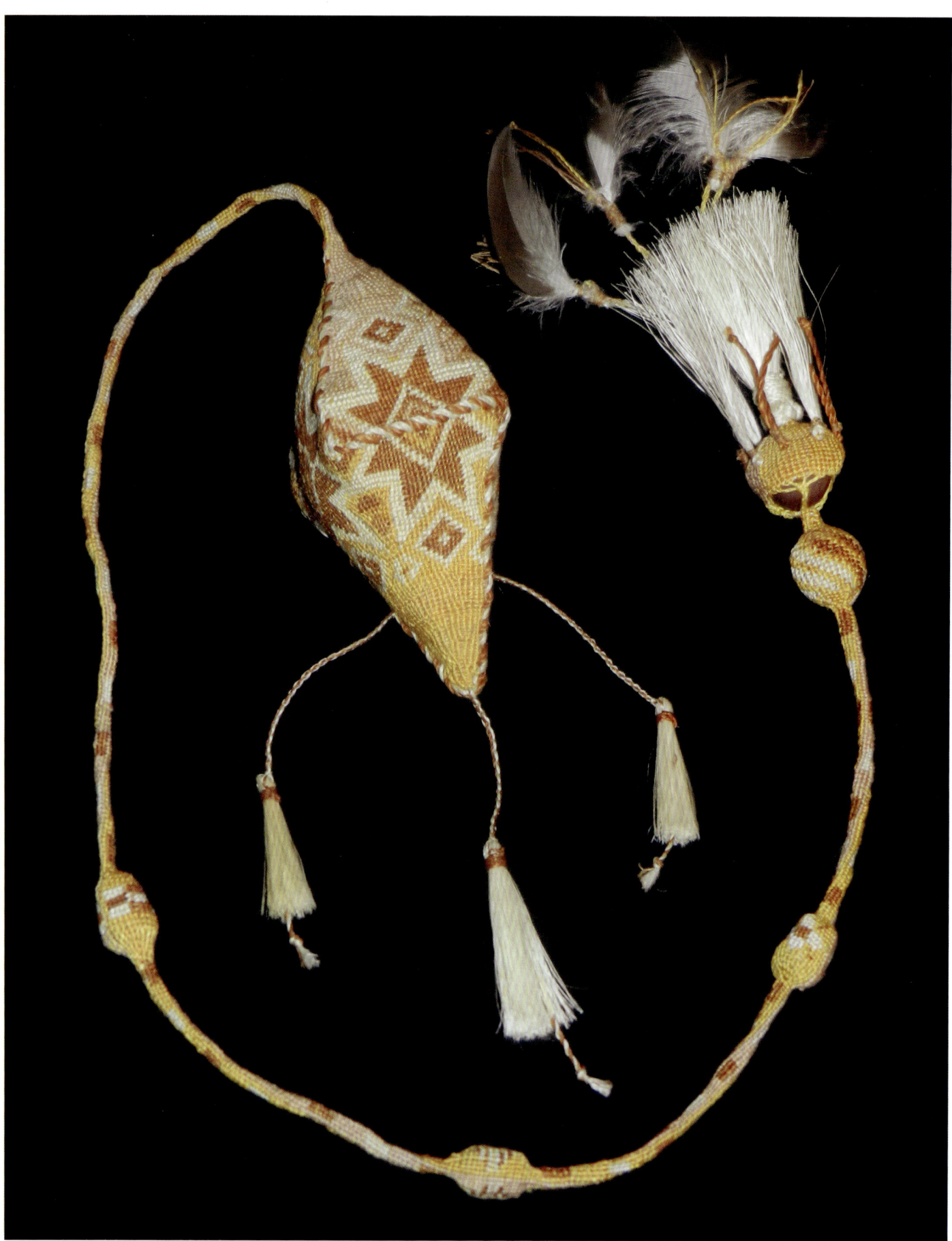

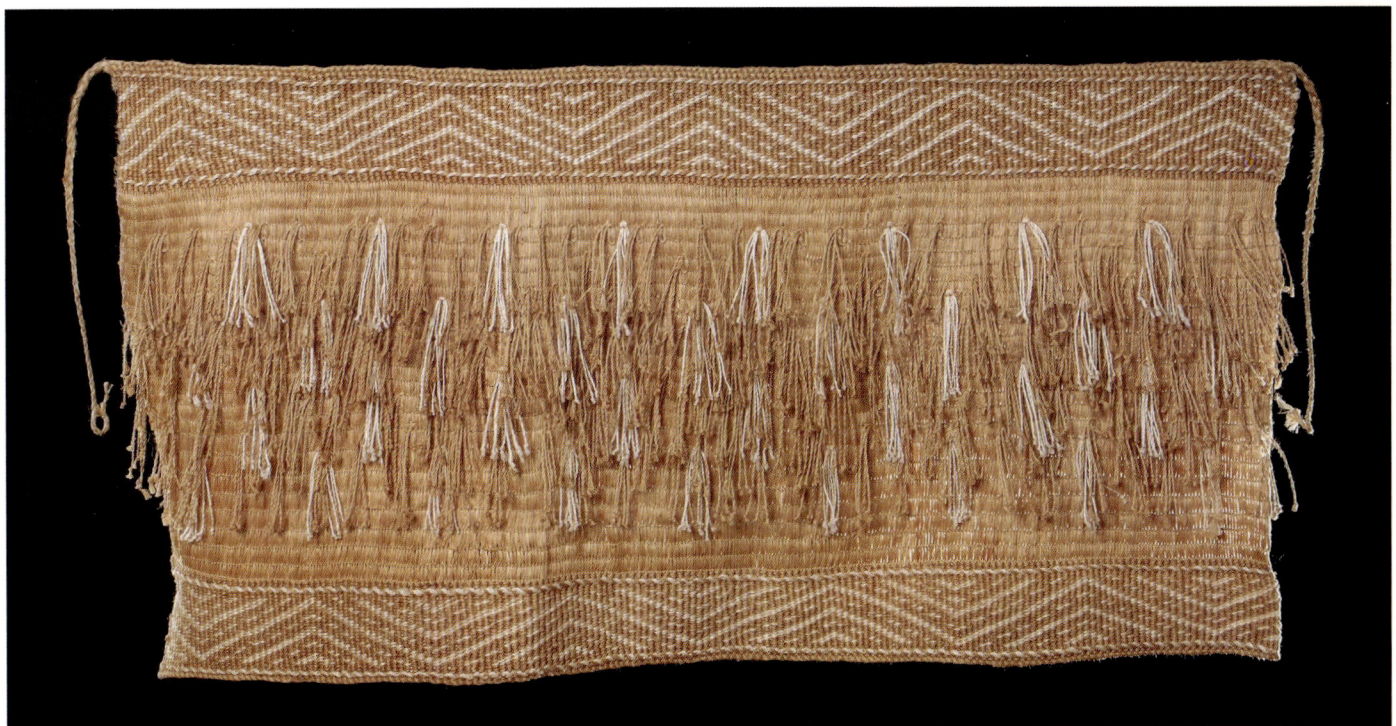

## Māori residencies funded through Te Waka Toi/Creative New Zealand

Māori artists have engaged with the international scene in ways other than exhibitions. Indigenous-focused events and residencies are crucial in promoting Māori art as intimately related to wider issues of culture and politics in the global Indigenous landscape. Māori artists have been actively seeking out opportunities to work alongside other Indigenous artists to form support networks in terms of the kaupapa of their work, as the experiences of Indigenous peoples are shared.

Creative New Zealand (CNZ) has funded a series of residencies across different Indigenous nations,[32] including one of the longest-running, the Toi Sqwigwialtxw Residency. Begun in 2006 in Washington State, this joint venture was initiated by arts advocate Elizabeth Ellis and painter Sandy Adsett when they were on Te Waka Toi, the Māori Arts Board of CNZ, and worked with the Longhouse Education and Cultural Center, Evergreen State College, in Olympia, Washington, led by its founder Tina Kuckkhan-Miller (Ojibwe).[33] Toi Māori (a branch of CNZ) also has an artist-in-residence programme as part of its Māori outreach to Native American artists; in 2017, for instance, carver Alex McCarty (Makah) spent two months in New Zealand. Māori recipients have included the carver Takirirangi Smith (2007), painter

Karl Rangikawhiti Leonard, *Rāpaki named Rongomai*, 2006
muka, Te Papa Tongarewa Museum of New Zealand, ME024024, purchased 2010

Opposite: Karl Rangikawhiti Leonard, *Te hononga o ngā wai – Waters meet*, 2012
muka, dogbane, eagle down; dyes – tanekaha, manono, harakeke; contains pipestone, riverstone, roadstone, sweetgrass and sage, private collection

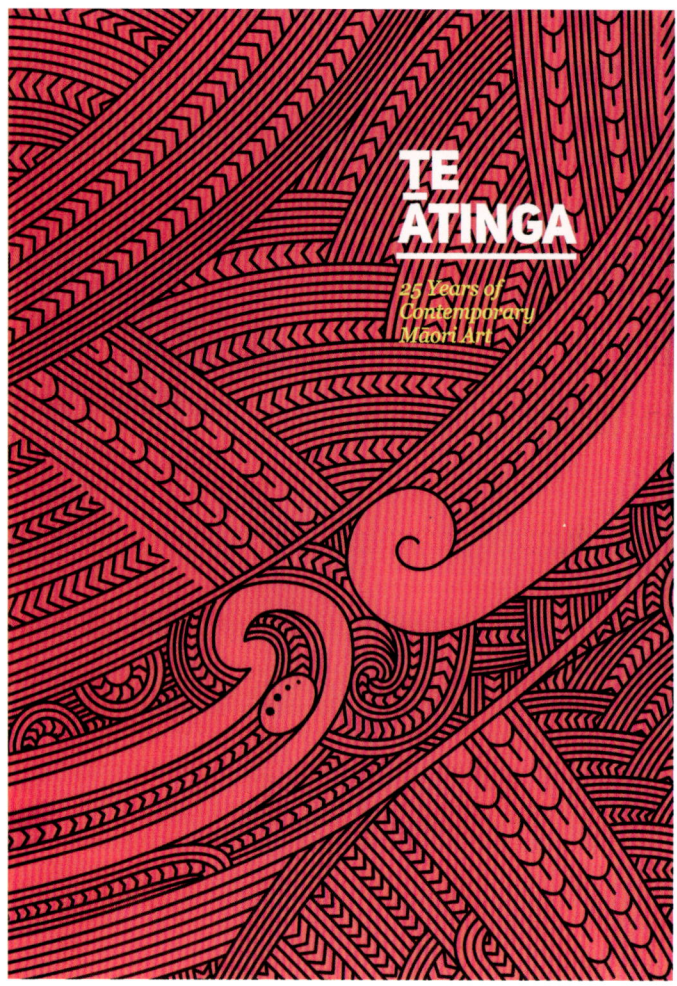

Cover of *Te Ātinga: 25 years of Contemporary Māori Art*, edited by curator-artist Nigel Borell (Toi Maori Aotearoa/Maori Art New Zealand and the Te Ātinga-Contemporary Visual Arts Committee, 2013).

June Northcroft Grant (2008), visual and performing artists Henare Tahuri (Ngāti Kahungunu, Ngāi Tūhoe) and Tāwera Tahuri (Ngā Ariki Kaipūtahi, Whakatōhea, Te Rarawa, Ngāti Uenuku, Tūwharetoa) (2010), and weaver Karl Leonard (2012), whose uncle was Kaka Niao, and who was trained as a carver by his father and another uncle; he was inspired by his grandmother Ranginui Parewahawaha Leonard, who was still weaving after she turned 100).[34] As a measure of the relationship, a carving house was opened at Evergreen College in April 2019; the design for the house was led by carver Lyonel Grant, with other work by Rangi Kipa. At the opening there was a special performance by Henare and Tāwera Tahuri. In doing so they reinforced the ways in which the connections between Indigenous artists remain strong.

CNZ and the Banff Centre for Arts and Creativity have partnered to offer Indigenous residency programmes for established Indigenous visual and performing artists at the centre in Canada. Over the years several Māori artists have taken part in the programme, including Natalie Robertson and Hemi Macgregor (2004), and Johnson Witehira and Rachael Rakena (2019). These residencies are now part of CNZ's recent Cultural and Art Form Exchange Programme.

There are few other Indigenous residencies. One at the University of Hawai'i at Manoa is offered every two years for five to ten weeks; CNZ covers the airfare, accommodation and expenses, including mentorship and networking. Before this was set up, the relationship between the University of Hawai'i and Māori had been initiated in some measure by Brett Graham, who studied for his MFA at the East–West Center at the university in 1989. Graham has since gone on to participate in residencies, in New York (2014) and at the University of Lethbridge, Canada (2016). Further placements are on a more ad hoc basis, initiated by overseas groups. In 2017, for instance, Charlotte Graham (Pare Hauraki, Pare Waikato) was funded by the Fundación Mar Adentro (a private foundation in Santiago) to go to southern Chile for a one-month residency at Bosque Pehuén, to connect with local Mapuche peoples. This was the result of the Art Te Manu Ka Tau: Flying Friends programme funded by CNZ, as part of which the Fundación's director was brought to New Zealand in 2015 to discuss the programme.

It is not only the artists who have these opportunities to work alongside Indigenous cousins. The Indigenous Curators Exchange was a three-year partnership between New Zealand, Canada and Australia, established in 2015 to 'share knowledge, cultural practice and networks'.[35] In that year a group of Aboriginal, Māori, First Nations and Sami curators met at the APT8 in Australia, followed by another hui in 2016 in New Zealand with thirteen curators, and in 2017 in Canada. Those involved are Megan Tamati-Quennell, Nigel Borell, Reuben Friend and Karl Chitham (director, Dowse Art Museum).[36] Most recently they have produced a book, *Sovereign Words: Indigenous Art, Curation and Criticism* (2018),[37] which examines the state of Indigeneity across the art and the museum world.

## Conclusion

When reflecting on the variety of activities in which Māori artists are engaged globally, it is important to place these within an Indigenous framework. Some of this kōrero is centred on the United Nations Declaration on the Rights of Indigenous Peoples (UNDRIP), 2007. Jolene Rickard has written of the implications of the declaration for Indigenous arts, and the ways in which it embodies notions of sovereignty that need to be integrated across all spheres of society.[38] New Zealand voted against the declaration in 2007, along with the United States and Australia, despite 144 of the 155 nation members of the UN supporting it. New Zealand has since changed its position, though controversially, when the then minister of Māori affairs, the Honourable Dr Pita Sharples, turned up at the UN Permanent Forum on Indigenous Peoples in New York and announced New Zealand's change of stance – confirmed later that day (20 April 2010) by the minister of justice at Parliament in Wellington.

One of the arguments of this book is for Māori art to be seen as part of a larger movement for and about Indigenous art. David Garneau argues that:[39]

> Indigenous criticism of Indigenous art begins with the knowledge that you are part of a community. Whatever you say or otherwise publish is delivered with care because you know that you will be held accountable by virtual neighbours. In Indigenous criticism of Indigenous art there is no critical distance of the Modernist sort.

The Māori world is anchored by whakawhanaungatanga – relationships between individuals and across communities. Indigenous art critics are often torn between expectations of their writing in a global art context, and expectations of supporting Māori. Indigenous art historians are not here merely to chart the history, but also to comment on it, and to consider it within wider ideas driven from our identity as Māori. Jim Vivieaere commented on this:

> Firstly 'outsider critics' tend to bypass, minimize, or stereotype the spiritual and cultural dimension of the art. Therefore the complexities, depths, and nuances of the artists' practices are misunderstood or unseen. Secondly, the very process of describing and engaging with the art is a similar kind of appropriation to so many other historical appropriations and thefts that there is a sense that this type of engagement should simply not occur.[40]

Contemporary artists today work in a fluid environment, where their horizons extend globally. The internet has enabled artworks and their makers to be known on an international stage as they are included on websites of galleries and dealers, blogged about by critics, and discussed in online research articles. Cheaper air travel and increased opportunities such as residencies have enabled artists to move around different countries, learning and sharing their practice and forging important relationships across cultures. This can lead to trans-Indigenous workshops and collaborations and gatherings. These are ongoing, and ensure that Māori artists keep the layers of Māori art constantly evolving.

In November 2019, the 9th International Indigenous Artists Gathering Pūhoro ō Mua, Pūhoro ki Tua, organised by Te Ātinga, took place at Tūrangawaewae Marae, Ngāruawāhia. There was an exhibition at Waikato Museum (24 November 2019–3 February 2020) curated by Nigel Borell and Leafa Wilson (Sāmoa, Vaimoso and Siumu villages), with daytrips on waka and to the Waitomo Caves. This was the latest in a series of wānanga that began in 1995 in Rotorua, and have been hosted in New Zealand (2000, 2005, 2010, 2014) and in the United States (2001, 2007, 2017).[41] Te Ātinga has started forays into art writing also, with the release of a book named after the group.[42] It was done, in part, to provide an insider's/artist's perspective of Māori art and – perhaps this is a shift that we might see more of – artists, increasingly with a postgraduate degree (such as Borell, Huhana Smith, Ngatai Taepa and Robert Jahnke), writing about their own practice from the perspective of the makers. Is this one strategy to increase the baseline of writing about Māori art? Let's hope so.

*Toi Te Mana* is deliberately subtitled 'An Indigenous History of Māori Art'. The aim has been to draw on values and concepts that anchor te ao Māori, and reinforce the ways in which art is a critical vehicle through which Māori have been able to promote and reflect change. Contemporary practice brings together Indigenous artists who are drawn together by virtue of shared experiences of living in countries that have a colonial past. This work is important, as it shapes Māori lives today, joining communities together to articulate and celebrate, to provoke and stimulate, to settle and reflect.

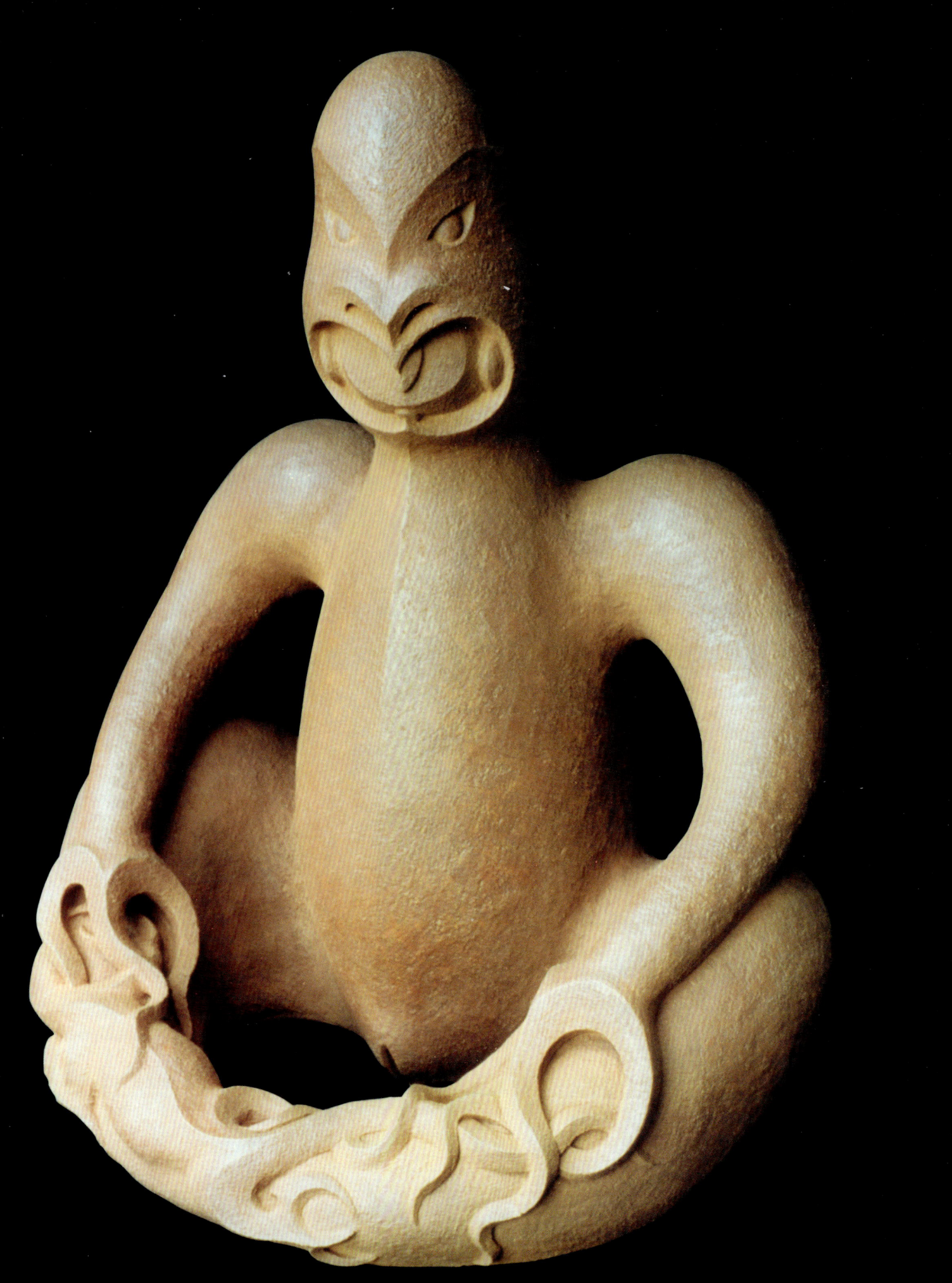

# NGĀ TAONGA UKU: MĀORI CERAMICISTS AND CLAY WORKERS

DEIDRE BROWN

The atua Tāne-nui-ā-rangi, who made the first woman, Hineahuone, from earth, was the first Māori clayworker. While there seems to be little evidence of early fired Māori ceramics, aside from some small balls of baked clay found at archaeological sites in Canterbury and Otago, contemporary Māori ceramicists have long looked to ancestral stories to create their whakapapa of practice. Among their pantheon of founding ancestors are the earth mother Papatūānuku, the guardian of fire Mahuika, and the atua of volcanoes Rūamoko. Kōkōwai, the most important pigment in customary Māori art, can be considered an early unfired precedent. The first contemporary Māori clayworks were possibly the clay pots made by children and photographed at Ngataki School in Northland in the mid-1950s, undertaken as part of the innovative arts curriculum developed by Gordon Tovey.[1] One of the Māori specialist arts advisors in this programme, Cath Brown, went on to make a career in ceramics, most notably for her *He Kākano* (seedpod) works that combine fibre art – a practice she learnt from Pine Taiapa's sisters during a 1960 arts-advisors training hui at Ruatōria – with ceramic 'seeds'. Other Māori artists have engaged with clay as part of their wider artistic practice, too, most notably Shona Rapira Davies for the 1982 *Ngā Mōrehu* installation and 1992 Te Aro Park project in Wellington.

Ngā Kaihanga Uku, a collective of Māori clayworkers, was established in 1987 by foundation members Paerau Corneal (Ngāti Tūwharetoa, Te Āti Haunui-a-Pāpārangi), Manos Nathan, Baye Riddell (Ngāti Porou, Te Whānau-a-Ruataupare), Wi Taepa and Colleen Waata Urlich. *Kurawaka*, curated by Megan Tamati-Quennell for the Dowse Art Museum in 1994, was the first major exhibition of their work. Waata Urlich, Manos Nathan and his brother Alex, who is a silversmith, all worked from their tribal base in the Waipoua Forest in Northland. There was no electricity, so they perfected low-tech methods to produce their ceramic works. Originally trained as a tohunga whakairo, Manos Nathan transferred his skills and knowledge to clay; as he said, 'I had no problem in putting the designs on to clay, but I wanted to find things that could be used within the culture … to imbue a non-traditional medium with integrity and to forge a link with Māori customs and values.'[2]

Taepa, too, has a carving background, and shifted from woodcarving to clay art for his rehabilitation work with youth offenders as a way of circumventing the cost of timber and the safety issues presented by chisels.[3] His is a highly organic response to clay that recognises its origins in the land through the forms he creates. Corneal was originally a weaver who moved to clay as a medium to express sculptural forms, specifically the female figure, created through a process of coiling.[4] Of all the Ngā Kaihanga Uku members, Waata Urlich had the earliest exposure to clay as a medium, beginning in the 1950s when she followed the recommendation of her clay teacher at Auckland Teachers' Training College and took additional art classes with Colin McCahon and Hamish Keith. Keith was working at the time on tableware with Barry Brickell, who was one of New Zealand's leading potters.[5] In 2002 she completed a master's of fine arts thesis at the University of Auckland that examined the influence of western Pacific Lapita pottery, with its distinctive stamped surfaces, on other Pacific arts including weaving and moko.[6] Her thesis thus connected the work of Māori ceramicists, trained in fibre and timber arts, to a tradition of claywork that originated on the other side of the Pacific, 3500 years earlier. Waata Urlich and other Ngā Kaihanga Uku members extended these connections by creating meaningful connections with Pacific, First Nations and Native American ceramicists that led to a series of reciprocal visits and workshops that have carried on after both Waata Urlich and Nathan died in 2015.[7] Exhibitions have also continued, and in 2020 Ngā Kaihanga Uku member Dorothy Waetford (Ngāti Wai, Ngāti Hine, Ngāpuhi) curated the

Manos Nathan, *Whakapakoko II, Nga Kaitiaki series 2*, 1998
private collection

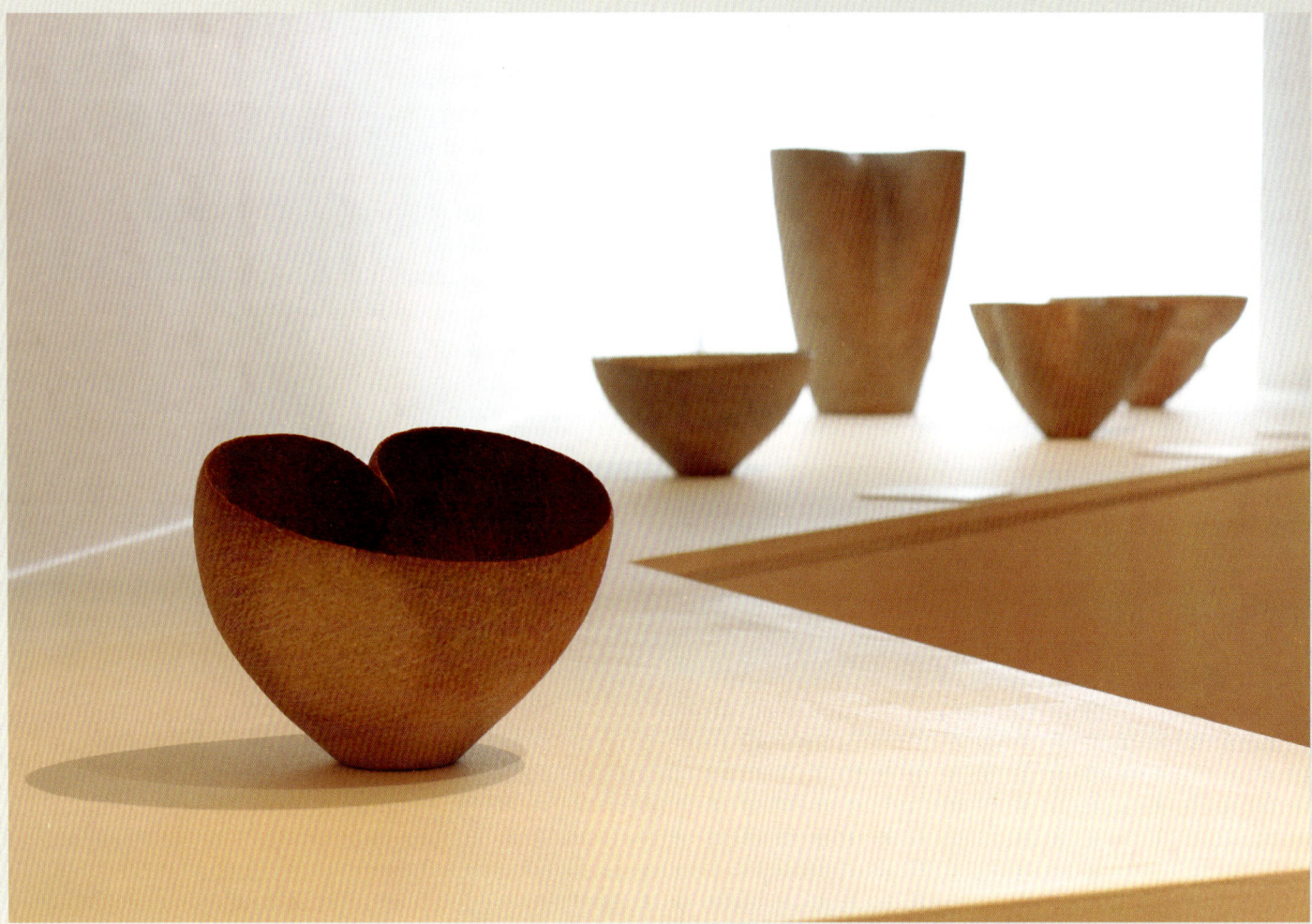

Hana Rakena, *Whenua Hou: New Māori Ceramics*, exhibition installation detail, 2016
photograph courtesy of Tauranga Art Gallery

group's *Ara Mai Nuku* exhibition as part of the New Zealand Festival of the Arts in Wellington. It featured new fired works by Riddell, Taepa, Carla Ruka (Ngāti Whātua, Ngā Puhi, Ngā Kiriporouri) and Amorangi Hikuroa and unfired works by Todd Douglas (Ngāpuhi), Noelle Jakeman (Ngāti Hine, Ngāpuhi, Ngāti Maniapoto, Tainui), Rhonda Halliday (Te Uri Taniwha, Ngāti Hineira, Ngāpuhi), Ida Edwards (Te Uriroroi, Te Hikutu, Ngāpuhi) and Waetford.

The 2016 exhibition *Whenua Hou: New Māori Ceramics*, curated by Karl Chitham and Kim Paton for Tauranga Art Gallery and Objectspace, Auckland, profiled a new generation of Māori ceramicists that includes Dan Couper (Ngāti Rongomaiwahine, Ngāti Kahungunu), Davina Duke (Ngāti Wai, Ngāpuhi, Ngāti Rehua, Patuharakeke), Stevei Houkāmau (Ngāti Porou, Te Whānau-ā-Apanui), Hera Johns (Ngāti Kahu), Tracy Keith, Jess Paraone (Ngāti Kawau, Kaitangata), Hana Rakena (Ngāpuhi, Ngāi Tahu) and Aaron Scythe (Mōrehu). The work is far more diverse in form than that of the founding members of Ngā Kaihanga Uku – probably because the earlier group worked more closely as a collective over many years. However, as the curators of *Whenua Hou* noted, these more recent ceramicists also make frequent reference to customary art practices such as whakairo rākau and moko in their works.[8] Māori ceramics, as a consequence, brings together multiple traditions of making, from the whakapapa of claywork, rediscovered by Waata Urlich and reimagined by Ngā Kaihanga Uku, to the wide variety of current expressions that reference the formalism of whakairo rākau, moko and fibre arts.

Opposite: **Colleen Waata Urlich**, *Hinaki—Eel trap, Kapowai series—Dragonfly Lake*, 2007
Whangārei Art Museum Te Manawa Toi

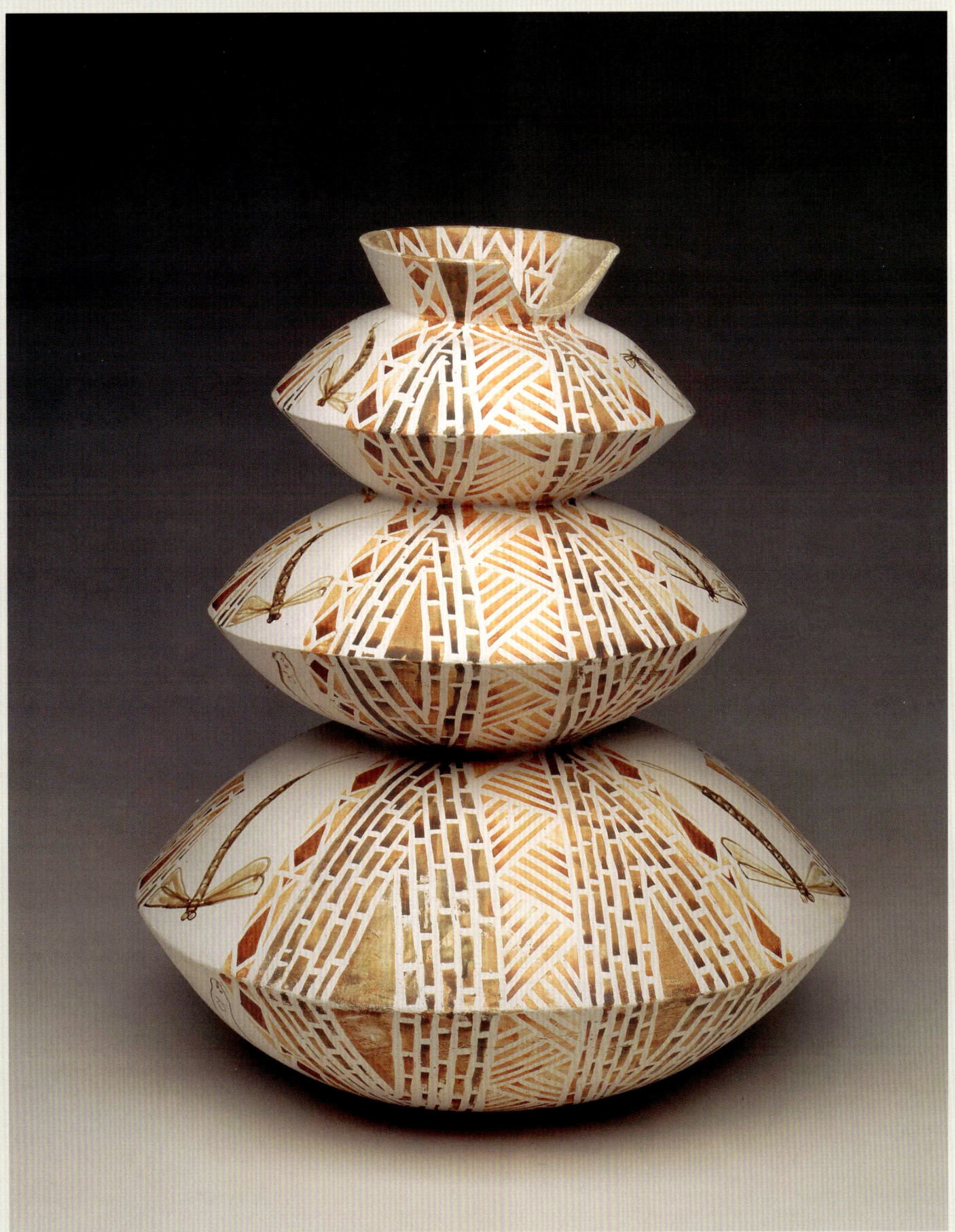

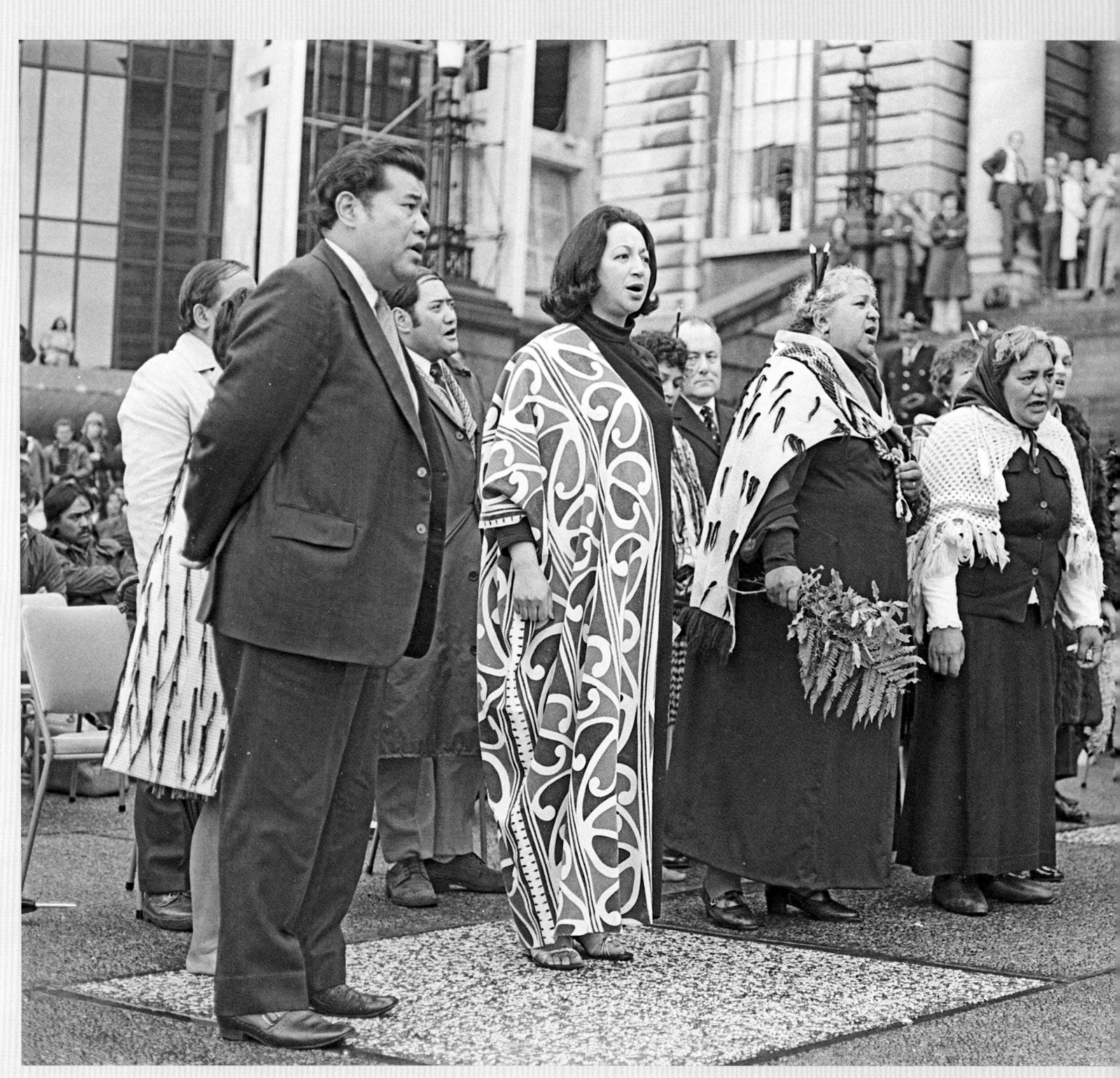

# CONTEMPORARY MĀORI CLOTHING
DEIDRE BROWN

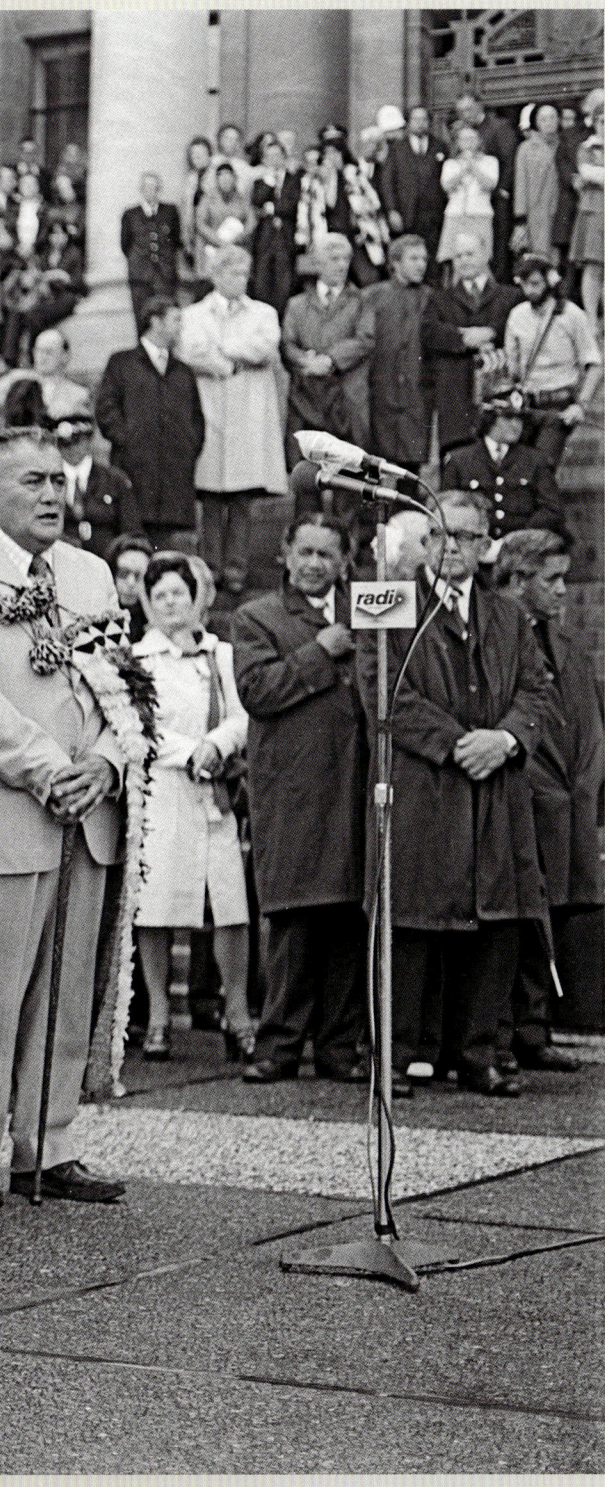

Whetū Tirikātene-Sullivan (second from left) outside Parliament in 1975, receiving Whina Cooper's hīkoi.
photograph by John Miller

Late-twentieth-century Māori fashion had no better ambassador than Whetū Tirikātene-Sullivan (Ngāi Tahu, Ngāti Kahungunu, 1932–2011), the first Māori woman cabinet minister, who was a Labour MP from 1967 to 1996. She was a talented seamstress: she learnt to design, sew and knit her own clothes from her grandmother Amiria Solomon, and by her teenage years was adapting this knowledge to incorporate Māori design elements into her clothes.[1]

Tirikātene-Sullivan's style was doubly unconventional. Her wardrobe had to reflect her status as a political leader at a time when there were few women in professional jobs and leadership positions, and it needed to express her personality as a contemporary Māori woman. Bold tāniko- and kōwhaiwhai-based prints dominated the fabric choices, some of which were designed by Māori modernist artist Sandy Adsett. A mangōpare design that Adsett created for her represented the tenaciousness she had demonstrated in her response to the Maori Affairs Amendment Act 1967.[2]

In 1972, she opened her own workshop and boutique, Ethnic Art Studio, in Wellington, which employed up to twenty crafters and designers. As her political work demanded more of her time, she began wearing clothes by other Māori designers such as Kura Ensor (Waikato-Tainui), who created the bold red, black and white 'Tania' dress that Tirikātene-Sullivan wore when she received Whina Cooper's hīkoi at Parliament in 1975.[3] Ensor had her own label called Gay '40s: she employed seventy people in her Takapuna workshop, where she designed high-end gowns for notable New Zealand personalities. She won several category awards in the Benson & Hedges Fashion Design Awards, her 'Tania' gown featured in the February 1975 Paris edition of *Vogue*, and her clothing was promoted in Paris and London by the New Zealand Wool Board.[4]

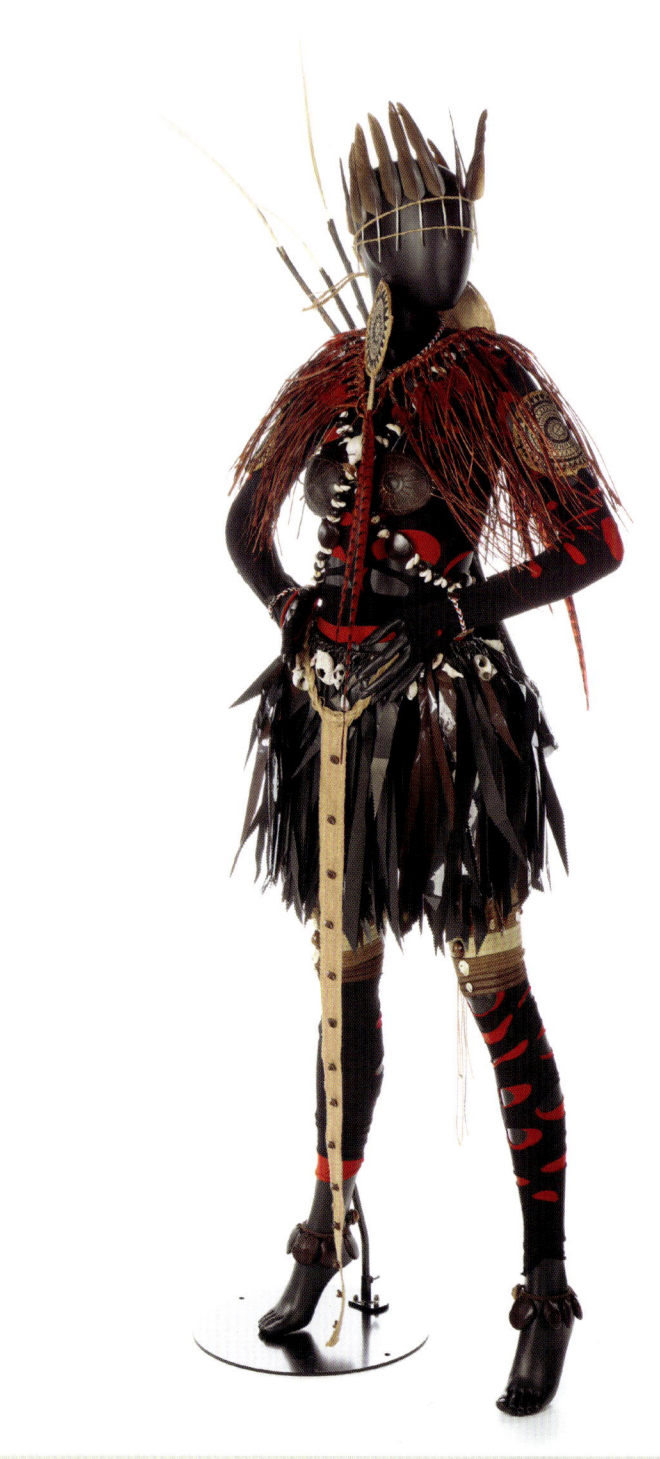

Since the 1990s, contemporary Māori fashion design has developed along two paths: one-off ensembles that are a comment on Māori life and identity today and can be considered art pieces in their own right; and custom-made and ready-to-wear designs for the commercial market. The Pacific Sisters collective developed contemporary Māori and Pacific clothing design, elevating it to a high art through their bespoke customary and urban streetwear-influenced costumes that are inspired by Indigenous futurism.[5] Their contribution to fashion and art was celebrated by the *Pacific Sisters: He Toa Tāera Fashion Activists* exhibition curated by Nina Tonga, which opened at Te Papa in 2018.

After the clothing industry was deregulated in the mid-1980s, clothing produced offshore flooded the Aotearoa New Zealand market, making it difficult for local designers to establish successful custom-made and ready-to-wear clothing businesses. In 2008, the Miromoda Indigenous Māori Fashion Apparel Board was established to assist aspiring Māori fashion designers and show their work locally and internationally.

According to the artists' statement: 'The 21st Sentry Cyber Sister guards the door to our whare. She is the determinator of all who enter. There is no room here for racism, trials and tribulations. Dedicated to the preservation of our tribal culture and our struggle towards self-determination. We recycle resources from our urban environment, traditional and contemporary fibres, to produce distressed deconstructed wearable art pieces that express our uniqueness as an urban tribe. While still following the paths created by our Ancestors. We are united in the cycle where our past meets our futures.'

**Pacific Sisters,** *21st Sentry Cyber Sister,* **1997**
Te Papa Tongarewa Museum of New Zealand, FE011080, purchased 1998

Kiri Nathan (Ngāpuhi, Ngāti Hine, Ngāti Maru, Ngāti Hauā) founded her own high-end label in 2010, after training in fashion design and customary and contemporary weaving. She combines these practices in clothes and body adornments (made by her husband Jason Nathan) that are sold in Auckland and shown on the runways of the New Zealand, Guangzhou and Fiji fashion weeks. Contemporary Māori clothing for men is still a developing field, with only a small number of designers, such as Te Ari Prendergast (Ngāi Tahu, Ngāti Porou, Te Whānau-ā-Apanui), catering to this market. All of these contemporary designers continue the kaupapa set down by Tirikātene-Sullivan of creating sophisticated, well-made clothing that exudes culture, context and strength.

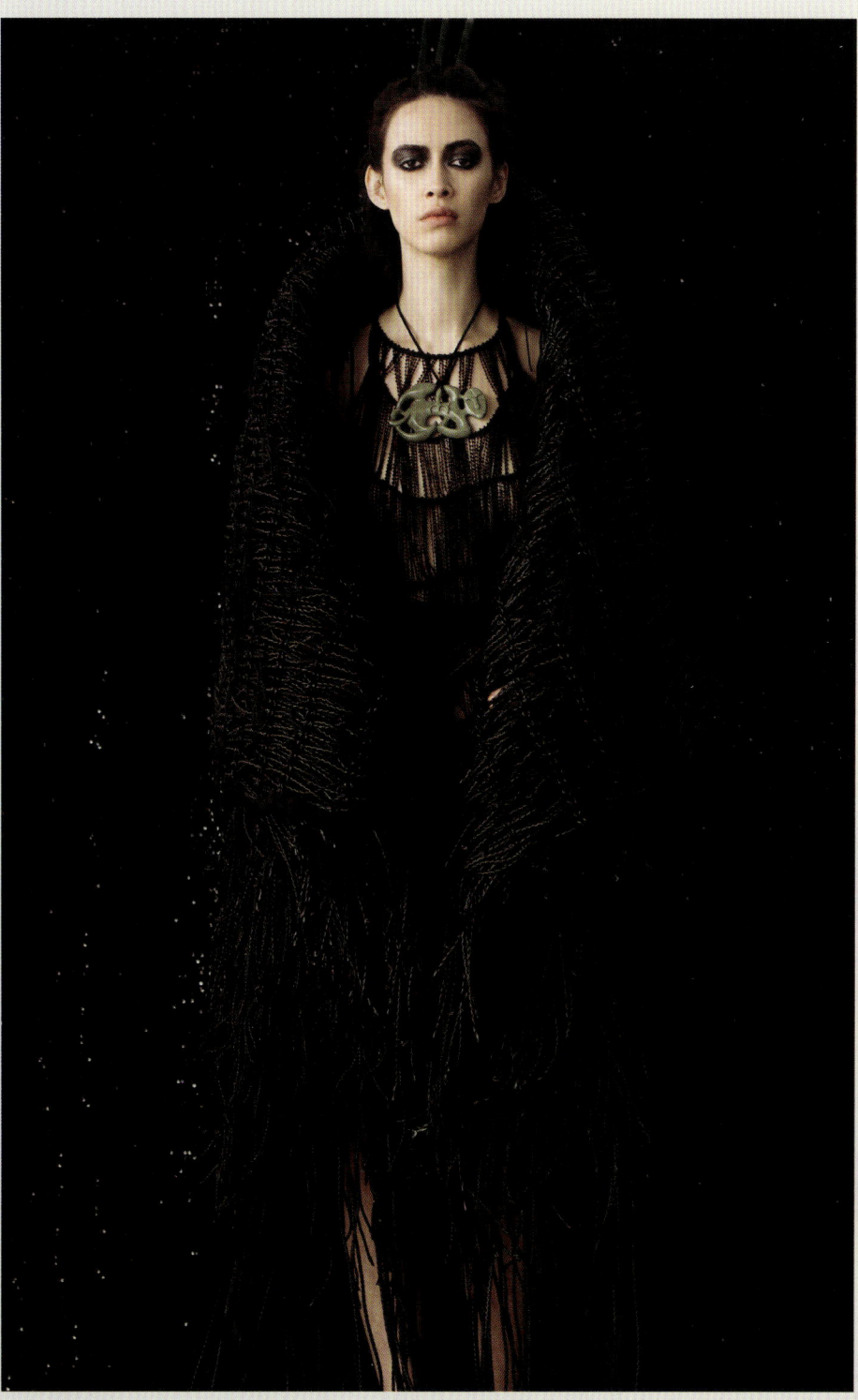

Kiri Nathan, black kākahu, modelled by Raina Masters.
photograph by David K. Shields

# ADVICE TO MĀORI ARTISTS
JONATHAN MANE-WHEOKI[1]

The art market in Aotearoa is, for a country with a small and not especially wealthy population, surprisingly buoyant, and some contemporary Māori artists have attained high critical recognition and enviable commercial success. But the market is limited and artists who wish to succeed in it must bear in mind some sobering considerations.

The competition is much fiercer than it used to be, and buyers and collectors are intelligent, sophisticated and discriminating. In the 1980s it was still the case that tertiary qualifications in fine arts were obtainable only from the universities of Auckland and Canterbury. However, an alternative to the individuality and competitiveness of the university system, which is repugnant to some Māori, has become available in other tertiary institutions: it is possible to study for a degree or diploma at regional polytechnics or wānanga. It used to be possible to compile a complete list of perhaps no more than fifty bona fide contemporary Māori art practitioners. Not anymore. There are now hundreds of young Māori art graduates; no one knows who they all are, and prospects for most of them, beyond teaching or supporting their art making by means of regular employment on jobs outside of the sector, are not very encouraging.

Although dealer galleries have proliferated in recent years, there is little point in unknown young artists trundling along portfolios of works to dealers in the expectation that their genius will be instantly recognised. The most prestigious dealers' 'books' are usually full and their exhibitions schedules planned a year ahead. There is a pecking order of dealer galleries and where you show and who you show with are important considerations. Better to try for a group showing in a well-regarded venue with like-minded, kindred artists, and slowly build up an exhibiting profile, than to go it alone in some makeshift out-of-the-way place that few potential buyers and no critics would visit.

Directors of public art galleries are very amenable to suggestions or proposals for exhibitions. While there will always be a place for the homespun, let's-awhi-everybody, art-society-ish, cobbled-together-at-the-last-minute exhibition, public art galleries are more interested in rigorously curated exhibitions constructed around concepts, themes or theses generated by contemporary art practice and issues. Directors have the ability and the experience to access funding or seek sponsorship or enter into partnership arrangements for projects they consider might attract an audience and from which prestige might accrue to their institution. Art galleries employ professional staff whose job it is to see that concepts are developed into exhibitions presented to the highest international standards the institution can muster, and to market the event. Unfortunately, few galleries have permanent, full-time Māori curatorial staff. Until this situation is rectified, Māori curatorial involvement in exhibition projects will continue to be on an ad hoc, contractual basis.

As part of the total exhibition 'package', a catalogue is essential both as a 'site' in which to expand on the theme or thesis, and as a journal of record. Too often in contemporary Māori art exhibitions the catalogue is the last thought of, instead of the first, and if there is a publication it appears after the exhibition has opened or even after it has closed! If the exhibition has a theme or a thesis the ideas need to be developed by a curatorial team in tandem with the actual selection of works over a generous lead-in time. A pool of Māori curatorial talent exists. The opportunities and the personnel are there. What are we waiting for?

It is important to be written about, in the public domain, in critical reviews, newspaper reports, and articles in such a journal as *Art New Zealand*. If you are an aspiring artist, where you are written about matters. You have arrived, internationally, when you are featured in *ArtAsiaPacific* and *World Art*. Who writes about you matters, too. The more authoritative the writer, the more respect the writer commands, the more seriously your work will be taken. In that such writing helps 'talk the market up', it can enhance the artist's prospects and translate into sales and commissions. Opportunities for writing are plentiful. Publications like *Art New Zealand*, for example, would probably carry more features on contemporary Māori art if more people were prepared to write them.

Art criticism is the new frontier for Māori artists – informed, intelligent, constructive criticism of well-thought-out, well-made original work that is able to withstand close scrutiny and bear comparison with the best of its kind. Critics are selective and will generally prefer to write about exhibitions that they perceive to be serious, that are held in prestigious art spaces and presented to high standards.

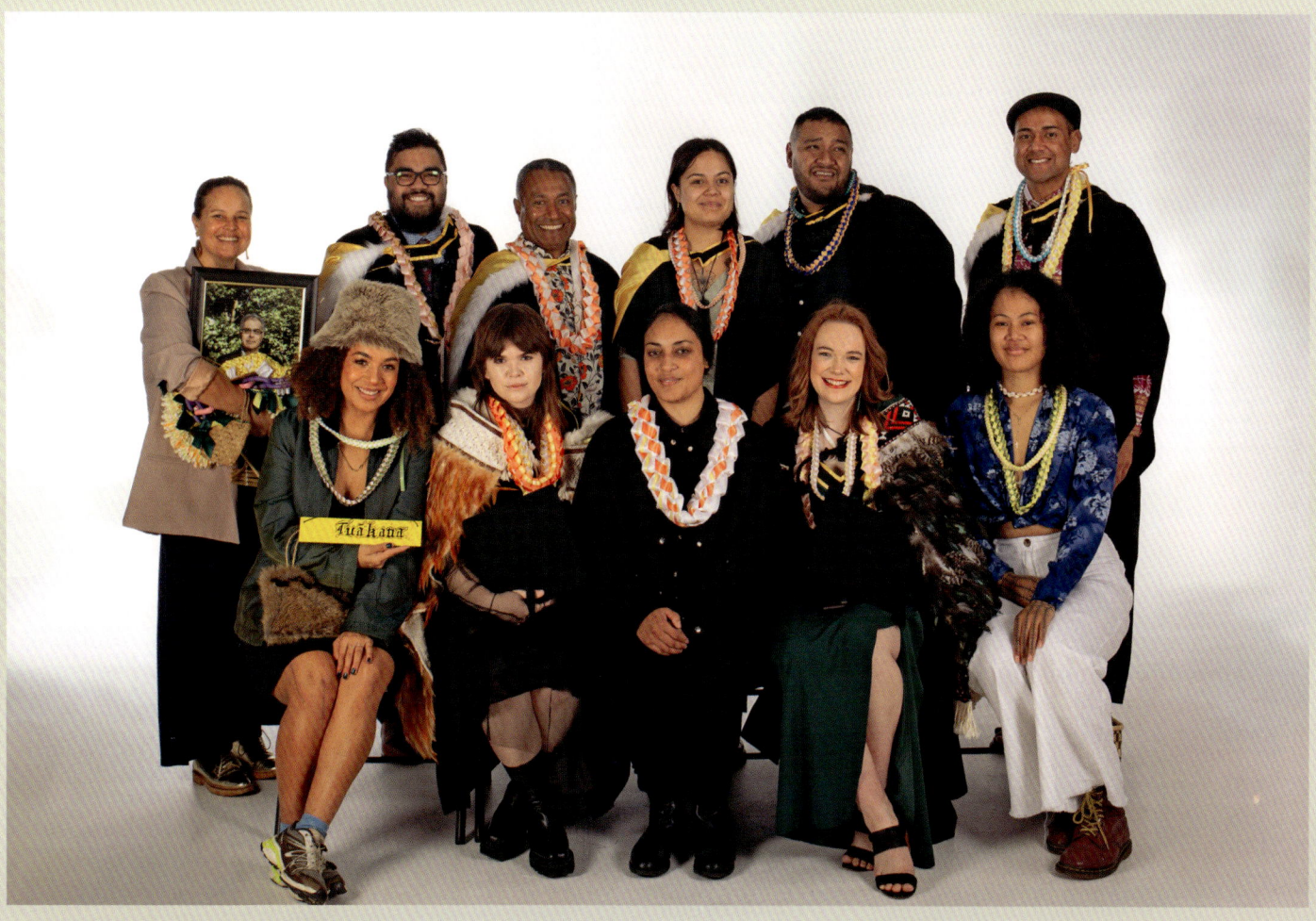

Since 2014, Māori and Pacific graduates from the Elam School of Fine Arts at the Waipapa Taumata Rau University of Auckland receive lei on their graduation, a tradition begun with the encouragement of Professor Jonathan Mane-Wheoki while head of the Elam School of Fine Arts. This photo shows 2021 graduates with their lei.

*Front row, left to right*: Nâāwié Tutugoro, Hannah Ireland, Salome Tanuvasa, Billie Bridges, Jasmine Tuia. Back row, left to right: Vaoala Olivia Blyth (organiser of the lei ceremony and shown here holding a photograph of Jonathan), Rodney Ah-Kan Mitasa, Ishmael Lotawa, Ashleigh Taupaki, Warren Paea, Pamata Toleafoa.

Olivia Blyth writes, 'Every year, [Jonathan] is part of the lei ceremony and is further adorned with a lei from each year. Hence he is laden with them after eight years of ceremonies. Whilst we are making the lei, or teaching about them, I talk about Jonathan, about who he was and what he did for us.'

# WHAKAMUTUNGA
## — CONCLUSION

*Toitū te whenua, toitū te tikanga, ka ora ngā toi.*

*When we hold fast to our land and values, our art flourishes.*

*Toi Te Mana* has been written to present our understanding of the history of our art so far to a wide audience. We would not be so whakahihi (arrogant) as to say that this is *the* art history made by Māori; rather, we present this as one story among others. In this book we have explored a myriad of art traditions, makers, materials and techniques, and in doing so we have argued for this field to be understood as forever shifting and changing in response to new ideas and pressures in our communities, tribal or artistic or otherwise. At times there have been conflicting stories or perspectives about history or treasures, but we recognise this as part and parcel of whakapapa, that there will sometimes be different understandings, perhaps even of the same event. In this book we have presented both (or more) to recognise that there is no one correct perspective on history: just as a kete may have many strands that ultimately come together, so too do our stories. We respect the fact that these stories have come through the whakapapa and we encourage this multiplicity of readings: oral histories and anthropology, for instance, give us alternative views of our whakapapa. Where are our beginnings – in Te Pō, or in the Pacific? Both are valid and need to be talked about together. The kōrero in the introduction discussed the purpose and position of this book within art histories. In examining the stories of art made by Māori from Polynesian arrival to the present day, and considering the fluidity and cyclical nature of these narratives, we have identified across all the kete three recurring, generative themes: whenua, tikanga and whakapapa.

### Whenua

The loss of whenua by land confiscation and sale to Pākehā in the nineteenth century, and consequent landscape modification, had a profound effect on the availability of materials and maintenance of lifeways required to create and support a vibrant artistic culture. Land alienation and unsustainable felling practices reduced access to and the availability of timber for whakairo rākau and whare construction. By the 1920s, the School of Maori Arts and Crafts struggled to source timber of adequate lengths for major structural members and had little choice but to use steel frameworks for some of its larger projects. Furthermore, the silting of waterways through deforestation and drainage of wetlands to create farmland diminished the supply of harakeke, raupō and toetoe, and this affected the supply of materials for whatu, raranga and tukutuku. While there were sufficient reserves of raupō and other thatch materials to build the large numbers of whare at Parihaka in the 1880s, by the start of the twentieth century these cladding materials had become harder to source. A century later and knowledge of whare raupō construction would be a distant childhood memory for the kaumātua who assisted Rau Hoskins and Carin Wilson to build their whare raupō at Whangaruru. Forests clearances and wetland drainage created land suitable for agriculture, an industry that many Māori men were drawn to in order to enter the paid economy from the mid-nineteenth century onwards. Life as a tohunga whakairo or tohunga tukutuku in a koha-based arts economy became less appealing and difficult to support financially, and by the early twentieth century Apirana Ngata and Te Rangi Hīroa were struggling to find experts in these fields. Until the opening of the School of Maori Arts and Crafts in 1927, the Rotorua tourism industry was perhaps the only employment sector where tohunga whakairo could maintain a living wage. Indeed, the need to earn money was also a factor in the increasing secularisation of some customary Māori arts, as it was difficult to maintain tapu when payment was noa.

Customary Māori arts survived in the pockets of land that remained in Māori ownership. Pātaka were still being built in areas where Māori lifeways could be maintained – particularly around hunting and preserving foods for storage. The distance between Māori communities on Māori land and Pākehā settlements was a factor in the survival of moko, which was worn by those Māori women whose lives had little intersection with the Pākehā world and its prejudices. Many Māori women in rural areas also retained the knowledge of raranga and whatu, which became more widely practised in the revival led by Rangimārie Hetet from the 1950s.

Some arts did not survive land loss. In South Canterbury and North Otago, rock art required seasonal hunting and gathering access to caves, plains and wetlands that quickly became private property with the arrival of European settlers. Land loss and initiatives to reclaim whenua have been important concepts and also purposes for contemporary Māori art and architecture from the 1970s onwards, and are as closely related to Māori renaissance activities as those from half a century before.

## Tikanga

While land was lost, tikanga – the customary outlook and practices that guide life and life's decisions – was steadfastly maintained across Māori communities and became a crucial source of inspiration for artists from the mid-nineteenth century onwards. This is clear from the earliest engagements with Pākehā and their media, beginning in 1793 with Tuki Tahua's egocentric map that showed the passage of pounamu from the south to the north, and the Māori Madonna and Child sculptures that sought to explicate Christianity within a Māori worldview. Some of the most critical choices around the retention of tikanga practices in art were made by the School of Maori Arts and Crafts. An early head tutor, Eramiha Kapua, retained the memorisation of designs, safe disposal of woodchips, gender separation and karakia recitation; other practices, though, were not kept, as Kapua believed that a contemporary workshop was safer if there were fewer tapu restrictions to transgress. The larger projects, of revitalising marae with whare whakairo and wharekai construction, ensured that the kawa of the marae was retained. The school's efforts and those of the Tūrangawaewae carving school and programmes run by the Taiapa brothers perpetuated these arts and customs and ensured that marae remain a bastion of customary arts and te reo Māori.

Elements of tikanga are apparent in the arts associated with the Rātana movement, which practised whakanoa to reduce the tapu of taonga placed in the whare Māori and maintained personification in its main buildings. When the Māori arts and crafts advisors gained Pine Taiapa's approval for their modernised art and educational practices – at the 1960 Ruatōria hui, the 1961 *The Arts of the Maori* book and the 1966 Hamilton Festival of Maori Arts exhibition – it meant they were working with the endorsement of the leading tohunga of the day. While this did not entirely avert criticism of their work by other Māori, it was a factor in emboldening many of them to address Māori themes and concepts in their work and to encourage teachers and students to do the same through the New Zealand educational curriculum. This flow-through of tikanga-based conceptual thinking was evident in the Māori art collectives, urban marae and tertiary training initiatives established from the 1970s onwards – and tikanga is a lens through which art historians and critics analyse and discuss Māori art today.

Taonga frequently circulated around and between districts to maintain utu balances were vital for Māori social order. Leaders like Te Rauparaha and Tītore could accumulate (by artistic patronage, inheritance and exchange) large collections of highly crafted taonga on behalf of their people as an expression of their rangatiratanga over considerable estates. These artworks acquired by utu, either through reciprocal exchange or through muru from other areas, were regarded as taonga through their association with particular rangatira and makers. The concept of taonga tuku iho, passed between leaders as well as down generations, is a better way of locating, understanding and valuing Māori art than simply identifying and appreciating the local 'style' in which they were made. Cultural knowledge and sovereign rights are thus embodied in these taonga, and their severance from the tuku iho process through seizure, concealment, destruction and storage in collections has had a negative effect on the kaitiakitanga and creation of taonga. Recent initiatives to reconnect museum-held taonga with Māori through research and creative activation processes are a small step towards restoring their currency within communities.

## Whakapapa

The central premise of *Toi Te Mana* is that Māori art is art made by Māori. The past two centuries have shown that even when whenua, tikanga and te reo are lost or under pressure, ancestry binds our people together. George Hubbard's resistance to tikanga-based curatorial propositions in his exhibitions in the 1990s emphasised the role of whakapapa in defining the identity of Māori artists even when those same artists regarded themselves as detribalised. Iwi-based exhibitions of contemporary Māori art still embraced artists who saw themselves in this way, as did curators who recognised that being raised in the Pākehā world was a fact of life for many urban Māori and tertiary-trained Māori artists. Exploration of a person's cultural self, with all of its complexities, became a theme in the work of the Young Guns generation; and for some, such as Shane Cotton and Peter Robinson, art has offered a way back into community.

Urbanisation and migration caused many Māori families to shed those elements of culture that could not so easily travel with them or find a space in the city, such as the whenua, marae and te reo Māori. Much of what was left to pass on to the next generation was that which resided within their hearts, hands and heads – waiata, oriori, mōteatea, waiata ā-ringa, kōrero tuku iho and whakapapa. Even with this little knowledge, some Māori in cities have been able to reclaim the arts associated with their culture, such as fibre art, kapa haka costume-making and kōwhaiwhai design and painting. The digital arts have allowed a much larger Māori world to be transported to new places: thus, for example, Lisa Reihana can physically and theoretically unpack the impact of the 1769 Cook voyage on Pacific peoples in venues across the world with data files and projectors.

## Wai 262 and beyond

Where to from here? *Ko Aotearoa Tēnei* – the report arising from the Wai 262 claim to the Waitangi Tribunal – offers one pathway forward, in which the nature and significance of taonga can be unpacked according to iwi and hapū imperatives. Iwi and hapū need to write their own art histories. The material they have gathered for their claims – oral evidence, taonga, historical narratives – holds much potential to write a more specific and nuanced history of their people, using the frameworks and terminology offered in *Toi Te Mana*. At their most potent, taonga are active and animate agents with their own mauri and have the mana to bring hapū and iwi together. The concepts of mana and tapu are implicit in taonga tuku iho and affect those who come into contact with them. They provide one method for considering the history of a place or time. By closely investigating the many facets of a taonga's whakapapa, researchers can uncover understandings of the people and their economic, political and artistic landscape. Detailed research on the wharenui Mātaatua (for Wai 46, the Ngāti Awa claim, 1993) and Te Hau ki Tūranga (for Wai 814, the Rongowhakaata claim, 2011) has shown how art histories have a contribution to make to iwi and hapū histories.

Another useful avenue for the future is for researchers fluent in te reo to examine Māori-language sources embedded in Native Land Court records and Māori newspapers, as well as mōteatea, whakataukī and other forms. The histories in these accounts can provide an intimate, iwi-centred form of mātauranga, activating voices long since quietened, with the power that specific terms and phrases can have to articulate ideas and concepts, people and taonga. In chapter 6, for instance, we began to unpack some of the practices around adornment such as mata whakarewa, as described by those who witnessed those wearing it. From this modest investigation we get a sense that there is a wealth of material that awaits those researchers with te reo.

Examining our art history through a different theoretical lens – such as feminist or Marxist – can enable other ways of understanding. While this book introduces aspects of these conceptual frameworks (acknowledging that they are based in Western Europe, primarily), more research is needed from these perspectives. So often the narrative has been written by men – initially Pākehā, and more recently also Māori. But this is changing, as this book shows. Tryphena Cracknell's article 'Wahine Mau Whao: A Woman's Hand to the Chisel',[1] which surveys Māori women carvers in the twentieth and twenty-first centuries, is an example of how this approach might look. Researching the economic aspect of Māori art would also be interesting: too few studies have examined patronage (payment and support for art projects). How were artists paid? What was their brief? How involved were the patrons in the style and final product of the project? Asking questions like these are another way to build resources on Māori art history.

The goal of *Toi Te Mana: An Indigenous History of Māori Art* has been to show the various ways in which Māori art has transformed, and continues to transform Māori people. These are complicated and constantly shifting: change characterises Māori art history rather than being an exception. The three kete strategy presented here is one approach we have used to shape our mātauranga to be easily understood. As authors, we want readers to leave the last page thinking about what they can do to continue what we pitched with Jonathan in 2014 as a 'global domination of Māori art history'. We still firmly believe this – and only wish Jonathan was here to see this moment. His whakaaro are infused through the chapters, and we know that he would be happy with what we have achieved here.

*Whāia te iti kahurangi, me tuohu koe
he maunga teitei.*

*Seek the treasure that you value most dearly,
and if you should bow your head, let it be
to a lofty mountain.*

# NGĀ PITOPITO KŌRERO – NOTES

### He kupu whakataki – Preface

1. See CIHA 2008 call for papers: www.migrationmuseums.org/web/index.php?page=crossing-cultures-conflict-migration-and-convergence; the outcomes from this debate are discussed in Jonathan Mane-Wheoki, 'Introduction: Indigeneity/Aboriginality, Art/Culture and Institutions', in Jaynie Anderson (ed.), *Crossing Cultures: Conflict, Migration and Convergence*, Miegunyah Press, Melbourne, 2009, pp. 770–72; Jonathan Mane-Wheoki, 'Art's Histories in Aotearoa New Zealand', *Journal of Art Historiography*, no. 4, June 2011, http://arthistoriography.wordpress.com/number-4-june-2011/

2. We have used Te Tiriti o Waitangi in preference to the Treaty of Waitangi as the former, written in te reo Māori, was the version signed by most Māori signatories. It is different to the English-language version, in wording and meaning. Te Tiriti o Waitangi is a partnership document between the Crown and Māori.

3. Waitangi Tribunal, *Ko Aotearoa Tēnei: A Report into Claims Concerning New Zealand Law and Policy Affecting Māori Culture and Identity, Report on Wai Claim 262*, Legislation Direct, Wellington, 2011.

4. Jonathan Mane-Wheoki, 'Out on His Own: Ralph Hotere and the Māori art movement', in Roger Taberner and Ronald Brownson (eds), *Hotere: Seminar Papers from 'Into the Black'*, Auckland Art Gallery, Auckland, 1998, p. 54.

5. Arapata Hakiwai, 'He Mana Taonga He Mana Tangata: Māori Taonga and the Politics of Māori Tribal Identity and Development', PhD thesis, Victoria University of Wellington, 2014, p. 2.

### Tīmatanga kōrero – Introduction

1. Maori Marsden, 'God, Man and Universe: A Maori View', in Maori Marsden (ed.), *The Woven Universe. Selected Writings of Rev. Maori Marsden*, Estate of Rev. Maori Marsden, Masterton, 2003, p. 20.

2. Ibid.

3. Margaret Orbell, *The Illustrated Encyclopedia of Maori Myth and Legend*, Canterbury University Press, Christchurch, 1996, p. 42.

4. Pakaariki Harrison, *Tane-nui-a-Rangi, Auckland University Marae*, University of Auckland, Auckland, 1991, p. 7.

5. Kahutoi Te Kanawa and John Turi-Tiakitai, 'Te Mana o te Kākahu: The Prestige of Cloaks', in Awhina Tamarapa (ed.), *Whatu Kākahu: Māori Cloaks*, Te Papa Press, Wellington, 2011, p. 23.

6. H. W. Williams also translates 'pūrākau' as 'ceremonies connected with making and launching a canoe'; Williams, *A Dictionary of Maori Language*, 7th edition, GP Publications, Wellington, 1991, p. 312.

7. Williams, *A Dictionary of Maori Language*, p. 181.

8. Kahutoi Te Kanawa, 'Toi Maramatanga: A Visual Māori Art Expression of Meaning', MA thesis, Auckland University of Technology, 2009, p. 51.

9. Rāwiri Taonui, 'Ranginui – the sky – Ranginui as knowledge and life', *Te Ara – the Encyclopedia of New Zealand*, www.TeAra.govt.nz/en/ranginui-the-sky/page-2

10. Ibid.

11. On the flipside, the term 'victimry' is used for those groups who have not been able to escape from the processes of colonisation, and who thus remain 'victims'. See Gerald Vizenor (ed.), *Survivance, Narratives of Native Presence*, University of Nebraska Press, Lincoln, 2008.

12. Puawai Cairns, 'Decolonise or Indigenise: Moving towards Sovereign Spaces and the Māorification of New Zealand Museology', Te Papa Tongarewa Museum of New Zealand, https://blog.tepapa.govt.nz/2020/02/10/decolonise-or-indigenise-moving-towards-sovereign-spaces-and-the-maorification-of-new-zealand-museology

13. Jonathan Mane-Wheoki, 'Mapping Contemporary Indigenous Art Post-*Les Magiciens de la Terre*', paper presented to '*Les Magiciens de la Terre*: A look back at a legendary exhibition' symposium, 27 March 2014, Centre Pompidou, Paris, n.p.

14. Jonathan Mane-Wheoki, '*Magiciens*'.

15. Mane-Wheoki was adamant that we should use a lower case 'm' for māori, up until the time of Te Tiriti o Waitangi at least, when the word was used to mean 'normal'. This was how Māori identified themselves in contrast (not in opposition) to 'pākehā', who were not the normal inhabitants of Aotearoa.

16. By authors such as Augustus Hamilton (1853–1913), Elsdon Best (1856–1931), Apirana Ngata (1874–1950), Te Rangi Hīroa (Sir Peter Buck) (1877–1951), Henry Skinner (1886–1978), Gilbert Archey (1890–1974), William Phillipps (1893–1967), Jock McEwen (1915–2010) and Roger Duff (1912–1978).

17. For example: David Simmons, *Whakairo: Maori Tribal Art*, Oxford University Press, Auckland, 1985; Hirini Moko Mead, *Toi Whakairo*, Reed, Auckland, 1986, and *Whatu Taniko*, Reed, Auckland, 1987; Mick Pendergrast, *Te Aho Tapu: The Sacred Thread*, University of Hawai'i Press, Honolulu, 1987; Roger Neich, *Carved Histories*, Auckland University Press, Auckland, 2003; Ngahuia Te Awekotuku with Linda Waimarie Nikora, *Mau Moko: The World of Māori Tattoo*, Penguin, Auckland, 2007; Deidre Brown, *Māori Architecture*, Raupō, Auckland, 2009.

18. Kelvin Day, *Māori Wood Carving of the Taranaki Region*, Reed, Auckland, 2001; Ngarino Ellis and Witi Ihimaera, *Te Ata: Māori Art from the East Coast, New Zealand*, Reed, Auckland, 2002; Deidre Brown, *Tai Tokerau Whakairo Rākau: Northland Māori Wood Carving*, Reed, Auckland, 2003; David Simmons, *Meeting Houses of Ngāti Porou*, Reed, Auckland, 2006; Ngarino Ellis and Deidre Brown (eds), *Te Puna: Māori Art from Tai Tokerau, Northland*, Reed, Auckland, 2007.

19. For example, Sidney (Hirini) Moko Mead, *Māori Art on the World Scene*, Matau, Wellington, 1997; Julie Paama-Pengelly, *Māori Art and Design*, New Holland, Auckland, 2010; D. C. Starzecka (ed.), *Maori: Art and Culture*, British Museum Press, London, 1996.

20. Roger Neich, *Painted Historie: Early Maori Figurative Painting*, Auckland University Press, Auckland, 1993; Ngahuia Te Awekotuku with Linda Waimarie Nikora, *Mau Moko*, Penguin, Auckland, 2007.

21. See Hirini Moko Mead, *Toi Whakairo: The Art of Māori Carving*, Reed, Auckland, 1995.

22. Hirini Moko Mead, 'Ka Tupu te Toi Whakairo ki Aotearoa: Becoming Maori Art', in *Te Maori: Maori Art from New Zealand Collections*, Abrams, New York, 1984, pp. 73–75.

23. Ibid., p. 75.

24. Patu Hohepa in Anne Salmond, *Between Worlds: Early Exchanges between Maori and Europeans 1773–1815*, Penguin, Auckland, 1997, p. 512.

25  Robert Jahnke, 'Maori Art Towards the Millennium', in Malcolm Mulholland (ed.), *State of the Māori Nation: Twenty-first Century Issues in Aotearoa*, Reed, Auckland, 2006, pp. 41–51.

26  The Māori collections of Te Papa Tongarewa Museum of New Zealand (Arapata Hakiwai and Huhana Smith, *Toi Ora*, Te Papa Press, Wellington, 2008); Auckland War Memorial Museum (Paul Tapsell, *Māori Treasures of New Zealand*, David Bateman, Auckland, 2006); British Museum (Dorota Starzecka [ed.], *Māori Collections of the British Museum*, British Museum Press, London, 2010); and Museum Volkenkunde, Leiden (Fanny Wonu Veys, *Mana Māori*, Leiden University Press, Leiden, 2010).

27  Mead, *Te Maori*; Starzecka (ed.), *Maori: Art and Culture*.

28  Sandy Adsett, Witi Ihimaera and Cliff Whiting, *Mataora: The Living Face*, Bateman, Auckland, 1996.

29  Huhana Smith (ed), *Taiāwhio* (*I* and *II*), Te Papa Press, Wellington, 2002 and 2007; Ngahiraka Mason, Ngarino Ellis, and Kahutoi Te Kanawa, *Pūrangiaho*, Auckland Art Gallery, Auckland, 2001.

30  Mead, *Te Maori*, p. 75.

31  Ngahuia Te Awekotuku, 'Art and the Spirit', *New Zealand Geographic,* 5, January–March 1990.

32  Elsdon Best, *Maori Religion and Mythology, Part 2,* Government Printer, Wellington, 1982, p. 48.

33  'Cultural Values Report prepared by Sophie McGregor and Cathy Begley on behalf of Te Runanga o Kaikoura in response to the Awatere Riverbed Activity Guidelines Document', 2014, p. 4.

34  See Dougal Austin, *Te Hei Tiki: An Enduring Treasure in a Cultural Continuum* (Te Papa Press, Wellington, 2019), for examples of this.

35  Mead, quoted in *Ko Aotearoa Tēnei: A Report into Claims Concerning New Zealand Law and Policy Affecting Māori Culture and Identity (Wai 262)*, Legislation Direct, vol. 1, p. 81.

36  See Apirana Ngata, *Ngā Mōteatea The Songs: Part One*, Auckland University Press, Auckland, 2004, waiata 60, line 11. Te Heuheu III Iwikau, 'A Lament for Te Heuheu (II) Tukino who was overwhelmed by a landslide'.

37  Ibid., waiata 75, lines 12–14, p. 255. Whakaawe, 'He Oriori/lament'.

38  Protected Objects Act 1975, www.legislation.govt.nz/act/public/1975/0041/latest/whole.html

39  Waitangi Tribunal, *Ko Aotearoa Tēnei (Wai 262),* 2011.

## PART 1 – TE KETE TUATEA

### 1  Ngā momo waka: Moana, migration and Māori

1  Raymond Firth, *Economics of the New Zealand Maori*, A. R. Shearer, Wellington, 1929, p. 242.

2  When Ngāti Porou people die, their body is carried by waka up their ancestral river Waiapu to the top of Mount Hikurangi, from where they go straight up to Rarohenga.

3  Atholl Anderson, Judith Binney and Aroha Harris (eds), *Tangata Whenua: An Illustrated History*, Bridget Williams Books, Wellington, 2014, p. 500, n. 3. Anderson references Te Aue Davis et al., *Nga Tohu Pumahara: The Survey Pegs of the Past: Understanding Maori Place Names*, NZ Geographic Board, Wellington, 1990.

4  Nicholas Thomas, Susanne Küchler and Lissant Bolton, 'Art, Trade and Exchange: New Guinea 1700–1900', in Peter Brunt and Nicholas Thomas, *Art in Oceania: A New History*, Thames and Hudson, London, 2012, p. 99.

5  Ibid.

6  Epeli Hauʻofa, 'Our Sea of Islands', *The Contemporary Pacific*, 6.1 (Spring 1994), pp. 148–61.

7  Te Matorohanga, 'The Lore of the Whare Wananga: Wahi II. Te Kauwae-Raro. Upoko III', *Journal of the Polynesian Society*, vol. 22, no. 87, 1913, pp. 109, 122.

8  Te Rangi Hiroa, *The Coming of the Maori*, Maori Purposes Fund Board, Wellington, 1949, p. 6.

9  Pakaariki Harrison, *Tane-nui-a-Rangi, Auckland University Marae*, University of Auckland, Auckland, 1991, p. 7.

10  Hoturoa Barclay-Kerr, 'Waka – canoes – Pacific origins', *Te Ara – the Encyclopedia of New Zealand*, www.TeAra.govt.nz/en/waka-canoes/page-1.

11  Te Rangi Hīroa, *Coming of the Maori*, p. 26.

12  See ibid., pp. 41–42 for a more detailed account.

13  Atholl Anderson, 'Changing Perspectives upon Maori Colonisation Voyaging', *Journal of the Royal Society*, vol. 47, no. 3, 2017, p. 28.

14  See Jeanette Wikaira, 'Early Observations of Sails in Aotearoa New Zealand', https://teraa.co.nz/2019/02/28/early-observations-of-sails-in-aotearoa-new-zealand/?fbclid=IwAR08rlPJKg8nlvxVQ4-n6_UVZK7cx0hlr_CAokGXA-YYnLBduNGY9L_PYYg

15  Te Rangi Hīroa, *Coming of the Maori*, p. 42; Apirana Ngata in A. H. Reed, *Treasury of Maori Exploration*, Reed, Auckland, 1977, p. 108; Anne Nelson, *Nga Waka Maori*, Macmillan, Auckland, 1991, p. 202.

16  Elsdon Best, 'Did Polynesian Voyagers know the double outrigger?', *Journal of the Polynesian Society*, vol. 32, 1923, p. 202.

17  Mere Whaanga, *A Carved Cloak for Tahu*, Auckland University Press, Auckland, 2004, p. 45.

18  Elizabeth Pishief and John Adam, *Te Tātua a Riukiuta: Three Kings Heritage Study*, Puketāpapa Local Board, Auckland Council, Auckland, 2015, p. 22.

19  Reed, *Treasury of Maori Exploration*, p. 74.

20  This is Wiremu Wi Hongi's account, in Jeffrey Sissons, Wiremu Wi Hongi and Pat Hohepa, *The Puriri Trees Are Laughing: A Political History of Ngāpuhi In the Inland Bay of Islands: A Report Submitted to the Social Sciences Research Fund Committee*, Polynesian Society, Auckland, 1987, p. 59.

21  Geoff Irwin, Dilys Johns, Richard G. J. Flay, Filippo Munari, Yun Sang and Tim Mackrell, 'A Review of the Archaeological Maori Canoes (waka) Reveals Changes in Sailing Technology and Maritime Communications in Aotearoa/New Zealand, AD 1300–1800', *Journal of Pacific Archaeology*, vol. 8, no. 2, 2017, p. 32.

22  Kelvin Day, *Maori Woodcarving of the Taranaki Region*, Reed, Auckland, 2001, p. 67. This is one of only eighty-eight carvings which Day was able to firmly ascribe to having been made in the Taranaki area (p. 117), the majority being by carvers from Te Ātiawa (p. 118).

23  For comparisons with other early prows see Irwin, Johns, et al., 'A Review of the Archaeological Maori Canoes', pp. 31–43.

24  Matthew Campbell, Beatrice Hudson, Jacqueline Craig, Arden Cruickshank, Louise Furey, Karen Greig, Andrew McAlister, Bruce Marshall, Reno Nims, Fiona Petchey, Tristan Russell, Danielle Trilford and Rod Wallace, 'The Long Bay Restaurant Site (R10/1374), Auckland, New Zealand, and the Archaeology of the Mid-15th Century in the Upper North Island', *Journal of Pacific Archaeology*, vol. 10, no. 2, 2019, pp. 39–40.

25  A. C. Haddon and J. Hornell, *Canoes of Oceania*, Bishop Museum Press, Honolulu, 1997, p. 200.

26  Gary Law, *Archaeology of the Bay of Plenty*, Department of Conservation, Wellington, 2008, p. 56.

27  W. J. Phillipps, 'The Rua Hoata Shelter, Waikato River', *Journal of the Polynesian Society,* vol. 56, no. 4, 1947, p. 337.

28  Gilbert Archey, 'Rock Shelter Drawings at Arapuni Gorge', *Journal of the Polynesian Society*, vol. 36, no. 144, 1927, p. 369.

29  See Jeff Evans, *Heke-Nuku-Mai-Nga-Iwi Busby: Not Here by Chance*, Huia Publishers, Wellington, 2015.

30  Pakaariki Harrison, *Nga Kete Wananga*, Manukau Institute of Technology, Auckland, 1999, p.21.

31  Pishief and Adam, *Three Kings*, p.36.

32 See Roger Neich, 'A Rare Form of Maori Tuere Canoe Prow from Opito, Coromandel Peninsula', *Records of the Auckland Museum*, 35, 1998, p. 8.

33 Many of these are now in museums overseas, including the British Museum (1900.7-21.1), Museum für Völkerkunde in Berlin (VI 165) and Museo Nazionale di Antropologia e Etnologia in Florence (32).

34 Roger Neich, 'Wood Carving', in Dorota Starzecka (ed.), *Maori: Art and Culture*, Trustees of the British Museum, London, 1996, pp. 69–113.

35 Apirana Ngata, *Ngā Mōteatea The Songs: Part Three*, Auckland University Press, Auckland, 2006, waiata 222, pp. 100–1.

36 Ibid., waiata 256, pp. 266–68.

37 Roger Neich, *Carved Histories: Rotorua Ngāti Tarawhai Woodcarving*, Auckland University Press, Auckland, 2002, p. 183.

38 Ibid., p. 319.

39 Ibid., p. 325.

40 Ibid., p. 327.

41 Halbert suggests that Matawhāiti was related to Rongowhaakata through marriage (in Rongowhakaata Halbert, *Horouta: The History of the Horouta Canoe, Gisborne and East Coast*, Oratia Books, Auckland, 2012, p. 91).

42 Mahumahu was the principal carver on House No. 2 at Rangihoua (Halbert, *Horouta*, p. 91).

43 *Tāheretikitiki II* was another of the older Tainui waka that was reworked by Poutapu. This waka was originally built in 1882 at Kaipara by Ngāti Whātua for their chief Paora Tūhaere of Ōrākei. This was unusual as most iwi had stopped building waka by this time. The majority of the waka had rotted away except for the main carvings which were stored away, and the tauihu was placed in Auckland Museum. In the early 1970s Poutapu directed the construction in an attempt to teach a new generation this important art tradition: he recognised he was not getting any younger. His work on this project was filmed and released as *Mana Waka* (www.nziff.co.nz/2011/archive/mana-waka). Piri Poutapu left Tūrangawaewae in 1944 after a dispute with Te Puea, and he did not return until after her death in 1952. In the meantime, the waka taua were not looked after and could no longer be used for formal occasions.

44 Inia's son, Inia Junior (1947–2018) was a carver, too, as is his son Renata.

45 For a great insight into this history, see *Waka: The Awakening Dream* (1990), www.nzonscreen.com/title/waka-the-awakening-dream-1990

46 For a first-person description of the emergence of PVS, see Ben Finney, 'Renaissance', in K. R. Howe (ed.), *Mana Waka: Voyages of the Ancestors*, David Bateman and Auckland War Memorial Museum, Auckland, 2006, pp. 288–333.

47 Finney, 'Renaissance', p. 310.

48 Whakataka-Brightwell was later commissioned by Te Rūnanga o Ngāti Porou to build a waka taua, named *Te Aio o Nukutaimemeha*. This was controversial, and ultimately the waka was never launched; it was left on land at Rangitukia at East Cape. In 2019 the waka was moved to Mount Hikurangi, where it lies near Māui's petrified waka of the same name.

## 2 Ngā toi whakairo: The arts of carving

1 This is based on the figures of 15,200 taonga overseas (Arapata Hakiwai, 'Te Toi Whakairo o Ngāti Kahungunu: The Carving Traditions of Ngāti Kahungunu', MA thesis, Victoria University, 2003), in addition to 30,000 in Te Papa, 10,000 in Auckland Museum and an estimated 2500 in regional museums, totalling 57,500. Of this figure, at least 70 percent would have been carved, giving us this figure of 40,250 – of which the vast majority would have been pre-1900. Most works in museums were collected during the nineteenth century, when museums in Europe sought out 'new' material freshly collected from voyages; it was also a time when the first museums in New Zealand sought to present a baseline of Māori carving: a pātaka, waka taua and whare whakairo.

2 H. T. Whatahoro, *The Lore of the Whare-wananga: Or Teachings of the Maori College on Religion*, Polynesian Society, New Plymouth, 1913, p. 26; Ranginui Walker, *Nga Pepa a Ranginui: The Walker Papers*, Penguin, Auckland, 1996, p. 33.

3 Elsdon Best, *Maori Religion and Mythology, Part 2*, Government Printer, Wellington, 1982, p. 375.

4 Pakaariki Harrison, *Tane-nui-a-Rangi, Auckland University Marae*, University of Auckland, Auckland, 1991, p. 21.

5 Hirini Moko Mead and Neil Grove, *Ngā Pēpeha a Ngā Tīpuna 4*, Victoria University of Wellington, Wellington, 1996, p. 325.

6 Arapata Hakiwai and John Terrell, *Ruatepupuke: A Māori Meeting House*, Field Museum, Chicago, 1994, p. 44.

7 Apirana Ngata, 'The Origin of Maori Carving, Part 1', *Te Ao Hou*, no. 22, April 1958, p. 35; translation by Ngarino Ellis in *A Whakapapa of Tradition: 100 Years of Ngati Porou Carving 1830–1930*, Auckland University Press, Auckland, 2016.

8 Ellis, *A Whakapapa*, p. 24.

9 Anaru Reedy, *Nga Korero a Mohi Ruatapu, Tohunga Rongonui o Ngati Porou*, Canterbury University Press, Christchurch, 1993, p. 159.

10 Harrison, *Tane-nui-a-Rangi*, p. 3.

11 Hakiwai and Terrell, *Ruatepupuke*, p. 44.

12 Ellis, *A Whakapapa*, p. 21.

13 Harrison, *Tane-nui-a-Rangi*, p. 22.

14 Caroline Phillips, Dilys Johns and Harry Allen, 'Why Did Maori Bury Artefacts in the Wetlands of Pre-contact Aotearoa/New Zealand?', *Journal of Wetland Archaeology*, vol. 2, no. 1, 2002, pp. 39–60.

15 Ibid., p. 54. This was a major site, by all accounts: 187 heru were found there, compared with only 32 at Ōruarangi, which was 'otherwise prolific' in terms of taonga (ibid., p. 45).

16 Te Rangi Hīroa, *The Coming of the Maori*, Maori Purposes Fund Board, Wellington, 1949, p. 55.

17 Pakaariki Harrison, Kahutoi Te Kanawa and Rawinia Higgins, 'Ngā Mahi Toi – The Arts', in Tānia Ka'ai (ed.), *Ki te Whaiao – An Introduction to Māori Culture and Society*, Pearson, Auckland, 2003, p. 120.

18 Other dog imagery can be found on nineteenth-century kumete (bowls): see Roger Neich, *Carved Histories: Rotorua Ngāti Tarawhai Woodcarving*, Auckland University Press, Auckland, 2002, pp. 236–41. The cave was uncovered in 1889 by the geologist and founder of Canterbury Museum, Julius von Haast; it also held an ama (outrigger), a carved paddle and a carved canoe bailer.

19 See Hirini Moko Mead, *Te Toi Whakairo: The Art of Maori Carving*, Reed, Auckland, 1995.

20 Mead identifies a relationship betweeen the Waimamaku waka tūpāpaku and Te Hau ki Tūranga, the Rongowhakaata house: *Toi Whakairo*, p. 25.

21 Mead, *Toi Whakairo*, p. 190.

22 Neich, *Carved Histories*, p. 332.

23 Bernie Kernot, 'Nga Tohunga Whakairo o Mua', in Sidney Moko Mead (ed.), *Te Maori: Maori Art from New Zealand Collections*, Heinemann, Auckland, 1984, pp. 138, 141.

24 Maori Studies Department, *Opening of Te Whakatuwheratanga o Te Tumu Herenga Waka, 6 Tihema 1986, Poneke, Te Whare Wananga o Wikitoria*, Victoria University of Wellington, Wellington, 1986, p. 36.

25 Hakiwai, 'Te Toi Whakairo', p. 170.

26 Mead (ed.), *Te Maori*, p. 218.

27 Hakiwai, 'Te Toi Whakairo', p. 230.

28 Jonathan Mane-Wheoki, ' : No Wai Tenei Whare Tupuna? A Report on Ngati Awa Claim (Wai 46)', Waitangi Tribunal, March 1993, p. 10.

29 'Pataka, The Maori Treasure Houses', *Te Ao Hou*, no. 40, September 1962, p. 32.

30 Kernot, 'Nga Tohunga Whakairo,' p. 150. Kernot was Neich's PhD supervisor at Victoria University of Wellington.

31 Terence Barrow, *A Guide to the Maori Meeting House 'Te Hau ki Turanga'*, National Museum, Wellington, 1976, p. 7.

32 Material from an unpublished manuscript on Tame Poata by Ngarino Ellis, 1988.

33  Roger Neich, 'Nineteenth to Mid-Twentieth Century Individual Maori Woodcarvers and the Known Works', *Records of Auckland Museum*, 41, 2004, 53–86.

34  Mere Whaanga, *A Carved Cloak for Tahu*, Auckland University Press, Auckland, 2004, p. 223.

35  Mereana Mokomoko, 'The Building of Hotunui, Whare Whakairo, W. H. Taipari's Carved House at Thames, 1878', *Transactions and Proceedings of the Royal Society of New Zealand*, 30, 1897, 41–44, p. 44.

36  W. J. Phillips and J. C. Wadmore, *The Great Carved House Mataatua of Whakatane*, Polynesian Society, Wellington, 1956, p. 33. Neich compiled a table of payments for Ngāti Tarawhai and Ngāti Pikiao canoe carvers (*Carved Histories*, pp. 180–81, table 4.1): pre-1823 the payment for a whole canoe might be two kahu kurī, but within ten years this had changed to three casks of powder and a gun. By the early 1850s this had shifted again – to cash, with payments expected or paid of £20–150.

37  Neich, *Carved Histories*, 325.

38  The taurapa of *Kahutiaterangi* is in Te Papa (ME014331).

39  Te Arawa (and others) reused components of Ngāpuhi waka taua in order to denigrate the mana of the original iwi. Roger Neich comments on the practice of reusing carvings: 'As with so many of these 1870s [Ngāti Tarawhai] houses, several disused war canoes were cut up to provide timber for the carvings in Houmaitawhiti.' *Carved Histories*, p. 325.

40  Taupō, with its geothermal activity, was another tourism hub, but there the tourism economy was run by former Pākehā soldiers rather than by Tūwharetoa. Paul Diamond, 'Te tāpoi Māori – Māori tourism', *Te Ara – the Encyclopedia of New Zealand*, www.TeAra.govt.nz/en/te-tapoi-maori-maori-tourism/print

41  Roger Neich, 'Te Rahui, Anaha Kepa', *Dictionary of New Zealand Biography*, first published in 1990, updated March 2011, *Te Ara – the Encyclopedia of New Zealand*, https://teara.govt.nz/en/biographies/1t61/te-rahui-anaha-kepa

42  Eva Garbutt, 'The Care of Living Objects: Caring for Rauru and Te Wharepuni a Maui in Germany', in Dean Sully (ed.), *Decolonising Conservation*, Left Coast Press, Walnut Creek, CA, 2007, p. 116.

43  Ōhinemutu was made from a façade of the house Ruhurahu from Orakei Korako, as well as other carvings.

44  Diamond, 'Te tāpoi Māori'.

45  Neich, 'Te Rahui, Ānaha Kēpa'.

46  https://thespinoff.co.nz/art/03-10-2019/things-i-learned-at-art-school-bob-jahnke/

### The Taiapa brothers: Carving in the twentieth century

1  Barney Christie, interview with Damian Skinner, 29 January 2003, Te Papa Tongarewa.

2  James Rickard, in Andrew Te Whaiti, *Te Puia: The Next 40 Years: Stories of those guiding the Maori Arts and Crafts Institute, Rotorua*, Open Polytechnic of New Zealand, Lower Hutt, 2005, p. 29.

3  R. Peter Walker-Taiapa, 'Biographical material relating to Pineamine Taiapa', Alexander Turnbull Library, MS-Papers-9104.

4  Pine Taiapa, 'The Significance and Stories of the Tukutuku Patterns – Ngati-Porou version', unpublished MS, undated, Ngarino Ellis collection.

5  'Interview with Pine Taiapa talking about Hinerupe Meeting House,' Ngā Taonga Sound and Vision, Recording 40734 (1965).

6  Pine Taiapa Interview Regarding Rongomaitapui Meeting House, Te Araroa 1965, Ngā Taonga Sound and Vision, Recording 40733 (1965).

7  Pine Taiapa – Tikitiki Church, Ngā Taonga Sound and Vision, Recording 40736 (1965).

8  Pine Taiapa – Porourangi Meeting House, Waiomatatini, Ngā Taonga Sound and Vision, Recording 40757, 40758 (1965).

9  Pine Taiapa IV – Talk on Rongomaianiwaniwa Meeting House, Ngā Taonga Sound and Vision, Recording 40864 (1965).

10  'Rotorua Maori Arts and Crafts Institute – Agendas and Minutes of Meetings, 1974–77'.

### Morelli and the nineteenth-century papahou artist

1  Roger Neich, 'Nineteenth and Mid-Twentieth Century Individual Maori Woodcarvers and the Known Works,' *Records of Auckland Museum*, 41, 2004, pp. 53–86.

2  The full list is: waka huia 1979.206, a, b; waka huia 1979.206.1341; waka huia 1979.206.1439; waka huia 1979.206.1635.

3  Roger Neich, 'Papahou and Wakahuia: Maori Treasure Boxes', in Chanel Clarke, Fuli Pereira and Nigel Prickett (eds), *Tradition and Change in Maori and Pacific Art: Essays by Roger Neich*, Auckland War Memorial Museum, Auckland, 2013, pp. 380–81.

4  Rosamund Currie, Glynn Davis, Catherine Elliot, Umaporn Kruekamwang and Raquel Pinto, 'Māori Treasure Box. Museum of London Accession Number Q100. The Thomas Layton Collection', Research Documentation Report, Institute of Archaeology, University College London, n.d., p. 10. This is a highly detailed report, which may be one model for future research into individual taonga – held overseas, at least.

5  'Overview of Papahou', Te Papa Tongarewa, https://collections.tepapa.govt.nz/topic/2407

6  X36780.1. It is 880mm long, 415mm wide and 250mm high; pre-1840.

### Māori art and archaeology

1  Joel Polack, *New Zealand: Being a Narrative of Travels and Adventures During a Residence in that Country Between the Years 1831 and 1837*, vol. 2, Richard Bentley, London, 1838, pp. 266–67.

2  Deidre Brown, *Tai Tokerau Whakairo Rākau: Northland Māori Wood Carving*, Reed, Auckland, 2003. Of the approximately one hundred whakairo rākau in New Zealand and overseas public museum collections that Brown could attribute with some certainty to Te Tai Tokerau, forty were waka kōiwi (called 'waka tūpāpaku' in the book).

3  Ibid., pp. 59–60.

4  Atholl Anderson, 'Pieces of the Past: AD 1200 to 1800', in Atholl Anderson, Judith Binney and Aroha Harris (eds), *Tangata Whenua: An Illustrated History*, Bridget Williams Books, Wellington, 2014, p. 78.

5  Atholl Anderson, 'Wairau Bar: Ancestors and Archaeology', in Anderson, Binney and Harris (eds), *Tangata Whenua*, pp. 100–1.

### 3  Ngā kākahu: Textiles

1  'He Waiata na Te Ranginui, Mo Te Kakahu Kore', in George Grey, *Ko nga Moteatea, me nga Hakirara o nga Maori*, Hon. Robert Stokes, Wellington, 1853, p. 200.

2  Translation by the authors.

3  Hirini Moko Mead, in *Traditional Maori Clothing: A Study of Technological and Functional Change*, Reed, Auckland, 1969, defines a 'hana' as an 'all white cape', pp. 117, 222.

4  Lisa McKendry, 'Māori Kākahu (Cloak) Fragments from Piha: Whakaari Pā', *Records of the Auckland Museum*, vol. 52 (2017), pp. 59–70.

5  Ibid., p. 63.

6  Ibid., p. 68.

7  Adrienne Rewi, 'Remnants of the Past: What Can Ancient Raranga Fragments Tell Us About Our Tīpuna?', *Te Karaka*, vol. 64, 21 December 2014, http://ngaitahu.iwi.nz/our_stories/remnants-past/

8  C. Jacomb, R. Walter. S. Easdale, D. Johns, D. O'Connell, D. Witter and A. Witter, 'A 15th Century Maori Textile Fragment from Kaitorete Spit, Canterbury, and the Evolution of Maori Weaving', *Journal of the Polynesian Society*, vol. 113, no. 3 (2004), pp. 291–96.

9  Rewi, 'Remnants'.

10  Te Rangi Hīroa, 'The Evolution of Maori Clothing', *Journal of the Polynesian Society*, vol. 33, no. 129, 1924, p. 32.

11  Ibid., p. 33.

12 Ibid., p. 34.

13 H. W. Williams, *A Dictionary of the Maori Language*, 7th edn, GP Publications, Wellington, 1991.

14 Te Rangi Hīroa, 'Maori Clothing', p. 34.

15 Joseph Hooker (ed.), *Journal of the Right Hon. Sir Joseph Banks*, Macmillan, New York, 1896, p. 206.

16 H. W. Williams translates 'paoi' as 'wooden beater for pounding fern root'.

17 Roger Neich and Mick Pendergrast, *Pacific Tapa*, University of Hawai'i Press, Honolulu, 2004, p. 89. See also Roger Neich, 'NZ Maori Barkcloth and Barckcloth Beaters', *Records of the Auckland Institute and Museum*, no. 33 (1996), pp. 111–58.

18 Neich and Pendergrast note that older examples from the ninth to the twelfth century have been found in Vaito'otia/Fa'ahia on Huahine in French Polynesia. These are 'fundamentally' different from paoi in their shaping and, as such, Neich and Pendergrast argue that there is no link between them: *Pacific Tapa*, p. 89.

19 Neich and Pendergrast, *Pacific Tapa*, p. 21.

20 William Colenso, 'Of Plants Formerly Cultivated For Their Textile Uses', *Transactions and Proceedings of the New Zealand Institute*, vol. 13, 1880, p. 18.

21 Patricia Te Arapo Wallace, 'Ko te Pūtaiao, te Ao o ngā Tūpuna. Ancestral Māori Scientific Practice', in Awhina Tamarapa (ed.), *Whatu Kākahu. Māori Cloaks*, Te Papa Press, Wellington, 2011, p. 47.

22 Mere Whaanga, *A Carved Cloak for Tahu*, Auckland University Press, Auckland, 2004, p. 48.

23 Ngahuia Te Awekotuku, 'We Will Become Ill if We Stop Weaving', *Mana Wahine Maori: Selected Writings on Maori Women's Art, Culture and Politics*, New Women's Press, Auckland, 1991, p. 119.

24 Diggeress Te Kanawa, *Weaving a Kākahu*, Bridget Williams Books in association with Aotearoa Moananui a Kiwa Weavers, Wellington, 1992, pp. 20–21. Erenora Puketapu-Hetet provides a clear table of the different dyes available and how they are used in *Maori Weaving*, Longman Paul, Auckland, 1989, pp. 16–17. Puketapu-Hetet was raised in the Waiwhetu community in Wellington, and learnt weaving by making tukutuku panels for the meeting house.

25 Mirama Evans and Ranui Ngarimu, *The Art of Māori Weaving*, Huia, Wellington, p. 111.

26 Puketapu-Hetet, *Maori Weaving*, p. 54.

27 Ngahuia Te Awekotuku, pers. comm, n.d.

28 Elsdon Best, *The Maori Canoe*, Board of Māori Ethnological Research for the Dominion Museum (Dominion Museum bulletin; no. 7), Wellington, 1925, p. 251.

29 Williams, *Dictionary*, p. 488.

30 Best, *The Maori Canoe*, p. 251.

31 Whaanga, *Carved Cloak*, pp. 63–64.

32 Other collections of the Forsters' are in the Sammlung für Völkerkunde in Göttingen, Germany (157 objects) and in Wörlitz, Germany (31 objects). See Adrienne Kaeppler, 'To attempt some new discoveries in that vast unknown tract', audio transcript, 2006, www.nma.gov.au/audio/captain-james-cook-series/transcripts/to-attempt-some-new-discoveries

33 Pitt Rivers Museum, Tātua 1886.1.1182, http://objects.prm.ox.ac.uk/pages/PRMUID25404.html

34 Williams, *Dictionary*, p. 395. There are other metaphorical references to tātua, for example in placenames such as Te Tātua a Riukiuta (a volcano in the Three Kings area of Auckland).

35 Whaanga, *Carved Cloak*, 88.

36 Williams, *Dictionary*, p. 395.

37 Te Rangi Hīroa, *The Coming of the Maori*, Maori Purposes Fund Board, Wellington, 1949, p. 175.

38 Paul Turnbull, www.nma.gov.au/audio/transcripts/cook/NMA_Turnbull_20060728.html

39 Williams, *Dictionary*, p. 442.

40 In Rangimārie Hetet and Rangituatahi Te Kanawa, *Aku Mahi Whatu Māori: My Art of Māori Weaving*, 1978, F15003, Ngā Taonga Sound and Vision, www.ngataonga.org.nz/collections/catalogue/catalogue-item?record_id=69704

41 Tamarapa, *Whatu Kākahu*, p. 11.

42 Ibid., p. 12.

43 Kahutoi Te Kanawa and John Turi-Tiakitai, 'Te Mana o te Kākahu: The Prestige of Cloaks', in Tamarapa, *Whatu Kākahu*, p. 21.

44 Tamarapa, *Whatu Kākahu*, p. 11.

45 Ibid., p. 163.

46 Ibid. Tōī was very versatile: the weaver could use the red midrib to make into tātua or for the designs on poi, and the leaves for binding a handle to an adze.

47 Hīroa, *Coming of the Maori*, p. 167.

48 https://collections.tepapa.govt.nz/object/381673

49 Best, 'The Art of the Whare Pora', *Transactions and Proceedings of the New Zealand Institute*, vol. 31, 1898, p. 644; see Hirini Mead, *Traditional Maori Clothing: A Study of Technological and Functional Change*, Reed, Auckland, 1969, pp. 46–48, for a more detailed discussion.

50 Mick Pendergrast, *Te Aho Tapu: The Sacred Thread*, University of Hawai'i Press, Honolulu, 1987, p. 93.

51 Roger Neich, Mick Pendergrast and Dorota Starzecka, *The Maori Collections of the British Museum*, British Museum Press, London, 2010, p. 117.

52 See Angas, 'Tara or Irirangi, Principal Chief of the Ngati Tai tribe', 1847 (Alexander Turnbull Library, PUBL-0014-34). Other examples, all from *The New Zealanders Illustrated* (Thomas McLean, London, 1847) include: plate 7 'Toenga', plate 9 'E Wai and Kahoki', and plate 22 'Children at the Boiling Springs'.

53 Te Rangi Hīroa, *Vikings of the Sunrise*, Frederick A. Stokes, New York, 1938, pp. 269–70.

54 Margery Blackman, 'Whatu: The Enclosing Threads', in Tamarapa, *Whatu Kākahu*, p. 91. Blackman cites D. R. Simmons, 'The Lake Hauroko Burial and the Evolution of Maori Clothing', *Records of the Otago Museum, Anthropology*, 5 (1968), pp. 4–6; M. M. Trotter, 'Investigations of a Maori Burial Cave on Mary Island, Lake Hauroko', *Records of the Canterbury Museum*, vol. 9, no. 2, 1972, pp. 113–28.

55 The word 'kura' has many meanings, all intertwined, including sacred, special, red.

56 Te Kanawa and Turi-Tiakitai, 'Te Mana o te Kākahu', in Tamarapa, *Whatu Kākahu*, p. 26.

57 Ibid., pp. 26, 28.

58 Hokimate Harwood, 'Identification and Description of Feathers in Te Papa's Māori cloaks', *Tuhinga* 22, 2011, 145–47, p. 126.

59 Te Kanawa, *Weaving a Kakahu*, p. 5.

60 Patricia Wallace, 'Ko te Pūtaiao, te Ao o ngā Tupuna: Ancestral Maori Scientific Practice', in Tamarapa, *Whatu Kākahu*, p. 57.

61 See Harwood, 'Identification and Description', p. 146.

62 Ibid.

63 Pendergrast, *Te Aho Tapu*, p. 9.

64 There was experimentation with feathers before this time: Cook collected two kākahu with huruhuru attached – one is in the Pitt Rivers Museum in Oxford (1886.21.18), and the other is in the Museum of Ethnology in Vienna, Austria. The former has only the quills left, as the barbs have disintegrated over time; the Austrian example shows sparse bundles of feathers which were widely spaced. See Raymond Firth, 'Maori Material in the Vienna Museum', *Journal of the Polynesian Society*, vol. 40, no. 159, 1931, pp. 95–102: Firth identified twenty-four cloaks in the Vienna collection, including 'a cloak with decoration of tufts of red feathers, several korowai, two kahu kuri, a cloak with mixed feather–wool decoration from "Te Uriohau tribe, Manakau" and a dog-skin cloak "hururiko" … the last mat of its kind among the savages of the King Country', p. 101. This 'hururiko' may be a misspelling of 'huru kuri', which was a rare type of dogskin cloak made solely from whole skins sewn together.

65 See Hirini Moko Mead, 'Clothing Fashions in Traditional Maori Society', in Mead, *Maori Art on the World Scene*, Ahua Design and Illustration, Wellington, 1997, pp. 96–101.

66 Maureen Lander, 'Te Ao Tawhito/Te Ao Hou: Entwined Threads of Tradition and Innovation', in Tamarapa, *Whatu Kākahu*, p. 66.

67 Ibid.

68 Margery Blackman, 'Whatu', in Tamarapa, *Whatu Kākahu*, p. 91. For more information on some of these cloaks see Stig Rydén, *The Banks Collection: An Episode in 18th-Century Anglo-Swedish Relations*, Ethnographical Museum of Sweden, Monograph Series no. 8, Stockholm, 1965; Wilfred Shawcross, 'The Cambridge University Collection of Maori Artefacts, Made on Captain Cook's First Voyage', *Journal of the Polynesian Society*, vol. 79, 1970, pp. 305–48; H. Ling Roth, *The Maori Mantle*, Bankfield Museum, Halifax, 1923. The British Museum alone has 159 Māori cloaks in its collection.

69 Vincent Malcolm-Buchanan, Ngahuia Te Awekotuku and Linda Waimarie Nikora, 'Cloaked in Life and Death: Korowai, Kaitiaki and Tangihanga', *MAI Journal*, vol. 1, no. 1, 2012, p. 53.

70 Toi Te Rito Maihi, 'The Meaning of Cloaks', www.youtube.com/watch?v=9mKiKYvcmpw

71 Whaanga, *Carved Cloak*, p. 70.

72 Mead, *Traditional Maori Clothing*, p. 175.

73 Ibid., pp. 24–25.

74 Ibid., p. 175.

75 Anya Mountain Hook, pers. comm., May 2019.

76 Marara Hook, pers. comm., May 2019.

77 Nepia Kaa, pers. comm., December 2019.

78 In 1947 the cloak and mere were placed in Te Papa by the Pitt–Porutu whānau. This is an example of the museum's continued custodianship on behalf of whānau.

79 Teremoana Sparks and W. H. Oliver, 'Te Rangitopeora', *Dictionary of New Zealand Biography, Te Ara – the Encyclopedia of New Zealand*, April 2012, https://teara.govt.nz/en/biographies/1t103/topeora-rangi-te-kuini

80 Hazel Petrie, *Outcasts of the Gods? The Struggle Over Slavery in Māori New Zealand*, Auckland University Press, Auckland, 2015, p. 103.

81 Elsdon Best, *Tuhoe, the children of the mist: a sketch of the origin, history, myths, and beliefs of the Tuhoe tribe of the Maori of New Zealand; with some account of other early tribes of the Bay of Plenty district*, Board of Maori Ethnological Research for the author, 1925, pp. 522–33.

82 Mead, *Traditional Maori Clothing*, p. 177.

83 Ibid.

84 Petrie, *Outcasts*, pp. 67–68. He would eventually find his way back to Kaiapoi, where he later became a renowned greenstone carver (p. 68).

85 Ngahuia Te Awekotuku, and Linda Waimarie Nikora, *Nga Taonga o Te Urewera. A Report Prepared for the Waitangi Tribunal's Urewera District Inquiry*, August 2003 (Wai 894, doc B6), p. 57.

86 Toi Te Rito Maihi, 'Ngā Aho', in Tamarapa, *Whatu Kākahu*, p. 41.

87 Whaanga, *Carved Cloak*, p. 223; see Rongowhakaata Halbert, *Horouta: The History of the Horouta Canoe, Gisborne and East Coast*, Oratia Books, Auckland, 2012, p. 90.

88 The waka was carved by Te Waaka Perohuka, Timoti Rangitotohuihara, Wiremu Te Keteiwi, Patorounu Pakapaka, Natanahira, Taumata and Mahumahu. In 1853 Perohuka presented the waka to Tāmati Wāka Nene and Patuone who, in exchange, sent him 'a piebald stallion called "Taika" (Tiger). The horse was later given to Tarakau, the builder of the famous canoe' (Thomas Lambert, *Pioneering Reminiscences of Old Wairoa*, Thomas Avery & Sons, New Plymouth, 1936, p. 162).

89 Apirana Ngata, 'The Origin of Maori Carving, Part 1', *Te Ao Hou*, no. 22, April 1958, p. 35.

90 Apirana Ngata (trans.), *Rauru Nui a Toi Lectures*, Department of Anthropology, Victoria University, Welington, 1972; translation by Ngarino Ellis in *A Whakapapa of Tradition: 100 Years of Ngati Porou Carving 1830–1930*, Auckland University Press, Auckland, 2016. For an extended analysis of the lament see Wayne Ngata, 'Te Waiata Tangi a Rangiuia', MA thesis, Massey University, 1993.

91 Ngata, *Rauru Nui*, p. 12.

92 'Keeping Alive Korowai Weaving', *New Zealand Crafts*, December 1982, p. 2.

93 In the first five years the league recruited over 4000 members, who were active in 300 branches across the country.

94 Kahutoi Te Kanawa, 'Te raranga me te whatu – Revival of Māori fibre work', *Te Ara – the Encyclopedia of New Zealand*, www.TeAra.govt.nz/en/te-raranga-me-te-whatu/page-5

95 'Keeping Alive Korowai Weaving', p. 3.

96 Atawhai Putaranui, 'Hetet, Rangimārie', *Dictionary of New Zealand Biography, Te Ara – the Encyclopedia of New Zealand*, August 2011, https://teara.govt.nz/en/biographies/5h18/hetet-rangimarie

97 Kahutoi Te Kanawa, 'Memories of Emily Rangitiaria Schuster', in Ane Tonga (ed.), *Te Ringa Rehe: The Legacy of Emily Schuster*, Rotorua Museum Te Whare Taonga o Te Arawa, Rotorua, 2017, p. 17.

98 Jim Schuster, 'Toku whaea, ko Emire: My mum, Emily', in Tonga, *Te Ringa Rehe*, p. 10.

99 Ibid., p. 14.

100 www.maoriart.org.nz/trrwoa.html

101 In 2010 the group hosted the Indigenous Weavers International Symposium in Rotorua.

102 Puketapu-Hetet, *Maori Weaving*, p. 55.

103 Te Kanawa, *Weaving a Kakahu*, p. 4.

104 Kahutoi Te Kanawa, 'Memories', p. 21.

105 Mick Pendergrast, *Te Aho Tapu: The Sacred Thread*, University of Hawai'i Press, Honolulu, 1987 and *Feathers and Fibre: A Survey of Traditional and Contemporary Maori Craft*, Penguin, Auckland, 1984.

### Tahuaroa, pākūwhā and hākari: The display and gifting of taonga

1 Toi Te Rito Maihi, 'Ngā Aho: Threads that join', in Awhina Tamarapa (ed.), *Whatu Kākahu: Māori Cloaks*, Te Papa Press, Wellington, 2011, p. 41.

2 Hirini Moko Mead, *Tikanga Māori: Living by Māori Values*, Huia, Wellington, 2019, p. 399.

3 Paula G. Rubel and Abraham Rosman, 'Potlatch and Hakari: An Analysis of Maori Society in Terms of the Potlatch Model', *Man*, vol. 6, no. 4 (December 1971), pp. 660–73.

4 Reverend William Yate described one tahuaroa in 1832: 'Went to Tahua Roa to Owaiawai [Ōhaeawai] with twenty-nine of our natives to a hahunga [bone-scraping ceremony]. About 5,000 persons were assembled together. There were three thousand bushels of *kumara* (sweet potatoes) for presents; two thousand more would be consumed: with 290 pigs, which had been killed for the occasion': William Yate, *Missionary Register for 1832*, Church Missionary Society, London, 1832, cited in Rubel and Rosman, p. 661. A. N. Brown described another tahuaroa: 'They have collected for the feast, six large albatrosses, nineteen calabashes of shark oil, several tons of fish, principally young sharks, which are esteemed by the natives as a great delicacy, upward of twenty thousand dried eels, a great number of hogs, and baskets of potatoes without number': A. N. Brown, *Church Missionary Record* (1838), Church Missionary Society, London, cited in Rubel and Rosman, p. 661.

5 See Mead, *Tikanga Māori*, pp. 329–31 for the details.

6 Mead, *Tikanga Māori*, p. 399.

7 Ibid., p. 197. One example was a pākūwhā in 1816 for Nohorua, Te Rauparaha's elder half-brother, who married a woman from Ngāti Rahiri, who sent waka filled with food to the wedding. However, the canoes met with disaster and all the food was ruined.

8 Elsdon Best, 'Maori Marriage Customs', *Transactions and Proceedings of the New Zealand Institute*, vol. 36, 1903, p. 46.

9 Raymond Firth, *Economics of the New Zealand Maori*, A. R. Shearer, Wellington, 1929, p. 305.

10 Mead, *Tikanga Māori*, p. 1978.

11  In 1835 Samuel Williams made an engraving of a tall series of stages, based on Yate's description: 'A stage erected for a New Zealand feast', Alexander Turnbull Library, PUBL-0101-139.

### Tihei mauri ora: The remaking of cloaks from museum collections

1  Jenny Ling, 'Modern day Māori cloak gifted to people of Hokianga', www.stuff.co.nz/auckland/local-news/northland/101588900/modern-day-maori-cloak-gifted-to-people-of-hokianga, 20 February, 2018.

2  Hamuera Robb, interview with Ngarino Ellis, 8 September 2020.

3  In January 2020 a Special Expert Commission in Russia could identify only forty-two taonga collected on this voyage, though Suvorova believes there are more. She identifies Toi Moko, for instance, as having been collected in 1820 and brought to Russia, and points to a newly discovered pare (lintel) discovered in the Russian Museum of Ethnography, which was not known to hold any Māori collection. See Olga Suvorova, 'Forgotten Taonga Māori in Russia: The 1820 Visit of the Bellingshausen-Lazarev Expedition to Queen Charlotte Sound,' *Te Kaharoa*, 13 (1), 2020, p. 32, https://doi.org/10.24135/tekaharoa.v15i1.295.

4  For more information, see Awhina Tamarapa (ed.), *Whatu Kākahu: Māori Cloaks*, Te Papa Press, Wellington, 2011, pp. 182–83.

5  Robb, interview with Ngarino Ellis.

6  See Pavel Mikhailov's drawings, 'South New Zealanders', 1820, in Suvorova, 'Forgotten Taonga Māori', fig. 9, p. 23. Note for example, Webber's drawing of chief Kahura in 1777 and Pavel Mikhailov's drawings of 'South New Zealanders, 1820'.

### 4  Ngā whare: Architecture

1  Mohi Tūrei, 'Takarakau', *Journal of the Polynesian Society*, vol. 22, no. 86, 1913, 6–66, pp. 63, 66.

2  William Marshall, *A Personal Narrative of Two Visits to New Zealand in His Majesty's Ship Alligator, AD 1834*, James Nisbet, London, 1841, p. 211.

3  B. F. Leach, H. M. Leach and R. G. Law, 'The Chronology of Pre-European Settlement in Palliser Bay, A Re-Evaluation of Radiocarbon Dating Fifty Years On', Heritage New Zealand digital library: Leach7, 2022, p. 52.

4  Janet Davidson, *The Prehistory of New Zealand*, Longman Paul, Auckland, 1984, p. 164.

5  No published information has as yet been found on the exact raranga and whatu techniques used in thatched architecture; however, Carin Wilson and Rau Hoskins have used whatu as binding in their whare raupō projects. See also Deidre Brown, 'Clothed not Clad: Māori Woven Architecture', *Celebration: Proceedings of the 22nd annual conference of the Society of Architectural Historians of Australia and New Zealand*, Napier, 2005, pp. 59–63.

6  W. J. Phillipps visited a house built of ponga logs with raupō interior linings in Kāwhia in the early twentieth century: Phillipps, *Maori Houses and Food Stores*, Government Printer, Wellington, 1952, p. 48.

7  Ibid., p. 24.

8  Raupo Houses Act 1842, www.nzlii.org/nz/legis/hist_act/rha18425v1842n17288/

9  Jarvis Hayman, 'Conflict in the Highlands: The Archaeology of the Scottish Highland Clearances', *Archaeological Review from Cambridge*, vol. 25, no. 1, 2010, 69–85, pp. 82, 83.

10  Rau Hoskins, 'A Māori Approach', *Advance*, Spring 2014, p. 9.

11  Hongi to Elsdon Best, 23 May 1912, in Best, *Maori Storehouses and Kindred Structures*, A. R. Shearer, Wellington, 1974, p. 34.

12  Paremata Māori, *Proceedings of the Third Kotahitanga Parliament April to May 1894*, Greytown, 1895, http://nzetc.victoria.ac.nz/tm/scholarly/tei-Kot1894Kore.html

13  Edward Jerningham Wakefield, *Adventure in New Zealand*, vol. 1, John Murray, London, 1845, p. 299.

14  Ambrosia Crum, 'Pataka: A Rare Survivor', MHerCons research report, University of Auckland, 2018, pp. 10–12.

15  There are many accounts describing the contents of pātaka and other storage structures; for one detailed description see Hongi in Best, *Maori Storehouses*, pp. 32–36.

16  James Herries Beattie and Atholl Anderson (eds), *Traditional Lifeways of the Southern Maori*, University of Otago Press, Dunedin, 1994, p. 44.

17  Crum, 'Pataka', p. 24.

18  Raymond Firth, 'Maori Store-houses of To-day', *Journal of the Royal Anthropological Institute of Great Britain and Ireland*, vol. 55, 1925, pp. 365, 370, 372.

19  Kahu in Harry Evison, *Te Wai Pounamu: The Greenstone Island, A History of the Southern Maori During the European Colonization of New Zealand*, Aoraki Press, Christchurch, 1993, p. 465.

20  Crum, 'Pataka', p. 19.

21  'Donald McLean papers', MS-Papers-0032-0387, Alexander Turnbull Library, Wellington.

22  James Schuster and Dean Whiting, 'Marae Conservation in Aotearoa', in Dean Sully (ed.), *Decolonising Conservation: Caring for Māori Meeting Houses Outside New Zealand*, Left Coast Press, Walnut Creek, CA, 2007, p. 74. This figure is based on marae listed on Māori Maps: it takes into account that some marae on the list do not have wharenui, and that not all marae have consented to be part of the Māori Maps project; https://maorimaps.com

23  For a complete discussion of pare composition, see Johnson Gordon Paul Witehira, 'Tārai Kōrero Toi: articulating a Māori design language', PhD thesis, Massey University, 2013, http://hdl.handle.net/10179/5213, pp. 83–136.

24  Jeremy Treadwell, 'Cosmology and Structure: the Tāhuhu in the 19th-century Whare Māori', *Journal of the Polynesian Society*, vol. 126, no. 1, 2017, p. 104; see also Richard Sundt, *Whare Karakia: Māori Church Building, Decoration and Ritual in Aotearoa New Zealand 1834–63*, Auckland University Press, Auckland, 2010.

25  Roger Neich, *Painted Histories: Early Maori Figurative Painting*, Auckland University Press, Auckland, 1993, p. 48.

26  Rongowhakaata Halbert in W. J. Phillipps, *Carved Maori Houses of the Eastern Districts of the North Island*, Harry H. Tombs, Wellington, 1944, p. 92.

27  See Te Rangi Hīroa, 'Maori Decorative Art: No. 1, House-panels', *Transactions and Proceeding of the New Zealand Institute*, vol. 53, 1920, 452–70, p. 465; for a detailed description on the evolution of kākaho and tukutuku linings see Ngapine Te Ao, 'The Legacy of Kākaho', in Ngarino Ellis and Witi Ihimaera (eds), *Te Ata: Māori Art from the East Coast, New Zealand*, Auckland, Reed, 2002.

28  Hīroa, 'Maori Decorative Art', p. 455.

29  Ibid., p. 457.

30  See Ngarino Ellis, 'Hoe Whakairo, Maori Painted and Carved Paddles 1769–1850', Master's thesis, University of Auckland, 1997, https://hdl.handle.net/2292/64515, p. 56.

31  Chris Jacomb, 'The Chronology of Moncks Cave, Canterbury, New Zealand', *Records of the Canterbury Museum*, vol. 22, 2008, 45–56, p. 55.

32  Neich, *Painted Histories*, p. 72.

33  See George French Angas's 1844 watercolours *Maketu house at Otawhao Pah* (Alexander Turnbull Library, PUBL-0014-25) and *Rangihaeata's celebrated house on the island of Mana* (Alexander Turnbull Library, PUBL-0014-04).

34  W. J. Phillipps, 'Carved Houses of Te Arawa', *Dominion Museum Records of Ethnology*, vol. 1, no. 1, 1946, 1–46, pp. 11–12.

35  Neich, *Painted Histories*.

36  H. W. Williams, 'Description of Maori Rafter Patterns', in Augustus Hamilton, *Maori Art*, Ferguson and Mitchell for the New Zealand Institute, Dunedin, 1957, pp. 117–18.

37  Hone Sadler in Treadwell, 'Cosmology and Structure', p. 101.

38  Mike Austin, 'Pacific Island Architecture', *Fabrications*, vol. 11, no. 2, 2001, 13–19, p. 13.

39  Treadwell, 'Cosmology and Structure', pp. 97, 99, 104.

40  Ibid., p. 115.

### Pakaariki Harrison, QSO (1928–2008)

1. Paki also made carvings for a house for urban Wellington Māori, but the house was never erected because of a lack of funds.
2. 'Creative NZ Scraps Maori Art Trademark Toi Iho', The Big Idea, www.thebigidea.nz/news/industry-news/2009/oct/62121-creative-nz-scraps-maori-art-trademark-toi-iho

### 5 Ngā toi whenua: Rock art

1. Gerard O'Regan, 'He Ana, He Whakairo: Examining Māori Belief of Place through the Archaeological Context of Rock Art', PhD thesis, University of Auckland, 2016, p. 14.
2. Ibid., p. 15.
3. Ibid., p. 16.
4. For a thorough interrogation of the contradictions and shortcomings of Aotearoa rock art research undertaken to the end of the 1980s, see O'Regan, 'He Ana, He Whakairo', pp. 14–30.
5. Ibid., p. 33.
6. Ibid., pp. 38–39.
7. Michael Trotter and Beverley McCulloch, *Prehistoric Rock Art of New Zealand*, A. H. and A. W. Reed, Auckland, 1971, p. 19.
8. Ian Barber and Justin Maxwell, 'Evaluating New Radiocarbon Dates from Midden Deposits near Moriori Tree Carvings, Rēkohu (Chatham Island)', *Journal of the Polynesian Society*, vol. 121, no. 1, March 2012, 33–50, p. 33.
9. O'Regan, 'He Ana, He Whakairo', p. 38.
10. Paul Horley and Georgia Lee, 'Painted and Carved House Embellishments at 'Orongo Village, Easter Island', *Rapa Nui Journal*, vol. 23, no. 2, 2009; Lee and Horley, 'Documentation of the Sacred Precinct of Mata Ngarau ('Orongo, Easter Island) in the Late 19th Century-Early 20th Century', *Journal of the Polynesian Society*, vol. 121, no. 4, 2012, 393–406, p. 394.
11. Beverley McCulloch, 'Maori Rock Drawings: A Matter of Interpretation', in *Maori Rock Drawings: The Theo Schoon Interpretations*, Robert McDougall Art Gallery, Christchurch, 1985.
12. Harry Evison, *Te Wai Pounamu: The Greenstone Island, A History of the Southern Maori During the European Colonization of New Zealand*, Aoraki Press, Christchurch, 1993, p. 12.
13. Nic Low, 'The First Language of Te Waipounamu', *Te Karaka*, no. 65, 2015, p. 33.
14. 'Te Ana Ngāi Tahu Māori Rock Art', www.teana.co.nz
15. O'Regan, 'He Ana, He Whakairo', p. 17.
16. Gilbert Archey, 'Rock Shelter Drawings at Arapuni Gorge', *Journal of the Polynesian Society*, vol. 36, no. 144, 1927, 369–371, p. 357; O'Regan, 'He Ana, He Whakairo', p. 18; W. J. Phillipps, 'The Rua Hoata Shelter, Waikato River', *Journal of the Polynesian Society*, vol. 56, no. 4, 1947, pp. 337–38; Trotter and McCulloch, *Prehistoric Rock Art*, p. 44.
17. Trotter and McCulloch, *Prehistoric Rock Art*, pp. 73, 75.
18. Ibid., p. 32.
19. Tahu Potiki, 'A Puzzling Absence', *Te Karaka*, no. 65, 2015, pp. 18–21; Trotter and McCulloch, *Prehistoric Rock Art*, p. 43.
20. Elsdon Best, 'Notes on Inscribed Stones of the Taranaki District', *Journal of the Polynesian Society*, vol. 36, no. 142, 1927, pp. 137–40; Michael Dunn, 'New Zealand Rock Shelter Art', *Art and Australia*, vol. 4, no. 1, 1966, p. 63; Harold Hamilton, 'The Kaingaroa Carvings', *Journal of the Polynesian Society*, vol. 34, no. 136, 1925, 356–62, p. 360; W. J. Phillipps, 'Note on a Carved Rock in Taranaki', *Journal of the Polynesian Society*, vol. 36, no. 142, 1927, 135–136, p. 135.
21. Trotter and McCulloch, *Prehistoric Rock Art*, p. 5.
22. Anderson, 'The Art of Concealment: Some Thoughts on South Island Māori Rock Drawings', in *Ka Tuhituhi o Nehera: The Drawings of Ancient Times*, National Museum of New Zealand, Wellington, 1988.
23. Ibid.
24. Kelly Keane-Tuala, 'Ngā manu – birds – Birds' names', *Te Ara – the Encyclopedia of New Zealand*, www.TeAra.govt.nz/en/nga-manu-birds/page-6
25. Michael Trotter, 'Foreword', *Maori Rock Drawings: The Theo Schoon Interpretations*, Robert McDougall Art Gallery, Christchurch, 1985.
26. Ibid.
27. Ibid., p. 11.
28. The drawings were still visible in the 1930s. Joel Polack, *New Zealand: Being a Narrative of Travels and Adventures During a Residence in that Country Between the Years 1831 and 1837*, vol. 2, Richard Bentley, London, 1838, pp. 135–36.
29. O'Regan, 'He Ana, He Whakairo', p. 196.
30. P. Pillay, G. O'Regan and J. Emmitt, 'A Locational Analysis of Rock Art in the North Island, Aotearoa New Zealand', *Journal of Pacific Archaeology*, 11 (1), 2020, pp. 71–82. Available at: https://pacificarchaeology.org/index.php/journal/article/view/300; Trotter and McCulloch, *Prehistoric Rock Art*, p. 2.
31. Trotter and McCulloch, Prehistoric Rock Art, p. 2.
32. Anderson, 'Art of Concealment'.
33. Gerard O'Regan, 'The Shifting Space of Ngāi Tahu Rock Art', in Geoffrey Clark, Foss Leach and Sue O'Connor (eds), *Islands of Inquiry: Colonisation, Seafaring and the Archaeology of Maritime Landscapes*, Australian National University Press, Canberra, 2008, p. 412.
34. Anderson, 'Art of Concealment'; Roger Duff, 'Maori Art in Rock Drawings', *New Zealand Arts Year Book*, no. 6, 1950, 6–11, p. 11.
35. Te Maire in James Herries Beattie, 'Traditions and Legends Collected from the Natives of Murihiku (Southland, New Zealand). Part VIII', *Journal of the Polynesian Society*, vol. 27, no. 107, 1918, 137–161, p. 156.
36. O'Regan, 'He Ana, He Whakairo', p. 12.
37. Walter Mantell, 'Address', *Transactions and Proceedings of the Royal Society of New Zealand 1868–1961*, vol. 1, 1868, p. 18.
38. Anderson, 'Art of Concealment'.
39. Theo Schoon, 'New Zealand's Oldest Art Galleries', *New Zealand Listener*, vol. 17, no. 429, 12 September 1947, pp. 6–7.
40. Duff, 'Maori Art', p. 7; 'More About Those Rock Drawings', *New Zealand Listener*, vol. 26, no. 661, 18 April 1952, p. 8; Neil Roberts, 'Maori Rock Drawing and Theo Schoon', in *Maori Rock Drawings: The Theo Schoon Interpretations*, Robert McDougall Art Gallery, Christchurch, 1985.
41. Tony Fomison, 'Theo Schoon and the Retouching of Rock Art,' *New Zealand Archaeological Association Newsletter*, vol. 30, no. 3, pp. 158–60; Michael Trotter and Beverley McCulloch, 'Frenchmans Gully and Theo Schoon,' *Archaeology in New Zealand*, vol. 43, no. 2, 2000, p. 146.
42. O'Regan, 'Shifting Space', p. 412.
43. Sally Blundell, 'How Do You Save Cave Drawings That Are Hundreds of Years Old from the Ravages of Time and Human Interaction?', *Te Karaka*, no. 49, 2010, p. 21.
44. 'The Ngāi Tahu claim', https://nzhistory.govt.nz/politics/treaty/the-treaty-in-practice/ngai-tahu (Ministry for Culture and Heritage).
45. 'Recording Rock Art', Te Rūnanga o Ngāi Tahu, 19 February 2015, https://ngaitahu.iwi.nz/our_stories/recording-rock-art/
46. 'Te Ana Ngāi Tahu Māori Rock Art', www.teana.co.nz
47. Gerard O'Regan, 'The History and Future of New Zealand Maori Rock Art: A Tribal Perspective', *Before Farming*, vol. 2003, no. 1, 2003, p. 1.
48. David Slack, 'A Sense of Time, Place and People: How the Passion to Preserve Rock Art Gathered Momentum', *Te Karaka*, no. 65, 2015, p. 32.
49. O'Regan, 'Shifting Space', pp. 413–14, 416.
50. The tapu motifs have, at various times, been taken from their landscape context and appropriated into sometimes egregious popular-culture noa contexts, such as graphic designs on Marmite jars, tea towels, placemats, postage stamps, glasses, Weetbix cereal cards and furniture fabric.

## 6 Ngā taonga o Wharawhara: Body adornment

1. Margaret Orbell, *The Illustrated Encyclopedia of Maori Myth and Legend*, Canterbury University Press, Christchurch, 1996, p. 33.

2. Eleanor Almeida and Eliza Macdonald, 'Summer Scholar Report 2019–20', University of Auckland, 2020, p. 20; Eliza Macdonald, 'Rakai Register online database', 2021, University of Auckland, collection of Ngarino Ellis.

3. Rawinia Higgins, 'He Tanga Ngutu, He Tuhoetanga te Mana Motuhake o te Ta Moko Wahine: The Identity Politics of Moko Kauae', PhD thesis, University of Otago, Dunedin, 2004, p. 34.

4. Ibid., p. 38.

5. Ibid., p. 32.

6. Ibid, pp. 39–40. Ngahuia Te Awekotuku identifies Tamanui-a-Raki from the South Island as another source for the origin of moko (*Mau Moko: The World of Māori Tattoo*, Penguin, Auckland, 2007, p. 14); Horatio Robley mentions a tipuna named Tama-nui-a-raki who also received 'permanent facial decoration' in the Underworld (in *Moko, Or, Maori Tattooing*, Chapman Hall, London, 1896, pp. 114–16).

7. Apirana Ngata, *Ngā Mōteatea The Songs: Part One*, Auckland University Press, Auckland, 2004, waiata 1, line 28.

8. Ibid., waiata 13, 'He Tangi mo Rangihiroa/A Lament for Te Rangihiroa', lines 2–3, pp. 48–49.

9. Ibid., waiata 5, line 17.

10. Ibid., waiata 33, lines 13–14.

11. Ibid, lines 18–19.

12. Ibid, waiata 54, 'He Tangi Mo Te Hiakai/A Lament for Te Hiakai', line 5, pp. 174–77.

13. Ben Finney, 'Ocean Sailing Canoes', in Kerry Howe (ed.), *Vaka Moana*, Auckland Museum and David Bateman, Auckland, 2006, p. 234.

14. Roger Neich and Fuli Pereira, *Pacific Jewelry and Adornment,* University of Hawai'i Press, Honolulu, 2004, p. 141.

15. Te Rangi Hīroa, *The Coming of the Maori*, Maori Purposes Fund Board, Wellington, 1949, p. 284.

16. Teone Tikau to Beattie, in James Herries Beattie and Atholl Anderson (eds), *Traditional Lifeways of the Southern Maori,* Otago University Press, Dunedin, 1994.

17. Beattie and Anderson, p. 241.

18. Apirana Ngata, *Ngā Mōteatea The Songs: Part Three*, Auckland University Press, Auckland, 2006, waiata 216, line 16.

19. Ibid., waiata 216, line 17.

20. Ibid., waiata 225, line 29.

21. Ngata, *Ngā Mōteatea The Songs: Part One*, waiata 51, line 6. See Ngarino Ellis, 'He Iti, He Pounamu: Lindauer and Personal Adornment' in Ngahiraka Mason (ed) *Gottfried Lindauer's New Zealand: The Māori Portraits*, Auckland University Press, Auckland, 2016, for a close analysis of adornment during the time of painter Gottfried Lindauer.

22. Keith St Cartmail, *The Art of Tonga*, Craig Potton, Nelson, 1997, pp. 101–2.

23. Neich and Pereira, *Pacific Jewelry*, p. 170.

24. See two whakapakoko (figures) in the British Museum, both 'masks' with teeth inserts (1854.12.29.91 #580, plate 108; 1944 OC.2.807 #581, plate 108). The explanatory text in Roger Neich, Mick Pendergrast and Dorota Starzecka, *The Maori Collections of the British Museum*, British Museum Press, London, 2010, p. 72, notes that 1854 was modelled on mokomokai (preserved heads). According to Neich, the 1854 figure is from the East Coast in the 1820s–1840s; the title is 'Whakapakoko rahui' in the Grey Collection. The 1944 example is in the Beasley Collection, made around the same time and place.

25. For a full report see http://objects.prm.ox.ac.uk/pages/PRMUID25949.html

26. At least twenty-two hei tiki were found there also; see Dougal Austin, *Te Hei Tiki: An Enduring Treasure in a Cultural Continuum*, Te Papa Press, Wellington, 2019, p. 59, and Roger Neich, *Pounamu*, David Bateman, Auckland, 1997, p. 8.

27. See Jane Reeves, 'Exiled for a Cause: Maori Prisoners in Dunedin', in M. Reilly and J. Thomson (eds), *When the Waves Rolled in Upon Us: Essays in Nineteenth-Century Maori History*, Otago University Press, Dunedin, 1999.

28. Justin J. Maxwell, Angela Middleton and Phil Latham, 'Victorian Era European Exploitation of Pounamu in Dunedin, New Zealand', *Journal of Pacific Archaeology*, vol. 6, no. 1, 2015, p. 59.

29. Jane Reeves, 'Maori Prisoners in Dunedin, 1869–1872 and 1879–1881: Exiled for a Cause', BA Hons thesis, University of Otago, 1989.

30. Te Awekotuku, *Mau Moko*, pp. 24–26. He was painted by Augustus Earle as 'A New Zealander', c.1827–1828. Te Awekotuku describes him as 'the tohunga ta moko of Kororareka [Bay of Islands]' on p. 24.

31. Wiremu Marsh Te Rangikaheke, 'Sir George Grey, Maori MS 89', New Zealand Electronic Text Collection, http://nzetc.victoria.ac.nz/tm/scholarly/tei-TeRSirG-t1-g1-t2.html

32. For the pūhoro design on a woman's neck, see Te Awekotuku, *Mau Moko*, p. 23.

33. See Ngarino Ellis, 'Ko Tō Ringa ki ngā Rākau ā te Pākehā? Drawings and Signatures of Moko by Māori in the Early 19th Century', *Journal of the Polynesian Society*, vol. 123, no. 1, 2014, pp 29–66, for a more detailed discussion and analysis of this process.

34. Wiremu Maihi Te Rangikaheke, 'Description of the ceremonies observed on the occasion of tattooing a chief and the method of performing the operation', 1850–4, GNZ MMSS 89, Grey NZ Collection, Maori Manuscripts, Auckland Libraries.

35. Renata Kawepo in William C. Cotton, Journal 1842–43, State Library of New South Wales.

36. See Amber Aranui, 'Te Hokinga Mai o ngā Tūpuna: Māori Perspectives of Repatriation and the Scientific Research of Ancestral Remains', PhD thesis, Victoria University, 2018; and Te Herekiekie Herewini, 'Toi Moko Tū Atu Toi Moko Tū Mai. The Trade and Repatriation of Toi Moko', PhD thesis, Victoria University, 2023.

37. Timothy Walker, 'Te Ropere, 1840–1930', Master's thesis, University of Auckland, 1985, p 182. See also Robley, *Moko*, p. 205.

38. Walker, p. 182. Purchased 1898; sold to the American Museum of Natural History in 1907.

39. Michael King, *Moko: Maori Tattooing in the 20th Century*, David Bateman, Auckland, 2008.

40. Te Awekotuku, *Mau Moko*, p. 80.

41. Edward Tregear, *Maori-Polynesian Comparative Dictionary*, Lyon and Blair, London, 1891, p. 40.

42. James Herries Beattie (ed.), *Tikao Talks*, Cadsonbury Publications, Christchurch, 2013, p. 151.

43. Apirana Ngata, *Ngā Mōteatea The Songs: Part Two,* Auckland University Press, Auckland, 2005, waiata 192, pp. 414–15.

44. Ngata, *Ngā Mōteatea The Songs: Part Three,* waiata 277, pp. 286–87.

45. Anne Salmond, *Hui: A Study of Maori Ceremonial Gatherings*, Reed, Auckland, 1975, p. 189.

46. Both are figured in Alison Jones and Kuni Kaa Jenkins's *Tuai: A Traveller in Two Worlds* (Bridget Williams Books, Wellington, 2017, pp. 215 and 216). Jones and Jenkins suggest the latter woman was a prisoner of war.

47. 'Women cutting themselves on arms for tears of blood. Mourning over the spear of a Ngaiterangi warrior killed 21 June '64 sketched by H. G. Robley it had been bought to family by a comrade. 1864.', Alexander Turnbull Library, A-080-015. Also see the Sydney Parkinson drawing in Anne Salmond, *Two Worlds: First Meetings between Māori and Europeans, 1642–1772*, Viking, Auckland, 1993, p. 217, of women possibly from the Far North with tangihaehae on their cheeks.

48. Alexander Turnbull Library, A-080-016.

49. Tarisi Vunidilo, 'The Exchange of Kula Feathers', in Karl Chitham, Kolokesa U Māhina-Tuai and Damian Skinner (eds), *Crafting Aotearoa*, Te Papa Press, Wellington, 2019, p. 39. Colonial administrators attempted to ban this trade in 1850 as they were concerned for the survival of

the birds. Despite this the Tongan royal family was able to access red feathers for the work they commissioned.

50  Beattie, *Tikao Talks*, p. 147.

51  Ngata, *Ngā Mōteatea The Songs: Part One*, waiata 13, pp. 48–49.

52  John White, *The Ancient History of the Maori*, Government Printer, vol. IV, Wellington, 1888, p. 107.

53  Noted by Pottier de l'Horne, in Robert McNab (ed.), *Extracts from the Journal of Pottier de l'Horne, First-Lieutenant on board the "Saint Jean Baptiste": Arrival in New Zealand*, John Mackay, Wellington, 1914, p. 279. Julien Crozet spent five weeks in the Bay of Islands in 1772: see Ling Roth (ed.), *Crozet's Voyage to Tasmania, New Zealand and the Ladrone Islands and the Philippines in the Years 1771–1772*, Truslove and Shirley, London, 1891, p. 37; and William Monkhouse in Poverty Bay and Anaura Bay: see J. C. Beaglehole (ed.), *The Journals of Captain James Cook*, vol. 1, Hakluyt Society, London, 1955, p. 586.

54  Monkhouse in J. C. Beaglehole (ed.), *The Endeavour Journals of Joseph Banks*, vol. I, Angus and Robertson, Sydney, 1962, p. 5.

55  See Anne Salmond, *Two Worlds: First Meetings between Māori and Europeans, 1642–1772*, Viking, Auckland, 1993, pp. 126–28, for a more detailed discussion of this moment.

56  Banks in J. C. Beaglehole (ed.), *Joseph Banks*, p. 406.

57  Salmond, *Two Worlds*, p. 142.

58  I. Ollivier, C. Hingley and J. Spencer, *Extracts from Journals Relating to the Visit to New Zealand of the French Ship St Jean Baptiste Under the Command of J. F. M. Surville*, Alexander Turnbull Endowment Trust with Indosuez NZ, Wellington, 1987, p. 67.

59  H. W. Williams, *A Dictionary of the Maori Language*, 7th edn, GP Publications, Wellington, 1991, pp. 448–49.

60  https://tairawhitimuseum.org.nz/acquisitions/showcase-10/

61  See Dougal Austin, *Hei Tiki: An Enduring Treasure in a Cultural Continuum*, Te Papa Press, Wellington, 2019, for a more thorough examination of this idea.

62  Janet Davidson, *The Prehistory of New Zealand*, Longman Paul, Auckland, 1984, p. 84.

63  Austin, *Hei Tiki*, p. 5.

64  Te Rangi Hīroa, *Coming of the Maori*; H. D. Skinner, *Comparatively Speaking: Studies in Pacific Material Culture, 1921–1972*, Otago University Press/John McIndoe, Dunedin, 1974.

65  Austin has identified a number of finer categories for these two main types.

66  Horatio Robley, *Pounamu, Notes on New Zealand Greenstone*, T. J. S. Guilford, London, 1915, p. 73.

67  http://collections.tepapa.govt.nz/object/58631

68  Ngata, *Ngā Mōteatea The Songs: Part One*, pp. 252–55. It is now in the British Museum: www.britishmuseum.org/collection/object/E_Oc1854-1229-10

69  See OLD 96, Museum of New Zealand, *Taonga Maori: Treasures of the New Zealand Maori People*, Australian Museum, Sydney, 1989, fig. 22, p. 69.

70  See AM192256, *Te Maori* catalogue, fig. 157.

71  There are a few other hei matau images with some reference to animal imagery: a number illustrated in Skinner show hei matau with one half in the hei matau 'hook' style while the other half is formed into a 'face': see figs 4.56, 4.57, 4.58 and 4.59, in H. D. Skinner, *Comparatively Speaking*, p. 61. Skinner describes these as a 'seal form' but they also relate to the hei tiki/hei matau above. Compare these pounamu examples with one from whalebone (fig. 4.112, Skinner, p. 73) where the face is clearly obvious (Otago Museum D.31.969).

72  'A man would often have a bunch of these *autui* suspended to his cloak in front, as an ornament. The *aurei* were small, oblong, flat pieces of whalebone, similar to the *kakara* fastened to a dog's neck when hunting the kiwi. Four or six of these *aurei* were fastened to a chief's cloak in front, so as to make a rattling sound as he moved': Elsdon Best, 'Kahu Kuri (Dogskin Cloaks)', *Transactions and Proceedings of the Royal Society of New Zealand*, vol. 31 (1898), pp. 644–45. For an example of a group of autui, see those in the collection of the National Museum of Ireland, Dublin (catalogue number 77, Stella Cherry, *Te Ao Maori: The Maori World*, National Museum of Ireland, Dublin, 1990, p. 50).

73  Elsdon Best, *The Maori as He Was: A Brief Account of Life as it Was in the Pre-European Days*, Dominion Museum, Wellington, 1934, p. 212.

74  Williams, *Dictionary*, p. 273.

75  Ibid., p. 211.

76  Best, *The Maori as He Was*, p. 212.

77  Quoted in ibid., p. 215.

78  Beaglehole, *Joseph Banks*, Vol. II, p. 17.

79  Best, *The Maori as He Was*, p. 215, quoting Arthur Thomson, a surgeon in 1850s New Zealand, and author of *The Story of New Zealand* (1859).

80  Te Rangikāheke, Wiremu Marsh, 'Sir George Grey, Maori MS 89', New Zealand Electronic Text Collection, http://nzetc.victoria.ac.nz/tm/scholarly/tei-TeRSirG-t1-g1-t2.html

81  George French Angas, *The New Zealanders Illustrated*, Thomas McLean, London, 1847, Plate XXXIII, 'Poahu and E Koti, Two lads of Poverty Bay,' p. 78.

82  Best, *The Maori as He Was*, p. 211.

83  Ibid., pp. 210–11.

84  Ibid., pp. 209, 211.

85  See Hirini Moko Mead, *Traditional Maori Clothing: A study of Technological and Functional Change*, Reed, Auckland, 1969, for more.

86  Beattie and Anderson, *Traditional Lifeways*, p. 242.

87  Best, *The Maori as He Was*, p. 211.

88  Atholl Anderson, 'Pieces of the Past, AD1200–1800', in Atholl Anderson, Judith Binney and Aroha Harris (eds), *Tangata Whenua: An Illustrated History*, Bridget Williams Books, Wellington, 2014, p. 94; see also Wilfred Shawcross, 'An Archaeological Assemblage of Maori Combs', *Journal of the Polynesian Society*, vol. 73, no. 4, 1964, 382–398, p. 382.

89  Wilfred Shawcross made an interesting discovery in her analysis of the Cook's First Voyage Collection in the Museum of Archaeology and Anthropology in Cambridge. She identified the wooden comb collected during the 1769–1771 voyage as correlating to those from Kauri Point, c.1550 ('The Cambridge University Collection of Maori Artefacts, Made on Captain Cook's First Voyage', *Journal of the Polynesian Society*, vol. 79, no. 3, September 1970, 305–348, p. 333). As heru were made by 'only a few highly skilled specialists' (p. 332), it is suggested that some of those heru not deposited at Kauri Point were in fact traded out of the area. Shawcross admits it is impossible from the explorers' journals to identify an exact point where the heru was obtained, but Cook spent at least a week in the Bay of Plenty area and it may have been on one of these days that the heru was traded for.

90  Sidney Moko Mead, 'The Origins of Māori Art: Explanations from Science', in Sidney Moko Mead, *Māori Art on the World Scene*, Ahua Design and Illustration, Wellington, 1997, pp. 33–34.

91  These were the most well-known names, but other terms have been used, including: waka kautuku (a kautuku is a type of rare feather), waka pare ('pare' refers to anything associated with the head), papa huia (huia feathers), and papa raukura.

92  Roger Neich, 'Powaka Whakairo: A Third Form of Maori Treasure Box', in Chanel Clarke, Fuli Pereira and Nigel Prickett (eds), *Tradition and Change in Maori and Pacific Art: Essays by Roger Neich*, Auckland War Memorial Museum, Auckland, 2013, p. 394.

93  Neich identified twenty powaka whakairo: seven in Auckland Museum and two in other museums in New Zealand, three in private collections, six in museum collections in England, one in Italy, plus three from written accounts. Many others have been described in museum records as 'tobacco containers' or 'cigar boxes'. Neich, 'Powaka Whakairo', p. 394; see also Roger Neich, 'Papahou and Waka Huia: Maori Treasure Boxes', in Clarke, Pereira and Prickett (eds), *Tradition and Change in Maori and Pacific Art*, pp. 376–91.

94 Ngahuia Te Awekotuku and Melody Thomas, 'BANG! Season 2, Episode 6: Takatapui', Radio New Zealand, 2 June 2018, www.rnz.co.nz/programmes/bang/story/2018651794/bang-season-2-episode-6-takatapui

95 Raymond Firth, *Economics of the New Zealand Maori*, A. R. Shearer, Wellington, 1929, p. 396.

96 Mākereti Papakura, *The Old Time Maori*, New Women's Press, Auckland, 1986, p. 323.

97 Pania Waaka, 'Hei Tiki and Issues of Representation Within Contemporary Māori Arts', *MAI Review* 1, 2007, p. 6.

98 See Ngahuia Te Awekotuku, 'Maori: People and Culture', in Dorothy Starzecka (ed.), *Maori: Art and Culture*, British Museum Press, London, 1996, p. 44.

99 Christopher B. Steiner, 'Body Personal and Body Politic: Adornment and Leadership in Cross-Cultural Perspective', *Anthropos*, 1990, p. 431; Terence S. Turner, 'The Social Skin', in J. Cherfas and R. Lewin (eds), *Not Work Alone: A Cross-Cultural View of Activities Superfluous to Survival*, Sage Publications, Beverly Hills, 1980, p. 112.

100 Mead, *Tikanga Māori*, pp. 392, 402.

### Areta Wilkinson

1 Wilkinson, 'Jewellery as Pepeha: Contemporary Jewellery Practice Informed by Māori Inquiry', PhD thesis, Massey University, 2014.

2 Warren Feeney, 'Christchurch Arts Festival: New exhibition aiming to change perceptions', *The Press*, 28 August 2017, www.stuff.co.nz/the-press/christchurch-life/art-and-stage/visual-art/96123970/christchurch-arts-festival-new-exhibition-aiming-to-change-perceptions

3 Mark Adams and Areta Wilkinson, *Repatriation*, Two Rooms, Ocula, https://ocula.com/art-galleries/two-rooms/exhibitions/repatriation/

4 Nigel Borell and Zara Stanhope, 'Areta Wilkinson', *APT 9: The 9th Asia Pacific Triennial of Contemporary Art*, Queensland Art Gallery and Gallery of Modern Art, Brisbane, 2018, p. 179.

5 Nigel Borell and Benjamin Lignel, 'In Conversation with Areta Wilkinson', *Art Jewellery Forum*, 23 September 2015, https://artjewelryforum.org/node/7135

### Pounamu

1 See Hirini Moko Mead, *Tikanga Māori: Living by Māori Values*, Huia, Wellington, 2019, pp. 182–84, for examples of tatau pounamu that have not worked.

2 H. G. Robley, *Pounamu, Notes on New Zealand Greenstone*, T. J .S. Guilford, London, 1915, p. 11.

## 7 Mana wāhine, mana tāne, mana takatāpui: Depicting gender in Māori art

1 The term 'takatāpui' here describes those from the LGBTQI+ community, though dictionaries often reduce this to lesbian or homosexual (P. M. Ryan, *The Raupō Dictionary of Modern Māori*, Raupo, Auckland, 2012, pp. 145, 160; also H. M. Ngata, *Maori-English Dictionary*, Learning Media, Wellington, 1993, translates 'homosexual' as 'tōingo, takāpui, takatāpui' (p. 207) and 'lesbian' as 'wahine takāpui' (p. 254). 'Tōingo', 'whakaeneene' and 'takāpui' for homosexual are not used as much today. 'Tapatāpui' also translates as 'bosom friend, intimate friend same sex' (Ryan, p. 72). More nuanced terms might also be found in older oral sources such as mōteatea, whakataukī and kōrero tuku iho (ancestral narratives).

2 Angela Ballara. 'Hinematioro', *Dictionary of New Zealand Biography*, first published in 1990. Te Ara – the Encyclopedia of New Zealand, https://teara.govt.nz/en/biographies/1h23/hinematioro

3 Gottfried Lindauer, *Rangi Topeora* (1915), Auckland Art Gallery.

4 Ngā mihi to Charlie Bluett (Te Runanga o Ngāti Awa) for details about Wairaka, the woman and the house.

5 H. G. Robley, *Moko, or, Maori Tattooing*, Chapman and Hall, London, 1896, p. 33.

6 Augustus Earle, '89. A New Zealander' (1832). See Ngahuia Te Awekotuku, *Mau Moko: The World of Māori Tattoo*, Penguin, Auckland, 2007, p. 25.

7 See Alison Jones and Kuni Kaa Jenkins, *He Kōrero: Words Between Us: First Māori–Pākehā Conversations on Paper*, Huia, Wellington, 2011, p. 101.

8 Charles Pratt Baker, 'Journal on a Journey to the East Coast 1861–2', Alexander Turnbull Library, qMS-0113, entry for 28 November.

9 There were three other moko practitioners active at this time: Te Aho Rangi Wharepu, Anaru Maxwell and Ngakau: Michael King, *Te Puea: A Life*, Hodder & Stoughton, Auckland, 1977; 4th illustrated edn, Reed Books, Auckland, 2003, p. 188.

10 See Anne Salmond, *Two Worlds: First Meetings between Māori and Europeans, 1642–1772*, Viking, Auckland, 1993, pp. 215, 217.

11 Apirana Ngata, *Ngā Mōteatea The Songs: Part Three*, Auckland University Press, Auckland, 2006, waiata 201, pp. 2–3.

12 www.maoritube.co.nz/people/paitangi-ostick-a-woman-ta-moko-artist-carver-painter-weaver-and-song-writer/

13 Roger Neich, 'Nineteenth to Mid-Twentieth Century Individual Maori Woodcarvers and the Known Works', *Records of Auckland Museum*, 41, 2004, pp. 53–86.

14 Apirana Ngata, *Rauru Nui a Toi Lectures*, lecture 4, Porourangi School of Maori Culture, 1944, pp. 10–11.

15 'New Schools for Old Crafts', *Te Ao Hou*, vol. 55, June 1966, p. 9.

16 Signalling a change, at the largest girls' school in Auckland (Westlake Girls' High School) in 2019, there were unprecedented numbers choosing 'hard tech' options, particularly in the senior school.

17 Judith Binney, 'The Heritage of Isaiah: Thomas Kendall and Maori Religion', *New Zealand Journal of History*, vol. 38, no. 2, 2004, p. 131.

18 See Ngahuia Te Awekotuku, 'He Reka Ano: Same Sex Lust and Loving in the Ancient Maori World', paper presented to Outlines Conference: Lesbian and Gay History in Aotearoa, Lesbian and Gay Archives of New Zealand, Wellington, 2003, cited in Clive Aspin and Jessica Hutchings, 'Reclaiming the Past to Inform the Future: Contemporary Views of Maori Sexuality', *Culture, Health and Sexuality*, vol. 9, no. 4, 2007, 415–27, p. 419.

19 Aspin and Hutchings, p. 419.

20 See Richard Sundt, *Whare Karakia: Māori Church Building, Decoration and Ritual in Aotearoa New Zealand 1834–63*, Auckland University Press, Auckland, 2010, for more details of Rukupō's work.

21 Ngahuia Te Awekotuku, 'Introduction', in Jordon Harris, *Takatāpui: A Place of Standing*, Oratia Media and the New Zealand AIDs Foundation, Auckland, 2016, pp. 38–39. See also Ngahuia Te Awekotuku's interview by Melody Thomas, *BANG! Season 2 Episode 6: Takatapui*, 2 June 2018, www.rnz.co.nz/programmes/bang/story/2018651794/bang-season-2-episode-6-takatapui

22 Robert Jahnke, 'He Tataitanga Ahua Toi: The House that Riwai Built, A Continuum of Māori Art', PhD thesis, Massey University, 2006, p. 113.

23 Elizabeth Kerekere, 'Part of the Whānau: The Emergence of Takatāpui Identity – He Whāriki Takatāpui', PhD thesis, Victoria University of Wellington, 2017, p. 178.

24 Roger Neich, *Carved Histories: Rotorua Ngāti Tarawhai Woodcarving*, Auckland University Press, Auckland, 2002, p. 281; see Appendix VIII for a more detailed discussion of these figures.

25 Neich, *Carved Histories*, fig 17.18.

26 Ngahuia Te Awekotuku, 'Hinemoa', *Journal of Lesbian Studies in Aotearoa/New Zealand*, vol. 5, 2001, pp. 1–11; she bases her interpretation on the writings of Te Rangikāheke.

27 Kerekere, 'Part of The Whānau', p. 21.

28 See Kerekere's thesis for insight into some of the challenges of being takatāpui in the twentieth and twenty-first centuries.

### Men and weaving

1. Vincent Buchanan-Malcolm, Ngahuia Te Awekotuku and Linda Waimarie Nikora, 'Cloaked in Life and Death: Korowai, Kaitiaki and Tangihanga', *MAI Journal*, vol. I, no. 1, p. 53, www.journal.mai.ac.nzisites/default/files/MAI_Journal_Vl %2C1_MalcolrnBuchanan_etal.pdf

2. See Elsdon Best, Notebooks, MS-Papers-1187-029, Alexander Turnbull Library, MS-Papers-1187-287.

3. The notebooks are now in Alexander Turnbull Library: Elsdon Best, Notebooks 1895-96, Alexander Turnbull Library, MS-Papers-l 187-113A.

4. Best wrote about these uhi: 'The Uhi-Maori, or Native Tattooing Instruments', *Journal of the Polynesian Society*, vol. 13, no.3, 1904, pp. 166–72.

5. www.creativenz.govt.nz/news/maori-weaver-selected-for-north-american-artist-residency. Many thanks to Karl Leonard for comments here.

## PART 2 – TE KETE TUAURI
### 8 Taonga, Māori and museums

1. Sidney Moko Mead and N. Grove, *Ngā Pēpeha a Ngā Tīpuna: The Sayings of the Ancestors*, Victoria University Press, Wellington, 2001.

2. Ngāti Tūmatakōkiri, 'First Encounter 375', https://sites.google.com/3ml.nz/ngati-tumatakokiri/home

3. *Te Tau Ihu o Te Waka a Maui: Report on Northern South Island Claims*, Waitangi Tribunal, Legislation Direct, Wellington, 2008, vol. 1, p. 166.

4. K. A. Simpson, 'Tasman, Abel Janszoon', *Dictionary of New Zealand Biography*, first published in 1990, updated August, 2019. *Te Ara – the Encyclopedia of New Zealand*, https://teara.govt.nz/en/biographies/1t17/tasman-abel-janszoon.

5. Anne Salmond, *Two Worlds: First Meetings between Māori and Europeans, 1642–1772*, Viking, Auckland, 1993, p. 81.

6. Ibid. The rest of the men swam to the *Heemskerck*.

7. Barry Barclay, 'Celebrating Fourth Cinema', *Illusions*, 35, 2003, pp. 7–11.

8. Tasman had visited in 1642 but did not land or collect anything while sailing around New Zealand.

9. Anita Herle, 'Whales Teeth, Turtle-shell Masks and Bits of String: Pacific Collections and Research at Cambridge', *Journal of Museum Ethnography*, no. 17, 2005, p. 36.

10. Peter Gathercole, 'Pacific Collections in the Cambridge University Museum', *Pacific Arts* 11/12, July 1995, p. 69. See also Adrienne Kaeppler, *Artificial Curiosities: An Exposition of Native Manufactures Collected on the Three Pacific Voyages of Captain James Cook, R.N.*, Bernice P. Bishop Museum Special Publication no. 65, Honolulu, 1978.

11. J. C. H. King, 'Sir Ashton Lever', in Hermione Waterfield and J. C. H. King (eds), *Provenance: Twelve Collectors of Ethnographic Art in England 1760–1990*, Somogy Éditions d'Art and the Barbier-Mueller Museum, Paris and Geneva, 2006, p. 28.

12. John White, *Ancient History of the Maori*, vol. V, Government Printer, Wellington, 1888, p. 130. Te Horeta was so upset at losing the nail/adze while at sea that he dived in to look for it, to no avail.

13. In J. A. Mackay, *Historic Poverty Bay and the East Coast, N.I., N.Z.*, Poverty Bay East Coast Centennial Council, Gisborne, 1966, p. 58.

14. Salmond, *Two Worlds*, p. 307.

15. Isabel Ollivier and Cheryl Hingley, *Extracts from Journals Relating to the Visit of the French Ship* St Jean Baptiste *in December 1769 under the Command of J. F. M. De Surville*, Alexander Turnbull Library Endowment Trust, Wellington, 1982, p. 167. For a more thorough discussion of this voyage see Salmond, *Two Worlds*, pp. 299–358.

16. Ollivier and Hingley, p. 125.

17. Ibid., p. 165.

18. Ibid., p. 67.

19. Ibid., p. 71.

20. Christian F. Feest, 'European Collecting of American Indian Artefacts and Art', *Journal of the History of Collections*, vol. 5, no. 1, 1993, pp. 1–11. For more on the Pacific MAA see Herle, 'Whales Teeth', pp. 32–57.

21. Jennifer Wagelie, 'Maori Art in America: The Display and Collection History of Maori Art in the United States, 1802–2006', PhD thesis, City University of New York, 2007, p. 28. See also Ernest S. Dodge, *The New Zealand Maori Collection in the Peabody Museum of Salem* (Peabody Museum, Salem, 1941), which reviews the collection in the Peabody Essex Museum. Two other museums also received early material from New Zealand: the Peabody Museum of Archaeology and Ethnology, Harvard University, Cambridge, Massachusetts, and the University of Pennsylvania Museum of Archaeology and Anthropology, Philadelphia, Pennsylvania.

22. Wagelie, p. 23.

23. See Deidre Brown, *Tai Tokerau Whakairo Rākau: Northland Māori Wood Carving*, Reed, Auckland, 2003, for further discussion.

24. See Maureen Lander and Amiria Salmond, 'Ancestral Threads: Seven Māori Cloaks', in Nicholas Thomas, Julie Adams, Billie Lythberg, Maia Nuku and Amiria Salmond (eds), *Artefacts of Encounter: Cook's Voyages, Colonial Collecting and Museum Histories*, Otago University Press, Dunedin, 2016, pp. 102–9.

25. There are a few exceptions, usually based on exhibitions. The Museum Volkenkunde in Leiden, The Netherlands, for instance, published a fully illustrated catalogue (Fanny Wonu Veys, *Mana Māori: The Power of New Zealand's First Inhabitants*, Leiden University Press, Leiden, 2010). Other museums are putting their collections online, such as the Musée du Quai Branly, Paris – see www.quaibranly.fr/en/explore-collections/base/Default/action/list/mode/b/?orderby=null&order=desc&category=all&&filters[]=maori%7C2&refreshFilters=true&refreshModePreview=true

26. See Elena Gover, 'Oceania in Russian History: Expeditions, Collections, Museums', in Lucie Carreau, Alison Clark, Alana Jelinek, Erna Lilje and Nicholas Thomas (eds), *Pacific Presences, vol. 1: Oceanic Art and European Museums*, Sidestone Press, Leiden, 2018, pp. 169–96; and Elena Gover, 'From Russia with Love: Nikolai Miklouho-Maclay's Pacific Collections', in Carreau et al. (eds), *Pacific Presences, vol. 2*, pp. 123–30.

27. Una Platts, *Nineteenth Century New Zealand Artists: A Guide & Handbook*, Avon Fine Prints, Christchurch, 1980.

28. See, for example, Fiona Pardington, *Portrait of a Life-cast of Matoua Tawai, Aotearoa New Zealand* (2010); *and Portrait of a Life-cast, possibly of Taha-tala [possibly Takatahara]* (2010), from the series *Āhua: A Beautiful Hesitation*.

29. Chazal was known for his reworking of the drawings made by Lejeune into watercolours, in preparation for these being remade into engravings: Platts, *Nineteenth Century New Zealand Artists*, p. 65.

30. These should be considered as a series of wars rather than a single long event. They began in the 1840s following the signing of Te Tiriti o Waitangi in the north, where Māori began challenging the assertion of sovereignty by English settlers, and ended in 1872 when Te Kooti Arikirangi escaped and settled near Te Kūiti.

31. For example, hei tiki were removed from Ruapekapeka pā in Northland in 1846 when it was stormed by 1400 colonial troops.

32. Ropoama Rakei to Governor Grey, GNZNA 265, Central City Library, Auckland, https://kura.aucklandlibraries.govt.nz/digital/collection/manuscripts/id/7105/

33. The New Zealand government confiscated Māori land and gave much of this land to settlers or to colonial soldiers as a reward for their service in the wars.

34. In 1886 Haast attended the Colonial and Indian Exhibition in London on behalf of the New Zealand government.

35. Fowler, *Te Mana o Turanga: The Story of the Carved House Te Mana o Turanga on the Whakato Marae at Manutuke Gisborne*, New Zealand Historic Places Trust, Wellington, 1974, p. 7.

36. James Fairchild, the captain of a steamer, had also offered to buy the house for £300 in 1864, possibly with the intention of selling it in London for an astronomical £1000. See Deidre Brown, 'Te Hau ki Turanga', *Journal of the Polynesian Society*, vol. 105, no. 1, 1996, pp. 7–26; *Turanga Tangata, Turanga Whenua: The Report on the Turanganui a Kiwa Claims*, Waitangi Tribunal Report for WAI 814, vol. 2, 2004.

37. Paul Tapsell, *Ko Tawa: Maori Treasures of New Zealand*, David Bateman, Auckland, 2006, p 67.

38. Paula Savage, 'Mair, Gilbert', *Dictionary of New Zealand Biography*, first published in 1990, updated January, 2012. *Te Ara – the Encyclopedia of New Zealand*, https://teara.govt.nz/en/biographies/1m4/mair-gilbert

39. Tapsell, Ko Tawa, pp. 85–86.

40. Roger Neich, Mick Pendergrast and Dorota Starzecka, *The Maori Collections of the British Museum*, British Museum Press, London, 2010, p. 23.

41. Letter from J. W. Williams, 20 January 1897, now in British Museum Archives, quoted in Neich, Pendergrast and Starzecka, *The Maori Collections of the British Museum*, p. 24.

42. Amiria Henare, *Museums, Anthropology and Imperial Exchange*, Cambridge University Press, New York, 2005, p. 115.

43. See ibid., p. 145.

44. One example is a Ngāti Toa kaukau (ear pendant) named Kaitangata, which is now in the collection of the British Museum (1855.5-14.1). Other taonga were presented to the City of Auckland (1893).

45. Hector was no longer responsible for the Geology section from 1892. Today only a late-nineteenth-century kiwi feather muff remains of his collection in Te Papa (ME0024137).

46. My thanks to the external reviewer for suggestions for this section.

47. Conal McCarthy, *Exhibiting Māori: A History of Colonial Cultures of Display*, Te Papa Press, Wellington, 2007, p. 33.

48. Noel Waite, 'Future Fairs: Industrial Exhibitions in New Zealand, 1865 to 1925', in Penny Sparke and Fiona Fisher (eds), *Routledge Companion to Design Studies*, Routledge, London and New York, 2019.

49. McCarthy, *Exhibiting Māori*, p. 38.

50. Eva Garbutt, 'The Care of Living Objects: Conserving Rauru and Te Wharepuni a Maui in Germany', in Dean Sully (ed.), *Decolonising Conservation*, Left Cross Press, Walnut Creek, CA, 2007, p. 114.

51. For more information see Nicholas Thomas and Mark Adams, *Rauru: Tene Waitere, Maori Carving, Colonial History*, Otago University Press, Dunedin, 2009; Roger Neich, *Carved Histories: Rotorua Ngāti Tarawhai Woodcarving*, Auckland University Press, Auckland, 2002.

52. The history of the house has been outlined by Rose Mohi, a descendant of the patron Takamoana, and Amber Aranui of Te Papa Tongarewa, in 'Te Whare o Heretaunga: A Journey of Rediscovery', *Tuhinga*, no. 31, 2020, pp. 42–55. The whare had earlier been described by Dimitri Anson, Otago Museum ('What's in a Name? The House Carvings that Dr Hocken Gave to the Otago Museum', *Journal of the Polynesian Society*, vol. 113, no. 1, March 2004, pp. 73–90). David Simmons had earlier incorrectly ascribed all these carvings to a meeting house he named Tumoanakotore: (Simmons, *Whakairo: Maori Tribal Art Styles*, Oxford University Press, Auckland, 1994, pp. 150–51).

53. See Elizabeth Pishief, 'Augustus Hamilton. Appropriation, Ownership and Authority', MA thesis, Massey University, 1998.

54. Anson, 'What's in a Name?', p. 73.

55. Another example of a house in a number of institutions is Rangitihi, which originally stood at Tāheke on Lake Rotoiti. Opened in the early 1870s, the house was dismantled in 1886 after the roof collapsed from the weight of ash from the Tarawera eruption. Gilbert Mair and Thomas Cheeseman, curator at Auckland Museum, organised for the house to be purchased by the museum in 1900, and some of the carvings were deposited there the following year. The pane (ridgepole in the porch) was cut in half: Auckland dealer Eric Craig obtained both halves in 1911, and sold them to W. D. Webster, a dealer in England: one part of the pane is now in the Miklukho-Maklay Institute of Anthropology and Ethnology in St Petersburg, Russia (1279.75), and the other half is in the Museum für Völkerkunde, Leipzig, Germany (P01775). See Neich, *Carved Histories*, p. 320.

56. Mohi and Aranui, 'Te Whare o Heretaunga', p. 51; see also 'Heretaunga Deed of Settlement Summary', www.govt.nz/browse/history-culture-and-heritage/treaty-settlements/find-a-treaty-settlement/heretaunga-tamatea/heretaunga-deed-of-settlement-summary

57. Douglas Cole, *Captured Heritage: The Scramble for Northwest Coast Artifacts*, University of British Columbia Press, Vancouver, BC, 2014.

58. Exhibitions were important sites in which Māori culture (rather than tribal culture) was augmented and heavily promoted, ostensibly to showcase the 'success' of colonisation. See Bernard Kernot, 'Maoriland Metaphors and the Model Pa', in John Mansfield Thomson (ed.), *Farewell Colonialism: The New Zealand International Exhibition, Christchurch 1906–07*, Dunmore Press, Palmerston North, 1998, pp. 61–78.

59. Neich, *Carved Histories*, p. 370.

60. McCarthy, *Exhibiting Māori*, p. 30.

61. Ibid.

### Tāngata mamae: The tragic story of Te Maro, Ranginui and Te Kuku

1. Isabel Ollivier and Cheryl Hingley, *Extracts from Journals Relating to the Visit of the French Ship* St Jean Baptiste *in December 1769 under the Command of J. F. M. De Surville*, Alexander Turnbull Library Endowment Trust, Wellington, 1982, p. 118.

2. For a more detailed account see R. R. D. Milligan, 'Ranginui, Captive Chief of Doubtless Bay, 1769', *Journal of the Polynesian Society*, vol. 67, no. 3, 1958, pp. 179–203.

3. Ibid., p. 186.

4. Pat Hohepa, 'My Musket, My Missionary, And My Mana', in Alex Calder, Jonathan Lamb and Bridget Orr (eds), *Voyages and Beaches: Pacific Encounters, 1769–1840*, University of Hawai'i Press, Honolulu, 1999, p. 195.

### Joseph Banks and the forty brass patu replicas

1. Jeremy Coote, 'Joseph Banks's Forty Brass Patus', *Journal of Museum Ethnography*, vol. 20, March 2008, p. 49.

2. Jennifer Newell, *Pacific Art in Detail*, Te Papa Press, Wellington, 2011, p. 126.

3. Nicholas Thomas, *Discoveries: The Voyages of Captain Cook*, Allen Lane, London, 2003, p. 66.

4. Te Papa, 'Biography of Joseph Banks', https://collections.tepapa.govt.nz/topic/574

5. When it was clear that Banks, his mentor, was not coming on the second voyage, Clerke asked if he could take some of the barrels of iron nails that Banks had commissioned as gifts.

6. Coote, 'Brass Patus', pp. 51–52.

7. Ibid., pp. 62–63.

8. Maria Wronska-Friend, 'From Shells to Ceramic: Colonial Replicas of Indigenous Valuables', *Journal of Museum Ethnography*, no. 28, 2015, p. 65.

9. Jeremy Coote, email to Ngarino Ellis, 14 January 2020.

### Tupaia

1. Joan Druett, 'Tupaia', *Dictionary of New Zealand Biography*, first published in 2017. *Te Ara – the Encyclopedia of New Zealand*, https://teara.govt.nz/en/biographies/6t2/tupaia

2. Letter from Joseph Banks to Dawson Turner, 1812. See www.bl.uk/the-voyages-of-captain-james-cook/articles/tupaia-the-navigator-priest-and-artist

3   Anne Salmond, 'Tupaia the Navigator, Priest and Artist', www.bl.uk/the-voyages-of-captain-james-cook/articles/tupaia-the-navigator-priest-and-artist. Salmond notes that Parkinson and Banks and others 'gathered' these designs on their own skin.

4   Joan Druett, *Tupaia: The Remarkable Story of Captain Cook's Polynesian Navigator*, Praeger, California, 2011; Anne Salmond, *Aphrodite's Island: The European Discovery of Tahiti*, Viking, Auckland, 2009.

5   Anne Salmond, *Two Worlds: First Meetings between Māori and Europeans, 1642–1772*, Viking, Auckland, 1993, p. 176. The practice of naming babies after important events is common in whānau, and even adults might change their name to commemorate an important event. In the nineteenth century many Māori adopted a surname or anglicised their Māori name.

### 9   Māori art and the Christian missions

1   Samuel Marsden, 'Observations on the Introduction of the Gospel into the South Sea Islands: Being my first visit to New Zealand in December 1814', in John Elder (ed.), *Letters and Journals of Samuel Marsden*, Coulls, Somerville Wilke, Dunedin, 1932, p. 93.

2   Ibid.

3   Exodus 33:7.

4   Te Rangi Hīroa, *The Coming of the Maori*, Maori Purposes Fund Board, Wellington, 1949, p. 343.

5   Roger Neich, *Carved Histories: Rotorua Ngāti Tarawhai Woodcarving*, Auckland University Press, Auckland, 2002, pp. 196–97.

6   Reverend Davies to Archdeacon Brown, 14 July 1845, in Alister Matheson, 'Catholic Missionaries at Maketu', *Historical Review*, vol. 57, no. 1, May 2009, 13–19, p. 16.

7   *Church Missionary Society Missionary Register*, Seeley, London, 1816, pp. 524–25.

8   Thomas Chapman, letter from Rotorua, Chapman MS 1: 198, Auckland War Memorial Museum Library, Auckland.

9   'Tauranga: Catholic Church at Otumoetai'; Lillian Keys, *Philip Viard: Bishop of Wellington*, Pegasus, Christchurch, 1968, p. 65.

10   Mānuka Hēnare, 'Māori Catholic Beginnings', in *The Visit of His Holiness Pope John Paul II, New Zealand, November 22–24*, Papal Visit Aotearoa, Wellington, 1986, pp. 14–15.

11   Jozef Penkowski, 'Pontifico Museo Missionario-Ethnologico', in *The Vatican Collections: The Papacy and Art*, Metropolitan Museum, New York, 1982, p. 227.

12   Jeffrey Sissons, *The Polynesian Iconoclasm: Religious Revolution and the Seasonality of Power*, Berghahn Books, New York, 2014.

13   Anegla Middleton, *Te Puna: A New Zealand Mission Station: Historical Archaeology in New Zealand*, Springer, New York and London, 2008, p. 176.

14   See Tanya Fitzgerald, 'Jumping the Fences: Māori Women's Resistance to Missionary Schooling in Northern New Zealand 1823–1835', International Standing Conference for the History of Education, 2000, http://unitec.researchbank.ac.nz/bitstream/handle/10652/1324/fulltext.pdf?sequence=1; Middleton, Te Puna, p. 177.

15   Ross Calman, 'Māori education – mātauranga – Māori church boarding schools', *Te Ara – the Encyclopedia of New Zealand*, www.TeAra.govt.nz/en/maori-education-matauranga/page-4; Hirini Kaa, 'Sex, Sin and Salvation: Māori Morality through a Christian Lens', *Te Pouhere Kōrero*, vol. 6, 2012, pp. 27–34; Zoe Laidlaw, '"Aunt Anna's Report": The Buxton Women and the Aborigines Select Committee, 1835–37', *The Journal of Imperial and Commonwealth History*, vol. 32, no 2, 2004, 1–28, p. 8.

16   Deidre Brown, *Tai Tokerau Whakairo Rākau: Northland Māori Wood Carving*, Reed, Auckland, 2003, pp. 150–89.

17   'Waitangi Carved Memorial Meeting House', Auckland Museum Library, Auckland; AM 45506, 5652-7, 5659 cards, Auckland Museum Ethnology Library, Auckland.

18   Joel Polack, *New Zealand: Being a Narrative of Travels and Adventures During a Residence in that Country Between the Years 1831 and 1837*, vol. 2, Richard Bentley, London, 1838, pp. 266–68.

19   Conrad Fristedt, *På forskningsfärd: Minnen från en tvåårig vistelse bland Ceylons tamiler och singhaleser, Australiens kannibaler och Nya Zeelands maorer*, Albert Bonnier, Stockholm, 1891, pp. 245–47; *Reiseerlebnisse eines Museumsdirektors: Gespräch mit Professor Dr. Schauinsland im Bremer Handelsmuseum*, broadcast in 1930 by the Bremen subsidiary of the North German Broadcasting Corporation (Norag); in Herbert Abel, *Vom Raritätenkabinett zum Bremer Überseemuseum. Die Geschichte einer hanseatischen Sammlung aus Übersee anlasslich ihres 75 jahrigen Bestehens (From the cabinet of rarities to the Überseemuseum of Bremen. The history of a Hanseatic collections from Obersee on the occasion of its 75th anniversary)*, Verlag Friedrich Röver, Bremen, 1970, p. 237.

20   Apirana Ngata to Harold Hamilton, 23 February 1934, 'Waima Carved Meeting House 1932–4', Series 51, no. 146, box 15, Māori Affairs Papers, National Archives, Wellington; Phillipps, *Carved Maori Houses of the Western and Northern Areas of New Zealand*, Government Printer, Wellington, 1955, p. 267.

21   Hong-key Yoon, 'The Sacred (Tapu) Complex in the Māori Settlements of the East Coast, New Zealand', *Journal of the Polynesian Society*, vol. 87, no. 2, 1978, pp. 115–24.

22   Ibid.

23   Charles Royal, *Rangiatea*, National Library of New Zealand and Te Ropu Whakahaere o Rangiatea, Wellington, 1997, pp. 16, 32.

24   Peter Shaw, *New Zealand Architecture — From Polynesian Beginnings to 1990*, Hodder and Stoughton, Auckland, 1991, p. 22.

25   Royal, *Rangiatea*, p. 19; Shaw, *New Zealand Architecture*, p. 22.

26   Roger Neich, *Painted Histories: Early Māori Figurative Painting*, Auckland University Press, Auckland, 1993, p. 38; Shaw, p. 22.

27   Neich, *Painted Histories*, p. 82; Francis Porter, *The Turanga Journals 1840–50: Letters and Journals of William and Jane Williams, Missionaries to Poverty Bay*, Victoria University Press, Wellington, 1974, pp. 229, 547.

28   Richard Sundt, *Whare Karakia: Māori Church Building, Decoration and Ritual in Aotearoa New Zealand 1834–63*, Auckland University Press, Auckland, 2010, pp. 113, 123; Leonard Williams, *East Coast (N.Z.) Historical Records, Poverty Bay Herald*, Gisborne, 1932, p. 20.

29   *Church Missionary Intelligencer*, vol. 2, 1852, p. 48.

30   Porter, *Turanga Journals*, p. 548.

31   Ibid., pp. 535–538.

32   Neich, *Painted Histories*, p. 86.

33   Porter, *Journals*, p. 589.

34   Warren Limbrick, 'George Augustus Selwyn', in W. H. Oliver (ed.), *Dictionary of New Zealand Biography 1769–1869*, Bridget Williams Books and the Department of Internal Affairs, Wellington, 1990, p. 387; Neil Benfell, *Mission and Moko, Aspects of the Work of the Church Missionary Society in New Zealand, 1814–1882*, Latimer Fellowship, Christchurch, 1992, p. 82.

35   'Parish Churches in New Zealand', *The Ecclesiologist*, vol. 1, no. 1, November 1841, pp. 4–5.

36   Ibid., p. 4.

37   Thomas Chapman, letter from Rotorua, Chapman MS1: 198, Auckland War Memorial Museum Library, Auckland; John Nicholas, *Narrative of a Voyage to New Zealand, Performed in the Years 1814 and 1815, in Company with the Rev. Samuel Marsden, Principal Chaplain of New South Wales*, James Black & Sons, London, 1817, pp. 17–18.

38   Hugh Rihari, pers. comm., 26 September 2017.

39   Philip Hansen King to James Blea, Te Puna, 18 May 1837, private collection.

40   Deidre Brown, *Outgoing CMS taonga inventory based on Marsden Online Archive missionary correspondence 1814–1820*, unpublished document, 2015.

41   Anne Salmond, *Tears of Rangi: Experiments Across Worlds*, Auckland University Press, Auckland, 2017, p. 166.

42 Théodore Vernes, *Exposition Universelle de 1867 à Paris*, Libraire de la Société des Gens de Lettres, Paris, 1867, p. 95.

43 Judith Binney, *The Legacy of Guilt: A Life of Thomas Kendall*, Bridget Williams Books, Wellington, 2005, p. 133. See Deidre Brown, 'Nukutawhiti Rediscovered: finding Thomas Kendall's 1823 Mariana consignment of whakairo rākau (Māori wood carvings)', *Waka Kuaka: Journal of the Polynesian Society*, vol. 132, no. 4, 2023, pp. 397–430.

44 Judith Binney, 'The Lost Drawing of Nukutawhiti', *New Zealand Journal of History*, vol. 14, no. 1, 1980, 3–24, pp. 3–14.

45 Salmond, *Tears*, p. 3.

46 Sissons, *Polynesian Iconoclasm*.

47 Frederick Williams, *Through Ninety Years, 1826–1916: Life and Work Among the Maoris in New Zealand*, Whitcombe & Tombs, Auckland, 1939, pp. 54–55.

48 Richard Altick, *The Shows of London*, Belknap Press, Cambridge, MA, 1978, p. 288.

49 Vernes, *Exposition Universelle*, pp. 65–70.

50 Alexander Maxwell and Evan Roberts, 'The Whangaroa Incident, 16 July 1824: A European–Māori Encounter and Its Many Incarnations', *Journal of Pacific History*, vol. 49, no. 1, 2014, 50–75, p. 54; Vernes, *Exposition Universelle*, p. 16.

51 Austin Friars, 'Catalogue of the Missionary Museum', 1826, British Library, 4766.e.19.[2.].

52 Rosemary Seton, 'Reconstructing the Museum of the London Missionary Society', *Material Religion*, vol. 8, no. 1, 2012, p. 99.

53 Ibid.

54 Meredith Lake, 'Samuel Marsden, Work and the Limits of Evangelical Humanitarianism', *History of Australia*, vol. 7, no. 3, 2010, 1–23, p. 13.

55 Laidlaw, '"Aunt Anna's Report"', pp. 3–4.

56 Thomas Fowell Buxton, *Report of the Parliamentary Select Committee on Aboriginal Tribes (British Settlements)*, William Ball, London, 1837.

57 See Vernes, *Exposition Universelle*.

58 Ibid.

59 'A Religious Department at the Paris Exposition', *Daily Alta California*, vol. 19, no. 7046, 9 January 1867, p. 6; Volker Barth, 'Displaying Normalisation: The Paris Universal Exhibition of 1867', *Journal of Historical Sociology*, vol. 20, no. 4, 2007, 462–485, p. 462.

60 Vernes, *Exposition Universelle*, object nos. 53–61, 713–16, 722, 724, 733, 756–7, 760, 762–3, 765, 768, 797, 799, 802, 804–5, 808–9, 852, 855–7, 862, 864, 880, 886, 892, 908, and 1197–1214.

61 'Merveilleusement sculptée' and 'travaillée avec soin', in Vernes, *Exposition Universelle*, p. 16.

62 '… exécutée avec des outils de pierre. Cet art est presque perdu en Nouvelle-Zélande', in Vernes, *Exposition Universelle*, p. 94.

63 Chris Wingfield, 'The Moving Objects of the London Missionary Society: An Experiment in Symmetrical Anthropology', PhD thesis, University of Birmingham, 2012, p. 190.

64 Brown, *Outgoing CMS Taonga*; Binney, *Legacy*, pp. 134–35.

65 *Musée des missions évangéliques, Exposition universelle, Paris, 1867*, https://rosettaapp.getty.edu/delivery/DeliveryManagerServlet?dps_pid=IE376162

66 'Items kept in CMS Museum', Cadbury Research Library, Birmingham, CMS/H/H30 E7/3, pp. 111–13. Three additional Māori items are listed as deposited or loaned by individuals who were not attached to the New Zealand mission.

67 Peter J. Lineham, 'Missions and missionaries – Decline of missionary influence', *Te Ara – the Encyclopedia of New Zealand*, www.TeAra.govt.nz/en/missions-and-missionaries/page-6

68 I am indebted to Dr Chris Wingfield, University of Cambridge, who in September 2015 explained to me the likely scenario for the dispersal of the CMS taonga Māori collection, based on his knowledge of the LMS Museum (DB). Unlike other CMS items from other parts of the world, no taonga Māori were transferred to London's Horniman Museum and British Museum when the remaining collection was deaccessioned in the mid-twentieth century.

69 Brown, 'Nukutawhiti', pp. 404–5.

70 Steven Hooper, 'Illustration of an Exhibition and Sale at the Wesleyan Centenary Hall', in Karen Jacobs, Chantal Knowles and Chris Wingfield (eds), *Trophies, Relics and Curios?: Missionary Heritage from Africa and the Pacific*, Sidestone Press, Leiden, 2013, pp. 46–48.

71 Angelyn Dries, 'The 1925 Vatican Mission Exposition and the Interface between Catholic Mission Theory and World Religions', *International Bulletin of Mission Research*, vol. 40, no. 2, 119–32, pp. 119–20.

72 Jeanette Greenfield, *The Return of Cultural Treasures*, Cambridge University Press, Cambridge, 1995, p. 94.

73 John Considine, *The Vatican Mission Exposition: A Window on the World*, Macmillan, New York, 1925, p. 124; Dries, 'The 1925 Vatican Mission', p. 122; 'Inauguration of the Marist Missions of Oceania at the Missionary Exhibition at the Vatican', *New Zealand Tablet*, vol. LII, no. 24, 1925, p. 13.

74 Greenfield, *Cultural Treasures*, p. 94.

75 Penkowski, 'Pontifico Museo', p. 227.

76 'The Museum of the London Missionary Society', *Illustrated London News*, 25 June 1859.

77 Jeffrey Auerbach and Peter Hoffenberg, *Britain, the Empire, and the World at the Great Exhibition of 1851*, Ashgate Publishing, Aldershot, England; Burlington, VT, 2008, pp. 81–85; Robert Ellis, *Official Descriptive and Illustrated Catalogue*, vol. 2, Spicer Brothers, London, 1861, pp. 1000–2; *International Exhibition 1862: Official Catalogue of the Industrial Art Department*, Truscott, Son and Simmons, London, c.1862, pp. 133–35; J. G. Knight, *The Australasian Colonies at the International Exhibition, London, 1862*, John Ferres, Government Printer, Melbourne, 1865, p. 75.

### Hongi Hika's self-portraits

1 Josiah Pratt to Samuel Marsden, 12 August 1815; Josiah Pratt to Thomas Kendall, 16 August 1815, Marsden Online Archive, https://marsdenarchive.otago.ac.nz/

2 Samuel Marsden to Josiah Pratt, 12 October 1814, Marsden Online Archive, https://marsdenarchive.otago.ac.nz/

3 Ibid.

4 See the spelling of Hare Hongi in the 1835 'He Whakaputanga o te Rangatiratanga of Nu Tirene: The Declaration of Independence', IA9-1, Archives New Zealand: Te Rua Mahara o te Kāwanatanga, Auckland, https://nzhistory.govt.nz/media/interactive/the-declaration-of-independence

5 Deidre Brown email correspondence with Judy Middleton, 15 and 16 October 2015.

6 Deidre Brown and Rebecca Conway, notes from an inspection of ETI.570 ('Hongi Hika' attributed wooden bust) by Dr Andrew Merchant, Faculty of Agriculture and Environment, University of Sydney, at Macleay Museum (now the Chau Chak Wing Museum), Sydney, 9 December 2015.

### Hone Heke's 'collar'

1 Frederick Williams, *Through Ninety Years, 1826–1916: Life and Work Among the Maoris in New Zealand*, Whitcombe & Tombs, Auckland, 1939, pp. 54–55.

2 David Hilliard, 'Bishop G.A. Selwyn and the Melanesian Mission', *New Zealand Journal of History*, vol. 4, no. 2, 1970, 120–137, p. 131; Museum of Archaeology and Anthropology, Cambridge, collection catalogue. The label affixed to the back of the catalogue card says: '1901.191 Bay of Island, New Zealand. Piece of Feather Collar given by the Chief "Heke" to Rev. William Nihill about 1845. Given by the Rev. John Still 1901.'

### He tikanga hōu? Figurative art in Rangitukia in 1838

1 Frances Porter, *The Turanga Journals 1840–50: Letters and Journals of William and Jane Williams, Missionaries to Poverty Bay*, Victoria University Press, Wellington, 1974, p. 40.

2 Tipiwhenua Kaa, *Piripi Taumata-a-kura Celebrations: 130 Years 1834–1964*, Waiapu Pastorate, Rangitukia, 1964, p. 2.

## 10 The art of utu

1. Matutaera Nihoniho, 'Uenuku or Kahukura: The Rainbow God of War', *Te Ao Hou*, no. 27, 1959, p. 66.

2. George Graham, 'Pare Hauraki-Pare Waikato: An old-time adage of the Hauraki and Waikato people, the origin thereof, and some of the significant history connected therewith as narrated to me by Wiremu Hoterene Taipari of Ngati Maru in 1887', *Journal of the Polynesian Society*, vol. 58, no. 2, 1949, 68–76, p. 76.

3. Awhina Tamarapa, 'Ngā Kākahu o Te Papa: The Cloaks of Te Papa', in Awhina Tamarapa (ed.), *Whatu Kākahu: Māori Cloaks*, Te Papa Press, Wellington, 2011, p. 111.

4. Paul Tapsell, 'The Flight of Pareraututu: An Investigation of *Taonga* from a Tribal Perspective', *Journal of the Polynesian Society*, vol. 106, no. 4, 1997, 323–374, p. 340.

5. Object file, cat. No. 812, Auckland Museum Ethnology Library, Auckland.

6. Patricia Wallace, 'Traditional Māori Dress: Rediscovering Forgotten Elements of Pre-1820 Practice,' PhD thesis, University of Canterbury, 2002, p. 149.

7. Thomas Lambert, *Pioneering Reminiscences of Old Wairoa*, Thomas Avery & Sons, New Plymouth, 1936, pp. 161–62.

8. Rongowhakaata Iwi Trust, 'Statement of Association', http://rongowhakaata.iwi.nz/wp-content/uploads/2010/12/Statement-of-Association-Te-Mana-Moana-o-Rongowhakaata.pdff, p. 16.

9. Mokomoko to Mair, 12 July 1897, in Mereana Mokomoko, 'The Building of Hotunui, Whare Whakairo, W. H. Taipari's Carved House at Thames, 1878', *Transactions and Proceedings of the Royal Society of New Zealand*, 30, 1897, pp. 41–44.

10. Tapsell, 'Flight of Pareraututu', p. 355.

11. Arini Loader, 'Origins and Establishment of Ngāti Raukawa', p. 77 ftnt 60, https://forms.justice.govt.nz/search/Documents/WT/wt_DOC_151826233/Wai%202200%2C%20H001.pdf

12. Te Waari Carkeek, 'In the Waitangi Tribunal', *Ngati Toa*, 9 June 2003, www.ngatitoa.iwi.nz/sitecontent/images/Folders/General/Te-Waari-Carkeek.pdf, p. 7; '"Tuhiwai" mere pounamu (nephrite weapon)', Te Papa, ME010922, https://collections.tepapa.govt.nz/object/71840

13. Steven Oliver, 'Te Rauparaha', *Dictionary of New Zealand Biography*, first published in 1990, *Te Ara – the Encyclopedia of New Zealand*, https://teara.govt.nz/en/biographies/1t74/te-rauparaha

14. Te Waari Carkeek, 'Te Rauparaha Part 2: South Island Raids and the Arrival of the "Tory"', *Te Ao Hou*, no. 31, June 1960, http://teaohou.natlib.govt.nz/journals/teaohou/issue/Mao31TeA/c9.html, p. 10.

15. Tamihana Te Rauparaha, *He Pukapuka Tātaku i ngā Mahi a Te Rauparaha Nui: A Record of the Life of the Great Te Rauparaha*, translated and edited by Ross Calman, Auckland University Press, Auckland, 2020, p. 145.

16. Te Rauparaha (Calman ed.), p. 147; Oliver, 'Te Rauparaha'.

17. Te Rauparaha (Calman ed.), pp. 149, 271.

18. Te Rauparaha in George Graham et al. 'Te Kaoreore: An Historic Mere-Pounamu of Ngati-Whakaue (Arawa): Its Origin and History as Narrated by Pirika Te Miroi Tiniraupeka (Ohinemutu, January, 1936.)', *Journal of the Polynesian Society*, vol. 52, no. 2, 1943, 46–64, p. 49.

19. Te Rauparaha (Calman ed.), pp. 7, 149.

20. Ron Crosby, *The Musket Wars: A History of Inter-Iwi Conflict 1806–1845*, Libro International, Auckland, 2012, pp. 237–42.

21. Oliver, 'Te Rauparaha'.

22. Te Rauparaha (Calman ed.), p. 271.

23. Mātene Te Whiwhi in 'Otaki Maori Land Court Minutebook' 2, 12 March 1874, Kete Horowhenua, https://horowhenua.kete.net.nz/item/19c851ed-1565-49bf-8277-2f346b9a0024#tab-item-description, p. 262.

24. Octavius Hadfield donated the carvings to Otago Museum on its founding in 1868, and in 1932 museum staff attached them to the hull of a Whanganui waka taua called *Te Paranihi*.

25. '"Tuhiwai" mere pounamu (nephrite weapon)', Te Papa Online Catalogue, https://collections.tepapa.govt.nz/object/71840

26. Editor's comment, *Te Ao Hou*, June 1963, p. 20; '"Tuhiwai"' – as above, Te Papa Online Catalogue.

27. Tessa Johnstone, 'Ngati Toa's Wealth of Objects', *Stuff*, 10 June 2014, www.stuff.co.nz/dominion-post/culture/10136743/Ngati-Toas-wealth-of-objects; '"Tuhiwai"', Te Papa Online Catalogue.

28. H. Campbell, 'Pine Spars and Plate Armour: Convicts and Colonists: H.M.S. *Buffalo* in the South Seas', *Auckland–Waikato Historical Journal*, vol. 52, no. 1, 1988, 6–11, p. 15.

29. Michael Roche, 'The Commodity Chain at the Periphery', in Christina Stringer and Richard Le Heron (eds), *Agri-Food Commodity, Chains and Globalising Networks*, Routledge, London and New York, 2016, p. 207; Geoff Park, *Forestry and Timber Trading in the Bay of Islands, 1769–1840*, Treaty of Waitangi Research Unit, Wellington, 2013, pp. 12–13.

30. Belle Sadler, letter to the British Museum, 8 July 1896, British Museum Archives.

31. Ibid. I thank Dr Billie Lythberg, University of Auckland, for her observations about these non-Māori items.

32. Tītore never travelled overseas, so it is likely that these non-Māori Pacific items were acquired by exchange with Pākehā or Māori who had similar contacts or had travelled to the Pacific Islands. Frederick Sadler does not appear to have travelled to either Fiji or Tonga, so a less likely scenario is that he had acquired these items and added them to his collection.

33. William Yate, 26 June 1834, in Philip Parkinson, 'Tuku: Gifts for a King and the Panoplies of Titore and Patuone', *Tuhinga*, no. 23, 2012, p. 57.

34. A few years earlier, Tītore and twelve other rangatira signed a letter appealing to King William IV for protection from France. Henry Williams, *The Early Journals of Henry Williams, Senior Missionary in New Zealand of the Church Missionary Society, 1826–40*, New Zealand Electronic Text Centre, Wellington, 2006, p. 192.

35. Frederick Sadler, 14 July 1836, in Parkinson, 'Tuku', p. 61.

36. Deidre Brown, 'Kings, Rangatira and Relationships: The Enduring Meanings of "Treasure" Exchanges between Māori and Europeans in 1830s Whangaroa', in Lucie Carreau, Alison Clark, Alana Jelinek, Erna Lilje and Nicholas Thomas (eds), *Pacific Presence, vol. 2: Oceanic Art and Museums*, Sidestone Press, Leiden, 2018, pp. 215–17; the suit of armour is still in Te Papa.

37. 'F. W. R. Sadler', SA Memory, State Library of South Australia, www.samemory.sa.gov.au/site/page.cfm?c=3547

38. My research was supported by a 2016–18 Pacific Presences Visiting Fellowship to the Museum of Archaeology and Anthropology, University of Cambridge.

39. Tapsell, 'Flight of Pareraututu', pp. 338, 342.

40. Annette Wilkes, 'Between People and Things: Understanding Violence and Theft in Early New Zealand Transactions', PhD thesis, University of Canterbury, 2013, p. 94. p. 94.

41. Tapsell, 'Flight of Pareraututu', p. 345.

## The Mātaatua wharenui

1. Sidney Moko Mead et. al, *Nga Karoretanga o Mataatua Whare. The Wanderings of the Carved House, Mataatua*. Research Report, No. 2. Whakatāne, 1990, p. 14.

2. George Preece, 'History of the Carved House "Mata[a]tua"', *Appendices to the Journal of the House of Representatives*, 1879, G.-4, p. 1.

3. Ibid.

4. 'A Present to the Queen: Loyalty of District Natives', *Bay of Plenty Times*, 18 March 1874.

5. Ibid.

## 11 Transforming cultures and traditions: New materials, ideas and technologies

1. There may be another instance in the Bay of Islands in 1840, though Roger Neich notes 'they are very indistinct': *Painted Histories: Early Maori Figurative Painting*, Auckland University Press, Auckland, 1993. p. 57.
2. Brian Flintoff, 'Māori musical instruments – taonga puoro', *Te Ara – the Encyclopedia of New Zealand*, www.TeAra.govt.nz/en/maori-musical-instruments-taonga-puoro
3. Vincent O'Malley, *The Meeting Place: Maori and Pakeha Encounters, 1642–1840*, Auckland University Press, Auckland, 2012, p. 32; Ling Roth, *Crozet's Voyage to Tasmania, New Zealand and the Ladrone Islands and the Philippines in the Years 1771–1772*, Truslove and Shirley, London, 1891, p. 27.
4. Judith Binney, 'Tuki's Universe', *New Zealand Journal of History*, vol. 38, no. 2, 2004, p. 223. Binney writes about some of the curious trading that occurred, stimulated by Māori of this period.
5. See Johnson Witehira's important article on this topic: 'Mana Matatuhi: A Survey of Maori Engagement with the Written and Printed Word', *Visible Language*, vol. 53, no. 1, 2019, pp. 77–109.
6. Ibid., p. 230.
7. Ibid.
8. Jeffrey Sissons, Wiremu Wi Hongi and Pat Hohepa, *The Puriri Trees Are Laughing: A Political History of Ngāpuhi in the Inland Bay of Islands: A Report Submitted to the Social Sciences Research Fund Committee*, Polynesian Society, Auckland, 1987, p. 37.
9. René Lesson, journal entry, as quoted in Alison Jones and Kuni Kaa Jenkins, *He Kōrero: Words Between Us: First Māori–Pākehā Conversations on Paper*, Huia, Wellington, 2011, p. 102.
10. See Witehira.
11. Atholl Anderson, *Welcome of Strangers: An Ethnohistory of Southern Maori A.D. 1650–1850*, Otago University Press, Dunedin, 1998, p. 200.
12. H. T. Whatahoro and S. P. Smith, *The Lore of the Whare Wananga*, Polynesian Society, New Plymouth, 1913. Smith explains that other aspects of the teaching – namely that it took place in a separate dedicated whare – remained the same. He wrote that this book was Te Whatahoro's manuscript of the accounts of both Te Mātorohanga and his 'confrère' Nēpia Pōhūhū (d.1882). Smith translated them, with help from Te Whatahoro. See also David Simmons, 'Te Mātorohanga, Moihi', https://teara.govt.nz/en/biographies/2t23/te-matorohanga-moihi
13. See Roger Neich, Mick Pendergrast and Dorota Starzecka, *The Maori Collections of the British Museum*, British Museum Press, London, 2010, p. 116.
14. Anderson, *Welcome of Strangers*, p. 75.
15. Ibid., p. 76.
16. Ibid., p. 92.
17. Ibid., p. 210.
18. Ibid., p. 210.
19. Ibid., p. 214.
20. Ibid., p. 127.
21. Ibid., p. 128.

### Moko signatures and tino rangatiratanga

1. Mānuka Hēnare, 'The Māori Leaders' Assembly, Kororipo Pā, 1831', in Judith Binney (ed.), *Te Kerikeri 1770–1850: The Meeting Pool*, Bridget Williams Books, Wellington, 2007, pp. 115–16.
2. Max Hailstone, 'Te Tiriti (The Treaty)', *Visible Language*, no. 27 (1993), pp. 302–19.
3. For a more detailed discussion see Ngarino Ellis, 'Ki Tō Ringa ki ngā Rākau ā te Pākehā? Drawings and Signatures of Moko by Māori in the Early Nineteenth Century', *Journal of the Polynesian Society*, vol. 123, no. 1, March 2014, pp. 29–67. The deed was later found to be unfair and illegal and was set aside.
4. Hēnare, 'The Māori Leaders' Assembly', pp. 115–16.
5. See Auckland Art Gallery, 'Whakamīharo Lindauer Online', www.lindaueronline.co.nz/artist/the-artist-gottfried-lindauer, for a discussion of this. Lindauer also depicted Kawepō with two eyes, whereas in real life he had only one. It is most likely that Lindauer based his painting of him on photographs, as Kawepō died in 1888 when Lindauer was only just starting to paint portraits of Māori. Lindauer was well known for using photographs as the source for his portraits of Māori.

### Early Māori drawings

1. Anne Salmond, *Between Worlds: Early Exchanges Between Maori and Pakeha 1773–1815*, Penguin, Auckland, 1997, p. 222.
2. Judith Binney, 'Ancestral Voices: Maori Prophet Leaders', in Keith Sinclair (ed.), *Oxford Illustrated History of New Zealand*, Oxford University Press, Auckland, 1990, p. 158.
3. Merata Kawharu, 'Ancestral Landscapes and World Heritage from a Māori Viewpoint', *Journal of the Polynesian Society.* vol. 118, no. 4, 2009, 317–338, p. 322.

### The second age of iron

1. Hongi Hika, quoted in Samuel Lee and Thomas Kendall (eds), *A Grammar and Vocabulary of the Language of New Zealand*, Church Missionary Society, London, 1820, p. 79.
2. Anne Salmond, *Between Worlds: Early Exchanges Between Maori and Pakeha 1773–1815*, Penguin, Auckland, 1997, pp. 327–29.
3. John Savage, *Some Account of New Zealand, Particularly the Bay of Islands and Surrounding Country*, J. Murray, London, 1807, p. 71.
4. John Nicholas, *Narrative of a Voyage to New Zealand, Performed in the Years 1814 and 1815, in Company with the Rev. Samuel Marsden, Principal Chaplain of New South Wales*, James Black & Sons, London, 1817, p. 48.
5. Deidre Brown, *Tai Tokerau Whakairo Rākau: Northland Māori Wood Carving*, Reed, Auckland, 2003, pp. 44–49.
6. Frankham, 'Weapon of Mass Destruction', *New Zealand Geographic*, no. 128, 2014, www.nzgeo.com/stories/weapon-of-mass-destruction/
7. I am in gratitude to Te Warihi Hetaraka for providing this information, April 2023.
8. Angela Middleton, *Pēwhairangi: Bay of Islands Missions and Māori 1814–1845*, Otago University Press, Dunedin, 2014, p. 259.

## 12 Ngā toi mōrehu: The arts of survival

1. Judith Binney, Vincent O'Malley and Alan Ward, 'The Coming of the Pakeha, 1820–40', in Atholl Anderson, Judith Binney and Aroha Harris (eds), *Tangata Whenua: An Illustrated History*, Bridget Williams Books, Wellington, 2014, pp. 213–17.
2. Judith Binney, Vincent O'Malley and Alan Ward, 'Rangatiratanga and Kawanatanga, 1840–1860', in Atholl Anderson, Judith Binney and Aroha Harris (eds), *Tangata Whenua: An Illustrated History*, Bridget Williams Books, Wellington, 2014, pp. 230–31.
3. Judith Binney, 'Kawanatanga and Rangatiratanga', in Judith Binney et. al. (eds), *The People and the Land*, Allen & Unwin, Wellington, 1993, p. 96.
4. Pātaka that have been attributed to the Ngā Pou o te Kīngitanga movement were built in Hāwera (1853), Ōtaki (1854), Whanganui (probably Pūtiki; n.d.), Pāpāwai (1855), Waiohiki (Taradale; c.1855), possibly Pūkawa (c.1855 or 1856; near Taupō) and Te Taitai (Taitā) (1856). The eighth is known only in narrative: Te Puea spoke of a pātaka that had been thrown into Lake Waikare to protect it from Ngāpuhi when they invaded the area in 1823; Brown, 'Nga Paremata Māori: The Architecture of Māori Nationalism', *Fabrications*, vol. 12, no. 2, 2002, 1–17, pp. 3–4.
5. A. R. Cairns, 'Wiremu Tako Ngatata', in W. H. Oliver (ed.), *Dictionary of New Zealand Biography 1769–1869*, vol. 1, Bridget Williams Books, Wellington, 1993, p. 314; Lindsay Cox, *Kotahitanga: The Search for Māori Political Unity*, Oxford University Press, Oxford, 1993, p. 45; W. J. Phillipps, *Maori Houses and Food Stores*, Government Printer, Wellington, 1952, pp. 107–8; John Te Herekiekie Grace, *Tuwharetoa: A History of the Maori People of the Taupo District*, Reed, Wellington, 1959, pp. 444–45; Elizabeth Hura, 'Te Heuheu

Tūkino III, Iwikau', *Dictionary of New Zealand Biography*, first published in 1990; *Te Ara – the Encyclopedia of New Zealand*, https://teara.govt.nz/en/biographies/1t32/te-heuheu-tukino-iii-iwikau; T. S. Grace, *A Pioneer Missionary Among the Maoris 1850–1879 – Being Letters and Journals of Thomas Samuel Grace*, G. H. Bennett & Co, Palmerston North, 1928, p. 75.

6  Cairns, 'Wiremu Tako Ngatata', p. 314; Phillipps, *Maori Houses*, pp. 107–8.

7  Roger Neich, 'The Māori House Down in the Garden: A Benign Colonial Response to Māori Art and the Māori Counter-Response', *Journal of the Polynesian Society*, vol. 112, no. 4, 2003, pp. 331–68, p. 348.

8  Cairns, 'Wiremu Tako Ngatata'.

9  Neich, 'Māori House', p. 348.

10  'Nuku Tewhatewha', Dowse Art Museum, http://dowse.org.nz/exhibitions/detail/nuku-tewhatewha

11  These tribespeople attending the 1854 hui were from Taranaki, Whanganui, Ngāti Raukawa, Ngāti Rauru and Ngāti Ruanui. Paul Clark, *Hauhau: The Pai Marire Search for Māori Identity*, Auckland University Press & Oxford University Press, Auckland, 1975, p. 18; Keith Sinclair, 'Te Tikanga Pekeke: The Maori Anti-Landselling Movements in Taranaki', in Peter Munz (ed.), *The Feel of Truth: Essays in New Zealand and Pacific History*, Reed, Wellington, 1969, p. 85; W. A. Quin, *The Story of Hawera*, C. O. Ekdahl, Hawera, 1904, p. 26; Richard Taylor, *The Past and Present of New Zealand – With its Prospects for the Future*, William Macintosh, London, 1868, p. 12; Tony Sole, *Ngāti Ruanui: A History*, Huia, Wellington, 2005, p. 218; James Cowan, *The New Zealand Wars: A History of the Maori Campaigns and the Pioneering Period, vol. 1, 1845–1864*, R. E. Owen, Wellington, 1955, p. 147.

12  Richard Taylor, *Te Ika a Maui, Or New Zealand and Its Inhabitants*, MacIntosh, London, 1870, p. 344.

13  Wī Tako paid for Te Puku Mahi Tamariki as headquarters for Te Ātiawa supporters of the King; Cairns, 'Wiremu Tako Ngatata', p. 314; A. R. Cairns, 'Ngātata, Wiremu Tako', *Dictionary of New Zealand Biography*, first published in 1990. *Te Ara – the Encyclopedia of New Zealand*, https://teara.govt.nz/en/biographies/1n10/ngatata-wiremu-tako; W. J. Phillipps, *Carved Maori Houses of Western and Northern Areas of New Zealand*, Government Printer, Wellington, 1955, p. 35.

14  'Fire Destroys Historic Hikurangi Meeting House', *Daily News*, 6 September 1976.

15  Bronwyn Elsmore, *Mana from Heaven – A Century of Maori Prophets in New Zealand*, Moana Press, Tauranga, 1989, p. 397.

16  Judith Binney, 'The Native Land Court and Maori Communities', in Judith Binney, Judith Bassett and Erik Olssen (eds), *The People and the Land*, Allen & Unwin, Wellington, 1993, p. 154; Robert Mahuta, 'Tukaroto Matutaera Potatau Te Wherowhero Tawhiao', in Claudia Orange (ed), *Dictionary of New Zealand Biography 1870–1900*, vol. 2, Bridget Williams Books and Department of Internal Affairs, Wellington, 1993, p. 509.

17  A. M. Latta, *Meeting of the Waters – The Story of Ngaruawahia*, Ngaruawahia Lions Club, Ngāruawāhia, 1980, pp. 153–54; John Wilson, 'The Māori Struggle for Mana Motuhake', *New Zealand Historic Places*, vol. 30, September 1990, p. 27; Binney, 'Native Land Court', p. 155; Michael King, *Te Puea: A Life*, Hodder & Stoughton, Auckland, 1977; 4th illustrated edn, Reed Books, Auckland 2003, p. 29; Tawhiao in Mahuta, p. 510.

18  Rahui Papa and Paul Meredith, 'Kīngitanga – the Māori King movement – Tāwhiao, 1860–1894', *Te Ara – the Encyclopedia of New Zealand*, www.TeAra.govt.nz/en/kingitanga-the-maori-king-movement/page-3

19  Judith Binney, 'Amalgamation and Separation', in Judith Binney, Judith Bassett and Erik Olssen (eds), *The People and the Land*, Allen & Unwin, Wellington, 1993, p. 205; King, *Te Puea*, p. 66; Pei Te Hurinui Jones, *King Potatau: An Account of the Life of Potatau Te Wherowhero, The First Maori King*, Polynesian Society, Wellington, 1959, p. 150.

20  John Cresswell, *Maori Meeting Houses of the North Island*, PCS Publications, Auckland, 1977, p. 36; King, *Te Puea*, p. 68; Phillipps, *Carved Maori Houses*, p. 211; Wilson, p. 27.

21  Judith Binney, 'Amalgamation and Separation', p. 205; King, *Te Puea*, p. 66; Jones, p. 150.

22  King, *Te Puea*, p. 102.

23  Phillipps, *Carved Maori Houses*, p. 216; *Weekly News*, 27 March 1919; Wilson, p. 28.

24  King, *Te Puea*, p. 103; Latta, p. 155.

25  Binney, 'Native Land Court', p. 157; Cox, p. 61.

26  Binney, 'Native Land Court', p. 160; King, *Maori: A Photographic and Social History*, Reed, Auckland, 1991, p. 160; Claudia Orange, *The Treaty of Waitangi*, Allen & Unwin, Port Nicholson Press and Historical Branch of the Department of Internal Affairs, Wellington, 1987, p. 223; Ranginui Walker, *Struggle Without End*, Penguin, Auckland, 1990, pp. 170–71.

27  Cox, p. 65; Roger Neich, *Painted Histories: Early Maori Figurative Painting*, Auckland University Press, Auckland, 1993, p. 117.

28  'Petition of Hare Hongi Hika', *Appendices to the Journals of the House of Representatives*, 1878, I-3, no. 139; 'Visit of his Excellency the Governor to the North', 1876, reprint from the *Daily Southern Cross*, Auckland, n.d., n.p.

29  Binney, 'Amalgamation and Separation', p. 158; Cox, p. 66; Orange, pp. 197–99, 201, 217, 231; Alan Ward, *A Show of Justice: Racial Amalgamation in Nineteenth Century New Zealand*, Auckland University Press and Oxford University Press, Auckland, 1983, p. 290; Edward Williams, 11 May 1880, *Appendices to the Journals of the House of Representatives*, G-4, no. 4, p. 3. The second Te Tiriti o Waitangi house collapsed during a storm in 1917: see *New Zealand Herald*, 30 March 1922.

30  Deidre Brown, 'Moorehu Architecture', PhD thesis, University of Auckland, 1997, pp. 285–86.

31  James Cowan, *The Maori, Yesterday and Today*, Whitcombe & Tombs, Christchurch, 1930, pp. 123–24; Neich, *Painted Histories*, p. 115; Phillipps, *Carved Maori Houses of the Eastern Districts of the North Island*, pp. 71, 95; Thomas Porter, *Major Ropata Wahawaha – The Story of his Life and Times*, Poverty Bay Herald, Gisborne, 1897, p. 30; *Poverty Bay Herald*, 2 March 1889.

32  Anne Salmond, *Hui: A Study of Maori Ceremonial Gatherings*, Reed, Auckland, 1975, p. 81; Peter Shaw, *New Zealand Architecture – From Polynesian Beginnings to 1990*, Hodder & Stoughton, Auckland, 1991, p. 56.

33  Judith Binney, *Redemption Songs: A Life of Te Kooti Arikirangi Te Turuki*, Auckland University Press, Auckland, 1995, p. 434.

34  William Greenwood, *Upraised Hand: The Spiritual Significance of the Rise of the Ringatu Faith*, Polynesian Society, Wellington, 1980, p. 58; Paroa Kurei in Binney, *Redemption Songs*, p. 382; Shaw, pp. 55–56; Te Kani Te Ua, *Echoes of the Pa: Proceedings of the Tairaawhiti Association*, Tairaawhiti Association, Gisborne, 1932, p. 14.

35  Binney, *Redemption Songs*, pp. 294, 519; Cairns in Allan North, 'Te Whai a Te Motu Meeting House, Ruatahuna', *Historical Review*, vol. 8, no. 1, 1965, p. 33.

36  Binney, *Redemption Songs*, p. 279.

37  Ibid., p. 275.

38  Gilbert Mair, 26 September 1873, *Appendices to the Journals of the House of Representatives*, G-2B, no. 1, p. 1, 1874.

39  Binney, *Redemption Songs*, p. 273; Neich, *Painted Histories*, p. 99.

40  Neich, *Painted Histories*, p. 178.

41  Binney, 'Amalgamation and Separation', p. 155; Neich, *Painted Histories*, p. 178; Phillipps, 'The Te Kuiti House', *Arts in New Zealand*, vol. 11, no. 2, 1938, 82–88, p. 87; David Simmons, *Whakairo: Maori Tribal Art Styles*, Oxford University Press, Auckland, 1994, p. 100.

42  Binney, *Redemption Songs*, p. 273.

43  Ibid., p. 329; 'Ruataupare, Kokohinau Marae', file ref. 8/17/4/17, rec. no. 72, 73 004, Marae Buildings Record Form, Heritage New Zealand Pouhere Taonga, Wellington.

44  M. Hunia, 'Memories of the Bay of Plenty Earthquake 1987', *20th Anniversary Earthquake Memories Project*, Sir James Fletcher Kawerau Museum, 2007.

45 'W. D.', 'Sketches in the King Country', *New Zealand Herald*, supplement, 26 May 1883.

46 Neich, *Painted Histories*, p. 28; Simmons, p. 137.

47 Hirini Moko Mead, *Te Toi Whakairo: The Art of Maori Carving*, Reed, Auckland, 1995, pp. 107–8; Simmons, *Whakairo*, p. 139.

48 Simmons, *Whakairo*, p. 137.

49 Neich, *Painted Histories*, pp. 119, 185.

50 Binney, *Redemption Songs*, p. 280; Neich, *Painted Histories*, p. 195.

51 Mead, *Te Toi Whakairo*, p. 104.

52 Mair, p. 1.

53 Neich, *Painted Histories*, pp. 181, 183.

54 Neich, *Painted Histories*, pp. 184–86; Phillipps, *Carved Maori Houses of the Eastern Districts*, p. 71; Monty Soutar, 9 November 1976, in 'Pakira, Waitahanui marae', file ref. 8/17/4/24, rec. no. 0038, Marae Buildings Record Form, Heritage New Zealand Pouhere Taonga, Wellington.

55 Binney, *Redemption Songs*, p. 280, caption pl. 2; Cowan, *The Maori, Yesterday and To-day*, pp. 168–70; Margaret Orbell, 'The Painted House at Putahi', *Te Ao Hou*, no. 46, March 1964, 32–36, pp. 32–33.

56 Binney, *Redemption Songs*, caption pl. 2; Neich, *Painted Histories*, p. 261.

57 Neich, *Painted Histories*, p. 192.

58 Binney, *Redemption Songs*, caption pl. 2.

59 Neich, *Painted Histories*, p. 192.

60 Binney, 'Amalgamation and Separation', p. 148; Edward Ellison, 'Sacred Stone Links Taranaki and Otago', *Historic Places*, no. 19, 1987, 7–11, pp. 7–8.

61 T. G. Hammond, 'Passing of Tohu', c.1907, MS Papers 4456-06, Manuscripts & Archives, Alexander Turnbull Library, Wellington, p. 2; Ailsa Smith, 'Tohu', Kakahi, in Claudia Orange (ed.), *Dictionary of New Zealand Biography 1870–1900*, vol. 2, Bridget Williams Books and Department of Internal Affairs Historical Branch, Wellington, 1993, p. 541; Tupatea Te Rongo and Te Kahu Pukoro in James Cowan, *The New Zealand Wars*, vol. 2, R. E. Owen, Government Printer, Wellington, 1956, pp. 23, 48.

62 Elsmore, p. 244; Hazel Riseborough, *Days of Darkness: Taranaki 1878–1884*, Allen & Unwin, Wellington, 1989, p. 1.

63 James Belich, *I Shall Not Die: Titokowaru's War, New Zealand 1868–1869*, Bridget Williams Books, Wellington, 1993, p. 285; Binney, 'Amalgamation and Separation', p. 148.

64 Keith Sinclair, *Kinds of Peace: Māori People After the Wars 1870–85*, Auckland University Press, Auckland, 1991, p. 84.

65 Binney, 'Amalgamation and Separation', p. 148; Cowan, *The New Zealand Wars*, vol. 2, pp. 481, 483.

66 Dick Scott, *The Parihaka Story*, Southern Cross, Auckland, 1954, p. 104.

67 Binney, 'Amalgamation and Separation', p. 149; Danny Keenan, 'Erueti Te Whiti-o-Rongomai', in Claudia Orange (ed), *Dictionary of New Zealand Biography 1870–1900*, vol. 2, Bridget Williams Books and Department of Internal Affairs Historical Branch, Wellington, 1993, p. 532.

68 Neville Peat, 'Rongo's Sacred Stone', *New Zealand Listener*, 8 August 1987, p. 31.

69 Deidre Brown, *Māori Architecture: From Fale to Wharenui and Beyond*, Raupo, Auckland, 2009, p. 71–79.

70 Captain L. F. Knollys, *Appendices to the Journals of the House of Representatives*, A-1, no. 38, en. 2, p. 26, 1881, p. 26; T. G. Hammond, 'Te Whiti and Parihaka', 1881, MS Papers 4456-01, Manuscripts & Archives, Alexander Turnbull Library, Wellington, pp. 15, 244.

71 William Marshall, *A Personal Narrative of Two Visits to New Zealand in His Majesty's Ship Alligator, AD 1834*, James Nisbet, London, 1841, p. 211.

72 Phillipps, *Maori Houses*, p. 24.

73 Phillipps visited a tree-fern house with raupō interior linings in Kāwhia in the early twentieth century. Phillipps, *Maori Houses*, p. 48.

74 Te Whiti in Phillipps, *Carved Maori Houses*, p. 117; Scott, p. 12.

75 'Illness at Parihaka', *Taranaki Herald*, 23 October 1884, p. 2.

76 Angela Wanhalla, 'Housing un/healthy bodies: Native housing surveys and Maori health in New Zealand 1930–45', *Health & History*, vol. 8, no. 1, 2006, 100–120, p. 115; James McLeod Henderson, 'Ratana', MA thesis, University of New Zealand, Auckland, 1955, p. 35.

77 Binney, 'Amalgamation and Separation', p. 147.

78 Barry Mitcalfe, *Maori Poetry*, Victoria University Press, Wellington, 1974, p. 121; Margaret Orbell, 'Te Waiata mo Te Whiti', *Tu Tangata*, no. 12, 1983, p. 9; Scott, *Parihaka Story*, appendix.

79 Binney, 'Amalgamation and Separation', p. 150.

80 Ibid., p. 149; Keith Sinclair, *Kinds of Peace: Maori People After the Wars 1870–85*, Auckland University Press, Auckland, 1991, p. 125.

81 King, *Maori*, p. 85; Scott, *Parihaka Story*, p. 135.

82 Binney, 'Amalgamation and Separation', p. 151; Cresswell, p. 105; Ministry of Works and Development, 'Rangi Kapuia Structural Report', file ref. 8/17/4/104, rec. no. 0130, 1987, Heritage New Zealand Pouhere Taonga, Wellington.

83 Negative, no. 12046 1/1, Alexander Turnbull Library, Wellington; Binney, 'Amalgamation and Separation', p. 151; *Wanganui Chronicle*, 26 August 1960; Dick Scott, *Ask That Mountain: The Story of Parihaka*, Southern Cross, Auckland, 1991, pp. 158, 174; A. J. Davis, 'Parihaka Paa: Housing Survey', 10 July 1956, acc. no. W2490, no. 34/3/98, box 15a, Maori Affairs Papers, National Archive, Wellington; Te Rangi Hiroa, 'The Taranaki Maoris: Te Whiti and Parihaka', Te Aute College Students' Association Conference, Napier, 1897.

84 Binney, 'Amalgamation and Separation', p. 151.

85 Hīroa, 'The Taranaki Maoris'; *New Zealand Times*, 29 March 1899, p. 2; Orbell, 'Te Waiata mo Te Whiti', p. 91; Scott, *Parihaka Story*, p. 134.

86 Ngarupoe Kohi in Hineani Melbourne, 'Recollections of Parihaka: Mrs. Ngarupoe Kohi (nee Paki) of Otorohunga', Maori Studies research essay, 6 February 2011, University of Auckland Māori Studies Library, Auckland; *New Zealand Times*, 29 March 1899, p. 2.

87 Hīroa, 'The Taranaki Maoris'.

88 Kohi in Melbourne.

89 Hīroa, 'The Taranaki Maoris'; *New Zealand Times*, 29 March 1899, p. 2; Scott, *Parihaka Story*, p. 134.

### Māori flags and banners

1 'United Tribes flag', Ministry for Culture and Heritage, https://mch.govt.nz/nz-identity-heritage/flags/united-tribes-flag https://mch.govt.nz/nz-identity-heritage/flags/united-tribes-flag

2 Charlotte Macdonald, Merimeri Penfold and Bridget Williams, *The Book of New Zealand Women*, Bridget Williams Books, Wellington, 1991, p. 531.

3 Steven Oliver, 'Te Kiri Karamū, Hēni', *Dictionary of New Zealand Biography*, first published in 1990. *Te Ara – the Encyclopedia of New Zealand*, https://teara.govt.nz/en/biographies/1t43/te-kiri-karamu-heni

4 Margaret Orbell, 'Maori Flags and Banners', *Te Ao Hou*, no. 50, 1965, 32–55, p. 34.

5 Judith Binney, 'Ancestral Voices: Maori Prophet Leaders', in Keith Sinclair (ed.), *Oxford Illustrated History of New Zealand*, Oxford University Press, Auckland, 1990, p. 129.

6 Paul Clark, *Hauhau: The Pai Marire Search for Maori Identity*, Auckland University Press and Oxford University Press, Auckland, 1975, p. 60.

7 James Cowan, *The Adventures of Kimble Bent*, Capper Press, Christchurch, 1911, p. 56.

8 Binney, 'Ancestral Voices', p. 134; Thomas Lambert, *The Story of Old Wairoa and the East Coast District, North Island, New Zealand*, Collins Somerville Wilkie, Dunedin, 1925, p. 484; Herbert Meade, *A Ride through the Disturbed Districts of New Zealand*, John Murray, London, 1870, p. 126.

9   Cowan, *Kimble Bent*, p. 56; Lindsay Head, 'The Gospel of Te Ua Haumene', *Journal of the Polynesian Society*, vol. 101, no. 1, 1992, 7–44, p. 37.

10  Cowan, *Kimble Bent*, p. 56; Orbell, p. 34; Robin Winks, 'The Doctrine of Hau-hauism', *Journal of the Polynesian Society*, vol. 62, no. 3, 1953, 209–10, p. 205.

11  James Cowan, *The New Zealand Wars*, vol. 2, R.E. Owen, Government Printer, Wellington, 1956, pp. 545–46.

12  Judith Binney, *Redemption Songs: A Life of Te Kooti Arikirangi Te Turuki*, Auckland University Press, Auckland, 1995, p. 133.

13  Ibid., p. 191.

14  E. E. Bush, 'Te Kooti Centenary Observance at Te Porere', *Te Ao Hou*, no. 69, 1970, 24–25, p. 24; Ormond Wilson, *War in the Tussock – Te Kooti and the Battle at Te Porere*, R. E. Owen, Government Printer, Wellington, 1961, p. 45.

15  Deidre Brown, *Māori Architecture: From Fale to Wharenui and Beyond*, Raupo, Auckland, 2009, pp. 69–70.

### 13  Ka whawhai tonu mātou: Taonga and museums since 1900

1   Ironically, at the exact time, Māori MPs were seeking to restrict the practices of a range of artists, most notably tohunga tā moko who used rongoā (remedies) as part of their practice. The 1907 Tohunga Suppression Act was seen by some as an attack on Māori artistic practices and, in particular, the work of tohunga tā moko. The Act, introduced by James Carroll (Ngāti Kahungunu) and supported by Apirana Ngata (Ngāti Porou), resulted in many tohunga not passing on their mātauranga to students, and ultimately it endangered art forms such as moko.

2   Auckland Institute & Museum, MS131, 11/2/2, 6 August 1901, in Pishief, 'Augustus Hamilton: Appropriation, Ownership and Authority', MA thesis, Massey University, 1998, p. 100.

3   'The Maori Gave His Best: Visit of TRH the Duke and Duchess of York, 1901', *Te Ao Hou*, Royal Tour, 1953, pp. 23–24. These gifts are now part of the Royal Collection Trust; a selection of taonga gifted to the British royal family feature on the RCT website: 'Maori Works of Art in the Royal Collection', www.rct.uk/collection/themes/trails/maori-works-of-art-in-the-royal-collection

4   MS131, in Pishief, p. 100.

5   Pishief, pp. 113–14. See also Roger Neich, *Carved Histories: Rotorua Ngati Tarawhai Woodcarving*, Auckland University Press, Auckland, 2002, pp. 332–33; Nicholas Thomas and Mark Adams, *Rauru: Tene Waitere, Maori Carving, Colonial History*, Otago University Press, Dunedin, 2009.

6   'Proposed Maori Museum', *Bay of Plenty Times*, 10 September 1902.

7   '"The Maori Antiquities Act, 1901" (Suggestions, Correspondence, etc. in Connection with)', *Appendix to the Journals of the House of Representatives*, 1902 Session I, G-08 Page 4, 1902, Session 1, G-08, p. 4.

8   Roger Neich (ed.), *The Oldman Collection of Polynesian Artifacts*, University of Hawai'i Press, Honolulu, 2004, p. v.

9   Ibid.

10  For more on this house see Damian Skinner, *The Carver and the Artist*, Auckland University Press, Auckland, 2008, pp. 27–41. Bernie Kernot identifies the main artists involved as Eramiha Kapua, Pine and Hone Taiapa, Iotua (Charles) Tuarau and Willie Marama (both from Rarotonga); the builder was Richard Wills, and the dimensions were decided by Ngata: 'Maori Buildings for the Centennial', in William Renwick (ed.), *Creating a National Spirit: Celebrating New Zealand's Centennial*, Victoria University Press, Wellington, 2004.

11  Deidre Brown, 'The Architecture of the School of Māori Arts and Crafts', *Journal of the Polynesian Society*, vol. 108, no. 3, 1999, pp. 241–76.

12  Conal McCarthy, *Museums and Māori: Heritage Professionals, Indigenous Collections, Current Practices*, Te Papa Press, Wellington, 2016, p. 36.

13  Leo Fowler, 'The East Coast Tribes Have a Modern Whare Wananga', *Te Ao Hou*, vol. 26, March 1959, pp. 24–27, http://teaohou.natlib.govt.nz/journals/teaohou/issue/Mao26TeA/c19.html

14  Ibid.

15  Ibid., pp. 25–26.

16  Miharaia Winiata, 'The Future of Maori Arts and Crafts', *Te Ao Hou*, no. 19, August 1957, pp. 29–35, http://teaohou.natlib.govt.nz/journals/teaohou/issue/Mao19TeA/c20.html

17  Ibid., p. 31.

18  'Maori Court at Wanganui Museum', *Te Ao Hou*, no. 64, September 1968, p. 32, http://teaohou.natlib.govt.nz/journals/teaohou/issue/Mao64TeA/c13.html.

19  Tribunal applications ask for either redress (where there is no acceptance that sovereignty was given to the Crown) or settlement (where it is accepted by iwi that their sovereignty was extinguished by signing the treaty).

20  Taniora Maxwell (Ngāi Tai, Ngāti Whātua) is currently writing an MA thesis on taonga returned to iwi through the settlement process at the University of Auckland.

21  Hugh Kawharu, 'Te Tiriti o Waitangi', https://waitangitribunal.govt.nz/treaty-of-waitangi/translation-of-te-reo-maori-text/.

22  *Te Roroa Report* (Wai 38), Waitangi Tribunal, 1992.

23  Ibid., p. 215.

24  Te Roroa Claims Settlement Act 2008, www.legislation.govt.nz/act/public/2008/0100/15.0/DLM1132303.html

25  Deidre Brown, 'Te Hau ki Turanga', *Journal of the Polynesian Society*, vol. 105, no. 1, 1996, pp. 7–26.

26  Jonathan Mane-Wheoki, 'Mataatua: No Wai Tenei Whare Tupuna? A Report on Ngati Awa Claim (Wai 46)', Waitangi Tribunal, March 1993. The chairman of the Ngāti Awa Trust Board had been tirelessly advocating for Mātaatua's return and was a pivotal figure here: see H. M. Mead, 'The Mataatua Declaration and the Case of the Carved Meeting House Mataatua', *University of British Columbia Law Review*, vol. 69, 1995, p. 69. For an overview, see Conal McCarthy, 'The Practice of Repatriation: A Case Study from New Zealand', in Louise Tythcott and Kostas Arvanitis (eds), *Museums and Restitution: New Practices, New Approaches*, Routledge, London and New York, 2014, pp. 71–84.

27  Assembly of First Nations and the Canadian Museums Association, 'Task Force Report on Museums and First Peoples', *Museum Anthropology*, vol. 16, no. 2, June 1992, https://anthrosource.onlinelibrary.wiley.com/doi/abs/10.1525/mua.1992.16.2.12

28  Native American Graves Protection and Repatriation Act 1990, www.nps.gov/subjects/nagpra/index.htm

29  Deidre Brown, 'Ko To Ringa ki nga Rakau a te Pākehā – Virtual Taonga Maori and Museums', *Visual Resources*, vol. 24, no. 1, 2008, pp. 59–75, www.tandfonline.com/doi/bs/10.10/01973760801892266; Wayne Ngata, Hera Ngata-Gibson and Amiria Salmond, 'Te Ataakura: Digital Taonga and Cultural Innovation', *Journal of Material Culture*, vol. 17, 2012, pp. 229–44; Cary Karp, 'Digital Heritage in Digital Museums', *Museum International*, vol. 66, 2014, pp. 157–62; Hēmi Whaanga et al., 'He Matapihi Mā Mua, Mō Muri: The Ethics, Processes, and Procedures Associated with the Digitization of Indigenous Knowledge: The Pei Jones Collection', *Cataloguing & Classification Quarterly*, vol. 53, no. 5–6, 2015, pp. 520–47.

30  Museums Aotearoa, 'Kāhui Kaitiaki Network', www.museumsaotearoa.org.nz/networks/k%C4%81hui-kaitiaki

31  'Virtual repatriation: a database of Māori taonga in overseas museums', led by Arapata Hakiwai from Te Papa, the National Museum of New Zealand; Digitisation & Research Part One: Arapata Hakiwai; www.maramatanga.ac.nz/node/1765

32  Linda Tuhiwai Smith, *Decolonizing Methodologies: Research and Indigenous Peoples*, Otago University Press, Dunedin, 2012.

33 Arapata Hakiwai, 'Te Toi Whakairo o Ngati Kahungunu: The Carving Traditions of Ngati Kahungunu,' MA thesis, Victoria University of Wellington, 2003.

### Trick or taonga: The mysterious case of the green-painted patu pora

1 'Cross-cultural Exchange between Māori and Europeans', Te Papa Tongarewa, https://collections.tepapa.govt.nz/topic/1080

2 John Nicholas, *Narrative of a Voyage to New Zealand, Performed in the Years 1814 and 1815, in Company with the Rev. Samuel Marsden, Principal Chaplain of New South Wales*, James Black & Sons, London, 1817, p. 134.

3 James Belich, *Making Peoples: A History of the New Zealanders From Polynesian Settlement to the End of the Nineteenth Century*, Penguin, Auckland, 1996, pp. 148–49.

4 I am indebted to Lucie Carreau for providing information about Beasley's purchase of the patu from her Beasley database. See also Bill Whelen, 'The Patu Pora, or Iron Hand Club, on Display in "Made in New Zealand"', Te Papa Tongarewa Archives, 6 September 2005.

5 Harry Beasley, 'Metal Mere', *Journal of the Polynesian Society*, 36, no. 143, 1927, pp. 297–98.

6 'Jamrach's', *Strand Magazine*, January–June 1891, p. 432. I am indebted to Eleanor Larrson for information about the Jamrach family business.

7 Lucie Carreau, email to Deidre Brown, 21 September 2015.

8 'Club (mere or patu pora)', Oc1944,02.821; 'Club (mere or patu pora)', Oc1944,02.822..JT.

### Fakes in the collection

1 H. D. Skinner, *Comparatively Speaking: Studies in Pacific Material Culture, 1921–1972*, Otago University Press/John McIndoe, Duendin, 1974, p. 188.

2 See Peter Gathercole, 'Obstacles to the Study of Maori Carving: The Collector, the Connoisseur, and the Faker', in C. Greenhaig and J. Megaw (eds), *Art in Society: Studies in Style, Culture and Aesthetics*, Duckworth, London, 1978, p. 282.

3 Dale F. Simpson Jr, 'Captain A. W. Fuller's Contribution to the Field Museum's Easter Island Collection', http://islandheritage.org/wordpress/wp-content/uploads/2010/06/RNJ_24_1_Simpson_Jr.pd

4 Robin Watt, 'James Edward Little's Forged Marquesan Stilt Steps', *Records of the National Museum of New Zealand*, vol. 2, no. 7, 1982, pp. 49–63.

5 'James Robieson', British Museum, www.britishmuseum.org/collection/term/BIOG127667

6 For more on these forgers, see Robin Watt, 'The Fake Maori Artefacts of James Edward Little and James Frank Robieson', PhD thesis, Victoria University of Wellington, 1990.

### Collecting the ancestors

1 While toi moko were mostly male, Aranui knows of a small number of female toi moko. Ngahuia Te Awekotuku notes that Horatio Robley drew one toi moko that he described as belonging to a woman, but that may be incorrect as it was based on the presence of fine features and long hair: see Te Awekotuku, *Mau Moko: The World of Māori Tattoo*, Penguin, Auckland, 2007. p. 78.

2 Paul Tapsell, 'The Flight of Pareraututu: An Investigation of *Taonga* from a Tribal Perspective', *Journal of the Polynesian Society*, vol. 106, no. 4, 1997, 323–374, pp. 347–48.

3 Also called mokomokai or upoko tuhi. Some make the distinction that mokomokai were those made from the heads of enemies; there was another term for those of ancestors. This has changed recently to reflect the understanding that they were all somebody's ancestor, whether enslaved or not.

4 Te Awekotuku, p. 48.

5 Robley also collected taonga Māori, some of which were later purchased by the British collector and dealer William O. Oldman (1879–1949), whose own collection was purchased by the New Zealand government in 1948 for £44,000. Oldman died a year later. The Oldman collection was subsequently distributed to a number of New Zealand museums, including Auckland, Canterbury and Otago. See 'The Oldman Collection: Maori Art in London', filmed by James Harris, NZ Film Unit, www.youtube.com/watch?v=mlststSsU-U

6 See 'Moko Mokai', *Bay of Plenty Times*, 26 October 1996, p. 35.

7 Elizabeth Ellis, pers. comm., November 2023.

### Enrico Giglioli and the taonga collection in the Pigorini National Museum of Prehistory and Ethnography, Rome

1 'Virtual repatriation: a database of Māori taonga in overseas museums', led by Arapata Hakiwai from Te Papa; Digitisation & Research Part One: Arapata Hakiwai; www.maramatanga.ac.nz/node/1765

2 Now known as Museo di Storia Naturale dell'Università di Firenze (Natural History Museum of the University of Florence).

3 Letter, Giglioli to Cheeseman, 19 November 1885, Auckland Museum, files MUS-2011-12.

4 Brian Gill, 'The Cheeseman-Giglioli Correspondence, and Museum Exchanges between Auckland and Florence, 1877–1904', *Archives of Natural History*, vol. 37, no. 1, 2010, p. 131.

5 Letter, Giglioli to Cheeseman, 13 January 1888, Auckland Museum Library files.

6 Florence has a good collection of taonga nonetheless, including a Ngāti Porou poupou from the 1870s and a rare kahu tetere whete – a cloak decorated with shoots of tetere whete moss (*Polytrichum commune*). Another example of this type of cloak is in Te Papa (ME000754).

## PART 3 — TE KETE ARONUI

### 14 The art of social reform: Te Puea, Ngata and Rātana

1 Deidre Brown, 'Moorehu Architecture', PhD thesis, University of Auckland, 1997, pp. 189–90.

2 Piri Poutapu, in Michael King, *Te Puea*, Sceptre, Auckland, 1990, p. 110.

3 Poutapu and Tumokai Katipa, in King, *Te Puea*, pp. 111–12.

4 Ann Parsonson, 'Hērangi, Te Kirihaehae Te Puea', *Dictionary of New Zealand Biography*, first published in 1996. *Te Ara – the Encyclopedia of New Zealand*, https://teara.govt.nz/en/biographies/3h17/herangi-te-kirihaehae-te-puea

5 Eric Ramsden, 'The Footstool of Old King Tawhiao', *Sun*, 10 September 1927.

6 Ibid.; Vernon Roberts, *Kohikohinga: Reminiscences and Reflections of Ropata*, Whitcombe & Tombs, Auckland, 1929, p. 320.

7 Michael King, 'A Place to Stand: A History of Turangawaewae Marae', in Isla Nottingham (ed.), Occasional Paper no. 15, University of Waikato, 1981, p. 13; Pei Te Hurinui Jones, *Turanga-waewae: Souvenir of Golden Jubilee 1921–1971*, Taumarunui, 1971, pp. 10–11, 14; Hērangi in King, *Te Puea*, p. 120.

8 Jones, *Turanga-waewae*, pp. 9, 13–14; Hērangi in King, *Te Puea*, p. 120.

9 John Cresswell, *Maori Meeting Houses of the North Island*, PCS Publications, Auckland, 1977, p. 31; W. J. Phillipps, *Carved Maori Houses of the Western and Northern Areas of New Zealand*, Government Printer, Wellington, 1955, p. 201; Hērangi in Roberts, p. 321.

10 King, *Te Puea*, p. 127; Patricia Sargison, *Notable Women in New Zealand Health*, Longman Paul, Auckland, 1993, p. 39; Jones, *Turanga-waewae*, pp. 13–15.

11 King, *Te Puea*, p. 128; Jones, *Turanga-waewae*, p. 15.

12 Hērangi to Ngata, September 1927, in King, *Te Puea*, p. 128.

13 Ngata to Buck, 17 August 1935, in M. P. K. Sorrenson (ed.), *Na To Hoa Aroha: From Your Dear Friend*, vol. 3, Auckland University Press, Auckland, 1987, p. 191; Jones, *Turanga-waewae*, p. 15.

14 Hērangi in King, *Te Puea*, pp. 138–39.

15 Hērangi to Ramsden, 8 December 1928, in 'Eric Ramsden – Correspondence 1927–29', MS Papers 196-167, Alexander Turnbull Library.

16. Ngata to Buck, 5 January 1929, in M. P. K. Sorrenson (ed.), *Na To Hoa Aroha: From Your Dear Friend*, vol. 1, Auckland University Press, Auckland, 1986, p. 171; Piri Poutapu in Phillipps, *Carved Maori Houses*, p. 203; Jones, *Turanga-waewae*, p. 25.

17. Poutapu in Phillipps, *Carved Maori Houses*, p. 203; Jones, *Turanga-waewae*, p. 25.

18. King, *Te Puea*, p. 147.

19. Patricia Adams, 'Marae Complexes', in Frances Porter (ed.), *Historic Buildings of New Zealand – North Island*, Historic Places Trust and Cassell New Zealand, 1983, p. 137; Poutapu in Phillipps, *Carved Maori Houses*, p. 203.

20. Ngata to Buck, 17 August 1935, in Sorrenson (ed.), *Na To Hoa Aroha*, vol. 3, p. 193; Poutapu in Phillipps, *Carved Maori Houses*, p. 203; Pei Te Hurinui Jones, *Mahinarangi: A Tainui Saga*, J. C. Ekdahl, Hawera, 1946, pp. 31, 33; Hērangi in Roberts, p. 322.

21. Jones, *Mahinarangi*, p. 31.

22. Katipa in King, *Te Puea*, p. 141.

23. King, *Te Puea*, p. 141.

24. Jones, *Mahinarangi*, p. 31.

25. Ibid., p. 30.

26. King, *Te Puea*, p. 146; Ngata to Buck, 17 August 1935, in Sorrenson (ed.), *Na To Hoa Aroha*, vol. 3, p. 193; Jones, 'Maori Kings', in E. G. Schwimmer (ed.), *Maori People in the Nineteen-Sixties – A Symposium*, Blackwood and Janet Paul, Auckland, 1968, p. 157.

27. Jones, *Turanga-waewae*, p. 27.

28. Ibid., pp. 25–29.

29. King, *Te Puea*, p. 145; Sorrenson (ed.), *Na To Hoa Aroha*, vol. 1, p. 32.

30. Hērangi in Roberts, p. 322.

31. Adams, p. 137; King, *Te Puea*, p. 146; Hērangi in Roberts, pp. 321–22.

32. King, *Te Puea*, p. 182.

33. William Worger, 'Te Puea Herangi, the Kiingitanga and Waikato', MA thesis, University of Auckland, 1975, p. 143.

34. King, *Te Puea*, p. 187; Ann Parsonson, 'Hērangi, Te Kirihaehae Te Puea', *Dictionary of New Zealand Biography*, first published in 1996. Te Ara – the Encyclopedia of New Zealand, https://teara.govt.nz/en/biographies/3h17/herangi-te-kirihaehae-te-puea

35. Ngata to Buck, 20 September 1930, in M. P. K. Sorrenson (ed.), *Na To Hoa Aroha: From Your Dear Friend*, vol. 2, Auckland University Press, Auckland, 1988, p. 56.

36. King, *Te Puea*, p. 182; Jones, *Turanga-waewae*, p. 26.

37. Poutapu, 'Maaoritanga English Transcription Tape'.

38. Ngata in Ramsden, 'Conversation with Sir Apirana Ngata'; Poutapu, 'Maaoritanga English Transcription Tape'.

39. Piri Poutapu, 'Maaoritanga English Transcription Tape', roll 165, folder 13, 'Michael King – Material', acc. 85-080-05, Manuscripts & Archives, Alexander Turnbull Library.

40. King, *Te Puea*, p. 183.

41. Poutapu in King, *Te Puea*, p. 184.

42. Ibid., p. 235; Phillipps, *Carved Maori Houses*, p. 237.

43. Eric Ramsden, 'The Ancient Art of the Carver', 15 June *Evening Post*, 1946.

44. King, *Te Puea*, pp. 235, 265.

45. Ibid., p. 184; Hērangi to Ramsden, 18 April 1935, 'Eric Ramsden – Te Puea's Correspondence', MS Papers 196-342, Manuscripts & Archives, Alexander Turnbull Library.

46. Hērangi to Ramsden, 2 November 1935, ibid.; King, *Te Puea*, pp. 184–85.

47. Ramsden, 'House for Maori King', article, c.1936, 'Eric Ramsden – Papers', MS Papers 196-394, Manuscripts and Archives, Alexander Turnbull Library; Jones, 'Maori Kings', p. 156; Jones, *Turanga-waewae*, p. 37.

48. A. M. Latta, *Meeting of the Waters – The Story of Ngaruawahia*, Ngaruawahia Lions Club, Ngāruawāhia, 1980, p. 144; Ramsden, 6 September 1946, 'Eric Ramsden – Notes', folder 13, 'Michael King – Material', acc. 85-080-05, Manuscripts and Archives, Alexander Turnbull Library.

49. 'Turongo house, Turangawaewae marae', rec. no. 0202, Marae Buildings Record Form, Heritage New Zealand Pouhere Taonga, Wellington.

50. McKay to Ramsden, 18 August 1936, in King, *Te Puea*, p. 185.

51. 'Turongo house'.

52. King, *Te Puea*, p. 186.

53. 'Turongo house'.

54. King, *Te Puea*, p. 186; Latta, p. 144.

55. Ramsden, 'Self-Sacrifice: Efforts by Maoris Building New House', article, 'Eric Ramsden – Papers', Alexander Turnbull Library.

56. Adams, p. 145.

57. Eugene Grayland, *Famous New Zealanders*, Whitcombe & Tombs, Christchurch, 1967, p. 145.

58. Korokī in King, *Te Puea*, p. 196.

59. Hērangi to Ramsden, 'Michael King – Material', Alexander Turnbull Library.

60. H. B. Turbott in I. L. G. Sutherland (ed.), *The Maori People Today — A General Survey*, New Zealand Institute of International Affairs and the New Zealand Council for Educational Research, Wellington, 1940, p. 244.

61. Ibid.; Michael King, *Māori: A Photographic and Social History*, Reed, Auckland, 1991, p. 106.

62. Roger Neich, *Carved Histories: Rotorua Ngati Tarawhai Woodcarving*, Auckland University Press, Auckland, 2002, pp. 293–95.

63. Apirana Ngata, 'Maori Arts and Crafts', in L. G. Sutherland (ed.), *The Maori People Today*, p. 322.

64. Deidre Brown, 'Moorehu Architecture', PhD thesis, University of Auckland, 1997, pp. 161–87, 327–72.

65. Apirana Ngata, 'Draft Statement of the Aims and Objectives of the Young Maori Party', Maori Purposes Fund Board Papers, MS-Papers 189, folder 11, Manuscripts and Archives, Alexander Turnbull Library.

66. Ngata to Buck, 17 August 1935, in Sorrenson (ed.), *Na To Hoa Aroha*, vol. 1, p. 193.

67. Peter Buck (Te Rangi Hīroa), 'Maori Decorative Art: No. 1, House-panels', *Transactions and Proceeding of the New Zealand Institute*, vol. 53, 1920, 452–70, pp. 452, 470.

68. Ngata in Sutherland, p. 323.

69. H. Balneavis to D. Ellison, 19 September 1935, 'Raukawa Carved Meeting House, Otaki, 1931–37', series 51, no. 132/1, box 13, Māori Affairs Papers, National Archives, Wellington.

70. Deidre Brown, 'The Architecture of the School of Maori Arts and Crafts', *Journal of the Polynesian Society*, vol. 108, no. 3, 1999, 241–76, pp. 263–64.

71. Roger Neich, 'Historical Change in Ngati Tarawhai Woodcarving Art', MA thesis, Victoria University, 1977, p. 124.

72. Poutapu, 'Maaoritanga English Transcription Tape'; Taiapa in Ngahuia Te Awekotuku, 'The Sociocultural Impact of Tourism on the Te Arawa People of Rotorua, New Zealand', PhD thesis, University of Waikato, 1981, pp. 212–13.

73. Erik Schwimmer, 'Building Art in the Maori Tradition: John Taiapa and the Carved Meeting House of Today', *Te Ao Hou*, no. 28, September 1959, 31–51, pp. 34, 50; Taiapa in Te Awekotuku, p. 213.

74. Apirana Ngata, 'The Origin of Maori Carving: Part 2', *Te Ao Hou*, no. 23, July 1958, 30–34, p. 31.

75. Ngata to Buck, 5 January 1929, in Sorrenson (ed.), *Na To Hoa Aroha*, vol. 1, p. 171; Ngata to Buck, 17 March 1934, in Sorrenson (ed.), *Na To Hoa Aroha*, vol. 3, p. 138; Ngata in Sutherland, p. 324.

76. Brown, 'School of Maori Arts and Crafts', p. 246.

77. Ngata in Sutherland, p. 325.

78. Ibid., p. 324.

79. Neich, 'Historical Change', p. 124; 'Ruaihona – 6th March 1993', Ruaihona Marae Committee, Te Teko, 1993, p. 51; Tuarau in Neich, 'Historical Change', p. 126.

80 David Simmons, *Whakairo: Maori Tribal Art Styles*, Oxford University Press, Auckland, 1994, p. 24.

81 Schwimmer, p. 34; Roger Neich, 'The Maori Carving Art of Tene Waitere, Traditionalist and Innovator', *Art New Zealand*, no. 57, Summer, 1990–91, pp. 74–75; Neich, 'Historical Change', p. 124.

82 Brown, 'Moorehu Architecture', p. 165; Ngata in Sutherland, p. 326.

83 Ngata to Buck, 5 January 1929, in Sorrenson (ed.), *Na To Hoa Aroha*, vol. 1, p. 172.

84 Brown, 'Moorehu Architecture', p. 166.

85 Ngata in Sutherland, pp. 326–27.

86 Ngata in 'Eric Ramsden – Apirana Ngata Articles', MS-Papers 196-380, Alexander Turnbull Library; Ngata in Sutherland, p. 326; W. J. Phillipps, 'Papers – Maori Carving', 1940–63, series 2, box 5, 164/79, Manuscript Archive, Canterbury Museum.

87 King, *Maori*, p. 126.

88 Brown, 'School of Maori Arts and Crafts', p. 261.

89 McEwen and Tuarau in Roger Neich, 'Jacob William Heberley of Wellington: A Maori Carver in a Changed World', *Records of the Auckland Institute and Museum*, vol. 28, 1991, 69–146, p. 137; Ngata to W. J. Phillipps, 31 October 1942, 'Apirana Ngata Papers', MS 1588, Manuscripts & Archives, Alexander Turnbull Library; Hirini Moko Mead, *Te Toi Whakairo: The Art of Maori Carving*, Reed, Auckland, 1995, p. 71; Phillipps, *Carved Maori Houses*, p. 103; 'Te Hau-ki-Turanga' brochure, Te Papa, Wellington, c.1993.

90 Ngata to Buck, 20 September 1935, Sorrenson (ed.), *Na To Hoa Aroha*, vol. 3, p. 201; Apirana Ngata, 'The Origin of Maori Carving: Part 1', *Te Ao Hou*, no. 22. April 1958, 30–41, p. 37; Roger Neich, *Carved Histories*, p. 241.

91 Brown, 'Moorehu Architecture', p. 170.

92 Brown, 'School of Maori Arts and Crafts', p. 252.

93 Brown, 'Moorehu Architecture', p. 464.

94 Te Awekotuku, p. 213.

95 Angela Ballara, 'Rātana, Tahupōtiki Wiremu', *Dictionary of New Zealand Biography*, first published in 1996. *Te Ara – the Encyclopedia of New Zealand*, https://teara.govt.nz/en/biographies/3r4/ratana-tahupotiki-wiremu, p. 417.

96 James McLeod Henderson, 'Ratana', MA thesis, University of New Zealand, Auckland, 1955, pp. 115–18; A. M. Linton to Whanganui Registrar, 5 October 1950, 'Raatana Paa – Part 1', acc. no. W2459, box 76, no. 30/3/179, Māori Affairs Papers, National Archives, Wellington.

97 Bruce Sedcole, 'A Temple for a Prophet: Rātana Architecture', BArch thesis, Victoria University, 1985, pp. 56, 70.

98 Peters in Sedcole, p. 26.

99 Manuao Aperahama, pers. comm., May 1992.

100 Cresswell, p. 110; Gary Herewini, pers. comm., April 1993.

101 Keith Newman writes that the carvings arrived at Rātana Pā in 1929 (*Rātana Revisited*, Raupo, Auckland, 2006, p. 68). William Phillipps dates their arrival to 1921 (*Carved Maori Houses*, p. 63).

102 *New Zealand Times*, 23 June 1924.

103 H. Pope, *Health for the Maori*, John McKay, Government Printer, Wellington, 1901, pp. 33, 68–69.

104 Henderson, p. 139; Te Whakaotinga Ronald Smith, *Te Omeka Pa: The Passing Years*, Te Omeka Marae Trustees, Tainui Press, Matamata, 1987, p. 10.

105 Smith, p. 15.

106 Ibid., p. 22.

107 Ibid., p. 18.

108 Henderson, p. 99; Rātana Church, 'Etahi mai on nga Whakaputanga', Etahi o Nga Akoranga series, typescript.

109 Henderson, p. 96; Ihimaera Ihimaera, unpublished manuscript.

### Te Araiteuru pā at the 1906 New Zealand International Exhibition

1 Amiria Henare (Salmond), *Museums, Anthropology and Imperial Exchange*, Cambridge University Press, New York, 2005, p. 220.

2 Ibid., p. 221; Augustus Hamilton, *Maori Art: The Art Workmanship of the Maori Race in New Zealand, 1896–1900*, New Zealand Institute, Wellington, 1901, accessed through https://books.google.co.nz/s?id=CaIaAAAAYAAJ&printsec=frontcover&source=gbs_ge_summary_r&cad=0#v=onepage&q&f=fals

3 Roger Neich, *Carved Histories: Rotorua Ngati Tarawhai Woodcarving*, Auckland University Press, Auckland, 2002, p. 339.

4 'New Zealand International Exhibition 1906', Christchurch City Libraries, http://christchurchcitylibraries.com/Heritage/Exhibitions/1906/Exhibits/TeAraiteuruPa/

5 Ian Church, 'Pukehika, Hōri' *Dictionary of New Zealand Biography*, first published in 1996. *Te Ara – the Encyclopedia of New Zealand*, https://teara.govt.nz/en/biographies/3p35/pukehika-hori

### 15 The emergence of contemporary Māori art 1950–1975

1 Alexander McLintock (ed.), *National Centennial Exhibition of New Zealand Art: Catalogue*, Wellington, Department of Internal Affairs, 1940, p. 7.

2 R. O. Ross, 'Maori Art', *Art in New Zealand*, vol. 16, no. 2, 1943, p. 12.

3 Apirana Ngata, Lindauer Art Gallery Visitors' Book, 26 June 1901, at www.aucklandartgallery.com/about/major-projects/lindauer-online?q=%2Fabout%2Fmajor-projects%2Flindauer-online

4 Stuart Bell Maclennan, 'Art in New Zealand: Survey, Trends, and Influences, 1938 to Present', in A. H. McLintock (ed.), *An Encyclopaedia of New Zealand*, originally published in 1966, *Te Ara – the Encyclopedia of New Zealand*, http://www.TeAra.govt.nz/en/1966/art-in-new-zealand/page-2

5 Jock McEwen, 'Maori Art', in A. H. McLintock (ed.), *An Encyclopaedia of New Zealand*, originally published in 1966, www.TeAra.govt.nz/en/1966/maori-art

6 'Personality Study: Muru Walters', *Te Ao Hou*, no. 35, June 1961, pp. 28–29, https://paperspast.natlib.govt.nz/periodicals/TAH196106.2.17

7 'H. M., Maori fullback goes in for abstract painting', *Auckland Star*, 10 June 1958, p. 1.

8 Ibid.

9 Mataira's 'sorrowing and Arab-like Christ' was singled out for mention for its 'haunting quality' (*Auckland Star*, 10 June 1958, p. 1). See 'painting of Christ as done by Ralph Hotere, art instructor at Kaikohe, and one of the more promising younger Maori artists', illustrated in *Te Ao Hou*, no. 29, 1959, p. 39, https://paperspast.natlib.govt.nz/periodicals/TAH195912.2.19

10 Arnold Wilson, 'Beginning to Bubble', *Landfall*, no. 185, April 1993, p. 26.

11 *Auckland Star*, 10 June 1958, p. 1.

12 Pākehā artists were, likewise, attempting to reconcile the Māori and the modern in their sculptures, including E. Mervyn Taylor, Alison Duff and Molly Macalister.

13 Selwyn Muru, *Te Hononga: The Confluence*, television documentary, Muru Art Film/Television New Zealand, 1990.

14 Adam Gifford, 'Strong Trap to Catch a Slippery Issue', *New Zealand Herald*, 24 May 2005, www.nzherald.co.nz/lifestyle/news/article.cfm?c_id=6&objectid=10127269

15 Rosemary Vincent, 'Selwyn Muru's Paintings Win Wide Acclaim', *Te Ao Hou*, no. 46, March 1964, 25–27, p. 25.

16 Ans Westra, 'Ngaruawahia Festival of the Arts', *Te Ao Hou*, no. 46, 1964, 28–29, p. 29. The Javanese-born Dutch artist Theo Schoon was the only Pākehā artist whose work was shown at the festival. Hotere was absent in Europe on a New Zealand Art Societies Fellowship. 'See Jonathan Mane-Wheoki, 'Out on His Own: Ralph Hotere and the Māori Art Movement', in Roger Taberner and Ronald Brownson (eds), *Hotere: Seminar Papers from* Into the Black, Auckland Art Gallery, Auckland, 1998, pp. 43–55.

17 'Talking of People', *Northern Advocate*, 25 January 1964, p. 2.

18 Foreword, Buck Nin and Baden Pere (eds), *New Zealand Maori Culture and the Contemporary Scene,* catalogue, Canterbury Museum, Christchurch, 1966.

19 Harry Dansey, 'Maori Artists Make Mark as Professionals', *Auckland Star*, 3 September 1966.

20 Nin and Pere.

21 Dansey.

22 'An Interview with Cliff Whiting', in Mary Barr (ed.), *Headlands: Thinking through New Zealand Art*, Museum of Contemporary Art, Sydney, 1992, p. 119.

23 Hirini Moko Mead to Jonathan Mane-Wheoki, pers. comm., 5 February 1999.

24 Ibid.

25 Ibid.

26 Jocelyn Tarrant, 'Selwyn Wilson: Artist and Teacher', *Te Ao Hou*, no. 41, December 1962, pp. 15–16.

27 Te Puoho Katene (Ngāti Toa, Te Ātiawa, 1927–2010) studied at the Canterbury University College School of Arts but left before he completed his qualification to study music at Victoria University in Wellington. He adorned the *Souvenir Programme* for the reception for South Island Armed Services personnel, held at Tuahiwi in March 1946, with Māori designs.

28 Tarrant, pp. 15–16.

29 'Personality Study', pp. 28–29.

30 Bridie Lonie and Marilynn Webb, *Prints & Pastels*, Otago University Press, Dunedin, 2004, p. 28.

31 Hirini Moko Mead to Jonathan Mane-Wheoki, pers. comm., 5 February 1999.

32 Darcy Nicholas and Keri Kaa, *Seven Maori Artists*, Government Printer, Wellington, 1986, p. 10.

33 *Auckland Star*, 10 June 1958, p. 1.

34 Matchitt said the experience of teaching and working with children had reawakened a creative urge in him. (Kāterina Mataira, *Maori Artists of the South Pacific*, New Zealand Maori Artists & Writers Society, Raglan, 1984, p. 43).

35 Wilson, p. 26.

36 Carol Henderson, *A Blaze of Colour: Gordon Tovey, Artist, Educator*, Hazard Press, Christchurch, 1998, p. 164.

37 Whiting recalls that 'working in conjunction with Pākehā, we weren't taught, we developed a Māori course': Barr, p. 119.

38 Henderson, p. 166.

39 'New Schools for Old Crafts', *Te Ao Hou*, no. 55, June 1966, p. 9.

40 Nicholas and Kaa, p. 11.

41 Barr, p. 120.

42 Kāterina Mataira, 'Modern Trends in Maori Art Forms', in Erik Schwimmer (ed.), *The Maori People in the Nineteen-Sixties*, Blackwood and Janet Paul, Auckland, 1968, p. 208.

43 Vincent, p. 27.

44 Nin and Pere.

45 Dansey.

46 Mark Young, *Painting 1950–1967*, Reed, Wellington, 1968, p. 32.

47 And in 1986 in the National Art Gallery's *Content/Context: A Survey of Recent New Zealand Art*.

48 Wilson, p. 23.

49 'Sculptor of Excellence', *Sunday Star*, 6 February 1994, p. C2.

50 Wilson, p. 26.

51 Nicholas and Kaa, p. 10.

52 Sydney Moko Mead, *Te Maori: Maori Art from New Zealand Collections*, Heinemann, Auckland, 1984, p. 75.

53 Nicholas and Kaa, p. 18.

54 Ibid.

55 Paratene Matchitt and Maia Matchitt, *Kohia ko Taikaka Anake*, video, Simon Nixon Productions, 1990.

56 Mataira, *Maori Artists*, p. 44; Matchitt, 'People are amazed. So am I', in Ian Wedde and Gregory Burke (eds), *Now! See! Hear! Art, Language, Translation*, Victoria University Press, Wellington, 1990, p. 245.

57 *Ascent: A Journal of the Arts in New Zealand*, vol. 1, no. 2, The Caxton Press, Christchurch, July 1968, p. 61.

58 Frank Takitaki Davis, 'Maori Art and Artists', *Education*, no. 9, 1976, p. 29. I am grateful to Robert Jahnke for drawing this reference to my attention.

59 This cohort of artists is increasingly referred to as the 'Taiapa Generation'.

### Oriwa Haddon (1898–1958)

1 Brian Sherriff, *A Pocket Reference to Old New Zealand Artists*, Te Rau Press, http://christchurchartgallery.org.nz/media/uploads/2014_02/PocketReference.pdf, p. 198.

2 Peter Lineham, 'Haddon, Ōriwa Tahupōtiki', *Dictionary of New Zealand Biography*, first published in 1998. *Te Ara – the Encyclopedia of New Zealand*, https://teara.govt.nz/en/biographies/4h2/haddon-oriwa-tahupotiki

3 A. H. McLintock, 'Oriwa T. Haddon', *National Centennial Exhibition of New Zealand Art Catalogue*, Department of Internal Affairs, Wellington, 1940, http://nzetc.victoria.ac.nz/tm/scholarly/tei-GovArt-t1-body-d2-d83.html; Lawlor, *New Zealand Artists' Annual*, 1929, https://catalogue.nla.gov.au/Record/3254875; Lawlor inscription on drawing archived as Haddon, 1932: 'Sweeps and Swipes: "What would you do if you won the 5000 pound sweep?" "Same as I'm doing now but prurry [sic] faster"', National Library of New Zealand, Wellington.

4 Elizabeth Hanson and Apirana Mahuika, 'Putiki and Waiapu Churches' in F. Porter (ed.), *Historic Buildings of New Zealand: North Island*, Historic Places Trust & Cassell, 1983, p. 205; Maxwell Smart, 'Maxwell Smart Speeches', typescript, MS papers 1008, folder 4, Manuscripts & Archives, Alexander Turnbull Library.

5 Greg McManus, CEO of Waitangi National Trust, to Jonathan Mane-Wheoki, pers. comm., n.d.

6 Sherriff, p. 11; The painting is now in the collection of Aotea Utanganui Museum of South Taranaki.

7 McLintock.

8 Lineham.

9 Lineham.

10 'Haere ki a Koutou Tipuna', *Te Ao Hou*, 1 October 1958, p. 3.

### Ramai Hayward (1916–2014)

1 Ramai Hayward was also known as Ramai Te Miha, Ramai Mawhinney, Patricia Rongomaitara Te Miha and Patricia Miller.

2 Katarina Hansard (née Ihaia; Ngāpuhi, ?–1906) may have been the first Māori studio-based photographer. She is claimed to have opened a studio in Kaikohe in 1893: see *New Zealand Herald*, 'Curator will focus on photographers of colonial times', 30 June 2000, www.nzherald.co.nz/nz/curator-will-focus-on-photographers-of-colonial-times/OX4DR5AFEG2DTZQUGP4E3PHEJQ/

3 Jacqueline Amoamo, 'Ramai Hayward: Photographer, Artist, Actress, Filmmaker: A Creative Life', in Sandra Coney (ed.), *Standing in the Sunshine: A History of New Zealand Women Since They Won the Vote*, Penguin, Auckland, 1993, p. 234.

4 John Sullivan to Jonathan Mane-Wheoki, pers. comm., n.d.

5 Deborah Shepard, *Between the Lives: Partners in Art*, Auckland University Press, Auckland, 2005, p. 119; 'Ramai Hayward: Biography', NZ On Screen, www.nzonscreen.com/profile/ramai-hayward/biography

6 Amoamo, p. 234.

7 Hayward in Tamara Martyn, 'Ramai Hayward', *Pacific Way*, December 1993, p. 22.

8 Amoamo, p. 234.

9 William Main, *New Zealand Photography from the 1840s to the Present*, Photoforum, Auckland, 1993, p. 46.

10  Hayward in Chas Toogood, *Koha: Ramai Hayward*, television documentary, Television New Zealand, 1989.

11  Ibid.

12  Jonathan Mane-Wheoki, *Te Puāwai o Ngāi Tahu: A New Flowering of Ngāi Tahu Art*, catalogue, Christchurch Art Gallery, 2003, p. 20; Amoamo, p. 234.

### Pauline Kahurangi Yearbury (1926–1977)

1  Ian Thwaites and Rie Fletcher, *We Learnt to See: Elam's Rutland Group 1935–1958: A Biographical Journey with Auckland Artists*, Pūriri Press, Auckland, 2004, p. 263.

2  Lynda Tyler, 'From the Collection', *Uninews*, vol. 44, 4, 2014, p. 10.

3  Thwaites and Fletcher, p. 264.

4  Tyler, p. 10.

5  'History of the Gallery: The Yearbury Colonial Gallery', South Sea Art, www.southseaart.co.nz/history.asp; Tyler, p. 10.

6  Pauline Yearbury, 'Earth and Sky', *New Zealand Home Journal*, September 1971.

### 16  Urban Māori art and architecture

1  Karen Scherer and Katherine Findlay, 'Waharoa', in *Aotea Centre Works of Art*, www.aucklandlive.co.nz/waharoa

2  Statistics New Zealand, 'How Is Our Maori Population Changing?', 2015.

3  Aroha Harris, *Hikoi: Forty Years of Maori Protest*, Huia, Wellington, 2004, pp. 10–31.

4  Merata Kawharu, *Maranga Mai! Te Reo and Marae in Crisis?*, Auckland University Press, Auckland, 2014, p. 5.

5  'Auckland's Community Centre', *Te Ao Hou*, vol. 40, 1962, pp. 25–29; Ngarimu Blair, 'Te Rimu Tahi: Ponsonby Road Master Plan/Māori Heritage Report', Auckland City Council, Auckland, 2013, p. 4; J. Sturm, 'The Ngatiponeke Young Maori Club', *Te Ao Hou*, vol. 12, 1955, pp. 29–32.

6  'Laying the Foundations', *Kōkiri*, vol. 15, August 2009, www.tpk.govt.nz/en/mo-te-puni-kokiri/kokiri-magazine/kokiri-15-2009/laying-the-foundations; 'Young Maoris Become Skilled Tradesmen', *Te Ao Hou*, no. 55, June 1966, p. 8.

7  Jan Bierman, 'If These Walls Could Talk …', *The Hobson*, September 2020, pp. 32–33; Emma Campbell, 'The Māori Hostel Movement', *Te Hau Kāinga*, 16 August 2020, www.maorihomefront.nz/en/whanau-stories/maori-hostels/?fbclid=IwAR15gyG0i8yosWAuX-qsLBZEgQoTZ3S7BsMieMIhUaJC3xlJUVyOiv0iXa0

8  Jonathan Mane-Wheoki, 'He Wahine Toa: Robyn Kahukiwa, Artist', in Robyn Kahukiwa, Hinemoa Hilliard, Edward Lucie-Smith and Jonathan Mane-Wheoki (eds), *The Art of Robyn Kahukiwa*, Reed, Auckland, 2005, p. 28.

9  Ibid., p. 27.

10  Ibid., pp. 29–30.

11  Karaka in Witi Ihimaera, 'Karaka', *Art New Zealand*, vol. 60, Spring 1991, p. 80.

12  Apirana Ngata to Eric Ramsden, 16 April 1947, 'Eric Ramsden–Apirana Ngata Correspondence', MS Papers 196, folder 376, Manuscripts and Archives, Alexander Turnbull Library.

13  Ivan Mercep, interview with Deidre Brown, July 2005.

14  *Tane-nui-a-Rangi*, University of Auckland, Auckland, 1988, p. 30.

15  *Te Whakatuwheratanga o Te Tumu Herenga Waka, 6 Tihema 1986, Poneke, Te Whare Wananga o Wikitoria*, Maori Studies Department, Victoria University of Wellington, Wellington, 1986; Deidre Brown, 'Nga Whare Matauranga Maori: The Recent History of Maori Tertiary Architecture', *Thresholds: Proceedings of Papers from the 16th SAHANZ Conference*, Hobart, 1999, pp. 19–24.

16  Deidre Brown, *Māori Architecture: From Fale to Wharenui and Beyond*, Raupo, Auckland, 2009, p. 135; Aroha Harris, 'Pipitea Pa', in Atholl Anderson, Judith Binney and Aroha Harris (eds), *Tangata Whenua: An Illustrated History*, Bridget Williams Books, Wellington, p. 219.

17  'Ngā Hau e Whā National Marae', Christchurch City Libraries, https://my.christchurchcitylibraries.com/nga-hau-e-wha-national-marae/#Aoraki

18  'Tapu Te Ranga Marae', www.taputeranga.Māori.nz/index.php

19  Kahukiwa, 'Artworks', www.taputeranga.Māori.nz/artworks.php; Karen McKenzie and Peter Mayo, 'Tapu Te Ranga – Whare Māori – Episode Excerpt', https://vimeo.com/54431474

20  'Ngā Hau e Whā National Marae'.

21  Lena Henry, 'Te Manaaki o te Marae: The Role of Marae in the Tāmaki Māori Housing Crisis', unpublished report, Building Better Homes, Towns and Cities National Science Challenge, 2018.

22  'Māori Leader in Western Australia Plans to Build Marae', Radio New Zealand, www.rnz.co.nz/news/te-manu-korihi/136428/maori-leader-in-western-australia-plans-to-build-marae; 'Council Knocks Back Sydney Marae Bid', Radio New Zealand, www.radionz.co.nz/news/te-manu-korihi/332898/council-knocks-back-sydney-marae-bid; Talisa Kupenga, 'Plans For First Marae in Australia Underway', Māori Television, www.Māoritelevision.com/news/regional/plans-first-marae-australia-underway

23  Ellen Anderson, 'Toenga o Te Aro', *Heritage New Zealand*, www.heritage.org.nz/the-list/details/7771

24  Morris Love, 'Te Āti Awa of Wellington – Migrations of the 1820s', *Te Ara – the Encyclopedia of New Zealand*, www.TeAra.govt.nz/en/artwork/1287/te-aro-pa-in-1842

25  Pamela Meekings-Stewart, *A Cat Among the Pigeons*, documentary, 1992, NZ on Screen, www.nzonscreen.com/title/a-cat-among-the-pigeons-1992

26  Camille Khouri, 'Justice and Emergency Services Precinct', *Architecture Now*, 19 June 2018, https://architecturenow.co.nz/articles/justice-and-emergency-services-precinct; Te Rūnanga o Ngāi Tahu, 'Ngāi Tūāhuriri/Ngāi Tahu Values Embedded in Te Omeka – Justice Precinct', 26 September 2017, https://ngaitahu.iwi.nz/our_stories/ngai-tuahuriringai-tahu-values-embedded-in-te-omeka-justice-precinct/

27  Jeremy Hansen, 'Toi Tū Toi Ora: Shane Cotton', https://britomart.org/shane-cotton/

28  Eke Panuku Development Auckland, '"Ko te toi ko au me te whenua" – Mahi Toi of the Waterfront', www.ekepanuku.co.nz/about/case-studies/ko-te-toi-ko-au-me-te-whenua-mahi-toi-of-the-waterfront/

### Street art

1  Tony Mitchell, 'Kia Kaha! (Be Strong!): Māori and Pacific Islander Hip-Hop in Aotearoa-New Zealand', in Tony Mitchell (ed.), *Global Noise: Rap and Hip Hop Outside the USA*, Wesleyan University Press, Middletown CT, 2001, p. 284.

2  Kerryn Pollock, 'Public and Street Art – Street Art', *Te Ara – the Encyclopedia of New Zealand*, 2014, www.TeAra.govt.nz/en/public-and-street-art/page-4

3  Ali Ikram, 'Tame Iti's Artistic Collaboration with Owen Dippie', *New Zealand Herald*, 13 February 2016, www.nzherald.co.nz/entertainment/news/article.cfm?c_id=1501119&objectid=11588624

4  Parkinson, 'First Instalment of Murals', *Gisborne Herald*, 27 April 2018, http://gisborneherald.co.nz/localnews/3342654-135/first-instalment-of-murals

5  Kim Parkinson, 'Latest Mural Represents Gisborne Region', *Gisborne Herald*, 17 September 2018, www.gisborneherald.co.nz/local-news/20180917/latest-mural-represents-gisborne-region

6  Te Kuru o te Marama Dewes, 'Mr G Sprays Community Pride Across NZ Rural Towns', *Te Ao Māori News*, 22 November 2017, https://teaoMāori.news/mr-g-sprays-community-pride-across-nz-rural-towns; www.charlesjaninewilliams.com

### 17  A new tradition or old disruption? Contemporary Māori exhibitions 1990–2021

1  Roma Potiki, 'Getting Brown in Hyper Town', in Mark Amery, Deidre Brown and Jonathan Mane-Wheoki (eds), *TechnoMaori*, City Gallery and Pātaka Porirua, Wellington and Lower Hutt, 2001 (CD-ROM).

2   Peter Brunt, 'Since *Choice!*', in Anna Smith and Lydia Wevers (eds), *On Display: New Essays in Cultural Studies*, Victoria University Press, Wellington, 2004, p. 235.

3   *Young Guns* was the name of a 1988 Hollywood movie and also the colloquial name for the New Zealand cricket team in the early 1990s, and was used to describe a generation of talented young people.

4   Brunt, p. 226.

5   Conal McCarthy, *Exhibiting Māori: A History of Colonial Cultures of Display*, Te Papa Press, Wellington, 2007, p. 163.

6   Jonathan Mane-Wheoki, 'The Resurgence of Māori Art: Conflicts and Continuities in the Eighties', *The Contemporary Pacific*, vol. 7, no. 1, 1995, 1–19, p. 2.

7   Anna-Marie White and Robert Leonard, 'George Hubbard: The Hand That Rocked the Cradle', *Reading Room: Politics in Denial*, vol. 8, 2018, p. 34; the *Choice!* curatorial statement by Hubbard and Craw was later published in *Antic*, 'Beyond Kia Ora: The Paraesthetics of *Choice!*', no. 8, December 1990, p. 28.

8   'Stop Making Sense: Documents', City Gallery, Wellington, https://citygallery.org.nz/documents/stop-making-sense-documents/

9   Brunt, p. 232; White and Leonard, pp. 43–47.

10  Brunt, p. 230.

11  Ibid., pp. 225–26.

12  Rangihīroa Panoho, *Whatu Aho Rua: A Weaving Together of Traditional and Contemporary Māori Art*, Tandanya Aboriginal Cultural Institute and the Sarjeant Gallery, Adelaide, 1991.

13  Ibid., p. 11.

14  Hubbard, in Jonathan Mane-Wheoki, 'Korurangi/Toihoukura: Brown Art in White Spaces', *Art New Zealand*, vol. 78, 1996, p. 43.

15  Alan Pearson, letter, *New Zealand Listener*, 28 October 1995, p. 14.

16  Maori Affairs Amendment Act 1974 (1974 No. 73), *New Zealand Legal Information Institute*, pp. 1708–50, www.nzlii.org/nz/legis/hist_act/maaa19741974n73232/, p. 1710.

17  Jonathan Mane-Wheoki, 'Cultural Safety: Contemporary New Zealand Art in Germany', *Art New Zealand*, no. 79, 1996, 66–69, p. 67.

18  Brunt, p. 232.

19  Taarati Taiaroa, 'The Development of the Māori Art Exhibition: A Typology?' MA thesis, University of Auckland, 2014, p. 71.

20  Ngahiraka Mason, 'Pūrangiaho Toku Mata', *Pūrangiaho Seeing Clearly*, Auckland Art Gallery, Auckland, 2001, p. 20.

21  Ngāi Tahu Strategic Plan 2025, https://ngaitahu.iwi.nz/wp-content/uploads/2013/06/NgaiTahu_20251.pdf

22  Moana Tipa, 'Ngāi Tahu Contemporary Visual Arts', www.moanatipa.com/Contemporary-Māori-Arts

23  The other artists included were Kerry Arlidge, Margaret Bond, Te Aritaua Brennan, Cath Brown, Bevan Climo, Priscilla Cowie, Janina Dell, Awatea Piripi Edwin, Manu Kincaid Edwin, Jacqueline Fraser, Turi Gibb, Anna Gorham, Christine Harvey, Chris Heaphy, Wanga Hebberd, Ross Hemera, Tahua Horomona, Teoti Jardine, Simon Kaan, Kirsten Kemp, Anthony Apirana Manuel, Hana Morgan, Ranui Ngarimu, Neil Pardington, Fiona Pardington, Peter K. Plumb, Rawinia Puna, Otene Rakena, Flora Mei Reiri, Jennifer Rendall, Nicola Reuben, Beverley Rhodes, Fayne Robinson, Peter Robinson, Irene Mura Schroder, Phyllis Smith, Wini Solomon, Kate Souness, Ramonda Te Maiharoa, Ngaio Te Ua, Reg Thompsett, Debbi Thyne, Maaka Tipa, Grace Voller, Metzger Whānau, Areta Wilkinson and Karl Wixon.

24  The artists included Cath Brown, Ewan Duff, Jacqueline Fraser, Ross Hemera, Simon Kaan, Heni Kerekere, Graham Metzger, Huhana Morgan, Fiona Pardington, Otene Rakena, Jenny Rendall, Peter Robinson, Keri Whaitiri and Areta Wilkinson. Moana Tipa, *Rukutia! Rukutia!*, Te Rūnanga o Ngāi Tahu & Christchurch Arts Festival, Christchurch, 1999.

25  Megan Tamati-Quennell, *Aukaha Kia Kaha: Strengthen the Bindings of the Earth, of the People, of the Soul*, Dunedin Public Art Gallery, Dunedin, 2000.

26  Taiaroa, p. 73. The artists included Cath Brown, Janina Dell, Simon Kaan, Kirsten Kemp, Ross Hemera, Chris Heaphy, Ranui Ngarimu, Reihana Parata, Fiona Pardington, Neil Pardington, Nathan Pohio, Rachael Rakena, Flora Mei Reiri, Jenny Rendall, Fayne Robinson and Areta Wilkinson.

27  Moana Tipa, 'Haumi e! Hui e! Taiki e!: Draw Together Affirm', *Te Karaka*, 2001, p. 27.

28  The artists included Cath Brown, Chris Heaphy, Ross Hemera, Lonnie Hutchinson, Simon Kaan, Fiona Pardington, Neil Pardington, Nathan Pohio, Rachael Rakena, Peter Robinson and Areta Wilkinson.

29  Jonathan Mane-Wheoki, Felicity Milburn and Megan Tamati-Quennell, 'Curatorial Summary', *Te Puawai o Ngai Tahu: Twelve Contemporary Ngai Tahu Artists*, Christchurch Art Gallery Te Puna o Waiwhetū, Christchurch, 2003, p. 8.

30  Artists included Ross Hemera, Lonnie Hutchinson, Simon Kaan, Ranui Ngarimu, Fiona Pardington, Neil Pardington, Nathan Pohio, Hana Rakena, Otene Rakena, Rachael Rakena, Jenny Rendall, Fayne Robinson, Areta Wilkinson and James York. The show was a response by the Rūnanga to the *Footprint of the Spirits: The Burrinja Collection* exhibition of Australian Aboriginal paintings which had toured to seven South Island galleries between 2002 and 2003. (Tipa, 'Ngai Tahi Contemporary Visual Arts'.)

31  Simon Kaan, 'Curatorial Comment', *Akona ki ngā Rekereke: Learning from the Knee*, Rūnanga o Ngai Tahu & Burrinja, Dandenong Ranges Community Cultural Centre, Melbourne, 2006, p. 5.

32  Hemara in Matt Philp, 'Expecting to Fly', *Te Karaka*, 5 April 2015, https://ngaitahu.iwi.nz/our_stories/expecting-to-fly/

33  'Gisborne iwi Rongowhakaata's exhibition at Te Papa', Ministry of Culture and Heritage, https://mch.govt.nz/gisborne-iwi-rongowhakaata%E2%80%99s-exhibition-te-papa

34  Taiaroa notes that 'remembering exhibition' is a term coined by Ressa Greenberg in 2009 to describe a curatorial fascination in Western Europe and North America at the time with memory and past exhibitions. Taiaroa, p. 82; Reesa Greenberg, 'Remembering Exhibitions: From Point to Line to Web', *Tate Papers*, no. 12, Autumn 2019, www.tate.org.uk/research/publications/tate-papers/12/remembering-exhibitions-from-point-to-line-to-web

35  Taiaroa, p. 83.

36  Ibid.

37  Ibid.

38  Ibid.

39  Sandy Adsett, Witi Ihimaera and Cliff Whiting, *Mataora: The Living Face*, Auckland, David Bateman, 1996.

### Māori architects and architectural designers

1   Martin Jones, 'St Augustine's Church (Anglican)', *Heritage New Zealand*, 2012, www.heritage.org.nz/the-list/details/4529

2   Jonathan Mane-Wheoki, 'Work of Māori Architects Adds to Our Heritage', *Historic Places*, no. 31, 1990, pp. 29–33, p. 31.

3   Lloyd Ashton, 'Much More Than Ornamental', *Mana*, no. 15, 1997, 39–45, pp. 41–42.

4   Mane-Wheoki, p. 30.

5   Russell Walden, 'Scott, John Colin', *Dictionary of New Zealand Biography*, first published in 2000. *Te Ara – the Encyclopedia of New Zealand*, https://teara.govt.nz/en/biographies/5s7/scott-john-colin

6   'Māori Battalion Hall: A Distinguished Building by a Gifted Architect', *Te Ao Hou*, no. 47, 1964, p. 33.

### Māori designers

1   Wilson in D. Wood, 'Interweaving in New Zealand Culture: A Design Case Study', *Journal of New Zealand Studies*, 17, 2014, 58–67, p. 64.

2   Cheryl Bernstein, 'Playing On', *Art, Life, TV, Etc.*, blog, 12 August 2009, http://cherylbernstein.blogspot.com/2009/08/playing-on.html

3   Ngahiraka Mason (ed.), *Five Māori Painters*, Auckland Art Gallery, Auckland, 2014.

4   Paola Trapani and Johnson Witehira, 'The Whakarare Typeface Project: When Culture-Specific Visual Design Brings Elements of Universal Value', *The Virtuous Circle Cumulus Conference*, Milan, 3–7 June 2015, 1–20, p. 7.

5   Johnson Witehira, 'Process', www.johnsonwitehira.studio/process.

### *Māori Moving Image* exhibition

1   Bridget Reweti and Melanie Oliver, 'Looking at 40 Years of Māori Moving Image Practice, Christchurch Art Gallery, https://christchurchartgallery.org.nz/bulletin/197/looking-at-forty-years-of-maori-moving-image-practt; see also Chevron Hassett, 'Into Te Ao Mārama', review of the show for *Pantograph Punch* (www.pantograph-punch.com).

2   Reweti and Oliver.

3   For a review of the exhibition, see Kirsty Baker, 'To Think about Fraught Things', *Art and Australia*, www.artandaustralia.com/online/online/discursions/think-about-fraught-things.html

4   The work was later exhibited at the City Gallery, Wellington in 2015, as part of a show with Susan Te Kahurangi King. Te Ao was born in Sydney. He is also a writer: see Murdoch Stephens and Shannon Te Ao, 'Unwelcome Guests: Hospitality, Asylum Seekers and Art at the 19th Biennale of Sydney', *Hospitality & Sydney*, vol. 4, no. 2, 2014, pp. 193–202.

5   Stephens and Te Ao, p. 199.

### Wairau Māori Art Gallery: The first public Māori art gallery

1   Wairau Māori Art Gallery, 'Exhibitions', https://en.wairaumaoriartgallery.co.nz/events/exhibitions/, accessed 20 March 2023.

2   Hundertwasser Art Centre, 'The History of the Hundertwaser Art Centre', www.hundertwasserartcentre.co.nz/about/hundertwasser-art-centre/the-history-of-hundertwasser-art-centre/

3   Jade Kake, 'We Are Still Here', *Pantograph Punch*, 14 March 2022, www.pantograph-punch.com/posts/puhi-ariki.

### 18  Māori art in Western Europe and Australia

1   Rachel Hand, interview with Deidre Brown, July 2016.

2   'Field notebooks and Index written by David Simmons, on his research trip to America and Canada 1973', MUS-2014-3, Auckland Museum Library; 'Original and photcopied works relating to David Simmons visits to Overseas Museums', MUS-2018-4, Auckland Museum Library; 'Field notebooks listing Maori Taonga in British and European Museums', MUS-2014-4, Auckland Museum Library.

3   Nicholas Thomas, interview with Deidre Brown, July 2016.

4   Adam Gifford, 'Man on a Pasifika Mission', *New Zealand Herald*, 21 November 2006, www.nzherald.co.nz/lifestyle/news/article.cfm?c_id=6&objectid=10411775; Nicholas Thomas, interview with Deidre Brown, July 2016.

5   Tipene O'Regan, 'A Vibrant Presence', *Te Karaka*, 18 July 2014, https://ngaitahu.iwi.nz/our_stories/vibrant-presence/

6   Dorota Starzecka (ed.), *Maori: Art and Culture*, David Bateman, Auckland, 1996.

7   Amiria Henare, Briar Wood, Maureen Lander and Kahutoi Te Kanawa, 'Visiting the House of Gifts: The 1998 "Māori" Exhibition at the British Museum', *Journal of New Zealand Literature*, no. 21, 2003, pp. 83–101.

8   Julie Adams, interview with Deidre Brown, July 2016.

9   Ibid.

10  Garth Cartwright, 'The Living and the Dead', *NZ Listener*, 23 February 2007, www.noted.co.nz/archive/listener-nz-2007/the-living-and-the-dead/

11  Rachel Hand, interview with Deidre Brown, July 2016; Raymond in Jennifer Dann, 'Twelve Questions: Rosanna Raymond on Fashion for Pacific Dance Festival', *New Zealand Herald*, 5 June 2018, www.nzherald.co.nz/entertainment/news/article.cfm?c_id=1501119&objectid=1206422

12  Cartwright.

13  'Power and Taboo: Sacred Objects from the Eastern Pacific', British Museum, www.britishmuseum.org/the_museum/london_exhibition_archive/archive_power_and_taboo.aspx

14  Julie Adams, interview with Deidre Brown, July 2016.

15  George Nuku, 'Perspicacité: The Art of George Nuku', *World Art*, vol. 1, no. 1, 2011, 67–73, p. 71.

16  Julie Adams, interview with Deidre Brown, July 2016.

17  Ibid.

18  They included Donna Campbell (Ngāpuhi, Ngāti Ruanui), Kewana Duncan (Ngāti Tara), Janine Clarkin (Ngāti Ranginui), Bethany Edmonds (Ngāti Kurī), Lonnie Hutchinson, Maureen Lander, Hemi Macgregor (Ngāti Kahungunu, Ngāi Tūhoe), Reuben Paterson, Louise Potiki-Bryant (Ngāi Tahu), Rachael Rakena, Lisa Reihana, Natalie Robertson, Suzanne Tamaki, Tracey Tawhiao (Ngāiterangi, Whakatōhea, Ngāti Tūwharetoa), Che Wilson and Wayne Youle.

19  Nuku in Anita Herle, 'Relational Objects: Connecting People and Things through Pasifika Styles', *International Journal of Cultural Property*, vol. 15, no. 2, 2008, 159–79, p. 176.

20  Rachel Hand, interview with Deidre Brown, July 2016.

21  *Current: Contemporary Art from New Zealand and the Pacific*, 23 June – 30 July 2011, www.octobergallery.co.uk/exhibitions/2011cur/index.shtml

22  Julie Adams, interview with Deidre Brown, July 2016.

23  Ibid.

24  Anita Herle, interview with Deidre Brown, July 2016.

25  Charles Stable, 'Maximum Intervention: Renewal of a Māori Waka by George Nuku and National Museums Scotland', *Journal of Conservation and Museum Studies*, vol. 10, no. 1, pp. 8–18, www.jcms-journal.com/articles/10.5334/jcms.1011202/#r1

26  Anita Herle, interview with Deidre Brown, July 2016.

27  Rosanna Raymond, artists' panel with Charmaine 'Ilaiu, Shigeyuki Kihara and Karamia Müller, *Pacific Arts Association Conference*, Musee du Quai Branly, Paris, 7 July 2007.

28  George Nuku and Karen Jacobs, 'An Artist's Perspective', *Journal of Museum Ethnography*, no. 21, March 2009, 127–138, p. 146.

29  Atholl Anderson and Peter White, 'Prehistoric Settlement on Norfolk Island and its Oceanic Context', *Records of the Australian Museum*, vol. 27, 2001, 135–41, p. 138.

30  June Northcroft-Grant, 'Papakura, Mākereti', *Dictionary of New Zealand Biography*, first published in 1996. *Te Ara – the Encyclopedia of New Zealand*, https://teara.govt.nz/en/biographies/3p5/papakura-makereti

31  Debrin Foxcroft, 'One in Six Māori Now Living in Australia, Research Shows', *Stuff*, www.stuff.co.nz/national/103712754/one-in-six-mori-now-living-in-australia-research-shows

32  Logan Metcalfe, Thelma Thomas and Keren Ruki, 'Cultural Collections Celebrate Waitangi Day', 15 February 2013, Australian Museum, https://australianmuseum.net.au/blog-archive/science/cultural-waitangi/

33  *Taonga Maori: Treasures of the New Zealand Maori People*, Australian Museum, Sydney, 1989, title verso page, p. 8; Jonathan Mane-Wheoki, 'The Resurgence of Māori Art: Conflicts and Continuities in the Eighties', *The Contemporary Pacific*, vol. 7, no. 1, 1995, 1–19, p. 1.

34  Rosalie Higson, 'Islands in the Stream', *The Australian*, 3 December 2007, www.theaustralian.com.au/arts/islands-in-the-stream/news-story/04b9f22853fe22c4b28979405a56e746

35  Ruki, interview with Diamond, in Claire Armstrong (ed.), *News from Islands*, Campbelltown Arts Centre, Sydney, 2007, p. 54.

36  Ibid, p. 55.

37  Ruki, artist statement, in Julie Gough (ed.), *Testing Ground*, Salamanca Arts Centre, Hobart, 2013, p. 31.

38  One third of Māori in Australia were born there, according to the 2011 Australian Census. Paul Hamer, 'Māori in Australia: an update from the 2011 Australian census and the 2011 New Zealand general election', working paper, 2012, 1–31, p. 10.

39  Léuli Eshrāghi, email communication to Deidre Brown, 7 December 2018; Tyson Campbell, www.tysoncampbell.info; James Tylor, biography, www.jamestylor.com

40  Anna Parlane, 'Kirsten Lyttle: *Digital Mana*', *Memo Review*, 25 February 2018, www.memoreview.net/blog/can-you-wear-a-digital-cloak-kirsten-lyttle-s-digital-mana-at-centre-for-contemporary-photography-by-anna-parlane

41  Māmari Stephens, 'The Long Shadow Over Our Marae', *e-Tangata*, 26 November 2017, https://e-tangata.co.nz/reflections/mamari-stephens-the-long-shadow-over-our-marae/; Talisa Kupenga, 'Plans for First Marae in Australia Underway', Māori Television, www.Māoritelevision.com/news/regional/plans-first-marae-australia-underway; Melissa Yeo, 'Plans for Australia's First Maori Marae Rejected', *Parramatta Advertiser*, 8 June 2017, www.dailytelegraph.com.au/newslocal/parramatta/plans-for-australias-first-Maori-marae-rejected/news-story/8131f645640f4360094b18c826439e04

### Ngāti Rānana and Hinemihi

1  Dean Sully, Rosanna Raymond and Anthony Hoete, 'Locating Hinemihi's People', *Journal of Material Culture*, vol. 19, no. 2, 2014.

2  'Inia's Carving Unveiled', *Te Ao Hou*, no. 72, January 1973, 39–41, p. 40.

3  A name celebrated in Alan Gallop's 1998 book about Hinemihi: *The House with the Golden Eyes: Unlocking the Secrets of Hinemihi, the Maori Meeting House from Te Wairoa and Clandon Park*, Running Horse Books, Middlesex, 1998.

4  Ambrosia Crum, Deidre Brown, Tumanako Fa'aui, Naomi Vallis and Jason Ingham, 'Seismic Retrofitting of Māori Wharenui in Aotearoa New Zealand', *Philosophical Transactions of the Royal Society*, vol. 337, no. 2155, 2019.

5  Dean Sully (ed.), *Decolonising Conservation: Caring for Maori Meeting Houses Outside of New Zealand*, Left Coast Press, California, 2007.

6  Neich, 'The Māori House Down in the Garden: A Benign Colonial Response to Māori Art and the Māori Counter-response', *Journal of the Polynesian Society*, vol. 112, no. 4, 2003, pp. 331–68.

7  Sully, Raymond and Hoete.

8  Both were graduates of Ngata's Maori Arts and Crafts Institute: Robert Rike (fourth-generation grandson of carver Tene Waitere) and Colin Tihi (third-generation grandson of Aporo Wharekaniwha).

9  Hoete has since returned to Aotearoa and works in the architecture programme at the University of Auckland.

10  Crum et al., p. 12.

11  'Hinemihi Survives Fire, But Taonga Destroyed', Radio New Zealand, 1 May 2015, www.rnz.co.nz/news/national/272521/hinemihi-survives-fire,-but-taonga-destroyed

### Māori art as a cultural property

1  Deidre Brown and George Nicholas, 'Protecting Indigenous Cultural Property in the Age of Digital Democracy: Institutional and communal responses to Canadian First Nations and Māori heritage concerns', *Journal of Material Culture*, vol. 17, no. 3, 2012, pp. 307–24.

2  For published engagement in this debate see: Elizabeth Eastmond, 'Ngahuia Te Awekotuku in Conversation with Elizabeth Eastmond and Priscilla Pitts', *Antic*, no. 1, 1986, pp. 44–55; Rangihīroa Panoho, 'Māori: At the Centre, on the Margins', in Mary Barr (ed), *Headlands: Thinking through New Zealand Art*, Museum of Contemporary Art, Sydney, 1992, pp. 122–34; and – written partly in reaction to the views expressed in these papers – Francis Pound, *Space Between: Pakeha Use of Maori Motifs in Modernist New Zealand Art*, Workshop Press, Auckland, 1994.

3  Patrick O'Keefe, 'First International Conference on the Cultural and Intellectual Property Rights of Indigenous Peoples', *International Journal of Cultural Property*, vol. 4, no. 2, 1995, pp. 388–96; Hirini Moko Mead, *Maori Art on the World Scene*, Ahua Design and Matau Associates, Wellington, 1997, pp. 213–19.

4  Waitangi Tribunal, *Ko Aotearoa Tenei: A Report into Claims Concerning New Zealand Law and Policy Affecting Māori Culture and Identity* (Wai 262), Legislation Direct, 2011.

5  This excerpt is a translation by Hugh Kawharu of the te reo version of Te Tiriti o Waitangi, which reads: 'te tino rangatiratanga o o ratou wenua o ratou kainga me o ratou taonga katoa.' www.waitangi-tribunal.govt.nz/treaty/english.asp; Waitangi Tribunal 'Kawharu Translation', https://waitangitribunal.govt.nz/treaty-of-waitangi/translation-of-te-reo-maori-text

6  *Ko Aotearoa Tenei*, p. 96.

7  Ibid., p. 44.

8  Ibid., pp. 74–76.

9  Ibid., pp. 93–96.

10  Deidre Brown is a member of the Māori Trademarks Advisory Committee. The comments in this paper do not necessarily reflect the views of the committee or the Intellectual Property Office of New Zealand.

11  'Toi Iho Artists', www.toiiho.co.nz/toi-iho-artists/

### 19  Haumi ē! Hui ē! Tāiki ē! Māori and Indigenous art on the global stage

1  Ngahiraka Mason, 'The State of Māori Art in an International Context', in *Sakahàn: International Indigenous Art*, National Gallery of Canada, Ottawa, 2013, p. 91.

2  Heather Igloliorte, Julie Nagam and Carla Taunton, 'Introduction: Transmissions. The Future Possibilities of Indigenous Digital and New Media Art', in *Public*, vol. 27, no. 54, Winter 2016, p. 5.

3  Gayatri Chakravorty Spivak, *In Other Worlds: Essays in Cultural Politics*, Methuen, New York, 1987, p. 205.

4  David Garneau, 'Indigenous Art: From Appreciation to Art Criticism', in *Sovereign Words: Indigenous Art, Curation and Criticism*, Valiz, Amsterdam, 2019, p. 320.

5  Linda Tuhiwai Smith, *Decolonizing Methodologies: Research and Indigenous Peoples*, Otago University Press, Dunedin, 2012, p. 108.

6  Donna Awatere, *Maori Sovereignty*, Broadsheet, Auckland, 1984, p. 34.

7  Tuhiwai Smith, p. 117, fig. 6.1.

8  Jolene Rickard, 'The Emergence of Global Indigenous Art', in *Sakahàn* , p. 54.

9  Chadwick Allen, *Trans-Indigenous: Methodologies for Global Native Literary Studies*, University of Minnesota Press, 2012, p. xiv.

10  'Indigenous_Trans Cultural', *Artlink,* issue 37, no. 2, June 2017, www.artlink.com.au/issues/3720/indigenous5Ftrans-cultural/

11  Ian McLean, 'Into the Transpocene: The Future of Indigenous Art', *Artlink*, issue 37, no. 2, June 2017, p. 29.

12  'Native American Scholarship and the Transnational Turn', *Cultural Studies Review*, vol. 15, no. 2, September 2009, pp. 122–23.

13  Candice Hopkins, 'On Other Pictures: Imperialism, Historical Amnesia and Mimesis', in *Sakahàn*, p. 22.

14  Hulleah J. Tsinhnahjinnie, 'When is a Photograph Worth a Thousand Words?', in Jane Alison (ed.), *Native Nations: Journeys in American Photography*, Barbican Art Gallery and Booth-Clibborn Editions, London, England, 1998, pp. 41–56; see also Henrietta Lidchi and Hulleah J. Tsinhnahjinnie, 'Introduction', in Lidchi and Tsinhnahjinnie (eds), *Visual Currencies: Reflections on Native Photography*, National Museum of Scotland, Edinburgh, 2009, p. xxiii.

15  Hulleah J. Tsinhnahjinnie, 'Dragonfly's Home', in *Visual Currencies: Reflections on Native Photography*, pp. 10, 11.

16  Jonathan Mane-Wheoki, 'Pompidou Centre Paper Version 5', unpublished draft. In his notes for his keynote at the twenty-fifth anniversary of the opening of that exhibition he provided a whakapapa of other related exhibitions right up to *Sakahàn* and the ways in which events (such as the 2008 CIHA conference) and international agreements (UN Declaration on the Rights of Indigenous Peoples) impacted on them.

17  Twenty years later, a group playfully called 'Bob's Mob' came together once again to celebrate twenty years since the founding of the Toioho programme. *Toioho XX: 20 Years of Māori Visual Art* (25–29 May 2016, Te Manawa Museum of Art, Science and History, Palmerston North) brought together over 150 alumni, alongside critics such as Cliff Whiting and Hirini Moko Mead.

18  Hirini Moko Mead, 'Māori Art Restructured, Reorganised, Re-examined and Reclaimed', *He Pukenga Kōrero*, vol. 2, no. 1, Kōanga/Spring 1996, pp. 3–4.

19  Nigel Reading and Gary Wyatt, *Manawa: Pacific Heartbeat: A Celebration of Contemporary Māori & Northwest Coast Art*, Raupo, Auckland, 2005, p. 4. More recently, Māori artists enjoyed their own exhibition there: *Wero: Pacific Challenge* (2014).

20  www.thepoiroom.co.nz

21  www.hetetschoolofmaoriart.com

22  See https://festpachawaii.org// for more information. The festival was postponed until June 2024 because of Covid-19.

23  https://creativenz.govt.nz/. The guidelines for the CNZ council which allocates the funding stipulate that there will be a minimum of four members with knowledge of Māori Arts, te ao Māori (a Māori world view) and tikanga Māori (Māori protocol and culture), appointed in consultation with the minister of Māori development; and two members with knowledge of the arts, and the traditions or cultures, of the Pacific Island peoples of New Zealand, appointed in consultation with the minister of Pacific peoples. CNZ covers flights, land transport, accommodation, meals and a per diem allowance. This funding has been criticised because of inequality with other arts bodies such as the New Zealand Ballet and the New Zealand Symphony Orchestra which, arguably, have more limited audiences, and ones that are typically in a higher socioeconomic sector.

24  An earlier version, *Bottled Ocean 2116*, was exhibited at Pātaka Art + Museum.

25  Nina Tonga graduated with a PhD in art history at Waipapa Taumata Rau University of Auckland in 2022, making her the first Tongan with this degree in New Zealand. Increasing numbers of Māori and Pacific students are enrolling in postgraduate courses and degrees in art history and related fields such as museums and cultural heritage, and Indigenous studies. At the University of Auckland alone in 2021 there were five Māori (Renee Hau, Sara Picard, Mia-Mae Taitimu-Stevens [Māori and Samoan], Taniora Maxwell, Talei Tu'inukuafe [Māori, Samoan and Fijian]).

26  Garnau, 'Indigenous Art', p. 321.

27  www.facebook.com/watch/?v=10155304917217873

28  www.creativenz.govt.nz/news/first-time-new-zealand-art-to-feature-at-international-documenta-exhibition.

29  Elisapeta Heta, 'E Moemoeā Tātou ka Taea: Māori Art and Artist Collectives in Aotearoa 1984–2014', MA thesis, University of Auckland, 2015.

30  www.mataahocollective.com/#/twp2012/

31  Hotere had previously been in Kassel in 1999 with Bill Culbert for the *Toi Toi Toi: Three Generations of Art from New Zealand* exhibition at the Museum Fridericianum. Jacqueline Fraser, Lisa Reihana and Peter Robinson were also there.

32  Many of these now fall under CNZ's Cultural and Artform Exchange Programme.

33  Interview with Elizabeth Ellis, 20 March 2019. Other residencies that were pitched unfortunately fell through, including at Sitka, Alaska, New Caledonia and at the National University of Sāmoa.

34  www.creativenz.govt.nz/news/maori-weaver-selected-for-north-american-artist-residency

35  www.australiacouncil.gov.au/international/first-nations-curators-exchange

36  For insights into this programme, see Megan Tamati-Quennell's 'Indigenous Art Curatorial Practice: Ideas and Observations': https://blog.tepapa.govt.nz/2016/04/07/indigenous-art-curatorial-practice-ideas-and-observations/. This builds on other programmes in those countries, such as the BlakLash projects; see: https://visualarts.net.au/nava-events/2018/blak-curatorial-exchange/)

37  Katya García-Antón (ed.), *Sovereign Words: Indigenous Art, Curation and Criticism*, Valiz, Amsterdam, 2019.

38  Jolene Rickard, 'The Emergence of Global Indigenous Art', in *Sakahàn*.

39  David Garneau, 'Can I Get a Witness? Indigenous Art Criticism', in *Sovereign Words: Indigenous Art, Curation and Criticism* p. 29.

40  Jim Vivieaere, 'When the Tuna Eats Its Tail: The Role of Critical Commentary in Relation to Aboriginal Art', in Lee-Ann Martin (ed.), *Making a Noise. Aboriginal Perspectives on Art, Art History, Critical Writing and Community*, Banff International Curatorial Centre, Banff, 2003, p. 151.

41  It was founded in 1987 by the stalwarts of contemporary Māori art: Sandy Adsett, Manos Nathan, Kura Te Waru Rewiri, Robyn Kahukiwa, Aromea Te Maipi and Ross Hemara.

42  *Te Ātinga: 25 Years of Contemporary Māori Art*, www.teatinga.com/site_files/14637/upload_files/teatinga_book.pdf?dl=1.

### Ngā taonga uku: Māori ceramicists and clay workers

1  'Gordon Tovey, art teacher specialists, and children making art', PAColl-10035-1, 1949–1998, Alexander Turnbull Library, Wellington.

2  Megan Tamati-Quennell (ed.), *Kurawaka*, Dowse Art Museum, Lower Hutt, 1994, p. 8.

3  Mark Hutchins, *Ukurere*, Pātaka Art + Museum, Porirua, 2013, p. 27.

4  Ibid., p. 23.

5  Ibid., p. 19.

6  Colleen Waata Urlich, 'Aho: the line that goes beyond the present to the past', MFA thesis, University of Auckland, 2002.

7  Bridget Reweti, 'A Hole in the Pocket', *Pantograph Punch*, 11 June 2018, www.pantograph-punch.com/post/hole-in-the-pocket

8  Karl Chitham and Kim Paton, 'Whenua Hou, New Māori Ceramics', Objectspace, www.objectspace.org.nz/exhibitions/whenua-hou-new-Māori-ceramics/

### Contemporary Māori clothing

1  Elizabeth Wratislau, 'A Signature Style', in Elizabeth Wratislau (ed.), *Whetu Tirikatene-Sullivan: Travel in Style*, MTG Hawke's Bay, Napier, 2014, pp. 10–11.

2  Tryphena Cracknell, 'He Whetu Marama', in *Whetu Tirikatene-Sullivan*, p. 60.

3  Ibid., p. 55.

4  Polished Pāua clippings archive, https://polishedpaua.tumblr.com/

5  Members of the Pacific Sisters collective included Lisa Reihana, Rosanna Raymond, Ani O'Neill, Suzanne Tamaki, Selina Haami, Niwhai Tupaea, Henzart @ Henry Ah-Foo Taripo, Feeonaa Wall and Jaunnie 'Ilolahia.

### Advice to Māori artists

1  Extract from Jonathan Mane-Wheoki, 'On the Brink', *Toi Māori* newsletter, 1999, n.p.

### Whakamutunga – Conclusion

1  *ATE Journal of Māori Art*, vol. 1, 2019, pp. 46–57.

# KUPUTAKA – GLOSSARY

| | |
|---|---|
| 'ahu 'ula | red-feather cape (Hawai'i) |
| ahi kā | long burning fires, signalling continuous occupation |
| aho | weft or sinistrals in weaving |
| āhua | shape |
| ama | outrigger on a waka |
| amo | upright support of the lower end of a bargeboard on the front of a wharenui |
| ariki | high-born chief, male or female |
| aroha | love, affection |
| ātea | area in front of a structure |
| atua | deity, ancestor with continuing influence |
| aurei | cloak pin |
| aute | paper mulberry, *Broussonetia papyrifera*; cloth made from the bark of this plant |
| autoru | small, round stone used in grinding pigments |
| āwheto | vegetable caterpillar, *Cordyceps robertsii*; used to create pigment for tā moko |
| epa | upright panel with a slanted top, at the inside corner of a wharenui's back or front walls |
| haehae | carved lines or ridges; incised lines on the skin |
| hāhi | church |
| hahunga | bone-scraping ceremony |
| hākari | feast; structure specially built to hold food |
| hākari taonga | feast at which taonga were displayed and exchanged |
| hana | dogskin cloak; to shine or glow |
| hangaroa | shell necklace or anklet |
| hapū | subtribe; pregnancy |
| hara | forbidden action, sin, infringement of tapu |
| hau | breath |
| hau kāinga | home community |
| haumi | early form of carving on the bow of a canoe |
| hei | neck adornment |
| hei kakī | neck adornment |
| hei tiki | neck pendant |
| hei tīpona | neck adornment |
| heke | rafter |
| heke tipi | half-boards that fit into the corners of the porch ceiling |
| heru | ornamental hair comb |
| hīkoi | land march |
| hīnaki | woven net |
| hinu | fat rendered from birds, used with pigments in dyeing |
| hoe | paddle |
| hoe whakairo | painted canoe paddle |
| hoeroa | long, curved weapon of whalebone |
| hui | meeting |
| hukahuka | rolled long tags used on korowai |
| hungahunga | flax fibre, used in mixing pigments |
| huruhuru | feathers |
| i ngā wā o mua | in the old days |
| 'i'iwi | scarlet Hawaiian honeycreeper |
| ihi | power, authority, essential force |
| ihopuni/ihupuni | dogskin cloak with darker fur around three sides |
| iwi | tribe |
| Iwirākau | ancestor credited with enlivening the art of carving in the Waiapu region, East Coast |
| kahu kiwi | kiwi-feather cloak |
| kahu koati | goat-hair cloak |
| kahu paetara | battens in a wharenui |
| kahu raurēkau | ear ornament made from strips of leaves of *Coprosma grandifolia* |
| kahu tetere whete | cloak decorated with moss shoots (*Polytrichum commune*) |
| kahu tōī | prestigious cloak made from leaves of mountain cabbage tree (*Cordyline indivisa*) |
| kahu waero | cloak made with long fur from white kurī |
| kai haukai | tribute |
| kai taonga | presentation of a gift |
| kaihautū | museum director, leader |

| | |
|---|---|
| kaikaranga | female callers welcoming visitors onto a marae |
| kaikōrero | orator |
| kaimoana | seafood |
| kaitaka | fine golden cloak with deep tāniko borders |
| kaitiaki | guardian |
| kaituki | time-caller on a waka, like a coxswain |
| kaiwhakaako | native teachers |
| kākā | bush parrot (*Nestor meridionalis*) |
| kākā pōria | ear ornament based on the bone or stone ring used around the leg of pet birds |
| kākaho | battens laid horizontally on the rafters to hold thatch made from toetoe stems |
| kākahu | dress cloak |
| kākahu kārure | dress cloak with kārure |
| kākahu raranga | plaited cloak |
| kākahu raranga pūputu | cloak made using a closely woven raranga technique |
| kākāpō | large green parrot (*Strigops habroptilus*) |
| kapeu | greenstone ear ornament with a curved end |
| kāraho | deck of waka |
| karakia | prayer |
| karamea | red pigment used in skin painting |
| kāretu | oil used to scent the body |
| kārure | twirled tassels used on cloaks |
| kauae | incised moko design on the chin |
| kaui tiki | fibre cord, used to suspend adornments |
| kaumātua | elder |
| kaupapa | main body of a woven cloak; also matter for discussion |
| kaupapa Māori | methodology promoted by Linda Tuhiwai Smith and others, which centres research by and for Māori using Māori ways of thinking, researching and writing |
| kawa | protocol |
| kawanga | opening (of a building) |
| kawe mate | ceremony to bring forth the spirit of the departed |
| kawei | lines of descent |
| kete | basket |
| kiore | Polynesian rat (*Rattus exulans*) |
| kirituhi | Māori designs inked on non-Māori |
| kōauau | sound instrument played with the lips |
| koha | gift, especially to maintain social relationships |
| kōhanga reo | Māori language nest |
| kōkau | plain, unadorned cloak |
| kōkiri | leatherjacket fish (*Meuschenia scaber*) |
| kōkōwai | red pigment |
| kōmaru | sail |
| kono | simple woven container |
| kōnunu | black flax cape |
| kope | ear adornment made from aute |
| kōpuru | oil used to scent the body |
| korari | canoes made from rushes |
| kōrere | broth feeder used in tā moko |
| kōrero pūrākau | narratives |
| kōrero tipuna | tradition |
| kōrero tuku iho | oral history, ancestral narratives |
| koropepe | spiral-shaped adornment |
| korowai | dress cloak adorned with hukahuka tags |
| koruru | carved face on the front gable of a wharenui |
| kōuma | breastplate |
| kōwhaiwhai | decorative patterns on house rafters |
| kōwhiti | Whanganui checkerboard tukutuku design |
| kuia | female elder |
| kūmara | sweet potato |
| kumete | bowl |
| kurī | Polynesian dog, now extinct (*Canis lupus familiaris*) |
| kuru | simple greenstone drop |
| kuru mahora | straight stone pendant |
| kuru papa | flattened form of the kapeu |
| kuru pounamu | greenstone adornment |
| kuta | sedge plant or rush (*Schoenoplectus lacustris*) |
| kūwaha | doorway, entrance |
| mahau | porch, veranda |
| mahinga kai | garden, cultivation, food-gathering place |
| māhiti | cloak decorated with dog's tails spaced out across the kaupapa |
| maihi | bargeboards descending from the tekoteko |
| mako, mako taniwha | tooth of a mako worn as an earring |
| mana | power, authority |
| mana Māori | Māori prestige |
| mana whenua | rights and responsibilities over land |
| manaaki | support |
| manaia | spiritual guardian, often shown as a beaked figure |
| mangōpare | kōwhaiwhai design that resembles a hammerhead shark |

| | | | |
|---|---|---|---|
| mangōroa | tukutuku design symbolising the Milky Way | ngārahu | pigment used for fine moko work (also ngārehu) |
| manu aute | kite made from aute | ngore | decorative pompoms |
| manu kōrero | speakers | ngū | octopus, squid, cuttlefish; also spiral moko pattern on the upper nose |
| manuhiri | guests, visitors | | |
| Manukura | upper parliamentary house in the Kauhanganui parliament | nguru | sound instrument played with the mouth or nose |
| marae | complex comprising meeting house at the very least | niho tangata | human teeth |
| | | niu | pole |
| marae ātea | courtyard in front of the chief's house | ohu | working bee |
| marakihau | sea monster design in wood carving and adornment | oko | container used for storing and grinding pigment used in tā moko |
| māramatanga | enlightenment | ope | group |
| māreikura | female supernatural being | pā | fortified settlement |
| māripi | cutting tool using sharks' teeth | pā maioro | a village defended by ramparts and stockades |
| maro | short, triangular-shaped kilt or apron | | |
| maro aute | apron | pā tūwatawata | fighting pā |
| maro kōpua | maro lined with dogskin and ornamented with pāua shell | paepae | porch, threshold |
| | | paepaeroa | kaitaka cloak where wefts are worn vertically |
| maroro | flying fish | | |
| mata kupenga | fishnet mesh design | paikea | whale |
| mata whakarewa | skin painting | pākati | notches |
| mataī | black pine (*Prumnopitys taxifolia*) | pākē kārure | waist garments featuring rolled cords |
| mataora | full-face moko | Pākehā | New Zealand European |
| Matariki | lower parliamentary house in the Kauhanganui parliament ; the constellation Pleiades | pākeke | elder (Ngāti Porou) |
| | | pākūhā | presentation of a gift; also known as pākūwhā |
| matau | fishhook | pākūwhā | ceremony carried out when a bride is formally handed over to her husband |
| mātauranga | knowledge, wisdom | | |
| matawhā | having four windows | | |
| mate ruahine | sickness caused by women | paoi | beater for making aute |
| mau taringa | ear adornments | papa | floor |
| maumahara | remembering | Papa, Papatūānuku | the earth mother |
| mauri | life force | papahou | rectangular treasure box |
| mihi | greeting, acknowledgement | pāraerae | footwear |
| mihi whakatau | welcome ceremony | parakawahia | blue earth used in skin painting |
| mokimoki | scented fern used in adornment (*Doodia mollis*) | parāoa | whale; whalebone |
| | | parata | carved face at the front of the waka taua |
| moko | designs inked on Māori skin | pare | lintel; headdress |
| moko kuri | early form of moko | pare kawakawa | headdress made from kawakawa (*Macropiper excelsum*), worn in mourning |
| mokomokai | preserved human head (also called toi moko) | | |
| mokopuna | grandchild/grandchildren | paru | iron rich mud used to colour textiles black |
| mōteatea | lament | | |
| mōtoi | earring made of pounamu or shark tooth | pātaka | raised, decorated food storehouse |
| muka | processed harakeke fibre | pātere | song of derision |
| mūmū | chequerboard tukutuku pattern | pātikitiki | flounder design used in weaving |
| muru | plundering another group's treasures; restitution | pātītī | hatchet, short-handled axe |
| | | patu | cleaver |
| | | patu aruhe | fernroot beater |

| | |
|---|---|
| patupaiarehe | fairy folk |
| pau | long ear ornament |
| pekapeka | adornment shaped like two bats back to back |
| pihepihe | shortened version of a kākahu |
| pīhere | moko design by the mouth |
| pīpīwharauroa | shining cuckoo (*Chrysococcyx lucidus*) |
| pītau | spiral; spiral-shaped prow on a waka |
| pito | afterbirth, navel |
| pōhoi | ear ornament consisting of a bunch of feathers or albatross down |
| pōhutukawa | tree with brilliant red flowers (*Metrosideros excelsa*) |
| pōkinikini | cylindrical dried strips of harakeke, used as decoration on cloaks |
| ponga | tree fern, silver fern (*Cyathea dealbata*) |
| pōngiangia | moko design of spirals on the nostrils |
| pono | truth |
| pora | panel of a whāriki |
| pōrera | fine kiekie mat, usually patterned |
| poro | toggle, as in adornment |
| poro-toroa | toggle made of albatross bone |
| pōtae tauā | hat worn in mourning |
| pou tahu | large post at the front internal wall of a meeting house |
| pou whakarae | large carved posts on the palisades of pā |
| pouaka whakairo | carved treasure box |
| pouākai | Haast's eagle (*Aquila moorei*) |
| pounamu | greenstone, nephrite |
| poupou | carved wall panels |
| poutokomanawa | central post in a meeting house |
| pou tuarongo | large post at the back internal wall of a meeting house |
| pōwhiri | welcome ceremony |
| puahi | cloak made from the skins from white kurī, cut into strips then attached to the kaupapa |
| puhi ki te kakara | placement of scented plumes on the body for adornment |
| pūhoro | elongated spiral pattern, representing speed and prowess |
| pukepoto | blue pigment used in skin painting |
| pūmanawa | leadership qualities |
| punga | anchor stone |
| pūrākau | oral histories |
| purapura whetū | multi-star tukutuku pattern |
| pūtātara | conch-shell trumpet |
| pūtōrino | large sound instrument |
| rā | sail |
| rākai | adorn, adornment |
| rākau hei tui | sharpened stick with a loop at the end for stitching tukutuku |
| rākau whakapapa | genealogical staff |
| rangatahi | youth |
| rangatira | chiefly person |
| rangatiratanga | chieftainship, right to exercise authority, autonomy |
| Rangitamaku | the eleventh heaven in Māori cosmology |
| raparapa | end of the maihi |
| raperape | buttock moko |
| raranga | plaiting |
| raranga pūputu | close plaiting technique |
| rauawa | side boards on a waka |
| raurākau | shrub with large leaves, also kanono (*Coprosma autumnalis, C. grandifolia*) |
| rāwhara, rā | sail on a waka |
| rei ika | stone pectoral adornment |
| rei niho | whale-tooth ornament |
| Rekohu | Chatham Islands |
| ritorito | fleur-de-lis-style design |
| riu | body |
| roimata | Te Arawa checkerboard tukutuku design |
| rongopai | settlement of disputes; also gospel |
| rōpū | performing group |
| roro | porch of a meeting house |
| tahua | heap, especially of food at a feast |
| tahuaroa | gifting ceremony |
| tāhuhu | ridgepole |
| taioma | white clay used in skin painting |
| takapapa | a mat on which to serve food |
| takapau | finely woven mat used for ceremonies |
| takapau wharenui | large woven mat, used in the tahuaroa ceremony |
| takarangi | pattern of double spirals |
| takatāpui | LGBTQIA+ person |
| takawaenga | arranged marriage |
| takere | hull of a waka |
| takitahi | one-over, one-under plaited design |
| Tānemahuta | deity of the forest |
| tangata whenua | people of the land |
| tangihaehae | laceration of the skin in mourning |
| tangihanga | funeral or death ceremony, lasting at least three days |
| tāniko | woven border of dress cloak |
| taonga | treasure, precious thing |

| | | | |
|---|---|---|---|
| taonga mokemoke | 'lonely treasures', those held in museums overseas | tikanga a iwi | tradition of a specific tribe |
| taonga pūoro | sound instruments | tino rangatiratanga | sovereignty |
| taonga tuku iho | treasures handed down from the ancestors | tīwhana | moko design on the forehead |
| | | toatoa | oil used to scent the body |
| taonga tūturu | taonga described by legislation (Protected Objects Act 1975) as relating to Māori culture, history, or society manufactured or modified in New Zealand by Māori, brought into New Zealand by Māori or used by Māori; and more than fifty years old | toetoe | native plant with long, grassy leaves with a fine, sharp edge and white plumes (*Austroderia* spp.) |
| | | tohunga | specialist, expert |
| | | tohunga ahurewa | religious expert |
| | | tohunga raranga | expert weaver |
| | | tohunga tā moko | moko expert |
| taowaru | notched surface pattern or a raised central line of carving, wiggly decorative surface design | tohunga tārai waka | expert canoe builder |
| | | tohunga whakairo | expert carver |
| tāpahu | dogskin war cloak | tōī | mountain cabbage tree (*Cordyline indivisa*) |
| tapu | sacredness | | |
| taramea | scented oils | toi moko | preserved heads of Māori |
| tareha | pigment used in skin painting | toki | axe |
| taro | root vegetable (*Colocasia esculenta*) | toki poutangata | ceremonial adze; a symbol of chieftainship |
| tataitanga āhua toi | stylistic lineage (term used by Robert Jahnke) | | |
| | | toko | mast on a waka |
| tatau pounamu | literally, greenstone door, metaphor for peace-making, especially through arranged marriage | tokotoko | orator's staff |
| | | tomo | betrothal ceremony |
| | | tōpuni | cloak decorated with stripes of white and black dog fur |
| tātua | belt; war belt (woven band of harakeke worn as armour) | | |
| | | toroa | southern royal albatross (*Dopmedea epomophora*) |
| tātua kōtara | plaited war belt | | |
| tātua pūpara | belt to hold valuables | tū | belt to which the maro was attached |
| tātua whara | plaited war belt | tū kāretu | belt made from kāretu (scented grass, *Hierochloe redolens*) |
| taua | war party, fighting force | | |
| tauihu | style of canoe prow | tū ure | tū worn to keep the ure erect |
| taumanu | thwarts of a canoe | tuakana | elder sibling or relative |
| taumata | speakers, especially during pōwhiri; panel of experts | tuere | style of canoe prow |
| | | tuhi kōhuru | diagonal lines of red in skin painting |
| taupō | reddish-brown clay used in skin painting | tuhi kōkihi | skin painting with red juice of berries of a plant found in damp places |
| tautarika | shark tooth earring; also aka tau, tautau | | |
| | | tuhi kōnekeneke | pattern of dots used in skin painting |
| tautoko | support | tuhi mareikura | horizontal lines of blue pigment in skin painting, also tuhi maraekura |
| te ao hurihuri | the turning world, i.e. the modern world | | |
| Te Ao Tūroa | the realm of earth and sky | tuhiwai | ritual of striking water |
| Te Rarohenga | the afterworld | Tūkākī | Te Whānau ā Apanui school of carving, named after an ancestor of the same name |
| te reo | Māori language | | |
| te tuhi mareikura | anointing the skin in adornment | | |
| te whare pora | metaphorical term for a space of learning about weaving | tuku iho | tradition |
| | | tukutuku | stitched wall panel in a wharenui |
| tekoteko | central figure on the top of the apex of the meeting house | tūmatakahuki | vertical rod used on tukutuku |
| | | tūpāpaku | deceased person |
| tī kōuka | cabbage tree (*Cordyline australis*) | tūporo haumi | method of joining stern and prow pieces of a canoe |
| tīenga | fine kiekie mat, usually patterned | | |
| tika | just, fair, right, correct | tūrangawaewae | literally, place to stand |
| tikanga | tradition, customs; protocols | | |

| | |
|---|---|
| tūrehu | spirit |
| turuki | ear adornment made from aute |
| turuturu | weaving peg |
| tūtaewhetū | blue clay used in skin painting |
| tuwhara | coarse mat used under a fine mat |
| uhi | chisel |
| unaunahi | fleur-de-lis-style design |
| ure | penis |
| urupā | burial ground, burial site |
| utu | revenge, reciprocity |
| waewaekoukou | climbing clubmoss, *Lycopodium yolubile*, used in headdresses worn in mourning |
| Waiapu | river and river catchment area on the East Coast |
| waiata | song |
| waiata ā-ringa | action song |
| wairuatanga | Māori spirituality |
| waka | canoe |
| waka hourua | double-hulled sailing canoe |
| waka huia | carved treasure container |
| waka kōpapa | Tainui style canoe used in racing |
| waka pahī | large, oceangoing waka |
| waka pūhara | canoe made of rushes (*Hierochloe redolens*) |
| waka taua | war canoe |
| waka tētē | seagoing canoe |
| waka tīwai | everyday canoes used on lakes and rivers |
| waka tūpāpaku | container used for the bones of ancestors |
| wana | inspire fear, awe; sublimity |
| wānanga | place of learning |
| wehi | fearsomeness |
| whaikōrero | oratory |
| whakaaro | thought, opinion |
| whakahihi | arrogance |
| whakairo | carving, decoration |
| whakairo rākau | wood carving |
| whakangau | final dressing of the wood by a carver |
| whakanoa | ritual cleansing, tapu removal |
| whakapakoko | statue, carved figure |
| whakapapa | lineage; genealogy |
| whakataukī | sayings, proverbs |
| whakateitei | personal treasures used as adornments |
| whakatūwhera | opening, e.g. of an exhibition |
| whakawae | window and door frames |
| whakawhiti | type of sail |
| whānau | family |
| whanaunga | relations |
| whanaungatanga | relationship, kinship |
| whao | chisel |
| wharau | shelter house, canoe shed |
| wharawhara | ancient expert in the art of decoration, i.e. a stylist |
| whare karakia | church or chapel |
| whare kāuta | cooking shed |
| whare ora | health centre |
| whare pākūwhā | house built for the pākūwhā ceremony |
| whare wānanga | school of learning |
| whare whakairo | decorated communal meeting house |
| whare whakamoemiti | house of praise in the Rātana church |
| whare rangatira | chief's house |
| wharekai | dining hall |
| wharenui | large house |
| wharepuni | sleeping houses, dormitories |
| whāriki | woven or plaited mat |
| whatārangi | platform |
| whatu | weaving |
| whatu aho pātahi | single-pair twining (weaving method) |
| whatu aho rua | double-pair twining (weaving method) |
| whatu porotaka | spool-shaped adornment |
| whenu | warp or dextrals in weaving |
| whenua | land; afterbirth |
| whetū mārama | star and moon symbol, used in the Rātana religion |
| whiri | braid |
| wīwī | native grass/rush; the name for several species of native plant which grow in stiff, rush-like clumps |

# RĀRANGI PUKAPUKA — SELECT BIBLIOGRAPHY

**Archives and manuscripts**

'Apirana Ngata Papers', MS 1588, Manuscripts & Archives, Alexander Turnbull Library, Wellington.

Baker, Charles Pratt, 'Journal of a Journey to the East Coast 1861–2', qMS-0113, Alexander Turnbull Library, Wellington.

Best, Elsdon, 'Notebooks 1895–96', MS-Papers-1187-113A, Alexander Turnbull Library, Wellington.

——, 'Notebooks, MS-Papers-1187-029', MS-Papers-1187-287, Alexander Turnbull Library, Wellington.

Brown, Deidre and Rebecca Conway, 'Notes from an inspection of ETI.570 ("Hongi Hika" attributed wooden bust) by Dr Andrew Merchant, Faculty of Agriculture and Environment, University of Sydney, at Macleay Museum, Sydney, 9 December 2015', unpublished document.

Brown, Deidre, 'Outgoing CMS taonga inventory based on Marsden Online Archive missionary correspondence 1814–1820', unpublished document, 2015.

Collection catalogue, Museum of Archaeology and Anthropology, Cambridge.

Cotton, William C., 'Journal. 1842–43', SAFE/DLMS 35, State Library of New South Wales.

Davis, A. J., 'Parihaka Paa – Housing Survey', 'Parihaka Paa 1950–59', 10 July 1956, acc. no. W2490, no. 34/3/98, box 15a, Maori Affairs Papers, Archives New Zealand, Wellington.

'Eric Ramsden – Apirana Ngata Articles', MS-Papers-196-380, Alexander Turnbull Library, Wellington.

'Eric Ramsden – Notes', 6 September 1946, folder 13, 'Michael King – Material', acc. 85-080-05, Alexander Turnbull Library, Wellington.

'Eric Ramsden – Papers', MS-Papers-196-394, Alexander Turnbull Library, Wellington.

'Eric Ramsden–Apirana Ngata Correspondence', MS-Papers-196-376, Alexander Turnbull Library, Wellington.

Ethnology Cards, AM 45506, 5652-7, 5659, Auckland Museum Ethnology Library, Auckland.

Friars, Austin, 'Catalogue of the Missionary Museum', 1826, 4766.e.19.[2], British Library.

Hammond, T. G., 'Te Whiti and Parihaka', 1881, MS-Papers-4456-01, Alexander Turnbull Library, Wellington.

——, 'Passing of Tohu', c.1907, MS-Papers-4456-06, Alexander Turnbull Library, Wellington.

Ihimaera, Ihimaera, unpublished manuscript, private collection.

'Items kept in CMS Museum', CMS/H/H30 E7/3, pp. 111–13, Cadbury Research Library, Birmingham.

Lythberg, Billie, 'Oceanic Collections in Italy', manuscript, author's files.

Ngata, Apirana, 'Draft Statement of the Aims and Objectives of the Young Maori Party', Maori Purposes Fund Board Papers, MS-Papers-189, folder 11, Manuscripts & Archives, Alexander Turnbull Library, Wellington.

——, entry, Lindauer Art Gallery Visitors' Book, Auckland Art Gallery, 26 June 1901.

Object file, cat. no. 812, Auckland Museum Ethnology Library, Auckland.

Otaki Maori Land Court Minutebook, 2–12 March 1874, pp. 261–71, Kete Horowhenua.

'Pakira, Waitahanui marae', file ref. 8/17/4/24, rec. no. 0038, Marae Buildings Record Form, Heritage New Zealand Pouhere Taonga, Wellington.

'Papawai Pa, Wairarapa 1934–35', no. 124, series 51, box 12, Maori Affairs Papers, Archives New Zealand, Wellington.

Phillipps, W. J., 'Papers – Maori Carving', 1940–1963, series 2, box 5, 164/79, Manuscript Archive, Canterbury Museum, Christchurch.

Poutapu, Piri, 'Maoritanga English Transcription Tape', roll 165, folder 13, 'Michael King – Material', acc. 85-080-05, Alexander Turnbull Library, Wellington.

Pratt, Josiah to Thomas Kendall, 12 and 16 August 1815, Marsden Online Archive.

Rakei, Ropoama to Governor Grey, GNZNA 265, Central City Library, Auckland.

Rātana Church, 'Etahi Mai o Nga Whakaputanga', Etahi o Nga Akoranga series, typescript.

'Raukawa Carved Meeting House, Otaki, 1931–37', series 51, no. 132/1, box 13, Maori Affairs Papers, Archives New Zealand, Wellington.

Robley, H. G., letter to the director, unarchived correspondence, Museum of Archaeology and Anthropology, University of Cambridge.

'Rotorua Maori Arts and Crafts Institute – Agendas and Minutes of Meetings, 1974–77', Archives New Zealand, Wellington.

'Ruaihona – 6th March 1993', Ruaihona Marae Committee, Te Teko, 1993.

'Ruataupare, Kokohinau marae', file ref. 8/17/4/17, rec. no. 72, 73 004, Marae Buildings Record Form, Heritage New Zealand Pouhere Taonga, Wellington.

Sadler, Belle, to the British Museum, 8 July 1896, British Museum Archives.

Sadler, Frederick, Memorandum, 14 July 1836, 209/2, p. 371, National Archives, Kew, London.

Simmons, David, 'Field notebooks and Index written by David Simmons, on his research trip to America and Canada 1973', MUS-2014-3, Auckland Museum Library.

——, 'Field notebooks listing Maori Taonga in British and European Museums', MUS-2014-4, Auckland Museum Library.

——, 'Original and photocopied works relating to David Simmons visits to Overseas Museums', MUS-2018-4, Auckland Museum Library.

Smart, Maxwell, 'Maxwell Smart Speeches', typescript, MS-Papers-1008, folder 4, Alexander Turnbull Library, Wellington.

Taiapa, Pine, 'The significance and stories of the tukutuku patterns – Ngati-Porou version', unpublished MS, undated, Ngarino Ellis collection.

Te Rangikaheke, Wiremu Marsh, 'Sir George Grey, Maori MS 89', digitised at New Zealand Electronic Text Collection.

'Turongo House, Turangawaewae Marae', rec. no. 0202, Marae Buildings Record Form, Heritage New Zealand Pouhere Taonga, Wellington.

'Waima Carved Meeting House 1932–4' Series 51, no. 146, box 15, Maori Affairs Papers, Archives New Zealand, Wellington.

'Waitangi Carved Memorial Meeting House (2), Description of the Carvings and Tukutuku Panels', MSS 771, Auckland Museum Library.

Walker-Taiapa, R. Peter, 'Biographical material relating to Pineamine Taiapa', MS-Papers-9104, Alexander Turnbull Library, Wellington.

Webster, William to Augustus Pitt-Rivers, 22 April 1896, B456, Salisbury and South Wiltshire Museum and Pitt-Rivers Manuscript Collection.

Yate, William, Journal and diary 1833–1845, MS-2544, Alexander Turnbull Library, Wellington.

### Books and book chapters

Adams, Patricia, 'Marae Complexes', in Frances Porter (ed.), *Historic Buildings of New Zealand – North Island*, Historic Places Trust & Cassell New Zealand, Wellington, 1983.

Adsett, Sandy, Witi Ihimaera and Cliff Whiting, *Mataora: The Living Face*, David Bateman, Auckland, 1996.

Alpers, O. T. J. and R. F. Irvine, *The Progress of New Zealand in the Century*, W. & R. Chambers, London, 1902.

Allen, Chadwick, *Trans-Indigenous: Methodologies for Global Native Literary Studies*, University of Minnesota Press, Minneapolis, MN, 2012.

Allingham, E. G., *Romance of the Rostrum*, H. F. & G. Witherby, London, 1924.

Altick, Richard, *The Shows of London*, Belknap Press, Cambridge, MA, 1978.

Amoamo, Jacqueline, 'Ramai Hayward: Photographer, Artist, Actress, Filmmaker: A Creative Life', in Sandra Coney (ed.), *Standing in the Sunshine: A History of New Zealand Women Since They Won the Vote*, Penguin, Auckland, 1993.

Andersen, Johannes, *Myths and Legends of the Pacific*, Farrar & Rinehart, New York, 1928.

Anderson, Atholl, Judith Binney and Aroha Harris (eds), *Tangata Whenua: An Illustrated History*, Bridget Williams Books, Wellington, 2014.

Anderson, Atholl, 'The Art of Concealment: Some Thoughts on South Island Maori Rock Drawings', in *Ka Tuhituhi o Nehera: The Drawings of Ancient Times*, National Museum of New Zealand, Wellington, 1988.

——, *The Welcome of Strangers: An Ethnohistory of Southern Maori A.D. 1650–1850*, Otago University Press, Dunedin, 1998.

——, 'Ancient Origins, 3000 BC–AD 1300', in Atholl Anderson, Judith Binney and Aroha Harris (eds), *Tangata Whenua: An Illustrated History*, Bridget Williams Books, Wellington, 2014.

——, 'Pieces of the Past: AD 1200 to 1800', in Atholl Anderson, Judith Binney and Aroha Harris (eds), *Tangata Whenua: An illustrated History*, Bridget Williams Books, Wellington, 2014.

——, 'Wairau Bar: Ancestors and Archaeology', in Atholl Anderson, Judith Binney and Aroha Harris (eds), *Tangata Whenua: An Illustrated History*, Bridget Williams Books, Wellington, 2014.

Angas, George French, *The New Zealanders Illustrated*, Thomas McLean, London, 1847.

Auerbach, Jeffrey and Peter Hoffenberg (eds), *Britain, the Empire, and the World at the Great Exhibition of 1851*, Ashgate Publishing Company, Farnham, 2008.

Austin, Dougal, *Te Hei Tiki: An Enduring Treasure in a Cultural Continuum*, Te Papa Press, Wellington, 2019.

Awatere, Donna, *Maori Sovereignty*, Broadsheet, Auckland, 1984.

Bagnall, A. G., *Old Greytown – The Story of the First Hundred Years of Greytown's Settlement 1854–1954*, Greytown Borough Council, Greytown, 1953.

Barr, Mary, *Content/Context: A Survey of Recent New Zealand Art*, National Art Gallery, Wellington, 1986.

—— (ed.), *Headlands: Thinking through New Zealand Art*, Museum of Contemporary Art, Sydney, 1992.

Barrow, Terrence, *A Guide to the Maori Meeting House 'Te Hau ki Turanga'*, National Museum, Wellington, 1976.

Barton, Gerry and David Reynolds, *Hotunui: The Restoration of a Meeting House*, Auckland Institute and Museum, Auckland, 1985.

Beaglehole, J. C. (ed.), *The Journals of Captain James Cook*, Hakluyt Society, London, 1955.

Beaglehole, J. C. (ed.), *The Endeavour Journals of Joseph Banks 1768–1771*, vol. 1, Angus and Robertson, Sydney, 1962.

Beattie, James Herries (ed.), *Tikao Talks*, Cadsonbury Publications, Christchurch, 2013.

Beattie, James Herries and Atholl Anderson (eds), *Traditional Lifeways of the Southern Maori*, Otago University Press, Dunedin, 1994.

Belich, James, *I Shall Not Die: Titokowaru's War, New Zealand 1868–1869*, Bridget Williams Books, Wellington, 1993.

——, *Making Peoples: A History of the New Zealanders from Polynesian Settlement to the End of the Nineteenth Century*, Penguin, Auckland, 1996.

Benfell, Neil, *Mission and Moko: Aspects of the Work of the Church Missionary Society in New Zealand, 1814–1882*, Latimer Fellowship, Christchurch, 1992.

Best, Elsdon, *The Maori: Volume 1*, Polynesian Society, Wellington, 1923.

——, *Tūhoe, The Children of the Mist: A sketch of the origin, history, myths, and beliefs of the Tūhoe tribe of the Māori of New Zealand; with some account of other early tribes of the Bay of Plenty district*, Board of Maori Ethnological Research for the author, 1925.

——, *The Maori Canoe*, Board of Māori Ethnological Research for the Dominion Museum (Dominion Museum Bulletin no. 7), Wellington, 1925.

——, *The Maori as He Was: A Brief Account of Life as It Was in the Pre-European Days*, Dominion Museum, Wellington, 1934.

——, *Maori Storehouses and Kindred Structures*, A. R. Shearer, Wellington, 1974.

——, *The Stone Implements of the Maori*, A. R. Shearer, Wellington, 1974.

——, *Maori Religion and Mythology, Part 2*, Government Printer, Wellington, 1982.

Binney, Judith, 'Ancestral Voices: Maori Prophet Leaders', in Keith Sinclair (ed.), *Oxford Illustrated History of New Zealand*, Oxford University Press, Auckland, 1990.

——, 'Amalgamation and Separation', in Judith Binney, Judith Bassett and Erik Olssen (eds), *The People and the Land / Te Tangata me te Whenua: An Illustrated History of New Zealand, 1820–1920*, Allen & Unwin, Wellington, 1993.

——, 'Kawanatanga and Rangatiratanga', in Judith Binney, Judith Bassett and Erik Olssen (eds), *The People and the Land / Te Tangata me te Whenua: An Illustrated History of New Zealand, 1820–1920*, Allen & Unwin, Wellington, 1993.

——, 'The Native Land Court and Maori Communities', in Judith Binney, Judith Bassett and Erik Olssen (eds), *The People and the Land / Te Tangata me te Whenua: An Illustrated History of New Zealand, 1820–1920*, Allen & Unwin, Wellington, 1993.

——, *Redemption Songs: A Life of Te Kooti Arikirangi Te Turuki*, Auckland University Press, Auckland, 1995.

——, *The Legacy of Guilt: A Life of Thomas Kendall*, Bridget Williams Books, Wellington, 2005 (reprint).

——, *Encircled Lands: Te Urewera, 1820–1921*, Bridget Williams Books, Wellington, 2009.

Binney, Judith, Vincent O'Malley and Alan Ward, 'The Coming of the Pakeha, 1820–40', in Atholl Anderson, Judith Binney and Aroha Harris (eds), *Tangata Whenua: An Illustrated History*, Bridget Williams Books, Wellington, 2014.

——, 'Rangatiratanga and Kawanatanga, 1840–1860', in Atholl Anderson, Judith Binney and Aroha Harris (eds), *Tangata Whenua: An Illustrated History*, Bridget Williams Books, Wellington, 2014.

Blank, Arapera, 'The Role and Status of Māori Women', in Arapera Blank, *For Someone I Love*, Anton Blank, Auckland, 2015.

Brougham, A. E and A. W. Reed, *Maori Proverbs*, A. H. & A. W. Reed, Auckland, 1975.

Brown, Deidre, *Tai Tokerau Whakairo Rākau: Northland Māori Wood Carving*, Reed, Auckland, 2003.

——, *Māori Architecture: From Fale to Wharenui and Beyond*, Raupo, Auckland, 2009.

——, 'Kings, Rangatira and Relationships: The Enduring Meanings of "Treasure" Exchanges between Māori and Europeans in 1830s Whangaroa', in Lucie Carreau, Alison Clark, Alana Jelinek, Erna Lilje and Nicholas Thomas (eds), *Pacific Presences, vol. 2: Oceanic Art and European Museums*, Sidestone Press, Leiden, 2018.

Brunt, Peter and Thomas, Nicholas, *Art in Oceania: A New History*, Thames and Hudson, London, 2012.

Buschmann, Rainer F., 'Oceania Collection in German Museums: Collections, Contexts, and Exhibits', in Lucie Carreau, Alison Clark, Alana Jelinek, Erna Lilje and Nicholas Thomas (eds), *Pacific Presences, vol. 1: Oceanic Art and European Museums*, Sidestone Press, Leiden, 2018.

Buxton, Thomas Fowell, *Report of the Parliamentary Select Committee on Aboriginal Tribes (British Settlements)*, William Ball, London, 1837.

Catholic Church, *Ko te Ako me te Karakia o te Hahi Katorika Romana*, He mea ta i te Perehi o te Epikopo Katorika, Kororāreka, 1847.

Cherry, Stella, *Te Ao Maori: The Maori World*, National Museum of Ireland, Dublin, 1990.

Church Missionary Society, *Missionary Register*, Seeley, London, 1816.

Clark, Paul, *Hauhau: The Pai Marire Search for Maori Identity*, Auckland University Press & Oxford University Press, Auckland, 1975.

Considine, John, *The Vatican Mission Exposition: A Window on the World*, Macmillan, New York, 1925.

Cowan, James, *The Adventures of Kimble Bent*, Capper Press, Christchurch, 1911.

——, *The Maori, Yesterday and To-day*, Whitcombe & Tombs, Christchurch, 1930.

——, *The New Zealand Wars: A History of the Maori Campaigns and the Pioneering Period, vol. 1, 1845–1864*, R. E. Owen, Wellington, 1955.

——, *The New Zealand Wars and the Pioneering Period, vol. 2*, R. E. Owen, Wellington, 1956.

Cox, Lindsay, *Kotahitanga: The Search for Maori Political Unity*, Oxford University Press, Oxford, 1993.

Cracknell, Tryphena, 'He Whetu Marama', in Elizabeth Wratislau (ed.), *Whetu Tirikatene-Sullivan: Travel in Style*, MTG Hawke's Bay, Napier, 2014.

Cresswell, John, *Maori Meeting Houses of the North Island*, PCS Publications, Auckland, 1977.

Crosby, Ron, *The Musket Wars: A History of Inter-Iwi Conflict 1806–1845*, Libro International, Auckland, 2012.

Cylcopedia Company, *The Cyclopedia of New Zealand (Taranaki, Hawke's Bay & Wellington Provincial Districts)*, Cyclopedia Company, Christchurch, 1908.

Davidson, Janet, *The Prehistory of New Zealand*, Longman Paul, Auckland, 1984.

Davis, Te Aue, Tipene O'Regan and John Wilson, *Nga Tohu Pumahara: The Survey Pegs of the Past: Understanding Maori Place Names*, New Zealand Geographic Board, Wellington, 1990.

Day, Kelvin, *Maori Woodcarving of the Taranaki Region*, Reed, Auckland, 2001.

Deloria, Vine Jr., 'Anthropologists Among Other Friends', in Vine Deloria Jr., *Custer Died for Your Sins: An Indian Manifesto*, University of Oklahoma Press, Norman, OK, 1969.

Diamond, Paul, *Makereti: Taking Māori to the World*, Random House, Auckland, 2007.

Dodge, Ernest S., *The New Zealand Maori Collection in the Peabody Museum of Salem*, Peabody Museum, Salem, MA, 1941.

Druett, Joan, *Tupaia: The Remarkable Story of Captain Cook's Polynesian Navigator*, Praeger, Westport, CA, 2011.

Duff, Roger, *The Moa Hunter Period of Maori Culture*, Whitcombe & Tombs, Wellington, 1950.

Ellis, Ngarino, 'He Iti, He Pounamu: Lindauer and Personal Adornment', in Ngahiraka Mason (ed.), *Gottfried Lindauer's New Zealand: The Māori Portraits*, Auckland University Press, 2016.

——, 'Looting and Theft in Colonial-Era Aotearoa/New Zealand,' in Arthur Tompkins (ed.), *Art Crime and Its Prevention: A Handbook for Collectors and Art Professionals*, Lund Humphries, London, 2016.

——, *A Whakapapa of Tradition: 100 Years of Ngati Porou Carving 1830–1930*, Auckland University Press, Auckland, 2016.

Ellis, Robert, *Official Descriptive and Illustrated Catalogue*, vol. 2, Spicer Brothers, London, 1861.

Elsmore, Bronwyn, *Mana From Heaven – A Century of Maori Prophets in New Zealand*, Moana Press, Tauranga, 1989.

Evans, Jeff, *Heke-Nuku-Mai-Nga-Iwi Busby: Not Here by Chance*, Huia, Wellington, 2015.

Evans, Miriama and Ranui Ngarimu, *The Art of Māori Weaving*, Huia, Wellington, 2005.

Evison, Harry, *Te Wai Pounamu: The Greenstone Island, A History of the Southern Maori During the European Colonization of New Zealand*, Aoraki Press, Christchurch, 1993.

Finney, Ben, 'Renaissance', in K. R. Howe (ed.), *Mana Waka: Voyages of the Ancestors*, David Bateman and Auckland War Memorial Museum, Auckland, 2006.

Firth, Raymond, *Economics of the New Zealand Maori*, A. R. Shearer, Wellington, 1929.

Fowler, Leo, *Te Mana o Turanga: The Story of the Carved House Te Mana o Turanga on the Whakato Marae at Manutuke Gisborne*, New Zealand Historic Places Trust, Wellington, 1974.

Fristedt, Conrad, *På Forskningsfärd. Minnen från en tvåårig vistelse bland Ceylons tamiler och singhaleser, Australiens kannibaler och Nya Zeelands maorer*, Albert Bonnier, Stockholm, 1891.

Gallop, Alan, *The House with the Golden Eyes: Unlocking the Secrets of Hinemihi, the Maori Meeting House from Te Wairoa and Clandon Park*, Running Horse Books, Middlesex, 1998.

Garbutt, Eva, 'The Care of Living Objects: Conserving Rauru and Te Warepuni a Maui in Germany', in Dean Sully (ed.), *Decolonising Conservation*, Left Cross Press, Walnut Creek, CA, 2007.

Garneau, David, 'Can I Get a Witness? Indigenous Art Criticism', in *Sovereign Words: Indigenous Art, Curation and Criticism*, Valiz, Amsterdam, 2018.

——, 'Indigenous Art: From Appreciation to Art Criticism', in *Sovereign Words: Indigenous Art, Curation and Criticism*, Valiz, Amsterdam, 2018.

Gathercole, Peter, 'Obstacles to the Study of Maori Carving: The Collector, the Connoisseur, and the Faker', in C. Greenhaig and J. Megaw (eds), *Art in Society: Studies in Style, Culture and Aesthetics*, Duckworth, London, 1978.

Gover, Elena, 'Oceania in Russian History: Expeditions, Collections, Museums', in Lucie Carreau, Alison Clark, Alana Jelinek, Erna Lilje and Nicholas Thomas (eds), *Pacific Presences, vol. 1: Oceanic Art and European Museums*, Sidestone Press, Leiden, 2018.

——, 'From Russia with Love: Nikolai Miklouho-Maclay's Pacific Collections', in Lucie Carreau, Alison Clark, Alana Jelinek, Erna Lilje and Nicholas Thomas (eds), *Pacific Presences, vol. 2: Oceanic Art and European Museums*, Sidestone Press, Leiden, 2018.

Grace, John Te Herekiekie, *Tuwharetoa: A History of the Maori People of the Taupo District*, Reed, Wellington, 1959.

Grace, T. S., *A Pioneer Missionary Among the Maoris 1850–1879 – Being Letters and Journals of Thomas Samuel Grace*, G. H. Bennett & Co, Palmerston North, 1928.

Grayland, Eugene, *Famous New Zealanders*, Whitcombe & Tombs, Christchurch, 1967.

Greenfield, Jeanette, *The Return of Cultural Treasures*, Cambridge University Press, Cambridge, 1995.

Greenwood, William, *Upraised Hand: The Spiritual Significance of the Rise of the Ringatu Faith*, Polynesian Society memoir, no. 21, Wellington, 1980.

Grey, George, *Ko nga Moteatea, me nga Hakirara o nga Maori*, Hon. Robert Stokes, Wellington, 1853.

Haddon, Alfred C. and James Hornell, *Canoes of Oceania*, Special Publications, Bernice P. Bishop Museum, Honolulu, 1936.

Haeata Māori Women's Art Collective, *Haeata Herstory 1985*, New Women's Press, Auckland, 1984.

Hakiwai, Arapata and John Terrell, *Ruatepupuke: A Maori Meeting House*, Field Museum, Chicago, 1994.

Halbert, Rongowhakaata, *Horouta: The History of the Horouta Canoe, Gisborne and East Coast*, Oratia Books, Auckland, 2012.

Hamilton, Augustus, *Maori Art: The Art Workmanship of the Maori Race in New Zealand, 1896–1900*, New Zealand Institute, Wellington, 1901.

Hanson, Elizabeth and Apirana Mahuika, 'Putiki and Waiapu Churches', in F. Porter (ed.), *Historic Buildings of New Zealand: North Island*, Historic Places Trust & Cassell, Wellington, 1983.

Harris, Aroha, *Hikoi: Forty Years of Maori Protest*, Huia, Wellington, 2004.

——, 'Pipitea Pa', in Atholl Anderson, Judith Binney and Aroha Harris (eds), *Tangata Whenua: An Illustrated History*, Bridget Williams Books, Wellington, 2014.

Harrison, Pakaariki, *Te Poho o Tipene*, St Stephen's School, Bombay, 1983.

——, *The Carving of Tane-nui-a-Rangi, Auckland University Marae*, University of Auckland, Auckland, 1991.

——, *Nga Kete Wananga*, Manukau Institute of Technology, Auckland, 1999.

Harrison, Pakaariki, Kahu Te Kanawa and Rawinia Higgins, 'Ngā Mahi Toi – The Arts', in Tānia Ka'ai (ed.), *Ki te Whaiao – An Introduction to Māori Culture and Society*, Pearson, Auckland, 2003.

Henare (Salmond), Amiria, *Museums, Anthropology and Imperial Exchange*, Cambridge University Press, New York, 2005.

Hēnare, Mānuka, 'Māori Catholic Beginnings', in *The Visit of His Holiness Pope John Paul II, New Zealand, November 22–24*, Papal Visit Aotearoa, Wellington, 1986.

——, 'The Māori Leaders' Assembly, Kororipo Pā, 1831', in Judith Binney (ed.), *Te Kerikeri 1770–1850: The Meeting Pool*, Bridget Williams Books, Wellington, 2007.

Henderson, Carol, *A Blaze of Colour: Gordon Tovey, Artist, Educator*, Hazard Press, Christchurch, 1998.

Henderson, James McLeod, *Ratana: The Man, the Church, the Political Movement*, Polynesian Society memoir, A. H. & A. W. Reed, Wellington, 1972.

Hīroa, Te Rangi [Peter Buck], *Vikings of the Sunrise*, Frederick A. Stokes, New York, 1938.

——, *The Coming of the Maori*, Maori Purposes Fund Board, Wellington, 1949.

Hohepa, Pat, 'My Musket, My Missionary, And My Mana', in Alex Calder, Jonathan Lamb and Bridget Orr (eds), *Voyages and Beaches: Pacific Encounters, 1769–1840*, University of Hawai'i Press, Honolulu, 1999.

Hooker, Joseph (ed.), *Journal of the Right Hon. Sir Joseph Banks*, Macmillan, New York, 1896.

Hooper, Steven, 'Illustration of an Exhibition and Sale at the Wesleyan Centenary Hall, United Kingdom', in Karen Jacobs, Chantal Knowles and Chris Wingfield (eds), *Trophies, Relics and Curios?: Missionary Heritage from Africa and the Pacific*, Sidestone Press, Leiden, 2013.

Hopkins, Candice, 'On Other Pictures: Imperialism, Historical Amnesia and Mimesis,' in *Sakahàn: International Indigenous Art*, National Gallery of Canada, Ottawa, 2013.

Howe, Kerry, 'The Last Frontier', in Kerry Howe (ed.), *Vaka Moana: Voyages of the Ancestors*, Auckland Museum and David Bateman, Auckland, 2006.

Hutchins, Mark, *Uku Rere*, Pataka Art + Museum, Porirua, 2013.

Jahnke, Robert, 'Maori Art Towards the Millennium', in Malcolm Mulholland (ed.), *State of the Māori Nation: Twenty-first Century Issues in Aotearoa*, Reed, Auckland, 2006.

Jones, Alison and Kuni Jenkins, *He Kōrero: Words Between Us: First Māori–Pākehā Conversations on Paper*, Huia, Wellington, 2011.

——, *Tuai: A Traveller in Two Worlds*, Bridget Williams Books, Wellington, 2017.

Jones, Pei Te Hurinui, *Mahinarangi: A Tainui Saga*, J. C. Ekdahl, Hawera, 1946.

——, *King Potatau: An Account of the Life of Potatau Te Wherowhero, The Frst Maori King*, Polynesian Society, Wellington, 1959.

——, 'Maori Kings', in E. G. Schwimmer (ed.), *Maori People in the Nineteen-Sixties – A Symposium*, Blackwood & Janet Paul, Auckland, 1968.

——, *Turanga-waewae: Souvenir of Golden Jubilee 1921–1971*, Taumarunui, 1971.

Jopson, Fraser W. and Craig R. McKibbin, *Moriori Tree Carvings, Chatham Islands: Close-range Photogrammetric Record and Survey*, Department of Conservation, Wellington, 2010.

Kaa, Tipiwhenua, *Piripi Taumata-a-kura Celebrations: 130 Years 1834–1964*, Waiapu Pastorate, Rangitukia, 1964.

Kaeppler, Adrienne, *Artificial Curiosities: An Exposition of Native Manufactures Collected on the Three Pacific Voyages of Captain James Cook, R.N.*, Bernice P. Bishop Museum Special Publication no. 65, Honolulu, 1978.

Kawharu, Merata, *Maranga Mai! Te Reo and Marae in Crisis?*, Auckland University Press, Auckland, 2014.

Kernot, Bernie, 'Nga Tohunga Whakairo o Mua', in Sidney Moko Mead (ed.), *Te Maori: Maori Art from New Zealand Collections*, Heinemann, Auckland, 1984.

——, 'Maoriland Metaphors and the Model Pa', in John Mansfield Thomson (ed.), *Farewell Colonialism: The New Zealand International Exhibition, Christchurch 1906–07*, Dunmore Press, Palmerston North, 1998.

Keys, Lillian, *Philip Viard: Bishop of Wellington*, Pegasus, Christchurch, 1968.

King, J. C. H., 'Sir Ashton Lever', in Hermione Waterfield and J. C. H. King (eds), *Provenance: Twelve Collectors of Ethnographic Art in England 1760–1990*, Somogy Éditions d'Art and the Barbier-Mueller Museum, Paris and Geneva, 2006.

Knight, John, *The Australasian Colonies at the International Exhibition, London, 1862*, John Ferres, Government Printer, Melbourne, 1865.

Lambert, Thomas, *The Story of Old Wairoa and the East Coast District, North Island, New Zealand*, Collins Somerville Wilkie, Dunedin, 1925.

——, *Pioneering Reminiscences of Old Wairoa*, Thomas Avery and Sons, New Plymouth, 1936.

Lander, Maureen, 'Te Ao Tawhito/Te Ao Hou: Entwined Threads of Tradition and Innovation', in Awhina Tamarapa (ed.), *Whatu Kākahu: Māori Cloaks*, Te Papa Press, Wellington, 2011.

Lander, Maureen and Amiria Salmond, 'Ancestral Threads: Seven Maori Cloaks', in Nicholas Thomas, Julie Adams, Billie Lythberg, Maia Nuku and Amiria Salmond (eds), *Artefacts of Encounter: Cook's Voyages, Colonial Collecting and Museum Histories*, Otago University Press, Dunedin, 2016.

Latta, A. M., *Meeting of the Waters – The Story of Ngaruawahia*, Ngaruawahia Lions Club, Ngāruawāhia, 1980.

Law, Gary, *Archaeology of the Bay of Plenty*, Department of Conservation, Wellington, 2008.

Lawlor, Pat, *New Zealand Artists' Annual*, Wellington, 1929.

Lee, Samuel and Thomas Kendall (eds), *A Grammar and Vocabulary of the Language of New Zealand*, Church Missionary Society, London, 1820.

Lidchi, Henrietta and Hulleah J. Tsinhnahjinnie, 'Introduction', in Henrietta Lidchi and Hulleah J. Tsinhnahjinnie (eds), *Visual Currencies: Reflections on Native Photography*, National Museum of Scotland, Edinburgh, 2009.

Lonie, Bridie and Marilynn Webb, *Prints & Pastels*, Otago University Press, Dunedin, 2004.

Macdonald, Charlotte, Merimeri Penfold and Bridget Williams, *The Book of New Zealand Women Ko Kui ma te Kaupapa*, Bridget Williams Books, Wellington, 1991.

Mackay, J. A., *Historic Poverty Bay and the East Coast, N.I., N.Z.*, Poverty Bay East Coast Centennial Council, Gisborne, 1966.

Maihi, Toi Te Rito, 'Ngā Aho: Threads that Join', in Awhina Tamarapa, *Whatu Kākahu: Māori Cloaks*, Te Papa Press, Wellington, 2011.

Main, William, *New Zealand Photography from the 1840s to the Present*, PhotoForum, Wellington, 1993.

Mane-Wheoki, Jonathan, 'He Wahine Toa: Robyn Kahukiwa, Artist', in Robyn Kahukiwa, Hinemoa Hilliard, Edward Lucie-Smith, and Jonathan Mane-Wheoki (eds), *The Art of Robyn Kahukiwa*, Reed, Auckland, 2005.

——, 'Introduction: Indigeneity/Aboriginality, Art/Culture and Institutions', in Jaynie Anderson (ed.), *Crossing Cultures: Conflict, Migration and Convergence*, Miegunyah Press, Melbourne, 2009, pp. 770–72.

Marsden, Maori, 'God, Man and Universe: A Maori View', in Maori Marsden (ed.), *The Woven Universe. Selected Writings of Rev. Maori Marsden*, Estate of Rev. Maori Marsden, Masterton, 2003.

Marsden, Samuel, 'Observations on the Introduction of the Gospel into the South Sea Islands: Being my First Visit to New Zealand in December 1814', in John Elder (ed.), *Letters and Journals of Samuel Marsden*, Coulls, Somerville, Wilke, Dunedin, 1932.

Marshall, William, *A Personal Narrative of Two Visits to New Zealand in His Majesty's Ship* Alligator, *AD 1834*, James Nisbet, London, 1841.

Mason, Ngahiraka, 'The State of Māori Art in an International Context', in *Sakahàn: International Indigenous Art*, National Gallery of Canada, Ottawa, 2013.

Mataira, Katerina, 'Modern Trends in Maori Art Forms', in Erik Schwimmer (ed.), *The Maori People in the Nineteen-Sixties*, Blackwood & Janet Paul, Auckland, 1968.

——, *Maori Artists of the South Pacific*, New Zealand Maori Artists & Writers Society, Raglan, 1984.

Matthews, Nathan and Karyn Paringatai, 'Nga Mahi Toi', in Tānia Ka'ai (ed.), *Ki Te Whaiao: An Introduction to Māori Culture and Society*, Pearson Longman, Auckland, 2004.

McCarthy, Conal, *Exhibiting Māori: A History of Colonial Cultures of Display*, Te Papa Press, Wellington, 2007.

——, 'The Practice of Repatriation: A Case Study from New Zealand', in Louise Tythcott and Kostas Arvanitis (eds), *Museums and Restitution: New Practices, New Approaches*, Routledge, London & New York, 2014.

——, *Museums and Māori: Heritage Professionals, Indigenous Collections, Current Practices*, Te Papa Press, Wellington, 2016.

McCulloch, Beverly, 'Maori Rock Drawings: A Matter of Interpretation', in *Maori Rock Drawings: The Theo Schoon Interpretations*, Robert McDougall Art Gallery, Christchurch, 1985.

McNab, Robert (ed.), *Extracts from the Journal of Pottier de l'Horne, First-Lieutenant on Board the "Saint Jean Baptiste": Arrival in New Zealand*, John Mackay, Wellington, 1914.

Mead, Hirini [Sidney] Moko, *Taniko Weaving: How to Make Maori Belts and Other Useful Articles*, Reed, Wellington, 1952.

——, *Traditional Maori Clothing: A Study of Technological and Functional Change*, Reed, Auckland, 1969.

——, *Te Maori: Māori Art from New Zealand Collections*, Harry Abrams, New York, 1984.

——, *Te Toi Whakairo: The Art of Maori Carving*, Reed Publishing, Auckland, 1995.

——, *Maori Art on the World Scene*, Ahua Design and Matau Associates, Wellington, 1997.

——, *Tikanga Māori: Living by Māori Values*, Huia, Wellington, 2019.

Mead, Hirini [Sidney] Moko (ed.), *Mataatua Wharenui: Te Whare i Hoki Mai*, Huia, Wellington, 2018.

Mead, H. M. and N. Grove, *Ngā Pēpeha a Ngā Tīpuna: The Sayings of the Ancestors*, Victoria University Press, Wellington, 2001.

Meade, Herbert, *A Ride through the Disturbed Districts of New Zealand*, John Murray, London, 1870.

Middleton, Angela, *Te Puna: A New Zealand Mission Station: Historical Archaeology in New Zealand*, Springer, New York & London, 2008.

——, *Pēwhairangi: Bay of Islands Missions and Māori 1814–1845*, Otago University Press, Dunedin, 2014.

*Missionary Register for 1832*, Church Missionary Society, London, 1832.

Mitcalfe, Barry, *Maori Poetry*, Victoria University Press, Wellington, 1974.

Mitchell, Tony, 'Kia Kaha! (Be Strong!): Māori and Pacific Islander Hip-Hop in Aotearoa-New Zealand', in Tony Mitchell (ed.), *Global Noise: Rap and Hip Hop Outside the USA*, Wesleyan University Press, Middletown, CT, 2001.

Neich, Roger, *Painted Histories: Early Maori Figurative Painting*, Auckland University Press, Auckland, 1993.

——, *Carved Histories: Rotorua Ngati Tarawhai Woodcarving*, Auckland University Press, Auckland, 2002.

——, 'Powaka Whakairo: A Third Form of Maori Treasure Box', in Chanel Clarke, Fuli Pereira and Nigel Prickett (eds), *Tradition and Change in Maori and Pacific Art: Essays by Roger Neich*, Auckland War Memorial Museum, Auckland, 2013.

——, 'Papahou and Wakahuia: Maori Treasure Boxes', in Chanel Clarke, Fuli Pereira and Nigel Prickett (eds), *Tradition and Change in Maori and Pacific Art: Essays by Roger Neich*, Auckland War Memorial Museum, Auckland, 2013.

Neich, Roger (ed.), *The Oldman Collection of Maori Artifacts*, University of Hawai'i Press, Honolulu, 2004.

Neich, Roger and Mick Pendergrast, *Pacific Tapa*, University of Hawai'i Press, Honolulu, 2004.

Neich, Roger, Mick Pendergrast and Dorota Starzecka, *The Maori Collections of the British Museum*, British Museum Press, London, 2010.

Nelson, Anne, *Nga Waka Maori*, Macmillan, Auckland, 1991.

Newell, Jennifer, *Pacific Art in Detail*, Te Papa Press, Wellington, 2011.

Newman, Keith, *Rātana Revisited*, Raupo, Auckland, 2006.

Ngata, Apirana, *Ngā Mōteatea: Traditional Song-poetry of the Maori*, Kiwi, Wellington, 1974.

Ngata, Apirana, trans. Pei Te Hurinui Jones, *Ngā Mōteatea The Songs: Part One*, Auckland University Press, Auckland, 2004.

——, *Ngā Mōteatea The Songs: Part Two*, Auckland University Press, Auckland, 2005.

——, *Ngā Mōteatea The Songs: Part Three*, Auckland University Press, Auckland, 2006.

Nicholas, Darcy and Keri Kaa, *Seven Maori Artists*, Government Printer, Wellington, 1986.

Nicholas, John, *Narrative of a Voyage to New Zealand, Performed in the Years 1814 and 1815, in Company with the Rev. Samuel Marsden, Principal Chaplain of New South Wales*, James Black & Sons, London, 1817.

O'Malley, Vincent, *The Meeting Place: Maori and Pakeha Encounters, 1642–1840*, Auckland University Press, Auckland, 2012.

——, *Haerenga: Early Māori Journeys Across the Globe*, Bridget Williams Books, Wellington, 2015.

O'Regan, Gerard, 'The Shifting Space of Ngāi Tahu Rock Art', in Geoffrey Clark, Foss Leach and Sue O'Connor (eds), *Islands of Inquiry: Colonisation, Seafaring and the Archaeology of Maritime Landscapes*, Australian National University Press, Canberra, 2008.

Ollivier, Isabel Cheryl and Hingley, *Extracts from Journals Relating to the Visit of the French Ship* St Jean Baptiste *in December 1769 under the Command of J. F. M. De Surville,* Alexander Turnbull Library Endowment Trust, Wellington, 1982.

Orange, Claudia, *The Treaty of Waitangi*, Allen & Unwin, Port Nicholson Press & Historical Branch of the Department of Internal Affairs, Wellington, 1987.

Orange, Claudia (ed.), *Dictionary of New Zealand Biography 1870–1900*, vol. 2, Bridget Williams Books & Department of Internal Affairs Historical Branch, Wellington, 1993.

Orbell, Margaret, *Waiata: Maori Songs in History*, Reed, Auckland, 1991.

——, *The Illustrated Encyclopedia of Maori Myth and Legend,* Canterbury University Press, Christchurch, 1996.

Panoho, Rangihīroa, 'Māori: At the Centre, on the Margins', in Mary Barr (ed.), *Headlands: Thinking Through New Zealand Art*, Museum of Contemporary Art, Sydney, 1992.

——, *Whatu Aho Rua: A Weaving Together of Traditional and Contemporary Māori Art*, Tandanya Aboriginal Cultural Institute & Sarjeant Gallery, Adelaide, 1991.

Papakura, Mākereti, *The Old Time Maori*, New Women's Press, Auckland, 1986.

Paremata Maori, *Te Nohonga Tuatahi o te Paremata Maori o Niu Tireni*, Webbe & Co, Ōtaki, 1892.

——, *Proceedings of the Third Kotahitanga Parliament, April to May 1894*, Greytown, 1895.

Park, Geoff, *Forestry and Timber Trading in the Bay of Islands, 1769–1840*, Treaty of Waitangi Research Unit, Wellington, 2013.

Parkinson, Stanfield (ed.), *A Journal of a Voyage to the South Seas, in His Majesty's ship, the* Endeavour: *Transcribed from the Papers of Sydney Parkinson*, Stanfield Parkinson, London, 1773.

Paterson, Lachy and Angela Wanhalla, *He Reo Wahine: Maori Women's Voices from the Nineteenth Century*, Auckland University Press, Auckland, 2018.

Pendergrast, Mick, *Te Aho Tapu: The Sacred Thread*, University of Hawai'i Press, Honolulu, 1987.

Penkowski, Jozef, 'Pontifico Museo Missionario-Ethnologico', in *The Vatican Collections: The Papacy and Art*, Metropolitan Museum, New York, 1982.

Petrie, Hazel, *Outcasts of the Gods? The Struggle Over Slavery in Māori New Zealand*, Auckland University Press, Auckland, 2015.

Phillipps, W. J., *Carved Maori Houses of the Eastern Districts of the North Island*, Harry H. Tombs, Wellington, 1944.

——, *Maori Houses and Food Stores*, Government Printer, Wellington, 1952.

——, *Carved Maori Houses of Western and Northern Areas of New Zealand*, Government Printer, Wellington, 1955.

Phillipps, W. J. and J. C. Wadmore, *The Great Carved House Mataatua of Whakatane*, Polynesian Society, Wellington, 1956.

Platts, Una, *Nineteenth Century New Zealand Artists: A Guide & Handbook*, Avon Fine Prints, Christchurch, 1980.

Pōhūhū, Nēpia, Memoir Supplement, *Te Wananga*, vol. 1, no. 2, Māori Purposes Fund Board, Wellington, 1930.

Polack, Joel, *New Zealand: Being a Narrative of Travels and Adventures During a Residence in that Country Between the Years 1831 and 1837*, vol. 2, Richard Bentley, London, 1838.

Pope, James H., *Health for the Maori*, John McKay, Government Printer, Wellington, 1901.

Porter, Frances, *The Turanga Journals 1840–50: Letters and Journals of William and Jane Williams, Missionaries to Poverty Bay*, Victoria University Press, Wellington, 1974.

Porter, Thomas, *Major Ropata Wahawaha – The Story of His Life and Times*, Poverty Bay Herald, Gisborne, 1897.

Pound, Francis, *Space Between: Pākehā Use of Māori Motifs in Modernist New Zealand Art*, Workshop Press, Auckland, 1994.

Puketapu-Hetet, Erenora, *Maori Weaving*, Longman Paul, Auckland, 1989.

Quin, W. A., *The Story of Hawera*, C. O. Ekdahl, Hawera, 1904.

*Rauru Nui a Toi Lectures*, Lecture 4, Department of Anthropology, Victoria University of Wellington, Wellington, 1972.

Reading, Nigel and Gary Wyatt, *Manawa: Pacific Heartbeat: A Celebration of Contemporary Māori & Northwest Coast Art*, Raupo, Auckland, 2005.

'Reiseerlebnisse eines Museumsdirektors: Gespräch mit Professor Dr. Schauinsland im Bremer Handelsmuseum (Travel Experiences of a Museum Director: Conversation with Professor Dr. Schauinsland in the Bremen Trade Museum, Broadcast in 1930 by the Bremen Subsidiary of the North German Broadcasting Corporation (Norag)', in Herbert Abel, *Vom Raritätenkabinett zum Bremer Überseemuseum. Die Geschichte einer Hanseatischen Sammlung aus Übersee Anlasslich ihres 75jahrigen Bestehens (From the Cabinet of Rarities to the Überseemuseum of Bremen. The History of a Hanseatic Collections from Obersee on the Occasion of its 75th Anniversary)*, Verlag Friedrich Röver, Bremen, 1970, p. 237.

Reed, A. H., *Treasury of Maori Exploration: Legends Relating to the First Polynesian Explorers of New Zealand*, A. H. & A. W. Reed, Wellington, 1977.

Reeves, Jane, 'Exiled for a Cause: Maori Prisoners in Dunedin', in M. Reilly and J. Thomson (eds), *When the Waves Rolled in Upon Us: Essays in Nineteenth-Century Maori History*, Otago University Press, Dunedin, 1999.

Renwick, William (ed.), *Creating a National Spirit: Celebrating New Zealand's Centennial*, Victoria University Press, Wellington, 2004.

Richards, Rhys, *Tracking Travelling Taonga: A Narrative Review of How Maori Items Got to London from 1798, to Salem in 1802, 1807 and 1812, and Elsewhere up to 1840*, Paremata Press, Wellington, 2015.

Rickard, Jolene, 'The Emergence of Global Indigenous Art', in *Sakahàn: International Indigenous Art*, National Gallery of Canada, Ottawa, 2013.

Riseborough, Hazel, *Days of Darkness: Taranaki 1878–1884*, Allen & Unwin, Wellington, 1989.

Roberts, Neil, 'Maori Rock Drawing and Theo Schoon', in *Maori Rock Drawings: The Theo Schoon Interpretations*, Robert McDougall Art Gallery, Christchurch, 1985.

Roberts, Vernon, *Kohikohinga: Reminiscences and Reflections of Ropata*, Whitcombe & Tombs, Auckland, 1929.

Robley, H. G., *Moko, or, Maori Tattooing*, Chapman and Hall, London, 1896.

——, *Pounamu: Notes on New Zealand Greenstone*, T. J. S. Guilford, London, 1915.

Roche, Michael, 'The Commodity Chain at the Periphery: The Spar Trade of Northern New Zealand in the Early 19th Century', in Christina Stringer and Richard Le Heron (eds), *Agri-Food Commodity, Chains and Globalising Networks*, Routledge, London and New York, 2016.

Roth, H. Ling, *The Maori Mantle*, Bankfield Museum, Halifax, 1923.

Roth, H. Ling (ed.), *Crozet's Voyage to Tasmania, New Zealand and the Ladrone Islands and the Philippines in the Years 1771–1772*, Truslove & Shirley, London, 1891.

Royal, Charles, *Rangiatea*, National Library of New Zealand and Te Ropu Whakahaere o Rangiatea, Wellington, 1997.

Ryan, P. M., *The Raupō Dictionary of Modern Māori*, Raupo, Auckland, 2012.

Rydén, Stig, *The Banks Collection: An Episode in 18th-Century Anglo-Swedish Relations*, Ethnographical Museum of Sweden, Monograph Series no. 8, Stockholm, 1963.

Saint Cartmail, Keith, *The Art of Tonga*, Craig Potton, Nelson, 1997.

Salmond, Anne, *Hui: A Study of Maori Ceremonial Gatherings*, Reed, Auckland, 1975.

——, *Two Worlds: First Meetings Between Māori and Europeans, 1642–1772*, Viking, Auckland, 1993.

——, *Between Worlds: Early Exchanges Between Maori and Pakeha 1773–1815*, Penguin, Auckland, 1997.

——, *Aphrodite's Island: The European Discovery of Tahiti*, Viking, Auckland, 2009.

——, *Tears of Rangi: Experiments Across the World*, Auckland University Press, Auckland, 2017.

Sargison, Patricia, *Notable Women in New Zealand Health*, Longman Paul, Auckland, 1993.

Savage, John, *Some Account of New Zealand, Particularly the Bay of Islands and Surrounding Country*, J. Murray, London, 1807.

Schuster, James and Dean Whiting, 'Marae Conservation in Aotearoa', in Dean Sully (ed.), *Decolonising Conservation: Caring for Māori Meeting Houses Outside New Zealand*, Left Coast Press, Walnut Creek, CA, 2007.

Schuster, James, 'Toku Whaea, ko Emire: My Mum, Emily', in Ane Tonga (ed.), *Te Ringa Rehe: The Legacy of Emily Schuster*, Rotorua Museum Te Whare Taonga o Te Arawa, Rotorua, 2017.

Scott, Dick, *The Parihaka Story*, Southern Cross, Auckland, 1954.

——, *Ask That Mountain: The Story of Parihaka*, Southern Cross, Auckland, 1991.

Shaw, Peter, *New Zealand Architecture — From Polynesian Beginnings to 1990*, Hodder & Stoughton, Auckland, 1991.

Shepard, Deborah, *Between the Lives: Partners in Art*, Auckland University Press, Auckland, 2005.

Sherriff, Brian, *A Pocket Reference to Old New Zealand Artists*, Te Rau Press, http://christchurchartgallery.org.nz/media/uploads/2014_02/PocketReference.pdf

Simmons, David, *Whakairo: Maori Tribal Art Styles*, Oxford University Press, Auckland, 1994.

Sinclair, Keith, *A History of New Zealand*, Penguin, Auckland, first published 1959, 1960.

——, 'Te Tikanga Pekeke: The Maori Anti-Landselling Movements in Taranaki', in Peter Munz (ed.), *The Feel of Truth: Essays in New Zealand and Pacific History*, Reed, Wellington, 1969.

——, *Kinds of Peace: Maori People After the Wars 1870–85*, Auckland University Press, Auckland, 1991.

Sissons, Jeffrey, *The Polynesian Iconoclasm: Religious Revolution and the Seasonality of Power*, Berghahn Books, New York, 2014.

Sissons, Jeffrey, Wiremu Wi Hongi and Pat Hohepa, *The Puriri Trees Are Laughing: A Political History of Ngāpuhi in the Inland

*Bay of Islands: A Report Submitted to the Social Sciences Research Fund Committee*, Polynesian Society, Auckland, 1987.

Skinner, Damian, *The Carver and the Artist*, Auckland University Press, Auckland, 2008.

Skinner, H. D., *Comparatively Speaking: Studies in Pacific Material Culture, 1921–1972*, Otago University Press/John McIndoe, Dunedin, 1974.

Smith, Huhana, *E Tu Ake: Māori Standing Strong*, Te Papa Press, Wellington, 2011.

Smith, Huhana (ed.), *Taiāwhio: Conversations with Contemporary Māori Artists*, Te Papa Press, Wellington, 2002.

Smith, Huhana (ed.), *Taiāwhio II: Contemporary Māori Artists, 18 New Conversations*, Te Papa Press, Wellington, 2007.

Smith, Te Whakaotinga Ronald, *Te Omeka Pa: The Passing Years*, Te Omeka Marae Trustees, Tainui Press, Matamata, 1987.

Sole, Tony, *Ngāti Ruanui: A History*, Huia, Wellington, 2005.

Sorrenson, M. P. K. (ed.), *Na To Hoa Aroha: From Your Dear Friend*, vol. 1, Auckland University Press, Auckland, 1986.

——, *Na To Hoa Aroha: From Your Dear Friend*, vol. 2, Auckland University Press, Auckland, 1988.

——, *Na To Hoa Aroha: From Your Dear Friend*, vol. 3, Auckland University Press, Auckland, 1988.

Spivak, Gayatri Chakravorty, *In Other Worlds: Essays in Cultural Politics*, Methuen, New York, 1987.

Stafford, Donald, *Te Arawa: A History of the Arawa People*, Reed, Auckland, 1994.

Starzecka, D. C. *Maori: Art and Culture*, British Museum Press, London, 1996.

Sully, Dean (ed.), *Decolonising Conservation: Caring for Māori Meeting Houses Outside of New Zealand*, Left Coast Press, Walnut Creek, CA, 2007.

Sundt, Richard, *Whare Karakia: Māori Church Building, Decoration and Ritual in Aotearoa New Zealand 1834–1863*, Auckland University Press, Auckland, 2010.

Tamarapa, Awhina (ed.), *Whatu Kākahu: Māori Cloaks*, Te Papa Press, Wellington, 2011.

——, 'Mere Ngareta's Kahu Kiwi', in Fiona McKergow and Kerry Taylor (eds), *Te Hao Nui – The Great Catch: Object Stories from Te Manawa*, Random House, Auckland, 2011.

——, 'Ngā Kākahu o Te Papa: The Cloaks of Te Papa', in Awhina Tamarapa (ed.), *Whatu Kākahu: Māori Cloaks*, Te Papa Press, Wellington, 2011.

Tamati-Quennell, Megan, *Aukaha Kia Kaha: Strengthen the Bindings of the Earth, of the People, of the Soul*, Dunedin Public Art Gallery, Dunedin, 2000.

Tamati-Quennell, Megan (ed.), *Kurawaka*, Dowse Art Museum, Lower Hutt, 1994.

Taonui, Rawiri, 'Polynesian Oral Traditions', in Kerry Howe (ed.), *Vaka Moana: Voyages of the Ancestors*, Auckland Museum and David Bateman, Auckland, 2006.

Tapsell, Paul, *Pukaki: A Comet Returns*, Raupo, Auckland, 2000.

——, *Ko Tawa: Maori Treasures of New Zealand*, David Bateman, Auckland, 2006.

Taylor, Richard, *The Past and Present of New Zealand – With Its Prospects for the Future*, William Macintosh, London, 1868.

——, *Te Ika a Maui: Or New Zealand and Its Inhabitants*, MacIntosh, London, 1870.

Te Ao, Ngapine, 'The Legacy of Kākaho', in Ngarino Ellis and Witi Ihimaera (eds), *Te Ata: Māori Art from the East Coast, New Zealand*, Auckland, Reed, 2002.

Te Awekotuku, Ngahuia, *Mana Wahine Maori: Selected Writings on Maori Women's Art, Culture and Politics*, New Women's Press, Auckland, 1991.

——, 'Ta Moko: Maori Tattoo', in Roger Blackley (ed.), *Goldie*, David Bateman, Auckland, 1997.

——, *Mau Moko: The World of Māori Tattoo*, Penguin, Auckland, 2007.

——, 'Introduction', in Jordon Harris, *Takatāpui: A Place of Standing*, Oratia Media and the New Zealand AIDS Foundation, Auckland, 2016.

Te Kanawa, Diggeress, *Weaving a Kakahu*, Bridget Williams Books in association with Aotearoa Moananui a Kiwa Weavers, Wellington, 1992.

Te Kanawa, Kahutoi, 'The Revered Whāriki: Traditional Māori Weaving', in Wulf Köpke and Bernd Schmelz (eds), *House Rauru: Masterpiece of the Māori*, Museum fur Volkerkunde, Hamburg, 2012.

——, 'Memories of Emily Rangitiaria Schuster', in Ane Tonga (ed.), *Te Ringa Rehe: The Legacy of Emily Schuster*, Rotorua Museum Te Whare Taonga o Te Arawa, Rotorua, 2017.

Te Kanawa, Kahutoi and John Turi-Tiakitai, 'Te Mana o te Kākahu: The Prestige of Cloaks', in Awhina Tamarapa (ed.), *Whatu Kākahu: Māori Cloaks*, Te Papa Press, Wellington, 2011.

Te Punga Somerville, Alice, *Once Were Pacific: Maori Connections to Oceania*, University of Minnesota Press, Minneapolis, MN, 2012.

Te Rauparaha, Tamihana, trans. and ed. Ross Calman, *He Pukapuka Tātaku i ngā Mahi a Te Rauparaha Nui: A Record of the Life of the Great Te Rauparaha*, Auckland University Press, Auckland, 2020.

Te Whaiti, Andrew, *Te Puia: The Next 40 Years: Stories of those Guiding the Maori Arts and Crafts Institute, Rotorua*, Open Polytechnic of New Zealand, Lower Hutt, 2005.

*Te Whakatuwheratanga o Te Tumu Herenga Waka, 6 Tihema 1986, Poneke, Te Whare Wananga o Wikitoria*, Maori Studies Department, Victoria University of Wellington, Wellington, 1986.

Thomas, Nicholas, *Discoveries: The Voyages of Captain Cook*, Allen Lane, London, 2003.

Thomas, Nicholas and Mark Adams, *Rauru: Tene Waitere, Maori Carving, Colonial History*, Otago University Press, Dunedin, 2009.

Thwaites, Ian and Rie Fletcher, *We Learnt to See: Elam's Rutland Group 1935–1958: A Biographical Journey with Auckland Artists*, Pūriri Press, Auckland, 2004.

Travers, W. T. L., *The Stirring Times of Te Rauparaha*, Wilson and Horton, Auckland, 1971.

Tregear, Edward, *Maori-Polynesian Comparative Dictionary*, Lyon and Blair, London, 1891.

Trotter, Michael, 'Foreword', in *Maori Rock Drawings: The Theo Schoon Interpretations*, Robert McDougall Art Gallery, Christchurch, 1985.

Trotter, Michael and Beverley McCulloch, *Prehistoric Rock Art of New Zealand*, A. H. & A. W. Reed, Auckland, 1971.

Tsinhnahjinnie, Hulleah J., 'When is a Photograph Worth a Thousand Words?', in Jane Alison (ed.), *Native Nations: Journeys in American Photography*, Barbican Art Gallery and Booth-Clibborn Editions, London, England, 1998.

——, 'Dragonfly's Home', in Henrietta Lidchi and Hulleah J. Tsinhnahjinnie (eds), *Visual Currencies: Reflections on Native Photography*, National Museum of Scotland, Edinburgh, 2009.

Tuhiwai Smith, Linda, *Decolonizing Methodologies: Research and Indigenous Peoples*, Otago University Press, Dunedin, 2012.

Turner, Terence, 'The Social Skin', in J. Cherfas and R. Lewin (eds), *Not Work Alone: A Cross-Cultural View of Activities Superfluous to Survival*. Sage Publications, Beverly Hills, CA, 1980.

University of Auckland, *Tane-nui-a-Rangi*, University of Auckland, 1988.

Vernes, Théodore, *Exposition Universelle de 1867 à Paris. Section des Missions Protestantes*, Libraire de la Société des Gens de Lettres, Paris, 1867.

Vivieaere, Jim, 'When the Tune Eats Its Tail: The Role of Critical Commentary in Relation to Aboriginal Art', in Lee-Ann Martin (ed.), *Making a Noise: Aboriginal Perspectives on Art, Art History, Critical Writing and Community*, Banff International Curatorial Centre, Banff, 2003.

Vunidilo, Tarisi, 'The Exchange of Kula Feathers', in Karl Chitham, Kolokesa U Māhina-Tuai and Damian Skinner (eds), *Crafting Aotearoa: A Cultural History of Making in New Zealand and the Wider Moana Oceania*, Te Papa Press, Wellington, 2019.

Waite, Noel, 'Future Fairs: Industrial Exhibitions in New Zealand, 1865 to 1925', in Penny Sparke and Fiona Fisher (eds), *Routledge Companion to Design Studies*, Routledge, London and New York, 2019.

Wakefield, Edward, *Adventure in New Zealand: From 1839 to 1844*, vol. 1, John Murray, London, 1845.

Walker, Ranginui, *Struggle Without End*, Penguin, Auckland, 1990.

——, 'The Meeting House', in Ranginui Walker (ed.), *Nga Pepa a Ranginui: The Walker Papers*, Penguin, Auckland, 1996.

Wallace, Patricia, 'Ko te Pūtaiao, te Ao o ngā Tūpuna: Ancestral Māori Scientific Practice', in Awhina Tamarapa (ed.), *Whatu Kākahu: Māori Cloaks*, Te Papa Press, Wellington, 2011.

Ward, Alan, *A Show of Justice: Racial Amalgamation in Nineteenth Century New Zealand*, Auckland University Press and Oxford University Press, Auckland, 1983.

Webb, Marilynn, *Prints & Pastels 1966–1990: Heartland*, Dunedin Public Art Gallery, Dunedin, 1992.

Wedde, Ian and Gregory Burke (eds), *Now! See! Hear! Art, Language, Translation*, Victoria University Press, Wellington, 1990.

Whaanga, Mere, *A Carved Cloak for Tahu*, Auckland University Press, Auckland, 2004.

Whatahoro, H. T. and S. P. Smith (trans.), *The Lore of the Whare-Wananga: Or Teachings of the Maori College on Religion*, Polynesian Society, New Plymouth, 1913.

White, John, *The Ancient History of the Maori*, vols 1–6, Government Printer, Wellington, 1887–90.

Williams, Frederick, *Through Ninety Years, 1826–1916: Life and Work among the Maoris in New Zealand*, Whitcombe & Tombs, Auckland, 1939.

Williams, H. W., 'Description of Maori Rafter Patterns', in Augustus Hamilton, *Maori Art*, Ferguson and Mitchell for the New Zealand Institute, Dunedin, 1957.

——, *A Dictionary of the Maori Language*, 7th edn, GP Publications, Wellington, 1991.

Williams, Henry, *The Early Journals of Henry Williams, Senior Missionary in New Zealand of the Church Missionary Society, 1826–40*, Pegasus Press, Christchurch, 1961.

Williams, Leonard, *East Coast (N.Z.) Historical Records*, Poverty Bay Herald, Gisborne, 1932.

Wilson, Ormond, *War in the Tussock – Te Kooti and the Battle at Te Porere*, R. E. Owen, Government Printer, Wellington, 1961.

Wonu Veys, Fanny, *Mana Māori: The Power of New Zealand's First Inhabitants*, Leiden University Press, Leiden, 2010.

Wratislau, Elizabeth, 'A Signature Style', in Elizabeth Wratislau (ed.) *Whetu Tirikatene-Sullivan: Travel in Style*, MTG Hawke's Bay, Napier, 2014.

Young, Mark, *Painting 1950–1967*, Reed, Wellington, 1968.

### Journal articles

Anderson, Atholl, 'Changing Perspectives upon Maori Colonisation Voyaging', *Journal of the Royal Society*, vol. 47, no. 3, 2017, pp. 222–31.

Anderson, Atholl and Peter White, 'Prehistoric Settlement on Norfolk Island and its Oceanic Context', *Records of the Australian Museum*, vol. 27, 2001, pp. 135–41.

Anson, Dimitri, 'What's in a Name? The House Carvings that Dr Hocken Gave to the Otago Museum', *Journal of the Polynesian Society*, vol. 113, no. 1, 2004, pp. 73–90.

Archey, Gilbert, 'Rock Shelter Drawings at Arapuni Gorge', *Journal of the Polynesian Society*, vol. 36, no. 144, 1927, pp. 369–71.

——, 'Wood Carving in the North Auckland Area', *Records of the Auckland Institute and Museum*, vol. 1, no. 4, 1933, pp. 209–18.

*Ascent: A Journal of the Arts in New Zealand*, vol. 1, no. 2, The Caxton Press, Christchurch, July 1968.

Ashton, Lloyd, 'Much more than Ornamental', *Mana*, no. 15, 1997, pp. 39–45.

Aspin, Clive and Jessica Hutchings, 'Reclaiming the Past to Inform the Future: Contemporary Views of Maori Sexuality', *Culture, Health and Sexuality*, vol. 9, no. 4, 2007, pp. 415–27.

'Auckland's Community Centre', *Te Ao Hou*, vol. 40, 1962, pp. 25–29.

Austin, Mike, 'Pacific Island Architecture', *Fabrications*, vol. 11, no. 2, 2001, pp. 13–19.

Baker, Kirsty, 'To Think about Fraught Things', *Art and Australia* online, 2018, www.artandaustralia.com/online/online/discursions/think-about-fraught-things.html

Barber, Ian and Justin Maxwell, 'Evaluating New Radiocarbon Dates from Midden Deposits near Morior Tree Carvings, Rēkohu (Chatham Island)', *Journal of the Polynesian Society*, vol. 121, no. 1, March 2012, pp. 33–50.

Barclay, Barry, 'Celebrating Fourth Cinema', *Illusions* 35, 2003, pp. 7–11.

Barth, Volker, 'Displaying Normalisation: The Paris Universal Exhibition of 1867', *Journal of Historical Sociology*, vol. 20, no. 4, 2007, pp. 462–85.

Beasley, Harry, 'Metal Mere', *Journal of the Polynesian Society*, vol. 36, no. 143, 1927, pp. 297–98.

Beattie, James Herries, 'Traditions and Legends Collected from the Natives of Murihiku (Southland, New Zealand), Part VIII', *Journal of the Polynesian Society*, vol. 27, no. 107, 1918, pp. 137–61.

Best, Elsdon, 'Kahu Kuri (Dogskin Cloaks)', *Transactions and Proceedings of the Royal Society of New Zealand*, vol. 31, 1898, pp. 644–45.

——, 'The Art of the Whare Pora', *Transactions and Proceedings of the New Zealand Institute*, vol. 31, 1898.

——, 'Notes on the Arts of War, Part VII,' *Journal of the Polynesian Society* vol. 12, no. 3, 1903, pp. 145–65.

——, 'Maori Marriage Customs', *Transactions and Proceedings of the New Zealand Institute*, vol. 36, 1903, pp. 14–67.

——, 'The Uhi-Maori, or Native Tattooing Instruments', *Journal of the Polynesian Society*, vol. 13, no. 3, 1904, pp. 166–72.

——, 'Did Polynesian Voyagers Know the Double Outrigger?', *Journal of the Polynesian Society*, vol. 32, no. 4, 1923, pp. 200–14.

——, 'Notes on Inscribed Stones of the Taranaki District', *Journal of the Polynesian Society*, vol. 36, no. 142, 1927, pp. 137–40.

Bierman, Jan, 'If These Walls Could Talk…', *The Hobson*, September 2020, pp. 32–33.

Binney, Judith, 'The Lost Drawing of Nukutawhiti', *New Zealand Journal of History*, vol. 14, no. 1, 1980, pp. 3–24.

——, 'The Heritage of Isaiah: Thomas Kendall and Maori Religion', *New Zealand Journal of History*, vol. 38, no. 2, 2004, pp. 127–53.

——, 'Tuki's Universe', *New Zealand Journal of History*, vol. 38, no. 2, 2004, pp. 215–32.

Blank, Arapera, 'Karanga Karanga', *Broadsheet*, no. 141, July/August 1986, pp. 35–36.

Blundell, Sally, 'How do you save cave drawings that are hundreds of years old from the ravages of time and human interaction?', *Te Karaka*, no. 49, 2010, p. 21.

Borell, Nigel and Benjamin Lignel, 'In Conversation with Areta Wilkinson', *Art Jewellery Forum*, 23 September 2015, https://artjewelryforum.org/interviews/in-conversation-with-areta-wilkinson/

Brown, Deidre, 'Te Hau ki Turanga', *Journal of the Polynesian Society*, vol. 105, no. 1, 1996, pp. 7–26.

——, 'The Architecture of the School of Maori Arts and Crafts', *Journal of the Polynesian Society*, vol. 108, no. 3, 1999, pp. 241–76.

——, 'Nga Paremata Māori: The Architecture of Māori Nationalism', *Fabrications*, vol. 12, no. 2, 2002, pp. 1–17.

——, 'Ko to Ringa ki nga Rakau a te Pākehā: Virtual Taonga Māori and Museums', *Visual Resources*, vol. 24, no. 1, 2008, pp. 59–75.

Brown, Deidre and George Nicholas, 'Protecting Indigenous Cultural Property in the Age of Digital Democracy: Institutional and Communal Responses to Canadian First Nations and Māori Heritage Concerns', *Journal of Material Culture*, vol. 17, no. 3, 2012, pp. 307–24.

Brunt, Peter, 'Since *Choice!*', in Anna Smith and Lydia Wevers (eds), *On Display: New Essays in Cultural Studies*, Victoria University Press, Wellington, 2004.

Bush, E. E., 'Te Kooti Centenary Observance at Te Porere', *Te Ao Hou*, no. 69, 1970, pp. 24–25.

Cairns, K., 'Papawai and the Maori Parliament', *New Zealand's Heritage*, 1971, pp. 1697–1701.

Campbell, H., 'Pine Spars and Plate Armour: Convicts and Colonists: H.M.S. *Buffalo* in the South Seas', *Auckland–Waikato Historical Journal*, vol. 52, no. 1, 1988, pp. 6–11.

Campbell, Matthew, Beatrice Hudson, Jacqueline Craig, Arden Cruickshank, Louise Furey, Karen Greig, Andrew McAlister, Bruce Marshall, Reno Nims, Fiona Petchey, Tristan Russell, Danielle Trilford and Rod Wallace, 'The Long Bay Restaurant Site (R10/1374), Auckland, New Zealand, and the Archaeology of the Mid-15th Century in the Upper North Island', *Journal of Pacific Archaeology*, vol. 10, no. 2, 2019, pp. 19–42.

Carkeek, Te Waari, 'Te Rauparaha Part 2: South Island Raids and the Arrival of the "Tory"', *Te Ao Hou*, no. 31, June 1960, pp. 10–14.

Cassels, Richard, 'Early Prehistoric Wooden Artefacts from the Waitore Site (N136/16), near Patea, Taranaki', *New Zealand Journal of Archaeology*, vol. 1, 1979, pp. 85–108.

*Church Missionary Intelligencer*, vol. 2, 1852.

Christian, Glenys, 'Keeping Alive Korowai Weaving', *New Zealand Crafts*, December 1982, pp. 2–4.

Colenso, William, 'Of Plants Formerly Cultivated for Their Textile Uses', *Transactions and Proceedings of the New Zealand Institute*, vol. 13, 1880.

Coote, Jeremy, 'Joseph Banks's Forty Brass Patus', *Journal of Museum Ethnography*, no. 20, March 2008, pp. 49–68.

Cracknell, Tryphena, 'Wahine Mau Whao: A Woman's Hand to the Chisel', *ATE Journal of Māori Art*, vol. 1, 2019, pp. 46–57.

Crum, Ambrosia, Deidre Brown, Tumanako Fa'aui, Naomi Vallis and Jason Ingham, 'Seismic Retrofitting of Māori Wharenui in Aotearoa New Zealand', *Philosophical Transactions of the Royal Society*, vol. 337, no. 2155, 2019.

Cull, Chloe, 'Themes in Māori Women's Art: How the Body "Speaks" Within the Work of Māori Women Artists of the Seventies and Eighties', *Oculus: Postgraduate Journal Visual Arts Research*, no. 5, pp. 1–15.

Davis, Frank Takitaki, 'Maori Art and Artists', *Education*, no. 9, 1976.

Downes, Thomas, 'Incised Designs Seen in a Cave near Waverley', *Journal of the Polynesian Society*, vol. 34, no. 135, 1925, pp. 252–58.

Dries, Angelyn, 'The 1925 Vatican Mission Exposition and the Interface between Catholic Mission Theory and World Religions', *International Bulletin of Mission Research*, vol. 40, no. 2, pp. 119–32.

Drummond, Janet, 'The Guardians of Papawai', *Historic Places*, vol. 63, 1997.

Duff, Roger, 'Maori Art in Rock Drawings', *New Zealand Arts Year Book*, no. 6, 1950, pp. 6–11.

Dunn, Michael, 'New Zealand Rock Shelter Art', *Art and Australia*, vol. 4, no. 1, 1966, pp. 54–66.

Eastmond, Elizabeth, 'Ngahuia Te Awekotuku in Conversation with Elizabeth Eastmond and Priscilla Pitts', *Antic*, no. 1, 1986, pp. 44–55.

'Editor's Comment', *Te Ao Hou*, June 1963.

Ellis, Ngarino, 'Ko Tō Ringa ki ngā Rākau ā te Pākehā? Drawings and Signatures of Moko by Māori in the Early 19th Century', *Journal of the Polynesian Society*, vol. 123, no. 1, 2014, pp. 29–66.

Ellison, Edward, 'Sacred Stone Links Taranaki and Otago', *Historic Places*, no. 19, 1987, pp. 7–11.

Feest, Christian, 'European Collecting of American Indian Artefacts and Art', *Journal of the History of Collections*, vol. 5, no. 1, 1993, pp. 1–11.

Firth, Raymond, 'Maori Store-houses of To-day', *Journal of the Royal Anthropological Institute of Great Britain and Ireland*, vol. 55, 1925.

——, 'Maori Material in the Vienna Museum', *Journal of the Polynesian Society*, vol. 40, no. 159, 1931, pp. 95–102.

Fomison, Tony, 'Theo Schoon and the Retouching of Rock Art', *New Zealand Archaeological Association Newsletter*, vol. 30, no. 3, pp. 158–60.

Fowler, Leo, 'The East Coast Tribes have a Modern Whare Wananga', *Te Ao Hou*, no. 26, 1959, pp. 24–27.

Frankham, James, 'Weapon of Mass Destruction', *New Zealand Geographic*, no. 128, 2014, www.nzgeo.com/stories/weapon-of-mass-destruction

Gathercole, Peter, 'Pacific Collections in the Cambridge University Museum', *Pacific Arts*, 11/12, July 1995.

Gill, Brian, 'The Cheeseman–Giglioli Correspondence, and Museum Exchanges between Auckland and Florence, 1877–1904', *Archives of Natural History*, vol. 37, no. 1, 2010, pp. 131–49.

Graham, George, 'Pare Hauraki-Pare Waikato: An Old-time Adage of the Hauraki and Waikato People, the Origin Thereof, and Some of the Significant History Connected Therewith as Narrated to Me by Wiremu Hoterene Taipari of Ngati Maru in 1887', *Journal of the Polynesian Society*, vol. 58, no. 2, 1949, pp. 68–76.

Graham, George, et al. 'Te Karoreore: An Historic Mere-Pounamu of Ngati-Whakaue (Arawa): Its Origin and History as Narrated by Pirika Te Miroi Tiniraupeka (Ohinemutu, January, 1936)', *Journal of the Polynesian Society*, vol. 52, no. 2, 1943, pp. 46–64.

Greenberg, Reesa, 'Remembering Exhibitions: From Point to Line to Web', *Tate Papers*, no. 12, Autumn 2019.

'Haere ki a Koutou Tipuna', *Te Ao Hou*, no. 24, 1 October 1958, p. 3.

Hailstone, Max, 'Te Tiriti (The Treaty)', *Visible Language*, vol. 27, 1993, pp. 302–19.

Hamilton, Harold, 'The Kaingaroa Carvings', *Journal of the Polynesian Society*, vol. 34, no. 136, 1925, pp. 356–62.

Harwood, Hokimate, 'Identification and Description of Feathers in Te Papa's Māori Cloaks', *Tuhinga*, no. 22, 2011, pp. 125–47.

Hayman, Jarvis, 'Conflict in the Highlands: The Archaeology of the Scottish Highland Clearances', *Archaeological Review from Cambridge*, vol. 25, no. 1, 2010, pp. 69–85.

Head, Lindsay, 'The Gospel of Te Ua Haumene', *Journal of the Polynesian Society*, vol. 101, no. 1, 1992, pp. 7–44.

Henare, Amiria, Briar Wood, Maureen Lander and Kahu Te Kanawa, 'Visiting the House of Gifts: The 1998 "Maori" Exhibition at the British Museum', *Journal of New Zealand Literature*, no. 21, 2003, pp. 83–101.

Herle, Anita, 'Whales Teeth, Turtle-shell Masks and Bits of String: Pacific Collections and Research at Cambridge', *Journal of Museum Ethnography*, no. 17, 2005, pp. 32–57.

——, 'Relational Objects: Connecting People and Things through Pasifika Styles', *International Journal of Cultural Property*, vol. 15, no. 2, 2008, pp. 159–79.

Hilliard, David, 'Bishop G. A. Selwyn and the Melanesian Mission', *New Zealand Journal of History*, vol. 4, no. 2, 1970, pp. 120–37.

Hīroa, Te Rangi [Peter Buck], 'Maori Decorative Art: No. 1, House-panels', *Transactions and Proceeding of the New Zealand Institute*, vol. 53, 1920, pp. 452–70.

——, 'The Evolution of Maori Clothing', *Journal of the Polynesian Society*, vol. 33, no. 129, 1924, pp. 24–47.

'Historic Papawai Pa', *Te Ao Hou*, no. 50, March 1965, pp. 36–42.

Horley, Paul and Georgia Lee, 'Painted and Carved House Embellishments at 'Orongo Village, Easter Island', *Rapa Nui Journal*, vol. 23, no. 2, 2009.

——, 'Documentation of the Sacred Precinct of Mata Ngarau ('Orongo, Easter Island) in the Late 19th Century–Early 20th Century', *Journal of the Polynesian Society*, vol. 121, no. 4, 2012, pp. 393–406.

Hoskins, Rau, 'A Māori Approach', *Advance*, Spring 2014, p. 9.

Hubbard, George and Robyn Craw, 'Beyond Kia Ora: The Paraesthetics of *Choice!*', *Antic*, no. 8, December 1990, p. 28.

Igloliorte, Heather, Julie Nagam and Carla Taunton, 'Introduction: Transmissions. The Future Possibilities of Indigenous Digital and New Media Art', *Public*, vol. 27, no. 54, Winter 2016, p. 5.

Ihimaera, Witi, 'Karaka', *Art New Zealand*, vol. 60, Spring 1991.

'Inauguration of the Marist Missions of Oceania at the Missionary Exhibition at the Vatican', *New Zealand Tablet*, vol. LII, issue. 24, 1925.

'Indigenous_Trans Cultural', *Artlink*, vol. 2, no. 37, June 2017.

'Inia's Carving Unveiled', *Te Ao Hou*, no. 72, January 1973, pp. 39–41.

Irwin, Geoff, Dilys Johns, Richard Flay, Filippo Munari, Yun Sang and Tim Mackrell, 'A Review of the Archaeological Māori Canoes (Waka) Reveals Changes in Sailing Technology and Maritime Communications in Aotearoa/New Zealand, AD 1300–1800', *Journal of Pacific Archaeology*, vol. 8, no. 2, 2017, pp. 31–43.

Jacomb, Chris, 'The Chronology of Moncks Cave, Canterbury, New Zealand', *Records of the Canterbury Museum*, vol. 22, 2008, pp. 45–56.

Jacomb, Chris, Richard Walter, Sheridan Easdale, Dilys Johns, David O'Connell, Dan Witter and Alison Witter, 'A 15th Century Māori Textile Fragment from Kaitorete Spit, Canterbury, and the Evolution of Māori Weaving', *Journal of the Polynesian Society*, vol. 113, no. 3, 2004, pp. 291–96.

Jefferson, Christina, 'The Dendroglyphs of the Chatham Islands', *Journal of the Polynesian Society*, vol. 64, no. 4, 1955, pp. 367–441.

Kaa, Hirini, 'Sex, Sin and Salvation: Māori Morality through a Christian Lens', *Te Pouhere Kōrero*, vol. 6, 2012, pp. 27–34.

Kawharu, Merata, 'Ancestral Landscapes and World Heritage from a Māori Viewpoint', *Journal of the Polynesian Society* vol. 118, no. 4, 2009, pp. 317–38.

Kernot, Bernie, 'Te Maori Te Hokinga Mai: Some Reflections', *Art Galleries and Museums Association of New Zealand Journal*, vol. 18, no. 2, 1987, pp. 3–7.

Khouri, Camille, 'Justice and Emergency Services Precinct', *Architecture Now*, 19 June 2018.

Laidlaw, Zoe, '"Aunt Anna's Report": The Buxton Women and the Aborigines Select Committee, 1835–37', *The Journal of Imperial and Commonwealth History*, vol. 32, no 2, 2004, pp. 1–28.

Lake, Meredith, 'Samuel Marsden, Work and the Limits of Evangelical Humanitarianism', *History of Australia*, vol. 7, no. 3, 2010, pp. 1–23.

Leach, B. F., H. M. Leach and R. G. Law, 'The Chronology of Pre-European Settlement in Palliser Bay, A Re-Evaluation of Radiocarbon Dating Fifty Years On', 2022, Heritage New Zealand digital library: Leach7.

Low, Nic, 'The First Language of Te Waipounamu', *Te Karaka*, no. 65, 2015.

Malcolm-Buchanan, Vincent, Ngahuia Te Awekotuku and Linda Waimarie Nikora, 'Cloaked in Life and Death: Korowai, Kaitiaki and Tangihanga', *MAI Journal*, vol. 1, no. 1, 2012, pp. 50–60.

Mallon, Sean, Rangi Te Kanawa, Rachael Collinge, Nirmala Balram, Grace Hutton, Te Waari Carkeek, Arapata Hakiwai, Emalani Case, Kawikaka'iulani Aipa and Kamalani Lapeliela, 'The 'Ahu 'Ula and Mahiole of Kalani'ōpu'u: A Journey of Chiefly Adornments', *Tuhinga*, no. 28, 2017, pp. 4–23.

Mane-Wheoki, Jonathan, 'Work of Māori Architects Adds to Our Heritage', *Historic Places*, no. 31, 1990, pp. 29–33.

——, 'The Resurgence of Māori Art: Conflicts and Continuities in the Eighties', *The Contemporary Pacific*, vol. 7, no. 1, 1995, pp. 1–19.

——, 'Korurangi/Toihoukura: Brown Art in White Spaces', *Art New Zealand*, vol. 78, 1996, p. 43.

——, 'Cultural Safety: Contemporary New Zealand Art in Germany', *Art New Zealand*, no. 79, 1996, pp. 66–69.

——, 'Art's Histories in Aotearoa New Zealand', *Journal of Art Historiography*, no. 4, June 2011, http://arthistoriography.wordpress.com/number-4-june-2011/

Mantell, Walter, 'Address', *Transactions and Proceedings of the Royal Society of New Zealand*, vol. 1, 1868.

'Maori Battalion Hall: A Distinguished Building by a Gifted Architect', *Te Ao Hou*, no. 47, 1964, p. 33.

'Maori Court at Wanganui Museum', *Te Ao Hou*, no. 64, September 1968, p. 32.

'The Maori Gave His Best: Visit of TRH the Duke and Duchess of York, 1901', *Te Ao Hou*, vol. 6, 1953, pp. 21–23.

Mataira, Katerina, 'Karanga Karanga', *Broadsheet*, no. 141, July/August 1986, p. 36.

Maxwell, Alexander and Evan Roberts, 'The Whangaroa Incident, 16 July 1824: A European–Māori Encounter and Its Many Incarnations', *Journal of Pacific History*, vol. 49, no. 1, 2014, pp. 50–75.

Maxwell, Justin J., Angela Middleton and Phil Latham, 'Victorian Era European Exploitation of Pounamu in Dunedin, New Zealand', *Journal of Pacific Archaeology*, vol. 6, no. 1, 2015.

McKendry, Lisa, 'Māori Kākahu (Cloak) Fragments from Piha: Whakaari Pā', *Records of the Auckland Museum*, vol. 52, 2017, pp. 59–70.

McLean, Ian, 'Into the Transpocene: The Future of Indigenous Art', *Artlink*, vol. 37, no. 2, June 2017, pp. 28–34.

Mead, Hirini [Sidney] Moko, 'The Mataatua Declaration and the case of the carved meeting house Mataatua', *University of British Columbia Law Review*, vol. 69, 1995.

Milligan, R. R. D., 'Ranginui, Captive Chief of Doubtless Bay, 1769', *Journal of the Polynesian Society*, vol. 67, no. 3, 1958, pp. 179–203.

Mokomoko, Mereana, 'The Building of Hotunui, Whare Whakairo, W. H. Taipari's Carved House at Thames, 1878', *Transactions and Proceedings of the Royal Society of New Zealand*, vol. 30, 1897, pp. 41–44.

Morris, Kate and Bill Anthes, '2017: Indigenous Futures', *Art Journal*, vol. 76, no. 2, 2017, pp. 6–9.

Neich, Roger, 'The Maori Carving Art of Tene Waitere, Traditionalist and Innovator', *Art New Zealand*, no. 57, Summer, 1990–1991.

——, 'Jacob William Heberley of Wellington: A Maori Carver in a Changed World', *Records of the Auckland Institute and Museum*, vol. 28, 1991, pp. 69–146.

——, 'New Zealand Maori Barkcloth and Barckcloth Beaters', *Records of the Auckland Institute and Museum*, vol. 33, 1996, pp. 111–58.

——, 'The Māori House Down in the Garden: A Benign Colonial Response to Māori Art and the Māori Counter-response', *Journal of the Polynesian Society*, vol. 112, no. 4, 2003, pp. 331–68.

——, 'Nineteenth to Mid-Twentieth Century Individual Maori Woodcarvers and the Known Works', *Records of Auckland Museum*, 41, 2004, pp. 53–86.

'New Schools for Old Crafts', *Te Ao Hou*, no. 55, June 1966, p. 9.

Ngata, Apirana, 'The Origin of Maori Carving: Part 1', *Te Ao Hou*, no. 22. April 1958, pp. 30–41.

——, 'The Origin of Maori Carving: Part 2', *Te Ao Hou*, no. 23, July 1958, pp. 30–34.

Ngata, Wayne, Hera Ngata-Gibson and Amiria Salmond, 'Te Ataakura: Digital Taonga and Cultural Innovation', *Journal of Material Culture*, vol. 17, 2012, pp. 229–44.

Nihoniho, Matutaera, 'Uenuku or Kahukura: The Rainbow God of War', *Te Ao Hou*, no. 27, 1959, p. 66.

North, Allan, 'Te Whai a Te Motu Meeting House, Ruatahuna', *Historical Review*, vol. 8, no. 1, 1965.

Nuku, George, 'Perspicacité: The Art of George Nuku', *World Art*, vol. 1, no. 1, 2011, pp. 67–73.

Nuku, George and Karen Jacobs, 'An Artist's Perspective', *Journal of Museum Ethnography*, no. 21, March 2009, pp. 127–38.

O'Keefe, Patrick J., 'First International Conference on the Cultural and Intellectual Property Rights of Indigenous Peoples', *International Journal of Cultural Property*, vol. 4, no. 2, 1995, pp. 388–96.

O'Regan, Gerard, 'The History and Future of New Zealand Maori Rock Art: A Tribal Perspective', *Before Farming*, vol. 1, 2003, pp. 1–9.

O'Regan, Tipene, 'A Vibrant Presence', *Te Karaka*, 18 July 2014.

Orbell, Margaret, 'The Painted House at Putahi', *Te Ao Hou*, no. 46, March 1964, pp. 32–36.

——, 'Maori Flags and Banners', *Te Ao Hou*, no. 50, 1965, pp. 32–55.

——, 'Te Waiata mo Te Whiti', *Tu Tangata*, no. 12, 1983.

'Parish Churches in New Zealand', *The Ecclesiologist*, vol. 1, no. 1, November 1841.

Parlane, Anna, 'Kirsten Lyttle: Digital Mana', *Memo Review*, 25 February 2018.

Parkinson, Philip, 'Tuku: Gifts for a King and the Panoplies of Titore and Patuone', *Tuhinga*, no. 23, 2012.

Parsonson, Ann, 'Parihaka – A Triumph of Maori Spirit' and 'Te Whiti – The Protector of his People', *New Zealand's Heritage*, Part 49, 1971.

'Pataka, The Maori Treasure Houses', *Te Ao Hou*, no. 40, September 1962, pp. 32–33.

'Personality Study: Muru Walters', *Te Ao Hou*, no. 35, June 1961, pp. 28–29.

Phillipps, W. J., 'Note on a Carved Rock in Taranaki', *Journal of the Polynesian Society*, vol. 36, no. 142, 1927, pp. 135–36.

——, 'The Te Kuiti House', *Art New Zealand*, vol. 11, no. 2, 1938, pp. 82–88.

——, 'Carved Houses of Te Arawa', *Dominion Museum Records of Ethnology*, vol. 1, no. 1, 1946, pp. 1–46.

——, 'The Rua Hoata Shelter, Waikato River', *Journal of the Polynesian Society*, vol. 56, no. 4, 1947, pp. 336–39.

Phillips, Caroline, Dilys Johns and Harry Allen, 'Why Did Māori Bury Artefacts in the Wetlands of Pre-Contact Aotearoa/New Zealand?' *Journal of Wetland Archaeology*, vol. 2, no. 1, 2002, pp. 39–60.

Philp, Matt, 'Expecting to Fly', *Te Karaka*, 5 April 2015.

Pillay, P., G. O'Regan and J. Emmitt, 'A Locational Analysis of Rock Art in the North Island, Aotearoa New Zealand', *Journal of Pacific Archaeology*, vol. 11, no. 1, 2020, pp. 71–82.

Pohawpatchoko, Calvin, Chip Colwell, Jami Powell and Jerry Lassos, 'Developing a Native Digital Voice: Technology and Inclusivity in Museums', *Museum Anthropology*, vol. 40, no. 1, Spring 2017, pp. 52–64.

Potiki, Tahu, 'A Puzzling Absence', *Te Karaka*, no. 65, 2015, pp. 18–21.

Rewi, Adrienne, 'Remnants of the Past. What Can Ancient Raranga Fragments Tell Us About Our Tīpuna?' *Te Karaka*, no. 64, 21 December 2014.

Reweti, Bridget and Melanie Oliver, 'Looking at Forty Years of Māori Moving Image Practice, Christchurch Art Gallery', *Bulletin*, 197, 19 August 2019.

Ross, R. O., 'Maori Art', *Art in New Zealand*, vol. 16, no. 2, 1943, p. 12.

Rubel, Paula G. and Abraham Rosman, 'Potlatch and Hakari: An Analysis of Maori Society in Terms of the Potlatch Model', *Man*, vol. 6, no. 4, December 1971, pp. 660–63.

Seton, Rosemary, 'Reconstructing the Museum of the London Missionary Society', *Material Religion*, vol. 8, no. 1, 2012.

Shawcross, Wilfred, 'An Archaeological Assemblage of Maori Combs', *Journal of the Polynesian Society*, vol. 73, no. 4, 1964, pp. 382–98.

——, 'The Cambridge University Collection of Maori Artefacts, Made on Captain Cook's First Voyage', *Journal of the Polynesian Society*, vol. 79, no. 3, September 1970, pp. 305–48.

Simmons, David, 'Maori Dog-Shaped Bowls', *Records of the Auckland Institute and Museum* vol. 21, 18 December 1984, pp. 51–60.

Sissons, Jeffrey, 'From Post to Pillar: God-Houses and Social Fields in Nineteenth-Century Rarotonga', *Journal of Material Culture*, vol. 12, no. 1, 2007, pp. 47–63.

Slack, David, 'A Sense of Time, Place and People: How the Passion to Preserve Rock Art Gathered Momentum', *Te Karaka*, no. 65, 2015.

Stable, Charles, 'Maximum Intervention: Renewal of a Māori Waka by George Nuku and National Museums Scotland', *Journal of Conservation and Museum Studies*, vol. 10, no. 1, pp. 8–18.

Steiner, Christopher B., 'Body Personal and Body Politic. Adornment and Leadership in Cross-Cultural Perspective', *Anthropos*, 1990, pp. 431–45.

Stephens, Māmari, 'The Long Shadow Over Our Marae', *e-Tangata*, 26 November 2017.

Stephens, Murdoch and Shannon Te Ao, 'Unwelcome Guests: Hospitality, Asylum Seekers and Art at the 19th Biennale of Sydney', *Hospitality & Sydney*, vol. 4, no. 2, 2014, pp. 193–202.

Sturm, J., 'The Ngatiponeke Young Maori Club', *Te Ao Hou*, vol. 12, 1955, pp. 29–32.

Sully, Dean, Rosanna Raymond and Anthony Hoete, 'Locating Hinemihi's People', *Journal of Material Culture*, vol. 19, no. 2, 2014.

Suvorova, Olga, 'Forgotten Taonga Māori in Russia: The 1820 Visit of the Bellingshausen-Lazarev Expedition to Queen Charlotte Sound', *Te Kaharoa*, vol. 13, no. 1, 2020.

Tapsell, Paul, 'The Flight of Pareraututu: An Investigation of *Taonga* from a Tribal Perspective', *Journal of the Polynesian Society*, vol. 106, no. 4, 1997, pp. 323–74.

Tarrant, Jocelyn, 'Selwyn Wilson: Artist and Teacher', *Te Ao Hou*, no. 41, December 1962, pp. 15–16.

Tau, Te Maire, 'The Discovery of Islands and the Stories of Settlement', *Thesis Eleven*, vol. 92, no. 1, 2008, pp. 11–28.

Te Awekotuku, Ngahuia, 'Art and the Spirit', *New Zealand Geographic*, 5, January–March 1990.

——, 'Hinemoa', *Journal of Lesbian Studies in Aotearoa/New Zealand*, vol. 5, 2001.

Te Matorohanga, 'The Lore of the Whare Wananga: Wahi II: Te Kauwae-Raro: Upoko III', *Journal of the Polynesian Society*, vol. 22, no. 87, 1913, pp. 107–33.

Tipa, Moana, 'Haumi e! Hui e! Taiki e!: Draw Together Affirm', *Te Karaka*, 2001.

Treadwell, Jeremy, 'Cosmology and Structure: The Tāhuhu in the 19th-Century Whare Māori. *Journal of the Polynesian Society*, vol. 126, no. 1, 2017, pp. 93–122.

Trotter, Michael and Beverley McCulloch, 'Frenchmans Gully and Theo Schoon', *Archaeology in New Zealand*, vol. 43, no. 2, 2000.

Tūrei, Mohi, 'Takarakau', *Journal of the Polynesian Society*, vol. 22, no. 86, 1913, pp. 6–66.

Tyler, Linda, 'From the Collection', *Uninews*, vol. 44, no. 4, 2014, p. 10.

Vincent, Rosemary, 'Selwyn Muru's Paintings Win Wide Acclaim', *Te Ao Hou*, no. 46, March 1964, pp. 25–27.

Waaka, Pania, 'Hei Tiki and Issues of Representation within Contemporary Māori Arts,' *MAI Review* 1, 2007, pp. 1–17.

Wanhalla, Angela, 'Housing Un/healthy Bodies: Native Housing Surveys and Maori Health in New Zealand 1930–45', *Health & History*, vol. 8, no. 1, 2006, pp. 100–20.

Warrior, Robert, 'Native American Scholarship and the Transnational Turn', *Cultural Studies Review*, vol. 15, no. 2, 2009, pp. 119–30.

Watt, Robin, 'James Edward Little's Forged Marquesan Stilt Steps', *Records of the National Museum of New Zealand*, vol. 2, no. 7, 1982, pp. 49–63.

Westra, Ans, 'Ngaruawahia Festival of the Arts', *Te Ao Hou*, no. 46, 1964, pp. 28–29.

Whaanga, Hēmi, David Bainbridge, Michela Anderson, and Korii Scrivener, 'He Matapihi Mā Mua, Mō Muri: The Ethics, Processes, and Procedures Associated with the Digitization of Indigenous Knowledge: The Pei Jones Collection', *Cataloguing & Classification Quarterly*, vol. 53, no. 5–6, 2015, pp. 520–47.

Whatahoro, H. T. and P. Smith, 'Te Kauwae-raro; Ara: nga Korero Tatai o Nehe a nga Ruanuku o te Whare-wānanga o te Tai-Rawhiti', *Journal of the Polynesian Society*, vol. 22, no. 88, 1913, pp. 169–218.

White, Anna-Marie and Robert Leonard, 'George Hubbard: The Hand that Rocked the Cradle', *Reading Room: Politics in Denial*, vol. 8, 2018.

Wilson, Arnold, 'Beginning to Bubble', *Landfall*, no. 185, April 1993, p. 26.

Wilson, John, 'The Maori Struggle for Mana Motuhake', *New Zealand Historic Places*, vol. 30, September 1990.

Winiata, Maharaia, 'The Future of Maori Arts and Crafts', *Te Ao Hou*, no. 19, August 1957, pp. 29–35.

Winks, Robin, 'The Doctrine of Hau-hauism', *Journal of the Polynesian Society*, vol. 62, no. 3, 1953, pp. 209–10.

Witehira, Johnson, 'Mana Matatuhi: A Survey of Maori Engagement with the Written and Printed Word', *Visible Language*, vol. 53, no. 1, 2019, pp. 77–109.

Wood, D., 'Interweaving in New Zealand Culture: A Design Case Study', *Journal of New Zealand Studies*, 17, 2014, pp. 58–72.

Wronska-Friend, Maria, 'From Shells to Ceramic: Colonial Replicas of Indigenous Valuables', *Journal of Museum Ethnography*, no. 28, 2015.

Yoon, Hong-key, 'The Sacred (Tapu) Complex in the Māori Settlements of the East Coast, New Zealand', *Journal of the Polynesian Society*, vol. 87, no. 2, 1978, pp. 115–24.

'Young Maoris Become Skilled Tradesmen', *Te Ao Hou*, no. 55, June 1966, pp. 7–9.

### Theses and research reports

Almeida, Eleanor and Eliza Macdonald, 'Summer Scholar Report 2019–20', University of Auckland, 2020.

Aranui, Amber, 'Te Hokinga Mai o Ngā Tūpuna: Māori Perspectives of Repatriation and the Scientific Research of Ancestral Remains', PhD thesis, Victoria University of Wellington, 2018.

Bennett, Te Arani, 'School Leadership for Māori Succeeding as Māori: A Mataatua Perspective', PhD thesis, University of Waikato, 2018.

Blair, Ngarimu, 'Te Rimu Tahi: Ponsonby Road Master Plan/Māori Heritage Report', Auckland City Council, 2013.

Brown, Deidre, 'Moorehu Architecture', PhD thesis, University of Auckland, 1997.

Carkeek, Te Waari, 'Brief of Evidence', 9 June 2003, Wai 207, Wai 785, Waitangi Tribunal.

Crum, Ambrosia, 'Pataka: A Rare Survivor', Master of Heritage Conservation research report, University of Auckland, 2018.

'Cultural Values Report Prepared by Sophie McGregor and Cathy Begley on Behalf of Te Runanga o Kaikoura in Response to the Awatere Riverbed Activity Guidelines Document', 2014.

Currie, Rosamund, Glynn Davis, Catherine Elliot, Umaporn Kruekamwang, and Raquel Pinto, 'Māori Treasure Box: Museum of London Accession Number Q100, The Thomas Layton Collection', research documentation report, Institute of Archaeology, University College London, n.d.

Ellis, Ngarino, 'Hoe Whakairo, Maori Painted and Carved Paddles 1769–1850', MA thesis, University of Auckland, 1997.

Furey, Louise, 'Hauraki Evidence for the Tauranga Moana Stage II Waitangi Tribunal Claim Hearings', brief of evidence, 0075, Annex A.

Hakiwai, Arapata, 'Te Toi Whakairo o Ngati Kahungunu: The Carving Traditions of Ngati Kahungunu', MA thesis, Victoria University of Wellington, 2003.

——, 'He Mana Taonga He Mana Tangata: Māori Taonga and the Politics of Māori Tribal Identity and Development', PhD thesis, Victoria University of Wellington, 2014.

Hamer, Paul, 'Māori in Australia: An Update from the 2011 Australian Census and the 2011 New Zealand General Election', working paper, 2012, pp. 1–31.

Henderson, James McLeod, 'Ratana', MA thesis, University of New Zealand, Auckland, 1955.

Henry, Lena, 'Te Manaaki o te Marae: The Role of Marae in the Tāmaki Māori Housing Crisis', unpublished report, Building Better Homes, Towns and Cities National Science Challenge, 2018.

Heta, Elisapeta, 'E Moemoeā Tātou ka Taea: Maori Art and Artist Collectives in Aotearoa 1984–2014', MA thesis, University of Auckland, 2015.

Higgins, Rawinia, 'He Tanga Ngutu, He Tuhoetanga te Mana Motuhake o te Ta Moko Wahine: The Identity Politics of Moko Kauae', PhD thesis, University of Otago, 2004.

'How Is Our Maori Population Changing?', Statistics New Zealand, 2015.

Jahnke, Robert, 'He Tataitanga Ahua Toi: The House that Riwai Built, A Continuum of Māori Art', PhD thesis, Massey University, 2006.

Kerekere, Elizabeth, 'Part of the Whānau: The Emergence of Takatāpui Identity – He Whāriki Takatāpui', PhD thesis, Victoria University of Wellington, 2017.

Loader, Arini, 'Origins and Establishment of Ngāti Raukawa', in Daphne Luke and Dr Fiona Te Momo (eds), *He Iti Nā Mōtai: Volume 1*, report commissioned by Te Hono ki Raukawa on behalf of Ngāti Raukawa ki te Tonga as part of the Wai 2200 Porirua ki Manawatū District Inquiry, 2019, pp. 48–131.

Mane-Wheoki, Jonathan, 'Pompidou Centre Paper Version 5', unpublished draft.

——, 'Mataatua: No Wai Tenei Whare Tupuna? A Report on Ngati Awa Claim (Wai 46)', Waitangi Tribunal, March 1993.

Mead, Sidney Moko, et. al, 'Nga Karoretanga o Mataatua Whare. The Wanderings of the Carved House, Mataatua', Research Report No. 2. Whakatāne, 1990.

Melbourne, Hineani, 'Recollections of Parihaka: Mrs. Ngarupoe Kohi (nee Paki) of Otorohunga', Maori studies research essay, 6 February 2011, Auckland University Māori Studies Library.

Ministry of Works and Development, 'Rangi Kapuia Structural Report', file ref. 8/17/4/104, rec. no. 0130, 1987, Heritage New Zealand Pouhere Taonga, Wellington.

Neich, Roger, 'Historical Change in Rotorua Ngati Tarawhai Woodcarving Art', MA thesis, Victoria University of Wellington, 1977.

Ngāi Tahu Strategic Plan 2025.

Ngata, Wayne, 'Te Waiata Tangi a Rangiuia', MA thesis, Massey University, 1993.

O'Regan, Gerard, 'He Ana, He Whakairo: Examining Māori Belief of Place through the Archaeological Context of Rock Art', PhD thesis, University of Auckland, 2016.

Pishief, Elizabeth, 'Augustus Hamilton: Appropriation, Ownership and Authority', MA thesis, Massey University, 1998.

Pishief, Elizabeth and John Adam, *Te Tātua a Riukiuta: Three Kings Heritage Study*, Puketāpapa Local Board, Auckland Council, Auckland, 2015.

Pryor Rodgers, Rata, 'The Connection of Māori to Whales', postgraduate certificate, University of Canterbury, 2017.

Rangihaeata, Kaikapo 'Nga Taonga no te Whenua o Potakataka', unpublished dissertation, University of Auckland, 2010.

Reeves, Jane, 'Maori Prisoners in Dunedin, 1869–1872 and 1879–1881: Exiled for a Cause', BA Hons thesis, University of Otago, 1989.

Sedcole, Bruce, 'A Temple for a Prophet: Rātana Architecture', BArch thesis, Victoria University of Wellington, 1985.

Taiaroa, Taarati, 'The Development of the Māori Art Exhibition: A Typology?' MA thesis, University of Auckland, 2014.

Taituha, Gloria, 'He Kākahu, he Korowai, he Kaitaka, he aha atu anō? The Significance of the Transmission of Māori Knowledge relating to Raranga and Whatu Muka in the Survival of Korowai in Ngāti Maniapoto in a Contemporary Context', MA thesis, Auckland University of Technology, 2014.

Te Awekotuku, Ngahuia and Linda Waimarie Nikora, 'Nga Taonga o Te Urewera. A Report Prepared for the Waitangi Tribunal's Urewera District Inquiry', August 2003 (Wai 894, doc B6).

Te Kanawa, Kahutoi, 'Toi Maramatanga: A Visual Māori Art Expression of Meaning', MA thesis, Auckland University of Technology, 2009.

Te Ratana, Rose, 'Ritual in the Making: A Critical Exploration of Ritual in Te Whare Pora', MA thesis, Auckland University of Technology, 2012.

'Te Roroa Report (Wai 38)', Waitangi Tribunal, 1992.

*Te Tau Ihu o te Waka a Maui: Report on Northern South Island Claims*, Waitangi Tribunal Report, Legislation Direct, Wellington, 2008.

Tu'inukuafe, Rameka, unpublished research paper.

'Turanga Tangata, Turanga Whenua: The Report on the Turanganui a Kiwa Claims', Waitangi Tribunal Report for Wai 814, vol. 2, 2004.

Waata Urlich, Colleen, 'Aho: The Line that Goes Beyond the Present to the Past', MFA thesis, University of Auckland, 2002.

Wagelie, Jennifer, 'Maori Art in America: The Display and Collection History of Maori Art in the United States, 1802–2006', PhD thesis, City University of New York, 2007.

Waitangi Tribunal, *Ko Aotearoa Tenei: A Report into Claims Concerning New Zealand Law and Policy Affecting Māori Culture and Identity* (Wai 262), Legislation Direct, 2011.

Wallace, Patricia, 'Traditional Māori Dress: Rediscovering Forgotten Elements of Pre-1820 Practice', PhD thesis, University of Canterbury, 2002.

Walker, Timothy, 'Te Ropere, 1840–1930', Master's thesis, University of Auckland, 1985.

Watt, Robyn, 'The Fake Maori Artefacts of James Edward Little and James Frank Robieson', PhD thesis, Victoria University of Wellington, 1990.

Whelen, Bill, 'The Patu Pora, or Iron Hand Club, on Display in "Made in New Zealand"', report, Te Papa Tongarewa Archives, 6 September 2005.

Wilkes, Annette, 'Between People and Things: Understanding Violence and Theft in Early New Zealand Transactions', PhD thesis, University of Canterbury, 2013.

Wilkinson, Areta, 'Jewellery as Pepeha: Contemporary Jewellery Practice Informed by Māori Inquiry', PhD thesis, Massey University, 2014.

Wingfield, Chris, 'The Moving Objects of the London Missionary Society: An Experiment in Symmetrical Anthropology', PhD thesis, University of Birmingham, 2012.

Witehira, Johnson Gordon Paul, 'Tārai Kōrero Toi: Articulating a Māori Design Language', PhD thesis, Massey University, 2013.

Worger, William, 'Te Puea Herangi, the Kiingitanga and Waikato', MA thesis, University of Auckland, 1975.

### Legislation and parliamentary debates

Knollys, Captain L. F., *Appendices to the Journals of the House of Representatives*, A-1, no. 38, en. 2, 1881, p. 26.

Mair, Gilbert, 26 September 1873, *Appendices to the Journals of the House of Representatives*, G-2B, no. 1, 1874, p. 1.

Maori Affairs Amendment Act 1974 (1974 No 73), New Zealand Legal Information Institute, pp. 1708–50.

'Petition of Hare Hongi Hika and Others', Reports of Native Affairs Committee, *Appendices to the Journals of the House of Representatives*, I-03, no. 139, 1878, p. 8.

Preece, George, 'History of the Carved House "Mata[a]tua"' *Appendices to the Journal of the House of Representatives*, G-4., 1879, p. 1.

Roberts, Lieut. Col., 17 April 1882, *Appendices to the Journals of the House of Representatives* G-3., 1882, p. 2.

'"The Maori Antiquities Act, 1901" (Suggestions, Correspondence, etc. in Connection with)', *Appendix to the Journals of the House of Representatives*, Session 1, G-08, 1902, p. 4.

Williams, Edward, 11 May 1880, *Appendices to the Journals of the House of Representatives* G-4, no. 4, 1880, p. 3.

### Exhibition catalogues and conference proceedings

Adams, Mark and Areta Wilkinson, *Repatriation*, Two Rooms, Ocula, https://ocula.com/art-galleries/two-rooms/exhibitions/repatriation/

Armstrong, Claire (ed.), *News from Islands*, Campbelltown Arts Centre, Sydney, 2007.

Bader, Hans-Dieter, Peter McCurdy and Jefferson Chapple, *Proceedings of the Waka Moana Symposium 1996: Voyages From the Past To the Future*, New Zealand National Maritime Museum, Te Papa National Services and the New Zealand National Commission of UNESCO, Auckland, 1999.

'Blak Curatorial Exchange', *National Association for the Visual Arts*, 28 August 2018, https://visualarts.net.au/nava-events/2018/blak-curatorial-exchange/

Borell, Nigel and Zara Stanhope, 'Areta Wilkinson', *APT 9: The 9th Asia Pacific Triennial of Contemporary Art*, Queensland Art Gallery and Gallery of Modern Art, Brisbane, 2018.

Brown, Deidre, 'Nga Whare Matauranga Maori: The Recent History of Maori Tertiary Architecture', *Thresholds: Proceedings of Papers from the 16th SAHANZ Conference*, Hobart, 1999, pp. 19–24.

———, 'Clothed not Clad: Maori Woven Architecture', *Celebration: Proceedings of the 22nd Annual Conference of the Society of Architectural Historians of Australia and New Zealand*, Napier, 2005, pp. 59–63.

Clarke, Chanel, 'Repatriation', presentation, University of Auckland, Auckland, 2014.

'Contemporary Māori Art of Aotearoa (New Zealand)', Spirit Wrestler Gallery, www.spiritwrestler.com/catalog/index.php?cPath=5 (site inactive).

'Current: Contemporary Art from New Zealand and the Pacific, 23 June–30 July 2011', www.octobergallery.co.uk/exhibitions/2011cur/index.shtml

'First Nations Curators Exchange', Australia Council for the Arts, www.australiacouncil.gov.au/international/first-nations-curators-exchange/ (link inactive).

Fitzgerald, Tanya, 'Jumping the Fences: Māori Women's Resistance to Missionary Schooling in Northern New Zealand 1823–1835', *International Standing Conference for the History of Education*, 2000.

Gathercole, Peter, 'The Maori Collection at the Cambridge University Museum of Archaeology and Anthropology', *Taonga Maori Conference*, Department of Internal Affairs, Wellington, 1990.

Gough, Julie (ed.), *Testing Ground*, Salamanca Arts Centre, Hobart, 2013.

Hīroa, Te Rangi [Peter Buck], 'The Taranaki Maoris: Te Whiti and Parihaka', Te Aute College Students' Association Conference, Napier, 1897.

Hunia, M., 'Memories of the Bay of Plenty Earthquake 1987', *20th Anniversary Earthquake Memories Project*, Sir James Fletcher Kawerau Museum, 2007.

*International Exhibition 1862: Official Catalogue of the Industrial Art Department*, Truscott, Son and Simmons, London, c.1862.

Kaan, Simon, 'Curatorial Comment', *Akona ki ngā Rekerekē: Learning From the Knee*, Rūnanga o Ngai Tahu and Burrinja, Dandenong Ranges Community Cultural Centre, Melbourne, 2006.

Kaeppler, Adrienne, 'To Attempt some New Discoveries in that Vast Unknown Tract', paper presented at Cook's Pacific Encounters symposium, National Museum of Australia, 28 July 2006.

'Ko te Pukapuka o te Tiriti o Kohimarama: Orakei, Akarana, 1889' (Cover title. Account of the proceedings of the hui at Ōerākei marae, Kohimarama, 27–29 March 1889), Auckland, 1889.

Mane-Wheoki, Jonathan, 'Out on His Own: Ralph Hotere and the Māori Art Movement', in Roger Taberner and Ronald Brownson (eds), *Hotere: Seminar Papers from Into the Black*, Auckland Art Gallery, Auckland, 1998, pp. 43–55.

———, *Te Puāwai o Ngāi Tahu: A New Flowering of Ngāi Tahu Art*, catalogue, Christchurch Art Gallery, 2003.

Mane-Wheoki, Jonathan, Felicity Milburn and Megan Tamati-Quennell, 'Curatorial Summary', *Te Puāwai o Ngāi Tahu: Twelve Contemporary Ngāi Tahu Artists*, Christchurch Art Gallery, Christchurch, 2003.

Mason, Ngahiraka, 'Five Māori Painters', Auckland Art Gallery, Auckland, 2014.

Mason, Ngahiraka, Ngarino Ellis and Kahu Te Kanawa, *Pūrangiaho: Seeing Clearly*, Auckland Art Gallery, Auckland, 2001.

McLintock, A. H. (ed.), *National Centennial Exhibition of New Zealand Art Catalogue*, Department of Internal Affairs, Wellington, 1940.

*Musée des Missions Évangéliques: Exposition Universelle, Paris, 1867*, Grassart, Paris, c.1867.

Ngata, Apirana, 'Rauru Nui a Toi', lecture 4, Porourangi School of Maori Culture, 1944.

Nin, Buck and Baden Pere (eds), *New Zealand Maori Culture and the Contemporary Scene*, catalogue, Canterbury Museum, Christchurch, 1966.

Potiki, Roma, 'Getting Brown in Hyper Town', in Mark Amery, Deidre Brown and Jonathan Mane-Wheoki (eds), *TechnoMaori*, City Gallery and Pataka Porirua, Wellington and Lower Hutt, 2001.

Ramsden, Irihapeti, Christian Lyndon and Keri Kaa, *Whakamamae*, catalogue produced with the support of the Maori and South Pacific Arts Council, Wellington, 1998.

Raymond, Rosanna, with Charmaine 'Ilaiu, Shigeyuki Kihara and Karamia Müller, artists' panel, Pacific Arts Association Conference, Musee du Quai Branly, Paris, 7 July 2007.

'Stop Making Sense: Documents', City Gallery, Wellington, 1995.

*Taonga Maori: Treasures of the New Zealand Maori People*, Australian Museum, Sydney, 1989.

Te Awekotuku, Ngahuia, 'He Reka Ano: Same Sex Lust and Loving in the Ancient Maori World', paper presented to Outlines Conference: Lesbian and Gay History in Aotearoa, Lesbian and Gay Archives of New Zealand, Wellington, 2003.

'Te Hau-ki-Turanga', brochure, Te Papa, Wellington, c.1993.

*Te Whakatuwheratanga o Te Tumu Herenga Waka, 6 Tihema 1986, Poneke, Te Whare Wananga o Wikitoria*, Maori Studies Department, Victoria University of Wellington, Wellington, 1986.

Te Ua, Te Kani, *Echoes of the Pa: Proceedings of the Tairaawhiti Association*, Tairaawhiti Association, Gisborne, 1932.

Tipa, Moana, *Rukutia! Rukutia!*, Te Rūnanga o Ngāi Tahu and Christchurch Arts Festival, Christchurch, 1999.

Trapani, Paola and Johnson Witehira, 'The Whakarare Typeface Project: When Culture-Specific Visual Design Brings Elements of Universal Value', *The Virtuous Circle Cumulus Conference*, Milan, 3–7 June 2015, pp. 1–20.

Turnbull, Paul, 'Encounters with Wondrous Things: The Historical Significance of the Cook–Forster Collection', *Cook's Pacific Encounters symposium*, 28 July 2006, National Museum of Australia, Canberra.

## Video and sound recordings

*Aku Mahi Whatu Māori: My Art of Māori Weaving*, 1978, F15003, Ngā Taonga Sound and Vision.

'Interview with Pine Taiapa Talking About Hinerupe Meeting House', 1965, recording 40734, Ngā Taonga Sound and Vision.

'Nathan Pohio Documenta 14 – Whakatau', Te Runanga of Ngai Tahu Facebook, www.facebook.com/watch/?v=10155304917217873

Maihi, Toi Te Rito, 'The Meaning of Cloaks', 5 June 2012, www.youtube.com/watch?v=9mKiKYvcmpw

Matchitt, Para and Maia Matchitt, *Kohia ko Taikaka Anake*, video, Simon Nixon Productions, 1990.

McKenzie, Karen and Peter Mayo, 'Tapu Te Ranga – Whare Māori – Episode Excerpt', https://vimeo.com/54431474

Meekings-Stewart, Pamela, 'A Cat Among the Pigeons', documentary, 1992, NZ on Screen.

Muru, Selwyn, *Te Hononga: The Confluence: From Stone Adze to Chainsaw*, Muru Art Film/Television New Zealand, 1990.

'Paitangi Ostick', Māoritube, www.maoritube.co.nz/people/paitangi-ostick-a-woman-ta-moko-artist-carver-painter-weaver-and-song-writer/

'Pine Taiapa – Porourangi Meeting House, Waiomatatini', recording 40757; 40758, 1965, Ngā Taonga Sound and Vision.

'Pine Taiapa – Tikitiki Church', recording 40736, 1965, Ngā Taonga Sound and Vision.

'Pine Taiapa Interview Regarding Rongomaitapui Meeting House, Te Araroa 1965', recording 40733, 1965, Ngā Taonga Sound and Vision.

'Pine Taiapa IV. Talk on Rongomaianiwaniwa Meeting House', recording 40864, 1965, Ngā Taonga Sound and Vision.

Skinner, Damian, Barney Christie oral history interview, 29 January 2003, CA000709/001/0006, Te Papa Tongarewa, Wellington.

'Tāhere Tikitiki – The Making of a Māori Canoe', documentary television series, National Film Unit, 1974.

Te Awekotuku, Ngahuia and Melody Thomas, 'BANG! Season 2, Episode 6: Takatapui', Radio New Zealand, 2 June 2018, www.rnz.co.nz/programmes/bang/story/2018651794/bang-season-2-episode-6-takatapui

'The Oldman Collection – Maori Art in London', NZ Film Unit, n.d., www.youtube.com/watch?v=mlststSsU-U

Toogood, Chas, *Koha: Ramai Hayward*, Television New Zealand, 1989.

*Waka: The Awakening Dream*, Nimrod Films, 1990.

*Whare Maori*, series 1, episode 7, Scottie Productions, 2011.

## Newspapers and other news sources

*Auckland Star*

*Bay of Plenty Times*

*Daily Alta California*

*Daily News*

*Daily Southern Cross*

*Gisborne Herald*

*Illustrated London News*

*Maori Women's Welfare League Newsletter*

*New Zealand Home Journal*

*New Zealand Times*

*Northern Advocate*

*NZ Listener*

*Pacific Way*

*Parramatta Advertiser*

*Poverty Bay Herald*

Radio New Zealand, www.radionz.co.nz

*Strand Magazine*, January–June 1891

Stuff, www.stuff.co.nz

*Sunday Star*

*Taranaki Herald*

Te Ao Māori News, www.teaonews.co.nz

*Te Paki-o-Matariki*

*The Australian*

*The New Zealand Herald*

*The Press*

The Spinoff, www.thespinoff.co.nz

*The Sun*

*Wanganui Chronicle*

*Weekly News*

## Websites

Art, Life, TV, Etc., http://cherylbernstein.blogspot.com

Auckland Live, www.aucklandlive.co.nz

Australian Museum, https://australianmuseum.net.au

British Library, www.bl.uk

British Museum, www.britishmuseum.org

Britomart, https://britomart.org

Charles and Janine Williams, www.charlesjaninewilliams.com

Christchurch City Libraries, http://christchurchcitylibraries.com

Creative New Zealand, www.creativenz.govt.nz

Eke Panuku Development Auckland, www.ekepanuku.co.nz

Evergreen State College, www.evergreen.edu

FestPac Hawaii, https://festpac-hawaii2020.org (link inactive)

Heritage New Zealand, www.heritage.org.nz

Hundertwasser Art Centre, www.hundertwasserartcentre.co.nz

Johnson Witehira, www.johnsonwitehira.studio

Mataaho Collective, www.mataahocollective.com

Ministry of Culture and Heritage, www.mch.govt.nz

Moana Tipa & Associates, www.moanatipa.com

New Zealand History, nzhistory.govt.nz

New Zealand on Screen, www.nzonscreen.com

Ngāi Tahu, https://ngaitahu.iwi.nz

Ngāti Toa, www.ngatitoa.iwi.nz

Ngāti Tūmatakōkiri First Encounter 375, https://sites.google.com/3ml.nz/ngati-tumatakokiri/home

Polished Pāua, https://polishedpaua.tumblr.com

Rongowhakaata Iwi Trust, http://rongowhakaata.iwi.nz

SA Memory, State Library of South Australia, www.samemory.sa.gov.au

Scape Public Art, www.scapepublicart.org.nz

Smithsonian Libraries, http://www.sil.si.edu

South Sea Art, www.southseaart.co.nz

Spirit Wrestler Gallery, www.spiritwrestler.com (link inactive)

Tahaa, www.tahaa.co.nz

Tapu-Te-Ranga Marae, www.taputeranga.Māori.nz (link inactive)

Te Ana Ngāi Tahu Māori Rock Art, www.teana.co.nz

Te Ara – the Encyclopedia of New Zealand, https://teara.govt.nz

Te Ātinga, www.teatinga.com

Te Hau Kāinga: The Māori Home Front, Campbell, Emma, www.maorihomefront.nz

Te Papa Tongarewa Museum of New Zealand blog, https://blog.tepapa.govt.nz

Te Papa Tongarewa Museum of New Zealand collections, https://collections.tepapa.govt.nz

Te Papa Tongarewa Museum of New Zealand, https://tepapa.govt.nz

Te Puni Kōkiri, www.tpk.govt.nz

Te Rā: The Māori Sail, https://teraa.co.nz

Te Rūnanga o Ngāi Tahu, https://ngaitahu.iwi.nz

The Big Idea, www.thebigidea.nz

The Dowse Art Museum, http://dowse.org.nz

*Pantograph Punch*, www.pantograph-punch.com

The Poi Room, www.thepoiroom.co.nz

Toi Iho, www.toiiho.co.nz

Toi Māori Aotearoa, www.maoriart.org.nz

Tyson Campbell, www.tysoncampbell.info

Wairau Māori Art Gallery, https://en.wairaumaoriartgallery.co.nz

Waitangi Tribunal, www.waitangitribunal.govt.nz

# KUPUTOHU — INDEX

Italicised page numbers refer to captions of illustrations. An endnote is indicated by a page number and 'n', followed by the note number, then by square brackets enclosing the page number of the reference in the text.

### A

Adams, Mark
  photogram works (with Wilkinson), 182, *183*
  *Whakapapa V* (with Wilkinson), *185*
adornments
  early styles, 149–50, *151*, 210
  in museum collections, 143
  Pacific antecedents of, 148–49, *151*, 154
  regional differences in, 149
  significance of, 143, 180–81
  wharawhara and, 145
  worn today, 143
  *see also* aurei; breastplates; ear adornments; head adornments; moko; neck adornments; skin painting
adornments, materials
  black ribbon, *153*
  bone, 148, *153*, 153, 162, 164–65, *165*, 268
  feathers, 148, *172*, 172, 278, *279*
  pounamu, 155, *162*, 164, 167, *168*, 172, 186, 222, *352*
  shell, *151*, *154*, 154
  stone, 153
  teeth, 148, *151*, *153*, 154, *155*, 222, *278*, *352*
  whalebone, *151*, 153
Adsett, Sandy
  as art teacher/advisor, 397, 399
  cultural identity, 404–5
  mangōpare design, 529
  *Mataora: The Living Face*, 12, 405, *464*, 464–65
advice to Māori artists, 532–33
Allen, Chadwick, 511, 517
Anderson, Atholl, 24, 138–39, 287, 290, 291
Angas, George French
  *Children at the boiling springs*, *94*
  drawings by, 32, 92, 366
  *Honi [Hone] Heke and Patuone*, *253*
  *House of Iwikau, brother of Te Heuheu*, *118*
  *Pepepe Church missionary station*, *231*
  *Poahu and E Koti*, *173*, 175
  portrait style of, 212
  *Suit of armour*, *268*
  *Te Heuheu & Hiwikau*, *92*
  *Te Moanaroa (Stephen). Te Awaitaia (William Naylor)*, *92*
  *Tukupoto at Kaitote, Tewherowhero's pah*, *109*
  *Whatas, or patukas*, *114*
Aniwaniwa Visitor Centre, *470*, 470, 471, 507
Aoraki (ancestor), 21–22
*Aotea* (waka), 22, 100, 263
Aotearoa Moananui a Kiwa Weavers, 101
Apanui, Wepiha, 54, 272
Araiteuru Marae, Dunedin, 425
Arapere, Reweti
  *Poropiti*, 457
archaeology
  excavations, 70, 74, 164
  Kauri Point finds, 43, 175, *178*, 178
  practices, 70, *71*, 216
  Wairau Bar finds, 70, *153*, 154, 186, 540n15[43]
Archey, Gilbert, 27
architecture, Māori
  ancestral narratives, 44
  Christianity influence, 237–40, 256–57
  colonisation impacts, 275, 290, 303, 322, 371
  Māori architects, 467, 469, 471–72, 474
  Rātana movement and, 376, 379, 382–83, 385
  Ringatū movement and, 311, 313–17
  role of tohunga whakairo, 41, 277, 424–25
  twentieth-century regulations, 37, 363, 371, 373, 423–25
  *see also* pātaka; urban marae; whare; whare whakairo
Arlidge, Clive, 397, 399
art history *see* European art history; Māori art history
art institutions in Aotearoa
  art galleries, 441–42, 532
  bicultural practice in, 441, 442, 447, 463, 512
  indigenisation of, 459, 465
  Māori advisory boards, 341
  Pākehā domination of, 405
  *see also* exhibitions of Māori art in Aotearoa
art writing, 465, 532
arts and crafts advisory service
  advisors, 398–99, 401–2, 525, 535, 561n37[401], 561n59[405]
  *Arts and Crafts of the Maori* (documentary), 408, 410
  *The Arts of the Maori* (book), 402, 535
Ashton, Arapeta, 102
Aspin, Clive, 192
Athfield, Ian, *109*, 472
aurei, *143*, *171*, 171, 267, *268*, 290, 353, 547n72[171]
Awanui (ancestor), 47
Awatere, Donna, 511

### B

Baker, Erena, 519
Banks, Joseph
  acquisitions, *196*, 208, 350
  and the brass patu, 224, *225*
  trading and warfare, 221–22, 550n5[224]
  observations recorded by, 76, 162, 175, 208
  Tupaia and, *227*, 551n3[226]
Barclay, Barry, 208
Barraud, Charles
  *Interior of Rangiatea Church at Otaki*, *236*
Barrett, Te Arani, *190*
Barry, James
  *Rev Thomas Kendall and the Maori chiefs Hongi and Waikato*, *82*
Beasley, Harry, 345, 347
Belich, James, 345
Bennet, George, 243, *251*
Bernstein, Cheryl, 478
Best, Elsdon, 87, 96, 175, 200
Binney, Judith, 241, 281
Birch, Israel Tangaroa
  *Ara-i-te-uru*, *456*, 458
  whakairo in Massey University wharekai, *109*
Bloomfield, William, 467
Borell, Nigel, 341, 456, 459, 516, *522*
breastplates, 26, 149–50, *151*, 154
Brennan, Ramari, 425
Brickell, Barry, 525
Brightwell, Taupuruariki (Ariki), 435
Brown, Cath, 397, *399*, 399, 459, 525
Brown, Deidre, 211, 337
Brunt, Peter, 442
Buck, Peter *see* Te Rangi Hīroa (Peter Buck)
Buller, Walter, *117*, 215, 334, 353
Busby, Hekenukumaingāiwi (Hec), 28, 36, *37*, 38, *39*
Buxton, Thomas Fowell, 244

### C

Campbell, Donna, *86*
Cape, Peter
  *New Zealand Painting Since 1960*, 420
Carroll, James, 333, 334, 557n1[333]
carvers
  contemporary artists, 61, 425, 490–91, 515–16
  customary community support for, 55
  individual styles, 66, 68
  innovative transferable skills of, 56–57, *59*, 112, 121, 256
  koha/payment, 54–55, 57, 100, 263, 535, 541n36[55]
  long-handled toki experts, 370, *386*, 386
  Mātaatua carvers on Ringatū whare, 311, 314
  Ngāti Porou carving lineage, 9
  numbers of in nineteenth century, 66, 191, 535
  rangatira as, 47, 49, 179
  tohunga whakairo (master carvers), 41, 56, 62, 425
  tools, 186, 278, 300, 370, 386

training, 51, 53, 57, 60, 62
unidentified artists, *66*, *66*, 68
women carvers, 28, 191–92, 537
work of, 51–52, 54–55, 57, 277, 535
*see also* whakairo artworks; whare whakairo
Catholic Church
exchange as a conversion tactic, 240
missionary attitudes to Māori art, 231, 233, *239*, 240
Ōtūmoetai Catholic chapel, *234*
Second Vatican Council (1962–1965), 233, 247
Society of Mary, 230
Vatican museum collections, 247
Whaiora Catholic marae, Ōtara, 128, 424
whare raupō chapel, *239*, 240
Chatham Islands, *29*, 29, *132*, 133, 215
Chazal, Antoine
*Toi, Roi des sauvages. Sauvage* (after Lejeune), 213, *214*, 549n29[213]
Cheeseman, Thomas, 353
Chitham, Karl, 341
Church Missionary Society (CMS)
attitudes to Māori art, 238–39, 240
chapels on the East Coast, 256–57, *257*
churches, *235*, *236*, *237*, 237–39, 256–57
exchange as a conversion tactic, 240–41
first mission stations, 230–31, 241, 281
gifts for patrons in Britain, 240, *241*
influence on colonial policy, 244
Māori converts, 241, 256
*Missionary Papers*, 250, *251*
museum collection in London, 240, 243, 245–46, *248*, 250, 552n68[246]
in New Zealand Wars, 303
waka chapels, *231*, 231
*see also* Kendall, Thomas; missionaries; Yate, William
Clarke, Cuthbert Charles, 104
Clarke, George, 478
Clayton, Te Hikapuhi Poihipi, 191
cloaks
archaeological finds, 74, 95
attachments, 74, 81, 91, 95–96
changing fashions, 87, 96–97, 277
as exchanges for waka, 31–32, 100, *262*, 263
exhibiting, 102
in gifting ceremonies, 104, *105*
incorporating text, *286*, 287, *288*, 288
kākahu raranga pūputu, 106, *107*
kōnunu, 106
and mana, 74, 96–97, 104, 261, 290
materials, 77, 80
museum collections, 102, 106
pihepihe, 74, 91
political value of, 98, 100
rāpaki, 91, 97, 277
symbolic role of, 97–98, 260–63
takitahi design, 21–22
and tangihanga practices, 98, 104, *105*, 260
*see also* kahu huruhuru; kahu kurī; kaitaka; korowai; patterns; whatu
clothing
adoption of European dress, *96*, 97, 234, 277, 290
changing fashions, 87, 96, 97

contemporary Māori clothing, 529–31
Coates, Isaac
*Cootia. Rauparaha's head wife*, 279
*Rangihaeata*, *172*, 279
*Rauparaha. Chief Capiti*, 279
Cole, Douglas, 219
Colenso, William, 76–77, 256, 284
collectives, artistic, 261, 458, 463, 519
Collinson, Thomas Bernard
*Huts and Waikanae Church*, 235
Colonial Museum, 214, 216, 334
*see also* Dominion Museum; Te Papa Tongarewa
colonisation
assimilationist policies, 219, 337
European values, 97, 192, 198, 234
historical amnesia and, 511
impacts on art, 5, 198–99, 205, 275, 290, 534–35
land alienation, 118, 127, 139, 205, 214, 215, 303, 333, 534–35
mass European immigration, 303
racial hierarchy and, 216, 247
resistance to, 5, 323, 509, 538n11[5]
*see also* decolonisation
Cook, James
expeditions of, 210
in *The Lighthouse / Tū Whenua-a-Kura* sculpture, 429, *431*
taonga collected by expedition members, 75, 97, *123*, 123, 164, *165*, 208, *209*, 211, 353, 542n64[96]
taonga distributed to recipients in England, 208–9
trading and warfare, 221–22
Tupaia and, 221, 226
*see also* Banks, Joseph; Forster, Johann Reinhold and Georg; Parkinson, Sydney
Cooper, Whina, 192, *416*, 416
Coote, Jeremy, 224
Corneal, Paerau, 525
Cotton, Shane
*Eden to Ohaeawai*, 452, *455*
exhibition at Wairau Māori Art Gallery, 483
*Lying in the Black Land*, 452, *455*
*Maunga*, *415*, 429
paintings in *Pūrangiaho*, 448
*Stelliferous Biblia XVI*, 452
and the Urban Generation, 438–39
*Whakapiri atu te whenua*, 440
works in exhibitions overseas, 513
Cowan, James, 329
Cracknell, Tryphena, 536–37
Crafts Council of New Zealand, 477
Creative New Zealand (CNZ)
funding for delegations, 515, 566n23[515]
marae rejuvenation, 61
residency programmes, 521–22, 566n32[521], 566n33[521]
Te Manu Ka Tau programme, 517, 522
Toi Iho trademark, 128–29, 505, *507*, 507
Crozet, Julien, 175, 278
cultural property, 477, *505*, 505, *507*, 507, 515, 547n50[141]
curatorial practice, 243, 335, 340, 441, 447, 450, 459, 465, 522, 532

**D**
Dansey, Harry, 397, 403
Davidson, Janet, 486
Davis, Te Aue, 91
de Sainson, Louis Auguste
*Neu Seeland. Hauptling von Houa-Houa*, *175*
de Surville, Jean François Marie, 162, 210, 221, *222*
Declaration of Independence *see* He Whakaputanga o te Rangatiratanga o Nu Tirene
Declaration on the Importance and Value of Universal Museums, 353
decolonisation, 6, 343, 431, 479, 493, 501, 511
dendroglyphs *see* rākau momori
Denton, Frank James
*Portrait of an unidentified Maori woman*, *282*
design-TRIBE, 474
Diamond, Jo, 494
Dippie, Owen
*Mural of Hokimoana Tawa* (with Iti), *433*, 435
Dominion Museum, 329, *336*, 338
*see also* Colonial Museum, Te Papa Tongarewa
Donne, T. E., 57
drawings by early Māori, 296, *297*, 493
Duff, Roger, 139
Dumoutier, Pierre-Marie Alexandre, 212–13
Dunn, Mike
*huri, ka huri, huri noa* (with Whaitiri), 449

**E**
ear adornments
kahu raurēkau, 172
kākā pōria, *162*, 164, *172*, 276
kapeu, *143*, *270*, *352*, 353
kaukau, 15, 550n44[215]
kuru mahora, 172
kuru papa, 172
kuru pounamu, 172, 222
mako pounamu, *155*
niho tangata, 222, *278*
objects introduced by Europeans, 175
pau, 172
pōhoi, 172, 278, *279*
tapa (aute), *75*, 75, 76, *143*, 172
whole bird wings, *173*
whole birds, 172, *177*
Earle, Augustus
*Amoko, Eana, Hepee*, 282
drawing of moko artist, 190
*Meeting of the artist and Hongi*, 243
*A tabood store-house*, 299
*Village of Parkuni*, 153
Edmunds, Bethany Matai, 488
Ellis, Elizabeth (née Mountain)
as art teacher/advisor, 397
documenting toi moko in Britain, 351
*Puke Huia*, 404
*Te Rawhiti Rakaumangamanga*, 404
on Te Waka Toi, 521
Ensor, Kura
'Tania' dress, *529*, 529
Eruera, Hemi, 38
European art history, 6, 7–8, 247
European modernists, 317, 391, 393, 395

European voyagers in eighteenth century, 210
*see also* Cook, James; de Surville, Jean
François Marie
exhibitions of Māori art in Aotearoa
    1865 New Zealand Exhibition, 217
    1906 New Zealand International
        Exhibition, 57, 217, *386*, 386
    1940 *National Centennial Exhibition of
        New Zealand Art*, 391
    1958 exhibition at Adult Education Centre,
        393
    1963 Maori Festival of the Arts, 395,
        561n16[395]
    1966 Festival of Maori Arts, 397
    Ahurei, 459
    *Akona ki ngā Rekereke*, 462, 563n30[462]
    *Ara Mai Nuku*, 526
    articulating continuity, 447, 449–51, 456
    *Aukaha*, 464
    *Aukaha Kia Kaha*, 460–61, 563n24[460]
    *Bottled Ocean 2118*, 516
    *Choice!*, 441–42, 512
    *Contemporary Maori Painting and
        Sculpture*, 396, 464
    *Cross-Pollination*, 512
    curatorial practice, 418, 438, 441, *443*, 457,
        463–64, 465, 532
    *E Ngā Uri Whakatupu Weaving Legacies*,
        102
    *The Earth Looks upon Us*, 480
    *Feathers and Fibre*, 102, *103*
    *Haumi e! Hui e! Taiki e!*, 461, 563n26[461]
    *Hiko! New Energies in Māori Art*, 446, 447,
        449–50
    *Kahu Ora – Living Cloaks*, 102
    Kāi Tahu Arts Festival, 460
    *Karanga Karanga*, 421
    *Kiss the Baby Goodbye*, 445
    *Ko Rongowhakaata*, 340, 463
    *Kohia ko Taikaka Anake*, *438*, 438–41, *439*
    *Korurangi*, 443
    *Kurawaka*, 525
    *Mana Tiriti*, 443
    *New Zealand Maori Culture and the
        Contemporary Scene*, 395, 397, 402–3,
        463–64
    *Māori Moving Image*, 480
    *Ngā Mahi o te Aka o Tūwhenua*, 463
    Ngāpuhi Festival, 459
    *Oceania*, 485
    *Old Lines/New Stock*, 445
    *Pacific Sisters*, 530
    *Paemanu: Nohoaka Toi*, 463
    *Paemanu: Tauraka Toi*, 463
    *Pu Manawa*, 439
    *Puhi Ariki*, *483*, 483
    *Pūrangiaho*, *448*, 450–52, 456
    'remembering exhibitions', 463–64,
        563n34[463]
    *Rukutia! Rukutia!*, 460, 563n23[460]
    Shane Cotton exhibition, 483
    *Te Aho Tapu*, 102, *103*
    *Te Maori*, 8, 12, 102, 339, 340, 357, 512
    Te Papa Tongarewa iwi exhibitions, 463
    *Te Puāwai o Ngāi Tahu*, 460, 461–62,
        563n28[461]
    *Te Ringa Rehe*, 101

    *Te Whanga a Reipae*, 483
    *Techno Māori*, *437*, *448*, 450
    *Tino Rakatirataka*, 460
    *Tohu Whakatipu*, 483
    *Toi Māori*, 102
    *Toi Tū Toi Ora*, 456–59
    *Whakamamae*, 421
    *Whatu Aho Rua*, 443–44
    *Whenua Hou*, 526
exhibitions of Māori art overseas
    1851 Great Exhibition, 217, 247
    1867 Paris Exposition Universelle, *244*,
        244–45, *248*
    1925 Vatican Missionary Exposition, 247
    in art galleries, 489, 491, 493
    Asia Pacific Triennial (APT), 494, 516
    *Current*, 489
    *documenta*, 517, 519
    *ethKnowcentrix*, 489
    *Fusion*, 513
    Gwangju Biennale, 516
    *Headlands*, 445
    Honolulu Biennale, 516
    *Indigenous Histories*, 516
    International Casablanca Biennale, 516
    *Les Magiciens de la Terre*, 512
    *Mana Māori*, 491
    *Manawa*, 513
    *Māori*, 486–87
    in museums, 485–89
    *Oceania*, 491, 493
    *Pacific Encounters*, 489, 490
    Pacific Wave festivals, 494
    *Pasifika Styles*, 102, 489, 490, 564n18[489]
    *Power and Taboo*, 488, 490
    *'Primitivism' in 20th Century Art*, 512
    *Sakahàn*, 517
    Sydney Biennale, 517
    *Taonga Maori*, 494
    *Toi Toi Toi*, 566n31[519]
    Venice Biennale, 493, 512–13, 516
    *Whakaahua*, 495

## F

Fairclough, John
    *Binary Strings* (with Lander), *448*, 450
fakes, 345, *347*, 347, *348*, 349
feathers
    in cloaks, 81, 95
    as ear adornments, 172, 278, *279*
    as head adornments, *143*, 148–49, *173*, 175,
        *177*, 284
    Heke's 'collar', 242, *252*, 252
    huia feathers, 77, 175, *177*
    puhi on waka taua, *30*, 30
    red feathers, 95, 148, 161, 542n55[95],
        547n49[161]
Finney, Ben, 33, 36
Firth, Raymond, 104
flags
    Aboriginal, *495*
    of Kīngitanga, *324*, 324, *326*
    of Pai Mārire, 324, *326*, 329
    symbols on, 329
    at tangihanga, *105*
    of Te Kooti, *326*, 329
    Tino Rangatiratanga flag, *329*, 329, *330–31*
    of the United Tribes, 292, *324*, 324

    Union Jack, 231, 242, 252, 329
    of Wī Tako Ngātata, *324*
Fleming, John
    *A World History of Art*, 8
Flintoff, Brian, 277
Foley, Jane (Hēni Pore), *324*
Fomison, Tony, 139, 422
Ford, John Bevan
    as art teacher/advisor, 397, 399
    at British Museum, 486, 488
    *Untitled*, 487
Forster, Johann Reinhold and Georg, 87, *144*,
    155, *278*, 542n32[87]
Fowler, Leo, 214, 337
Fraser, Jacqueline
    *Bi-Polar* (with Robinson), 516
    and the Urban Generation, 438–39
French explorers, 210, 221
Friedlander, Marti
    *Moko* (book, with King), 159–60
Fuller, Alfred W. F., 334, 347
funerary practices *see* tangihanga and burial
    practices

## G

Garneau, David, 509, 517, 523
Gehry, Frank, 472
gender and sexuality depictions in art
    censoring of, *117*, 117, *192*, *194*, 198
    fertility and procreation, *117*, 117, 193, *196*,
        *197*, 198
    gendered carving, *190*, 193, *196*, *197*, 199
    takatāpui and heterosexual activity,
        179–80, 189, 193, *194*, *195*, 198, 548n1[189]
gender roles
    complementarity of customary roles, 189,
        262–63
    European heteropatriarchy, 97, 189, 234–35
    European values in education, 192, 198,
        234–35, 548n16[192]
    in peacemaking, 259–60
    in production of art, 92, 189–91, 198–99,
        200, 262
George, Darryn
    *Konae Korero #2*, 458
    *The Lambs' Book of Life (Folder Wall)*, 429
    *New Generation*, 446
    painting strategies, 449
Giglioli, Enrico Hillyer, *170*, *352*, 353
Gilfillan, John Alexander
    *Honi [Hone] Heke* (after Merrett), 255
Gilsemans, Isaack
    sketches of waka, 24, 84
    *A view of the Murderers' Bay*, *206*, 207–8
Goldie, Charles
    *The Arrival of the Maoris* (with Steele), 36
    *The Calm Close of Valour's Various Day*, 284
Gombrich, Ernst
    *The Story of Art*, 8
Gordine, Stacy
    *Hei Tiki Ruatepupuke*, 11
    *Mako Pounamu Earrings*, 155
Grace, Patricia
    *Wahine Toa* (book, with Kahukiwa), 420
Graham, Brett
    *Aniwaniwa* (with Rakena), 516
    *Aukaha* exhibition, 464
    *Kahukura*, 443

*Maungārongo ki te Whenua Maungārongo ki te Tangata*, 322
residencies, 522
*U.F.O.B* (with Rakena), 512–13, *513*
and the Urban Generation, 438, 440
*Wasteland*, 509
Graham, Charlotte, 522
Graham, Fred
as art teacher/advisor, 397, 399
and 'the class of '66', 464
*Whiti te Ra*, 396
Grant, June Northcroft, 513
Grant, Lyonel, 127, 488, 522
Grant, T. J.
watercolour of pou, 198
Gray, John
City to Sea Bridge (with R. Thompson and Matchitt), 472
Great Exhibition, London (1851), 217, 247
Green, Ayesha
*Mum (May 1985)*, 458
greenstone *see* pounamu
Gregg, Kirsty, 449
Grey, George, 15, 157, 171, 215–16, 423, 550n44[215]
Grimwood, Andrew
*Flights and Fancies* (illustrated by Haddon), 406

## H

Haast, Julius von, 214, 353, 550n34[214]
Haast's eagle, 137
Haddon, Edward Oliver *see* Haddon, Oriwa Tahupōtiki
Haddon, Olivia
*Te Rongopai*, 446, 447, *448*, 449
Haddon, Oriwa Tahupōtiki, 406
in 1940 exhibition, 391
painting of arrival of Turi (with Hay-Campbell), 406, *407*, 561n6[406]
*Signing of the Treaty of Waitangi*, 406, *407*
Hadfield, Octavius, 235, 238, 553n24[266]
Haeata Collective
*Hineteiwaiwa te Whare*, 11
and *Mana Tiriti* exhibition, 443
hairstyles, *96*, *144*, 175, *175*, *178*
haka, 207, 256, 368
hākari
*Feast at the Bay of Islands* (Oliver), *110*
kai haukai, 291
stages for display of, 544n11[104]
tahuaroa, 104, 543n4[104]
Hakiwai, Arapata, 341, 342, 486
Hall, Xoë
Wakefield Street i-Site mural, *435*
Hamilton, Augustus
*Art Workmanship of the Maori Race* (Hamilton), 370, 386
roles of, 217, 219, 333, 370
Hamilton, Harold, 369, 376
Hanan, Ralph, 338
Hansard, Katarina (née Ihaia), 561n2[408]
Hansen, Eugene
*Some Kind of Vague Landscape*, 446, 449
Hapeta, Dean, 415
harakeke, 2–3, 38, 77, 80, 97, 127
Harawira-Havili, Anikaaro, 191
Harrison, Ngahuia, 480

Harrison, Pakaariki (Paki), 128–29
carving work, 128, 545n1[128]
and Ivan Mercep, 424–25
on manaia, 46
photograph of, *129*
and Pine Taiapa, 61, 128
Tāne-nui-ā-rangi, *4*, *9*, 424–25
on Tangaroa, 43
on waka taua, 29
Harvey, Christine, 191
Harwood, Hokimate, 84, 95–96
Hauhau *see* Pai Mārire
Hau'ofa, Epeli, 24
Haupapa, Rotohiko, 62, 363, 370
Hauwaho, Sam, 61
Hay-Campbell, Charles Duncan
painting of arrival of Turi (with Haddon), *407*, 561n6[406]
Hayward, Ramai Rongomaitara (née Te Miha/Miller)
as artist and photographer, 392, 408, 410, 561n1[408]
*Arts and Crafts of the Maori*, 408, 410
*Inside Red China*, 408
movie posters by, *410*, 477
photograph of, *408*
*Rewi's Last Stand*, 408
*To Love a Maori*, 410
Hayward, Rudall, 408, 410
He Whakaputanga o te Rangatiratanga o Nu Tirene, 285, 292
head adornments
of feathers, 95, *143*, 148–49, *173*, 175, *177*, *284*
pare kawakawa, *148*, 148
purposes of, 175
*see also* heru
Heaphy, Charles
*Rangiaeata*, *172*, 279
Heaphy, Chris
*Te Ika a Maui & Te Waka a Maui*, 462
Hector, James, 213, 216, 550n45[216]
hei *see* neck adornments
hei tiki
acquired by Enrico Giglioli, *170*
archaeological finds, 155
carvings with, *167*
from contemporary materials, 171
looting by colonial troops, 549n31[213]
made from human skulls, 165
in museum collections, *167*, 167
from Ngāti Ruanui, *352*
of pounamu, 164, 167, *168*, 212, *268*
with red wax eyes, 245, *246*
symbolism of, 167
Te Maungārongo, 170, *171*
types of, 165, 547n65[167]
Whakatere-kohukohu, 15, 171
Heke, Hone, 15, 171, 242, 252, *253*, *254*, 255
Hemara, Ross, 463–64
Hēnare, Mānuka, 233, 292
Henare, Te Hemo Ata
*Ka Nukunuku! Ka Nekeneke!*, 483
Henry, William (Bill), 397
Heperi, Pita Te Hoe, 32
Hērangi, Tāmati, 366
Hērangi, Te Puea

Māori housing, 112, 360, *367*, *368*, 368
photograph of, *359*
Te Pou o Mangatawhiri concert party, 361, 363
Tūrangawaewae carving school, 127, 359, 364, 366
Tūrangawaewae House, 307, *308*
Tūrangawaewae Marae, 54, 192, 360–61, 363–64, 366–67
waka taua, 32, *33*, 37
whakatauākī of, 359
Herewini, Te Herekiekie, 351
heru
found at Kauri Point, 43, 175, *178*, 178, 540n15[43], 547n89[178]
Paikea pūrākau about, 145
purposes of, 175
of whalebone, *144*, 175, *178*, 222
of wood, *143*, *144*, *178*, *179*
Heta, Elisapeta, 474
Heta, Te Motu, 307
Hetaraka, Riini, *190*
Hetet, Rangi, 61, 64
Hetet, Rangimārie, 3, 80, 87, 100–101, *443*, 494
Hetet, Veranoa, 81, 103, 514
Hetet School of Māori Art, 61, 103
Hewson, Charles George
*Sketch of flags*, 324
Higgins, Rawinia, 145, 480
Hinemoa and Tūtānekai, 198
Hinenuitepō, 9, 41, 199, 235, 420
Hineteiwaiwa, 89, 167
Hīngāngāroa, 42, 52, 191
Hīona building, Maungapōhatu, *328*, 329
Hitchens, Dion
*Manaaki Patupaiarehe*, *452*, 452
HMS *Buffalo*, 267–68, *268*, *270*, 271
Hoani Waititi Marae, *424*, 424
Hocken, Thomas, 213, 216–17, 219
Hodges, William, 209
hoe, 26, *123*, 123, 158, 290
Hoete, Anthony, 503, 565n9[503]
Hoete, Graham (Mr G), 435
Hohepa, Patu, 9, 222
Holmes, Tommy, 36
Hongi Hika
carved self-portrait, 250, *251*
and the CMS, 250, 284
death of, 243, 285
in England, *82*, 261, 284
and iron, 298
*Meeting of the artist and Hongi* (Earle), 243
military raids, 15, 31, 98, *243*, 256
*Rev Thomas Kendall and the Maori chiefs Hongi and Waikato* (Barry), *82*
and taonga, 15, 171, *242*, 242
Hopkins, Candice, 511
*Horouta* (waka), 24
Hoskins, Rau, 112, *113*
Hotere, Ralph
as art teacher/advisor, 399
*Black Paintings* series, *403*, 457, 519
cultural identity, 405
at *documenta*, 517, 519, 566n31[519]
early exhibitions, 393, 397, 401
*Malady Panels*, 519
*Still life*, 391

Hotere, Ralph (*cont.*)
  study in Europe, 403
  untitled pencil sketch of a girl, *401*
Hovell, John, 61, 128, 129, 424
Hubbard, George, 441–42, 444, 512, 536
Hudson, Sarah, 519
Hügel, Carl von, *276*, *488*
Hundertwasser, Friedensreich, 483
Hutchings, Jessica, 192
Hutchinson, Lonnie
  hanging cutouts, 452
  *Hoa Kōhine (Girlfriend)*, 199
  *Kahu Matarau*, 429
  *Light My Fire*, 519
  *Pikihuia i te Ao, i te Pō*, 429
  *Sista7*, 460

## I

identity
  as artist v. as Māori artist, 405, 512
  co-option of urban African American culture, 433
  as hapū or iwi, 121, 459, 536
  as Indigenous, 7, 357, 440, 499, 509, 511
  as Māori, 143, 160, 181, 445, 494–95, 515
  as Māori Australians, 495
  moko and, 292
  as pantribal, 121, 303–4, 311, 369
  as part of a collective, 405, *440*, 458, 509, 512, 519
Igloliorte, Heather, 509
Indigeneity, 6–7, 357, 440, 499, 509, 511, 523
Indigenous Curators Exchange, 522
Insley, Tere, 474
  C Company Maori Battalion Memorial House, *475*
International Casablanca Biennale in Morocco, 516
International Indigenous Artists Gathering, 523, 566n41[523]
Iranui, 191
iron trade
  nails, 209, *246*, 278, 298
  tools, 298, *299*, 300
Iti, Ana, 480
Iti, Tame
  *Mural of Hokimoana Tawa, Tāneatua* (with Dippie), *433*, 435

## J

Jackson, Margaret, 106
Jackson, Moana, 6
Jacomb, Chris, 74
Jahnke, Robert
  on contemporary Māori art, 487
  on Māori art history, 11, 340
  and Massey University wharekai, *109*
  on pare, 198
  *Ripeka* series, 458
  *Te Utu: The Battle of the Gods*, 480
  and Waipiro Bay marae, 61
  *Whenua Kore*, 457
Jessop, Esther (née Kerr), 501
Jessop, Jeff, 501
Jones, Con Te Rata, 199
Jones, Owen
  *Grammar of Ornament*, 370

## K

Kaan, Simon
  *Ka Waka Tipuraka*, 460
  on Ngāi Tahu artists, 462
Kae, 43, 112, 117
kahu huruhuru
  in European museums, 542n64[96]
  gifted to Elsdon Best by Tūtakangahau, 95–96
  *Kahu huruhuru featuring the Australian Aboriginal flag* (Tahana), *495*
  kahu kiwi, 14–15, 95, 503
  kahu kura, 95, 287, *288*, 542n55[95]
  numbers of feathers used, 95
  in roimata toroa pattern, *72*
  *see also* cloaks; feathers
kahu koati, *275*, *279*, *280*
kahu kurī
  as ceremonial wear, *143*, 210
  in European museums, 542n64[96]
  huru kurī, 542n64[96]
  kahu waero, *92*, 279
  and Kaihuānga feud, 290
  making of, 92, 200
  *Te Kahumamae o Pareraututu*, *261*, 261–62, 271, 350
  *Tuhono te Karangarua* (Ruki), *494*, *495*
  types of, 92, 279, 290
  used by Te Rangitopeora to claim a lover, 98
  value of, 263, 279, 541n36[55]
  *see also* cloaks; kurī
kahu tōī, *79*, 80, *90*, *91*
Kahukiwa, Robyn
  as art teacher/advisor, 418–19, *419*
  *The Choice*, *419*, 419
  *Hineteiwaiwa*, *12*
  and mana wāhine, 199, 420
  paintings in Tapu Te Ranga Marae, 426
  *Tihe Mauri Ora*, *419*, 419
  *Wahine Toa* (book, with Grace), 420
  *Wahine Toa* exhibition, 420
  *Whakamamae* exhibition, *421*
Kahungunu (ancestor), 47, 75, 87, 191
Kaika, Rua, 36
Kaimoana, Wiremu, 314
kaitaka
  as armour, 260
  incorporating text, 288
  kaitaka huaki, 92, *94*, 106, 281, *286*
  kaitaka mai muka, *209*
  kaitaka paepaeroa, *2*, 92, *259*, *260*
  kaitaka pātea, 92
  Karamaene, 32, 100, 263
  superseded by korowai, 81, 275
  used by Ruhia Pōrutu to save McKenzie, 98, *259*, *260*, 260
  worn around the shoulders, 222
  *see also* cloaks; whatu
kākahu *see* cloaks
Kake, Jade, 483
kapa haka costumes, 91–92, 141, 164, 181
Kapua, Eramiha, 32, 62, 370–71, 386, 535, 557n10[337]
Kapua, Neke, 57, 217, 386
Kapua, Tene, 386
Karaka, Emily
  political issues, 420, 422
  *Polynesian Potae*, 456
  *Pot of Honey*, 456
  *Race Relations*, *422*, *423*
karakia significance, 3, 22, 42, 51, *71*
Karamu, Heni Te Kiri *see* Foley, Jane
Karanga Aotearoa repatriation programme, 351
Katene, Te Puoho, 561n27[399]
Kaupapa Waka (Project Canoe) initiative, 33, 61
Kauri, Karauria, 198–99, 287, *335*
Kawepō, Rēnata, 159, 292, *293*, 554n5[292]
Kawharu, Freda (née Rankin)
  as art teacher/advisor, 397
  *Gothic Tracery*, 397
Kawharu, Hugh, 338
Kawharu, Merata, 296
Keith, Hamish, 525
Kemara, Irini, *284*
Kendall, Thomas, *82*, 192, *241*, 241–42, 249, 250, 281
Kereama, Kelly, 469
Kereama, Waka, 54, 364
Kerekere, Elizabeth, 198
Kernot, Bernie, 51, 340
kete
  kete pukirikiri, *85*
  kete whakairo, *1*, 84, *201*
  kete whakapuareare, *79*, *103*
  types of, 84
  *see also* patterns; raranga
kiekie, 3, 74, 80, 84, 91, 123
Kihara, Shigeyuki, 489
King, Michael
  *Moko* (book, with Friedlander), 159–60
King, Philip Hansen, 240
Kīngitanga
  building wharenui and wharekai, 306, 364
  establishment and development of, 304, 306–7, 555n11[306]
  flags, *324*, 324, *326*
  invasion and confiscation of land of, 359–60, 423
  Kauhanganui buildings, 304, *306*, 307, *308*
  Korokī (King), 366, 367
  Mahuta (King), 307, *308*
  Ngā Pou o te Kīngitanga pātaka, 304, 306
  Pōtatau Te Wherowhero (King), *109*, 292, 303, 306, 423
  Tāwhiao (King), 170, 307, 313, 366
  Te Paki o Matariki coat of arms, *363*, 363
  Te Puea *see* Hērangi, Te Puea
  Te Rata (King), 307
  *see also* Tūrangawaewae
Kipa, Rangi
  carving work overseas, 513, 522
  *Haukura*, *1*, 171
  working on Te Papa artwork, *514*
Kirkwood, Te Rongo, 102
kōkōwai, 74, *75*, 80–81, *82*, 95, *118*, 525
Kokowai, Te Warihi, 300
Kopua, Mark, 145
Korokoro, portraits of, *295*
korowai
  with hukahuka, 81, 92, *94*, *284*
  with kārure, 81, *82*, 92

with ngore, 81, *92*, *94*, *96*, 281
*see also* cloaks; whatu
koru designs
  appropriation of, 477, 505
  in carving, 45
  in kōwhaiwhai, *123*, 125
  in moko, 158, 285
  in rock art, *131*, *134*, 137
Kotahitanga Parliament (Paremata Māori), 112, *114*, 304, 309, *310*, 311
kōuma, 26, 149–50, *151*
kōwhaiwhai
  artists, 61, 125–26
  on hoe, *123*, 123
  innovation in, 125, 129
  kiwi embryo design, *140*
  koru design, *123*, 125
  origins and development of, 123, 125, 256, 277
  pītau a manaia design, 238
Kukutai, Jimmy, 32
kumete, *50*, *58*, *59*, 193, *215*
Kupe, 22, 24
Kurahaupō (iwi), 106
*Kurahaupō* (waka), 24
Kurei, Te Waka, 238
kurī, 92, 96, 216, 279
Kururangi, Mere, 399

## L

Lander, Maureen
  *Atapō* (with Mataaho Collective), 458–59, *519*
  in Australia, 499
  *Binary Strings* (with Fairclough), *448*, 450
  *Hongi's Red Cloak – Deconstructed*, *82*
  and research, 102, 103
  *Wai o te Marama*, 458
  on weavers, 97
Lapita culture, *22*, 23, 525
Lardelli, Derek, 191
Laws, George, 119
Lejeune, Jules
  drawings, 160, *161*, *214*, 549n29[213]
  *Ecao. Jeune fille de la Nouvelle Zélande*, *282*
Lemon, Norman, 397
Leonard, Karl Rangikawhiti
  background, 200
  *Mississippi, te awa kai kete*, *201*
  *Rāpaki named Rongomai*, *201*, 521
  *Te hononga o ngā wai*, 521
Lilo, Janet
  *SHIFT #*, 480
Lindauer, Gottfried
  *Tomika Te Mutu*, *177*
  use of photographs, 554n5[292]
Lindt, John William, *117*
literacy
  impacts of, 281, 284–87, 292, 478
  incorporation of text in artworks, 121, 138, 287
  *Woman and child* (Merrett), *282*
Little, James Edward, *347*, 347
Locke, Samuel, 214
Lodge, Mere (née Harrison)
  in 1966 Festival of Maori Arts, 397
  *Mata Whenua*, 399
  *Te Toka-a-Torea*, 399

London Missionary Society (LMS), *242*, 243–45, *244*, *246*, 247, *249*
Lyttle, Kirsten
  *Gundulu/Emu Kākahu huruhuru*, 497
  *Major Mitchell's Cockatoo*, 496
  *Whakaahua* exhibition, 495

## M

Maclennan, Stewart Bell, 392
Madonna and Child carvings, 158, 192–93, *228*, *232*, 233, *448*, 450–51
Māhinaarangi and Tūrongo (ancestors), 313, 366
Mahuika, 189, 199, 298
Mahumahu, 32, 540n42[32]
Mahupuku, Tamahau, 334
Mahuta, Pōtatau Te Wherowhero, 307, *308*
Mair, Gilbert
  taonga collected by, 56, *117*, 214–15, *215*, 233, 262, 271, 329, 550n55[219]
  *Te Kooti's flag, Te Wepu*, 326
mana
  displayed by architecture, 51, 55, 109, 119, 127, 238
  mana takatāpui, 199
  mana tangata, 51, 54–55, 97, 290
  mana wāhine, 28, 190, 192, 199
  mana whenua, 14, 45, 121, 431
  of taonga, 14, 74, 84, 98, 100, 104, 259–61, 263–64, 271
Mane-Wheoki, Jonathan
  advice to Māori artists, 532
  on contemporary Māori art, 357, 441, 445, 449–50
  and Elam students, 533
  *Hiko!* exhibition, 447, 449
  on Indigeneity, 7, 538n15[7]
  on Indigenous art, 512, 566n16[512]
  and Māori art history, 9, 439
  in *New Zealand Maori Culture and the Contemporary Scene*, 397
  on Mātaatua whare, 272, 339
  on Robyn Kahukiwa, 419
Maniapoto, Moana, 146
Mantell, Walter, 139
Manutuke church, *237*, 237–39
Maori and South Pacific Arts Council (MASPAC), 101, 512
Maori Antiquities Act (1901), 333, 334, 370
Māori architects, 467, 469, 471–72, 474
Māori art history
  1920s and '30s revival of customary art, 368–71, 392
  1970s cultural renaissance, 405, 416–17, 456
  contemporary art as a disruption, 9, 404, 438, 441–43, 447
  continuity of customary and contemporary art, 437–38, 444–45, 447, 456, 462, 463, 563n28[461]
  defining contemporary Māori art, 511–12
  defining Māori art, 9, 12, 444, 447
  digital turn, 449–50
  early historians' assumptions, 8, 242, 247
  emergence of contemporary Māori art movement, 401, 403
  ethnographic artefacts v. fine arts, 8, 11–12, 340, 391, 493–94, 538n16[8]

  expressionism, 418, 422
  future research directions, 536–37
  Māori modernists, 412, 442, 458, 465, 468
  Mead's time periods, 8
  postmodernism, 438–40, 459, 563n3[438]
  publications, 12, 464–65, *522*, 522
  reconciling Māori and modern, 393, 395, 403, 437, 560n12[395]
  resistance to modernism, 60, 404
  turning points in, 11, 148, 340, 376, 391, 437, 464, 512
Māori Art Market (MAM), 514
Maori Artists and Writers Association, 405, 456
Māori artists' characteristics
  acting as agents of change, 28, 57, 275, 509, 523, 537
  communal approach, 54, 370, 405, 458, 519, 532
  creative use of new materials, 278, 281, *285*, 298, 463
  treating artworks as the ancestor depicted, 15, 292, 519
Māori ceramicists, 525–26
Māori civil rights movement, *416*, 416, 418, 420
Māori curators, 340, 465, 512, 522, 532
Māori designers, 477–79, 529
Māori population
  in Australia, 357, 416, 485, 493, 565n38[495]
  health of, 186, 318, 359, 360
  urbanisation, 405, 415–16, 536
Maori Representation Act (1867), 309
Maori Women's Welfare League, 101, 370, 543n93[101]
marae, 119, 126, 303, 369, 373, 426–27, 535, 544n22[119]
*see also* urban marae
Marama, Willie, 557n10[337]
Marion du Fresne, Marc-Joseph, 210
maro, 81, 87, *88*, 277
Marsden, Hiraina, *329*, 329
Marsden, Māori, 1
Marsden, Samuel, 230–31, 241, *242*, 242, 243–44, 250
Marsters, Cori Buster, 200
Mason, Ngahiraka, 450, 509
mata whakarewa *see* skin painting
Mataaho Collective
  *Atapō* (with Lander), 458–59, *519*
  *Kiko Moana*, *485*, 519
  members of, *519*, 519
  *Takapau*, 516, 519
  *Te Whare Pora*, 519
Mātaatua Declaration, 505
*Matahourua* (waka), 22, 24
Mataira, Katerina, 393, 397, 399, 402
Matakohe Architecture and Urbanism, 474
Mataora and Niwareka, 145
*Mataora: The Living Face* (book, Adsett et al., editors), 12, 405, *464*, 464–65
Matchitt, Gina
  *Praying Madonna Nike*, *451*
Matchitt, Paratene
  in 1963 Maori Festival of Arts, *394*, 395
  as art teacher/advisor, 397, 399, 561n34[401]

Matchitt, Paratene (*cont.*)
   City to Sea Bridge (with R. Thompson and Gray), 472
   and contemporary art, 60
   at *Contemporary Maori Painting and Sculpture* exhibition, *396*
   *Te Wepu Assemblage*, *326*
   *Whiti te ra*, *393*
mau taringa *see* ear adornments
Māui, *9*, 21, 41, 145, 171, 189, 235, 298
Maungapōhatu, *328*, 329
Maupakanga, Rānui, 32
mauri, 14, *45*, 45, 263–64, 536
Maxwell, Taniora, 557n20[338]
McCahon, Colin
   *I am*, *440*
   as an influence on other artists, 418, 419, 422, *445*, 525
   and misappropriation of Māori symbolism, 505
   *Urewera Mural*, *507*
McCarthy, Conal, 217, 219, 337
McEwen, Jock, 392
McKendry, Lisa, 74
McKenzie, Thomas Wilmor, *98*, 98, *259*, 260
McKirdy, Aaron, 478
McLean, Ian, 511
McLintock, Alexander, 391
McMillan, Larissa, 341
Mead, Hirini Moko
   on carving styles, 8, 46, 178, 540n20[47]
   on contemporary art, 8–9, 404
   and cultural property, 505
   on defining Māori art, 12, 512, 515
   on garments and adornments, 96–97, 98, 175, 178
   on rangatira, 49
   on taha wairua, 14
   on taonga gifting ceremonies, 104
   and *Te Maori* exhibition, 340
   on teaching art, 398, 401
Meade, Herbert George Phillip
   *Pai Marire karakia*, *326*
meeting houses by name
   Aoraki, *424*, 425
   Arohanui ki te Tangata, 61
   Hau Te Ana Nui o Tangaroa, *53*, 214, 337
   Hikurangi, 277, 306
   Hinemihi, *501*, *502*, 503
   Hinenuitepō, 200
   Hotunui, *52*, 55, 263, 287
   Houmaitawhiti, 55
   Kahurānaki I, 51
   Māhinaarangi, *360*, *363*, 363–64
   Mātaatua, *52*, *272*, *273*, 339–40, 382, 493, 505, 536
   Matukurua, 128
   Ngā Tokotoru, 54
   Nuku Te Apiapi, 57
   Ōhinemutu, 57, 541n43[57]
   Porourangi, 62, 193, 277, 287
   Rākairoa, 128–29
   Rangikurukuru, 191
   Rangitihi, 31, 57, 550n55[219]
   Rauru, 51, 57, 217, 334, 503
   Rongopai, 311, 316–17
   Ruataupare, 314
   Ruatepupuke II, *41*, 43, *124*, 217, 503
   Ruatepupuke III, 373
   Taiporohenui, 306
   Tākitimu, *315*, 334, *371*
   Tama ki Hikurangi, *315*, 316, 317
   Tamatekapua, 56
   Tāne-nui-ā-rangi, *4*, *9*, 101, 128, *424*, 424
   Tānewhirinaki, 311, 314
   Tāpeka, 64
   Te Aroha o Rongoheikume, 101
   Te Aroha o te Iwi Māori, 503
   Te Hau ki Tūranga, 11, 53, *120*, 123, 193, 198, 209, 214, 237, 339–40, 374, 376, 463, 536, 550n36[214]
   Te Ika a Māui, 379
   Te Kete Uruuru Matua, 128
   Te Ngākau Māhaki, 127
   Te Otawhao, 128
   Te Poho o Rāwiri, *372–73*, 373
   Te Poho o Tipene, 128
   Te Puawai o Te Arawa, *117*, 117
   Te Rauru, *493*
   Te Tiriti o Waitangi, *309*, 309, 311, 555n29[311]
   Te Tokanganui a Noho, *312–13*, 313, 315–16
   Te Tumu Herenga Waka, 199
   Te Wai o Pāoa, 128
   Te Waiariki, 128
   Te Waipounamu, *310*
   Te Whai a te Motu, *315*, 316
   Te Whaioranga o Te Whaiao, *109*
   Te Whare o Heretaunga, 217, *219*, 219, 550n52[217]
   Te Whare o Rangi, *63*, 128
   Te Wharepuni-a-Māui, 57, 217, 386, 503
   Te Whatu Manawa Māoritanga o Rehua, *140*, 141
   Tokopikowhakahau, 31, 57
   Wairaka, *190*, 190
   whare rūnanga at Waitangi, 337, 391, 557n10[337]
   *see also* whare whakairo
Melbourne, Hirini, 277
Mercep, Ivan, 424
mere pounamu
   belonging to Te Rauparaha, 264, *265*, 265–66, *266*
   carried by rangatira, *98*, 98, *143*, 221
   exchanged in peace negotiations, 186, 263, 266
   exchanged in trade with Europeans, 210
   gifts to Europeans, *242*, 242, 266, 268
Merrett, Joseph Jenner
   *Group of Maori Women*, *148*
   *Group of Maoris*, *213*
   *Hannah and Mary*, *96*
   *Hone Heke and his Wife Harriet with Four Attendants*, *255*
   *Johny Heke & wife*, *253*
   portrait style of, 212
   *The warrior chieftains of New Zealand*, *253*
   *Woman and child*, *282*
Meurant, Ross, 420
Miller, John Frederick (English artist)
   *A chest of New Zealand* (with Ralph), *180*
Miller, John (photographer)
   *The Launch of Ngatokimatawhaorua*, *483*
   photographs in *Pūrangiaho*, 456
Miromoda Indigenous Māori Fashion Apparel Board, 530
missionaries
   attitudes to Māori art, 192–93, 233, 238–40, 249
   collecting of taonga, 192, 240–42
   European patrons of, 240, 246
   first mission stations, 230–31, *231*, 237, 241
   and heteropatriarchy, 189, 192, 548n16[192]
   influence on Māori practices, 159, 160, 233–35, 238
   and literacy, 281
   Māori converts, 231, 243–44, 256
   rangatira patrons of, 237–38
   waka chapels, *231*, 231, 249
   *see also* Church Missionary Society (CMS); Kendall, Thomas; Williams, William; Yate, William
Moerewa, 26
Mohi, Rose, 219
moko
   contemporary reasons for taking moko, 160, 191
   impact of 1907 Tohunga Suppression Act, 159
   indicating mana and identity, 157–58, 193, 292
   and kirituhi on non-Māori, 12, 160, 515
   kōrere, *156*, 157
   mataora (moko kanohi, full-face design), 158, 193, 233, 250, *251*, 290, *295*
   moko kauae, *55*, 158, 159–60, 191, 535
   Ngāi Tahu styles, 292
   oral histories about, 145, 546n6[145]
   Pacific antecedents of, 157
   pūhoro (half-face moko), *222*, 222
   recorded in drawings, 159, 292, *293*
   signatures derived from, 159, 213, 284–85, 292
   tapu process of, 157
   and tattooed text, 190–91, *282*, *284*, 285
   tohunga tā moko, 53–54, 157, 159, 190–91, 515, 548n9[191], 557n1[333]
   tools and pigments for, 157, 515
   traditional designs, 145, 157–59, *158*, 164, 191, 221
   women with full-face moko, 158, 193, 233, 290
mokomokai *see* toi moko
Mokomokai Education Trust, 351
Mokomoko, Mereana, 55, 263
Monkman, Kent
   *The Four Continents*, 511
Morelli, Giovanni, 66, 68
Mount Tarawera eruption, 503
Mountain, Elizabeth *see* Ellis, Elizabeth (née Mountain)
muka, 2–3, 74, 172, 240
   *see also* raranga; whatu
Munn, Linda, *329*, 329
Murirangawhenua, 21, 189
Muriwai, *190*, 190
Muru, Bill, 361
Muru, Pero, 361
Muru, Selwyn
   in early exhibitions, 395, 397
   *Kohatu*, *141*
   *Te Waharoa o Aotea*, *415*, 415

on traditional Māori art, 402
*Untitled Taupiri Mountain*, 403
museum collections in Aotearoa
  Auckland Museum, 540n1[41]
  Colonial Museum in Wellington, 214, 216, 334
  curators, 335, 340, 341, 463
  Māori involvement, 217, 337, 338, 340, 341–42
  in nineteenth century, 215–17, 550n58[219]
  proposals for a national Māori museum, 334
  repatriation of taonga, 338–40, 353, 491
  as research and inspiration, 62, 91, 236, 337–38, 370
  Te Papa Tongarewa, 340, 351, 463, 465, *514*, 540n1[41]
  *see also* exhibitions of Māori art in Aotearoa
museum collections overseas
  activation of taonga and contemporary art, 485, 487, 489, 491, 499
  in Australia, 494
  exchange/trade between museums, 219, 353
  exhibitions of taonga, *244*, 244–45, 247, *248*, 485–89
  in mission museums, 243–47, 249
  in non-English-speaking countries, *270*, 353, 549n25[212]
  numbers of taonga in, 342, 540n1[41]
  online access to, 341, 343, 353
  reconnecting communities and taonga, 341, 343, 353, 485–86, 487
  repatriation of taonga, 343, 351, 353, 491
  as research and inspiration, 102, 106, 181, 343, 485–86
  in Russia, 106, 212, 544n3[106], 550n55[219]
  tikanga practices in, 340, 351
  toi moko in, 351
  in United States, 211, 217, 549n21[211]
  in Western Europe, 208, 210, 215, 217, *248*, 334, 353, 486, 493, 550n55[219]
  *see also* exhibitions of Māori art overseas

# N
nākahi drawing, 296, *297*
Nathan, Alex, 513, 525
Nathan, Kiri
  black kākahu, *531*, 531
Nathan, Manos
  *Ngā Kaihanga Uku*, 525
  *Whakapakoko II, Nga Kaitiaki series 2*, *525*
National Art Gallery, 441, 442
*Native Christian church at Turanga* (unknown artist), *237*
neck adornments
  hei matau, 164, 171, *186*, 547n71[171]
  of human teeth, *148*
  kākā pōria, *162*, 164, 277
  of moa bones, *153*, 153
  of paua shell, *148*
  pekapeka, 149, 164, *276*, 277
  reels, *47*, 153
  rei ika, 46
  rei niho, 46, *47*, 149, *151*
  rei puta, *143*, 164, *165*, 222
  of sharks' teeth, *148*
  of tusk shell, *154*, 154, *155*, 155
  of whale teeth, 148, *153*, 164
  *see also* hei tiki
Neich, Roger
  on carving, 54, 66, 68, 179, 191, 198, 486
  on collectors, 215, 334
  *Painted Histories*, 8, *440*
  on waka taua/tuere, 30, 31
Nelson, Charles, 31, 51, 57
Nene, Tāmati Wāka, 32, *110*, 285
Netana, Te Rangitu, 515
New Zealand International Exhibition (1882), 219
New Zealand International Exhibition in Christchurch (1906), 57, 217, *386*, 386, *388*
New Zealand Maori Artists and Writers Association, 405, 456
New Zealand Māori Arts and Crafts Institute, 38, 60, 61, 101, 103, 404, 477, 514
New Zealand Wars
  battle of Gate Pā, *324*
  and confiscation of land, 214, 307, 423, 549n33[214]
  destruction of whare, waka and pātaka, 21, 31, 119, 214, 304, 423
  duration of, 205, 549n30[213]
  looting of taonga, 119, 213–14, 549n31[213]
Newell, Jenny, 224
Ngā Aho, 477
Ngā Hau e Whā marae, *424*, 425, *426*, 427
Ngā Kaihanga Uku, 525–26
ngā kete e toru, 3, 5, 18
Ngā Puna Waihanga, 405, 456, 512
Ngāi Tahu
  arts community, 459–60, 462–63
  Māori Rock Art Project, 139, 141
  and Ngā Hau e Whā marae, 425
  Paemanu Rōpū, 463
  and pounamu, 14, 186, 264
  and Te Rauparaha, 264–67
  Te Waka o Aoraki, 21–22
  Treaty settlement, 139
Ngāi Tūhoe, 98, 100, 435, 470
Ngāiterangi, 159, 175, *177*, 263
Ngākaho, Tāmati, *53*, 214
Ngāpuhi
  Ngāpuhi Festival, 459
  prisoners of war in, 31, 157, 190, 256
  and role of taonga in peacemaking, 98, 171, 186
  waka taua, 31, 56
  *see also* Heke, Hone; Hongi Hika
Ngareta, Mere, 15
Ngarimu, Ranui, 84, *86*
Ngata, Apirana
  on art, 56, 392
  marae and land development schemes, 62, 359, 369, 373
  revival of customary arts, 334, 368–71, 373–74, 375
  and School of Māori Arts and Crafts, 368–71, 373–76, 386
  and Te Araiteuru Pā, 386
  tukutuku, 62, *80*, 199, *335*
  and Tūrangawaewae Marae, 363, 366
  waiata, haka and whaikōrero, 170, *368*, 369
  whare rūnanga at Waitangi, 337, *368*, 557n10[337]
Ngata, Arihia, 363
Ngatai, Hoani, 53, *124*
Ngātata, Wī Tako, 304, *324*, 555n13[306]
Ngāti Awa
  carvers, 47, *52*, 55
  Mātaatua whare, 3, 52, *272*, 272, 339–40, 382, 493, 505, 536
Ngāti Porou
  Mount Hikurangi, 21, 539n2[21], 540n48[36]
  names of meeting houses, 192, 287
  Paikea, 23, 145, 175
  whakapapa of carving, 9, 43
Ngāti Rānana, 357, 485, 487, 489, 501, *502*, 503
Ngāti Tarāwhai carvers, 31, 47, 53, 57, 219, 386
Ngāti Te Ata, 32
Ngatoto, Hone, 62, *65*, 369
nguru, *212*, 277
Nicholas, Henriata, 191
Nicholas, John Liddiard, 298
Nihoniho, Matutaera (Tuta), 14, 76, 84, 87, 259
nīkau whare *see* thatch
Nikora, Linda Waimarie
  *Mau Moko* (book, with Te Awekotuku), 8
Nin, Buck
  *The canoe prow*, 394
  *New Zealand Maori Culture and the Contemporary Scene* exhibition, 395, 397, 402–3
*Nlle Zélandaise de 20 à 22 ans* (attributed to Lejeune), *161*
Nuku, George
  adornments made from Perspex, 171
  *Bottled Ocean 2118* collaboration, 516
  in Europe, 61, 487–91, *488*, 515–16
  *Outer Space Marae*, *488*, 489, 491
  Perspex additions to *Te Tuhono*, *491*, 491
Nukunuku, Te Iwingaro, *103*
Nukutawhiti, 22, 24, *33*, 45, 241
Nunes, Keone, 191, 515
Nunns, Richard, 277

# O
Oldman, William, *248*, 334, 347, 558n5[350]
Oliver, Richard
  *Feast at the Bay of Islands*, *110*
O'Neill, Ani
  *Kua Marino Te Tai*, 519
online presence of Māori art, 343, 514
Onslow, William, 503
oral histories
  adornments in, 15, 145
  aute in, 75
  building houses in, 45
  carving in, 42–43
  moko in, 145, 546n6[145]
  pounamu in, 2
  women's role in, 190, 199
  waka in, 21–22, 24, 26
  celestial narratives, 1, 3, 21, 41, 126, 189
  differing narratives, 2
  *see also* waiata
O'Regan, Gerard, 70, 133, 139, 141, 341
O'Regan, Tipene, 486

O'Reilly, Ron, 405
Ostick, Paitangi, 191
Ōtaki church, 237–38

## P

*Pa, Te Aro* (unknown artist), *428*, 428
Paama-Pengelly, Julie
    *Māori Art and Design*, 12
Pacific Arts Association, 353, 490, 491
Pacific Arts Festivals, 515
Pacific Ocean, 22–24, 32, 36, 161, 509
Pacific Sisters collective
    *21st Sentry Cyber Sister*, 530
    *He Toa Tāera Fashion Activists* exhibition, 530, 566n5[530]
Pahewa, Dawn and Edna, 101
Pai Mārire, 296, 324, *326*, 329
    *see also* Te Ua Haumēne
Paitini, Makurata, 287, *288*
Pakira, 191
Panoho, Rangihīroa
    on customary and contemporary art, 443–44
    *Māori Art*, 12
    on misappropriation of cultural property, 505
    *Whatu Aho Rua* exhibition, 443–44
paoi, 76, *77*, 542n16[76], 542n18[76]
Papakura, Mākereti (Guide Maggie), 89, 180–81, *493*, 493
Papawai pā, Wairarapa, *310*
Parangi, Tamati, 31, 263
Paraone, Jess
    *Kete Rosebud*, 85
Pardington, Fiona
    *Davis Kea Wings (above)*, *456*
    museum research by, 181
    *Nabokov's Blues*, *513*
    reimaging of life-casts, 213
Pardington, Neil
    *Five Māori Painters* typeface, *478*, 479
    Parihaka typeface (with McKirdy and Clarke), *478*, 478
    *Taonga Māori Store #2, Whanganui Regional Museum*, *332*
    *Taonga Māori Store #3, Whanganui Regional Museum*, *342*
Parekōwhai, Michael
    *The Bosom of Abraham*, 452, *453*
    *The English Channel*, *431*
    *On First Looking into Chapman's Homer*, *516*
    *The Indefinite Article*, *440*
    *Kiss The Baby Goodbye*, *446*
    *The Lighthouse / Tū Whenua-a-Kura*, 428–29, *430*, 431
    *Mimi*, *445*
    *The Story of a New Zealand River*, 452, *453*
    and the Urban Generation, 438–39
Paremata Māori (Kotahitanga Parliament), 112, *114*, 304, 309, *310*, 311
Parerautūtu, *261*, 261–62, 271, 350
Parihaka before the invasion
    destruction of, 304, 317–19
    passive resistance, 317
    prisoners from, 157, 317
    Te Whiti's house, *319*, 319
    village whare, *302*, 316, 317–18

Parihaka reconstruction
    colonial style buildings, 304, *320*, *321*, 322–23
    dining hall, *320*, *321*, 323
    Tohu Kākahi's house, *320*, 323
Parkinson, Sydney
    drawings, 24, 30, *75*, 84, 191, 208, 212
    *The heads of six men*, 175, *177*
    *A New Zealand war canoe*, *22*
    *A New Zealand warrior in his proper dress*, *143*
    *Portrait of a New Zealand Man*, *221*
    *Portrait of Otegoowgoow*, *222*
paru, *80*, 80, 91
pātaka
    carving of, 112, *118*, 193, *299*, 300
    decreasing need for, 117–18, 275
    depictions of, *114*, *117*, 241, *299*
    epa of, 49
    as food stores, *117*, 117, 119
    Hīnana ki uta, Hīnana ki tai, *305*
    Ngā Pou o te Kīngitanga, 119, 304, *306*, 554n4[304]
    Nuku Tewhatewha, *305*, 306
    purposes of, 52, 109, 112, 119
    at Te Araiteuru, *386*, 388
    Te Puawai o Te Arawa, *117*, 117, 119
    Te Tairuku Potaka, 198
    Te Tākinga, *117*
    uncarved pātaka, *117*, 117–18
    whata, 118
Paterson, Reuben
    *The Kaiahuwhenua and his Three Sons*, *452*, 452
    *Te Pūtahitanga ō Rehua*, *457*
patterns, decorative
    mūmū, 106
    pātikitiki, 81
    poutama, *1*, *2*, *94*, *201*, *472*
    purapura whetū, 81, 238
    roimata toroa, *72*, 123
    in tukutuku, 121–23
patu aruhe, *242*, 243
patu ōnewa, 212, *244*
patu parāoa, 217, *270*, 271
patu pora, *345*, 345
Patuone, Eruera Maihi, 32, *253*, 268, 285
Paul, Nova, 480
Pearson, Alan, 444–45
Pendergrast, Mick
    *Feathers and Fibre* exhibition, 102, *103*
    on fibre arts, 486
    *Te Aho Tapu* exhibition, 102, *103*
Pere, Baden, 395, 402–3
Pere, Wi, 316–17
Perohuka, Te Waaka, 31–32, 54–55, 100, *262*, 263, 543n88[100]
Phillipps, William, 27, 335
Piailug, Mau, 36
pigments
    for moko, 157
    for rock art, 135, *136*
    for skin painting, 162
    for textiles, 80–81
Pigorini National Museum, 270, 352, 353
Pihama, Leonie, 340
Pihopa, Te Tuhi, 200

pīngao, 80, 87, 91, 123
Pipitea Marae, 425
Pishief, Elizabeth, 334
piupiu, *91*, 91–92, 277, *284*
plaster life-casts, 212–13
Poata, Tame, 53–54, *55*
Pohio, Nathan
    at Auckland Art Gallery, 341
    *Raise the anchor*, *517*, 517, 519
    *Sleeper 1999*, *460*
    *Takiroa, takinui* (with Rakena), *463*
poi tāniko, 200
Polack, Joel, 84, 277
Polynesia Tatau tattoo convention, 515
Polynesian Voyaging Society, 36
Pōmare, Māui, 351, 360
Pompallier, Jean Baptiste François, 233
Pope, James
    *Health for the Maori*, *318*, 382
Pore, Hēni, *324*
Porter, Thomas, 55
portraits of Māori, 212–13, 222, 250, 277, 292, 392
    *see also* Angas, George French; Coates, Isaac; Goldie, Charles; Heaphy, Charles; Lindauer, Gottfried; Merrett, Joseph Jenner
Pōrutu, Ruhia, *98*, 98, *259*, *260*, 260, 543n78[98]
Potiki, Roma, 437
pounamu
    adornments, 155, *162*, 164, 167, *168*, 172, 186, 222, *352*
    ancestral narratives, 2
    carvers, 157, 543n84[98]
    tools made of, 186, 300
    trade, 186, 264–65, 268, 281, 291, 296, 335
    value, 180, 186
    *see also* mere pounamu; tatau pounamu
Poutapu, Piri, 32, 54, 361, 364, 366, 370, 540n43[32]
Pouwhare, Robert
    *Raupatu, Te Kaea and The Waiohou Fraud*, 443
Preece, George, 272
Prendergast, Te Ari, 531
Prince, Diane
    paintings in Tapu Te Ranga Marae, 426
    *Untitled* wall sculpture, *442*, 443
Project Employment Programme weaving schemes, 101
Protected Objects Act (1975), 15
Pukehika, Hōri, *386*, 386
Puketapu-Hetet, Erenora, 81, 103, 542n24[80]

## R

rā, *22*, 24, 28, 84, *86*, 87, 290
rain capes, *75*, 79, 80, 81, 89, *90*, 91, 97
rain cloaks, 91
rākai *see* adornments
rākau momori, *132*, 133, 215
Rakena, Hana
    *Whenua Hou* installation detail, *526*
Rakena, Otene, 461
Rakena, Rachael
    *Aniwaniwa* (with Graham), *516*
    *Takiroa, takinui* (with Pohio), *463*
    *U.F.O.B* (with Graham), 512–13, *513*

Ralph, Richard
   *A chest of New Zealand* (with Miller), *180*
Ramsden, Irihapeti
   *150 Years of Dirty Laundry* (with Reid), *445*
rangatira
   attributes of, 47, 49, 51
   carving, 56, 179
   commissioning works, 6, 54–56, 121, 127, 290, 304
   exchange of taonga, 100, 259, 263–67, 535
   mana of, 28, 51, 97
Rangi (tohunga tā moko), 157, 190
Rangiātea church, Ōtaki, 81, *236*, 237–38, 257
Rangikatia, Hone, 256
Ranginui (Ngāti Kahu chief), 221, *222*
Ranginui and Papatūānuku (ancestors), 1–2, *4*, 126
Rangitukia chapels, 256
Rapira Davies, Shona
   *Nga Morehu (The Survivors)*, *421*, 525
   Te Aro Park project, *428*, 428, 525
raranga
   products of, 84, 87, 106
   techniques, 81, 87, 106
   *see also* kete; rā; tātua; textiles; whāriki
Rātana, Tahupōtiki Wiremu, 376, 379, 382–83, 385
Rātana movement
   alliance with Labour Party, 383
   architectural design, 376, 385
   Ōmeka hall, Matamata, 383, *384*
   pan-tribalism, 382, 385
   whare whakamoemiti, 376, *379*, 379
   whetū mārama motifs, 329, 376
Rātana Pā
   Manuao, *384*, 385
   Temepara, *328*, 329, 376, *377*
   Whare Māori, 379, 382, *383*
raupō whare *see* thatch
Raymond, Rosanna, 487–91
Reid, Papaarangi
   *150 Years of Dirty Laundry* (with Ramsden), *445*
Reihana, Lisa
   *Dandy*, *189*, 488
   *Digital Marae*, 452, *455*, 489, *495*
   *Diva*, *7*
   *Emissaries*, 516
   *ethKnowcentrix* poster, *488*
   *He Tautoko*, *488*, 491
   *Hinepūkohurangi*, 452, *455*
   *Ihi*, *458*
   *Marakihau*, 452, *455*
   *in Pursuit of Venus [infected]*, *173*, 480, *511*, 511
   *Tai Whetuki*, 480
   *Tauira*, 439, *440*
   and the Urban Generation, 438
   *Wog Features*, *439*
Rēkohu Chatham Islands, *29*, 29, *132*, 133, 215
Rewa, 285
Reweti, Bridget, 480, 519
Rewiri, Kura Te Waru *see* Te Waru Rewiri, Kura
Richardson, William, *211*, 211,
Richardson, William Putnam, 211, *212*

Richmond, James, 214
Rickard, James, 61
Rickard, Jolene, 511, 523
Riddell, Baye, 525
Rihari, Hugh, *71*
Rika-Heke, Makere, 70
Ringatū movement
   architecture of, 311, 313–17, 323
   carving and painting style, *313*, 314–17, *315*
   flags, *326*, 329
   Kīngitanga connections, 313–14
   Te Kooti, 311
Ririnui, Te Atiwei
   *Poutama*, *201*
   *Poutama Ahurewa*, *1*
Robb, Hamuera, 106
Robieson, James Frank, *348*, 349
Robinson, Peter
   *Bi-Polar* (with Fraser), 516
   *Boy Am I Scarred Eh*, *437*
   *I Am I, I Am Not I*, *451*, 451
   *Māori Have Rights Too!*, *461*
   series in *Toi Tū Toi Ora*, *457*
   *Strategic Plan*, *451*, 451
   *Untitled*, *445*
   and the Urban Generation, 438–39
Robley, Horatio Gordon
   collecting taonga, 246–47, *248*, 350, 353, 558n5[350]
   drawings, 159, 386, 558n1[350]
   *Ngaiterangi woman with curious tattooing*, 159
   *Pataka*, *117*
   *Roman Catholic chapel Otumoetai*, *233*, *235*
   'Tangi at Matapihi', 160
   *Woman of the Ngaiterangi Tribe*, 159
   *Women cutting themselves*, 160, *161*
rock art
   animal themes, *134*, 135, *136*, 137, *140*
   attributed to Tupaia, 138, 545n28[138]
   damage to, 139, 463
   decline of the practice, 139, 535
   evidence of European contact, *134*, 138, 138
   as inspiration for artists, *141*, 141
   interpretations of, 139
   koru and spiral details, 137
   large works, *136*, 138
   pigments for, 135, *136*
   purposes, 133, 139, 141
   at Rapanui Easter Island, *132*, 133
   at Rēkohu Chatham Islands, *132*, 133
   tapu of, 139
   tiki themes (human forms), *131*, *136*, 137
   waka and ship themes, 27–28, *134*, *138*, 138
rock art sites
   distribution, *131*, 131, 133, 139
   Kaingaroa, *134*
   'Orongo, Rapanui, *132*
   Te Ana a Nunuku cave, Rēkohu, *132*
   types, 135, 138
   Waitaki, *134*, *136*, *138*, 138, 463
Rongomātāne, 126
Rongowhakaata, 237, 238, 263, 339–40, 463
Rōpiha, Hori, 51
Ross, R. O., 391

Royal, Wiremu (Bill), *467*
Royal Connection Trust, 557n3[334]
Royal Doulton Maori Ware, *507*
Rua, John, 425
Rua Kēnana, *328*, 329
Ruanui, 45
Ruatara, 230–31
Ruatepupuke (ancestor), 9, *11*, 42–43
Rūaumoko, 145
Rudofsky, Bernard
   *Architecture Without Architects*, 426
Ruki, Keren
   *Cultural Safety Vest*, *496*
   *A Place to Stand*, 494–95
   *Tuhono te Karangarua*, 494, *495*
Rukupō, Raharuhi
   church at Manutuke, 192, *237*, 238
   Te Hau ki Tūranga, 11, 53, *120*, 121, 198, 209, 214, 287, 333

## S

sails, *22*, 24, 28, 84, *86*, 87, 290
Salmond, Amiria, 386
Salmond, Anne, 207, 210, 226
Savage, Paula, 214–15
School of Maori Arts and Crafts
   adherence to tradition, 62, 123, 125, 127, 369–70, 386, 442, 534
   carving, 101, 127, 236
   closing of, 60, 376
   establishment of, 57, 62, 368–69
   instructors, 32, 62, 101, 370
   kōwhaiwhai, 125
   museum research, 236, 370
   projects, 60, 64, 128, 368–69, 373, 376
   tikanga practices, 371, 535
   trainees, 54, 62, 128, 364, 369
   tukutuku programme, *120*, 123, 199, 370
Schoon, Theo
   in 1963 Maori Festival of Arts, 560n16[395]
   on rock art, 139
   *Untitled*, 505, *507*
Schuster, Emily, 101, *102*
Schuster, James, 101, 200, 503
Scott, John
   Aniwaniwa Visitor Centre, *470*, 471, *471*
   Futuna Chapel, *468*, 469
   Maori Battalion Memorial Community Centre, *468*, 469
   residential designs, 469
Selwyn, George Augustus
   and church design, 239–40
   *Natives assembled to celebrate the Lord's Supper*, 231
Sharples, Pita, 523
Simmons, David, 8, 486
skin painting, 161–62, 164
Skinner, Henry Devenish, 165, 219
Smith, Catherine, 84, *86*
Smith, Huhana, *464*, 465
Smith, Jan, *329*, 329
Smith, Linda Tuhiwai, 342, 511
Smith, Takirirangi, 38
Snowden, Sonya
   *Tatai Whetu ki te Rangi*, *85*
*Sovereign Words: Indigenous Art, Curation and Criticism* (book), 522

Spirit Wrestler Gallery, 513
Spivak, Gayatri Chakravorty, 509
Spöring, Herman, 30, 208
St Mary's Church, Tikitiki, 62
Stable, Charles, 491
Steele, John Louis
    *The Arrival of the Maoris* (with Goldie), 36
Steiner, Christopher, 180
Stewart, Bruce, 426
street art, 433, 435
suit of armour for Tītore, *268*, 268
Sullivan, Robert
    excerpt from 'He Kohatu Iti', 131
Surville, Jean François Marie de, 210, 221
Szabo, Kat, *252*

**T**
Taahu, Hone, *53*, 53, 214
Taepa, Kereama
    *Pākati Pakemana*, 457
Taepa, Ngataiharuru, *109*, 452, 458
Taepa, Wi, 525
Tahana, Rehutai
    *Kahu huruhuru featuring the Australian Aboriginal flag*, 495
Taiapa, Hone, 60, 61, 62, 370, 557n10[337]
Taiapa, Pine, 62, 64
    bridging the customary and the modern, 405, 424, 535
    photographs of, *80*, *403*
    projects, 62, *65*, 557n10[337]
    teaching, 43, 60–61, 62, 64, *80*, 128, 191, 370
    tukutuku, 64, *80*
    on women carvers, 401–2
Taiaroa, Taarati, 341, 463–64, 563n34[463]
*Taiāwhio* (book, H. Smith et al., editors), 12, *464*, 465
*Taiāwhio II* (book, H. Smith et al., editors), *464*, 465
Taingakawa, Tupu, 307
*Tainui* (waka), *360*, 363
Taipari, Wirope Hotereni, 55, 263
Takahanga Marae
    *Te Kūwaha o Wharetutu* (with Whiting), 486, *487*
takatāpui, 5, 180, 189, 193, 198, 548n1[189]
*Tākitimu* (waka), 24
Tako, Wī, 304, 555n13[306]
Tamarapa, Awhina, 87, 89, *464*
Tamatea, Patoromu, *58*, 193
Tamati, Hukuhuku, 191
Tamati-Quennell, Megan, 341, 461
Tamihana, Wiremu *see* Te Waharoa, Wiremu Tamihana Tarapīpipi
Tāne (atua), *3*, *4*, 29, 41–42, 126, 525
Tangaroa (atua), 41, 43
tangihaehae, 160–61, *161*, 290
tangihanga and burial practices
    hahunga ceremonies, 160, 162
    hei tiki and, 167
    kawe mate, 160
    korowai and, 97–98, 104, 260
    pare kawakawa, *148*, 148
    pōtae tauā, 200
    tahuaroa ceremonies, 104, *105*
    tangihaehae, 160–61
    toi moko as reminders, 350

waka kōiwi, 70, 235
whakairo mate, 235
Tāngonge, 45
tāniko, 87, *94*, 200
taonga
    alienation of, 333–34, 337–38, 353
    calls for return, 333, 337, 343
    collectors, 214–15, 217, 334
    looting of, 119, 213–14, 236, 338, 549n31[213]
    mana of, 14, 74, 84, 98, 100, 104, 167, 205, 259–61, *263*, 536
    muru of, 259, 271, 290
    provenance, 68, *69*, 219
    repatriation, 219, 338–40, 343, 353, 491
    taonga tuku iho definitions, 14–15, 182, 292, 535–36
    trading, 208, 219, 334
taonga gifting practices
    forming alliances with non-Māori, 240, 242, 267–68, *270*, 271, 333–34
    hākari taonga, 104, 544n11[104]
    kai haukai, 291
    pākūwhā, 104, 543n7[104]
    peace negotiations, 98, 100, 170–71, 186, 259–60, 263, *265*, 266–67, 272
    tahuaroa, 96, 104, *105*, 543n4[104]
    utu exchanges, 31–32, 55, 100, 205, 259, 263, 268, 271, 535, 543n88[100]
taonga pūoro
    kōauau, *50*, *143*, 198, *268*, *276*, *278*
    nguru, *212*
    revival of interest in, 277
ta'ovala, 79
tapa (aute), 74–77, *75*, 172, 226, 542n16[76], 542n18[76]
Tapsell, Paul, 92, 214–15
tapu
    of moko, 14
    of rangatira, 290
    removal of, 55, 138, 139, 198, 241, 259, 379
    of toi moko, 351
    of waka taua, 28, 29
    of whare whakairo, 363
Tapu Te Ranga Marae, 425–26, *426*
Tarakau, Te Waaka, 31, 100, 263, 540n41[31]
Taroi, Wero, 503
Tasman, Abel, 84, 207, 549n8[208]
Tasman and Ngāti Tūmatakōkiri engagement, *206*, 207–8, 549n6[207]
tatau pounamu, 186, 259, 260, 264–67, 272
tātua, 87, *88*, *143*, 542n34[87]
Taumata a Kura, Piripi, 256
Tāwhiao (Tukaroto Matutaera Pōtatau Te Wherowhero), 170, 307, 313, 366
Taylor, Richard
    *A chapel in the valley of Waiapu*, 257
Te Amo, 31, 53
Te Ao, Ngapine Tamihana (née Allen), 9, 463
Te Ao, Shannon
    *okea uruoatia (never say die)*, 480
    *Two shoots that stretch far out*, 480, *481*, 564n4[480]
Te Araiteuru Pā, 386
Te Arawa (iwi), 56, 123, 215, 263
*Te Arawa*, 24
Te Aro Park, *428*, 428
Te Ataotū, 98, 543n84[98]

*Te Ātinga* (book, Borell et al., editors), 512, *522*, 523
*Te Aurere*, 36, *37*, 38
Te Awekotuku, Ngahuia
    on clothing and adornment, 14, 97, 486
    on cultural property, 505
    on gender and sexuality, 180, 193, 198
    on korowai, 37
    *Mana Wahine Maori*, 422, *423*
    *Mau Moko* (with Nikora), 8
    on toi moko, 350
Te Hamaiwaho, Apanui, 52, 263, 287
Te Hāpuku, 51, 292
Te Hau ki Tūranga, 11, 53, *120*, 123, 193, 198, 209, 214, 237, 339–40, 374, 376, 463, 536, 550n36[214]
Te Heuheu Tūkino III, Iwikau, 15, *92*, *118*, 304, *305*
Te Heuheu Tūkino IV, Horonuku, 304, *305*
Te Horeta, 209, 549n12[209]
Te Kāhui Toi, *109*
Te Kahumamae o Pareraututu, *261*, 261–62, 271, 350
Te Kanawa, Diggeress, 3, 80, 95, 100–101, *102*, 405
Te Kanawa, Kahutoi, 2, 3, 95, 102, *103*, 450
Te Kiri, Nichola, 181
Te Kooti Arikirangi Te Tūruki
    and Ringatū faith, 311
    and Te Maungārongo hei tiki, 170
    Te Wepu flag, *326*, 329
    wharenui design, 277, 304, 311, *313*
Te Kuku, *222*, 222
Te Kumeroa, Aporo, 287
Te Maihāroa, Hipa, 138
*Te Maori* exhibition, 8, 12, 102, 339, 340, 357, 512
Te Maro, 221
Te Mātorohanga, 287, 554n12[287]
Te Moananui a Kiwa, 22–24, 32, 36, 161, 509
Te Morenga's self-portrait, *293*
Te Mutu, Tomika, *177*
Te Ohaki Maori Village and Crafts Centre, 101
Te Pahi, 261, 298
Te Papa Tongarewa, 339, 351, 463, 543n78[98]
    *see also* Colonial Museum; Dominion Museum
Te Pehi Kupe, 146, 292
Te Pohoi, Paratene, 263
Te Puea *see* Hērangi, Te Puea
Te Puea Marae, 423, 427
Te Puia, 38, 60, 61, 101, 103, 404, 477, 514
Te Rāhui, Ānaha, 31, *50*, *57*, *59*, 121, 217, 349
Te Raihi, Tamatekapua, 370
Te Rangi Hīroa (Peter Buck)
    on hei tiki, 164–65
    on hieke rain capes, 91
    on *Kurahaupō*, 24
    on red feathers, 95
    and Te Araiteuru, 386
    on tukutuku, 121, *335*, 369
Te Rangihaeata portraits, *172*, *279*
Te Rangikāheke, Wiremu Maihi, 49, 159, 175
Te Rangitopeora, 98, 189
Te Rarawa, 45
Te Ratana, Saffronn, *109*, 452

Te Rauparaha
    and CMS churches, 81, *235*, *236*, 238
    portrait by Coates, *279*
    pounamu and, 170, 264–67, *265*
    South Island expeditions, 98, 170, 264–67, *265*
    waka taua of, *56*, 265
Te Rito Maihi, Toi, 97, 100, 458
Te Rito school of weaving, 101, 103
Te Roopu Raranga Whatu o Aotearoa, 101, 200, 543n101[101]
Te Tau, Terri, 519
Te Tii Marae, Waitangi, *309*, 309, 311
Te Tuiti-Moeroa, *49*
Te Ua Haumēne, 324, 329
Te Uhi a Mataora collective, 515
Te Waharoa, Wiremu Tamihana Tarapīpipi, 304, 307
Te Waru Rewiri, Kura
    background, 422
    *The Covenant*, 422, *423*
    *Nga Tohu o Te Tiriti*, 422
    Te Aro Park project, *428*
    *Te Kahurangi*, 422, *423*
    *Whenua, Wahine, Whenua*, 456
Te Whakatatare o te Rangi, 209
Te Whanarere, Te Hareti, *117*
Te Whata, Kohuru, 235–36
Te Whatahoro, Hoani, 287, 554n12[287]
Te Wherowhero, Pōtatau, 292, 303, 306, 423
Te Wherowhero, Tukaroto Matutaera Pōtatau (Tāwhiao), 170, 307, 313, 366
Te Whiti o Rongomai, 304, 317, *319*, 319, *322*, 322–23, 353
Te Wiata, Īnia (Te Iwiata), 32, 366, *500*, 501, 503, 540n44[33]
Teimana, Pikau, *284*
tertiary art education
    Māori Adult Education classes, 2, 337–38
    museum studies, 342
    university programmes, 60, 103, 512, 515, 532, 533, 566n17[512], 566n25[516]
    wānanga programmes, 103, 443, 459, 515, 532
textiles
    archaeological finds, 74, *85*, 95
    dyes, 80–81, 542n24[80]
    items made by men, 200
    materials, 77, 80
    *see also* cloaks; kaitaka; kete; korowai; rain capes; tukutuku; whāriki
thatch
    government objections to, 111–12, 318–19
    materials for, 534
    Raupo Houses Act (1842), 111
    thatched roofs, 111
    as wall linings, *368*, 544n6[111], 556n73[318]
    whare nīkau, 112, *113*
    whare raupō, 112, *113*, *239*, 256, 318
    whatu techniques for, 544n5[111]
Thomas, Nicholas, 23, 224
Thompson, Nainoa, 36, 38
Thompson, Rewi, 233, 472, *473*
tī kōuka, 80
tikanga, 5, 14, 22, 45, 204, 371, 428, 444, 535–36

Tikao, Teone Taare, 149, 160, 161, 175
time as a non-linear continuum, 1, 9, 182, 263–64
Tinirau, 43, 112, 117
tino rangatiratanga
    flag, *329*, 329
    as opposed to biculturalism, 459, 465, 471
    self-determining authority, 205, 285, 303, 523
    sovereignty as a concept, 511
Tiria Hōri, 386
Tirikatene-Sullivan, Whetū, *529*, 529
Tiriti o Waitangi
    Article Two, 338, 505, 565n5[505]
    commemorations, 32, 33, 61, 337, 391, 406, 437
    guaranteed rights, 81
    principles, 341
    signatures on, 285, 292
    *see also* meeting houses by name: Te Tiriti o Waitangi
Tītore, 267–68, *268*, 271
TOA Architects
    Te Taumata o Kupe, Te Mahurehure Marae, 474, *475*
Tohu Kākahi, 304, 317, *320*, *322*, 322–23
tohunga, 233, 234, 249, 323
Tohunga Suppression Act (1907), 159, 557n1[333]
tōī, 79, 80, *90*, 91, 542n46[91]
Toi, Gordon
    *Mataora*, 146
Toi Iho trademark, 128–29, 505, *507*, 507
Toi Māori trust, 514
toi moko, 98, 159, 350–51, 353, 558n1[350], 558n3[350]
Toia, Roi, 513
Toka, Henare, 337–38
Toka, Mere, 2, 337–38
toki
    long-handled toki, 370, *386*, 386
    making ancestral waka, 24, 26
    of pounamu, 2, 26, 167, 300
    toki kakauroa, 300
    toki poutangata, 209
    Whakarau, 221
Tonga, Nina, 516, 566n25[516]
Topia, Heni (Jane), 191
Tovey, Gordon
    arts and crafts advisory service, 398, 525
    *The Arts of the Maori*, 402, 535
    and the 'Tovey Generation', 405
Trade Marks Act (2002), 507
Treadwell, Jeremy, 126
Treaty of Waitangi *see* Tiriti o Waitangi
tree carvings *see* rākau momori
Tregear, Edward, 160
Tsinhnahjinnie, Hulleah J., 511
tū, 87
Tuai, 213, *214*, 294, *295*
Tuarau, Iotua (Charles), 557n10[337]
Tūhaere, Paora, 32, 540n43[32]
Tūhoe, 98, 100, 272, 459, 471
Tuki Tahua, 296, 297
tukutuku
    artists, 62, 92, *120*, 198–99, *335*, 535
    development of, 121, 123, 277
    incorporating names, 287

    panel with poutama design, *2*
    Pine Taiapa's research of, 64
    *see also* patterns
Tūmatauenga, 30, 126
Tupaia, 226
    'A Maori man and Joseph Banks', *227*
    map drawn by, *25*, 226
    relationship with Māori, 92, *123*, 138, 221, 226
Tupu, Tania, 181
Tūrangawaewae
    carving school, 127, 359, 364, 366
    Māhinaarangi, *360*, 361, *363*, 363–64
    Regatta, *33*, 37
    Tūrangawaewae House, 307, *308*
    Tūrongo House, 33, *365*, 366–67
    village facilities, 360–61
Tūrei, Mohi, 256
Turei, Raukura, 480
Turi, 22, 26, 45, 100, 263
Turi-Tiakitai, John, 2, 95
Turnbull, Alexander, 215
Twomey, Āwhina, 341
Tylor, James
    drawn and photographic works, 516
    *Tā Moko (More Than Skin Deep)*, 498

## U

Ūawa, 138, 226, 263
Uenuku, 14, *45*, 45
United Nations Declaration on the Rights of Indigenous Peoples (UNDRIP), 523
upoko tuhi *see* toi moko
urban Māori
    Auckland Maori Community Centre, *417*, 417
    challenges and issues, 416, 429, 499
    large-scale urban artworks, 415, 428–30
    migration to cities, 127, 357, 405, 415–17, 431
    Ngati Poneke Young Maori Club, 417
urban marae, 423–27

## V

Venice Biennale, 493, 512–13, 516
Vivieaere, Jim, 486, 523

## W

Waata Urlich, Colleen, 525
    *Hinaki—Eel trap, Kapowai series—Dragonfly Lake*, *526*
Waetford, Dorothy, 525–26
Wagelie, Jennifer, 211
waiata
    carving in, 42
    cloaks in, 2, 73–74, 95, 100
    'E Tū' (Hapeta), 415
    hei tiki in, 170–71
    'Moko' (Maniapoto), 146
    'Repatriation' (Herbs), 341
    tangihaehae in, 160
    waka in, 30
Waikanae church, *235*, 237–38
Waikato-Tainui
    carving style, 32, 363–64, 370
    invasion of lands, 359–60, 423
    Uenuku and, 14, *44*, 45
    *see also* Kīngitanga

Waipapa Marae, 4, 9, 101, 128, *424*, 424
Wairau Bar archaeological finds, 70, *153*, 154, 186
Wairau Māori Art Gallery, 483
wairua, 14, 264
Waitangi Tribunal
    Flora and Fauna Wai 262 claim, 15, 505, 536
    Ngāti Awa Wai 46 claim, 272, 339–40, 536
    Rongowhakaata Wai 814 claim, 339–40, 536
    Te Roroa Wai 38 claim, 338–39
    work of, 338, 557n19[338]
Waitere, Tene, *56*, 57, 101, 217, 349, 386, *493*, 503
waka
    ancestral waka, 22, 24, 26, 100, 263, 360
    changing styles of, 23, 27–28, 31, 37, 290
    haumi prows, 24, 26–27, *27*, 49
    lashing holes, *25*, 26
    oceangoing waka, 21, 24, 26, 36, *37*
    oldest surviving hull, *25*, 26
    oral histories, 21–22, 24, 26, 30
    paddles (hoe), 26, *123*, 123, 158, 290
    rock art drawings of, 27–28
    sail technology, 22, 24, 28, 84, *86*, 87, 290
    single-hull waka, 27–31
    taurapa sternposts, 24, 26
    waka ama, 24, 37
    waka builders, 22, 24, 26, 29
    waka kōpapa, 37
    waka kōrari (pūhara), 28, *29*
    waka tētē, 28
    waka tīwai, 28
    *see also* waka taua
waka hourua revival
    *Hawaiki-nui*, 36
    *Hinemoana*, 21
    *Hōkūle'a*, 36, 38
    *Tairāwhiti*, 21
    *Te Aurere*, 36, *37*, 38
waka taua
    community investment in, 28–29
    construction of, 29, *30*
    and inter-hapū warfare, 21, 31, 56, 264
    *A New Zealand war canoe* (Parkinson), 22
    recycling of carvings, 31, 55, 541n39[56]
    revival in 1930s, 31–33
    symbolism of, 29–30, 56–57
    tauihu (pītau) prows, 26, 30, 210, 241, *248*, *265*, 428
    taurapa, 30, *56*, 56, 210, *265*, 491
    tuere prows, 30, 540n33[30]
    whare/waka design relationship, 29, 56, 109, 123, 157, 275
waka taua by name
    *Kahutiaterangi*, *56*, 56, 541n38[56]
    *Ngātokimatwhaorua*, 32, *33*, 36, 38
    *Rangimārie*, 38
    *Taheretikitiki*, 30, 386
    *Taheretikitiki II*, 32–33, 540n43[32]
    *Te Aio o Nukutaimemeha*, 540n48[36]
    *Te Aniwaniwa*, 61
    *Te Rangatahi* (Tākitimu), 32, *33*
    *Te Raukura*, 61
    *Te Toki a Tāpiri*, 31–32, 100, *262*, 263, 423, 543n88[100]

*Te Tuhono*, 491
*Te Winika*, 32–33
*Tūmanako* (Aotea), 32
*Uerangi*, 38
*Waikahua*, 265, *266*, 553n24[266]
Wallace, Patricia Te Arapo, 77, 106
Walters, Gordon
    *Kahukura*, 446
    *Painting No. 1*, *505*, 505
    and rock art, 139
Walters, Muru
    as art teacher/advisor, 399
    *Blue Faces*, 393
Warren, John, 307, *308*
Warrior, Robert, 511
weapons, traditional
    pātītī, *280*, *300*, 300
    taiaha, 160, *161*, 270, 300
    tewhatewha, *143*, 215
    toki kakauroa, 300
    *see also* patu ōnewa, patu parāoa
weavers
    associations of, 101
    exhibitions, 101–2
    experimentation by, 81, 91, 97, 281, *286*, 287, *289*
    men as, 200
    study of overseas collections, 102
    training of, 89, 101, 103
    *see also* cloaks; kaitaka; korowai; muka; patterns; raranga; whatu
Webb, Marilynn
    as art teacher/advisor, 399
    *Going Through Fiordland Suite No 15*, *459*
Webster, Kohe, 36
Wentworth Indenture, 292
Wesleyan Methodist Missionary Society (WMS), 230, 240, 243, 247
Whaanga, Mere, 24, 84, 87, 97
Whaiora Marae, 424
Whaitiri, Keri
    *Hohoko: Trading Terms*, 449
    *huri, ka huri, huri noa* (with Dunn), 449
whakairo artworks
    amo, *219*
    carved handles, 209, *280*, 298
    koruru, *167*
    kūwaha pātaka, *248*
    papahou, 51, *66*, 68–69, *69*, *181*, *194*, *241*
    pare, 198, *211*, 211
    poupou, *196*, *197*, *219*, 287
    poutokomanawa, *41*
    powaka whakairo, 179, 547n93[179]
    tauihu, 26, 30, 210, 241, *248*, *265*, 428
    taurapa, 30, *56*, 56, 210, *265*, 491
    tekoteko, *197*, *232*, *276*
    upoko whakairo, *251*
    waharoa, *388*
    waka huia, *50*, 178–79, 193, *194*, *195*, 547n91[179]
    waka kōiwi, 70, 235
    waka tūpāpaku, 47, 338
    *see also* carvers
whakairo motifs
    animal imagery, 24, 26, 46, 117, 540n18[46]
    double spirals (takarangi spirals), 30, *49*, 68
    human figures, 30, 45, 46–47, 68, 238

    manaia, 26–27, *27*, 42, 43, 45–46, 100, 238
    mata kupenga, 30, *49*, 192
    piko-o-rauru spirals, *181*
    sexual imagery, 117, 117, *118*, 179–80, 192
    taniwha, 32, 363, 366
    taowaru, 42, 100
    taratara ā Kae, 43, 112, 117
    unaunahi, *49*, 68
whakairo rākau
    buried in wetlands, 43, 45
    origins of, 41–43
    tapu of, 51, 263, 311, 366
    tools, 27, 209, 278, *299*, 300, 386
    as transitional markers between tapu and noa, 241
    volume of works, 41, 540n1[41]
    works made for sale, 57, *59*, 193, 219, 541n40[57]
    *see also* carvers
whakairo styles
    central North Island and East Coast style, 47
    of individual carvers, 51, 66
    Mead's analysis, 46, 540n20[47]
    northern and Taranaki style, 47, *49*, 68, *181*, 236, *322*, 370, 539n22[26]
    Ringatū style, 314–16
    Waikato style, 363–64, 370
whakapakoko, 46, 75, *216*, 216, 546n24[154]
whakapapa
    expressed in whare whakairo, 121, 126, 315
    and identity, 129, 536
    and Māori art practice, 3, 14, 18, 463
    and multiple understandings, 43, 534
    in Rākairoa whare, 129
    of taonga, 31–32, 68
Whakataka-Brightwell, Matahi Avauli, 36, 540n48[36]
whalers and sealers, 210–11, 290
whare
    construction of, 111, *124*, 318
    incorporating Pākehā elements, 290, *367*, *368*
    kākaho wall linings, 111, 121, 123, 306, 359, 371
    parts of, *118*
    ponga walls with raupō linings, 318, 556n73[318]
    tāhuhu, 41, 56, *124*, 126–27, 275
    waka/whare design relationships, 29, 56, 109, 123, 127, 275
    whare kāuta (whare umu), 109, 112, *114*
    whare rangatira, 275, 277
    wharekai, *109*, *320*, *321*, 323, 374
    wharepuni, *109*, *110*, 111–12, *118*, 318, 323, 544n5[111], 544n6[111]
    *see also* meeting houses by name; whare whakairo
whare wānanga, 22, 42, 51, 62, 287
whare whakairo
    archaeological records of, 45, 46
    construction of, *124*, 127, 424–25
    figurative paintings in, 257, *315*, 315–16
    functions of, 119, 121, 311
    meanings and symbolism of, 126–27, 198, 424–25
    named after ancestors, 126, 192, 287

opening ceremonies, 55, 198, 263, 311, 363, *368*
origins and development, 43, 119, 121, 127, 275
polychromatic painting in, *313*, 314, 370
revitalisation of, 369–70, 376
twentieth-century innovations, 371, 373–74, 424–25
*see also* meeting houses by name
wharepū *see* pātaka
Wharepu, Te Aho o Te Rangi, *284*
whāriki, 81, 84, 104
Whātonga, 24, 42
whatu
  and Te Whare Pora, 89
  techniques, 74, 81, 87, 89
  turuturu, 87, *88*
  twentieth-century rejuvenation, 100–101
  *see also* cloaks; kaitaka; korowai; muka; textiles
whenua
  alienation of, 214, 292, 307, 423, 549n33[214]
  importance of, 14
  land loss consequences, 127, 139, 205, 214, 215, 303, 333, 534–35
  Native Land Court, 121
whītau *see* muka
Whiting, Cliff
  as art teacher/advisor, 397, 399, 402, 561n37[401]
  at *Contemporary Maori Painting and Sculpture* exhibition, *396*
  on European-influenced works, 401
  on resistance to Māori modernism, 404
  *Te Ao o Ngā Atua*, 60
  *Te Kūwaha o Wharetutu* (with Takahanga Marae), 486, *487*
  *Te Wehenga o Rangi rāua ko Papa*, 4
  on Tovey, 398
  work on fibreboard, 61
Wilkinson, Areta, 182
  *Hine-Āhua and Huiarei (toggle)*, *183*
  making *Whakapapa I*, *184*
  *Moa Hunter Fashions*, 182, *185*
  photogram works (with Adams), 182, *183*
  *Star Whata: Space Odyssey 2021*, *140*, 140
  *Vertebra I, II, III*, *183*
  *Whakapapa V* (with Adams), *185*
William IV, King of England, 267–68, 285, 292, 553n34[268]
Williams, Charles (PHAT1), 435
Williams, Herbert, 126, 162
Williams, Janine (Lady Diva), 435
Williams, Joseph Walter, 215
Williams, Samuel, *236*, 238, 544n11[104]
Williams, William, *237*, 238–39, 256–57
Wills, Richard, *371*
Wilson, Arnold Manaaki
  as art teacher/advisor, 401
  on community expectations v. art school training, 403–4
  in *New Zealand Maori Culture and the Contemporary Scene*, 397
  *Mihaia te Tuatahi*, *393*
  photograph of, *401*
  on reconciling traditional and modern art, 60, 393, 395

Wilson, Carin
  *Boardroom Table and Chairs*, *477*
  *Royal Pain in the Arse*, *477*
Wilson, Selwyn
  as art teacher/advisor, 393, 398–99
  *Figure study*, *398*
  *Study of a head*, *398*
Winiata, Maharaia, 337–38
Wirihana, Christina Hurihia
  in Australia, 499
  *Reflections of Kete Kai*, *79*
Witehira, Johnson
  billboards in Times Square, New York, *479*, 479
  on tattooed text, 285
  Whakarare typeface, *479*, 479
Witter, Dan and Alison, 74
Wood, Cecil, 424
Wright, Louise, 474

# Y

Yate, William, 104, 172, 256, 543n4[104]
Yearbury, Jim, 412
Yearbury, Pauline Kahurangi (née Blomfield)
  as Māori trailblazer, 6, 392
  *The Children of Rangi and Papa*, *412*
  *Tane Makes the First Woman*, *412*